# Twentieth-Century
# Literary Criticism

# Guide to Gale Literary Criticism Series

| For criticism on | Consult these Gale series |
| --- | --- |
| Authors now living or who died after December 31, 1959 | *CONTEMPORARY LITERARY CRITICISM (CLC)* |
| Authors who died between 1900 and 1959 | *TWENTIETH-CENTURY LITERARY CRITICISM (TCLC)* |
| Authors who died between 1800 and 1899 | *NINETEENTH-CENTURY LITERATURE CRITICISM (NCLC)* |
| Authors who died between 1400 and 1799 | *LITERATURE CRITICISM FROM 1400 TO 1800 (LC)* <br><br> *SHAKESPEAREAN CRITICISM (SC)* |
| Authors who died before 1400 | *CLASSICAL AND MEDIEVAL LITERATURE CRITICISM (CMLC)* |
| Authors of books for children and young adults | *CHILDREN'S LITERATURE REVIEW (CLR)* |
| Dramatists | *DRAMA CRITICISM (DC)* |
| Poets | *POETRY CRITICISM (PC)* |
| Short story writers | *SHORT STORY CRITICISM (SSC)* |
| Black writers of the past two hundred years | *BLACK LITERATURE CRITICISM (BLC)* |
| Hispanic writers of the late nineteenth and twentieth centuries | *HISPANIC LITERATURE CRITICISM (HLC)* |
| Native North American writers and orators of the eighteenth, nineteenth, and twentieth centuries | *NATIVE NORTH AMERICAN LITERATURE (NNAL)* |
| Major authors from the Renaissance to the present | *WORLD LITERATURE CRITICISM, 1500 TO THE PRESENT (WLC)* |

ISSN 0276-8178

Volume 80

# Twentieth-Century Literary Criticism

**Excerpts from Criticism of the
Works of Novelists, Poets, Playwrights,
Short Story Writers, and Other Creative Writers
Who Lived between 1900 and 1960,
from the First Published Critical
Appraisals to Current Evaluations**

Jennifer Baise
*Editor*

Thomas Ligotti
*Associate Editor*

GALE

DETROIT • LONDON

**STAFF**

Jennifer Baise, *Editor*

Thomas Ligotti, *Associate Editor*

Susan Trosky, *Permissions Manager*
Kimberly F. Smilay, *Permissions Specialist*
Sarah R. Chesney, Steve Cusack, Kelly A. Quin, *Permissions Associates*
Sandy Gore, *Permissions Assistant*

Victoria B. Cariappa, *Research Manager*
Michele P. LaMeau, Andrew Guy Malonis, Barbara McNeil, Gary J. Oudersluys, Maureen Richards, *Research Specialists*
Julia C. Daniel, Jeffrey Daniels, Tamara C. Nott, Tracie A. Richardson, Norma Sawaya,
Cheryl L. Warnock, *Research Associates*
Corrine Stocker, *Research Assistant*

Mary Beth Trimper, *Production Director*
Deborah L. Milliken, *Production Assistant*

Gary Leach, *Graphic Artist*
Randy Bassett, *Image Database Supervisor*
Robert Duncan, Michael Logusz, *Imaging Specialists*
Pamela Reed, *Imaging Coordinator*

Library of Congress Catalog Card Number 76-46132
ISBN 0-7876-2740-2
ISSN 0276-8178

Printed in the United States of America
10  9  8  7  6  5  4  3  2  1

# Contents

Preface   vii

Acknowledgments   xi

# Preface

Since its inception more than fifteen years ago, *Twentieth-Century Literary Criticism* has been purchased and used by nearly 10,000 school, public, and college or university libraries. *TCLC* has covered more than 500 authors, representing 58 nationalities, and over 25,000 titles. No other reference source has surveyed the critical response to twentieth-century authors and literature as thoroughly as *TCLC*. In the words of one reviewer, "there is nothing comparable available." *TCLC* "is a gold mine of information—dates, pseudonyms, biographical information, and criticism from books and periodicals—which many libraries would have difficulty assembling on their own."

## Scope of the Series

*TCLC* is designed to serve as an introduction to authors who died between 1900 and 1960 and to the most significant interpretations of these author's works. The great poets, novelists, short story writers, playwrights, and philosophers of this period are frequently studied in high school and college literature courses. In organizing and excerpting the vast amount of critical material written on these authors, *TCLC* helps students develop valuable insight into literary history, promotes a better understanding of the texts, and sparks ideas for papers and assignments. Each entry in *TCLC* presents a comprehensive survey of an author's career or an individual work of literature and provides the user with a multiplicity of interpretations and assessments. Such variety allows students to pursue their own interests; furthermore, it fosters an awareness that literature is dynamic and responsive to many different opinions.

Every fourth volume of *TCLC* is devoted to literary topics. These topic entries widen the focus of the series from individual authors to such broader subjects as literary movements, prominent themes in twentieth-century literature, literary reaction to political and historical events, significant eras in literary history, prominent literary anniversaries, and the literatures of cultures that are often overlooked by English-speaking readers.

*TCLC* is designed as a companion series to Gale's *Contemporary Literary Criticism,* which reprints commentary on authors now living or who have died since 1960. Because of the different periods under consideration, there is no duplication of material between *CLC* and *TCLC*. For additional information about *CLC* and Gale's other criticism titles, users should consult the Guide to Gale Literary Criticism Series preceding the title page in this volume.

## Coverage

Each volume of *TCLC* is carefully compiled to present:

- criticism of authors, or literary topics, representing a variety of genres and nationalities

- both major and lesser-known writers and literary works of the period

- 6-12 authors or 3-6 topics per volume

- individual entries that survey critical response to each author's work or each topic in literary history, including early criticism to reflect initial reactions; later criticism to represent any rise or decline in reputation; and current retrospective analyses.

## Organization of This Book

An author entry consists of the following elements: author heading, biographical and critical introduction, list of principal works, excerpts of criticism (each preceded by an annotation and a bibliographic citation), and a bibliography of further reading.

- The **Author Heading** consists of the name under which the author most commonly wrote, followed by birth and death dates. If an author wrote consistently under a pseudonym, the pseudonym will be listed in the author heading and the real name given in parentheses on the first line of the biographical and critical introduction. Also located at the beginning of the introduction to the author entry are any name variations under which an author wrote, including transliterated forms for authors whose languages use nonroman alphabets.

- The **Biographical and Critical Introduction** outlines the author's life and career, as well as the critical issues surrounding his or her work. References to past volumes of *TCLC* are provided at the beginning of the introduction. Additional sources of information in other biographical and critical reference series published by Gale, including *Short Story Criticism, Children's Literature Review, Contemporary Authors, Dictionary of Literary Biography,* and *Something about the Author,* are listed in a box at the end of the entry.

- Some *TCLC* entries include **Portraits** of the author. Entries also may contain reproductions of materials pertinent to an author's career, including manuscript pages, title pages, dust jackets, letters, and drawings, as well as photographs of important people, places, and events in an author's life.

- The **List of Principal Works** is chronological by date of first book publication and identifies the genre of each work. In the case of foreign authors with both foreign-language publications and English translations, the title and date of the first English-language edition are given in brackets. Unless otherwise indicated, dramas are dated by first performance, not first publication.

- Critical excerpts are prefaced by **Annotations** providing the reader with information about both the critic and the criticism that follows. Included are the critic's reputation, individual approach to literary criticism, and particular expertise in an author's works. Also noted are the relative importance of a work of criticism, the scope of the excerpt, and the growth of critical controversy or changes in critical trends regarding an author. In some cases, these annotations cross-reference excerpts by critics who discuss each other's commentary.

- A complete **Bibliographic Citation** designed to facilitate location of the original essay or book precedes each piece of criticism.

- Criticism is arranged chronologically in each author entry to provide a perspective on changes in critical evaluation over the years. All titles of works by the author featured in the entry are printed in boldface type to enable the user to easily locate discussion of particular works. Also for purposes of easier identification, the critic's name and the publication date of the essay are given at the beginning of each piece of criticism. Unsigned criticism is preceded by the title of the journal in which it appeared. Some of the excerpts in *TCLC* also contain translated material. Unless otherwise noted, translations in brackets are by the editors; translations in parentheses or continuous with the text are by the critic. Publication information (such as footnotes or page and line references to specific editions of works) have been deleted at the editor's discretion to provide smoother reading of the text.

- An annotated list of **Further Reading** appearing at the end of each author entry suggests secondary sources on the author. In some cases it includes essays for which the editors could not obtain reprint rights.

## Cumulative Indexes

- Each volume of *TCLC* contains a cumulative **Author Index** listing all authors who have appeared in Gale's Literary Criticism Series, along with cross references to such biographical series as *Contemporary Authors* and *Dictionary of Literary Biography.* For readers' convenience, a complete list of Gale titles included appears on the first page of the author index. Useful for locating authors within the various series, this index is particularly valuable for those authors who are identified by a certain period but who, because of their death dates, are placed in another, or for those authors whose careers span two periods. For example, F. Scott Fitzgerald is found in *TCLC,* yet a writer often associated with him, Ernest Hemingway, is found in *CLC.*

- Each *TCLC* volume includes a cumulative **Nationality Index** which lists all authors who have appeared in *TCLC* volumes, arranged alphabetically under their respective nationalities, as well as Topics volume entries devoted to particular national literatures.

- Each new volume in Gale's Literary Criticism Series includes a cumulative **Topic Index,** which lists all literary topics treated in *NCLC, TCLC, LC 1400-1800,* and the *CLC* yearbook.

- Each new volume of *TCLC,* with the exception of the Topics volumes, includes a **Title Index** listing the titles of all literary works discussed in the volume. In response to numerous suggestions from librarians, Gale has also produced a **Special Paperbound Edition** of the *TCLC* title index. This annual cumulation lists all titles discussed in the series since its inception and is issued with the first volume of *TCLC* published each year. Additional copies of the index are available on request. Librarians and patrons will welcome this separate index; it saves shelf space, is easy to use, and is recyclable upon receipt of the following year's cumulation. Titles discussed in the Topics volume entries are not included *TCLC* cumulative index.

# Citing Twentieth-Century Literary Criticism

When writing papers, students who quote directly from any volume in Gale's literary Criticism Series may use the following general forms to footnote reprinted criticism. The first example pertains to materials drawn from periodicals, the second to material reprinted from books.

[1]William H. Slavick, "Going to School to DuBose Heyward," *The Harlem Renaissance Re-examined,* (AMS Press, 1987); excerpted and reprinted in *Twentieth-Century Literary Criticism,* Vol. 59, ed. Jennifer Gariepy (Detroit: Gale Research, 1995), pp. 94-105.

[2]George Orwell, "Reflections on Gandhi," *Partisan Review,* 6 (Winter 1949), pp. 85-92; excerpted and reprinted in *Twentieth-Century Literary Criticism,* Vol. 59, ed. Jennifer Gariepy (Detroit: Gale Research, 1995), pp. 40-3.

# Suggestions Are Welcome

In response to suggestions, several features have been added to *TCLC* since the series began, including annotations to excerpted criticism, a cumulative index to authors in all Gale literary criticism series, entries devoted to criticism on a single work by a major author, more extensive illustrations, and a title index listing all literary works discussed in the series since its inception.

Readers who wish to suggest authors or topics to appear in future volumes, or who have other suggestions, are cordially invited to write the editors.

# Acknowledgments

The editors wish to thank the copyright holders of the excerpted criticism included in this volume and the permissions managers of many book and magazine publishing companies for assisting us in securing reproduction rights. We are also grateful to the staffs of the Detroit Public Library, the Library of Congress, the University of Detroit Mercy Library, Wayne State University Purdy/Kresge Library Complex, and the University of Michigan Libraries for making their resources available to us. Following is a list of the copyright holders who have granted us permission to reproduce material in this volume of *TCLC*. Every effort has been made to trace copyright, but if omissions have been made, please let us know.

## COPYRIGHTED EXCERPTS IN *TCLC*, VOLUME 80, WERE REPRODUCED FROM THE FOLLOWING PERIODICALS:

*American Jewish History*, v. 71, September, 1981. Reproduced by permission.—*American Literature*, v. XXXIX, March, 1967. Copyright © 1967 by Duke University Press, Durham, NC. Reproduced by permission.—*The American Scholar*, v. 9, Spring , 1940; v. 48, Winter, 1978/79. Copyright © 1940, 1978 by the United Chapters of the Phi Beta Kappa Society. Both reproduced by permission of the publisher.—*American Quarterly*, v. 44, March, 1992. © 1992. Reproduced by permission of The Johns Hopkins University Press.—*American Studies*, v. 20. Spring, 1979, for "Jacob Riis and the Jews: The Ambivalent Quest for Community" by Louis Fried. Copyright © Mid-American Studies Association, 1979. Reprinted by permission of the publisher.—*Ariel: A Review of International English Literature*, v. 17, October, 1986. Copyright © 1986 The Board of Governors, The University of Calgary. Reproduced by permission of the publisher.—*The Arizona Quarterly*, v. 37, Autumn, 1981. Copyright © 1981 by the Regents of the University of Arizona. Reproduced by permission of the publisher.—*Biography: An Interdisciplinary Quarterly* , v. 6, Spring, 1983. Copyright © 1983 by the Biographical Research Center. All rights reserved. Reproduced by permission.—*Comparative Literature Studies*, v. 22, Spring, 1985. Copyright © 1985 by The Pennsylvania State University. Reproduced by permission of The Pennsylvania State University Press.—*Current History*, v. 6, January, 1944. Copyright, 1944, by Current History, Inc. Reproduced by permission of the publisher.—*Genre*, v. XI, Winter, 1978 for "The 'Super Historical' Sense of Hart Crane's The Bridge" by John Carlos Rowe. Reproduced by permission of the publisher and the author.—*Hispania*, v. 55, May, 1972, for "The Function of Myth in the Plays of Xavier Villaurrutia" by Sandra M. Cypess. © 1972 The American Association of Teachers of Spanish and Portuguese, Inc. Reproduced by permission of the publisher and the author.—*Indian and Foreign Review*, Vol. 17, January 1-15, 1980.—*Journal of Modern Literature*, v. 17, Summer, 1990. Reproduced by permission.—*Journal of Popular Film and Television*, v. 14, Summer, 1986. Copyright © 1986 Helen Dwight Reid Educational Foundation. Reproduced with permission of the Helen Dwight Reid Educational Foundation, published by Heldref Publications, 1319 18th Street NW, Washington, DC 20036-1802.—*Journal of South Asian Literature*, v. XIII, Fall, 1977. Reproduced by permission.—*Latin American Literary Review*, v. 22, July-December, 1994. Reproduced by permission.—*Latin American Theatre Review*, v. 3, Fall, 1969. Copyright 1969 by the Center of Latin American Studies, The University of Kansas, Lawrence, KS 66045, U.S.A. Reproduced by permission.—*The Midwest Quarterly*, v. XXVI, Winter, 1985. Copyright © 1985 by The Midwest Quarterly, Pittsburg State University. Reproduced by permission.—*Modern Philology*, v. 90, August, 1992, for "Ezra Pound, Yone Noguchi, and Imagism" by Yoshinobu Hakutani. Copyright © 1992 by The University of Chicago. All rights reserved. Reproduced by permission of the publisher and the author.—*Modernist Studies*, v. 3, 1979, for "A Divided Self: The Poetic Responsibility of Hart Crane with Respect to 'The Bridge'" by Joseph Schwartz. Reproduced by permission of the author.—*National Review*, v. XX, April 23, 1968. Copyright © 1968 by National Review, Inc, 215 Lexington Avenue. New York, NY 10016. Reproduced by permission.—*The New York Review of Books*, v. 21, October 31, 1974. Copyright © 1974 Nyrev, Inc. Reproduced with permission from The New York Review of Books.—*Political Science Quarterly*, v. LVIII, September, 1943. Copyright 1943, renewed 1971 by the editors of the Political Science Quarterly . Reproduced by permission.—*Raritan: A Quarterly Review*, v. 8, Spring and Summer, 1989 for "Back Home Again in India: Hart Crane's 'The Bridge'" by John T. Irwin. Copyright © 1989 by Raritan: A Quarterly Review. Reproduced by permission.—*South Atlantic Review*, v. 54, January, 1989. Copyright © 1989 by the South Atlantic Modern Language Association. Reproduced by permission.—*The Sewanee Review*, v. LXXXIX, Spring, 1981. Copyright © 1981 Malcolm Cowley. Reproduced with the permission of The Sewanee Review.—*The Southern Review*, Louisiana State University, v. V, Autumn, 1939, for "Henry and Brooks Adams: Parallels to Two Generations" by R. P. Blackmur. Copyright 1939, renewed © 1967. Reproduced by permission of the Estate of R. P. Blackmur./ v. 20, January, 1984 for "Toward a Poetics of Technology: Hart Crane and the American Sublime" by Tom Chaffin. Copyright © 1984, by Tom Chaffin. Reproduced by permission of the author.—*Thalia*, v. VIII, Fall-Winter, 1985. Copyright © 1985 by Jacqueline Tavernier-Courbin. Reproduced by permission.—*Twentieth Century Literature*, v. 26, Fall, 1980. Copyright © 1980, Hofstra University Press. Reproduced by permission.

# Brooks Adams

## 1848-1927

(Full name Henry Brooks Adams) American historian.

## INTRODUCTION

A noted historian of the late-nineteenth and early-twentieth centuries, Adams is primarily remembered for his exploration of the rise and fall of world civilizations based upon their relation to the major paths of economic exchange. Adams's body of work—characterized by his deep pessimism and anti-Semitism—represents his attempt to establish a cyclical view of history based in part upon the natural laws of thermodynamics, which he believed governed social and economic development and decline. Early in his career, Adams generated controversy for his attacks on New England's religious forefathers, whom he believed to be the antithesis of democratic leaders. In his later writings, Adams exhibited an increasing bitterness, reflecting his belief that the energy of the United States had been spent, and that the nation had succumbed to materialism and greed. During his life, Adams was also an outspoken advocate for converting the United States' economy from the gold standard to bimetallism—the use of both silver and gold as standards.

### Biographical Information

The youngest of six children of Charles Francis Adams and Abigail Brooks Adams, Adams belonged to a dynasty of prominent American political thinkers. His great-grandfather John Adams and his grandfather John Quincy Adams were presidents of the United States. His father was the 1848 Free Soil candidate for U.S. vice president; he ran on the same ticket as Martin Van Buren. Charles Adams was also named minister to Great Britain during the U.S. Civil War by President Abraham Lincoln. Adams's older brother was Henry Adams, whose literary legacy includes his autobiography *The Education of Henry Adams,* the novel *Democracy,* and a nine-volume *History of the Administrations of Jefferson and Madison.* Two other brothers, Charles and John Quincy, also enjoyed modest fame. Adams attended English schools and graduated from Harvard in 1870. He completed one year of study at Harvard Law School, and passed the bar examinations without obtaining a law degree. His family's wealth enabled Brooks Adams to pursue his writing career unencumbered by financial concerns. Adams practiced law for a brief period before leaving for Europe with his father. During his adult life, Adams traveled extensively throughout Europe, the Middle East and India. From 1904 to 1911 he lectured at the Boston University School of Law.

### Major Works

Adams published several articles and reviews before his first history, *The Emancipation of Massachusetts* (1887). In it, Adams attacked the hagiographic depictions of the Protestant forefathers of New England. He argued that previous depictions of early New England founders were untrue and that, instead of fostering democratic virtues, the founders engendered a climate of religious intolerance. The book was perceived as controversial in its time, and much was made of the unbalanced nature of Adams's presentation. Adams's defended his work to Henry Cabot Lodge: "It is really not a history of Mass. but a metaphysical and philosophical inquiry as to the actions of the human mind in the progress of civilization; illustrated by the history of a small community isolated and allowed to work itself free. This is not an attempt to break down the Puritans or to abuse the clergy, but to follow out the action of the human mind as we do of the human body. I believe they and we are subject to the same laws." While declaring his premise sound for the original, Adams added a 168-page preface to his 1919 revision, which many critics believe refutes the theories of his original manuscript.

In his next major work, *The Law of Civilization and Decay: An Essay on History* (1895), Adams examined the control of economic power and its effect on history, politics, culture, and religion. Adams posited that the cyclical nature of centralization and stagnation was governed by physical laws. Civilization, wrote Adams, followed a set pattern of stages: energy-gathering, which incorporated imagination, war and conquest; centralization and the accumulation of wealth; and usurpation of energy by capitalists. Once economic power is centralized in a civilization, greed becomes predominant, leading to stagnation in all elements of society. Adams supported his thesis using ancient Rome, Medieval Europe, and Imperial Britain as examples. When economic power became centralized in any of these areas, stagnation set in and this power moved elsewhere. While finding Adams's methodology unsystematic, critics received *The Law of Civilization and Decay* positively. The perception that Adams was disenfranchised from American capitalism and was predicting the eventual demise of the U.S. economy was reinforced by his subsequent efforts. *America's Economic Superiority* (1900), *The New Empire* (1902), and *The Theory of Social Revolutions* (1913) continued his theories into economic history. He also wrote the preface to brother Henry Adams's *The Degradation of the Democratic Dogma* (1920).

# PRINCIPAL WORKS

*The Emancipation of Massachusetts* (history) 1887
*The Law of Civilization and Decay: An Essay on History* (history) 1895
*America's Economic Superiority* (history) 1900
*The New Empire* (history) 1902
*The Theory of Social Revolutions* (history) 1913

# CRITICISM

## The Yale Review (review date 1896)

SOURCE: A review of *The Law of Civilization and Decay,* in *The Yale Review,* 1896, pp. 451-53.

[*In the following excerpt, the reviewer finds Adams's* The Law of Civilization and Decay *a flawed yet valuable work in determining historical patterns.*]

Reference was made in a notice of Kidd's *Social Evolution* in the third volume of this Review, to the probability that we should have many attempts in the next few years to construct a philosophy of history on the basis of our existing knowledge. The present attempt is by the historian of the ***Emancipation of Massachusetts.*** Any one who thinks it possible for the present age to produce a final philosophy of history, would derive much instruction by reading this book and Mr. Kidd's together.

The term "science" of history rather than "philosophy" must be applied to the attempt, if we speak strictly. It opens—to give the order of the author's thought rather than of his statement—with three fundamental assumptions. First, actions of every kind are manifestations of material energy, and are controlled by its laws. Second, human history, as one of the "outlets through which solar energy is dissipated," is governed by fixed laws. Third, among human actions, thoughts or "intellectual phenomena," are those which determine the course of history. Starting with these propositions assumed, the science of history is developed in this way. The first controlling intellectual conception is fear. This leads to religious, military, and artistic types of civilization, and, in richly endowed races, to an accumulation of energy in the form of capital. As this accumulation takes place, the race passes into the second stage, and greed succeeds fear as the determining idea. This leads to economic organization in which capital tends to become supreme, to the decay of the earlier types of civilization, to the waste of energy through competition, and, as this can no longer be reproduced under a capitalistic organization, to the disintegration of society, from which there can be no return except through an infusion of fresh barbarian blood, that is, through a renewal of the earlier types of civilization.

The author's treatment of Roman history may serve as an example. The Romans, when they first appear in history, are of a martial type just passing into an economic. As they had no adaptation either to commerce or to manufactures, but only to agriculture, greed with them took the form of usury. This produced a society divided into two classes, creditor and debtor. As society consolidated and centralized itself, the power of the former increased and the pressure upon the latter became heavier, until at last the reproduction of energy ceased, that is, less was produced than was dissipated. Then society, which reached its greatest centralization under the Caesars, disintegrated, the barbarian took possession of the world, and the middle ages began. In these a return took place to an imaginative and military type of civilization, similar to that from which the Romans had earlier emerged.

The doctrine is a thoroughgoing and ideally complete pessimism. We stand in our own age, upon the verge of another disintegration of society like that which befell Rome, from which the world can hope to emerge upon a new round of the same sort only by the infusion of barbarian blood from some source. But it does not appear from anything in the book that this fate can make the slightest difference to those whom it overtakes, or to the human race as a whole. The only movement for mankind is this ceaseless round, every stage of which is deplorably bad, and is constantly changing into another just as bad.

The fatal defect of the book is that it follows but a single thread through the course of history. It must be recognized, however, as a valuable contribution to the science of history. Especially noteworthy are the author's keenness of insight and freshness of interpretation. His power of combination is less evident, but the future worker in this field will have to reckon with Mr. Adams's reading of the economic movements of history.

In closing one cannot forbear to quote two passages, of which many might be selected throughout the book, to show its character as a "tract for the times." These are from the chapter on Rome:

> "It appears to be a natural law that when social development has reached a certain stage, and capital has accumulated sufficiently, the class which has had the capacity to absorb it shall try to enhance the value of their property by legislation. This is done most easily by reducing the quantity of the currency, which is a legal tender for the payment of debts. A currency obviously gains in power as it shrinks in volume, and the usurers of Constantinople intuitively condensed to the utmost that of the empire. After the insolvency under Elagabalus, payments were exacted by gold in weight, and as it grew scarcer its value rose when measured in commodities."

> "When wealth became force, the female might be as strong as the male; therefore she was emancipated. Through easy divorce she came to stand on an equality with the man in the marriage contract. She controlled her own property, because she could defend it; and as she had power, she exercised political privileges. . . . When force reached the stage where it expressed itself exclusively through money, the governing class ceased to be chosen because they were valiant or eloquent, artistic, learned, or devout, and were selected solely because they had the faculty of acquiring and keeping wealth."

### *Journal of Political Economy* (review date 1902)

SOURCE: A review of *The New Empire*, in *Journal of Political Economy*, 1902, pp. 314-17.

[*In the following excerpt, the reviewer unfavorably assesses Adams's* The New Empire.]

Pursuing a line of argument already worked out in his *Law of Civilization and Decay,* Mr. Adams offers an explanation, a theory it may be called, of the rise and decline of successive "empires" from the dawn of history to the present. The objective point of the argument is to account for the present, or imminent, supremacy of America as an imperial power. This supremacy has, in Mr. Adams's mind, all the certainty of an accomplished fact. While it takes the form of a political supremacy, its substantial ground is the commercial leadership of the new imperial organization; the reason for commercial leadership being, in its turn, the possession of superior material resources, particularly mineral resources, together with the convergence of trade routes upon the territory in which the seat of empire lies.

Mr. Adams's explanation of the growth of imperial power, in all ages, is altogether a geographical one. From the beginning trade routes have determined where accumulations of wealth would occur, and they have thereby determined where the greater masses of population would congregate and so where the seat of political power would be found. Whereas, trade routes have largely been determined by the *provenance* of the minerals most useful or most sought after at the time. Within historical times this means the metals—the precious metals primarily, and secondarily that one of the useful metals which has for the time chiefly served the industrial arts. Today it is steel and coal. In the early times, before navigation developed, the trade routes lay overland, chiefly between the east and the west of Asia; and where these overland routes converged the ancient cities and the ancient monarchies grew up—as Egypt, Babylonia, or Persia—and power shifted from the one to the other as the path of commerce shifted. Later, when great improvements in navigation had taken place, the sea routes gradually supplanted the land routes, and the question of empire became a question of the convergence of the routes of maritime commerce. Today these routes cross and blend within the domain of the United States, and radiate from this as a center, at the same time that this domain contains the largest, most valuable, and most available supply of the mineral wealth upon which the fortunes of commerce ultimately hang. Mr. Adams also finds that in some way, mysterious so far as his discussion goes, energy springs up where the trade routes cross, and slackens abruptly when the routes depart. So that now, for some half-a-dozen years past, America holds over all competitors in point of energetic and sagacious administration.

Cogent as Mr. Adams's presentation of the case is, it has an air of one sidedness, in that it neglects other than geographical factors; and even within the range of geographical factors it places the emphasis almost exclusively on the circumstances which condition commerce, as contrasted with other economic factors. It may be noted, for instance, that the element of race is left out; whereas it would not be a hopeless task to construct an equally plausible theory of the facts considered by Mr. Adams on grounds of race alone. It may also be noted that so striking a case as that of China does not come within the explanation offered. China has all the mineral resources on which Mr. Adams throws emphasis; her territory lies also at the meeting of the overland and the maritime routes of the East; the Chinese people have from time immemorial been highly skilled and diligent workmen; but, great as China has been, she has never taken the leadership except locally; the industrial revolution did not come through Chinese initiative; the development of navigation and the expansion of modern commerce are not due to Chinese enterprise and ingenuity, although the material circumstances have, on Mr.

Adams's theory, for some thousands of years apparently favored the rise of China to the position of an all-dominating world-power.

### The American Political Science Review (review date 1914)

SOURCE: A review of *The Theory of Social Revolutions*, in *The American Political Science Review*, Vol. VIII, No. 1, February, 1914, pp. 131-32.

[*In the following excerpt, the reviewer finds Adams's methodology in* The Theory of Social Revolutions *flawed but intellectually stimulating.*]

This work [*The Theory of Social Revolutions*] while filled with errors and hasty generalizations, possesses the quality of stimulating thought. Mr. Adams' primary contention is one against judicial authority in political matters. He contends that "no court can, because of the nature of its being, effectively check a popular majority acting through a coördinate legislative assembly. . . . The only result of an attempt and failure is to bring courts of justice into odium or contempt, and in any event to make them objects of attack by a dominant social force in order to use them as an instrument. . . . Hence in periods of change, when alone serious clashes between legislatures and courts are likely to occur, as the social equilibrium shifts the legislature almost certainly will reflect the rising, the court the sinking power" (pp. 76, 77).

Mr. Adams regards the courts as properly a group of passionless persons administering a body of abstract principles (pp. 76, 81), and insists that our system has made the courts largely bodies for the registration in law of the dominant economic and social interests of the community (pp. 89-131). "In fine," he says, "whenever pressure has reached a given intensity, on one pretext or another, courts have enforced or dispensed with constitutional limitations with quite as much facility as have legislatures, and for the same reasons." In this view the author is to a large extent right, as he is also in the position that courts must in the long run fail whenever they seek to interpose constitutional barriers against legislation approved by the better judgment of the community (p. 111).

The author assumes that "those who, at any given time, are the strongest in any civilization, will be those who are at once the ruling class, those who own most property, and those who have most influence on legislation" (p. 132). Capitalism, in his view, has been this dominant force in the community, and now as it is losing its power, seeks to entrench itself behind political courts. Mr. Adams thinks that such a policy may prove disadvantageous to capital, in that with a change of power, the political court will be employed as an instrument against capital itself. This contention he seeks to illustrate by a lengthy discussion of political tribunals during the French revolution.

Mr. Adams is probably correct in his contentions that our courts have too much political power and that such power will tend to be employed in the manner approved by the dominant sentiment of the community at any one time. But he seems to be clearly in error in regarding law as properly a body of abstract principles divorced from political principles and administered by a group of passionless persons. So long as society is developing, law also must develop, and in any system of government those who administer the law will be influenced by social changes and will themselves serve to some extent at least as instruments for the adaptation of law to those changes. A system of courts absolutely free from political and social influences would be equally as harmful as a system dominated by such influences.

### Stuart P. Sherman (essay date 1920)

SOURCE: "Evolution in the Adams Family," in *The Nation*, New York, Vol. CX, No. 2858, April 10, 1920, pp. 473-77.

[*In the following excerpt, Sherman examines the genealogy of political and historical thought among members of Adams's family.*]

Brooks Adams apologizes for the inadequacy of his introduction to his brother's philosophical remains on the ground that the publishers hurried him, saying that if he did not get the book out within the year it would have lost its interest. Of course the readers who take up *The Education of Henry Adams* because it is the sensation of the hour will soon drop away, perhaps have already done so; but interest in the Adamses, so long quiescent, so piquantly reawakened at the end of the fourth eminent generation, is likely to hold more serious readers for some time to come. Henry has thrown out challenges which the indolent reviewer cannot lightly answer nor easily ignore. What shall be done with that profoundly pessimistic theory of the "degradation of energy"—a degradation alleged to be discoverable in the universe, in democracy, and even in that incorruptible stronghold of pure virtue, the Adams family? Every one who has sat blithely down to read "The Education," much more to review it, must have discovered that it is only the last or the latest chapter of a "continued story." It is a lure leading into a vast literary edifice, built by successive generations, which one must at least casually explore before one can conceive what was the heritage of Henry Adams, or can guess whether the family's energy suffered degradation when it produced him.

One who wishes to measure the decline from the source must begin with *The Works of John Adams* in ten volumes, edited by his grandson Charles Francis Adams I, and including a diary so fascinating and so important that one marvels that American students of letters are not occasionally sent to it rather than to Pepys or Evelyn. One should follow this up with the charming letters of John's wife, Abigail, also edited by Charles Francis I in

1841—a classic which would be in the American Everyman if our publishers fostered American as carefully as they foster English traditions. For John Quincy Adams, we have his own "Memoirs" in twelve volumes, being portions of that famous diary of which he said: "There has perhaps not been another individual of the human race whose daily existence from early childhood to fourscore years has been noted down with his own hand so minutely as mine"; also a separate volume called *Life in a New England Town,* being his diary while a student in the office of Theophilus Parsons at Newburyport. One may perhaps pass Charles Francis I with his life by Charles Francis II. Then one descends to the fourth generation, and reads the *Autobiography* of Charles Francis II, published in 1916, a notable book with interest not at all dependent upon reflected story. Of Brooks Adams one must read at least **The Emancipation of Massachusetts** and the introduction to *The Degradation of Democratic Dogma;* and then one is tantalized on into **The Law of Civilization and Decay, America's Economic Supremacy,** and **The Theory of Social Revolutions.** Finally one approaches Henry's *Education* not quite unprepared and not overlooking the fact that, besides biographies of Gallatin and Randolph, he wrote what has been called "incomparably the best" history of the administrations of Jefferson and Madison in nine volumes distinguished by lucid impartiality, "Mont Saint Michel and Chartres," an interpretation of the twelfth century as impressive in height and span as the great cathedral which Adams takes as the symbol of his thought.

Historians, of course, are familiar with all these paths; I should like, however, to commend them a little to gentler and less learned readers. Taken not as material for history but as the story of four generations of great personalities, living always near the centre of American life, the Adams annals surpass anything we have produced in fiction. One may plunge into them as into the Comédie Humaine of Balzac or Zola's Rougon-Macquart series and happily lose contact with the world, which, if we may believe Brooks Adams, *ultimus Romanorum,* is going so fatally to the dogs. Perhaps an Adams of the present day must come forth from the study of his heredity, environment, and education with a conviction that he is an automaton, moved forward by the convergence of "lines of force," and that he is a poorer automaton than his grandfather. But for my part, I have emerged from these narratives much braced by contact with the stout, proud, purposeful Adams will, and with an impression that their latest pessimistic theories are poorly supported by their facts.

The Adams pessimism has a certain tonic quality due to its origin in the Adams sense for standards. The three Adonises, Charles Francis, Brooks, and Henry, have humiliated themselves all their lives by walking back and forth before the portraits of their statesman ancestors and measuring their altitude against that of the friends of Washington. An Adams should always be in the grand style. So history presents them to the young imagination:

Plutarchan heroes, august republicans, ever engaged in some public act or gesture such as Benjamin West liked to spread on his canvases—drafting the Declaration of Independence, presenting credentials to George III, signing the Monroe doctrine, fulminating against the annexation of Texas, or penning the famous dispatch to Lord Russell: "It would be superfluous to point out to your lordship that this is war."

For an Adams, who needs a bit of humility, it no doubt is wholesome to dwell on the superiority of his forefathers; but for the democrat, who needs a bit of encouragement, it is equally wholesome to reflect that John Adams represents a distinct "variation" of species. The family had been in America a hundred years before the grand style began to develop. In the words of Charles Francis I, "Three long successive generations and more than a century of time passed away, during which Gray's elegy in the country churchyard relates the whole substance of their history." If we can only understand the processes by which John was transformed from a small farmer's son to President of the United States, the evolution of the rest of the family will be as easy to follow as the transmission of wealth. Now, John's emergence is singularly devoid of miraculous aspects, and it is therefore of practical interest to the democrat.

John abandoned the pitchfork and varied his species by taking two steps which in those days were calculated to put him in the governing class. He went to Harvard—a course which may still be imitated, but which in 1755, when the total population of the colonies only equalled that of one of our great cities, set a man far more distinctly in a class by himself than it does today, and marked him for a professional career. Second, after an insignificant interval of school teaching, he studied law in the office of Rufus Putnam, and thus entered a still smaller class, carefully restricted by limitation of the number of apprentices that could be taken in any office. At the same time he began keeping a diary, a habit which it is now the custom to ridicule.

What strikes one about John's diary in his years of adolescence is that he uses it as an instrument for marking his intellectual progress and getting himself in hand, neither of which is a morbid activity. He notes that he is of an amorous temperament and that his thoughts are liable to be "called off from law by a girl, a pipe, a poem, a love-letter, a Spectator, a play, etc., etc." But *studia in mores abeunt;* and year after year he is digging away tenaciously and purposefully at studies which communicate a masculine vigor to the mind; and he is reading, with instant application to his own future, authors that are still capable of putting a flame of ambition in a young man's vitals.

The breadth and humanity of an old-fashioned program of reading for the bar may be suggested by one of his entries at the age of twenty-three:

> Labor to get distinct ideas of law, right, wrong, justice, equity; search for them in your own mind,

in Roman, Grecian, French, English treatises of natural, civil, common, statute law; aim at an exact knowledge of the nature, end, and means of government; compare the different forms of it with each other, and each of them with their effects on public and private happiness. Study Seneca, Cicero, and all other good moral writers; study Montesquieu, Bolingbroke, Vinnius, &c., and all other good civil writers.

He enjoins it upon himself to observe the arts of popularity in the tavern, town-meeting, the training field, and the meeting-house, though it must be added that none of his line mastered these arts. He frequents the courts, converses with successful men, records a public-spirited act of Franklin's, and surmises after an hour's talk at Mayor Gardener's that "the design of Christianity was not to make men good riddle-solvers or good mystery-mongers but good men, good magistrates." After a bit of dawdling, he tells himself that "twenty-five years of the animal life is a great proportion to be spent to so little purpose." He vows to read twelve hours a day. He cries to himself: "Let love and vanity be extinguished, and the great passions of ambition, patriotism, break out and burn. Let little objects be neglected and forgot, and great ones engross, arouse, and exalt my soul." Such temper issued from that diet of lion's marrow, that energetic digestion of law and classical literature!

The only miraculous aspect of the variation effected in this generation was that such a man as John Adams should have found such a wife as Abigail Smith, a woman descended from the religious aristocrats of New England, and her husband's equal in heart and mind. Her descendants of the present day would say that predetermined lines of force—theological and legal—converged here to strengthen the social position of John and to insure the production of John Quincy; but that is not the way most men think of their wooing. Abigail had no formal schooling; yet, as "female" education went in those days, it mattered little. She was obviously the "product" of that family culture and social discipline which, at their best, render formal schooling almost superfluous. She had the gaiety of good breeding, the effusion of quick emotions, and that fundamental firmness of character which is developed by a consciousness that one was born in the right class. From books, from table-talk, from the men and women who frequented her home, not least from her lover, she had derived the views of the classical mid-eighteenth century, with just a premonitory flush of romantic enthusiasm; she had become familiar with public affairs; she had acquired the tone and carriage, she had breathed in the great spirit, of such a woman as Cato would have a Roman wife and mother.

Emerson cherished the thought of writing an American Plutarch. In such a book we should have a picture of Abigail managing her husband's estate in Braintree while he is at the Congress in Philadelphia—through pestilence, siege, battles, and famine-prices not venturing to ask a word of his return, lest she perturb a mind occupied with public business. We should have her reply at a later period to one who asked whether she would have consented to her husband's going to France, had she known that he was to be absent so long:

> I recollected myself a moment, and then spoke the real dictates of my heart. "If I had known, sir, that Mr. Adams could have effected what he has done, I would not only have submitted to the absence I have endured, painful as it has been, but I would not have opposed it, even though three years should be added to the number (which Heaven avert). I find a pleasure in being able to sacrifice my selfish passions to the general good and in imitating the example which has taught me to consider myself and family but as the small dust of the scale when compared with the great community."

We should see her called from her farm to be the first American lady at the English Court. We should remark that she finds the best manners in England in the home of the Bishop of St. Asaph, old friend of her adored Franklin, where, by the way, she meets those dangerous English radicals Priestley and Price. And with the warmth of fond native prejudice, we should adore her for writing home:

> Do you know that European birds have not half the melody of ours? Nor is their fruit half so sweet, nor their flowers half so fragrant, nor their manners half so pure, nor their people half so virtuous; *but keep this to yourself, or I shall be thought more than half deficient in understanding and taste.*

In the jargon of Brooks and Henry, as I have remarked, irresistible "lines of force" converge for the education of the second generation. More humanly speaking, the ambition of John, the tenderness and pride of Abigail, unite above the cradle of John Quincy, and most intelligently conspire to give him what he later was to recognize as "an unparalleled education." "It should be your care and mine," John writes to his wife, "to elevate the minds of our children, and exalt their courage, to accelerate and animate their industry and activity." It is the fashion nowadays to assert, against the evidence of history, that great men in their critical hours are unconscious of their greatness; but these Adamses assuredly knew what they were about. With the fullest recognition that her boy's father and his friends are living classics, she writes:

> Glory, my son, in a country which has given birth to characters, both in the civil and military departments, which may vie with the wisdom and valor of antiquity. As an immediate descendant of one of these characters, may you be led to that disinterested patriotism and that noble love of country which will teach you to despise wealth, pomp, and equipage as mere external advantages, which cannot add to the internal excellence of your mind, or compensate for the want of integrity and virtue.

Of course John Quincy was to use the "external advantages" which his mother a little hastily urged him to despise. By working twelve hours a day at the law, John Adams had raised the family from the ground up to a point at which he could give to the educational processes of his son a tremendous expansion and acceleration. At an age when John had been helping his father on the farm, from eleven to fourteen, John Quincy, son of the peace commissioner, was studying in Paris or Leyden, or travelling in Russia as private secretary to the American Envoy. He acquired history, diplomacy, geography as he acquired his French—by what we call in the case of the last, "the natural method." It cannot be too much emphasized that from the second, third, and fourth generations the family and its connections were in positions to provide a liberal education without resort to a university. Before John Quincy went to Harvard he had assisted in negotiating the treaty of peace between his country and Great Britain. The whole matter of external advantages may be summed up in a picture of the boy at the age of eleven returning from France in a ship with the French ambassador the Chevalier de la Luzerne, and his secretary M. Marbois, the three lying side by side on their cots and thus portrayed by the boy's proud father:

> The Ambassador reading out loud, in Blackstone's Discourse at his entrance on his Professorship of the Common Law at the University, and my son correcting the pronunciation of every word and syllable and letter. The Ambassador said he was astonished at my son's knowledge; that he was a master of his own tongue, like a professor. M. Marbois said, Your son teaches us more than you; he has *point de grâces, point d'éloges.*

Charles Francis II, who knew his grandfather only in his old age, says that he was not of a "holiday temperament"; but the diary of his life in Newburyport shows a fairly festive young Puritan, tempted like his father before him to frequent truancies from the law, reading *Tom Jones* and Rousseau's *Confessions,* shooting, playing the flute, visiting, frequently dancing till three, occasionally drinking till dawn, and regretting it for three days afterward. His social position was secure, his experience and attainments already notable, his career marked out, the reflected glamour of paternal glory gratifying; perhaps he asked himself why he should not rest on his oars while his contemporaries were catching up. Such considerations may occur to an Adams, but they do not remain with him. His ambition widens with his culture. He begins on the verge of manhood to pant for distinction, bids farewell to the revellers, girds up his loins, and strikes into his pace.

John Quincy had found his stride when he wrote to his father from London, December 29, 1795:

> When I am clearly convinced that my duty commands me to act, if the love of ease, or the love of life, or the love of fame itself, dear as it is, could arrest my hand, or give me a moment's hesitation in the choice, I should certainly be fit for no situation of public trust whatever. . . . So much for the principle. But I may go a little further. The struggle against a popular clamor is not without its charms in my mind.

In the next year, following the example of John Wesley, he began rising at four o'clock; and so eager was his mind, so tireless his industry, so completely had he taken himself in hand that he rose not later than four-thirty for the next fifty years—fifty years spent almost without interruption in public service, fighting the Jacksonian democrats, fighting for internal improvements, fighting the extension of slavery, fighting for free speech till he sank in harness in his eighty-first year on the floor of the House of Representatives.

His training in law and diplomacy had fitted him for statesmanship, and as a statesman chiefly he lives. But Brooks Adams makes much of his philosophical temper and his talent for scientific investigation. For our purposes it is important also to note that he had a marked taste for literature, as the vast memoirs bear witness. In his old age he spoke of the "ecstasy of delight" with which he had heard a choir singing his version of the 65th Psalm as surpassing all the pleasure he had received in the whole course of his life from the praise of mortal men. His literary and his political aspirations were intimately associated. He had hoped that his diary would rank next to the Holy Scriptures as the record of one who "by the irresistible power of genius and the irrepressible energy of will and the favor of Almighty God" had "banished war and slavery from the face of the earth forever."

Charles Francis I, perhaps not the most ambitious of John Quincy's children, was the only one that survived him; he must therefore be our representative of the third generation. We may, however, pass lightly over him, because though an eminent, sturdy, and capable man he repeats in general the formative processes and the careers of his predecessors without any singular distinction or deviation from type. His richness of educational opportunity may be summarized by saying that he learned French at St. Petersburg, where his father was minister, spent several years at a school in England, passed through the Boston Latin School and Harvard, and studied law and observed public men from the White House in the administration of his father and in the palmy days of Jackson, Clay, and Webster. Possibly if the father had retired after his defeat for reëlection in 1828, Charles Francis might have felt more distinctly called to advance the Adams banner; but the almost immediate return of the ex-president, plunging into his long Congressional career, preëmpted the field. Charles went to Boston, engaged in business, served for several years in the legislature, was elected to Congress in 1859, and crowned his achievements in the period of the Civil War by staunchly and successfully representing the Union in his ministry to Great Britain.

Coming now to the representatives of the fourth generation who made their careers after the war, we confront once more the three Adonises who more or less darkly despair of the Republic and of the future of the Adams line; Henry, Brooks, and Charles Francis II. All three were bred in the traditions of the great family, inherited its culture and social advantages, became conscious of an obligation to distinguish themselves, strove to keep pace with the new nation which the war had created, and all three, rendering an account of their adventures, intimate a degree of failure and rail at their education as inadequately adapting them to their circumstances. As a matter of fact they fell short of the glory of their ancestors in that no one of them held public office of first-rate national importance. But on the other hand none of them really competed with his illustrious predecessors. Each of them developed marked variations from the ante-bellum type, in one case so marked as to constitute a new species. If the ancestral energy is degraded, it is none the less abundantly present in them all.

Charles Francis II, the least highly individualized of the trio, was the one who most conspicuously fell into the stride of the new industrial, expansive America. At his graduation from Harvard in 1856 he had discovered no remarkable aptitude—for which he blames his teachers—and so gravitated into a law office. At the outbreak of the war it slowly occurred to him to enlist; but once in, he enjoyed the hard athletic life, and developed a drillmaster's pride in his company and in his regiment, at the head of which he rode into burning Richmond. His military duties disclosed to him his talent for organization, and also the disquieting fact that famous fighters and great organizers were frequently beneath his standard for gentlemen; Grant, for example, "was a man of coarse fibre, and did not impress with a sense of character." But the war had toughened his own fibre; and when it was over he turned to the study of railroads as the biggest enterprise of the new era, wrote his "Chapters of Erie," became a member of the Massachusetts Board of Railroad Commissioners, which was created largely through his instrumentality, and crowned his professional career with the presidency of the Union Pacific. He was perhaps the first Adams who looked West with any special interest. His flash of genius was divining the future importance of Kansas City. The business success on which he plumes himself is his organization of the Kansas City Stock Yards Company, which, under his forty-year headship, increased its capitalization from $100,000 to over ten millions, and earned annually above $1,200,000. He does not blush to declare that he also organized in Kansas City another enterprise which made in one year "twelve dividends of ten per cent each." The big business men, however, like the big generals, disappointed him socially: "Not one that I have ever known would I care to meet again, either in this world or the next." Having made, as the vulgar say, his "pile," this well-bred, energetic Massachusetts business man withdrew from the ungentlemanly world of business, moved from Quincy, the home of his ancestors, to Lincoln, because the former residence had become too "suburban"; and devoted his leisure to writing his memoirs, criticizing Harvard, and composing communications to the Massachusetts Historical Society. At the age of fifty-five he burned his diary, full till then with the expectation that he might accomplish something notable; and in his Autobiography, with the tang of the new Adams humility, he declares: "I now humbly thank fortune that I have almost got through life without making a conspicuous ass of myself."

Brooks Adams also set out as a lawyer, but he seems to have retired much earlier into authorship. His writing is less perspicuous and well-ordered than that of his brother Charles; but that is partly because he has more ideas and more difficult ones. Brooks is a restless-minded lawyer of a not unfamiliar type, who turns here and there for something "craggy" upon which to wreak his excess of mental energy; and so he becomes amateur-historian, amateur-economist, amateur-philosopher. The antiquarianism of historical societies is a bit too tame for his temper. Like his brother Henry, and indeed in collaboration with him, he seeks a law connecting phenomena, and in search of it ransacks history. He imagines and declares that he has made his mind passive to the lessons of facts and that his results are scientific; but the truth is that he is a dogmatic materialist, an infatuated mechanist, who, when he has formulated an hypothesis, sees nothing between earth and heaven and the first Adam and the last Adams but the proof of it.

Like his grandfather he finds a certain charm in an unpopular position. Sitting in the neighborhood of Plymouth Rock, he discovers that the scutcheon of his Puritan fore-fathers blushes with the blood of Quakers and Anabaptists; and in his *Emancipation of Massachusetts,* Puritan as he is, he remorselessly prosecutes them as selfish and blood-thirsty hypocrites. Looking further into history, he concludes that the same indictment can be brought against all religious societies and organizations from the time of Moses down; for the facts constrain him to believe that the two master passions of man are Fear and Greed. If he refrains from censure, it is because he holds that mental as well as physical phenomena are determined as fatally as the earth moves round the sun. The examination of long periods of history impresses him with "the exceedingly small part played by conscious thought in moulding the fates of men." He applies the doctrine of manifest destiny in the most fatalistic sense to the Philippine Islands and to capitalistic society, which, however, seems to him on the point of disintegration into a condition from which it can only be revivified by an "infusion of barbarian blood."

Brooks attributes many of his views to Henry and undertakes to interpret him; but temperamentally he is not qualified to understand him. He admits indeed that there were crypts in his brother which he had never entered. Chief of these was the unfathomable crypt of his skepticism. By contact with Mill, Comte, Darwin, Spencer, all the Adamses of the fourth generation had been emancipated from their attenuated hereditary belief in a beneficent over-ruling Providence. But Charles Francis II and Brooks recommitted themselves without reservation to the overweening positivism of mid-century "scientific" philosophy. Henry alone refuses to surrender. A wily, experienced wrestler, returning again and again to grapple with the Time-Spirit, at the end of each bout he eludes the adversary; and at the moment one expects to see him thrown, suddenly he has vanished, he has fled through centuries falling about him like autumn leaves, and from somewhere in the Middle Ages, near some old shrine of the Virgin, one hears the sound of mocking laughter. It is the free spirit, eternally seeking.

Henry was, I think, a great man and the only great Adams of his generation. All the other Adamses had been men of action tinctured with letters. Henry alone definitely renounced action and turned the full current of the ancestral energy to letters. By so doing he established a new standard of achievement for the Adams line; and in consequence, of course, for the rest of us. Up to the time of the Civil War there had been for them but one field of glory, the political arena, and one standard of achievement, national administration. After the war Charles Francis II tried to be great in "big business," but in the Adams sense "failed" because his culture was of no use there. Brooks tried for greatness in naturalistic philosophy, but found that his creed ignobly reduced all heroes to automata. But Henry, without otherwise committing himself, sought to comprehend and to represent his world, and he achieved greatness. Like yet unlike his ancestors who were painted by Copley and Stuart, he is in the grand style.

"The Education of Henry Adams" marks with precision the hour when its author became conscious of his variation. It was in England, towards the close of the war, where as secretary to his father he had exhausted all the excitements of the diplomatic "game," and London society had begun to pall, and loitering in Italy had ceased to charm, yet he was collecting bric-à-brac and sketches by the old masters and becoming attached to his habits and his hansom cabs, and was in a fair way to become one of those dilettantish, blasé young Americans of the period whom Henry James has preserved like pressed flowers for posterity. It was after Sir Charles Lyell and the evolutionists had set him off on a new quest for a "father"— it mattered not, he said, "whether the father breathed through lungs, or walked on fins, or on feet." It was in that summer hour, characteristically marked by him with its picturesque accessories, when he had wandered to Wenlock Edge in Shropshire, and, throwing himself on the grass where he could look across the Marches to the mountains of Wales, thus meditated on the new theory:

> Natural selection seemed a dogma to be put in the place of the Athanasian creed; it was a form of religious hope; a promise of ultimate perfection. Adams wished no better; he warmly sympathized in the object; but when he came to ask himself what he truly thought, he felt that he had no Faith; that whenever the next new hobby should be brought out, he should surely drop off Darwinism like a monkey from a perch; that the idea of one Form, Law, Order, or Sequence had no more value for him than the idea of none; that what he valued most was Motion, and that what attracted his mind was Change. . . . Henry Adams was the first in an infinite series to discover and admit to himself that he really did not care whether truth was, or was not, true. He did not even care that it should be proved true, unless the process were new and amusing. He was a Darwinian for fun.

From that moment, literature was the one career for Henry, and all his overtures were failures till he discovered it. He returned to America, indeed, with the Emersonian resolution that "the current of his time was to be his current, lead where it might." He went to Washington, as a member of the governing class should do, and while waiting for an opportunity to serve the incoming administration of Grant, offered himself on long argumentative walks as the anvil for Sumner's hammer. The announcement of Grant's cabinet, however, as he explains the matter, closed for him the door of political opportunity. A revolution had taken place which had made him appear "an estray of the fifties, a belated reveller, a scholar-gipsy." Coal, iron, and steam had supplanted agriculture, hand-work, and learning. "His world was dead. Not a Polish Jew fresh from Warsaw or Cracow—not a furtive Yacoob or Ysaac—but had a keener instinct, an intenser energy and a freer hand than he—American of Americans, with Heaven knew how many Puritans and Patriots behind him, and an education that had cost a civil war." And so Henry drifted into his antiquarian professorship at Harvard, cut loose from that and wrote his great history of Jefferson and Madison, and only returned to Washington to watch the spectacle, and to sit in his windows with John Hay, laughing at Presidents, and mocking the runner's heat.

Where was the bold energy of the first and second Adams that broke down barred doors of opportunity and found a "charm" in contending against a powerful opposition? Transmuted by the accumulated culture of the Adams family education, not wasted. The mockery and the pervasive irony, so seductive in the "Autobiography," spring from no sense of essentially depleted energy in the author; on the contrary they have their origin in a really exuberant sense of spiritual superiority. Adams after Adams has seen himself outshone, in the popular estimate, by vulgar "democratical" men, by rising men of the "people," whom he has half or wholly despised—by Franklin, by Paine, by Jefferson, by Jackson, by Lincoln, by Grant. But when John Quincy was defeated by Jackson, though he thought God had abandoned America, he felt himself still high priest. And though Henry thought the progress of evolution from Washington to Grant sufficient to upset Darwin, and though he regarded Grant as a man who should have lived in a cave and worn skins, he reinstated Darwin in the next breath; for he would not have changed places with Washington; he regarded Washington himself as but a cave man in comparison with Henry Adams! In revulsion from a world bent on making twelve dividends of ten per cent in a year and spending them for it knew not what, the Adams energy in him had been diverted to the production of a human measure of civilization; to a register of the value of art and social life and manners and those other by-products of coal and iron which the Philistines of every age rate as superfluous things; to a search finally, to an inquiry all the way from Kelvin to the Virgin of Chartres, for some principle of Unity, for some overarching splendor to illumine the gray twilight of an industrial democracy. He did not find it, but the quest was glorious.

Henry Adams was an egotist. Granted. But what an egotist! Not since Byron

> bore
> With haughty scorn which mock'd the smart
> Through Europe to the Ætolian shore
> The pageant of his bleeding heart—

not since the days of "Childe Harold" have we had so superb an egotist in literature, so splendidly in revolt, so masterly in self-portraiture, so romantically posed among the lights and shadows of history, against the ruins of time. Let us forget and forgive the unfeeling cynic who inquired "If a Congressman is a hog, what is a Senator?" Let us remember the poet who felt the "overpowering beauty and sweetness of the Maryland autumn" and the "intermixture of delicate grace and passionate depravity that marked the Maryland May." Let us fix our gaze on the Pilgrim receiving the news of the blowing up of the Maine as he watches the sun set across the Nile at Assouan:

One leant on a fragment of column in the great hall at Karnak and watched a jackal creep down the débris of ruin. The jackal's ancestors had surely crept up the same wall when it was building. What was his view about the value of silence? One lay in the sands and watched the expression of the Sphinx. Brooks Adams had taught him that the relation between civilizations was that of trade. Henry wandered, or was storm-driven, down the coast. He tried to trace out the ancient harbor of Ephesus. He went over to Athens, picked up Rockhill, and searched for the harbor of Tiryns; together they went on to Constantinople and studied the great walls of Constantine and the greater domes of Justinian. *His hobby had turned into a camel, and he hoped, if he rode long enough in silence, that at last he might come on a city of thought along the great highways of exchange.*

**Worthington C. Ford (essay date 1927)**

SOURCE: "Brooks Adams," in *The Harvard Graduates' Magazine,* Vol. 35, No. 140, June, 1927, pp. 615-27.

[*In the following excerpt, Ford surveys Adams's major works.*]

Brooks Adams, born at Quincy, Massachusetts, June 24, 1848, died at Boston, February 13, 1927. He was the youngest son of Charles Francis Adams and Abigail Brooks, daughter of Peter Chardon Brooks. After some years in English schools, his father being the American Minister to the Court of St. James's, he was prepared for Harvard College by Professor Ephraim Whitman Gurney, later to be professor of history in the University. Graduating in 1870, he passed one year in the Harvard Law School, but was taken by his father to Geneva to serve as his Secretary during the Alabama Claims Arbitration. In 1873 he was admitted to the Suffolk bar. It was characteristic of him to take an office in a building other than

that where his father and brothers were, and to remain alone, forming no law partnerships, except for a single year, when he was associated with William S. Macfarlane, who removed to New York. In 1883, after having practically retired from active practice, he joined his brothers in the Adams Building, 23 Court Street, and later followed them to the India Building, 84 State Street, Boston.

What turned him to historical writing can only be conjectured. In 1885 he wrote to Charles Deane: "I am for my sins, trying to write something about this State [Massachusetts]. There are, of course, to a man so ignorant of church history, in particular, as I, a number of points I should much like to get cleared up, on which I can't find much light in the books." A more probable cause than that which he assigned was an inherited interest in history and the example of his brothers. Charles Francis Adams had printed in an edition of half a dozen copies his *Episodes of New England History,* afterwards developed into "Three Episodes of Massachusetts History," and had recently completed his well edited edition of Morton's *New English Canaan.* Henry had already shown his bent by his four volumes of the "Life" and "Writings of Albert Gallatin," the first contribution in his notable historical series. With leisure on his hands and with such examples before him it was only natural for Brooks to enter the same field. His first book attracted more general attention than he could have anticipated, but awakened no greater hostility than he could have hoped for. It struck a somewhat new note in Massachusetts historical writing.

The merit of the ***Emancipation of Massachusetts*** lies in its vigorous denunciation of certain phases of colonial history and its promise of a new weighing of authorities. It cannot be said that the chapters hang together, for each is rather a separate essay. Nor can it be admitted that the writer discovered hitherto unknown facts, or developed a vitally novel interpretation of known facts. The reader is left in doubt what was the "emancipation" and how or by whom emancipation, if any, was accomplished. The defects of presentation did not in any degree make the work less readable or timely. The overpraise of the Puritan, the unbroken laudation of the early New Englanders, had reached an absurd degree and an attack, resting upon a good use of recognized authorities, came as a welcome relief. The smug self-satisfaction that pervaded the historical writing of the day received a shock which obliged a reconsideration of a blind worship of certain idols and a clinging to carefully nursed prejudices. That the blow came from an Adams made it the more telling, for the Adams tribe were all rebels on proper occasions. From that day the filiopietistic school of history was laughed out of court. Too much credit cannot be given to the native writer who attacked that preposterous structure. It crumbled at the first blow.

A critic suggested that the book showed that Adams had in him the making of a novelist, and instanced the opposite case of Motley, who began as a novelist and ended as a historian. The suggestion was not unkind, for imagination is as useful in good history as in a good novel. Adams's imagination enabled him to conceive a theory of historical interpretation; its limitations prevented a full fruition in application. A single idea colored all the chapters and became somewhat monotonous. The same fault affected his *Law of Civilization and Decay,* published in 1896, put forth as a product of the *Emancipation.* From the religious experience of New England he went back to the Reformation, and thence through the school-men and crusades. "I thus became convinced that religious enthusiasm, which, by stimulating the pilgrimage, restored communication between the Bosphorus and the Rhine, was the power which produced the accelerated movement culminating in modern civilization."[1] Commerce was antagonistic to the imagination, and the medium by which commerce expressed itself he found in its coinage or money. Convinced that conscious thought played an exceedingly small part in moulding the fate of men, he believed that as the external world changed only those survived whose nervous system—he used also the word mind—was adapted to the conditions to which they were born. Finally, he perceived that "the intellectual phenomena under examination fell into a series which seemed to correspond, somewhat closely, with the laws which are supposed to regulate the movements of the material universe." History then must be governed by law. As the law of force and energy is of universal application in nature, animal life being one of the outlets through which solar energy is dissipated, human societies differ among themselves in proportion as they are endowed by nature with energy. He coined terms which recur again and again throughout the book—the velocity of social movement in any community is proportionate to its energy and mass; its centralization is proportionate to its velocity; "therefore, as human movement is accelerated, societies centralize." His conclusion preached downright fatalism:

> In proportion as movement accelerates societies consolidate, and as societies consolidate they pass through a profound intellectual change. Energy ceases to find vent through the imagination, and takes the form of capital; hence as civilizations advance, the imaginative temperament tends to disappear, while the economic instinct is fostered, and thus substantially new varieties of men come to possess the world.

> Nothing so portentous overhangs humanity as this mysterious and relentless acceleration of movement, which changes methods of competition and alters paths of trade; for by it countless millions of men and women are foredoomed to happiness or misery, as certainly as the beasts and trees, which have flourished in the wilderness, and are destined to vanish when the soil is subdued by man.[2]

In spite of this dominant note the study of the rise and fall of trade, the routes it followed and the media of exchange, is valuable and brilliantly written. Rarely has an economic treatise been set forth in so attractive yet irritating a form.

It is worthy of record that the book was reviewed in *The Forum* by Theodore Roosevelt, who characteristically expressed the warmest admiration with emphatic dissent from parts of the thesis. Somewhat to his amusement Roosevelt was attacked for "having dealt too gently with Brooks," the seasoned Charles A. Dana being one of the objectors. In a letter to Senator Lodge, Roosevelt expresses himself, as was his wont, freely: "Brooks Adams's theories are beautiful, but in practice they mean a simple dishonesty, and a dishonest nation does not stand much higher than a dishonest man."[3] The method of the *Emancipation* had been extended to the wider field of world history. The constantly repeated phrases seemed to force the acceptance of his theme as a well-established historical law—almost axiomatic. Although the book reached a second issue, it never had the influence it deserved and for a peculiar reason, not necessarily inherent. It appeared when the acrimonious contest on monetary standards divided the country and those who favored silver found in it a support to their contention that a period of contraction of the currency was a period of suffering, and that the bankers, having the power to enforce contraction, used that power tyrannically. The "mighty engine of a single standard" favored the bankers. That application of his studies raised a prejudice against the book, an unexpected political intervention. To attribute the study and much of the form it took to his brother Henry would not be far out of the way, for Henry believed in silver and in an even more general and radical dissipation of energy than Brooks had suggested. Writing of the "panic" of 1893 Henry said:

> For the first time in several years he saw much of his brother Brooks in Quincy, and was surprised to find him absorbed in the same perplexities. Brooks was then a man of forty-five years old; a strong writer and a vigorous thinker who irritated too many Boston conventions ever to suit the atmosphere; but the two brothers could talk to each other without atmosphere and were used to audiences of one. Brooks had discovered or developed a law of history that civilization followed the exchanges, and having worked it out for the Mediterranean was working it out for the Atlantic. Everything American, as well as most things European and Asiatic became unstable by this law, seeking new equilibrium and compelled to find it. Loving paradox, Brooks, with the advantages of ten years' study, had swept away much rubbish in the effort to build up a new line of thought for himself, but he found that no paradox compared with that of daily events. The facts were constantly outrunning his thoughts. The instability was greater than he calculated; the speed of acceleration passed bounds. Among other general rules he laid down the paradox that, in the social disequilibrium between capital and labor, the logical outcome was not collectivism, but anarchism; and Henry made note of it for study.[4]

The note of social hopelessness ruled Brooks from that time. It was the year after the issue of the *Law of Civilization and Decay* that I first met Mr. Adams—a legacy of his brother Henry, when Brooks occupied for one winter the house on H Street, at this moment being torn down to make room for a modern office building. I was in charge of the national commercial statistics and had come to know Henry intimately, through a common interest in the balance-of-trade conundrum—insoluble except by way of generals, not by actual statistics. Brooks's problem involved wider considerations. He was already preaching the unholy domination of the bankers and the assured, any, imminent downfall of Europe—a universal cataclysm which economically foreshadowed a day of judgment. His first note to me, dated May 14, 1897, contained the sentences: "I am full of gloomy fears. I do not know where we are going, nor do I see any light ahead. There seems to me to be no headway on the ship and that we are going on the rocks. I hope I may be wrong." If that hope ever took shape he never confessed to entertaining it. His earnestness, his wide reading, his unusual interpretation of usual data, and his unshakable certainty, were extremely interesting to a mere statistician, whose occupation was to gather unlimited tables of figures for others to misinterpret. From that time I saw much of him, read letters from many parts of the world to his brother Henry, and myself corresponded freely with him, and the drift of his endeavor tended in one direction—to warn of the end of the economic world. His best writings treated of that subject and the deepening shadows of his convictions placed him in the van of pessimists.

In 1900 he published ***America's Economic Supremacy,*** a special study of the last three years of the decade but east in the mold of the ***Law of Civilization and Decay.*** The international center of empire and wealth was moving from England westward and the instinctive effort of humanity to adjust itself to the new conditions had caused the unrest that prevailed in Europe and in Asia. Even should the seat of wealth and power rest for a time in America the industrial development of Asia might prove the stronger and in the end become the more important factor. American social and political institutions, he thought, were ill-adapted to meet such a contest or responsibility successfully. Much of his speculation, rather loosely supported by figures, has been disproved by events; the essay on **"Natural Selection in Literature,"** being a comparison between Scott and Dickens based upon a social change, is extremely suggestive as a critical excursion and may be remembered. "What divided Dickens from the men of letters who had preceded him was the gulf which divided Cobden from Chatham. Dickens was the child, the creation, of the 'Industrial Revolution.'"[5]

Not satisfied with what he had written on trade routes and their influence on civilization, and having gone more deeply into the subject by consulting European libraries, he published in 1902 ***The New Empire.*** It was not so much an expansion of his theory, for he had already covered in outline the world on the subject, as a closer presentation of a phase. The note struck in the preface gave his idea of his undertaking: "All my observations lead me to the conclusion that geographical conditions have exercised a great, possibly a preponderating, influence over man's destiny. I am convinced that neither history nor economics can be intelligently studied without a constant reference to the geographical surroundings which have affected different nations." The influence of environment, geographical or other, was no novelty, however imperfectly the governing principles had been defined. But when Adams baldly stated that in the decade before 1900 "the seat of energy has migrated from Europe to America" and insisted upon "American supremacy," he went beyond what the facts justified. He himself qualified his own statements. If American corporations, thanks to applied science, had shown unequaled economy and energy in administration, the national government showed signs of decrepitude. All administrative systems tend to become rigid, "more especially political systems, because they are most cumbersome." On the other hand, nature is in eternal movement; unless the government adapts itself to change catastrophe follows. The British nation suffered through intellectual rigidity. If America should become the "new empire," it must be an enormous complex mass, "to be administered only by means of a cheap, elastic, and simple machinery; an old and clumsy mechanism must, sooner or later, collapse, and in sinking may involve a civilization."[6] To reach that conclusion the history of the known world had been related and the reader, rather disturbed by his breathless career through the ages, is not quite convinced that the remedy, suggested rather than imposed, will answer to the undeniably able exposition of the past.

Continuing his studies Adams published in 1913 his ***Theory of Social Revolutions.*** The idea pervading the book may be thus briefly sketched. Civilization is nearly synonymous with centralization; but social consolidation (he changes the word) implies an equivalent capacity for administration. Revolutions have for the most part supervened on administrative difficulties. A new mind, formed or aided by triumphant science, rises through social revolution and a redistribution of property. The capitalistic class, in control, showed an absence of success in government, believed it could purchase all it wanted—courts, legislatures and elections—and was precipitating a conflict, instead of establishing an adjustment. It was a lawless class, unequal in mind to cope with the extremely complex administration of modern industrial civilization. Without a great change the capitalist will decline and capital become fugitive.[7]

There was another feature to his activities which, had it been cultivated, held promise of more permanent results—his studies in legal history. His active law practice ceased after 1881 and was never renewed until he became a lecturer in the Boston University School of Law in 1904, a position he held for seven years. His colleague, in a sense his master, was Melville M. Bigelow, of whom he said: "More learned lawyers doubtless have lived than was Mr. Bigelow. I do not dispute the fact. But if so I have never met them."[8] In that surrounding he might have formed a permanent place, for it was both congenial and centered his reading. Lecturing stimulated him and his students, to such a degree that a trustee of the University regarded him as dangerous and secured his dismissal. That he held the attention of his hearers goes without saying; he enjoyed the contact as much as they. He embodied fragments of his lectures in two chapters of *Centralization and the Law* on "The Nature of Law—Methods and Aims of legal education" and "Law under Inequality; Monopoly." A brief essay on **"Unity of Law"** he contributed to the *Bulletin* of the Boston University School of Law. More important, and better examples of his manner of weaving his social and historical studies into a presentation of a legal argument, were two printed papers.

In 1910 he printed his brief in the case of the City of Spokane *vs.* Northern Pacific Railway under the title *Railways as Public Agents: A Study in Sovereignty,* the contention being that "uncontrolled methods of monopolistic administration of railways, which have hitherto been tolerated in the United States, are incompatible with the continuance of constitutional government." There is also in print a brief of unknown date on the French Spoliation Claims, which contains much historical reference and should be read in connection with his more careful presentation of the historical facts in *The Convention of 1800 with France.*[9] As a member of the Massachusetts Constitutional Convention of 1917 he made an address in favor of the Initiative and Referendum, and he spoke rather as a student of past history than as a lawyer, and the connection with the Initiative was of the slightest. It became in the end a reassertion of the need of collective administration. Mr. Albert E. Pillsbury writes of that incident: "He talked political philosophy to the members, who listened respectfully, but most of them with the amused curiosity of a child at the appearance of a new and strange animal. His voice and vote were given for the Initiative and Referendum, which seemed inconsistent with his lack of faith in democracy, but he privately defended his position on the ground that the measure would furnish a safety-valve against the oppressions of capital."[10] This naturally leads to the position he held in matters of government.

Democracy has come to have many meanings and, like most political terms of frequent use, has no accepted definition. American democracy, in origin, development and present status, challenges controversy whenever used to buttress a cause or disprove an opposing argument. The subject occupied much of Adams's speculation in his later years. However absorbed in studying world conditions the great experiment of a government by the people in America offered what might almost be termed an inherited problem. John and John Quincy Adams could be eloquent on the efforts they had made to direct a republic and the trials to which they had been subjected at the hands of a democracy, and the second half of the nineteenth century had greatly complicated its operations. Brooks had already shown at full length the rule of the money power, tracing its history from the eleventh century; he watched the progress of the mad war and the apparent justification of his worst fears on the social instability of Europe; and he brooded in doubt of the ability of the American people to hold their own in the face of

such a visitation and its probable permanent results. In an address, June 17, 1916, he made the statement that to him "it seems far from improbable that we shall find to our sorrow, when the present conflict has closed, our fortunes to have been more deeply concerned in the readjustment impending than were the fortunes of many of the nations already fighting." Using the rise of trade paths and facilities as a measure he showed how little coherence in political thought could be found in our history, how state and section had maintained conflicting interests and opinions which even the establishing of unquestioned nationality by the Civil War could not harmonize. To him the conclusion was inevitable: that the largest and richest nation of the world had lost in its collective energy in thought and action. He had occasion in the same year to speak on **"The Revolt of Modern Democracy against Standards of Duty"** before the American Academy of Arts and Letters. He assumed that no national civilization can cohere against those enemies which must certainly beset it, if it fail to recognize as its primary standard of duty the obligation of the individual man and woman to sacrifice themselves for the whole community in time of need. He then pointed out how far the Americans had gone in opposing what they believed to be the "tyranny of self-sacrifice." Reverting to his earlier train of ideas he again expressed his belief that "we Americans are nearly incapable of continuous collective thought except at long intervals under the severest tension." The particular, the selfish interest, dominated the collective interest. "Democratic ideal" was only a phrase to express our renunciation as a nation to all standards of duty, and the substitution therefor of a reference to private judgment.

So unfavorable an opinion of the rule of the people could easily be discounted by objecting to its source and its expression. Yet inheritance and provocative language the rather insisted upon the fundamental truth of the indictment. What replies were made drifted into that wordy laudation of democracy which has been such an obstacle to clear thinking and statistics of progress reached nowhere in the face of a wrecked Europe and the notorious trend towards selfishness in America. What may be regarded as Brooks Adams's final word on the subject took the form of an introduction to Henry Adams's *Letter to American Teachers of History,* reprinted in 1920 with the title **"The Degradation of the Democratic Dogma."** He abated in no respect his dark explanations of the past and gloomier foreboding for the future, but he supported them by the lives and opinions of his grandfather, John Quincy Adams, and of his brother Henry. The degradation of energy applied to the intellect as well as to nature, and Democracy, an infinite mass of conflicting minds and of conflicting interests, "loses in collective intellectual energy in proportion to the perfection of its expansion. . . . I hope I have set forth his [Henry's] doctrines of modern social movement with sufficient clearness to indicate his meaning." The manifold applications to stated phases of that movement can only be appreciated by reading all that he has written. That he had no large following need not be matter for surprise; that he had earnest admirers was certain.

It is obvious that Mr. Adams exhausted his views on social movement and administration in his *Law of Civilization and Decay* and his later outpourings repeated rather than really enlarged his outlook. He received recognition abroad in greater measure than at home. The *Law of Civilization,* with added matter, was translated into French and German; the *Economic Supremacy* appeared in German and the *New Empire* in German and Russian translations. He commented on the little attention he thought his writings had received in the United States and, with a note of bitterness, noted how often his researches and theories, and even his set examples, were quoted without credit. Every writer has much the same feeling. Dealing with what is current he expresses only what is in the air, open to any other observer who gives it attention. Adams's strength was in his presentation of the past—the far past—and his earlier methods gave good results, putting in a connected and attractive form what was not readily accessible, or what had been buried in the overpowering learning of foreign, chiefly German, authors. Those same methods held danger. He would strike off an opinion on a present social phase, based on economic facts, as conspicuous as it was true, a brilliant summary of complicated relations. A little later he would have carried the question to the seventeenth century, linking it with legal or monied incidents of that time, still maintaining his thesis and strengthening it by apposite arguments. Yet later he had reached the middle ages, Rome, Greece, Egypt and the dawn of civilization, still searching, still convinced, but having lost the original question. It was no longer an explanation of immediate social ill, but the history of the development of an idea. To a certain point he carried us with him, unquestioning and wondering; but the fated break came; some wide chasm overleaped by a flash of perception beyond our mentality, and we saw him disappear in the beginnings of things, now wholly separated from his original proposition, but enthusiastic in plotting connection and sequence that held out the promise of an all-inclusive generalization. That it should also be all conclusive, final, seemed of secondary moment.

In reviewing the writings of Mr. Adams the impression grows that his message, as he conceived it, was neither novel nor complete. A custom by long usage grows into a law, and a generalization may in time come to be accepted as a law. The *law* of civilization put forth by Adams in 1896 again appeared twenty-three years later as a *theory* of social revolutions. Details had been dropped and new illustrations added. No change of terms could conceal the fact that the earlier note was repeated in the later year, but the change from law to theory seems to suggest doubt on his own part. The persistence of the note through all his writings gives a certain consistency to the product, while emphasizing the real restrictions of his conclusions. His chapters have substance and show sound reading; his explanations of social movement and disturbance are suggestive. That he had a true remedy for social ills cannot be admitted, and much of his speculation went by the board after 1914. It is difficult to make a true appreciation of his life work. His influence was felt by few, but it was a select few.

He was in a sense proud of his ancestry, proud of the "Old House" at Quincy and its contents, and proud of his father's achievements. He rather resented criticism of the presidents and opposed an extensive biography of his father. Not oversympathetic with any of his brothers he disliked to listen to praise of them. It was a form of jealousy, unconscious, for he looked upon himself as holding a distinct position and expected others to recognize it. Charles Francis and Henry had inherited from John Quincy Adams—the one in his active interest in public questions, the other in his taste for science. John Adams had been a great lawyer, and from him Brooks claimed to derive his characteristics. Teaching law would have been a profession, for the search after general principles fascinated him; but the practice of law in these days is quite another matter from its practice in the Massachusetts of the eighteenth century. The union of law and revolution in John Adams differed entirely from the same union in Brooks Adams. The unrest of modern conditions was reflected in the restlessness of Brooks's mind. Its fineness and inheritance were wasted on questions of secondary import. Public employment might have concentrated this energy and made it of public service, but the opportunity never came.

With all his eager participation in modern life he had a strong regard for earlier beliefs and practices. He harked back to the first days of New England when he rose in the Stone Church at Quincy and made public profession of his faith. There was no wish to be peculiar; the act was wholly spontaneous, sincere, intended to serve as an example as well as an effort to bring back into use a once honored custom. We could have looked for such an act from many others rather than from him. Again heredity may explain. John Quincy Adams lived a life of deep religious conviction and wrote letters to his son on the study of the Bible, which passed through many editions and are still to be met.[11] Charles Francis Adams, the elder, entertained a faith undisturbed by the advance of science which so often took the shape of attacks on revealed religion. The form of Brooks's confession would have surprised his forbears, yet it merely denounced the appeal on moral questions to private judgment as leading to "an emasculated church, a renunciation of the old canons of duty, and an impotent administration of justice." Neither science nor philosophy had offered explanations or substitutes, and, renouncing the agnosticism of his youth, he accepted the ecclesiastical tradition. "Lord, I believe, help thou mine unbelief."

He married, September 7, 1889, Evelyn Davis, daughter of Admiral Charles Henry Davis and Harriette Blake Mills, and a sister of Mrs. Henry Cabot Lodge. She died December 14, 1926. After his marriage he passed his summers in the "Old House" at Quincy and after 1910 his winters at 33 Chestnut Street, Boston. In both homes he and his wife had an appropriate setting of family portraits, old china and silver. The man who wrote the *Emancipation* which shocked the older generation was the same man who amused a younger generation—and himself—thirty-three years later, in making Moses a vulgar magician and suicide. In the last chapter we forget the printed extravagances and remember the man of brilliant though ungoverned mind, the framer of dazzling pictures and remarkable generalizations, the host of aggressive and stimulating conversation, never so well pleased as when he felt you in opposition, and the friend whose demands were large, but whose compensation in suggestion and direction was larger. He was the last of his generation, contributing his accentuated personality in the group of four notably individual brothers.

NOTES

[1] *Law,* VI.

[2] *Law,* 297.

[3] *Correspondence of Roosevelt and Lodge,* 1, 231. See also his rather pertinent comparison between Brooks Adams's conclusions and those of Gustav Le Bon on p. 218.

[4] *Education of Henry Adams,* 338.

[5] *America's Economic Supremacy,* 139.

[6] *The New Empire,* 211.

[7] The concluding chapter of the work has been summarized.

[8] *Proceedings,* LIV, 293.

[9] *Proceedings,* XL, 377.

[10] *Boston Evening Transcript,* February 14, 1927.

[11] "It is said that one of the best readers in his time was the late President John Quincy Adams. I have heard that no man could read the Bible with such powerful effect." (Emerson on "Eloquence," in *Letters and Social Aims.*)

## R. P. Blackmur (essay date 1939)

SOURCE: "Henry and Brooks Adams: Parallels to Two Generations," in *The Southern Review,* Vol. V, No. 2, Autumn, 1939, pp. 308-34.

[*In the following excerpt, Blackmur explores the combined influence that brothers Henry and Brooks exerted over the study of history.*]

The greater reputation and the imaginative character of his work have made Henry Adams' name more familiar and more significant than that of his brother Brooks. Actually each inseminated the other; their thought along certain lines was coöperative, and it is impossible to deal fairly with the political and energetic ideas which occupied Henry Adams towards the end of his life—from 1893 to the end—without considering them in connection with those of Brooks Adams. It is here proposed to lay down the pattern of that connection and to underline the significance of its product.

The relationship between the two brothers is probably best expressed by accepting the statements of each that he was much indebted to the other, and that each was irritated by the other. Each, we might say, irritated the other into intellectual motion. Friction ignites like materials best; if the mode is primitive, it is yet reliable. Similarly, complements are most often produced from unanimities struck, least often from disparities felt; which is the very feeling of obfuscation. The brothers made no war in their attitudes towards history and thought: each saw himself dappled in the other. The single predominance Henry had over Brooks was personal; that of the older brother; and was the effect of those initial years when Henry had taken Brooks in charge, not only holding but asserting responsibility for him, at Harvard and afterwards. Otherwise they were on a level, and played participating parts. Brooks we commonly think of as more brilliant and more erratic than Henry, but we do not therefore think of Henry as sounder or straighter in line. The distinction—and here we get our sense of the complementary—is that Brooks tended to leap ahead of the logic that carried him along, where Henry endeavored to work always into the imagination that sustained him. For Brooks, facts might lose themselves in the pattern of law, and the pattern exclude all that did not fit it. For Henry, facts as such were nothing; the value they illustrated, the meaning they illuminated, everything. Brooks conned his trade routes and the statistics of price, and produced a theory of economic force. Henry kept magnets on his desk and meditated the lines of force, attractive and repellent, between them as if they made the ineluctable image of value, or even principle, itself. Yet John La Farge could complain: "Adams, you reason too much." Yet Brooks could make in the second edition of *The Emancipation of Massachusetts,* a vivid dramatic picture of Moses as a focused image of force. It was a matter of emphasis; each brother was attracted to the other's mode of approach as securing what he himself lacked to make, say, reason divine, or divination reasonable.

It was Henry's luck, just the luck of being on the imaginative side of the equilibrium, to come nearer the double virtue than Brooks. *Mont Saint Michel and Chartres* has its value for us precisely because it is a work of divination dressed out or enacted in the mode of the rational imagination; which is to say, the value is lasting. *The Law of Civilization and Decay,* perhaps Brooks Adams' strongest book, has a different value, not imaginative at all, but speculative, logical, statistical: it is an example of the forcible application of a set of ideas to history—to life in perspective—valuable just so long as the reader can persuade himself to entertain that set of ideas. Brooks had imagination, like Henry, but he used it conceptually, before he wrote; Henry put his imagination in his book: so that the book seems finally, as we think of it, to divine its own substance. It is the difference between the artist and the lawyer, who may be equally eloquent; but of whom the second excites you to a verdict where the first persuades you of a substance. You use Brooks Adams and you proceed; you use Henry and he participates in your sensibility ever afterwards.

But this is to speak on the high level, without regard to the motives and manners that bring us there, or the chance that richens sensibility. There are quotidian levels in the intellectual life no less intellectual for that. The everyday work of the mind is much the same—conditioned by the job in hand and by the appropriate tradition—without regard to the high product, if any appear. Thus we find the "help" which Henry extended to Brooks only different in particulars from that which Brooks probably gave Henry: all help on the common level, and not at all, so far as the evidence goes, the high creative help to which Brooks attested in **"The Heritage of Henry Adams."** Each brother stood on his own feet, rather conspicuously so to an outsider, and each thought that he himself did all the leaning upon the other. The James brothers, William and Henry, could only with less justice have thought the same in their own case: *The Sacred Fount* might be held one of the *Varieties of Religious Experience.* What we have really, in either set of brothers, is something like a pair of perpendicular parallels making a pointed arch in infinity—with infinity, though always out of sight, never altogether far off.

Returning to our common level—to the evidence of help given Brooks by Henry—there are copies of the first and second editions of *The Law of Civilization and Decay* in the Massachusetts Historical Society, both annotated by Henry Adams. Both sets of annotations start out to do a complete job—a page by page examination and citation—and both peter out rapidly after the first chapter has been gone through. Two things are remarkable. One is that none of Henry's notes are meant to affect either the thesis of the book or its substantial development, but merely to elucidate and document. The other is the witness they afford to the tenacity with which Henry hung on to his classical reading. There are specific references to Juvenal, Josephus, Martial, Pliny, Tacitus, Varro, Suetonius, Dio Cassius, Propertius, Petronius, Horace, and Lucian. Some of the notes run to inserts of several closely written pages on such subjects as the economic effects of the great Roman estates in the early empire (*Latifundia perdidere Italiam*), the *Lex Julia*, the *cheapness* of Roman legions, on money, taxes and the extent of wealth, and on the triumph of Civil over Military power as the crown of Civilization. There are besides, of course, many short notes of emendation and condensation. Some of these were used in the French translation, but the only important suggestion of which Brooks took advantage was that an entire chapter be given to art. The conclusion to the second edition is tantamount to such a chapter. Otherwise there are a few notes, here and there, far more characteristic of Henry's own interest and bias than of Brooks'. For instance, there is a note on page 186 of the second edition to the effect that when the imaginative mind is dominant, we have "cobblers interested in angels," while when the economic mind is dominant, religion becomes a trade and we see "every priest a huckster"; which is Henry's comment on Brooks' discussion of Lollardy and the discarding of the miracle as an economic medium "because the miracle was costly and yielded an uncertain return." Again, there is a note to page 365 in the same edition where Brooks compares the skepticism since 1789 in Paris with the skepticism of imperial Rome, of which the earlier produced a new religion and the latter has not. Apparently, wrote Henry, no further development of religion is possible in line with the further centralization which has occurred since 1789. There has been no invasion, no freshening of the blood, by emotional barbarians—though Nazi Germany in 1939 might offer a potential in that direction. One could have wished Henry had developed his notion as a kind of anachronistic footnote to his study of the Virgin of Chartres as an imaginative centralization of force.

But wishes are prone to proliferation. What these notes show is the literal independence of Brooks' book and thought. They prove what Henry had already declared in a letter written when Brooks, apparently, sent him the proof sheets of the first edition in the spring of 1895. First he refused the dedication to himself—because it was not needed, because it might hint that the book was really his, and because "the book is wholly, absolutely, and exclusively yours. Not a thought in it has any parentage of mine." Later in the same letter he insists that Brooks strike all the egoism out of his preface that he could reach. "You should be able to get all the literary advantage that the pronouns *I, me,* and *my* can give, by restricting yourself to a definite scale, say once on an average of five lines." Henry Adams understood that the best criticism is *primarily* directed at craft, for there, in craft, all values lie. Perhaps also he had forgotten, in the instance, that he was no longer the professor and editor of twenty years earlier, no longer addressing his pupil and contributor, Cabot Lodge.

Reverting to our figure of the perpendicular parallels making a pointed arch in infinity, is not centralization the pointing word, the jointing notion, with which the brothers were, in their context, obsessed, and which gave them motive and manner for thinking in concert? They had seen in their own youth an unprecedented centralization of social power in the new hands of industry, and they saw it now, in their crop time or age, proceed at an accelerated pace to a still closer concentration in the hands of what we call the finance-capitalists, and what the Adams brothers called indifferently goldbugs, jews, or usurers. The sight was all the more poignant to them, and pressed harder upon their vigil, because it had occurred at the expense of everything they stood for and had hoped, almost by birthright, to participate in—at least in America—a responsible, stable society governed by intelligence under the democratic vision. The Adamses were eighteenth-century men; rationalists; believers in knowledge and the discipline that flowed from knowledge; but American not English eighteenth century in their bias, and in America Massachusetts men not Virginian: that is to say moralists, inheritors of the Puritan scruple and the Christian ethic, quite used to wrestling equally with God and the Devil, but wrestling with the Idea, in their day, rather than the person of each. It was this modified inheritance and this reduced habit that kept them free of both intolerance and easy tolerance, of traditionalism and enthusiasm; which kept their minds open and active upon the old principles, maintaining sturdy integrities even in rebellion and dismay; but which yet, in dilution though it was and lacking, as we say, in personality, prevented them from finding twentieth-century society acceptable, live in it as they must and for the most part thoroughly did. The eighteenth-century mind unqualified did well enough; it merely became more worldly—lost the ability to care along with treasures to cherish—like John Hay; but the eighteenth century infected with Massachusetts, so far as it claimed survival at all claimed care its own, and what it could not care for reacted violently against, including sometimes the burden of inheritance.

Thus the mind faced with an unacceptable order—an order irresponsible to eighteenth-century principles however modified by twentieth-century theory—bent in two directions, either to the past, not for escape but refreshment, or to a special and punitive picture of the present almost, so inviting is the prospect of inevitable destruction, as refreshing as the contemplation of the high past. No mind can avoid, at some point of dissatisfaction, resort to magic; for what is the resort to conscience, even, but the application of the extreme rationalized form of magic; but since magic is universal in thought, we need keep only one eye on it. Here we need merely observe that Brooks and Henry Adams chose that type of magic appropriate to their special heritage. To the new form of economic centralization which he called multiplicity Henry Adams responded by invoking the extreme imaginative centralization symbolized by the Virgin of Chartres, which he called unity: the invocation was an act of imagination. Brooks responded by demonstrating through what he understood to be the logic—the Laws—of history, that the new centralization was self-destructive and represented civilization in an advanced state of decay; an act of intellect.

The brothers sympathized with each other's views—Henry perhaps sympathizing more with Brooks' destructive logic than Brooks was able to sympathize with Henry's refreshing imagination. We, today, may sympathize with both, as their predicament like their principles—their engaging values—remain some part of our own. We, the best of us, no more than they, seem able to bend either imagination or intellect directly to express the society in which we live, nor discern in what shape or pattern its unity lies. The difficulties are no less now than a generation ago; indeed, we may be pleased to call them greater; for the plain fact is that our society, measured by its own reduced aspirations, is unacceptable at more points to us than it was to the Adamses. The velocity of society has already become, as Henry Adams prophesied, too great for our intellects to cope with: we cower in a new and private dark as we barefaced move willy-nilly. Or so we choose to feel in most of our distinguished poetry and fiction and art. The mood was as common to the Adamses as to us; even a Bostonian in the mood would sympathize with what Henry wrote Brooks after a visit to Coutances in the fall of 1895:

> I have rarely felt New England at its highest ideal power as it appeared to me, beatified and glorified, in the Cathedral of Coutances. Since then our ancestors have steadily declined and run out until we have reached pretty near the bottom. They have played their little part according to the schedule. They have lost their religion, their art and their military tastes. They cannot now comprehend the meaning of what they did at Mont St. Michel. They have kept only the qualities which were most useful, with a dull instinct recalling dead associations. So we get Boston.

What Brooks may have written Henry in private does not appear to have survived, but it could hardly have been more despondent, or put with more relish, than many of his published statements. An extreme instance may be found at the end of the preface to the second edition of *The Law of Civilization and Decay:*

> In this last stage of consolidation, the economic, and, perhaps, the scientific intellect is propagated, while the imagination fades, and the emotional, the martial, and the artistic types of manhood decay. When a social velocity has been attained at which the waste of energetic material is so great that the martial and imaginative stocks fail to reproduce themselves, intensifying competition appears to generate two extreme economic types,—the usurer in his most formidable aspect, and the peasant whose nervous system is best adapted to thrive on scanty nutriment. At length a point must be reached when pressure can go no further, and then, perhaps, one of two results may follow: A stationary period may supervene, which may last until ended by war, by exhaustion, or by both combined, as seems to have been the case with the Eastern Empire; or, as in the Western, disintegration may set in, the civilized population may perish, and a reversion may take place to a primitive form of organism.

The prospect seems inviting just so long as it seems inevitable. Intellect and imagination—the actuality of life—supervened upon the Adamses, as upon everybody. They were persuaded to react practically to the society about them, as no doubt they were "persuaded" to react to walnuts and kittens. Who intervenes, who persuades—what is the *vis a tergo*—what made Hamlet soliloquize—is of no importance except as a matter of principle; what counts is the value, and the value is all walnuts and kittens. Adams felt himself, once, "a kitten in walnuts," and may have felt himself something of the sort again when he wrote Brooks in the summer of 1905 to hold his tongue rather than make panacea. Panacea is all principle and no value.

> Your social impasse [he went on] merely reflects the position of human thought altogether. No matter

where you follow it, you reach the same diffusion. Chemistry would tell you the same; Physics the same; your own mind, the same. You will make matters worse by meddling with the United States Constitution or any other relic of ancient order. Within thirty years, man himself must make a big jump or break his neck. He must develope new mental powers or perish. He has set in motion energies which he cannot control. It is he, you must develope, not the law or the machine.

Man is the value *and* the valuer; society is moral; morals imaginative; and imagination, in the end, the sole persuader: its effort is, to keep up with what happens willy-nilly—with the product of the machine and the prediction, as Justice Holmes put it, of the law. The lag in general imagination is appreciable. We see today as ruin, always; we see everywhere about us, on *this* day, imagination turning to violence in its desperation to catch up: violence or retreat, for retreat is a kind of inner violence that must terminate equally in dismay. The individual who does keep up, or tries to keep up, does so most often by the partial subterfuge of forcing his imagination emphatically upon those aspects of life which only seem to have changed, but which beneath their current formularies have not stirred a hair to the weather: he is religious, he brings the past up to the present. He controls all that has not altered. It is his imagination that keeps us going whether we catch up or not. But he lacks both candor and sophistication: the candor to see new energies as transforming, not his principles, but his values; the sophistication to distinguish or to unite, as the case calls, the new effects and the old emotions. Hence he cannot see, even if he wants to, what it is which he wishes to catch up with. It is this lack, one observes—not either conservatism or reformism—that is the vitiating defect both of the Churchman and the old-fashioned liberal. Add candor, add sophistication, and in so far as your mixture is justly proportioned, you will have an imagination free enough, *disponible* enough, and with labor informed enough, to react directly and continuously upon society in motion, no matter what the velocity or what the bearing. The type is rare. It is always ahead of its generation; and indeed, regardless how far back you go for your example, ahead of any generation. The Montaigne of *An Apology for Raimond Sebond* is one example; André Gide may turn out another; and in our own country, barring those occasions when partisan zeal overtakes him, there is possibly Kenneth Burke. The type is rare, in pure form unavailable; for the mixture, or confederation of elements, is never altogether justly proportioned. It was not so in Henry Adams—rather less still in Brooks; we may put it—to make it simple—that Henry showed more sophistication than candor, and that in Brooks candor sometimes outran sophistication and came out bald. To say that is easy, if not quite simple; it is to say that Henry sometimes forgot what he was driving at, and that Brooks sometimes drove the point of his pen harder than its holder would bear. Thus Henry declined an honorary degree at Harvard on the ground of a sprained ankle. Thus Brooks, when President Eliot mildly observed to him after an address at the Law School that he apparently did not overcherish democracy, responded abruptly in his harsh, full-carrying voice: "Do you think I'm a damned fool?"

Such ease is facile—as President Eliot would have been the first to acknowledge; it explains nothing but itself. What is wanted here is not an explanation but a measure of dependability—of penetration—of value, in the persistent activity of the Adams mind. The matter of heresy, of deviation from its own norm, is trivial in perspective; the actual movement of mind within its field, the evidence of keeping up here, of lagging there, of going offside somewhere else, is precisely what we want to take count of. We should be preoccupied at this point with Henry Adams busy discerning values in American society and attempting to develop, not laws or machines, but the mind of the men who made them. There is no accurate measure for the activity of mind except through citation and summary based on the citation. The hundred and forty odd letters to Brooks from 1895 to 1914 which have survived, make, taken together with other cognate letters, a unified and consistent picture of Henry Adams' reaction to finance and politics in the large sense: they sit in the general, shifting picture, an emphasis of long moment—as it were accidentally predominant—in the vast mass of disparate interests that go to make up the unity of an active mind. We see, as we read, the portrait grow. That is, if we cite well, the summary will take care of itself.

The clue, the focus of vision, the attractive force—whatever it is that arrests attention upon a feature, is double, even multiple. Multiplicity, in character, is but the cumulus of felt duplicity: duplicity become pattern; spinning become weaving. As Adams said, "the scientific synthesis commonly called Unity was the scientific analysis commonly called Multiplicity." Character in action was like matter at heart—pure motion, as Adams thought, or, as it may better be put, pure pattern. One part of the clue is the fragment of vegetative pattern which Henry and Brooks saw together. "Apropos to our—or rather your—garden!" Henry wrote Brooks in the spring of 1898, and went on:

> Reflecting at Cairo, Thebes, Baalbeck, Damascus, Smyrna, and Ephesus—alas I did not get to Antioch or Aleppo—on your wording of your Law, it seemed to me to come out, in its first equation thus, in the fewest possible words:
>
> All Civilisation is Centralisation.
>
> All Centralisation is Economy.
>
> Therefore all Civilisation is the survival of the most economical (cheapest).
>
> Darwin called it fittest, and one sense fittest is the fittest word. Unfortunately it is always relative, and therefore liable to misunderstanding.
>
> Your other formula is more difficult:
>
> Under an economical centralisation, Asia is cheaper

than Europe.

The world tends to economical centralisation.

Therefore Asia tends to survive, and Europe to perish.

The most brilliant part of your theory, however, is its application to thought as well as to economy. Nothing has struck me so much as its application to religions. The obvious economy of monotheism as compared with polytheism explains why the two sole monotheistic religions developed on the edges of the two great channels of trade, one at Jerusalem, the other at Mecca. You have already applied the theory to the reformation, but you have not casually, and, as it were carelessly thrown out the suggestion that atheism is still cheaper than reformed religion.

Part of the necessary comment here is contained in the next excerpt, from a letter written two years later from Washington, March 4, 1900. "As to your request about your book, I have nothing to suggest. I should try to eliminate from it everything that shows prejudice for or against any state of society. As it implies for its thesis the general law that mankind is irresponsible—a sort of vegetable growth—there is no reason for approving or disapproving his action." So much for comment; the letter proceeds: "If the imagination is too costly and wasteful for a true economic society, it is not the fault of the society. To me, the new economical law brings or ought to bring us back to the same state of mind as resulted from the old religious law,—that of profound helplessness and dependence on an infinite force that is to us incomprehensible and omnipotent." It should be observed that in an unpublished part of this letter, Adams remarked that the Adams dogmatism was certainly odious, and added, "but it was not extravagant until we made it a record. The world is going so fast, now, that dogmatism or marked individuality has become economically unprofitable and socially obstructive."

The attitude was as significant as the idea, and prior to it. The truth of Adams' observation is immaterial; the significance is in the feeling that it was both unprofitable and obstructive to show as different or to apply conviction. One felt weakness in difference, quicksand under conviction. Conformity was no better if there was no conviction to conform to, no individual to make the assent; conformity was a levelling down, out of sight and out of date: old age come on ahead of itself. Adams had written it all out to his brother in December, 1899, from Paris, and the passage is worth quoting, as an act of conformity *in extremis*.

I am sorry to hear of your anxieties. Whether they are harder to bear in one place than another I do not know. One always hopes that home is best in trouble; but I never found it to make much difference. What one really wants is youth, and what one really loses is years. Life becomes at last a mere piece of acting. One goes on by habit, playing more or less clumsily that one is still alive. It is

ludicrous and at times humiliating, but there is a certain style in it which youth has not. We become all, more or less, gentlemen; we are *ancien régime;* we learn to smile when gout racks us. We make clever speeches which rhyme with paresis,—or do not, for paresis has a short *ê*. We get out of bed in the morning all broken up, without nerves, color or temper, and by noon we are joking with young women about the play. One lives in constant company with diseased hearts, livers, kidneys and lungs; one shakes hands with certain death at closer embrace every day; one sees paralysis in every feature and feels it in every muscle; all one's functions relax their action every day; and, what is worse, one's grasp on the interests of life relax with the physical relaxation; and, through it all, we improve; our manners acquire refinement; our sympathies grow wider; our youthful self-consciousness disappears; very ordinary men and women are found to have charm; our appreciations have weight; we should almost get to respect ourselves if we knew of anything human to respect; so we affect to respect the conventions, and we ask only to be classed as a style.

Understanding, observation, memory are steady forms of gout; Adams might have crowned his dramatic fable, and without diluting an ounce of its persuasiveness, had he added the remarks on stoicism which he sent to Margaret Chanler ten years later from Paris, September 9, 1909. His friend Bay Lodge had recently died. "Well! being a poor bit of materialised *Energetik,* I have no resource but the old one, taught by one's brothers in childhood—to grin and bear it; nor is this refuge much ennobled by calling it stoicism. The defect in this old remedy is that it helps others not at all, and oneself only by a sort of moral suicide."

The stoic style wore better, like any mask, for being seen through; one could adjust one's inner features, without embarrassing one's privacy, to meet the smart of what one saw. Stoicism, then, was no protection beyond the small haven of manners; better, it was a weapon and a blind, to be used precisely by being thrown off—all the more disarmingly effective because, as a rule, no one realized until too late it was not still up.

From time to time Adams threw it off as discreetly and with as much form—the stoicism of art—as possible; and persuaded his brother to do likewise. Arguing, first, the advantage of holding one's tongue: "Yet silence is a sort of truth, and equally virulent," Adams went on, in a letter of November 1, 1910, from Paris: "Should I do better by jumping with the tide, and accepting communism and anarchism as our evident goal—not perhaps as the object of human and other energy, but as its legitimate end . . . ? Very clever men have done so, and are doing it. Why not we? Is there any form of doing it in good faith? St. Augustine and St. Jerome found a way. I can't."

This was written at the end, or nearly the end, of a long submission to the political dilemma of the times, Adams' times and our own. It is Adams' idiosyncrasy that he thought of St. Augustine, who envisaged the City of God, St. Jerome, who expounded the scriptures to widows and young ladies, and Symmachus—earlier in the same letter—who was a rock-bottom honest conservative and a great praiser of gone times: all men who got into trouble, with themselves and their friends, over their propulsive convictions. It may be our idiosyncrasy that we think of no one, and regard ourselves as self-propelled. Presumably, the idiosyncrasy of human intelligence itself is at stake. Yet the choice was clear and, as always, already made, beyond repair: open only to execution and interpretation. Twelve years earlier, in May, 1898, Adams was in Budapest, and wrote his brother Brooks what he saw: it was the same question that was implied. Budapest was the first place he had ever struck that really led to Russia and the future.

> The present Hungary is the child of State-Socialism in a most intelligent and practical form. In principle there is no apparent limit to its application. . . . What is more curious, the result seems to be reasonably consistent with a degree of individual energy and character. As one form of future society, it deserves a little attention, especially in connection with Russia; and, as it represents to me the possible future with which I sincerely wish I may have nothing to do, I recommend it to your notice. To me it seems to demonstrate that the axiom of what we are civil enough to call progress, has got to be:—All monopolies will be assumed by the State; as a corollary to the proposition that the common interest is supreme over the individual.

> Enough of that! I touch on it only with reference to the next Presidential campaign, which, if you feel obliged to take part in, you must lift off from silver, and lift in to Socialism. Not that I love Socialism any better than I do Capitalism, or any other Ism, but I know only one law of political or historical morality, and that is that the form of Society which survives is always in the Right; and therefore a statesman is obliged to follow it, unless he leads. Progress is Economy! Socialism is merely a new application of Economy, which must go on until Competition puts an end to further Economies, or the whole world becomes one Socialistic Society and rots out. One need not love Socialism in order to point out the logical necessity for Society to march that way; and the wisdom of doing it intelligently if it is to do it at all.

These statements perhaps represent Henry Adams' most candid—and least sophisticated—reaction to the political society of his time. They are not isolated statements—but chosen from many; nor are they shots in the superficial dark; nor middle-class maundering liberalism. If there was a myth to which Henry Adams surrendered himself, it was that he was by right, by duty—what he called *corvée*—and potentially by ability, a member of the governing class. The family gocart was properly the governing gocart. That what he thought of as the governing class was permanently out of power only made the problem more acute and intensified the responsibility of independent thought. In a way, the mind could better afford responsibility out of power than in. For the mind has always independent means, ample for every emergency except the management of irresponsible power; which is why in the careers of statesmen we see conviction disappear for the term of office, only to reappear in retirement quite unimpaired: a principle of comment altogether as applicable to Neville Chamberlain as to Léon Blum, to De Valera as to Roosevelt, to Lenin as to Cardenas. The power of office, let alone the power of the man, is seldom equal to the power confronted and as a rule disintegrates before it. Henry Adams in making out his rough socialist position was making out, as much as anything, a case for the only possible vitalization of the governing class that he could see. Every other position constituted a more or less abject surrender to the money power; a surrender upon which every president since Lincoln had battened, just as the money power had battened on presidents. Socialism as framed was meant precisely to control the money power through absorption. So far, Socialism was the only means of control that went further than compromise. No government that was at the conspicuous mercy of the bankers, as Grant's had been, and Cleveland's, and Roosevelt's, could fairly be said to govern. No nation that could be victimized by a pressure put upon gold in London or Paris could be said to be free. There was, in short, no such thing as political independence at home or abroad, unless there was financial independence.

For a long time Adams thought financial independence could be obtained through free silver or, perhaps, paper. That is, he thought the virulence of the goldbug could be destroyed by setting a silver beetle or a paper wasp—or both—at its side. But he never thought the problem could be solved the other way around (unless one solved it by calling it insoluble): by surrendering political power to the money power in the hope that financiers would suddenly become governors, that is to say, responsible. The protective system which the money power had forced into the tariff—to such an extent that the words had become synonymous—showed to him as "a display of frantic lust for unbridled and irresponsible power." Again, in a letter to Brooks from Paris, September 20, 1910, the following sentences occur:

> Your argument, like mine, goes to wreck on our system of protection. . . . Railways, trusts, banking-system, manufacturers, capital and labor, all rest on the principle of monopoly which you are attacking in one of its outposts. . . . The suggestion that these great corporate organisms, which now perform all the vital functions of our social life, should behave themselves decently, gives away our contention that they have no right to exist. Nor am I prepared to admit that more decency can be attained through a legislature made up of similar people exercising similar illegal powers. . . . All we can hope to do is to teach men manners in wielding power, and I'll bet you ten to one, on the Day of Judgment, that we shall fail. St. Peter will feel our pockets at the door, and charge us prohibitive rates for the inside journey to the New Jerusalem.

Furthermore, Adams believed neither in the intelligence nor in the courage of the money power, a distrust he expressed most forcibly in his letter to Brooks from Washington, February 18, 1896.

> You fear the usurer, but one of the profoundest of your many observations is that the usurer is an imbecile politician. The old mercantile pirate was a great one. Even the manufacturer was an able one. But the usurer is a coward and narrow-minded. All through the world's history, he has ended as a victim or as a tool. I have watched him the last year. He has no brains, no education and no courage. He is a liar and an area-thief, but not a conqueror or a pirate. He has, within six months, broken down in Armenia, Abyssynia, and even in Cuba and the Transvaal. He stands helpless today before every one of the great political and economical questions of the world. If these questions are to be settled at all, they must be settled by political processes.

Forty-odd years of further concentration of the money power have only added application to Adams' observations. Had it occurred to him to put it that as a tool the usurer is manipulated by his own folly—that is, by the operation of inadequate instincts—and that in his cowardice he is driven to stir up trouble, the story in that quarter would be complete. The same years and an analogous concentration of social and extrasocial energies controlled—or milked without control—by the usurers, have added little to the political story. The problem, the aggravations, and the solutions remain unaltered—even in urgency. It needs a date and an identification to mark the following as inappropriate to the American scene in the early summer of 1939 instead of the spring of 1906. "The President shows evident fatigue. Everyone seems to admit that both parties are wrecked. As long as Roosevelt is on their backs they will stay wrecked. Afterwards they will begin again, no doubt with a new socialist element, as in Europe. Fisher Ames, a hundred years ago, said that our system was a raft on the Connecticutt river. One's feet were always under water, but the raft couldn't sink." Hitler and Mussolini and Franco were unforeseeable; as manners worse than those of Wall Street and State Street were unimaginable. The point here is in Adams' doubtful emphasis on "a new socialist element." In a letter to Ward Thoron, July 3, 1911, he made—as he said, with folded hands and wearing yellow glasses—the emphasis clear: We have not yet recognized socialism as a religion; but we must. Religion was, for Adams, a means of focusing energy: energy seen as motive forces. Everything lay in the seeing.

On the practical level Adams saw it plain. It was no good, as he wrote Brooks, to stick to silver; to stick, that is, to the palliative reform of the money power, which would at best merely reduce the abuse of energy by doubling the means of irresponsible manipulation. In theory one would check the other, like Congress and the Supreme Court. The first thing was to get at the energy itself where it actually furnished handles—types of mind—for control; then to remove those controls from the possibility of abuse. There is a passage in the *Education* (pages 421-22), which may be accepted, as perhaps the letters cannot, as more than tentative, where Adams lifted off the means of silver and on to the means of socialism.

> The work of domestic progress is done by masses of mechanical power—steam, electric, furnace, or other—which have to be controlled by a score or two of individuals who have shown capacity to manage it. The work of internal government has become the task of controlling these men, who are socially as remote as the heathen gods, alone worth knowing, but never known, and who could tell nothing of political value if you skinned them alive. Most of them have nothing to tell, but are forces as dumb as their dynamos, absorbed in the development or economy of power. They are trustees for the public, and whenever society assumes the property, it must confer on them that title; but the power will remain as before, whoever manages it, and will then control society without appeal, as it controls its stokers and pit-men. Modern politics is, at bottom, a struggle not of men but of forces. The men become every year more and more creatures of force, massed about central power-houses. The conflict is no longer between the men, but between the motors that drive the men, and the men tend to succumb to their own motive forces.

What Adams is saying will become more pointed if three or four sentences from Brooks Adams' *Theory of Social Revolutions* are put beside it to show the same problem from another angle.

> Since those are strongest through whom nature finds it, for the time being, easiest to vent her energy, and as the whole universe is in ceaseless change, it follows that the composition of ruling classes is never constant, but shifts to correspond with the shifting environment. When this movement is so rapid that men cannot adapt themselves to it, we call the phenomenon a revolution. . . . A ruling class is seldom conscious of its own decay, and most of the worst catastrophes of history have been caused by an obstinate resistance to change when resistance was no longer possible [page 132].

> Social consolidation implies an equivalent capacity for administration. I take it to be an axiom, that perfection in administration must be commensurate to the bulk and momentum of the mass to be administered, otherwise the centrifugal will overcome the centripetal force, and the mass will disintegrate. In other words, civilization would dissolve. It is in dealing with administration, as I apprehend, that civilizations have usually, though not always, broken down, for it has been on admin-istrative difficulties that revolutions have for the most part supervened [page 204].

> The rise of a new governing class is always synonymous with a social revolution and a redistribution of property [page 205].

The Adams brothers worked, as we have said, in vigorous parallel to make a pointed arch in infinity. Being short of it, infinity need not concern us except as a prospect. What the Adamses said in effect was: that in fact a revolution had taken place in both the structure and energetic development of American society; that the historical American political mode was inadequate to the task of administering the conflict of new forces; that the money power had taken advantage of the weakness of government to assert, and exert, for itself, irresponsible sovereign powers; and that the resumption of sovereignty by government could evidently only occur through a combination of political concentration equal to the energetic concentration and the rise of an administrative class capable of controlling the expression of energy through the political process. Henry Adams roughly and from time to time, with varying doubt and distrust, assented to socialism as the necessary means. Brooks Adams seemingly did not commit himself to the word; he was content to demonstrate that what we call capitalistic control was incompetent to its task—that whereas "through applied science infinite forces have been domesticated" yet "our laws and institutions have remained, in substance, constant," and that, "as a result, society has been squeezed, as it were, from its rigid eighteenth-century legal shell, and has passed into a fourth dimension of space, where it performs its most important functions beyond the cognizance of the law, which remains in a space of but three dimensions." (*Theory of Social Revolutions,* pages 11-12.) There is little difference in the substance of argument, and only a difference of a point or two in the angle of vision: the difference, as much as anything, in the degree of sophistication. Brooks Adams was a lawyer and tended to see the administrative problem of society as a matter of mechanical law: a generalization of facts. Henry Adams was in some species a man of imagination, and saw the administrative problem as *analogous* to the fictions of physics: as generalizations of facts in terms of a policy. Where one brother ignored the connections, the other insisted upon them. It will be made plain below how much the distinction was worth.

Here there is room for a perspective down the avenue of another fiction, already mentioned, to which the brothers resorted as they thought by necessity, and which they came to belabor rather than discard, since it could not be ignored: the fiction of money as stored energy. If the perspective is digressive, desultory, *deraciné*—so is the human mind that entertains it. Here it is, in the form of a sentence extracted from some fragmentary undated notes addressed to Brooks: "It seems to me, therefore, that what I miss is a paragraph explaining that, among the many forms of machinery which society has used for its concentrating process, money, like coal or iron, is particularly important, and like railroads, particularly sensitive to manipulation." These words appear to make a self-evident statement of fact; even the suggestion that it could be explained or developed in a paragraph seems innocuous—assuming that common sense were used, a mere modest understatement of the space needed. Regrettably Brooks Adams' response is unavailable; and there is no such paragraph in his published work. Nor should it have been expected; for the self-evidential veil be-

comes transparent to a sharp look and shows through to a substantial confusion. In the consideration of money as stored energy the important thing is the difference, not the similarity, between it and coal or iron or railroads: the difference is that money is a representative fiction not a substance, and as it varies infinitely in the degree of representativeness so it is subject to infinite manipulation. In times of what is called financial crisis such as 1893, 1907, 1929, or 1933, it is clear that the representative value is at its lowest and the manipulative value at the highest; in other words political sovereignty is vestigial—only enough to make money considered as negotiable contract enforceable at law—and extralegal sovereignty nearly omnipotent. The bankruptcy law is a palliative attempt to restore political sovereignty; which is cutthroat economy at best—and usually cuts the wrong throats. The trouble lies in the universally accredited fiction that money is itself a form of energy; society believes in money as it once believed in miracles—up to the point of desperation. One would say that money like miracles became too expensive the moment its control became irresponsible: when it ceased being representative and became privileged property: an incorporeal hereditament administered as a right: that is to say, when society ceased controlling a responsible fiction and lay helpless before what it took to be an irresponsible fact. If you find society from millionaire to mudslinger asserting that money and coal may have an equivalence in stored energy varying only with the relative efficiency of manipulation—the furnace or the banking system—it will do you no good to point out that where coal stores heat gold in itself is almost cold, colder than paper for example, and that no amount of efficiency will extract work from it without a preponderant supply of gratuitous faith. No one will believe you; and in practice—so prone are we to prefer the agency of the miraculous at the focus of reason—you will not believe yourself—not all the time; hardly ever at the moment of decision or action. It may be laid down as almost an axiom that the attractive force of society over the independent mind is greatest where expressed in fictions that have lost their basis in actual behavior and have become merely rational formulae. The mind, as Henry Adams said, resorts to reason for want of training; and the mind is trained least in the basis of the fictions upon which it depends, most in the rationale of their execution. Hence the best minds, accepting perforce for reaction the reasons of society, tend as La Farge said Adams did, to reason too much. Reason seems centripetal, in its long succumbing; direct reaction, in all its lonely valor, centrifugal.

Henry Adams reasoned too much about money; it was a lifelong habit begun during the financial crisis after the Civil War—reflected in his three essays: "The Bank of England Restriction," "The Legal-Tender Act," and "The New York Gold Conspiracy"—and pursued necessarily in his account of the struggle over the United States Bank in the *Life of Gallatin,* and also, of course, in the relevant chapters in the *History.* What we are concerned with here has nothing to do with any historical question of financial policy; we are concerned just with the effect upon Adams of his obsession from 1895 to 1910 with the international exchanges and the manipulation of prices by the bankers and brokers: with the intellectual effect, that is, of his excessive addiction to the fiction of money as stored energy. In extreme form the effect showed in sentences like the following: "The imminent peril of the finances of the world weighs on my mind more than anything else. I do not see how Russia, which is quite mad and without a government, can avoid a bankruptcy which will, for the time, drag France, England, Germany under water, as well as ourselves." Again: "If Gage can let her [England] have a hundred millions of gold now, he can carry her and Russia over, till the gold mines are re-opened. Otherwise I can see no chance that England can maintain her credit, and for at least five years she has kept her head above water only by credit. She has been insolvent since 1895."

The secret of Adams' exaggerated fears—which commonly overtook him, as he said, every fall—lay entirely in the circumstance that he reasoned, almost unquestioningly, on other men's premises—the very men whom he hated and distrusted most, the brokers and usurers of New York, London, Paris, and Berlin. He took foreign exchange, trade balances, and the supply of gold with the utmost seriousness as the very outward form of the fluid energy he was most concerned to handle. The usurped power of a monstrous administrative fiction seemed to him, as it every day seems to everybody, its convulsions no less acceptable than those of the weather, the necessary and sovereign power. Had he reflected at the right moments—the exact moments when society failed of its logical collapse—it must have appeared that the "finances of the world" alone were in peril of life; the money power might ruin society but could not destroy it; for at the moment of destruction belief in the money power faltered short of the enacting trust. Historically the reflection was common, and always sound; Adams himself had made it of post-Napoleonic England, of Madison's finance of 1815, and of the Legal Tender crisis after the Civil War. His brother Brooks had made it all along in his discussions of usury from Rome to the Rothschilds. But he did not catch up with his own history during the American financial impasse from 1893 to 1905. The Klondike and South Africa acted as brakes to the movement of thought exactly as they perpetuated, by staving off gold-bankruptcy, the goldbug himself. The rescue of the bankers, no matter how often enacted, seemed the salvation of society—which, indeed, to the bankers it was. Had the rescue been political, as in 1933, instead of metallic as in 1898, or military as in 1914 and now again perhaps as in 1939, it would have been more difficult to confuse the fate of society with the solvency of its masters. As Mill told the young man who portrayed England in ruins, there is an inexhaustible amount of ruin in society. It is the instruments of control that are subject to destruction, never the energy controlled that dies; for the instruments are all fictions—conventions, contracts—and all invariably come to be framed against the public interest. If stoicism, as Adams said, is moral suicide, social suicide consists in putting up with fictions whose

sole sanction lies in the credulity they command when the faith that inspired them is gone.

Adams knew all about the gone faith, but he put up with the persistent form as the path of least resistance: the path of inattention which consists in absorption in logical reason. Hence he saw, rightly, society everywhere committing suicide, or, worse, achieving apathy, according to the rules of its logic: for the most part in dogmatic ignorance of its action. Money was everywhere held the cohesive of civilization and lessened every other value, stultifying the energies it fed on. The movement of money was life. Whether you liked it or not, the movement of international exchanges and the disequilibria called trade balances, showed you what movement there was. If you could trace the motion, you could leave what moved—and what ran the motor—out of account. So Adams thought; and for about ten years he tried to think in the terms on which businessmen believed they acted; very much as "everybody" tried to think in America from 1929 to 1934. He tackled the trade balances in particular and attempted to make them tell a connected and complete story. Mr. Worthington C. Ford, then statistician of the State Department, tried to help him, for five years through 1898 supplying him with the best figures and the best comment obtainable. Breakfast or dinner two or three times a week while Adams was in Washington gave opportunity for conversation devoted exclusively to the exchanges of money and trade. The story was disconnected, incomplete, and pointed always to chaos.

"The whole thing is one vast structure of debt and fraud. The Church never was as rotten as the stock-exchange now is. The State never could be as hollow a fraud as our system of credit." "The single point which now stands ahead of us as the centre of the next chaos . . . is the money-lending system which has ruled us so long." More specifically on the interpretation of trade balances:

> The substance is that in twenty five years a favorable balance of 25 [millions] has been converted into an unfavorable balance of 150. . . . Last year we ran twenty millions or more behind the average of the previous five years. . . . We have just made a gift of five millions to Wall Street to carry us for three months. We propose to contract our basis of credit, if necessary, two hundred and fifty millions or more to save the Treasury at the expense of our industries. . . . In London they told me that this process could hardly last beyond April. To give a date for future events is always dangerous, but to me it seems clear that we are already keeping ourselves afloat only by the most desperate expedients, and that, if we carry over till the next harvest we shall be lucky—or unlucky, for I do not know which dilemma is worst.

So to Mr. Ford, February 9, 1897. By the end of November, 1898, the story had evidently changed—in immediate direction if not in goal. The collapse of Spain had left, both Henry and Brooks Adams saw, America economically supreme: an economic revolution of the first magnitude. It seemed to Henry that there was a choice open, and he wrote to Mr. Ford:

> The effect of the vast inflow of wealth on our domestic social condition, is another matter about which I prefer to shut my cowardly eyes. The future must bury its own dead, me among the rest. Sooner or later we must all rot, I suppose, and in the meanwhile our society can get no small amusement out of its ripeness. There will be a rich field for intelligent socialist changes, and a still richer one for thievery and private greed.

Writing again to Mr. Ford a few weeks later, December 19, 1898, Adams got away from the immediate and subjective relation to money and into the more objective reach of historical thought:

> The economical theory of history requires the extinction of the wasteful, and the substitution of the cheaper forms of life, until the forms become too cheap to survive; but we have reached the point where cheapness can only be reached by a social system growing rapidly more and more socialistic. Plutocracies are wasteful, and yet we are building up the greatest plutocracies that ever existed. If you are right, government has now got to feed on accumulated capital, which will speedily bring about the Russian millenium of a centralised, despotic socialism.

It seems superfluous to remark on the application of these sentences to the deficit-budgetary system current by force since 1930; but if Adams could ignore his own conclusions in practice, so can we. His letter immediately returns to the consideration of trade balances.

> The British trade return for November is again deplorable, and that for the eleven months is awful. France, this year, is apparently running behind. Russia can no longer borrow in Europe, and wants to borrow of us, with the pledge to spend all the loan here. In short, I have terrible qualms about the bottom of that European money bar'l as our next general election approaches. . . . The problem is certainly calculated to set the whole menagerie to chewing its tails in religious silence.

The point of the intellectual consequences of Adams' addiction to the fiction of money as stored energy should be by now clear. Precisely as the system failed in responsible representation so did the deductions logically drawn from watching its operation. Logic like instinct is only good in closed circuits of circumstances—those which formulated the logic or accreted the instinct—and in altered circumstances neither is apt except to the unchanged residues. So long as Adams applied the logic of the money system he was unable adequately to react to the energies of which the system had usurped the control: the actual energies in coal and rail-road and dynamo; and the partial reaction alone afforded came out wrong or desperate or blank. Precisely, on the other hand, as he ignored the system—ignored the whole comedy of the everyday considerations upon which men apparently acted—he came out astonishingly close to seeing the terms and scope of the political problem of his day and our own: the problem of administering infinite and diverse energies by finite mind so as to make a social unity. Thus in the letters we see the alternate crotchety pessimism of dismayed reason and the exhilaration of direct reaction which is quite beyond pessimism or reason or dismay. By April, 1906, the last operative traces of the addiction to the money fiction were gone; what remained were but the signs of quotidian discomfiture at the itch. Give up the jabber about MONEY, he wrote his brother Brooks on the 12th of that month. "What I see is POWER. Abolish money; power remains."

In such guise, with metonymous thinking put aside, the problem, if not the solution, was mud-plain. On March 23, 1906, he wrote Gaskell in much the same terms he had written to Brooks a year before on the necessity of developing new mental powers to encompass the new machines. Repetition is the simplest and most emphatic emphasis and is the least expensive persuader we can employ here.

> What is the end of doubling up our steam and electric power every five years to infinity if we don't increase our thought power? As I see it, the society of today shows no more thought power than in our youth, though it showed precious little then. To me, the whole lesson lies in this experiment. Can our society double up its mind-capacity? It must do it or die; and I see no reason why it may not widen its consciousness of complex conditions far enough to escape wreck; but it must hurry. Our power is always running ahead of our mind.

It must still hurry. The usurped predominance of money over power persisted, and persists; it is still necessary to reduce the terms of administrative measures, however otherwise conceived—in the public interest, say—to the terms of the money interest before they can be effectuated. Political thought remains permissive rather than sovereign; stultified at heart. Brooks Adams, in **"The Heritage of Henry Adams,"** published in 1919 as an introduction to Henry's "Letter to Teachers" and "Phase," felt compelled to deal with the usurper as practical sovereign. "Great Britain and America," he said, "like the parts of some gigantic saurian which has been severed in a prehistoric contest, seem half unconsciously to be trying to unite in an economic organism, perhaps to be controlled by a syndicate of bankers who will direct the movements of the putative governments of this enormous aggregation of vested interests independent of the popular will."

The arc of digression is closed, and we are returned with all the more force to what underlay it all along: the effort to give up the jabber about money, and seize on power. Because money had usurped power, money must needs be dethroned before political sovereignty could be restored. Because the new energies had led of necessity to new and intense concentrations—industrial cities, monopolies, powerhouses—only by an equivalent concentration of political power could sovereignty—even if otherwise achieved—be administered. To repeat all consciously and with even more emphasis in this repetition than the last, as there is more repeated—the necessities were equal by observation. Put morally, which is here to say politically, the whole necessity was to recognize your fate in order to achieve your character. It was not a matter of logic, which may always be satisfied, but of need, which is always come short of. The proximate satisfaction of need, as Adams saw it predicted by the character of society, could only be secured by state monopoly of all private monopolies and all aggregates of energy which tended towards private monopoly. Monopoly is the very name for public interest. The strategy and tactics of public monopoly constitute the administrative theory called socialism or communism—though they had as well, until they acquire religious aspirations or imaginative vision, be called the theory of government, without qualification. This language will not of course be found either in Adams' letters or in his books; but it may be argued that it flows naturally from the consideration of the material cited from Henry and Brooks: it is the summary that it makes for itself.

It should be added that this account of the Adams brothers' direct response to the politico-economic impasse of their times and ours is not in any way meant to express their predilection. It does not follow that one desiderates what one perceives to be predetermined. Brooks, as we said, did not use the word socialism; he distrusted the innate as well as the practical ability of any form of democratic electorate almost as much as he distrusted the intelligence of the bankers; he claimed that his thought expressed the necessity of mechanical law. Henry resorted to the word and program of socialism because he thought they expressed the natural and necessary next stage of society, and not because he *liked* the prospect. He did not; he disliked and detested it only less than he did the prospect of the usurer. Both socialism and usury represented forms of rot; both were levellers, disintegrators, cheapeners of the energies they sought to control; both prevented the imagination—or so he most often thought. Socialism was one peg cheaper than the bourgeoisie—where usury was, as plutocracy, the extreme of waste. Usury was usurpation; socialism was politics. With the strong political bias which he had inherited and cultivated as a *corvée,* he made the choice of socialism. "The socialist society of the immediate future," he wrote Gaskell in March, 1910, "is the end of possible evolution or forward movement on any lines now known to us." Knowing that, he could not do other than think it through.

That was the *corvée* of the politically minded man. Being also an imaginative man and greatly desirous of being a scientific historian, his next effort was to find some concept of physical energy which should lift the socialist phase of society to the imaginative plane where it might show its meaning as unity, even if the meaning were fatal. For there must be a policy of the imagination no less than a policy of the state.

## Charles A. Madison (essay date 1940)

SOURCE: "Brooks Adams, Caustic Cassandra," in *The American Scholar,* Vol. 9, No. 2, Spring, 1940, pp. 214-27,

[*In the following excerpt, Madison offers a survey of Adams's major works and political concerns.*]

Brooks Adams is, a dozen years after his death, a truly forgotten man. A test poll of twenty-five college graduates of various ages and interests elicited the fact that less than a third were able to identify him and that only one, a writer on legal history, was familiar with some of his writings. Nor is this surprising. His radical social and economic views had early antagonized the class to which he belonged, and throughout his mature years he was scorned (by those who knew what he stood for) as the last and least worthy of the captious Adams tribe. His books, readily appreciated in England and translated into French, German and Russian were ignored by most of the important American periodicals and disregarded by the leaders of public opinion. Consequently they had few readers. When he died in 1927 his passing received scant public notice. The incisive obituary paragraph in the New York *Nation* and the commendable brief memoir by his friend Worthington Chauncey Ford were the only items to mark the event. The living generation of Americans, on the verge of the economic catastrophe which he more than anyone had clearly foreseen and had tried so valiantly to forestall, knew not the name of Brooks Adams.

Yet this youngest son of Charles Francis Adams was in some essential respects the most original and profound member of our most distinguished family. His contribution to the culture of his time appears the more significant if viewed from the vantage point of his background and personality. With a grandfather and great-grandfather past Presidents of the United States, with his father the extraordinarily capable ambassador to Great Britain during the crucial Civil War period, with the leading men of England and America frequenting his home on an intimate basis, Brooks could not but grow up intensely proud of being an Adams. Nor was this empty conceit. He and his brothers more than justified their acute sense of self-importance. In the words of the late Professor Vernon Parrington, "Intellectually curious, given to rationalism, retaining much of the eighteenth-century solidity of intellect and honest realism, refusing to barter principle for the good will of men, the Adams line produced no more characteristic offshoots than came in the fourth generation." But if the reverse of the picture is less attractive it is no less authentic. According to James Russell Lowell "the Adamses have a genius for saying even a gracious thing in an ungracious way." From John down they have indulged in self-dramatization, have placed themselves in leading positions, exaggerated the animus of their opponents and accepted misunderstanding and disapproval with injured hauteur. None of the exceptionally able sons of Charles Francis Adams would stoop to fit himself to the political hurly-burly of the post-Civil War period;

dignified, disdainful, dissentient, each sooner or later sought upon Clio's deep bosom the solace needed by their aggrieved vanity.

Brooks was a thoroughbred Adams. Proud of his obviously distinguished lineage although he sometimes derided it, certain of his high intellectual capacities, possessed of an acute social conscience, he was at the same time extremely shy, as much the prig as his brother Henry (both of them, according to the latter, "were used to audiences of one") and readily suspicious of the motives of others. Brought up by a father whose puritanic severity had made the childhood of his sons monotonous and dreary, Brooks remained to the end overserious and zealous for the sanctity of truth and justice. As his brother Henry wrote him in 1910, "I have known you for sixty-odd years, and since you were a baby, I've never known you when you weren't making yourself miserable over the failings of the universe. It has been your amusement, and a very good one."

Like the other Adamses ever since John, Brooks studied at Harvard and became a lawyer. Jealous of his considerably older brothers and wishing to make his way unaided, he opened an office for himself and for eight years he waited for a practice which failed to materialize. It was not that he was deficient in his equipment as a lawyer; his knowledge of the law in time became immense and incisive. Nor was it a lack of the will to succeed; the idea of failure was obnoxious to his inflated vanity. He soon perceived, however, that even less than his brothers could he adjust himself to the grasping and unscrupulous ways of his contemporaries. "Brooks," wrote his brother Henry, "irritated too many Boston conventions ever to suit the atmosphere." Before long State Street became to Brooks, even more than to the other Adamses, the symbol of all that was crass and iniquitous. Since he had early inherited from his maternal grandfather enough money to keep him in comfort for the rest of his days he decided in 1881 to close his law offices and to turn his mind, even as his brothers had done, to the study of history.

In 1886, after years of intensive reading and hard thinking, Adams completed his first historical work, *The Emancipation of Massachusetts.* The book aroused considerable controversy and was damned and praised with equal promptitude. It was in truth an iconoclastic examination of our colonial past—the first work in that field to treat persons and events with the factual objectivity of the seasoned scholar rather than with the smug self-satisfaction of the sentimental chronicler. As such it struck a body blow against the carefully-nourished prejudices that pervaded the historical writing of the period. "From that day," Mr. Ford testified, "the filiopietistic school of history was laughed out of court."

If documentary evidence forms the basis of the book, its spirit throbs with a passion for the freedom of the mind. With the unmitigated severity of the crusading prosecutor Adams, who was shocked to find the early history of his native state compounded of intolerance and cruelty, un-folded the horrible record of persecution and repression, of flogging and burning, of greed and cupidity. He had nothing but scorn for a clergy who had perverted the Puritan Commonwealth—child of the Reformation and predicated on the assertion of the freedom of the mind—into a "cesspool of iniquity" more intolerable than the one from which they had fled. Nor had he anything to retract when he issued a new edition some thirty years later. He regretted somewhat only the "acrimonious tone" of certain passages. For what he found in early Massachusetts was a duplication of previous periods in history during which the clergy exercised temporal power.

> The power of the priesthood lies in submission to a creed. . . . The horrors of the Inquisition, the Massacre of St. Bartholomew, the atrocities of Laud, the abominations of the Scotch Kirk, the persecution of the Quakers had one object—the enslavement of the mind.

In chapter after chapter Adams relates in factual detail how, in the fanatic pursuit of conformity, the Puritan clergy and elders, basing their criminal code on Pentateuch law, cruelly persecuted Anabaptists, Quakers, witches and religious liberals and turned their parishioners into neurotic censors and vindictive zealots. The leaders are etched in acid. Governor Winthrop, John Cotton, the Mathers—these and numerous others are quoted to their own condemnation as cruel and conceited bigots. Increase Mather is pictured as having "an inordinate love of money and flattery," a preacher who "delighted to blazon himself as Christ's foremost champion in the land." And of Cotton Mather's pious attempts to justify the burning of witches Adams remarks, "It is not credible that an educated and a sane man could ever have honestly believed in the absurd stuff which he produced as evidence of the supernatural." Father and son are quoted at length on their opposition to Leverett's appointment to the presidency of Harvard, and only after reading their epistles to Governor Dudley and their diary notations can one appreciate Adams' pleasure in their discomfiture—"But these venomous priests had tried their fangs upon a resolute and able man. Dudley shook them off like vermin."

Having noted that the dominance and decline of the Puritan priesthood followed a fairly common trend in the history of social development, Adams devoted the next decade of his life to the evidence that enabled him to write his most original contribution, *The Law of Civilization and Decay.* In 1893, four years before the volume was actually published, his brother Henry, then his intimate companion, commented in a letter, "Loving paradox, Brooks, with the advantages of ten years' study, had swept away much rubbish in the effort to build up a new line of thought for himself, but he found that no paradox compared with that of daily events. The facts were constantly overrunning his thoughts." And having read the final version of the manuscript, Henry wrote to his brother, "You have struck out of it pretty much all that was personally offensive, and left only generalities which no one need resent . . . all I can say is that, if I wanted to write any book, it would be the one you have written." This last remark, incidentally, should set at rest the common assumption that Henry and not Brooks was the first American to develop as a law of history the theory that "civilization followed the exchanges."

This law is largely based on an intensive study of trade routes and the shifting centers of civilization. It assumes that civilization is the product of social concentration, constantly seeking a new equilibrium and compelled to find it; that it moves always from decentralization to centralization and back again to decentralization. A corollary of the law pertains to the conspicuous roles played by man's two basic drives, fear and greed, during the different periods of civilization.

> In the earlier stages of concentration, fear appears to be the channel through which energy finds the readiest outlet; accordingly, in primitive and scattered communities, the imagination is vivid, and the mental types are religious, military, artistic. As consolidation advances, fear yields to greed, and the economic organism tends to supersede the emotional and the martial.

While fear holds sway the sacred caste is the characteristic ruling class; when greed motivates social behavior, supremacy passes to a moneyed oligarchy.

To prove the validity of this law Adams traces in vivid detail the development of European civilization from the earliest times to the present—and in passing offers pointed illustrations and shrewd observations which even more than the law itself illumine the dark recesses of human nature. He examines the rise and decline of the various centers of population and demonstrates the similarity in each instance in the elements of growth and decay. In our own era, with which the book is most concerned, the fall of Rome initiated a period of decentralization which lasted a thousand years—a millennium during which men were motivated by the fear of the invisible and consequently were dominated by the organized clergy. With the development of trade and science, however, fear gave way to greed and in time resulted in the Reformation, the separation of church and state, and the supremacy of the moneyed classes. England, having gone farthest along the path of concentration, best illustrates this constant flux:

> Gradually energy vented itself more and more freely through these merchants, until they became the ruling power in England, their government lasting from 1688 to 1815. At length they fell through the very brilliancy of their genius. The wealth they amassed so rapidly, accumulated, until it prevailed over all other forms of force, and by so doing raised another variety of man to power. These last were the modern bankers. With the advent of the bankers a profound change came over civilization, for contraction began. Self-interest had from the outset taught the producer that, to prosper, he should deal in wares which tended rather to rise than to fall in value, relatively to corn. The opposite

instinct possessed the usurer; he found that he grew rich when money appreciated, or when the borrower had to part with more property to pay his debt when it fell due, than the cash lent him would have brought on the day the obligation was contracted.

Another corollary of the law is the relative character of law itself. "Law is merely the expression of the will of the strongest for the time being, and therefore laws have no fixity, but shift from generation to generation." At each stage of civilization the class in power has always sought to perpetuate itself by means of legislation. When the imagination is vivid and fear holds sway over the minds of men, ecclesiastical law prevails. As trade develops and competition sharpens, civil codes are drawn up

> for the enforcement of contracts and the protection of the creditor class. The more society consolidates, the more legislation is controlled by the wealthy, and at length the representatives of the monied class acquire that absolute power once wielded by the Roman pro-consul and now exercised by the modern magistrate.

When *The Law of Civilization and Decay* was published in 1897 the author's views on the then-embittered silver question obscured the great merits of the book. Because Adams advocated bimetallism his work was attacked and deprecated when it was not deliberately ignored. The one important exception was Theodore Roosevelt's extended review in *The Forum.* Although Roosevelt was expected by his friends to demolish the book, and he certainly disapproved strongly of Adams' political and economic radicalism, he was urbane enough to find the volume "a marvel of compressed statement" and a distinguished contribution to the philosophy of history. Although he objected, more or less justifiably, to a number of statements made by the author he readily admitted his scholarly approach and deep sympathy:

> Through the cold impartiality with which he strives to work merely as a recorder of facts, there break through now and then flashes of pent-up wrath and vehement scorn for all that is mean and petty in a purely materialistic, purely capitalistic, civilization.

In *America's Economic Supremacy* and *The New Empire,* collections of essays published in 1900 and 1902 respectively, Brooks Adams pursues his study of the flux of civilization, but with special reference to modern economic concentration and to the sudden emergence of the United States as a world power. Main trade routes are again examined in great detail and their obvious effect upon the flow of social activity is indicated. Adams is here acutely interested in the problem of the transmission of energy from one center of concentration to another. He demonstrates effectively, decades before the appearance of Spengler's work on the decline of Western civilization, the constant movement of power and empire from east to west, from south to north, until they have gone half around the earth and have at the turn of the 20th century established themselves in the United States. After considering all the available facts he points out that the centers of concentration have developed in places containing an abundance of food and useful metals and that when these means of wealth are depleted the seat of power migrates to a more suitable location. In this respect he was also among the first to develop the effect of geography on politics. "I am convinced that neither history nor economics can be intelligently studied without a constant reference to the geographical surroundings which have affected different nations."

Having traced the past movement of empire from one center of concentration to another Adams proceeded to analyze economic conditions in Europe during the final quarter of the last century. France he found definitely in eclipse after the war with Prussia, and Germany in his view lacked the resources required for world dominance. Of Russia he was less certain. A vast country, potentially capable of great economic development, it could be impelled in that direction only by the cataclysm of social revolution. In the light of what has actually happened his perspicacity is of special interest—"What a social revolution in Russia would portend transcends human foresight but probably its effect would be felt throughout the world." England, having maintained the seat of wealth and power for more than a century, he believed definitely on the decline. In his opinion Englishmen were exerting less initiative, less energy; were depending too much on the income from their colonies; were indulging themselves to the point of mental inertia. In the United States, on the contrary, the ascending curve of power was clearly evident. In every field of major economic endeavor American enterprise and American wealth dwarfed the efforts of competing countries.

What impressed Adams most about this transfer of "the seat of energy" was the extraordinary velocity of its migration. "A change of equilibrium," he pointed out, "has heretofore occupied at least the span of a human lifetime, so that a new generation has gradually become habituated to the novel environment. In this instance the revolution came so suddenly that few realized its presence before it ended." For this reason he regarded the rapid rise of his native land to industrial and business supremacy with grave apprehension. He knew the type of men who headed the gigantic corporations and huge banking establishments and he did not trust them. Aware also that "prosperity had always borne within itself the seeds of its own decay" he could not help fearing that the cupidity of our business leaders would either bring on a social revolution or hasten the migration of economic power from our shores to the next "seat of energy" across the Pacific. "Supremacy," he reflected, "has always entailed its sacrifices as well as its triumphs, and fortune has seldom smiled on those who beside being energetic and industrious, have not been armed, organized, and bold."

The problem of America's destiny perturbed Brooks Adams so acutely that he could not refrain from pondering it for years on end. In an article published in 1910 he writes:

> Within the last decade, step by step and very reluctantly, I have been led to suspect that not only the tranquility of life, but the coherence of society itself, may hinge upon our ability to modify, more or less radically, our method of thinking, and, as I tend toward this conclusion, I look at these questions more seriously. . . . We are abundantly inventive and can create wealth, but we cannot control the energy which we liberate. Why we fail is the problem which perplexes me.

Continuing his study of the greatly-increased velocity of our economic concentration, and being only too familiar with the type of mind of our leading "malefactors of wealth," he was led gradually and unwillingly to the conclusion that, unless we exercised our best intelligence, "the expansion of the social core within would induce an explosion which we call a revolution."

In 1913 he published the result of this cogitation and research in a volume entitled *The Theory of Social Revolutions.* Applying his law of civilization and decay to contemporary conditions he argues cogently that our present rulers, the capitalists, are incapable of coping with the complex problem of democratic government and must be deprived of their dominant position. His analysis of our modern economic system, to which he devotes a good part of the book, is detailed and incisive, if somewhat oversimplified—as when he insists that our economy is under the complete control of a small group of men concentrated near the tip of Manhattan:

> Since 1871, while the area within which competition is possible has been kept constant by the tariff, capital has accumulated and has been concentrated and volatilized until, within the republic, substantially all prices are fixed by a vast moneyed class. This class, obeying what amounts to being a single volition, has its heart in Wall Street, and pervades every corner of the Union.

Not that Adams condemned this development of monopolies; on the contrary, as an economic scientist he regarded it as a "vital principle of our civilization" which could not be eliminated without undermining our economic system. But he could not abide the predatory capitalists who were exploiting the various monopolies for their own selfish ends.

> The modern capitalist not only thinks in terms of money, but he thinks in terms of money more exclusively than the French aristocrat or lawyer ever thought in terms of caste. . . . He may sell his services to whom he pleases and at what price may suit him, and if by so doing he ruins men and cities, it is nothing to him. He is not responsible, for he is not a trustee for the public.

Brooks Adams' indictment of the capitalist class is thorough and devastating—he sees it as a crass, greedy, unprincipled and unsocial body of men, without vision or the capacity for leadership, clinging desperately and defiantly to the economic power thrust upon them by the sudden and fortuitous change in "the seat of energy." As an example of the capitalist's blindness Adams points to his stupid scorn for the very laws enacted for his safeguard. "In spite of his vulnerability, he is of all citizens the most lawless. He appears to assume that the law will always be enforced, when he has need of it, by some special personnel whose duty lies that way, while he may evade the law, when convenient, or bring it into contempt, with impunity." But Adams finds the capitalist's failure to emerge out of his narrow role as the exploiter of money and men, to become a power for good over the nation as a whole, an even more glaring deficiency:

> From the days of William the Conqueror to our own, the great soldier has been, very commonly, a famous statesman also, but I do not now remember, in English or American history, a single capitalist who has earned eminence for comprehensive statesmanship. . . . Certainly, so far as I am aware, no capitalist has ever acquired such influence over his contemporaries, as has been attained with apparent ease by men like Cromwell, Washington, or even Jackson.

Step by step the argument leads to the inevitable conclusion that the capitalist class had, like all the ruling groups in the past, served its social purpose while advancing along the path to power and that, like the earlier ruling groups, it had been "stricken with fatuity" once it reached the crest. Adams avers:

> Privileged classes have seldom the intelligence to protect themselves by adaptation when nature turns against them, and, up to the present moment, the old privileged class in the United States has shown little promise of being an exception to the rule. . . . It is hard to resist the persuasion that unless capital can, in the immediate future, generate an intellectual energy, beyond the sphere of its specialized calling, very much in excess of any intellectual energy of which it has hitherto given promise, and unless it can besides rise to an appre-ciation of diverse social conditions, as well as to a level of political sagacity, far higher than it has attained within recent years, its relative power in the community must decline.

He has not the slightest doubt, of course, that the capitalist class would neither discover within itself the intelligence and the ability with which to perpetuate its power nor submit peacefully to the group destined to supplant it. He feared therefore that the resulting struggle for power would be as radical and calamitous as all previous similar contests, since "the rise of a new governing class is always synonymous with a social revolution and a redistribution of property."

Brooks Adams was equally outspoken in his censure of the politico-economic nature of our court system. Long before J. Allen Smith and Charles A. Beard he described the class bias of our Constitution and the special interpretation given it by lawyers elevated by the group in power. In this book he offers a wealth of irrefutable evidence to the effect not only that our federal courts function politically but that their political character had been given them deliberately at the beginning of our national existence. At the time the Constitution was under discussion, he explains, this compromise had seemed the only feasible solution of the impasse between the frail federal republic and the jealous and obstinate states. As a consequence of this adjustment the courts have arrogated to themselves the right to control the political branches of the government. He contends:

> Under the American system the Constitution, or fundamental law, is expounded by judges, and this function which, in essence, is political, has brought precisely that duality of pressure on the bench which it has been the labor of a hundred generations of our ancestors to remove. On the whole the result has been not to elevate politics, but to lower the courts to the political level.

He cites numerous instances, from the case of *Marbury vs. Madison* down, to indicate how often the judiciary has interfered with the will of Congress in favor of a special class; and maintains that a society organized under the modern scientific conditions which have created trusts and monopolies out of the essentials of life cannot indefinitely be "administered under an effete code of law."

> Law is the frame which contains society, as its banks contain a river; and if the flow of a river be increased a thousandfold, the banks must be altered to correspond, or there will be flood overwhelming in proportion to the uncontrollable energy generated. . . . Courts, I need hardly say, cannot control nature, though by trying to do so they may, like the Parliament of Paris, create a friction which shall induce an appalling catastrophe.

Eager to circumvent the danger threatening the country, Adams became wrathful at the thought that those best able to save it were instead selfishly bent on maintaining the status quo. Himself a member of a family of lawyers and a profound student of the law, he excoriated the limited and rigid mentality of the legal practitioners who were more interested in benefiting their clients than in upholding the law, and who employed their ingenuity and cunning in behalf of the capitalists bent on aggrandizement. It is this type of lawyer, he argued, who has deliberately turned the Constitution into a fetish (as if it had "some inherent and marvellous virtue by which it can arrest the march of omnipotent Nature") in order to make it a bulwark against the attempts of the people to adapt their economy to changing conditions.

Brooks Adams was preoccupied throughout his mature years with the basic problem of our industrial civilization: how to adjust modern society to the ever-increasing velocity of economic concentration. The more he dug into the origins of our economy, the more he observed its effect upon the mass of mankind, the more he was persuaded that capitalism must be superseded by a system of government more in keeping with our scientific centralization if we are to avoid an internal explosion and maintain our world supremacy. Knowing that every ruling class is struck blind once it has passed the crest of its upward curve, he was full of foreboding. "I am full of gloomy fears," he wrote to Mr. Ford in 1897, the year in which his book *The Law of Civilization and Decay* was published, "I do not know where we are going, nor do I see any light ahead. There seems to me to be no headway on the ship, and that we are going on the rocks. I hope I may be wrong." Further research in the fields of economics and politics only intensified his premonitions, and in *The Theory of Social Revolutions* he exerted his brilliant powers of analysis and generalization, as well as his natural capacity for invective, to make clear to his countrymen the inherent faults of our system of government and their urgent need of a remedy.

It is easy to dismiss his admonitions as the alarms of a disgruntled pessimist, as some have done, or to decry his indictment of capitalism as an arraignment from a pseudo-socialist. Brooks Adams was neither. He had an extraordinary familiarity with the law and a thorough and profound knowledge of the history of civilization. In addition he was moved in all things by a passion for social justice, by an intense devotion to truth. Motivated in all his writings by an acute puritanic conscience, he propounded his views of civilization, and of own economy, with the force of utter conviction. If, in his eagerness to generalize and to express himself emphatically, his conclusions were at times too sweeping, his basic assumptions are as valid today as when they were first made. Indeed his original and acute intellect perceived trends and relationships long before they became obvious to his contemporaries. Again, although he was certainly familiar with the works of the leading socialistic writers and although the Marxian theory of history was really, according to his brother Henry, the foundation for Brooks' later historical views, the similarity was only coincidental. He had too keen and unequivocal a mind to absorb the ideas of another uncritically. Politically he was, if anything, "a Jeffersonian Jacksonian Bryonian democrat" (to quote the words of his favorite brother) and a passionate admirer of Washington, "the whole man—in brief, he was a true descendant of the Adamses who had helped build our nation and who had had the courage to prefer truth and honesty to the good will of men. And if his animadversions upon our state of society offended those in power—men who were getting what they could for themselves and let "the public be damned"—with the result that his books went quickly out of print and are today practically unobtainable and unknown, the loss is all the more our own.

**Donald J. Pierce (review date 1943)**

SOURCE: A review of *The Law of Civilization and Decay: An Essay on History*, by Brooks Adams, in *Political Science Quarterly*, Vol. LVIII, No. 3, September, 1943, pp. 457-58.

[*In the following excerpt, Pierce favorably reviews* The Law of Civilization and Decay.]

It might be thought unnecessary to describe the contents of a book which was first published almost half a century ago, which appeared in two foreign languages and in several editions and reprints, and which is declared by Mr. Charles A. Beard, who now introduces it, to be "among the outstanding documents of intellectual history in the United States and, in a way, the Western World"; yet the reviewer knew a young historian a few years ago who had recently finished writing a volume on the decline of ancient Rome and had never heard of Brooks Adams' thesis. There are some books which run so counter to the prevailing tendencies, or influences, of the society in which they appear, that it is possible, in spite of the many great qualities that they may possess, for something approaching a conspiracy of silence to develop against them and gradually bury them in oblivion. It is impossible to know to what extent, if at all, the present study was subjected to such a process; but there can be little doubt that many of its pronouncements are of the kind that would certainly have aroused during recent decades a wide and deep hostility.

The theme of *The Law of Civilization and Decay* is the course of history from the days of the Roman Republic down to the nineties of the last century; yet less emphasis is placed upon the occurrences that actually make up that course than upon the nature of the course itself, and the reasons why it prevailed. Thus there are vast stretches and regions of history, even within the selected field, to which little or no reference is made; and only those sections of the historical process are described which seemed to the author most clearly to illustrate the nature and tendencies of the process as a whole. The events dealt with are indicated by the titles of the chapters: "The Romans", "The Middle Age", "The First Crusade", "The Second Crusade", "The Fall of Constantinople", "The Suppression of the Temple", "The English Reformation", "The Suppression of the Convents", "The Eviction of the Yeomen", "Spain and India", "Modern Centralization". But throughout these chapters much of the space is given over to a description and discussion of the theory which is being brought out or maintained; and a final chapter, "Conclusion", is similarly divided between fact and theory. Perhaps a historical work of this kind, in which occurrences are presented essentially with a view to expounding and emphasizing certain principles, might best be described as "a philosophy of history".

What makes the volume interesting and valuable today, however, is not so much the "philosophy" which was ostensibly its main purpose, as the history which was utilized to support the theory. It is still probably true that, for the vast majority of people who in one way or another come into contact with history as it may be studied and known, many of those events which are most significant for a true understanding of the past remain hidden, or are so misrepresented by various "interpretations" as to lose most of their real significance; and to no class of events is this observation more applicable than to those which belong to what is generally called the "economic" sphere. It was in such happenings, largely connected with the ownership and operation of various forms of wealth, that Brooks Adams sought to discover a formula or "law" to account for the main course of history down to his own time; and the facts which he utilized to carry out his purpose are still well worth the concentrated attention of all students who would attempt to know how the present state of mankind came about, and especially of those who have been partially befogged by various "official" histories.

Unfortunately much of the theory of the book tends to defeat what must have been the fundamental purpose of the author; namely, to use the past as a guide or a warning for the future. A contemptuous repudiation of religion as magic, superstition or greed is not likely to inspire confidence in an author among logical-minded readers; and an explanation of the course of history which ascribes all change to the operation of inexorable "natural laws" contains its own refutation. Everyone has a religion, even if it be only a worship of self, or a machine or "the laws of nature"; and if human conduct is inevitable, so, too, are explanations of history, and truth and falsity do not exist.

Such weaknesses, however, may be ascribed largely to Brooks Adams' background and environment and the age in which he lived. They should not be allowed to detract unduly from the real greatness of his work which was undoubtedly inspired by honest motives and which was carried through painstakingly and brilliantly. Merely as evidence in the history of ideas in the late nineteenth and early twentieth centuries the *Law* is well worth reading, and this value is greatly enhanced in the present edition by Mr. Beard's masterly Introduction.

**Rushton Coulborn (review date 1943)**

SOURCE: A review of *The Law of Civilization and Decay: An Essay on History*, in *American Historical Review*, Vol. 49, No. 1, October, 1943, pp. 77-78.

[*In the following excerpt, Coulborn favorably reviews* The Law of Civilization and Decay, *but finds much of its research and conclusions dated.*]

The republication of Brooks Adams' theory of history [*The Law of Civilization and Decay: An Essay on History*] is an event of importance to historians. Mr. Alfred Knopf judged such an event timely. Dr. Charles A. Beard judged Brooks Adams' work the best lesson from the American classics for the present generation of historians. By this judgment and by his introduction Dr. Beard repeats the attempt made by Brooks Adams' more distinguished brother Henry, half a century ago, to persuade American historians to take their profession seriously and address themselves to the problem Brooks Adams faced.

Brooks Adams explained history as a cyclical process, each civilization—the term not defined—beginning in an age of dispersion and proceeding into an age of concentration. In the first age, the first phase of the cycle, institutions are loose and weak and the "imaginative man" leads society, expressing himself in religion and in war; fear is the dominant urge in this age. In the second age, the second phase of the cycle, there is a process of centralization and the "economic man" attains to leadership, expressing himself in science and in business, especially in currency manipulation; greed has now become the dominant urge. The "law" of civilization compels a society to move from the first into the second phase of the cycle and then, continuing to operate, becomes a law of decay, as economic man, in his climactic type, the "usurer," gradually starves his fellows until their vitality is destroyed. Thereupon new "races" appear and the cyclical process is repeated *ad infinitum.* This theory Brooks Adams applied to the Graeco-Roman and Western civilizations.

Some of his contemporaries received Brooks Adams' sally politely—for example, the reviewer in this journal (see *Am. Hist. Rev.*, I, 568). But it did not convert the profession; the same reviewer gently recommended further "minute study" of the "fall of Rome" before "any very complete work . . . upon the general course of history" was undertaken. Since that time Brooks's problem, the meaning of history, has been treated by some foreign scholars, few of them professional historians.

There are important parts of Brooks's argument which have been put out of court by the increase of knowledge since his time, but there are other parts still well worthy of comparison with the products of more recent thinkers. As a determinist and a vitalist Brooks Adams anticipated Spengler, as Dr. Beard notices (pp. 3-4). Today there is a strong reaction against determinism which tends to result in vitalism becoming humanistic. But Brooks's treatment of economic matters, which Henry Adams thought akin to Marx's treatment, has recently been fairly closely paralleled by Ralph Turner in his anthropological-economic interpretation of history (see *Am. Hist. Rev.*, XLVII, 810). Brooks's "usurer" is one type of what Ortega y Gasset calls the "mass-man," when the mass-man rises to power. The first phase of Brooks's cycle is equivalent to Toynbee's "universal church" and, though vaguer, is perhaps by the same token truer to the facts. Brooks's description of the two phases of his cycle is not impressive when compared with modern definitions of culture by categories, as made, for example, by MacIver or the Webers. Nevertheless, the two-phase cycle itself, which goes back to Vico, still seems to the reviewer preferable to Sorokin's three-phase cycle.

Whatever crudities and positive errors there may be in Brooks Adams' theory, he did face the supreme problem of the historian. And, if this last statement be regarded as one of opinion, the opinion is shared by Dr. Beard, by Toynbee, and presumably by most of the other scholars mentioned above. Dr. Beard says in his introduction (p.

4) that "all great human causes turn on theories of history, that all the modern revolutions which have shaken the world have been inspired by theories of history. Every piece of philosophic, economic or political writing either presents such a theory or rests upon assumptions, articulate or tacit, derived from it." In the present era of wars, revolutions, and other social struggles, then, Brooks Adams brings a pertinent message to historians.

Finally, *The Law of Civilization and Decay* presents an instructive example of the relation between the events and conditions of a period of history and the serious historiography of that period. Dr. Beard's introduction demonstrates that relation at length. He has used in part the evidence of unpublished material, namely Henry Adams' annotations upon the manuscripts made before publication of the New York and Paris editions and several letters of Brooks and Henry made available by Mr. Henry Adams of Boston, nephew of the brothers. From this portion of the introduction a thoughtful historian has an admirable opportunity to deduce the true meaning of the duty of objectivity. He may perhaps measure his own professional qualifications by his ability to make the deduction.

It is fair to add—since there is here much praise of Brooks Adams—that contemporary historians may take warning from what may be called the "romance" of Brooks's conclusion. There were, in fact, three rather different conclusions, respectively in the English, American, and French editions! (The conclusions are stated in the respective prefaces, not in the last chapter.) Now Newton (so far as is known to the reviewer) did not publish three editions of the *Principia* having three different conclusions: the apple did not shoot up to heaven, nor did it fly off tangentially to the east; it fell only and always to the ground. At least, the contrast shows that Dr. Beard is right when he says that *The Law of Civilization and Decay* is no law; at most, it shows that Benedetto Croce is right—but I cannot believe that he *is* altogether right—when he says that the historian should not seek to be a prophet.

## Harry Elmer Barnes (essay date 1944)

SOURCE: "Brooks Adams on World Utopia," in *Current History*, Vol. 6, No. 29, January, 1944, pp. 1-6.

[*In the following excerpt, Barnes examines the intellectual background of Adams's* The Law of Civilization and Decay.]

The air is full of planning for the future happy state of mankind. Glimpses of Utopia are everywhere in evidence. Glib and hopeful books on "The United States of the World" are being written by Clement Wood and others. The speedy installation of a strong and durable international political order and plenty of milk for the Hottentots are being freely predicted.

Personally, all this suits me perfectly and I hope that these rosy dreams may quickly come true. But we all want to know what the prospects are that they may do so. Actually, the world was never in a more chaotic and unpredictable condition. We may attain Utopia, but it is also possible that we may temporarily revert to barbarism instead. We need light as well as heat. We should pay attention to the skeptics as well as the optimists.

In this search for light and balance we may profitably turn to the one American philosopher who has dealt with the history and destiny of man in a profound, searching and skeptical fashion, namely, Mr. Brooks Adams, author of the now historic book, *The Law of Civilization and Decay,* first published in 1895.

Brooks Adams was hardly the first American writer to suggest a philosophy of history. Before him, William T. Harris and Josiah Royce had expounded the doctrines of Hegel, John William Draper had brought over from England the historical philosophy of Henry Thomas Buckle, and John Fiske had applied the evolutionary doctrine of Spencer and others to historical developments. But Mr. Adams was the first American writer to formulate a comprehensive and original philosophy of history, and to write a book to expound and illustrate it.

The numerous and far-reaching historical changes of our time and the great uncertainties of the social future make it a highly timely enterprise to bring out a new printing of this classic work, which sought to discover whether there is any law of historical development and, if so, what it is. We may, therefore, feel much indebted to Alfred Knopf for issuing an attractively printed new edition, based on the version published by the Macmillan Company in 1896, the book having been first published in England.

Scarcely less valuable than the new edition itself is the long introduction of over fifty pages by Charles Austin Beard, which combines textual scholarship with interpretative genius. The introduction is devoted to the intellectual and personal basis of Mr. Adams' theory of history, to the relative influence of Brooks and Henry Adams in developing it, to the nature and growth of the theory through the several editions of the book, and to an examination of its validity and of the permanent value of the discussion which the book provoked.

Perhaps the most valuable and original portion of Professor Beard's introduction is his account of the origins and development of Mr. Adams' trend of thought and of the intellectual relations between Brooks Adams and his more famous brother, Henry Adams. Because of Henry Adams' well known concern with the philosophy of history, it has been widely believed that Henry really suggested the theory which runs through his brother's book, and then Brooks merely dug about in historical materials to document the notion.

THE AGE OF FEAR

The exact reverse appears to be true. Henry Adams seems to have had no interest in the philosophy of history until 1893, when Brooks propounded to him the doctrines that underlie *The Law of Civilization and Decay.* Doctor Beard believes, and the evidence seems conclusive, that Henry Adams' writings on the philosophy of history, especially his well known efforts to interpret historical development in terms of thermo-dynamics, were almost entirely the outgrowth of his discussions with Brooks Adams following 1893. So it was Brooks who made a philosopher out of Henry, rather than the reverse. It may be, however, that Henry's over-ecstatic notions about medieval art, architecture and culture had no little influence upon Brooks' conviction that the age of fear is highly conducive to works of imagination and art.

Brooks Adams' philosophy of history was built up gradually as a result of a number of lines of thought. His original and daring study of colonial New England impressed him with the hitherto generally neglected economic factors in the Protestant Reformation. Reflecting upon the then popular Darwinism and Spencerianism, Adams became skeptical of the dogma of universal and unilateral progress. The dramatic importance and immediacy of financial and monetary problems in the early 'nineties, emphasized the potent rôle of capitalism and finance throughout the course of history. These lines of thought converged to give him his philosophy of history.

Brooks Adams' conception of the evolution and destiny of human civilization may be briefly summarized about as follows: The history of mankind is, in the most profound sense, the human manifestation of dynamic cosmic energy. The actions of all animal societies, including the human race, are refined and secondary expressions of solar energy. The historical evolution of our race and human culture constitutes a mental progression from Barbarism (dispersion) to Civilization (concentration), and then a reversion to Barbarism and Anarchy.

In the case of the human race, cosmic energy expresses itself chiefly through mental activity. In the era of Barbarism, *Fear* is the dominating mental trait and produces the *imaginative mind.* This manifests itself in war, conquest and other deeds of virility, in notable works of art, and in the storing up of wealth through conquest. When enough wealth has been accumulated, *Greed* gains ascendancy over Fear and produces the *economic mind.*

In this second main era of cultural evolution, which Adams calls Civilization, economic activities dominate, taking the form of plutocratic capitalism and the exploitation of society by the money-changers. Morale, racial virility, art and social institutions tend to decay as a result of this corrosive process, fathered by the bourgeoisie, and the net result is an inevitable return to Barbarism.

Anarchy rather than collectivism and a world-state would, thus, appear to be the next stage of human experience. Mr. Adams' own summary of this dolorous outlook, for at least the immediate future of the human race, is well stated in the following paragraphs:

"However large may be the store of energy accumulated by conquest, a race must, sooner or later, reach the limit of its martial energy, when it must enter on the phase of economic competition. But, as the economic organism radically differs from the emotional and martial, the effect of economic competition has been, perhaps invariably, to dissipate the energy amassed by war."

"When surplus energy has accumulated in such bulk as to preponderate over productive energy, it becomes the controlling social force. Thenceforward, capital is autocratic, and energy vents itself through those organisms best fitted to give expression to the power of capital. In this last stage of consolidation, the economic, and, perhaps, the scientific intellect is propagated, while the imagination fades, and the emotional, the martial and the artistic types of manhood decay. When a social velocity has been attained at which the waste of energetic material is so great that the martial and imaginative stocks fail to reproduce themselves, intensifying competition appears to generate two extreme eco-nomic types—the usurer in his most formidable aspect, and the peasant whose nervous system is best adapted to thrive on scanty nutriment. At length a point must be reached when pressure can go no further, and then, perhaps, one of two results may follow: A stationary period may supervene, which may last until ended by war, by exhaustion, or by both combined, as seems to have been the case with the Eastern Empire: or, as in the Western, disintegration may set it the civilized population may perish, and a reversion may take place to a primitive form of organism."

"The evidence, however, seems to point to the conclusion that, when a highly centralized society disintegrates, under the pressure of economic competition, it is because the energy of the race has been exhausted. Consequently, the survivors of such a community lack the power necessary for renewed concentration, and must probably remain inert until supplied with fresh energetic material by the infusion of barbarian blood."

ADAMS' EXAMPLE

To illustrate his theory of history, Mr. Adams turned especially to the "fall" of Rome, the Protestant Reformation and the British Empire. His theory of the dominant influence of money power led him to lay special stress upon the rôle of the monetary exchanges in each of these epochs of history. The tyranny of the usurer brought about the fall of Rome and the reversion to medievalism, where the revived régime of Fear encouraged war and creative artistic achievements. The Reformation renewed the tendency towards centralization, with mankind becoming once more primarily concerned about economic matters, promoted the growth of capitalism and produced a return to the dominion of Greed and the economic mind, which had earlier doomed Rome. England, through the combined impact of the Reformation and imperial expansion, represented the most extreme triumph of these centralizing and financial tendencies which are, according to Mr. Adams, ultimately to return society once more to Anarchy, Fear and Barbarism.

Mr. Adams takes a strong position against the current assumption in our optimistic circles that humanity can—indeed, must—pass on from Civilization to Utopia. He contends that the status of Rome at its height and of England at the close of the nineteenth century represents the highest level that man can reasonably hope to attain. He holds that the evidence in both time and space is overwhelming on this point:

> "Such uniformity of development in the most distant times, and among the most divergent peoples, points to a progressive law of civilization, each stage of progress being marked by certain intellectual, moral, and physical changes. As the attack in war masters the defence, and the combative instinct becomes unnecessary to the preservation of life, the economic supersedes the martial mind, being superior in bread-winning. As velocity augments and competition intensifies, nature begins to sift the economic minds themselves, culling a favoured aristocracy of the craftiest and the subtlest types; choosing, for example, the Armenian in Byzantium, the Marwari in India, and the Jew in London. Conversely, as the costly nervous system of the soldier becomes an encumbrance, organisms, which can exist on less, successively supplant each other, until the limit of endurance is reached. Thus the Slavs exterminated the Greeks in Thrace and Macedonia, the Mahrattas and the Moslems dwindle before the low caste tribes of India, and the instinct of self-preservation has taught white races to resist an influx of Chinese. When nature has finished this double task, civilization has reached its zenith. Humanity can ascend no higher."

If we accept Mr. Adams' line of historical reasoning neither world organization nor Utopia lies ahead of us. Rather, an ominous prospect of cultural and institutional disintegration lies in the offing. Indeed, the second World War may be hastening us in this direction with unprecedented speed. If this unhappy destiny of the race is not inevitable, it is surely sufficiently possible to warrant our reckoning with its implications and taking what steps we may to avert its realization.

We may agree with Professor Beard that Mr. Adams' theory of history is highly stimulating, if not always borne out by the facts, though his emphasis upon the economic aspects of the Reformation is in accord with later scholarship. If few take seriously any longer the cynical theory of history, it is also true that discriminating students no longer accept the idea of inevitable, universal and unilateral progress.

Most historians today would reverse Mr. Adams' emphasis upon the creative factors in history. Fear seems far more likely to breed intolerance, stagnation, superstition and violence, than notable cultural achievements. On the other hand, commerce is regarded as one of the great civilizing agencies of history. The expansion of Europe and Commercial Revolution after 1450 are looked upon as the most dynamic forces in creating modern civilization, just as Periclean Athens was the product of temporary commercial dominion and prosperity. Capitalism has, assuredly, produced plenty of exploitation and waste, but Soviet Russia demonstrates that the outcome of this may not be a return to primitive barbarism.

TECHNOLOGY UNDERESTIMATED

But perhaps the main weakness in Mr. Adams' approach to history is his relative neglect of the technological elements in human destiny. Our modern empire of machines renders the comparison of our age with any earlier period highly misleading in many respects. Even the fall of Rome depended more upon technological factors, such as inadequate communication and transportation, than upon the monetary trends and practices.

In dealing with money and finance, Mr. Adams erred in reading back the finance capitalism that was just getting established in his own time into periods of history where it scarcely existed. His theory is much more cogent in helping us to understand American history between the two World Wars than in throwing light upon the fall of Rome. It may, indeed, be more relevant to the destiny of twentieth-century culture and institutions than to the ancient and early modern cultures to which Adams chiefly applied his doctrine.

At any rate, it is probably better for an historian to think hard, even if he sometimes thinks wrong, than it is for him to store away his mental equipment and plod along as a dull, if prolific, copyist and recording clerk. The method of Brooks Adams is as important and useful to historians as that of Leopold von Ranke.

Despite Mr. Adams' failure adequately to consider the technological factors in history and the novelty of our own material culture, his pessimistic outlook may be justified. We cannot be certain that history will not vindicate his predictions. Most of us insist upon living in a sort of fool's paradise, maintaining that we are so highly civilized that we could not possibly revert to barbarism. We know that the enlightened Greeks and Romans lost their civilization, but no such calamity, it is said, could possibly descend upon us. Our civilization is too highly developed and well buttressed.

The historian of culture quickly senses the fallacy in this argument. In every respect, except for science and machinery, the Greeks and Romans were more highly civilized than we are. Our superiority in science and machinery is an asset, to be sure, but it is such only if used wisely and for the benefit of mankind. In our artificially maintained scarcity economy, efficient machinery can close more factories—and more speedily—than the cruder industrial mechanisms of earlier day. And events since September, 1939, amply demonstrate what science and machinery, unrestrainedly placed at the service of Mars, can accomplish in the way of hitherto unimaginable destruction of life and property. Giant air bombers, massive tanks, submarines, heavy artillery, machine guns and rocket bombs can obliterate civilization far more quickly and successfully than the javelin, broadsword and battle-axe.

In other words, our marvelous science, machinery, and armaments, if used unwisely, can consign our culture to a more inevitable and speedier oblivion than the rudimentary science, machinery, and weapons which were at the disposal of the Greeks and Romans. It is obvious, therefore, that not only can we lose our civilization, but in an even more catastrophic manner than in ancient days. The glory that was Greece and the grandeur that was Rome expired, so to speak, relatively slowly and gently. Our civilization may die a violent and rapid death. Indeed, it almost inevitably will do so unless we can plan a social and international order which will enable us to use our newly-acquired science and machinery for the benefit rather than the impoverishment and destruction of humanity.

## Daniel Aaron (essay date 1948)

SOURCE: "The Unusable Man: An Essay on the Mind of Brooks Adams," in *The New England Quarterly,* Vol. XXI, No. 1, March, 1948, pp. 3-33.

[*In the following excerpt, Aaron surveys Adams's work and intellectual development.*]

I

Brooks Adams has been dead for more than twenty years now, but there are still many people in Boston and Cambridge who remember this eccentric and arrogant man, the last of the children of Charles Francis Adams to survive. His nephews and nieces recall his gruff manner and his penchant for saying shocking things at dinner parties, his love of argument, his endless jaunts to watering spas, his fondness for the Scottish lays he compelled his niece Abigail Adams to memorize. To some people, it seems, he was known as a crank, "that damned fool, Brooks," and Boston never quite accepted the man whom, during the fiery days of '96, it had ostracized as a dangerous incendiary. Even his brother Henry, certainly closer to Brooks than to any other member of his family, saw a mulish streak in the youngest Adams, and continually cautioned him not to kick so violently against the obnoxious aspects of American life they both loathed but to which Henry had become resigned.

Brooks never became resigned to anything, no matter how vehemently he boasted to Henry that he had. He remained the rebel, the unreconstructed individualist, knowing all the time that he was an anachronism, an "unusable man," as his niece put it, preaching to uncomprehending ears. The few times in his life when he did manage to interest a small audience always astonished him, and he would sometimes announce with a curious air of triumph to Cabot Lodge or to Henry that he was not

a maniac. "I feel I am not mad," he wrote to Lodge in 1894 as if to reassure himself. "I am after all like other men. I am not the victim of an illusion. I am not a man with a maggot in my brain—and all the years when I have been wandering from New York to Jerusalem speculating on the causes which seemed to be crushing the world, I have not been morbid, crazy or ill." This is the cry of the "unusable man," the prophet in the wilderness, and it is only after we have discovered more about this misplaced American that we can understand his despair. It is agonizing to believe that one has a revelation that one's contemporaries are incapable of responding to, and Brooks Adams's eccentricity and neuroticism were aggravated if not actually produced by what he chose to regard as the blockheadedness of his fellow citizens.

Adams took some consolation in the thought that posterity might find some merit in his views and even wrote to Henry in a moment of pride, "I shouldn't wonder if I had quite a reputation after I'm dead," but his recognition has come slowly. It is ironic that Vernon Louis Parrington, whose political philosophy he would have found completely repugnant, should be one of the first to write favorably about him. Parrington's essay was genial but thoroughly misleading, and most of his successors have erred in taking literally Henry's joking reference to his brother as a "Jeffersonian Jacksonian Bryonian democrat," a judgment which clashes with almost everything Brooks Adams ever wrote. While an immense literature has grown up about Henry, Brooks (if we except the valuable introduction by Charles Beard to *The Law of Civilization and Decay* and R. P. Blackmur's perceptive essay which appeared some years ago in *The Southern Review*) has received only the most cursory treatment and that of a very inferior sort.

That Adams might be a more considerable person than the historians had supposed was made clear in Mr. Blackmur's essay and also in the few pages which Mr. Matthew Josephson devoted to Adams in his book, *The President Makers* (1940), where he appears for the first time as a flamboyant and somewhat sinister figure. The quotations Mr. Josephson cites from Adams's letters to Theodore Roosevelt reveal the imperialist and the Darwinian, the snob and the frustrated aristocrat. According to Mr. Josephson, Brooks Adams had become, after a brief flirtation with political reform, the historical theoretician and international strategist for the younger group of statesmen who came into power during McKinley's administration. Adams's speculations on trade routes, international exchanges, and the historical responsibilities of peoples were extremely congenial to men like Roosevelt, Lodge, and Beveridge, and although Mr. Josephson makes far too much of Adams's influence, he is correct in pointing out the similarity between the ideas of Adams and the neo-Hamiltonian expansionists who were cheered by America's reviving nationalism and who sought to substitute the martial values for the spirit-destroying materialism of plutocrat and socialist. Roosevelt and Lodge shared Adams's distaste for what T.R. called "the lawless capitalist" and "the Debsite type of anticapitalist." They too believed in the "Stewardship" principle, in the desirability of a public-spirited but aristocratic élite of skilled administrators representing the nation as a whole and jealous of its honor.

It is rather surprising that Adams's geopolitical speculations have not attracted more attention during the last decade (Harper's recent reissue of *America's Economic Supremacy* seems a little belated) for Adams was one of the first American strategists of *Realpolitik* to be taken seriously by the Germans, and his remarks upon America's place in the world and her future course with Russia make less eccentric reading to us than they did to his provincial contemporaries. It seems likely, however, that as his papers become available, he will become less important as an authority on the dynamics of international change and more interesting as a kind of American phenomenon, a complement to his brother Henry whose ideas he helped to shape and who furnished him, in turn, with his only sympathetic audience.

II

From his birth in 1847 until his death eighty years later, Adams lived a life that was not, on the surface at least, very different from the lives of his older brothers; that is, he was graduated from Harvard College, married well, travelled extensively, and wrote from time to time on public issues. But he seems to have been a chronically dissatisfied man, conducting a one-man mutiny against the world as he found it. He never attained the popular success of his brothers Charles and John Quincy, to whom apparently he never felt particularly drawn, nor could he acquire the disciplined resignation of Henry who taught himself to stare into the horrid abyss of the future without quivering.

As a young man Brooks hoped for political preferment or at least for some post of power and authority, and persisted in his ambitions for a much longer time than Henry. With the retirement of his father from politics, he lost for a time his last intimate connection with the men guiding American affairs, and it was not until Lodge and Roosevelt came into the ascendant during the nineties and Henry began to move in the Washington orbit that he once again found access to the inner circle. Out of office himself, he still had the pleasure of knowing and advising men who were in. He enjoyed playing the rôle of the amateur statesman and offered his ideas and services to properly oriented people in Washington who had the wit to appreciate his expert counsel. It is not too much to say that Adams's pessimism about the future of the country fluctuated with his friends' political successes and failures.

During his early years after his father had returned from his post as Minister to England, Adams practised law, served as private secretary to his father when the latter represented the United States on the Alabama Claims Commission, and married the sister of Mrs. Henry Cabot Lodge. For a short time he flirted with the Mugwump reformers, but he quickly repudiated their ideals as sen-

timental and unrealistic, and from the nineties on, he developed his particular brand of romantic conservatism which distinguished his writings from this time until his death.

We cannot be sure what influences or forces changed Adams from a genteel reformer to a hard-headed geopolitician, but this much seems clear. After his marriage he retired from the active practice of law and began to write history. Fortunately for him he was not obliged to earn his living, for, as he remarked to Henry, he was too original a person to survive in a world that protected a man only if he joined a guild and listened to him only if his ideas were stolen. The reception of his first book, *The Emancipation of Massachusetts* (1887) convinced him that the public was far stupider than he had dreamed possible, and from this time on he played the misunderstood prophet with gusto. Ostensibly the book was a ferocious attack on the Puritan founders of Massachusetts Bay whom Adams excoriated as monsters, sadists, and hypocrites. So, at least, Boston interpreted the book. But Adams, in letters to Cabot Lodge, Henry Adams, and William James protested that such was not his intention at all. "What I feel the lack of," he wrote to Lodge, "is appreciation of the unity of cause and effect in the notices I see of my book. It is really not a history of Mass. but a meta-physical and philosophical inquiry as to the actions of the human mind in the progress of civilization; illustrated by the history of a small community isolated and allowed to work itself free." He insisted that he could have done the same for any other similar community: "This is not an attempt to break down the Puritans or to abuse the clergy, but to follow out the action of the human mind as we do of the human body. I believe they and we are subject to the same laws."

Whether or not Adams was justified in censuring his audience or in confiding to Henry that no one seemed bright enough to review him, his explanations to his friends clearly show that already he was thinking along the lines he was to develop most completely in *The Law of Civilization and Decay* (1895). He was attempting to show, as he told William James, "that mind and matter obey the same laws and are therefore probably the same thing." In this same letter he outlined one of his cardinal theories and defended his historical approach:

> My dear sir, the deepest passion of the human mind is fear. Fear of the unseen, the spiritual world, represented by the priest; fear of the tangible world, represented by the soldier. It is the conflict between these forces which has made civilization. And it is the way in which the problem has worked itself out which interests me. . . . If you mean I have given a side, it is very true; I can't conceive what is meant by impartial history, any more than impartial science. There are a set of facts; your business is to state them accurately and then criticise the evidence, and draw a conclusion; and at the same time, if you can, throw in enough interest to sugar-coat the pill. I have tried to show what I believe to be the crucial point of a certain

phase of development, and then to show that what is true of this is universally true. . . . I have perhaps erred in making the story too personal, but the temptation to try to interest your audience, I admit, is too strong for me; and I can't resist the desire to make all the men and women as real to other people as they are to me.

The explanation to James is most revealing, for it helps to show what prompted Brooks Adams to apply his theory on a larger scale as well as offering a hint of what he took to be the function of the historian.

The initial result of his first political fiasco was to send him to Europe and to a set of experiences which he later cherished as the most rewarding of his life. Europe, the Near East, and afterwards India not only confirmed and expanded the ideas he first propounded in America but opened up the endless vistas of a past which even his mercenary and vulgar contemporaries, he told Henry, could not desecrate. In 1888 he began his introduction to the middle ages, his discovery of the meaning of the Gothic, and what he described to Henry as "the heart of the great imaginative past." At a cathedral in Le Mans, the meaning of the mass and the medieval spirit struck him with a strange intensity, and it was here that he received the impetus to go on to Jerusalem; to Syria, and to see "what it was that made the crusades" and "the remains of the age of faith." In Jerusalem, at Beaufort, at the Krals, and "most of all it may be," he reminisced to his brother, "in that tenderest of human buildings, the cathedral of the Templars at Tortosa, I suppose I had an intenser emotion than I could ever have again."

Out of these experiences came *The Law of Civilization and Decay,* perhaps his greatest book and as much a glorification of the pre-industrial age of fear and of the imagination as it was a demonstration of the inexorable movements of the trade routes and money centers. Simultaneously with this sudden and ravishing illumination came the numbing realization of what it all portended. In the past he read the degeneration of the present and glimpsed the chaos toward which he saw his own world rapidly heading. The revelation heightened his nostalgia for an age forever closed, and increased his disgust for the age in which he found himself entrapped. His subsequent writing can be understood only in the light of this dilemma.

Long before his European adventure, Adams indicated that his sympathies lay with the obsolescent standards of a defunct past rather than with the capitalistic ethic of his own America. As early as 1874, he confessed a strong distaste for Benjamin Franklin's doctrines of self interest. "No man who has elevated ideas of morality," he wrote to Lodge, "is willing to put the duty he is under to keep his word of honour to the account of profit and loss." Franklin's morality was perfectly suited to

> counter jumpers but well I know that George Washington would never have indulged in any such calculation nor yet would have been proud to

become the preacher of such small ware if he had. I never said Franklin wasn't useful—so is the constable and so are your account books—but you don't set the constable by the side of your God nor make a bible of your ledger—though many folks have no other.

These assumptions he developed more fully some years later in a remarkable essay on Scott and Dickens in which Adams made out his case for the pre-industrial man.

According to Adams, Scott expressed the ideals of the non-economic man while Dickens spoke for the economic man. Scott's heroes, and we may assume they are Adams's too, are extremely brave, hold honor more precious than life, display the utmost naïveté about money matters, and cling fervently to an ethic which, on the eve of the industrial period, is becoming obsolescent. The soldier-hero, the religious enthusiast, the loyal retainer (creatures of the age of fear) are ennobled by Scott, and the attributes which characterize them, he believes, derive from a decentralized, rural, policeless society. Only the courageous and the physically strong can flourish in this kind of world. But when these conditions disappear, Adams continues, with the rise of the industrial community in the eighteenth century, a new and timid social stratum comes to power (creatures of the age of greed), differing from the preceding one as the organism of the ox from the wolf. Charles Dickens is its chronicler. Where the antique world of Scott had singled out courage as the "essential quality of the ruling class," in Dickens's novels the prevailing trait is a kind of scaredness, the fear of a timid class that has applied craft and guile to the struggle for survival rather than valor. "Accordingly," Adams concludes, "when Dickens wished to personify force, he never did so through the soldier, or the swordsman but through the attorney, the detective, or the usurer."

Beginning with *The Law of Civilization and Decay* and continuing in books, articles, and letters, Adams ranged the idealized types from the age of faith against the mercenary and unheroic figures of his own day. He deplored this world of Dickens, a world devoid of statesmanship, of art, of manners, of adventure, even while he traced its inevitability. Hence his attacks against plutocrats, bankers, Jews—collectively subsumed in the word "goldbug," the quintessence of everything vile and rotten in his generation.

The "gold-bug" for both Brooks and Henry was an epithet and conveyed no exact designation. The gold-bug or Jew or banker (he used the words interchangeably) embodied the spirit of the modern, the genii of money. Essentially they were poetic conceptions personifying the forces of commerce. In his more rational moments, he recognized that "to hate the gold-bug is not the attitude of the historian. The gold-bug sucks because he is a goldbug, and nature causes him to suck." He also knew perfectly well, as Henry did, that the family income depended on the sovereignty and well-being of the moneychangers. But history had also persuaded him that the money power had poisoned his world. "I never should have hated Wall Street as I do," he wrote to Henry in 1896, "if I had not just dug the facts out of history, and convinced myself that it is the final result of the corruptest society which ever trod the earth. I tell you Rome was a blessed garden of paradise beside the rotten, unsexed, swindling, lying Jews, represented by J. P. Morgan and the gang who have been manipulating our country for the last four years." This is a romantic statement and typical of the naïve over-simplifications to which so-called "realists" are often susceptible. That a money power existed, that it exerted an influence dangerous to a democratic people was certainly true, and many thousands of Adams's contemporaries agreed with this view, but Brooks, and Henry too, attributed to international finance an almost occult energy and pervasiveness which hardly differed from the fantasies of the primitive populists they ridiculed.

Brooks Adams's mightiest effort to overcome the legions of gold came in 1896, when he lent some tangible and much moral support to the Democrats. He had spent the last year in India studying reverently, almost ecstatically, the vestiges of a warlike, poetic, and imaginative culture. Modern India, with its crumbling shrines, its commercialized temples, its vulgar, arrogant officialdom epitomized for him the deteriorating effects of the money economy on human institutions, and he returned to Quincy full of resolves to strike at gold if the opportunity arose.

The campaign of 1896 seemed to offer that opportunity. In a long and interesting series of letters, Brooks recounted to Henry what he later referred to as the last great servile insurrection. It was characteristic of Adams that he should quixotically associate himself with the Nebraska farmers (a group as obsolete, he believed, as the Templars and the English monks) while at the same time having no respect for the populists or their candidate Bryan, "one of the very most empty, foolish, and vain youths, ever put in a great crisis by an unkind nature." He informed his brother that the election of Bryan would mean revolution, for the bankers would never let him assume office even granting the remote possibility that he could win the election. Bryan was only a clever agitator, he reported to Henry, with no understanding of economics, and he early came to the conclusion "that the Republicans had better win" over the "honest incompetents" of the silver movement. Adams had everything to lose by a Bryan victory. The Adams's estate had gone on the rocks in '93, and a democratic administration, as he told Henry, "would disarrange many things which have taken me three long, harassing years to get in order." Adams had backed the conservative movement within the Democratic camp, but he was not prepared to support actively "a raving Populist stump speaker" and his bob-tail following.

Believing as he did that the country and the family fortunes would remain safer with McKinley as president, Adams could still enjoy the spectacle of the struggle ("it is like a cold bath, it is like looking into a heavy surf where you know you must plunge") and take the most exquisite pleasure in the consternation of the gold-bugs. The Republicans, moving "in their course like a squad of police against a mob" had everything on their side. Mark Hanna, Adams mentioned to his brother, took two millions out of one Boston office building alone during the first week of August 1896. And yet the Democrats, lacking "ability, or judgment, or capacity of any kind" and led by an "empty vessel" still managed to keep the election in doubt and terrify business. The violence of the agrarian storm astonished him:

> I have never seen so impressive a sight as the election. A rising of miserable bankrupt farmers, and day labourers led by a newspaper reporter, have made the greatest fight against the organised capital of the world that has ever been made this century—or perhaps ever. . . . No money, no press, no leaders, no organization. Amidst abuse, ridicule, intimidation, bribery—against forces so powerful and so subtle that they reach the bravest and most honest men in the country.

Brooks, as a gesture, sent money to Chicago and induced Henry to do the same, but he reluctantly reached the conclusion that the gold-bug must retain control until the inevitable rot should set in. "Henceforth," he wrote to Henry, "the old travesty of popular government must be abandoned and the plutocracy must govern under its true colors." Nature had so constituted the gold-bug mentality that it alone could survive; the rest were mere anachronisms, the rejected, animals "who might have done well in the glacial or the torrid or some other age, but who can't live now." And the worst of the defeat, Adams lamented, was the absolute impossibility of a renaissance:

> Out of it all observe, that for the first time in human history there is not one ennobling instinct. There is not a barbarian anywhere sighing a chant of war and faith, there is not a soldier to sacrifice himself for an ideal. How can we hope to see a new world, a new civilization, or a new life. To my mind we are at the end; and the one thing I thank God for is that we have no children.

III

During the exciting days of '96, Adams had been reflecting on other subjects besides silver and gold, and in the closing years of the century, he continued his European travels, watched carefully what he believed to be the signs of decay in the British empire, studied the campaigns of Napoleon, for whom he developed an intense admiration, and scrutinized the great Russian state sprawling to the eastward. It was at this time that he thought through the ideas embodied in his next books, *America's Economic Supremacy* (1900) and *The New Empire* (1902). These ideas can be reduced to the following axioms: (1) that "man is an automatic animal moving along the paths of least resistance" without will and dominated by forces over which he has no control, and that what is true of men is true of nations; (2) that "by nature, man is lazy, working only under compulsion," and that "when he is strong he will always live, as far as he can, upon the labour or the property of the weak"; (3) that the history of nations is simply the success or failure of adaptation (the flexible live; the rigid die) and that "intellectual variations are the effect of an attempt at adaptation to changing external conditions of life"; (4) that since the life of nations centers around the fiercest competition (with war as the extreme form) and since nations "must float with the tide," it is foolish for men to talk of "keeping free from intanglements. Nature is omnipotent." Nations either respond to challenges or decline. There is no standing still.

The corollary economic laws worked out by Adams made national survival depend upon energy and mass, or, to put it in another way, upon concentration and the cheap and efficient administration of large units. "From the retail store to the empire," he wrote, "success in modern life lies in concentration. The active and economical organisms survive: the slow and costly perish." Throughout the history of man, Adams decided, civilizations have expanded or receded according to their control of trade routes and their access to mineral deposits; but military and commercial successes frequently destroyed national traits responsible for engendering these successes, and newer and more virile nations rose upon the ruins of the old. As society comes to be organized into "denser masses," he reasoned, the "more vigorous and economical" unit "destroys the less active and more wasteful." Hence the modern state, if it is to survive, must move in the direction of collectivism, whether private or state. Political principles for the realist become less important than success in underselling one's rival. Victory in the war of trade depends, in turn, upon ready access to raw materials and a cheap efficient administration.

> Political principles are but a conventional dial on whose face the hands revolve which mark the movement of the mechanism within. Most governments and many codes have been adored as emanating from the deity. All were ephemeral, and all which survived their purpose became a jest or a curse to the children of the worshippers; things to be cast aside like worn-out garments.

Adams's attitude toward governments rested finally upon the degree to which they could exploit material and human resources and survive in the continuous struggle between nations. To see him solely as an anti-plutocrat and a radical, as some have done, is to over-simplify as well as to misconstrue his true position. The clue to his character and the explanation for his various stands are suggested by his dual rôle of romantic and conservative. In the first, he glorified the pre-industrial man, lashed out against the money-power, and identified himself with the obsolete organisms who retained the vestigial attributes of the age of faith. In the second, he played the ambitious opportunist, the lover of power, the geopolitical schemer mapping the course of his country's destiny and bolstering the *status quo*. These two seemingly antithetic guises were actually complementary.

As a historian and a realist, Adams knew that to protest against the change in the character of society was foolish, and that the sensible man adjusted himself even in a world for which he felt himself unsuited. He saw no reason why he should make himself a martyr to gold. "Only those who have a faith to die for want to suffer," he wrote to Henry who needed no convincing. "I see no future to this thing but a long, sordid, slow, grind lasting, may be, indefinitely, with no hope of anything better, and no prospect of what you call anarchy, even supposing anarchy an agreeable condition." The wise strategy for the philosopher in a dying world was to survive as comfortably as he could. "If I believed in a god, or a future, in a cause, in human virtue right or wrong, it would be another thing; but I have not enough lust for martyrdom to want to devote myself to misery simply for the sake of suffering." One did not have to make one's peace with the gold-bug to endure in his society.

Given the stupidity of the average man, certainly one of Adams's primary postulates, and the iron laws of history, the sheer task of staying alive was difficult enough to preoccupy any man. He knew for certain that the world was disintegrating, and he had no faith, as we have seen, in man's ability even to comprehend the complexities of modern living. Man moved instinctively toward self-gratification by the shortest possible route, the "human mind so constituted that whatever benefits an individual seems to that individual to benefit the race." What his grandfather had discovered about the people who spurned his services, Adams professed to have discovered about his own generation: that the American people rejected the great dream of his idol, George Washington, of a "constructive civilization," that science and education only aggravated the problem since man was not, as John Quincy Adams at first hopefully surmised, an intelligent rational animal. Science only permitted man to "control without understanding." It hastened the process of disintegration since "an education of conservation was contrary to the instinct of greed which dominated the democratic mind, and compelled it to insist on the pillage of the public by the private man." With such human stuff to work with, no government could evolve "capable of conducting a complex organism on scientific principles." Democracy was by its very nature disintegrative, "an infinite mass of conflicting minds and of conflicting interests, which, by the persistent action of such a solvent as the modern or competitive industrial system, becomes resolved into what is, in substance, a vapor which loses its collective intellectual energy in proportion to the perfection of its expansion."

These conclusions (which illustrate again the Adams brothers' fondness for applying the second law of thermodynamics to human institutions) spelled ultimate disaster for the race; but Brooks nevertheless felt that a strategy might be worked out whereby America's prosperity and potential supremacy could be at least temporarily sustained and which could once more revive the old heroic virtues. As a property holder and a gentleman he opposed the thrusts of populism, socialism, and trades unionism. As a statesman and an economist, on the other hand, he saw the policies of the plutocracy, with their unintelligent domination of the banks and the courts, as suicidally stupid and leading straight to revolution. His criticism of the rich, therefore, must in no sense be interpreted as adventures in muckraking, but as warnings to a class in danger of being overthrown by forces within and without. Most of his writings after 1896 should be seen as lectures to the members of his own class on the tactics of survival. Governments, he says, are not accidents but growths "which may be consciously fostered and stimulated, or smothered, according as more or less intelligence is generated in the collective brain." In modern society their duration depends upon the successful application of Adams's talismans: consolidation, conservation, administration.

Adams's domestic ideas were radical enough to anger most of the conservatives, but as he turned more and more to the international scene around the turn of the century, an apparent inconsistency began to appear in his writings which disturbed even Henry, always in close rapport with his brother. Adams had started as a young man in the Mugwump camp and had worked with the New England reformers of the "Goo Goo" variety. He had refused to support James G. Blaine, "the continental liar from state of Maine," and for some time had plumped for Cleveland, a conservative Democrat who wanted, as Adams saw it, to scale down a revolution-provoking tariff and maintain sound money. He came out flatly at this time against the McKinley tariff as a device by capitalists to destroy capitalism; for it was the oppressive protective duties, he felt, that indirectly lured the ignorant into supporting confiscatory and socialistic financial schemes like the unlimited coinage of silver. Harrison in 1892 he labeled a gold-bug. Cleveland steered a path between socialism and plutocracy, and Adams supported him for that reason. And then, rather dramatically, Brooks Adams, the anti-gold bug, the secret sympathizer of the populists, the man who wanted to see McKinley hanged in front of the White House, became one of the Republican administration's strong supporters.

Actually the shift was not so bewildering as an innocent populist who had read *The Law of Civilization and Decay* as an anti-gold bug tract might have supposed, and Henry, out of sympathy with Brooks's new jingoistic phase, need not have been surprised. This book, as Adams pointed out to Lodge in 1894, did trace "the origin, rise, and despotism of the gold bug," but he advocated no heretical monetary theories and had seen silver as a feasible solution only in so far as it might be controlled by conservative business men in the Democratic party. Adams feared revolution in 1896 and thought that an intelligently controlled silver policy might reduce its threat by relieving the impoverished farmers. His pamphlet on the gold standard published in that year (described by Samuel Bowles of the influential *Springfield Republican* as "perhaps the most insidious and powerful argument ever made in demonstration of the ruinous consequences of silver demonetization") provided useful

ammunition for the anti-gold bugs. But he found no difficulty in coming to terms with the other side a few years later, because his own friends, the imperialists, were moving into positions of power. The war with Spain had alleviated the pressure at home by opening up new markets. Surplus production could now be handled without tampering with the monetary system. Adams announced his change of views at a press interview in 1898:

> The party (he was quoted as saying) which takes advantage of the opportunity afforded now for the nation to advance and takes its place as a power in the world, is bound to be victorious, no matter what its name, and the men and parties who are content to stand still, and who cannot see that the country has outgrown the system of government which did very well a century ago, will be swept aside. I believe in the war . . . and in the policy of expansion which it forced the nation. I am an expansionist, an "imperialist," if you please, and I presume I may be willing to go farther in this line than anybody else in Massachusetts, with, perhaps, a few exceptions.

Certain world patterns were beginning to take shape that called for a different strategy. From 1898 to 1912 Adams was eager to provide it.

IV

From his studies and travels, Adams became convinced by the early nineties that the old European balance of power was beginning to shift. Watching the money centers moving further westward from Lombard Street to Wall Street, always a sign of impending convulsion and revolution in Adams's prognosis, he calculated that the United States stood at last upon the threshold of a new era. By 1897 (a crucial date in the Adams's chronology when Pittsburgh steel began to undersell European steel) America was on its way to becoming the greatest creditor nation in the world. The rapid liquidation of British assets abroad—the dissolution of the British empire was a favorite theme of both Brooks and Henry—had placed tremendous demands upon the supply of American specie. But owing to the superb and remarkably efficient reorganization of American industry through the great trusts, we met our obligations and then proceeded to undersell Europe. In addition to our clearly superior manufacturing facilities and our rich endowments of natural resources, especially the all-important minerals, our prohibitive tariff, formerly assailed by Adams, permitted us to pay for the losses suffered temporarily in the trade invasion abroad. We were carrying on the war of commerce with commendable energy, impoverishing European farmers, reducing the profits of Europe's industry, excluding large potentially productive areas from European penetration, and, in general, making our position economically unassailable.

For the moment Adams could support the party of the plutocrats and the trusts. "The trust must be accepted," he said in 1901, "as the corner stone of modern civilization, and the movement toward the trust must gather momentum until the limit of possible economies has been reached." Not only did he feel that the trust produced more cheaply and efficiently than small concerns, reducing waste and providing low prices for the consumer, but he saw the trust also as a form of western collectivism which would meet the challenge of the collectivist peoples of the East. He summarized his ideas when he wrote to Lodge:

> I must honestly and seriously believe that we are now on the great struggle for our national supremacy, which means our existence. I believe, from years I have given to the study of these matters in many countries, that we must be masters or we must break down. We must become so organized that we can handle great concerns and vast forces cheaper and better than others. It is fate. It is destiny. I believe that, unsatisfactory in many ways as our present system is, the overthrow of McKinley, or even the failure to strengthen his administration, would be a blow to our national life.

After his conversion to McKinleyism in 1900, he saw no reason why McKinley's administration should not go down "as the turning point in our history. As the moment when we won the great prize. I do believe," he assured his friend Lodge, "that we may dominate the world, as no nation has dominated it in recent time." In this happy and aggressive frame of mind, the country's prospects looked particularly good. To Henry he wrote:

> I look forward to the next ten years as probably the culminating period of America. The period which will hereafter be looked back upon as the grand time. We shall likely enough, be greater later, but it is the dawn which is always golden. The first taste of power is always the sweetest.

His temporary good spirits did not delude him into the belief that America's ultimate future was any brighter, "but the bloom," he concluded, "will last our time. We have vitality enough for one generation at least—perhaps more. And we shant last that long." A trip to Spokane in the spring of 1901 provided more evidence of America's incredible energy:

> The journey was tiresome (he wrote to Henry) but very interesting. I came home straight, and sat most of the time in an observation car. It is no use for the world to kick, the stream is too strong, nothing can resist it. Beginning on the crest of the rockies the tide flows down into the Mississippi valley, and then across to the eastern mountains in an ever increasing flood, with an ever heightening velocity. At last you come to the lakes and Buffalo. There, I take it, modern civilization reaches its focus. No movement can keep pace with the demand; no power can be found vast enough. . . . No one who has watched that torrent from its source on the Divide to its discharge in New York Bay can, I think, help feeling the hour of the old world has struck.

Confident in America's destiny, close to his friends Lodge and Roosevelt, and eager to receive information or offer what he considered to be sound advice, his utterances took on a magniloquence, a bellicosity, and a fervor which he showed neither before nor after.

Both Roosevelt and Lodge understood geographical necessities; they shared Adams's distaste for plutocrats and socialists and appreciated the soldierly virtues. But it was Roosevelt who seemed particularly attuned to Adams's aggressive message and who most clearly reflected the influence of his scholarly friend. From the time of Roosevelt's sympathetic review of *The Law of Civilization and Decay* until the days of the Bull Moose party, Adams closely followed T.R.'s career. He had sympathized with Roosevelt's ambitions in 1896, for Roosevelt too felt the pain and frustration in a gold-bug age, and he had advised his friend to sell himself. "It is of course a poetical conception to fight and die for what is right, what is pure and true and noble, but after all is it not the dream of a poet, or at least a poetic age? Is not to live the first, the most pressing demand of nature; and to live must we not bend to nature? Can anything be wrong for us to do which is imperiously demanded by the instinct of self-preservation?" After Roosevelt had temporized with Wall Street and found himself by accident in the White House, Adams congratulated his protégé as the new Caesar:

> "Thou hast it now: king, Cawdor, Glamis, all—" The world can give no more. You hold a place greater than Trajan's, for you are the embodiment of a power not only vaster than the power of the Empire, but vaster than men have ever known.
>
> You have too the last and rarest prize, for you have an opportunity. You will always stand as the President who began the contest for supremacy of America against the eastern continent.

Roosevelt, in short, was to carry out the policies of McKinley whose death Adams deeply regretted, and whom he now described as the best president since Lincoln. McKinley had kept pace with the times, changing his cabinet after the war, reorganizing the army, checking Russia and Germany in the east without causing a panic, and revising America's trade policy. Roosevelt must continue and implement these achievements or we were doomed. This was to be the theme on which he continually harped to the new president and which lay behind all of his subsequent counsel, both on foreign and domestic relations.

Dreams of peace, Adams had long argued, were the will o' the wisps luring nations to destruction. Human destiny called for war. Nations destroyed or were in turn destroyed. Our trade methods actually despoiled the world, whether or not they were intentionally devised to do so, and if we meant to retain our commercial hegemony, we had to face the facts. If we played the braggart, "rich, aggressive, and unarmed," we would most certainly be stripped by our adversaries; nor could we cautiously withdraw. "If we retreat from our positions," he wrote Henry in 1901, "we might keep the peace, but I fancy our retreat would mark our culmination. It would mark the point you are always speculating about when America would be overweighted by the combination of all Asia from the Atlantic to the Pacific. It would be all Asia then, Europe would be absorbed." For the certain success of the new American push, Adams added one more proviso. Our political administration would have to be as flexible, up-to-date, and energetic as our economic; our political machinery would have to be recast into a cheaper, more elastic, and simpler form. Finally, we would have to develop a new kind of administrator, well-trained, audacious, and disinterested.

Now by their very natures, the rulers of American society were specialists whose skill in aggrandizing themselves and whose heroic devotion to their own interests incapacitated them for public service. The ideal administrator represented no special interest but all the interests, and his mind was not bounded by the narrow concerns which made the capitalist unfit to rule a vast, complex, and centralized economy. Unfortunately, America, said Adams, had no administrators, and in 1903 his letters to Henry are filled with apprehensive references to this dearth of trained personnel:

> We need a new deal of men and we need it very bad, and everyone agrees with it. Only we can't raise the men. . . . As I see it, everything is ripening for a plunge. We must have a new deal, we must have new methods, we must suppress the states, and have a centralized administration, or we shall wobble over. The most conservative as well as the most radical seem to agree to this.

Adams used the analogy of the "new high steel building" to suggest the powerful, compact, administrative system he had in mind. "Our whole civilization," he warned, "must consolidate to match the high building."

> In daily life we have outgrown the specialist, and for that reason the specialist fails and is a positive danger. We are now attempting to produce the generalizing mind. We are attacking administration scientifically. If we succeed in training the next generation right, and their nervous systems do not give way under the strain, we shall, likely enough, pull through and land a big fish . . . the change is represented by the steel cage of thirty or forty stories. Everything has to pass onto the basis of steel from a basis of brick and stone. It means a social revolution going down to the family and up to the government.

An intelligent administration subordinated the indispensable monopolies to the service of the state, obviating the necessity of a biased judiciary (which hastened the movement toward revolution), and taught the people how to obey and take responsibility. Adams's dream envisioned a kind of modified state socialism, run along the lines of a big modern corporation, with a trained and conservative élite solidly in control, a powerful but amenable industrial aristocracy, and an orderly responsible electorate. "The older I grow," he wrote to Henry, "the more I am convinced that the administrative mind is the highest vehicle of energy, and that is what makes the power of the soldier, for the soldier must also be an administrator." The time was rapidly approaching, he hazarded with more prophetic insight than he usually showed, "when we shall be reorganized by soldiers." From 1900 his cry was for discipline—a disciplined Business, a disciplined Nation, a disciplined Home. "Life is tolerable," he concluded, "under any form of orderly government."

Adams placed his hope in Roosevelt as the man who might bring about the necessary administrative reforms. He welcomed his incumbency and remained in close touch with him until T.R.'s death. Roosevelt, he thought, at least approximated the ideal type of administrator, despite his occasional aberrations, his volatility, and his penchant for addressing hard-bitten party men as if they were Groton boys. He too shared Adams's disgust for "moral platitudinizing" about war ("hogwash without admixture," Adams called it) and feared the loss of national virility if the feminists had their way. Adams backed Roosevelt, admitting all of the latter's limitations, not only because of his sincerity and honesty, but because Roosevelt represented the kind of intelligent conservatism which, through limited concessions to reform, would preserve their class and protect the country. Writing to the President in 1903 about the railroad problem, he remarked:

> I think all conservative men owe you and the Attorney-General a great debt—for it is your policy or State ownership. There is no middle course. In a word, to live, this country must keep open the big highways leading west, at equitable rates, and must command the terminus in Asia—if we fail in this we shall break down.

Throughout Roosevelt's administration, Adams constantly advised him on the railroad issue. His own affairs happened to be involved here, but he saw the arrogant and irresponsible practices of the roads, supported by what he regarded as a stupid and reactionary judiciary, as an invitation to social convulsion as well as an injurious blow to our foreign interests. "I apprehend that we are entering on a social revolution," he wrote Roosevelt in 1906, "which must either wreck or reorganize our society. The community, or the monopoly must control prices, and therefor all wealth." Under Taft, Adams was now certain, the gold-bugs had regained lost ground; it was for this reason that, in 1912, he urged his friend to seek a third term and save the country. "This two term business," he agreed with his grandfather, was "vicious and preposterous Jeffersonian rot," and as Roosevelt seemed to respond to Adams's ideas, he grew more excited about his campaign for re-election. He warned Roosevelt that he was attempting to defeat the strongest and best defended entrenchment in the world and that the gold-bugs would treat him no better than an anarchist. But then, he concluded, "it has always been so":

> I think I know this thing to the bottom. What I

want, and have always wanted, is order and authority, and we can have neither unless the law is equally enforced. Capitalism, as always, seeks unequal enforcement of the law—or privilege. Just now, to get privilege, they use the courts, as they are using the Commerce Court to upset the Interstate Commerce Commission. To attain this immediate end they expose the courts to popular attack, as the vested slave interest did the Dred Scott Case. Capital always will. But in so doing it undermines the foundation of order. It works chaos. And chaos is straight before us.

These ideas he presented in greater detail in his *Theory of Social Revolutions* (1913) which reflected the 1912 campaign as *The Law of Civilization and Decay* embodied the issues of '96. As Adams saw it, Roosevelt's job, if elected, was to rebuild a broken-down administrative system, unable to cope with modern complexities, in a scientific way. He could not succeed by making emotional speeches against the bosses. Bryan and his followers had failed in a similar contest because they relied too much on emotion, and Roosevelt's task was immeasurably more difficult than Bryan's.

The question (he told Roosevelt) is whether we can construct a central administration strong enough to coerce those special interests, or whether they can prevent such a consolidation. Call it what you will: empire, dictatorship, republic, or anything else, we have the same problem which Caesar had in Rome when he suppressed the plundering gang of senators led by Brutus, who murdered him for it. We must have a power strong enough to make all the interests equal before the law, or we must dissolve into chaos. All of these special interests are now banded against you in Chicago and they are capable of anything, including murder.

After Roosevelt failed to win the Republican nomination at Chicago, Adams advised him not to run independently and to bide his time, but to Henry he confided his disappointment. Roosevelt had tried hard, but his mind was not elastic and he never fully understood the issues; with a tenth of Caesar's ability he faced problems ten times as difficult. Adams found the emotion of the Bull Moose crusade extremely distasteful, and the antics of Roosevelt and his followers reminded him of "these volatilized women who run about in motors and can't keep still." Henry was sure by this time that Roosevelt's mind had "disintegrated like the mind of the country," but Brooks still believed that some use remained in his erratic friend even though Teddy made "plenty of mistakes" and was "as headstrong as a mule."

Adams had never really approved Roosevelt's brief alliance with the progressives ("They do not know what they want and, if they were told what must be done, they would run like rabbits"), but as Roosevelt moved back again to reality and began his crusade against Wilson and unpreparedness, Adams warmed up considerably. The war he had predicted in 1903 had already embroiled Europe and threatened to drag in the United States. American participation at this time would be disastrous,

he told Roosevelt in 1914, because only by remaining neutral could we reconstruct our obsolete political system and defend ourselves. A German victory he thought preferable to an English, "for Germany will not dare attack us with the English fleet on her flank, whereas England, I suspect, if she has the better, must control our competition on the sea if she is to carry her debt and feed her people." The Germans, at least, might teach our plutocrats and our mercenary proletariat that "we men owe a paramount duty to our country." Our salvation lay in substituting for the money standard of Wall Street the military standards of West Point.

By 1916 Roosevelt's chances for the presidency were slim, but Adams thought he might carry enough influence to have himself appointed Secretary of War or see to it that a man like Leonard Wood got the job. He wanted to see a series of military schools on the order of West Point set up all over the country in which "obedience, duty, and self-sacrifice" would be taught "on a great scale." If Roosevelt succeeded in this all-important assignment, which was nothing less than changing the moral values of people raised for two generations on the gospel that money is the chief end in life, he would have made his greatest contribution to the nation. "Our troubles," according to Adams, "now arise from the false standards of our people. Is it not logical for men to reason that if money is the only end in life, then peace at any price is a sound policy?"

Roosevelt, however, could not prevent the re-election of Wilson, the president who had become for Adams a "flagrant ass" and the symbol of our national disunity. He detected the hand of his old enemies, the Bankers, behind the League of Nations and suspected that Mr. Schiff was "somewhere near the focus of the hell-broth." Adams should have realized by this time that his recommendations had little chance of being taken seriously, but he could not resist the temptation to preach in spite of Henry's pointed remarks that he avoid didacticism; he still felt obliged to warn his uncomprehending and bemused contemporaries. In the debates of the Massachusetts Constitutional Convention in 1917 and 1918, he unfolded all of his favorite arguments and admonitions: the necessity of national supremacy and the subordination of all special interests to the collective will; the dangers which would follow from our failure to collectivize in the face of European tendencies; the tyranny of the courts as brakes on progress; the importance of a flexible bureaucracy which could administer without obstruction ("All modern government means administration, and that is all it does mean"); the certainty that "everything is to be cured by the concentration of power in some one who really will protect the whole community, the interest of all of us"; the natural inequality of men and the inevitable concomitant, competition; the necessity of recasting our society and girding ourselves for the future struggle which is most certain to occur.

These ideas, amusingly and sometimes brilliantly elaborated in the Massachusetts debates, drew polite applause but no one pretended to know what he was talking about. Only one person really understood Adams's remarks, the person who had provided his first and most sympathetic audience—his brother Henry.

V

Henry had been following Brooks's strenuous theorizings from the beginning and had found little to disagree with. Always more reserved and skeptical, if no less pessimistic than Brooks, he still found his brother's economic analyses stimulating and instructive; indeed, his own thinking was frequently so similar that it is sometimes hard to discover what brother anticipated the other. Although Henry refused to take credit for the ideas in *The Law of Civilization and Decay,* he exhibits many of Brooks's pet preconceptions, not only his loathing for the gold-bugs, Jews, and socialists, but his views on the inevitability of some kind of state socialism. Both brothers predicted the bankruptcy of England, Henry with more regret, for he did not share Brooks's inveterate hatred of England or accept his vision of an American empire. America, he felt, could not manage its own concerns, much less the world's (a view which Brooks returned to), and Henry preferred to see Germany and Russia direct the machine after Britain went under. But Henry's geopolitical speculations resemble Brooks's in large part (he too believed "that superiority depends . . . on geography, geology and race energy"), and he accepted unchanged Brooks's hypothesis of civilization:

> All Civilization is Centralisation.
> All Centralization is Economy
> Therefore all Civilization is the survival
> of the most economical (cheapest)

Henry's heavy correspondence with Brooks, earnest for the most part and without the veneer of flippancy that characterized most of his other correspondence, is merely one indication of their close intellectual relationship. "We are too much alike, and agree too well in our ideas," Henry remarked to a friend. "We have nothing to give each other." Both used different methods to approach identical ends and acted upon each other as counter irritants or whetstones. Each submitted favorite hypotheses to the other and criticized each other's ideas with brotherly candor.

Brooks had a younger brother's respect for Henry's genius and the highest admiration for his literary talents. *Mont St. Michel and Chartres* he called "the best literary production of America, if not Europe, at least upwards for two generations," and he took a family pride in this "gem of thought, of taste, of execution" which redeemed his generation. "I perhaps alone of living men can appreciate fully all that you have there," he wrote to Henry, "for I have lived with the crusaders and the schoolmen." Of the *Education* he was less certain although he allowed that it was perhaps "the broadest and, in many ways, the best thing you have ever done." His criticisms or recommendations seem a little cryptic to the outsider, but ap-

parently he felt that Henry had not written the last half on the scale of the first and had "tried to relieve the shadow." Brooks may have meant by this last remark that the "failure" of Henry's life was not seen clearly enough as an individual reflection of a general predicament: man's tragic inability to adapt himself in a changing universe. Such a meaning is certainly suggested in Brooks's reply to Henry after receiving his essay on "Phase." Here he recommended that the *Education* be rewritten on the basis of this radical theorem:

> You have at last overcome your obstacle. Here is unity whereby to measure your diversity. The theorem which should precede the experiment. Your education has been the search for the "new mind." The contrast you wish to draw is the absolute gap between the thing nature demands and the human effort. If you can strip from your book all semblance of personal irritation against individuals, eliminate the apparent effort to write fragments of biography, and raise the story of your life to the level in dignity of the vast conception against which you are to measure the result, you will have created one of the master-pieces of literature, psychology and history. But I can only say again to you what I have said before . . . that this is a huge and awful tragedy.

Henry had begun to complain to Brooks in 1908 about failing powers of mind, and his brother's praise and encouragement must have been especially welcome. Brooks assured him that his work had steadily improved and that his best work, like his grandfather's, had been done after sixty. "The only trouble with you," he wrote, "is the trouble he felt and we all feel, that is an increase of mental power as the bodily power declines. I suffer from that myself."

As for himself, Adams noted that he was losing his "faculty of expression" and that he could not rid himself "of that rigid, didactic and school-mam manner, which drives me to frenzy but which holds me like a vice." Certainly Henry wrote far better than Brooks. He was more successful in presenting systematically and meticulously his well-considered ideas, sustained, as Mr. R. P. Blackmur says, by an all-pervasive imagination. But it should be added that Brooks knew perfectly well the strength and limitation of his method. Always deferring to Henry and regarding him as one of the greatest minds of his age, he nevertheless stoutly defended his own kind of writing against his brother's criticisms. He never thought of his books as being history or literature in the strict sense. They were written for an "occasion," for crises, and the times were too crucial to allow him the luxury of being a mere chronicler. History for him had no particular interest unless a practical lesson could be extracted from it:

> I try to present a method, not an historical study. I use history as little as possible, and only as illustration. Anyone can gather facts if they only have a plan upon which to arrange them. Hence I have a perfectly plain task, very narrowly limited. I have to state a theory or a method. I have to

illustrate it enough to be understood. . . . I have to take a definite starting point, and I have to deduce a practical conclusion bearing on our daily life. I have last of all to be ready at the precise moment when the catastrophe is impending evidently—or I shant be read.

Henry and Brooks clearly differed in method—Brooks choosing to be didactic and active, Henry non-committal and passive, but they saw eye to eye on laws of social change and the probable future of the world.

After Henry's stroke and gradual debilitation, Brooks foresaw his brother's death and recoiled from the prospect of being left alone, the last of his generation. Writing to Henry in the spring of 1915, he reminisced:

> And as I look back through the long series of years to the days when I was a schoolboy and you used to take me to walk in England, more than fifty years ago, I wonder more day by day what it has all been about and why I am here at all. You have been closer to me than any other man, I suppose, and I cannot with equanimity contemplate parting with you. At this moment my whole life rises before me. I am a coward. I do not want to stay till the last. You must wait and keep me company.

A few months later he wrote almost shyly:

> You have helped both of us over many a wet place in our path. . . . It is my birthday—so I may be forgiven an emotion. You always were the best of us four brothers—you are so still now that we are reduced to two. I wish I could have done more to justify my life—but I think I have done nearly my best—good or bad, the best part has been yours ever since I was a boy. And now, as an old man, I look at your worth and thank God that you have redeemed our generation.

Brooks's last tribute to Henry was his long introduction to the latter's *Degradation of the Democratic Dogma* in which he reiterated his and Henry's theory of exhaustion of resources by waste and its human equivalent. The introduction was mainly an account of John Quincy Adams and, by indirection, of Brooks himself, for he had come gradually to identify his own career with that of his grandfather. In 1909, while he was preparing a biography of John Quincy Adams that he never published, he wrote to Henry that Washington and their grandfather were

> the only two men who ever conceived of America as a unity and tried practically to realise their idea. They failed and with them our civilization has failed. Adams stood alone because no one else saw the sequence of relations. He felt this and the sense of failure made him bitter and morbid.

Brooks and Henry, facing the same problem, had failed too. No one ever understood their grandfather, Brooks concluded, and "no one will ever understand us—but he was right: and we are right."

Brooks Adams died in 1927, the same arrogant, blunt, audacious man that he always was, with a few years to spare before the crackup he anticipated and had hoped to escape. With him died his prejudices that were later to crop up in uglier forms and his yet unfulfilled predictions. He had wanted to serve his countrymen, for he never seemed quite able to resign himself to the pessimistic implications of his own message, but they neither responded to his promise of national glory nor to his threats of disaster. He had much to suggest which was pertinent and valuable, but he always stood aloof from the democracy he wanted to save and believed that men were "doomed eternally and hopelessly to contend" against a blind and purposeless universe. And yet he did not gloat over the world's destruction as Henry Adams liked to do. He made a great show of being fatalistic and of enjoying the twilight before the *Gotterdammerung,* but behind the façade of scientific detachment can be discerned a prevailing sympathy for man in his uneven contest with nature.

## Don M. Wolfe (essay date 1957)

SOURCE: "Brooks Adams: Human Nature in the Decay of Civilization," in *The Image of Man in America,* Southern Methodist University Press, 1957, pp. 239-48.

*[In the following excerpt, Wolfe critiques Adams's approach to historical theory.]*

> "Perhaps Caesar's army was the best an ancient general ever put in the field, and yet it was filled with barbarians. All his legions were raised north of the Po, and most of them, including the tenth, north of the Alps."
>
> —Adams

The historian, like the novelist and the economist, scatters through his pages colors and forms of his portrait of the nature of man, a portrait often painted in the image of himself. The more complex and many-sided the historian, the more contradictory his image of human nature. In his *History,* Henry Adams pictured man more as an energy-using and energy-producing organism than as one fixed and limited by heredity. When Charles Beard defined history as "the interplay of *ideas* and *interests* in the time-stream," he suggested the power of the human mind to absorb and act upon ideas even when they are in conflict with economic self-interest. At the end of Beard's life, his image of man was more complex than in his earliest books, when economic self-interest was to him always dominant over the dreams and visions of youth. In a search for the realities of human nature, none of us is without his myths; for myths and poetry must precede any science, and as yet we have only glimmerings of a science of man.

Like his brother Henry, Brooks Adams grew up with many high hopes for the race of man in a democratic society. But in 1880, at the age of thirty-two, Brooks suffered a nervous breakdown "which only good fortune prevented from turning out tragically for me." From this time forth, Brooks Adams believed man to be

> a pure automaton, who is moved along the paths of least resistance by forces over which he has no control . . . I reverted to the pure Calvinistic philosophy. As I perceived that the strongest of human passions are fear and greed, I inferred that so much and no more might be expected . . . from any automaton so actuated.[1]

By the word "forces" in the statement above, Adams means environmental forces in the main. But when he speaks of fear and greed, he considers them to be the products of heredity. Hence, though Adams is deterministic, his image of man is confused and contradictory. To him the social principle of competition arises from the inborn passions of "greed, avarice, and cruelty"; these passions do not emerge from the necessities of competition. Indeed, from the time of his nervous breakdown onward, Adams thought of every civilization as embodying two principles in conflict: "the law, or the moral principle, and the flesh, or the evil principle," the latter exemplified in the practices of competition. As he grew older, Adams leaned more and more heavily upon Rom. 7:14-24 as the central explanation of human nature. Like St. Paul he would say, "I delight in the law of God after the inward man: But I see another law in my members, warring against the law of my mind." The union of mind and flesh is necessary to life, yet perpetually a chaos. As no equilibrium can ever emerge between mind and flesh in the nature of man, so no harmony can fix itself permanently in a social organism. In a democracy, moreover, the greed and avarice of human nature are released at an accelerated pace in the ceaselessly grinding mills of heightened competition.[2]

This view of man is pervasive and persistent in Adams' works, though not always dominant. However diligently Adams aspired to view the world through the eyes of science, he succeeded least when he was formulating his image of the nature of man. Had he kept his image of man in focus, Brooks Adams could not have written his classics of social analysis. In the midst of his evidence his theory of human nature collapses and disappears. But when he writes his prefaces, his theory of man magically comes whole again. In one of his earliest works, *The Emancipation of Massachusetts* (1886), he makes no mention of St. Paul; but many years later (1919), in a revised edition, he makes St. Paul the center of his theory, with no changes in the work itself. In *Degradation,* which also appeared in 1919, he again quotes St. Paul to the Romans on man's inner chaos. In *The New Empire* (1903) and *The Theory of Social Revolutions* (1913), Adams view of human nature appears only obliquely. But the essentials of his portrait had already appeared with startling fulness in his preface to *The Law of Civilization and Decay* (1895), which Adams wrote "to show how strong hereditary personal characteristics are." This work we must examine closely for the strokes and shadings it added to his portrait of the nature of man.

II

Whereas Henry Adams sought to make history conform to a mathematical formula, Brooks searched for the constants of social change from the appearance of a strong agricultural economy to its disintegration. In his classic, *The Law of Civilization and Decay,* he describes a cycle of events which he believes to be inevitable. The original strength of every country, according to Adams, lies with its farming population. It was only by means of the farming population that Rome could recruit soldiers to expand its empire. As long as the population of free farmers was prosperous and sufficient, Rome could fill its legions with first-rate soldiers. Then, as the wealth of Rome increased, her rich men bought huge tracts of land on which they planted slaves taken in the wars. The free farmers, unable to compete with slave labor, were forced to mortgage their farms at exorbitant interest and finally lost their property to the usurers and bankers of the city. Then, as the free farmers forsook the land, Rome's strength declined, and the legions which were victorious, like those of Julius Caesar, were recruited from the barbarians of the empire's frontiers.

With the destruction of the free farmer, Rome's military power declined and her art decayed. Riches, not victory, usury, not oratory, became the central quest of Rome's young men. With the decline of the farming population, the family also disintegrated. As the free farmer was the bulwark of the army, so was he also the main support of the family as a stabilizing institution. To Brooks Adams a free farming population, a martial spirit, a religious fervor, an instinct for art, and family solidarity are the main props of a strong society. When these elements disappear, the civilization inevitably decays. This cycle of strength and decay Brooks Adams traces in Rome, England, and India, drawing conclusions also from the France of the nineteenth century and the America of the twentieth.

In praising *The Law of Civilization and Decay,* Henry Adams wrote, "It is the first time that serious history has ever been written. He has done for it what only the greatest men do; he has created a startling generalisation which reduces all history to a scientific formula." A cycle of events, however often repeated, cannot, however, be called a scientific formula. One may ask, for example, in Brooks Adams' law, why was it that Rome allowed its free farmers to be destroyed by its rich men? Was it inevitable that Rome should make no laws for the protection of its free farmers? In fact, Adams himself describes a period of revolt against the moneyed oligarchy in which the dictator Camillus was forced to agree to the passage of the Licinian Laws, which provided for a redistribution of the public land to the debtor class—land which had been seized in war and appropriated by the patricians. In Adams' words,

> Licinius obtained a statute by which back payments of interest should be applied to extinguishing the principal of debts, and balances then remaining

due should be liquidated in three annual installments. He also limited the quantity of the public domain which could be held by any individual, and directed that the residue which remained after the reduction of all estates to that standard should be distributed in five-acre lots.[3]

The impact of the Licinian Laws was, according to Brooks Adams, so revolutionary as to justify describing it as "the conquest of Italy." It was only after the passage of the Licinian Laws that Rome gained sufficient strength to conquer Carthage and Macedon.

Just how this revolutionary era in which the free farmer and the debtor class were favored by new laws is a part of the predictable law of civilization and decay Brooks Adams fails to explain. A cycle of history may be repeated a number of times without justifying an appraisal of its events as a law. One might as well say that wherever land is denuded of trees or washed by water, erosion takes place. It is true that an effect follows from a given cause, but it is not true that the cause is inevitably repeated. Indeed Brooks Adams' own illustration of the Licinian Laws shows that the reversal of the so-called law of civilization and decay was precisely the action which permitted Rome's greatest expansion. Hence for Henry Adams to call the tracing of such a cycle of events a science of history is like calling war an inevitable extension of belligerent human nature. Henry, indeed, afterward recognized the fallacy of his own high praise when he wrote to Brooks: "You with your lawyer's method, only state sequence of fact, and explain no causes?"

III

In *The Law of Civilization and Decay,* one of Brooks Adams' crucial generalizations about the nature of man runs as follows:

> Like other personal characteristics, the peculiarities of the mind are apparently strongly hereditary, and, if these instincts be transmitted from generation to generation, it is plain that, as the external world changes, those who receive this heritage must rise or fall in the social scale, according as their nervous system is well or ill adapted to the conditions to which they are born.[4]

What Adams means by the term "peculiarities of mind" he does not elaborate, but throughout his masterpiece one may find such terms as "the imaginative type," "essentially martial race," "imaginative blood," and "Latin mind." If these are the peculiarities of mind to which Adams refers, most psychologists and all anthropologists today would call his assumption an utter myth, though it is true that we do not yet possess either quantitative or qualitative proof that such a thing as "the Latin mind" does not exist.

Another generalization upon which Adams bases his conclusions is this:

> Thought is one of the manifestations of human energy, and among the earlier and simpler phases of

thought, two stand conspicuous—Fear and Greed. Fear, which, by stimulating the imagination, creates a belief in an invisible world, and ultimately develops a priesthood; and Greed, which dissipates energy in war and trade.[5]

Though Adams does not claim in this passage that fear and greed are inherited traits, we know from later statements that he accepted them as such. From fear comes imagination, which in turn produces mental casts that are not only religious, but military and artistic. As long as fear dominates society, the family, the army, and the church are strong. But when greed dominates, and commerce thrives, a new type of man appears whose main interests are economic and scientific; then art and religion decay, and the family declines.

According to Adams, when a nation has disintegrated through the concentration of capital in a few hands, through the growth of the population unfitted for war or art, and through depletion of its farming manhood, the only possible remedy is an invasion which supplies "fresh energetic material by the infusion of barbarian blood." This crucial statement shows that Adams regarded involuntary eugenics, not a redistribution of wealth and opportunity, as the only hope for the strengthening of race. The cycle Adams describes he was certain is irreversible by the growth of social intelligence or an economic revolution such as that set in motion by the Licinian Laws. A population in which families grow smaller and smaller and manhood less martial cannot, in Adams' opinion, rejuvenate itself. If Adams had read Henry George's explanation of the decline of civilizations as proportionate to the progressive denial of equality, he gives no evidence in *The Law.* To Adams society was an organism, with a birth, growth, and decline; to George society had no fixed life cycle; it was a grouping of social forces in which the amenities and creativity of civilization would inevitably expand with the extension of economic opportunity to larger and larger numbers. Adams, however, always returns to his central thesis that barbarian blood rejuvenates a people.

Since Adams regarded England and America as far advanced economic societies, he expected a breakdown in Western civilization by 1985. The dark races, he asserted, were gaining on us. England was a bankers' civilization in which, to Adams, the London Jew was a symbol of the dominance of the economic mind. In 1896 he wrote, "England is as much governed by the Jews of Berlin, Paris, and New York as she is by her native growth. It is in the nature of a vast syndicate, and by control of London, they control the world." It was in vain that Theodore Roosevelt reminded Adams that America and England were still producing a vast number of first-rate fighting men despite the centralization of wealth and the concentration of American civilization in larger and larger cities.

IV

In his analysis of the dispersion of human energy, Brooks Adams, like Henry, begins with the assumption that all energy is derived from the sun and that human life is one form of animal life by which solar energy is released. From this statement one might assume that Brooks believed those societies most exposed to the sun or eating foods grown by its warmth would have the greatest energy. On the contrary, however, Adams' thesis is that societies have differing reservoirs of energy "in proportion as nature has endowed them, more or less abundantly, with energetic material." What energetic material consists of Adams does not explain; but it is apparent that to him human energies derive from genetic determinants rather than from proper foods or a hardy outdoor life.

In neither Adams' day nor our own do we have any scientific data on the transmission of energy by genetic means, except for sexual energy, the quantitative potential of which, on the basis of the Kinsey analysis, appears to be hereditary. But a great mass of evidence exists to show that human energies depend primarily upon work habits and the quality and quantity of food to which one is accustomed. In one brilliant study alone, Josué de Castro's *The Geography of Hunger,* we have ample proof that the energies of two-thirds of the world's people are depleted daily for lack of food. To what extent psychological forces deplete or replenish human energies no one yet knows, though William James has explored the topic with brilliant insight in "The Energies of Men." Brooks Adams does not touch this thorny problem; he is content with the inheritance of "energetic material" and the assumption that an exhausted and decaying society can be rejuvenated only through the "infusion of barbarian blood."

Brooks Adams' picture of human nature is filled, then, with grotesque inaccuracies unchallenged in the main by his contemporaries and undiluted by decades of ruthless self-inspection. To correct his image of man in a less mythical direction, Brooks needed the medical training of Oliver Wendell Holmes or William James or the earthy realism of John Dewey. Even the crude Abraham Lincoln, with no access to the wealth of Boston's learning, produced a more consistent and realistic picture of man than did Brooks Adams. If Lincoln was a determinist, he recognized, as Brooks did not, causes and effects as distinguished from patterns; whereas Lincoln was rationalistic in his determinism, Brooks put his faith in the inner chaos of flesh and spirit. To Lincoln's mind, the energies of men expanded with the conviction that their hopes had a realistic basis in the conditions of society; that too was determinism. But to Brooks Adams the expansion of democracy could only mean the expansion of greed and fear and the victories of the flesh, whatever the small triumphs of benevolence along the way.

Even Henry Adams held a more dispassionate view of the nature of man than his brother Brooks. In the writing of history, Henry achieved a detachment from himself that was not possible for Brooks; as Ed Howe said, Henry could "sit on the fence and watch himself go by." Whereas, in his study of the Licinian Laws, Brooks shows no realization whatever that Rome's success thereafter was due to the expansion of opportunity for the small farmer, and the corresponding release of energies hitherto imprisoned by despair, Henry Adams shows an acute awareness of the torrents of American energy, "like the blast of a furnace," when men understood that economic and political betterment waited only upon their labor. In a sense his history of America represented to Henry Adams and his readers the plasticity and variability of the nature of man; whereas to Brooks *The Law of Civilization and Decay* embodied his belief that greed and fear are so fixed in human nature as to prevail ultimately over all hostile forces. But whereas Henry's picture of man in his masterpiece represents a kind of dispassionate agnosticism about man's nature, Brooks's *Law* is a doleful repetition of the failure of man to achieve emancipation from his innate greed and fear.

Fortunately, however, the most significant aspects of *The Law* do not derive from the crude anthropology of its author. Nothing that Henry Adams wrote is a more brilliant synthesis of social forces than *The Law;* indeed, Brooks's masterpiece abounds with facts, insights, and parallels unique in their coherence and force among American historians. Brooks's analysis of the concentration of wealth and power as concurrent with the decline of the farming population is always informed and pithy: "For many years farming land has fallen throughout the West, as it fell in Italy in the time of Pliny. Everywhere, as under Trajan, the peasantry are distressed; everywhere they migrate to the cities, as they did when Rome repudiated the denarius." No American historian has used statistics with more dramatic timeliness: "In 1789 the average French family consisted of 4.2 children. In 1891 it had fallen to 2.1, and since 1890, the deaths seem to have equalled the births." On some problems, it is true, Brooks has a blindness hardly comprehensible: art to him is an expression of the imaginative and martial age, not the commercial. Hence he is forced to omit the glories of Florence in the time of Michelangelo and the art of Amsterdam in the time of Rembrandt. But no historian can see the world whole, and Brooks was catholic and brilliant in his use of diverse original sources. To write his classic, Brooks was forced to detach himself from the limitations of his training as an Adams, a lawyer, a member of the privileged rich. From his image of man however, Brooks could not escape; indeed, he never doubted the accuracy of his portrait.

NOTES

[1] Henry Adams, *The Degradation of the Democratic Dogma* (New York, 1919), pp. vii-viii. See Arthur F. Beringause, *Brooks Adams, A Biography* (New York: Alfred A. Knopf, 1955), p. 373.

[2] *The Emancipation of Massachusetts* (New York, 1919), p. 5; *Degradation* (1919), pp. 85, 105.

[3] *The Law of Civilization and Decay* (New York: Vintage Books, 1955), pp. 16-17.

[4] *Ibid.,* pp. 4-5.

[5] *Ibid.,* p. 6.

### Frederic Cople Jaher (essay date 1964)

SOURCE: "Brooks Adams: Belligerent Brahmin," in *Doubters and Dissenters: Cataclysmic Thought in America, 1885-1918,* The Free Press of Glencoe, 1964, pp. 158-87.

*[In the following excerpt, Jaher surveys Adams's career and examines claims that Adams was an anti-Semite.]*

It was Brooks Adams's misfortune to be born in 1848. Had he lived a generation earlier or later he would have been a far happier man. Adams would then have escaped the frustration of estrangement from American life, the painful memory of decaying Brahmin prestige and power, and the obstacle of an unadaptable aristocratic outlook.

Patrician privilege, however, was still undisputed when the youngest son of Charles Francis Adams was born. Old families still counted, Irish immigrants had not yet overrun Boston, and Peter Charendon Brooks, the lad's merchant grandfather, was one of the richest men in the area. Massachusetts Whiggery, whether Conscience or Cotton, wielded a mighty influence, and Sumner and Webster were still names to be reckoned with. The Adamses too retained their public position. It was only a few years since old John Quincy had won fame defending liberty in the House of Representatives, and his son bid fair to take his place. Intellectually, Boston was the national hub. Transcendentalism was in its prime, and Lowell, Longfellow, and Parkman had barely embarked on their great careers. The great tragedy of this fourth Adams generation was that it was born into such a society and forced to make its way in a world where New York bankers, western writers, and urban politicians held sway.

Brooks Adams grew up unaware that he was enjoying the Indian summer of his class, with no hint of his later irascibility and despondency. Charles Francis Adams regarded his son as a "good . . . boy . . . with a very fine disposition."[1] Brooks fully reciprocated this paternal pride and affection. Even late in life he retained fond memories of his father and thought him "the most remarkable man I have ever known."

Adams's only really difficult boyhood experience was living at an English private school. Most of his classmates, sons of aristocrats, were Confederate sympathizers and did not welcome the American ambassador's son. Many years later, he remembered experiencing "their feelings in all their crudity" and hearing "the North vilified or ridiculed, . . ."[2] This unfortunate sojourn among the young "gentry" may have influenced his dislike for England and his contempt for European aristocracy.

In 1866, like the scions of most other prosperous and prominent Bostonians, Brooks Adams enrolled in Harvard College. He was quite similar to hundreds of other undergraduates, and certainly his college days indicated no later moroseness. Adams rowed in regattas, played in the productions of the Hasty Pudding, was admitted to the highly coveted Porcellian Club, and indulged in several collegiate pranks. As a senior, he looked back on those days and could not "help thinking how lucky I have been."

While at Harvard, Brooks developed the interests and attitudes that marked his mature years. The Adamses' testy individuality appeared early; even in college he wanted to go his own way. He complained about living with his brother Charles because "I am second fiddle and I like to play my own fiddle my own way. . . ."[3] Another family trait, passion for self-improvement, developed during his undergraduate years. "I despise an idle man, or rather clubmen, more than any being I know," he wrote to his father in 1868, "and would rather be anything than that."[4] Lasting intellectual interests, particularly in medieval history, were formed in these years. Politically, too, Brooks was absorbing ideas that would determine his future course. Taking a Brahmin's dim view of Andrew Johnson's administration, he commented sardonically that "our politics seem to me to be getting more and more muddy and beautifully worse, and hold out rich promises of, in the end, managing to bring us to the ardently desired point of having no politics at all."[5]

In 1874, after having been graduated, taking a law degree, and acting as his father's private secretary at the Alabama Claims Arbitration, Brooks Adams made his political debut. He started out as a conventional patrician reformer, becoming active in the Commonwealth Club, a Mugwump organization run by his brother Henry and made up of young bluebloods like Henry Cabot Lodge and Moorfield Storey. During the next several years, the fledgling reformer conscientiously fought the good fight and followed his elders out of the Republican Party.

Brooks was orthodox in those days. Like many other young aristocrats, he saw himself as a Brahmin St. George entering politics to slay the dragon of corruption. Certainly there was plenty of evil to combat, and who else but an Adams should lead the crusade? In July, 1874, he wrote an article for Henry's *North American Review* expressing the views of the conservative reformers. "Grantism" represented the ultimate corruption, the national nadir, as a witless President and a lawless Congress plundered the country. The blame, this young élitist thought, lay in "the naked rule of numbers" through which "majorities are manufactured by demagogues craftily manipulating the least intelligent portion of society." To Mugwump Brooks Adams, "a government by a corrupt civil service, with demagogues manipulating caucuses, is ruin!" In the nation's dire need, he proposed to "cut the evil at the root." These were brave words, but in reality his solution did not differ from the superficial suggestions of other genteel reformers. The "root" was a shallow, if troublesome, growth of a "feeble executive, a corrupt civil service and the caucus system." His cure, therefore, was correspondingly bland. Measures like the election of a strong president to curb Congress, the end of rotation in office, and the protection of minorities from demagogic "thralldom" were to bring America again to full bloom.[6] During these years, Brooks was the blueblood reformer. Mugwumpery was to him, as to Henry, a vehicle for asserting aristocratic élitism by fighting the influence of business and numbers in politics.

Although his political opinions later changed, Adams formulated some permanent principles in this period. A glimpse of things to come was contained in his review of James Fitzjames Stephen's *Liberty, Equality, Fraternity.* In this article, he exhibited his preference for the realist—"Mr. Stephens . . . an active, ambitious lawyer, accustomed to deal with men and facts as they actually exist, [who] looks on life as a long struggle, in which the prizes are to the strong and wise,"—to "Mr. Mill, the highly trained, speculative philosopher, with a passion for doctoring society of all its ills, real and imaginary, [who] was apt in his great longing to bring all the world to something nearer his ideal to forget and ignore any practical difficulties . . . which might stand in his way." Adams fired away at the British liberal, maintaining that every "election [is] but an appeal to force." "Fraternity is simply a nauseous lie,—men are not brothers," he said, curtly dismissing the Christian ethic that he felt underlay Mill's politics. Much sounder, Brooks thought, was the doctrine "that in the end the battle must always be to the strong, and the race to the swift; and that the strong man will always rule the weak; by persuasion if possible, but if necessary by force. Nothing can alter the order of nature."[7] Darwinian pragmatism, the foundation of Adams's emphasis on *real politik* and of his contempt for muddleheaded, sentimental liberals, appeared even at the heyday of his membership in a group with more than its share of the visionary and the tenderhearted.

Other blocks in the Adams edifice (perhaps sepulchre is a better word) were added during these years. In 1879, he first suggested a cyclical theory of history. This idea, later to become his explanation for the rise and fall of world empires, appeared in rudimentary form in his "plague on both your houses" attitude toward class conflict. "The rich man," he wrote Henry Cabot Lodge, "has had his fling for a thousand years and while he was the stronger he led his poorer neighbors the devil's own dance, and if they didn't like it, he struck an iron spike into them." But "he prodded once too often, and . . . the poor man got the rich man by the throat and cut his stupid head off, and served him right." Since the French Revolution, however, we had completed the circle, and now the poor man was growing as "greedy and silly as the nobles did."[8]

These somber thoughts, which he refined in the next several years, generated Adams's theory of social revolutions. His old belief about ruling groups establishing themselves by force became the basic premise of a class-conflict theory. Revolutions were caused by the "drifting of power from class to class, and the effort of the new class to assert itself."[9] This analysis was the embryo of future works. Perhaps already lurking in Brooks's mind was the notion that the passing of his own class might lead to such an uprising.

Changes in Adams's personality occurred concomitantly with conceptual developments. A bitter, quarrelsome adult replaced the agreeable youth. Charles Francis noticed as early as 1877 that his son was "singularly brusque in his manners."[10] Outsiders also saw the change. Mrs. Duncan Cryder, who had known him "as a young boy, when . . . he was friendly and pleasant," now found him "full of gloom."[11] Some of his acerbity was due to his hairline defeat for the state legislature in 1877. No doubt the decline of Massachusetts Mugwumps and his father's death also contributed to the transformation— and there were rumors of a broken romance. Brooks seemed aware of what was happening to him and communicated some of this negativism in a letter to Lodge. He wondered how he could ever have "enjoyed the life" of travel. Musing on his present dissatisfied state, he concluded that "after all the years make a difference in the way a man looks at the world."[12]

Disappointed in politics and dissatisfied with himself, Adams turned scholar. The first fruit of his new vocation was *The Emancipation of Massachusetts,* a study of the Bay Colony Puritans. His purpose in this, as in all future, works was "to set forth a scientific theory of history" by applying "certain general laws to a particular phase of development."[13] Thus, in 1887, he began his lifelong quest for "general laws" based on historical facts. Ultimately it would lead him to view history as a cycle in which all civilizations were doomed to catastrophic ends.

The law investigated in *The Emancipation* was the motive power of fear. In seventeenth-century New England, a "spiritual oligarchy" buttressed its position with "superstitious terrors." When the Puritan ministry was threatened by eighteenth-century rationalism, it became bigoted and reactionary. Progressive enlightenment and reactionary prejudice then locked horns in "the fiercest battle of mankind; the heroic struggle to break down the sacerdotal barrier, to popularize knowledge and to liberate the mind." In Massachusetts, free inquiry, "that constitutional system which is the root of our national life," triumphed. So complete had been the victory that "wheresoever on this continent blood shall flow in defense of personal freedom, there must the sons of Massachusetts surely be."

Adams outraged fellow Brahmins by calling their ancestors "cruel bigots," men who shrank "from no deed of blood to guard the interests of their order."[14] He claimed, contrary to everything his class had been taught, that only in spite of their Puritan forefathers had liberty found a refuge in America. Despite Brooks's rejection of the past, however, he had not yet broken with the present.

Behind his ancestral scorn lay an optimistic belief in the inseparability of progress, virtue, liberty, and truth and in the destiny of America to be their champion.

Despite its patriotic ending, ***The Emancipation*** was taken to task for bias and inaccuracy. Unfortunately, criticism drove the youngest Adams to castigation rather than to investigation. Rejected by readers and experts, he became contemptuous. Alienation expressed itself in diatribes against the opposition. "My estimation of popular intelligence has fallen," he defensively wrote to Henry. "I used to think you were wrong for the language you used to use about popular criticism and popular estimations of work but I give in, you are right."[15] The critical barbs sank deeply, intensifying his isolation. Never again would Brooks write a book so hopeful about America.

The turbulent Nineties gave Brooks a public cause on which to vent his personal bitterness. Trouble was in the air in 1892, and the always apprehensive Adams quickly sniffed it. Strikes, agrarian political insurgence, and the emergence of giant corporations made him doubt the future. "Between the tariff and the trust," he wrote, "we are approaching something akin to a social revolution; for government by capital must necessarily be government by a minority and a government by a minority is a reversal of what we have had hitherto." Plutocratic government, he warned, would result in class conflict. Such a "state of affairs" could last, at best, "twenty five years," and then "we shall be in a social revolution of which no man can see the end."

Adams's rhetoric was radical, but his message was still conservative. After all, was it not natural for a Brahmin merchant's grandson to attack the high tariff, and blame industrialists and bankers for social and economic unrest? Brooks's essential moderation can be seen in his election plea for 1892. Amid "the mutterings of the storm," he called for "the defeat of Mr. Harrison." Cleveland's victory was vital because it would destroy the tariff that "holds together the great moneyed combination" and draw labor and capital "into violent collision."[16] Revolutionaries do not flock to Mugwumps like Grover Cleveland, nor do they congratulate Republican friends on winning Senate seats.[17]

Despite Adams's faith, Cleveland did not save the nation. Within a year after his triumph, bankruptcy threatened the Adams family. Although failure was avoided, the brothers suffered considerable "care and anxiety."[18] Harrowing experience now reinforced Adams's inherited dislike for bankers and businessmen. After such painful personal proof of their determination to crush him and his fellows, he became their intractable enemy.

During the misery of 1893, Brooks Adams began the ***Law of Civilization And Decay,*** the first full statement of his pessimistic philosophy. Adams sought to trace the development and decline of society with scientific principles of force and energy. According to these principles, communal growth and decay involved "oscillations between barbarism and civilization, or what amounts to the same thing . . . movements from a condition of physical dispersion to one of concentration." In the primitive state of dispersion, fear is the major manifestation of human energy. Fear, stimulating the imagination, stems from the need for self-defense. Hence, "religious, military, [and] artistic" types characterize the initial stages of society. The advance of civilization entails a "consolidation of energy" by which "fear yields to greed, and the economic organism tends to supersede the emotional and martial." The degree and rate of centralization depend upon the abundance of energy in any given society. Thus the growth and scope of civilization is proportionate to the flow of energy.

Having analyzed the principles of progress, Adams went on to describe its process. Through this discussion, he formulated his doctrine of the rise and fall of civilizations. In daily living, a richly endowed society does "not expend all its energy," but stores a "surplus . . . in the shape of wealth." Wealth, however, is accumulated by conquest, and "a race must, sooner or later, reach the limit of its martial energy." These limits are reached when "surplus energy" preponderates "over productive energy," i.e., when capitalists triumph over priests, artists, and soldiers.

When capital prevails, economic competition is substituted for war. Soldiers and farmers, creators of surplus energy, are ill adapted to the new style of life and give way to the parasitical "usurer." Since businessmen, unlike martial types, do not produce, "the effect of economic competition has been, perhaps invariably to dissipate the energy amassed by war." Consequently, the rule of bankers is as temporary as that of their predecessors. If war does not destroy the pacifistic "economic organism," it sinks more slowly "because the energy of the race has been exhausted." Thus "by war, by exhaustion or by both combined, . . . disintegration may set in, the civilization may perish, and a reversion may take place to a primitive form of organism."

Although the Adamses had a dramatic and personal vision of doom not unlike those of Donnelly and London, they also formulated a philosophical system of catastrophe. Brooks Adams's doctrine of disaster rested upon an impossible attempt to combine three contradictory ideas. He explained social growth through Darwinian concepts but attributed society's destruction to the triumph of the fittest. The organism that would finally survive the struggle for existence would doom civilization by dissipating vital energy. Disintegration, however, actually would resuscitate the race and reverse the decline. Once civilization had fallen, energy-gathering types would reappear and initiate a new society, which would itself go through the inevitable cycle of development, deterioration, and destruction. Evolution became a popular way to explain the emergence of America and to rationalize the triumph of corporation owners. Adams, as an aristocrat, resisted the social implications of Darwinism because America's growth drew the nation away from Brahmin values and because the Algeristic myth of business success underscored his own failure to achieve life goals. Thermodynamics and the cyclical theory of history provided a framework with which to use evolutionary ideas while escaping their unfavorable implications. This fusion of theories enabled Brooks to reject the captain of industry as nature's fittest organism and to deny that archaic types hindered survival. According to his application of the Second Law of Thermodynamics, commercial organisms dissipated energy, and aristocratic types created it. Consequently, the victory of industrial titans involved the decline of civilization.

Adams derived only limited gratification from contradicting the theory that posited his class as atavistic. Although asserting the relevance of aristocrats to American society, he also accepted the thesis that the old must give way before the new. Brooks believed enough in evolution and the success myth to block his own wholesale rejection of these ideas. His thesis therefore, by admitting defeat, yielded only the negative satisfaction of withholding the spoils of victory. The triumph of his own class was impossible because it had not adjusted; the triumph of its displacers entailed society's disintegration. Only the theory of fatalistic cycles could resolve these clashing claims of relevance and legitimacy. Brooks Adams received some grim hope from seeing in the commercial élite's supremacy society's eventual reversion to a state of savagery where warriors and churchmen would prevail. In this way, the subjugation of the aristocrat would guarantee his return.

After conceptualizing his theory of energy cycles in general terms, Adams applied it to modern times. When Europe emerged from the Dark Ages, capitalism enabled men to accumulate surpluses and delegate their defense to others. Physical force was transmuted "into money and this process went on until individual strength or courage ceased to have importance." The mercantile triumphed over the martial way of life. The merchants, however, then gave way to modern bankers. These parasites who lived off other men's labor constricted the flow of currency so that money appreciated and "the borrowers had to part with more property to pay his debt when it fell due."

To Brooks Adams, Mayer Rothschild, the Jewish banker, epitomized the new group. According to Brooks, Rothschild's last words, uttered to his son as he lay dying, were: "You will soon be rich among the richest, and the world will belong to you." Nathan, who succeeded Mayer to the Rothschild empire, was sketched with the acid of an aristocrat's pen. He "had no tastes, either literary, social or artistic; in his manner and address he seemed to delight in displaying his thorough disregard of all the courtesies and amenities of civilized life; . . . Extremely ostentatious, though without delicacy or appreciation." Adams was trying to even the score of 1893 by attacking with rapier finesse the business blunderbuss that had almost annihilated him.

With the bankers' victory, gold had become supreme. As a result, credit was "manipulated by a handful of men" who had financially enslaved the debtor. Even the triumphant capitalist system, however, "bears within it the seeds of its own decay." In their unquenchable desire for markets and cheap labor, the magnates had opened up the East. Easterners, once mechanized, could undersell western businessmen. Greed, which impelled capitalism's triumph, would destroy it.

Apart from economic strangulation, modern civilization was threatened with biological extinction. In a centralized capitalistic society, the family was losing its economic and social significance, marriage was no longer sacred, and children had become a burden. Consequently, reproduction was declining, and, since modern society had no revitalizing "supply of barbaric life," race suicide was a likely prospect.[19] For Brooks, the decline of that basic aristocratic institution, the patriarchal family unit, meant society's disintegration.

Adams turned history into a treadmill. There were stages but no progress, Darwinian conflict but no evolution to higher types. He acknowledged the financiers' success in the struggle for existence, but evolution did not seem to him a progressive process. Compared to previous aristocracies, the banker was dull, cowardly, and uncultured. Even though he disagreed with its positive conclusions, Brooks borrowed much from Darwinism. The human situation was conceived in terms of constant change, adaptation through necessity, and conflict for survival. Substituted for the tenet of growth to higher levels, however, was an endless repetition of triumph alternating with defeat. There was a ceiling to any society's development, and, when it was reached, the pendulum would always swing the other way. Decline, ending in disaster, would occur, and another civilization would rise to go through the inevitable cycle.

Doubtless Adams's portrayal of the financier was colored by a combination of his experience in 1893, a Brahmin bias against the *bourgeoisie,* and the traditional Adams animus for State Street. Like Henry, Brooks chronicled the emergence of the class that had displaced his own and took grim satisfaction in discovering the sources of its eventual disintegration. He, too, linked capitalistic deterioration with its divergence from the patrician style of life. Both brothers saw in the gross manners, pervasive materialism, and artistic inarticulateness of the businessman his ultimate destruction. To these aristocrats, taste meant energy, and sensibility meant survival.

There was another theme in Brooks's treatise, a theme far different in context, though not in content, from that of the alienated aristocrat. It was a long way from Boston to Nininger City, and an Adams could never be confused with a Donnelly, but nevertheless they shared a common grievance against commercial interests. Brahmin Brooks Adams agreed with the Populists in attributing to the financiers a tight money policy deliberately aimed at crushing producers. He joined the farmers in condemning "usurers" whose only activity in the economy was to destroy it by their own greed. The aristocrat and the agrarians held a common opinion of the materialism and cowardice of the dominant class. As members of disaffected groups, even their cataclysmic outlook was similar. They both predicted that the élite, through its insatiable greed, would doom itself and all civilization.

Adams did not restrict himself to deploring capitalistic depredations, however. He attempted by political agitation to redress the balance between Wall Street and Beacon Street and sought revenge against the bankers who had made him so miserable in 1893. In 1894, he fought business with bimetallism as earlier he had opposed it through the tariff. With Francis A. Walker, Brahmin economist and President of Massachusetts Institute of Technology, and Benjamin Andrew, President of Brown University, he formed the International Bimetallists, an organization that advocated the use of both silver and gold for an international money standard.

Brooks opened his campaign with **"The Gold Standard,"** a pamphlet written in 1894. Devaluation of silver, he argued, had brought depression and dissension. If the silver solution was not immediately implemented, Adams characteristically foresaw catastrophe. Nihilism "in Russia, agrarian insurrection in Italy; anarchism in France and Spain; socialism in England and Germany" were warnings of what could happen here under the gold standard.[20]

Brooks Adams was becoming more radical. Even though he was a moderate silverite compared to the westerners, still the money issue, in the Populist context, was much hotter than civil-service reform or tariff reduction. Its potential explosiveness did not bother Adams in 1894, and 1895, and the campaign acted as a tonic. For years, he had "been preaching disaster and . . . suffering under the thing which is hardest to bear, the conspiracy of silence, and the being set aside as a harmless crank." But the popularity of **"The Gold Standard"** made people think of him as they did of other men. Approbation was particularly gratifying because it came from his own class. "I admit to being frankly more pleased at your letter," he told Lodge, "and one or two others I have received, than I have been at anything since Mrs. Adams told me she would marry me."

Although buoyed up by approval and resolving to fight hard, he remained convinced that the bankers would win. "Between you and me," he vowed to Lodge, "I think the end is near, but I am in the popular side of this fight and I mean to fight to the last."[21]

These were brave words, but Adams did not "fight to the last." Within a year of its unfurling, he hauled down his flag. In June, 1895, gratified at prospective recovery, he took comfort that "the bankers themselves are perfectly assured." Impressed by "Morgan's pool" which stopped the drain of gold, he admitted that "as for myself I am desperately anxious for the success of Morgan. Everything I am interested in hangs on that and I admit I cannot contemplate the collapse of the corner with equanim-

ity." The possibility of another recession made "silver agitation . . . the worst thing for us, and the whole country. . . . If silver is to come it had best come naturally. . . . Not through a political, semi-revolutionary agitation, which would prostrate all values for several years."[22] Brooks, after all, was bound hand and foot to the master class. Whenever opposition got too radical or too threatening or whenever his own finances were in danger, he retreated behind the battlements of the bankers and rallied to the standard of the dollar sign. Henry was right, when many years later while commenting on his brother's cataclysmic predictions, he claimed that Brooks confused personal interests with political perceptions.[23]

An Adams, however, could not forever live in peace with a Morgan. "I can't disguise from myself that the victory of capital . . . will lead to anything but disaster to us," he wrote to Henry. "I can see no glimmer in the future, less than a year ago, far less than in 1893."[24]

With a vision of ultimate doom weighing on his mind, Brooks entered the campaign of 1896. At Chicago, he steered clear of both radicals and eastern bankers and supported the conservative silverite, Henry M. Teller. When Bryan was nominated, however, Brooks switched parties. Bryan's election, he feared, "would mean revolution and probably armed revolution." But Adams was not like other self-righteous McKinleyites who regarded the Nebraskan as the devil's latest disciple. If Bryan meant revolution and confiscation to Brooks Adams, McKinley meant oppression and depression. No matter who won, Adams would lose. Whether Bryan "is or [is] not [elected] appears to me to be the end of the Republic, or very near it."[25]

When the "Great Commoner" went down to defeat, there were no cries of joy or jeers of derision from Adams. McKinley was not his savior, nor had Bryan been an object of his hatred. Sensing an affinity of basic outlook and seeing another vestige of civilization destroyed by the modern machine age, he had a word of condolence for followers of a lost cause not unlike his own. Never had he seen so impressive a sight as this election—"a rising of miserable, bankrupt farmers, and day laborers, led by a newspaper reporter, have made the greatest fight against the organized capital of the world that has been made this century—or perhaps ever."[26]

When the brief elation of 1894 had passed, Adams reprinted *The Law Of Civilization And Decay.* The second edition, which came out in 1896, reflected his more pessimistic mood. A study of science and society had convinced him that man was but a plaything of fate. Determinism, the natural outgrowth of his worship for objective, scientific laws, was an admission of inability to cope with modern forces. This confession was emphasized by his personalized version of the Darwinian principle that anachronisms go under in the struggle for survival.

> Like other personal characteristics, the peculiarities of the mind are apparently strongly hereditary, and,

if these instincts be transmitted from generation to generation, it is plain that, as the external world changes, those who receive this heritage must rise or fall in the social scale, according as their nervous system is well or ill adapted to the condition to which they are born. Nothing is commoner, for example, than to find families who have been famous in one century sinking into obscurity in the next, not because the children have degenerated, but because a certain field of activity which afforded full scope, has been closed against their offspring.[27]

What could Adams do? What could anyone born past his time do but wait for the inexorable laws of civilization to sentence him to oblivion?

Adams's pessimism, which culminated in the despair of 1896, was partly due to the cool reception of his books. Brooks's moods always fluctuated with his own image in the public eye. The great tragedy of his life, as in the lives of his ancestors, was his failure to receive plaudits from the populace. Rejection resulted in alienation, in the construction of a barrier between himself and humanity. Call it weakness, hurt pride, paranoia, or perverse self-isolation. However it is labeled, Adams's attitude defined his relationship with the world. Sometimes it appeared as self-pity, as when he wrote to Cecil Spring Rice, then a comparative stranger, "My dear fellow, I'm a crank; very few human beings can endure to have me near them, but I like to be with you, and I suppose I like to be with those who are sympathetic, the more since they are so few."[28] Less hesitant with Henry, he unburdened himself of a mixture of pity and pride, of paranoia and outraged justice:

> I cannot disguise from myself, that for me too my race is run. I have nothing more to hope from the world. Here I am really an outcast. I hardly think you can appreciate not only how completely I am alone, but how I am shunned. I am treated as a man with a mark. As for a hearing I shall never have one, and now my strongest wish is to escape somewhere where I shall forget and be forgotten . . . this winter has been almost more than my nerves can stand; I am beginning to be frightened, . . . [29]

Sometimes the syndrome was dominated by anger. He raged at those who refused to accept him, and hell could have had few furies more bitter than Brooks Adams scorned:

> I don't care a damn for this country, or indeed for anything much except to get out of it at least for awhile, or at least out of Boston; Boston the modern Sodom. . . . Oh Henry; Oh my dear, what a bloody fool your brother has been ever since he was born, and he has lain in the gates of the rich like Lazarus. Why do I want to print a silly book that no one will read, and that I shall be cursed for, and laughed at for, by every chuckle headed gold bug who will be told by a reviewer that at last I have done the thing everyone was waiting for me to do. Proved myself insane.[30]

By 1896, with western radicals moving into the silver crusade, Adams had no more stomach for the fight on "the popular side." The allies of 1894 had departed leaving him "but one lonely man against whom all society is banded. . . . to crush me, to ridicule and suppress me." The "weight of this monied mass" was on him and all he wanted was "to escape from the whole thing." As Henry had been disillusioned with Grantism, Brooks discovered that "I am not made for this fight. It is folly in me to enter it."[31]

Defenseless and exposed, the silver moment having failed him, Adams could find no new source of strength, no belief behind which to seek shelter. "If I believed in a god, in a future, in a cause, in human virtue, right or wrong, in an ultimate transfiguration of the human race," he wailed to Henry.[32] But there was no cause and there was no belief—there was only loneliness.

Brooks inherited the family propensity for turning private reverses into cosmic catastrophes. If Adams had been crushed by money-grubbing philistines, then the whole world would share this defeat. Amid his own disappointment, "The country . . . seemed . . . utterly barren," without "one ennobling instinct." Society was "at the end," he thought, "and the one thing" he found gratifying was "that we have no children."[33] The Adams habit of amplifying personal setbacks into national crises deflected guilt by placing the burden of failure upon society. Seeking relief from defeat by reading global misfortune into unsettling experiences was a characteristic response among cataclysmists.

Mutual moroseness made Henry and Brooks partners in misery. Having similar values and reactions, they pooled their emotional resources to compensate each other for wounds received from an unfeeling world. One conviction they held in common was a dislike for Jews. Brooks matched Henry's bigotry, bitterly condemning Jewry as the embodiment of the master class. A bit of free-silver anti-Semitism must have rubbed off, for he thought "the pure Jew," a "pure concentrated gold bug," a villainous parasite living off the hard earned gains of the producing class.[34] Through "a vast syndicate," the Hebrews controlled London and thereby "the world."[35] This vision of the conspiratorial Jew holding the globe in his mercenary grasp revealed Brooks's alienation from the contemporary era. The Jew symbolized both betrayal and the advent of financial capitalism. In arguing that the Jews had become supreme, Adams proclaimed his own displacement by business.

His estrangement also manifested itself in a longing for the past. Medieval history had been Brooks's favorite period since his youth. He eagerly responded to his elder brother's interest now that Henry, drawn by a similar need, was immersed in the Middle Ages. "I am delighted to hear that you have been making a Gothic pilgrimage," he told his brother. "On the whole, the parts of my life which I look back to with the greatest delight are those I have spent among the churches and castles of the

Middle Ages." Like Henry, he had been overwhelmed by the cathedral where he "really and truly did believe the miracle, and . . . sat and blubbered in the nave and knelt at the elevation." The "Gothic is the greatest emotional stimulant in the world. I am of it, I understand it, I know how those men felt, and I am in feeling absolutely one with St. Anselm, or Godfrey de Bouillon."[36] The twelfth century, an age unsullied by commonness, became a refuge for alienated aristocrats.

Despair drove Brooks Adams abroad in 1895, but his spirits were not raised by the trip, and he surveyed foreign lands with the same scorn as his own. A journey to India brought forth strident racism and an almost Nietzschean contempt for the weak. "To the Western mind, the mind of the conquering race, . . . The Indians are slaves." Instead of exhibiting the conquerors' vitality, they only "endure—endure beyond all belief." In Anglo-Saxon freebooters like Adams, pacifism invoked instinctive contempt. Even racism, which had compensated inferiority feelings in so many others, did not bring comfort, however. Inert India, for Adams, was an example to nations like the United States of what happens when "the fighting races, the manly, bold and noble races, the only men who have ever done anything worth doing, have been annihilated, evicted from their lands, wiped out, and their place . . . taken by a mixed mass of usurers."[37]

Adams's foreign trip initiated a crusade that occupied his remaining years. America's world position concerned him greatly, and he felt that the course of empire was the only route to national power. Geopolitics had fascinated Brooks for some time. As early as publication of *The Law Of Civilization and Decay,* he had believed that trade routes, access to markets, and ability to undersell competitors were the vital sinews of a country's strength. The visit to India, by awakening racism and expectations of an East-West conflict, stimulated his imperialist thinking. By January, 1896, he was sure that the United States was in a death battle for world supremacy that would end in defeat if the magnates continued to dominate soldiers and luxury to undermine Spartan living standards. Without soldiers or cheap goods, the West could neither conquer nor compete with the East. To Adams, the situation bore "every mark of premature decay." He gave Europe three generations and the rest of the "system" until the "twenty-first century" before total disintegration.[38]

After 1896, Adams embraced imperialism. The silver crusade had ended dismally, and there was no better way to regain public favor than to court the present popular passion. Furthermore, expansion not only had mass appeal but one's closest friends advocated it. Imperialism, however, meant something more to Adams than a vehicle by which to win congenial companionship and popular approval. It engaged his interests, embodied his ideals, and thrilled every fiber of his being. Initially opposed by business, it was, for Brooks, another way to combat commercial encroachment. Through the quest for empire, he

idealized force and deified the warrior. Thus he hoped to reinforce those vital qualities that he saw being undermined in the modern era. In addition, belief in racist expansion compensated for patrician decline. If the Brahmin élite had been displaced, at least he could still be part of the sovereign race. The cause also appealed intellectually; it furnished a global program corresponding to the world outlook for which Adams pleaded. Finally, the belligerency inevitable in imperialism was a fitting climax to the conflict of a Darwinian society. In mind and in spirit, if ever a man was suited to an idea, Brooks Adams was suited to imperialism.

At first, Brooks treated foreign prospects as glumly as he had domestic problems. America's commitment to empire, the Spanish-American War, was greeted with the usual pessimism. "I am in despair," he wrote Henry, "to have this silly business forced on us, where we can gain neither glory nor profit . . ." He fretted about the nation's finances and military ability and about his own bank account.[39] As Brooks put it, however, nothing "lays me out" like a victory. Accordingly, after Manila, he adjudged "our world position" much improved.[40] But global strategy was not nearly as thrilling as the specific exploits of America's forces. Adams, brimming with pride over victory, retracted his long standing accusation that the country was under the golden thumb of the financiers. "I have often told you that the old tradition was dead," he said to his young niece, "that the world was the Jews and that State Street and ignominy were all that was left us now. I was wrong. The old tradition lives. Gentlemen still survive."[41] The war meant America's rebirth and Adams's own resurgence. "Taking Boston, in general," he gleefully remarked, "it is beginning, if you can believe such a thing, to trifle with our notions."[42]

The conflict intensified Adams's nationalism. Conscious of being on the popular side for once, Brooks proudly proclaimed that "I am an expansionist, and an 'imperialist,' if you please, and I presume I may be willing to go farther in this line than anybody else in Massachusetts, with perhaps, a few exceptions."[43] Victory made him wave the flag even more grandly. Prewar despair had disappeared, and the new century dawned optimistically on an Adams who believed the nation's pre-eminence to be at most only a few years away.

Adams's next book, *America's Economic Supremacy,* developed the argument for America's assumption of world power. The Panic of 1893, once a source of dismay, had actually brought about the nation's economic supremacy. Driven by depression to undersell Europe, America had turned the Continent into a market and had become leader of the western coalition against Germany and Russia. The outcome of the struggle between Orient and Occident would be decided in Asian markets. Due to recent territorial acquisitions, the United States had only to drop its isolationistic traditions, and hegemony would easily be secured. The Teutonic-Slavic combination, once quite formidable, was, in Adams's *fin de siècle* optimism, bankrupt and obsolescent.

In order to sustain its position, the nation had to adjust to changing conditions. Success in modern life meant economy, activity, and centralization. Business, above all other contemporary forces, had met these demands. Corporate efficiency had enabled America to undersell other countries and capture international markets. Since empire was the political counterpart of the trust, Adams, by advocating one, had come to support the other. The combination of personal prosperity, the imperialist crusade, and capitalistic support of military conquests had caused him to repudiate his former antipathy toward the corporations.

Adams remained sanguine for the next few years. *America's Economic Supremacy* sold widely and was respected in the right circles. For once, Brooks was accepted by the influential intelligentsia. "Opinion is running . . . strong with the new movement," he wrote. "As I happen to be pretty widely identified with the new departure it naturally makes a change in my position; and to my intense astonishment, I find myself, for the first time in my life, growing actually popular."[44]

These already high spirits soared at Roosevelt's accession. With Theodore as President and Cabot running Congress, it seemed for a time as if the commercial tide had been rolled back, as if America's destiny was once again being guided by aristocrats who believed in action, imagination, and expansion. At last, Brooks Adams would have a hand in national policy. A lifetime of hungering for recognition, of being frustrated by issuing clarion calls that bounced back as empty echoes, seemed to be over. Only a few months before Brooks received his great chance, Henry attested to his brother's craving for power. He pointed out that his own displacement was as nothing compared to that of "poor Brooks," who was "the real sacrifice, for he was ambitious."[45] A truer comparison between the brothers has never been made. Henry had relaxed his grip on the twentieth century and was sinking into the passive romanticism of Virgin adoration, while Brooks still tried to make his way in this world. Long after one Adams had given up, the other, still driven by a Puritan conscience and a reformer's energy, eagerly grasped his final chance for power. At last, his ambition was to be realized. "Thou hast it now: King, Cawdor, Glamis, the world can give no more," Brooks cried perhaps a bit vicariously to Roosevelt. So inspired was he in his fight for Roosevelt that he lauded him as greater than the greatest Roman emperor. "Hail Caesar!" Hail Theodore!—"The President who began the contest for the supremacy of America against the eastern continent."[46]

Brooks was deliriously happy in the months following the inauguration. Anticipating a Roman triumph, he willingly forgot years of iconoclasm and embraced values upon which he had previously spat. Now "that we have the world at our feet," he was "for the new world. . . . electric cars, mobiles, plutocracy and all." After all, he reasoned, "I don't live but once, and when one is dead its for a long time and a nation is only great once. One might

as well try to cut off a hunk of fat, even if you don't like a particular kind."[47] Adams, like Donnelly, was the marginal man—condemning what he really wanted and praising a way of life that was at best a consolation for what he could not have. Usually, he posed as the lonely aristocrat, the forgotten man martyred by his age, but when ambition beckoned, he became a modern man. How the tune changed when success was the piper!

America was the macrocosm of Adams' euphoria, and he well-nigh burst with national pride. America's "enemies were either foolish or bewildered." For the "first time," Brooks felt "that for us is the earth and the fullness thereof."[48] Utopia never meant much to Henry Adams. After Mugwumpery failed, he awaited an adverse fate. For activists like Brooks Adams and Ignatius Donnelly, however, resignation was impossible. As changes in personal fortune triggered elation or depression, their visions of the future fluctuated between wish-fulfillment and wish-destruction. In the all-or-nothing-world of these cataclysmists, utopia alternated with disaster.

Adams's nationalism was not notable for its uniqueness. Like a thousand other patriots before and after, he called for a native culture and was thrilled by any display of national power. Military glory became more of an obsession than ever before. "As to me there is nothing so magnificent as the soldier's death," he said at a veteran's memorial service. "War may be terrible, but it is also beneficent, for it has given us the noblest type of manhood that, I believe, the race has ever known. It has given us the American soldier."[49] The man on horseback, whether twelfth-century knight or twentieth-century warrior, was always Brooks's hero.

Even those hopeful times, however, were not without problems. Believing war to be "the ultimate form of economic competition," Adams anticipated that America's prosperity would invite strife. Germany and Russia could not be squeezed out without violence, and, as a last resort, they would start a "war to the death,—a struggle no longer against single nations, but against a continent."[50]

The danger of impending conflict seemed to escape most citizens. By being woefully unprepared, inadequately armed, and pacifistic the people indicated that they had not "maturely considered" their position in the power struggle and were still hampered with "old prejudices" against making war and conquering territory. The worship of force that led Brooks Adams to admire uniforms also convinced him that an "opulent, unarmed" America was putting a "premium" on European aggression.[51]

Another weakness was our decentralized and disorganized government. Survival depended upon organizing for cheap production, but even in a hopeful mood Adams doubted whether there could be such consolidation to capture foreign markets. Although the country's industries were expanding, "administrative power does not grow with the mass." Haphazard organization was unable to manage the unprecedented mass and accelerated energy created by science and competition. Already "society is quivering under the strain," a "social reorganization must take place, or something would give way."[52]

By 1904, these doubts had undermined Brooks's confidence. Business, once the force behind national greatness, now symptomized administrative inefficiency. In order to establish an adequate measure of government control over commerce, he re-engaged the vested interests. Adams's campaign for railroad rate regulation was carried out in the same moderate fashion as his previous reform efforts. Brooks did not cross the Rubicon of radicalism by demanding state ownership, but, in true Progressive style, he rapped errant corporations across their greedy hands with the rule of law. He asserted that transportation should be regulated by government because travel on highways is a "public trust" and railroad monopolies were setting "arbitrary" rates that taxed people far in excess of a fair return. Therefore, the railroad was violating one of the most sacred Progressive canons, "equality before the law." But for Adams, "sovereignty" was even more important than equity. If the government did not act, private corporations would encroach upon its powers, subvert the law, and seize control of the nation. Then the state "will have become a formal instrument serving as a mask to protect a sovereign oligarchy," and the capitalists would absorb "the whole national wealth." These two essentials of Progressivism, equality before the law and the public sovereignty, had to be maintained—otherwise "constitutional government" would be destroyed. On its ruins would arise the bugaboo of all middle class reform—the threat of violent conflict between those who had too much and those who had nothing. "The worst convulsions which have rent society," he warned, touching Progressivism's most responsive chord, "have been caused by the effort of the weak to free themselves from unequal exactions imposed by the strong."[53]

Brooks was thoroughly imbued with the spirit of New Nationalism. He recognized the value of trusts and even advocated more economic concentration, but he never forgot the difference between good and bad corporations. He worshipped neither Adam Smith nor Andrew Carnegie. If free enterprise would destroy our economy because it was inefficient and antiquated, monopoly would strangle it through greed and corruption.

Adams regarded his skirmish with the railroads as part of a general offensive Roosevelt had mounted against the vested interests. Although victorious in his own battle, he was disconsolate because the campaign on Capitol Hill seemed lost. The honeymoon of 1901-1903 was over. Capital had vanquished even his idol, the Lochinvar of the upper class, Theodore Roosevelt. "The magnates have won," he told Henry. "You are now to have Mr. Morgan and his hired hands owning the Senate, the Senate really naming the judges, and the judges executing the orders of the Senate." Anticipation of business rule awakened cataclysmic thoughts dormant since Roosevelt's accession. Once again, Adams doubted the duration of "this system."[54]

Underlying the gloom of these years was keen disappointment at being denied the recognition he so eagerly desired. "Ten years ago," Brooks once remarked, "I admit, I should have liked to hold office, but a man cannot be young forever, nor can he be Jack of all trades." To this disclaimer, however, he added, "I have turned toward writing, not from choice, but from necessity." But even if he is taken at his word about holding office, there was still the attraction of moving behind the facade of titles to grasp real power. By 1902, any hopes along this line had also been dashed. After having "had a good look at Washington," he was sure that, although "they are willing enough to use me, and take my ideas when convenient . . . they don't want me about."[55] Deprivation of a long awaited and ardently sought after reward raised old suspicions of persecution. Others would "steal" from him, they would get "money" and "fame" properly his.[56] Being shunted aside just when he expected his hour to strike brought back the old depressing sense of worthlessness. Once more he felt "nothing one does matters very much one way or the other." Effort made no difference in an "age notable for the way it could ignore."[57]

Depressed by Roosevelt's failure to halt business, disappointed at not having an official role, and watching his contemporaries disappear through the attrition of old age, Adams sank into cataclysmic thoughts. As a result of Russia's defeat in 1905, he was sure Europe would collapse, thus precipitating the final "struggle."[58] In 1906, he set the date for international catastrophe in 1925, but two years later, after being "shaken most uncomfortably," he doubted whether disaster would hold off that long.[59]

As the present grew more forbidding, the past became more precious. Increasingly conscious of the passing of his class, Adams indulged in a sentimental requiem with his equally nostalgic brother: "Almost the worst is that I feel as if we were the last of it. I'm afraid the next generation knows little and cares less for the things we cared for."[60] Brooks spent summers in the "Old House" at Quincy and decided to turn it into a memorial. He collected all the Adams memorabilia and, in a fit of ancestral possessiveness, prevailed upon his brothers to prevent family papers from being scrutinized by eyes that were not Adamses.' Adoration of the past extended to early heroes like Washington but concentrated chiefly on his own famous forebears. One offering of this worship was a biography of his grandfather. In such esteem did Brooks hold John Quincy, however, that, always prejudiced against family studies and doubting whether his own did full justice to its subject, he withheld publication.

A deep urge to establish continuity with the past is readily apparent in this work. John and John Quincy Adams are portrayed as having the same values, suffering the same slights, and enduring the same emotional anguish as their descendant. They, too, led thoroughly miserable lives, and their discouragement stemmed from the same source—popular rejection. Brooks saw his grandfather very much in his own image. To him, John Quincy

Adams was the last of a species, the vestige of a vanishing society. John Quincy "belonged to a dying civilization," an era that "cherished antiquated standards of right and wrong." These virtues made him ineffectual against "the Jacksonian faction" and so he was swept aside in the triumph of a corrupted democracy.

Beliefs, as well as moods, were shared by the men. John Quincy had had little use for businessmen and was so resented that "the wealthy manufacturers of the North. . . . thought him a semidemented incendiary." As an expansionistic Secretary of State, he had had the astounding foresight to realize that "the equilibrium of human society" was moving across the Atlantic. The Adamses, agreeing on national destiny, were also in accord on the means of its implementation. John Adams and his son had advocated a strong military establishment. They represented "the nation militant," basing "their whole theory of life upon the necessity of the use of physical force."

The author's feelings of persecution were projected on the figures in this biography. His grandfather and great-grandfather appeared as the innocent objects of vicious opprobrium. Criticism against John Adams must have been "engendered by personal malice, since no one any longer attempts to dispute the purity or wisdom of his acts." His son, John Quincy Adams, despite great vilification, "was the last and perhaps the extremest specimen of an illustrious race of patriots and statesmen."[61]

Brooks now completely identified with his ancestors. Writing to Henry in 1909, he said of their grandfather and of themselves: "No one ever understood him, no one will ever understand us—but he was right and we are right." "Adams was heavy, I am heavy. We are what we are, we cannot be changed." In the defeat of John Quincy Adams, he read the doom of America: "Washington and he were the only two men who conceived of America as a unity and tried practically to realize their ideas. They failed and with them our civilization has failed."[62] Eighty years after that misfortune, another family failure had occurred. Once again, an Adams was scorned when he tried to point out the road to salvation. Indeed, one wonders to which Adams Brooks was referring in 1909.

Brooks had previously been ambivalent toward the past. His early book, *The Emancipation of Massachusetts*, was filled with ancestral criticism. At times, when he seemed to be moving in harmony with the dominant modern forces, Adams praised the present. But now that his star had definitely set, comfort lay only in the past. Unfulfilled ambition made only those things never contested seem worthy of winning.

Advancing age and contemplation of family tradition made Adams more conscious of class ties. He was even pained by the death throes of foreign aristocrats. A Tory setback in the elections of 1910 occasioned regret that England's "landed aristocracy" had not lasted "for my time." Their defeat meant "that the whole world is to be swept away before my eyes." It saddened him to realize

that all is "gone, everything I love or understand or respect, is dead with the wild animals, and the country and poetry, and color and form." For him, perhaps, it was also "time . . . to die."[63] America's failure to halt business encroachment made him feel even more strongly the deposition of "an old ruling class whose power is broken, whose privileges are being taken away, who is facing an economic position with which they admit they cannot deal, and who is half wild with fear of attack."[64] It was the twilight of the gods for Brooks, as he praised Oliver Wendell Holmes for being "the last of the great race who have had at once the taste and the power to do them [make speeches] perfectly. Like poetry it dies with us."[65] Even taste, that last refuge of the patricians, was being destroyed by the onslaught of the ascending class.

Disappointments in the Roosevelt era turned the aggressive seeker after power into the victimized old man. Feebleness partly excused failure, and guilt was neutralized by a withdrawal from society. Nostalgia for the past and martyrdom in the present—such self-dramatization was all that remained after a life of defeat. The passing of his class convinced Brooks that disintegration was imminent, and he vied with Henry for the most pessimistic formulation of the Second Law of Thermodynamics. "I have reached precisely your conclusions," he wrote, "except that I incline to think that energy is absolutely lost and that it is not degraded." He was morally certain that "men are losing energy—mental energy I mean and very fast."[66] "The only question" now "is one of time," and even twenty-five years was "too long."[67]

Adams's cataclysmic mood varied. At times he felt himself yielding "to the depression of age." Catastrophe had become a "fixed idea," and he began "to fear lest . . . it makes me doubt my own balance. I talk and think of little else."[68] Unfortunately, these fruitful introspections disappeared as others came to share his outlook. As always, acceptance dissolved his self-doubt. Gratified at being "actually accepted as orthodox and conservative," Brooks suddenly discovered that "I have more than I ever deserved."[69] He had become "an exceptionally happy man, . . . happier than I have ever been," even if "the atmosphere about us is so charged with an indescribably sickening decay that it is very hard to resist depression." Thought the old crowd was dying, and "we have not much further to go," Adams found "this satisfaction, thank God! At least I have lived. I have known the old world. I have loved, and hoped and believed . . . the deluge may come—but we have lived."[70]

Did this euphoria amid disaster mean that his gloomy prophecies had been a pose? Brooks's intimates sometimes thought so. "I have known you for sixty-odd years," wrote Henry, "and since you were a baby I've never known you when you weren't making yourself miserable over the failings of the universe. It has been your amusement, and a very good one."[71] Such an estimation is substantiated by his chameleon moods, in which somber expectations alternated with personal elation. But, even if Adams was not above gilding the lily or using the world as a stage for his own tragedy, a genuine atmosphere of despair hung about him. There was nothing of the *poseur* in these words of regret at his inability to commit himself to an ideal or cause:

> I wish I could have faith in Christ. It is sad to have no inner light as we near the end and I have none. I cannot care, as you do, for the race in general. I am no philanthropist. My nature, my race, my blood confines my affections and bounds my interests. If they are doomed I care not for the future. It is too cold for me. For me, the world dies with them. Very seriously, I envy you who can find consolation in the stars, as I envy men like Newman, who can find rest in the Church.[72]

While in this somber mood, Adams wrote *The Theory Of Social Revolutions.* In his other works, he had debated the people's willingness to administer energy released by modern science and business. In the new book, a veritable graveyard of abandoned hopes, he questioned whether "finite minds" ever have the capacity to organize such boundless forces. The discrepancy between organization and production of energy, only a danger in 1904, had already enabled the capitalists to seize "sovereignty." Once in command, the magnates had shown themselves unscrupulously greedy, bankrupting debtors and twisting the laws to serve their ends. To protect themselves from corporate servitude, workers had formed unions. Now the two groups were squaring off for a battle that "may at any moment, shatter the social system; while under our laws and institutions, society is helpless." At one time, he had believed there was a chance capitalists could apply economic centralization to administration; now he concluded that specialization would prevent them from functioning outside of business. Paradoxically, the very specialization that had enabled captains of industry to seize power might be their undoing. Unless the vested interests became more responsible and adapted to new social demands, they would go the way of previous élites. Brooks warns that "the experience of the English speaking race" included a violent upheaval "about every three generations."[73] According to his calculations, capitalists had taken control around 1865, approximately two generations before. There was little time left.

In the *Theory Of Social Revolutions,* the final formulation of Brooks Adams's philosophy, Progressivism is fused with Darwinian determinism. Unlike Henry, who emphasized the laws of thermodynamics, Brooks clung to the Darwinian framework throughout his lifetime. Perhaps the younger Adams held onto the doctrine of evolution because he still struggled to survive in the modern world long after his brother had surrendered. Since business had failed to adapt, it must abdicate sovereignty or be annihilated. Some power must be found to mediate between management and labor, to suppress revolutionary forces by establishing the supremacy of law. To Adams's Progressive mind, only government could ensure equity. Roosevelt's Square Deal offered society its last chance to avoid becoming a jungle in which the struggle for existence could only go against its unfit leaders.

World War I confirmed Brooks's conviction that catastrophe was inevitable. In this cataclysmic mood, Adams published an article designed to crush the false illusions of our civilization. "No society," he asserted, "ever has succeeded or ever can succeed, in realizing any ideal or abstraction whatever, because, . . . the interposition of the flesh makes impossible the fulfillment of the law. And yet to-day our democratic society gravely proposes to cause infinite nature to permit man to live in peace." "Unable to reconcile himself to the calamities of his lot" the selfish American dreams "that he may escape self-denial and hardship by omitting those duties which entail a sacrifice." Brooks demanded that these delusions cease and that mankind face up to the fact that it was an atom of "measureless space . . . never being at rest, never in perfect equilibrium, but assuming forms which have the aspect of competing selfishly with each other." In such a cosmos, man could never achieve any goal, let alone the ideals of peace and freedom.

Adams vented his distaste for modern America by bitterly assailing democracy. Popular rule was actually a conspiracy of "recklessness and self-complacency" against "the common safety." It exalted "the individual" over the necessity for community cooperation. Without discipline, "even an approximation to order, justice, mercy, peace, or any of the ideals is impossible."[74] Even survival was impossible in a society atomized and immobilized by the centrifugal force of human selfishness. Shortly, Brooks expected, a "more cohesive and intelligent organism . . . shall spring upon us and rend us as the strong have always rent those wretched . . . feeble creatures who are cursed with an abortive development."[75]

Disgust for democracy was consistent with the Calvinist creed that attracted Adams in his later years. Submersion in family history and a confession of faith at the First Parish Church on November 11, 1914 (an adherence to an Old Puritan custom), were signs of his tapping of ancestral roots. Henry fled to history in order to escape his conscience, but Brooks embraced the past to reaffirm a rigid moral code. The elder brother pleaded for mercy; the younger demanded retribution. Brooks embraced the communitarian and even the authoritarian aspects of Protestantism. "No society like anything which we or our ancestors have known, can cohere without a faith in revealed religion," were the words of his confession.[76] "Perfection," to the new saint, presupposed "a code of moral standards" that would provide barriers against selfish irresponsibility. Sensual desire offered one challenge, but the real task was to overcome the sin of pride. Adams echoed his stern-visaged Puritan fathers by declaring that man's "greatest enemy is always his own vanity and self esteem," his refusal "to admit his own intellectual impotence in the face of the infinite, and endure with resignation his destiny. He is always aspiring to dominate nature and is always suffering defeat." "Democracy," reveling in "personal liberty," encourages rebellion against proper restraint and enables lust and pride to master men.[77] What could be more reminiscent of Governor John Winthrop's distinction between "Civil Liberty" and "Natural Liberty" than Brooks Adams's **"Can War Be Done Away With?"**

Adams's antidemocratic diatribe reflected his alienation from contemporary America. A "growing reluctance to express my views in public," evidenced the distance between him and his fellow citizens. "So far sundered from most of" his countrymen did he find himself, that he shrank "exceedingly from thrusting on them opinions which will give offense, or more likely still, excite derision."[78] Brooks was reluctant to express himself because the country's basic ideal was the source of all his problems. Democracy created an open society, which permitted the wrong people to eclipse the Brahmin élite. By substituting change for permanence, individualism for community, and anarchy for order, popular rule upset aristocratic calculations and turned patrician virtues into weaknesses.

The war was not a pleasant period for Adams. In 1915, his brother Charles's death triggered another wave of despondency. "Good luck has followed him to the end," he wrote Henry. "I wish I dared to hope that a like passage might be mine." Death in the family accentuated the emptiness of life. As Brooks looked "back through the long series of years," he wondered "more day by day what it has all been about and why I am here at all."[79] His depression was so overwhelming that the old stimulants failed to raise his spirits. America's triumphs did not "lay him out" as lesser victories had done twenty years earlier. Even long-awaited election to public office—that of delegate from Quincy to the Massachusetts Constitutional Convention of 1917-1919—failed to encourage him.

In 1918, Adams was struck an even more crushing blow in the death of Henry. When his brother died, he wrote to Holmes bemoaning the loss that "nothing can ever . . . make good." From boyhood, Henry had "filled a place in my life which was all his own and now, I frankly admit that, reason with oneself as I may, I cannot pull myself together at all—I do not suppose I ever shall be able to."[80]

Adams entered his last productive year with a heavy heart. His first venture was a new edition of ***The Emancipation of Massachusetts.*** The preface to this reprint sharply pointed up the differences between the old man of 1919 and the youthful optimist of 1887. Adams professed amazement that he had once maintained "the Twelfth and Thirteenth centuries" to be "as contrasted with the Nineteenth, ages of intellectual torpor." The venerable pessimist was startled by "the self-satisfied . . . finality of my conclusions." He renounced an earlier confidence in progress and repudiated any past belief in the order of the universe or the unity of science. In a passage similar to Henry's *Education* he recanted his former faith: "Each day I live I am less able to withstand the suspicion that the universe, far from being an expression of law originating in a single primary cause, is a chaos which admits of reaching no equilibrium and in which man is doomed eternally and hopelessly." As society

sank deeper into directionless anarchy, an acceleration of energy was hastening our doom. Signs of disaster abounded. Imminent defeat by Asia, disorganized administration, and the triumph of desire over discipline all indicated that "democracy in America has conspicuously and decisively failed" and that "capitalistic civilization, . . . is nearing an end."[81]

Brooks's last publication was, fittingly, an introduction to Henry's *Degradation Of The Democratic Dogma.* Henry's work on the cataclysmic implications of the Second Law of Thermodynamics was in keeping with his mood. Characteristic also was Adams's lengthy discourse on the family. In this last projection of himself onto the past, he portrayed his grandfather as a tragic hero betrayed by the "Democratic Dogma." John Quincy embodied all the noble ideals, he was enlightened, rational, scientific, patriotic, and incorruptible. Yet in the end, these very merits led to his rejection. Trapped by virtue, he was lost in a struggle with slick charlatans who capitalized on the common man's selfishness. To Brooks Adams, John Quincy was a lion amid jackals. But a whole pack of jackals is too much even for a lion.

Brooks Adams was sure that in resisting the allurements of the harlot democracy, he had avoided his grandfather's failure. He too had "inherited a belief in the great democratic dogma" but had "learned . . . to look on man, . . . as a pure automaton, who is moved along the paths of least resistance by forces over which he had no control. In short, I reverted to the pure Calvinistic philosophy." Fortified by Calvinism, Brooks skirted the pitfalls of his ancestor. He realized "that the strongest of human passions [are]—fear and greed," and he put no more faith in chaotic science.[82] Above all, Brooks was wary of democracy. This system, the child of idealism, science, and free will, had inherited all their faults. It was steeped in chaos and complexity. Democracy had deified competition and surrendered to selfishness. Adams could take pride in the fact that he had not yielded to the blandishments of popular rule. But even an arid pride is not satisfied by avoiding defeat, especially at the price of not entering the fray. His was still a Calvinistic pride to be gratified only when the millennium arrived. On that glorious day, when "the ultimate conclusion came," when "social war, or massacre" would end democracy, Brooks Adams and his kin would sit at the right hand of God.[83] In spite of this grim triumph, however, the grandson shared in his grandfather's downfall. It was clear that he too had been beaten, for he would hardly demand vengeance for a defeat that he had not suffered. Nonetheless, Adams called for the judgment day and claimed justice. He did not really, however, want them at all, for in his innermost heart, a voice plaintively cried for mercy.

Oliver Wendell Holmes once said that, although "I have known him [Brooks Adams] from boyhood. . . . yet I still don't quite know what to think."[84] These words are heartening to those who study Brooks Adams and also do not "quite know what to think." From the complex personality and the diverse moods, however, some basic emotional patterns do emerge. Clearly, his doubts about himself and his country rose out of status anxiety. Adams, keenly aware of belonging to a declining class, evinced the self doubt and ineffectuality that often accompany social displacement. A life that did not fulfill the promise of its birthright of national leadership must have been a nightmare of failure. Out of such feelings came the authoritarian conviction that man could neither master his fate nor be autonomous without sinning. The dead weight of the past was a staggering handicap for Brooks, and his whole life was a struggle to prevent himself from buckling under. Restlessness and *ennui,* anti-Semitism and imperialism, escape through Calvinism or cataclysmism were all attempts to lay down this burden. But Adams was too proud, too sensitive, and too intelligent to forget his legacy, and through the pathetic rationalizations and self-deceptions there frequently flashed insights that revealed painful awareness of his predicament. "I apprehend that I approach pretty nearly being utterly without a use in the world I live in," he told Henry in 1901. "It is a sign that the blood is exhausted, and that we have come to the end. Apparently our generation was all right. We seemed to have ability, energy and opportunity, and yet we all have tried and have not suited ourselves or anybody else."[85]

It was one thing to admit ineffectuality, but it would be asking too much of any human being that he shoulder full responsibility for a lost life. Brooks admitted to being an anachronism, but he never forgave the society that had made him one. Of all human conditions, irrelevance is the hardest to bear and the most difficult for its sufferer to forgive. The longer Brooks was ignored in his own time, the more he professed to scorn the present and to admire the past. When the present grew so unbearable that the divergence between the two could no longer be spanned, it followed that the modern era had to be destroyed. Lacking virtue, which meant not appreciating an Adams, twentieth-century society could not survive. The bitterest charges, the most dire accusations, were hurled against the pre-emptors. The Jew, the banker, and the industrialist were held responsible for society's miserable state because they typified contemporary culture. They had driven the Adamses from their perch; they were interlopers destroying America's native aristocracy. Not knowing the past, not having shared in building the present, their ravenous hands mercilessly tore civilization apart. But Brooks, angry at being displaced, would be revenged. In his own alienation, the new leaders became aliens; his own guilt for failure would be purged by society's destruction.

Since Adams had been born at the juncture of the present and the past, since he existed in the twentieth century but really lived in the eighteenth, he was deeply divided. Inability to come to terms with himself and his age caused contradictions in his thought and behavior. He could plead for centralization, expansion, and adjustment while claiming that preindustrial traits were necessary for adaptation. Ultimately, despite his commitment to modern times, he chose the past and rejected the magnates in favor of aristocrats like George Washington, John Quincy Adams, and Theodore Roosevelt. Great discrepancies also appeared between his diagnoses of radical social ills and his prescriptions for superficial nostrums. Despite his cataclysmic predictions, Adams was almost as much a Mugwump while he called himself a Progressive as when he agitated for civil-service reform in the 1870's. The challenge of science also stirred irreconcilable notions. Brooks argued repeatedly that the application of scientific principles to social problems was our only salvation. Yet, at the end of his life, he embraced Calvinism and claimed that science was leading us to chaos.

Adams's values were as much at war as his ideas. Although asserting aristocratic obsolescence, he trusted only Roosevelt and Lodge. Professing to be a rigid determinist, he spent his life trying to divert the nation from its fate. Thus despite his claim of amoral pragmatism, he would up condemning America for its sinfulness.

His conflicting moods, values, and ideas were the results of a divided personality. A lifetime of dismal prophecy did not prevent his friends from thinking him something of a *poseur*. Nor did frustration at not being taken seriously prevent him from playing the "crank." Rather, it led to a transparent disdain for humanity that showed that he had been cut to the quick by lack of recognition.

Interminable contradictions were created by a deeply dissatisfied, doubt-ridden existence. In desperation, Brooks sought solace by suppressing the warring elements within him. Authority in any form, but chiefly military or religious, promised peace. Democracy, on the other hand, was feared and hated because it preached autonomy for one who craved discipline to curb his clashing emotions. Even the relief of losing his individuality was denied him, however. Adams was unable to fall back on the religion of his forefathers although he had made a confession of their faith. How could one believe in a god who escaped his responsibility by allowing "young men to grow old?" How could one love a god who left one's life in "a devilish turmoil."[86] That was life for Brooks Adams—"a devilish turmoil." He was at war with society and at war with himself, and his great tragedy was that he could achieve neither victory nor peace.

NOTES

[1] Charles Francis Adams, Sr., "Diary," June 24, 1861, microfilmed Adams Papers, Widener Library (Cambridge). Cf. December 19, 1871.

[2] Brooks Adams, "The Seizure of the Laird Rams," *Proceedings: Massachusetts Historical Society,* XLV (December, 1911), 243-244, 247.

[3] Adams to C. F. Adams, January 26, 1868, Adams Papers.

[4] Adams to C. F. Adams, March 24, 1868, Adams Papers.

[5] Adams to C. F. Adams, February 24, 1868, Adams Papers.

[6] Adams, "The Platform of the New Party," *North American Review,* CXIX (July, 1874), 47, 60, 60-61.

[7] Adams, "Review Of James Fitzjames Stephen's *Liberty, Equality, Fraternity,*" *North American Review,* CXVIII (April, 1874), 445, 447.

[8] Adams to Henry Cabot Lodge, August 20, 1879. All letters to Lodge cited here are in the Lodge Papers, Massachusetts Historical Society.

[9] Adams, "The Last Stage of English Whiggery," *Atlantic Monthly,* XLVII (April, 1881), 569.

[10] C. F. Adams, "Diary," July 21, 1877.

[11] Mrs. Duncan Cryden, quoted in Arthur F. Beringause, *Brooks Adams* (Alfred A. Knopf: New York, 1955), pp. 71-72.

[12] Adams to Lodge, September 4, 1881.

[13] Adams to H. Adams, March 7, 1887. Unless otherwise noted, Adams's letters are from Houghton Library (Cambridge).

[14] Adams, *The Emancipation of Massachusetts* (Houghton Mifflin Co.: Boston, 1887), pp. 42, 363-364, 40.

[15] Adams to H. Adams, March 11, 1887.

[16] Adams, *The Plutocratic Revolution* (New England Tariff Reform League: Boston, 1892), pp. 1-2, 4.

[17] Adams to Lodge, November 23, 1892.

[18] Adams to H. Adams, January 4, 1893.

[19] Adams, *The Law of Civilization and Decay,* (2nd ed., Alfred A. Knopf: New York, 1943), pp. 58-59, 60, 184, 303, 304-305; 326, 328-329, 336-339.

[20] Adams, *The Gold Standard: An Historical Study* (New England News Co.: Boston, 1894), p. 34.

[21] Adams to Lodge, May 6, 1894.

[22] Adams to H. Adams, June 24, 1895, Adams Papers, Massachusetts Historical Society. Cf. Adams to H. Adams, October 28, 1896, Adams Papers.

[23] H. Adams to Elizabeth Cameron, September 5, 1917, quoted in Worthington Chauncy Ford, ed., *The Letters of Henry Adams: 1892-1918,* II (Houghton Mifflin Co.: Boston, 1938), 645.

[24] Adams to H. Adams, April 22, 1896.

[25] Adams to H. Adams, July 12, 1896.

[26] Adams to H. Adams, October 31, 1896.

[27] Adams, *Law,* pp. 58-59.

[28] Adams to Cecil Spring Rice, June, 1888, quoted in Stephen Gwynn, ed., *The Letters and Friendships of Cecil Spring Rice,* I (Constable and Co.: London, 1929), 97.

[29] Adams to H. Adams, February 2, 1895.

[30] Adams to H. Adams, May 14, 1895.

[31] Adams to H. Adams, June 24, 1895, Massachusetts Historical Society. Cf. Adams to H. Adams, September 21, 1895; Adams to H. Adams, October 13, 1895; Adams to H. Adams, August 17, 1896; Adams to H. Adams, November 15, 1896.

[32] Adams to H. Adams, September 9, 1896.

[33] Adams to H. Adams, August 17, 1896. Cf. Adams to H. Adams, August 25, 1896; October 15, 1896.

[34] Adams to H. Adams, October 15, 1896; Adams to H. Adams, March 25, 1896.

[35] Adams to H. Adams, July 26, 1896.

[36] Adams to H. Adams, September 21, 1895.

[37] Adams to H. Adams, December 23, 1895.

[38] Adams to H. Adams, March 7, 1896.

[39] Adams to H. Adams, February 27, 1898; Adams to H. Adams, April 29, 1898.

[40] Adams to H. Adams, May 22, 1898; Adams to Abigail Homans, April 26, 1898.

[41] Adams to Abigail Homans, May 25, 1898.

[42] Adams to H. Adams, May 22, 1899. Cf. Adams to A. Homans, May 25, 1898.

[43] Adams, *Springfield Republican,* September 20, 1898, quoted in Daniel Aaron, *Men of Good Hope* (Oxford University Press: New York, 1951), p. 267.

[44] Adams to H. Adams, October 13, 1901. Cf. Adams to H. Adams, April 30, 1901.

[45] Adams to Mrs. Cameron, February 3, 1901, quoted in Ford, *op. cit.,* II, 313.

[46] Adams to Theodore Roosevelt, September 12, 1901, quoted in Beringause, *op. cit.,* p. 203.

[47] Adams, to H. Adams, October 13, 1901.

[48] Adams to Lodge, March 27, 1901.

[49] Adams, "Address at the Memorial Service to Lieutenant Edward Bumpus," *Boston Evening Transcript,* October 16, 1901, p. 9. Cf. Adams to Holmes, April 13, 1902; Adams, "Address at the Reform Club Dinner," *The American Architect,* LXXIV December 28, 1901), 99-100.

[50] Adams, "The New Industrial Revolution," *Atlantic,* LXXVII, (February, 1901), 165. Cf. "War and Economic Competition," *Scribner's Magazine,* XXXI (March, 1902), 352; Adams to H. Adams, July 5, 1901; July 27, 1901; September 12, 1902.

[51] Adams, "Reciprocity or the Alternative," *Atlantic,* LXXVIII (August, 1901), 153-155; "War as the Ultimate Form of Economic Competition," *Proceedings: American Naval Institute* (December, 1903), 829-881; "Economic Conditions for Future Defense," *Atlantic,* XCII (November, 1903), 632-649.

[52] Adams to H. Adams, September 26, 1902; Adams to H. Adams, December 11, 1902.

[53] Adams, *Railways as Public Agents: A Study in Sovereignty* (Plimpton Press: Boston, 1910), pp. 53-54, 136-138, 143, 144. Cf. Adams to Henry Teller, December 19, 1907.

[54] Adams to H. Adams, April 10, 1906.

[55] Adams to H. Adams, April 28, 1902.

[56] Adams to H. Adams, February 3, 1903.

[57] Adams to H. Adams, October 6, 1904.

[58] Adams to H. Adams, July 2, 1905.

[59] Adams to H. Adams, January 9, 1906; Adams to H. Adams, April 15, 1908.

[60] Adams to H. Adams, January 1, 1908. Cf. Adams to H. Adams, January 9, 1906; May 21, 1905.

[61] Adams, "John Quincy Adams" (1909), Unpublished ms. in the Massachusetts Historical Society, pp. 165, 396, 564-565, 299, 256, 80, 406.

[62] Adams to H. Adams, March 6, 1909. Cf. Adams to H. Adams, January 28, 1910.

[63] Adams to H. Adams, January 28, 1910.

[64] Adams to H. Adams, November 12, 1910. Cf. Adams to H. Adams, April 9, 1911.

[65] Adams to Holmes, June 29, 1911, private collection of Mark DeWolfe Howe, Harvard Law School.

[66] Adams to H. Adams, March 1, 1910.

[67] Adams to H. March 2, 1910.

[68] Adams to H. Adams, March 10, 1910; Adams to H. Adams, April 5, 1910.

[69] Adams to H. Adams, October 22, 1910; Adams to H. Adams, November 12, 1912.

[70] Adams to H. Adams, April 9, 1911.

[71] Adams to B. Adams, January 30, 1910, quoted in Ford, *op. cit.,* II, 532. Cf. Theodore Roosevelt to John Hay, May 3, 1897, quoted in Elting Morison, ed., *The Letters of Theodore Roosevelt,* I (Harvard University Press: Cambridge, 1951), 609; Oliver Wendell Holmes to Sir Frederick Pollack, August 9, 1897, quoted in Mark DeWolfe Howe, ed., *Holmes-Pollack Letters,* II (Harvard University Press: Cambridge, 1941), 76.

[72] Adams to Holmes, March 9, 1913, private collection of Mark DeWolfe Howe.

[73] Adams, *The Theory of Social Revolutions* (The Macmillan Co.: New York, 1913), pp. 3-4, 17-19, 27-30, 6-7. Cf. Adams, "The Collapse of Capitalistic Government," *Atlantic,* CXI (April, 1913), 433-444.

[74] Adams, "Can War Be Done Away With," *Publications: American Sociological Society,* X (December, 1915), 104, 104-105, 104, 105-106.

[75] Adams, "The American Democratic Ideal," *Yale Review,* V (January, 1916), 233.

[76] Adams, quoted in Mark DeWolfe Howe, *Who Lived Here* (Little, Brown and Co.: Boston, 1952), p. 12.

[77] Adams, "Can War Be Done Away With," pp. 106, 115, 106.

[78] Adams, "Democratic Ideal," p. 225.

[79] Adams to H. Adams, March 20, 1915.

[80] Adams to Holmes, April 18, 1918, private collection of Mark DeWolfe Howe.

[81] Adams, *The Emancipation of Massachusetts* (Houghton Mifflin Co.: Boston, 1919), pp. 152, 166-167. Cf. Adams, "Collective Thinking in America," *Yale Review,* VIII (April, 1919), 623-640.

[82] Adams, "Introductory Note," in H. Adams, *The Degradation of the Democratic Dogma* (The Macmillan Co.: New York, 1919), pp. v-vi, vii, viii.

[83] Adams, "The Heritage of Henry Adams," *Ibid.,* p. 121.

[84] Holmes to Pollack, May 25, 1906, quoted in Howe, ed., *Holmes-Pollack Letters,* II, 123.

[85] Adams to H. Adams, July 5, 1901. Cf. Adams to H. Adams,

[86] Adams to Mark DeWolfe Howe, June 22, 1921. December 21, 1899.

## Mina J. Carson (essay date 1983)

SOURCE: "The Evolution of Brooks Adams," in *Biography: An Interdisciplinary Quarterly*, Vol. 6, No. 2, Spring, 1983, pp. 95-112.

[*In the following excerpt, Carson surveys Adams's body of work, which she characterizes as born out of his politically conservative background.*]

Brooks Adams generally appears in the history of American thought as Henry Adams's cranky younger brother, an eccentric misanthrope who reputedly began each day "by singing a song of his own invention, which consisted entirely of three repeated words: 'God damn it! God damn it! God damn it!'" In a less apocryphal vein is the recognition that *The Education of Henry Adams* was fertilized by Brooks Adams's audacious attempt to forge theoretical order from material and spiritual chaos.[1] For Henry Adams, the century ended on a note of Darwin-induced despair. In contrast, Brooks Adams's personal odyssey in the decade of 1893 to 1903 traced an arc from apocalyptic despair to progressive optimism and nationalistic celebration.

Brooks Adams might well merit attention solely for the insights his career offers into the crucial social and intellectual movements of the turn of the century: "genteel reform" politics, Free Silver, scientific historiography, Anglo-Saxonism, imperialism, and the Progressive movement toward rational, scientific government. Ultimately more compelling, however, is the question of the man himself. In reconciling the apparent contradictions of his thought and career, the historian is drawn into a recapitulation of Adams's own search for order—and perhaps, too, to a reaffirmation of the qualities that constitute the kind of intellectual heroism Adams celebrated, and may be said in his queer, crabbed way to have embodied.

The youngest child of Charles Francis and Abigail Brooks Adams, Brooks Adams was trained in the law, in the family tradition. Although he began his career in 1872 determined to be a lawyer in more than name only, politics and quarterly journalism soon encroached on his legal practice. An attack of "nervous illness" in 1881 forced Adams to curtail his practice almost completely, and he turned to writing, traveling, and caring for his refractory health.[2] In 1895, after several years of restless travel and reflection, he produced his *magnum opus*, *The Law of Civilization and Decay*. Surveying western civilization through cycles of growth, centralization and decay from the Roman Republic through modern Britain, Adams formulated a theory of the rise and decline of empire, based on a hypothesis of the alternating dominance of two "types" of men: the economic and the military-religious. The immediate impetus for this undertaking was Adams's sympathy with the silver cause, bred of the personal and national trauma of the panic of 1893. His conviction that the gold standard was imposed on society by greedy capitalists led him by degrees to examine the patterns of economic power and policy through world history. A deeper strain emerged from his lifelong fascination with the Middle Ages. His interpretation enthroned the ideals he saw as represented by the monk and the crusader, and cast "economic man"—the merchant, the entrepreneur, the banker—as history's Antichrist.

Through the late 1890's Adams watched with horror and then with exhilaration as the old world crumbled and a new global order seemed to emerge, with the United States gravitating to its natural position as a young and vigorous world power. Adams ruptured his fifteen-year liaison with the Democrats in 1900 to join the Republican party in what he hoped would be an attempt to forge a rational bond between big business and strong government in service of a newly mobilized society rising from the ashes of *laissez-faire* drift. After the accession of his friend and ideological ally, Theodore Roosevelt, Adams stepped into his long-coveted role of gadfly to the great. In 1903 he accepted a lectureship in constitutional law at Boston University, and in 1907, representing the city of Spokane, he prosecuted James J. Hill for monopolistic railroad practices. Beginning with *The New Empire* (1903), he devoted the rest of his writing career to elaborating his belief that in mass education, purposive centralization, and expert administration lay the keys to national and global progress.

How can we understand Adams's abrupt truce with modern capitalist society? It seems anomalous that a man in love with the superstitious, idealistic, static world view supremely represented to the Victorians by the Middle Ages should suddenly join hands with a dynamic, iconoclastic movement born of the complexities of a technological society. To get at such an understanding, we must discern the "logic" of events as it revealed itself to Adams in the course of this tumultuous *fin-de-siècle* decade. In tracing the evolution of his thought it becomes apparent that his drive to interpret his world was fueled by a rich and complex set of personal impulses. Even more intricately than most intellectuals, he saw his personal history as bound up and played out in the history of his times.

I.

Ten years older than Brooks, Henry Adams early took it upon himself to act as his brother's intellectual cicerone. "[We] ought to try our hardest to tolerate the child, who is really a first-rate little fellow . . . That boy's disposition will either make something of him or kill him," Henry wrote to Charles Francis, Jr., in 1858.[3] Henry was probably the single greatest influence on Brooks's life and thought, and their early relationship set the tone for a continuing, if erratic, closeness. As they grew older,

Brooks came to use Henry as his favorite sounding board; characteristic was his claim in reference to the manuscript of *The Law* in 1894: "There is no one else whom I care to consult at all."[4]

It is hardly surprising, then, that Brooks seems to have derived little from his Harvard years except a confirmation of his nascent interest in the Middle Ages. "I don't know how it is," he wrote his father in 1868, "but I find, and always have found, that medieval history was more to my taste than either Greek, or Roman, just as I can't help confessing to myself that a Gothic cathedral, or ruined castle, pleases me more than a Roman ruin. . . ."[5] As a first-year student at Harvard Law School, Brooks took up residence in Harvard Square with Henry, who had just been appointed professor of medieval history.[6] A year later, Brooks's legal education as well as his informal exposure to Henry's ideas were interrupted by his father's summons to act as his private secretary at the Alabama Claims Commission in Geneva. When he returned to America in 1872, Brooks was admitted to the bar in Suffolk County.[7]

As a student, Brooks Adams had joined the Commonwealth Club, a political reform organization founded by one of his brother's first students, Henry Cabot Lodge.[8] Now a young lawyer, he joined Lodge and Henry Adams in Carl Schurz's Republican reform movement, taking up his pen to promote the "new party" in 1874. His brother's *North American Review* printed this patrician battle cry: "The system now developing falls little short of placing absolute power in the hands of demagogues who use corruption as a means of controlling ignorant votes, since their fixed policy is to exclude integrity and intelligence from politics, and to rule by an appeal to folly and to fraud."[9]

His early articles testify that Adams found congenial the mugwumps' distinctive brand of conservatism tinged with panic. His appeals to "citizens of influence" to stem the ugly tide of political corruption were reinforced by urgent warnings of impending doom. "America has been wildly drifting for the past ten years . . . Nothing but a penetrating sense of their danger can save the people from having a dire choice thrust upon them,—the choice between anarchy and disintegration, or force."[10] For the first time Adams sounded the Cassandran prophecy that would characterize his writings until the end of the century. The other note struck by reform Republicanism which carried lasting resonance for Adams was that of the irresponsible, uncultured soullessness of the creatures of new wealth.[11] In 1884 Adams bolted the Republican party for the haven provided by the Cleveland Democrats, where he sheltered, though increasingly uncomfortably, for the next sixteen years.

In a review of Trevelyan's *Early History of Charles James Fox* in 1881, Adams first revealed his attraction to overarching theories of historical process. In the course of defending the historical triumph of free competition, he espoused a theory of historical determinism in which the weak inevitably yield to the strong.

> It is the shifting of power from class to class, and the effort of the new force to assert itself, that causes revolutions. Thus in the last century the power has passed from the few to the many, the centre of gravity had shifted, the whole social fabric was rotten, and was doomed to fall with a crash, because the feeble were in authority, and the weak cannot control the strong.[12]

Here in embryonic form first appears the strange mixture of Darwinism, physical metaphor, and economic determinism that would stamp Adams's subsequent work as both heavily derivative and peculiarly his own.

The professional leisure enforced by his illness in the 1880's gave Adams the opportunity to undertake his first full-length monograph, a work on early Massachusetts history solicited by Houghton, Mifflin for their Commonwealth series.[13] Adams seized this opportunity to test and elaborate some of his earlier speculations on the broad processes of history. *The Emancipation of Massachusetts* portrays the gradual erosion of the all-encompassing power of the early Massachusetts Bay clergy, and the tenacious and sometimes brutal resistance they offered to incursions on their dominion. In Adams's hands, Puritan Massachusetts became a battleground of competing historical forces, personified by human actors in the grip of the impersonal workings of "natural" law: "Like all phenomena of nature, the action of the mind is obedient to law; the cause is followed by the consequence with the precision that the earth moves round the sun, and impelled by this resistless power his destiny is wrought out by man."[14]

The heroes of Adams's scientific saga were those who did battle against the small, closed, priest-ridden society, manifesting the courage "to break down the sacerdotal barrier, to popularize knowledge, and to liberate the mind. . . ."[15] We are confronted by the anomalous spectacle of libertarian protest impelled by "that automatic, yet resistless, machinery which produces innovation"[16]; Adams's equation of the unhindered operation of the mechanistic laws of the mind with the growth of freedom of thought. This contradiction, as well as his condemnation of the "priestly caste," vanish from his later work. Time, reflection, and disillusionment would conspire to produce theoretical consistency.

In a note defending his work against the historian Charles Deane's criticism, Adams protested: "My book is not a history; it is not intended for one. It is an attempt to set forth a scientific theory of history which happens to be taken from Massachusetts, but which might as well be taken from India."[17] Deane was not the only critic to fail to recognize Adams's purpose. His first major brush with an uncomprehending public dismayed Adams ("my estimate of popular intelligence has fallen," he wrote sourly[18]), and he turned to Henry for solace. "You my dear fellow, are, permit me to say, almost the only man, who has understood the point. . . ."[19] That people were not "brighter than they are" would continue to be Adams's lament for at least another decade, as he delved further into the processes of history and became convinced of the impending doom of western civilization.

II.

Although he had early shown a capacity for unorthodox thought, Brooks Adams was a political conservative and a strong-government man by heritage and by inclination. Until 1892 he had found the well-trodden path of the eastern reform movement quite sufficient to his ideological needs.

After Cleveland's election, however, conditions rapidly deteriorated and carried Adams's convictions with them. The panic in 1893 greatly affected the Adams family fortune, much of which was tied up in bank and property interests in Kansas City and Spokane. After an anxious summer together in the Old House in Quincy, the Adams brothers were relieved to see the bulk of their estate escape from jeopardy.[20] This personal scare as well as the broader social convulsions he observed prompted Adams to rethink his views on the gold standard, which seemed directly responsible for the panic. Characteristically quick to act on a new conviction, by November he had enlisted several of his academic acquaintances and launched a fragile bark christened "International Bimetallists"—an implicit disowning of the inflammatory "free silver" cognomen.[21] Though the group quickly foundered, Adams himself spoke and wrote actively for the silver cause through the election of 1896—although near the end he faltered, rather frightened by his Bryanite bedfellows. For Adams, silver had become not only a respectable cause but also the only rational economic policy.[22]

Though his ardor for silver coincided neatly with contemporary conditions, Adams portrayed it as the practical culmination of his study and reflection since *The Emancipation of Massachusetts.* After his first book, he had "read theology backward to the schoolmen and the crusades," then traveled to Europe, studying "countless churches and castles and battlefields" in pursuit of evidence to support his evolving theory of the action of natural law upon the human mind.[23] As Adams wandered back through the ages, the religious man persisted in his scheme, but his character and role in world history changed fundamentally as Adams's demonology shifted to include and finally center on "economic man." Later he recalled the "shock of surprise" he felt, standing like a latterday Gibbon amidst the ruins of Baalbek, when he realized that the competition between free and slave labor and Roman industrial inferiority "caused a contraction of the currency, and a consequent fall in prices by reason of a drain of silver to the East, and in this way brought on the panic . . . followed by the adulteration of the denarius under Nero."[24]

If we are to rely on Adams's memory, then, his researches had shown up the hazards of monometallism even before the current panic hit. "The question with me was, how fully was I justified in applying these admitted facts of history to the crisis of 1893."[25] At the Quincy house that summer, Henry was treated to the outlines of Brooks's theory in the earliest manuscript of *The Law of Civilization and Decay.* "Brooks was then a man of forty-five years old," Henry recalled in his *Education,* "a strong writer and a vigorous thinker who irritated too many Boston conventions ever to suit the atmosphere; but the two brothers could talk to each other without atmosphere and were used to audiences of one."[26] Henry was impressed with the manuscript, as Brooks tells it, but he warned against publication. "I know not if you have any political or other ambitions, but this will be their death blow. The gold-bugs will never forgive you. You are monkeying with a dynamo."[27]

Undeterred—perhaps even a little pleased—by Henry's grim warning, Brooks continued his work. In 1895 he judged his book ready for the press and placed it with the London firm of Swan Sonnenschein.[28] But at the last moment he panicked. "Oh Henry," he cried,

> oh my dear, what a bloody fool your brother has been ever since he was born—what a fool he is now, even now when all the donkeys have kicked him, and he has lain in the gates of the rich like Lazarus. Why do I want to print a silly book that no one will read, and that I shall be cursed for, and laughed at for, by every chuckle-headed gold-bug. . . ."[29]

*The Law of Civilization and Decay* hardly succeeds as a comprehensive theory of the rise and decline of civilizations. It is flawed from the start in its foundation on arbitrary and indefensible propositions. Yet it is nonetheless a "powerful and melancholy book," as Theodore Roosevelt called it[30]: a cry of despair masquerading as dispassionate scientific theory. As such, it recalls much of both the academic and apocalyptic literature of its era; but it achieves a singular lyricism and intensity.[31] Civilizations are born in barbarian innocence, raise their superstitious monuments to an omnipotent God, expand in pursuit of trade, centralize around capitals of commerce, and finally, having sacrificed military strength to wealth, crumble under a fresh onslaught of barbarian force.

Adams would have resented the accusation that *The Law* is no "law." He took great care to lay out the theoretical underpinnings of his work in a preface. These were, once again, compounded of transpositions of physical and biological theory into the social realm and a strange mixture of economic and psychological determinism. Launching his argument with the *a priori* assertion that instinct rather than conscious thought determines men's actions, Adams observes that these controlling instincts "divide men into species distinct enough to cause opposite effects under identical conditions." His empirical observations of the artistic and cultural expressions of past societies led him to conclude that these "species" must somehow alternate in periods of social dominance.[32]

In order to fit these observations into a systematic scheme of social change, Adams had to suggest a viable sequence of cause and effect. This he finally borrowed from the physical realm. "The theory is based upon the accepted scientific principle that the law of force and energy is of universal application in nature, and that animal life is one of the outlets through which solar energy is dissipated."[33] The most common human outlets of this fixed store of energy were the mental states of Fear and Greed, which in a weirdly animistic historical synopsis Adams portrayed as somehow "possessing" and creating his dominant social types. "In the earlier stages of concentration, fear appears to be the channel through which energy finds the readiest outlet; accordingly, in primitive and scattered communities, the imagination is vivid, and the mental types produced are religious, military, artistic. As consolidation advances, fear yields to greed, and the economic organism tends to supersede the emotional and martial."[34]

This shotgun wedding of the physico-biological and social realms is resoundingly Spencerian; but two things must be noted. First, it is difficult to establish Adams's direct debt to Spencer, though inconceivable that he was unfamiliar with Spencer's work. Secondly, their origin is less important than the use to which Adams bent these ideas. At this point in his evolution, Adams substituted an emphasis on "economic" for Spencer's preferred "industrial" society. While Spencer stressed the development of scientific and technical modes of thought as concomitants of this phase of social evolution, Adams pointed to the commercial or "economic" impulse as critical in shaping a centralized, industrial society. As Henry Adams most succinctly summarized Brooks's theory, "Civilization followed the exchanges."[35]

Adams's personal financial worries must in part account for the attention he gave in *The Law* to those he deemed responsible for the recent national catastrophe: the bankers and the brokers—"economic man" epitomized. Yet Adams's animus had deeper roots, as might be guessed from the vehemence of much of his personal correspondence of the early 1890's. "I tell you," he wrote to Henry, "Rome was a blessed garden of paradise beside the rotten, unsexed, swindling, lying Jews, represented by P. Morgan and the gang who have been manipulating our country for the last four years."[36] Here Adams only reflected, albeit with marked violence, one ugly strain of the rhetoric of his time, which depicted conspiracy and manipulation behind every social and economic fluctuation, masterminded by an international community of Jewish bankers and businessmen.[37] This paranoia, fully shared by Henry Adams, was further fed by the "Mugwump mentality," hostile to what it perceived as the crudity and cultural ignorance of the industrial *nouveaux riches*. But Adams's prejudices and hatreds took on a distinctive coloration from the particular ideal he erected in opposition to the "economic man." "To me, the Gothic is the greatest emotional stimulant in the world. I am of it, I understand it, I know how those men felt, and I am in feeling absolutely at one with Saint Anselm, or

Godfrey de Bouillon."[38] Though Adams came of age during the American Gothic revival, and, through Henry and some of his friends, must have been exposed to the debates that accompanied Ruskin's reception in this country, his chief attraction to the Gothic was neither specifically aesthetic nor religious, but rather broadly nostalgic.[39] Again, Adams absorbed and then refracted this cultural strain through the lens of his unique world view. The ideals that the Gothic represented for him were not reproducible in or adaptable to the modern age; in fact, they stood in the historical memory as wrenching harbingers of inevitable decay. "There is not a barbarian anywhere singing a chant of war and faith, there is not a savage to build a natural hut, there is not a soldier to sacrifice himself for an ideal. To my mind we are at the end."[40]

Indeed, *The Law* ends with a prophecy of doom. The cycle would not swing round once again. The acceleration of consolidation, due to the development of modern technology and communication, coupled with the decreasing fecundity of what he called "the more costly races,"[41] generated two extreme types: the Western usurer, and the Eastern peasant bred to live on the scantiest nutriment. Their inevitable clash could only result in the victory of the "simpler organism" and the destruction of Western economic society.[42]

Reviewers were for the most part polite, praising *The Law*'s "depth," "originality," and "keenness of insight."[43] The public received *The Law* more favorably than either Brooks or Henry had hoped, buying out the first printing in three months.[44] Henry, busy circulating the book among his friends, wrote to Brooks in January 1896: "Of course it scares everybody. My only astonishment is that so far no one has ventured to attack it. . . . The British-American calico-school of civilization must be moribund when it does not take up such a challenge."[45] A month later Henry reported to Brooks, still in Europe, that his narrower message was also being heard: "[A] speech of Senator Mitchell of Oregon, Jan. 30, [gives] you a big puff . . . and the puff direct, even from a silver senator, has the merit of costing nothing."[46]

Henry himself was proud of his brother and more than superficially impressed. What the reviewers said hardly mattered, for to him there was not one competent to judge the book on its merits. To a friend Henry wrote that *The Law* had become "my Gospel of anarchy."[47]

III.

"I have never seen so impressive a sight as this election," wrote Brooks Adams in 1896. "A rising of miserable, bankrupt farmers, and day laborers, led by a newspaper reporter, have made the greatest fight against the organized capital of the world that has been made in this century—or perhaps ever."[48] As a Democrat and a silver man never quite reconciled to private citizenship, Adams took a nominal stance for Bryan that year, though his conservative instincts rebelled. He probably viewed McKinley's victory with some relief.[49]

By 1897 Adams had gravitated both socially and ideologically toward the small group of men who would occupy the center of his orbit for the next decade. One bright spot of his short sojourn in Washington that year was his frequent lunches with Theodore Roosevelt. "I am immensely fond of him. He is, I believe, one of the very few sincere men I ever met in my life."[50] Roosevelt's extensive review of *The Law of Civilization and Decay* in the *Forum* in January 1897 had been sensitive to Adams's purpose. Though objecting to its pessimistic determinism, Roosevelt responded strongly to *The Law*'s faintly jingoistic prophecies of decay: the fear that America might become nothing better than a nation of "hucksters," the weakness of the martial spirit among modern Americans, and the danger of "race suicide"— the failure of virility among the more "highly civilized" races. While acknowledging the alarming accuracy of some of Adams's observations, though, he ultimately declined to join in a gloomy prognosis of the nation's destiny.[51] In fact, Roosevelt wrote privately to Cecil Spring Rice, sometimes he wasn't certain that Adams was "quite right in his head."[52]

Such was the politician's reaction to the theorist. Adams, on the other hand, admired the successful New Yorker. In 1896, playing Cicero to Roosevelt's Pompey, he had written: "I have watched your career with deep interest. You may remember a year ago in Washington, *I told you to sell.* . . . You are an adventurer and you have but one thing to sell—your sword."[53] His advice to Roosevelt (superfluous, of course) reflected Adams's own ambivalence toward the sordid spectacle of contemporary American politics. Aloofness had its charms; but it also might be seen to reflect a kind of eviscerated moralism which Adams increasingly disdained. Was there not an equal moral courage in fighting it out in the midst of the fray?

Unfortunately, Adams's intermittent temptations to come out swinging had always had to contend with his basic temperamental unfitness for active politics. Henry once assessed the situation candidly: "Brooks is too brutal, too blatant, too emphatic, and too intensely set on one line alone . . . to please any large number of people."[54] In the late 1890's, however, Brooks Adams's visits to the nation's capital grew longer and more frequent. The pace of global events accelerated his intimacy with Roosevelt and Lodge, gave a new slant to his theoretical work, and offered an entrée into the highest government circles peculiarly fashioned to his talents and his temperament.

The Spanish-American War was the turning point. Word of the sinking of the *Maine* convinced him that at last the end had come. "I think we all feel as if we stood on the brink of a gulf. . . ."[55] When war was declared, he hurried to Washington. "Poor Teddy has been quite carried off his legs," he wrote with amusement; yet he himself was not immune to the atavistic appeal of war preparations.[56]

In fact, as he wrote to his niece in France, the soldiers had won his "heart of hearts."

> I have often told you that the old tradition was dead, that the world was the Jews, and that State Street and ignominy were all that was left us now. I was wrong. The old tradition still lives. Gentlemen still survive. Men whom I verily believe to be as fine a type as ever marched with Godfrey de Bouillon, or sailed with Drake.[57]

The victory at Manila was exhilarating and challenging. Adams took the plunge into imperialism. The annexation of the Philippines, "which is what we all have our hearts set on," was the manifest destiny of a new naval and commercial power. The pieces had fallen into place, and he discerned a pattern in the seemingly chaotic expansion of American influence. This realization coincided with his own sudden elevation to new respect. "Last year," he wrote to Henry, "if you remember, Roosevelt, Cabot, and others thought my views extreme. Roosevelt has thought it worth while to apologize to me . . . and to tell me that all I ever said fell behind the truth."[58]

Adams laid out his new ideas in a series of articles in 1898 and 1899. Building upon the groundwork of *The Law* in charting the global flow of goods and capital, Adams added a new dimension, military power, to his geopolitical schema. The Spanish-American War had been but the last in a series of shocks necessary to break up the old world order established at Waterloo. "[D]isintegration is sweeping capital and industry in opposite directions from their former centres,—to the east from Paris, and to the west from London." France had "amalgamated" with the newly-consolidated Russian empire in self-defense. In counterbalance to the eastward tendency of French capital was the new westward orientation of Great Britain, which might be "not inaptly described as a fortified outpost of the Anglo-Saxon race, overlooking the eastern continent and resting upon America."[59]

Vital to Adams's main conclusion was the development of the China trade. He joined Alfred Thayer Mahan in urging Anglo-American cooperation in the commercial exploitation of the East. Competition might lead to war; alliance between these maritime powers would, in the event of war, lead to certain victory. "Anglo-Saxons have little to fear in a trial of strength; for they have been the most successful of adventurers."[60]

Undergirding his advocacy of a new departure in American foreign policy was a new morality: "necessitarianism," as Henry Adams dubbed it, or the futility of men's resistance to the inexorable laws of nature.[61] "It is vain that men talk of keeping free from entanglements," Brooks wrote. "Nature is omnipotent; and nations must flow with the tide. Whither the exchanges flow, they must follow; and they will follow as long as their vitality endures."[62] This was the old determinism of *The Law,* but with a new twist. As long as the tide must flow, it was better to ride it than be swept under. Adams had put forward a new and sophisticated version of Manifest Destiny: a concise and well-formulated melding of the ragged ends of expansionist arguments for retaining the Philippines. America was to be the seat of a new empire, an "Anglo-Saxon coalition" stretching from China to the British isles and "encompass[ing] the Indian ocean as though it were a lake, much as the Romans encompassed the Mediterranean."[63]

Adams found an eager audience in the claque of ardent imperialists which had grown to include, not only Lodge and Roosevelt, but also Albert J. Beveridge, Mark Hanna, and of course John Hay.[64] Pleased by the attention and influence he now seemed to command among prominent Republicans, Brooks Adams was increasingly discomfited by his formal alliance with the Democratic party. In 1900 temptation proved too strong, and Adams bolted to McKinley (and his young running-mate, Roosevelt) just in time for the election.[65] Once more he indulged the vain hope that his vocal support might issue in some tangible reward, writing to Henry in November, "I am going to Washington to show myself for a week or two before I begin the work of the winter."[66]

His hopeful self-display did him no apparent good at that time; but with McKinley's assassination came his chance at last to play the kind of role he had envisioned for himself back in 1896. "Thou hast it now," he wrote dramatically to the new President in September 1901: "King, Cawdor, Glamis, the world can give no more. . . . You will always stand as the President who began the contest for supremacy of America against the eastern continent."[67]

Roosevelt did turn to Brooks Adams, among others, for advice on his new position.[68] Flattered—indeed, elated—Adams bid farewell to the years of crying in the wilderness. He gloated to Henry, "I find myself, for the first time in my life, growing actually popular." That did it. "[B]y God, I like it. I'm in for the new world. I go with it, electric cars, mobiles, plutocracy, and all. One don't live but once, when one is dead its for a long time, and a nation is only great once."[69]

Now ensconced to his satisfaction close to the seat of power, Adams turned to the task of completing and perfecting his transformed vision of the world's future and America's destiny in it. In the summer of 1902 he pulled together and recast his recent articles as ***The New Empire,*** a forcible statement of his thought as it had evolved since the Spanish war. If not as powerful as ***The Law of Civilization and Decay, The New Empire*** rested on a firmer and more closely reasoned theoretical foundation. More important, Adams had found a way to abrogate ***The Law.***

Man's history had been shaped and punctuated by the rise and dissolution of empires. An empire rose invariably at the crossroads of trade and could be loosely defined as a seat of commercial exchange politically guided by some form of administrative organism. Empires fell

through starvation or defeat, supplanted in commercial dominance by a competitor's superior economic administration or vanquished in a military contest for trade outlets. In either case, at fault was the doctrinal, intellectual, or administrative rigidity of the defeated. They had failed to adapt to the ever-changing demands of nature.[70]

In one neat formula, Adams had finally explained to his own satisfaction all the eccentrics who had refused to fit into his vision of world history: the Puritan clergy of New England, the medieval schoolmen, modern Harvard professors. All had been victims of intellectual rigidity: a stubborn insistence on the superiority of *a priori* doctrine of some sort to the irresistible mandates of an unreasoning Nature. This type of mind was dangerous, posing a threat to "progress" as Adams had come to define it. "This temper of mind is conservatism. It resists change instinctively and not intelligently, and it is this conservatism which largely causes those violent explosions of pent-up energy which we term revolutions."[71]

The key to survival was adaptibility, a set of mind which must be fostered in whole populations through systematic education. "Man cannot shape his own environment, but he alone of all animals can consciously adapt himself to the demands of nature. He does so by education. . . . Intellectual flexibility may be developed as readily as intellectual rigidity."[72] For Adams, the backbone of such training was the scientific method. It alone drew its generalizations exclusively from fact; it alone maintained an openness to constant adjustment. This mode of thought Adams called "generalization."[73] In contemporary America, the scientific schools had outstripped the traditional liberal colleges in preparing young minds to deal effectively with the world. As "the offspring of the Church and the daughter of the medieval convent," the liberal college purveyed a form of education shackled by outworn ethical assumptions. Conversely, the process as well as the content of "scientific education" trained for adaptation.[74]

In this focus on process, Adams had refined "necessitarianism" into an ethic of success for its own sake. In doing so, he had also finally cast aside the lifelong prejudices that had shaped ***The Law of Civilization and Decay.*** The cultural sterility of the greedy capitalist now gave way in his rhetoric to the superiority of the "trust" as tending toward the epitome of economic efficiency, "eliminating double profits, surplus wages, and needless rent."[75] National survival depended on external strength, which was only insured by internal cohesion brought about by the acceleration of the natural movement of society toward consolidation. But far from endorsing a random agglomeration of wealth sanctioned by a *laissez-faire* philosophy, Adams envisioned a concomitant strengthening of the state's administrative organs to deal with the ramifications of economic growth. "[A]dministration by masses is cheaper than administration by detail. Masses take the form of corporations . . . and if our political institutions are ill-adapted to their propagation and development, then political institutions must be readjusted, or the probability is that the whole fabric of society will be shattered by the dislocation of the economic system."[76]

Thus while never relinquishing a certain fatalistic determinism, Adams pointed the way to a planned society. Like Darwin, he rejected the notion of a law of continual progress to mitigate the unfeeling harshness of nature. What science and technology could do for man would not be done automatically and would never finally arrest the dislocation of society by chance and nature. But, though man could only cushion the shocks of nature, he should do so, through the concerted actions of public and private agencies in developing a "cheap, elastic, and simple machinery" of administration. Process, not principle, mattered now to Adams; the good was the successful. "[T]here is but one great boon which the passing generation can confer upon its successors: it can aid them to ameliorate that servitude to tradition which has so often retarded submission to the inevitable until too late."[77]

Adams had arrived by his unique route at the point where much of contemporary American political thought was converging. He joined the ranks of the technocrats of the Progressive era: believers in government by scientific principles, a bureaucracy of experts, the promotion of process as ideal.[78] Adams had rejected the notion of progress—yet his new program assumed the possibility of some sort of progress. He had rejected reason as a primary force in human affairs—yet what but reason informed the concept of the "generalizing mind"? Finally he had explicitly rejected the possibility of absolute moral values. Yet implicit in *The New Empire,* behind the impersonal, technocratic façade, was the belief that human life should not be unnecessarily harsh or tragic.

IV.

Clues to a resolution of the apparent contradictions in Brooks Adams's thought and life may be sought at several levels. At bottom, however, is an irresolvable paradox in Adams's self-consciousness: the search for an identity that contended, on the one hand, against his personal *anomie,* his sense of being purposelessly adrift in time, and on the other, against his rootedness in a family tradition that spanned and colored the history of his nation.

"I belong to an archaic type," he once wrote to Henry.[79] He felt isolated in history, passionately at one with Godfrey de Bouillon and the doomed crusaders. "Even the artists, men like LaFarge, don't see the heart of the great imaginative past. They see a building, a color, a combination of technical effects. They don't see the passion that this meant, and they don't feel that awful tragedy, which is the sum of life. The agony of consciousness."[80] History weighed heavily on Adams. The tragedy was the inexorable passage of time that confounded stasis and brought ruin to those who sought to fix their lives on an unchanging ideal. Adams's natural enemies were the unthinking creatures of time: those who had no consciousness of what they destroyed in passage. The ar-

chaic idealist joined the Boston patrician in Adams in condemning the Gilded Age capitalist. Brute insensitivity was the spiritual hallmark of the economic man. If Adams was misunderstood it was the result of being dropped into a crass age. "I am jealous of strangers—they don't see the pictures I do, and if ever I try to show them they only stare. . . . To make public is to vulgarize."[81]

Adams had a more palpable claim to archaism, as the scion of a long prominent family, now fallen in fortune not, apparently, because of any failure of natural talent and energy, but because the times had passed it by. Brooks Adams shared his brother Henry's obsessive concern with the metaphysics of the family annals. It is not surprising that both turned—protesting all the way—to the study and writing of history.

Perhaps it was egotistical in the Adams brothers to perceive in the fate of their family larger issues that merited the world's attention. But there is really no gainsaying their positive, indelible, and fundamentally accurate assumption that they were somehow special—so special that even original and successful careers as historians, editors, lawyers, and consultants to the powerful could not erase a lingering sense of failure. "I apprehend," wrote Brooks to Henry, "that I approach pretty nearly being utterly without a use in the world I live in. It is a sign that the blood is exhausted and that we have come to an end. Apparently our generation was all right. We seemed to have ability, energy, and opportunity, and yet we have all tried and have not suited ourselves or anybody else."[82]

The manifest futility of laying blame for this impotence wholly on society or on oneself led Brooks Adams to a belief in social Darwinism. Certain abilities, and the "types" who possessed them, would atrophy as civilization lost its use for them. That this scheme of evolution was nonteleological rendered resistance or blame even more pointless. Even scientists admitted, in the laws of thermodynamics, that anarchy ruled in the universe. One man had little recourse against relentless natural law.

But there is a paradox in Adams's reverence for his forebears. They did not stand as symbols of a static set of ideals. John Adams was a leader of the Revolutionary generation, and John Quincy Adams a prophet of the union of government and science. In 1919, after Henry's death, Brooks gathered together a few of his brother's last essays and published them with a long introduction entitled **"The Heritage of Henry Adams."** In it he tried to sketch the lines of thought that proved Henry to be the direct intellectual descendant of John Quincy Adams. His grandfather's chief contribution to American democracy had been his tireless, thankless work in the causes of scientific education and scientific government in the United States. His ideal was democracy as an evolutionary vehicle, a form of government and social order that would free man's instinct toward progress and open the opportunity of education and advancement to all. Instead, he had seen the beginning of the "degradation of the democratic dogma" with Jackson's election and had lived to foresee the dissolution of the Union in civil war. According to his grandson, Adams had fallen victim to "that fallacy which underlies the whole theory of modern democracy—that it is possible by education to stimulate the selfish instinct of competition . . . so as to coincide with the moral principle that all should labor for the common good."[83] And Henry Adams, sitting in the gallery of Congress in 1869, had "blushed for himself" when he heard the list of names for Grant's new cabinet. "He understood at length, as his ancestor had learned, that mankind does not advance by his own unaided efforts, and competition, toward perfection."[84]

Brooks Adams came to read a pattern in his family's history: worldly success disguising ultimate failure. Of John Adams he once wrote: "The old man's judgment and instinct was better than Washington's—his fault was that he was so unequal."[85] This is an infinitely expressive statement. John Adams had been unappreciated because he had been misunderstood; John Quincy Adams had exhausted himself in the cause of science and American progress; even Brooks's father, Charles Francis Adams, had been left alone to handle the crisis in Anglo-American relations during the Civil War. For Brooks, the record was both tragic and proud. One family, generation after generation, had struggled toward unity and progress against the mechanical laws of nature, and of human nature, which dictated chaos and disintegration.

By 1919, seven years before his own death, Brooks Adams had not only become once more disillusioned with American democracy, but he had become fully conscious of his place in the family tradition. **"The Heritage of Henry Adams"** is not only the articulation, but to a great extent the invention, of that tradition. The task of making order from chaos had come full circle in being written out in family history.

But what had John Quincy Adams to do with Godfrey de Bouillon? The most suggestive answer perhaps is that to Brooks Adams they were both heroes: not simply personal heroes, worthy of emulation, but rather heroes of a passion for unity, doing battle against a chaotic and amoral world. It was that quest for unity that Adams had celebrated, and mourned, in the "religious man" of *The Law of Civilization and Decay*: that "ecstatic dream, which some twelfth-century monk cut into the stones of the sanctuary. . . ."[86] It is no wonder that, viewing the callous insensitivity of economic society to the wreckage of what was to him the sublimest beauty man had conceived and erected on earth, Adams should pass harsh judgment on human nature and on history.

As a young man he had worked for reform within the Republican party, but the reform movement had collapsed under the weight of an apparently hopeless corruption. As a slightly older man he had witnessed the social distress caused by an economic policy dictated by politics and blind greed. It was not just Adams as Boston

Brahmin or even as Gothic aesthete who warred against the politicians and capitalists of the Gilded Age. He perceived in the politics and culture of his era the subtle, killing anarchy of drift, and he rebelled against it from the start. Even after repeated rebuffs, he never really abandoned the role of seer-cum-minister to the American people. Behind the dark fatalism of *The Law of Civilization and Decay* lay, in the herculean task he had set himself, the same quest for overarching system, explanation, rationale.

So when, in the heady years following the defeat of Spain, he sat down to draw the blueprint of a new American supremacy, Adams himself had not fundamentally changed, although his immediate attitudes toward his country and his world had. Certainly it is hard to pierce the tough armor he had forged for himself by the beginning of the new century, when he wrote, "There is but one logic, the logic of the real—there is but one moral, the moral of success. I can see no other."[87] But in his culminating concept of the "generalizing mind," one perceives not only a fundamental reaffirmation of the role of reason in human destiny, but also an essentially moral response to the cruel amorality of nature's laws. As an Adams, Brooks was taking up the fallen standard: an heroic role that he understood himself only years later, but that, despite the cynicism and disillusionment of the previous decade, was at one with both his training and his nature.

A cynic and an idealist, a misanthrope and a reformer, Adams was a man of contradictions, explicable only in terms of his unique mind and temperament. He is a remarkable study in the individual's compulsion to bend and interpret his world in the light of his deepest personal needs. At the same time, Adams had an undeniable impact, however diluted, on his times; and he did not stand alone in the intense mixture of anguish and exhilaration with which he met the turbulent end of the century.

NOTES

For their helpful comments on this and an earlier version of this essay, the author wishes to thank Donald Fleming, James Turner and Helena Wall.

All letters from Brooks Adams to Henry Adams, unless otherwise noted, are from the Adams Collection in the Houghton Library at Harvard University, and are cited here by permission of the Houghton Library and the Massachusetts Historical Society.

[1] The story of Adams's private matins is offered by David Hackett Fischer in *Historians' Fallacies: Toward a Logic of Historical Thought* (New York: Harper & Row, 1970), p. 139. Two excellent essays on Adams's thought are Daniel Aaron, "The Unusable Man: An Essay on the Thought of Brooks Adams," *The New England Quarterly* 21 (March 1948), 3-33; and William Appleman Williams, "Brooks Adams and American Ex-

pansion," *The New England Quarterly* 25 (June 1952), 217-232.

² There are two full-length biographical studies of Brooks Adams. The better one is Arthur Beringause, *Brooks Adams. A Biography* (New York: Alfred A. Knopf, 1955). An earlier study is Thornton Anderson, *Brooks Adams. Constructive Conservative* (Ithaca: Cornell University Press, 1951).

³ Worthington Chaucey Ford, *Letters of Henry Adams,* 2 vols. (Boston: Houghton Mifflin Co., 1938), 1:10.

⁴ Brooks Adams to Henry Adams, 14 November 1894 (hereafter cited as BA to HA).

⁵ Brooks Adams to Charles Francis Adams, 24 March 1868. Quoted by Beringause, p. 45.

⁶ Henry Adams, *The Education of Henry Adams* (New York: Modern Library, 1931), pp. 302-304.

⁷ Beringause, pp. 50-53.

⁸ Beringause, p. 49; Alden Hatch, *The Lodges of Massachusetts* (New York: Hawthorn Books, Inc., 1973), pp. 28-29.

⁹ Brooks Adams, "The Platform of the New Party," *North American Review* 119 (July 1874), 43.

¹⁰ Brooks Adams, "Oppressive Taxation and Its Remedy," *Atlantic Monthly* 42 (December 1878), 765-767; "The Platform of the New Party," p. 60.

¹¹ See John G. Sproat, *"The Best Men": Liberal Reformers in the Gilded Age* (New York: Oxford University Press, 1968), esp. pp. 150-151.

¹² Brooks Adams, "The Last State of English Whiggery," *Atlantic Monthly* 47 (April 1881), 569.

¹³ Beringause, pp. 77-78.

¹⁴ Brooks Adams, *The Emancipation of Massachusetts* (Cambridge, Mass.: The Riverside Press, 1887), p. 41.

¹⁵ *Emancipation,* p. 42.

¹⁶ *Emancipation,* p. 363.

¹⁷ Brooks Adams to Charles Deane, 26 January 1887. Charles Deane Collection, Massachusetts Historical Society.

¹⁸ BA to HA, 11 March 1887.

¹⁹ BA to HA, 7 March 1887.

²⁰ Beringause, p. 102; Ernest Samuels, *Henry Adams. The Major Phase* (Cambridge: The Belknap Press of the Harvard University Press, 1964), p. 116.

²¹ Adams rounded up Francis Amasa Walker of MIT and F. Benjamin Andrews of Brown University, among others. BA to HA, 25 November 1893.

²² Among Adams's efforts during this period was a popular pamphlet, *The Gold Standard. An Historical Study* (Boston: A. Mudge & Son, printer, 1894). A revised edition took the reader . . . *To April 1895* (Washington, D.C.: R. Beall, [1895]).

²³ Brooks Adams, "The Heritage of Henry Adams," introduction to Henry Adams, *The Degradation of the Democratic Dogma* (New York: The MacMillan Co., 1919), p. 88.

²⁴ "The Heritage of Henry Adams," p. 89.

²⁵ "The Heritage of Henry Adams," p. 95.

²⁶ *The Education of Henry Adams,* pp. 338-339.

²⁷ "The Heritage of Henry Adams," p. 90.

²⁸ BA to HA, 9 May 1894; Beringause, p. 115.

²⁹ BA to HA, 14 May 1895.

³⁰ Theodore Roosevelt, review of *The Law of Civilization and Decay, Forum* 22 (January 1897), 575.

³¹ Among studies dealing with the literature of the 1890's, see Larzer Ziff, *The American 1890's: Life and Times of a Lost Generation* (New York: The Viking Press, 1968), esp. pp. 206-228. Dorothy Ross has written a fascinating and provocative article delineating a movement from millennial to historicist perceptions of social change in American *fin-de-siècle* writing: see "The Liberal Tradition Revisited and the Republican Tradition Addressed," in John Higham and Paul Conkin, eds., *New Directions in American Intellectual History* (Baltimore: The Johns Hopkins University Press, 1979), pp. 116-131.

³² Brooks Adams, *The Law of Civilization and Decay* (New York: Alfred A. Knopf, 1943), p. 58. This edition contains an excellent introduction by Charles A. Beard.

³³ *The Law,* p. 59.

³⁴ *The Law,* p. 60.

³⁵ *The Education of Henry Adams,* p. 339.

³⁶ BA to HA, 10 October 1896.

³⁷ Among the studies that deal with this phenomenon, two stand out: Hannah Arendt, *The Origins of Totalitarianism* (New York: Harcourt Brace Jovanovich, 1973), and Norman Cohn, *Warrant for Genocide: The Myth of the Jewish World Conspiracy and the Protocols of the Elders of Zion* (London: Eyre & Spottiswoode, 1967). For a lurid picture of Henry Adams as an anti-Semite, see

Barbara Miller Solomon, *Ancestors and Immigrants. A Changing New England Tradition* (Chicago: The University of Chicago Press, 1972), pp. 38-41.

[38] BA to HA, 21 September 1895.

[39] See Roger B. Stein, *John Ruskin and Aesthetic Thought in America* (Cambridge: Harvard University Press, 1967), esp. ch. 4, pp. 157-186.

[40] BA to HA, 17 August 1896.

[41] This alarmist argument, which ultimately fed the eugenics movement, struck a chord in many contemporaries, notably Theodore Roosevelt. See his review of *The Law* in *Forum* 22 (January 1897), 586-587; also a letter from Roosevelt to Cecil Spring Rice, 5 August 1896, in Elting E. Morison, ed., *The Letters of Theodore Roosevelt*, 8 vols. (Cambridge: Harvard University Press, 1951), 1:554. For secondary commentary, see John Higham, *Strangers in the Land. Patterns of American Nativism, 1860-1925* (New York: Atheneum, 1969), esp. pp. 150-153; Richard Hofstadter, *Social Darwinism in American Thought* (Boston: Beacon Press, 1955), pp. 175-184; Solomon, *Ancestors and Immigrants*, esp. pp. 59-81.

[42] *The Law*, pp. 332-333.

[43] See, for example, G.B.A., review of *The Law of Civilization and Decay*, *Yale Review* 4 (February 1896), 451-453; also John L. Stewart, review of *The Law of Civilization and Decay*, *Annals of the American Academy of Political and Social Science* 8 (July 1896), 163-167. This was a thoughtful and more critical assessment.

[44] Beringause, p. 130.

[45] HA to BA, 24 January 1896.

[46] HA to BA, 7 February 1896.

[47] HA to Elizabeth Cameron, Ford, ed., *Letters of Henry Adams*, 2:76; also see HA to Sir Robert Cunliffe, *Letters of Henry Adams*, 2:91.

[48] BA to HA, 31 October 1896.

[49] See BA to HA, 12 July, 9 August, 6 September, 12 September 1896; also Samuels, *Henry Adams. The Major Phase*, p. 169.

[50] BA to HA, 29 April 1897. Theodore Roosevelt and the Adams brothers made their first social contacts through Henry Cabot Lodge. In 1889, Brooks Adams added family to old school ties when he married Lodge's sister-in-law, Evelyn Davis (after thoughtfully warning her that he was "eccentric to the point of madness"). In the same year Theodore Roosevelt came to Washington as Civil Service Commissioner. He and Lodge had become political allies in 1884 when both refused to join the patrician stampede out of the Republican party after Blaine's nomination. Now that residual political enmities had cooled, Roosevelt and the Adamses took each other's personal measure at the Lodges' house in the capital. See Beringause, p. 95; Henry Dean Cater, *Henry Adams and His Friends: A Collection of His Unpublished Letters* (Boston: Houghton Mifflin Company, 1947), lxci-lxvii; Ford, ed., *Letters of Henry Adams*, 1:398; Matthew Josephson, *The President Makers: The Culture of Politics and Leadership in an Age of Enlightenment, 1896-1919* (New York: Harcourt, Brace and Company, 1940), esp. pp. 42-45.

[51] Theodore Roosevelt, review of *The Law of Civilization and Decay*, *Forum* 22 (January 1897), 575-589.

[52] "For Heaven's sake don't quote this, as I am very fond of all the family." Roosevelt to Spring Rice, 29 May 1897, Morison, ed., *Letters of Theodore Roosevelt*, 1:620.

[53] BA to Roosevelt, 25 February 1896. Quoted by Matthew Josephson, *The President Makers*, p. 26.

[54] HA to Elizabeth Cameron, 12 January 1902, Ford, ed., *Letters of Henry Adams*, 2:367.

[55] BA to HA, 20 February 1898.

[56] BA to HA, 29 April 1898.

[57] BA to Abigail Adams, 25 May 1898, Adams Collection, Houghton Library, Harvard University.

[58] BA to HA, 22 May 1898.

[59] Brooks Adams, "The Spanish War and the Equilibrium of the World," in *America's Economic Supremacy* (New York: The MacMillan Co., 1900), p. 10.

[60] "Spanish War," p. 24; see also Alfred Thayer Mahan, *Lessons of the War with Spain and Other Articles* (Boston: Little, Brown, and Company, 1899), vii-xi.

[61] HA to BA, 20 August 1899, in Harold Dean Cater, ed., *Henry Adams and His Friends* (Boston: Houghton Mifflin Co., 1947), p. 473.

[62] "The Spanish War," p. 23.

[63] "The Spanish War," p. 25.

[64] See Walter LaFeber, *The New Empire. An Interpretation of American Expansion, 1860-1898* (Ithaca: Cornell University Press, 1963), pp. 85-101; Williams, "Brooks Adams and American Expansion," pp. 217-232; Marilyn Blatt Young, "American Expansion, 1870-1900: The Far East," in Barton J. Bernstein, ed., *Towards a New Past* (New York: Vintage Books, 1969), pp. 176-183.

[65] BA to HA, 26 November 1899, 19 July 1900.

[66] BA to HA, 13 November 1900.

[67] BA to Roosevelt, 21 September 1901, quoted in Beringause, p. 204.

[68] Beringause, pp. 204, 216-217.

[69] BA to HA, 13 October 1901.

[70] Brooks Adams, *The New Empire* (New York: The MacMillan Co., 1903).

[71] *The New Empire,* xiii.

[72] *The New Empire,* xvi.

[73] *The New Empire,* xxviii.

[74] *The New Empire,* xxiv.

[75] Brooks Adams, "The New Industrial Revolution," *The Atlantic Monthly* 88 (February 1901), 165.

[76] *The New Empire,* xxxiii.

[77] *The New Empire,* p. 211.

[78] For a concise statement of the new political ideal, see Robert, H. Wiebe, *The Search for Order, 1877-1920* (New York: Hill and Wang, 1967), p. 161.

[79] BA to HA, 15 January 1897.

[80] BA to HA, 13 October 1895.

[81] BA to HA, 22 April 1896.

[82] BA to HA, 5 July 1901.

[83] "The Heritage of Henry Adams," pp. 78-79.

[84] "The Heritage of Henry Adams," p. 109.

[85] BA to HA, 6 October 1904.

[86] *The Law,* p. 349.

[87] BA to HA, 28 February 1901.

---

# FURTHER READING

## Biography

Beringause, Arthur F. *Brooks Adams: A Biography.* New York: Alfred A. Knopf, 1955, 404 pp.
    Defends Adams as a philosophical progenitor of Os-

wald Spengler, author of *The Decline of Western Civilization*, and credits Adams as the first historian to apply a scientific formula to the explanation of history.

Nagle, Paul C. *Descent from Glory: Four Generations of the John Adams Family.* New York: Oxford University Press, 1983, 400 p.
    Examines the dynamics of the Adams's dynasty, and dedicates a chapter to Brooks Adams.

## Criticism

Aaron, Daniel. "Theodore Roosevelt and Brooks Adams: Pseudo-Progressives." In *Men of Good Hope: A Story of American Progressives,* pp. 245-80. New York: Oxford University Press, 1951.
    Positions Adams and Roosevelt at the forefront of the American Progressive Movement, and enumerates varying critical assessments of Adams's career. The essay also includes a useful, lengthy biographical discussion of Adams, and quotes liberally from his letters and essays.

Aiken, Conrad. A review of *The Emancipation of Massachusetts,* by Brooks Adams, and *The Degradation of History,* by Henry Adams. In his *A Reviewer's ABC,* pp. 115-20. New York: Meridian Books, 1958.
    In his 1920 review of the revised *The Emancipation of Massachusetts* and Henry Adams's *The Degradation of History,* Aikens finds that both brothers attempted to bring order to what they believed to be the inherent chaos of the degradation of society.

Anderson, Thornton. *Brooks Adams: Constructive Conservative.* New York: Cornell University Press, 1951, 250 p.
    Examines Adams's conservatism in light of his personality, which Anderson describes as shy among people but passionate among ideas.

Brooks, Van Wyck. "The Adamses." In *New England: Indian Summer,* pp. 485-502. New York: E. P. Dutton, 1950.
    Discusses Adams's disgust for "an age in which pig-iron was more important than poetry," and presents a concise overview of Adams's theories in *The Law of Civilization and Decay.*

Childs, Marquis W. "Evaluation." In *America's Economic Supremacy* by Brooks Adams, pp. 1-60. New York: Harper & Brothers, 1947.
    Observes that Adams presented a topical antidote to U.S. fin-de-siècle optimism, and that Adams's theories remained sound in 1947.

Clark, J. B. "America's Economic Supremacy." *Political Science Quarterly*, Vol. XVI, No. 1 (March 1901): 142-44.
    Grapples with Adams's demand for imperialist expansion to acquire China and its vast resources.

Loos, Isaac, "The Theory of Social Revolution." *The American Journal of Sociology*, Vol. XIX, No. 6 (May 1914): 842-44.
    Questions the validity of Adams's assertions that human society operates as a living organism, and challenges the facts employed by Adams to support his theories.

Madison, Charles A. "Brooks Adams: Jeremian Critic of Capitalism." In *Critics & Crusaders: A Century of American Protest,* pp. 285-307. New York: Henry Holt, 1947.
    Declares *The Law of Civilization and Decay* a "work of seminal influence," and assesses Adams as "the most original and profound member" of the Adams family. Madison also associates Adams's theories with the socialist writings of Karl Marx.

"The New Empire." *The Yale Review* (Feb. 1903): 421-23.
    Challenges Adams's scholarship and his use of uncredited sources, finally discounting *The New Empire* as "hurriedly written and ill-constructed; regarded even as fiction, it is dull."

**Additional coverage of Brooks's life and career is contained in the following sources published by Gale Research:** *Contemporary Authors,* **Vol. 123, and** *Dictionary of Literary Biography,* **Vol. 47**

# The Bridge

## Hart Crane

(Full name Harold Hart Crane) American poet and essayist.

## INTRODUCTION

Although he left only a small body of work, Crane is important as a lyric poet in the tradition of the romantic visionary as exemplified by such other poets as William Blake, Samuel Taylor Coleridge, Charles Baudelaire, and Walt Whitman. Crane's greatest contribution to this tradition is his epic poem *The Bridge* (1930), in which he attempted to delineate a mythic vision of the American experience through his primary symbol, the Brooklyn Bridge, an engineering marvel of the time that many people considered to represent the promise of America.

### Biographical Information

Born in Garrettsville, Ohio, Crane was the only child of a wealthy candy manufacturer. His mother had a history of mental illness, and in 1908, when she entered a sanatorium to recover from a nervous breakdown, Crane was sent to Cleveland to live with his maternal grandmother. There he enrolled in East High School in 1914, undertaking a program that emphasized English literature and composition, mathematics, and foreign languages. While his formal education was frequently disrupted by family conflicts and long vacations with relatives, Crane pursued a course of independent reading that included classic literature as well as contemporary avant-garde literary journals, and at this time he began writing poetry. After the separation of his parents in 1916, he moved to New York City, originally to study with a tutor to prepare for entrance into Columbia University. Instead, Crane wrote poems that were published in New York magazines during the next few years and worked in advertising and at various other jobs. Crane's first major poem, "The Marriage of Helen and Faustus," was published in 1923, and during this year he began work on *The Bridge*. In 1925 Crane was able to further pursue his literary endeavors as a result of a grant from Otto Kahn, a financier and patron of the arts. Crane's first collection of poetry, *White Buildings*, was published the following year, and he completed a substantial portion of *The Bridge*—an undertaking that was to preoccupy him for seven years—while living at his grandmother's plantation on the Isle of Pines near Cuba. Using an inheritance from his grandmother's estate, Crane traveled to Paris in 1929. There he met Harry and Caresse Crosby, the owners of the Black Sun Press, which published the first edition of *The Bridge* the following year. After Crane was awarded a Guggenheim Fellowship in 1931, he moved to Mexico City but produced little writing there that was to his satisfaction. Feeling alienated

from friends and family and convinced his poetic abilities were waning, Crane began indulging in alcohol and homosexual exploits on a regular basis. In April of 1932, while returning to New York City on a ship, Crane jumped overboard after a night of heavy drinking, and his body was never recovered.

### Major Themes

Crane originally conceived of *The Bridge* as a poem about equal in length to his "The Marriage of Helen and Faustus," and intended it to be published in his first volume of poetry. But, returning to it repeatedly over seven years, Crane gradually expanded the scope and themes of the poem until it grew to its final epic length. Written as a refutation of the pessimism he found in T. S. Eliot's epic modernist poem *The Waste Land*, *The Bridge* is intended to create an American mythology—in the spirit of Ralph Waldo Emerson and Walt Whitman—built around its central image, the Brooklyn Bridge. Organized into eight major sections–"Ave Maria," "Powhatan's Daughter," "Cutty Sark," "Cape Hatteras," "Three Songs,"

"Quaker Hill," "The Tunnel," and "Atlantis"—as well as an opening "Proem" to the Brooklyn Bridge, the poem contains references to and meditations on historical and fictional figures significant to the founding and development of America, including Christopher Columbus, Pocahontas, the Wright brothers, and Rip Van Winkle. But despite Crane's hope of creating an epic vision for the country, *The Bridge* is ultimately considered to be the portrayal of a spiritualquest for a new mythic vision, and thus its major theme is the quest itself and the necessity for an intense examination of experience by every individual. Whether or not the quest succeeds in providing a new vision is of secondary importance. Joseph Miller wrote of *The Bridge*: "Brooklyn Bridge itself, the controlling symbol of the poem, with which it begins and ends, is at the same time a historical object, a work of art, a product of modern technology, and a perfect metaphor for the desire, the spiritual ambitions, and the unifying and reconciling aspirations of American idealism."

## Critical Reception

Upon publication, *The Bridge* was met with limited praise and much confusion from critics. While some commentators, especially those associated with the New Criticism movement, recognized noteworthy individual passages, most found the poem lacking in formal unity or logical exposition and deemed its symbolic structure incoherent and poorly executed. Others asserted that Crane's limited formal education resulted in social analysis and criticism that display a deficient knowledge of the American past. Since the 1960s, however, critics have reassessed the poem. While most agree that as an epic expression of American history and an affirmative myth of American experience the poem fails, many have argued that *The Bridge* succeeds admirably as the depiction of the spiritual quest in America and is a major achievement in many of its sections as well as an important contribution to American literature.

---

# CRITICISM

## Waldo Frank (essay date 1933)

SOURCE: An introduction to *The Bridge: A Poem by Hart Crane,* Liveright, 1933, pp. xvii-xxxvi.

[*In the following essay, Frank discusses the ways in which Crane represents the quintessential poet of modern America.*]

*A*

Agrarian America had a common culture, which was both the fruit and the carrier of what I have called elsewhere "the great tradition" [*The Re-discovery of America*]. This tradition rose in the Mediterranean world with the will of

Egypt, Israel and Greece, to recreate the individual and the group in the image of values called divine. The same will established Catholic Europe, and when it failed (producing nonetheless what came to be the national European cultures), the great tradition survived. It survived in the Europe of Renaissance, Reformation, Revolution. With the Puritans, it was formally transplanted to the North American seaboard. Roger Williams, Thomas Hooker, Jonathan Edwards; later, in a more narrow sense, Jefferson, Madison, Adams, carried on the great tradition, with the same tools, on the same intellectual and economic terms, that had been brought from Europe and that had failed in Europe. It was transplanted, it was not transfigured. But before the final defeat of its Puritan avatar—a defeat ensured by the disappearance of our agrarian economy, the great tradition had borne fruit in two general forms. The first was the ideological art of what Lewis Mumford calls the Golden Day: a prophetic art of poets so diverse as Emerson, Thoreau, Poe, whose vision was one of Possibility and whose doom, since its premise was a disappearing world, was to remain suspended in the thin air of aspiration. The second was within the lives of the common people. Acceptance of the ideal of the great tradition had its effect upon their character; and this humbler achievement is recorded, perhaps finally, in the poems of Robert Frost. Frost's art, unlike Whitman's or Melville's, is one of Probability. It gives us not a vision, but *persons*. They are frustrated, poor, often mad. They face grimly their resurgent hills, knowing the failure of their lives to enact the beauty of their great tradition. Yet their dwelling within it for many generations, their acceptance of its will for their own, has given them even in defeat a fibre of strength, a smoldering spark of victory; and it is this in the verse of Frost that makes it poetry of a high order.

Frost's record (*North of Boston,* 1914; *Mountain Interval,* 1916) was already madewhen the United States entered the War; and the War brought final ruin to the American culture of "free" individuals living for the most part on farms, whose beauty Frost recorded. The tradition which had tempered the persons in Frost's poems had already, before the Civil War, sung its last high Word in the old terms that were valid from Plato to Fichte. And this too was fitting, for the Civil War prepared the doom which the World War completed, of our agrarian class-culture. But the great tradition, unbroken from Hermes Trismegistus and Moses, does not die. In a society transfigured by new scientific and economic forces, it too must be transfigured. The literature and philosophy of the past hundred years reveal many efforts at this transfiguration: in this common purpose, Marx and Nietzsche are brothers. The poetry of Whitman was still founded on the substances of the old order. The poetry of Hart Crane is a deliberate continuance of the great tradition in terms of our industrialized world.

If we bear in mind this purpose of Crane's work, we shall be better prepared to understand his methods, his content, his obscurity. We shall, of course, not seek the clear forms of a poet of Probability, like Frost. But we shall, also, not too widely trust Crane's kinship with the poets of the Emersonian era, whose tradition he immediately continues. They were all, like Crane, bards of Possibility rather than scribes of realisation. Yet they relied upon inherited forms . . . forms emotional, ethical, social, intellectual and religious, transplanted from Europe and not too deliquescent for their uses. Whitman's apocalypse rested on the politics of Jefferson and on the economics of the physiocrats of France. Emerson was content with the ideology of Plato and Buddha, his own class world not too radically differing from theirs. Even Emily Dickinson based her explosive doubts upon the permanent premise of a sheltered private garden, to which such as she could always meditatively retire. These conventional assumptions gave to these poets an accessible and communicable form; for we too have been nurtured on the words of that old order. But in Crane, none of the ideal landmarks, none of the formal securities, survive; therefore his language problem—the poet's need to find words at once to create and to communicate his vision— is acute. Crane, who began to write while Frost was perfecting his story, lived, instinctively at first, then with poignant awareness, in a world whose cant outlines of person, class, creed, value—still clear, however weak, in Emerson's Boston, Whitman's New York, Poe's Richmond—had dissolved. His vision was the timeless One of all the seers, and it binds him to the great tradition; but because of the time that fleshed him and that he needed, to substance his vision, he could not employ traditional concretions. He began, naked and brave, in a cultural chaos; and his attempt, with sound materials, to achieve poetic form, was ever close to chaos. What is clear in Crane, besides the intensity and the traditionalism of his creative will, is the impact of inchoate forces through which he rose to utterance. Cities, machines, the warring hungers of lonely and herded men, the passions released from defeated loyalties, were ever near to overwhelm the poet. To master them, he must form his Word unaided. In his lack of valid terms to express his relationship with life, Crane was a true culture-child; more completely than either Emily Dickinson or Blake, he was a child of modern man.

*B*

Harold Hart Crane was born in Garrettsville, Ohio, July 21, 1899. His parents, Clarence Arthur Crane and Grace Hart, were of the pioneer stock that trekked in covered wagons from New England to the Western Reserve. But his grandparents, on both sides, had already shifted from the farm to small town business; and Clarence A. Crane became a wealthy candy manufacturer in Cleveland. Here, the poet, an only child, lived from his tenth year. At thirteen, he was composing verse; at sixteen, in the words of Gorham Munson, [in *Destinstions*] "he was writing on a level that Amy Lowell never rose from." In the winter of 1916, he went with his mother, who soon separated from her husband, to the Isle of Pines, south of Cuba, where his grandfather Hart had a fruit ranch; and this journey, which gave him his first experience of the sea, was cardinal in his growth. The following year, he

was in New York; in contact with Margaret Anderson and Jane Heap, editors of *The Little Review;* tutoring for college; writing; already passionately and rather wildly living. At this time, two almost mutually exclusive tendencies divided the American literary scene. One was centered byEzra Pound, Alfred Kreymborg, the imagists, Harriet Monroe's *Poetry* and *The Little Review;* the other was grouped about *The Seven Arts.* Young Crane was in vital touch with both. He was reading Marlowe, Donne, Rimbaud, Laforgue; but he was also finding inspiration in Whitman, Sherwood Anderson and Melville. His action, when the United States lurched into war, reveals the complexity of his interests. He decided not to go to college, and by his own choice, returned to Cleveland, to work as a common laborer in a munition plant and a shipyard on the Lake. He loved machines, the earth-tang of the workers. He was no poet in an ivory tower. But he also loved music; he wanted time to write, to meditate, to read. The conflict of desires led him, perhaps, to accept what seemed a comfortable compromise; a job in the candy business of his father where he hoped to find some leisure without losing contact with the industrial world.

The elder Crane seems to have been a man of turbulent and twisted power, tough-fibred and wholly loyal to the gods of Commerce. He was sincerely outraged by the jest of fortune which had given him a poet for a son. Doubtless, he was bitter at his one child's siding with the mother in the family conflict; but under all, there was a secret emotional bond between the two, making for the ricochet of antagonism and attraction that lasted between them until the father's death, a year before the poet's. The candy magnate set to work to drive the "poetry nonsense" out of his boy. Hart became a candy salesman behind a counter, a soda-jerker, a shipping clerk. He received a minimum wage. Trusted employees were detailed to spy on him lest he read "poetry books" during work hours. Hart Crane escaped several times from the paternal yoke, usually to advertising jobs near home or in New York. And at last, in 1920, he decided to break with both Cleveland and his father.

His exquisite balance of nerves was already permanently impaired. The youthful poet, who had left a comfortable household to live with machines and rough men, who had shouldered "the curse of sundered parentage," [*The Bridge*] who had tasted the strong drink of literature and war, carried within him a burden intricate and heavy, a burden hard to hold in equilibrium. Doubtless, the chaos of his personal life led him to rationalise that accessible tangent ease from the strain of balance, which excess use of alcohol invited. Yet there was a deeper cause for the dis-equilibrium which, when Crane was thirty-two, was finally to break him from his love of life and destroy him.

Crane was a mystic. The mystic is a man who *knows*, by immediate experience, the organic continuity between his self and the cosmos. This experience, which is the normal fruit of sensitivity, becomes intense in a man whose native energy is great; and lest it turn into an overwhelming, shattering burden, it must be ruthlessly disciplined and ordered. The easiest defense from this mystic burden is of course the common one of denying the mystic experience altogether. An anti-mystical age like ours is simply one so innerly resourceless that it solves, by negation and aggressive repression, the problem of organic continuity between the self and a seemingly chaotic world—thus perpetuating the inward-and-outward chaos. The true solution is too arduous for most men: by self-knowledge and self-discipline, it is to achieve within one's self a stable nucleus to bear and finally transfigure the world's impinging chaos. For the nucleus within the self, as it is gradually revealed, is impersonal and cosmic; is indeed the dynamic key to order in the "outward" world. By this synthesis of his own burden, the mystic escapes from destruction and becomes a master. Crane did not personally achieve it. Yet he was too virile to deny the experience of continuity; he let the world pour in; and since his nuclear self was not disciplined to detachment from his nerves and passions, he lived exacerbated in a constant swing between ecstasy and exhaustion. Therefore, he needed the tangent release of excess drink and sexual indulgence.

The poet was clearer and shrewder than the man. His mind, grown strong, sought a poetic principle to integrate the exuberant flood of his impressions. The important poems, anterior to **The Bridge,** and written between his nineteenth and his twenty-fifth year, reveal this quest but not the finding. As Allen Tate points out in his Introduction to **White Buildings** (1926), "a suitable theme" is lacking. The themes of these poems are high enough. But, to quote Mr. Tate again: "A series of Imagist poems is a series of worlds. The poems of Hart Crane arefacets of a single vision; they refer to a central imagination, a single evaluating power, which is at once the motive of the poetry and the form of its realisation." This central imagination, wanting the unitary principle or theme, wavers and breaks; turns back upon itself instead of mastering the envisaged substance of the poem. That is why, in this first group, a fragmentary part of a poem is sometimes greater than the whole. And that is why it is at times impossible to transpose a series of images into the sense- and thought-sequence that originally moved the poet and that must be perceived in order to move the reader. The mediate principle, conterminous with both the absolute image-logic of the poem and the thought-logic of the poet, and illuminating the latter in the former, is imperfect. The first lines of his **White Buildings**

> As silent as a mirror is believed
> Realities plunge in silence by . . .

are a superb expression of chaos, and of the poet's need to integrate this chaos within the active mirror of self. Page after page, "realities plunge by," only ephemerally framed in a mirroring mood which alas! at once melts, itself, into the turbulent procession. Objective reality exists in these poems only as an oblique moving-inward to the poet's mood. But the mood is never, as in imagist or romantic verse, given for and as itself. It is given only as a moving-outward toward the objective world. Each

lyric is a diapason between two integers of a continuous one. But the integers (subjective and objective) are almost never clear; the sole clarity is the balance of antithetical movements. This makes of the poem an abstract, wavering, æsthetic body. There is not yet, as in the later work, a conscious, substantiated theme or principle of vision to stratify the interacting parts of the poem into an immobile whole. But in the final six lyrics **"Voyages"**) there is the beginning of a synthesis attained by the symbolic use of the Sea. The turbulent experiences of Crane's childhood and youth are merged into a litany of the Sea.

> You must not cross nor ever trust beyond it
> Spry cordage of your bodies to caresses
> Too lichen-faithful from too wide a breast.
> The bottom of the sea is cruel.

> —And yet this great wink of eternity,
> Of rimless floods, unfettered leewardings,
> Samite sheeted and processioned where
> Her undinal vast belly moonward bends,
> Laughing the rapt inflections of our love;

> Take this Sea, whose diapason knells
> On scrolls of silver snowy sentences,
> The sceptred terror of whose sessions rends
> As her demeanors motion well or ill,
> All but the pieties of lovers' bands.

Here is the Sea, objective, huge, hostile, encompassing, maternal.

> —As if too brittle or too clear to touch!
> The cables of our sleep so swiftly filed,
> Already hang, shred ends from remembered stars.
> One frozen, trackless smile . . . What words
> Can strangle this deaf moonlight? For we
> Are overtaken. Now no cry, no sword
> Can fasten or deflect this tidal wedge,
> Slow tyranny of moonlight, moonlight loved
> And changed. . . .

And

> *. . . Blue latitudes and levels of your eyes,—*

here, as William Carlos Williams has noted, is the Sea giving to the poet'slove its rhythm and very substance.

Crane is using the symbol of the Sea as a principle of unity and release from the contradictions of personal existence; much as D. H. Lawrence used the symbol of perfect sexual union. Both, as poetic instruments for solving the mystic's burden, are romantic and unreal; both denote a return to a "beginning" before the life of reason, and a unity won by the refusal of human consciousness. Lawrence was satisfied with his symbol. Not Crane. His intellect was more robust, his art more rigorous. Crane knew the Sea—source of life, first Mother—as death to man; and that to woo it was death. **White Buildings** closes on the note of surrender. But the poet is ready to begin his quest again for a theme that shall integrate, not destroy, the multiple human world he loves.

In 1924, the poems of *White Buildings* written but unpublished, Crane was living at 110 Columbia Heights, Brooklyn, in range of the Harbor, the Bridge, the sea-sounds:

> *Gongs in white surplices, beshrouded wails,*
> *Far strum of fog horns. . . .*

And now the integrating theme came to him. By the fall of 1925, he had achieved the pattern of his Poem. He was working as a writer of advertising copy. He appealed successfully to Otto H. Kahn (his father, after he left Cleveland, gave him no financial assistance until the last years when his son's fame began to impress him); and with a generous purse he went to the Isle of Pines; then to Paris, Marseilles, writing and—at intervals—rather riotously living. The Poem was completed in December, 1929. In the interim, Crane had learned that the house where the vision of *The Bridge* first came to him and where he finished it, was once the property of Washington Roebling, and that the very room in which Crane lived had been employed by the paralysed engineer of Brooklyn Bridge as an observation tower to watch its construction. In the year when Crane first found his theme, Lewis Mumford was prophetically writing:

> . . . beyond any other aspect of New York, I think, the Brooklyn Bridge has been a source of joy and inspiration to the artist. . . . All that the age had just cause for pride in—its advances in science, its skill in handling iron, its personal heroism in the face of dangerous industrial processes, its willingness to attempt the untried and the impossible—came to head in the Brooklyn Bridge. [*Sticks and Stones*]

*The Bridge* was published in April, 1930 (a limited first edition, inscribed to Otto H. Kahn, was issued earlier in Paris by the Black Sun Press). In 1931, Crane received a fellowship from the Guggenheim Foundation, and went to Mexico; his plan being to write a poem on the history of Montezuma, a variation on the American theme which *The Bridge* stated.

The principle that Hart Crane had sought, to make him master of his sense of immediate continuity with a world overwhelmingly chaotic, gave him *The Bridge.* But in actual life, it did not sustain him. He had a literary method to apply the principle to his vision; he had no psychological method to apply it to his person. The symbol of the Sea—theme of retreat into the unity of immersion and of dissolution—still bespoke him, as it had finally bespoken the love experience in *White Buildings. The Bridge,* with its challenging synthesis of life, wherein all the modern multiverse is accepted and transfigured without loss into One, could not hold its poet. The poems later than *The Bridge,* despite their technical perfection, mark a retreat from the high position of that Poem back to the mood of *White Buildings*—a return from grappling with the elements of the industrial world back to the primal Mother world whose symbol is the tropic Sea.

It was not accidental that Crane's tender friendships were with boys who followed the Sea. And drink was the Sea's coadjutor; for it gave Crane release not, as with most men, from the burden of *separateness* from life, but from the more intolerable burden of *continuity* with life's chaos. The Sea had ebbed, while he stood high above it on his mythic Bridge; now again it was rising.

> Here waves climb into dusk on gleaming mail;
> Invisible valves of the sea—locks, tendons
> Crested and creeping, troughing corridors . . .

Nor was it accidental that Crane now chose to go to Mexico, where for a thousand years a cult of Death—personal immolation in a Nature ruthless and terrible as the Sea—has been practiced by a folk of genius.

While Crane sailed to Mexico, I was writing:

> Perhaps the earth of Mexico conspired to create the tragic mood of the Aztec, and to fulfill it in the Conquest from which modern Mexico was born. It is an earth unwieldy to man's pleasure. Titanic and volcanic mountains, mesetas of thin air, exuberant valleys, burning deserts, encourage a culture not smiling but extreme, from tears to frenzied laughter. This earth is a tyrant; it exiles valley from valley, it begrudges loam for corn or overwhelms it with torrential rains. Man is a stranger within it, and yet he loves it like a goddess, radiant, cruel, suddenly indulgent, in whose house he must serve forever. It is no mystery that in such an earth man should have built temples of blood or possessed his life in contemplation of a loveliness deadly as fire and distant as the stars.
>
> But this man was still man. In a hostile and adorable world, man's and woman's love of life breathed on. . . . [*America Hispana*]

The second paragraph refers to the Mexico of Revolution—"the will of Mexico to be free of its death and of a beauty that flowers in death"; the first describes the Mexico that now possessed Hart Crane. The periodicity of his excesses grew swifter; the crystal intervening times when he could write were crowded out. Crane fought death in Mexico. But on his return to New York, to the modern chaos, there was the Sea: and he could not resist it.

On April 27, 1932, a few moments before noon, he walked to the stern of the *Orizaba.* The boat was about three hundred miles north of Havana, leaving the warm waters which fifteen years before he had first known. He took off his coat, quietly, and leaped.

*C*

The beauty of most of Crane's lyrics and of many passages in *The Bridge* seems to me to be inviolable. If I begin to analyse this conviction, I am brought first to the poetic texture. Its traditional base is complex. Here is a music plainly related to the Elizabethans. And here, also, is a sturdy lilt, like the march of those equal children of the Elizabethans—the pioneers. Although Crane describes a modern cabaret,

> *Brazen hypnotics glitter here;*
> *Glee shifts from foot to foot . . .*

always, there is this homely metronomic, linking him to his fathers. Hence the organic soundness of the verse. Its livingness it owes to the dimension of variant emergence from the traditional music—like the emergence of our industrial world from the base of old America. Indeed, the entire intellectual and spiritual content of Crane's verse, and of Crane the child of modern man, could be derived from a study of his typical texture. And this is earnest of his importance.

But an analysis of Crane's poetics does not belong in a brief introduction. More fitting, perhaps, will be a swift outline of the action of *The Bridge,* if it help the reader to give his whole attention at once to that Poem's inner substance.

The will of Crane in *The Bridge* becomes deliberately myth-making. But this will, as we have seen, is born of a desperate, personal need: the poet *must* create order from the chaos with which his associative genius overwhelms him. The Poem retains the personal origin of its own will. The revelation of *The Bridge,* as myth and principle, comes to a person in the course of his day's business; and that person is the poet. In this sense, *The Bridge* is allied to the *Commedia* ofDante who also, in response to desperate need, takes a journey in the course of which his need finds consummation.

Lest the analogy be misleading, I immediately amend it. Dante's cosmos, imaged in an age of cultural maturity, when the life of man was coterminous with his vision, contains Time and persons: only in the ecstatic last scenes of the *Paradiso* are they momently merged and lost. Therefore, the line of Dante's Poem is always clear, being forth and back in Time: and the focus of the action is always cogent, being the person of the Poet with whom the reader can readily graph points of reference. Crane's cosmos (for reasons which we examined when we called Crane a child of modern man, a poet innocent of culture-words) has no Time: and his person-sense is vacillant and evanescent. Crane's journey is that of an individual unsure of his own form and lost to Time. This difference at once clarifies the disadvantageous æsthetic of *The Bridge,* as compared with that of broadly analogous Poems of cosmic search, like the *Commedia* or *Don Quixote.* It exemplifies the rôle played by the cultural epoch in the creation of even the most personal work of genius.

In **"Proem,"** the poet exhorts the object of his choice—the Bridge. It shall synthesise the world of chaos. It joins city, river, and sea; man made it with his new Hand, the machine. And parabolawise, it shall now vault the continent and, transmuted, reach that inward heaven which is the fulfillment of man's need of order. Part One, **"Ave**

**Maria,"** is the vision of Columbus, mystic navigator who mapped his voyage in Isaiah, seeking to weld the world's riven halves into one. But this Columbus is scarcely a person; he is suffused in his history and his ocean; his will is more substantial than his eye. Nor does he live in Time. Part Two, **"Powhatan's Daughter"** (the Indian Princess is the flesh of America, the American earth, and mother of our dream), begins the recital of the poet's journey which in turn traces in extension (as Columbus in essence) the myth's trajectory. The poet awakes in his room above the Harbor, beside his lover. Risen (taking the harbor and the sea-sounds with him), he walks through the lowly Brooklyn streets: but walks with his cultural past: Pizzaro, Cortés, Priscilla, and now Rip Van Winkle whose eyes, fresh from sleep, will abide the poet's as they approach the transfigured world of today. He descends the subway that tunnels the East River (the Bridge is above); and now the subway is a river "leaping" from Far Rockaway to Golden Gate. A river of steel rails at first, bearing westward America's urban civilisation ("Stick your patent name on a signboard") and waking as it runs the burdened trudge of pioneers and all their worlds of factory and song. The patterning march of the American settlers traces the body, gradually, of Pocahontas; the flow of continent and man becomes the Great River; the huge travail of continental life, after the white man and before him, is borne southward, "meeting the Gulf." Powhatan's daughter, America's flesh, dances and the flesh becomes spirit. Dances the poet's boyhood memories of star and lake, of "sleek boat nibbling margin grass"; dances at last into the life of an Indiana mother, home from a frustrate trek to California for gold, who is bidding her son farewell; he is going east again to follow the sea. ("Write me from Rio.")

There are no persons in the universe, barely emergent from chaos, of Hart Crane; and this first crystallisation—the prairie mother—is the first weak block in the Poem's structure. Now with Part Three, **"Cutty Sark,"** the physical course of the poet (the subway ride has exploded into the cosmic implications of the River) returns to view, but blurred. The poet is in South Street, Manhattan, near midnight: he is carousing with a sailor who brings him, in snatches of song, Leviathan, Plato, Stamboul—and the dim harbinger of Atlantis. "I started walking home across the Bridge"; and there, in the hallucinatory parade of clippers who once winked round the Horn "bright skysails ticketing the Line," the poet is out again, now seaward.

Part Four, **"Cape Hatteras,"** is the turning point of the Poem. Thus far, we have seen the individual forms of the poet's crowded day melt into widening, deepening cycles of association. Columbus into the destiny and will of the Atlantic: two lovers into the harbor, the harbor into the sea: a subway into a transcontinental railroad, into a continent, into a River; the River into the Gulf; the Indianprincess into the Earth Mother and her dance into the tumult and traffic of the nation; ribald South Street into a vision—while the Bridge brings the clippers that bring China—of Atlantis. Now, the movement turns back toward crystallisation. **"Cape Hatteras"** at first invokes the geologic age that lifted the Appalachians above the waters; the cosmic struggle sharpens into the birth of the airplane—industrial America; the "red, eternal flesh of Pocahontas" gives us, finally, Walt Whitman. "Years of the Modern! Propulsions toward what capes?" The Saunterer on the Open Road takes the hand of the poet. Part Five, **"Three Songs,"** is a pause for humbler music, upon the variable theme of woman. Part Six, **"Quaker Hill,"** is an attempt to focus the cosmic journey once more upon the person of the poet. In my judgment, it fails for the same basic reasons. And now, Part Seven, **"The Tunnel,"** runs swift and fatefully to the climax. The poet, in mid air at midnight, leaves the Bridge; he "comes down to earth" and returns home as he had left, by subway. This unreal collapse of bridge into subway has meaning. The subway is the tunnel; is the whole life of the city entextured of all the images created by the Poem, all the previous apparitions of earth and sun. The tunnel is America, and is a kind of hell. But it has dynamic direction, it is moving! In the plunging subway darkness, appears Poe:

> *And why do I often meet your visage here,*
> *Your eyes like agate lanterns . . . ?*

If the reader understands Poe, he will understand the apparition. Of all the classic poets of the great tradition in America, Poe—perhaps the least as artist—was the most advanced, the most prophetic as thinker. All, as we have noted, were content more or less with the merely transplanted terms of an agrarian culture. Only Poe guessed the transfiguring effect of the Machine upon the forms of human life, upon the very concept of the person. The Tunnel gives us man in his industrial hell which the machine—his hand and heart—has made; now let the machine be his godlike Hand to uplift him! The plunging subway shall merge with the vaulting bridge. Whitman gives the vision; Poe, however vaguely, the method. The final part, **"Atlantis,"** is a transposed return to the beginning. The Bridge, in Time, has linked Atlantis with Cathay. Now it becomes an absolute experience. Like any human event, *fully known,* it links man instantaneously, "beyond time," with the Truth.

*D*

The structural pattern of ***The Bridge*** is superb: a man moves of a morning from Brooklyn to Manhattan, returns at midnight, each stage of his course adumbrating, by the mystic law of continuity, into American figures with cosmic overtones; and all caught up in a mythic bridge whose functional span is a parabola and an immediate act of vision. The flaw lies in the weakness of the personal crystallisation upon which the vision rests, as the Bridge is spanned upon its piers. This flaw gets into the idiom and texture. Sometimes the image blurs, the sequence breaks, the plethora of words is blinding. There is even, in the development of certain figures, a tendency toward inflation which one is tempted to connect with the febrile, false ebullience of the American epoch (1924-1929) in which the Poem was written. Yet the concept is sound; the poet's genius has on the whole equalled his ambition.

Even the failings in execution, since they are due to weakness of the personal focus, help to express the epoch; for it is in the understanding and creating of *persons* that our rapidly collectivising age is poorest.

Crane's myth must, of course, not be confused with the myth as we find it in Homer or the Bible or the Nibelungen. The Bridge is not a particularised being to be popularly sung; it is a conceptual symbol to be *used.* And the fact that this symbol begins as a man-constructed thing is of the essence of its truth for our instrumental age. From a machine-made entity, the Poem makes the Bridge into a machine. But it has beauty. This means that through the men who built it, the life of America has flowed into the Bridge—the life of our past *and our future.* A cosmic content has given beauty to the Bridge; now it must give it a poetic function. From being a machine of body, it becomes an instrument of spirit. *The Bridge is matter made into human action.*

We may confidently say that this message of ***The Bridge*** will be more comprehensible in the future (not in the immediate future), when the functionally limited materialism of our collectivist era has, through success, grown inadequate to the deepened needs of a mankind released from economic insecurity and prepared, by leisure, for regeneration. For even as necessity, today and tomorrow, drives most men to think collectively in order that they may survive; necessity, day after tomorrow, will drive men to think personally (poetically, cosmically), in order that their survival may have meaning. When the collectivist era has done its work—the abolition of economic classes and of animal want—men will turn, as only the privileged of the past could ever turn, toward the discovery of Man.

But when that time comes, the message of ***The Bridge*** will be taken for granted; it will be too obvious, even as today it is too obscure, for general interest. The revelation in Crane's poems, however, of a man who through the immediate conduit of his senses experienced the organic unity between his self, the objective world, and the cosmos, will be accepted as a great human value. And the poems, whose very texture reveals and sings this man, will be remembered.

### Bernice Slote (essay date 1958)

SOURCE: "The Structure of Hart Crane's 'The Bridge'," in the *University of Kansas City Review,* Vol. 24, March, 1958, pp. 225-38.

[*In the following essay, Slote defends* The Bridge *against critical charges of lacking structure, noting in particular Crane's own assertion that the poem is symphonic in structure rather than adhering to a traditional narrative form.*]

Because contemporary literature has offered few enough long poems, it is unfortunate that Hart Crane's ***The Bridge***[1] has been generally held unworthy as a whole, though poetically rich in texture. While many have believed in the poem, following the favorable tone of Malcolm Cowley's early review,[2] critical judgments have been cut more generally from the whole cloth of the Tate-Winters "archetypal" pattern.[3] Crane's long poem is ironically and somewhat sadly viewed as a shape without form, a bridge with uncertain connections, as chaos come again and lost Atlantis doubly lost. But there are signs that this both puzzling and brilliant poem is being reconsidered,[4] and in that spirit I should like to offer a skeleton design for a unified *Bridge,* a design on Crane's own terms.

From one position, and with one type of critical glass, *The Bridge* does certainly seem to be a series of unrelated poems in which disillusion makes a shambles of a hope brighter than its logic. But approaching the poem from another position with the glass in a somewhat different focus, adjusted to Crane's conceptions, the elements fall into place. First, Crane thought of *The Bridge* as a complex symphonic structure with intricate repetitions of form within the whole, rather than an epic with the usual narrative logic.[5] Although complicated, it is "one poem" with an "integrated unity and development"[6] in which "motives and situations recur" throughout.[7] Secondly, as Crane said, he was writing in an affirmative rather than a negative tradition: "The poem, as a whole, is, I think, an affirmation of experience, and to that extent is 'positive' rather than 'negative' in the sense that *The Waste Land* is negative."[8] He saw in the poetry of *The Waste Land* "complete renunciation," and preferred to identify himself with others of a "new vitality" and vision.[9]

And finally, in this affirmative tradition Crane used the point of view, the poetic theory, and the specific patterns of Walt Whitman, with whom he repeatedly and explicitly aligned himself, and whom he knew in part through Waldo Frank. In a letter to Munson, he said, "I begin to feel myself directly connected with "Whitman. I feel myself in currents that are positively awesome in their extent and possibilities."[10] This identification is made clearer in *The Bridge,* in which he takes Whitman as guide: "My hand/in yours,/Walt Whitman—/so—" Here, of course, is the key. Since Crane so clearly took the Whitman position, he will be misunderstood as long as that position is misunderstood. If Whitman is seen as a bubbling exploiter of American chauvinism, *The Bridge* will seem like a hapless panegyric of American history and science, with many of the individual poems obviously unconnected. If, however, Whitman is seen as a deeply spiritual thinker, a mystic of cosmic consciousness (as he was to Waldo Frank and to Crane), the pattern in *The Bridge* has a chance to come into focus.[11] And it is critical here to note that whatever any one else may think of Whitman, Crane considered him a mystic of a particular oneness. The shape of *The Bridge* derives from that principle.

THE PATTERN OF *THE BRIDGE*

Crane's invocation to the bridge concludes: "And of the curveship lend a myth to God." Here, I believe, he has

given the essential symbol and the essential form of the poem. In statement, structure, and idea, the curve or the arch—with its implied completed circle and its mystical direction—is the image which informs and illuminates *The Bridge.* Moreover, the sections of the poem are composed in united curves of space, time, and spiritual movement so that the whole is rounded into one. Although Crane uses the thematic curve repeatedly, it will be possible here to describe only the very general framework of the poem, with something of the origin and meaning of that structure. Others have noted the appearance of curves in *The Bridge;* I wish to go further in suggesting that the basic design of body and meaning depends upon that form.

*The Bridge* is divided into two parts, the first half including the **"Proem,"** **"Ave Maria,"** **"Powhatan's Daughter,"** and **"Cutty Sark."** The second section begins with **"Cape Hatteras"** as theme, and continues through **"Three Songs,"** **"Quaker Hill,"** **"The Tunnel,"** and **"Atlantis."** This division is Crane's own, for in asking his publisher to place a photograph ("of the barges and tug") between the **"Cutty Sark"** section and **"Cape Hatteras,"** he wrote: "That is the 'center' of the book, both physically and symbolically."[12] The first half explores the fused past and present of America and the meaning of self. It is the realization of identity, or position in time and space. The second half is the movement to spiritual vision, or the journey of the soul.

The structural curves of *The Bridge* are on three levels—space, time, and psychological action—and are accented by innumerable visual repetitions. In the first half, the space curve begins in mid-ocean (**"Ave Maria"**), moves to the bridge and city (**"Harbor Dawn"**), through subway and highway west (**"Van Winkle"**), across the land and down the river (**"The River"**), up the Appalachian river and to the far west (**"The Dance"**), back from the west and down the river again to the sea (**"Indiana"**), and returns in **"Cutty Sark"** to city, sea, and bridge. The time curve uses the present as a base, with a simultaneous historical movement from Columbus (**"Ave Maria"**) to present consciousness (**"Harbor Dawn"**), exploration and settlement (**"Van Winkle"** and **"The River"**), the ancient Indian world (**"The Dance"**), and a return through pioneers (**"Indiana"**) to the invocation of whaling ships at the close of **"Cutty Sark."** These passages also suggest the cyclic life movement from birth to maturity to old age, with life and land encircled by the farther reaches of being suggested by the sea.

In the second half, **"Cape Hatteras"** first ties the identity of the self-America to the dilemma of human failure after aspiration. Then begins a dramatization, in three inverted curves, of action which moves in a fall from illusion, through purgatorial punishment and evil, to the upward aspiring climb toward a mystic end. The first curve is a thematic statement in **"Cape Hatteras"** in which Whitman is chosen as the Vergil to lead the protagonist from death to soaring flight (and this is Whitman the mystic, not Whitman the so-called American optimist). The second curve is that of **"Three Songs,"** in which the sexual or female principle is traced from death (or sterility) to life. And the final curve is the larger involvement of man dramatized through the failure of **"Quaker Hill,"** the hell of **"The Tunnel,"** and the final vision of **"Atlantis."** Around these sections is a space arc, from the sea of **"Southern Cross,"** through the city's depths and heights, and back to bridge and sea at the close.

This general pattern of *The Bridge* can be verified by letting the imaginationmove rapidly through the course of the action. How those arcs of movement derive from the original image of Brooklyn Bridge, and how they function symbolically, will be considered further.

THE IMAGED CURVE: ORIGIN AND USE

Brooklyn Bridge, the initial image, is a suspension bridge, its main line tracing across and through two stolid piers in a shallow curve to the land on either side. From the tops of the piers fall cables in three inverted arches, one half-moon in the center and two slighter curves at the ends. In the piers are openings arched like Gothic windows. It is this symmetry of substance and grace, beaded with lights by night, gull-circled by day, holding at once both stillness and movement, that aroused Crane's most mystical imagination.

One of the best descriptions of its quality he found in a painting and an essay by Joseph Stella, to whom Crane wrote of the coincidence that "you . . . have had the same sentiments regarding Brooklyn Bridge which inspired the main theme and pattern of my poem."[13] Stella's essay describes the bridge as

> a weird metallic Apparition under a metallic sky, out of proportion with the winged lightness of its arch, traced for the conjunction of WORLDS, supported by the massive dark towers dominating the surrounding tumult of the surging skyscrapers with their gothic majesty sealed in the purity of their arches, the cables, like divine messages from above, transmitted to the vibrating coils, cutting and dividing into innumerable musical spaces the nude immensity of the sky; it impressed me as the shrine containing all the efforts of the new civilization of AMERICA—the eloquent meeting point of all the forces arising in a superb assertion of their powers, in APOTHEOSIS . . . [14]

In Stella's painting[15] two of the arched openings of a pier are at the forefront of a vista of cables in sweeping curves, and are crossed by circles of light and brighter arcs against the distant perpendicular lines of the steel city. It is important to note that Stella's response to the bridge emphasized not the steel power of the scientific bridge, but the mystical movement and music of its lines, its *curveship.*

In Crane's poem, the visual curveship of the bridge as theme is stated in the last line of the poem, **"To Brook-** lyn Bridge."** The culmination of the visual images is in the last section, **"Atlantis,"** where the shape sustains "the arching path Upwards" which blends into "One arc synoptic of all tides below . . ." Here are the "arching strands of song" and its "lariat sweep" which imply the rainbow's arch of promise as "Deity's glittering Pledge."

But the immediate visual curves of the bridge are only thematic beginnings, even as the gods who take on mortal forms must then use the mythic word and act. The arch of the mind and emotions of the man who follows the curve of the bridge is the kinetic image that is also important to the effect of the poem. "All architecture is what you do to it when you look upon it," wrote Walt Whitman in "A Song for Occupations."[16] The lines continue,

> (Did you think it was in the white or gray stone? or the lines of the arches and cornices?)

> All music is what awakes from you when you are reminded by the instruments . . . (I,263)

Whitman turned the arena of the poem from the page to the person, the variable poetic movements tracing their own designs in the consciousness.

Crane, too, in a letter to Harriet Monroe, said that he considered the *effect* of images in series the only essential logic in his poetry and the source of its meaning.[17] That he deliberately tried to make the motion of the curve organic in *The Bridge* is indicated in a letter to Waldo Frank:

> I have attempted to induce the same feelings of elation, etc.—like beingcarried forward and upward simultaneously—both in imagery, rhythm and repetition, that one experiences in walking across my beloved Brooklyn Bridge.[18]

"Motion forward and upward" is reinforced by the use of words like "sweep," "flight of strings," "spiring cordage," "ascends," "leap and converge." From the seagull's flight "with inviolate curve" to the last ring of rainbows, the curveship of *The Bridge* projects into parabolas of imaginative movement in time and space that fit the action and the idea of the poem into a single comprehensible pattern. The meaning of that curved pattern can be traced first in Whitman.

BACKGROUNDS IN WHITMAN

Crane's indebtedness to Whitman for theme and image in *The Bridge* can be observed in the rather obvious parallels in "Crossing Brooklyn Ferry," "Passage to India," and "Song of the Universal"; in Crane's explicit alignment with Whitman in **"Cape Hatteras";** and in the similarity of their ideas. Although it is not my intention to explore completely the relationships in the poetry of Crane and Whitman, it is necessary to show something of their likeness. Both were mystics, and Crane felt drawn into the currents of the larger tradition to which both belonged—the affirmation of a spiritualized cosmic union.

That others thought of Whitman as a blatant exploiter of the glories of America and the mass disturbed Crane, as he wrote despairingly to Tate:

> as you, like so many others, never seem to have read his *Democratic Vistas* and other statements sharply decrying the materialism, industrialism, etc., of which you name him the guilty and hysterical spokesman, there isn't much use in my tabulating the qualified, yet persistent reasons I have for my admiration of him, and my allegiance to the positive and universal tendencies implicit in nearly all his best work.[19]

These "positive and universal tendencies" form a conception of a mystic totality in which opposites are paradoxically identified: body and spirit, past and present, good and evil. The parabolas of mystic evolution, the encirclement of all experience as necessary to the generation of a spiritual force, the movement of consciousness which in its very kinetic poise also unites man and the cosmos—these central conceptions in Whitman's poetry help to explain the essential form of Crane's bridge.

The union, totality, and inclusion suggested by the curve or the circle are also Whitman's, whose "vast similitude" spans and encloses life and death and time. (II,22) Equating the spiritual and physical (I,105), Whitman saw the body as identity and selfhood, and the threshold for a complete consummation in the mystic vision. The wholeness of the cosmos is the true good; therefore, the "devilish and the dark" are also a part of "earth's orbic scheme," the "Rounded Catalogue Divine Complete." (III,23) In the mystic evolution, Whitman wrote in "Song of the Universal," not only the right is justified, but "what we call evil" is "also justified." From "the huge festering trunk, from craft and guile and tears," health and joy emerge. In the affirmative acceptance of experience, all things have their place. (I,277)

Whitman's "mystic evolution" is the upward, spiral lift of generation and fulfillment towards immortality, or spiritual essence, the Cathay or Atlantis which Crane uses as symbolic end. And when Crane says of Whitman,

> something green,
> Beyond all sesames of science was thy choice
> Wherewith to bind us throbbing with one
>   voice,

he could have been reading directly from Whitman's "Song of the Universal":

> Yet again, lo! the soul, above all science,
> For it has history gather'd like husks around
>   the globe.

and "In spiral routes by long detours," the real to the ideal tends. (I,276-277) There are ever the "Eidolons,"

> growth, the rounding of the circle,
> Ever the summit and the merge at last . . .
>
>                                     (I,6)

The scheme of the cosmos and man's green force within it is marked by movement—the span of consciousness on Whitman's open road, passage to India and more than India: "Are they wings plumed indeed for such far flights?" (II,196) Crane's flight of the gull, the eagle, and "Easters of speeding light" repeat the upward and outward aspiring of the arch.

The paradox of balance and movement at one in the span of Crane's bridge suggests Whitman's idea of the poet whose immediate eye becomes the ever-present moving consciousness which unites past and present with one look and sees in diversity a spiritual whole. Whitman speaks of the "full-grown poet" standing between the round globe of Nature and the Soul of man, holding each by the hand, blending and reconciling the two. (III,18) And in "Passage to India" the poet is seen as an instrument of divine union:

This end—the union of separations and discordances—is part of the "more than India" to which Whitman's poetry set sail.

Crane saw in his own function as poet the same joining of diversity in the creation of a whole. "What I am really handling," he wrote to Otto Kahn, "is the Myth of America. Thousands of strands have had to be searched for, sorted and interwoven."[20] What implications, then, do Whitman's ideas of spiritual totality and force have for an understanding of Crane's **"Myth of America,"** a myth which also belongs to the older poet? The relationship is clearly intended, as Crane writes in **"Cape Hatteras"**:

> Our Meistersinger, thou set breath in steel;
> And it was thou who on the boldest heel
> Stood up and flung the span on even wing
> Of that great Bridge, our Myth, whereof
>   I sing!

Both the life in the object (the breath in steel) and the shape of the idea make the span possible. This body-spirit of the myth of America Whitman emphatically articulated. It was most clearly *not* a celebration of the present glories, power, and scientific achievements of America, either in Whitman's day or very soon to come. As Crane observed, in *Democratic Vistas* Whitman agonized over the failures, the weakness, the slow maturing of America:

> I say we had best look our times and lands searchingly in the face, like a physician diagnosing some deep disease. Never was there, perhaps, more hollowness at heart than at present, and here in the United States. (V,61)

He found the apparently successful New World democracy "an almost complete failure in its social aspects, and in really grand religious, moral, literary, and esthetic results." (V,63) Crane was often disillusioned, as his letters show, but Whitman more than matched him in despair:

We sail a dangerous sea of seething currents, cross
and under-currents, vortices—all so dark, untried—
and whither shall we turn? (V,144)

However, the dark moods are matched with more knowledgeable insights:

> Thought you greatness was to ripen for you like a
> pear? If you would have greatness, know that you
> must conquer it through ages, centuries—must pay
> for it with a proportionate price. (V,145)

These are the hard views of America that Crane found in
*Democratic Vistas.* If Whitman could feel in "Thou
Mother with Thy Equal Brood" an "ominous
greatnessevil as well as good," (II,239) his own mythic
bridge must be of something other than chauvinistic steel.

For Whitman, the "Myth of America" was the possible
spiritual fulfillment of its people (who are its individuals), a fulfillment hoped for, believed in, but not yet accomplished. It was the whole structure and act of a human society moving toward brotherhood and complete
selfhood. The story of America's past could be only the
statement of its birth-pangs and its peculiar identity, but
there was also the certainty that if ever a people might
reach a state of spiritual force, it might well be America
where there already existed a symbolic union and a kind
of Adamic "new earth" whose strength might nourish the
seed of perfection. Thus a celebration of America's
present could be in truth the celebration of the life force
and its potency.

It is clear in all of Whitman's writing that he believed the
greatness possible for America must include spiritual
unity and aspiration. Both individualism and brotherhood
are to be

> vitalized by religion . . . breathing into the proud,
> material tissues, the breath of life. For I say at the
> core of democracy, finally, is the religious element
> . . . Nor may the scheme step forth, clothed in
> resplendent beauty and command, till these, bearing
> the best, the latest fruit, the spiritual, shall fully
> appear. (V,80)

If there is no spiritualization, "we are on the road to a
destiny . . . of the fabled damned." (V,147) In the
"Notes" to his *Preface, 1876,* Whitman spoke of "the
ultimate Democratic purports" as "the ethereal and spiritual ones." (V,194) In the poems of "death, immortality,
and a free entrance into the spiritual world" he wished
"to set the keystone to my democracy's enduring arch."
(V,195) The central poem in this group is "Passage to
India," almost a prototype for *The Bridge.*

Crane wrote in his essay, **"Modern Poetry,"** that
Whitman

> better than any other, was able to coordinate those
> forces in America which seem most intractable,
> fusing them into a universal vision which takes on
> additional significance as time goes on.[21]

In relation to Whitman's "universal vision," America is
not great in herself, but she may *become* great through
the fulfillment of the scheme, and the search of the soul
through time and space is the most significant part of the
myth of America. As Whitman wrote in "Song of the
Universal,"

> And thou America,
> For the scheme's culmination, its thought
>   and its reality,
> For these (not for thyself) thou hast ar-
>   rived.
>
> (I,278)

America is second; the "mystic ensemble," the "plan of
Thee enclosed in Time and Space" (I,278) is first. The
end (India? Cathay?) is the spiritual end, and *it* will give
the glory to America if the ship of the soul can sail far
enough into the mystery of that ethered sea.

To conceive of the Whitman-Crane myth of America as
even partially a glorification of science or the machine
age is to miss the point again. If science is praised, it is
as a means, not as a final glory, just as all that is physical
is good because it is a way of becoming. In **"Modern
Poetry"** Crane is clearly saying that science is to be
used, not defined—to be blended, not isolated. This is
only the most practical of poetic views, when a twentieth
century poet wishes to speak with some contemporaneity.
He must of course use the mechanical manifestations of
his own time. But when he also wishes to speak in the
eternal, spiritual present, he turns more especially to that
"something green," beyond all sesames of science. The
"rebound seed" wielded by Whitmaninvolves generation
and the cyclic meaning of life: the circle which spans,
encompasses, and identifies birth and death, space and
time, past and present, flesh and spirit, good and evil.
Because it is the core of Whitman's meaning, the principle of such a cosmic union cannot be ignored in determining the symbolic bridge of Crane, whose allegiance
was to "the positive and universal tendencies" in
Whitman's work.

THE SYMBOLIC CURVE

What, then, is involved in the curveship of Crane's
bridge, the shape which can "lend a myth to God"? A
form that includes, unites, and completes is performing a
spiritual act; or, to paraphrase Crane's line further, spiritual action is the myth of God and it can be represented
physically in the symbolic curve and circle. Crane's
bridge, both visual object and course of action, *means*
whatever its lines trace upon the consciousness. These
traceries are, first, the sense of wholeness; and, second,
the sense of lift and resolution, or its reverse in fall and
recovery.

The curves and circles of Crane's bridge perform the
ancient ritual of eternity: what is whole, total, and perfect
is circumscribed with unending motion; what is divided is
made one. The bridge is called "one arc synoptic of all
tides below." Elements that are unlike or separate can in

this one structure be tied together and made one identity: the two shores of Here and There, of Now and Then—Space in the enclosure of the arc, and Time in the going across. The piers of the bridge are heavy and rooted in earth, but its upward curves are of the air. In some of his first versions of **"Atlantis,"** Crane described the bridge

> Whose alignment rears from equal out to
>     equal,
> Yielding mutual assumption on its arches
> Fused and veering to the measure of our
>     arms . . . [22]

The form has feet on the ground and head in the air, even as Crane in those early versions represented the poet-speaker as standing on the bridge with arms

> That open to project a salient disk
> That winds the moon and midnight in one
>     face.[23]

These first drafts of the poem are significant only in that they show by more direct image and statement something of Crane's later, and more subtle, mystic synthesis.

Both wholeness and resolution are represented in the peak of balance at the center of the arch, where the double thrust of two halves are fused into one. This is the highest moment of the curve, and the point of vision. Such a fusion blends into the symbolism of sexual union and fulfillment of the life force, much as D. H. Lawrence used the image of the male and female joined to make a spiritual whole. For example, the arch to Will Brangwen in *The Rainbow* "leapt up from the plain of earth," until with it he

> leaped clear into the darkness above, to the fecundity
> and the unique mystery, to the touch, the clasp, the
> consummation, the climax of eternity, the apex of
> the arch.[24]

At the same "climax of eternity" Whitman had placed his keystone of democracy's arch—the poems of spiritual vision—and here the "Eidolon" circle found its "summit and the merge at last . . ." (I,6) Such a "merge" or union of duality holds the paradox of "kinetic poise" in the structure of the bridge (both object and poem), where motion is caught in the moment of fulfillment. The creative force toward completion is also a part of spiritual experience.

Another important element in the curveship of the bridge is the kind of wholeness in which man meets the elemental world and rounds act and being to nature's creative force and mysterious darkness. Waldo Frank, Crane's friend and critic, gave in a 1925 essay called "Straight Streets"[25] an analysis which could well be related to Crane's conception of the curve. "The curve is the way of acceptance: the angle is the way of resistance," said Frank. Nature is "the sinuous, rounded being," exterior and interior:

> Man's mind moves in curves. His thoughts arch,
> vault, melt into reverie. Dream and sense swerve

into each other. His heart, too, is full of arcuations. And the heart's desires are parabolas.

Frank saw in the highest Indian culture a kind of sophisticated primitivism which has learned to follow the curve of nature:

> The Indian culture began when his innate spiritual
> and intellectual values formed a solution with the
> world about him: his culture was achieved when
> the responses between his soul and the world had
> rounded into a unified *life* which expressed both
> fully.

The curve is here the tracery of a kind of ultimate cultural health, suggesting man's acceptance of his place in the wholeness of life. As Whitman saw in all living things "in them and myself the same old law," (I,48) and all things a part of the scheme, the ensemble, so man joins with the curve of acceptance. The "identification of yourself with *all of life*" was to Crane happiness, related to "the true idea of God."[26]

The concept of the whole, of unified duality, is dramatized in another way by the act of the curve whose lines go in continuous upward and downward movements—or which fall from high, and out of descent create another rising force. These are patterns of the journey of the soul in its struggle with the unwieldy, unequal, and fragmentary forms of mortal experience that must be reconciled before the final vision is attained. Both the lines of Crane's physical bridge and the movement of imaginative action in the poetic bridge turn to the same thematic key: that the whole form can exist only *because* it has joined division, diversity, and motion; and that such an identity has a living dimension which can touch an infinite spiritual power.

CURVESHIP IN *THE BRIDGE*

Two elements of meaning and form in the curveship of *The Bridge* can be considered representative of the body of the poem: the union of duality, and spiritual realization through that duality. For whatever chaos Crane may personally represent, his poetic vision did seize upon this kind of wholeness, and he dramatized it in the curved union, the encircling lines of *The Bridge*.

To achieve an identity, man or America is shown in the first half of *The Bridge* to be contained in time and space, aware of what is incomplete and mortal and envisioning the eternal. Thematic imagery in the **"Proem"** introduces the "inviolate curve" of the gull's flight, repeated later in the "unfractioned idiom" of the bridge. At the close of the **"Proem,"** the descending sweep of the vaulting curve is invoked to link the man standing by the shadowy pier to the initial skyward flight. Here two elements of the bridge—its root in earth and its lift to air—are joined in the imagery of the poem. By shadow, the darkened city, and the snow that "submerges an iron year," the **"Proem"** further implies the duality of darkness and light, of death and generation, that the curveship of the bridge can include and unify.

In the mid-ocean of **"Ave Maria,"** looking both forward and back to the hoped-for Cathay and the discovered continent, the ship of Columbus links past and present and moves into the "steep savannahs" of the double Word: "Eden and the enchained Sepulchre." These oppositions of life and death, or the corollary of time-eternity and body-spirit, are repeated throughout the poem. What Crane called the "sea swell crescendo" of **"Ave Maria"** culminates in a vision beyond the waves' green towers in night and chaos, but this spiritual vision comes down to rest in naked kingdoms of the trembling heart, the movement here paralleling theturn at the close of the **"Proem,"** in which the down-sweeping curve of the bridge is to touch the man who waits in its shadow.

The central figure of **"Powhatan's Daughter"** is Pocahontas, the natural body of America and a symbol of fertility and the life-force. In this section is performed the ritual of union with nature and the sexual-physical as a progress toward spiritual identity. This principle is the same as Whitman's identification of body and soul and Waldo Frank's curve of acceptance. This element of earth and the flesh is the physical half of duality, and its complete acceptance is necessary for any final mystic vision. When the drama of **"Powhatan's Daughter"** explores the body of America, the land symbolizes the physical and creative body of man as much as Pocahontas symbolizes the soil of natural America. In history, the complete realization of the body of America is through its exploration in space and time, and this narrative line is traced in the five sections of **"Powhatan's Daughter,"** but with a fusion of present and past so that all of it happens in a simultaneous grasp of consciousness. Crane wanted to show "the continuous and living evidence of the past in the inmost vital substance of the present."[27]

Throughout the drama of movement over America, described in **"Powhatan's Daughter,"** there is a consciousness of the natural world, "a body under the wide rain," but its meaning is evanescent, and the "iron dealt cleavage" of an age that has nearly obliterated the natural union of physical and spiritual needs to be joined. As the time-river blends into sea and prefigures the eternal Atlantis, so in the Indian world of **"The Dance"** Maquokeeta is phoenix-like brought out of time, and the nature-figure of Pocahontas fulfills the cyclic body-life. Here Crane also uses the serpent-time and eagle-space duality. The separation of white and Indian culture is a corollary of the cleavage which has denied the natural and primitive reality and thus a spiritual wholeness. But in a possible union of nature and man, best demonstrated in the cyclic, generative, fertility principle, time and eternity may also be reconciled, as well as time and space: "The serpent with the eagle in the boughs." Thus the white mother of **"Indiana"** takes on the nature symbolism of Pocahontas, and the son continues to sea in man's perpetual search.

In **"Cutty Sark"** the fugue of time (the derelict sailor) and eternity (Atlantis out of the pianola song) prepares the protagonist for a union of the real and present walk across the bridge and the phantasy of whalers and clipper ships, whose quest joins the dreams of India, Cathay, and Melville's elusive whale. But identity and selfhood are made of these very contradictions: the real and the visionary, time and mortality bound in the visible land surrounded by eternal seas where may lie the mystic rose of Atlantis.

The drama of spiritual vision, the journey of the soul, is demonstrated in the second half of *The Bridge* as a downward and upward curve: the fall from the attempted ideal, and the re-trial through chaos and the stark ugliness which is part of the human commitment to the flesh and mortality. But it is through this very death that the upward lift to mystical fulfillment is achieved, as light is known by darkness. This configuration can be seen most completely in the details of **"Cape Hatteras,"** the ode to Whitman which Crane said was a two years' effort at a synthesis of his theme.[28]

The first scene of **"Cape Hatteras"** ("Imponderable the dinosaur/sinks slow") suggests the turning of the earth (the sinking eastern Cape, the rising western range) and the simultaneous recession of the primitive creature into the past. At the center of this natural machine is the dynamo of flux and creative energy, and (known, too, by Whitman) the natural body of America in Pocahontas, which still lives under the surface structures. Whatever has been discovered in space and time is reduced finally to the contained view of the past-reversed self; but the circle of infinity, the crucible of endless or unconquered space, has eternal motion for the "free ways still ahead!" Here Whitman is taken for the Vergil to conduct the soul upon the search for infinity, spiritual knowledge to be gained through eyes that know the full acceptance of the great cyclic mystery—"Sea eyes and tidal, undenying, bright with Myth!"

Turning again to the pattern of the search, Crane introduces the dynamo of earth's creative force as the "nasal whine of power" in the air-conquering machine. Through a violent re-creation of the physical force of the airplane, the reader is careened upward to splinter the yet "unvanquished space." Lines move up, like hurtling javelins, above the lightning, yet the ascensions are aimed farther still: in the wrist (the blood-pulse) of the symbolic flyer is yet the charge "To conjugate infinity's dim marge—" In the images of the poem, the man-machine is forced downward before it reaches the heights of infinity, and with the "skull's deep, sure reprieve" all movement twists in spirals downward in the falling curve, crashing the brave attempt into debris.

This tracing of a curve across symbolic skies has very little significance as a eulogy of air-power. Rather, it is the image of the human situation diagrammed in the language of the modern world. It is the way a poet of the machine age would tell the story of Icarus. The climb toward infinity is also a kind of voyage, with air taking the place of sea, and airplane of ship, but the old trial toward "something beyond" and the mortal failure—perhaps in death—are again dramatized. The last part of **"Cape Hatteras"** shows the way in which the ascending curve can rise out of the "beached heap of high bravery" by Hatteras. From Whitman and his prophetic voice, ascensions hover, and with belief in the "rebound seed," with "pure impulse inbred? To answer deepest soundings/ O, upward from the dead/ Thou bringest tally . . ."

Whitman's song has known both heights and depths of experience, the whole arc. He has kept the meaning of death, and has given to the speaker the meaning of the seasonal cycle of life, in which gold autumn (or death) "crowned the trembling hill." Whitman is clearly used as a messianic, prophetic figure whose spiritual force and understanding could create the true bridge to infinity, "set breath in steel" and fling the span of the mythic bridge, or set the pattern for the ascending, encircling movement toward a spiritual fulfillment. Because Whitman has passed the barrier of death (both actually and in the poetic vision), he can lead out of the debris of mortal failure to the farthest space of consciousness. Movement ascends

> launched in abysmal cupolas of space,
> Toward endless terminals, Easters of speed-
> ing light—

The final "curveship" is the rainbow's arch that

> shimmeringly stands
> Above the Cape's ghoul-mound . . .

So the poet-speaker takes the hand of Whitman, the Vergil who can lead the soul on its necessary road.

**"Cape Hatteras"** presents a pattern which is to be retraced in other symbols in the remaining section of the poem. Here it is shown in the physical terms of air-flight and destruction. But it is out of the total experience of both high and low that the final ascending "passage" is possible. This is the journey of the soul to the mystic end, as it goes through the flesh, the evil, and the death which are the necessary parts of mortality. To think of the structure of **"Cape Hatteras"** as showing, first, the human condition; second, the human failure; and third, the rise to infinity through the way set down by Whitman, will give it a consistent form. As a miscellaneous praise of geology, or of science, or of Whitman, it will be a fumbling, sentimental effort. But Crane's two years of work on it as a synthesis are justified when it is seen as the diagram, the visualization, of a kind of modern *Commedia*.

The falling-rising curve of **"Three Songs"** enacts the life-giving, spiritualizing force of the sexual principle, uniting the dualities of male and female, fertility and sterility, lust and idealized love. Recognizing defeat through Eve, who brought death into the world, life is reborn by the acceptance of the flesh and generation, begun at its

lowest form in Magdalen and rising to the idealized reality of Mary. The visual curve drops from the heights of the Southern Cross, to the dark waters, and up through dance hall and streets to the nickel-dime tower. In a similar curve, **"Atlantis"** is attained by way of the fallen ideal of **"Quaker Hill"** and the darkness of **"The Tunnel."** The visual descent is in the autumn leaves of **"Quaker Hill"** which leads farther into the depths of the subway and up to the bridge, at last a symphony whose leap is the circle of "the lark's return," which holds "in single chrysalis the many twain," and from whose curveship springs a mystical rainbow-prophecy.

The last four lines of **"Atlantis"** epitomize the three directives in Crane with which this paper began: the symphonic form, a positive spiritual belief, and this affirmation in the design of Whitman's cosmic unity:

> —One Song, one Bridge of Fire! Is it Cathay,
> Now pity steeps the grass and rainbows ring
> The serpent with the eagle in the leaves . . . ?
> Whispers antiphonal in azure swing.

The bridge is one being of music and fire. Themes of the serpent and the eagle, time and space, are bound by rings of rainbows while "pity steeps the grass," recalling Whitman's microcosm of the *Leaves* infused by love. But to the question, "Is it Cathay . . . ?" the answers are dual, antiphonal. The point of stillness out of movement is not yet gained, for whispers swing somewhere in the blue. Yet "swing" suggests the balanced poise of the present, whose moment of Here and Now is what we know of the bridge of consciousness.

In fact, both sections of **The Bridge** end in questions. "Is it Cathay?" is matched at the end of the first half (at the close of **"Cutty Sark"**) with the elusive quest of the whaling ships, and of "You rivals two—/Taeping?/ Ariel?" Both Leviathan and Atlantis are legendary objects of search, strangely shrouded in the mysteries of the sea, and their ambiguity adds to the unanswered questions. But neither did Whitman arrive at India in his voyage. "Passage to India" ends with the "daring joy" of sailing farther and farther on the seas of God. This swing between mythic object and immediate action reinforces the ambivalence which enters into much of the symbolic bridge, as the present moment joins past and future and identity fuses the separations. Here is the center of the "oneness" or acceptance which Crane celebrates, and which the curveship of the bridge dramatizes.

THE LOGIC OF METAPHOR

The structural unity of Crane's **The Bridge** is more logically fulfilled in the poem than most criticism has been willing to allow. But the glass must, of course, be turned to more than the function of the visual object. As an identity of idea, movement, and form, the "bridge" operates in a kind of psychological logic, or what Crane called the "logic of metaphor."[29] Curves and arches are traced in a multitude of visual ways, but the reader must also feel himself lifted, poised, or ascending physically and emotionally; and he must see both action and concept rounded to each other. Because Crane assumed that the imagination of the reader would follow the "emotional dynamics" of the metaphor, the shape of the bridge has its own logic in the context of the poem, and comes alive in the sensibility of the reader. One of Whitman's statements on poetry will have a particular significance here:

> Poetic style, when address'd to the soul, is less definite form, outline, sculpture, and becomes vista, music, half-tints, and even less than half-tints. True it may be architecture; but again it may be the forest wildwood, or the best effect thereof, at twilight, the waving oaks and cedars in the wind, and the impalpable odor. (V,202-203)

The architecture of **The Bridge** is the curve of union. But in the farther vistas opened by that curve blend circles upon circles, parabolas like petals that compose at last the impalpable flower of eternity.

[1] *The Collected Poems of Hart Crane,* ed. with Introd. by Waldo Frank (NewYork, 1946).

[2] "A Preface to Hart Crane," *New Republic,* LVII (23 April 1930), 276-277.

[3] Allen Tate, "A Distinguished Poet," *The Hound and Horn,* III (July-Sept. 1930), 580-585, and Yvor Winters, "The Progress of Hart Crane," *Poetry: A Magazine of Verse,* XXXVI (June 1930), 153-165.

[4] Two significant articles are Stanley K. Coffman, Jr., "Symbolism in *The Bridge,*" *PMLA,* LXVI (March 1951), 65-77, and John R. Willingham, "'Three Songs' of Hart Crane's *The Bridge:* A Reconsideration," *American Literature,* XXVII (March 1955), 62-68.

[5] Letter to Gorham Munson (18 Feb. 1923), in *The Letters of Hart Crane,* ed. Brom Weber (New York, 1952), p. 125. All references to Crane's letters are to pages in this edition.

[6] Letter to Herbert Weinstock (22 April 1930), p. 350.

[7] Letter to Waldo Frank (23 Aug. 1926), p. 275.

[8] Letter to Selden Rodman (22 May 1930), p. 351.

[9] Letter to Waldo Frank (27 Feb. 1923), p. 127.

[10] (2 March 1923), p. 128.

[11] For a view of mysticism in Whitman, see James E. Miller, Jr., "'Song of Myself' As Inverted Mystical Experience," *PMLA,* LXX (Sept. 1955), 636-661.

[12] Letter to Caresse Crosby (26 Dec. 1929), p. 347.

[13] (24 Jan. 1929), p. 334.

[14] Joseph Stella, "The Brooklyn Bridge," *transition,* 16-17 (June 1929), 87-88; reprinted from a monograph, *New York,* privately issued by Joseph Stella.

[15] *Ibid.,* facing p. 88.

[16] *The Complete Writings of Walt Whitman,* ed. R. M. Bucke et al., 10 vols. (New York, 1902), I, 263. All references to Whitman are to this edition and will be indicated in the text with volume and page.

[17] "A Discussion with Hart Crane," *Poetry: A Magazine of Verse,* XXIX (Oct. 1926), 34-41.

[18] (18 Jan. 1926), p. 232.

[19] (13 July 1930), p. 354.

[20] (12 Sept. 1927), p. 305.

> All these separations and gaps shall be taken up and hook'd and linked together,
>
> Nature and Man shall be disjoin'd and diffused no more,
>
> The true son of God shall absolutely fuse them. (II,191)

[21] *The Collected Poems of Hart Crane,* p. 179.

[22] Lines sent to Alfred Stieglitz (4 July 1923), in Brom Weber, *Hart Crane* (New York, 1948), p. 426.

[23] *Ibid.*

[24] D. H. Lawrence, *The Rainbow* (London, 1955), p. 199.

[25] *In the American Jungle* (New York, 1937), pp. 123-127.

[26] Letter to Charlotte Rychtarik (21 July 1923), p. 140.

[27] Letter to Otto H. Kahn (12 Sept. 1927), p. 305.

[28] Letter to Caresse Crosby (17 Sept. 1929), p. 346.

[29] General Aims and Theories," in Philip Horton, *Hart Crane* (New York, 1937), p. 327 (App. I). See also Crane's letter to Harriet Monroe in *Poetry,* XXIX, 35-36.

### Joseph J. Arpad (essay date 1967)

SOURCE: "Hart Crane's Myth: The Brooklyn Bridge," in *American Literature,* Vol. XXXIX, No. 1, March, 1967, pp. 75-86.

[*In the following essay, Arpad attempts to "uncover the Platonic sources" for Crane's "myth of the Brooklyn Bridge."*]

One striking feature of Hart Crane's *The Bridge* is the poet's seemingly unorthodox conception of myth. Although several scholars have made known Crane's use of myth, they have not concerned themselves with exposing the poem as myth—an idea explicit in its dedicatory proem. Furthermore, although various critics have been successful in establishing Crane as a poet by equating his Platonic idealism with romantic mysticism, this approach has not proved precise enough to lend total coherence to the symbolism, the metaphysical imagery, and the structure of the poem, nor in particular, to explain the poet's use of the term *myth*.[1] By emphasizing, however, Crane's Platonism—by opposing it to notions of romantic mysticism—one may gain this needed insight, and in so doing, add meaning to Crane's poetic principle "the logic of metaphor," establish a structure for *The Bridge,* and uncover the Platonic sources for his myth of the Brooklyn Bridge.

I

Although the Platonic implications of Crane's poetry have received due critical attention, the exact nature and extent of the Platonic influence has not been adequately explored. Philip Horton, for example, Crane's first biographer, noted that an early influence on Crane was the "Ion" section of Plato's *Dialogues,* where Socrates argued the necessity of madness in a true poet, an idea the young poet found impressive enough to underline doubly in red ink. On such evidence, Horton and others have reasoned Crane adhered to the Platonic conception of the poet, the poet as mystic, who creates from hallucinations and narcotic dreams, who cannot create unless he is inspired and possessed, no longer in his right mind.[2] This observation may be true for Crane's early poetry, but later, Crane came to reject the validity of Plato's analysis. In 1926, in a letter to Gorham Munson, he articulated his "logic of metaphor" principle, a new direction in his poetic theory, one that did not deny Plato's general thesis, but instead, redefined the poet's technique of acquiring knowledge as identical with the Platonic philosopher's.[3]

Plato, it may be recalled, held there were two kinds of extrasensory vision: dream-visions, the insights of poets; and Idea-visions, the insights of philosophers. Since neither of these corresponded to ordinary sensory perception, the poet and the philosopher must appear equally "possessed" to the common man. If, however, Plato's ideal state were ever to become fact, the common man would have to be persuaded to accept philosophic vision as more valid than his own. To prevent confusion, Plato banished poets from the ideal state; their dream-visions had no validity, being only imitation, a product of the imagination, the lowest form of cognizance. The philosopher's Idea-vision, however, was a product of "rational intuition" (*noesis*), the highest form of cognizance; his was a "synoptic view" of experience which allowed him to perceive the universal Form or Idea in particular objects or events.[4]

In his letter to Munson, Crane argued that in banishing poets from the ideal state, Plato had been merely acting in self-defense. According to Crane, both the poet and the philosopher attained truth through a synoptic view of experience. The only difference was in the kinds of truth acquired—one, a poetic truth, the other, philosophic—and there was no reason to believe, the techniques of vision being the same, that one was more valid than the other.[5] Thus, for expository purposes, Crane's "logic of metaphor" may be equated with Plato's philosophic method of perceiving universal Forms or Ideas, the "synoptic view" of experience. This approach acts toward clarifying certain problems which have frustrated attempts to explicate *The Bridge.*

The first of these is the poet's disturbing use of the word *myth.* In the last stanza of **"Proem: To Brooklyn Bridge,"** the poet invokes the bridge to "descend / And of the curveship lend a myth to God."[6] The idea of the Brooklyn Bridge, specifically the curves of the bridge, lending a "myth" to God does not readily agree with the traditional sense of *myth,* meaning a story or narrative.[7] Yet, it does correlate with the Platonic sense of myth. *Platonic myths* were not stories but philosophic expositions of Ideas. Throughout the *Dialogues,* Plato made little apparent distinction between the Greek words *mythos* and *logos;* the stories he told were both the ideal and the philosophic exposition of the ideal. The "accounts" were narrative syllogisms, logical progressions of insights, pressed forward by the Platonic dialogues. But since, for Plato, all insights were visions of forms or images, the dialectical progressions were actually of images, not words.[8] Crane recognized this as closely approximating the "qualitative progression" of images found in lyric poetry; the Platonic philosopher, like the lyric poet, attained his vision of truth through a logic of imagery—in Crane's terms, a "logic of metaphor."[9] Thus, it was perfectly appropriate to have the Brooklyn Bridge "lend a myth to God." In Crane's poetic vision, the bridge embodied an absolute Form or Idea (its curveship) which could only be comprehended through a lyrical progression of images; the poem itself was a record of that progression and was, in the Platonic sense, a myth.

A second implication of Crane's Platonic "logic" is that the absolute Form or Idea, which the poet envisions in the Brooklyn Bridge, exists in the bridge itself—not in the poet's imagination or in any narcotic dream-vision.[10] Crane was particularly aware of the Brooklyn Bridge as a formal work of art.[11] Not only did he study the bridge's architecture, he also investigated the biography of John Roebling, the designer of the bridge, to discover his aesthetic theory of art.

Roebling, a German immigrant, had been a student and friend of philosopher Georg Hegel while studying at the Royal Polytechnical Institute in Berlin. It was there that Roebling first viewed a suspension bridge, a small span suspended by four chains across the Regnitz River at Bamber. For Roebling, the logic of the "miracle bridge" must have appeared remarkably compatible with Hegel's philosophic dialectic; it was a perfect synthesis of antithetical elements, of opposing forces, the chains in tension, the towers in compression, uniting to form a coherent structure of surprising strength. As a consequence, Roebling dedicated his entire life to perfecting the form of suspension bridges, a task which culminated in the design for the Brooklyn Bridge.[12]

The Brooklyn Bridge is a thoroughgoing architectural statement of the Hegelian thesis-antithesis-synthesis. Against the massive granite towers, a stone architecture of the past with Gothic arches and shadowy solids, stands the spidery web of steel, an architecture of the future, light, airy, a composition of voids rather than solids.[13] But more important, for Crane at least, was one other aspect: the bridge is actually two bridges in one. Unlike more modern suspension bridges which have only two suspending cables, the Brooklyn Bridge has four.[14] The New York–bound roadway is suspended separately with its own set of cables; it is thus a distinct unit, apart from the Brooklyn-bound roadway. The towers which lift the cables at each side of the river are the unifying medium of the bridge; although their twin arches reveal the duality of the bridge, they embrace the separate roadways in a common wall of granite, effecting the appearance of one bridge. When these aspects are considered in relation to the more obviously contrasting configurations of the bridge's curves—the rising and falling arcs of the bridge's cables versus the broad arc of the bridge's floor—the overall effect of the bridge's formal artistry becomes apparent: a distinctive tone, texture, tension, and rhythm attained through a synthesis of antithetical elements.

This inherent synthetic form is of course apparent through a common sensory vision of the bridge. As Crane's poetic theory suggests, though, the full exposition of the bridge's absolute form, the ultimate Idea of the bridge, can only come from the poet-philosopher's Idea-vision, his synoptic insight into the bridge's ultimate reality. The poem, *The Bridge,* is an attempt to do just that, to expose the metaphysical form or idea of the Brooklyn Bridge's physical form. Characteristic of the bridge itself, the metaphysical imagery and symbolism are synthetic, as these lines from **"Proem"** indicate: "O harp and altar, of the fury fused, / (How could mere toil align thy choiring strings!)"; the poet envisions the bridge's cables as a harp, the granite towers as an altar, and wonders at their amazing synthesis. As a consequence, the imagery and symbolism create a dialectic, in both the Hegelian and Platonic senses, and thus function as the raw material for the poetic myth, the lyric progression toward an absolute poetic truth.

II

The final value, therefore, of recognizing Crane's Platonism is that it suggests a coherent form for *The Bridge,* a logical structuring of ideas and imagery.[15] Crane began his poem in 1923, writing to his friends that he was building a bridge that would synthesize the American experience.[16] Three years later, his bridge, his poem, was barely out of the planning stage; he had written slightly more

than eighty lines, a bare semblance of what now appears as the conclusion, Part VIII, the Atlantis section.[17] Then, suddenly, late in July, 1926, work began in earnest. Starting with the prologue, **"Proem: To Brooklyn Bridge,"** Crane wrote approximately one-half the entire poem in a matter of months. To Waldo Frank, the poet explained his previous difficulty: "I didn't realize that a bridge is begun from the two ends at once. . . . "[18] As this remark suggests (and the early revisions of **"Atlantis"** indicate), the poet was having difficulty in establishing a dialectic from which he might draw a synthesis. He found inspiration for the dialectic in two Platonic myths: the Atlantis myth, which forms the basis for the final section of the poem, and the myth of the cave, which forms the basis for the prologue.[19]

The Atlantis myth, though only a fragment, embodied sufficient material to suggest a poetic analogy with modern America.[20] The Brooklyn Bridge, the longest and highest span of its time, a great engineering spectacle, a monument and symbol of America's scientific and technological advance, readily suggested the Great Bridge of Atlantis. It, more than any other form, structure, or idea, represented what was good and beautiful in a materialistic culture, an industrial age. In Part III, **"Cutty Sark,"** Crane developed this analogy into a poetic image, "ATLANTIS ROSE";[21] in Part VIII, **"Atlantis,"** he elaborated the image, developing "ROSE" into "Anemone." In this context, *rose* had dual meaning: first, a flower, the traditional symbol of beauty; and second, resurrection, a divine second chance. America, the image of Atlantis, was to rise magnificently from the floor of the Atlantic, manifesting absolute beauty and perfection, establishing once again a lost Adamic Eden.

It should be noted here that the Atlantis fable was for Plato a national myth, created to expose a national ideal, not an individual one.[22] Similarly, for Crane, *The Bridge* was originally to be a national myth, embodying a national ideal, the absolute Idea of America. In this sense, Crane's original intent was epic, and as an epic poet he felt a commitment to sing the national ideal, regardless of whether he himself embraced it as his own.[23] Here, of course, lay the problem: the national ideal in America was not identical with the poetic ideal; indeed, the two were in direct conflict. The national ideal saw beauty, good, and truth only in material objects, the physical reality; the poetic ideal saw these in spiritual objects, the non-physical reality. Thus, Crane found himself taking an absurd poetic stance: singing the glory that was America, not by celebrating the spirit of that country as embodied in a national hero, butinstead, by holding up for public acclaim a non-spiritual, though magnificent, physical object, the Brooklyn Bridge. To square himself with his poetic tradition, Crane adapted Plato's myth of the cave.

Often referred to as the "allegory" of the cave, the Platonic myth was created to expose an individual ideal, the Idea of the philosopher.[24] As Crane had stated earlier in his letter to Munson, this was also the poetic ideal, the

Idea of the poet. Thus, in **"Proem,"** the poet states (stanza three):

> I think of cinemas, panoramic sleights
> With multitudes bent toward some flashing scene
> Never disclosed, but hastened to again,
> Foretold to other eyes on the same screen.

The "cinemas" are described as "panoramic sleights"—that is, as panoramas of sly artifice, like the shadows on the wall of the cave. "Multitudes" are "bent toward" these shadows, but the reality is "never disclosed" except to "other eyes," the eyes of Crane's poet-philosopher. Here, then, is a direct allusion to the Platonic myth.[25] Another is the fifth stanza:

> Out of some subway scuttle, cell or loft
> A bedlamite speeds to thy parapets,
> Tilting there momently, shrill shirt ballooning,
> A jest falls from the speechless caravan.

The poet sees in this suicidal attempt a re-creation of Plato's warning to the would-be philosopher. Out of the subway scuttle (the subway itself, a tunnel, remarkably similar to Plato's description of the cave), a man "speeds" to the parapets of the bridge, as though escaping from some imprisonment (suggested by "cell").[26] Standing upon the parapet, the man hesitates, as though blinded and confused by what he sees on the other side. The words "tilting," "momently," and "jest" suggest his fate: having been blinded by what he has seen, the man is unwilling to consummate his escape by jumping; instead, he is suspended there, "tilting" back and forth "momently" (not momentarily), as though vacillating between two worlds, both of which he can no longer comprehend. The witnesses to his act (the "caravan") are "speechless"; yet, at least one of them finds opportunity to ridicule him for destroying his vision ("a jest falls . . .").

With these allusions in mind, it is possible to explicate briefly the prologue, eliminating several obscurities otherwise encountered. The passage opens with the poet exclaiming: "How many dawns" has he observed the seagull, "chill from his rippling rest," suspend himself high over the "chained bay waters" and then swoop downward with "inviolate curve."[27] The vision of the seagull's flight is "apparitional" to the poet, as though a dream. Yet, it is not. He thinks of a scene recalling Plato's distinction between shadows and reality and recognizes that the flight of the bird describes a form which he sees also in the Brooklyn Bridge, the "inviolate curves" of the bridge's cables. This form is actually an idea: the "Liberty" of the seagull's flight and the "freedom" implicit in the architecture of the bridge. In contrast with these comparatively serene images of freedom, the poet sees a third: the freedom the bedlamite attains in speeding to the parapets of the bridge—a rather ominous freedom, for it does not appear to be freedom at all, but instead, a kind of paralysis, a pitiful alienation from both the worlds of reality and of shadows.

Then, a strange phenomenon occurs (stanza six):

> Down Wall, from girder into street noon leaks,
> A rip-tooth of the sky's acetylene;
> All afternoon the cloud-flown derricks turn . . .
> Thy cables breathe the North Atlantic still.

If one observes the towers of the bridge at noon, one will notice a pattern of light and shadows which appears to "leak" down the granite walls, suggesting the jagged blast ("a rip-tooth") of an acetylene lamp or torch. But "Wall" is capitalized, like "Liberty" in stanza one, indicating an absolute quality or idea; in the context of the bridge's architecture, the granite walls represent unity, a fusion of the bridge's duality. "Acetylene," too, connotes not only a brilliant light, but also a cutting action. This impression is augmented by "rip-tooth," indicating something vicious that can rive the bridge in two. Yet, later in **"Proem"** (stanza eight), the bridge is envisioned as "harp and altar, of the fury fused," suggesting a welding action. Thus, the general impression of stanza six is that the bridge has survived a trial by fire: the same force (the blast of brilliant light) that would divide, can also unify, that would destroy, can also create.[28] The specific reference is to the bedlamite who, like the bridge, is in the act of being riven in two, torn between two worlds. But in the general context of the prologue, the acetylene image may be viewed as symbolic of a bright new truth—specifically, scientific knowledge and industrial advance. The bedlamite then becomes representative of modern man, torn between two worlds, the old world of Nature which science has destroyed, and the new world of science which he cannot yet fully comprehend. The bridge's ability to survive this divisive force serves as an example: man's world too will remain unified, even in the light of this new truth. Modern man, like the bedlamite, has only to endure his fate; like the bridge itself, he must remain suspended between antithetical forces which would destroy his precarious balance.

The remainder of **"Proem"** is the poet's affirmation of how a vision of the bridge's absolute form or idea (though as "obscure as that heaven of the Jews") may assist man in enduring his fate, may lead him eventually to see the ultimate reality. First, the bridge offers man an anonymous embrace ("Accolade thou dost bestow . . ."); it shares his fate of being suspended between two worlds. Second, the bridge has the ability to "condense eternity"; since it is a synthesis of the old and the new, it offers man the opportunity to perceive these in a shade, a form, familiar to his vision. Finally, the bridge "lends a myth to God"—myth, not in the sense of story, but as *logos,* the philosophic Word. In Christian terms, the Word has been identified with Christ, the Virgin Mary, the Church, and the Gospel; in all instances, the Word has been both a vision of God and an intermediary means of attaining a vision of God. In Crane's terms, the Brooklyn Bridge had been given this function in the modern world.

Thus, by envisioning the Brooklyn Bridge as *logos,* as a Platonic myth, Crane was able to justify his celebration of a physical object in the epic tradition; the bridge was not only the material ideal of a nation, but also the spiritual ideal of the individual. ***The Bridge*** exists as literally suspended between these two points: the prologue, where the individual ideal is exposed, and Part VIII, where the national ideal is evoked. What occurs in the middle is a series of ideas experienced by the poet while contemplating the bridge. Each section, therefore, embodies some essential of the bridge's ultimate meaning. Part I, for example, **"Ave Maria,"** has Columbus establishing a bridge between the old world and the new, doing so through the intercession of the Virgin Mary. Furthermore, the ideas expressed in each section are seldom parallel, nor even antithetical, but are often differing insights into the bridge's ultimate reality. Part IV, for example, **"Cape Hatteras,"** expands upon the "curveship" of the bridge, the poet seeing the same curves in the geographical shape of the cape, jutting out into the ocean, as well as in the flight of the airplane, first achieved at Kitty Hawk. In contrast, Part VII, **"The Tunnel,"** expands upon the cave myth, the poet seeing there in the subway the apparition of Edgar Allan Poe, another "bedlamite" who escaped the shadows only to become blinded by the bright reality. As a result of all this, there is no linear progression of ideas or images throughout the poem. Instead, the progression is accumulative, each subsequent section adding new insights into the bridge's meaning, producing increments of knowledge for the poet, so that by Part VIII, the Atlantis section, the poet has gained an awareness by which he can finally realize a synthesis of his initial dialectic, the conflict between the individual and the national ideals.

The "logic" of ***The Bridge,*** therefore, exists not in a syllogistic structuring of the poem, but in the qualitative logic (the *logos*) embodied in the bridge itself. The bridge is made an object of contemplation, with the poem existing as a record of that contemplation. The poetic technique is neither mystical nor dream-visionary, but represents a poetic adaptation of Platonic philosophy.

¹ For the rationalist critique of Crane as a romantic mystic, see, for example, R. P. Blackmur, *Form and Value in Modern Poetry* (New York, 1957), pp. 269-286; Allen Tate, *Collected Essays* (Denver, 1959), pp. 225-237, 528-531; and Yvor Winters, *In Defense of Reason* (Denver, 1947), pp. 577-603. For a sympathetic treatment, see Sister M. Bernetta Quinn, *The Metamorphic Tradition in Modern Poetry* (New Brunswick, N. J., 1955), pp. 147-167. L. S. Dembo, in *Hart Crane's Sanskrit Charge: A Study of "The Bridge"* (Ithaca, N. Y., 1960), among others, has attempted a definition of Crane's use of *myth,* but in terms of romantic mysticism.

² Philip Horton, *Hart Crane: The Life of an American Poet* (New York, 1937), p. 31 *et passim*. See also Brom Weber, *Hart Crane: A Biographical and Critical Study* (New York, 1948), pp. 150-163, and Alan Trachtenberg, *Brooklyn Bridge, Fact and Symbol* (New York, 1965), p. 148-149 n., who argue the influence of P. D. Ouspensky's Neoplatonic mysticism on Crane's poetry.

³ *The Letters of Hart Crane, 1916-1932*, ed. Brom Weber (New York, 1952), pp. 237-240. See also Crane's unpublished essay, "General Aims and Theories," and his letter to Harriet Monroe, in Horton, pp. 323-334.

⁴ *The Republic of Plato,* trans. Francis M. Cornford (New York, 1945), pp. 221-226.

⁵ *Letters,* pp. 238-239. Crane felt the articulation of these ideas was a significant mark in his development as a poet; he chided Munson for failing to recognize the new "logic" of his poetry, for allowing "too many extra-literary impressions of me" to shape his criticism of the poet.

⁶ *The Complete Poems of Hart Crane,* ed. Waldo Frank (Garden City, N. Y., 1958); all quotations are from this text.

⁷ See, for example, Weber, *Crane*, pp. 321-329. Roy Harvey Pearce, *The Continuity of American Poetry* (Princeton, 1961), pp. 101-111, and Dembo, pp. 9-10, equate Crane's use of myth with *logos,* or the Word; Pearce, however, tends to interpret *Word* literally, finally equating it with language; Dembo emphasizes the mystical sense of *Word,* not the Platonic. For other interpretations, see, for example, Howard Moss, "Disorder as Myth: Hart Crane's *The Bridge,*" *Poetry,* LXII, 32-45 (April, 1943), and Deena Posy Metzger, "Hart Crane's *The Bridge:* The Myth Active," *Arizona Quarterly,* XX, 36-46 (Spring, 1964).

⁸ J. A. Stewart, *The Myths of Plato* (London and New York, 1905), pp. 20-39. Crane may have been familiar with this standard work. See also his letter to Gorham Munson, Dec. 10, 1923, on his reading of Walter Pater's *Plato and Platonism,* a work he admired more than Pater's *The Renaissance* (*Letters,* p. 161).

⁹ *Letters,* pp. 238-239, and Horton, pp. 326-327, 330-333. The term "qualitative progression" is Kenneth Burke's: *Counter-Statement* (New York, 1931), pp. 157-159. Crane and Burke, of course, were friends, Crane being particularly appreciative of Burke's critical theories (*Letters,* pp. 103-104 *et passim*).

¹⁰ In Part VIII, for example, the poet invokes the "intrinsic Myth" of the bridge. The influence of Pater may be seen here: *Plato and Platonism* (New York, 1905), pp. 134-155. For sources of Crane's "power in repose" and the Platonism of the Atlantis section, see Pater's chapters on the Platonic doctrines of motion, rest, and numbers (pp. 1-65).

¹¹ For Crane's appreciation of art, note especially his relationship with Alfred Stieglitz (Horton, pp. 152-154, and *Letters, passim*). See also Gordon Grigsby, "The Photographs in the First Edition of *The Bridge,*" *Texas Studies in Literature and Language,* IV, 5-11 (Spring, 1962).

[12] D. B. Steinman, *The Builders of the Bridge: The Story of John Roebling and His Son* (New York, 1950), pp. 12-14, and especially Roebling's "A Metaphysical Essay on the Nature of Matter and of Spirit," pp. 128-130. Crane had negotiated without success to be the official Roebling biographer (*Letters,* pp. 293-294).

[13] Lewis Mumford, *Sticks and Stones* (New York, 1924), pp. 114-117.

[14] The Manhattan Bridge, immediately adjacent to the Brooklyn Bridge, also has four cables; it was completed in 1909. The reduction to two cables came with improvements in the tensile strength of steel—e.g., the Golden Gate Bridge.

[15] See also John Unterecker, "The Architecture of *The Bridge,*" *Wisconsin Studies in Contemporary Literature,* III, 5-20 (Spring-Summer, 1962).

[16] *Letters,* pp. 124, 127, 223, and esp. p. 319, where Crane defines *logos* in terms of a "substantial synthesis."

[17] Weber, *Crane,* pp. 425-440.

[18] *Letters,* p. 270. Completed by the end of the year were "Ave Maria," "Cutty Sark," "The Tunnel," "Atlantis," and parts of "Powhatan's Daughter." Crane's poetic fecundity may have been triggered by the death of Washington Roebling, July 21, 1926; he sent "Proem" ("my little dedication") to Waldo Frank on or about July 24, 1926 (*Letters,* p. 267).

[19] Trachtenberg, pp. 161-164, argues effectively that Crane relied on the Platonic version of the popular Atlantis myth; he mentions Crane's use of the cave myth only in passing (p. 154).

[20] The myth postulated an island-continent in the western Atlantic Ocean, geographically isolated by several concentric rings of sea and land. The inhabitants of the island, guided by their god Poseidon, eventually overcame their insularity, first, by inventing boats, and second, by constructing a Great Bridge, of such length that it reached from the inner island to the outermost ring of land, and of such height that ships could sail under it with ease. Thus freed, the inhabitants of Atlantis became a powerful nation, using the knowledge bestowed by Poseidon to create a bright materialistic culture in the West. See the "Timaeus" and "Critias" sections of *The Dialogues of Plato,* trans. B. Jowett (4th ed.; Oxford, 1953), III, 631-639, 781-804.

[21] Crane claimed this section was the center of the work, "both physically and symbolically" (*Letters,* p. 347).

[22] Stewart, pp. 451-456.

[23] On the epic intent of Crane's poem, see *Letters,* pp. 304-309, and Pearce, pp. 61-62 *et passim.*

[24] Stewart, pp. 245-253, 451-456. Though the myth is well known, it is useful here for purposes of analysis to note its outstanding features. Men were compared with prisoners in a cave, shackled facing a wall, their backs to the light, unable to see themselves or anyone else; they observed only the shadows of things on the wall. The philosopher was compared with one who left the cave, came to know things as they really were, and returning to the cave, could recognize the reality of things by their shadows. The myth included a warning to those who would become philosophers. The light in the cave was produced by a brilliant flame situated behind a parapet. People behind the parapet manipulated figurines above their heads, producing the shadows on the wall of the cave. If one of the men were ever set free and allowed to witness the machinery, he would not comprehend what he saw, for he knew only the world of shadows. Furthermore, if the man were to rush to the parapet, not allowing his eyes to become accustomed to the light, he would no doubt be blinded by the brilliant flame. He might then prefer to return to his chains and the comfortable world of shadows; but being blinded, he would no longer comprehend the shadows either. Thus, the escaped prisoner would find himself in a frustrating state, caught between two worlds, neither of which he could comprehend. As a consequence, he would no doubt experience the ridicule of the other prisoners for having tried to see the light, only to have his vision destroyed (Cornford, pp. 227-235).

[25] Coincidentally, Cornford, in his translation of the myth, notes: "A modernPlato would compare his Cave to an underground cinema . . ." (p. 228).

[26] When *The Bridge* was written, the subway still traversed the Brooklyn Bridge. See Crane's letter to his mother, May 11, 1924, where he described the lights of the elevated trains on the bridge (*Letters,* p. 183).

[27] "Chained bay waters" refers to the "chain bridge"—i.e., the Brooklyn Bridge.

[28] "Cloud-flown derricks" has caused some difficulty in interpretation (see, for example, Dembo, p. 50 n.); actually, it probably refers to a common scene along the docks under the bridge, as the tall booms (the "derricks") of the unloading equipment turn "all afternoon," enveloped in clouds of vapor from their steam-driven engines. For a description of such a scene, see Crane's letter to his mother, Oct. 21, 1924 (*Letters,* p. 192). In a general sense, then, the line merely represents a passage of time, during which normal activities continue.

I should like to emphasize here the general nature of this explication. I believe it is consistent with Crane's poetic technique (i.e., his Platonism) that any one of his poetic images may have several particular referents. For example, "Down Wall, from girder into street noon leaks" may refer to the brilliant slice of light that penetrates at noon through the division between the roadways into the street below, where the bridge "leaps over the edge of the street" (*Letters*, p. 181). It may also refer to Wall Street, where, because the buildings are so tall and the streets so narrow, only at noon can the sun penetrate into the street below. These complement, however, rather than supplant the general poetic image: the first reaffirms the impression of an attack on the bridge's unity; the second, the reference to Wall Street, identifies one symbol of America's materialistic culture with another, the Brooklyn Bridge. By concentrating on the general poetic image, I do not intend to deny the richness of Crane's symbolist technique.

## R. W. Butterfield (essay date 1969)

SOURCE: "The Writing of 'The Bridge': 1923-1929," in *The Broken Arc: A Study of Hart Crane*, Oliver & Boyd, 1969, pp. 121-51.

[*In the following essay, Butterfield attempts to account for the disunity within* The Bridge *by examining the circumstances surrounding its composition.*]

> I am perfectly sure that [*The Bridge*] will be finished within a year.[1] (Crane—Jul. 21, 1923)

The usual criticism of *The Bridge* is that, while many of the separate parts are of an astonishing power and beauty, the whole lacks order, unity, and coherence. In the last few years there have been several attempts to point out various principles of organisation, but by the majority of careful readers the poem is still regarded as disjunct. That *The Bridge* does contain serious internal contradictions seems indisputable. Some of these contradictions can, however, be accounted for by an exploration of the circumstances of its composition over a period of seven years. During this time Crane changed from the excited, confident adolescent who had just completed **"For the Marriage of Faustus and Helen"** into the prematurely aged libertine who could hardly discipline himself to write the poem's final sections.

In February 1923 the idea had taken shape in Crane's mind of "a new longish poem under the title of *The Bridge* which carries on further the tendencies manifest in 'F and H'".[2] This statement suggests that initially his poem was to be yet another projection of the will from the real to the ideal, and that the particular American situation was secondary. Very soon, however, we have evidence of an ambition to unify the American experience. These four lines were sent to Allen Tate:

> Macadam, gun grey as the tunny's pelt,
> Leaps from Far Rockaway to Golden Gate,
> For first it was the road, the road only
> We heeded in joint piracy and pushed.[3]

And in greater detail he explained to Gorham Munson:

> Very roughly, it concerns a mystical synthesis of "America". History and fact, location, etc., all have to be transfigured into abstract form that would

almost function independently of its subject matter. The initial impulses of "our people" will have to be gathered up toward the climax of the bridge, symbol of our constructive future, our unique identity, in which is included also our scientific hopes and achievements of the future.[4]

*The Bridge* is to be a consensus of past American experience guiding the present towards "our constructive future". A Nietzschean assertion of the will and the Platonic resolution of fragmented reality are now conjoined with a sense of national destiny, learnt from Whitman through Munson and Waldo Frank.[5] Fired by the ecstatic love affair which he was enjoying at this time, Crane's optimistic idealism spreads from a narrow vision of a merely personal destination until it covers the whole horizon of America. His own quest was now identified with that of America, on her road to becoming, as Whitman had expressed it, "divine Mother not only of material but spiritual worlds, in ceaseless succession through time".[6] "I have lost the last shreds of philosophical pessimism", he announced in March.[7] *The Bridge* was thus conceived as a testament of unwavering optimism—an optimism which was not directed towards any particular end, but which was a state of mind; and consequently it was the exultant finale, later to be entitled **"Atlantis"**, which absorbed all his energies at the beginning. The rest was to be a record of the unbroken, upward ascent to that climax. Here then are the seeds of the first internal confusion; originally Crane did not prepare for a journey through the hells of **"Southern Cross"** and **"The Tunnel"**.

After a three months' lull, while he sampled the delights and excitements of his escape from the provinces into New York, in July he found himself driven again before a storm of irresistible creative force, and variant drafts of the final section were dispatched to Alfred Stieglitz and Charlotte Rychtarik. Ouspensky and Blake had now contributed their part to the span of the bridge, and Crane's letter to Stieglitz was a rhapsodic improvisation upon the theme of Ouspensky's "new order of consciousness", and of Blake's dictum that "what is now proved was once only imagined".[8] "*The Bridge* seems to me so beautiful . . . sheer ecstasy", he confided to Charlotte Rychtarik.[9] So far all was going smoothly, with regard to both the poem's conception and its composition. *The Bridge* was to be a celebration of personal and national aspiration towards some kind of constructive future, "that fills us and renews us as a sun".[10] He was "perfectly sure that it will be finished within a year".[11] There seemed to be no impediments, practical or intellectual, in July 1923.

Yet, within a month he had lost grip of the poem and was not to regain any semblance of control for almost three years. On 25 August, tormented by the heat, he had already "been in such despair about *The Bridge* for some time".[12] And though the winter passed with few references to the poem, we are left in no doubt that he was deeply troubled by his inability to make any progress, when we hear him exclaiming to Charlotte Rychtarik in

March that "I would to God that I could get more done on my poem, to be called *The Bridge*".[13] It was in April 1924 that he both entered upon the love affair which inspired the **"Voyages"** sequence and took up residence at 110 Columbia Heights, overlooking Brooklyn Harbour. This happy love relationship gave a serenity to his gaze as he looked out over the Brooklyn water-front; and undoubtedly it was at this time, and in the autumn when he was at work upon **"Voyages"**, that there came to him many of the impressions and images which were later to find their way into **"Proem: To Brooklyn Bridge"** and **"The Harbor Dawn"**.[14] But of concerted work upon *The Bridge* there was none; merely a frustrated, petulant reminder to his mother in September, from the cage of a time-consuming job, that "a poem like [*The Bridge*] needs unbroken time and extensive concentration, and my present routine of life permits me only fragments".[15] Apart from such lamentations, there is hardly a mention of *The Bridge* in his correspondence until in desperation he approached Otto Kahn inDecember 1925.

During these two and a half years the poem had become something of a white elephant. His desire to write "a great American poem" was known to all his friends, who were continually curious about its progress. But, driven by the need to earn a living, he could find no time to work consistently upon it, only plenty of time in which to be depressed by its fragmentary condition. When he wrote his letter to Kahn, seeking means of escaping that economic enslavement which he felt must be the primary cause of the poem's failure to progress, he pleaded:

> I have had to work at it very intermittently, between night and morning, and while shorter efforts can be more successfully completed under such crippling circumstances, a larger conception such as this poem, *The Bridge,* aiming as it does to enunciate a new cultural synthesis of values in terms of our America, requires a more steady application and less interruption than my circumstances have yet granted me to give it.[16]

This letter was successful in obtaining from Kahn the generous loan of $2,000 which enabled him to retreat to a haven in the country. Here, relieved of economic pressure, within a very short time he was busily revising the final section and wrestling with **"Ave Maria"**. The bridge as symbol had already developed some of its multiplicity, and with only **"Atlantis"** in any state of completion it had become "a ship, a world, a woman, a tremendous harp".[17] All of these symbolic strands would have to be woven into the whole.

Throughout the early months of 1926 he stuck limpet-like to the poem and on 18 March sent a further progress report to Otto Kahn. There was still very little of *The Bridge* visible, only "about one hundred lines": but he had now a much clearer idea than previously of how the poem was to proceed section by section, and of the thematic part that each section was to play:

> . . . . Mid-ocean is where the poem begins. It

concludes at midnight—at the center of Brooklyn Bridge. Strangely enough that final section of the poem has been the first to be completed,—yet there's a logic to it after all; it is the mystic consummation toward which all the other sections of the poem converge. Their contents are implicit in its summary. . . .

> There are so many interlocking elements and symbols at work throughout *The Bridge* that it is next to impossible to describe it without resorting to the actual metaphors of the poem. Roughly, however, it is based on the conquest of space and knowledge. The theme of "Cathay" (its riches, etc.) ultimately is transmuted into a symbol of consciousness, knowledge, spiritual unity. A rather religious motivation, albeit not Presbyterian. The following notation is a very rough abbreviation of the subject matter of the several sections:

> I. Columbus—Conquest of space, chaos.

> II. Pocahontas—The natural body of America—fertility, etc.

> III. Whitman—The spiritual body of America. (A dialogue between Whitman and a dying soldier in a Washington hospital; the infraction of physical death, disunity, on the concept of immortality.)

> IV. John Brown.

> (Negro porter on Calgary Express making up berths and singing to himself (a jazz form for this) of his sweetheart and the death of John Brown, alternately.)

> V. Subway—The encroachment of machinery on humanity; a kind of purgatory in relation to the open sky of the last section.

> VI. The Bridge—A sweeping dithyramb in which the Bridge becomes the symbol of consciousness spanning time and space.

> The first and last sections are composed of blank verse with occasional rhymesfor accentuation. The verbal dynamics used and the spacious periodicity of the rhythm result in. an unusually symphonic form. What forms I shall use for the other sections will have to be determined when I come to grips with their respective themes. . . .

> As I cannot think of my work in terms of time I cannot gauge when it will be completed, probably by next December, however.[18]

*The Bridge* is to record "the conquest of space and knowledge", and will become "a symbol of consciousness, knowledge, spiritual unity . . . spanning time and space". The direction of the poem is still towards "the height beyond despair", a journey undertaken still in the evident company of Nietzsche, Plato, Ouspensky, Blake, and Whitman. But unable, with any intellectual integrity, to disregard the private hells he had so often visited during the last three years, Crane has made arrangements for a ride on the purgatorial subway.

This explanation of aims was sent to Kahn in the third week of March. During the remainder of his stay at Patterson he felt the poem gradually eluding his grasp, until by the end of April he was approaching a desperation about the project as acute as ever before. After his row with the Tates, he set sail for the Isle of Pines, in the hope that a complete change of scenery might stimulate his poetic nerve. If he could not write his poem in the time of economic freedom which Kahn's loan had granted him, it would never be written. He had for too long consoled himself with the belief that all he needed was time. He muttered ominously to the Rychtariks: "I realise it's hard for [my mother] to think of me as so far way [on the Isle of Pines]—but I'll be still farther away, I think, if my *Bridge* breaks down entirely".[19] Something substantial had to be produced very soon if Crane was not to collapse into a dangerous and total despair. He was saved from such a descent into the depths by an unprecedented fluidity of poetic invention in the third week of July. Within a month he rescued *The Bridge* from impending oblivion and wrote almost half of one of the major long poems of the century.

At this point it would seem appropriate to turn from the circumstances of the poem's composition and to look at some of the works from which Crane drew ideas for the construction of his bridge; for by July 1926, he had absorbed all the influences, conscious and unconscious, sympathetic and antipathetic, which had effect upon the development of his poem.

His thought had for so long been imbued with Platonic, Nietzschean, Ouspenskian, and Blakeian elements that nothing that is not repetitive can be added. All of these teachers play as large a part in the conception of *The Bridge,* as they have played in the making of the shorter, lyric poems. Inspired by an Ouspenskian optimism and a Blakeian vision, the protagonist drives himself across the bridge with a Nietzschean exercise of the will towards the divine harmony of **"Atlantis"**, which takes its epigraph from Plato's *Symposium.* In these respects the psychological and metaphysical premises supporting *The Bridge* are no different from those on which were founded the poems of *White Buildings.*

The full impact of Whitman, however, has so far not been felt. Crane had long thought himself "directly connected" with Whitman, but apart from **"Voyages"**, which have certain affinities with "Out of the Cradle Endlessly Rocking", the self-involved lyrics of *White Buildings* were only peripherally influenced by the singer of nineteenth-century "Modern Man". *The Bridge* was a different matter altogether.

Crane was thoroughly familiar with the whole of *Leaves of Grass,*[20] but he was most clearly indebted to the imagery and symbolic devices of "Crossing Brooklyn Ferry" and "When Lilacs Last in the Dooryard Bloom'd", and to some of the assumptions of "Passage to India" and of the prose essay, *Democratic Vistas.* Crane's poem opens

with a seagull gradually disappearing from sight into the upper air:

> How many dawns, chill from his rippling rest
> The seagull's wings shall dip and pivot him,
> Shedding white rings of tumult, building high
> Over the chained bay waters Liberty—
> Then, with inviolate curve, forsake our eyes
> As apparitional as sails that cross
> Some page of figures to be filed away. . . .

Traversing the same stretch of river in "Crossing Brooklyn Ferry", Whitman

> Watched the Twelfth-month seagulls, saw them high in
> the air floating with motionless wings, oscillating their
> bodies,
> Saw how the glistening yellow lit up parts of their bodies
> and left the rest in strong shadow,
> Saw the slow-wheeling circles and the gradual edging
> toward the south. . . .

And playing a similar part to **"The Tunnel"** in *The Bridge* is the sixth section of Whitman's poem, where he confesses to times of doubt, despair with self, and spiritual defeat:

> It is not upon you alone the dark patches fall,
> The dark threw its patches down upon me also,
> The best I had done seem'd to me blank and suspicious,
> My great thoughts as I supposed them, were they not in
> reality meagre?
> Nor is it you alone who know what it is to be evil,
> I am he who knew what it was to be evil. . . .

From "When Lilacs Last in the Dooryard Bloom'd" Crane must have derived not only particular elements (the star, bird, flower, and song, which are common to both poems), but also and especially the intricate symbolic and imagistic organisation. In an exactly similar manner at the conclusion of each poem are these elements gathered up and "twined" together in a transcendent unity. Whitman exults over the

> Lilac and star and bird twined with the chant of my soul,
> There in the fragrant pines and the cedars dusk and dim.

Likewise (though with significantly less certainty) does Crane address his prayer

> So to thine Everpresence, beyond time,
> Like spears ensanguined of one tolling star
> That bleeds infinity—the orphic strings,
> Sidereal phalanxes, leap and converge:
> —One Song, one Bridge of Fire! Is it Cathay,
> Now pity steeps the grass and rainbows ring
> The serpent with the eagle in the leaves . . . ?

Whispers antiphonal in azure swing.

With *Democratic Vistas* **The Bridge** shares an urgent optimism in spite of a like conviction that there was never "more hollowness at heart than at present";[21] it answers Whitman's call for "a class of bards who will, now and ever, . . . link and tally the rational physical being of man, with the ensembles of time and space"; it obeys his imperative that "faith, very old, now scared away by science, must be restored, brought back by the very power that caused her departure"; and finally, it attempts to build that path, proclaimed in the closing sentences of the essay, "upward into superior realms", where America will be "divine Mother not only of material but spiritual worlds, in ceaseless succession through time". To some extent **The Bridge** was written by one half-believing that he was the "divine literatus", to whom in *Democratic Vistas* Whitman had played John the Baptist.

As for "Passage to India", it is almost a preliminary abstract of **The Bridge**—withthe conspicuous omission of the infernal chapters. **"Cape Hatteras"**, whose epigraph is taken from "Passage to India", is the section most obviously inspired by the earlier poem. It concludes with Whitman taking Crane by the hand, just as Whitman in his own poem had dreamed of the time when "the Elder Brother found,/ The Younger melts in fondness in his arms". But similarities are not limited to **"Cape Hatteras"**, which after all is intended as a kind of beatification of the Good Gray Poet.

Whitman had begun "Passage to India",

> Singing my days,
> Singing the great achievements of the present,
> Singing the strong light works of engineers,
> Our modern wonders, (the antique ponderous
>     Seven
>   outvied),
> In the Old World the east the Suez canal,
> The New by its mighty railroad spann'd,
> The seas inlaid with eloquent gentle wires;
> Yet first to sound, and ever sound, the cry with
>     thee O soul,
> The Past! The Past! The Past!

Crane's Bridge has as its centrepiece Roebling's great achievement of strong and graceful engineering, and from there plunges westwards into the continent by a mighty railroad in search of the past. Whitman continues to evoke

> Not you alone proud truths of the world,
> Not you alone ye facts of modern science,
> But myths and fables of eld, Asia's, Africa's
>     fables . . .

Likewise, Crane pays heed not only to the "facts of modern science" in **"Cape Hatteras"**, but also in **"Powhatan's Daughter"** attempts to recapture the "fables of eld", the myths of those Indians who were thought by the first discoverers to be inhabitants of Asia.

Again, Whitman depicts Columbus as "a visionary,/ With majestic limbs and pious beaming eyes". It is the same Columbus who gazes out towards Spain in **"Ave Maria"**. But Whitman, for all his experience of the Civil War and his warnings against corruption and betrayal sounded in *Democratic Vistas*, had been able to believe that America was still true to Columbus's vision:

> Ah, Genoese thy dream! thy dream!
> Centuries after thou art laid in thy grave,
> The shore thou foundest verifies thy dream.

For Crane, who half a century later had often felt "disgust at America and everything in it",[22] there could be no such certainty; and this is the point at which Whitman's influence upon Crane's poem becomes very much a complicating factor.

"Passage to India" was impelled by an optimism, unadulterated and unqualified, and by a faith in movement for movement's sake. The poem concludes with an exhortation to

> Sail forth—steer for the deep waters only,
> Reckless O soul, exploring, I with thee, and thou
>     with me,
> For we are bound where mariner has not yet dared
>     to go,
> And we will risk the ship, ourselves and all.
> O my brave soul!
> O farther farther sail!
> O daring joy, but safe! are they not all the seas of
>     God?
> O farther, farther, farther sail!

This invocation presumes a state of continual progress—progress undefined, unspecified, outwards, upwards, farther.[23] In the spring of 1923, when **The Bridge** was first mooted and when Crane felt that he had "lost the last shreds of philosophical pessimism", such a perspective of history was wholly attractive tohim. In **The Bridge,** as the first manuscript drafts demonstrate, he intended to sail farther, farther, farther, to "India" or "Cathay". And over the six and a half years of the poem's composition he never seriously doubted that this was the way the poem should end.

Yet in these years, Whitman's exhortations notwithstanding, the shore Columbus found had often, against Crane's explicit philosophical will, verified a nightmare rather than a dream. In consequence, before Cathay was reached, the dictates of psychological reality demanded a trial by agony in the tunnel of Hades. In **The Bridge** the journey into the tunnel is all too convincing; it seems the necessary and only possible direction for Crane's twentieth-century America; it is a metaphor for Crane's personal, real, and incontrovertible experience. Conversely, the emergence from the tunnel fails to convince, save as a miracle of wish-fulfilment, because it answers only to the requirements of a philosophical optimism that was no longer immediately available to Crane. This makes for a crucial flaw in **The Bridge;** and the flaw is the result of a man trying to write a poem to a programme, dictated by another, in which he could not fully believe. If Whitman may take credit for providing much of the pattern and overall conception of *The Bridge,* the simplistic progressivism of "Passage to India" is also partly to blame for the most serious internal contradiction in Crane's poem.

Whitman was not, of course, Crane's sole guide in the writing of his poem. As soon as Kahn's loan had allowed him to engage in the leisurely planning of his project, he set out on a course of systematic reading, always with one eye on his notebook for *The Bridge.* "I've read considerably", he told Munson in March 1926:

> Prescott's *Ferdinand and Isabella, Journal of Columbus,* a book on Magellan by Hildebrand (this was rather inexcusable), Melville's delightful *White Jacket* as well as a marvelously illustrated book on whaling and whaling ships, published by the Marine Research Society, Salem, Mass. . . . In the midst of my readings of *Science and the Modern World,* Whitehead,—along comes *Virgin Spain.* I'm about half way through this at present and feel like telegraphing Waldo [Frank] my immediate uncontrolled and unstinted enthusiasm. As prose it certainly is his climax of excellence—and as a document of the epic one of the most lively testaments ever written. I had been dwelling with a good deal of surprise in a pleasant conviction that Lawrence's *Plumed Serpent* was a masterpiece of racial description. It certainly is vividly beautiful, its landscapes, theatrical vistas, etc.—but Waldo's work is a world of true reality—his ritual is not a mere invention.[24]

**"Ave Maria",** in both its narrative framework and its vocabulary, draws heavily upon Prescott and upon Columbus's *Journal;* and in **"Cutty Sark"** the sailor in his drunken meanderings babbles of desolate coasts and lifeless expanses of sea not unknown to Melville in fact or in imagination. From Whitehead Crane drew no details of his poem or of his thought to which we can point with accuracy: but the mathematician-philosopher's general thesis—his substitution of a monistic "organism" for a dualistic concept of mind and matter—must have been reassuring to a man continually perplexed and tortured by dualism.

More directly influential was Lawrence, **"Powhatan's Daughter"** obviously being written by a man familiar with both *The Plumed Serpent* and *Studies in Classic American Literature.* In the latter work it is particularly the two chapters on Cooper that are of relevance. At times here Lawrence exactly describes the reasons for and the nature of the quest that the protagonist undertakes in **"The River"** and **"The Dance":**

> Not that the Red Indian will ever possess the broad lands of America. At least I presume not. But his ghost will.
>
> The Red Man died hating the white man. What remnant of him lives, lives hating the white man. Go near the Indians, and you must feel it. As far as we are concerned, the Red Man is subtly and unremittingly diabolic. Even when he doesn't know it. He is dispossessed in life, and unforgiving. He doesn't believe in usand our civilisation, and so is our mystic enemy, for we push him off the face of the earth. . . .
>
> The moment the last nuclei of Red life break up in America, then the white men will have to reckon with the full force of the demon of the continent. At present the demon of the place and the unappeased ghosts of the dead Indians act within the unconscious or under-conscious soul of the white American, causing the great American grouch, the Orestes-like frenzy of restlessness in the Yankee soul, the inner malaise which amounts almost to madness sometimes.[25]
>
> Yet one day the demons of America must be placated, the ghosts must be appeased, the Spirit of Place atoned for. Then the true passionate love for American Soil will appear. As yet, there is too much menace in the landscape.
>
> But probably, one day America will be as beautiful in actuality as it is in Cooper. Not yet, however. When the factories have fallen down again.[26]

On other occasions he lays his finger very nearly upon one of the fundamental contradictions which undermined Crane's poem—and indeed more than his poem:

> The white man's mind and soul are divided between these two things: innocence and lust, the Spirit and Sensuality. Sensuality always carries a stigma, and is therefore more deeply desired, or lusted after. But spirituality alone gives the sense of uplift, exaltation, and "winged life", with the inevitable reaction into sin and spite. So the white man is divided against himself. He plays off one side of himself against the other side, till it is really a tale told by an idiot, and nauseating.[27]

If such a paragraph cannot properly be classified as influential, it does in retrospect appear as a disturbingly accurate prediction.

It is to Frank, however, that Crane owes greatest debt, and not so much to *Virgin Spain* as to an earlier work, *Our America,* which he had first read several years beforehand.[28] Isolated ideas from Frank's effulgent rhapsody on medieval Spain undoubtedly affected Crane deeply. For instance, Frank's notion of a bridge as "a force lifting the broken things of Spain in a great dance Godward"[29] effectively describes the function that Crane's Brooklyn Bridge is intended to possess in contemporary America. And the dialogue between Cervantes and Columbus, with which *Virgin Spain* closes, is one that Crane frequently conducted within himself.[30] It is an argument between a despair over all things American, voiced by the pessimistic Cervantes, and Columbus's refusal to give up hope. *The Bridge,* with **"The Tunnel"** opening on to **"Atlantis",** continues this tense debate.

Nonetheless, it is to *Our America* that **The Bridge** is chiefly similar, not merely in details, but in premise, substance, and design. In both works there is the same sense of the "body of America" and of the need to rediscover a blood-consciousness of it such as the Indians supposedly had felt. To this end Crane wrote **"Powhatan's Daughter"**, and Frank advised his readers to

> Try, as you read these pages about the spirit of our world, to bear in mind [its] body. . . . America is a land with a shrieking rhythm. . . . Centuries ago, a balance to this autochthonous rapture was achieved in the Indian civilisation.[31]

And in his chapter, "The Land of Buried Cultures", Frank predicts the annihilation of the proud Indian in a passage that might well serve as a gloss to Crane's **"The Dance"**:

> The Indian will be destroyed. . . . [But] he withdraws forever farther within himself. He makes his sanctuary of silent meditation deeper from the encroachment of the hostile human world. And holding up his head, he meets the storm.[32]

As for Whitman, he is as important a symbol of faith and purpose to Frankas he is to Crane in **"Cape Hatteras"**:

> America therefore is holy land to us. Not because Whitman stood upon it, but because we have faith that there is meaning in the fact that Whitman stood upon it.[33]

Turning to the twentieth century, we find that, like Crane, Frank believes that from the dark night of the national soul there is yet possibility of a triumphant emergence, for Chicago (his equivalent to Crane's Manhattan) "is still fluent, still chaotic, [but] in the black industrial cloak are still interstices of light". Despair has "not altogether won".[34] Crane's visionary **"Atlantis"**, his celebration of spiritual victory in the midst of this black industrial chaos, has its parallel in *Our America* in a composite of numerous, scattered ideas—of America as the new "mystic word" (*cf.* Crane's "multitudinous Verb"), as a country "consciously engaged in spiritual pioneering", and as a land of poets and seers whose sacred duty it is "to lift America into self knowledge that shall be luminous so that she may shine, vibrant so that she may be articulate".[35] Finally, there is a similarity of most general intention. It was Frank's aim in writing his history "to suggest a vast movement by scanty lines that shall somehow catch up the density of life between them".[36] Crane's historical lines were so scanty as to omit all mention of the War of Independence and almost all of the Civil War, but somewhere in the vast movement the density of past and present life was caught.

There are certainly sharp differences between these two men in a number of respects. Crane, for instance, is considerably less moralistic than Frank and less convinced of the efficacy of any kind of social revolution; and America's Jewish heritage plays no vital role in *The Bridge,* as it does in *Our America.* But these differences apart, the two works read almost as if they were entries for some literary prize in either prose or verse under the title of "The Myth of America".

Another entry for this hypothetical competition might have been William Carlos Williams's *In the American Grain,* which had been published in 1925. Crane, perhaps conscious of the extent to which **The Bridge** had already followed the pattern of another man's work, namely *Our America,* postponed reading it until Autumn, 1926, when "I felt my own way cleared beyond chance of confusions incident to reading a book so intimate to my theme".[37] He went on to say how interested he was "to note that he puts Poe and his 'character' in the same position as I had *symbolised* for him in **'The Tunnel'** section". Having chosen Poe as archetypal prisoner in a mechanised hell, he was perhaps thinking in particular of this paragraph from *In the American Grain:*

> It is especially in the poetry where 'death looks gigantically down' that the horror of the formless resistance which opposed, maddened, destroyed him has forced its character into the air, the wind, the blessed galleries of paradise, above a morose, dead world, peopled by shadows and silence, and despair—It is the compelling force of his isolation.[38]

If the similarity in their treatments of Poe was coincidental, it seems certain that in one respect Crane was indebted to Williams at least for reassurance. Williams's chapter, "De Soto and the New World", is presented in the form of a love-skirmish between an enthralled De Soto and an irresistible "She", the feminine spirit of the continent. The continent is a temptress, a fatal woman who beckons an insatiable and obsessed De Soto deeper and deeper into her Indian womb, where finally, unvanquished, she destroys the Spaniard. From **"Harbor Dawn"** to **"The Dance"** the protagonist of **The Bridge** is engaged in a like infatuated pursuit of the female continental body, until he too is consumed in her fiery, Indian embrace. Since these sections were all composed or radically revised after Crane's reading of *In the American Grain,* it seems reasonable to suppose that they were influenced conceptually by Williams's "De Soto and the New World".[39]

There is one thinker whose part in the building of **The Bridge** must be mentioned, although his writings acted less as an inspiration towards the exultant climaxthan as an impediment. This was Oswald Spengler, whose *Decline of the West* Crane seems to have dipped into from time to time throughout his life.

The history of Crane's reactions to Spengler demonstrates how completely intellectual systems were for him but the objectifications of emotional states. When all was well with the world, he was only too delighted to have Spengler's pessimistic thesis of cultural decay refuted. In January 1927 he was expressing his gratitude to Frank for "your review of Spengler. It's a magnificent rebuttal of the man's psychology."[40] The sigh of relief audible here suggests the fateful attraction Spengler's ideas had for Crane in times of emotional distress, when the ecstatic upper air was obscured from view. He was most susceptible in periods of creative drought. Thus was he captured by Spengler in June 1926, on the Isle of Pines. Once again it was Frank who was asked to overhear his confusion:

> At times it seems demonstrable that Spengler is quite right. At present—I'm writing nothing—would that I were an efficient factory of some kind! . . . I think that the artist more and more licks his own vomit, mistaking it for the common diet. He amuses himself that way in a culture without faith and convictions—but he might as well be in elfin land with a hop pipe in his mouth. . . . No, *The Bridge* isn't very flamboyant these days.[41]

A letter written the very next day to the same correspondent has more to say about his poem's temporary lack of flamboyance:

> The form of [*The Bridge*] rises out of a past that so overwhelms the present with its worth and vision that I'm at a loss to explain my delusion that there exist any real links between that past and a future destiny worthy of it. The "destiny" is long since completed, perhaps the little last section of my poem is a hangover echo of it—but it hangs suspended somewhere in ether like an Absalom by his hair. The bridge as a symbol today has no significance beyond an economical approach to shorter hours, quicker lunches, behaviorism and toothpicks.[42]

In such moments Crane sees with a painful clarity the fissure in the plan, let alone the completed work, of *The Bridge.* The present, which seemed squalid and trivial to him, broke the link between his idealised past of Pocahontas and Whitman and his future with its promise of Cathay. There was no way of relating the reality of contemporary America with its envisaged ideal. If this "new cultural synthesis of values in terms of our America" were to omit all reference to the infernal regions of America and of his American self, the poem would be merely a complacent, compensatory, and sentimental dream. Yet if the protagonist were to visit the depths, as for the poem to be valid he must, there would be no means of emergence save on the wings of the idealist's will to aspire—wings manufactured not in the reality of the depths but in the visionary world of the imagination. The real and the ideal could not be bridged, as they had not been even in his early adolescence, when he had written poems alternately ecstatic and despairing.

Spengler was not, of course, responsible for this schism. He had not made miserable Crane's childhood, just as that childhood's moments of joy and release had not been learnt from Whitman. But what Spengler did was to provide some sort of explanatory system or rationale at times when the path of vision was hidden. However, just as

there was no emotional balance in Crane's life, only violent alternations, so there was no synthesis of Spengler and Whitman. Depression sank Crane in the horrors of the material world, where he took a masochistic delight in being a dedicated Spenglerian; when the depression lifted, Spengler faded in the bright Whitmanic dawn. Thus in *The Bridge* one might say that Spengler led Crane into **"The Tunnel"**. Somewhere in that subterranean purgatory Spengler vanished from Crane's sight. But he vanished only in the sense that Crane had shut his eyes to external reality; it was in the world of an inward vision that the poet made passage to Cathay.[43]

For two months after his arrival on the Isle of Pines Crane was held in the grip of this Spenglerian pessimism. He was immensely excited by the more luscious aspects of tropical scenery, and by the heightened effects of sea and sky: but,since he was unable to continue work on *The Bridge,* his predominant state of mind was analogous less to the exotic Isle of Pines than to its barren neighbour, Grand Cayman, which he visited in the middle of June, to find it "flat and steaming under black clouds of mosquitoes, and not a square inch of screening on the island".[44] At this time Crane felt himself being reduced inexorably to a similar, devitalised condition. "I have not been able to write one line since I came", he told a friend at the beginning of July. "The mind is completely befogged by the heat . . . I've lost all faith in my material".[45] This letter ended with an abject submission to a hedonistic nihilism: "Let my lusts be my ruin, since all else is a fake and mockery". It seemed that a poet and his major poem had both evaporated in the tropical heat.

Then suddenly, a miracle . . . a creative downpour. The lull of months, the unfulfilled promise of years, came to an end in a furious storm of poetic activity. On 24 July, a poet reborn and saved, he began his letter to Waldo Frank: "Hail brother! I feel an absolute music in the air again, and some tremendous rondure floating somewhere";[46] and in the month that followed he was constantly at work either on *The Bridge* or on several fine, short lyrics capturing the spiritual atmosphere of the tropics. Never before or again was Crane driven by so powerful a creative force. "I'm simply immersed in work to my neck, eating, 'sleeping', and breathing it", he told his mother.[47] With Frank at this time he kept up a stream of correspondence, a description of work in progress, that rivalled the flow of his poetry: "I feel as though I were dancing on dynamite these days—so absolute and elaborated has become the conception. All sections moving forward now at once! I didn't realise that a bridge is begun from the two ends at once."[48] And on another occasion there came to him this marvellous image of the earlier stages of the creative process: "It is very pleasant to lie awake—just half awake—and listen. I have the most speechless and glorious dreams meanwhile. Sometimes words come and go, presented like a rose that yields only its light, never its complete form."[49]

This spell in a creator's paradise lasted a little over a month. By the end of August seven sections were either complete or awaiting revision of only minor details: "Proem", "Ave Maria", "Cutty Sark", "Southern Cross", "National Winter Garden", "The Tunnel", and "Atlantis". In addition, "The Dance" and "Virginia" were written at least in part at this time. "Indiana" was conceived, and there is also a reference to a "Calgary Express" as being "largely finished".[50]

By September 1926 Crane had good cause to be exhilarated and hopeful. He had written the major part of *The Bridge,* and if the co-ordination of the whole was still an achievement for the future, he felt that so far "what has been done . . . is superb".[51] All the completed sections had been written out of a necessity to create and in obedience to an internally-directed imperative, not out of a necessity to implement a theoretical programme, like some of the later work. Now he believed he could finish the poem by the following May (1927);[52] and there was no strong reason to suppose that the remaining sections, now merely links, would not fall into shape and place with a similar ease and assurance.

In the autumn he returned first to New York, and then to Patterson. Summer's deluge of creativity was over, but it had left him with a conviction that if it could happen once it could happen a second time. "I'm not worried", he asserted to Frank in November. "I know too well what I want to do now, even if it doesn't spill over for months and months. It must 'spill', you know."[53] Yet within a month, with an abrupt swing of the emotional pendulum, he was deposited once more in a pit of dejection. He recanted his so recent confidence and confessed to a fear that "it may be too late, already, for me to complete the conception [of *The Bridge*]. My mind is about as clear as dirty dishwater."[54]

What had happened was that he had once again become enmeshed in a web of chaos, emanating from his mother. Her problem at the moment was that after only seven months her second marriage was ending in divorce.[55] "It is a very melancholy Christmas for all of us . . . I am certainly anything but joyful" observed Crane, in a tone less of sympathetic sorrow than of weary disillusionment with her whom he had once described as a queen of the spirit.[56] It would be wrong to suggestthat either this unhappy turn of events or the general painful relations that he had with his mother during the next two years was any kind of direct impediment to the progress of *The Bridge.* But in times of inactivity, as in this last month of 1926, any sympathy was accentuated, any depression aggravated, and any reserve strength sapped by the considerable emotional demands made on him by his mother.

A slight counterbalance to the damage wrought by family confusions was provided by the publication in December of *White Buildings.* Crane was delighted to find that nearly all the reviews were favourable;[57] and what gave him particular pleasure—the New World still seeking the approval of the Old—was the unexpectedly enthusiastic notice in *The Times Literary Supplement.*[58] Of the literary journals, only *The Dial* had important reservations.[59] It

was a most encouraging reception for a first book of poems, and it certainly helped him resist any acute despair during the early months of 1927.

In these months, between trips from Patterson to New York in search of excessive or eccentric pleasures, Crane was working off and on at *The Bridge.* By February he had added to the previous sections "The Harbor Dawn" and "The Dance". Over the next three months he managed to write little and by May could no longer hide from himself the fear that he might be losing sight of the grand conception of his poem. He announced to his mother that "this next month must see something accomplished on *The Bridge* or I shall be completely discouraged".[60] Something *was* accomplished within that month, and July saw the completion of "Van Winkle" and "The River", on which section he had "worked harder and longer . . . than any other".[61] Twelve of the eventual fifteen sections were now finished and had been submitted for publication as single poems to a number of literary magazines.[62] He knew that there remained to write only "Indiana", "Cape Hatteras", and whatever would come as the link between "Three Songs" and "The Tunnel".[63] It seemed that at the latest he could "get it all done by December".[64]

When he approached Otto Kahn for a further loan in September, he told him that, "although I have found the subject to be vaster than I had at first realised, I am still highly confident of its final articulation into a continuous and eloquent span".[65] But in fact, even at the time of writing this letter, he was already climbing down from those heights of confidence. The major portion and the finest parts of *The Bridge* had been written in the twelve months that ended in July 1927. Temporary doubts there had been, but he had managed to maintain conceptual and structural command of his poem. Thereafter, he lost control, purpose, and direction in both his poetry and his personal life. Between the summer of 1927 and the summer of 1929 he wrote practically nothing, in verse or in prose, within or without *The Bridge.* He slipped from an irritable lethargy into a self-destructive irresponsibility, until he became a man living continually on the crumbling edge of disaster.

One of the factors contributing to this collapse was undoubtedly the fact that soon after his return to the United States in the autumn of 1926 his sense of economic and social dislocation once again became acute. He was unqualified for any work, such as school or university teaching, which might have allowed him extended periods of time in which to concentrate on writing. And though he had become, as he reminded Kahn, "a perfectly good advertising writer",[66] employment of this kind always exhausted him physically and mentally, so that consistent work on a large project was impossible. Kahn's loan had been the key out of this economic prison, and at least for the months of July and August 1926 this freedom had paid handsome dividends. However, Crane soon found that this liberty was not without its peculiar disadvantages. Such was his temperament that when poetry was not forthcoming, he faced within himself only a huge and intolerable emptiness, which even a copywriter's project might have enabled him temporarily to ignore. How pitifully ironic, and yet how comprehensible, that so often after entering the haven of Kahn's patronage, he recorded a desire to return to the cage of a daily job.

During his stay at Patterson from November 1926 to September 1927 Crane was always well-warmed and well-nourished, and bridge-building proceeded in fits and starts. But he could never quite stifle the anxiety (one of increasing vehemenceas the completion date of *The Bridge* was postponed from the autumn to December to the spring of 1928) about what would happen to both himself and his poem when the money ran out in the near future. He was the recipient of a small monthly cheque from his father, but the amount was essentially in the nature of an increment rather than of an income. Hence, throughout these months there are continual references in his letters to the necessity of finding a job; and hence, in September he approached Kahn again for a loan of "800 or 1,000 dollars". However, he was fully aware that any such loan would not alleviate his sense of social displacement. When unable to write, alone with a blank page, he would still feel that he was the inhabitant of a social limbo. He was caught in a cleft stick: equipped only for jobs which sapped his energies or which did not give him time to write poetry; outside the bondage of a job, doomed, when not writing, to feel totally superfluous, day in, week out. He saw himself as the text-book example of the romantic artist estranged from society, and it was as this representative displaced artist that he scolded Yvor Winters, who had demanded that the poet become again "the complete man", and take "his ethical place" as a functional member of society:

> You need a good drubbing for all your recent easy talk. . . . As a matter of fact I'm all too ready to concede that there are several other careers more engaging to follow than that of poetry. But the circumstances of one's birth, the conduct of one's parents, the current economic structure of society and a thousand other local factors have as much or more to say about successions to such occupations, the naive volitions of the poet to the contrary. I agree with you, of course, that the poet should in as large a measure as possible adjust himself to society. But the question always will remain as to how far the conscience is justified in compromising with the age's demands.[67]

Thus, in 1927, in that America whose myth he claimed to be composing, the mythmaker found himself socially irrelevant. From Patterson, during the spring and summer, whenever the frustration and the weight of superfluity became unbearable, he escaped to lose himself in delirious pleasure in the bars and along the waterfronts of New York. Sobriety meant only a despair with all things American, and he admitted

> How futile I feel most of the time, no matter what I do or conceive of doing, even. Part of the disease of modern consciousness, I suppose. There is no standard of values in the modern world—it's mostly

slop, priggishness, and sentimentality.[68]

By September, with the day of financial reckoning approaching, rather than work in America his sights were set on Mexico or Mallorca.[69] In the end he took a job as secretary to a stockbroker, that foremost contributor to the design of the "diseased" American twentieth century, and in November accompanied his new employer to Los Angeles, a city which by its fiercer critics has been seen as the apotheosis of "slop and sentimentality". This particular employment was not likely, for long, to solve his profound inner confusions about the artist in contemporary America.

He remained in Southern California for six months until May 1928. Only three of these were spent in the singularly undemanding employ of the stockbroker, Mr Herbert Wise. Thereafter he lingered in the area "with the hope of securing some 'literary' connection with the movies".[70] But the attempts to establish such a connexion were very half-hearted, and the hope therefore unfulfilled.

In all, this stay on the West Coast was little short of disastrous. Within two weeks he had found that "one can't seem to wake up here without the spur of scotch or gin".[71] He might have added that, let alone wake up, he could not continue through the day without incessant alcoholic spurs. Unfortunately, he did not confine his drinking to the comparative safety of a private residence, but wandered to the sailors' bars on the San Pedro waterfront. It was on one such excursion in March that Crane and a friend were beaten up and robbed of all they possessed. The quieter moments snatched from drinking and the seeking out of agreeable sailors Crane appears to have spent reading. There was more fiction on his reading-list than usual, but his chief joy was the discovery of Hopkins'spoetry, which "terribly excited" him and affected the revision of what was ultimately his most Hopkinsesque poem, **"The Hurricane"**.[72] But of progress on *The Bridge* there was none. "Writing is next to impossible", he told Malcolm Cowley.[73] All he could do was to put the poem out of mind with alcohol and with the frantic pursuit of physical pleasure. Sobriety brought in the personal foreground only contemplation of prospective failure, and on the horizon a broken vista of moral chaos in that country his poem was to celebrate. As he wrote to Gorham Munson, when congratulating him on the publication of his *Destinations*:

> The spiritual disintegration of our period becomes more painful to me every day, so much so that I now find myself baulked by doubt at the validity of practically every metaphor I coin.[74]

If Southern California was America's future, he could not "imagine ever having anything to say . . . except in vituperation of the scene itself".[75]

By the time he left California it was a full nine months since he had added so much as a word to the twelve disjunct sections of *The Bridge*. He was now blind to the vision that had originally inspired the poem, and deaf to that "absolute music" he had heard on the Isle of Pines. He had lost confidence in his own poetic abilities and lost belief in the subject of his poem. *The Bridge* rose out of his mind's barren plateau, magnificent, useless.

He returned to New York by way of New Orleans in the middle of May, embarrassed by his renowned but uncompleted poem, and still claiming to his friends that it would be finished during the summer.[76] But the depths of the hopelessness to which he had in fact sunk can be gauged from his confession to Wilbur Underwood that "there's nothing left to struggle for except 'respectability'. Occasionally some sailor gives me a jolt—but I guess I'm getting old."[77] The summer saw neither the completion of *The Bridge* nor an improvement in his general emotional state. "What a hell the last two years have been", was his verdict in October. "I haven't had a creative thought for so long that I feel quite lost."[78]

As usual economics had been one of the engines of this hell. Any remnants of energy and enthusiasm vanished as he tramped New York's humid streets in search of work. A cheque from his father helped him out in August, and in the autumn he obtained in succession temporary jobs in a bookshop and an advertising agency.[79] But such an existence afforded him none of the security required for consistent work on a long poem.

This security was not even achieved in September when his beloved grandmother died, leaving him a bequest of $5,000. It was true that for the first time in his life he had behind him a considerable sum of money, which was unquestionably his own rather than a loan from a patron or a gift with invisible strings from his father. But the complications attendant upon the receiving of this inheritance effectively sabotaged any stability which the bequest ought to have brought.

Over the past two years Crane had become increasingly irked by his mother's possessiveness and by her desire to dominate and mould him in every way possible. This irritation had become acute in Hollywood, where she had joined him, and where later in relief he had left her. Obviously, if Crane had not been bound to his mother at a very deep emotional level, he could long before have severed the relationship, or, preferably, have guided it into happier, healthier channels. But neither of these courses had he been capable of taking.

His grandmother's bequest brought matters to a head. Crane was perhaps indelicately, though understandably, eager to obtain the money. His mother was anxious lest her son's economic independence might strain the last threads of her hold over him. In Hollywood, she postponed signing the papers that would facilitate the release of the money, while, apparently feigning illness, she tried to coax him Westwards. In New York, Crane between drinking-bouts posted urgent demands for money to her and to the Trust Company. The affair deteriorated into a ferocious exchange of fantastic threats, until at length in

November Crane, realising that in their relationship were mutually destructive elements that could not be exorcised, resolved never to see his mother again.[80] He informed anaunt that he was

> now making a strong effort to discipline myself against the obsession with this and other wasteful family problems that have robbed me of my vitality during these last twenty years—unmanned me time and again . . . I won't be dragged into hell—and live there forever for anybody's joke—not even my mother's.[81]

In the end Crane obtained the money; and in December, with America offering only memories of intellectual confusion and emotional torment, he set sail for Europe. If his first aim in going was merely to put unpleasantness behind him, his second was of course to find somewhere he could work quietly on his poem. But the effort involved 'in cutting a particularly strong umbilical cord and in terminating the closest, if most contorted, relationship of his life proved to have left him little energy to spare for anything as demanding as *The Bridge*.

After a few days in London, he made the obligatory 1920s pilgrimage to Paris, where he was soon in touch with a large number to literary figures, French, English, and American. His chief interest, however, was in those who gave the wildest parties and who were most liberal with their whisky; and in Paris in 1929, for an expatriate American artist, there was one man who was unrivalled in these respects. This was Harry Crosby, millionaire, gambler, poet, amateur airman, and, most significant for Crane, publisher of de luxe editions. In the midst of a whirl of alcoholic activity Crane showed the completed sections of *The Bridge* to Crosby and his wife, Caresse. The Crosbys were so impressed with what they read that they begged Crane to let them publish immediately. And Crane agreed, so pessimistic was he now about the return of his poetic gifts, and so eager to be free of his burden. He was also tempted by the superb edition promised him; at least the volume might be a beautiful work of the printer's art, even if the contents were no more than a splendid wreck of literature.[82] An explanation of his decision to Isidor Schneider demonstrates the extent to which in him despair had turned into an intellectually dishonest nonchalance:

> I haven't so far completed so much as one additional section to *The Bridge*. It's coming out this fall in Paris, regardless. . . . If it eventuates that I have the wit or inspiration to add to it later—such additions can be incorporated in some later edition. I've alternated between embarrassment and indifference for so long that when the Crosbys urged me to let them have it, declaring that it reads well enough as it is, I gave in. Malcolm Cowley advised as much before I left America, so I feel there may be some justification. The poems, arranged as you may remember, do have I think, a certain progression. And maybe the gaps are more evident to me than to others.[83]

With these timid qualifications Crane launched his poem. *The Bridge* was given into the hands of its prospective publishers, not because its author wished to publish a book, merely because he wished to get rid of it.

After a gregarious, hectic spring in Paris, Crane travelled to the South of France in April. But the self-confrontation which a quiet solitude imposed upon him he could stand for only three weeks, before he was off again exploring the delights of the port of Marseilles. Back in Paris in July he was arrested for playing the leading part in a café brawl, and, after continuing the battle with the police, he was jailed and later fined. This fine exhausted the last of the money he had taken to Europe. Harry Crosby bought him a boat-ticket, and he sailed back to the United States, having written nothing during seven months in Europe. It was now six and a half years since he had begun *The Bridge,* three years since he had done any consistent work on it, and two years since he had written more than a "scratch note" for it.

Then, suddenly, in August 1929, in Patterson and Brooklyn, he was back at work on the poem in one last attempt to rescue it from the public show of fragmented disunity to which he had doomed it by his agreement to publish. He was writing now under no such inspiration as had magically come to him on the Isle of Pines; he was writing to fill in the gaps and to beat a publisher's dead-line. Small wonder that much of what he wrote at this time lacks the rhythmic flexibility andthe figurative flamboyance of the earlier sections; or that **"Cape Hatteras"** deteriorates into bombast and a shrill hysteria, as he strains every nerve to simulate an ecstasy which he no longer felt, but which the structure of the poem demanded at that point.

First came the gloss notes for **"Ave Maria"** and **"Powhatan's Daughter"**, which he thought would be "a great help in binding together the general theme".[84] Then he was co-ordinating various jottings he had made for **"Cape Hatteras"** and adding much that was new, until in September it looked "pretty good" to him.[85] **"Indiana"** and **"Quaker Hill"** were in progress, and on 17 September he predicted that he was within a week of finishing. But, sure enough, even at this stage his estimate was self-deceptive, and it was a full three months before on 26 December he was able to announce that "I'm hastily enclosing the final version of **'Quaker Hill'**, which ends my writing on *The Bridge*".[86] In these three months the American economy had collapsed, and Harry Crosby had killed himself, leaving his wife to discharge the publishing commitments of The Black Sun Press. But at least, in the midst of these national and individual disasters, there was something to be relieved about: *The Bridge* was finished.

It was just under seven years between the conception of *The Bridge* and its completion. In February 1923 Crane had been the messenger of a free-wheeling optimism, with an intermittently megalomaniac confidence in his mission and in his poetic genius; in 1929 he was a self-contemptuous alcoholic, whose erotic ecstasies had become self-consciously barbaric lusts, whose only certainty was of his own failure and loss of talent, and whose "philosophic optimism" had been routed by a more or less steady conviction of general spiritual disintegration. The man who completed the poem shared few beliefs and attitudes with the man who had begun it. It is hardly surprising that the poem is not conspicuous for its coherence, its internal logic, and its consistency of development.

[1] *Letters,* p. 141.

[2] *Letters,* p. 118. "F and H" is of course Crane's abbreviation for his "For the Marriage of Faustus and Helen".

[3] *Op. cit.,* p. 123. The first two lines of the verse quoted, with but one word altered ("belt" substituted for "pelt"), became the opening lines of "Van Winkle".

[4] *Op. cit.,* p. 124.

[5] See letter to Gorham Munson of 2 Mar. 1923 (*Letters,* p. 128): "Since my reading of you and Frank (I recently bought *City Block*) I begin to feel myself directly connected with Whitman".

[6] The quoted words are from the final sentence of *Democratic Vistas*.

[7] *Letters,* p. 129.

[8] *Op. cit.,* pp. 137-9.

[9] *Op. cit.,* pp. 139-42.

[10] The quoted words constitute a line from early drafts of the final section, later dropped. See Weber, *Hart Crane,* p. 427.

[11] *Letters,* p. 141.

[12] *Op. cit.,* p. 145.

[13] *Op. cit.,* p. 178.

[14] *Op. cit.,* pp. 181-3, 192, 198.

[15] *Op. cit.,* p. 191.

[16] *Op. cit.,* p. 223.

[17] *Op. cit.,* p. 232.

[18] *Op. cit.,* pp. 240-2. It will be noted that as yet there is no conception of the "Proem", and that the proposed Whitman and John Brown sections disappear, their places being taken by "Cutty Sark", "Cape Hatteras", "Three Songs", and "Quaker Hill". Of course, Whitman remains thematically central both to "Cape Hatteras" and to *The Bridge* as a whole, and the Calgary Express was

presumably rendered superfluous by the Twentieth Century Express of "The River" section.

[19] *Op. cit.,* p. 250.

[20] For instance, see his remark to Allen Tate (*Letters,* p. 354): "You've heard me roar at too many of Whitman's lines to doubt that I can spot his worst, I'm sure."

[21] In this paragraph the four quoted phrases or sentences from *Democratic Vistas* are to be found in Whitman, *Prose Works:* Vol. 11, *Collect and Other Prose,* New York, 1964, respectively on pp. 369, 421, 421, 426.

[22] *Letters,* p. 62.

[23] Yvor Winters, *In Defense of Reason,* New York, 1947, p. 589, writing in a similar context on Whitman's influence on Crane, summarises Whitman's lesson, not unfairly, as follows: "We have no way of determining where we are going, but we should keep moving at all costs and as fast as possible; we have faith in progress."

[24] *Letters,* pp. 235-6.

[25] D. H. Lawrence, *Studies in Classic American Literature.* New York, 1951, p. 44. The work was first published in 1923.

[26] *Op. cit.,* p. 60.

[27] *Op. cit.,* p. 72.

[28] Crane had read *Our America* as long ago as December 1919 (see *Letters,* pp. 26-7). He commented at that time: "Waldo Frank's book IS a pessimistic analysis. The worst of it is, he has hit the truth so many times." But its "extreme national consciousness" troubled one who was still the composer chiefly of intensely personal lyrics.

[29] Waldo Frank, *Virgin Spain: Scenes from the Spiritual Drama of a Great People.* New York, 1926, p. 9.

[30] *Op. cit.,* pp. 295-301. Of course, I do not mean to imply that Frank invented the dialogue. It is almost as old as the colonisation of America. But Frank's re-enactment of it assuredly impressed Crane, whose Columbus is also the spokesman of hope and faith.

[31] Waldo Frank, *Our America.* New York, 1919, p. 5.

[32] *Op. cit.,* p. 116.

[33] *Op. cit.,* p. 204.

[34] *Op. cit.,* p. 123.

[35] *Op. cit.,* pp. 3-10, passim.

[36] *Op. cit.,* p. 7.

[37] *Letters,* pp. 277-8.

[38] William Carlos Williams, *In the American Grain.* New York, (New Directions) 1956, p. 231.

[39] The epigraph which Crane chose for "Powhatan's Daughter" is from William Strachey's *The Historie of Travaile into Virginia Britannia.* However, almost certainly Crane did not take it from the original, but from the extract quoted by Williams in his chapter, "The May-pole at Merrymount".

[40] *Letters,* p. 285.

[41] *Op. cit.,* p. 259.

[42] *Op. cit.,* p. 261.

[43] Weber, *Hart Crane,* p. 286, suggests that Spengler was also sympathetic to Crane on account of his "high regard for the technique of analogy as a means of understanding", and for his "contempt for 'reason and cognition' and the importance he attached to 'intuitive perception' as the only means of comprehending metaphysical reality and the human future".

[44] *Letters,* p. 258.

[45] *Op. cit.,* p. 264.

[46] *Op. cit.,* p. 267.

[47] *Op. cit.,* p. 269.

[48] *Op. cit.,* p. 270.

[49] *Op. cit.,* pp. 272-3.

[50] *Op. cit.,* p. 272. "Calgary Express" was probably later incorporated into the first part of "The River".

[51] *Op. cit.,* p. 276.

[52] *Op. cit.,* pp. 269-70.

[53] *Op. cit.,* p. 277.

[54] *Op. cit.,* p. 280.

[55] The divorce was eventually granted, in his mother's favour, in the spring of 1927.

[56] *Letters,* p. 280.

[57] See letter to Waldo Frank (*Letters,* p. 285): "*WB's* is getting—or is going to get—wonderful reviews. Not to mention yours [in *The New Republic*], there's a great explosion coming from Yvor Winters in *The Dial;* another from Mark Van Doren (of all the unexpected!) in *The Nation* this week. Seligmann has written a sincere and just estimate in the *Sun;* Josephson in the *Herald-Tribune;* Mcleish in *Poetry . . .*"

[58] *T.L.S.*, 24 Feb. 1927. See *Letters*, p. 295: "Altogether it's the most satisfactory newspaper mention we have had".

[59] *The Dial*, LXXXII (February 1927), Crane was castigated for affectation of idiom, self-conscious preciosity, intellectual fakery, and an inability to write a satisfactory, complete poem. However, even here his blank verse measure was commended, but this slight qualification of disapproval was not enough to satisfy Crane, and he spent much of the spring railing at editors, in particular MarianneMoore of *The Dial*. For instance, see *Letters*, p. 289.

[60] *Letters*, p. 297.

[61] *Op. cit.*, p. 303.

[62] By 1928 eleven of the twelve sections had been published: "Proem: To Brooklyn Bridge" in *The Dial*, June 1927; "Ave Maria" in *The American Caravan*, 1927; "The Harbor Dawn" in *Transition*, No. 3, (1927); "Van Winkle" in *Transition*, No. 7, (1927); "The River" in *2nd American Caravan*, 1928; "The Dance" in *The Dial*, October 1927; "Cutty Sark" in *Transition*, No. 3 (1927); "Three Songs" in *The Calendar*, 1927; and "The Tunnel" in *The Criterion*, November 1927. Only "Atlantis" awaited the publication of *The Bridge*.

[63] See Weber, *Hart Crane*, p. 370: "Crane probably wrote ['Quaker Hill'] to take the place of three projected sections that were never completed—'The Cyder Flask', 'Calgary Express', and '1927 Whistles!'"

[64] *Letters*, p. 303.

[65] *Op. cit.*, p. 308.

[66] *Ibid.*

[67] This very interesting letter (*Letters*, pp. 298-302) should be read in its entirety. In addition to the extract cited, it contains discussions of "wholeness of personality", the artist's moral responsibilities, the homosexual artist, the structural weaknesses in Crane's poetry, and its metaphysical qualities.

[68] Letter to Wilbur Underwood, reprinted in Horton, *Hart Crane*, p. 235.

[69] See *Letters*, p. 309.

[70] *Op. cit.*, p. 318.

[71] *Op. cit.*, p. 312.

[72] *Op. cit.*, p. 317.

[73] *Op. cit.*, p. 314.

[74] *Op. cit.*, p. 323.

[75] *Op. cit.*, p. 325.

[76] *Ibid.*

[77] Letter reprinted in Horton, *Hart Crane*, p. 245. It is worth noting that he was still under thirty!

[78] *Letters*, p. 329.

[79] Relations with his father improved as those with his mother deteriorated, not to the extent, however, of allowing him, even when virtually penniless, to accept a job his father had offered him. He was still too fearful of any emotional entanglements such a situation might entail.

[80] He kept this resolve never to see her again. His mother lived on until 30 Jul. 1947.

[81] Letter reprinted in Horton, *Hart Crane*, pp. 248-9. See Horton, pp. 246-51, for a considerably more detailed account of this whole tawdry wrangle. Horton is as usual unduly generous towards Crane's mother.

[82] The frontispiece was to have been a reproduction of Joseph Stella's paintingof Brooklyn Bridge, of which Crane wrote to Stella (*Letters*, pp. 333-4): "It is a remarkable coincidence that I should, years later, have discovered that another person, by whom I mean you, should have had the same sentiments regarding Brooklyn Bridge which inspired the main theme and pattern of my poem." Eventually, instead of Stella's painting, three fine photographs by Walker Evans graced the Paris edition.

[83] *Letters*, p. 340.

[84] *Op. cit.*, p. 343.

[85] *Op. cit.*, p. 345.

[86] *Op. cit.*, p. 347.

## John Carlos Rowe (essay date 1978)

SOURCE: "The 'Super Historical' Sense of Hart Crane's *The Bridge*," in *Genre*, Vol. XI, Winter, 1978, pp. 597-625.

[*In the following essay, Rowe examines the "anti-poetic" nature of the primary symbol of the bridge.*]

> Art has the opposite effect to history; and only, perhaps, if history suffers transformation into a pure work of art, can it preserve instincts or arouse them. Such history would be quite against the analytical and inartistic tendencies of our time, and even be considered false. But the history that merely destroys without any impulse to construct will in the long run make its instruments tired of life; for such men destroy illusions, and "he who destroys illusions in himself and others is punished by the ultimate tyrant, Nature."

By the word "unhistorical" I mean the power, the art, of *forgetting* and of drawing a limited horizon round oneself. I call the power "super-historical" which turns the eyes from the process of becoming to that which gives existence an eternal and stable character—to art and religion.

—Nietzsche, *The Use and Abuse of History*
(1874)

Even more explicitly than Williams' *Paterson* or Eliot's *The Waste Land*, Crane's **The Bridge** seems to establish its proper poetic site. Everything in the poem refers quite clearly to the "bridge" as the central poetic *telos*. As a poetic symbol, the "bridge" appears to be even more fundamentally grounded in the particular and local than Williams' Paterson, New Jersey. The poet who announces his subject to be a "city" speaks already of his own selective reading of a topography—architecture, history, population—that is notoriously difficult to chart. The Brooklyn Bridge, however, is sufficiently modern and particular to be encompassed in a single visionary act; the imagination is capable to the task of conceptualizing at least this beginning: the bridge as artifact. Even acknowledging Whitman's "Crossing Brooklyn Ferry," the reader shares Crane's sense of the bridge as initially "anti-poetic," in itself a stout, graceless structure with hardly the "curveship" of loftier bridges. And yet nothing in the poem is more problematic than this apparently sharp particularity of Crane's central symbol. The bridge is the desired condition, the Word that redeems the words, the Atlantis of the imagination; this mythic bridge seems the antithesis of the homely, commercial bridge out of which it is shaped. It is, of course, characteristic of Crane's method to make "A grail of laughter of an empty ash can" or to transform the mechanized destruction of the technological age into "Easters of speeding light—/ Vast engines outward veering with seraphic grace. . . . "[1] But Crane's extended mediation on the poetic conception of "bridging"—of poetry as a spiritual "bridging"—is not to be explained fully by his tendency to metamorphose substantial facts into spiritual metaphors. The very "anti-poetic" character of Crane's central symbol offers us an entrance into this concept of "bridging," because to "bridge" is always to declare the emptiness of the pure act and its dependence upon the abyss to be spanned.

And yet in this poem, "bridging" itself is the proper poetic site, the nothingness on which the poem is based and toward which it moves. We are accustomed to think of a *telos* in spatial metaphors as a site at the end of a journey; the bridge is the "between," an Atlantis or utopia that measures the distance separating the voyager's origins and ends. Does the bridge mark an arrival or a departure? For Crane, it serves both purposes at once; it is an approach toward Atlantis in the very act of leaving the corruptions of American history behind. But this is not quite correct, because the bridge is neither arrival nor departure, but the waiting hesitation between, a "no-place" where origins and ends are determined. Heidegger uses the metaphor of the bridge in a similar fashion to represent that poetic thinking whereby man measures his dwelling on the earth and in time:

> The bridge swings over the stream "with ease and power." It does not just connect banks that are already there. The banks emerge as banks only as the bridge crosses the stream. The bridge designedly causes them to lie across from each other. One side is set off against the other by the bridge. Nor do the banks stretch along the stream as indifferent border strips of the dry land. With the banks, the bridge brings to the stream the one and the other expanse of the landscape lying behind them. It brings stream and bank and land into each other's neighborhood. The bridge *gathers* the earth as landscape around the stream. Thus it guides and attends the stream through the meadows. Resting upright in the stream's bed, the bridge-piers bear the swing of the arches that leave the stream's waters to run their course. . . . Even where the bridge covers the stream, it holds its flow up to the sky by taking it for a moment under the vaulted gateway and then setting it free once more.[2]

There is no "between" to measure temporal sites before there is a bridge, before the poet has fissured the naive continuity of past, present, and future. On the metaphysical axis, the division of man and the gods has no meaning until there is this "between," until there is some *need for* or *will toward* a bridge that measures this distance.

Crane's poem is full of mythical sites, all of which seem to be synthesized in the same goal. Yet, there is a difference between Atlantis and Cathay; Atlantis represents the "between" and thus its impossibility as a transcendental site or Belle Isle. Atlantis is the "between" that elsewhere is figured as the bridge or the sea:

> O Thou who sleepest on Thyself, apart
> Like ocean athwart lanes of death and birth,
> And all the eddying breath between dost search
> Cruelly with love thy parable of man,—
> Inquisitor! incognizable Word
> Of Eden and the enchained Sepulchre,
> Into thy steep savannahs, burning blue,
> Utter to loneliness the sail is true.
>
> ["**Ave Maria**"]

Columbus discovers his New World in neither Cathay nor America, but in his voyaging between the Old World and the New.[3] The divinity that Columbus invokes is represented by the "teeming span" of the sea and the "orbic wake of thy once whirling feet. . . . " "Cathay" may be the "word" that Columbus brings back to Court, but he already anticipates the ways in which that word will be corrupted:

> —Yet no delirium of jewels! O Fernando,
> Take of that eastern shore, this western sea,
> Yet yield thy God's, thy Virgin's charity!
>
> —Rush down the plenitude, and you shall see
> Isaiah counting famine on this lee!

Yet, Columbus' warnings can have no value for those who have not endured the spiritual *rite de passage* of the voyage, which is accomplished as much by the imagination of the explorer as by his starry navigation. Only in this "between"may the dream of Cathay be truly measured: "For here between two worlds, another, harsh, / This third, of water,. . . . "

Columbus' warning that we must not "Rush down the plenitude" of the New World anticipates Crane's general critique of modern American history, which finds its "civilized" origin in Fernando's impulse toward exploitation. For Crane, American history has not constructed that living "bridge" of the present that would measure the relations of past and future, man and the gods. Epitomizing modern historical movement, the 20th-Century Limited of **"The River"** employs its speed to give the illusion of the particular and manifold converging in a debased unity.[4] Train and River, train *as* river, achieve the same poetic destiny in the **"Gulf,"** which represents in this section of the poem only the destructive element of the sea. In **"Ave Maria,"** the sea threatens death but also promises discovery and thus serves as that space in which man "ventures" his being. In **"The River,"** there are no tidal movements to the modern flow that ends only in the boundless sea:

> The River, spreading, flows—and spends your
>     dream.
> What are you, lost within this tideless spell?
> You are your father's father, and the stream—
> A liquid theme that floating niggers swell.

When Crane writes, "You are your father's father," he is not referring to the sort of poetic inversion of genealogy that Stephen Dedalus discusses in *Ulysses.* Crane's lines betray no sense of the poetic genius as "the father of all his race" and thus his father's father, even though this Joycean notion has some similarities with Crane's own poetic goals elsewhere in *The Bridge.* In this river, "you are your father's father," because all proper historical and ontological distinctions have been blurred and confused. The goal of the river merely parodies the poet's own spiritual aim to discover something that endures, a center that will hold:

> Poised wholly on its dream, a mustard glow
> Tortured with history, its one will—flow!
> —The Passion spreads in wide tongues, choked
>     and
>   slow,
> Meeting the Gulf, hosannas silently below.

In **"Cape Hatteras,"** Crane expresses the destructive will of modern history in terms of a literal assault on heaven. The "new verities" and "new inklings" that hum in the "dynamos" define the "blind ecstasy" of a will to destroy life as a system of differences. Crane links the modern worship of sheer Power to the human yearning to overcome spatiotemporal bonds. Crane's argument in this section recalls Nietzsche's definition of "nihilism" as the hatred (*ressentiment*) of life itself that compels man to invert his creative powers into a will to nothingness:

> The history of philosophy is a secret raging against the pre-conditions of life, against the value feelings of life, against partisanship in favor of life. Philosophers have never hesitated to affirm a world provided it contradicted this world and furnished them with a pretext for speaking ill of this world. It has been hitherto the grand school of slander; and it has imposed itself to such an extent that today our science, which proclaims itself the advocate of life, has accepted the basic slanderous position and treated this world as apparent, this chain of causes as merely phenomenal. What is it really that hates here?[5]

Whitman's "eyes, like the Great Navigator's without ship," represent a mythic vision in direct opposition to modern man's sight of himself as a fully determined creature: "Seeing himself an atom in a shroud—/ Man hears himself an engine in a cloud!" What Whitman "sees" is quite predictably the rich variety of a world that urban man is rapidly obliterating:

> Gleam from the great stones of each prison crypt
> Of canyoned traffic . . . Confronting the
>     Exchange,
> Surviving in a world of stocks,—they also range
> Across the hills where second timber strays
> Back over Connecticut farms, abandoned
>     pastures,—
> Sea eyes and tidal, undenying, bright with myth!

Whitman's vision is "tidal, undenying, bright with myth," because it brings society and nature into dynamic relation. For Crane, Whitman's attention to the particularities of human and natural experience is a poetic mode of "bridging" that he himself would approximate. Whitman does not offer a simple pastoral escape from social corruptions, but he "confronts" the Exchange and still "survives" "in a world of stocks."

In a similar sense, Crane does not want to eliminate modern technology, but merely deromanticize the myth of the machine by appropriating man's mechanical inventions to serve his spiritual needs: "Machinery will tend to lose its sensational glamour and appear in its true subsidiary order in human life as use and continual poetic allusion subdue its novelty. . . . The power and beauty of machinery . . . can not act creatively in our lives until, like the unconscious, nervous responses of our bodies, its connotations emanate from within—forming as spontaneous a terminology of poetic reference as the bucolic world of pasture, plow, and barn."[6] Like Emerson, Crane considers man to be the poetic interpreter of nature's hieroglyphic script, and by means of his interpretations man liberates nature to its own creative, metamorphic powers. Man "improves upon" nature only by allowing nature to realize its spirituality in and through the project of human be-ing in the world:

> Stars scribble on our eyes the frosty sagas,
> The gleaming cantos of unvanquished space . . .

. . . . .

> Remember, Falcon-Ace,
> Thou hast there in thy wrist a Sanskrit charge
> To conjugate infinity's dim marge—
> Anew . . . !

The very pulse of man, the throb of his blood in the wrist, is a "Sanskrit charge" to mark this between of the earth and the sky, of beings and Being, that constitutes man's being in time.

Modern man has lost the poet's sense of this "measure-taking" of man and nature, city and country. Crane's aviators recall only ironically the visionary flights of Columbus or Whitman in "Passage to India." The planes themselves figure the destruction that man has brought upon his own nature in trying to "splinter Space" and thus destroy the "between" that is invoked by the poet as the true ontological bridge. The battle is initially represented as an attack by the aviators on the clouds themselves, recalling the Titans' vain assaults on heaven: "Up-chartered choristers of their own speeding / They, cavalcade on escapade, sheer Cumulus—/ Lay siege and hurdle Cirrus down the skies!" But the real war is conducted by man against his own nature. The downward spirals of the planes suggest a dance, but one that only ironically recalls the rhythms of life and death in **"The Dance."** Here we have only a *danse macabre*:

> Giddily spiralled
>          gauntlets, upturned, unlooping
> In guerilla sleights, trapped in combustion gyr-
> Ing, dance and curdled depth
>             down whizzing
> Zodiacs, dashed
>       (now nearing fast the Cape!)
>         down the gravitation's
>           vortex into crashed
> . . . . dispersion . . . into mashed and shapeless
>    de-
>     bris. . . .
> By Hatteras bunched the beached heap of high
>    bravery!

The predominant alliteration in these final lines suggests the ironic unity that the planes have achieved in their "dispersion." Crane struggles to bring destruction and creation, death and birth, into some new relation, which reveals his Romantic impulse to find order in and through dialectical differences. Thus Whitman holds the "heights" most surely "at junctions elegiac, there, of speed / With vast eternity." Crane finds "eternity" only in the "junction" of death and life, past and future, that enables man to measure his relation to Being and to time. Whitman is the father of "our Myth," whose "boldest heel" echoes Elohim's "sounding heel" in **"Ave Maria,"** but not for reasons of his originality or transcending genius: "Not greatest, thou,—not first, nor last,—but near / And onward yielding past my utmost year." Whitman provides the poet with his own imaginative eucharist (*Panis Angelicus*), because like the hoboes of **"The River"** and the "mendicants in public places" he partici-

pates in the "dayspring's spreading arc." As the poet who celebrates man's temporal situation as the proper site of his spiritual dwelling, Whitman serves as Crane's democratic muse: "Whitman . . . better than any other, was able to coördinate those forces in America which seem most intractable, fusing them into a universal vision which takes on additional significance as time goes on."[7]

The rapid pace of the modern world is based on the destruction of time and thus the destruction of the earth as such: "Years of the Modern! Propulsions toward what capes?" The poet's purpose is to reappropriate the misdirected energy of the modern age in order to establish an authentic human community on earth and in time. Crane wrote to Waldo Frank: "The validity of a work of art is situated in contemporary reality to the extent that the artist must honestly anticipate the realization of his vision in 'action' (as an actively operating principle of communal works and faith), and I don't mean by this that his procedure requires any bona finde evidences directly and personally signalled, nor even any physical signs or portents."[8] Modern America pits history against nature; technological man is never "timely" for Crane, because he destroys the very ground of "time" that is the tidal and seasonal movements of the body of nature. The pioneers initiate this historical destruction of what is most "timely" in themselves:

> A dream called Eldorado was his town,
>   It rose up shambling in the nuggets' wake,
> It had no charter but a promised crown
>    Of claims to stake.

The "charter" for this dream is a crown of thorns that promises the crucifixion of nature and the barren spoils reaped by her murderers:

> But we,—too late, too early, howsoever—
>   Won nothing out of fifty-nine—those years—
> But gilded promise, yielded to us never,
>    And barren tears . . .

The mother's appeal to her first-born son, the voyager, is to "come back to Indiana—not too late!" The "timeliness" of the poet is his discovery of human being in time and the nature of that being as a function of the earth's time and man's dwelling in it. What Heidegger writes of Rilke seems equally appropriate for Crane in this context: "What Rilke calls Nature is not contrasted with history. Above all, it is not intended as the subject matter of natural science. Nor is Nature opposed to art. It is the ground for history and art and nature in the narrower sense. In the word Nature as used here, there echoes still the earlier word *phusis*, equated also with *zoe*, which we translate 'life.' In early thought, however, the nature of life is not conceived in biological terms, but as the *phusis*, that which arises. In line 8 of our poem, 'Nature' is also called 'Life.' Nature, Life here designate Being in the sense of all beings as a whole."[9]

Crane's poet and voyager resist technological man's lust for dominion and self-assertion by submitting themselves to the natural energies that define them. The Dionysian ritual of **"The Dance"** is the poet's effort to experience the Willof nature in itself as a creative principle, an intoxicating power that negates the determinism of the modern age. Crane quite explicitly approximates Nietzsche's sense of the revel as a sudden liberation:

> Now the slave emerges as a freeman; all the rigid, hostile walls which either necessity or despotism has erected between men are shattered. Now that the gospel of universal harmony is sounded, each individual becomes not only reconciled to his fellow but actually at one with him—as though the veil of Maya had been torn apart and there remained only shreds floating before the vision of mystical Oneness. Man now expresses himself through song and dance as the member of a higher community; he has forgotten how to walk, how to speak, and is on the brink of taking wing as he dances.[10]

This is the self-abrogating freedom that Crane had attempted to express in **"The Wine Menagerie,"** in which the surfaces of an artificial world are rent to reveal:

> New thresholds, new anatomies! Wine talons
> Build freedom up about me and distill
> This competence—to travel in a tear
> Sparkling alone, within another's will.

In **"The Dance,"** this Dionysian power achieves its highest expression in the rhythms of apparently intractable forces. The poet becomes Maquokeeta, his enemies, Pocahontas, and the very earth that their rituals of procreation and destruction celebrate. The poet identifies himself with the body of America as he measures the rhythms of the seasons, which are invoked as the basis for that time in which man lives truly:

> Thewed of the levin, thunder-shod and lean,
> Lo, through what infinite seasons dost thou
>     gaze—
> Across what bivouacs of thine angered slain,
> And see'st thy bride immortal in the maize!
>
> Totem and fire-gall, slumbering pyramid—
> Though other calendars now stack the sky,
> Thy freedom is her largesse, Prince, and hid
> On paths thou knewest best to claim her by.

The discovery of this natural time, of man's "timeliness," involves a form of forgetting as well. It seems especially ironic that *The Bridge* should be counted a failure for being insufficiently "historical," because Crane's very effort to transform American history is also an attempt to destroy the hold of that history on contemporary man.[11] **"Van Winkle"** makes explicit Crane's desire to liberate America from its imprisonment in "what was":

> *And Rip forgot the office hours,*
>     *and he forgot the pay;*
> *Van Winkle sweeps a tenement*
>     *way down on Avenue A,—*

Like the hoboes and mendicants outside of time, Van Winkle escapes the historical determinants of a culture that lives in the evasive future of unrealizable dreams. Memory as well can serve to alienate man from his present and condemn him to an anguished, life-denying nostalgia for what is lost:

> So memory, that strikes a rhyme out of a box,
> Or splits a random smell of flowers through
>     glass—
> Is it the whip stripped from the lilac tree
> One day in spring that my father took to me,
> Or is it the Sabbatical, unconscious smile
> My mother almost brought me once from church
> And once only, as I recall—?

Whether it be the father's "whip" or the mother's "Sabbatical, unconscioussmile," the poet's memory of punishment or unrealized love only corrupts the present and saps his will. The rush to obliterate the present in **"The River"** is shown to be as much a function of an overly historical culture as of an excessively progressive culture: both destroy "time" as Crane understands it. As Nietzsche writes in *The Use and Abuse of History:*

> One who cannot leave himself behind on the threshold of the moment and forget the past, who cannot stand on a single point, like a goddess of victory, without fear or giddiness, will never know what happiness is; and, worse still, will never do anything to make others happy. The extreme case would be the man without any power to forget who is condemned to see "becoming" everywhere. Such a man no longer believes in himself or his own existence; he sees everything fly past in an eternal succession and loses himself in the stream of becoming. At last, like the logical disciple of Heraclitus, he will hardly dare to raise his finger. Forgetfulness is a property of all action, just as not only light but darkness is bound up with the life of every organism.[12]

Interpretations of *The Bridge* that attempt to read it according to traditional models for an historical or mythic consciousness fail to recognize that the poem itself is an extended attack on the very idea of American history, whose obsession with the past or future has exhausted the synergy of the present:

> Macadam, gun-grey as the tunny's belt,
> Leaps from Far Rockaway to Golden Gate. . . .
> Keep hold of that nickel for car-change, Rip,—
> Have you got your *"Times"*—?
> And hurry along, Van Winkle—it's getting late!

Characteristically doubling his key images in order to emphasize the differences between the superficiality of urban life and the poet's spiritual vision, Crane uses these lines proleptically to anticipate the more authentic harmony of time and space in **"The Dance":**

> We danced, O Brave, we danced beyond their
>     farms,
> In cobalt desert closures made our vows . . .

Now is the strong prayer folded in thine arms,
The serpent with the eagle in the boughs.

And this coupling of time and space in the dance is ech-oed later in Crane's renewed sense of Whitman's "Open Road": "To course that span of consciousness thou'st named / The Open Road—thy vision is reclaimed! / What heritage thou'st signalled to our hands!" (**"Cape Hatteras"**). Crane's very poetic style relies on ironic allusions, doubled images, and prolepses to suggest the "temporality" of the poem as bridge in the very rhythms of writing. The origins and ends of the poem are made to serve the architecture that constitutes the present of the poetic activity: "For poetry is an architectural art, based not on Evolution or the idea of progress, but on the ar-ticulation of the contemporary human consciousness *sub specie aeternitatis,* and inclusive of all readjustments incident to science and other shifting factors related to that consciousness."[13]

The past—the lost mythic impulse, the corruptions of the pioneers, Whitman's prophetic vision—and the future—the acceleration of man's self-destruction, the poet's own aim to restore an American *mythos*—are appropriately divided within themselves by positive and negative po-tentialities. The poet brings these potentialities into relief by attempting to employ them in his own architecture by forgetting, recalling, metamorphosing, and prophesying. Thus the "between" of the bridge realizes itself as a "measure-taking" of human being in the present by means of its own mode of poetic appropriation.[14] Unlike the antiquarians who live only to deny life for the sake of the dead past or the "egoists" who yearn for a utopia in re-venge against their time-bound existences, Crane's poet builds that present in which the past and future assume a meaningful relation to life. Like Nietzsche, Crane recog-nizes the dangers of an "excess of history" that threaten man's fundamental need to live in a world of time: "If there is no constructive impulse behind the historical one, if the clearance of rubbish is not merely to leave the ground free for the hopeful living future to build its house, if justice alone be supreme, the creative instinct is sapped and discouraged."[15]

Crane's architecture of the "contemporary conscious-ness" is based on the creative energy of the body, which in his moments of greatest Dionysian intoxication the poet experiences as both vast natural forces and man's own sexual potency.[16] Like Williams, Crane insists upon "No ideas but in things" and attempts to renew contact with natural things by using poetic language to produce certain affective resonances, "like the unconscious ner-vous responses of our bodies," in which "connotations emanate from within."[17] Poetry is thus a spontaneous dance in which man expresses and celebrates his most fundamental needs, desires, and drives. "Spontaneity" for Crane, however, is not merely the uncontrolled overflow of powerful feelings; the poet must first break down those intervening fictions that "splinter space" or split "a random smell of flowers through glass." In **"Modern Poetry,"** Crane tries to argue against the "familiar con-tention that science is inimical to poetry" by insisting upon their different epistemologies: "That 'truth' which science pursues is radically different from the metaphori-cal, extra-logical 'truth' of the poet."[18] Yet, *The Bridge* makes it clear that the poet "can absorb the machine" only by violating scientific categories with his own mode of poetic thinking. The dislocations of the poem follow the "logic of metaphor" to expose the superficiality of certain modes of causal and intentional thinking that govern modern man's historical determinism. The mod-ern historian records selected "events" to give the illu-sion of coherence and order; Crane *uses* experience to inspire that poetry through which man expresses his be-ing. Like Williams in *Spring and All,* Crane struggles to "raise to some approximate co-extension with the uni-verse" wherein the poet learns: "To perfect the ability to record at the moment when consciousness is enlarged by the sympathies and the unity of imagination which the imagination gives, to practice skill in recording the force moving, then to know it, in the largeness of its propor-tions."[19]

Thus Crane's poetic "object" is not an empirical "thing" purified of ideas, but the thing-in-itself: the creative force in which natural and verbal signs originate and endure. Most often critics have assumed Crane's Logos or "incognizable Word" to be an ineffable spiritual unity for which the poet vainly strives. But Crane's Word is the measure-taking of poetry that constitutes the present of the "between," the bridge. Word, Myth, Bridge, Atlantis—these apparently transcendent ideals or su-preme fictions are defined repeatedly as metaphors for the differential energy governing man's being in the sea-sonal timeliness of the world:

> Swift peal of *secular* light, *intrinsic* Myth
> Whose fell unshadow is death's utter wound,—
> O River-throated—iridescently upborne
> Through the bright *drench* and *fabric of our veins;*
> With white escarpments swinging into light,
> Sustained in tears the cities are endowed
> And justified conclamant with *ripe fields*
> *Revolving* through their *harvests* in *sweet torment.*
> 　　　　　　　　["Atlantis," my italics]

The terrible brightness ("fell unshadow") of this Myth is "death's utter wound," because the Myth establishes the enduring nature of man's dwelling on earth. The Myth is in time and of time rather than an effort to escape time, and thus it is a figure for that energy of creation and destruction in which life itself is preserved as a system of differences. Everything converges only ironically:

> Into what multitudinous Verb the suns
> And synergy of waters ever fuse, recast
> In myriad syllables,—Psalm of Cathay!
> O Love, thy white, pervasive Paradigm . . . !

As Pearce and others have suggested, the "multitudinous Verb" is language itself: "The power of human agency is imputed to things which don't actually have them. But don't they really? Crane is asking. Isn't the whole of reality chargedwith the power of agency? And isn't it the peculiar burden of language to reveal that power to us—that power which will prove to be ours, since it is our language? Man, through language, is maker and master of all he surveys, including himself."[20] Yet, Pearce has described the language of technology that betrays man's lust for dominion and assertion over the earth; this is hardly the language of being that Crane would have speak man into his true human dwelling. By the very nature of its inherent differences, this primal language can never be commanded by a single agent or subject. The earth is that "multitudinous Verb" in which "the suns and synergy of waters ever fuse" and thus the Logos that is defined both by fusion and dispersion. As Emerson writes in "The Poet," "we participate the invention of nature" by sharing in this creative enterprise and bringing ourselves and nature into more authentic and vital relation.[21] It is emphatically *not* "our language" that Crane invokes with his Word, but the language of the earth that ought to speak *through* us. The Dionysian energy of nature is never commanded by our words; indeed, in his moments of greatest intoxication, Crane's poet achieves his most profound visions by virtue of his loss of self.[22] Liberated from his historical and physical particularity, the poet becomes his various personae in the poem and ultimately fuses with the bridge as poetic act. As Nietzsche puts it: "No longer the *artist*, he has himself become a *work of art*: the productive power of the whole universe is now manifest in his transport, to the glorious satisfaction of the primordial One. The finest clay, the most precious marble—man—is here kneaded and hewn, and the chisel blows of the Dionysiac world artist are accompanied by the cry of the Eleusinian mystagogues: 'Do you fall on your knees, multitudes, do you divine your creator?'"[23] Crane's "primordial One" is the energy of differences, never a synthesis that would destroy those tensive and productive relations.

Throughout ***The Bridge,*** Crane's various avatars of the feminine principle represent a creativity and fecundity that are coupled properly with destruction and death. Pocahontas focuses these various elements of creative potential; she is the figure of a certain historical "bridge" that measures "the conflict between the two races in this dance" as well as a "common basis of our meeting" as "a star that hangs between day and night."[24] As Crane suggests in his explanatory letter to Kahn, Pocahontas inhabits "the twilight's dim perpetual throne" because she is the measure of time's measuring, the essence of temporality that is the body of the Continent. Relating "day and night" as the poet struggles to measure past and future, she incarnates the differences of the earth's language. She is the goddess of fertility (Ceres) as well as the perpetually unravished "virgin" bride, the "'well-featured but wanton yong girle'" of the epigraph as well as a goddess of sheer nothingness:

> High unto Labrador the sun strikes free
> Her speechless dream of snow, and stirred again,
> She is the torrent and the singing tree;
> And she is virgin to the last of men . . .

These lines echo **"North Labrador,"** in which the "eternal movement toward nothing represents the inhuman remorselessness of Nature"[25]:

> "Has no one come here to win you,
> Or left you with the faintest blush
> Upon your glittering breasts?
> Have you no memories, O Darkly Bright?"

Coupled with Maquokeeta as well as with the "torrent and the singing tree," this cold goddess becomes part of nature's creative power. Crane's "glacier woman" is "squired" "down the sky" to run "the neighing canyons all the spring" as a fertility goddess: "She spouted arms; she rose with maize—to die." Leibowitz may consider Crane's images of cold northern climes as metaphors for nature's blindness to man, but for Crane this will to nothingness is the proper complement of nature's will to survive. Crane's cold goddess certainly betokens death as absolute, but also signifies the power of negation that man may employ creatively to forget the past in order to act or to lose himself and therefore to experience the wholeness of Being.

All the other women in ***The Bridge*** are measured in terms of Pocahontas' capacity to preserve the differential energy of nature. The mother's "Sabbatical, unconscious smile" "flickered through the snow screen" and "Did not return with the kiss in the hall." Here the coldness of the "snow screen" is associated with the smile that does "not return"; the mother is a reminder not only of the son's alienation from his family but from that history characterized by its evanescence and unfulfilled dreams. On the other hand, the goddess of the Continent gives of herself always anew in her seasonal and geographical variety:

> Youngsters with eyes like fjords, old reprobates
> With racetrack jargon,—dotting immensity
> They lurk across her, knowing her yonder breast
> Snow-silvered, sumac-stained or smoky blue—
> Is past the valley-sleepers, south or west.
> **["The River"]**

The poverty of the mother's love is measured against this bounty of the earth that always exceeds our desires, always escapes "the print that bound her name." The unrealized "Sabbatical, unconscious smile" of the mother in **"Van Winkle"** is redeemed in **"Indiana"** by "A homeless squaw," "passing on a stumbling jade." Everything about this squaw suggests the differences ennobled in Pocahontas by the poet but degraded by civilized man:

> Perhaps a halfbreed. On her slender back
>   She cradled a babe's body, riding without rein.
> Her eyes, strange for an Indian's, were not black
>   But sharp with pain
> And like twin stars.

The mother's smile is almost brought to the son "only once, as I recall," but here the gesture of the pioneer woman, who holds up her son to this "halfbreed," is rewarded by "that smile across her shoulder" that "Will still endear her."

The eyes of these mythic women are compared often with the stars, a motif that is made even more explicit in **"Southern Cross,"** in which the poet attempts to create his own image of creativity: "Eve—wraith of my unloved seed!" The "nameless Woman of the South," however, is part of the namelessness of God, whose very silence is known only in the various and conflicting interpretations to which it gives birth. Like the other lyrics in **"Three Songs,"** **"Southern Cross"** explores the discrepancy between the ideal and the poet's false conception of that ideal.[26] As Thomas Vogler suggests: "The consummation the poet desires is doomed, even before he considers the problem of naming the woman, for she is apart, 'High, cool, / wide from the slowly smoldering fire / Of lower heavens,—.' The distance and high coolness, can imply the separation between fallen man and Eve in the garden."[27] Yet in spite of the poet's false conception of her, the "woman" of **"Southern Cross"** recalls quite clearly the mythic complex of differences that Pocahontas represents. The Southern Cross is, of course, a star formation that aids navigators, and the poet employs this notion to metaphorize the Cross as a woman of both heaven and earth. The feminine principle of nature's creative energy is celebrated variously as "simian Venus, homeless Eve," fallen from her starry height only to be figured in the "long wake of phosphor, / iridescent / Furrow of all our travel" of the sea below, in which she is both violated and realized:

> And the wash—
> All night the water combed you with black
> Insolence. You crept out shimmering,
>     accomplished.
> Water rattled that stinging coil, your
> Rehearsed hair—docile, alas, from many arms.

The "nameless woman of the South" is a composite of "Eve! Magdalene! / or Mary"; she is whore and virgin, sea-siren and "Madre María" of the "mantle's ageless blue," temporal woman and eternal goddess. Becoming visible only against the darkness of the night or the blackness of the sea, the starry light of this goddess accomplishes that confrontation of differences that is Crane's own aim as the conjugator of infinity's dim marge. If the poet in this song fails to preserve or even incarnate his vision, then he fails by virtue of his incapacity to accept the "illogic" of what *is:* the contradictions that define his muse. The poet confesses in the opening lines: "I wanted you, nameless Woman of the South, / No wraith, but utterly—as still more alone / The Southern Cross takes night / And lifts her girdles from her, one by one—/ High, cool, / wide from the slowly smoldering fire / Of lower heavens,—/ vaporous scars!"[28] The poet's desire for the utter possession of this nameless divinity implicates him in the modern technological urge for dominion over nature's energies. For Crane, the principle of divinity cannot be preserved in its heavenly height and coldness, but is realized only as it descends as "fire" and "blood" in the sea's "long wake of phosphor."[29]

The two other songs suggest the ways in which the poet's desire "utterly" to possess the essential energy of nature reflects the modern age's burlesque of life. All the sexual imagery in **"National Winter Garden"** leads toward an empty consummation: "The world's one flagrant, sweating cinch." As the title of this poem suggests, this hot jazz world is in fact a cold and lifeless realm that only mimes the Dionysian intoxication of **"The Dance."** The purpose of this sexual rite is the destruction of proportions and relations: "legs waken salads in the brain" and the dancer, despite her glittering garb, is "whiter than snow" and reveals a "sandstone grey between." The climax of the dance is in fact a complete collapse that repudiates the rich vitality of sexuality it presumes to celebrate:

> We wait that writhing pool, her pearls collapsed,
> —All but her belly buried in the floor;
> And the lewd trounce of a final muted beat!
> We flee her spasm through a fleshless door. . . .

The music here is "A tom-tom scrimmage with a somewhere violin, / Some cheapest echo of them all—begins," which is hardly the jazz-poetry of the roof-top garden scene in **"For the Marriage of Faustus and Helen":**

> Where cuckoos clucked to finches
> Above the deft catastrophes of drums.
> While titters hailed the groans of death
> Beneath gyrating awnings I have seen
> The incunabula of the divine grotesque.
> This music has a reassuring way.

In **"Faustus and Helen,"** the jazz approximates the "measure-taking" of the poet, who enables us to confront death with a Chaplinesque pirouetting, an ecstasy of life that acknowledges change and mortality as the very resources of our intoxication. In **"National Winter Garden,"** the dancer enables us to be "reborn" only by exposing to us the emptiness and futility of our desires for fulfillment that she represents:

> Yet, to the empty trapeze of your flesh,
> O Magdalene, each comes back to die alone.
> Then you, the burlesque of our lust—and faith,
> Lug us back lifeward—bone by infant bone.

**"Virginia"** burlesques the poet's desire for the divine, which in **"Southern Cross"** he can see in the phosphor wake only as a "fallen Eve." Trying to transmute the quotidian and meretricious world of the modern into the place of some renewed spirituality, the poet ends only by increasing the distance between the secular and divine. Once again, the poet frustrates and corrupts his vision by seeking to possess it totally, to "name" it: "O blue-eyed Mary with the claret scarf, / Saturday Mary, mine!" Degraded to an office girl mockingly adorned with the colors of heaven and earth, Crane's goddess is reduced to an object for the lust of the boss or the poet. By way of contrast, we might recall **"The Dance,"** in which heaven's blue and earth's red are brought into an active relation: "Now snaps the flint in every tooth; red fangs / And splay tongues thinly busy the blue air." The image of the serpent snapping the air represents that "margin" or "between" of the earth and the sky that Crane seeks to determine. Brought into relation by the dance, the earth and the sky are only further divided in **"Virginia"**: "O Mary, leaning from the high wheat tower, / Let down your golden hair" and "Out of the way-up nickel-dime tower shine, / Cathedral Mary, / shine!—." And yet this poem suggests a method whereby the poet might begin to "absorb" modern urban life in his larger mythic vision. Crane had a preference for the word "synergy," which is a medical term that describes the correlated action of different parts of the body to produce a complex movement. In this lyric, Crane extends his social criticism but also offers the reader a series of images that seem modern equivalents of the synergetic rhythms of **"The Dance"**:

> It's high carillon
> From the popcorn bells!
> Pigeons by the million—
> And Spring in Prince Street
> Where green figs gleam
> By oyster shells!

The suggestive sexuality of the figs and oysters is complemented by the poetic contiguity of what is still ripening ("green figs") and what has been used ("oyster shells"). What is to come "gleams" only in relation to what has been, the imagistic coupling itself constituting the sexual potency of the present. The poet discovers a threshold of myth in the very "logic" of his metaphors, which begin to invade the city and displace modern man's sense of his contingent existence. The metropolitan god seems to be Chance—"Crap-shooting gangs in Bleecker reign,"[30] but the poet buries Chance in the luxuriant flowers of his own imaginative vision, which seems to initiate some renewed contact between man and nature:

> High in the noon of May
> On cornices of daffodils
> The slender violets stray.
> Crap-shooting gangs in Bleecker reign,
> Peonies with pony manes—
> Forget-me-nots at windowpanes. . . .

Thus Crane's goddess in *The Bridge* ought to be understood as the principle of differences, Dionysian energy, or *synergos* that is figured in the central symbol of the bridge itself.[31] The double movement of the poem's imagery relies upon the differences between the past and the future, the earth/sea and heaven/sky, death and renewal that are the main thematic co-ordinates of the poem. Crane's aim is to employ this stylistic tension as a sort of subliminal reinforcement of his main argument. The present is not merely a vanishing moment in a progressive or regressive series of events; the present is not an experience that is recorded passively by the poet. The present is an architecture: an active measuring of the past in terms of the future as well as an appropriation of the monuments of the past and our desires for the future for use in the construction of a site for human dwelling. Crane criticizes the modern age for pursuing an historical course that is itself the destruction of "history" as the basis for man's spiritual dwelling on earth. As we have seen, everything in this modern world is a rush toward the satisfaction of desire, the collapsing of distances, and the annihilation of nature. The poet implicates himself in this desperate desire to escape life and deny the differences whereby he is constituted. Man's desire to "possess" the "nameless" reveals his hatred of life in his struggle to arrest the perpetual metamorphoses whereby "living" as such is preserved.

In similar terms, Heidegger distinguishes the building that enables man to reveal his own nature and destiny as the one who dwells on the earth from mere construction for its own sake. The engineering of commercial bridges for mere movement and transport aims secretly at the destruction of space and the obliteration of boundaries. There is an ironic "bridge" of telecommunication wires in **"The River"**: "The last bear, shot drinking in the Dakotas / Loped under wires that span the mountain stream. / Keen instruments, strung to a vastprecision / Bind town to town and dream to ticking dream." For Crane and Heidegger, however, the poetic bridge involves that constructive act in which space, as both ontological and historical, achieves its proper dimensions:

> Only things that are locations in this manner allow for spaces. What the word for space, *Raum, Rum,* designates is said by its ancient meaning. *Raum* means a place cleared or freed for settlement or lodging. A space is something that has been made room for, something that is cleared and free, namely within a boundary, Greek *peras*. A boundary is not that at which something stops but, as the Greeks recognized, the boundary is that from which something *begins its presencing*. That is why the concept is that of *horismos,* that is, the horizon, the boundary. Space is in essence that for which room has been made, that which is let into its bounds. That for which room is made is always granted and hence joined, that is, gathered, by virtue of a location, that is, by such a thing as the bridge. *Accordingly, spaces receive their being from locations and not from "space."*[32]

For Crane, the old Quaker Meeting House established such a space of human dwelling, but as "the New Avalon Hotel" that spiritual space becomes a metaphor for modern man's perpetual homelessness in what Henry James termed this "hotel-civilization":

> This was the Promised Land, and still it is
> To the persuasive suburban land agent
> In bootleg roadhouses where the gin fizz
> Bubbles in time to Hollywood's new love-nest
>         pageant.
> Fresh from the radio in the old Meeting House
> (Now the New Avalon Hotel) volcanoes roar
> A welcome to highsteppers that no mouse
> Who saw the Friends there ever heard before.

Thus the poet descends in **"The Tunnel"** to an underground world in which this modern frenzy is reduced to an infernal "unity": "The monotone / of motion is the sound / of other faces, also underground—." Repeating the strains of the 20th-Century Limited, the subway train objectifies what modern America has been accomplishing: the denial of the earth and man's life in it. The Daemonic force of the modern age intends the very destruction of time: "the muffled slaughter of a day in birth—/ O cruelly to inoculate the brinking dawn / With antennae toward worlds that glow and sink;—." One must be careful in reading these extremely condensed lines to follow Crane's poetic logic or else mistake the syntactic subject or antecedent. Vogler reads these lines in terms of the poet's desire for vision: "His vision of 'worlds that glow and sink' is balanced on a 'brinking dawn' that can never become full day."[33] But the agent of this stanza is the Daemon of the subway, a sort of infernal Underpower. This Daemon "inoculates" the "brinking dawn," which in the natural world measures diurnal time, with "antennae toward worlds that glow and sink." Crane plays upon the root of the verb "inoculate," *in* (in) + *oculus* (eye), perhaps to suggest the Cyclopean eye of the subway train as a sort of surrogate sun. "Inoculation" is also a botanical term for the engrafting of an eye or bud from one plant to another. The poet has been moving toward an imaginative mode of appropriation whereby he might "graft" the objects of the urban world back onto the natural, organic stalk; but in the subway, he himself tracks the inverted appropriation of nature by this technological culture. The "day in birth" illuminates only the decline of the West: "worlds that glow and sink."

The Daemon of **"The Tunnel"** subordinates the life of this subterranean antiterra to its own blind will:

> O caught like pennies beneath soot and steam,
> Kiss of our agony thou gatherest;
> Condensed, thou takest all—shrill ganglia
> Impassioned with some song we fail to keep.

Ironically anticipating the concluding lines of this section, in which the spiritual gathering of the Logos is invoked, this Daemon gathers the "kiss of our agony" only to "condense" it unto itself, a nerve center ("shrill ganglia")driven by its own destructive force. The resurrection of the poet from this world is expressed in images that begin to restore the proportions and boundaries of the natural world:

> And yet, like Lazarus, to feel the slope,
> The sod and billow breaking,—lifting ground,
> —A sound of waters bending astride the sky
> Unceasing with some Word that will not die . . . !

The poet himself intones a song that displaces the nervous tremors of the subway's noise and that we *cannot* fail to keep, because it is in its very nature "some Word that will not die." The world to which he returns still remains inverted, but he has initiated his return by establishing the familiar loci of natural energies: the sod of the prairies, the billows of the sea, the sky of the divine, and the language that binds men to these elements.

Everything in *The Bridge* is defined in relation to the central figuration of the bridge itself as the "measure-taking" of human beings and Being. Most critics read the "Atlantis" of the poem to be a sort of fictive ideal that governs the human voyage in a world that has lost any contact with true divinity. Unquestionably, Crane himself is driven by this desire for an impossible consummation and to create some "nameless" presence in which all things would be reconciled. Yet like Poe in *Eureka,* Crane recognizes that such divinity may be known only in its dispersed variety and that the purity of the "white, pervasive Paradigm" in itself is merely a cold abstraction.[34] Crane introduces **"Atlantis"** with a passage from Plato that suggests "harmony and system" might govern ideally the dissonance of temporal life, but Crane himself makes this Platonic vision of perfection serve man's tragic *agon.* The "bridge" of **"Atlantis"** mocks abstract idealism with Nietzschean discords: "In order to understand the difficult phenomenon of Dionysiac art directly, we must now attend to the supreme significance of *musical dissonance.* The delight created by tragic myth has the same origin as the delight dissonance in music creates. The primal Dionysiac delight, experienced even in the presence of pain, is the source common to both music and tragic myth."[35] Nietzsche argues that the "anti-Dionysiac" artist "tried to resolve the tragic dissonance" and thus followed the scientific faith "that the world can be corrected through knowledge and that life should be guided by science; that it is actually in a position to confine man within the narrow circle of soluble tasks, where he can say cheerfully to life: 'I want you. You are worth knowing.'"[36] We have already seen how such a theory of knowledge as possession represents the will to destruction that characterizes the modern age.

Giving up the desire to "represent" or "understand" the divine energy that pervades all things but which in itself remains a nameless abstraction, Crane turns instead to the poetic "performance" wherein Being is enabled to "speak" in and through men.[37] The dissonance of the performance expresses the living and present man in his *radical* becoming: not man's anxious and passive submission to the fleeting moment but his willful participation in life's creative energy. What speaks through man also speaks in nature; it is language, but not merely the words of *homo faber.* What speaks is the nature of language, the creative principle that remains in itself nameless only to appear in its various avatars: Dionysus, Woman, Will, Sea, Dance, Bridge. The creative energy that is given poetic voice in *The Bridge* is thus never reducible to a single name; it endures by virtue of its transformations and manifests itself in its very dismemberment. As Heidegger writes: "Because man *is,* in his enduring dimension, his being must now and again be measured out. That requires a measure which involves at once the whole dimension in one. To discern this measure, to gauge it as the measure, and to accept it as the measure, means for the poet to make poetry. Poetry is this measure-taking—its taking, indeed, for the dwelling of man."[38] Poetry affirms the enduring in man's being by commanding the repeated measure-taking whereby man's being is made to appear. Crane begins his poem with the clear aim of establishing or recovering that which is enduring in human nature: "a myth to God," "Unfractioned idiom, immaculate sigh of stars," "condense eternity." But what endures is finally the bridge that actively measures the relations of life and death, beings and Being, time and eternity.

Like Nietzsche's Eternal Recurrence, Crane's bridge affirms life's creative energy in its manifold differences as that which endures and recurs. As Heidegger reads Nietzsche: "Eternal Recurrence is the inexhaustible fullness of joyful-painful life."[39] We have argued that Crane attacks modern America for its secret aversion to time, for its desire to escape the transience of the present in lust for the future or nostalgia for the past. Thus Crane's modern characters are never "timely," but always "too late" or "too early." *The Bridge* is "unhistorical" in its effort to "forget" the historical burden that compels man to hate his own existence; *The Bridge* is "super-historical" in its effort to affirm human and natural transience as that radical becoming "which gives existence an eternal and stable character." This is precisely what the "hypothesis" of Nietzsche's Eternal Recurrence offers man as a joyful wisdom.[40] Heidegger's reading is again useful: "This *yes* to time is the will that would have transience abide, would not have it degraded to nihility. But how can transience abide? Only in such a way that, as transience, it does not just constantly pass, but always comes to be. It would abide only in such a way that transience and what ceases to be return as the selfsame in its coming."[41] The "failure" of Crane's vision in *The Bridge* has been stressed by critics who cannot untangle the man's biography from his poetic aims. The anxiety of the poem is inescapable, but it functions as the other pole of the joyous intoxication that syncopates the dissonance. Crane wrote to Selden Rodman: "The poem, as a whole, is, I think, an affirmation of experience, and to that extent is 'positive' rather than 'negative' in the sense that *The Waste Land* is negative."[42] *The Bridge* is an effort to affirm experience and discover within man's temporal environment the creative resource that would redeem us from our homeless longing for some desert Belle Isle.

Joseph Riddel has suggested that the poem's very structure and movement express something akin to Nietzsche's Eternal Recurrence. Although he emphasizes the anguish of the poet's necessary repetitions, Riddel recognizes that Crane wants to transform "history's incessant motion into the myth of an on-going cycle, realized through the voice of the Dionysian self. Crane indicates, thereby, that the cycle (and history) is manifest only in the coming and going of the individual self—the poet as word and as flesh, the poet as sufferer returned again and again to the deathly landscape of history's changes and the perfidies attendant upon his role as the keeper of the Word, the ground of being."[43] In "Atlantis," the bridge itself becomes a hieroglyph whose "reading" now and again constitutes the visionary act of poetry. The "inviolate curve" of the "seagull's wings" in **"To Brooklyn Bridge"** is associated at the end with the "eyes" of the poet and reader:

> Sheerly the eyes, like seagulls stung with rime—

> Slit and propelled by glistening fins of light—
> Pick biting way up towering looms that press
> Sidelong with flight of blade on tendon blade
> —Tomorrows into yesteryear—and link
> What cipher-script of time no traveller reads
> But who, through smoking pyres of love and death,
> Searches the timeless laugh of mythic spears.

Crane's imagery stresses the violation of the "inviolate curve" by relying on such words as "stung," "slit," "fins," "pick biting way," "blade on tendon blade." The violation of the pure white Paradigm is the very process of the poem and the act that resituates the Ideal within the transience of the world. The bridge thus leads us "from time's realm" only to return us more fully to time; the bridge is that measure of the "between" wherein time and space achieve their natures. The "Everpresence, beyond time" is the creative energy that endures only within the movements of human time and that is manifest only in the dissonance of its Word as words. The poet knows the "Cathay" that marks the end of voyaging has been displaced by Atlantis, the "between" of the bridge, that measures man's voyaging as his proper site, his true dwelling on the earth:

> Is it Cathay,
> Now pity steeps the grass and rainbows ring
> The serpent with the eagle in the leaves . . . ?
> Whispers antiphonal in azure swing.

Zarathustra's own image for the wisdom of Eternal Recurrence—the eagle with the serpent—replaces the original dream of Cathay.[44] And in Crane's last words, the dissonant method of the poem is condensed as the final symbol of the vernal bridge.

Critics frequently conclude that Crane expresses in *The Bridge* a desire for mythic vision that is never achieved and by its nature unrealizable. Yet, *The Bridge* does achieve its "vision" of the divine repeatedly, but systematically dismantles its epiphanies in order to repeat and renew them. Each of the individual poems has its visionary moment, although few achieve the ecstatic intoxication of **"The Dance"** or the incantatory enthusiasm of **"Ave Maria."** Yet even in those poems that seem most concerned with modern America's corruptions, such as **"National Winter Garden"** or **"The Tunnel,"** there are moments in which negativity is transformed into poetic knowledge and insight. Each poem enacts the dissonance that governs the entire work, repeating not only key images and themes but also recalling the differential energy that governs man's being. As Riddel argues: "Crane's long poems do not develop, they recur. They pivot upon the external event, which the poet is constantly reliving. The persona of *The Bridge* is no protagonist, is involved in no *agon* except the recurrent event of his quest and failure."[45] Viewed in this way, Crane's "epic" differs fundamentally from those long poems that rely on a progressive, episodic structure to direct the educational process of a protagonsit or hero. **"Atlantis"** is neither the *telos* of the poem nor the poet's final confession of defeat and yearning, but the dissonant chord in which the dance of the poem is made to endure in its repetition.

1 Quotations from Crane's poetry are made from *The Complete Poems and Selected Letters of Hart Crane*, cd. Brom Weber (Garden City, N.Y.: Doubleday and Co., Inc., 1966), unless indicated otherwise in the notes.

2 Martin Heidegger, "Building, Dwelling, Thinking," in *Poetry, Language, Thought,* trans. Albert Hofstadter (New York: Harper and Row, 1971), p. 152.

3 This view inverts Brom Weber's reading of Atlantis and Cathay in *Hart Crane: A Biographical and Critical Study* (New York: The Bodley Press, 1948), p. 377: "Atlantis, like Cathay, is an ideal. But whereas Cathay is for us an unsullied symbol, Atlantis is a symbol of the triumph of the material over the spirit. The juxtaposition of these two ideals leads to a transference of the fuller implications of Atlantis to Cathay."

4 Crane wrote to Waldo Frank, *The Letters of Hart Crane: 1916-1932,* ed. Brom Weber (Berkeley: Univ. of California Press, 1952), p. 261: "The bridge as a symbol today has no significance beyond an economic approach to shorter hours, quicker lunches, behaviorism and tooth-picks."

5 Friedrich Nietzsche, *The Will to Power,* trans. Walter Kaufmann and R. J. Hollingdale, ed. Walter Kaufmann (New York: Random House, 19567), # 461, pp. 253-54. Nietzsche offers many similar outbursts against this "priestly" abnegation of life throughout his writings.

6 "Modern Poetry," in *The Complete Poems and Selected Letters,* p. 262.

7 Ibid., p. 263.

8 *Letters of Hart Crane,* p. 260.

9 Heidegger, "What Are Poets For?" in *Poetry, Language, Thought,* p. 101.

10 Nietzsche, *The Birth of Tragedy,* in *The Birth of Tragedy and The Genealogy of Morals,* trans. Francis Golffing (Garden City, N.Y.: Doubleday and Co., Inc., 1956), p. 23.

11 Among others, see Brom Weber, *Hart Crane,* p. 325: "Yet history and science were the two most important ingredients in a project which united past and present, ideas with machinery. Because he was unable to cope with these subjects, *The Bridge* was fated to fall to pieces as an organic structure."

12 Nietzsche, *The Use and Abuse of History,* trans. Adrian Collins, rev. ed. (Indianapolis, Ind.: Bobbs-Merrill Educational Publishing, 1957), pp. 6-7.

13 "Modern Poetry," p. 260.

14 As Crane explained "Powhatan's Daughter" to Otto Kahn, *Letters of Hart Crane,* p. 305: "It seemed altogether ineffective from the poetic standpoint to approach this material from the purely chronological angle. . . . One can get that viewpoint in any history primer. What I am after is an assimilation of this experience, a more organic panorama, showing the continuous and living evidence of the past in the inmost vital substance of the present."

15 *The Use and Abuse of History,* p. 42.

16 Crane's emphasis on the body and affective response recalls Nietzsche's repeated insistence that we return to "biology" as the extra-moral base for values. For example, see *The Will to Power,* # 532, p. 289; "Essential: to start from the *body* and employ it as a guide. It is the much richer phenomenon, which allows of clearer observation. Belief in the body is better established than belief in the spirit."

17 "Modern Poetry," p. 262. See also Crane's letter to Gorham Munson, *Letters of Hart Crane,* p. 125: "And I am even more grateful for your very rich suggestions best stated in your *Frank Study* on the treatment of mechanical manifestations of today as subject for lyrical, dramatic, and even epic poetry. You must already notice that influence in 'F and H.' It is to figure even larger in *The Bridge.* The field of possibilities literally glitters all around one with the perception and vocabulary to pick out significant details and digest them into something emotional."

18 "Modern Poetry," p. 262.

19 William Carlos Williams, *Spring and All,* in *Imaginations,* ed. Webster Schott (New York: New Directions, 1970), pp. 105, 120.

20 Roy Harvey Pearce, *The Continuity of American Poetry* (Princeton, N.J.: Princeton Univ. Press, 1961), p. 110.

21 Emerson, "The Poet," in *Essays, Second Series,* vol. III in *The Works of Ralph Waldo Emerson,* 14 vols. (Boston, Mass.: Houghton, Mifflin and Co., 1883), p. 29: "The pairing of the birds is an idyl, not tedious as our idyls are; a tempest is a rough ode, without falsehood or rant; a summer, with its harvest sown, reaped, and stored, is an epic song, subordinating how many admirably executed parts. Why should not the symmetry and truth that modulate these, glide into our spirits, and we participate the invention of nature?"

22 See Joseph Riddel, "Hart Crane's Poetics of Failure," *ELH,* 33 (1966), 486: "Like Dionysus, the poet must not possess but be possessed, and realize himself in losing himself."

23 *Birth of Tragedy,* p. 24.

24 Letter to Otto Kahn, *Letters of Hart Crane,* p. 307.

[25] Herbert Leibowitz, *Hart Crane: An Introduction to the Poetry* (New York: Columbia Univ. Press, 1968), p. 32.

[26] Samuel Hazo, *Hart Crane: An Introduction and Interpretation* (New York: Barnes and Noble, Inc., 1963), p. 106, interprets the personification of Southern Cross as the "'bride' of 'The Dance'" degraded to "an anonymous prostitute who 'liftsher girdles from her, one by one,' until the poet's 'mind is churned to spittle, whispering hell.'" Actually, the antecedent of "her" in the poem is "night," not "The Southern Cross." The rising of the Southern Cross "lifts" the night's "girdles," as if this starry illumination were a liberation of the night from utter obscurity. Hazo is properly sensitive to the sexual suggestiveness of girdles being lifted, but "Southern Cross" is a "prostitute" in this poem only insofar as "she" is made to serve the transcendental ideals of the poet, who wants her "utterly" and "as still more alone" as well as "High, cool."

[27] Thomas Vogler, *Preludes to Vision: The Epic Venture in Blake, Wordsworth, Keats, and Hart Crane* (Berkeley: Univ. of California Press, 1971), p. 177.

[28] Crane's association of his lost desire with the rising of the Southern Cross recalls Melville's "Crossing the Tropics," in which the sailor/poet recalls his bride at home in a similar fashion:

> While now the Pole Star sinks from sight
>   The Southern Cross it climbs the sky;
> But losing thee, my love, my light,
> O bride but for one bridal night,
>   The loss no rising joys supply.

In the last lines, the poet suggests that his wandering and desire have condemned him to a sort of eternal limbo:

> O love, O love, these oceans vast:
> Love, love, it is as death were past!

From *Collected Poems of Herman Melville*, ed. Howard P. Vincent (Chicago, Ill.: Hendricks House, 1947), p. 202.

[29] Crane suggests this quite clearly in the seventh poem in *Ten Unpublished Poems* (New York: Gotham Book Mart, 1972), n. p.:

> I rob my breast to reach those altitudes—
> Abstractions to meet the meaningless concussion
>   of
> Pure heights—Infinity resides below . . .
> The obelisk of plain infinity founders below
> My vision is a grandiose dilemma.

[30] The "Crap-shooting gangs" echo the lines in "At Melville's Tomb":

> The dice of drowned men's bones he saw
>   bequeath
> An embassy. Their numbers as he watched,
> Beat on the dusty shore and were obscured.

See Crane's commentary on these lines in his letter to Harriet Monroe, in *Complete Poems and Selected Letters*, p. 238: "These being the bones of dead men who never completed their voyage, it seems legitimate to refer to them as the only surviving evidence of certain messages undelivered, mute evidence of certain things, experiences that the dead mariners might have had to deliver. Dice as a symbol of chance and circumstance is also implied." Is this modern Manhattan composed of the scattered shards of the message Columbus failed to deliver?

[31] This reading of the differential structure of Crane's "Woman" explores only one such image-motif in the poem. Many other recurrent images in the poem follow a similar pattern, which is also evident in Crane's other poems. Riddel discusses such dualisms as Dionysus/Christ as reflections of such basic psychic differences as id/ego. His discussion of Crane's use of the serpent is exemplary: "Moreover, the complex associations of the immortal serpent, the sexual serpent, the serpent of intellect and time, and the serpentine dance of Dionysus begin to accumulate upon the double vision of the sacrificial and the generative act" (p. 488).

[32] Heidegger, "Building, Dwelling, Thinking," p. 154.

[33] Vogler, p. 190.

[34] Riddel, p. 483: "The poem aspires toward the tranquillity and silence of 'belle isle' (monistic union), but the language ironically will not let go, and ultimately disdains the end in which it would consume itself."

[35] *Birth of Tragedy,* p. 143.

[36] Ibid., pp. 107, 108.

[37] See *Birth of Tragedy,* p. 55: "We all talk about poetry so abstractly because we all tend to be indifferent poets. At bottom the esthetic phenomenon is quite simple: all one needs in order to be a poet is the ability to have a lively action going on before one continually, to live surrounded by hosts of spirits. To be a dramatist all one needs is the urge to transform oneself and speak out of strange bodies and souls." Riddel, p. 483, argues that Crane's poem "achieves, or seeks to, an intensity of rhythm and movement that overrides intellect and purifies it."

[38] Heidegger, "' . . . Poetically Man Dwells . . . '" in *Poetry, Language, Thought,* pp. 223-24.

[39] Heidegger, "Who Is Nietzsche's Zarathustra?" trans. Bernd Magnus, in *The New Nietzsche: Contemporary Styles of Interpretation,* ed. David B. Allison (New York: Dell Publishing Co., Inc., 1977), p. 69.

[40] Nietzsche's clearest exposition of Eternal Recurrence is given in *The Gay Science,* trans. Walter Kaufmann (New York: Random House, 1974), especially # 341, pp.

273-74. Nietzsche poses the eternal return of the same as an hypothetical question designed to elicit man's affirmation or negation of life; he does *not* offer the concept as a "theory of history," as many commentators have suggested: "What, if some day or night a daemon were to steal after you into your loneliest loneliness and say to you: "This life as you now live it and have lived it, you will have to live once more and innumerable times more; and there will be nothing new in it, but every pain and every joy and every thought and sigh and everything unutterably small or great in your life will have to return to you, all in the same succession and sequence—even ·this spider and this moonlight between the trees, and even this moment and I myself. The eternal hourglass of existence is turned upside down again and again, and you with it, speak of dust!' Would you not throw yourself down and gnash your teeth and curse the demon who spoke thus? Or have you once experienced a tremendous moment when you would have answered him: 'You are a god and never have I heard anything more divine.'"

⁴¹ Heidegger, "Who Is Nietzsche's Zarathustra?," p. 74.

⁴² *Letters of Hart Crane,* p. 351.

⁴³ Riddel, p. 492.

⁴⁴ Nietzsche, *Thus Spoke Zarathustra,* in *The Portable Nietzsche,* ed. and trans. Walter Kaufmann (New York: The Viking Press, 1968), p. 137.

⁴⁵ Riddel, p. 482.

## Joseph Schwartz (essay date 1979)

SOURCE: "A Divided Self: The Poetic Responsibility of Hart Crane with Respect to 'The Bridge'," in *Modernist Studies,* Vol. 3, No. 1, 1979, pp. 3-18.

[*In the following essay, Schwartz explains the fragmentation of* The Bridge *by discussing the ways in which Crane's temperament and training were actually unsuitable to the writing of such a poem.*]

I would like to consider the question of how Hart Crane came to think of himselfas the kind of poet who could undertake the composition of *The Bridge.* By temperament, education, and heritage Crane was the worst equipped of poets to undertake an exhaustive meditation upon the nature of the modern with its implications of a maturing technological culture. Constitutionally unable to apprehend the world as a whole, he had no enthusiasm for cosmic poetic designs or programs. He was expressive not topical by nature. Yet he found himself gradually being cast (and casting himself) in the role of Walt Whitman's successor. How this came to happen remains an essential question for the reader of his enormous, fragmented poem. Considering this question will make us better able to appreciate the essential indecision of the poet, and it may help explain the vacillation between

poetic and rhetoric in the poem itself. Largely because of the strength of its parts, *The Bridge* remains one of the most significant literary efforts thus far to come to terms with modernism; it stands as a magnificent and instructive wreck on the path of one's progress toward an understanding of our age.

My concern, however, is directly with Crane's divided self rather than with the poem. My effort will be to trace how the divided self came about. My thesis is simply that Crane was essentially one kind of poet and that he tried, because of a variety of pressures, to become another kind of poet. He did not slowly evolve or mature or change— all words conventionally used to describe the development of writers. He undertook a willful arbitrary shift; he was uncomfortable with it, and he did not persist in it.¹ It will be necessary first of all to sketch briefly the essential poetic sensibility of Crane, a point easily documented. Then, at more length, I would like to come to grips directly with the question of how he came to think of himself as Whitman's heir.

Allen Tate has perceptively particularized the essential character of Crane's poetic sensibility, and it is a good place to begin: "locked-in sensibility" and "insulated egoism." Crane's derangement and disorder, in contrast to that of Rimbaud, was original and fundamental. It is Tate's view that Rimbaud cultivated derangement, working at achieving disorder within the context of a milieu in which an implicit order still existed. He struggled against the intellectual order he inherited. By Crane's time, the derangement of the intellectual systems of modernism had already taken place, and he had to struggle with the problem of finding some principle of order. For Crane, disorder was natural and fundamental; his poetic perception of this condition marks "the special quality of his mind that belongs particularly to our time."² Although the romantic cosmology of *The Bridge* made Crane a symbol of the apotheosis of the romantic spirit in our century, essentially his romanticism was not at all cosmic in its outreach, but personal and lyric, characterized by the richest intensity, best sustained, if at all, in short stabs at the feel of things—the poems in *White Buildings* and many of the individual parts of *The Bridge.* "I write damned little because I am interested in recording certain sensations, very rigidly chosen, with an eye for what according to my taste and sum of prejudices seem suitable to—or intense enough—for verse."³ "God save me from a Messianic predisposition!" (To Herbert Weinstock, April 22, 1930). His tortured diction, private imagery, and personal habit of metaphor, in such vivid contrast to Whitman's simple rhetorical speaking-out, were essential to the character of his poetic mind. Crane was aware of this bent both before and after he had completed *The Bridge.* He complained to Tate about critics who were not looking for poetry, but for some grand design. "They are . . . in pursuit of some cure-all." Poetry is truer to itself when it does not attempt to sum up the universe. Crane admitted that he was unable to write such verse: "My vision of poetry *is* too personal to 'answer the call.' And if I ever write any more verse it will probably be at least as personal as the idiom of **White Buildings** whether anyone cares to look at it or not" (To Allen Tate, July 13, 1930). Three letters should be considered here to better understand Crane's perception of himself as "too personal," the standard by which other influences must be judged.

After Gorham Munson wrote "Hart Crane: Young Titan in the Sacred Wood," an essay on Crane in which he decreed a social and speculative function for the poet, and wanted poetry to have the character of philosophy (or science), Crane objected: "Poetry . . . is simply the *concrete evidence* of *experience* of a recognition (*knowledge* if you like). It can give you a *ratio* of fact and experience, and in this sense it is both perception and thing perceived, according as it approaches a significant articulation or not. This is its reality, its fact, *being*." He accused Munson of wanting some kind of exact ethical formula or moral classification for poetry and insisted that this goal made poetry subordinate to science or philosophy. While Crane asserted that he was not opposing any new synthesis that would provide a consistent philosophical and moral approach for his time, he maintained that he was not attempting through poetry to delineate any such system. ("My vision of poetry is too personal to 'answer the call.'") Do not propose a goal "for me which I have no idea of nor interest in following. Either you find my work poetic or not, but if you propose for it such ends as poetry organically escapes, it seems to me as Allen [Tate] said, that you as a critic of literature are working into a confusion of categories" (March 17, 1926).

In a letter to Yvor Winters Crane made a related point. Winters had articulated the theory of the poet as the complete man, using this theory to point out inadequacies in Crane's work. Crane referred to Munson and other of his friends who had been "stricken with the same urge"— an urge for a grand design—and they had "rushed into the portals of the famous Gurdjieff Institute and have since put themselves through all sorts of hindu antics, songs, dances, incantations, psychic sessions, etc., so that now, presumably the left lobes of their brains and the right lobes respectively function . . . in perfect unison." Crane explained that he could not become enthusiastic about their methods, but was careful to indicate that he was not identifying Winters' advice with their practice. He insisted, however, that he did not aspire toward the "rather classical characteristics that you cite as desirable" for the poet. "This is not to say that I don't 'envy' the man who attains them, but rather that I have long since abandoned *that* field—and I doubt if I were ever born to achieve . . . those richer syntheses of consciousness that we both agree in classing as supreme, at least the attitude of a Shakespeare or a Chaucer is not mine by organic rights, and why try to fool myself that I possess that type of vision when I obviously do not!" He begged not to be credited with ambitions that he did not have. He insisted that he would try to develop as poet but that he could not develop into the kind of poet Winters praised, using the method which Winters recommended. The letter is a pas-

sionate outburst of a highly personalistic poet who had no metaphysical base on which to rest and did not much care. "If you knew how little a metaphysician I am in a scholastic sense of the term, you would scarcely attribute such a conscious method to my poems . . . as you do. I am an utter ignoramus in that whole subject, have never read Kant, Descartes or other doctors. It's all an accident as far as my style goes" (May 29, 1927).

The third letter, to Isidor Schneider, reinforces the point. He laments the fact that he does not have the scientific and metaphysical training to appreciate and judge the encyclopedias of the future by Whitehead, Bradley, and Wyndham Lewis. The only one he had been able to understand was Spengler. They were too formidable for him to master because of their statistics, allusions, threats, and labyrinth of abstractions. He would give them up in defense of his own writing, since

> all they really net me is a constant paralysis and distraction. I think this unmitigated concern with the future is one of the most discouraging symptoms of the chaos of our age, however worthy the ethical concerns may be. It seems as though the imagination has ceased all attempts at any creative activity—and had become simply a great bulging eye ogling the foetus of the next century (March 29, 1928).[4]

This letter to Schneider, like the one to Winters, is especially interesting because Crane was under great pressure at this time to construct some grand design to give order, form, and authority to the still incomplete **Bridge.**

It is, thus, easy to understand why Crane's romanticism could find suitable expression only in the intense lyrics which were his highly personal response to the chaos that reality seemed to be. Commencing with his shattered sense of family, the normal props that lead to security and synthesis were unavailable tohim. No significant coherent religious view of things was offered to him, a deficiency especially important to remember for a poet who had a profound religious need. Further, he had no education to speak of—that is, the kind of education a poet making a major attempt at synthesis would have to have. This is what Allen Tate meant when he described Crane as one of the most ignorant men he ever knew. His letters show that though he read widely, he read impulsively and only along the narrow avenues he himself picked out. The reading, for example, that he did to provide himself with background for the historical motifs of **The Bridge** was improvised at best. Frederick Hoffman's point is worth repeating: "He had no acquaintance with a systematic body of knowledge through which his tentative convictions could be translated."[5] "The tragic quandry (or agon) of the modern world," Crane wrote to Munson, "derives from the paradoxes that an inadequate system of rationality forces on the living consciousness." He disavowed any attempt "through poetry to delineate any such system" (March 17, 1926). He did not have, and he seemed not to want to have, the poise one would need to look at things steadily and whole, to keep anxiety and turbulence under that tense control needed by the speculative poet. Rather, he used his anxiety and turbulence as fuel for the creation of a certain kind of lyric. We know from Philip Horton's biography that Crane was so highly impressed with the following passage from Plato's *The Ion* that he marked it with red in his copy.

> For all good poets, epic as well as lyric, compose their beautiful poems not by art, but because they are inspired and possessed. . . . Lyric poets are not in their right minds when they are composing their beautiful strains: but when falling under the power of music and meter they are inspired and possessed. . . .

A passage from *The Phaedrus,* also heavily underscored by Crane, is likewise to the point. It is Socrates' observation that the poet who is not possessed by madness is no poet, that the poetry of sane men "is beaten hollow by the poetry of madmen." Early in his career, sporadically thereafter, and ultimately, he believed his mission as a poet was to celebrate his personal consciousness of some undefined absolute which he thought he apprehended in rare moments of poetic consciousness. Locked in his own sensibility, Crane used the fragmented character of reality as the "splendid waste" out of which he fashioned his ecstatic lyric cries moment by moment (when the moment was right).

The division in Crane's poetic sensibility came about when one group of his friends encouraged him to invent a form of experience—a grand design, a system, a synthesis of consciousness—that would give comprehensive meaning to an otherwise fragmented and chaotic reality through a programmatic scheme. The destructive tension between these competing views of his function divided his energies and was responsible, in part, for his agonizing life as a poet from the time he first conceived the idea of **The Bridge** until it was finally published.

The most influential of this group of friends was Waldo Frank. Although Crane had known Gorham Munson for some time, and although the influence of Frank and Munson became somewhat intertwined in its impact upon Crane, it was not until the correspondence with Frank and the meeting with him that the ideas about to be considered started to take serious hold of him.[6] In 1922 he had written scornfully to Munson, "will radios, flying machines, and cinemas have such a great effect on poetry in the end?" (April 19, 1922). Approximately one year later he was saying (again to Munson): "the more I think about my **Bridge** poem the more thrilling its symbolic possibilities become, and since my reading of you and Frank . . . I begin to feel myself directly connected with Whitman. I feel myself in currents that are positively awesome in their extent and possibilities. . . . " He was excited by these new possibilities, since the modern artist most needs vision to go along with his gigantic assimilative capacity. He had lost the shreds of philosophical pessimism and felt himself fit to become "a suitable Pindar for the dawn of the machine age" (March 2, 1923). The influence of Waldo Frank had begun to make itself felt.

When Crane first read *Our America* in 1919 he thought it pessimistic, and was bothered by Frank's "extreme national consciousness." He felt in contrast to Frank that writers succeeded because of their "natural unconsciousness combinedwith great sensitiveness." Frank's "thoroughly logical or propagandistic" mind annoyed him. Yet, he noted that Frank had hit the truth many time (To Gorham Munson, December 13, 1919). Though the book was too rhapsodical and a bit "pathetic," there was meat in it and it was stimulating (To Gorham Munson, December 27, 1919). Frank's comments cannot be ignored (To Gorham Munson, March 6, 1920). After reading *Rahab,* he thought Frank a real artist, except for the slight touch of sentimentality to his mysticism, sincere, and "certainly in the front line" (To Gorham Munson, August-September, 1922).[7]

In the summer of 1922 Munson was completing his study of the novels of Waldo Frank, Crane worked on a jacket blurb for Munson's book, and planned to write a short review of it for the *Double Dealer*. He became closely acquainted with Frank's ideas and with Munson's analysis of them. In the fall of 1922 he read Frank's short story "Hope" in *Secession* and found it "so fine" that he could not keep from writing him an enthusiastic letter of extravagant praise. About a month later Frank commented on **"For the Marriage of Faustus and Helen"** in the most flattering terms in his reply to Crane. Crane's subsequent letter in (February 27, 1923) is almost ecstatically appreciative of Frank's notice.

> It is a new feeling and a glorious one, to have one's inmost delicate intentions so fully recognized as your last letter to me attested. . . . I am certain that a number of us at last have some kind of community of interests . . . something better than a mere clique. It is a consciousness of something more vital than stylistic questions and "taste," it is a vision, and a vision alone that not only America needs, but the whole world.

Crane then asked Munson to set up a meeting with Frank; Munson arranged a luncheon when Crane came to New York in the spring of 1923. After this first meeting Crane wrote to Frank that "yours is the most vital consciousness in America and that potentially I have responses which might prove interesting, even valuable to us both" (Easter 1923). Just before this meeting with Frank, Crane had written to Charmion Weigand, "I cry for a positive attitude!" (January 30, 1923).

Frank did offer a positive attitude made up of many strands consciously worked into a systemic program, but many of the strands had been available to Crane from others: Munson, Lewis Mumford, Van Wyck Brooks, Plato, Nietzsche, P. D. Ouspensky, and Whitman. Perhaps it is impossible to determine finally why Frank in particular was such a catalyst for Crane. It may have been personal charisma of some kind. Frank was influential in a way quite different from Tate, Kenneth Burke, Malcolm Cowley, or others who might have been expected to fill this role. "I'm glad to know that **The Bridge** is fulfilling your utmost intuitions; for an intuition it undoubtedly was. . . . What I should have done without your love and most distinguished understanding is hard to say, but there is no earthly benefit for which I would exchange it" (To Waldo Frank, August 19, 1926). Crane might have been speaking of Frank's poem, or better of an agreement they might have had that Frank mined the ore while Crane shaped it. Crane quarreled with almost all of his friends, at times bitterly; he never quarreled with Frank.[8] He was of course flattered by Frank's attention, since Frank was already a well-respected intellectual and the author of four novels. His earnest Americanism, his strong emphasis on the significance of Whitman, especially the *Democratic Vistas,* his belief that American poets were meant to be makers of myth and pioneers of the spirit, and his Ouspensky-like "mysticism" represented a combination of qualities, some of which had previously engaged Crane's own interest. Whatever the causes, it was Frank principally who influenced Crane to see the incipient *The Bridge* as a vehicle for the expression of some grand design. Although the "vision" which Crane had described to Frank was never eliminated from the poem, it now had to share the poem with something more systematic than Crane had ever tried before and in which he did not maintain a sustained interest. The "vision" would be extensively modified by the "thoroughly logical and propagandistic" mind of Waldo Frank.

Frank was much more inclined than Crane to be systematic; he had come home from Europe determined to formulate some grand design, guided in part by the work of Anatole France. Western civilization was in a near-chaotic state of irreversible decline. This condition, however, was a sign that a rebirth of culture would begin in the soil of the new world. Since Frank was committed to the creation of a grand design, and since he had such a strong view of the necessity for the improvement of life that this design could bring, he gave prime attention to the role of the poet as the voice through which this system would be given articulation. The social function of the poet became preeminent; his energies must become Whitmanian in the service of mankind. He was able finally to accept the machine, integrating it into his system but less crudely than Munson suggested in *Waldo Frank, A Study.* Just as primitive man had to undergo a profound psychological revolution in learning that a simple tool could be an extension of his personal will, so too man in a machine culture would have to learn that the machine adumbrated the will of the age. The elements of life contained in the machine must be fused into a higher synthesis. In this way the mechanized world could express man's joy and pride.[9]

For Frank, Whitman was of singular significance, perhaps even the cornerstone upon which the design could be built. Above all writers, Whitman had a sense of the cosmic whole; he naturalized it in his poetry by showing an organic connection between inner vision and external reality. And in *Democratic Vistas* he had given scope to his ideas of human brotherhood, modern democracy, and vigorous individualism as the principal impulses of a new organic American culture which rejected the old values of the European past. Whitman found the materials for a new culture in his univocal mystic vision. He saw in American history a "new order of consciousness" which pointed toward a purposeful evolution which was no longer dualistic but integrated.[10] Frank, following the example of Whitman, rejected both transcendentalism and materialism ("The Modern Distemper"), accepting the unity of spirit and matter only. The poet must be prophet and mystic in bringing this message to his time. National self-consciousness, created by the poet, is the beginning of greatness. When Crane wrote **"Modern Poetry"** (1930), he was using Frank's ideas and vocabulary. "[Whitman] better than any other was able to coordinate those forces in America that seem most intractable, fusing them into a universal vision which takes on an additional significance as times go on." Whitman, it seems, became for Frank the "great bulging eye ogling the foetus of the next century."

Crane was ready for Frank's design: "I cry for a positive attitude!" It brought many things of interest to Crane into a seemingly respectable intellectual whole. Whereas Crane was confused by competing philosophies and would remain essentially so, Frank was boldly putting them together. He convinced Crane of the validity of a myth of America, understood in Whitman's terms as assimilating the full extent of modernism, which we can fairly call our technological culture.[11] Frank was formulating an aesthetic and a mysticism that would embrace the machine age. After a period of despair over the condition of modern life, he began to rediscover the American dream especially in terms of the scientific achievement of the machine age.[12] On the other hand, Crane, somewhat influenced by P. D. Ouspensky's *Tertium Organum,* had profoundly doubted the ideal of progress in the material order.[13] Ouspensky's dreary prose highlighted certain ideas (borrowed from William James) which Crane found corroborative "of several experiences in consciousness that I have had" and undoubtedly corroborative of what he had already discovered in Blake and some others (To Allen Tate, February 15, 1923). Humanity was decaying spiritually under the onslaught of scientific materialism. A new order of consciousness was the hope of the future. Ultimate realities in the noumenal world will be realized by the pure intuitive consciousness of the mind itself. Since poetry is the most effective means of revealing these spiritual realities, the poet must be a visionary. Now, however, inspired by Whitman and Waldo Frank to a new belief in the potentialities of America, he laid Ouspensky's pseudo-mysticism over the accomplishments of the modern world in an attempt to get at what Whitman had been celebrating earlier. For a moment, then, he seemed to have reconciled the ideal and the real, the flesh and the spirit.[14] He would shape experience outside his consciousness according to the possibility of the new "spiritual values" offered by Frank.

Crane addressed himself directly and at length to the problem of poetry and the machine age in his essay **"Modern Poetry."** The machine, firmly entrenched in modern life, has produced challenging responsibilities for the poet. Poetry willfail its contemporary function if it cannot "acclimatize" it naturally. The poet must have the capacity to surrender temporarily "to the sensations of urban life." Science has now become the "uncanonized deity of the times"—one of the "fundamental factors" of our time along with the machine, as important to the modern poet as religion had been to Dante and Milton. As a result, Whitman had become the most "typical and valid expression of the American *psychosis*" because he was able to integrate the forces of his time into a coherent vision,[15] a view of Whitman that came directly from Frank. The challenge to Crane of what Frank found in Whitman is seen in a passage from the 1855 "Preface" to *Leaves of Grass,* a passage which compares strikingly with parts of Crane's essay.

> The direct trial of him who would be the greatest poet is today. If he does not flood himself with the immediate age as with vast oceanic tides . . . and if he does not attract his own land body and soul to himself and hang on its neck with incomparable love and plunge his semitic muscle into its merits and demerits . . . and if he is not himself the age transfigured—let him merge in the general run and wait its development.

Despite Crane's natural antipathy for becoming a public voice to express the age, he was moved by Frank's vision. It should be noted in passing that fellow romantics such as Wordsworth, Emerson, and Shelley had written prose much like Crane's **"Modern Poetry."** The very simplicity of the machine as a symbol of progress, as Henry Adams noted, accounted for its astonishing power, the same argument John Stuart Mill had made in his commentary on de Tocqueville. Further, the attempt Crane made was quite in accord with the times, this strange marriage of experience and subjectivity so characteristic of modernism. His hope of combining personalism with a form of experience to create a single mythology of American history had been justified by Nietzsche long before when he had indicated that even philosophies of history would be personalistic: behind every observation is an eye. Malinowski had asserted that the religious life depends upon man's sense of the difference between the sacred and the secular ("these Godless days!" Crane had lamented). Since this simple distinction had broken down, perhaps one could discover that the secular was itself sacred. One is reminded of F. N. Cornford's rich suggestion that when a culture loses confidence in God, the sense of the sacred is transferred first to philosophy and then to science.

Crane in search of a form for his vision was attracted easily enough to the promise of science and technology.[16] "We are not sure where this will lead, but after the complete renunciation symbolized in *The Waste Land* and, though less, in *Ulysses* we have sensed some new vitality" (To Waldo Frank, February 27, 1923). Culturally the promise of technology was filled with an immediate and apparent hope. That there would be necessarily a tremendous gap between what one expected of technology and

what one would get made little difference. The expectations for technology in the nineteenth and twentieth centuries, before the present current of disillusion set in, were profound. The ultimate hope was that in the long run everybody would be relieved of problems and shortages that throughout history had made human life seem a trial. Only a generation ago, John Maynard Keynes held out this promise for all of us. If one could see spiritual forces at work in technology and connect this insight with the past and future of America, then one had seemingly a metaphysical base for hope and something to celebrate. "I want to keep saying YES to everything" (To Charlotte Rychtarik, September 23, 1923).

A brief account of the composition of *The Bridge* will document the extent of Crane's conversion, and will also reveal the troubled effort he made to force this view on his reluctant genius. On February 6, 1923 in separate letters to Gorham Munson and Allen Tate, Crane first mentioned *The Bridge* as yet too vague and nebulous in his mind to discuss in any detail. The initial conception, however, was meant to carry on the tendencies manifest in **"Faustus and Helen"** which he described later in **"General Aims and Theories"** as an attempt to discover an absolute conception of beauty the Greeks had in the midst of the "seething, confused cosmos of today." By February 18 he was prepared to go into more detail about the poem in a letter to Munson. *The Bridge* was now to be "a mystical synthesis" of America. Up to this point fewer than a dozen lines had beenwritten. Especially important in this letter is his reference to Munson's study of Frank. America's constructive future and unique identity would have to include our scientific achievements of the future. Although his ambition might be finally impossible, he noted that he was planning a symphonic form about as long as **"Faustus and Helen":** "And I am even more grateful for your very rich suggestions best stated in your *Frank Study* on the treatment of mechanical manifestations of today as subject for lyrical, dramatic, and even epic poetry. You must already notice that influence in "F and H." It is to figure even larger in *The Bridge*" (February 18, 1923).

I think we can infer that the Frank influence had made itself felt; Crane even began to see **"Faustus and Helen"** through these eyes. In a letter to Munson a few weeks later the "symbolic possibilities" of *The Bridge* were connected "directly with Whitman" through his reading of Frank (March 2, 1923). After meeting with Frank, he mentioned the "new consciousness" in his correspondence with Charlotte Rychtarik (April 13, 1923). By June 5 he was ready to begin again on the poem. In a letter to Alfred Stieglitz "the new consciousness" became the "higher tranquility"—the point arrived at when the terror of experience reaches a climax of intensity indicating that a new and higher stage of development will come. This was Frank's theory of the way civilization advances. Differing early versions of **"Atlantis"** were sent to Stieglitz and Charlotte Rychtarik on July 4 and July 21. Crane called it ecstatic poetry, "written verse by verse in the most tremendous emotional exaltations I have ever felt." By August the moment of visionary exaltation either was gone or had been exhausted; Crane confessed to Stieglitz that his mind was like dough and that *The Bridge* was "far away" (August 11, 1923). During this time he was in despair over the poem; only a tentative draft of **"Atlantis"** was finished (August 25, 1923). He wrote to Stieglitz in October voicing his hope that the poem soon would be finished so that it could be included in his first volume of poems.

The next mention of the poem in his letters was not until seven months later, March 5, 1924: "I would to God that I could get more done on my poem. . . . " He wrote to his mother on May 11, 1924 that it would be sometime before the poem could be completed. In another letter to his mother he indicated that he was still thinking of it as the final poem for his first volume: "But a long poem like that needs unbroken time and extensive concentration, and my present routine of life permits me only fragments" (September 23, 1924). The poem was not mentioned in his letters again until over a year later, December 3, 1925, when he requested a subsidy from Otto Kahn. It was by this time no longer thought of as a final poem for his first volume. The vague conception was still indebted to Frank-Whitman—"to enunciate a new cultural synthesis of values in terms of our America." (Notice the echo of Frank's *Our America*.) He was given $2,000. On January 18 he sent a revision of **"Atlantis"** to Waldo Frank. For almost three years that section had been *The Bridge* a section most congenial to his conception of himself as a poet of lyric vision. He mentioned to Frank that he was working at **"Ave Maria."** By March his mood had radically altered as he confessed to the Rychtariks and to Munson:

> At times the project seems hopeless, horribly so; and then suddenly something happens inside one, and the theme and the substance of the conception seem brilliantly real, more so than ever! At least, *at worst,* the poem will be a *huge* failure! (To the Rychtariks, March 2, 1926)

> As Waldo may have mentioned, the finale of *The Bridge* is written, the other five or six parts are in feverish embryo. They will require at least a year more for completion; however bad this work may be, it ought to be hugely and unforgivably, distinguishedly bad. In a way it's a test of materials as much as a test of one's imagination. (To Gorham Munson, March 5, 1926)

Since he felt that Otto Kahn expected a report from him, he sent him on March 18 an outline for the poem. At this time only the **"Atlantis"** section had been finished. Three of the projected sections would be completed eventually, a fourth changed radically, and a fifth dropped altogether. A few days later he sent the first verse of **"Ave Maria"** to Frank and told him as well how magnificent *Virgin Spain* was and how it was something of a prelude for his intentions in *The Bridge.*

In May Frank accompanied him to the Isle of Pines and stayed with him for about two weeks. Refreshed, it seems, by the change of scene. Crane started to write verse again, but made no progress on *The Bridge.* He then read Oswald Spengler's *Decline of the West* and sent Frank one of his most significant letters. It was a full-bodied critique of the underlying base of a poem not yet written, a prophetic criticism which anticipated the objections of his most perceptive contemporaries to the completed poem when it finally appeared. The letter must be quoted in detail.

> Emotionally I should like to write *The Bridge;* intellectually judged the whole theme and project seems more and more absurd. A fear of personal impotence in this matter wouldn't affect me half so much as the convictions that arise from other sources. . . . I had what I thought were authentic materials that would have been a pleasurable-agony of wrestling, eventuating or not in perfection—at least being worthy of the most supreme efforts I could muster.

> These "materials" were valid to me to the extent that I presumed them to be (articulate or not) at least organic and active factors in the experience and perceptions of our common race, time and belief. The very idea of a bridge, of course, is a form peculiarly dependent on such spiritual convictions. It is an act of faith besides being a communication. The symbols of reality necessary to articulate the span—may not exist where we expected them, however. By which I mean that however great their subjective significance to me is concerned—these forms, materials, dynamics are simply non-existence in the world. I may amuse and delight and flatter myself as much as I please—but I an only evading a recognition and playing Don Quixote in an immorally conscious way.

> The form of my poem rises out of a past that so overwhelms the present with its worth and vision that I'm at a loss to explain my delusion that there exist any real links between that past and a future destiny worthy of it. The "destiny" is long since completed, perhaps the little last section of my poem ["Atlantis"] is a hangover echo of it—but it hangs suspended somewhere in ether like an Absalom by his hair. The bridge as a symbol today has no significance beyond an economical approach to shorter hours, quicker lunches, behaviourism, and toothpicks. . . . If only America were half as worthy today to be spoken of as Whitman spoke of it 50 years ago there might be something for me to say—not that Whitman received or required any tangible proof of his intimations, but that time has shown how increasingly lonely and ineffectual his confidence stands. (June 20, 1926)

By July 24, however, he was almost frenetically at work on different parts of the poem, beginning one of the most productive periods of his entire career. Yet by the end of August the ecstatic, feverish mood was gone and progress on the poem came to a standstill. During this brief period he completed **"To Brooklyn Bridge," "Ave Maria," "Cutty Sark," "Three Songs," "The Tunnel," "The Dance,"** and a revision of **"Atlantis."** In his August 19 letter to Frank, Crane suggested that his reading of Spengler's "stupendous" book acted as a negative catalyst because it forced him to find a positive centre of action. He assured Frank that he had recaptured their vision. I think Crane was right in seeing Spengler as a catalyst, but I do not think he was a negative catalyst. If we look with care at the sections completed, with the exception of **"Atlantis,"** we will notice that they reflect with great accuracy the mood of his June 20 letter expressing his immediate reaction to Spengler's work. The form of these poems does rise out of a past that overwhelms the present with its worth. No real links are forged between that past and any future destiny worthy of it. The overwhelming impression of the poems is that the worth of the past serves as a means of embarrassing the hopeless present. That present is represented by the bedlamite of **"To Brooklyn Bridge,"** the horrors of **"The Tunnel"** without its falsely intruded stanza, and the drunken sailor of **"Citty Sark."** Whitman's confidence does indeed seem "lonely and ineffectual." The paradox appears to be that Spengler somewhat directly inspired, willy-nilly, some of the most elegantly fashioned sections of *The Bridge.*

During November and December of 1926 he wrote to various friends that he hoped to finish the poem shortly. He was confident and waiting for it to spill over. "I am not worried." And then this very enlightening observation to his mother: "Am making as much effort as possible to free my imagination and work the little time that is now left me on my *Bridge* poem. So much is expected of me via that poem—that if I fail on it I shall become a laughing stock and my career closed" (December 22, 1926). This seems to indicate that the poem conceived as a whole had become a burden to him. He recognized the existence of external pressures forcing him to complete a poem for which he was having difficulty finding a centre. That he saw the already completed poems as discrete and not dependent upon some whole can be deduced from the way he submitted them for publication. In no instance did he hedge the submission with any indication that this was work-in-progress. On January 24, 1927 he submitted **"Cutty Sark"** and **"Harbor Dawn"** along with **"O Carib Isle"** to Edgell Rickword for publication in *The Calendar,* noting the marine emphasis in the three of them as justifying this multiple submission. He submitted **"Van Winkle"** and **"Harbor Dawn"** to *New Republic,* but they were rejected. On March 19 he wrote to his mother that **"Ave Maria"** would soon be coming out in *The American Caravan* and *The Dial* had accepted **"The Dance."** On March 27 he cheerfully reported to Tate that Harriet Monroe had accepted **"Cutty Sark"** for *Poetry.*

Although he wrote to both his mother and father in May telling them of the urgency he felt to get the poem finished, he confessed that nothing much was getting done. On July 4, however, he did send a copy of the newly completed **"The River"** to Mrs. Simpson. In his lengthy progress report to Otto Kahn (September 12, 1927) he discussed **"To Brooklyn Bridge," "Ave Maria," "Harbor Dawn," "Van Winkle," "The River," "The Dance," "In-**

diana," as yet incomplete, **"Cutty Sark,"** and the not-yet started **"Cape Hatteras."** He petitioned for more money in order to have the leisure to complete this "symphony with an epic theme." In his present state of mind progress on the poem was impossible. Almost a year later (March 28, 1929) in a letter to Isidor Schneider, Crane contended that he might have the nerve to continue on *The Bridge* if he could get certain things sorted out in his mind. He seemed troubled by the "new encyclopedias of the future" which every intellectual seemed obliged to publish. In June he wrote to Frank that he hoped to complete the poem in the coming summer. I do not think that a complete poem, as he and Frank were seeing the poem, would ever have been finished if Harry and Caresse Crosby had not offered early in 1929 to publish it. His May 1, 1929 letter to Schneider pretty well summarized the difficulties he had in the composing of the poem since that spurt of energy in 1926. Although he had not completed any additional sections of the poem, he announced the fall Paris publication. With Whitman's *Leaves of Grass* in mind, he planned such additions, if they eventuated, for some later edition.

> I've alternated between embarrassment and indifference for so long that when the Crosbys urged me to let them have it, declaring that it reads well enough as it already is, I gave in. Malcolm [Cowley] advised as much before I left America, so I feel there may be some justification. The poems, arranged as you may remember, do have I think, a certain progression. And maybe the gaps are more evident to me than to others . . . indeed, they must be.

His description of the work as a series of poems with a "certain progression" is telling, I think.

After the Crosbys' offer, however, he was forced to face the fact that the whole was unsatisfactory. There was something missing. So Crane turned rather desperately, the evidence seems to indicate, to the composition of **"Cape Hatteras."**[17] He regarded this section as crucial— "According to *my* ideas of *The Bridge* this edition wouldn't be complete or even representative without it" (To Caresse Crosby, September 6, 1929). **"Cape Hatteras"** was his last attempt to find a center and thus a subject for his poem. That is why Whitman became so important for this section, "a kind of ode to Whitman." Some final definition of his elusive visionary idea was absolutely necessary, as he confessed to CaresseCrosby. If we can entertain the theory that the newest part of a growing poem (for example, *The Bridge,* "Ash Wednesday") reveals most clearly its principle of unity because it is the part most immediate to the resolving motive of synthesis, then a reading of **"Cape Hatteras"** is especially instructive. As George Williamson put it, "the parts that are not published until the new composition appears commonly afford the best insight into the character of such poems."[18] There is substantial agreement among many readers that this section is the singular failure in the poem. Its inflated bombast is an unconscious confession that his attempt for *The Bridge* as a whole to capture the positive aspects of the modern technological world had failed. **"Cape Hatteras"** was Crane's final opportunity to put into *The Bridge* the ideas of Walt Whitman. It was the place for a specification of what, precisely, Whitman's univocal view of death and life meant and how it solved the problem which Spengler presented to Crane in his analysis of death and destruction. "This man [Spengler] is certainly fallible in plenty of ways but much of his evidence is convincing—and is there any good evidence forthcoming from the world in general that the artist isn't completely out of a job?" (To Waldo Frank, June 20, 1926). Frank's position had been that Whitman, specifically, was the best possible evidence that the artist in the modern world was not only *not* out of a job but desperately needed. In an earlier plan for *The Bridge* Crane wanted to present in a central section of the poem those principles of Whitman, "The Spiritual Body of America," which when spoken would illuminate the meaningful unity of death and life. He wanted to avoid basing his view on the historical "character" of Whitman.[19] In **"Cape Hatteras,"** however, whatever Whitman stands for remains vague and unarticulated. Instead the historical character is thrust on the scene in a way that Allen Tate rightly characterized as sentimental.

The poem, considered as a single work, was at least completed, though it would be somewhat revised for the Liveright edition. The mixture of a powerfully self-centered lyric imagination with what Crane hoped would be an epic of national consciousness organized around a controlling idea would have to stand. The publication of the poem made the curious mixture permanent. As a result the brilliant success of so many sections of the poem would always be in a peculiar way altered by being considered as parts of an unstable whole. The already completed sections would gain nothing by being linked with **"Cape Hatteras"** and **"Quaker Hill."** At least the struggle, if not resolved, was ended. Crane's fears concerning the poem's unity and development were well-founded. This is not to speak of the failure of most of the poems, published separately, which make up *The Bridge.* These poems, with the exception of **"Indiana," "Quaker Hill,"** and **"Cape Hatteras"** are among the most brilliant in the history of modern literature. We sometimes forget that Crane's established and eminent reputation among his most perceptive contemporaries was based on the poems in *White Buildings* and the individually published poems which were eventually brought together in *The Bridge.* What **"Cape Hatteras"** (and **"Quaker Hill"**) finally revealed was the failure of the design and intention of the new poem which tried to use previously published materials—poems which had their own autonomy built into their very structure.

Crane persisted over a period of six years attempting to make *The Bridge* into something it could not become. His frequent announcements concerning the scope of the poem made the whole effort a public affair, and he was bothered by this since he felt his inability to complete it would mark him as a failure. All of his friends as well as the literary establishment had been made fully aware of

his ambitions. Not strangely for Crane, he also felt an obligation to Otto Kahn for his financial assistance. More important, however, was the compelling indebtedness he felt to Frank, an indebtedness that was the result of an extraordinary closeness. The effect of this was a reluctance to disappoint Frank. But it must be said again that what Frank offered him had a very powerful appeal to Crane. Always veering toward disaster, Crane was conscious of being inadequate in one way or another. Since Frank viewed him as an extraordinary poet with a cosmic vision, Crane was more than merely flattered. He was being offered by his father figure a towering vision of the function of the poet, a vision different from the ones Crane got from Tate or Yvor Winters. Instead of being cautioned to discipline his gift, he was encouraged by Frank to plunge boldly ahead, ridingthe whirlwind of his temperament, opening himself to the subjective visions which Frank misread as potentially cosmic. Whereas Crane saw himself finally as the poet of *White Buildings,* Frank encouraged him to see himself as a universal cosmic seer. Crane, always uneasy with any definition of his self, was eager to accept these new terms. A child reared in the shade, Crane thought he had a vision of the sun. His romantic impulse would conquer the world out here by imagining it into being on his terms—"the egotistical sublime." In this way Crane could catch the ineffable in the splendor of his apocalyptic vision. He could luxuriate in an order created by his own conceptions. He could will his ideas into existence and structure the world as a mirror of his own consciousness.

While Crane intended, insofar as his intentions were ever consistent, to make a poetic myth from the materials of history, it was really a metaphysical myth he sought—the kind of myth which no man can both create and believe in—"lend a myth to God."[20] Crane's sense of the "tragic quandary (or agon) of the modern world" was caused by his sense of the failure of any value system available to him. We live in a culture, he wrote to his mother, "without faith and conviction"; hence "at times it seems demonstrable that Spengler is quite right" (June 1, 1926). There are so few common terms that are solid enough to "ring with any vibration or spiritual conviction." The great mythologies of the past, even the Church, he lamented, are no longer able to sustain one.[21] The times are so bewildering, he wrote to Frank, that there seems nothing to fight for. "In some ways," he repeated, "Spengler must have been right" (February 19, 1931). "The spiritual disintegration of our period becomes more painful to me every day" (To Gorham Munson, April 17, 1928). His conception of *The Bridge* was finally Promethean in that he had to start afresh with his own consciousness—the intractable ego—the pathetic reduction of the egotistical sublime. What T. S. Eliot said of D. H. Lawrence might well be applied to Crane: an extreme personality, a man of fitful insights rather than ratiocinative powers.

The enthusiasm of 1923 had not been sustained, nor was the form of experience he tried to master and accept of any enduring value. The brief success of the summer of 1926, a result of reading Spengler, was never repeated, and Crane's confidence in his poem never fully returned. He was, at best, an uneasy Promethean. He was perhaps overly-conscious of the regular and terrible failures of his ego, a problem surely exacerbated by his unhappy experience in composing *The Bridge*. I do not mean to underestimate the urgent need he felt to create a new myth. His genuine and sensitive experience of the void moved him deeply and explains the compensatory attempt to satisfy this need. This was not a need, however, that could be satisfied by the symbolic uses of imaginative thought which is the very stuff of poetry. "Man is man because he can recognize supernatural realities, not because he can invent them."[22] The search that best explains the fragmentary character of *The Bridge* was for something else, for a metaphysical myth quickened by faith (and by faith alone) which can nourish the soul. Such myths, Jacques Maritain has explained, have no force except through the faith man has in them. Crane himself experienced this attempt and this failure throughout the history of the composition of *The Bridge,* as his letters show. The man kept pushing the poet to provide a belief in which the man could put his trust. The poet tried vainly again and again (the ever-shifting center of the poem) to satisfy the man. What Crane seemed to know intuitively (he certainly *experienced* it) was that the man must provide the poet with a vital belief. "Metaphysical myths are needed by poetry, but they cannot be provided by poetry."[23] If he had been satisfied with the new myth Frank had encouraged him to invent, he would have brought his poem to its conclusion without that agonizing doubt about its very conception which marks its history. Crane had agreed with Yvor Winters that there was a need for some kind of order, but he was not finally at ease with the design offered him by Waldo Frank. His search for unity without an adequate base in some certitude that went beyond his own invention of it had been a failure.

One of the most significant sentences Crane ever wrote, and it is at the base of my speculations, is one to Waldo Frank in a letter of June 20, 1926: "The Romantic attitude must at least have the background of an age of faith, whether approved or disapproved no matter." I think Crane was accurate when he described himself as "only a disappointed Romantic after all" (To Waldo Frank, February 19, 1931). Crane's romantic egoism was not cosmic enough to sustain the composition of the kind of poem he forced *The Bridge* to be. Although he was compelled to peer into the void, he could not believe in the myth he had created to rescue him from it. The modern world (and it would have been any world that Crane lived in) was nothing more than a season in hell. He invented a fiction he hoped would release him from the prison of his own sensibility and unite him instead with the body (Pocahantas-Whitman) of America.[24] And although he struggled desperately to sing a myth out of this imagined fiction, he was at bottom convinced of the profound spiritual disorder of his time. He had hoped with *The Bridge* to answer what he thought was the "complete renunciation symbolized in *The Waste Land,*" but his experience in composing the poem was instead a demonstration of T. S. Eliot's premise that the individual consciousness could

not create its own world. At his best Crane depended upon the intensity of sensations to re-create single moments in the stream of sensation. His world had no center, and the effort he made to find one failed, creating the divided self fatal to his poetic sensibility. The bridging metaphor, where he was most at home poetically, was not the organizing center of a comprehensive philosophy. Because Crane was typical of the rootless spiritual life of modernism, his attempt to be the spokesman for the integrated culture of a future he forced himself to envision was doomed from the start.

NOTES

[1] Consider the implications, relevant only in small part to my thesis, of this insight of Katherine Anne Porter. This event took place in Mexico near the end of his life. "Later, drunk, he would weep and shout, shaking his fist, 'I am Baudelaire, I am Whitman, I am Christopher Marlowe, I am Christ' but never once did I hear him say he was Hart Crane." John Unterecker, *Voyager, A Life of Hart Crane* (New York, 1969), p. 659.

[2] "Hart Crane," *Essays of Four Decades* (New York, 1970), p. 310.

[3] To Yvor Winters. May 29, 1927. *The Letters of Hart Crane 1916-1932,* ed. Brom Weber (Berkeley and Los Angeles, 1965). Since there are other editions of the letters, I will insert the date of the letter referred to and the name of the person to whom the letter is addressed parenthetically immediately after the citation when necessary for the convenience of the reader.

[4] " . . . this 'future' is, of course, the name of the entire disease" (To Gorham Munson, April 17, 1928).

[5] *The Twenties* (New York, 1962), p. 257.

[6] Robert L. Perry's *The Shared Vision of Waldo Frank and Hart Crane* (Lincoln, Nebraska, 1966) suggests some topics which might be explored in more depth in future studies.

[7] Despite his early reservations about *Our America,* and I have no reason to believe he reread it later, it seemed to have made a deep impression on Crane. Someone should study with care the many echoes of *Our America* in *The Bridge*. Almost all of the ideas in *The Bridge* first appeared there; even the correspondences in diction is striking.

[8] On the other hand, Crane was well aware of the fact that Frank was almost alone in his enthusiasm for the epic design of *The Bridge*. Tate, Slater Brown, and Cowley (to mention only a few) had made their uneasiness with the Whitman business well known to Crane. In his April 11, 1926 letter to the Rychtariks, he is quite candid in observing that "people like Frnak will probably like it— that is, they'll be interested in the content and presentation, but most of my younger associates and friends will

probably be pretty doubtful about it" (Unterecker, p. 442).

[9] "Frank has the real mystic's vision. His apprehensions astonish me" (To Allen Tate, February 15, 1923).

[10] "*Democratic Vistas* is quite clearly our greatest book of social criticism as *Leaves of Grass* is our greatest poem." *Our America* (New York, 1919), p. 205.

[11] Before the influence of Frank took hold, Whitman had been one of the many poets Crane admired. The letters do not reveal that he was special as, say, Eliot and Blake were special to him. However, after he began to feel the impact of Frank he could write, "I begin to feel myself directly connected with Whitman" (To Gorham Munson, March 2, 1923).

[12] Frank argued that "we lack an instinctive metaphysical consciousness to make us master and absorb it—to fuse the machine with all its elements of will and act into our own expression" (*The New Republic,* November 18, 1925). Probably this essay and Munson's *Waldo Frank* influenced the ideas and diction of Crane's "Modern Poetry" written for *Revolt in the Arts* (1930), a collection edited by Oliver Sayler devoted to a consideration of the place of the machine in the modern arts.

[13] Philip Horton has indicated that Ouspensky's *Tertium Organum* "became a common bible for the small group" led by Frank which included, besides Crane, Munson and Jean Toomer. During 1923 the four of them met frequently and discussed "the new slope of consciousness." When Munson and Toomer fell under the influence of the Russian spiritualist, Gurdjieff, with whom Ouspensky allied himself, the group lost its tight unity because Crane was unable to commit himself as a disciple. He was already Frank's disciple, and Frank had nothing to do with Gurdjieff. *Hart Crane: The Life of an American Poet* (New York, 1937), pp. 154-156.

[14] "He [Crane] had no politics, and he missed it. Spengler's *Decline of the West* greatly disturbed him because he needed to know it to be wrong. And I recall a letter Hart wrote urging me to answer it. . . . There was no room in the universe of the grim old Prussian for the hot, hopeful parabolas of Crane or other apocalyptic poets in verse and prose. *He needed reassurance, and I seemed able to give it.*" (Emphasis added.) Waldo Frank, *Memoirs of Waldo Frank,* ed. Alan Trachtenberg (University of Massachusetts Press, 1973), pp. 241-242.

[15] "Modern Poetry," *The Complete Poems and Selected Letters and Prose of Hart Crane,* ed. Brom Weber (New York, 1966), pp. 261-263.

[16] In two early reviews, before he came under the influence of Frank and Munson, Crane blamed science and technology for the disintegration of culture and of men within that culture. See "The Ghetto and Other Poems by Lola Ridge," *The Pagan,* 3 (January, 1919), 55-56, and his review of Sherwood Anderson's *Poor White* in *The Double Dealer,* 2 (July, 1921), 42-45.

[17] Actually "Quaker Hill" was the last part finished, but Crane admitted that it was not "one of the major sections of the poem; it is rather by way of an 'accent mark' that it is valuable at all" (To Caresse Crosby, December 26, 1929). It does, however, raise precisely the same problem that "Cape Hatteras" does, and the two parts might well be considered together in making the point.

[18] *A Reader's Guide to T. S. Eliot* (New York, 1957), p. 190.

[19] Brom Weber, *Hart Crane* (New York, 1948), p. 260.

[20] "The effort of a poet to create new metaphysical myths of his own invention, for the sake of his work as a poet, is self-contradictory, since, having invented them, he cannot believe in them. A man lost in the night might as well invent an imaginary moon because he needs to have his way lighted." Jacques Maritain, *Creative Intuition in Art and Poetry* (New York, 1953), pp. 180-181.

[21] "General Aims and Theories," *The Complete Poems and Selected Letters and Prose of Hart Crane,* ed. Brom Weber (New York, 1966), p. 218.

[22] T.S. Eliot, "Second Thoughts about Humanism," *Selected Essays* (New York, 1950), p. 433.

[23] Maritain, p. 181.

[24] Allen Tate forecast this failure in his "Introduction" to *White Buildings* in a comment written when only a small part of *The Bridge* was in manuscript: "Whitman's range was possible in an America of prophecy; Crane's America is materially the same, but it approaches a balance of forces; it is a realization; and the poet, confronted with a complex present experience, gains in intensity what he loses in range. The great proportions of the myth have collapsed in its reality. Crane's poetry is a concentration of certain phases of the Whitman substance, the fragments of the myth."

## Roger Ramsey (essay date 1980)

SOURCE: "A Poetics for 'The Bridge'," in *Twentieth Century Literature,* Vol. 26, No. 3, Fall, 1980, pp. 278-93.

[*In the following essay, Ramsey argues that readers must have a clear idea of the poetics of* The Bridge *in order to appreciate Crane's genius.*]

The criticism of Hart Crane's **The Bridge** has generally dealt out the opinion that Crane was, as James Russell Lowell called Shakespeare, "an inspired idiot." No one can be satisfied with the poem, but no one can let it alone either; no one (almost) can find the large truth in it that

Crane claims to have attempted, and yet most readers find intermittent excellence, calling it with Allen Tate "a collection of lyrics, the best of which are not surpassed by anything in American literature."[1] The designation of the poem as a failure rests on the imputation of a "myth" or "vision" structure for *The Bridge,* an idea abetted by Crane himself in several letters. The correspondence of this vision to Whitman's—again supported by letters—has been the subject of many studies and is generally felt to be fundamental. But whereas Whitman has succeeded, Crane has failed in his mythmaking—and this for a variety of reasons, it is argued, mostly structural (or personal).

I will not be able to answer all the critics as I make my way to my own subject—the punning in *The Bridge*—but a few facts, both internal and external to the poem, may be surveyed. First is the insubstantiality of Crane in his letters. On no modern poem, surely, has the intentional fallacy had more deleterious effect than on *The Bridge.* Like those mean spirits who dismiss Shakespeare's first fourteen sonnets because there is a subtext of financial request, the Tate and Winters crew (their *many* followers, in spirit if not in opinion) adduce from "friendship" and the letters and even gossip that Crane was too uneducated, too unstable, too drunk, too this and that *ever* to have accomplished what he set out to do; and what he set out to do we know from the letters as well. It must be admitted that Crane has played into their hands, but it must also be acknowledged that Crane was trying in these letters to convince others—including a patron, shades of Shakespeare!—of the work's importance. They are not to be trusted as guide or gloss.[2]

The only relevant data we can learn from the letters are that the individual poems were not written continuously, that the poet abandoned the project for three years, and that the final order—indeed the final selection—was hasty and almost offhanded. These facts argue neither for epic intention in the poem nor for a consistent myth or steady vision. In fact, in the poem we find too many lulls and low points, a lack of narrative, not even a clear, pervasive persona to carry the burden of vision. It is simply not fair to demand something that neither the poem nor its crafting suggest.

Another pervasive critical collapse, besides intentional fallacy, is the *kind* of structure demanded of *The Bridge.* I have yet to find a critic who even acknowledges this demand. We have continuously required the form of *The Bridge* to be Aristotelian. It is not. There is, as Northrop Frye says, "a distinction between two views of literature that has run all through the history of criticism."

> These two views are the aesthetic and the creative, the Aristotelian and the Longinian, the view of literature as product and the view of literature as process. For Aristotle, the poem is a *techne* or aesthetic artifact: he is, as a critic, mainly interested in the more objective fictional forms, and his central conception is catharsis.[3]

Frye then explains catharsis. But his explanation of Longinus is what interests us here:

> Just as catharsis is the central conception of the Aristotelian approach to literature, so ecstasis or absorption is the central conception of the Longinian approach. This is a state of identification in which the reader, the poem, and sometimes, at least ideally, the poet also, are involved. We say reader, because the Longinian conception is primarily that of a thematic or individualized response: it is more useful for lyrics, just as the Aristotelian one is more useful for plays.[4]

I think it is self-evident that what we have been asking of *The Bridge* is catharsis, but what *The Bridge* provides is ecstasis.

The issue is clarified by Frye when he later synopsizes the two critical approaches in the appreciation of the Bible as literature:

> The Bible may thus be examined from an aesthetic or Aristotelian point of view as a single form, as a story in which pity and terror, which in this context are the knowledge of good and evil, are raised and cast out. Or it may be examined from a Longinian point of view as a series of ecstatic moments or points of expanding apprehension. . . . [5]

Since I believe *The Bridge* offers just such "points of expanding apprehension" instead of a "story" with cathartic effect, the critical task is to locate those points, study them, and evaluate their effects, not to complain of incoherent narrative or inconsistent "myth." If there is a chartable "form" in *The Bridge,* it will be rhythmical only.

There will be themes in such a poem, of course, but the real interest is in the accomplishment of that "state" in which reader, poem, and poet are identified. This is attachment, not the cathartic detachment; it is transubstantiative, not consubstantiative. It is also entirely subjective, for who can say that a reader is involved but that reader? But it is probably possible to agree on which moments *seem* ecstatic on the basis of technique alone. That is, these moments are characterized not by understanding (as is catharsis, the detached experience) but by intensity. The moment is not emotional (as is catharsis: pity and terror) but rather spiritual, which it will be allowed often seems to transcend the understandable. Thus, the language of such moments may involve the reader in ways he cannot entirely explain; the resultant "obscurity" (with which Crane is usually charged) is thereby a necessity, not an excrescence.

Now, I am no more friend to obscurity than any other modern critic, but I am arguing only that in the Longinian approach it can be seen to be functional. If I seem to be unclear myself, it is at least partly due to a lack of Longinian vocabulary; one wishes for *half* the literature on ecstasis that there is on catharsis! I hope only to have established that there *is* an approach to the sublimities of *The Bridge;* this is not special pleading and the poem will fail or succeed on its own merits. But the fact that we have been applying inadequate (Crane's "intentions") and inappropriate (Aristotelian) criteria to the poem has kept us from appreciating what it *is.*

What *is The Bridge?* It is, I believe, a lyric (for which, as Frye says, the Longinian approach is most appropriate) and more specifically a religious lyric. The substantive assignment is too complex to take up here except to remind ourselves that the Longinian view does not expect a narrative (or *epos* form) and that the definition of lyric offered by Frye is "an associative rhetorical process, most of it below the threshold of consciousness, a chaos of paranomasia, sound-links, ambiguous sense-links, and memory-links very like that of the dream."[6] This reminds us instantly of *The Bridge.* Once we shed the demand for amyth, we recognize the truth of the matter: Crane is at play in the field of words. The impulse of *The Bridge* is allowed its rein and the result, if I may be so bold, is delight. That harried myth and Crane's own pretensions become, in the Longinus lyric, irrelevant.

By the modifier, *religious,* I mean ritualized ecstasy. If Crane is at play, he is seriously at play.[7] Again, the critical absorption of ritual into literature is too complex for this essay, but a crucial point may be made here. The "myth critics" are all—to my knowledge—Aristotelians; that is, they look for pattern and cathartic effect. Their point of view is essentially that of the observer—they are consubstantiative. They might ask, What is the effect of the death of the god on me? Looked at from a Longinian perspective, however, the question changes. It becomes, How does it feel to die as a god? The issue is transubstantiative. The point of view is not that of the society, but rather that of the god. The viewer of the god's death is absorbed *into* the god (who is also the land itself). This is exactly the *moment* of ecstasis. So the Aristotelian myth critic speaks of pattern and effect (*epos* and catharsis), the Longinian critic of the intensity of the moment. Again as Frye says, the reader (viewer, society) and the poem (the *meaning* of the experience, the resurrection of the land through sacrifice) and ideally the poet (the god) are one at such moments of ecstasis. Thus, I believe, in the large sense *The Bridge* is religious, not in an Aristotelian, spectator way, but in a Longinian, participator way. It is a transubstantiative poem.

The further religious question in *The Bridge* needs some definition. Clearly, the question is not what Crane believes in. That is irrelevant, for it posits a spectator, it detaches. From a Longinian point of view, it is fruitless to ask a reader to interpret symbols; symbols require us to acknowledge a this and a that, the image itself and its intellectual content. Consequently, there is an aesthetic distance (which, as Frye says, is synonymous with Aristotelian catharsis). But distance is the enemy of ecstasis. We proceed, inexorably it seems, to another outlandish conclusion: there are no important symbols in *The Bridge.*

That is, the god really dies and the god is I. Thus it is, as others have recognized (having *participated* in the poem and the poet), the fullest ecstasy and climax of the poem (meaning not a narrative climax, but the "highest" point) is the heartrending line, "I could not pick the arrows from my side." At once is the poet (Crane), the poem (Maquokeeta here), and the reader (through the rhetoric of first person) united. The god *is* poet, poem, and I. It is belief incarnate, the wafer on the tongue, ecstasis.

Intensity is here achieved by stunning understatement, not unlike Othello's final speech which begins, "Soft you." It is so unexpected that it jars the emotions loose. And as a technique in *The Bridge,* it is almost unprecedented; in **"The Dance"** section it is utterly unpredictable. For the power of understatement one is led to Herbert and Vaughan, poets whom Crane knew and associated in a particular context, which I want to take up now. But first to reiterate the position I have outlined: there are no symbols in *The Bridge* because the purpose is not to make *something other* but to invite participation; the transubstantiative imperative is to identify the thing with the maker and the participant; thus symbol is irrelevant. Somehow, the poem, the poet, and the reader must become one. Here it is understatement, but that is not characteristic of the poem; the poem generally hits its "high" moments with such multiplex language that it initially seems obscure, crabbed in rhythm, and undecipherable.

The language does not remind one of Whitman. This is, I hope, the last of my outlandish assertions. Whitman is not Crane's master. I don't know if one can speak of a "master" for Crane's poetics, but one can certainly speak of affiliates. Whitman, for all of Crane's accommodation in his letters, has exactly nothing to do with Crane's language. If there is a Whitman influence, as many have argued and as would seem only decent since he is invoked in *The Bridge,* it is on that irrelevant "myth" that has occupied so much printed space. We have seen that there is no "myth," not in the sense of pattern. There is, however,religion in the sense of ecstatic moment, not a steady vision but "visions," not a philosophy but an apprehension, fitfully perceived. And this perception, for a poet as god, is in language. Crane's language is condensed and ambiguous, a "shorthand" as Crane called it. Whitman's language is expansive, almost discursive, denotative.

No, it isn't Whitman whom Crane most resembles; it is Hopkins. The field for commentary is wide open. R. W. B. Lewis, in his useful book on Crane, dismisses Hopkins in a footnote, and L. S. Dembo doesn't raise the ghost at all. But it is Hopkins about whom Crane was most excited during the years of the writing of *The Bridge,* as Unterecker tells us: "Before he returned Winters's copy of the poems, he made typewritten copies of a number of them and even committed several—including 'The Wreck of the Deutschland'—to memory."[8] The year is 1927, and Crane's enthusiasm—always mercurial—does not diminish. The amazing thing is that the critics have not made the connection; even Yvor Winters himself, who loaned the book of poems to Crane, does not make the obvious connection; he says, "He [meaning Hopkins] violates grammar as he sees fit, mainly to gain results which he considers more valuable than grammar: striking epithets and striking phonic effects,"[9] but he does not associate this technique with Crane; indeed he berates Crane for the very same qualities.

So much for the critics. Crane and Hopkins—not Crane and Whitman—should be studied together because of predispositions: to a poetics, to an "ecstatics," and to a simple love of language. In addition, Crane and the Jesuit priest share a commitment to what the priest called "inscape," the utter reality of a thing in its full thingness, and "instress," the making real of such a thing. The primary difference—Crane admits "I am not as original in some of my stylisms as I had thought I was"[10] after reading Hopkins—is in the source of reality: for Hopkins it is God and for Crane it is the imagination. A full study of these two poets, a needed study, would not of course be so superficial.

I begin to move into more familiar territory when I make the last of my basic assertions. Crane's poem posits no god; instead, it is the ecstatic ritual of confirming the Word. And ultimately, in spite of certain misdirections, the word is neither "Cathay" nor even "bridge." The Word is word. In the word is all the intensity of belief and ecstatic identification; in the word is salvation itself. That this idea is already available to Crane students will be evidenced by these quotations from major studies:

> *The Bridge* is not a naive attempt to set up a national myth based on technology for its own sake, but an account of the exiled poet's quest for a logos in which the Absolute that he has known in his imagination will be made intelligible to the world. . . . The "logic of metaphor" was simply the written form of the "bright logic" of the imagination, the crucial sign stated, the Word made words.[11]

> The plot of *The Bridge* is the gradual permeation of an entire culture by the power of poetic vision— by that ever-pursuing, periodically defeated but always self-renewing visionary imagination. . . . [12]

> The creative act itself is the true subject of these poems, the life of the poet-quester-visionary-lover-seeker whose role is as futile, yet as necessary, to himself as Sisyphus'.[13]

In addition, there is the precise assertion by Barbara Herman—in the best study of Crane's language—that "Crane's language more than depended upon his philosophy; it was his philosophy."[14] In exact accord with my own conclusions, but without the Longinian underpinning, Herman believes that Crane thought of words as things, as actualities in the way that witch doctors believe in words, almost magical incantations; that Crane "became the figure of the twentieth century priest, investing his words with magic properties, erecting with them, either the Word or words, his frail bulwark against chaos and dissolution."[15] She also gives credence to Crane's own formal statement of poetics, which has nothing to do with mythmaking in the Aristotelian sense but only with the power of words. **"General Aims and Theories"** is, unlike the letters, a public and worked-outprogram; thus the notions of the "logic of metaphor" (associational meaning of words) and the "dynamics of inferential mention" (allusiveness, primarily) may be valued by the critic. It will be noted, however, that his entire "poetic" has to do with word color and potential sense; it has nothing to do with *epos,* mythmaking, or even structure. A most fertile suggestion is Herman's: "The unit was the word, and, like the spot of color in pointillism, that word could be altered in various ways by the other words placed around it."[16]

Here we see that the Word is—dare one say?—sacramental. This idea may help us to see, in "Atlantis," why the apostrophe reads

> —O Choir, translating time
> Into what multitudinous Verb the suns
> And synergy of waters ever fuse, recast
> In myriad syllables,—Psalm of Cathay!

The Word is not Cathay, obviously, but "Psalm of Cathay"—the singing *is* the religious experience. This makes the singer (priest in Miss Herman's vocabulary but god and king in archetypal terms) the center of the sacrament, his song (*The Bridge*) the sacrament in myriad syllables, and the choir (readers) the celebrants. And finally, all the conceptions that I feel are necessary to a proper, fair, and useful reading of the poem fall into place.

We are to begin by looking for ecstasis, moments of intense identification, poem with poet with reader. These moments may be, at least initially, obscure because the language itself will be intense (or stunningly understated). The poem itself will be lyrical and religious and, at these ecstatic moments, it will be transubstantiative; in this it reminds us of Hopkins rather than Whitman. But it is not a symbolic poem because the Word is word, not some other (such as Hopkins' God). Therefore, the participation of the reader is with the poet as poet (the god of the language) and the Word as word itself. Again, this is understood to occur at moments, not continuously.

A final apology for dragging the reader over familiar terrain. I have not seen these precepts gathered together cogently in any of the criticism on Hart Crane and I have felt that the poem has been dealt with unfairly because of it. Here, major ideas have been shamelessly summarized for what I hope is a sound purpose: to provide a poetics for *The Bridge.*

Since the poem is not symbolic (since it refers not outside itself but to itself) it calls attention to its own devices. This self-consciousness has often been distracting to critics who want a myth, but if the Word is sacramental it must call attention to itself. Thus we get a language which both Glauco Cambon and Joseph Riddel have characterized as "violent."[17] It is a good term, entirely appropriate to the moment of ecstasis (the god dies, after all). Other characterizations include Cambon's "accumulated paroxysm" and "forest of baroque exclamations" (on the same page!),[18] R. P. Blackmur's "sweeping, discrete, indicative, anecdotal language,"[19] David Bulwer Lutyens' "a kind of inspired telegraphese."[20] Crane himself, in his **"General Aims and Theories,"** speaks of "the logic of metaphor"—as well as "shorthand" in a letter—and in *The Bridge* itself he offers "unfractioned idiom" and "sanskrit charge." Clearly the language calls to us.

If not symbolic, then, what is it? I am struck—after due study and the shock of crabbed rhythms and oddness has worn off—with the absence of simile. The manifold likenesses in the poem are all demanded; whereas a simile is an instruction to notice a likeness, the metaphor is an injunction. The difference—I am delighted to discover after all these years—is precisely the difference between consubstantiation (the simile, the symbol) and transubstantiation (the metaphor). The first requires aesthetic distance, the latter participation; the first insists on likeness, the latter suggests identity. It follows that when one interprets a metaphor, he participates in the poem (by identifying the likeness); one merely acknowledges a simile. Thus it is consistent with the poetic outlined that *The Bridge* is devoid of simile and packed with metaphor; it requiresparticipation.

It is time to quote Longinus on language:

> There are, it may be said, five principal sources of elevated language. . . . First and most important is the power of forming great conceptions. . . . Secondly, there is vehement and inspired passion. These two components of the sublime are for the most part innate. Those which remain are partly the product of art. The due formation of figures deals with two sorts of figures, first those of thought and secondly those of expression. Next there is noble diction, which in turn comprises choice of words, and use of metaphors, and elaboration of language. The fifth cause of elevation . . . is dignified and elevated composition. . . . [21]

For Aristotle, language was "embellishment"; catharsis was achieved by action. But for Longinus language "elevates"; ecstasis is achieved by choice of words. If the poet innately has the first two powers—conceptual and passionate—then by artifice he can create the "elevation," the moment of expanded apprehension. The metaphor is the figure Longinus indicates and the only undebatable qualification for such artifice. Whether Crane is capable of "figures" of thought, noble diction, or dignified composition is therefore moot. Whether he is capable of metaphor is not.

Metaphor—implied likeness—is basic to many figures of speech: personification, metonymy, synecdoche, paradox, oxymoron, etc. But we are looking for that figure which most intensifies the likeness so as to make it an identity, intense and immediate. Only that will satisfy our need for the ecstatic moment. That figure is the pun. For the pun integrates two ideas into the same sound. The symbol merely integrates two ideas into the same notion; and the simile merely insists on integration. It is the immediacy of the pun that allows it its special effect. The pun tries— as Lewis says of the **"Atlantis"** section—"to say everything at once."[22] This is the linguistic equivalent of transubstantiation. With the pun the author (god/poet) does two things at once (dies/is resurrected); the reader makes this possible by responding to the pun in its twofold meaning at the same moment; and the ecstasy is achieved instantaneously. The pun says, This is my body and my blood; I died, I live. Both ideas—whether ironic (to an atheist) or celebratory (to a believer)—are implicated in the one word—logos, Christ, or—for Crane—word itself, "multitudinous Verb."

This is a good deal to argue for the infamous pun, whose history is not pretty. It is certainly a frequent device in *The Bridge,* although the critics have on the whole ignored it (except for some local effects) or summarized it and thus left the reader without bearings. Yet it is a potent literacy device (re: Joyce) and to a Longinian approach quite perfect for instant, intense apprehension. For an Aristotelian—or neoclassicist—it is quite indecorous, however; here, for instance, is Dr. Johnson sitting in judgment on Shakespeare's puns:

> A quibble is to *Shakespeare,* what luminous vapours are to the traveller; he follows it at all adventures; it is sure to lead him out of his way, and sure to engulf him in the mire. It has some malignant power over his mind, and its fascinations are irresistible. . . . A quibble is the golden apple for which he will always turn aside from his career, or stoop from his elevation. A quibble, poor and barren as it is, gave him such delight, that he was content to purchase it, by the sacrifice of reason, propriety and truth. A quibble was to him the fatal *Cleopatra* for which he lost the world, and was content to lose it.[23]

It's a wonder the pun did not disappear from the very vocabulary, so felicitous is the Doctor's damning phrase. One is almost convinced (like a Polonius): 'Tis very like Cleopatra! But the pun did not die with the Queen of Egypt; it lived to relish "infinite variety" in English poetry.

Coleridge, on the other hand, recognized Shakespeare's puns as intensifiers and—whether in comic or serious moods—most would agree. In our time, a close critic of Shakespeare can write:

> By means of the multiplicity of meanings characteristic of the pun, Shakespeare is able to let his characters understand each other in different degrees. The characters may talk with each other and really believe that they understand each other. But the true (hidden) meaning of the one is not grasped by the other. The

audience, however, may well understand it.[24]

In other words, the pun has gained recognition as functional, either as intensifier or a key to dramatic irony. And these are the very fundamental uses of the pun in Crane.

I say "very fundamental" because William Empson has argued seven types of ambiguity in which the pun figures prominently. To involve ourselves in his sensibility would be to lose track of our prey, except perhaps to note that Empson's definition of the third type of ambiguity is what is meant here by the pun: "when two ideas, which are connected only by being both relevant in the context, can be given in one word simultaneously."[25] He goes on to distinguish this from the fourth type, in which we encounter "a more complicated state of mind in the author."[26] an assertion rather appropriate to Crane (Empson analyzes a poem by Hopkins in this section), but the third type offers a clear perspective from which to view the common pun.

The common pun—or an aspect of paronomasia, the wordplay which is identified with the lyric—is of three typical kinds: derivations, homophones, and compressed metaphors (often fossilized). One might include those words which strongly suggest others, such as the **"Proem"**'s *unfractioned*—which suggests not-fractioned (as in mathematics), not fractured, and not refracted (as in optics)—and I have no objection to calling these semi-puns, but they resemble metonymy and I will not discuss them.

Although the pun shares with simile and symbol the aspect of likeness, its special feature is simultaneity, as Empson suggests. This feature is not foreign to Crane criticism. R. W. B. Lewis says of the **"Atlantis"** section, "The almost overpowering difficulty is rather that this is a work of total synthesis, one which at every point is trying . . . to say everything at once."[27] Coffman early commented on the "multiple values of the most efficient of Crane's images,"[28] and Herman says that the puns "were a method of loading his words with implications and disparate meanings; sometimes with ironic context . . . sometimes packed with emotional implications. . . . [29]

This simultaneity at first suggested to me a structure for *The Bridge,* something—perhaps—like Arpad's platonic notion that "the bridge was not only the material ideal of a nation, but also the spiritual ideal of the individual"[30] or Eugene Paul Nassar's general view that it is a poem "which dramatizes a dualistic experience of life,"[31] or something dealing with the imagery of doubleness, from "twin monoliths" to "biplane" to "whispers antiphonal." But that leads to no Aristotelian structure. Neither does the hopeful but vapid assertion which one reads over and over again, that (in this case, Lewis) the dual vision has led to "a visionary wedding of the timeless and the temporal, the ideal and the actual,"[32] an idea variously adumbrated.

That *kind* of structure is not forthcoming from the poem. What actually happens to the reader is that *at moments* he feels some identity between two "things," some immediateness. If the poet is in control, these are moments of ecstatic understanding, the fullest possible participation in the poem. At such a moment the poet-god has uttered a word-death which absorbs the reader-communicant. No amount of exegesis after the fact will substitute for that moment, that participation. So Lewis is somewhat justified in apologizing for the "critical betrayal" of analysis when he looks at the word *curveship* at the end of **"Proem"**:

> It is almost a critical betrayal to dismantle the word "curveship," so many of the ingredients of "Proem" has it fused and with such finality; but it secretes too ingenious a pun not to remark upon it. The "curve" in the coined word relates the bridge's arching curve to the inviolate curve by which the sea gull, at dawn, had forsaken our eyes; and it thus suggests that the lost morning vision may—by means of the bridge and of what the bridge has been made torepresent—yet be recovered. The second syllable recalls the sails that had similarly been glimpsed and had vanished; while it also adds dignity to the object addressed. . . . But Crane perhaps knew that the word "ship" is equivalent to the word "nave" in religious architecture—from the Latin word *navis.* The nave is the central passage or path across which the believer moves to come into God's presence at the altar; by its etymology, it is therefore both the way and the vessel which carries the believer along the way.[33]

Far from being a "critical betrayal," this is what I believe the Crane critic *must* do (and with no apologies or hesitations about whether Crane knew Latin or not). For I am convinced there is no Aristotelian, primary or previous structure, only such chosen words which intermittently drive us deeply into the poetic process itself: the relationship between words, the possibilities of words.

The real "betrayal" in Lewis' words is not the exegesis itself, but the distance he tries to establish. It is *his* self-consciousness that is so inappropriate here (although understandable because it is after the fact); this is not the communicant's or the Longinus response. What he says is—in the proper perspective—"the mind is transported into word associations because of the pun." One wishes the critic could be so humble as to admit this. We remember that the Longinian approach requires subjectivity.

I chose the word *curveship* for focus not only because of its ingenuity, but because it focuses the critical issue. The word has been the jumping-off place for those who trace the "curve" imagery throughout *The Bridge* and find there the coherence which the Aristotelian demands of art. For instance, in a sensitive and valuable essay, Stanley K. Coffman finds the curve the primary image:

> The bridge thus speaks, through this one of its properties, a universal geometry, an "unfractioned idiom," and argues, by what can best be called a logic of metaphor, the fundamental point which

the poem was to present: its man-made configuration, repeated by nature, is given a kind of divinity, and the mathematical thinking which planned it a like sanctity.[34]

One is grateful for such a statement, for it challenges the reader to think through the poem, even though it cannot finally be adopted. So, too, for a list of "thematic anticipations" which Frederick J. Hoffman provides in his book, *The Twenties*.[35] And the same is true for any concentration on language interworking in Crane. Yet the various explanations have been unconvincing simply because they are detached; because they preconceive the poem's function as pattern, the poem as *techne*. It is not finally satisfactory with Crane to objectify the poem. This would seem to be the critic's aesthetic, not the poet's.

Freed from the myth and Aristotelian ideas of structure, the critic should be allowed (or required, rather) to respond with intimacy and with faith in the poetic process. For the reader who perceives the pun, there is immediate delight; this would seem to be the value of the "thesaurus effect"—it rewards the reader as well as the poet. Crane's shorthand is for those who can read shorthand. It is not required of the poet that he be democratic, that his vision be available to all, or that his effects be common. Stanley K. Coffman is an inspired reader in this sense; he may project onto the poem more form than it can admit of, but he is ready to follow the signs and participate in the workings of the poem. He too recognizes the nature of the pun:

> One more instance of Crane's use of white, to illustrate further the multiple values of his imagery. . . . In "**Atlantis**" the stars ring the Bridge in a "*palladium* helm." Silver-white *palladium* from the vocabulary of science carries out, of course, Crane's effort to express the natural in the vocabulary of his age (with *helm*, it gives new expression to the old); it is an element which is rare, costly; it is malleable and fuses more readily than the others of its group—all properties which support and enlarge the meaning of the central symbol to which it is related through its color and its use here with *star*. It was, in fact, named for an asteroid, which in turn took its name from Pallas Athene. *Palladium* also denotes a statue of Athene, in particular one on thecitadel of Troy which was supposed to guarantee the safety of the city, and by extension applies to anything that is said to ensure protection: a further passage from palladium to the Bridge, and additional evidence of the remarkable strength of Crane's epithets.[36]

This is true Crane criticism—in spite of the pointless "central symbol" business. Coffman here participates in the choice of the word *palladium* in just the way the poet does; thus there is true communion between poet, reader, and word. It is just what the Longinian critic must do.

Not every word of *The Bridge* creates such ecstasis. How could it? Prolonged ecstasy is called madness. One can-

not be at the "high" point constantly because it would no longer be the "high" point. A rhythm of stress and unstress is required, which may suggest the value of such "low-stress" poems as "**Harbor Dawn,**" "**Indiana,**" and "**Three Songs.**" But *The Bridge* signals such moments more often than most poems—thus the "violence" of its language. We are forced to communion by the language.

When to praise and when to condemn? For me that is the crucial issue of critical application. If the reader does not recognize what Lewis and Coffman do in the puns on *curveship* and *palladium,* how is he to appreciate fully, participate fully, in the language (subject *and* object of *The Bridge*)? Since the approach is subjective of necessity (Longinian, lyrical, religious) what can determine the excellencies and what the failures of the poem? Only personal response? Surely more is required of any adequate reader. I have quoted Lewis and Coffman at length because I think that is what is required: thorough, even creative investigation of the language. Instead of imposing myth or vision or even pattern on the poem, he must be open to it, to be response-able, to take the color and meanings as its wafer and wine. No doubt there are meager moments in *The Bridge* and even trivial puns, but in the larger rhythm it is the accomplishment of the ecstastic moments that counts, that makes the poem the achievement it is. Only an appropriate poetics is needed to appreciate that.

And that's where I want to end. On the accomplishment and the plain, simple/complex *work* that goes into it. Hart Crane was no "inspired idiot." He was, to adjust an earlier idea, at *work* in the field of words. He was a professional poet. Malcolm Cowley tells an almost funny story about Crane choosing a word for the great lyric, "**Voyages II.**" The word is the celebrated *spindrift*, which is unimprovable in its context. Crane is paging through a dictionary, his eye falls on the word, and he instantly recognizes it as the perfect word for the line: "The seal's wide spindrift gaze toward paradise."[37] This I call an almost funny story because it causes some unease in the critic. If the word did not come *out of* the poet, can it be truly his? Is it talent or genius to find a word in a dictionary? This is pointless unease. The fact is that when we encounter the word—in its sounds, meanings, and relationships to other words—we discover it, just as the poet did. The form of *The Bridge* is just this process. And Hart Crane, like Gerard Manley Hopkins, was that kind of poet, a professional ecstatic.

NOTES

[1] Allen Tate, *Man of Letters in the Modern World* (Cleveland: World, 1955), p. 290.

[2] See Crane's letter to Harriet Monroe for another, more humble Crane: "The execution is another matter, and you must be accorded a superior judgment to mine in that regard." (In Brom Weber, ed., *The Complete Poems and Selected Letters and Prose of Hart Crane* [New York: Doubleday Anchor, 1966, p. 240].)

[3] Northrop Frye, *Anatomy of Criticism: Four Essays* (Princeton: Princeton Univ. Press, 1957), p. 66.

[4] *Ibid.,* p. 67.

[5] *Ibid.,* p. 326.

[6] *Ibid.,* pp. 271-72.

[7] Frye usefully says, "a good deal of sacred literature is written in a style full of puns and verbal echoes," *ibid.,* p. 294.

[8] John Unterecker, *Voyager: A Life of Hart Crane* (New York: Farrar, Straus and Giroux, 1969), pp. 528-29.

[9] Yvor Winters, *On Modern Poets* (New York: Meridian Books, 1959; originally 1943), p. 174.

[10] Unterecker, *Voyager: A Life of Hart Crane,* p. 526. A passage from a general, brief study of Hopkins will relate his affiliation with Crane: "What Hopkins provides is not exposition, reflection, and argument but a succession of spontaneously engendered feelings, concentrated by scenes, some narrated, some enacted, and uttered in language and imagery thick with implication, 'manifold' in suggestion—to adopt a crucial adjective from T. E. Hulme, the theorist of the Imagist movement—which in its own fashion led the 'twenties in search of the 'intensive manifold,' of intensity as opposed to amplitude, of impact rather than exposition" (Francis Noel Lees, *Gerard Manley Hopkins,* New York: Columbia Univ. Press, 1966, pp. 13-14).

[11] L. S. Dembo, *Hart Crane's Sanskrit Charge: A Study of* The Bridge (Ithaca, N.Y.: Cornell Univ. Press, 1960), p. 9 and p. 34).

[12] R. W. B. Lewis, *The Poetry of Hart Crane* (Princeton: Princeton Univ. Press, 1967), p. 382.

[13] Joseph Riddel, "Hart Crane's Poetics of Failure," *ELH,* 33, no. 4 (Dec. 1966), 478.

[14] Barbara Herman, "The Language of Hart Crane," *Sewanee Review,* 58 (1950), 52.

[15] *Ibid.,* p. 54.

[16] *Ibid.,* p. 61.

[17] Glauco Cambon, *The Inclusive Flame* (Bloomington: Indiana Univ. Press, 1963), p. 134, and Riddel, "Hart Crane's Poetics of Failure," p. 486.

[18] Cambon, *The Inclusive Flame,* p. 164.

[19] R. P. Blackmur, *Language as Gesture* (New York: Harcourt Brace, 1952), p. 305.

[20] David Bulwer Lutyens, *The Creative Encounter* (London: Secker & Warburg, 1960), p. 99.

[21] Bernard F. Dukore, *Dramatic Theory and Criticism* (New York: Holt, Rinehart, and Winston, 1974), p. 79.

[22] Lewis, *The Poetry of Hart Crane,* p. 370.

[23] Walter Raleigh, ed., *Johnson on Shakespeare* (Oxford: Oxford Univ. Press, 1908), pp. 23-24.

[24] W. H. Clemens, *The Development of Shakespeare's Imagery* (London, 1951; rpt. Cambridge: Harvard Univ. Press, 1951), pp. 91-92.

[25] William Empson, *Seven Types of Ambiguity* (London: Chatto and Windus, 1956), p. 102.

[26] *Ibid.,* p. 133.

[27] Lewis, *The Poetry of Hart Crane,* p. 370.

[28] Stanley K. Coffman, "Symbolism in *The Bridge,*" *PMLA,* 66 (Mar. 1951), 70.

[29] Herman, "The Language of Hart Crane," p. 63.

[30] Joseph J. Arpad, "Hart Crane's Platonic Myth: The Brooklyn Bridge," *American Literature,* 39, no. 1 (Mar. 1967), 85.

[31] Eugene Paul Nassar, *The Rape of Cinderella* (Bloomington: Indiana Univ. Press, 1970), p. 144.

[32] Lewis, *The Poetry of Hart Crane,* p. 369.

[33] *Ibid.,* pp. 254-55.

[34] Coffman, "Symbolism in *The Bridge,*" p. 67.

[35] Frederick J. Hoffman, *The Twenties: American Writing in the Postwar Decade,* rev. ed. (New York: The Free Press, 1962), p. 264n.

[36] Coffman, "Symbolism in *The Bridge,*" p. 72.

[37] Malcolm Cowley, *Exile's Return* (New York: Viking Press, 1951), pp. 229-30.

**Malcolm Cowley (essay date 1981)**

SOURCE: "Two Views of 'The Bridge'," in *The Sewanee Review,* Vol. LXXXIX, No. 2, Spring, 1981, pp. 191-205.

[*In the following essay, Cowley explains what he sees as two different ways to read* The Bridge: *"integrationists," who assert that the poem has a unified plot and vision, and "dispersionists," who believe that the poem is inherently and deliberately fragmented.*]

Fifty years after the book was first published, little doubt remains that Hart Crane's **The Bridge** is a monument of American poetry. Among the longer poetic works I should place it below Whitman's "Song of Myself," but above almost everything else; and this is a judgment shared by many critics. The argument that continues to rage is about where its principal virtue lies. Should we reread it now as something unified, a special type of epic, or is it an aggregation of fifteen lyrics, most of them having a rather distant kinship with the others? Is the whole greater than the sum of its parts, or are a few of the parts greater than the whole?

In this argument the two opposing schools might be called the integrationists and the dispersionists. R.W.B. Lewis is an outstanding member of the first school. In *The Poetry of Hart Crane* he asserts that *The Bridge* has a unified plot, which is "the gradual permeation of an entire culture by the power of poetic vision." But is that a plot, strictly speaking, or is it something else, a theme with variations? In the other camp Brom Weber might be cited as an extreme dispersionist. "Nothing useful can be accomplished," he says in his *Hart Crane*, "by persisting in the consideration of *The Bridge* as a unified poem. . . . [It] is a collection of individual lyrics of varying quality." Its readers should "cease mourning the failure of *The Bridge* as a whole"—something that Weber takes for granted—"and begin acclaiming Crane for the poetic achievements which are lavishly strewn throughout its length."

Might it be that both sides are partly right in their opposite contentions? *The Bridge* does have a unity based on the poet's vision of the complete work; mark down a score for Lewis and his side. Each of the fifteen lyrics does embody parts of that vision, and each of them states or restates themes that are also sounded in other lyrics, thus creating a web of interconnections, as in a symphony. The vision is personal, however, and almost impossible to paraphrase. Sometimes it falters, with the result that the separate lyrics, or movements in the symphony, are of strikingly uneven value; Brom Weber was right about that, as almost everyone agrees. *The Bridge* might have seemed an even greater poem if two or three of them had been omitted.

Does it follow that the work as a whole is a failure? The answer must be a firm Yes and a firm No. Obviously *The Bridge* falls short of the author's sweeping conception. Crane, as he often explained, was undertaking to create a myth of America, a "mystical synthesis" of our past, present, and future. Success in such a venture is impossible; to fashion that myth of America will never be more than a Faustian dream. Crane was, if you will, a Faustian character, a heaven-stormer bent on rising above the human condition by magic and force of will, and if necessary by selling his soul. Even if his goal had been attainable, he was doomed to fall short of it by American realities, in which, as he often said, he was "caught like a rat in a trap."

He was also doomed by the strengths and failings of his character. He had vision, energy, obdurate patience—genius, in a word; he had a magnificent sense of rhythm; but also he had limited knowledge and something less

than the immense stamina required for the completion of his task. Eventually he was worn out by his efforts (and of course by the debaucheries that he regarded as a necessary part of them). He abandoned the poem—that is the proper word here—a month before it was published in February 1930. But can one say that *The Bridge* was a failure except in his own Faustian terms? Hasn't the partially realized dream a grandeur of its own, like a crusader's castle that looms above a squalid village in Lebanon? Already *The Bridge* has survived its author by half a century. It will continue to live by virtue of its bold conception, the splendor of its language, and the almost complete rightness of some of its parts. As compared with other American poets of his time, Crane was an heroic success.

II

How *The Bridge* was written is a story that has to be told again. It casts light on the extraordinary qualities of the work and on why they are absent from some passages.

The project was conceived in the first week of February 1923, when Crane was working for an advertising agency in Cleveland. It was mentioned February 6 in letters he wrote to his friends Gorham Munson and Allen Tate. "I'm already started on a new poem, *The Bridge*," he said in the letter to Tate, "which continues the tendencies that are evident in 'Faustus and Helen,' but it's too vague and nebulous yet to talk about." Two weeks later he was ready to say more, in a letter to Munson:

> I am too much interested in this *Bridge* thing lately to write letters, ads, or anything. It is just beginning to take the least outline,—and the more outline the conception of the thing takes,—the more its final difficulties appal me. . . . Very roughly, it concerns a mystical synthesis of "America." History and fact, location, etc., all have to be transfigured into abstract form that would almost function independently of its subject matter. The initial impulses of "our people" will have to be gathered up toward the climax of the bridge, symbol of our constructive future, our unique identity, in which is included also our scientific hopes and achievements of the future. The mystic portent of all this is already flocking through my mind . . . but the actual statement of the thing, the marshalling of the forces, will take me months, at best, and I may have to give it up entirely before that; it may be too impossible an ambition. But if I do succeed, such a waving of banners, such an ascent of towers, such dancing, etc., will never before have been put down on paper!

Already he had started work on **"Atlantis,"** which was to be the concluding section of the poem. But that waving of banners and ascent of towers had to be deferred when Crane lost his job in Cleveland and moved to New York. There, in the midst of distractions—looking for a job then finding it, sitting late in speakeasies, and roaming the city with exciting new friends—he had little time for the intense concentration that the poem required. He kept working on it, sometimes with a feeling of exaltation, but progress was slow. In the spring of 1924 it was halted altogether by his falling in love and writing his **"Voyages"** as a celebration. Again progress was halted when he decided to put together a book of shorter poems to precede *The Bridge;* he agonized over details. "I've spent all of today at one or two stubborn lines," he told a friend.

In December 1925 the financier Otto Kahn made him a grant of (eventually) two thousand dollars, and Hart went to the country to spend the winter with Allen and Caroline Tate, in an old house near Patterson, New York. During the next four months he wrote another draft of **"Atlantis"** and made a good start on **"Ave María"**—jumping to the other end of his bridge—but more of his time was spent reading, and reading closely. Some of the authors were Melville, Prescott, Columbus (for the journals), and Alfred North Whitehead, each of whom would contribute something to his planned work. The plan itself was the principal achievement of those months. Now he saw more clearly what he hoped to write, if he could find the mood to write it.

The mood suddenly appeared in the last ten days of July 1926, when he was living in a house that his grandmother owned on the Isle of Pines. "Hail Brother!" he wrote on July 24 to his friend and mentor Waldo Frank. "I feel an absolute music in the air again and some tremendous rondure floating somewhere." He had just completed his Proem, **"To Brooklyn Bridge,"** started earlier that summer, and was busy revising, once again, **"Atlantis"** and **"Ave María."** It was the beginning of the thirty-odd days that biographers call his *mensis mirabilis.* "I feel as though I were dancing on dynamite these days," he told Frank at the beginning of August, "—so absolute and elaborated has become the conception. All sections moving forward now at once!" Before the end of the month he had written something like two-thirds of *The Bridge* as it was finally published. Of course the materials had been patiently assembled, and he was chiefly waiting for the moment when they would put themselves together. But some productions of that miraculous month were completely new: **"Cutty Sark"** and **"Three Songs";** and he had also written a number of lyrics that would be included in his posthumous sheaf of poems, *Key West.* Then, at the end of August, he had to rest, and he rewarded himself with a week in Havana that included an affair with a young Cuban sailor.

Those days on the Isle of Pines had been the climax of his creative life. Most of the symphony or cycle was completed by that time, but there were revisions to be made and there were missing sections that he regarded as essential. He worked on some of these after returning to the old house near Patterson. By the middle of July 1927 he had completed three of them, including **"The River,"** which I think is the best of all. But it was to be the last of his greater poems—except for **"The Broken Tower,"** written shortly before his death.

In September, before setting out to look for a job in the city, Hart wrote a very long letter to his benefactor Otto Kahn. The letter boasted of what he had so far accomplished and apologized for his delay in completing *The Bridge.* "It has taken a great deal of energy," he said, "—which has not been so difficult to summon as the necessary patience to wait, simply wait much of the time—until my instincts assured me that I had assembled my materials in proper order for a final welding into their natural form." Hart had always waited for those moments of confident inspiration and had tried to induce them by drinking, music, dancing, copulation, and anything else that might give him an overarching vision of his materials. It was all part of his system for producing masterpieces.

The letter continued: "Each section of the entire poem has presented its own unique problem of form, not alone in relation to the materials embodied within its separate confines, but also in relation to the other parts, *in series,* of the major design of the entire poem. Each is a separate canvas, as it were, yet none yields its entire significance when seen apart from the others." Hart himself was a resolute integrationist. He offered notes on several of the finished sections "as a comment on my architectural method," then went on to the still unwritten **"Cape Hatteras."** "It will be a kind of ode to Whitman," he said. "I am working on it as much as possible now. It presents very formidable problems, as, indeed, all the sections have." He was determined to complete not only **"Hatteras"** but the whole grand work as soon as possible. "If I could work in Mexico or Mallorca this winter," he said, "I could have *The Bridge* finished by next spring. But that is a speculation which depends entirely on your interest."

Kahn did show interest and offered a further loan, but *The Bridge* wasn't finished that winter, which Hart spent in California, or the following summer, when he returned to the old house near Patterson. His life was becoming more and more disordered, and his friends were disturbed by signs of physical deterioration. In December 1928 he received a legacy of five thousand dollars from his grandmother's estate and sailed for Europe. There he plunged into wilder revels, this time in the company of wealthy new friends, Harry and Caresse Crosby, who admired his poems and applauded his follies. They gave him a room to write in, at the old mill they had leased near Paris, and for a time he made some progress on **"Cape Hatteras."** The Crosbys undertook to publish *The Bridge* at their Black Sun Press, and finally Caresse, who could lay down the law in her mild way, told him that she would go ahead with the book, on schedule, whether or not Hart supplied the missing sections. It would be a great poem, she said, even without them. Hart was almost persuaded, but then, begging for time, he insisted that three more sections would be required to carry out his plan.

When he sailed home at the end of July, after spending a week in jail as the sequel to a brawl outside a Montparnasse café, Hart was determined to finish *The Bridge* at any cost. It had become a test of himself and the supreme justification he might offer to others for his apparently wasted years. He could no longer afford to "wait, simply wait much of the time" for the moment when his materials assembled themselves; now he had to summon the moment by force of will. Drunk or sober, but mostly sober, he reworked **"Cape Hatteras"** and finished it by the middle of September. The other two missing sections had been sketched out, and he told Caresse in a letter that they might be ready the following week. Then suddenly he found himself unable to write anything whatever, and he began to drink heavily out of desperation.

The next three months were a series of battles with himself in which he was usually but not always defeated. There were nights when he telephoned wildly for help and a trusted friend, usually Lorna Dietz or Peggy Robson, came to sit at his bedside while he threshed about in delirium tremens. There were days and even weeks when he applied himself to the poems in a sober frenzy. **"Indiana"** was finished after one of those weeks. It went off to the Crosbys with apologies for the "letdown" of its language—but, Hart added, "It does round out the [**"Powhatan's Daughter"**] cycle, at least historically and psychologically."

With only one more section to finish, Hart should have been confident. Instead he fell into a period of despair and sought refuge at his father's house in Ohio. He was cheerful there until a threatened visit from his mother, with whom he had bitterly quarreled, sent him scuttling back to Brooklyn. Just as he was beginning to work seriously on the last section, **"Quaker Hill,"** the Crosbys appeared, bringing with them a round of parties. Hart was devoted to both the Crosbys, and he was deeply shaken by Harry's unexpected suicide, on the evening of December 10. Nevertheless he went back to work, by now in a dogged fashion. All of *The Bridge* was in type except for that last poem. Caresse, before sailing back to France alone, had promised to publish the book in February if she received a final manuscript of **"Quaker Hill"** by New Year's Day. Hart mailed it in time to catch the *Mauretania* on December 26. The great project had been completed in five weeks less than seven years.

Much as one admires Hart for having won that battle against his personal devils, one can't help asking whether those last two poems were worth the torments they inflicted on him. **"Indiana"** is flat and forced. It does provide a transition between two better sections, **"The Dance"** and **"Cutty Sark,"** but not in the right manner. Lines such as "Lit with love shine" and "Will still endear her" belong in a musichall ballad. **"Quaker Hill"** also has a function that it performs not too effectively. It deals with the decay of New England, which, the poet felt, wasinvolved with his own decay. On the whole it is better than **"Indiana"** and it has a very few memorable lines—among them "Shoulder the curse of sundered parentage," which applies so well to Hart—but most of the verse is tired. Only the last two stanzas rise to the level of his best work.

**"Cape Hatteras,"** the section he finished in September of that year after struggling over it since 1927, has more to be said in its favor. It was part of his original conception; without it *The Bridge* would not have seemed to him complete. It embodies his complicated attitude toward American technology: first, admiration for its achievements and for the sheer beauty of machinery (including such items as ball bearings that revolve "In oilrinsed circles of blind ecstasy"); then, second, dismay at the dismal way of life that technology imposes on us, leading as it does to war in the skies; and finally the hope that technology will somehow be redeemed and spiritualized by a new race of poets, with Whitman, not Virgil, as their guide through the American inferno. **"Cape Hatteras"** has a sounder structure than most critics have been willing to admit, but it also has more ineptitudes of rhyme and image. Especially I am haunted by Hart's vision of a huge dirigible with landing decks, an aerial supership that would serve as mother vessel for whole squadrons of fighter planes. Hart was proud of that vision, and I remember his declaiming the passage, just after he had written it during a week spent at the old house near Patterson:

> While Cetus-like, O thou Dirigible, enormous
>     Lounger
> Of pendulous auroral beaches,—satellited wide
> By convoy planes, moonferrets that rejoin thee
> On fleeing balconies as thou dost glide,
> —Hast splintered space!

Yes, we applauded the lines, but with a sense of uneasiness about his picture of wars to come. Of course he was writing in 1929, eight years before the *Hindenburg* burst into flames at Lakewood and ended the era of huge dirigibles. Hart was vaunting himself as a futurist, a breed to whom the future is seldom kind. What seems less pardonable as one rereads the passage is the Elizabethan bombast, with all those capital letters and that high thee-thouing of a ballroom as if it were a divinity. **"Cape Hatteras"** is the section most often cited by those who insist that Hart's grand project was a failure. Still, the section had to be written. It sweeps along and—contrary to the judgment of some critics—almost reaches its goal. Continually it teeters on the edge of greatness, but at the risk of stumbling into absurdity.

III

I don't like to align myself with the dispersionists, who are so often blind to implications and interconnections, but still I feel relief in passing from **"Cape Hatteras"** to the indubitably great sections of *The Bridge,* all finished by 1927. The great sections are **"Ave María," "The River," "The Dance," "The Tunnel,"** and **"Atlantis";** the nearly great are **"To Brooklyn Bridge," "The Harbor Dawn,"** and **"Cutty Sark."** Each of these—including those I call "nearly great"—is not only successful in itself, having solved a special problem of form, but is also a contribution, as Hart rightly insisted, to "the major design of the entire poem." Each has the rich illogic of metaphor that marked his writing, as well as an extraordinary range of vocabulary. To put the revelations of modern music into words, Hart said in an early letter to Gorham Munson, "one needs to *ransack* the vocabularies of Shakespeare, Jonson, Webster (for theirs were the richest) and add on scientific, street and counter, and psychological terms, etc. Yet I claim such things can be done!" He had said in a still earlier letter: "One must be drenched in words, literally soaked with them to have the right ones form themselves into the proper pattern at the right moment."

One aspect of his vocabulary was the special effort he made to find concrete verbs of action that would vivify his images. There is a simple example early in the Proem, **"To Brooklyn Bridge."** The noonday sun *leaks* into the downtown canyons, where—in a noun so vigorous as to have the effect of a verb, it becomes "A rip-tooth of the sky's acetylene." Near the end of the same poem one admires theline "Already snow *submerges* an iron year." (The italics in these and later quotations are mine.) In the first stanza of **"Van Winkle,"** a highway does not merely cross the continent; it "*Leaps* from Far Rockaway to Golden Gate." "And when the caribou *slant down* for salt," Hart writes in **"The Dance,"** creating an image mostly with the one word *slant*. Another stanza in the same poem contains ten verbs, of which seven are in the imperative mood:

> *Dance,* Maquokeeta! snake that lives before,
> That casts his pelt and lives beyond! *Sprout,* horn!
> *Spark,* tooth! Medicine man, *relent, restore*—
> *Lie* to us,—*dance* us back the primal morn!

Of course Crane's magical use of language is not confined to verbs. Sometimes an adverb is the key to a phrase, as in two other lines from **"The Dance"**: "Now lie *incorrigibly* what years between . . ." and "Fall, Sachem, *strictly* as the tamarack." *Strictly* is exactly the word for the fall of a conifer, just as *tamarack,* an Algonquian word, is a proper choice for the tree. Crane's adjectives are never wasted and are sometimes aptly new, as in "Preparing *penguin* flexions of the arms"—this in **"The Tunnel,"** where "The subway yawns the quickest promise home." As for his nouns, when they are most abstract he likes to combine them with a concrete verb. Thus he says of his tramps in **"The River"** that "*dotting immensity/*They *lurk* across her, knowing her yonder breast."

Still it is the verbs that best reveal the intensity of his feelings or the simple accuracy of his perceptions. In the dementia of the subway he comes to suspect that love is only "a burnt match *skating* in a urinal"; it is the *skating* that makes the phrase unforgettable. In **"The River"** Crane is less agonized and more observing. Thus he notes that the taillights of an express train "*wizen* and *converge, slip-/ping* gimleted and neatly out of sight." He says of the hoboes watching the Limited as they "*ploddingly*" follow the tracks:

> Caboose-like they go *ruminating* through
> Ohio, Indiana—blind baggage—
> To Cheyenne *tagging* . . . Maybe Kalamazoo.

Except for the rhyme that last word isn't quite right, having been abused by stand-up comics; but Crane is usually adept with place-names and their connotations. Far Rockaway, Golden Gate, Gravesend Manor (this last as a destination for people buried in the subway): each of these names serves one of his purposes. As for a town mentioned by the hoboes who used to follow the railroad tracks—

> "There's no place like Booneville though,
>     Buddy,"
> One said, excising a last burr from his vest,
> "—For early trouting."

Crane is trying to suggest a parallel between the hoboes and the American pioneers, and Booneville has the right echo for that. "Excising a last burr" is a modest but perfect phrase. When he comments on the hoboes as a group

> Each seemed a child, like me, on a loose perch,
> Holding to childhood like some termless play.
> John, Jake or Charley, hopping the slow freight
> —Memphis to Tallahassee—riding the rods,
> Blind fists of nothing, humpty-dumpty clods.

I could go on quoting from **"The River,"** which is the section in which Crane best combined his accurate observation, his ear for idiom, and his broader vision of the American continent. It is also the longest section, except for **"Cape Hatteras,"** and it is soundly constructed from the first to the last of its 144 lines; Crane had a gift for building with large blocks. The first of those blocks, in **"The River,"** is the shortest; it is a passage of twenty-three lines. Hart described it in that famous letter to Otto Kahn, where he said that it is "an intentional burlesque on the cultural confusion of the present—a conglomeration of noises analogous to the strident impression of a fast express rushing by. The rhythm is jazz." In the second block, this one of forty-eight lines, "the rhythm settles down to a steady pedestrian gait, like that of wanderers plodding along. My tramps are psychological vessels, also. Their wanderings, as you will notice, carry the reader into interior after interior, finally to the great River." There follows a transitional passage of forty-one lines in a more elevated tone; it brings in suggestions of an earlier world, especially when "Trains sounding the long blizzards out" are transformed into "Papooses crying on the wind's long mane." The last block, in eight rhymed quatrains, is a solemn hymn to the River:

> You will not hear it as the sea; even stone
> Is not more hushed by gravity . . . But slow,
> As loth to take more tribute—sliding prone
> As one whose eyes were buried long ago. . . .

IV

I have always been stirred by those final quatrains, and the impression they made on me was deepened by a remembered circumstance. Early in October 1930, with Peggy, my first wife, I took passage on a freighter bound from New Orleans to Vera Cruz. We would be spending five or six hours on the Mississippi, I was told, before reaching the Gulf. I looked forward to those hours as I recalled Hart's poem. But the autumn day was ending without a sunset, and I could see little from the deck except a monotonous wall of forest to the westward and, if I walked to the bow, another wall to the east unbroken by villages or plantations. To soothe my disappointment I kept repeating lines from Hart's hymn:

> Down two more turns the Mississippi pours
> (Anon tall ironsides up from salt lagoons)
> And flows within itself, heaps itself free.
> All fades but one thin skyline 'round . . . Ahead
> No embrace opens but the stinging sea;
> The River lifts itself from its long bed. . . .

The last of these lines, in its marriage of image and sound, impressed me as one of the greater lines in English poetry. I kept watching for the moment when the River would lift itself as if to embrace the Gulf, but it moved on in level silence. Gradually night fell. Then there was a light off the bow and I knew we were sliding out to sea, if only by the slap of little waves against the hull. I thought of Hart and his more poignant vision. I hadn't seen much of him the previous summer, though I heard that he was dejected after publication of *The Bridge* and unfavorable reviews by two or three of his respected friends. What would he do next?

Three years before, when he wrote **"The River,"** he still hadn't seen the Mississippi except from transcontinental trains. In 1928, however, he had at last sailed from New Orleans on a steamer bound for New York. "The boat ride down the Delta," he reported in a letter to his father, "was one of the great days of my life. It was a place I had so often imagined and, as you know, written about in the River section of *The Bridge*. There is something tragically beautiful about the scene, the great, magnificent Father of Waters pouring itself at last into the oblivion of the Gulf." Hart had a gift that most of us lack, for first imagining a scene and then at last, when he beheld it, infusing the reality with his grand vision. I can picture him standing at the rail as he repeated his final majestic lines:

> The River lifts itself from its long bed,
>
> Poised wholly on its dream, a mustard glow
> Tortured with history, its one will—flow!
> —The Passion spreads in wide tongues, choked
>   and slow,
> Meeting the Gulf, hosannas silently below.

My own disappointing voyage down the Mississippi and across the Gulf was to have its importance in his life. I enjoyed Mexico City more than I did the River, and in March of the following year, when Hart was awarded a Guggenheim fellowship, I suggested that he too might enjoy it instead of going to France as he had originally planned. It was dangerous advice in the circumstances, but Hart accepted it. Meanwhile my first marriage had broken up, and Peggy also went to Mexico, in June, to establish residence for a divorce. Hart lived wildly in Mexico City, and then in December he became Peggy's lover. To celebrate the change in his life, he wrote his last great poem, **"The Broken Tower."** On their return voyage to New York he committed suicide.

## Michael Sharp (essay date 1981)

SOURCE: "Theme and Free Variation: The Scoring of Hart Crane's 'The Bridge' ," in *The Arizona Quarterly*, Vol. 37, No. 3, Autumn, 1981, pp. 197-213.

[*In the following essay, Sharp considers* The Bridge *as a piece of modern music.*]

In a letter to Gorham Munson, Hart Crane wrote:

> Modern music almost drives me crazy! I went to hear D'Indy's *II Symphony* last night and my hair stood on end at its revelations. To get those, and others of men like Strauss, Ravel, Scriabin, and Bloch into *words,* one needs to *ransack* the vocabularies of Shakespeare, Jonson, Webster (for theirs were the richest) and add on scientific, street and counter, and psychological terms, etc. Yet I claim such things can be done![1]

The reference to Vincent d'Indy and "Modern music" is helpful as a starting point to the understanding of Crane's long poem *The Bridge* (1930). D'Indy was the influential director of Paris's Schola Cantorum, founded in 1894, whose "musico-mystical-aesthetic-regime" trained musicians in Gregorian chant and counterpoint.[2] He was also the composer of the *Istar Variations* (1897), in which he modified the variation, as a restatement of a musical theme, by transferring the theme from its usual place at the beginning of a composition to the end. This innovation paved the way for composers like Reger and Richard Strauss to write free variations in which the structural outlines of a theme were almost unrecognizable.

The *Istar Variations,* which begins with a complex variation and ends with a simple theme in octaves, is similar in structure to *The Bridge* in that the latter is developed through various stages of complexity which culminate in the harmonious statement of **"Atlantis,"** the eighth variation of the poem. That the structure of *The Bridge* is a free variation on a theme is evidenced by the apparent disharmony of its development. There is no tight structure or forward movement as there is in Eliot's *The Waste Land* (1922); rather, the poem develops a-chronologically through verbal plainsong and cadence, cacophony and discord. Unlike the atonality of Schoenberg, which attuned to the dissonance of things, Crane argued for the possibility of the ideal by scoring a song of joy. Like his mentors, Blake and Whitman, however, he realized that harmony was not merely a reconciliation of opposites; this much he had learned from Plato's *Symposium*:

> . . . harmony is composed of differing notes of higher or lower pitch which disagreed once, but are now reconciled by the art of music; for if the

higher and lower notes still disagreed, there could be no harmony,—clearly not. For harmony is a symphony, and symphony is an agreement; but an agreement of disagreements while they disagree there cannot be; you cannot harmonize that which disagrees.

Music was a great love of Hart Crane. In 1920, Ernest Bloch became the Director of the Cleveland Institute of Music; he also conducted the institute's orchestra. After seeing Bloch conduct his *Trois Poèmes Juifs,* Crane wrote that it was "magnificent enough for Solomon to have marched & sung to," and of the maestro he said: "I occasionally pass him on the streets or in the aisles of the auditorium, and realize that genius, after all, may walk in Cleveland" (*Letters,* p. 82).

Crane was part of a group which met periodically at the Cleveland Institute of Music. There, he became friends with Jean Binet, a professor of Eurhythmics, who was "a remarkable and inspired amateur pianist, playing Erik Satie, Ravel, etc., to perfection" (*Letters,* p. 66). While in Cleveland, Crane attended a concert every other week, and when he moved away from Ohio, his musical interests aggrandized. In his letters are mentioned Chopin ballades, Scriabin preludes, Debussy's *Dr. Gradus ad Parnassum,* Isadora Duncan dancing to Tschaikovsky's *Pathetique,* a new Victrola on which he listened to Wagner's *The Meistersingers* overture. He also knew the modern music of Bartok, Varèse, Bax, Casella, Szymanowski, and Schoenberg. The latter, he wrote, "is my preference among them all as being the only one who approached the magnificence of Bloch's work as I still remember it from Cleveland performances" (*Letters,* p. 177). At a party in New York, he met Aaron Copland, who in 1944 composed the ballet *Appalachian Spring,* whose title is from **"The Dance."** He met Edgar Varèse in Paris, and while in California he took a liking to Brahms and Beethoven (*Letters,* p. 316). In 1925, he saw Stravinsky conduct but was disappointed because the *Sacre du Printemps* was not included on the program. "I don't care," he wrote, "for what I heard of his *latest work.* Indeed, the *Petrouchka* was the only fine thing on his program" (*Letters,* p. 200).

Crane's taste was not only for classical music; he also liked popular jazz and ethnic music. While in Mexico, the native canciones and the local singers intrigued him. One song, *Las Mañanitas,* he liked particularly, going so far as to say that it "might have been composed by Bach" (*Letters,* p. 408). While he was writing *The Bridge,* he would turn up the volume on his phonograph and compose to the "Brazen hypnotics"[3] of jazz, or Wagner, or Scriabin. In the light of his musical interests, it is appropriate that *The Bridge* was to be "a symphony with an epic theme" (*Letters,* p. 309).

There is in *The Bridge* a harmonizing scheme which is complemented by the aims of the American composers Charles Ives and Aaron Copland. Ives's intention was to "make anew the toughness, power, copiousness, triviality

and grandeur of the American scene and the American spirit."[4] While he did not believe that the real and the ideal could be reconciled in temporality, he insisted that it was the duty of all to attempt such a reconciliation. In order to create a new New World, man must reforge his own individual spirit to reforge society. Copland, on the other hand, sought to reintegrate in his music the broken fragments of the present. His compositions grew out of the mechanical world of the twentieth century, the heir of Ives's traditional America. Consequently, Copland's music is of the city, Ives's of the garden. In *The Bridge,* Hart Crane set out to unify these two disparate elements in a verbal score in which the Brooklyn Bridge, like Schoenberg's twelve-tone row, became a means to faith—the Word from which society might derive sustenance and life.

As suggested, *The Bridge* is a free variation on a theme of the Brooklyn Bridge. It is *free* in the sense that it does not conform to a strict horizontal time sequence. When Crane chose to present a historical analogy, he used the new cinematic technique of flashback. This did not, however, affect the form which is as rigid as a musical score.

The impetus for the form came from the Brooklyn Bridge itself. From the window of his apartment at 110 Columbia Heights, Brooklyn, Crane could see the Manhattan skyline. The roof, which was accessible to him, afforded a panoramic view of John Roebling's masterpiece. Roebling, whom Crane called "a true Spenglerian hero" in a letter to Allen Tate, had been a student and friend of the philosopher Georg Hegel (*Letters,* p. 293). As a result of this friendship, the Brooklyn Bridge is "a thoroughgoing architectural statement of the Hegelian thesis-antithesis-synthesis."[5] This synthesis of antithetical elements, of stone and steel, allowed Crane to compose a poem which conformed to the "One arc synoptic" (**"Atlantis"**) of the Brooklyn Bridge.

That Crane saw the synthesis of his bridge as "synoptic" is no accident, lendingas it does a further dimension to the poem. Just as the first three books of the New Testament are closely related, each presenting a similar account of the birth, death, and resurrection of Christ, so Crane's poem presents a very definite scheme which is both religious and philosophic. Contained within the symbolic design of Hegelian philosophy and religious belief is the American past, present, and projected future. Using the past as his thesis, the antithesis of the present becomes a synthesis in which the future is projected as a harmony of the past and the present. The "triple-noted clause" of **"Quaker Hill"** becomes, for example, a single word, a single song, and a single myth, connected grammatically by a "multitudinous Verb" (**"Atlantis"**) which ultimately links the past and the present to a polyphony which sounds the future. The Brooklyn Bridge is the "harp and altar, of the fury fused" (**"To Brooklyn Bridge"**) whereby this syntactical harmony is achieved.

There are in *The Bridge* nearly two hundred direct or indirect references to sound and music; over ten musical instruments are mentioned specifically by name. The poem, preceded by an introductory proem or prelude, is written in eight sections. Until Chopin changed the nature of the prelude, its purpose was to introduce the theme of a liturgical ceremony or other composition, usually a fugue or a suite. The remaining eight sections of the poem may be seen equally as a verbal octet which develops the theme or, more appropriately, a motet for eight voices. The latter was the most important form of early polyphonic music in the Middle Ages and the Renaissance. Whereas, originally it was an unaccompanied choral composition based on a Latin sacred text, it was adapted over the centuries to accommodate the secular and, in the case of French motets, the licentious. The analogy between *The Bridge* and the Latin motet is not too gratuitous because the latter was a perfect expression of the sacred and the secular which voiced, for example, the universalism of Thomas Aquinas. This sacro-secularism became, in essence, the stuff of Hart Crane's Americanism.

In writing an eight-part motet, which is also a free variation on a theme, Crane broke all musical rules. In this, his experiments are closer to those of John Cage than Josquin des Pres. While musical influence is pervasive in *The Bridge,* Crane's use of it was not confined to the hymns of "choristers" (**"Cape Hatteras"**) or the cadenzas of "a somewhere violin" (**"National Winter Garden"**). His musical ear was also able to tune natural and mechanical sound into words. By incorporating these various sounds, he was able to compose a pastiche whereby each period in the poem could be easily identified by its own particular music. For example, the Indian past of the continent is suggested by the sounds of the earth; the times of the first explorers by the Angelus (**"Ave Maria"**). The music of the twentieth century, on the other hand, is one of syncopating jazz and throbbing machine.

The analogy between Roebling's bridge and Hegel's triad is useful because it helps to notate the variations at work in Crane's poem.[6] As suggested, **"To Brooklyn Bridge"** is a prelude to the composition; similarly, **"Ave Maria"** is an aubade, **"Cape Hatteras"** a nocturne, and **"Atlantis"** a serenade which becomes, in Wallace Stevens's words, "a chant of paradise."[7] It is in these terms that I wish to discuss *The Bridge.*

By coincidence, in Charles Ives's orchestral piece *The Unanswered Question* (1908), a solo trumpet, representing the artist, questions the nature of being. The response is a polytonal mockery of the trumpet's phrase. The artist, however, is undeterred, and the piece ends with the original question. In other words, the artist can transcend chaos even though he may not know the answer to his question. In **"To Brooklyn Bridge,"** the poet determines to provide the answer to such a question. He emerges from the twentieth-century cave in which multitudes of his fellowmen bend hypnotically "toward some flashing scene" on which nothing is "disclosed." As a man "elect," in the Platonic and Romantic sense, the poet—the "other eyes"—realizes that he must make something of being in time in order to help the apparently hopeless urban bedlamites in their plight. Consequently, he sees the bridge, as only see-ers can, not simply as evidence of American technological ingenuity, but as a "harp and altar, of the fury fused." As a poet, he knows that it is his task to "align" the bridge's "choiringstrings." The resultant "Unfractioned idiom" of his song, it is hoped, will inspire Americans to live, like Camus's Sisyphus, with dignity and purpose. Like Dante in the dark wood, the poet waits under the bridge's "shadow by the piers," for only "in darkness is . . . [its] shadow clear." Like Orpheus the harpist, he will tune the bridge so that its "curveship lend a myth to God."

In **"Ave Maria,"** the theme established in the proem is implicit only in the sense that Columbus bridged the Atlantic by crossing from the Old World to the New. In this the poem is a variation on the theme and an aubade in that it celebrates the morning of the New World. En route for Spain, Columbus knows that he has seen "what no perjured breath / Of clown nor sage can riddle or gainsay." Consequently, he brings back to Ferdinand and Isabella what he believes is "Cathay." As the ships come in sight of land, some sailors sing an Angelus while gathered around a mast. The Angelus, in accord with the aubade, is a devotional prayer sung at morning, as well as at noon and in the evening, to commemorate the Annunciation. In this case, perhaps, the secular intrudes as the incarnation of the New World is praised. The fact that the voyagers have been returned safely from the "passage to the Chan" is celebrated sacredly by the chanting of a Te Deum. Despite the praise and thanksgiving, the **"Ave Maria"** variation introduces an idée fixe which remains a subtheme of the poem. In discovering the New World, Columbus warns:

> —Yet no delirium of jewels! O Fernando,
> Take of that eastern shore, this western sea,
> Yet yield thy God's, thy Virgin's charity!
> —Rush down the plenitude, and you shall see
> Isaiah counting famine on this lee!

The time between morning and noon, between **"Ave Maria"** and **"Cape Hatteras,"** is devoted to chronological flashbacks in which the Indian past of the continent and the white man's misuse of the New World are evoked. In **"The Harbor Dawn"** (another aubade?), it is obvious that contemporary Americans have paid little attention to Columbus's warning. Asleep with a woman in a room in New York's dockland, the poet dreams of Pocahontas, his symbolic emanation of primal America. The dream affords "Insistently through sleep—a tide of voices." These are "signals dispersed in veils," warning the poet, perhaps, to transcribe the sounds of the past. In a Rossetti-ish lyric, Pocahontas is celebrated:

> *your hands within my hands are deeds;*
> *my tongue upon your throat—singing*
> *arms close; eyes wide, undoubtful*
> > *dark*
> > > *drink the dawn—*

*a forest shudders in your hair!*

Despite these "Soft sleeves of sound," the modern world clamors for attention; outside the room, trucks lumber, engines throb, drunks howl. The virgin land is no longer "naked as she was" because "all the fort over" industrial America reverberates rapaciously.

The variation **"Van Winkle"** argues that "it's getting late," that things are falling apart: the "iron year" of the proem has clamped down on the land. "A hurdy-gurdy," once composed for by Haydn and Vivaldi, has degenerated into a street instrument which "grinds—/ Down gold arpeggios mile on mile." Despite this, "The grind-organ says . . . Remember, remember . . . Recall—recall." It is time, the poet warns, to get the *"Times"* before chaos comes.

In order to fully understand the *"Times,"* the poet must journey into the mythic past to transcribe and "recall" the sound and timbre of the continent for modern ears. This he does by taking a train into the Mississippi heartland of America. **"The River"** is to Hart Crane what *The Water Music* was to Handel: it is a brilliant evocation of "a world of whistles, wires and steam" which comprised "the telegraphic night" of twentieth-century America. To his benefactor Otto Kahn, Crane wrote:

> The extravagance of the first twenty-three lines of this section is an intentional burlesque on the cultural confusion of the present—a great conglomeration of noises analogous to the strident impression of a fast express rushing by. The rhythm is jazz. (*Letters*, p. 306)

While the jazz is hard to scan, the "whistling" of the Twentieth Century Limited and the broken conversations of the hoboes, together with the cinematographic effect of the train speeding past "Tintex—Japalac—Certainteed Overalls ads," convey a society hell-bent on destruction. And so it will destroy itself if it does not slow down to hear again the sounds of its past. As long as the twentieth century rushes by "Papooses crying on the wind's long mane" and drowns the screams of "redskin dynasties," then the "iron" will always deal "cleavage." The "liquid theme that floating niggers swell" will and does subsume all.

In **"The Dance,"** the poet journeys into the Indian past; in a triumph of the imagination, he transcends time—"the village"—for space—"dogwood." In this primal chant, the poet travels by canoe and foot, takes "the portage climb," gains "the ledge," speeds over "many bluffs, tarns, streams" until he comes to the "Grey tepees." In this savage world, there is no music except that of Nature and the Indians' "black drums." "A cyclone threshes in the turbine crest" describes the "eagle feathers" of the Sachem's headdress. When Maquokeeta and Pocahontas dance, fingers whistle, leaves crash, the dance moans, lightning twangs, flint snaps, "red fangs / And splay tongues thinly busy the blue air." As the dance tarantellas into a frenzy, the poet adds his voice to the primitive rite:

> Dance, Maquokeeta! snake that lives before,
> That casts his pelt, and lives beyond! Sprout,
>   horn!
> Spark, tooth! Medicine-man, relent, restore—
> Lie to us,—dance us back the tribal morn!

After this Adamic plea, the poet throws himself into the ceremony and dies at the stake, hedgehogged like St. Sebastian by a hundred "arrows." From the experience, he discovers that while he cannot be both Indian and white man, the two can learn from each other. "Thewed of the levin, thunder-shod and lean," the poet sees the continent as a "bride immortal in the maize." America becomes "the torrent and the singing tree. / . . . virgin to the last of men. . . . " Having discovered that his "freedom is her largesse," that there is "sibilance" in her hair, he knows that "The serpent" and "the eagle" can coexist. In essence, **"The Dance"** is a ritual folk chant in which Indian, white man, land, and the age are reborn and the poet has a new song to sing.

While **"Indiana"** has been called an unsuccessful attempt to bridge the granting of America by the Indian to the white man, simply because the latter appropriated it unmercilessly, the poem does, nevertheless, provide a means for the poet to bring his song to the modern world. The "bison thunder" and the tempting "golden syllables" of fool's gold do not detain the poet in "A dream called Eldorado." Nothing was won "out of fifty-nine" and the poet leaves, like Melville's Ishmael, for the sea. The pioneer-woman who narrates this variation warns that her son, in this case the poet, will be "a ranger to the end." But unlike Robert in Eugene O'Neill's *Beyond the Horizon*, the poet will go beyond to "Where gold is true" and bridge the ocean to a new Atlantis.

In a letter to Otto Kahn, in which he set out his plan of *The Bridge,* Crane wrote of the next variation:

> **"Cutty Sark"** is built on the plan of a *fugue.* Two "voices"—that of the world of Time, and that of the world of Eternity—are interwoven in the action. The Atlantis theme (that of Eternity) is the transmuted voice of the nickel-slot pianola, and this voice alternates with that of the derelict sailor and the description of the action. The airy regatta of phantom clipper ships seen from Brooklyn Bridge on the way home is quite effective, I think. It was a pleasure to use historical names for these lovely ghosts. Music still haunts their names long after the wind has left their sails. (*Letters*, pp. 307-08)

"Cutty Sark" is a verbal fugue which is written in contrapuntal style and consists of *three* voices: the poet's, the sailor's, and the singer's. As a fugue it introduces the theme of Atlantis. Whereas the poem does not begin with the theme, it is repeated throughout. Between each restatement, the counterpoint is divided into the respective voices of the poet and the sailor.

The part of the sailor is itself attuned to a contrapuntal variation in that he speaks of the past and the present. Of the latter, the reader learns that he cannot comprehend time and, "beating time" with "bony hands," he laments that "that / damned white Arctic killed" his time. He is unable to live on land, but, like Coleridge's Ancient Mariner, he has seen what others do not see. Consequently, he is trapped in time and condemned to wander, telling his tale to whoever is caught by his hypnotic "GREEN—/ eyes."

Scored against the ex-whaler's part is the song "Stamboul Nights" which is "jogged" out on "the nickel-in-the-slot piano." Crane had read Plato's *Critias,* in which Atlantis is described as an imperfect utopia. Regardless of this, the submerged city became his ideal for a new America. The title of the song is related to the myth in that Istanbul stands on the Golden Horn and the citadel of Atlantis was encased with gold. But here the analogy ends, and the song encourages that America "Sing!" an ideal song which will transmute iron into gold, which will counterpoint the anthem that climaxes *The Bridge.* The poet's "clipper dreams" which conclude **"Cutty Sark"** affirm the great days of American mercantile expansionism. With this recitative, counterpointed by the sea-shanty "Sweet opium and tea, Yoho!" the poet is able to start "walking home across the Bridge. . . . "

**"Cape Hatteras"** is the center of Hart Crane's poem. It is not only a lauda to modern America and a panegyric to Walt Whitman, but also a nocturne in which the melody—that of technological achievement—is played over by a broken chord accompaniment—that of a restatement of Columbus's warning. If **"Ave Maria"** represented the morning of the New World, then **"Cape Hatteras"** represents its noon. The poem presents America at its zenith, the still point from which no advance is possible. The sound of the continent is no longer thunder or plainsong but industrial boom. In a passage that might have been penned by Marinetti and the Futurists, Crane scored the cacophony of this world:

> The nasal whine of power whips a new universe . . .
> Where spouting pillars spoor the evening sky,
> Under the looming stacks of the gigantic power
>     house
> Stars prick the eyes with sharp ammoniac
>     proverbs,
> New verities, new inklings in the velvet hummed
> Of dynamos, where hearing's leash is strummed . . .
>
> Power's script,—wound, bobbin-bound, refined—
> Is stropped to the slap of belts on booming spools,
>     spurred
> Into the bulging bouillon, harnessed jelly of the
>     stars.
> Towards what? The forked crash of split thunder
>     parts
> Our hearing momentwise; but fast in whirling
>     armatures,
> As bright as frogs' eyes, giggling in the girth
> Of steely gizzards—axle-bound, confined
> In coiled precision, bunched in mutual glee
> The bearings glint,—O murmurless and shined
> In oilrinsed circles of blind ecstasy!

The time is 1903, when from "Kill Devils Hill at Kitty Hawk" in North Carolina, "Two brothers in their twin-ship left the dune." These were the "windwrestlers" Orville and Wilbur Wright, whose power-driven biplane revolutionized aeronautics and then wrote the "prophetic script" from which "The soul, by naphtha fledged into new reaches." But this invention, like the discovery of the New World, has been misused: it has been "employed to fly / War's fiery kennel." "Each plane" became, during the Great War, "a hurtling javelin of winged ordnance." Just as Columbus warned Ferdinand, so the poet advises that the "Upchartered choristers" who "splintered space" must determine the zenith of America, not its nadir:

> . . . Remember, Falcon-Ace,
> Thou hast there in thy wrist a Sanskrit charge
> To conjugate infinity's dim marge—
> Anew . . . !

In the immoderately Baroque eulogy to Whitman, Crane projected the "Ascensions" of his mentor into the persona of his poet. Whitman, whose "wand" had beaten "a song" in the nineteenth century, was for Crane the epitome of "living brotherhood" and champion of the "Years of the Modern." As a mythmaker, Whitman saw himself as the means (a bridge?) whereby ecstatic union with all things was possible, that he was, indeed, "Our Meistersinger" who, "Beyond all sesames of science," was able to "bind us throbbing with one voice." By invoking the spirit of Whitman, by partaking of the *"Panis Angelicus,"* the poet can "span on even wing" that "great Bridge" of which he sings.

The **"Three Songs"** are a variation on the effects of a New World which has been un-paradised by generations of modern men. As emanations of Pocahontas, the symbol of that Edenic world, Eve, Magdalene, and Mary are a trio as off-key as "SCIENCE—COMMERCE and the HOLYGHOST" (**"The River"**). As the epigraph from Marlowe suggests, the poet must bridge the past with the present in the same way that Leander swam the Hellespont to re-sing Hero. Only in the unification of Abydos and Sestos could the lovers hope for a future. Each of the songs in Section V is a variation on a theme of America.

In **"Southern Cross,"** Eve is "gardenless"; she is "homeless" in a "whispering hell" of a world whose disharmony is strummed on "Windswept guitars." As a symbol of the continent, she is innocence undone: a spent woman of "many arms." Now "docile," she is at the mercy of a tuneless age.

In **"National Winter Garden,"** Magdalene is a whore who burlesques her dignity by stripping to "A tom-tom scrimmage with a somewhere violin." Beneath America's "ruby" and "emerald sheen" there is an "empty trapeze" of "flesh."

**"Virginia,"** on the other hand, presents a land whose "high carillon" is rung on "popcorn bells." Cacophony, it is stressed, has tolled the continent into soundlessness. In a wry inversion, the prostitution of America has created a chastity so tight that Mary, like Rapunzel, is unable to let her hair down and show off her real beauty. But there is in the final admonition "shine!" a distant echo of the exhortations "flow!" (**"The River"**) and "Sing!" (**"Cutty Sark"**). It is, after all, "Spring in Prince Street," and there is hope of the summer yet to be.

In **"Quaker Hill,"** the poet travels to New England which was, for the Founding Fathers, "the Promised Land." Instead, he discovers that, as Columbus warned, "plenitude" (**"Ave Maria"**) has been rushed down: the old "Meeting House" has become the "New Avalon Hotel." To the "persuasive suburban land agent" and the "highsteppers" this *is* paradise, an elysium of "gin fizz" and golf, dirty weekends and "plaid plusfours." In an allusion to the *Purgatorio,* "the borders of three states" and the "four horizons that no one relates" suggest that the three Theological virtues of faith, hope, and charity, and the four Cardinal virtues of prudence, justice, temperance, and fortitude, synonymous with Puritanism, are no more.[8] The volcanic roar of the radio and an unconcerned Babbittry sound the dissonant "famine" (**"Ave Maria"**) of the day. The poet is unable, in Emily Dickinson's phrase, to see "New Englandly" and exclaims: "Where are my kinsmen and the patriarch race?" Despite the razzmatazz of Prohibition America, the poet never loses sight of the ideal:

> . . . Yes, while the heart is
> wrung,
> Arise—yes, take this sheaf of dust upon your
> tongue!
> In one last angelus lift throbbing throat—
> Listen, transmuting silence with that stilly note
> Of pain that Emily, that Isadora knew!

He has learned, particularly from Emily Dickinson, that joy is often the result of pain; consequently, the bridging of America will be achieved out of discord and cadence. In order to re-sound the "triple-noted clause" he must, like Orpheus, descend into the underworld.

**"The Tunnel"** is Hart Crane's variation on the dark night of the soul. The poem is a polytextual borrowing from mythology, Dante, and Poe, who appears as a symbol of the crucified artist. To all intents and purposes, "the garden" of America is "dead." The city has become a Baudelairean hell. To escape the "Performances, assortments, résumés" of this urban inferno, the poet takes the subway from Manhattan under the East River to the Brooklyn side of the bridge. Once in a subway car, "the overtone of motion / underground, the monotone / of motion is the sound / of other faces, also underground" prepare the poet for the staccato conversations of his fellow passengers:

> "Let's have a pencil Jimmy—living now
> at Floral Park
> Flatbush—on the fourth of July—
> like a pigeon's muddy dream—potatoes

> to dig in the field—travlin the town—too—
> night after night—the Culver line—the
> girls all shaping up—it used to be—"

Just what "used to be" is lost as "tongues recant like beaten weather vanes." "Repetition freezes" as an enraged obligato jars above the other broken descant:

> " . . . if
> you don't like my gate why did you
> swing on it, why *didja*
> swing on it
> anyhow—"

The poet hears "The phonographs of hades" and as the journey continues he confronts yet another emanation of Pocahontas. This time it is a "Wop washerwoman" who may also be a variation on Columbus's "Madre Maria." Whoever she is, she has no influence in this subutopian world where "the Daemon" rules. This specter, an inversion perhaps of Eurydice, whose "hideous laughter is a bellows mirth," does not cause the poet to turn. In a Christian conversion, he becomes "like Lazarus" determined to ascend and emerges on the other side, like Leander, "Impassioned with some song," with "some Word that will not die." As suggested by the epigraph from Blake's "Morning," the poet has found "the Western path / Right thro' the Gates of Wrath."

So far, Crane has demonstrated that his duty as a poet was to remind the present of the usable past. By scoring the two into concord, he was able to compose **"Atlantis,"** the ultimate harmony of *The Bridge,* of which R.W.B. Lewis has written:

> **"Atlantis"** is Crane's supreme apocalypse of imagination, the revelation of universal radiance and harmony, of a world transfigured; a revelation begotten and (for the brief duration of the poem) sustained by the sheer power of poetic vision.[9]

In the musical structure of *The Bridge,* **"Atlantis"** is an evening serenade which courts the ideal. But it is as a "Psalm of Cathay"—not the "poetic rant of an extravagant order" that Lewis suggests—that the bridging of the real with the ideal is celebrated.[10] Just as Atlantis's circle of islands was bridged so that all the inhabitants could be in communion with the citadel, so the poet used Brooklyn Bridge as his sacred object, his "palladium helm of stars," to harmonize the sounds of the past and the present into a polyphonic whole. As such, this poem is the 'musica futuristica' of *The Bridge.*

**"Atlantis"** is the "One Song" which makes *The Bridge* a single structured composition. It celebrates the replacement of the "ROSE" (**"Cutty Sark"**) by the "Anemone," the "whitest flower." But is it Cathay? Has the poet brought back "The Chan's great continent" (**"Ave Maria"**)? As far as the poet is concerned, one may assume, Cathay *is;* the poem is testament to this. As far as the reader is concerned, he can only take the poet's word. The "Atlantis" section does, after all, conclude in oracular promise as "Whispers antiphonal in azure swing." As in the rustling of leaves at Delphi signifying prophecy, so there is in *The Bridge* a suggestion of the "Sibylline voices" that "flicker" as if "a god were issue of the strings" (**"Atlantis"**).

The place of the poet's ideal, whether it be Atlantis or Cathay, is a land of music which is, in Plato's epigraph, "the knowledge of that which relates to love in harmony and system." It is also, as Lewis suggests, "the domain of love."[11] In Plato's *Symposium,* Eryximachus, in reminding the group that it is impossible to harmonize that which disagrees, argues:

> In like manner rhythm is compounded of elements short and long, once differing and now in accord; which accordance, as in the former instance, medicine, so in all these other cases, music implants, making love and unison grow among them; and thus music, too, is concerned with the principles of love in their application to harmony and rhythm.

In order to achieve this, a good artist is required. The physician concludes with the insight that, as in music, the *fairness* of the muse Urania and the *vulgarity* of the muse Polyhymnia are both present in love.

In *The Bridge,* it was Hart Crane's personal aim to show that America could be reconciled imaginatively into a symphonic agreement. That he used musical and aural influences in the poem is evidence of that aim. As such, *The Bridge* is is no cozy celestial hymn; like many of Emily Dickinson's poems it constructs a bridge for the reader to take on a journey of self-exploration. As indicated by the epigraph from Isadora Duncan's autobiography that prefaces **"Quaker Hill,"** Crane knew that "no ideals have ever been fully successful on this earth." Consequently, he scored an exhortation, from personal experience, that Americans at least attempt to rearrange the present dissonance by sounding out the tonality of the past. "A white hunter," to use Gertrude Stein's maxim, may be "nearly crazy,"[12] but he is more likely to be in tune with his world than "the Czars / Of golf" (**"Quaker Hill"**).

*The Bridge* is, then, a polytextual variation which harmonizes the solution of one man's quest as a possible paradigm for individual or national exploration. It is *not* the "Answerer of all" (**"Atlantis"**), but a theme and free variation whereby questions are elicited.

[1]*The Letters of Hart Crane 1916-1932,* ed. Brom Weber (New York: Hermitage House, 1952), pp. 128-29. Further references will be included in the text and cited as *Letters.*

[2]Gilbert Chase, *America's Music: From the Pilgrims to the Present,* rev. 2d ed. (New York: McGraw-Hill Book Company, 1966), p. 631.

[3]From "For the Marriage of Faustus and Helen," pt. II, *The Complete Poems and Selected Letters and Prose of Hart Crane,* ed. Brom Weber (New York: Liveright Publishing Corporation, 1966). All citations to Crane's poetry are to this edition.

[4]Wilfrid Mellers, *Music in a New Found Land: Themes and Developments in the History of American Music* (London: Barrie and Rockliff, 1964), p. 102.

[5] Joseph J. Arpad, "Hart Crane's Platonic Myth: The Brooklyn Bridge," *American Literature,* 39 (1967), 78-79.

[6] A triad is also a chord of three notes consisting of a root and the third and the fifth above it.

[7] From Wallace Steven's "Sunday Morning," stanza VII.

[8] Before descending into the Flowering Valley, Dante looks at the south pole and sees three stars (the three Theological virtues). These have replaced the four stars (the four Cardinal virtues) which he had seen at dawn. See *Purgatorio* VIII. 88-93.

[9] *The Poetry of Hart Crane: A Critical Study* (Princeton: Princeton University Press, 1967), pp. 365-66.

[10] Lewis, p. 366.

[11] Lewis, p. 372.

[12] From "Objects" in Gertrude Stein, *Tender Buttons* (New York: Claire-Marie, 1914), p. 27. (Rpt. New York: Haskell House Publishers Ltd., 1970.)

## Alan Trachtenberg (essay date 1981)

SOURCE: "Cultural Revisions in the Twenties: Brooklyn Bridge as "Usable Past"," in *The American Self: Myth, Ideology and Popular Culture,* edited by Sam B. Girgus, University of New Mexico Press, 1981, pp. 58-75.

[*In the following essay, Trachtenberg discusses* The Bridge *as a landmark of the 1920s cultural and aesthetic vision.*]

Hart Crane's *The Bridge* (1930) has its origins in the twenties. As much autobiography as "myth of America," the poem belongs not only to the decade's syncopated tempos and aesthetic entrancements, but as well to its deep changes and conflicts. The poet's own life in these years of encroaching mechanization, standardization, and consumer capitalism, is the historical ground of the poem, a ground too rarely allowed more than passing notice in criticism. It is characteristic of our criticism that it knows less about history than it does about literary forms and influences, and knowing less about the ground of art, it inevitably knows less about the ideas that inform works of art, and the intrinsic powers that reside within them. We know that the twenties brought a renascence into American art, a flourishing of energies that had been launched in the previous decade. We know too little, however, of how those energies confronted new social and cultural formations, how they were shaped by struggles of artists to realize visions antithetical to their times, especially to the behavioristic model which in these years established itself in the media, in advertising, and in popular and academic social thought.[1]

The twenties witnessed a flowering of literary and artistic experiment, an assimilation of European modernism, of Surrealism and Dada, and the achievement of a new speech in the poetry of Pound, Eliot, Frost, Stevens, and Williams. Crane himself breathed deeply in this atmosphere of aesthetic excitement, of jostling manifestoes and doctrines, and *The Bridge* might be read, as Frederick Hoffman shows, as a typical document of experimentation.[2] But we need also a way of reading the poem, and understanding the aesthetic production of the period in general, as embodying a resistance to what Crane and other artists perceived as the ultimate menace of modern bourgeois society: its assault on the realm of autonomy, on the very sources of art. For the first time in American life, at least in such coherent form, art began to appear as a separate realm: not merely a vehicle for criticism, but an alternative way of life.

The implicit ambition of modernist art in the twenties was to open a space for itself (as for the daily life of artists and a new intelligentsia in Bohemian colonies) within the larger culture, a culture in which older patterns of gentility and puritan moralism were adapting themselves to new social demands of consumership and technological change. Crane's poem has yet another emphasis, an additional ambition: to alter the larger culture itself, to revise its sense of itself, its dominant values, and especially its idea of its history. As a revisionary epic, *The Bridge* shares a common project with works of criticism and cultural history by Waldo Frank, Van Wyck Brooks, Lewis Mumford, Paul Rosenfield, and especially William Carlos Williams—the project of creating a "usable past."[3] Crane's is the epic statement of this concerted effort, at the heart of which lay (even in the more conventional historical writings of Lewis Mumford) a vision of an aesthetic self, a poetic sensibility, as the true mediator of a true cultural history. How else are we to understand the epic scale of *The Bridge* except as the effort of the poet to discover *himself* in all of American history, from Columbus's voyage to the western settlement, from the building of Brooklyn Bridge to invention of the airplane? To discover himself as the redemptive poetic consciousness of the history as a whole, as a totality. Revision of history becomes a mode of self-discovery and self-possession. The poem, like Williams' project to "re-name the things seen" in *In The American Grain* (1925), is a deliberate act of such revision, a rethinking and recasting of the past into a future represented by the poet's present.

*The Bridge* strives for transcendence, for a conversion of the everyday into the spiritual, of modern American into a symbol of a new consciousness. Or, in terms the great Dutch historian Johan Huizinga used in his account of the

way of life he found in American in 1926, to transform the "transitive culture" of "This, Here, and Soon," into a "transcendental culture."[4] Crane's method of transcendence is the Romantic fusion of self and world, the planting of the self at the center of his world. His nameless narrator is a Crispin, searching to become "the intelligence of his soil,/The sovereign ghost." Crane performed his quest without Stevens' muted comedy of the voyaging imagination, and his poem now seems less reflective upon the dilemmas of the artist in an inhospitable environment (Stevens' comedian learns eventually that "his soil is man's intelligence./That's better.") than a pained reflection of them. The poem insists upon the sovereignty of art, and although its confidence suffers often against appalling evidence of murderous engines, rigid buildings, and the mental prison of billboards and airwaves, it never pauses to question its own aesthetic ideology. Where Stevens investigates and redefines the imagination's ground in reality, Crane defends and asserts the primacy of a Romantic relation to the world as the premise of his "usable past." His stance is defensive without secondary defenses: his singer either floats or sinks, and his world either glows in the radiance of art or dies in the "muffled slaughter of a day in birth."

*The Bridge* belongs to the twenties also by virtue of what Huizinga might call a "higher naivete": its hope for a purely aesthetic transformation of a world already remade, reconstituted by industrial and corporate capitalism into mechanized space and time. The poem concedes a fully technologized and rationalized world (only fleeting visions of Indian voluptuousness, of "ancient men . . . hobo-trekkers," and of resolute but defeated artists like Melville and Dickinson, evoke historical alternatives to the "elevators [that] drop us from our day"), and its ringing optimism in the final section (only momentarily qualified by the final question: "Is it Cathay . . . ?") seems willed, more programmatic than earned by the cumulative energies of the poem. The hopefulness of the opening prayer ("lend a myth to God")—which has nothing in common with the "transitive" optimism of Overstreet and the hucksters of the age—is charged with aesthetic power precisely because it encloses an anxiety that continues to live irrepressibly throughout the poem. Thus the poem's naivete is "higher," a higher mode of aspiration than the surrender to environment and to machine in the name of adjustment, maturity, and progress everywhere urged in the larger culture.

Crane's defense of art is a defense of an idea of culture, an alternative culture of aesthetic modes of experience. The entire poem, and his entire "usable past" project, rests upon the "naive" belief that such forms might appropriate the machine and subordinate its mechanicalness to human spirituality. His machines are not forms of exploitation or stolen labor power, but modes of experience, capable of aesthetic redemption. Crane's symbol of such a possibility, symbol and pledge of its historical imminence, is of course, Brooklyn Bridge: the paradigmatic structure of an older urban modernity, itself a fusion of science and love, technology and art. The choice of this bridge was not arbitrary; other artists chose it as well in the same years as an arch emblem of modernity.[5] Crane's bridge, like the poem, belongs to the decade. The coincidence of what I am calling re-visions of Brooklyn Bridge in these years, and what lay behind that coincidence, is the phenomenon of cultural revision I will explore here. My own method will be a reconstruction of consciousness: an attempt to recover thesubjective features of the bridge's remarkable hold upon the imagination in the twenties. My purpose is to begin to uncover motives and intentions invested in the revisionary project Crane shared with other aspiring form makers in the twenties: to see if and how their efforts at making a "usable past" suggest a useful lesson for us.

"TO BE, GREAT BRIDGE, IN VISION BOUND OF THEE"

Imagine yourself midway. How you arrive is of no account. Here the looming form takes command, governs every neural response. This visual and kinetic surrender begins what we can call the classic moment of Brooklyn Bridge: the classic moment in the imagination of the bridge. The self is obliterated to a bare eye bound in space. Everything else falls away. Mere walking ceases, and crossing begins: the bridge sweeps the body into the modulated measures of an upward passage, and sweeps the eye into new harmonies of motion and sound. Midway, above, alone. Joseph Stella recounts:

> Many nights I stood on the bridge—and in the middle alone—lost—a defenceless prey to the surrounding swarming darkness—crushed by the mountainous black impenetrability of the skyscrapers—here and there lights resembling suspended falls of astral bodies or fantastic splendors of remote rites—shaken by the underground tumult of trains in perpetual motion, like the blood in the arteries—at times, ringing as alarm in a tempest, the shrill sulphurous voice of the trolley wires—now and then strange moanings of appeal from tug boats, guessed more than seen, through the infernal recesses below—I felt deeply moved, as if on the threshold of a new religion or in the presence of a new DIVINITY.[6]

Alone with the bridge: and walking, the city man's customary slice through dense space, ceases, and *crossing,* the act of piety, devotion, belief, begins. The bridge is now a threshold to a new realm, "as though a god were issue of the strings." "And midway on that structure," writes Hart Crane in his first composed lines, later canceled, toward *The Bridge:* "And midway on that structure I would stand/ One moment, not as diver, but with arms/ That open to project a disk's resilience/ Winding the sun and planets in its face."[7] The classic moment achieves its classic form in the opening stanza of the final poem of *The Bridge:*

> Through the bound cables strands, the arching
>    path
> Upward, veering with light, the flight of strings—
> Taut miles of shuttling moonlight syncopate
> The whispered rush, telepathy of wires.
> Up the index of night, granite and steel—

> Transparent meshes—fleckless the gleaming
>    staves—
> Sibylline voices flicker, waveringly stream
> As though a god were issue of the strings . . .[8]

But surely Crane and Stella and their coreligionists of the bridge in the twenties were not the first to walk across the structure—only the first to single out that experience and build another structure upon it: the first to *imagine* the bridge in this way: or to make a walk across the bridge an intensified moment in their imagination of what it was like to be alive in America in their day. Others had walked before. Why now does the walk seem a momentous crossing? Why, say, from 1917 to 1930 does the classic moment dominate the imagination of the bridge, as it appears, at least, in painting, photographs, fiction, criticism and poetry?

Let us first understand more precisely the meaning of the classic moment—its historical meaning, its place in the history and in the celebration of the history of Brooklyn Bridge. A usual way of speaking is to say that Crane and Stella and others are part of the history of the bridge: their celebrations additional data in a list of celebrations, reaching from at least the Opening Ceremonies and surrounding hoopla to what promises to come at the hundredth anniversary. We might also say that this history, engaging as it does both an object and responses to it (or a fact and symbolic interpretations of it), belongs to another, broader history: a phase or chapter in the history of the coming of the modern, of the big industrial city, of new styles and new materials of building—and of making artworks. In the usual way of speaking, the classicmoment takes its place as another item to be classified, another response to the bridge and to what it manifestly represents: the stage of urban modernity in the history of American life.

Further: taken as a response to a significance-laden object, the classic moment might be classified as one among many indices to what we call culture: meaning, in normal usage, an interior realm where personal need meets exterior value, combining into a shared picture of the world. We might then study the classic moment and other individual responses to the bridge, along with the bridge itself, to piece together a picture of culture: the object of our scholarship, perhaps our admiration and nostalgia.

But there is a flaw in this way of speaking and of thinking. As Emerson might say, it leaves history *outside* of me. Culture is not merely the object of my attention, but *how* I attend to anything, the form and style of my attending, as well as the ingrained decision itself about what is worth attending to. What remains simply an object in my field of vision is not yet part of me, not yet culture: or, if I see something as existing only as an object-in-the world, and do not see that my own way of seeing affects my perception of the object, then I am not yet aware of how deeply cultural a creature I am.

The classic moment is a moment of profound subjectivity, even of privacy. Yet it is profoundly cultural—all the more cultural, all the more profound to the extent that it subjectivizes the bridge itself—that it re-sees or revises the bridge. Through its power of communication the classic moment has revised the bridge for us: not so much into a specific revision, a specific image, but into an unforgettable lesson that *any* seeing of the bridge, through personal experience or historical document, is a re-seeing, a revision that constitutes and reveals our own cultural being. Does the bridge as a thing have a history apart from a chronicle of *physical* revision? Any thing is historical only in the role it plays in the life, the total life, of the people it serves. Thus the classic moment is a paradigm of the making of the bridge into a historical object. Granted, this seems to insist upon a paradox, for what is the classic moment of lonely suspension upon the form of the bridge but a severing of ties, a breaking of connections with history? The paradox dissolves, however, when we recognize, as I hope we shall, that the severance is only apparent, a precondition thought necessary by a surprising number of people in the same period for a re-connection with history. Typified by the walk that becomes a crossing, the classic moment is an imaginative history: a discovery that the making of a history is radically subjective, yet (another function of bridging) capable of being shared. To study the classic moment is to study the making of Brooklyn Bridge into history and into culture. It is not another datum we are after, but the most essential fact of Brooklyn Bridge: its role as an event, a symbolic act, in the imagination.

"SOME SPLINTERED GARLAND FOR THE SEER."

"Beyond any other aspect of New York," wrote Lewis Mumford in *Sticks and Stones* (1924), "the Brooklyn Bridge has been a source of joy and inspiration to the artist." The appeal lay in the visual elegance of the structure: "the strong lines of the bridge," as Mumford writes, "and the beautiful curve described by its suspended cables," and especially the steel work and "the architectural beauty of its patterns." Brooklyn Bridge was among those "great bridges" that surpassed the more "grotesque and barbarous" features of the first age of industrial building and survived as "enduring monuments." "To this day they communicate a feeling of dignity, stability, and unwavering poise."[9]

Dignity, stability, and poise describe well the feeling one has in the paintings of the bridge by Jonas Lie, by Twachtman and Childe Hassam and Bellows and Joseph Pennell—and are not at odds with, but by themselves inadequate to describe the effects of the much different painterly intentions of John Marin, Albert Gleizes, and Joseph Stella. At the time Mumford wrote, a change was already in process in the representation of the bridge in painting—a change measured by the eruption into American painting of modernist styles such as cubism, fauvism, and futurism, but also indicative of a change in the kind of appreciation artists felt for the bridge. We might, of course, consider the change in appreciation and feeling aseffects of the changed notion of what a painting is and how its framed composition relates to an ostensible subject in the world, but that would be to assign to style or mode the power of causing changes in feeling. Feeling and style more likely arise from a common source, and the new styles might also be taken as "answerable" to a new set of feelings and circumstances. Did futurism by itself instigate the revised vision of the bridge in works by Marin and Stella, or did it provide elements of a vocabulary that answered to the revised relation of artist to bridge?

A full cultural history would have to take into account the subtle interplay of forces that intersect and become palpable in any single expression. Here we are looking for the origins or the ground of a changed relation to the bridge I am calling the classic moment: the moment on the bridge when *walking* crosses over to *crossing*. In 1954 Mumford comments in a new preface to *Sticks and Stones* on the fact that he and Hart Crane were at work on their respective treatments of the bridge at the same time: "Our common appreciation of this great work of art became part of a wider movement, which owes so much to the polarizing effect of *The Seven Arts* and *The New Republic,* the working toward the creation of a 'usable past' for our country."[10] Common to the appreciation of the "wider movement" as well as of Crane and Mumford (and we include Mumford's own long-unknown but recently restored and published play of 1925-27, *The Builders of the Bridge*) was some variant of the classic moment, the momentous walk and the eye-crossing at midway. Mumford's reference to "usable past" suggests a focus to bring that moment into relation with a common cultural project of the period.

Consider the innocent walk. To cross the bridge on foot, on the elevated promenade, is to know the bridge from the inside: to discover that it has an inside, or a siding of crossing cables and stays which construct the illusion of an enclosure. For the first thirty years or so the bridge was predominantly a walkway: walking across the bridge was the common way of using it. Walking across, getting to and fro, from home to work and back, was a way of marking a precious transition. Rarely were you alone. The bridge, like a boulevard, provided company. There are written records of the innocent pleasure of this promenade, but we no longer read them; they lie buried in old reportage and letters to the editor of the nineties and the turn of the century. But photographs made for stereoscopic parlor viewing tell of the charm of a walk on the bridge, on the civic parade ground in the sky.

This is an older vision of Brooklyn Bridge, before vehicular traffic surpassed the volume of pedestrian traffic in 1916. An older bridge, and its place in the imagination shows it whole, complete, a unitary thing: a bridge between two places, the separate roadways (for walkers and for riders) together serving the multiple needs of city life. The bridge would meet the "interests of the community as well as of the Bridge Company," Roebling explained in his master plan of 1869: a roadway for vehicles and an elevated boardwalk to "allow people of leisure, and old and young invalids, to promenade over the Bridge on fine days, in order to enjoy the beautiful views and the pure air." And in the older vision the towers, "its most conspicuous features," still serve, as Roebling promised, "as landmarks to the adjoining cities . . . entitled to be ranked as national monuments."[12] They stood high above the city, as yet without the defiant challenge of skyscrapers. And thus the older bridge appealed to the eye—an older eye, too, we might say, which saw the world itself as whole, compact, reliable, in a manner much like Roebling's own confident vision. The dominant vision before, say, 1912 was lateral and iconic: a public bridge seen from some clear and impersonal perspective everyone would recognize.

Walking the bridge then must have seemed in its very commonness not especially worthy of remarkable comment. The midway vision, the eye-crossing along mystic strings, had not yet emerged, as true as it might have been to the feelings of midnight crossers, divers, lovers, and other bedlamites. Still thinking of it as contemporary, not a survival of the past (as it appeared to Mumford and his generation) but an immediate forerunner, virtually a breeder of new bridges, new constructions, writers of the Progressive period appropriated the bridge in its monumentality. For Ernest Poole in *The Harbor* (1915) it is the "Great Bridge," whose "sweeping arch . . . seemed high as the clouds." The novel sets the hopes represented by harbor and bridge, hopes "of the power of mind over matter, and of the mighty speeding up of a world civilization and peace, a successful world, strong, broad, tolerant," against the realities of class conflict and social unrest.[13] The sweeping bridge remains an emblem of hope. As it does in an obscure but intriguing verse drama published in 1913 by the avant-garde house of Mitchell Kennerley. The play, *The Bridge,* by one Dorothy Landers Beall, is also torn by conflict, between rich and poor, workers and owners, and projects a union of the selfless engineer and the passionate settlement-house worker as a solution to the rifts of the age. Brooklyn Bridge here is "Long Bridge," the sovereign spirit of bridges as such, and it inspires the young engineer to persist in his struggle with the elements, and with labor agitators and crooked businessmen, to raise a new bridge alongside the old. The doubts and anguish of his beloved Hilda give way when she hears "The Spirit of the Bridge" explain:

> Do you not see grave bridges, free suspensions,
> All woven, builded, swinging in the sunlight
> Over the bitter streams of old neglect,
> Like a glad-going company of workers
> Linking the separate and the little-souled,
> The great, the tiny, the unfortunate.

The play concludes with a shining reconciliation between the engineer and his workers, to the tune of Hilda's bright song: "Quick, O Bridge—rise surely—/ Bridges—world-Bridges, span like sympathy,/ Till there are left no bitter gulfs to pass!"[14]

From an icon of public reconciliation to a private event of mystical eye-crossing: this passage, which occurred

between 1912 and 1915, marks a rupture between the old bridge and the new, a rupture at least in the kind of joy and inspiration the bridge offered to artists. As we know, the whole cultural past of America itself took on a new and oppressive look to a growing number of young Americans in the same years, the years of the Armory Show (1913), of Van Wyck Brooks' *America's Coming of Age* (1915), and of *The Seven Arts* (1917-18). One of the modes of the new look of things, the new look *at the* world, was deconstructive: the old integrity of vision, of seeing, begins to dissolve. Marin's swift expressions of visible urban energy in his views of the bridge of 1912 and 1913 are symptoms as well as acute modernist achievements. "I see great forces at work," Marin wrote in the exhibition catalogue to his 1913 show at "291":

> great movements; the large buildings and the small buildings; the warring of the great and small; influences of one mass on another greater or smaller mass. Feelings are aroused which give me the desire to express the reaction of these "pull forces," those influences which play with one another; great masses pulling smaller masses, each subject in some degree to the other's power. . . . And so I try to express graphically what a great city is doing.[15]

A new idea of the modern itself appears here, in Marin's revisions of the bridge and in his words: a nervous tropism toward the abstract yet concretely emotional structures lurking within the changing city and bursting the seams of conventional realism: the mode not only of earlier representations of the bridge, but correspondingly of the actual making of the original bridge itself.

An impulse to revise, to remake, arose in these years in literary and artistic circles in New York: an impulse that found one coherent expression in a new attention to the American cultural heritage. Sensing a creative anarchy in the American scene—"the sudden unbottling of elements that have had not opportunity to develop freely in the open"—Van Wyck Brooks in 1918 deplored "the lack of any sense of inherited resources" to fertilize and tutor the energies of the young. What passed for culture—the genteel collocations of the chiefly European "best that had been thought and said," and the severely bowdlerized and domesticated version of American literature—had discredited itself, largely by its blatant subservience to the powers of business and industry in this period of heightened conflict. As a result, Brooks wrote, "the present is a void, and the American writer floats in that void because the past that survives in the common mind of the present is a past without living value. But is this the only possible past? If we need another past so badly, is it inconceivable that we might discover one, that we might even invent one?"[16] Brooks' call for the invention of a "usable past," a past that would answer the question, "What is important for us?", led to the breaking of new ground in literary study and, especially in the work of Lewis Mumford in the 1920s, in the study of the tangible past in architecture and building. It was under the aegis of this impulse to invent, to remake, to discover and forge alternatives to the lame and pallid and defunct culture of their fathers that Brooklyn Bridge appeared in the 1920s as a survival, a *historic* monument, a link with valuable cultural forces of the past. Crane's use of the bridge as in part a scaffolding for a reconstruction of the cultural past, a retelling of American history, falls properly under the heading of Brooks' "usable past." Part of the attention to Brooklyn Bridge in the period derives from this collective project of discovery, invention, and reconstruction.

But describing it in this way, as invention and revision, we make the project seem too calculating, too programmatic; we miss its urgency and inner sense of need. To look at Brooklyn Bridge and to see it as a monument of industrial heroism and creativity is one thing; to walk across the bridge and take possession of it in a radically subjective way, the way of the classic moment, is another. Is there a continuity of need between the two ways?

Consider in Waldo Frank's novel of 1917, *The Unwelcome Man,* the first instance in literature of the classic moment:

> Before him swept the bridge. He felt that every cable of the web-like maze was vibrant with stress and strain. With these things he was alone. Yet he felt no insecurity, such as the crowds inspired. Beyond, through the net-work of steel, huddled Brooklyn. And below his very feet, tumbled together as if some giant had tipped the city eastward and sent all the houses pell-mell toward the down-tilted corner, lay the wharves and slums of Manhattan. It seemed to Quincy that he was being caught upon a monstrous swing and swept with its pulsed lilt above the grovelling life of the metropolis. Suddenly, the fancy flashed upon him that from his perch of shivering steel the power should indeed come to poise and judge the swarm above which he rocked. The bridge that reeled beyond him seemed an arbiter. It bound the city. It must know the city's soul since it was so close to the city's breath. In its throbbing cables there must be a message. In its lacings and filigrees of steel, there must be subtle words! . . . [17]

What are the novel elements here? The hero is alone on the bridge, in a solitude more consoling than the isolation of the city crowds. The bridge permits him to enact his true condition: alone, separate from the shabby and groveling city, poised above, prepared for an access of power lost to him on the streets, in the crowds. The bridge is an arbiter; it stands above; it binds; it judges. And it has a message, a word, which the hero almost hears.

But he rejects the bridge's demanding message, and in the passage that follows he descends the bridge's "unattainable pathway," moves in a panic through the narrow streets, in an effort to "escape the omnipresent Bridge." "Crowds jostled him; cars clashed; machines were braying, shuttling. The taste of New York was bitter on his lips." "Under the Bridge itself he went—looming above him like a curse." Frank made clear the cause of his hero's malaise: he could not face the need to struggle for personal liberation, to find a perspective in which to reconcile the ugliness of the manifest city with the beauty of its wholeness and its potentiality. The bridge offers such a perspective: not merely as a physical platform but as a message, a word.

Frank described his hero as a victim of "the culture of industrialism," and Brooks saw the novel as proof of John Stuart Mill's prediction that industrialism would lead to "an appalling deficiency of human preferences." In the same year Brooks published an essay in *The Seven Arts* called "The Culture of Industrialism," an essay which, like Frank's novel, sheds light on the inner needs of the quest for a "usable past." "The world over," he wrote, "the industrial process has devitalized men and produced a poor quality of human nature." Industrialism has ruptured the fabric of life; it has cut off sources of nourishment from traditional culture, and has demeaned the orthodox "high" culture by turning it over to "the prig and the aesthete." In Europe at least some vestige of the traditional culture remains, and "a long line of great rebels"—Nietzsche, Renan, Morris, Rodin, Marx, Mill— have kept it alive by reacting "violently" against the "desiccating influences" of industrialism. "They have made it impossible for men to forget the degradation of society and the poverty of their lives and built a bridge between the greatness of the few in the past and the greatness of the man, perhaps, in the future."[18] While here in America, "our disbelief in experience, our habitual repression of the creative instinct with its consequent overstimulation of the possessive instinct, has made it impossible for us to take advantage of the treasure our own life has yielded." "The real work of criticism in this country," Brooks continues, is "to begin *low,*" to find and accept "our own lowest common denominator." Then, he concludes in another image suggesting a bridge, a joining of forces around a vital center:

> As soon as the foundations of our life have been reconstructed and made solid on the basis of our own experience, all these extraneous, ill-regulated forces will rally about their newly found center; they will fit in, each where it belongs, contributing to the essential architecture of our life. Then, and only then, shall we cease to be a blind, selfish, disorderly people; we shall become a luminous people, dwelling in the light and sharing our light.[19]

## "O THOU STEELED COGNIZANCE"

And Crane, in the final walk, the crossing-into-light that concludes *The Bridge:*

> And on, obliquely up bright carrier bars
> New octaves trestle the twin monoliths
> Beyond whose frosted capes the moon bequeaths
> Two worlds of sleep (O arching strands of song!)—
> Onward and up the crystal-flooded aisle
> White tempest nets file upward, upward ring
> With silver terraces the humming spars,
> The loft of vision, palladium helm of stars.

The concluding poem, Crane had written to his patron, Otto Kahn, in 1926, would be "a sweeping dithyramb in which the Bridge becomes the symbol of consciousness spanning time and space."[20] And a year later, ten years after Brooks' call for a new structure of experience, a "newly found center," again to Otto Kahn, regarding the kind of "history" the poem will be: "What I am after is an assimilation of this experience [American history], a more organic panorama, showing the continuous and living evidence of the past in the inmost vital substance of the present."[21] What he is after is "usable past," an act of *bridging* past and present in a more vital connection than orthodox histories provide.

The coincidence of the figure or trope of bridging in Crane and Brooks is not remarkable: it is a common rhetorical figure for transcendence through connection. Crane's writings, his poetry and prose, are rife with such crossings. But the coincidence of *need,* the sense of inner division that needs healing, especially a division, a breach that feels both personal and cultural at once: so personal and so cultural that the solution to the problem of "America" appears as the form of the solution to the problem of *being:* this is worth remarking as a deep feature of the age, or of the life of its estranged and unhappy artists and intellectuals. Especially for Crane, a personal divided consciousness—the "curse of sundered parentage"—became the scene for a symbolic action, a bridging, of cultural consequence. The poem would perform his "essential architecture" doubly or trebly: it would reconnect the American present to the American past in a new, "vital" way; it would reconnect the poet to his personal experience; and it would, by the fusion of these two goals, build a bridge between the poet and his people: between poetry as such and "America." And this theory of multiple connection descends into Crane's poetics, into the very performance and "synergies" of his poetic language.

Among the meanings of Crane's bridge, then, is the rhetorical trope of "bridging," the *act* of crossing over. A bridge crosses and unites; it mediates, like the priestly function in the word *pontiff:* mediates between here and there, now and to come. In this function alone, apart from its concreteness as Brooklyn Bridge, the bridge provides fusion, transcendence, healing. It promises connection: simultaneously to earth, here-and-now, and to a realm beyond, a connection that transforms the here-and-now itself into a meaningful pattern of details. In its immediacy as *at once* bound and unbound, it promises new power of experience.

"History and fact, location, etc.," Crane wrote to Gorham Munson in 1923, "all have to be transfigured into abstract form that would almost function independently of its subject matter."[22] Transfiguration is a phase of the bridging act, and the achievement of the "abstract form"—the form of bridge—is its culmination, for now the transcending act can perform its ultimate work: making it possible to see and to experience each discrete detail of "history and fact" as connected to all others, as

constituting one totality, which can be named Bridge, and which in its oneness can be named also as One, Thou steeled Cognizance, Deity's glittering Pledge: As though a god were issue of the strings. . . .

But the bridge is also Brooklyn Bridge, a shuttle between two mundane places, an instrument, as Crane put it in a famous despairing letter to Waldo Frank in 1926, of "shorter hours, quicker lunches, behaviorism and toothpicks."[23] Can such a bridge, a crude servant of capitalism, also serve the bridging function, the crossing over that the poet needs? Crane stalled in the making of his poem when this question occurred to him. And the completed poem, with its final apparent apotheosis of the bridge, has troubled many readers as embodying an aesthetic flaw: a confusion of the real bridge, in its multiplicity of function, with the imaginary bridge of transcendence. Does it matter, it is asked, that the bridge of the poem is Brooklyn Bridge? Are we not concerned after all with the revisionary powers and practices of the imagination, not with the bridge of granite and steel, but the bridge of metaphor: not with Roebling's bridge but with Hart's?

The question turns on whether Hart's bridge is a symbol, or a symbolic act: a thing or an event. Consider the striking coincidence between Crane's bridge and Stella's. Some scholars have asked whether Stella's canvases, the *Brooklyn Bridge* of 1917-18 and the bridge panel of *New York Interpreted,* of 1922 might not have influenced Crane. Certainly Crane himself was taken with the coincidence of "sentiments" when he wrote to Stella in 1929, and he thought to include one of the paintings (exactly which one remains unclear) as frontispiece to the Black Sun edition of **The Bridge.** The plan collapsed, apparently for technical reasons, and the poem appeared in 1930 with three tactfully placed photographs by Crane's friend Walker Evans.

The question whether the painter's vision has priority to the poet's must now take into account the contribution of the photographer to the poem. Is the poet's bridge a symbol in the sense of an icon, a physical "shrine," as Stella described his first painting, a symbolic "meeting point of all forces arising in a superb assertion of their powers, in APOTHEOSIS?" It is noteworthy that John Marin considered Stella's painting excessively formalistic: having no more relation with the actual bridge "than if he had put up some street cables and things in his studio—painted a rather beautiful thing and called it the 'Bridge.'"[24] Marin misses the *experience* of the bridge, precisely what he himself attempted to capture and convey in his *The Red Sun, Brooklyn Bridge,* of 1922. Stella's paintings, in fact, in their stylization project an idea of bridge linked only by iconic association to the specific Brooklyn Bridge. Partly he calls up associations with popular imagery of the bridge. Although the compositions are dynamic, the geometric formality of the icon freezes the bridge into a static image of towers, arches, and cables. The action of the paintings is not so much *crossing* as *recognizing,* and in the recognition, enhancing the actual bridge with heroic energies, *raising* the bridge above the common experience of it. We look *up* to Stella's bridge, as a figurative projection and elevation of the familiar bridge.

Crane, too, in his program for the poem, speaks of the bridge as a "climax," a "symbol of our constructive future, our unique identity, in which is included also our scientific hopes and achievements of the future." Much of the worry critics have displayed toward the poem comes from taking this early (1923) statement too literally. In fact the bridge does not appear anywhere in the poem as a symbol of this sort, a sign which stands for the abstraction "America." Apart from the transfiguration of details of the bridge (through Crane's "logic of metaphor") into elements of the poem's governing "abstract form"—the curve becomes a "curveship," for example, and the span of steel a "cognizance,"—the bridge always appears in its aspect as Brooklyn Bridge: a shuttle for traffic ("Again the traffic lights that skim thy swift/ Unfractioned idiom . . ."), a parapet for bedlamites, a pier under which the poet waits in the bridge's shadow, a walkway ("I started walking home across the Bridge") from which the poet has a vision of clipper ships—and on which he walks his final walk and crossing into a vision of Oneness that *may* be "Cathay." And Evans' photographs reinforce and elaborate the implications of this literalness of Brooklyn Bridge in the poem.

At the time Evans lived near Crane on Brooklyn Heights, and also knew the bridge as a walker. Presumably at Crane's behest or encouragement, tacit or otherwise, Evans took along a hand camera on one or two of his strolls, and although he published only three of the images in the Black Sun edition, and another (very close to the first Black Sun image) as frontispiece to the first American edition (Boni & Livright, 1930), the entire group (at least those images that survive) make up an ensemble with a consistent inner conception. First, they represent an original photographic representation of the bridge, breaking decisively from the lateral or heroic or iconic views of earlier serious photographers like Coburn or the clichés of commercial views. The view from beneath, of the dark underside of the bridge's floor pinned against the sky, was entirely novel, with no predecessors at all in the popular or naive iconology of the bridge. But the originality of the group lies not only in composition. The bridge here is viewed freshly, in a series of images, as the experience of a specific eye; the vision of each print is the vision of all: a visual possession of the bridge as someone's—a walker's—palpable experience.

The three images accompanying the poem suggest a remarkable coincidence of vision. The first, which faces the opening lines of **"Proem,"** shows the bridge from underneath; the second, dead midway during the poem, faces the lines in **"Cutty Sark"** in which the poet, walking home across the bridge, envisions a fleet of sailing ships: the exquisite framing of coal barges and tugboat in the photograph works as counterpoint to the poet's fantasy: grounding it in the literal (though aesthetically transformed) experience recorded in the photograph. The

final image faces the concluding lines of **"Atlantis,"** where the poet crosses and asks of the transfigured towers and cables and meshwork, "Is it Cathay?" The swinging antiphonal whispers of the last line awaken the lines of the photograph, and together, words and image, ground the question in the living, kinetic experience of crossing the bridge. The poem is then framed by two images *of* the bridge, and punctuated at mid-point by an image *from* the bridge. We begin and conclude with Brooklyn Bridge: beginning low, under its piers, and concluding high, eye-crossing amidst the pattern of cables, tower, and stays on the walkway.[25]

The photographs achieve what Stella's paintings would not: they mediate, or connect, or *bridge* the poem to the real bridge. They keep before us shifting images of that bridge as the poet's object in the poem—as what he is aware of. Moreover, taken as rhetoric, far more understatedly than Stella's images do, they connect the reader's experience of a real bridge, a specific bridge, with the bridge and the bridging of the poem. They assist the communication of the poem—and reveal what kind of communication Crane wished the poem to achieve.

> And Thee, across the harbor, silver-paced
> As though the sun took step of thee, yet left
> Some motion ever unspent in thy stride,—
> Implicitly thy freedom staying thee!

Here, in the opening view of the bridge, it lies across the harbor, anobject of the poet's vision. It is external to him, yet focuses his attention. As an object in **"Proem"** it reveals itself as possessing a place, a set of connections and relations: to the city, the cinema, office buildings, Wall Street, traffic. Yet it looms above just as it remains connected, and bespeaks a pledge, a promise, that its "curveship" might "lend a myth to God." The curveship and the promise were already prefigured in the "inviolate curve" of the seagull's wings in stanza 1 (but they flicker and are gone), and especially in the progress of the sun crossing the diagonal stays seeming to *take step* of the bridge, to climb its ascending cables. The motion of sun, free yet restrained by the form of the bridge—bound yet unbound—prefigures the poet's own walk in the concluding section of the poem.

The motion, the walk, the crossing into a visionary vision: these compel the recognition that the bridge is not merely an object, but also a subject, a Thee. Possessed by the kinetic eye and thus transfigured into a personal event, animated by the poet's eye-crossing, it performs the act of bestowing upon the poet what he most urgently needs: the kind of centrality that will make his recovery of experience—personal and historical experience—possible. The pledge of the bridge is not simply (or not at all) to yield *itself* to the properly devout poet: it promises, in short, a "usable past," and in the fullest, deepest, life-giving sense of the word, it promises "culture."

Simultaneously springing from a ground and joining, the bridge as symbolic act is the very act of culture itself, as

Crane and his colleagues understood the term: culture not as a set of objects but culture as an ongoing process of mergings, makings, and crossings toward a totality. The bridge offers what Crane in his programmatic statement of 1924-25, **"General Aims and Theories,"** called "an absolute experience, an experience that will engross the total faculties of the spectator." Such totalizing endows the spectator with centrality: he is the focal point, the organizing center of his own experience. Nothing is superfluous, nothing is missing: "Our imagination is unable to suggest a further detail consistent with the design of the aesthetic whole."

"And I have been able to give freedom and life which was acknowledged in the ecstasy of walking hand in hand across the most beautiful bridge of the world," Crane wrote in 1924, about crossing the bridge with a lover, "the cables enclosing us and pulling us upward in such a dance as I have never walked and never can walk with another."[26]

> As soon as the foundations of our life have been reconstructed and made solid on the basis of our own experience, all these extraneous, ill-regulated forces will rally about their newly found center; they will fit in, each where it belongs, contributing to the essential architecture of our life. Then, and only then, shall we cease to be a blind, selfish, disorderly people; we shall become a luminous people, dwelling in the light and sharing our light.

The evangelical, apocalyptic accents of Brooks' bridging vision come to a fruition in Crane's poem. The poem is not "about" Brooklyn Bridge. It translates the bridge into culture, into the simultaneous possession of world and self the vision of which served Crane and his fellow artists as their high alternative to American "normalcy." The vision still lives in the poem, even if the anticipated luminosity (or even the hope of it) has long since dimmed in the culture: lives not only as a vestige of what historians have called the first decade of our own times, but perhaps also as an inducement. As excessive, exaggerated, and, in their own way, blind to the real possibilities of their everyday culture as Crane and others may have been, they were the first in our era to understand that revision in the light of a universal idea (their "America") was the central condition for a living culture. Insofar as we concern ourselves not only with their vision but with what they failed to see, their enterprise might yet succeed as our own "usable past."

NOTES

[1] These terms are prominent in Johan Huizinga's observations, in *America: A Dutch Historian's Vision, from Afar and Near* (New York, 1972). I have also profited a great deal from the discussion of technological and economic changes in the 1920s in Martin J. Sklar, "On the Proletarian Revolution and the End of Political-Economic Society," *Radical America* 3, no. 3 (May-June 1969): 1-41.

[2] Frederick Hoffman, *The Twenties* (New York, 1955), pp. 163-239.

[3] See Lewis Mumford, "Prelude to the Present," in *Interpretations and Forecasts, 1922-1972* (New York, 1973), pp. 110-21. Also, Alan Trachtenberg, ed., *Critics of Culture* (New York, 1976).

[4] Huizinga, *America,* p. 283.

[5] Alan Trachtenberg, *Brooklyn Bridge: Fact and Symbol* (New York, 1965), surveys much of the relevant material.

[6] Quoted in Irma Jaffe, *Joseph Stella* (New York, 1970), p. 58.

[7] Quoted in Brom Weber, *Hart Crane* (New York, 1948), p. 425.

[8] Brom Weber, ed., *The Complete Poems and Selected Letters and Prose of Hart Crane* (New York, 1966), p. 114.

[9] Lewis Mumford, *Sticks and Stones* (New York, 1924), pp. 115-16.

[10] Ibid.

[11] Quoted in Trachtenberg, *Brooklyn Bridge,* p. 74.

[12] Ibid., p. 79.

[13] Ernest Poole, *The Harbor* (New York, 1915), p. 193.

[14] Dorothy Landers Beall, *The Bridge and Other Poems* (New York, 1913), pp. 13-131.

[15] Quoted in Sheldon Reich, *John Marin: A Stylistic Analysis and Catalogue Raisonné* (University of Arizona Press, 1970), pp. 54-55.

[16] Clair Sprague, ed., *Van Wyck Brooks: The Early Years* (New York, 1968), p. 223.

[17] Waldo Frank, *The Unwelcome Man* (New York, 1917), pp. 167-69.

[18] Sprague, ed., *Van Wyck Brooks,* p. 199.

[19] Ibid., p. 202.

[20] Brom Weber, ed., *The Letters of Hart Crane* (New York, 1952), p. 241.

[21] Ibid., p. 305.

[22] Ibid., p. 124.

[23] Ibid., p. 261.

[24] Reich, *John Marin,* p. 148.

[25] For an interesting discussion of the function of the Evans photographs, see Gordon K. Grigsby, "Photo-

graphs in the First Edition of *The Bridge*," *Texas Studies in Language and Literature* 4(1962):4-11. A more general, and suggestive, essay on the appeal of photography to Crane, is F. Richard Thomas, "Hart Crane, Alfred Stieglitz, and Camera Photography," *Centennial Review,* 1977, pp. 294-309.

[26] Weber, ed., *Letters,* p. 181.

## Tom Chaffin (essay date 1984)

SOURCE: "Toward a Poetics of Technology: Hart Crane and the American Sublime," in *The Southern Review,* Vol. 20, No. 1, January, 1984, pp. 68-81.

[*In the following essay, Chaffin contends that* The Bridge *is most properly read as exemplary of representations of the sublime in American literature.*]

To his critics, Hart Crane remains an inspired but troublesome poet—one whose reach, in the end, far exceeded his grasp. Particularly vexing to assayers of his poetic legacy has been *The Bridge,* Crane's intended magnum opus, which was published in 1930, two years before his suicide.

While critics have come to acknowledge the breadth and uneven brilliance of some of the poem's fine lyrical passages, they also generally lament it as one of the more hubristic acts of poetic enterprise in American literature. "Perhaps none in our time has failed more gloriously," says Hyatt Waggoner in a 1950 study. Even Crane's friend Allen Tate, who praises several sections of the poem, finally rejects the whole as incoherent. "The episodes of *The Bridge,*" Tate writes in a 1930 essay that remains the most incisive criticism of the poem, "follow out of no inherent necessity in the theme, for they are arbitrary, and appear not organically but analogously."

More recently, others have argued that criticism of *The Bridge* as a failed epic misses the point. In a recent letter to the author, Crane biographer John Unterecker argues that the poet's correspondence suggests that Crane never intended to write an epic poem, and that the work should not be judged as such. Rather, Crane "was interested in writing a long poem that suggested some of the variety of an American experience—an experience sometimes celebratory, sometimes caught up in chaos, sometimes sentimental, sometimes comic." The structure of the poem, Unterecker maintains, was historical, not epic, in intention. "An epic becomes a single statement. He was interested in various approaches to a statement." To Unterecker, *The Bridge* should be approached as one would come to a long poem by Yeats or Roethke: "In such a poem, the sections have an oblique relation to one another, frequently accompanied by a shift in tone—so that the critic looking for *a* tone to the poem is instantly doomed."

While it would be a mistake to suggest that a single tone or locale dominates *The Bridge,* Crane's correspondence and subsequent criticism do suggest a central concern—one Whitmanian in nature and Modernist in approach. Of all the sections of *The Bridge,* the "Cape Hatteras" section most explicitly addresses this Whitmanian and Modernist agenda. The seven-page "Cape Hatteras" section, which Crane himself calls a sort of ode to Whitman, is the longest in the poem and also the one most engaged in issues of modern civilization—technology, war, the alienation of the human spirit.

Other sections of *The Bridge* (e.g., "To Brooklyn Bridge," "The Tunnel," "Atlantis," to name a few) speak to these modern and Modernist concerns. "Cape Hatteras," however, for all its flaws, is Crane's most dramatic frontal assault on the field of modern consciousness, his boldest journey into the miasma of twentieth-century anxiety. In "Cape Hatteras," Sherman Paul writes in *Hart's Bridge,* "doubt is transformed, cosmos restored, and the poet is prepared to journey onward into the future."

Admiration of Crane's courage abounds in Paul's praise of "Cape Hatteras." He suggests that the poem can only be as brave as the poet's risk in creating it: "The poem—and the act of writing it, living in it—is a gathering of faith." Paul's description of "Cape Hatteras"—the work *and* its creation—in terms of the author's personal risk is striking but not without precedent in the criticism of art that derives its strength not from irony but from the sublime. Writing on the physical and moral courage of Frederick Church, the nineteenth-century critic Henry Tuckerman alludes to the *plein air* painter's willingness to "risk life and limb" at "great cost of fatigue and exposure" in order to paint erupting volcanoes and other acts of nature.

Putting aside the structural debate, I believe that much of the confusion surrounding *The Bridge* can be resolved if the poem is read not as a failed epic but as a poem that, for good or ill, derives much of its force from the tradition of the sublime—a tradition usually more often alluded to in British than in American criticism. Crane sought in *The Bridge* to bring to bear on contemporary American life a vision commensurate with Whitman's—a faith that sought its main strength not in irony but in the sublime.

And nowhere is Crane's sublimity more manifest than in "Cape Hatteras." The poet foundered here just as surely as earlier voyagers who met their fate on the wind-thrashed shores of Hatteras. There is, however, a consolation: an examination of the wreckage of Crane's Hatteras transit can offer insight into just what that doomed reach was attempting to grasp. Such an examination can also place Hart Crane in his proper context in the history of American letters—as a Modernist, as a poet of the city, as a direct descendant of Walt Whitman, and, most critically, as the poet who pushed nineteenth-century poetics as far into the twentieth century as they would reach. First, however, one must revisit some old ground.

THE COPERNICAN REVOLUTION OF EDMUND BURKE

To appreciate the full breadth of the sublime and its interpretation from British Romantics down to Whitman and Crane, one turns back to the doctrine's seminal propagandist, Edmund Burke. In 1757, Burke published the essay *A Philosophical Enquiry into the Origin of Our Ideas of the Sublime and Beautiful,* which was to bear heavily on the aesthetic doctrines of Kant, Lessing, and Coleridge, among others in the late eighteenth century. The essay suggests a new way of understanding sensibility. Burke distinguishes between the "positive pleasures" of the "beautiful," on the one hand, and the "delight" that arises from the diminution of pain, on the other. The latter concept, upon which his book focuses, arises from a desire for self-preservation and is to Burke the most intense of human experiences. The condition that leads to this "delight" he calls the "sublime." In his *Enquiry,* Burke describes the sublime specifically as that mental transaction in which the mind confronts stimuli so terrible or awesome or "obscure" that it is, to use a term from M. D. Uroff's excellent *Hart Crane: The Patterns of His Poetry,* "impinged upon." Burke describes it:

> In this case the mind is so entirely filled with its object that it cannot entertain any other, nor by consequence, reason on that object which employs it.

The sublime, then, is that state of mind in which the subject is "beside himself." In another passage, Burke emphasizes the symbolic violence implicit in his conception of the sublime—a trait important to bear in mind when considering Crane. Burke speaks of a sort of Dionysian surrender to that which is terrible or overwhelming. In the presence of the "Godhead":

> We shrink into the minuteness of our own nature, and are in this manner, annihilated before him. And though a consideration of his other attributes may relieve in some measure our apprehension, yet no conviction of the justice with which it is exercised, nor the mercy with which it is tempered removes the terror that naturally arises from a force which nothing can withstand.

Burke's reference to an awe that arises from a "terror which nothing can withstand" resonates in romantic literature from Wordsworth's "Lines Written on Westminster Bridge" to Whitman's "On the Beach at Night" (one of Whitman's strongest invocations of the Burkean sublime). For Burke, "force," power, and the sublime form a natural equation. In the *Enquiry,* he writes, "I know of nothing sublime which is not some modification of power."

Again, here, it remains critical to bear in mind that Burke's is not a religious vision. While his reference to "the Godhead" suggests that the terrible powers of nature originate from the "force" of a divine entity, the sublime is not a religious transaction. Rather, the sublime is a phenomenal act in which "the mind is hurried out of it-self, by a croud of great and confused images, which affect because they are crouded and confused." Burke assigns no moral judgment to theact. The overload of sensible images affects simply because the images are "crouded and confused," not because they are redemptive or punitive in any religious scheme of nature.

In considering Crane, it is worth remembering that Burke describes the sublime as a function not of nature but of the mind. In exploring the sublime in the context of Modernist, urban-oriented poetry, keep in mind that if to some readers the proper locus of the sublime is nature, the connection they make is historic, not semantic. If the term "sublime" brings to mind the mountains of Wordsworth, the violent seascapes of Turner, remember that Burke himself never restricts the sublime to the domain of nature. His is a psychological, not a geographical concept.

In the *Enquiry,* Burke offers a metaphor in the language of eighteenth-century introspective psychology: he speaks of a very specific phenomenal "transaction." This condition—the sublime—involves an overload of sensible material, an "annihilation of the self," and a correlate restoration of equilibrium, of "delight," to use Burke's term.

In this context, Ernest Lee Tuveson writes in *The Imagination as a Means of Grace* that Burke's essay "appeared as perhaps the first substantial effort to construct a system of aesthetics in the strict sense of the word." According to Tuveson, Burke rejected "the whole doctrine of the final cause for pleasures of the imagination."

As Immanuel Kant, in his 1787 *Critique of Pure Reason,* rebelled against the dominant rationalism of his day and sought, through his own "Copernican Revolution," to restore man to his position as the final arbiter of experience, so Burke rebelled against the Lockeian rationalism of his day and sought a way to speak of aesthetic experience without referring to "final causes" or to an objective universe. Tuveson sees Burke, in this mode, as a "radical skeptic" who sought to "bring the philosophy of aesthetics up to a level with that of physical science." Burke's most critical departure from the rational spirit of his day, Tuveson argues, was his eschewing of final causes—or references to God in an objective universe—in explaining the nature of man's reaction to sensible material. "Burke found that aesthetic sensibility is simply a byproduct of the simple sensations. . . . Burke accounts for aesthetic responses by reducing them to the status of feelings which accompany the original sensations; we feel not only heat and cold but the sublime and beautiful as well . . . the aesthetic is thus physiological."

Burke's "Copernican Revolution," in the history of ideas, removes the a priori as a necessary component of aesthetic theory. He creates the first "pure" aesthetic doctrine. As a correlative, Burke shifts the locus of aesthetics from the object to the subject. He writes that poetry and rhetoric should "display rather the effect of things on the mind of the speaker, or of others, than to present a clear idea of the things in themselves." This reorientation anticipates an observation made by Crane's mentor Whitman in "A Song of Occupations": "All architecture is what you do to it when you look upon it." In the same vein, Crane asks, "Did one look at what one saw/Or did one see what one looked at?" To Tuveson, this shift from the objective to the subjective engenders a new task for the artist and poet: "His business is now rather the re-creation of what happens in the mind during the aesthetic experience than the direct occasioning of that experience." In line with this task, Crane writes to Harriet Monroe that he considers the effects of images on the mind to be the only essential logic to his poems.

It is this kind of aesthetic prescience on Burke's part that led Tuveson to call the *Enquiry* the first truly modern work on aesthetics—"modern not only in machinery but in spirit as well."

TOWARD AN AMERICAN SUBLIME: WHITMAN'S PASSAGE, CRANE'S BRIDGE

Problematic to any consideration of Crane as a poet of the sublime is the looseness with which the term "sublime" has been used—when it has been used at all—in American literature and criticism. Roderick Nash, in his *Wilderness and the American Mind,* describes an early American interest in the doctrines of Burke but adds that by the late nineteenth century the terms "beautiful" and "sublime" were "applied so indiscriminately as to lose meaning." Josephine Miles, unique in the attention she gives to the sublime in American literature, describes in her 1963 *Kenyon Review* article, "Hart Crane and the Poetry of Praise," a long-standing bias against the sublime and in favor of irony.

> American criticism has held sublimity in check. Especially recently, but throughout our history, our critics have been ironists, or have spoken from a cooler English point of view. Most of the new critics are anti-sublime poets and theorists.

This critical inattention notwithstanding, Miles argues that the sublime in America, from the eighteenth century on, has enjoyed a healthy popularity among American poets, from Whittier and Bradstreet to Whitman and Crane. Ironically, Miles claims, the Johnsonian skeptics who opposed Burke's doctrine in England found no constituency in the New World. Rather, "the natural bounty of America—its 'purple mountains' majesty and spacious skies'—afforded unlimited opportunities for a poetry of the sublime." From the beginning of the American republic, Miles writes, the sublime nourished the American cult of nature and met the poetic demands of a literature that desired to celebrate "a special time and place, America, when universality, not specialness, was great and noble." In America, "the sublime found soil fertile for rich growth, with growing transcendentalism and modern imagism not stays but aids."

In this tradition, Miles views Crane's spiritual mentor, Whitman, as the great bard of the American sublime—as a poet "more visionary, more adjectival, more cumulative and harmonic than any other poet in English. . . . " Miles breaks away from Burke's philosophical definition and defines the sublime in America as a rhetorical tradition, a poetry of praise.

> This American poetry of praise has a long free-cadenced line, full of silences, symbols, and implications. It has a cumulative structure, building up to a height of force and feeling, whether in imprecation or in rhapsody. It has a phraseology of resounding height and of warm responsive sense, suggestive of heights beyond the reach of form or reason.

To deliver this American sublime, Miles says, such poets as Crane and Whitman rely on "verbs of bodily motion, nouns of natural motion and power, adjectives of positive intensity." Certainly the opening verses of *The Bridge* bear her out:

> How many dawns, chill from his rippling rest
> The seagull's wings shall dip and pivot him,
> Shedding white rings of tumult, building high
> Over the chained bay waters Liberty—

Crane's use of such words as "dawn, chill, rippling, dip, pivot, shedding, building, chained," and, finally, **"Liberty,"** create a vibrant, muscular syntax and musical assonance every bit as graceful as the bridge the poem will celebrate.

Now consider these lines from **"Cape Hatteras":**

> Stars scribble on our eyes the frosty sagas,
> The gleaming cantos of unvanquished space . . .
> O sinewy silver biplane, nudging the wind's
>         withers!
> There, from Kill Devils Hill at Kitty Hawk
> Two brothers in their twinship left the dune;
> Warping the gale, the Wright windwrestlers
>         veered
> Capeward, then blading the wind's flank, banked
>         and
>             spun.
> What ciphers risen from prophetic script,
> What marathons new-set between the stars!
> The soul, by naphtha fledged into new reaches
> Already knows the closer clasp of Mars,—
> New latitudes, unknotting, soon give place
> To what fierce schedules, rife of doom apace!

This tribute to another kind of Icarus soars with the same breathless lyricism—"Stars scribble frosty sagas / gleaming cantos, unvanquished space / nudging wind's withers / Warping the gale, windwrestlers veered / blading, banked, spun / ciphers risen / The soul fledged / New latitudes unknotting . . ." The two passages use similar rhetorical strategies—but to different ends. The former is, indeed, a poetry of praise. The latter suggests something more foreboding: naphtha is a colorless and very volatile petroleum distillate. Crane's admiration for the

Wright Brothers as they "warp the gale" is paled by a Burkean sense of doom. The airplane is a logos of a technological carnage; a "cipher risen from prophetic script" meeting its historic "fierce schedules," it promises "doom apace."

One stanza celebrates the beauty and strength of a seagull and, by implication, a triumph of modern architecture—the Brooklyn Bridge. The other celebrates the flight of the Wright Brothers and, by implication, the future of modern aviation and technology. What, then, is the difference? Both employ a muscular syntax and a diction worthy of their subjects. Both speak in a voice of awe—and therein lies the difference between the two passages. The former accommodates Miles's poetry-of-praise criterion. The latter expresses a certain kind of awestruck praise, but it is a praise overpowered by augury, by fear—by the Burkean sublime. **"Cape Hatteras"** approaches the limits of Miles's definition of the American sublime.

Though Miles's isolation of the sublime as a critical strain in American poetry is salutary, her definition of the term falls short of accommodating the Burkean one. It turns on a common ambiguity, described by Benedetto Croce in his classic *Aesthetics.* "What is the sublime?" he asked rhetorically.

> The unexpected affirmation of an overwhelming moral force: that is one definition. But the other is equally good, which recognizes the sublime also where the force which affirms itself is certainly overwhelming, but immoral and destructive.

Miles's "American Sublime" clearly partakes more of Croce's former definition than of his latter, with its Burkean resonances. Obviously, some of the vitality of the Burkean sublime is leached away when it associates with a panegyric celebration of nature, with its implicit Whitmanian pantheism. A sense of what may be regained when the sublime rejects a decidedly referential aesthetic is conveyed by Wallace Stevens in "On the Road Home." Here, fecundity is restored when the referential aesthetic is discarded:

> It was when I said,
> "There is no such thing as the truth"
> That the grapes seemed fatter.
> The fox ran out of his hole.

Barbara Novak, in *Nature and Culture: American Landscape and Painting 1825-1875,* describes a similar process in the development of American landscape painting during the latter half of the nineteenth century. This period, says Novak, saw American landscape painting move *away from* the "old" sublime of Burke toward the newer "Christianized" sublime of Emerson and the Luminist painters. This transit from the old to the new in sublime art may be seen in the work of Thomas Cole, Frederick Church, and others associated with the Hudson Valley School.

Novak notes that many of the large-scale works of these artists are almost histrionic in their use of color, and

heavily invested with the "labor trail" of the artist—manifest in the heavy brush strokes and in the artist's compulsion to depict himself within the composition. (No *sprezzatura* here!) Choice of subject matter also betrays this labor trail. Paintings of exotic scenes—exploding volcanoes, frigid icebergs, and the like—conveyed the artist's personal risk in the pursuit of his art. Such risk suggests a sense of mission on the artist's part, draws attention to his self-assigned role as mediator between nature and viewer, and, finally, puts the artist—not God—at the sublime center of the phenomenon depicted in the composition.

Increasingly, however, this Burkean sublime was crowded out, Novak says. A new Christianized sublime was nourished by a growing transcendentalism and a tendency of artists to conceive of natural phenomena (volcanoes, icebergs, etc.) as merely revelatory of a living deity—a living deity within a universe of His own ordering. Burke's terrible sublime gave way to the blandishments of Emersonian idealism. In the terms of the Wallace Stevens poem, the fox ran back into the hole—and the sublime became panegyric, an art that praised rather than feared nature.

Out of this shift came the Luminists. Such painters as Church and John Kensett turned their energies toward smaller canvases, works with delicate—almost Oriental—brush strokes. These paintings celebrated tranquility, not turmoil, in nature.

For Novak, Church and Albert Bierstadt stand as transitional figures between these two traditions of the sublime in American landscape art, and their use of light is instructive:

> In all instances, the spirituality of light signals the newly Christianized sublime. In the large paintings by Church and Bierstadt light moves, consumes, agitates and drowns. In its striving it is Gothic. . . . In the smaller, luminist paintings, also executed occasionally by Church and Bierstadt, light, because of its silent, *unstirring* energy, causes the universe, as Emerson would have it, to become "transparent, and the light of higher laws than its own" to shine through it.

Again, it is not important here to decide which of these two senses of the sublime—as defined by Novak, Miles, or Croce—is the most authentic. The point is that various meanings have been historically attached to the word sublime and that the term's utility as a critical lens is directly related to the precision with which it is used.

TOWARD A TECHNOLOGICAL SUBLIME: AMMONIAC PROVERBS

Miles identifies the American sublime with the pastoral poetics of Walt Whitman and his pantheistic praise of "the traits of natural divine endowment." Crane, she suggests, stands clearly in this panegyric tradition. She cites Crane's **"Voyages,"** section II, with its Whitmanian echoes of the poet stalking the lonely beaches: "Take this sea, whose diapason knells,/On scrolls of silver snowy sentences. . . . " There are similar passages in *The Bridge.* Lines from the section called **"The Dance"** bring to mind the sympathetic Whitman who "skirted" Sierras with his palm:

> O Appalachian Spring! I gained the ledge;
> Steep, inaccessible smile that eastward bends
> And northward reaches in that violet wedge
> Of Adirondack!—wisped of azure wands.

Miles correctly isolates in Crane a Whitmanian celebration of "suns and waves, seas and bodies, hands and waters, stars and meadows. . . . " To be sure, Crane's debt to his taskmaster was great. It was Whitman who located the city for Crane as the locus of fecundity for modern romantic poetry and, indirectly, for Modernism. With regard to Crane's "logic of metaphor," it was Whitman, along with the French Imagists, who, in the words of critic James E. Miller, Jr., "turned the arena of the poem from the page to the person, the variable poetic movements tracing their own designs in the consciousness." And, finally, it was Whitman to whom Crane looked for the epic reach of his poetic vision—as Whitman had demanded, "Arouse! for you must justify me. . . . "

With regard to the sublime in the poems of Whitman and Crane, however, much remains unanswered in Miles's conception of the sublime. Yes, Crane, in many passages, does bear witness to Whitman's pantheism ("She ran the neighing canyons all the spring; / She spouted arms; she rose with maize. . . . ") Crane's pathetic fallacy of "Pocahontas" stands clearly in the chthonic tradition of Whitman's 1860 "Songs of Parting" ("Of seeds dropping into the ground, of birth / Of the steady concentration of America, inland, upward, to impregnable and swarming places. . . . ") But *The Bridge* reveals another, more problematic, legacy of Whitman. It is the Whitman of what Leo Marx has called "the technological sublime." It is the Whitman who took up Emerson's call that American poetry should "sing" the city and industrialism as well as the "open road" of nature. Emerson declares:

> Readers of poetry see the factory-village and the railway and fancy that the poetry of the landscape is broken up by these; for these works are not yet consecrated in their reading; but the poet sees them fall within the great Order not less than the beehive of the spider's geometrical web.

Whitman's acceptance of Emerson's challenge is clear when he speaks of his poetic scheme to celebrate the industrial conversion of the North American continent. From his 1871 "Song of the Exposition";

> Mightier than Egypt's tombs,
> Fairer than Grecia's, Roma's temples,
> Prouder than Milan's statued, spired cathedral,
> More picturesque than Rhenish castle-keeps,
> We plan even now to raise, beyond them all,
> Thy great cathedral sacred industry, no tomb,
> A keep for life for practical convention.

In the same vein, consider these lines from the **"Cape Hatteras"** section of *The Bridge:*

> The nasal whine of power whips a new universe . . .
> Where spouting pillars spoor the evening sky,
> Under the looming stacks of the gigantic power
>   house
> Stars prick the eyes with sharp ammoniac
>   proverbs,
> New verities, new inklings in the velvet hummed.

In Crane's affirmation of "the nasal whine of power" that "whips a new universe," he shares Whitman's uncritical acceptance of a teeming industrialism. But while Whitman speaks of the "picturesque cathedral of industry" in classical aesthetic terms—the terms of Henry Adams' "Virgin"—Crane's "nasal whine" has more foreboding discords. It is a notion of the sublime that comes closer to Burke's doctrine of transfiguration—and Adams' "Dynamo."

While Whitman seeks to subsume the city and industrialism into classical aesthetic schemes, Crane describes a "nasal whine of power," a new and darker force unleashed on civilization that alludes more to Adams' explication of the "Dynamo," or the pre-Luminist sublime, than to any rhetorical poetry of praise. To Miles, the sublime is a rhetorical strategy by which the poet embarks on panegyric flights. While Crane, as has been said, surely partakes of this variety of the sublime, he does not take it into the city. Although there are moments of pastoral calm in Crane's celebration of the natural world, moments that accommodate Miles's and the Luminists' panegyric sublime, his portraits of the city bespeak a far more portentous situation. "I know of nothing sublime which is not some modification of power," wrote Burke. And so, Crane's "cyclone of the turbine crest" is a force that "whips, spouts, looms, and pricks." It is a force that, in turn, offers "new verities, new inklings," but that must first annihilate that which it will transform—must "prick the eyes with sharp ammoniac proverbs."

Similarly, it is a sublime that appropriates the severities of Novak's pre-Luminist Burkean sublime of nature ("suspenseful, attended by terror and dread, and often interrupted by the uproar of cataracts, earthquakes, fires,storms, thunder and volcanoes") and translates them into the violent imagery and rough-edged diction of modern technology:

> Slit the sky's pancreas of foaming anthracite
> Toward thee, O Corsair of the typhoon,—pilot,
>   hear!
> Thine eyes bicarbonated white by speed, O
>   Skygak, see
> How from thy path above the levin's lance
> Thou sowest doom thou hast nor time nor chance
> To reckon—as thy stilly eyes partake
> What alcohol of space . . . !

Uroff, in her discussion of Crane's debt to the French Imagists, implicitly acknowledges the Burkean *modus operandi* employed in this passage from **"Cape Hatteras."** "The image of razing, burning, and breaking apart is central to Crane's imagination. Violence is deeply ingrained in his imagination. . . . He is possessed by emotions which overpower him, and only as they expand themselves, only as they exhaust him, is he purified of them." This, of course, is the same Crane who in 1923 wrote to his mother, "Suffering is a real purification . . . without a certain measure of which any true happiness cannot be realized." If, as Crane claimed, he was in a "direct line with Whitman," it was the Whitman who had forsaken pastoral romanticism to bring his faith to the city rather than the one who demanded, "Give Me the Splendid Silent Sun."

THE BROKEN WORLD

There are moments when *The Bridge* sings with the clear assurance promised in Whitman's "Song of the Open Road": "It is safe, I have tried it." Such sections as **"To Brooklyn Bridge," "Van Winkle,"** and **"The Dance"** bear muscular witness to the poetic project proposed by Whitman in 1855: "Poets to come! . . . Arouse! for you must justify me." But when Crane in **"Cape Hatteras"** answers, "The Open Road—thy vision is reclaimed!" he is unconvincing. When Crane, in this critical section of *The Bridge,* takes Whitman's faith to the cutting edge of history, he becomes undone. The "Open Road's" transit into the consciousness of the twentieth century takes Crane to the brink of self-parody in Whitmanian excess.

Having eschewed Ransomian "aesthetic distance"—the trope of irony—Crane was left to fend for himself in the overwhelming, complex, and often contradictory milieu he confronted. Having rejected irony as a breaking of faith with Whitman—recall Crane's criticism of the "pessimism" of Eliot's *Waste Land*—Crane embraced, via the French Imagists, the terrible sublime of Edmund Burke's *Enquiry.* This contradiction between two senses of the sublime—one pastoral-oriented and a rhetoric of praise, the other urban-oriented and a doctrine of transfiguration—is given voice in Whitman's "Give Me the Splendid Silent Sun." But while Whitman in 1865 could play safely with such ambivalences, by the time of Crane's maturation as poet, the stakes were higher.

The closing of the American frontier in the late nineteenth century, and the fragmentation of American social and political institutions in the wake of World War I, continued to undermine the easy optimism of past doctrines of the New Jerusalem, Manifest Destiny, American Progressivism, and faith in new technologies. Just as Whitman, by the time of his 1871 *Democratic Vistas,* had sensed a betrayal of the American destiny he had celebrated in the early editions of *Leaves of Grass,* so it is worth bearing in mind that Crane published *The Bridge* almost sixty years after Whitman's own renunciation of the epic vision that Crane sought to bring to fruition. It was a calculus of pessimism reflected by Modernist literature.

In *Dionysus and the City,* Monroe K. Spears praises the iconoclastic vitality of the early Modernists—Nietzsche, Samuel Butler, the early Pound—"which seems to come from the release of pent-up energies." But, Spears adds:

> In time the sense of emancipation tends to grow uncertain of itself: Whitman's "Years of the modern! Years of the Unperformed!" becomes Hart Crane's "Years of the Modern! Propulsions toward what Capes?"

Spears's comments echo Crane's own doubts. In a 1926 letter to Waldo Frank, Crane wonders if "America were half as worthy today to be spoken of as Whitman spoke of it fifty years ago." The irony here is that "fifty years ago" Whitman had already abandoned the optimism he projected in the 1855 edition of *Leaves.* Allen Tate, in his 1930 essay on *The Bridge,* ponders the deterioration of Crane's vision.

> Crane had, in his later work, no individual consciousness: the hard form style of "Praise for an Urn" which is based on a clear-cut perception of moral relations, and upon their ultimate inviolability, begins to disappear. When the poet goes out into the world he finds that the simplicity of a child's world has no universal applicability.

Crane's "child's world" was the one he inherited from the early Whitman—the world of Miles's "American Sublime." It was the mythopoeic world of nature that was to be praised—not feared because it was overwhelming. And it was Crane's fate to take this naive doctrine to a technological and mostly urban landscape that, as Tate aptly puts it, could no longer support the romantic poetry to which Crane's vision aspired: Whitman's masthemmed Manhatta had become the cobalt-blue nightmare of the Precisionists, his Open Road a slit sky of foaming anthracite. As gifted as Crane was, as worthy a project as he embraced, its ultimate risk could not be supported by the consciousness born of his time and place.

**Margaret Dickie (essay date 1986)**

SOURCE: "The Bridge," in *On the Modernist Long Poem,* University of Iowa Press, pp. 47-67.

*[In the following essay, Dickie discusses the problems Crane encountered in dealing with the form of the long modernist poem.]*

It is hazardous to begin writing a long poem at the end, and all the more so with a long poem that will rely on the poet's moments of inspiration. Hart Crane's difficulties in writing *The Bridge* may be traced to this peculiar method of composition and to the assumptions about form that it embodies. Crane finished the final section of *The Bridge* first, and he called it **"Atlantis."** With that section completed, it was hard to begin the poem, harder still because Crane saw the ending as "symphonic in including the convergence of all the strands separately detailed in antecedent sections of the poem—Columbus, conquests of water, land, etc., Pokahantus, subways, offices, etc., etc." (LHC 232). To begin at the end, where Poe thought all works of art should begin, placed almost insurmountable restrictions on the unwritten long poem; and Crane's completion of **"Atlantis,"** a poem on which he had been working for three years, brought his writing on *The Bridge* to a temporary halt. **"Atlantis"** was the ending for a beginning that Crane could not imagine, and when he recommenced work on the long poem again some months later, he wrote a poem that essentially recasts **"Atlantis"**—**"To Brooklyn Bridge."** Then his writing stopped again. Eventually he resumed work on the poem, and, hedged in by a beginning balanced and doubled by the ending, Crane in one summer wrote most of the intervening sections.

In a different way from Eliot, Crane started his long poem too early, before he had prepared himself to write it. He imagined both that the long poem would come to him and that he could block it out first. He prepared an outline of the poem, and *The Bridge* emerged from a struggle between its inspired moments of composition and a preliminary plan. The plan proved to be an obstruction as well as an aid, encouraging creation but encouraging also the insights that made the plan unworkable. This long poem has always posed the problem of its organizational principle. If *The Waste Land* suffered from a dilatory composition and a structure realized only in the middle of the composition, *The Bridge* may suggest the problems presented by a plan developed fully prior to composition. The composition of *The Bridge* suggests that a predetermined structure can restrain the clarity of expression it is designed to serve.[1]

Crane's peculiarly deterministic method of writing reveals an uncertainty about the long form and an anxiety about how to channel his creative impetuosity into a sustained work. These fears he attempted to allay by methods that were destined to intensify them. But this narrative of composition also indicates the importance of such antagonistic creative habits. *The Bridge* develops by evading its supposed purposes.

It is not surprising, then, that the poem has always appeared to be a structural puzzle. Crane's first critics judged the poem brilliant in parts but inadequate as a total work. Later readers found the poem as a whole sturdy, but identified some sections as weak. Still later, the failure or success of the larger structure was seen as of one piece with the failure or success of the individual sections. One critic has argued that "Crane's long poems do not develop, they recur," and the problems of organization that such a "poetics of failure" requires manifest themselves both in the part and in the whole.[2] Thus, questions of organization—always the first and most crucial points of debate for a long poem—have tended to force the very judgment from which they have arisen.

Actually, Crane himself was his first negative critic. Even before he had written anything but the ending of *The Bridge,* he began to suspect that he would not be able to construct the long poem, not because his own creative powers were inadequate, but because he could find no material on which to exercise them. It is a curious complaint for a poet committed to inspiration and to art as creation rather than imitation. Still, he commented, "intellectually judged the whole theme and project seems more and more absurd." And he goes on to say: "The symbols of reality necessary to articulate the span—may not exist where you expected them, however. By which I mean that however great their subjective significance to me is concerned—these forms, materials, dynamics are simply non-existent in the world" (LHC 261). And once he had finished the poem, he admitted to Allen Tate, "My vision of poetry *is* too personal to 'answer the call'" (LHC 353).

His sense of failure, early and late, stemmed from what he imagined was a failure of vision. Like Pound, Crane judged himself by his ability to see a unified meaning within the fragments of history. For him, the poem was to be a vision of synthesis or wholeness: "a mystical synthesis of 'America,'" "a symbol of consciousness, knowledge, spiritual unity," the "Myth of America" (LHC 124, 241, 305). And like Pound too, he underestimated the power of his creative strength to vindicate history by revising it. But his stated ambition toward a synthesis is much more conservative than the poem he actually wrote. His aspirations here call for a fixed form that was always at odds both with the proliferation of material on which it was imposed and with his own febrile creative energy.

Starting at the end became a persistent strategy by which Crane could satisfy his need for synthesis, and at the same time give free expression to a creative resistance to closure. The poem as a whole, its sections, and even its lines appear consistently to start at the end. For example, the final section, **"Atlantis,"** opens with a vision of the whole bridge ("bound cable strands, the arching path") and a vision of wholeness ("Sibylline voices flicker, waveringly stream / As though a god were issue of the strings. . . . "). It ends at the beginning with that vision just about to be accomplished ("the orphic strings, / Sidereal phalanxes, leap and converge") and with a questioning of vision ("Is it Cathay, / Now pity steeps the grass and rainbows ring / The serpent with the eagle in the leaves . . . ?"). Stanza after stanza opens with an image of wholeness and moves to more tentative images: "bound cable strands" and "voices flicker," "hails, farewells" and "splintered in the straits," "Swift peal of secular light" and "harvests in sweet torment," "thine Everpresence" and "Whispers antiphonal." Even individual lines open and end in that way: "One arc synoptic of all tides below," "In single chrysalis the many twain," "O Answerer of all,—Anemone." The synopsis, singleness, answer, must be inevitably broken down into parts.

This poem and the larger poem which it launched develop neither by "symphonic convergence," nor by synthesis, nor by unifying strands. Both **"Atlantis"** and *The Bridge* set out an image of completion or wholeness, and then proceed to break itdown. This method operates at every level of the poem, from section to stanza to line to word combinations. Typically, the most complete form precedes its parts, and the parts, once they are enumerated, do not fit neatly together as a whole. Despite Crane's desire to affirm and unify, his poem tends to question and disassemble.

Crane's visionary inclinations, what R. W. B. Lewis has called his "apocalyptic *hope*,"[3] are usually cited as reasons for the discrepancy between the poem he imagined and the one he actually was able to write. As his comments to Frank that are quoted above suggest, when Crane despaired he seemed to despair of constructing the bridge between the real world and his image of it, of finding materials to embody his vision. Yet, the actual narrative of composition as well as the poem that emerged from it do not support this view.

Almost from the beginning and certainly as soon as he had completed **"Atlantis,"** Crane had a sense of the whole poem and the experiences that would form it. In an early letter to his benefactor, Otto Kahn, he laid out the sections that were to comprise **The Bridge** which, with the exception of the John Brown part and the two sections written last, he then proceeded to write. He had the evidence from history already sorted out, and he had also clearly established the symbolic significance of figures such as Columbus and Pocahontas. Nor were modern examples lacking from this early summary. He could already identify the subway section as "a kind of purgatory in relation to the open sky of last section" (LHC 241). There may be a certain visionary element in this outline, even a naive optimism about the creative process that lay ahead, but this scaffolding of the poem does not indicate a mind anxious for material to embody an idea. Nor was Crane misled about the symbolic significance of any element in the projected poem. Here, as in the finished poem, Pocahontas stands for "the natural body of America-fertility," and Columbus and Whitman are likewise accurately identified (LHC 241).

It might be argued that Crane's poem had been overdetermined, too clearly thought out before it was written through. But his difficulties in actually writing the poem would suggest otherwise. He composed in fits of inspiration that were in some minor way controlled by the plan, threatening to subvert its dominance and yet dependent on it too. For example, the climax of "Atlantis" is suspended at the end, but **The Bridge** does not develop by careful stages of increasing intensity up to this poem, which Crane described as a "sweeping dithyramb in which the Bridge becomes the symbol of consciousness spanning time and space" (LHC 241). Nor is there any gradual movement toward that ending. Sections do not build on one another; individual sections do not work toward affirmative conclusions. Yet the movement is not aleatory, because the composition appears to depend on this initiating structure which was there to encourage the poet when his inspiration flagged. Crane struggled through vision and revision to write a long poem that would fit

between the ecstatic ending and beginning that, in their finish, offered no principle of development except the possibility that they could be repeated, dismantled, or recreated.

The ambition to project a long poem was fixed by the poet's fear of inadequacy, which inspired a too elaborate conception of the task ahead; this in turn created a failure of expression, so that Crane was always working at odds with himself. He explained his method to Kahn: "Naturally I am encountering many unexpected formal difficulties in satisfying my conception, especially as one's original idea has a way of enlarging steadily under the spur of daily concentration on minute details of execution" (LHC 241). The discrepancy is between the whole and the parts, between the colossal conception of wholeness, completion, and ending, and the proliferating parts needed to make up that idea. But, as the narrative of the poem's composition reveals, Crane made the middle sections of the poem not only difficult to write but impossible even as an experiment in composition. Every section had to be wedged between the unity of beginning and end. Each part would threaten the whole and keep open the hazards of long form, even as the poem lengthened out. No bridges, the sections of **The Bridge** deny their connective functions as they vie for autonomy within the poem's larger structure.

This process of development differentiates **The Bridge** from most poems which gaintheir length from some generative process. Because Crane starts his poem with a finished structure, the Brooklyn Bridge, "Answerer of all," **"Atlantis,"** he has no way of generating a poem. Even when the poem undoes its end and moves toward origins, it either appropriates them or it denies their validity, destroying not only the idea of progress but the possibility of long form. For example, in the actual image of the bridge, Crane hears "labyrinthine mouths of history / Pouring reply," "Jason! hesting Shout!," "Beams yelling Aeolus," all voices from antiquity still present in the bridge, which is then identified as "O Choir, translating time." Thus, mythic origins are incorporated into the technological end, not superseded by it. At other points in **"Atlantis,"** Crane seems anxious to envision the end as obviating or excusing the beginning, as he says:

> Migrations that must needs void memory,
> Inventions that cobblestone the heart,—
> Unspeakable Thou Bridge to Thee, O Love.
> Thy pardon for this history, whitest Flower.

To conceive of the bridge in these two ways is to make links with the past either unnecessary or impossible, and in either case it prevents any poetic development based on generation. In order to write a long poem at all from this beginning, Crane had to keep repeating the ending, enlarging it with details, as he said, in a process which might be called degenerative form. He did not work toward wholeness and completion, but rather away from them, toward endlessly proliferating parts.

Crane's problems with form, which appear to derive from a too rigidly and extravagantly conceived whole, have their origin in his early uncertainty about representation. The drafts of **"Atlantis"** suggest that Crane wanted to represent the bridge as evidence of wholeness in the broken modern world, but he had not decided whether meaning inhered in the structure, was measured by it, played through it, or whether the bridge simply pointed to some vision beyond itself.[4] In worksheets of the spring and summer of 1926, Crane tries out these possibilities by changing prepositions:

> [with] [its]
> And through the cordage, notching *its white* call
> [after]
> Arch *into* arch, from seamless tides below,
> [With]
> *Their* labyrinthine mouths of history.[5]

The "cordage notching with its call" implies some progression just as "arch *after* arch" does, but this possibility is written out in the final choice, "One arc synoptic of all tides below." Again, in this same draft, the important fourth stanza deals directly with the question of vision, and it locates the source of vision not in the bridge, as in the final version, but in dreams:

> and *soar* [thread] [delve]
> [cipher curves]
> With *curves* of sleep *into* what *lakes* what skies
> contain
> The mythic laugh of spears.[6]

Questions of whether to use *up* or *of* or *with* plagued Crane throughout the drafts. In some sense, the final version refused to settle definitely on one location. The vision was "*through* the bound cable strands," "*Up* the index of night," "*Onward* and *up*," but also "*In* myriad syllables," "*In* single chrysalis," and finally, "*To* wrapt inception" "*through* blinding cables." Vision seems to run *through* the bridge, *upward* from it, *toward* an "Everpresence, *beyond* time" (italics mine). Thus, the significance of the bridge is never clear; meaning inheres in it and beyond it. By seeing the bridge both as a man-made creation of wholeness and the sign by which such wholeness "beyond time" could be apprehended, Crane created a structure false to the actual fact from which this symbol was abstracted and false also to the radical energy that inspired Crane's long poem. Crane made his bridge an icon—harp, altar, pledge, myth—but no bridge. And by calling the bridge "Answerer of all," he gave his poem a resolute closure and a preordained order that his creative proclivities could never sustain.

His was not an imagination either satisfied with or longing for answers or the forms that answers would contain. In **"The Broken Tower,"** one of the last poems he wrote, he finally acknowledged that his song was a "long-scattered score / Of broken intervals," the song made when "the bells break down their tower; / And swing I know not where." It is the radical energies which these bells represent, energies that will not be contained in

towers or rigid forms, that inspired Crane's poetry from beginning to end. But in undertaking to write **The Bridge,** Crane attempted to channel these disruptive energies into an essentially conservative form and end.

The impulse to write the great myth of America came from Crane's reading of *The Waste Land,* among other sources. After Eliot's "perfection of death—nothing is possible in motion but a resurrection of some kind," Crane wrote (LHC 115). And a few months later, he elaborated this notion in a letter to Alfred Stieglitz, whose work he admired: "The city is a place of 'brokenness,' of drama; but when a certain development in this intensity is reached a new stage is created, or must be, arbitrarily, or there is a foreshortening, a loss and a premature disintegration of experience" (LHC 138).

Crane's initial aim was to locate what he calls here variously "spiritual events," "resurrection," a "new stage," in some relation to the new forms of the modern city. His ambition would always be toward the whole, a conversion of parts into wholes. Thus, the Brooklyn Bridge becomes "steeled Cognizance," "intrinsic Myth," "Deity's glittering Pledge," "whitest Flower." This willed equivalence is another manifestation of beginning at the end. But such a method is not without its hazards. In equating nature, technology, and the supernatural, Crane mended the "brokenness" of the modern city by denying the city's modernity and history. Renaming the bridge, Crane not only denied its bridgeship but left himself no space in which to write his poem.

Crane seemed to be aware of the disparity between a vision that is apprehended as complete in itself and a poem that remained to be written. In **"Atlantis,"** in the very heart of his ecstasy, he says,

> O Choir, translating time
> Into what multitudinous Verb the suns
> And synergy of waters ever fuse, recast
> In myriad syllables,—Psalm of Cathay!

The exact mood is hard to grasp here largely because the verb moves in at least two directions. The "Choir" seems to be in apposition to the Bridge, which is addressed in the line before, and thus we may read these lines as affirming the bridge's connective quality and fusing powers: time and verb, sun and water or sky and earth. But the phrasing unsettles that confidence: "Into what multitudinous Verb" might be followed by a question mark. Here it is in the form of an exclamation, but an exclamation with a question: the poet cannot imagine, can only marvel at whatever will be produced by this fusion. The lines then go on into the imperative: "recast/In myriad syllables." The translation and fusion appear to be reversed here, and one "multitudinous Verb" is itself to be translated into "myriad syllables." In turn, these syllables are to be translated into the "Psalm of Cathay." So the single and the many, the whole and the part, fuse and refuse to adhere in these lines.

Crane was committed to the "Vision-of-the-Voyage," the "Verb," the "Psalm," to the whole; and these lines, in their refusal to parse, testify to his desire for that wholeness in every word, every line, every stanza, and yet such a desire had a destabilizing effect on connections of words or lines into a total structure. The poem that remained for Crane to write had to be constructed word by word, and his real task was to negotiate between whole and part, something that was impossible if every part were conceived as a whole. As the poet leaves "the haven" of the bridge in **"Atlantis,"** he cannot relinquish this vision of wholeness. He does not go far before he sees "still the circular, indubitable frieze / Of heaven's meditation." Although "Eyes stammer through the pangs ofdust and steel," they see *still* the "indubitable frieze." They cannot see parts; they can see only the whole, "one song devoutly binds." Such evidence cannot compose a poem, or rather it does not lead to any indication of the poem's constituent parts. Significantly here the poet imagines that he "backward fled" to "time's end." The direction of the flight is accurate; he must go back to the beginning in order to trace the process by which "time" was translated into a "Verb." But his destination, "at time's end," is peculiar if prophetic of Crane's paradoxical backward flight to the end from this magnificent early conclusion.

The experience of the backward flight in these lines of **"Atlantis"** is simply an optical illusion. The poet imagines himself on a boat leaving the harbor, although he experiences it as the harbor itself moving: "harbor lanterns backward fled the keel." But the optical illusion embodies a persistent way of seeing. As he wrote various sections of the poem, Crane moved away from his ending, and his vision of the bridge as an icon faded in the process. He came to the end of time, his own time and that of his poem, by a creative withdrawal from his initiating impulse. Far from leading up to the ending, the poem was written away from it.

The route was not entirely direct, as the order of composition of the actual sections clearly indicates. Crane moved back and forth, writing in the summer of 1926 the first section and the final version of the last, then going back in time to **"Cutty Sark," "Ave Maria,"** and **"The Dance,"** then forward to the present in **"The Tunnel," "Three Songs,"** and **"Harbor Dawn,"** and then both back and forward again to start work on **"The River."** This order is all the more curious because Crane had already established whether each section would fit into the final structure, and it would have been possible to write each in the sequence in which it was to appear. In fact, Crane himself seemed struck by the wayward progress of his work, writing to Waldo Frank, "All sections moving forward now at once! I didn't realize that a bridge is begun from the two ends at once," and later, "I skip from one section to another now like a sky-gack [*sic*] or girderjack" (LHC 270, 272). He concluded his remarks to Frank: "The accumulation of impressions and concepts gathered the last several years and constantly repressed by immediate circumstances are having a chance to func-tion, I believe. And nothing but this large form would hold them without the violence that mar [*sic*] so much of my previous, more casual work" (LHC 272).

Crane's statement is interesting for its curious insistence both on an organizing larger form and the free functioning of concepts. Large form, in Crane's view, would not do violence to impressions; only casual work, by which Crane seems to mean shorter work without the design of *The Bridge,* violates. He is simply describing here the freedom and expansiveness he felt in writing a long poem. But these comments also reveal a certain ambivalence toward form: it should contain an accumulation of impressions but not be casual; it should order but not violate. The parts of *The Bridge* would not have been written without a conception of the whole, and yet the whole was never fully composed of the parts.

With these conflicting views, Crane could of course justify writing the sections in any order they "popped out," as he described his creative process. He could write as he was inspired to write, and still compose parts of a preplanned poem; he could be both Whitman and Poe. But *The Bridge* was neither conceived nor written as an open-ended poem in the style of *Leaves of Grass.* From the very start, Crane knew where he was going and toward what end, and individual sections were written to be placed into a predetermined scheme. At the same time, Poe's carefully plotted poem could not serve Crane as a model, committed as he was to inspiration and to the simultaneous creation of all parts.

Crane's method of composition indicates another curious byproduct of his degenerative form. He seemed to work in double sets, as if one expression inspired its opposite and peculiarly related form. After writing the last and first sections, he wrote another double set—**"Ave Maria,"** the beginning of American history, and **"The Tunnel,"** the end or present day. He then moved further toward the center of the poem to a set of love poems—**"The Dance,"** a hymn to the fertile Indian princess and an invocation to historical origins, and its opposite, **"Three Songs,"** a trilogy on the sterility of modern love. The sectionsthus balance each other and forestall the poem's forward movement: the despair and weak faith of **"The Tunnel"** correspond to the faith and fear of **"Ave Maria,"** and the lust of **"The Three Songs"** responds to the passion of **"The Dance."** The desire to state and restate and unstate, to project one vision and then imagine an alternate and contradictory vision, indicates some of Crane's hesitancy about a developing structure, a doubt at the heart of his celebratory faith, a self-fulfilling fear of failure.

The sustained period of work on *The Bridge* in 1926 produced the poem's second section, **"Ave Maria,"** which offered a possibility for locating the origin of Crane's subject in Columbus' voyage of discovery. Here is where the history began. However, Crane does not start at the beginning, but surprisingly neither does he start at the end, although he imagines Columbus himself imagining that he has discovered not America but "Cathay,"

"Indian emperies," "The Chan's great continent." In short, Crane's Columbus identifies his discovery as the end he had set out to find. Crane locates Columbus not at the actual moment of discovery or at the moment of triumphant return to Spain, but rather in mid-ocean, terrified that the weather or a mutinous crew will not allow him to return with the "word."

Thus placing Columbus, Crane eases into the central section of his poem with a tentative confidence that Columbus, like the poet, has "seen now what no perjured breath / Of clown nor sage can riddle or gainsay." But within that confidence, there is also the unmasking fear about his powers to express it. More than that, Crane places Columbus in mid-ocean and thus in time, fitting appropriately between origin and end. Columbus is most anxious there, counting time, "biding the moon/Till dawn should clear that dim frontier," noting its passage, "Some Angelus environs the cordage tree," and marveling at "all that amplitude that time explores." In mid-ocean, Columbus also juggles space; he stands between the Old World, land of his birth, his own origins, from which his visions made him an exile, and the New World, his land by discovery but from which he is also exiled by his misapprehension of it as Cathay.

If Columbus' voyage is to mark the beginning of Crane's myth of America, his location in mid-ocean announces Crane's retreat from the end, although it clearly articulates his reticence about origins. The myth of America did not begin during Columbus' return voyage to the Old World, nor did it begin in his fears that he would not complete his round trip; it was rather an idea in Columbus' mind or even before him in the hopes of a generation of navigators. These moments are given scant notice in "Ave Maria." Nor does Crane ever develop the moment when Columbus returns to Spain to announce his finding, a moment that is another potential origin for the myth of America.

Refusing a vision of the beginning, Crane places Columbus in mid-ocean, on this middle ground where he can deny the whole and recant the dream that had impelled him to search for it. He admits that the God he worships both contains and withholds the truth of man's origins and his destiny: "incognizable Word / Of Eden and the enchained sepulchre."[7] So God's purpose is and is not revealed, and at the end Columbus withdraws into that incognizance. He had opened with a petition for a safe return, but he ends with a plea for "still one shore beyond desire." And then he breaks off with fragments: "Beyond / And kingdoms," a repetition of the *Te Deum,* and an appeal to the "Hand of Fire."

Just as there is no real beginning for this great voyage of discovery and no origin of the myth of America in the poem, so right here with Columbus Crane begins to deny the end. He leaves Columbus dangling in mid-ocean yet yearning for still more because he himself cannot close the poem. Columbus' anxiety here about a safe return as well as his willingness to journey forever mark the first

stages of the poet's retreat from the idea of completion that was so affirmatively set forth in **"Atlantis"** and **"Proem."** **"Ave Maria"** acknowledges more fully than any other section the time and space between beginning and end, but in so doing it becomes entranced with its own inbetweenness, longs to perpetuate that and not to be a connective link pointing to other destinies. Crane's Columbus does not want to round out the journey, complete the circle, affirm the whole; he longs only for more, a vision "beyond desire," "Beyond."

This section was composed with **"The Tunnel,"** the section that leads into **"Atlantis"** in the finished work just as **"Ave Maria"** had led out of **"Proem."** The double set reveals Crane's refusal to develop his long poem and his engagement with obsessive repetitions of points. Despite obvious differences, the two sections share the journey motif and the concluding image, "O Thou Hand of Fire," "O Hand of Fire." The journey of the modern subway rider, like that of the great navigator, is not completed. Although he gets to the East River, the modern traveller does not seem to have arrived at any destination. For him the journey has been "cruelly to inoculate the brinking dawn / With antennae toward worlds that glow and sink," a kind of demonic version of Columbus' "one shore beyond desire." Yet, despite this despair, he, like Columbus, is "Impassioned with some song we fail to keep," "some Word that will not die." The ending of the poem contains these mutually exclusive emotions. The subway rider seems to give up, admitting,

> Here at the waters' edge the hands drop memory;
> Shadowless in that abyss they unaccounting lie.
> How far away the star has pooled the sea—
> Or shall the hands be drawn away, to die?

He has come to the eastern shore, the beginning of history and the point from which America, the subject of *The Bridge,* was launched. In this movement backward, however, he reaches an "abyss," not a point from which to start but a centripetal force preventing any beginning—time's end, in fact. The hands that "drop memory" lose the power to write, to "account" for time and to count it. But with the question mark the poem negates such an ending, and from this lowest point it moves to the final lines: "Kiss of our agony Thou gatherest / O Hand of Fire / gatherest." The prayer in the end echoes Columbus' final prayer for "one shore beyond desire," for a continuation of voyaging, of writing, of gathering, and again Crane appears to be retreating from the vision of **"Atlantis"** even as this poem leads into it.

One indication of this retreat is the poem's obsession with beginning, despite its ending and its own position at the present day or end of American history as Crane saw it. The first scene projects a play opening: "Someday by heart you'll learn each famous sight / And watch the curtain lift in hell's despite." From here, the speaker is launched on a series of journeys, leaving with "a subscription praise / for what time slays." He cannot decide whether to ride or walk, feeling trapped either way in some kind of restricted form ("boxed alone a second, eyes take fright"). When he does move, he comes to a dead end, fleeing the call girl who calls out, "if / you don't like my gate why did you / swing on it." He moves along, meets Poe, whom he identifies with "Death, aloft," sees he is destined for "Gravesend Manor," but keeps on going toward morning imagined as "the muffled slaughter of a day in birth."

Thus, the beginning is made into the end; dawn is identified with a world of waste, evidence of time's degenerative process. The "burnt match skating in a urinal," "Newspapers wing, revolve and wing," the "tugboat, wheezing wreaths of steam," "the oily tympanum of waters," all detail a world that is used up, run down, begrimed. Language, too, seems to be part of this general decay. The people who speak throughout this section repeat themselves, use only cliches or degraded language. Crane says:

> Our tongues recant like beaten weather vanes.
> This answer lives like verdigris, like hair
> Beyond extinction, surcease of the bone;
> And repetition freezes.

The answer at this point is not the "Answerer of all," but rather is identified with death and decay.

Recanting the affirmation of **"Atlantis,"** Crane is forced here to acknowledge the corrosive power of time. Time does not fuse; it disintegrates. It provides no bridge from one point to another. The poem can offer now no pardon for history, no excuse even for its own composition. The poet is isolated, alone, and hislanguage fragments: "Tossed from the coil of ticking towers. . . . Tomorrow, / And to be. . . . / Here by the River that is East." Unable to locate himself in time, even cast out from time, he loses all direction. Still, **"The Tunnel"** does not end with these images of dispersal, dislocation, uncertainty, but rather with the poet's desire to gather up again, gather himself, his poem, to be returned to the coil of time, his hand in the hand of God. The great despair in this section is balanced by a desperate hope in the end, and once again the poet's genius at taking things apart reveals itself. He can undo even his own despair.

Composed in the same creative spurt as **"The Tunnel"** was **"The Dance,"** the only part of the long central section, **"Powhatan's Daughter,"** to be completed in these early stages of writing in the summer of 1926. It was a remarkable feat of creation to move from the fragmented utterance of **"The Tunnel"** to the formal organization of **"The Dance."** But this narrative of composition sets off **"The Dance"** from the other parts of **"Powhatan's Daughter"** and indicates that here too Crane started at the end he hoped he would achieve.

**"The Harbor Dawn"** and **"The River,"** the first and third poems in **"Powhatan's Daughter,"** were started, but they were not completed until the next summer, when Crane also worked on **"Van Winkle"**; and **"Indiana,"** the final poem in that section, was one of the last to be composed. **"Powhatan's Daughter"** can be read, as it is published, as a journey back in time to the Indian and in space to the Mississippi, and then forward again to the pioneers and movement once more east. But it may also be read in the order of its composition as it charts the degenerative stages in Crane's inspiration.

**"The Dance"** belongs to the initiatory vision evident in **"Atlantis"** and **"Proem,"** still there in **"Ave Maria,"** and fainter still in **"The Tunnel."** Like Columbus, Pocahontas offered Crane a marvelous opportunity from history, a real person in whom to locate his understanding of the myth of America. Crane's use of Pocahontas suggests that in his earliest inspiration he worked from historical figures, trying to make his poem close to reality. But even here, the impulse was thwarted. Crane did not take advantage of the known facts about Pocahontas the historical personage.

The real story of **"The Dance"** is Crane's own search for "Mythical brows we saw retiring." Typically, these mythical brows of winter king and glacier woman are retiring or fleeing backward. They are "loth" but "destined" in their flight, the speaker acknowledges, as if his acquaintance with them were intimate or rather, since he uses the first person plural, as if they were figures well known to the community. These mythic figures seem also to beckon to those they have left as "Greeting they sped us, on the arrow's oath." So the poet is encouraged in his pursuit of them. But somehow, between the retirement and the present, "lie incorrigibly what years between." As always in Crane, the time scheme here is confusing, as the speaker seems to be witness both to the past and to the present. The Indian and his nature gods have gone, "destined" by the course of history to depart, so we may assume that their departure is "incorrigible." Yet they appear to the poet "loth" to go, and he sets out to reclaim them, to rewrite their ending.

He charts his search in carefully rhymed quatrains, as if such hypnotic regularity would itself restore the Indian gods. And in fact it does, as through it he approaches the Indian dance: "its rhythm drew, /—Siphoned the black pool from the heart's hot root." He is mesmerized by Maquokeeta's tranced performance, urging him on:

> Dance, Maquokeeta! snake that lives before,
> That casts his pelt, and lives beyond! Sprout,
>    horn!
> Spark, tooth! Medicine-man, relent, restore—
> Lie to us,—dance us back the tribal morn!

This is a pivotal stanza in **"The Dance"** and in the composition of *The Bridge* because it carries the burden of Crane's desperate desire to get back to the beginning which he now realizes he can never accomplish.

Up to this point in **"The Dance,"** and in fact in *The Bridge,* the speaker has been outward-bound, on an open-ended search for something identified here as

Pocahontas, for the magic that will restore not only her presence but a sense of history itself to a world which has been cut off from such knowledge. In this poem the search ends, or at least the speaker imagines its ending, as a backward dance to the tribal morn. But to get there, time itself, embodied now in the serpent figure Maquokeeta, must "relent." To get back to the beginning, the speaker must deny history, and to deny history is, the speaker blurts out, a lie. This dilemma is deepened by Crane's method of composition. Crane cannot trace to its origin the splendor of **"Atlantis."** It remained as resistant to discovery or analysis as Pocahontas. Thus, the narrative of the poem's composition traces the inadequacy of the poem's narrative.

Time, Crane discovers, will not relent. To identify with the Indian as the speaker does ("I, too, was liege / To rainbows currying each pulsant bone") is also to identify with his death. To separate himself from such a fate is to undercut the confidence of the end: "We danced, O Brave, we danced beyond their farms." The affirmative vision of **"Atlantis"** cannot hold up against time—either the history the poem relates or the history of the poem itself as the poet moves through various stages of composition.

The point at which the speaker says to Maquokeeta, "Lie to us," cannot be glossed adequately as an appeal to the sacred lie—something like Wallace Stevens' "supreme fiction"—as R. W. B. Lewis does. This is largely because Crane has been too earnestly negotiating with history and with what he calls "Cognizance," "some Word that will not die," and these references must reverberate through that phrase.[8] To equate lies with the backward dance is to acknowledge the fact of history. The tribal morn cannot be restored except through a lie, and as the poem itself proves, a lie about the very history that it invokes.[9]

But the implications of this discovery were treacherous for the poet of a visionary synthesis. If past and present can be equated, time itself made to relent, and history rewritten so that the Indian still dances beyond his fate, then the poet's invocations to images of wholeness here and throughout *The Bridge* must rely on an equally false equivalence. Between the "steeled Cognizance" and the "incognizable Word," there would thus be no difference. The "Unfractioned idiom" would exist only in fractioned idiom. Cognizance would be equivalent to incognizance, and incognizance to cognizance. If we can deny what we know and claim what we cannot know, the very act of naming is called into jeopardy. By identifying with the Indian, Crane hoped to restore the beginning, but in doing so, he cancelled out the very notion of beginning and end.

Crane might have stopped his composition here. But it is a testament to the tenacity of his longing for long form that he moved on to write the next section, **"Three Songs,"** poems about modern women, figures who are in their minimalization of the female principle the obverse of Pocahontas and yet doomed to suffer the same fate of

cancellation. In **"Southern Cross,"** the first of the three songs, the poet's search for the Indian princess and all she embodied has dwindled into a lustful yearning for some "nameless Woman." Identity becomes the issue here as he is willing to assign her any name: "Eve! Magdalene! / or Mary, you? / Whatever call—falls vainly on the wave." In **"National Winter Garden,"** the lust remains undifferentiated: "You pick your blonde out neatly through the smoke. / Always you wait for someone else though, always—." And in **"Virginia,"** although the girl is called Mary, she seems to be a multifaceted girl, at once just a date, "Saturday Mary, mine!" and then a Rapunzel figure, "Mary, leaning from the high wheat tower," and finally the virgin, "Cathedral Mary." Here in this section are all the faces of women: Eve, Magdalene, Mary. But, as with all faces and names, they are one—the object of the poet's intense but fruitless longing for the capacity to possess them through naming.

Names, both as links and as points of differentiation, had concerned Crane from the beginning of his work on *The Bridge* in the creative frenzy of the first summer.[10] To name is to possess whole, Crane imagined then, but he was to discover the fragility of such aspirations. **"Cutty Sark,"** located in thepublished work between two sections on pioneers that were almost the last parts written (**"Indiana"** and **"Cape Hatteras"**), takes its themes and concerns from the poems just discussed that were written during the same period. Something of the atmosphere of **"National Winter Garden"** is evident in the bar scene, "the / swinging summer entrances to cooler hells." And Pocahontas' spring is here in the "skilful savage sea-girls / that bloomed in the spring." But two larger issues that came to obsess Crane as he worked on the parts of *The Bridge* take over **"Cutty Sark."** The process of writing had led Crane from vision to verb, from large structures to small components, as he turned his concern first to names and then to time, or to time as it issues from names.

The frame of the poem is a song from the nickelodeon, "Stamboul Nights," heard in a modern bar by a drunken sailor who recalls there his own past and the American past of the clipper ships and their explorations of the Orient. Time blurs in this drunken reverie, chiefly by a free association of names. "Stamboul Nights" recalls *"Stamboul Rose,"* who becomes not just some pickup in a port but *Rose of Stamboul O coral Queen—/ teased remnants of the skeletons of cities."* This evocation of lost cities brings up Atlantis, a reminder for the poet at least of just how far he has moved from the fabled end that he had posited at the beginning of his poem. But Atlantis is introduced with the notion that in the mind of this drunken sailor the mere passage of time "may start some white machine that sings," send him into dawn, while his companion "started walking home across the Bridge." In this moment of composition, the poet writes himself back to his original structure, now irremediably altered in his imagination.

The last part of **"Cutty Sark"** is a series of catalogues—first a catalogue of reasons for trade with China ("Blithe

Yankee vanities, turreted sprites, winged / British repartees"), then a catalogue of locations en route ("the Line," "the Horn / to Frisco, Melbourne"), then the names of ships themselves (*Thermopylae, Black Prince, Flying Cloud,*" "*Rainbow, Leander,*" "*Taeping,*" "*Ariel*"), names with their own histories, we might note. As a way of organizing, the catalogue is inclusive without being explanatory. It is also a form that equates everything; here reasons for trading, shipping routes, ships themselves, are all given the same treatment. Thus, the differentiation that names afford is minimized. And despite the range of historical references in the names of the ships, time itself as a divisive strategy seems to be cancelled. Just as the sailor is "not much good at time any more" since that "damned white Arctic killed my time," so the appearance here in the twentieth century of the clipper-ship era seems to attest to the obliteration of time in the mind of the poet, who does not even attempt to connect this vision with the scene in the bar, but simply attaches it here to the end of the poem.

In explaining this poem to Otto Kahn, Crane acknowledged his persistent method by saying the poem "starts in the present and 'progresses backwards.'"

> "Cutty Sark" is built on the plan of a *fugue.* Two "voices"—that of the world of Time, and that of the world of Eternity—are interwoven in the action. The Atlantis theme (that of Eternity) is the transmuted voice of the nickel-slot pianola, and this voice alternates with that of the derelict sailor and the description of the action. The airy regatta of phantom clipper ships seen from Brooklyn Bridge on the way home is quite effective, I think. It was a pleasure to use historical names for these lovely ghosts. Music still haunts their names long after the wind has left their sails. (LHC 307-8)

Most curious here is Crane's notion that names evoke history, or rather that the music of names outlasts their references. Names that can slip from one context to another may not serve as reliable links in any structure, and names that have a layered context may end up meaning so many things that they serve no particular connective function.

"Cutty Sark" has seldom been read as one of the strongest sections of *The Bridge,* yet it was written right after the very powerful "Ave Maria." Along with "The Dance," these poems are Crane's first efforts to deal with points in American history, to find some connection between the present and the past, to locate theorigin of the "Atlantis" vision in time and space. Yet they also undercut their connections, resist their purpose, and remain suspended in a drunken haze or frenzied trance.

As Crane moved in toward the center of his long poem in that first burst of creativity, starting "The Harbor Dawn" and "The River" before he put his work aside, he moved further and further away from the power that in "Atlantis" he called "arching strands of song." The "many twain" that he was moved to embody in "single chrysalis" in that final section pulled apart as he wrote. The poet seemed conscious in mid-poem of the need to bring various strands together, and he tries to compensate for the dispersal of his poem by imagining his task as an act of weaving: in "Cutty Sark" dreams "weave the rose," or "weave / those bright designs the trade winds drive," or in "The Harbor Dawn" the speaker urges the "blessed" one beside him to "weave us into day." Like Melville's weaver god, this figure is unseen but felt, her "signals dispersed in veils." However, her mysterious and fleeting presence mirrors the mystery of those activities—so central now to Crane—of weaving, uniting, completing.

As the last great section of *The Bridge* to be written, "The River" is the most desperate in its desire to weave the various strands of the poem together, the most far-ranging in the material it includes, but it is also the most revisionary. In the Mississippi River, Crane finds at last the image that will serve his purposes. It is not the bridge, not even *a* bridge. But as an energy and force, it is a more appropriate image for what Crane now sees he can do with the subject he has set himself. As he comes into the image very gradually and tentatively, almost as if he were afraid of it, he is possessed by a language that can serve him. But if his comments to Kahn are any indication, Crane seemed almost totally oblivious to the power of this most powerful section of *The Bridge.* He felt that he had simply approached the Indian world which, he claims, "emerges with a full orchestra in the succeeding dance" (LHC 307). In many ways, "The River" is a more elaborate and powerful version of "The Dance." Here there is no false equivalence, but a slow, gradual, and steady movement from one time to an earlier time.

The section opens with what Crane identified as jazz rhythm, always his favorite notion of how to embody speed, but this section is more significant for its obsession with names than for its rhythms. Here Crane opens with a list of trade names—labels: "Tintex—Japalac—Certain-teed Overalls ads." Yet, he concludes immediately, with all the labels we are still unable to find meaning, to read sermons in "RUNning brooks." Such names do not signify anything, especially now fifty years after the poem was written. Only the poem's hobos who are left behind by the train, which is called significantly the Twentieth-Century Limited, know names that are attached to meaning: "watermelon days," "Booneville" for early trouting. Their wisdom stems from experience, not from reading, and from a true knowledge of time. They can identify differences in time and space. For such travellers willing to abandon themselves to the continent, the midnights are "rumorous," and dreams "beyond the print that bound her name." All that has been taken in by the word will become "Dead echoes!" in comparison to the touch of "her body." As the gloss notes indicate, the land must be approached by getting away from names or renaming, *"knowing her without name" "nor the myths of her fathers."* Typically, Crane undercuts his poem's purpose in his acceptance of namelessness, mythlessness, and yet he continues to name and to search for myths.

To make this contact, the "Pullman breakfasters" are urged to "lean from the window," "gaze absently below," "turn again and sniff once more—look see." In this movement toward the river, the travellers also relinquish themselves to time: "For you, too, feed the River timelessly. / And few evade full measure of their fate"; "Down, down—born pioneers in time's despite." The movement continues its downward plunge into the earth, "Damp tonnage and alluvial march of days," "O quarrying passion, undertowed sunlight!"

The Mississippi River has become here the model of signification that the bridge, as Crane conceived of it, never could be. In Crane's terms, the bridge was a completed structure, a symbol of completion and wholeness, a sign of man's ability to conceive of such a view, but in its iconicity not very useful as a model for a long poem's structure. By contrast, the river spreads, flows, lengthens, throbs, "heaps itself free," fades, "lifts itself from its long bed," moves always by "its one will—flow!" In the strong final image, the river reveals its power as arising from its progress, its length and slowness, its accession to time:

> —The Passion spreads in wide tongues, choked and slow,
> Meeting the Gulf, hosannas silently below.

These lines are puzzling. But they pay tribute to difference, to difficulty, to two forces meeting, and to silence. In short, they acknowledge meaning as something achieved through time and space. The "Passion" has tongues and presumably speaks; and, identified as it is here with the Mississippi River and with time as well as space, it suggests that only by acknowledging and not obliterating the course of time and our own implication in it can we sing. In this sense, these silent hosannas recall Columbus' *Te Deum* as a hymn of praise that is also in part a plea for continuation. Almost finished with his long poem, Crane at this point could acknowledge time and change, the time he had taken in getting to **"The River"** and time as an avenue to meaning. This section marks Crane's slow progression toward meaning not given at the beginning but achieved in the writing, an idea he dismissed at the beginning of his writing and resisted until it alone would provide him with some consolation.

The long poem has become the product of various stages of composition—the opening poet declaring the sufficiency of beginning and the concluding poet acknowledging the triumph of the end. But because Crane wrote the poem in a different sequence from the one which we read, the beginning sufficiency comes to the readers at the end, when it has been seriously undercut by the actual final composition. Once Crane found the image that would serve him as a structural model, the river gathering strength as it goes, he did not go on to write better than he ever had before. It must be admitted that **"The River"** marked the end of Crane's great productivity. He neither went back to revise sections written earlier nor was he able to project better sections still ahead. He finished **"The River"** in 1927 along with **"Van Winkle."** **"Van Winkle"** is not a major contribution to the long poem, although it is a fuller acknowledgment of time than Crane had achieved before.

The three remaining sections of *The Bridge* were not written until 1929, under the compulsion to finish inspired by an offer from Harry and Caresse Crosby, editors of the Black Sun Press, to publish the entire poem. These sections, **"Cape Hatteras," "Quaker Hill,"** and **"Indiana,"** are generally judged the weakest in the long poem, evidence that the progress of the poem exacted a toll on the poet's creative energies. The various ways in which these poems are overwritten suggest the extent to which Crane was straining at the end, trying desperately to pull the whole poem together or at least to fill in the gaps. But each of these poems reveals some knowledge of what had gone wrong. Behind the bombast and repetition of **"Cape Hatteras,"** means by which Crane hoped to cover the emptiness of its subject, the poet is remarkably candid. He says, to his predecessor, for example, "Walt, tell me, Walt Whitman, if infinity / Be still the same as when you walked the beach." It is a despairing plea, a desire to escape his task on the grounds of the monstrosity of historical development, but it is also a concession to time and the fantastic differences it could produce. At the end of **"Cape Hatteras,"** Crane insists on both the "Open Road" and the "rainbow's arch," the extended, extending journey and the finished form, ambitions reminiscent of Columbus' mutually exclusive desires to return home and to keep on voyaging.

In contrast to **"Cape Hatteras"** and its inflated language, "Indiana" is rigidly controlled in binding rhyme schemes, artificial sentence structures, and sentimentalized scenes. The plea is the mother's regressive wish to bind her son to her through need and guilt and pity. Still, despite the wordiness of this poem, the mother here, like the poet, has learned a healthy disrespect for words, taken in as she has been by a "dream called Eldorado." Coming back from the barren pioneering venture with her newly born son, she meets an Indian squaw withher baby, and she offers her own baby as an emblem of their common condition and "Knew that mere words could not have brought us nearer." Disappointed, still she has gained a wisdom that stems from love itself and not from words. Just as she holds up her baby for the Indian to see, so she trusts her son to write to her: "you'll keep your pledge; / I know your word!"

If **"Cape Hatteras"** is bombastic and "Indiana" sentimental, then **"Quaker Hill"** veers between self-pity and excessive cynicism. It may be, as the quotation from Isadora Duncan states, that *"no ideals have ever been fully successful on this earth,"* but the disappointment is expressed in terms that are too cynical, as Crane concludes, "This was the Promised Land, and still it is / To the persuasive suburban land agent." The view here is only of death: "High from the central cupola, they say / One's glance could cross the borders of three states; / But

I have seen death's stare in slow survey." He suffers the ending, "In one last angelus lift throbbing throat—/ Listen, transmuting silence with that stilly note // Of pain that Emily, that Isadora knew!"

For the poet who had started out with the assurance that "one song devoutly binds—/ The vernal strophe chimes from deathless strings," this is a terrible end. The choir translating time has lost its power. The song which had been identified at the beginning of Crane's enterprise with the bridge, with arching strands, "One arc synoptic," with connections and completion, has been reduced to a "stilly note." Crane's last angelus is a pained and minimal effort, one note rather than a song that binds. Surprisingly, though, this note is echoed by "That triple-noted clause" of the "whip-poor-will," and so desperate is Crane's need that the bird's song, even in its dying fall, "unhusks the heart of fright."

From **"Atlantis"** to **"Quaker Hill,"** the progress of the actual composition of *The Bridge* has charted a gradual diminishment of vision, a dispersal of energy, a dismantling of the whole structure. The vision in **"Quaker Hill"** belongs only to the cows: "Perspective never withers from *their* eyes" (italics mine), Crane says, as a corrective to his former hopes. The old hotel still stands on top of Quaker Hill, its broken windows "like eyes that still uphold some dream." In this landscape, "resigned factions of the dead preside." The elements that came together in **"Atlantis"** are all separate here. The past and the present are irreparably divided as time has turned the "old Meeting House" into the "New Avalon Hotel," "highsteppers" replace the "Friends," "Powitzky" takes over from "Adams." The poet finally admits that the "slain Iroquois" and "scalped Yankees" are not one identity but two, and he must "Shoulder the curse of sundered parentage" "With birthright by blackmail." He is left now with "the arrant page / That unfolds a new destiny to fill." The "arrant page" of the poem has wandered away from the "clear direction" promised in **"Atlantis."** The "orphic strings" do not "leap and converge" at this end as they promised to do at the beginning. And the poet has no time to "fulfill" his "new destiny," finished as he is with the structure he had set out years before that had completely drained his creative energies.

*The Bridge* as Crane wrote it and *The Bridge* as we read it are quite different structures. The first closes on a "stilly note / Of pain," the second on "One Song, one Bridge of Fire!" Crane stood by his original structure as the years went by, and as he produced within it a series of sections that threatened its stability. As published, *The Bridge* can hardly be read as a sequence, if we mean by that term a series with continuity and connection. It moves erratically through history from Columbus to the present and then back into the far past of the Indian and up again to the near past of the pioneer and the clipper ships, and forward into World War I and the subway. And even within these sections, the movement is back and forth, Walt Whitman and Edgar Allan Poe appearing in the modern world as the poet merges into the old world.

But, as planned and published, *The Bridge* seems to be designed to affirm unity and wholeness while accommodating certain historical points, or rather an interpretation of American history as itself unified and whole. In the plan, the affirmation and the proof were one. This overall structure had necessarily to be abandoned as soon as Crane began to focus on all the sections between beginning and end. If they were to be written, they had to be differentiated, separated from the wholeness and unity, and made particular. Thus differentiated, they were either not part of the whole, since no principle of unity was acknowledged, or they were only part of an overdetermined unity where one word, one time, one event, was the same as any other. The vision of **"Atlantis"** and **"Proem"** did not acknowledge time, either the time of American history or the time of the poem's composition.[11] It was the middle sections of *The Bridge,* as they negotiated with historical moments and their own creative history, that had to wedge open a space for themselves in the larger structure. In the process they threatened the unity, the equivalence of beginning and end, but they made the long poem possible. Without the original plan, the individual sections might never have been written or, if written, might have simply proliferated to no end, so that Crane's original determination did, provide some stability. However, had the original idea not been held in abeyance, shifted around, bypassed, or dismantled at points, the long poem would not have been written. As this narrative of composition suggests, *The Bridge* degenerated in vision and in verbal power, but it also grew through the means of such degenerative form.

NOTES

[1] See the letter to Otto Kahn, March 18, 1926, which outlines the poem and explains the "interlocking elements and symbols at work" in the poem, in LHC, 240-42. The critical debate over *The Bridge* goes back to its early reviewers—Allen Tate and Yvor Winters, among others—who had praised Crane's first volume of poetry, *White Buildings,* but found *The Bridge* a failure. See Tate's "Hart Crane," in *Reactionary Essays on Poetry and Ideas* (New York: Charles Scribner's Sons, 1936), 26-42, and Winters, "The Progress of Hart Crane," *Poetry* 36 (June 1930): 153-65. The discussion continues in John Unterecker's "The Architecture of *The Bridge,*" *Wisconsin Studies in Contemporary Literature* 3 (Spring-Summer 1962): 5-20; Donald Pease's "Blake, Crane, Whitman, and Modernism: A Poetics of Pure Possibility," *PMLA* 96 (January 1981): 64-85; Suzanne Clark Doeren, "Theory of Culture, Brooklyn Bridge, and Hart Crane's Rhetoric of Memory," *MMLA Bulletin* 15 (Spring 1982): 18-28.

[2] Joseph Riddel, "Hart Crane's Poetics of Failure," *ELH* 33 (December 1966): 482.

[3] R. W. B. Lewis, "Days of Wrath and Laughter," in *Trials of the Word* (New Haven: Yale University Press, 1965), 202.

[4] See the drafts of "Atlantis" in Brom Weber, *Hart Crane* (New York: The Bodley Press, 1948), Appendix C, 425-40.

[5] Weber, 432-33.

[6] Weber, 437.

[7] R. W. B. Lewis makes this point in *The Poetry of Hart Crane* (Princeton: Princeton University Press, 1967), 265.

[8] Lewis, 311-12.

[9] See Eric J. Sundquist, "Bringing Home the Word: Magic, Lies, and Silence in Hart Crane," *ELH* 44 (Summer 1977): 376-99, for a psychoanalytic reading of this passage and the whole poem. Sundquist reads the poem as the story of "the sacrifice of ancestral fathers with one eye toward sexual reunion with a maternal, *free* origin, the other toward the *debt* aroused by the parricide necessary to an acquisition of power over that origin" (376).

[10] Crane's fascination with names and puns is discussed by John Irwin, "Naming Names: Hart Crane's 'Logic of Metaphor,'" *The Southern Review* 11 (April 1975): 284-99, and by Roger Ramsey, "A Poetics for *The Bridge,*" *Twentieth Century Literature* 26 (Fall 1980): 278-93.

[11] John Carlos Rowe develops the Nietzschean bias in Crane's treatment of history in "The 'Super-Historical' Sense of Hart Crane's *The Bridge,*" *Genre* 11 (Winter1978): 597-625.

### Susan M. Schultz (essay date 1989)

SOURCE: "The Success of Failure: Hart Crane's Revisions of Whitman and Eliot in 'The Bridge'," in *South Atlantic Review,* Vol. 54, No. 1, January, 1989, pp. 55-70.

[*In the following essay, Schultz considers the use Crane made of the works T. S. Eliot and Walt Whitman in writing* The Bridge.]

Hart Crane composed *The Bridge* during the seven years between 1923 and 1930. His ambitions for the poem were enormous: it was to be nothing less than what he called, in letters to his patron otto Kahn, "a new cultural synthesis of values in terms of our America" (*Letters* 223) and "an epic of the modern consciousness" (308). The very scope of his ambition threatened the project with failure, and the last sections that Crane wrote, including **"The Tunnel"** (1926) and **"Cape Hatteras"** (1929), deal very directly with poetic ambition and failure.[1] In a 20 June 1926 letter to Waldo Frank, Crane

expressed the fear that he was deluding himself in finding links between the past and the future. He directed his most damning criticism, however, at the symbol of the bridge itself: "The bridge as a symbol today has no significance beyond an economical approach to shorter hours, quicker lunches, behaviorism and toothpicks" (261). Later in that letter he asserts bitterly, "A bridge will be written in some kind of style and form, at worst it will be something as good as advertising copy" (262). These harsh self-criticisms sound painfully like those that greeted **The Bridge** on its completion, charges by Crane's friends, Allen Tate and Yvor Winters among others, that the poem failed as an epic, that it was incoherent.[2] Yet there is a larger problem hidden behind these value judgments, for whether or not one considers **The Bridge** to be a failure, its main subject *is* failure.[1] The poem's major figures—Columbus (who failed to find the passage to India), Rip Van Winkle, the mother in **"Indiana,"** the sailor in **"Cutty Sark,"** and the women of the **"Three Songs"**—are all failures. Crane's obsession with failure, at the time of the letter to Frank, came in part out of his reading of Oswald Spengler's *Decline of the West.*[4] More importantly, American cultural criticism of the time took America's failings as its principle subject. When Crane read Waldo Frank's *Our America* on its publication in 1919, he remarked both on the pessimism—and the truth—of Frank's analysis (*Letters* 26). And Frank's polemic was but one of many similar tracts, including the 1922 symposium, *Civilization in the United States.* Crane's poem, composed over seven years of the decade, in some ways shares the temper of the times. Yet what makes **The Bridge** so radical is its uncompromising refusal to hold to that temper.

"The Waste Land," published in 1922, elaborated a modernist poetics of failure. About Eliot, Crane felt persistently ambivalent: "There is no one writing in English who can command so much respect, to my mind, as Eliot," Crane wrote. "However, I take Eliot as a point of departure toward an almost complete reverse of direction. His pessimism is amply justified, in his own case" (114). **The Bridge** is Crane's response to "The Waste Land"—he considered his poem to be "an affirmation of experience," in opposition to the "negative" posed by Eliot (351). Crane's poem also responds, by extension, to the poet himself, nursing doubts about his ability to justify the ecstatic praise of **"Atlantis."** (That section, written first, was meant all along to be placed last in **The Bridge.**) In positioning himself against Eliot, Crane joined the league of Walt Whitman, for whom he wrote **"Cape Hatteras."** But Crane recognized Whitman to be a complicated and complicating figure, and he was aware that Whitman's perception of American possibilities had altered over time; the Whitman of *Democratic Vistas* is far more pessimistic than the Whitman of "Song of Myself," as Crane acknowledged in a 1930 letter to Allen Tate (353-54). So Crane, in **The Bridge,** had not only to overturn Eliot's negations, but he had also to address himself to the Whitman who writes in *Democratic Vistas* that the United States could "prove the most tremendous failure of time" (930).

Crane's purpose in addressing Whitman in **"Cape Hatteras"** and in echoing and responding to "The Waste Land" in **"The Tunnel,"** is twofold, for Whitman and Eliot conflate Crane's mythical and his poetic concerns. I argue in the first part of this essay that in **"Cape Hatteras"** Crane seeks (with difficulty) to reaffirm Whitman's vision of America. He does so dialectically, testing that vision against a grimmer contemporary reality and a grimmer poetics. Having reaffirmed the vision at the end of **"Cape Hatteras,"** Crane tests it once again, and more severely, in the most Eliotic sections of *The Bridge.* **"The Tunnel"** is the last of a pessimistic series of poems (including the **"Three Songs"** and **"Quaker Hill"**) that form a link between **"Cape Hatteras"** and **"Atlantis."** I argue in the second section of the essay that Crane finds an alternative to Eliot in Edgar Allan Poe.

To a certain extent Crane exalts failure, making it the subject of his myth. But for Crane, as for Waldo Frank in *Our America,* failure can be sacred if it denotes a failure of "material ends" (Frank 146). The myth that Crane tells involves literal quests for riches (from Columbus's to that of the mother in **"Indiana"**). The failure of that myth, and of Eliot's myth of negation, is necessary before the poet is able to revive America's spiritual possibilities, and the myth that Whitman created.

I

The connections between Whitman and Crane have often been noted but rarely discussed in detail. One important exception is Donald Pease's revision of Harold Bloom's theory of influence, which he applies to Crane's assimilations of Whitman. In *The Anxiety of Influence* Bloom argues a jealous relation between the younger and the older poet, the younger writing by aggressively misreading his predecessor. Pease, to the contrary, finds Crane's attitude toward Whitman to be less anxious. He locates a better parallel in Blake's use of Milton: in the epic, "Milton," the older poet enters Blake's foot. Pease emphasizes the kind of re-visionism that reaffirms: "Crane feels his freedom compromised by the very discourse intended to express it, and he attempts to write his way out of the modernist dilemma through a *re*-vision of the poetry of his British ancestor William Blake and his American predecessor Walt Whitman" (Pease 193). Pease's argument, which is in many ways a compelling one, looks past Crane's genuine criticism of Whitman toward the reaffirmations that conclude **"Cape Hatteras."** But Whitman's vision *had* failed. The ways in which Crane works through that failure, and toward a re-vision of Whitman, is the subject of my discussion of the poem: my conclusion resembles Pease's, but I see the process as more complicated, and Crane as more ambivalent, than he does.

Crane's attempt to write an American myth was complicated by America's history, which had left Whitman a lonely and ineffectual myth-maker. His reaffirmation of Whitman's faith required an overturning of history, or the "apocalyptical method," that Waldo Frank described in

his 1929 book, *The Re-discovery of America*[5]: "The ideal forms we have inherited are finally dissolved; therefore the message of our fathers, based on those forms, must be transfigured by us, ere we can use it. To our tragic artists there remains only the *apocalyptic method . . .* this direct recreation of a formal world from the stuffs within us" (140).

The apocalyptic method provides a way to reconstruct history by overturning it, recreating Platonic forms from within, or lending a myth back to God, as in **"To Brooklyn Bridge."** To overturn history is, for Crane, also to overturn Whitman, for Whitman is at once a formidable historical figure and the author of a powerful interpretation of history, that is, "the message of our fathers." Crane's rewriting of Whitman in **"Cape Hatteras"** is a necessary prelude to Whitman's rebirth within Crane. The overturning, if you will, is Bloomian, the rebirth, Peasian.

In a 1926 letter to Waldo Frank, Crane presented Whitman as a solitary figure who had in many ways been proven wrong by history: "If only America were half as worthy today to be spoken of as Whitman spoke of it fifty years ago there might be something for me to say—not that Whitman received or required any tangible proof of his intimations, but that time has shown how increasingly lonely andineffectual his confidence stands" (*Letters* 261-62). This passage reveals at least as much about Crane's fear that his own confidence was ungrounded as it does about Whitman, for his criticism of Whitman is also a warning to himself: "Well, perhaps I need a little more skepticism to put me right on *The Bridge* again" (*Letters* 262). This skepticism acts as a kind of homeopathic cure: by looking critically at Whitman, Crane will free himself to write. Crane inscribes his demystification of Whitman into **"Cape Hatteras,"** situating him as a lonely and ineffectual seer whose gleaming eyes foreshadow Edgar Allan Poe's "agate lanterns" in **"The Tunnel":**

> O Saunterer on free ways still ahead!
> Not this our empire yet, but labyrinth
> Wherein your eyes, like the Great Navigator's
>     without ship,
> Gleam from the great stones of each prison crypt
> Of canyoned traffic . . .

We recall that Columbus—the Great Navigator—retained his belief that he had discovered Cathay in the face of evidence to the contrary. Tzvetan Todorov describes Columbus's strategy of interpretation as one that guarantees his failure to see through self-delusion.[6] Columbus's failure to recognize that what he saw was other than what he believed found a parallel in Crane's fear that his poetic project was based on illusion. An earlier reference to the labyrinth helps to illuminate this point, as it concerns the poet's fear that he will not be able to see beyond himself:

> What whisperings of far watches on the main
> Relapsing into silence, while time clears

Our lenses, lifts a focus, resurrects
A periscope to glimpse what joys or pain
Our eyes can share or answer—then deflects
Us, shunting to a labyrinth submersed
Where each sees only his dim past reversed . . .

The poet's problem is like that of Columbus and Whitman: these seers are threatened by a solipsism that causes them to see only what they want to see. Seeing is necessarily artificial, governed by time, and only occasionally open to the counter-response of the outside world. Crane pursues his examination of sight in what follows, again linking Whitman to Columbus:

> . . . Confronting the Exchange,
> Surviving in a world of stocks,—they also range
> Across the hills where second timber strays
> Back over Connecticut farms, abandoned
>         pastures,—
> Sea eyes and tidal, undenying, bright with myth!

These "undenying" eyes, which are like Columbus's "sea eyes," look beyond, without taking into consideration the failed foreground. The eyes that are "bright with myth" are self-deluding; neither Columbus nor Whitman explains what *is:* failure cannot change their myths, because they cannot see it. In offering a corrective, Crane presents himself as a poet who can look failure in the eye and go beyond it.

Although Crane knew of Whitman's change of heart in *Democratic Vistas,* his portrait in **"Cape Hatteras"** is of the earlier, more optimistic bard. In preliminary sketches of **The Bridge** Crane intended to write a dialogue between Whitman and a dying soldier during the Civil War; he meant to follow that with an exploration of "the infraction of physical death, disunity, on the concept of immortality" (*Letters* 241). That sketch offers far less drama than does the final version of the poem, for it sets up a symmetry between Whitman's vision and national experience. In the **"Cape Hatteras"** that we read, Whitman's vision is less inclusive; he largely fails to see the disunity that surrounds him. Crane devotes only seven lines to Whitman's war experience and his "memories of vigils, bloody, by that Cape," then abruptly shifts to a lyrical passage concerning his own discovery of Whitman's poetry. Whitman is, instead, "Our Meistersinger," the originator of the myth that Crane purports to carry on. But as the master singer, the first author of "that great Bridge, our Myth," he is also a poet whose vision has failed in history.

Crane's critical voice in this section speaks loudest in his revision of the myth of flight, which relates to Crane's larger concern with Whitman. As L. S. Dembo and others have pointed out, Crane was influenced by Eugene Jolas's manifesto of Verticalism, a rewriting of the ancient myth of flight, which attributed divine qualities to the airplane.[7] Crane takes the "marvellous of the skies" from the manifesto, but rewrites the myth of Icarus, including his fall—now a crash. The greatest fall surveyed by Crane, however, is that of modern science that was so beloved by Whitman. Ironically, Crane directs his critique of modernity at a poem written previously, that is, Whitman's "Years of the Modern." Crane boldly steals phrases from Whitman's poem and wrenches them out of context with the verve of Eliot raiding the word-hoard in "The Waste Land." "Years of the Modern" is indeed an optimistic catalogue ("Years of the modern! years of the unperform'd! / Your horizon rises, I see it parting away for more august dramas, . . .") that continues:

> Years prophetical! the space ahead as I walk, as I
>         vainly try
>      to pierce it, is full of phantoms,
> Unborn deeds, things soon to be, project their
>         shapes
>      around me,
> This incredible rush and heat, this strange ecstatic
>      fever of
>      dreams O years!
> Your dreams O years, how they penetrate through
>      me! (I
>      know not whether I sleep or wake;)
> The perform'd America and Europe grow dim,
>      retiring in
>      shadow behind me,
> The unperform'd, more gigantic than ever,
>      advance, advance
>      upon me.
>
>                                               (598)

For Whitman the more august dramas are imminent, though as yet unperformed. Crane's use of Whitman's material, however, sheds a new light on the "years of the unperform'd,"—a period that extended from the inception of Whitman's vision to that of his own. This period, however, left "unperformed" Whitman's prophetic myth. Where Whitman typically discounts time (as he does most flagrantly in "Crossing Brooklyn Ferry"), Crane here insists on its passage. Crane's myth of flight, like Whitman's myth, cannot survive time's withering. Whitman himself flies metaphorically and timelessly in "Song of Myself," when he writes in section 49:

> I ascend from the moon, I ascend from the night,
> I perceive that the ghastly glimmer is noonday
>      sunbeams
>      reflected,
> And debouch to the steady and central from the
>      offspring
>      great or small.
>
>                                               (246)

But he can only ascend in Crane after that poet has shown the failure of the myth of flight. The juxtaposition of sections of **"Cape Hatteras"** devoted to Whitman and those devoted to the plane crash strongly suggest that Crane is describing the failure of Whitman's myth in the destruction caused by World War I. This is also Whitman's crash, which is necessary so that Whitman can be reborn in Crane. But for Crane, this destruction—of the plane and of the myth of flight—is part of a redemptive process—"The benediction of the shell's deep, sure reprieve!"—because that destruction allows for rebirth, reascension. The immediate aftermath of the crash is indeed Whitman's ascension in Crane:

> But who has held the heights more sure than thou,
> O Walt!—Ascensions of thee hover in me now
> As thou at junctions elegiac, there, of speed
> With vast eternity, dost wield the rebound seed!

After the destructions wrought by history, Whitman's myth is reborn. The poem all along stutters with direct quotation, including, "Years of the Modern," "The Open Road," "Recorders Ages Hence," and many other direct and indirect allusions.[8] But now Crane takes on Whitman's words as affirmations, looking past science toward a mathematics of the word ("New integers of Roman, Viking Celt") whose mathematician is Whitman. For Crane inheritance raises the problem of repetition and, more specifically, the danger that he, the poet, will fall into his inheritance, the voice of another poet. In **"Cape Hatteras"** Crane positively courts this danger, asserting his community of vision with Whitman by way of inventive plagiarism: he writes long lines suggestive of the older poet. But the effect of the quotations, even where he most affirms his connection to Whitman (as in the quotation above), is quite opposite to that of his predecessor, for Crane uses Whitman's words in a new context, and uses rhyme ("like Alexander Pope in a mild frenzy"[9]). The repeated words and phrases affirm identity: they work oddly with Crane's claim that he is one with Whitman and that their visions are inseparable. Yet the rhyming works against Crane's claim. He repeats, while asserting his originality, just as he pays homage in a later poem to Emily Dickinson without imitating her style. And Crane's use of enjambment allows for a reading of the following lines as a recollection of his own ascension into poetic power, as though to read Whitman were to become identical with him:

> As vibrantly I following down Sequoia alleys
> Heard thunder's eloquence through green arcades
> Set trumpets breathing in each clump and grass
>     tuft—'til
> Gold autumn, captured, crowned the trembling
>     hill!

Both the "I" and the "trumpets" share the verb "set," so that Crane shares the thunder's trumpeting—that of nature and of Whitman.

If the initial movement in the poem is of a poet who depends on Whitman even as he gains power by way of the elder poet, then its final movement makes Whitman dependent on Crane: his ascent is predicated upon Crane's power to record it. True, the end of the poem affirms Whitman's vision, but it also lays Crane's claim that Whitman is afoot again precisely because Crane has him by the hand:

>             yes, Walt,
> Afoot again, and onward without halt,—
> Not soon, nor suddenly,—no, never to let go
>     My hand
>         in yours,

> Walt Whitman—
>         so—

These lines establish sublime counterparts to those that end **"Van Winkle,"** where the poet gains authority over his myth, guiding Rip into the subway. They indicate the poet's self-confidence not so much by virtue of his belonging in Whitman's company, but Whitman's belonging in his. Whitman's "Passage to India" is the source of Crane's epigraph to **"Cape Hatteras"**: *"The seas all crossed, / westered the capes, the voyage done. . . . "*[10] It is concerned with the poet's relation to another creator, in Whitman's case God. In the eighth section of Whitman's poem—**"Cape Hatteras"** is the eighth section of **The Bridge,** excluding the **"Proem"**—Whitman bids his soul take ship, "launch out on trackless seas," and mount toward God, who is referred to parenthetically as "the Comrade perfect." If God is the perfect creator, Whitman is more perfect:

> Thou pulse—thou motive of the stars, suns,
>     systems,
> That, circling, move in order, safe, harmonious,
> Athwart the shapeless vastnesses of space,
> How should I think, how breathe a single breath,
>     how
>     speak, if, out of myself,
> I could not launch, to those, superior universes?
>                                        (538)

Whitman's mastering soul journeys until it greets God as a brother. The following lines include those that Crane uses as his headnote:

> Reckoning ahead O soul, when thou, the time
>     achiev'd,
> The seas all cross'd, weather'd the cape, the
>     voyage done,
> Surrounded, copest, frontest God, yieldest, the
>     aim attain'd
> As fill'd with friendship, love complete, the Elder
>     Brother
>         found,
> The Younger melts in fondness in his arms.

Just as Whitman's voyage ends with God, so his voyage may be said to end with Crane in **"Cape Hatteras."** Whitman's voyage has been accomplished and, at the same time, begun anew in Crane's poem: "recorders ages hence" will confront not only Whitman, but a Crane who has been strengthened by his encounter with him. The elder brother it is, who finds the younger one. "Recorders" may in fact read Whitman through Crane's lens. The bridge between them, like Crane's other bridges, asserts independence and difference even as it asserts identity; it is like the image of a vase whose two sides are human profiles—we see now the one, now the other, but we know that they originate from the same object. Whitman's "Recorders Ages Hence" also ends with an image of a bridge, the spanning of two friends' shoulders by their outstretched arms:

> Whose happiest days were far away through
>     fields, in woods,

> on hills, he and another wandering hand in
> 　hand, they
> 　　twain apart from other men,
> Who oft as he saunter'd the streets curv'd with his
> 　arm the
> 　　shoulder of his friend, while the arm of his
> 　friend rested
> 　　upon him also.
>
> (276).

The strength of **"Cape Hatteras"** lies in Crane's translation of Whitman into the modern idiom: he reads Whitman's optimism through the pessimistic tonalities of *Democratic Vistas* and, as we shall see, those of T. S. Eliot. By including the airplane's flight and fall, Crane reworks Whitman's myth to include failure. But in so doing he also clears the ground for rebirth, and re-claims possibility out of the unperformed visions of the past and the present. Crane's reading of Whitman is a loving one, but it is also in some sense an Eliotic one, setting Whitman's vision against that of the "Waste Land" of World War I.

II

Crane's discomfort with Whitman, as we have seen, was due to the insufficient strength of his myth in the face of history; his discomfort with T. S. Eliot was due to that poet's negative vision. If Crane felt the need to reconcile Whitman's optimism with the fact of failure, he also felt compelled to use Eliot as the representative of modern failure and to go beyond him, to "launch into praise," as he told Tate (*Letters* 94). If Walt ascends in Crane's **"Cape Hatteras,"** then in **"The Tunnel"** Crane ascends in Eliot, showing a way through what he termed Eliot's "absolute *impasse*" (*Letters* 90). Crane's imitation of Eliot's language and style is in some sense a sincere form of flattery, for Crane genuinely admired Eliot's skill. But more importantly, Crane uses Eliot as a negative example: he states ironically, in a letter quoted previously, that pessimism is justified in Eliot's case, but not in his own. Whereas Eliot has succeeded brilliantly in portraying failure, Crane asserts that he will risk failing in order to point the way past "The Waste Land." Crane was not alone in his emotional reaction against Eliot's poem; William Carlos Williams was also among those who felt betrayed by the poem. He compared its impact to that of "an atom bomb" (*Autobiography* 174). Williams—and Crane—countered Eliot's example by asserting the primacy of American literature, whose founding father they considered to be Edgar Allan Poe. "The Waste Land" struck them as a poem more British than American. Poe, unlike Eliot, had had a failed career, but he had introduced what Waldo Frank called "the apocalyptic method" to literature. As Williams writes in *In the American Grain,* he "[drove] to destroy, to annihilate the copied, the slavish, the FALSE literature around him" (223). Poe serves both Williams and Crane as the model of an original poet who is not afraid to write against the kind of poetry that seems to him "untrue." Williams's choice of Poe as the American original seems surprising, as does Crane's acceptance of that choice: surely both derive more from Whitman than from Poe.[11] But their choiceis, in a curious way, quite apt; if Poe's influence was nothing if indirect on his American followers, he did exert a significant influence on European writers. Those writers, in their turn, influenced T. S. Eliot. In the context of **"The Tunnel,"** therefore, Poe is at once identified with Eliot—in his role as Daemon and failed truth-teller—and with an alternative to Eliot. Certainly in what Williams called Poe's "anger to sweep out the unoriginal . . . to destroy, to annihilate the copied," we may be tempted to see an antidote to Eliot's quotations of a tradition less American than European.

The voice of Eliot describes Hell in *The Bridge.* It speaks loudest when Crane guides us into the tunnel that owes both its sound and its subject to "The Waste Land." Crane does not address Eliot as directly as he addresses Whitman; there is no ascent of Eliot in Crane, although his presence in the poem is inescapable. Sherman Paul notes the Eliotic tenor of **"The Tunnel,"** and its resemblances to the Faustus and Helen poem.[12] An astonishing number of details in Crane's poem refer to Eliot: the poet's punning hesitancy ("You shall search them all. / Someday by heart you'll learn each famous sight"; "Or can't you quite make up your mind to ride"); and his odd anatomical descriptions ("This answer lives like verdigris, like hair / Beyond extinction, surcease of the bone"). Toward the end of the poem, the poet addresses the Daemon as one who "spoon[s] us out more liquid than the dim / Locution of the eldest star,"—an echo of Prufrock's coffee spoons that measure out our lives. The dialogue, as Sherman Paul points out, is derived from the pub scene in "The Waste Land," and its unhappy sexuality. Paul compares the poet's voice to that of Prufrock talking to himself, including a reference to himself as Lazarus, but he does not develop Crane's obvious relationship to Eliot. The Eliotic tone of this poem is appropriate, because this section is the poem's nadir; the necessary Inferno to precede the Paradise that is portrayed in **"Atlantis."**

Crane described **"The Tunnel"** section of *The Bridge* in a letter of August, 1923 to Waldo Frank as something of a catharsis: "It's rather ghastly, almost surgery—and, oddly almost all from the notes and stitches I have written while swinging on the strap at late midnights going home" (*Letters* 274-75). The words of the poem seem at once part of his flesh (the pun on "stitches") and taken out of his body ("surgery"): the implications are not of healing, but as "ghastly" as the discovery of Poe "swinging on the strap" in **"The Tunnel."** Crane's pain at severing himself from Eliot is understandable, in view of the fact that he had advised Tate to "[absorb] him enough [that] we can trust ourselves as never before, in the air or on the sea" (*Letters* 90).

Poe's failure to be appreciated in his lifetime probably spoke to Crane's own fears about the lack of readers. Like Eliot, Poe is a negative bridge, as evidenced in one stanza from Poe's poem "To One in Paradise," that Williams, incidentally, thought to be his best work:

Ah, dream too bright to last!
    Ah, starry Hope! that didst arise
But to be overcast!
    A voice from out the Future cries,
"On, on!"—but o'er the Past
    (Dim gulf!) my spirit hovering lies
Mute, motionless, aghast!

(31)

This passage is starkly reminiscent of Crane's doubt, referred to earlier, that he could find legitimate links between the past and the future. The contrast to Whitman's brotherly spanning of time and space is considerable. In **"The Tunnel,"** the death that looks down looks through Poe's ghostly image and toward the poet:

    —And did their riding eyes right through your
        side,
    And did their eyes like unwashed platters ride?
    And Death, aloft,—gigantically down
    Probing through you—toward me, O evermore!

Crane's question for Poe reflects his fear that Poe, like Faustus, was not averse to selling his soul:

    And when they dragged your retching flesh,
    Your trembling hands that night through
        Baltimore—
    That last night on the ballot rounds, did you
    Shaking, did you deny the ticket, Poe?

The question is based on a story that Poe, on the night of his death, had been paid to vote fraudulently; if he had done so, his act would have represented a negation of the American myth, and of the myth of the artist as truth-teller. But Poe appears in Crane's poem, not only because of his failures, or his blindness, but because he founded a national literature.[13] Poe thus becomes an ambivalent figure, at once failing and affirming, helping to bridge the gap between what America is and what it might be.

Poe remains in the underworld of the tunnel; the vehicle of birth is Lazarus, a figure derived both from Eliot's "The Love Song of J. Alfred Prufrock" and the Bible. The poet's identification with Prufrock is not accidental; to one of Prufrock's many questions—"And would it have been worth it, after all, / . . . / To say: 'I am Lazarus, come from the dead, / Come back to tell you all, I shall tell you all'—" he replies, like a daring Prufrock:

    And yet, like Lazarus, to feel the slope,
    The sod and billow breaking,—lifting ground,
    —A sound of waters bending astride the sky
    Unceasing with some Word that will not die . . . !

This Lazarus is the envoy of the poem's final word; he brings the word from below, as the poet has promised to "lend a myth to God" and reverse the traditional route of the word.

**"The Tunnel"** concludes with "hands [that] drop memory," and with memory comes the loss of all in the poem that is

Eliot or Whitman. There is a new world—national and poetic—to be discovered in the poem's final section, **"Atlantis." "Atlantis,"** despite its strainings after sublimity, contains no echoes of either poet; its voice and praise are those of Hart Crane. Its conclusion—"Is it Cathay[?] . . . / Whispers antiphonal in azure swing"—seems oddly hesitant. Taken, however, as the poet's final act of revision, the last lines make brilliant sense, swinging between the sheer transcendence of Whitman's vision and the depressing gravity of the Eliotic conversations in **"The Tunnel."**

Hart Crane builds a bridge between himself, Whitman, and Eliot; he is finally able to speak his own vision only because he has answered to theirs.[14] His myth of America is powerful, not only for what it says about the nation, but also for what it says about America's poets. He is not afraid to face national and poetic failures and to show them not as an end, but rather as a means toward a more positive beginning. Crane's lesson, that the poet must risk failure, perhaps fail, in order to show us how to praise, is an important one. He perhaps feared that he might embody what Joseph Riddel (writing on "The Broken Tower") calls "the pathetic gesture of a man dying into his work" (91); but the sublimity of failure assured him of a certain heroism.

NOTES

[1] See Edward Brunner on the textual history of *The Bridge*. Brunner sees no conflict between Crane and Whitman and claims that they possessed "identical values." I see Crane's attitude toward Whitman as more ambivalent and interesting: thus I also consider "Cape Hatteras" to be more important to *The Bridge* than Brunner does.

[2] Early critics of Crane's work (Allen Tate, Yvor Winters, R. P. Blackmur) concentrated on the poet's failure, however splendid (they never question his great talent). Only in the 1960s did critics begin to assume Crane's excellence and control of his vision. The affirmative critics include L. S. Dembo (*SanskritCharge*), R. W. B. Lewis, Sherman Paul, M. D. Uroff, and Robert Combs.

[3] Joseph Riddel emphasizes the self-sacrificial quality of Crane's work, and the inevitable failure of any attempt "to purify himself virtually into the form of a poem" (92). Riddel addresses himself more to the failure of the man than of the poetry itself. My argument limits itself to the poetry.

[4] Crane mentioned Spengler often in the letters he wrote while he was at work on *The Bridge*. In 1931, after he had finished the poem, he wrote Waldo Frank: "Present day America seems a long way off from the destiny I fancied when I wrote that poem. In some ways Spengler must have been right" (*Letters* 366).

[5] Waldo Frank was not alone in his interest in apocalypse. D. H. Lawrence and W. B. Yeats wrote, respec-

tively, a book (*Apocalypse,* published in 1931) and several late poems, including "Byzantium" (1932) and "Lapis Lazuli" (1938), on the subject.

[6] See Todorov 14-33. Robert Combs, who argues that Crane uses romantic irony, writes: "Columbus had not, as he thought, found Cathay. He says that being proved right nearly drove him mad with joy, but we know that he was *not* right. So we see the sense of value again as glorious and ridiculous" (116). I agree, although I think we see Columbus as misguided, rather than "ridiculous."

[7] See L. S. Dembo, "Hart Crane's 'Verticalist' Poem." Uroff discusses the theme of flight (114-52), but she assumes Crane's unambivalent stance toward Whitman. Tom Chaffin makes the same attempt with his more recent interpretation of Crane's technological sublime.

[8] R. W. B. Lewis enumerates Crane's debts to Whitman in "Cape Hatteras" (328). On Whitman and Crane see also Bernice Slote's chapter in *Start with the Sun* (137-65).

[9] The phrase is R. W. B. Lewis's (328).

[10] Crane was also capable of spoofing the poem, as he does in "America's Plutonic Ecstasies," a Cummings-esque poem about laxatives.

[11] William Carlos Williams's *In the American Grain,* although it is a prose work, is similar to *The Bridge* in its concentration on American failures, and in its glorification of them. Crane's claim to have read the book after he had completed *The Bridge* is probably disingenuous: "I put off reading it, you know," he wrote Waldo Frank in 1926, "until I felt my own way cleared beyond chance of confusions incident to reading a book so intimate to my theme. I was so interested to note that he puts Poe and his 'character' in the same position I had *symbolized* for him in 'The Tunnel'" (*Letters* 277-78). Actually, Crane most likely read excerpts from the book as they were published in journals. Joseph E. Slate notes that one chapter of *In the American Grain* appeared in the January, 1923 *Broom* alongside Crane's "The Springs of Guilty Song" (490). John Unterecker, who also believes that Williams influenced Crane, reported that Crane had invited Williams and his wife to the party he threw for Harry Crosby, "because Crane had [I suspect] used a passage from *In the American Grain* to link 'Ave Maria' and the opening sections of 'Powhatan's Daughter'" (608-09).

[12] Sherman Paul briefly discusses Crane's debt to Eliot in "The Tunnel" (265). See also Herbert Leibowitz (123 ff). John Irwin argues: "Setting out to confute Eliot's pessimistic rule, Crane found himself in danger of becoming an example of that rule" (184).

[13] Crane borrows from two sources in his lines about Poe. "—And did their riding eyes right through your side, / And did their eyes like unwashed platters ride?" echoes the lines with which Blake begins his poem on Milton:

"And did those feet in ancient time, / Walk upon Englands mountains green" (95). The lines that follow, "And Death, aloft,—gigantically down / Probing through you—toward me, O evermore!" (the last word is an echo of "nevermore") are derived from Poe and were transmitted through Williams's *In the American Grain* (see page 231).

[14] Whitman and Eliot are not, after all, without their affinities. Prufrock's invitation, "Let us go then, you and I," parodies Whitman's self-assured, "And what I assume you shall assume." "The Waste Land" is itself a dry variant of Whitman's "As I Ebb'd with the Ocean of Life": "I too am but a trail of drift and debris, / I too leave little wrecks upon you, you fish-shaped island." Whitman continues, "Tufts of straw, sands, fragments, / Buoy'd hither from many moods, one contradicting another . . ." (395-96).

WORKS CITED

Blackmur, R. P. "New Thresholds, New Anatomies: Notes on a Text of Hart Crane." *Modern Critical Views: Hart Crane.* Ed. Harold Bloom. New York: Chelsea, 1986. 17-30.

Blake, William. *The Complete Poetry and Prose.* Ed. David V. Erdman. Garden City. NY: Anchor, 1982.

Bloom, Harold. *The Anxiety of Influence.* New York: Oxford UP, 1973.

Brunner, Edward. *Hart Crane and the Making of The Bridge.* Urbana: U of Illinois P, 1985.

Chaffin, Tom. "Toward a Poetics of Technology: Hart Crane and the American Sublime." *Southern Review* 20 (January 1984): 68-81.

Coffman, Stanley K., Jr. "Symbolism in *The Bridge,*" *PMLA* 66 (1951): 65-77.

Combs, Robert. *Vision of the Voyage: Hart Crane and the Psychology of Romanticism.* Memphis: Memphis State UP, 1978.

Crane, Hart. *The Complete Poems and Selected Letters and Prose of Hart Crane.* Ed. Brom Weber. Garden City, NY: Anchor, 1966.

———. *The Letters of Hart Crane: 1916-1932.* Ed. Brom Weber. Berkeley: U of California P, 1965.

Dembo, L. S. *Hart Crane's "Sanskrit Charge": A Study of "The Bridge".* Ithaca: Cornell UP, 1960.

———. "Hart Crane's 'Verticalist' Poem." *American Literature,* 40 (March 1968): 77-91.

Edelman, Lee. *Transmemberment of Song: Hart Crane's Anatomies of Rhetoric and Desire.* Stanford: Stanford UP, 1987.

Eliot, T. S. *Collected Poems: 1909-1962.* New York: Harcourt, 1970.

Frank, Waldo. *Our America.* New York: Boni, 1919.

————. *The Rediscovery of America: An Introduction to a Philosophy of American Life.* New York: Scribner's, 1929.

Irwin, John. "Figurations of the Writer's Death: Freud and Hart Crane." *Modern Critical Views: Hart Crane.* Ed. Harold Bloom. New York: Chelsea, 1986. 155-188.

Leibowitz, Herbert. *Hart Crane: An Introduction to the Poetry.* New York: Columbia UP, 1968.

Lewis, R. W. B. *The Poetry of Hart Crane: A Critical Study.* Princeton: Princeton UP, 1967.

Miller, James E., Jr., Karl Shapiro, and Bernice Slote, eds. *Start with the Sun: Studies in the Whitman Tradition.* Lincoln: U of Nebraska P, 1960.

Paul, Sherman. *Hart's Bridge.* Chicago: U of Illinois P, 1972.

Pease, Donald. "Blake, Crane, Whitman, and Modernism: A Poetics of Pure Possibility." *Modern Critical Views: Hart Crane.* Ed. Harold Bloom. New York: Chelsea, 1986. 189-220.

Poe, Edgar Allen. *The Complete Poems of Edgar Allen Poe.* Ed. J. H. Whitty. Boston: Houghton, 1917.

Riddel, Joseph. "Hart Crane's Poetics of Failure." *Modern Critical Views: Hart Crane.* Ed. Harold Bloom. New York: Chelsea, 1986. 91-110.

Stearns, Harold, E., ed. *Civilization in the United States: An Inquiry by Thirty Americans.* New York: Harcourt, 1922.

Tate, Allen. "Forward." *White Buildings,* by Hart Crane. New York: Boni, 1926.

Todorov, Tzvetan. *The Conquest of America: The Question of the Other.* New York: Harper, 1984.

Unterecker, John. *Voyager: A Life of Hart Crane.* New York: Farrar, 1969.

Uroff, M. D. *Hart Crane: The Patterns of His Poetry.* Chicago: U of Illinois P, 1974.

Whitman, Walt. *Complete Poetry and Selected Prose.* Ed. Justin Kaplan. New York: Library of America, 1982.

Williams, William Carlos. *Autobiography.* New York: New Directions, 1967.

————. *In the American Grain.* New York: New Directions, 1956.

Winters, Yvor. *In Defense of Reason.* New York: Swallow, 1947.

Yeats, William Butler. *Selected Poems and Two Plays of William Butler Yeats.* Ed. M. L. Rosenthal. New York: Collier, 1968.

## Warner Berthoff (essay date 1989)

SOURCE: "'The Bridge': "Too Impossible An Ambition?"" in *Hart Crane: A Re-Introduction,* University of Minnesota Press, 1989, pp. 83-109; 121-23.

[*In the following essay, Berthoff uses other criticism and Crane's own correspondence to evaluate the success or failure of* The Bridge.]

No one now pays much attention to Edgar Allan Poe's famous pronouncement, delivered in the apprehensive dawn of literary modernism, that given natural limits to human responsiveness there can be no such thing as a satisfactory long poem; only short compositions machined to produce a single affective impression can be admired straight through. Yet understanding Poe's peremptory rule for what it was, a one-sided, problem-solving response to the pre-modernist breakdown of classical-humanist norms of use and value (and to the underlying redistribution of cultural authority), we may have to grant that something oddly like its model of performative excellence still thrives among us. Our newest academic criticism, grown aggressively skeptical and subtilizing in addressing literary *texts,* appears correspondingly uncertain in its dealings with the entirety of literary *works.* In the transactions of imaginative literature the first indeterminacy, the unreliability hardest to correct for—to apply terms now much in vogue—appear to be our own. Faced with work that merely by reason of length has to be talked about abstractly and summarizingly, and that in the singularity of its actual making would resist descriptive reconstruction in any case, we retreat to favored presuppositions about its essential office and use. We hypothesize for it some preemptive single line of meaning, the hermeneutic counterpart to Poe's affective uniformity; we extract some dominant configuration of expressive reference (or aporia-creating nonreference), and we pin critical description to that. An anticipatory and, in the event, totalizing textual positivism becomes our fallback position, our means of staying in business—on our own declared terms.

In the case of *The Bridge,* the "long lyric poem, with interrelated sections" (as Hart Crane would finally describe it) that in 1930 became his second published volume, it may be argued that two presuppositions in particular have regularly worked to distract appreciation.[1] The first of these controlled much of the early commentary; fixing on the poem's synoptic canvass of American history and myth, it is the view that success or failure in *The Bridge* necessarily depends on the coherence of its imaginative rendering of the totality of American experience, from a mythic past to the incitements and confusions of the present age. This was Allen Tate's tactical premise, and it effectively prejudged the poem's main purpose as one incapable of realization. "We know," Tate wrote, "that Crane's [subject] is the greatness of America." But this sublime subject is simply not "structurally clarified." Nor could it have been, the implication is, since it is, a priori, a subject "capable of elucidation neither on the logical plane nor in terms of a generally known idea of America." As a result the symbolism of the poem's central argument, including the grand figure of the bridge itself, is undelivered: "The historical plot of the poem, which is the groundwork on which the symbolic bridge stands, is arbitrary and broken."[2]

Admittedly this way of reading and judging *The Bridge* can be supported by several of Crane's own explanatory formulations—"Very roughly, it concerns a mystical synthesis of 'America'" (February 18, 1923); "a new cultural synthesis in terms of our America" (December 3, 1925); "What I am really handling, you see, is the Myth of America" (September 12, 1927). With each of these statements we need to take some account of the occasion. They mainly come (like the first, to Gorham Munson) at *The Bridge*'s excited inception early in 1923, which was also the moment of Crane's least qualified adherence to his New York friends' campaign for a "new consciousness," a national reawakening, or else (like the next two) in letters to Otto Kahn outlining objectively impressive reasons for Kahn's continuing support.[3] By contrast, when Crane is writing about *The Bridge* to Yvor Winters theme and argumentative intention, if discussed at all, are made secondary to performative issues. A letter, for instance, in which Crane takes up Winters's evident skepticism about "modern epics" puts its answering emphasis on the compositional effort to release the "true luminous reality" of his chosen materials—"I'm engrossed in a thousand problems of form and material all at once these days" (November 15, 1926). This letter's point of arrival has already been noted; it is the postulation of that ideal moment "when one's work suddenly stands up, separate and moving of itself with its own sudden life." As with the lyrics of *White Buildings* what most absorbed Crane, once settled on his poem's basic program, was pursuit of this clinching autonomy of statement, this specifically poetic authenticity. In a subsequent letter he reports to Winters the pleasure he takes, with what has so far got written of *The Bridge,* in "'pottering' over such sections as have seemed to lack a final sense of conviction" (March 6, 1927).

The second main presupposition, building on a contrary sense that the historical material is incidental to an essentially private psychodrama, fixes on the poet's own omnipresent role as his poem's burdened and questing protagonist. In this view *The Bridge* is to be read as product and record of an exemplary progression, achieved or aborted, toward subjective fulfillment or wholeness.

Some such conception is implicit in the title, "The Long Way Home," chosen by Sherman Paul for his strongly affirmative 120-page reenactment of the poem's structured advance, and has been worked through with stricter insistence in Edward Brunner's detailed study of the progressive "making" of *The Bridge.* It is Brunner's contention that the poem's proper design, free of needless additions Crane forced himself to write after losing confidence in what he had completed by the winter of 1926-1927, is that of a "developing narrative . . . in which the poet continually [comes] up against examples of his own inadequacy and struggle[s] to work beyond them" (*Splendid Failure,* 183). This view also has documentary support. Writing to Munson in April of 1926, with the whole enterprise still in suspension, Crane appears to recognize that all the imaged expansions attaching to his central bridge symbol may themselves have become a blocking factor, and that creative "fusion" will depend on the complementary release of somethingprivate or personal. "I'm afraid I've so systematically objectified my theme and its details that the necessary 'subjective lymph and sinew' is frozen" (April 5, 1926).

The most persuasive commentaries on *The Bridge*—and both Paul's and Brunner's are, within their premises, vigorously persuasive—are likely in some fashion to combine these evaluative presuppositions. What links them is the assumption that the main work of the poem is to enact a substantial and continuous referential argument; consequently criticism's concern must be to find out whether and by what means the argument, as staged, coheres. But this may be a guardian's concern more than it is the poet's own (beyond the commonsense notion that any practice of a valued art is worth testing against the demands of some subject or occasion of major consequence). Whatever the subject, the poet's immediate question is likely to be closer to the question Emily Dickinson put to the Boston literary eminence who was her one solicited reader. "Are you too deeply occupied," she famously asked Colonel Higginson, "to say if my verse is alive?" If the work is not performatively "alive," no structure or plot will save it and certainly no affectation of moral, psychological, historical wisdom. (Isn't this after all the point of Henry James's sly fable, "The Figure in the Carpet," with its mockery of misdirected critical inquisitiveness?) "A literary creation can appeal to us in all sorts of ways," Pasternak wrote in *Doctor Zhivago* (IX, 4), "by its theme, subject, situations, characters. But above all it appeals to us by the presence in it of art," the least particle of which "outweighs all the other ingredients in significance and turns out to be the essence, the heart and soul of the work."

For Hart Crane, at any rate, the project of *The Bridge,* which sprang into his mind in February of 1923 in the compounded excitement of driving **"Faustus and Helen"** to completion and inwardly preparing what then seemed a final drastic break from Cleveland, was first of all a conscious putting at risk of his own passionate vocation. Preoccupied from the start with the job of transmuting "history and fact, location, etc. . . . into abstract form that would almost function independently of its subject matter," he warily acknowledged that "the actual statement of the thing, the marshalling of the forces, will take me months, at best"—in the end it took him six and a half interrupted years—"and I may have to give it up entirely before that; it may be too impossible an ambition" (February 18, 1923). But at every stage of his work on *The Bridge* and through every interruption he understood it as a critical test of the conception of poetry he had begun to realize in the early 1920s and had powerfully reaffirmed in his best work of 1924-1925, most of all in **"Voyages II"** and **"V," "At Melville's Tomb,"** and **"Repose of Rivers."** Arguably it is in this particular sense that John Unterecker was most right in observing that Crane never deviated from his initial vision of the poem (Unterecker, 279).

[A third presupposition about *The Bridge,* where it is not simply a version of the second autobiographic one, is a presupposition bound to flourish during an interval that finds Wallace Stevens widely promoted as our era's best model for a major, a "strong," poetry. It is that poetry itself is the subject and problematic protagonist of a poem which still, in this view, is judged to succeed or fail by virtue of its running action or "plot." R. W. B. Lewis has summed up such readings as well as anyone: "The plot of *The Bridge* is the gradual permeation of an entire culture by the power of poetic vision" (Lewis, 382). Recognizing an arbitrariness in the poem's over-all design—"nothing in [Crane's] conception dictates the exact order or the exact number of its parts'—Lewis appeals effectively to Kenneth Burke's postulation of "repetitive" as against "conventional" (i.e., narrative or dramatic) form. The poem's separate parts, though not insistently sequential, do "'speak to one another' and 'open out' into each other." Yet the argument as made still requires notions of "progression" or "accumulation" and the steady building of something called "momentum," until at last "beauty and harmony have come again . . . and the poem is done." An initial question about this argument and its plangent conclusion has to be whether or not it was preordained by a particular reader's desire for it or expectation of something like it in any grandly accomplished poem.]

On the issue of how most advantageously to frame this ambitious test—what materials to fill his poem out with, what order to follow, and even what voice or speaking presence to use in different parts—Crane changed his mind and plans more than once. In mid-1923, with one high-flown fragment of forty-three lines on paper, he spoke of a poem roughly "four or five times" longer (that is, half again as long as **"Faustus and Helen"**), to be written throughout in the same exalted idiom. Expecting to finish it "within a year," he saw it as rounding out his first collection: "I am especially anxious to finish it . . . because then I shall have all my best things brought out in book form" (July 21, 1923). Early in 1926, with a "finale" still the one drafted section, he was again projecting not more than "five or six" additional parts (March 5, 1926). Some parts of *The Bridge,* which runs

as printed to eight numbered sections and fifteen separate poems, seem not to have been planned at all. Writing to Waldo Frank in the bounteous late summer of 1926, Crane describes two of the **"Three Songs"** as having suddenly "popped out" (August 12, 1926); no section with that name appears in the detailed outline drawn up a few months earlier for Otto Kahn (March 18, 1926). A section given the title "John Brown" and later "Calgary Express," described in mid-August of 1926 as "largely finished," disappeared from the poem between the winter of 1926-27, when it was listed in a plan sent to Yvor Winters, and the next summer. (Elements of this, possibly whole stanzas, survive in **"The River,"** written during June and July of 1927, but the notion that it would take in, by way of a sleeping-car porter's ruminations, "the whole racial history of the Negro in America" has effectively vanished.) A short section called "The Mango Tree," marked as "completed" in the same numbered plan, also got dropped early in 1927.[4]

What all this reasonably suggests is that the final organization and sequence of *The Bridge* are in some considerable measure accidental. Crane might well defend his work-in-progress, against self-doubt as much as anything, by appealing to conceptions of an "organic" ordering and "fusion" (November 15, 1926, and *passim*) and of a full "assimilation" and "final welding" of all elements (September 12, 1927). Yet it seems likely enough that in different circumstances additional lyric sections might have been added at any of several points in the final design. Similarly we can imagine judging the achievement of the poem more or less as we do now if certain of its fifteen composed parts had never existed; these include not only a late addition like **"Indiana"** but sections as commonly admired as **"The Harbor Dawn," "Van Winkle," "Cutty Sark,"** or **"Three Songs."** Fairly obviously not too much of the poem we now read could be removed or go unreplaced without damage to the whole. A certain amplitude and duration are essential, however achieved. Indeed, these properties—amplitude, abundance, variety, mass, duration—have as much to do with the poem's success as, within rough limits, any particular selection of materials and episodes. There are self-evident reasons why the prayerful soliloquy given to Columbus in "Ave Maria" stands near the beginning, and the sonnet-length coda appended to "The Tunnel" and leading us back to the river and the harbor's edge makes a suitable transition to the soaring "Atlantis" hymn with which the poem ends. (This coda's final broken outcry as well as other lines toward the end of **"The Tunnel"** were brought over in the summer of 1926 from the draft of **"Atlantis"** Crane had shown Waldo Frank the previous January: see Brom Weber, *Hart Crane,* Appendix C.) But for *The Bridge* as a whole only the two formal hymns which initiate and conclude the poem's design are strictly mandated in Crane's determining conception and are positioned where they have to be.[5]

Otherwise it would need only to be a "large form," as in the rush of its realization he wrote Frank (August 12, 1926). Nothing but that would provide space for all the violently tensile "impressions and concepts" he felt himself once again handling freely and openly. The imaginative data most important to him invariably came to him in radical doubleness, the fear of their dissolution inwrought in the excitement and startled joy of receiving them; and an "architectural" poetry as Crane conceived of it was one that above all found expressive room, in the part and in the whole, for each of these determining propulsions. Taking the argument one step further, we might also say that this relative unconcern for any strict program of thematic progression, this macro-organizational casualness and openness, proved fundamental in the creation of a poetry embodying that "fulness, of experience" Robert Lowell would attributeto Crane's work, that power to speak from "the center of things" without getting "sidetracked" even by the most chaotic incentives.

Such freedom brought with it its own intensifications. Crane wrote again to Frank during that same breakthrough summer of his delight at the recurrences materializing within his poem's fast-shifting panorama of "motives and situations." It seemed to him that "every circumstance and incident" were now, at last, "flock[ing] toward a positive center of action, control and beauty" (August 19 and 23, 1926). In discouragement he might speak, as he had done six weeks earlier, of losing "all faith in my material" (early July 1926).[6] But the faith needed to sustain him through *The Bridge* would be that faith in his own released powers which his best earlier lyric verse had confirmed him in and that only the renewed act of writing—as when, that summer, he felt himself "dancing on dynamite," with "all sections moving forward now at once"—could keep alive for him.

2

All this is not to say that the material particulars of *The Bridge*—"history and fact, location, etc."—were not calculatingly chosen and sorted out. One circumstance that made immediately plausible the idea of combining episodes from a reimagined American past with events and passions out of contemporary life was simply the wide currency projects of a comparable sort already had in the literary adventuring of 1918 and after. Writings on comprehensive national themes by the literary generation just ahead of Crane's—the critical manifestoes of Van Wyck Brooks, Waldo Frank's visionary propagandizing, Mencken's public diatribes, the controversies over issues in cultural and institutional life occupying journals like *The New Republic, The Seven Arts,* and *The Dial*—gained new urgency and point from the traumas of the war experience and the rapid dissolution of the Progressive era's long festival of public hopefulness. What was now set in motion for imaginative and polemical writing alike was nothing less than a prolonged national self-audit, a prophetic reexamination of American behavior in relation to its known historical origins.

After 1918 poets, novelists, historians, publicists and policy lobbyists all were enlisted, in one or another fashion, into this collective undertaking. Its mark is on every

kind of imaginative project. These were the years of grandscale revisionist histories like the Beards' *Rise of American Civilization* and V. L. Parrington's *Main Currents in American Thought;* of biographies as iconoclastic as Brook's *The Ordeal of Mark Twain* or as lavishly mythicizing as Carl Sandburg's *Abraham Lincoln* (too "milk sick" in its manner for Crane's taste: letter to Winters, October 5, 1926); of Dreiser's elegiac *Twelve Men* and the poignant inquest of Anderson's *Winesburg, Ohio* (a "chapter in the Bible of [America's] consciousness," Crane wrote at twenty in *The Pagan;* "America should read this book on her knees"); of Harold Stearns's acerbic symposium *Civilization in the United States* in 1923; of Gertrude Stein's *The Making of Americans* and of the parabolic narrative climaxes, each one New York-centered, of Cummings's *The Enormous Room,* Fitzgerald's *The Great Gatsby,* Edmund Wilson's *I Thought of Daisy;* of Paul Rosenfeld's celebrative *Port of New York* and Alfred Stieglitz's continuing promotion at Gallery 291 of a city-based art keyed to an unprecedented social reality (it was in writing to Stieglitz that Crane defined the contemporary city as "a place of 'brokenness'" where either "a new stage is created, or must be, arbitrarily, or there is a foreshortening, a loss and a premature disintegration of experience": July 4, 1923); of Dos Passos's cinematic *Manhattan Transfer,* with childhood delights and fears presented as continuous with the headlined violences of contemporary city life; of the visionary representationalism, in painting metropolitan scenes, of John Sloan, Edward Hopper, Stuart Davis, and of Joseph Stella, whose abstractive series on the Brooklyn Bridge dates from the beginning of the '20s; of, further along, the inception of "epic" undertakings like Stephen Benet's *John Brown's Body,* Dos Passos's *U. S. A.,* MacLeish's *Conquistador,* also of the American cantos of Pound's master effort; and of (not least pertinent to the sensibility at work in *The Bridge*) the new seriousness and generosity in such appraisals of popular and indigenous culture as Gilbert Seldes's *The Seven Lively Arts,* Constance Rourke's *Trumpets of Jubilee* and its successors, and the ethnographer John Collier'sexplorations, beginning in 1923, of American Indian consciousness.

Crane had, characteristically, his own rationale for what he was attempting. "I *must,* perforce, use the materials of the time," he told Yvor Winters, "or the terms of my material will lack edge,—reality" (February 26, 1927). We may understand this working principle as including, for any artist, not only what he himself has known directly but the materials and themes shared with his most adventurous contemporaries. What Crane took from the literary climate of the mid-1920s thus included the conviction that his poem's "conquest of consciousness" would remain substantially incomplete if it did not reach out to encompass collective and historical actions and memories. To such an end American materials will serve an American poet not, as he wrote in **"General Aims and Theories,"** because "America has any so-called par value as a state or as a group of people" but because, being more deeply instinctive with him and at the same time already having a certain formalized acceptance, they can better help achieve an effectively "autonomous" construct, a poem moving out on "an orbit or predetermined direction of its own." (This is a view of the relation between poetic authority and popular attitudes and conventions that becomes less paradoxical-sounding the more you think it through.)

One new work in particular by an American contemporary, the set of historiographic re-creations William Carlos Williams published in *In the American Grain* (1925), struck Crane as coming so near his scheme for *The Bridge* that he made a point of standing off from it. So at least he told Winters a year after its publication: "I don't want to read *In the American Grain* until I get through with Bridge" (November 12, 1926). Nine days later he seems to have read Williams's book after all, telling Waldo Frank it was "an achievement that I'd be proud of" (November 21, 1926):

> A most important and *sincere* book. I'm very enthusiastic—I put off reading it, you know, until I felt my own way cleared beyond chance of confusions incident to reading a book so intimate to my theme. I was so interested to note that he puts Poe and his "character" in the same position as I had *symbolized* for him in **"The Tunnel"** section.[7]

But an authorial persona figures in the various chapters of *In the American Grain* as recorder and commentator rather than as an integrally dramatized participant; delivering revisionist judgements about America's historical past and its legacy *is* Williams's organizing pursoe. And since our first concern with *The Bridge* is not its textual foundations but its performative logic or *combinatoire*, there seems to me a more immediate interest in putting beside it an earlier specifically poetic American precedent, the 1855 poem of Walt Whitman's that we now know as "The Sleepers."

In a long poem meant—among other motives at work in *The Bridge*'s making—to show past and present bound into a living continuum it is hardly surprising to find Whitman as, under his own name, a solicited elder presence. The poem's fourth numbered section, **"Cape Hatteras,"** was planned, so Crane told Otto Kahn, as "a kind of ode to Whitman" (September 12, 1927); in it, besides explicit references to particular titles and phrasings—"Children of Adam," "Recorders Ages Hence," Paumanok, "Out of the Cradle," "Years of the Modern," "Song of the Open Road"—Whitman is projected as the master maker and originator of Crane's leading symbol. The oddly stilted lines clinching this tribute conclude an unusual stanza in heroic couplets:

> Our Meistersinger, thou set breath in steel;
> And it was thou who on the boldest heel
> Stood up and flung the span on even wing
> Of that great Bridge, our Myth, whereof I sing!

*The Bridge* carries no overt allusion to "The Sleepers," which in any case is a noticeably shorter poem and comes into the 1855 *Leaves of Grass* as a kind of nighttime

supplement to "Song of Myself" (to give this much longer section of *Leaves* its final title). But "The Sleepers" constitutes a self-completing unitwithin the larger work, and what directly links it to *The Bridge* is Whitman's introduction into it of a series of episodes from past American life and history, to complement and extend his poetry's regular fusion of first-person rhapsody and the generic experience presenting itself to his imaginative witness.[8]

The framing action of "The Sleepers" is the poet's night journey through the gathered democracy of human sleep, where all alike—the comfortable and the afflicted, old and young, male and female, murderer and murdered, the new-born and the dying—come to rest under his assimilative gaze. Lines of brooding sympathy with all human suffering co-exist with lines of rough-neck ebullience and a startling erotic candor (this particularly in an eleven-line passage, completing what is now the poem's long first section, that directly mimes sexual dreaming: "O hotcheeked and blushing . . ."—lines withdrawn from more circumspect later printings). But my immediate concern is with the series of historical and quasihistorical scenes filling out the middle sections of "The Sleepers." These are, first of all, scenes of defeat and loss, of suffering and sorrow, and of the end of things or at the least of an inexorable attenuation of life's promises—though in the peaceable kingdom of the poem's closing passage all souls are envisioned as waking again to full life in the "invigoration" and "chemistry" of the night. In this expressive emphasis Whitman anticipated an intuition fundamental to *The Bridge*'s panoramic unfolding: that a significant public myth, irrepressible as it may be in its self-engendering power of renewal, may gain final clarification as much through an accounting of those excluded from its promise as in representations of those most eloquent in proclaiming it.

So in the second section of "The Sleepers" the poet, his communing self turned passive and elegiac, enters in imaginative preparation the bodies of an aged woman and of a sleepless and grieving widow, then becomes no more than a blank shroud in an underground coffin; but in the third and fourth sections he is a watcher again as, in succession, a "gigantic" swimmer and (in what is specified as a "past-reading") a battered ship move from the open sea to destruction on rocky shores. In the section following we enter the specifically historical past, with two episodes from the American Revolution. The first of these presents the hero Washington—not in glowing defiance as in Blake's *America* but after the defeat at Brooklyn—grieving at the slaughter of his young troops; in the second he relinquishes command at the war's end and, embracing one by one his weeping officers, bids good-bye to the disbanding army. The next section, the sixth, divides in the 1855 text into two distinct parts. There is first a story recalled by the poet's mother from girl-hood when a solitary Indian woman came to her family's house one early morning—a figure beautiful, mysterious, with "free and elastic step"—but went away in mid-afternoon and "never came nor was heard of there again"; then a strange intense passage in which the poet, identifying himself as "Lucifer" ("Black Lucifer" in a draft fragment), speaks as a slave, curses the man who has "defiled" him, and ends transformed into an agent of preternatural revenge:

> Now the vast dusk bulk that is the whale's bulk . .
> . it seems mine,
> Warily, sportsman! though I lie so sleepy and
> sluggish, my tap is death.

Deftly here the two great institutional crimes in America's long history, genocide and race slavery, have been given their place, too, along with a premonition of grim consequences still to be enacted, in the poem's synoptic myth.

The climactic seventh section of "The Sleepers," which now follows, is equally remarkable. A quick return to happier matters—a "show" (appropriate formal word) of love and summer, light and air, autumn harvest and filled barns—expands into a more comprehensive vision of "elements" merging back into some primal wholeness, and then, abruptly, of fugitive uprooted souls returning in their dreams to a life and world irrevocably lost to them:

> . . . the immigrant is back beyond months and
> years;
> The poor Irishman lives in the simple house of his
> childhood, with
> wellknown neighbors and faces,
> They warmly welcome him, he is barefoot again,
> he forgets he is well off,
> The Dutchman voyages home. . . .

—so the vision develops, in Whitmanesque amplitude and detail, of a nation of exiles and strangers whose single dream is strikingly antithetical to the one commonly professed. Beneath our sanctified American dream, "The Sleepers" acknowledges at this interior climax, lies the American sadness, the broken life of contrary passions and sorrows that only the poet's own reconciling pledge ("I swear they are averaged now") can imagine restoring to equity and wholeness.[9] And since this controlling vision is one revealed in its completeness at every stage of American history, the form chosen for presenting it is not a continuous narrative but what may properly be called a lyric pageant, in which an emblazoned succession of independent yet concordant scenes of past and present life is framed between opening and closing attestations by the pageant-master poet himself. As with *The Bridge* the order of the scenes is not strictly binding, and we can imagine a greater or lesser number of them. What counts is a certain affective range and mass in the full sequence. Despite all obvious differences in scale "The Sleepers," so described, may be read, I would say, as a confirming anticipation of the performative architecture worked out for *The Bridge.*

3

Lyric pageant, lyric suite on epideictic (or celebratory) materials and themes: a genre classification of *The Bridge,* if one is wanted, has only to take account of Crane's faithfulness to his own mastered style of intensifying lyric apostrophe and at the same time his extension of this style to the scale of the collective and historical. The poet's work of "analysis and discovery" moves out not only onto a broader stage but one—that of the continuing "matter of America"—already foregrounded in his first audience's expectation.[10] It must be granted that certain of the formal claims Crane himself advanced in support of his grand effort have been as prejudicial to judgment as were certain of Whitman's brasher self-promotions, though we may note again that past the moment of inception in February of 1923 it is mainly in reports to Otto Kahn that claims to an "epic" form and "symphonic" organization are pressed into service. ("It is at least a symphony with an epic theme," Crane wrote his benefactor on September 12, 1927, in the course of asking for a further subsidy.) By Ezra Pound's bluff definition of epic—"a poem including history"—*The Bridge*'s qualifications are unimpeachable.[11] But a straightforward remark earlier in the same letter to Otto Kahn, commenting on the "unique problem of form" presented by each section, comes nearer to describing what we are actually given in *The Bridge.* "Each [section] is a separate canvas," Crane explains, even though "none yields its entire significance" unless seen in relation to the others. The poem will hold us more by the displayed inventiveness of its successive parts, the autonomy and force of their separate execution, than by any fully constituted and sustained action or theme.[12]

The felt continuity of *The Bridge* is thus first of all in the recurrence across richly varied materials of a consistent intensity of lyric (apostrophic) statement. In each section of the poem, figures and forms of affective energy—confident or despairing, guileless or corrupted, prolific or devouring (Blake's words seem directly appropriate here), but all attached firmly to a real temporal and historical world—are put in relation to some actively responsive matrix of being (sometimes represented as a particular woman); and in each section the encounter moves across, as its reciprocal dynamic develops, to a particular tableau or voiced pledge not of resolution but of full continuing engagement. Throughout *The Bridge* what is felt as the theme beneath the theme is, in a word, power—and is not this the theme or subject presenting itself for realization in any major art? Certainly, so Crane himself had come to believe, it is the matter vitally at issue in both the artist's and the true scientist's creative passion. The imaginative strength of *The Bridge,* in this view, develops from its concrete rendering of the inflections of power in power's three great identifiable modes—in the universals of human self-being and of human love's literally ecstatic conviction, in all existence as phenomenally apprehended, and in the singular occurrences of a given people's recoverable history—in each mode to be validated by the refiguring power of the poet's own abstractive and formalizing language.

So in each section of *The Bridge* we are summoned into a contestation of invoked powers. (Audibly summoned in the exclamatory syntax opening several early sections: "How many dawns . . . ," "Be with me, Luis de San Angel, now—," "Stick your patent name on a signboard/ brother—".) Some essential contrariety, some reflexive opposition of self-legitimizing protagonists or life-agencies—they may be wholly natural, or suprapersonal— becomes the center of reference in a formalized enactment of promise and frustration, or postponement; of joining and sundering—kinesthetic patterns carrying the flow and recoil of feeling throughout the poem; of convergences and severances that, deriving with equal force from the condition of all existence, remain equally active in the voiced reconciliation or stasis each section contrives at its end.[13] Coincidentally some provisionally recuperative scene flashes forth in each section that is never fully realized—or, in a phrase from the dedicatory opening, "never disclosed"—in the ideal of itself which draws thought after it, though that ideal remains unimpaired as a locus of imaginative attraction. In a double sense possibilities of "epic" consummation do pull this poetry forward and are undiminished by being always and necessarily deferred; their reality to the imagination is in the affective desiring that irrepressibly generates them. Thus in the poem's specifically historical moments and episodes the progression is toward some restored communion of purpose and, specifically, some right way of occupying the collective estate (for which the land, the continent itself, is a primary symbol) and of entering all the occasions of its distinguishing history; here, too, consummations are felt as immanent that are never once and for all "disclosed" but always again "foretold," with unabated power to undiminished expectation.

[The part given in *The Bridge* to music and dance, the purest of our formalizations of power and desire, is scarcely accidental. Musical figures and references—assimilative harmonies, ritual chants, discords that "part / Our hearing"—enter every section of the poem, from the Angelus and Te Deum of **"Ave Maria"** (not to mention the "water-swell rhythm" Crane claimed for this section: July 26, 1926) to the industrial world's "nasal whine of power" in **"Cape Hatteras"** and the burlesque show's "tom-tom scrimmage" in **"National Winter Garden."** In **"The Harbor Dawn"** we hear of gong warnings, singing sirens (a calculated pun, surely), the "far strum of fog horns," and the lovers' own "singing arms"; in **"Van Winkle"** a grinding hurdy-gurdy; in **"The River"** the nostalgic songs of hoboes, road gangs, steamboat men; in **"The Dance"** the pounded rhythms of a tribal rite; in **"Cutty Sark"** a nickel-in-the-slot pianola balanced by the litany of clipper-ship names ("Music still haunts [them]," Crane told Otto Kahn); in **"Cape Hatteras"** Whitman's conglomerate singing, correlative with gypsy songs and bird notes, over against modern radio static and the hum of dynamos; in each of the **"Three Songs"** the eponymous form itself; in **"Quaker Hill"** hotel dance music against the whippoorwill's pastoral augury of fear and pain; in the subway plunge of **"The Tunnel,"** hell's own phonographs and the "serenade" of screeching equipment; and at both ends of the poem's pageantry the choiring wind-harp rapturously invoked as an avatar of the bridge itself. (The epigraph from Plato introducing **"Atlantis,"** *The Bridge*'s final section, makes explicit music's supervisory role.) By Crane's own account different sections of the poem imitate particular musical forms. **"Cutty Sark,"** he told Kahn, "is built on the plan of a fugue" with "two 'voices' . . . interwoven in the action" (September 12, 1927), while to Winters he spoke of **"The River"** as composing a "hieratic largo"—"It is *timed* insofar as I have been able to time it, every word and beat is measured and weighed," to the end of "slightly vary[ing] a continuous and (I think) desirable underlying monotony of rhythm" (July 5, 1927). This line of consideration may also put us on somewhat better terms with **"Indiana,"** commonly disparaged as abjectly sentimental. With its rhymed and typographically staggered quatrains this lyric section points us formally toward the mode of folksong and popular ballad; so it announces itself in the opening verse as a song and continues to the end with the abstracting intimacy of voice characteristic of ballad recitative as a mode.]

The "field of possibilities" opened through the figure and symbol of the bridge virtually exploded once Crane hit on it—its "mystic possibilities" he was pleased to say in the excitement of beginning to track them. But some of his anticipatory claims for it have, again, proved more distracting than helpful. Neither his initial projection, in letters, of the bridge itself as "symbol of our constructive future, our unique identity . . . also our scientific hopes and achievements of the future" (February 18, 1923) nor his identification of it three years later, still with only one section written, as "a ship, a world, a woman, a tremendous harp" (January 18, 1926) is immediately useful in entering the poem Crane actually wrote. The real solidity of the bridge figure is that as directly invoked it never ceases to be concretely and circumstantially itself. (In the Black Sun printing of *The Bridge* Walker Evans's three sharp angled photographs reinforce this concreteness.) With Hart Crane at his best there is always something representationally solid and self-organizing to fix attention, and to answer factually the question "What *might* the Brooklyn Bridge be taken as symbolizing?" can give us as much purchase as we need on the imaginative contexts the poem works to re-establish.

As a visible structure of steel and stone joining two divided sectors of a huge modern city across, day and night, a free space of sky and flowing waters, the bridge is at once an extraordinary feat of industrial engineering and, in the boldness of its conception, an equally extraordinary imaginative act. Its stone towers and metal cables lift skyward with a geometric grace that for grandeur and erected strength matches anything to be found either in nature or in past history. Yet its practical service is merely to speed up the daily traffic of a mechanized civilization, a frantic new iron age—and to furnish a superior platform for this civilization's bedlamites and suicides. So perceived, the bridge looms as both a master trope for all adventuring, all crossing or abrogating of boundaries, all imaginative voyaging, and as an icon of the fatality hanging over any passionately risked human undertaking.

How this title metaphor rides over the whole poem and what actions and correlations attach to it are epitomized in the opening hymn **"To Brooklyn Bridge"**—"almost the best thing I've ever written," Crane jubilantly told Waldo Frank at the moment of completing it (July 24, 1926).[14] Simply the first four of its eleven vividly sequenced stanzas form an introductory synopsis of algebraic precision and elegance. The dawn arc of a seagull's tumultuous flight—high over "chained bay waters" to the monument to Liberty it seems itself to have raised up—remains as an inviolate apparition above the business files, plunging elevators, and movie-house phantasms of the mechanized city world and leads thought directly back to the arching freedom of the bridge itself; in the "ever unspent" motion of the bridge's huge stride even the sun discovers its daily orbit. More of any day's common events synecdochally follow. A suicide climbs the bridge's heights and jumps (in a line, however—"A jest falls from the speechless caravan"—somewhat too nearly recalling the feature-journalism ironies of O. Henry's storytelling; it does not seem to me this poem's best moment). Then the immense system of light and air that Brooklyn Bridge shares with lower Manhattan's office towers and oceanic outlook organizes a vividly concrete stanza—

> Down Wall, from girder into street noon leaks,
> A rip-tooth of the sky's acetylene;
> All afternoon the cloud-flown derricks turn . . .
> Thy cables breathe the North Atlantic still.

—a stanza also continuing the dialectic of incandescent violence and some saving antithesis, of power gone amok and the unreduced promise of transcendence.

The animate suggestion in "breathe" cues, through the next two stanzas, attributions to the bridge of godlike powers and, coordinately, a shift in voicing from awed description to supplication:

> O harp and altar, of the fury fused,
> (How could mere toil align thy choiring strings!)
> Terrific threshold of the prophet's pledge,
> Prayer of pariah, and the lover's cry,—[15]

A final quatrain, besides outlining the historical geography still to be explored of river, sea, and the "prairies' dreaming sod," resumes and completes this transformation into prayer—but not before we are given two more stanza-long projections of the bridge's iconographic import: how it compacts within itself the contraries of wholeness and brokenness, timeless expectancy and the self-consuming rush of human life; how in particular its "Everpresence" (to bring down another name for it from the poem's final section) mediates the unceasing agon of this rapid-transit, office-block world. Characteristically these two stanzas' descriptive precision and (never to be overlooked with Hart Crane) metrical, syntactical, idiomatic firmness serve to anchor in common fact and common apprehension the dedication's closing movement:

> Again the traffic lights that skim thy swift
> Unfractioned idiom, immaculate sigh of stars,

> Beading thy path—condense eternity:
> And we have seen night lifted in thine arms.

> Under thy shadow by the piers I waited;
> Only in darkness is thy shadow clear.
> The City's fiery parcels all undone,
> Already snow submerges an iron year . . .

This dedicatory section's final lines, fixing again on the bridge's geometric grandeur, form a hyperbole that brings to a climax the poet-supplicant's rapt absorption. "And of the curveship lend a myth to God"—it is a patently risky formulation. But against arguments that this is empty rhetoric, or blasphemy, or both, ordinary rules of expressive context and progression surely allow us to read this closure dramatistically and provisionally rather than as a statement of Crane's own settled belief or even of his determining purpose in writing *The Bridge.* What it enacts is a certain state of mind, that one in which the category of the sacred forces itself back into conscious experience.

4

**"Ave Maria,"** first in *The Bridge*'s main sequence of episodes and panels, exemplifies Crane's stated ambition to show "the continuous and living evidence of the past in the inmost vital substance of the present" (September 12, 1927). In constructing it he worked directly from Columbus's printed journal, among other textual resources. This section's prosodic form—a series of intermittently rhymed pentameter octaves, breaking off at the end into a staggered couplet of exclamation—has a formality appropriate to its conventionally heroic subject. Staged as a recollective meditation and concluding prayer, it places its speaking protagonist not at the high moment of new-world landfall but on the voyage back into the skepticisms and treacheries of imperial Europe. The recollective first part's climaxes do come, though, in recreating the great moment when visionary belief was staggeringly confirmed—

> . . . Then faith, not fear
> Nigh surged me witless. . . . Hearing the surf
> near—
> I, wonder-breathing, kept the watch,—saw
> The first palm chevron the first lighted hill.

—then in evoking in mid-ocean, suspended between the old and new land worlds, "this third, of water," signifying in its self-sufficient immensity the sum of all that bewilderingly "tests" the "word" of our faith yet also promises completion and wholeness, a final rounding into light:

> Series on series [of waves], infinite,—till eyes
> Starved wide on blackened tides, accrete—enclose
> This turning rondure whole, this crescent ring
> Sun-cusped and zoned with modulated fire. . . .

The title **"Ave Maria"** notwithstanding, the sustained prayer that forms this section's second part is directed not to Mary but to an ocean god of "plenitude" and "holocaust" combined, one of whose avatars is the creative-destructive fire made visible to Columbus in his ship's corposants and in the "garnet" flare of Teneriffe's volcanic cone. The consummation liturgically unfolded—"Hushed gleaming fields and pendant seething wheat/ Of knowledge"—is thus as harrowing as any invoked apocalypse:

> And kingdoms
>           naked in the
>                     trembling heart—
>     Te Deum laudamus
>           O Thou Hand of Fire

Columbus, his voyage itself a bridge flung out across space and time, is made to speak here for every passionate discoverer and bridge-maker, not least of course for the poet himself in his imaginative adventuring.

The longest numbered section, **"Powhatan's Daughter,"** now follows. Designed, so Crane told Waldo Frank, to serve his poem as a "basic center and antecedent of all motion" (August 3, 1926), its five subsections fill out nearly a third of *The Bridge*'s printed text. More than elsewhere we seem to follow a narrative though not a chronological sequence, an impression sharpened by the running series of marginal glosses subjoined to this but (except for a single notation at the start of **"Ave Maria"**) to no other part of the poem. The Indian princess Pocahontas, in Crane's synopsis to Otto Kahn, stands for the "physical body of the continent" and is the matrix of life and potentiality to be explored and, ideally, reawakened in every event this long section recovers and celebrates. As such she is apparently one with the unnamed "she" of the glosses: the "woman with us in the dawn," the woman whose "chieftain lover" still "haunts the lakes and hills." Hers is the "body under the wide rain" known to the continental drifters of **"The River"** and to the poet himself in his journeying, and she is the grieving bride in the ritual exorcism of temporality and death re-enacted in **"The Dance"**—"on the pure mythical and smoky soil at last," as Crane explained things to Kahn.

**"Powhatan's Daughter"** begins, however, with two poems drawing us back into the contemporary city scene. Against a confused early morning medley of dockside and harbor noise—"a tide of voices," "a drunken stevedore's howl and thud," "soft sleeves of sound," "signals dispersed in veils"—the second-person protagonist of **"The Harbor Dawn"** lies with an unnamed lover, watched over (the gloss tells us) by a woman-figure's ghostly presence.[16] Then in **"Van Winkle"** fragments of a disorienting metropolitan day are played off against the childhood remembrances stirred up by a handorgan's casual drone—schoolroom lessons about story-book heroes, backyard games edging into scariness, a father's punishment, a mother's tantalizingly withdrawn smile. These two lyric cameos make self-contained interludes within the longer poem; neither seems essential to its advancing structure. But each brings forward the same abstract oppositions—of near and remote, center and circumference,

private feeling and the historical world's collective intrusions—that play across *The Bridge* as a whole. Each hints at continental expansions (the last dawn star beckons the lovers of **"The Harbor Dawn"** to some western hill, the macadam pavements of **"Van Winkle"** stretch in fact to the Golden Gate); each advances formally by the same kaleidoscope rhythm of notation, the same quickened sequence of dissolves from one evocative phrasing to the next. Together these sections compose a double overture to the panoramic design of **"The River,"** the staccato opening lines of which follow directly from the accelerated beat and excited verbs ("Keep hold," "Have you got," "hurry along") of **"Van Winkle"**'s closing stanza.

Beyond question **"The River"** is the showpiece of **"Powhatan's Daughter,"** if not of the poem as a whole. Crane himself wrote, at the moment of finishing it, "I think I have worked harder and longer on this section of *The Bridge* than any other" (July 4, 1927). To Winters, the next day, he summed up its organizing intention, which was "to tell the pioneer experience backward"; that is, to re-create from the perspective of the present the full succession of the North American continent's life-in-history. Accordingly this section moves from the commercialized "wilderness of freight and rails" that 1920s hoboes now wanderacross, the contemporary landscape of advertising billboards and telegraph wires stringing "town to town and dream to ticking dream," back to earlier epochs of "axe and powder horn," vanished Indian dynasties, and—still deeper in aboriginal time, or timelessness—the vast processes of geologic accumulation from which everything else in the continent's evolving life takes its rise:

> Damp tonnage and alluvial march of days—
> Nights turbid, vascular with silted shale
> And roots surrendered down of moraine clays:
> The Mississippi drinks the farthest dale.
> O quarrying passion, undertowed sunlight! . . .

There are too many comparable expressive figurings in **"The River"** to do justice to in a summary account. Repeatedly single lines or line pairings bring theme and occasion into precise idiomatic focus; so the poem's temporal counterpointing of short-run agitations and long slow unfoldings is neatly caught up in a description of men who "take their liquor slow—and count / . . . The river's minute by the far brook's year." The cumulative power of this section is twofold. In part it is in the hieroglyphic scene-painting—inscribed slogans, place-names of rivers and railroad stops, mythologic presences underground—and in the names, acts, and chanted songs of those whose childlike "bird-wit" penetrates to elemental meanings:

> Time's rendings, time's blendings they construe
> As final reckonings of fire and snow. . . .

Lost to any comfortably organized or purposeful future ("Blind fists of nothing, humpty-dumpty clods"), it is these derelict wanderers who nevertheless "touch something like a key perhaps":

—They know a body under the wide rain.

They also know sudden death: a stanza that Winters at his dourest continued to find affecting gives us, in the two lines evoking the railroad hobo "Dan Midland—jolted from the cold brake-beam," a figure as memorable in his fugitive appearance as *Moby-Dick*'s Bulkington.[17] But equally the power of **"The River"** develops through its graduated cadences and rhythms, above all in the movement through the middle part of it from slow-paced pentameter stanzas of eight to ten firmly rhymed lines (with one stanza of double length) into the full solemnity of its eight closing quatrains. These, rhymed throughout in heavy long-voweled monosyllables, re-enact the great river's heraldic passage (carrying with it the lives of all who live in its wide basin) downward into the receiving and answering ocean:

> And flows within itself, heaps itself free.
> All fades but one thin skyline 'round . . . Ahead
> No embrace opens but the stinging sea;
> The River lifts itself from its long bed,
>
> Poised wholly on its dream, a mustard glow
> Tortured with history, its one will—flow!
> —The Passion spreads in wide tongues, choked
>     and slow,
> Meeting the Gulf, hosannas silently below.

Intimations midway in **"The River"** of what Crane identified to Otto Kahn as "the primal world of the Indian" (September 12, 1927) now open out into the re-created tribal ritual and frenzy of **"The Dance."** Here a structure of continuous narrative encloses the descriptive fantastications meant to enact a metamorphic reconvergence of the white and red races and through this a reconciliation with the physical continent's dangerously autochthonous powers. "Grey tepees tufting the blue knolls ahead, / Smoke swirling through the yellow chestnut glade . . . / A distant cloud, a thunder-bud—it grew, / That blanket of the skies: the padded foot / Within,—I heard it; 'til its rhythm drew,/—Siphoned the black pool from the heart's hot root!": though prosodically **"The Dance"**continues with the pentameter quatrains used for the measured close of **"The River,"** an audibly different syntax and voicing give it what Crane especially wanted for it, a contrasted rhythm of its own—"a rapid foot-beat," he explained to Yvor Winters (July 5, 1927).

Appropriately, in this context, *The Bridge*'s symbolism of eagle and serpent—soaring conquests of space and the unappeasable bite of time—comes front and center in **"The Dance"** and remains to complete the shift, once more, to prayer and resolution in its closing lines:

> The serpent with the eagle in the boughs.

Only, perhaps, an element of artificiality not in the Indian fiction itself but in its staged development qualifies admiration. Details of the central episode seem a touch too schematic, its symbolic furnishing too methodically inscribed. But if **"The Dance"** risks factitiousness, it is not

in the way both Winters and Allen Tate asserted in fastening on one line in particular as clear evidence of Crane's imaginative confusion (or false faith). This is the line concluding a stanza spoken directly by the poem's entranced protagonist to his Indian counterpart: "Lie to us,—dance us back the tribal morn!" Surely this is to be understood as rising out of the dramatized frenzy of the narrative moment rather than as (so Winters described it in reviewing *The Bridge*) a desperate maneuver to compensate for "the inadequacy of [Crane's own] belief." Crane, in his reply, made a last attempt to straighten matters out and to remind Winters that dramatic poetry especially is, after all, a fabrication in appropriate words of imaginable states and conditions of consciousness. "All I am saying," Crane wrote back about the line in question, "amounts in substance to this: 'Mimic the scene of yesterday; I want to see how it looked'" (June 4, 1930).[18]

The Indian material may nevertheless be the element in *The Bridge*'s basic program requiring the greatest, or least rewarding, suspension of disbelief. In the text of **"Indiana"** (one of the three sections not written out until late in 1929, it completes **"Powhatan's Daughter"**) the one passage that does seem misconceived is a four-stanza interpolation in which the bereft pioneer woman who speaks, or sings, this poem remembers a speechless exchange of glances with an Indian mother along the trail back from the delusions of the Gold Rush:

> . . . I suddenly the bolder
> Knew that mere words could not have brought us
>     nearer.
> She nodded—and that smile across her shoulder
>     Will still endear her . . .

Knowing that this interpolation was meant to continue the Pocahontas symbolism and its "absorption into 'our contemporary veins'" (as Crane told Harry and Caresse Crosby: October 29, 1929) is no great help in getting through it. Yet in gauging Crane's working intentions with **"Indiana"** some credit should be allowed the poem's singular verse form. As already noted, its rhymed quatrains—second and fourth lines indented and the fourth elliptically shortened—appear on the page as an adaptation of the regular balladnarrative stanza, and the poem itself follows a ballad or folksong scenario. The woman speaker, her husband long dead from his own disappointed wandering, grieves at the absence in turn of her son; old now, she remembers past events and at the end pleads for his return home.

It is an archetypal story—Frost's "The Black Cottage" offers another version of it—and though so far as I know no particular precedent has been suggested as Crane's model or source, it remains as alive as ever to popular consciousness.[19] As, again, briefly in **"Cutty Sark"** and in the third of the **"Three Songs"**—

> O rain at seven,
> Pay-check at eleven—
> Keep smiling the boss away . . .

—borrowing popular song-forms would seem to have an appropriate place inCrane's effort after the widest possible "scope of implication" (in a key phrase from the essay **"Modern Poetry"**). Demonstrating correspondences with popular tradition does not of itself salvage an ill-written performance—to cite Ezra Pound's stern rule in *ABC of Reading:* "When the writing is masterly one does NOT have to excuse it or to hunt up the reason for perpetuating the flaw"—and **"Indiana"** does show a more than usual, or more than usually unrevised, improvisation and haste. But the Indian-woman episode apart, the pioneer mother's complaint is effective enough in crossing tiredness and resignation with strokes of bitter wit—

> We found God lavish there in Colorado
>   But passing sly.

—and its direct closing appeal for her boy's return structurally anticipates the reversed appeal, the poet's appeal to his spiritual predecessor Whitman, which will end the long **"Cape Hatteras"** section, soon to follow.

5

**"Cutty Sark,"** the next numbered section of *The Bridge,* repeats the progression backward in time from present disorders to the heraldry of a heroic past, represented here (as Crane described the poem in his September 1927 letter to Otto Kahn) in a "regatta of phantom clippershipships seen from Brooklyn Bridge." The burned-out sailor whose reminiscences, delivered to banal piano accompaniment, dispatch the poet-speaker into the city night and his bridge walk home derives from more than one literary source. Melville's derelict sea-wanderers, Baudelaire's *matelot ivrogne,* characters in Eugene O'Neill's sea plays for the Provincetown Players have been suggested, and Crane himself, delighted with his newly drafted poem, dropped an allusion to "Herr Freud" in identifying this uncanny interlocutor as "an old man of the sea" (July 29, 1926). Only a little longer than **"The Harbor Dawn"** and **"Van Winkle,"** **"Cutty Sark,"** too, takes its place in *The Bridge* as a self-contained interlude, though correspondences with other sections are easy enough to spot in its phrasing and imagery. Possibly this is why Yvor Winters exempted it from the general charge of chaos and failure. An "almost incomparably skillful dance of shadows," Winters called it, for once as fulsomely approving in 1930 as he seems to have been on first reading this and other sections of *The Bridge* three and a half years before.

Winter's comparable praise of **"Southern Cross"**—to look past **"Cape Hatteras"** for a moment to the mid-ocean phantasmagoria of this first of the **"Three Songs"**—may again reflect its relative independence of other sections. (The kinesthetically vigorous satire of **"National Winter Garden,"** second in this group, Winters spoke of as only a further instance of Crane's "faults of rhetoric.") Both individually and as a numbered section the **"Three Songs"** are incidental to *The Bridge's*

main advance but complement its working dialectic of interwoven contraries. These short poems are addressed in succession to the feminine archetypes given their ultimate names early in **"Southern Cross"** ("Eve! Magdalene! / or Mary, you?") and call forth, particularly the first and second, both preternatural threats and terrors and the irrepressible resurgence of human desiring—for spiritual transcendence, for the actual consummations of bone and flesh. The third and slightest, **"Virginia,"** is merely—but thoroughly—charming, finding its "blue-eyed Mary" in a dime-store tower (the Woolworth "cathedral," as commonly identified in the 1910s and 1920s) high above springtime flower vendors, "[c]rap-shooting gangs," and Eliotesque "oyster shells" in the downtown streets.

**"Cape Hatteras,"** its more than two hundred lines making it nearly as long as the whole of "The Sleepers," is a different affair altogether, composing both the compositional center of *The Bridge* and its most argued-over major section. It is another of those that Crane completed only in the final rush to publication in 1929. In several ways it seems marked by haste and expressive forcing—in its turbulent language and stretched-out lines, its noisy simulations of industrial and martial violence, its contraction at intervals into sheer percussiveness:

> Power's script,—wound, bobbin-bound, refined—
> Is stropped to the slap of belts on booming spools, spurred
> Into the bulging bouillon, harnessed jelly of the stars.
> Towards what? The forked crash of split thunder parts
> Our hearing momentwise. . . .

Something of what R. P. Blackmur, writing about the problems of judgment posed by Yeats's later practice, shrewdly called "ad libbing"—when "the artist poaches most on his resources," his stock and manner of performative contrivance—comes into **"Cape Hatteras"** with particular prominence. Yet the main scheme is solid and clear. From the perspective (introducing, again, a geologic framing) of that point on the continent's margin from which early in our century the first airship took off, this section's alternating "we" and "I" look out across the full expanse of time and space that has precipitated the world we know, above all the world of 1914-1918, and in what was planned from the start as "a kind of ode to Whitman" (September 12, 1927) the question is asked: Is our collective future what yours was, Walt, when you sang on through the massacres of that earlier war? Successive long stanzas of **"Cape Hatteras"** enact the modern forms of blinding, death-dealing human motion: in the sky, in industrial plants, in the armed battle fleets now set loose in the air and on the sea. The long closing appeal to Whitman—which incidentally produces one antithetical sixteen-line cadenza ("Cowslip and shadblow . . .") that strikes me as remarkably foreshadowing, even with its two extra lines, the irregular "sonnet" structure Robert Lowell would devise for the poetry of *Note-*

*book* and *History*—ends with a fine resolving simplicity in a final typographically divided four-stress line gesture:

> Afoot again, and onward without halt,—
> Not soon, nor suddenly,—no, never to let go
>   My hand
>     in yours,
>       Walt Whitman—
>         so—

In his anxiety to "get the 5-year load of The Bridge off my shoulders" ("You can't imagine how insufferably ponderous it has seemed, yes, more than once": October 29, 1929), Crane was sensitive to the danger of some final botch. But in sending off a last revised segment of **"Quaker Hill,"** the poem's sixth numbered section, he was more dismissive than the case requires. "[It] is not, after all," he wrote in a covering letter, "one of the major sections of the poem; it is rather by way of an 'accent mark' that it is valuable at all" (December 26, 1929). **"Quaker Hill"** is more substantial than that. Its compact succession of rhymed octaves draws out (with a caricaturing humor not quite overdone in its detail of proper names; an actual Mrs. Powitzki had been a Patterson, New York neighbor of Crane's) the ironic contrasts of past and present on a patch of historic ground now thoroughly suburbanized. Within this enclave of golf courses, antique-hunting, and real estate deals only the poet still sees, behind everything, "death's stare in slow survey." The legacy of the vanished Quakers, and of clashing Iroquois and Yankee, remains only in the whippoorwill's note of pain, though two embattled artists, the poet Emily Dickinson and the dancer Isadora Duncan, are remembered in the closing stanza as having known such meanings. The observing poet's own stake in the matter is caught up in directly autobiographical lines that condense a lifetime's private torment. I must, he writes—

> Shoulder the curse of sundered parentage,
> Wait for the postman driving from Birch Hill
> With birthright by blackmail . . .

—a turn into self-dramatization that carries across the elegiac close of **"Quaker Hill"** to the full-scale encounter of **"The Tunnel,"** the staged journey through an underworld of brokenness and death that now follows and that antithetically clears the way to *The Bridge*'s rhapsodic climax in **"Atlantis."**

**"The Tunnel"** owes not a little of its shadow play of metropolitan dissonance anddisorder to the precedent of "The Waste Land."[20] Language and figured allusion together cue us to this section's manner of unfolding. Its opening words are explicit about what is to be presented:

> Performances, assortments, résumés—
> Up Times Square to Columbus Circle lights
> Channel the congresses, nightly sessions,
> Refractions of the thousand theatres, faces—
> Mysterious kitchens. . . . You shall search them
>   all.

As if speaking to some other self that is also his own inmost being, the poet's scene-setting voice warns of nightmarish entrapments, in "interborough fissures of the mind" or simply in an entryway's revolving door—

> Where boxed alone a second, eyes take fright

—it transmits fragments of mindless subway chatter that are crystallized in time by sheer repetition—

> " . . . it's half past six she said—if
> you don't like my gate why did you
> swing on it, why *didja*
> swing on it
> anyhow—"

—and, in a resumption of the basic pentameter cadence, it summons up yet one more ghostly forebear from past history, the death-haunted visage of Poe:

> Your eyes like agate lanterns—on and on
> Below the toothpaste and the dandruff ads. . . .

Poetically **"The Tunnel"** is up and down, offering both brilliantly particular snapshots of city demoralization ("love" reduced here to a "burnt match skating in a urinal") and the turgidness of one late stanza of panicked exclamation ("Daemon . . . / O cruelly to inoculate the brinking dawn / With antennae toward worlds . . . ," etc.) before returning its protagonist, "like Lazarus," to open air and the miraculously recovered promise of the bridge-vision itself:

> —A sound of waters bending astride the sky
> Unceasing with some Word that will not die . . . !

Once more the poem's furthest projections are secured by a preliminary concreteness of notation; so the closing appeal to some ingathering "Hand of Fire" (the poem's "Daemon" transformed?) develops metaphorically from coasting lights and a tugboat's "steam" and "galvanic blare" in the lines just preceding.

"Atlantis," the final section of *The Bridge* though the first to have been drafted, was in Crane's mind all along as his point of arrival. More or less from the start this section was planned (in the words of his March 1926 outline to Otto Kahn) as "a sweeping dithyramb in which the Bridge becomes the symbol of consciousness spanning time and space." Add to this formulation the theme of love in its Dantesque power of reconciliation and renewal, and we have the interior climax of the eighth of its irregularly rhymed octaves, in the opening phrase of which the bridge receives—among all the other names now chanted out: "Tall Vision-of-the-Voyage," "Choir," "Psalm of Cathay," love's "Paradigm," "intrinsic myth," "Deity's glittering Pledge," "Flower," "Answerer," "Anemone," "Everpresence," "Song"—that one name ("steeled Cognizance") that rises directly from its erected structure:

> O Thou steeled Cognizance whose leap commits
> The agile precincts of the lark's return;

Within whose lariat sweep encinctured sing
In single chrysalis the many twain,—
Of stars Thou art the stitch and stallion glow
And like an organ, Thou, with sound of doom—
Sight, sound and flesh Thou leadest from time's
    realm
As love strikes clear direction for the helm.[21]

In the apprehension Crane means at this climax to impose, there is no opposition finally between knowledge and love, or between human enterprise and the forms of the created world—both of them double, both harboring the hope of an ultimate reconvergence.

Except in the upward thrust of its prepositions and adverbs—"Through the bound cable strands," "Up the index of night," "And on, obliquely up . . . ," "Onward and up the crystal-flooded aisle / White tempest nets file upward . . ."—**"Atlantis"** develops no forwarding action other than the poet's own lyric repetitions of prayer and praise. Its metaphoric complication has one fixed theme and is all to one end, a final concentrated celebration of the bridge presence itself as benedictory icon of all human striving:

> . . . iridescently upborne
> Through the bright drench and fabric of our veins. . . .

Journeys go off from it to new consummations ("We left the haven hanging in the night—"); eyes that open to its full luminousness must accept the stinging pain and severing violence ("blade on tendon blade") that always for Crane are inseparable from fulfillment; but the bridge itself remains "beyond time," its changeless arc "synoptic of all tides below," its "antiphonal" song justifying ("in azure swing") the historical world's self-renewing torment.

Planning as late as March of 1926 to make Columbus's soliloquy **The Bridge**'s opening section, Crane seems to have considered giving this paired finale the title "Cathay," and "Cathay" remains a primary name in the **"Atlantis"** section for the prophetically restored cities—their "white escarpments swinging into light"—which will be the issue of the bridge's rainbow covenant. Even the draft sent to Waldo Frank on August 3, 1926, though the accompanying letter calls it **"Atlantis,"** nowhere uses the name itself; this late draft lacks the entire penultimate stanza in which, in the published text, the word **"Atlantis"** is finally sounded. But at the start of that Isle of Pines summer Crane had reported to Patterson friends his excitement over Lewis Spence's *Atlantis in America,* a book ("the last . . . out on the subject": May 22, 1926) which *The Criterion* had reviewed in its January 1926 number; and the Blakean myth of a city-state of timeless artistry and wisdom reborn from ocean chaos seems in due course to have struck him as nearer his poem's imaginative grounding than the Columbian legend of great riches hidden away in remote regions of the earth. At any rate, in this penultimate stanza whose addition completed the poem we now read, it is to an

Atlantidean avatar of the bridge that the poet's own covenanting prayer goes up:

> Atlantis,—hold thy floating singer late!

Are we to think of it as after all "too impossible an ambition," as in a first exuberant outlining of "this **Bridge** thing" (February 18, 1923) Crane conceded to Gorham Munson that it might prove to be? No more so, I would say, than of any other imaginative venture strong enough to create for its readers as it moves forward an ideal conception of some "absolute" fulfillment, to use the heuristic word Crane himself risked deploying in **"General Aims and Theories."** What is not seriously in question is **The Bridge**'s demonstrated power to impose its singularly contrived expressiveness on our own sense of, at once—so far as we remain concerned with either matter—the continuing possibilities of poetry and the continuing task of recovering a measure of humane control over our common, our revolutionary, history. Not less than, say, Yeats's Byzantium poems and indeed the whole body of Yeats's work involved with the fantastications of *A Vision,* Crane's poem fixes itself in consciousness both through the figurative authority of its master image and through the surprising fitness and force—the delivered eloquence—of, again and again, individual lines and stanzas, beginnings and endings, self-confirming phrase cadences and a fresh renaming and reordering of recognizable experience. Poetry's value to us is, at best, only exemplary orvirtual. The one trustworthy measure of its success is whether we do or do not discover its achieved forms to have become an available and availing part of our own language-framed apprehension of things, our living collaborations of insight and judgment. The test with Hart Crane is simply to find out, in coming to know his work, whether some such consequence does actually follow.

NOTES

[1] The classifying phrase comes by way of Crane's concern, in replying to Yvor Winters's disparaging review, to detach his poem from the genre of *epic* and from useless comparisons with Homer, Dante, and Virgil. Though Crane is engaged here in special pleading, his counterarguments strike home. Winters *had,* once more, allowed "notions about the author's personality to blur the text"; he *was* now bound on a course shaped by considerations outside the distinctive province of poetry. For Crane's reply see Vivian H. Pemberton, "Hart Crane and Yvor Winters, Rebuttal and Review: A New Crane Letter," *American Literature,* May 1978, 276-81; reprinted, with the review itself, in *Critical Essays on Hart Crane,* ed. David R. Clark (1982), 102-14.

[2] "Hart Crane," in *On the Limits of Poetry* (1948), 225-37.

[3] Similarly it was to the author of *Our America* that, with his poem surging ahead, Crane wrote on August 19, 1926, of his excitement at realizing concretely "how

much of the past is living [in the present] under only slightly altered form, even in machinery and such-like."

[4] A "little unconscious calligramme on the mango tree" sent to Waldo Frank on May 22, 1926, was the one new poem Crane managed to write during his first fortnight on Isle of Pines. Whether it is identical with the poem mentioned to Winters, or with the irregular prose poem printed under the same title in *transition* in 1929 and posthumously in the *Key West* group, is uncertain.

Crane's synopsis of "Calgary Express," as planned, is given in Brom Weber's biography (p. 261).

[5] Once Crane's ambitions for *The Bridge* were at last being realized, his comments shifted to, among other concerns, the danger of following too strictly determined a scheme. Writing to Winters, who, though praising the sections Crane had sent him, was already worrying about the poem's over-all unity and logical coherence, Crane responded defensively: "The logical progression of the Bridge is well in my mind. But one has to fight even that. At least one has to be ready to doubt its validity thoroughly" at every fresh return of imaginative "temperature" or "fusion" (March 19, 1927).

[6] Interestingly, in writing this not to Waldo Frank but to Wilbur Underwood, the confidant of his private doings, Crane's definition of "my material" is not "this myth of America" but "'human nature' or what you will."

[7] As Sherman Paul notes, however, Williams's Columbus chapter—most of it presented, like "Ave Maria," in Columbus's voice—had appeared in *Broom* in March 1923, where Crane is not likely to have missed it. Its closing prayer, addressed to the Mother of God, conceivably influenced Crane's choice of title. Also, besides the presence in both *In the American Grain* and *The Bridge* of figures like Poe, De Soto, and the vaudeville clown Bert Williams, there is the prose epigraph to "Powhatan's Daughter"—a historical text (by William Strachey, on the colonization of Virginia) either lifted directly from William's "May-pole at Merrymount" chapter or transcribed from Kay Boyle's review of Williams's book in *transition,* April 1927.

[8] Untitled in 1855, "The Sleepers" was called "Night Poem" in the 1856 expansion of *Leaves of Grass* and in 1860 "Sleep-Chasings," when it was pushed back to the end of an again much enlarged collection. Under its final title it remains hidden away in the supplementary final third of the bulky post-1870 pritings of *Leaves of Grass.* But interestingly, as regards *The Bridge,* it is placed just after the poems "Passage to India" and "Prayer of Columbus."

[9] The passage may give us as good a way as any of glossing Crane's remark, in "Modern Poetry," that in Whitman is to be found the best expression of the "American psychosis," the permanent intractability of the forces determining our national existence. Whether or not Crane took special note of "The Sleepers" he knew that

Whitman's legacy was something more than an uncritical public boosterism, and temperately suggested to Allen Tate, who shared Winters's prejudice against Whitman, that he read the explicit attack in *Democratic Vistas* on those American characteristics ("materialism, industrialism, etc.") "of which you name him the guilty and hysterical spokesman" (July 13, 1930).

[10] R. P. Blackmur, in 1935, oddly considered it a self-evident mark of "failure" that *The Bridge* compels readers to "supply from outside the poem, and with the help of clues only," a "controlling" part of its meaning. So far had principled commentary, in the formative years of the New Criticism, absorbed the modernist *telos* of an absolute creative autonomy. But in the real transactions of literary history what accessible poem does otherwise? The matter is simply that the reader, too, becomes a contributing maker of the poem's presumptive significance. Blackmur himself, writing soon after about Yeats's final phase, put it down as the plainest of critical truths that all poetry "must be conceived as the manipulation of conventions that the reader will, or will not, take for granted," however the poet's "mastery of language" may have transformed these conventionalized formulations and meanings. See "New Thresholds, New Anatomies: Notes on a Text of Hart Crane" (1935) and "The Later Poetry of W. B. Yeats" (1936), in *Form and Value in Modern Poetry* (1957).

[11] *ABC of Reading* (1934), 46.

[12] But the amplitude and variousness of expression and imputed action in *The Bridge* do have their cumulative effect, an effect only increased in the perspective of later poetic history. "Judged by the standards of epic greatness," A. Alvarez bluntly declared in 1957, "[Crane's] failure is not in doubt," but in the next breath he was obliged to acknowledge—against, specifically, the undoubted "wit and temperance" of the later Wallace Stevens—the "more vivid range of experience" in Crane's writing (*The Shaping Spirit,* 110). And David Perkins, closing his comprehensive history of modern poetry in English with a generous appreciation of James Merrill's *Sandover* triology (a work establishing Merrill as "one of the most moving, imaginative, and ambitious of living poets"), matter-of-factly notes for comparison not only the superior "intensity" of *The Bridge* but the distinctively "wide and various" world Crane's poem persuasively unfolds (*A History of Modern Poetry: Modernism and After* [1987], 659).

[13] With an eye on the same structural features Mutlu Konuk Blasing, composing a "typology of the generic rhetorics of American poetry," speaks of "the diacritical interplay of fusion and diffusion" in Crane's lyric art and of *The Bridge*'s extension of this interplay to include historical time: *American Poetry: The Rhetoric of its Forms* (1987), 188-89.

[14] *The Dial,* never without skepticism in dealing with Crane, accepted this section at once for its June 1927 issue.

To be entirely accurate, *The Bridge* as a whole opens, following its title page and a grateful dedication to Otto Kahn, with an epigraph from an understated verse in the Book of Job: "From going to and fro in the earth, and from walking up and down in it." Sherman Paul, virtually alone in commenting on this, notes its fitness—it is Satan's brazen answer to God's question, Whence comest thou?—to the world of experience the poem consistently discloses.

[15] A reading preoccupied with archetypes and universals can make much of the sequence *prophet, pariah,* and *lover.* Harold Bloom, translating directly into allegory, identifies these with Dionysus, Ananke, and Eros—"the full triad of the Orphic destiny": "Introduction," *Hart Crane: Modern Critical Views,* ed. Harold Bloom (1986), 8.

[16] Except perhaps as a kind of tonal shading the "symbolism of the life and ages of man" that Crane, writing to Otto Kahn, claimed to have woven into this poem's "love-motif" (September 12, 1927) seems unregistered in the descriptive delicacy of its actual language.

[17] Yvor Winters, *In Defense of Reason* (1947), 92n.

[18] One line in "The Dance" which, ever since Winters called it "worthy of Racine" and later "one of the purest and most moving lines of our time," has repeatedly been cited as an instance of Crane's genuine mastery may also be an instance of his responsiveness to the best verse cadences in the work of his major contemporaries. Coming at the same frenzied climax, the line in question—"I could not pick the arrows from my side"—exactly reproduces the decisive simplicity of statement that Frost had put at the rhetorical center of "After Apple-Picking" (therefore of all of *North of Boston*): "I cannot rub the strangeness from my sight."

[19] Two fittingly sentimental versions of the same fable that could be heard half a century after *The Bridge* are the folksong-like "Sonny's Dream," which Jean Redpath popularized (and could find no author for), and Commander Cody's poignant rap-ballad "Mama Hated Diesels," written by Kevin "Blackie" Farrell. The refrain of "Sonny's Dream," like the whole of "Indiana," is in the woman's own voice: "Sonny, don't go away,/I'm here all alone." It is a song whose intervals, Jean Redpath remarks, "go straight for the tear ducts." The narrative in "Mama Hated Diesels" is delivered instead by the son, standing alone with the preacher by his mother's grave and telling the forlorn tale of how in time she lost both husband and son to the romance, trucker's version, of the open American road.

In Crane's fullest description of *The Bridge* (September 12, 1927) "Indiana," not yet written, was projected as the monologue of a farmer failed in the Gold Rush and saying farewell to his departing son, but with the dead mother's part in the story carrying its own symbolic import.

[20] Eliot's continuing interest in dramatic immediacy and demotic speech may well have been the particular spur to his accepting "The Tunnel" for *The Criterion.* During 1926 and 1927 he was publishing in *Criterion* his own dramatized "Sweeney" fragments.

[21] In the virtually complete draft of "Atlantis" sent to Waldo Frank on August 3, 1926, this stanza opens: "O Thou, carved cognizance. . . . " The shift to "steeled" is, all in all, an extraordinarily advantageous improvement. So, too, was omitting the comma after "Thou."

## John T. Irwin (essay date 1990)

SOURCE: "Back Home Again in India: Hart Crane's 'The Bridge'," in *Romantic Revolutions: Criticism and Theory,* edited by Kenneth R Johnson, Gilbert Chaitin, Karen Hanson, and Herbert Marks, Indiana University Press, 1990, pp. 269-96.

[*In the following essay, Irwin focuses on the question of self and national origin in the "Indiana" section of* The Bridge.]

Several years ago I published a book called *American Hieroglyphics,* that dealt with the influence of the decipherment of the Egyptian hieroglyphics on the literature of the American Renaissance and used this rather specialized area of inquiry as a means of raising larger questions about the figuration of the self and the search for origins in that form of late romanticism that is nineteenth-century American symbolism. It is this question of origins and their figuration, as posed in the writings of the American Renaissance, that I would like to pursue here into twentieth-century American poetry. One of the most common poetic figures in the English romantic tradition for the quest for origins (whether the origin of the self, of language, or of the human) is, of course, the search for the source of a river. In the wake of the publication of Sir James Bruce's *Travels to Discover the Source of the Nile* (1790), this figure for the pursuit of origins appears in works as various as Shelley's *Alastor,* Coleridge's "Kubla Khan," Book 6 of Wordsworth's *The Prelude,* and George Darley's *Nepenthe,* to name a few. In the American Renaissance the most striking examples of the figure are found in the works of Poe, whether in the unfinished *The Journal of Julius Rodman* (about a man who explores the Louisiana Territory ten years before Lewis and Clark, looking for, among other things, the source of the Mississippi) or in *The Narrative of A. Gordon Pym* (about a journey to the polar abyss). One might wonder for a moment what a journey to the polar abyss has to do with the search for the source of a river. The trope linking the two derives from the classical notion of the ultimate circularity of the waters of the earth: the notion that the waters of the oceans flow into the earth through openings at the poles, travel through subterranean passages to the equator, where they issue forth in springs and fountains that are the sources of great rivers that in turn flow back to the seas and thence to the polar abysses. As in any circular system, origin and end coincide, so that the search for the source of a great river can be approached from the opposite direction through a voyage to the polar abyss. (We might recall in this regard that in Book 6 of *The Prelude* Wordsworth correctly locates the source of the Nile in Abyssinia, and that in *Pym* the languages which the hero encounters in the vicinity of the polar abyss—Arabic, Coptic, and Ethiopic—are the languages of the Nile valley.)

Perhaps the most notable use of this romantic trope in twentieth-century American poetry occurs in Hart Crane's *The Bridge,* an epic representation of the search for American origins. Part of the poem's action involves a phantasized journey by its speaker back in time to the pre-Columbian world of the Indians to observe a primal scene of origin in which a people and a land are joined in the sacred marriage of the Indian chief Maquokeeta (whose name means "Big River") and the maiden Pocahontas, symbol of the virgin continent. And the metaphoric vehicle for this return to origin is the speaker's journey down the Mississippi River to the abyss of the Gulf. In his role as native son imaginatively present at, imaginatively participating in, the generation of the American self, Crane found that the work of depicting a primal scene of national origin inevitably involved for him a reassessment of the emotions associated with his personal origin, an examination of the way in which his stormy relationship with his parents affected his imagining of that central scene in which the seminal river pours into the abyss. That Crane understood this quest as a romantic project is clear from his 1930 response to Allen Tate's review of the poem: "The fact that you posit *The Bridge* at the end of a tradition of romanticism may prove to have been an accurate prophecy, but I don't yet feel that such a statement can be taken as a foregone conclusion. A great deal of romanticism may persist—of the sort to deserve serious consideration."[1]

In pursuing this inquiry into the figuration of origins in *The Bridge,* I want to focus in particular on the **"Indiana"** section of the poem. In his 1927 letter to his benefactor Otto Kahn, which outlines the plan and progress of *The Bridge,* Crane, noting that the **"Indiana"** section "is not complete as yet," describes it as "the monologue of an Indiana farmer; time, about 1960. He has failed in the gold-rush and is returned to till the soil. His monologue is a farewell to his son, who is leaving for a life on the sea. It is a lyrical summary of the period of conquest, and his wife, the mother who died on the way back from the gold-rush, is alluded to in a way which implies her succession to the nature-symbolism of Pocahontas" (*L,* 307). What interests us in this description of **"Indiana"** is that the roles assigned to the father and mother in this section as it was conceived in 1927 are reversed in the published version of 1930. In its completed form **"Indiana"** is the monologue not of a father but of a mother: it is the wife of the Indiana farmer who bids farewell to her son as he leaves for a life on the sea. And, conversely, the parent who dies on the way back from the gold rush is the father rather than the mother. The question, then, is what oc-

curred during the two-year period between Crane's description of "Indiana" in the letter to Kahn and the completion of the poem, to cause this reversal in the roles that had originally been projected for the father and mother.

We know that the single most important event in Crane's personal life during this period was the definitive break he made with his mother in the spring of 1928 and the subsequent reversal in his long-standing opposing attitudes toward his parents. Since at least late adolescence Crane had been close to his mother, who, seeing her own "artistic" temperament reborn in her son, encouraged his poetic career, and either at odds with or estranged from his father, for whom success in business was an ideal inherited from his own father that he had tried to pass on to his son, an ideal in relation to which Hart could never be anything but a failure. When Grace and Clarence Crane's marriage began to fall apart, their son became both a prize to be won and a weapon to be wielded in the battle between them. Crane's alliance with his mother lasted from the time of his parents' divorce in 1917 until the early months of 1928, even though his precarious finances required that he remain on civil terms with Clarence Crane (or C. A. as he was called), to whom he periodically applied for loans. At this period Crane and his mother were both living in Los Angeles. Hart was acting as secretary and companion to Herbert Wise, and Grace was staying with her ailing mother in a bungalow in Hollywood. In February 1928, Hart, perhaps in response to Grace's requests that he introduce her to his Hollywood friends or fearing that she might hear of his escapades, told his mother that he was a homosexual. There are conflicting reports about Grace's immediate reaction to the news, but Crane told a friend that she was "visibly upset" and that "for days afterward she seemed to him cold and contemptuous."[2] Whatever the truth was, the disclosure of his homosexuality placed an enormous strain on his relationship with his mother, a strain that was soon compounded when, after quitting his job with Wise at the end of February, Crane moved in with his mother and grandmother in mid-March. His grandmother was dying, and Hart spent part of each day serving as her nurse and companion while at the same time coping with his mother's own "nervous collapse." For the next two months the relationship between Hart and Grace steadily worsened. Unterecker describes Crane's

> growing conviction that his mother's love for him
> had degenerated into a brutal possessiveness. . . .
> Not only did he discover that Grace was jealous of
> his love for his grandmother; he also discovered—
> recalling his past—a lifelong pattern of jealousy:
> Grace "guarding" him from any deep affection for
> his father, for his other relatives, for the girls whom,
> in a more conventional boyhood, he might have come
> to love. . . . She would never voluntarily, he felt,
> allow him to love anyone other than her; nor, he
> was sure, would she ever allow him a life substantially
> independent of her. (p. 540)

By the end of May 1928, Crane was desperate to leave, and after packing surreptitiously for a week, he stole away from the bungalow in the dead of night heading for New York, never to see his mother again. If, as Emerson says, poets write with actions as well as with words, then the route that Crane chose in leaving his mother to return to the east was a symbolic statement whose gloss is to be found in *The Bridge.* After traveling by train from Los Angeles to New Orleans, he continued by ship through the Gulf of Mexico and up the East Coast to New York. In a letter dated June 14, 1928, written to his father after his return, he gave some indication of the significance of this journey in his description of a day he spent in New Orleans: "The boat ride down the delta of the Mississippi (we were from 10 till 5 p.m. completing it) was one of the great days of my life. It was a place I had so often imagined and, as you know, written about in my River section of *The Bridge.* There is something tragically beautiful about the scene, the great, magnificent Father of Waters pouring itself at last into the oblivion of the Gulf!"[3] In recounting his boat ride on "the great, magnificent Father of Waters" to his own father, Crane evokes this transitional place he "had so often imagined," this threshold where the seminal river pours itself into the oblivion of the gulf, as a "tragically beautiful . . . scene"—a primal scene in a Oedipal tragedy, I would suggest. Pausing in New Orleans at mid-continent, midway in his flight from his mother, Crane recalled the "River section of *The Bridge*" and the quester's imaginative identification with the hobo Dan Midland, whose body was cast into the Mississippi to descend to the submarine, amniotic world of the Gulf. He may have sensed even then that his eastward flight from his mother would turn out to be a circular journey like all of those in *The Bridge,* a journey whose turnings would finally bring him back to the oblivion of the Gulf four years later.

In spite of periodic setbacks, Hart's relationship with his father improved steadily after his break with Grace. Hart's new sense of the way in which his mother had turned him against his father was matched by a new willingness onClarence Crane's part to admit that his own life was no model for his son's. In July 1928, the elder Crane wrote Hart:

> You and I agree now as never before that your father has made a failure of his life because he has paid too much attention to hard work and not enough to play. I have been too ambitious for things that really did not amount to anything at all. . . . It was born in my father to be saving and energetic. All of my younger life he kept me at it until I got the same impression of things . . . so I kept at it and kept at it. . . . Now, I don't want you to do this way, for I have lived to see the folly of it all. . . . I think you write well, and unquestionably have better than an average ability for it, but no business is any good unless it pays a dividend and if writing does not pay a dividend then you have to do something else. . . . I cannot tell you what to do. On that subject my advice has been all wrong for many years. (*L,* 627-29).

But while Crane grew closer to his father, he became increasingly hostile toward his mother, until the one he had always loved best came to seem his nemesis. Unterecker describes the elaborate precautions that Crane took during the rest of his life to keep his mother from learning of his whereabouts: "Each flight—prompted always by terror that she might persuade him to return—led to an orgy of drunken escape and complex moves from place to place as, swearing friends to secrecy, he attempted to cover his trail. . . . So long as she lived, he felt, she would continue to hunt him down" (p. 542). It is significant that while Crane was working on *The Bridge* and its vision of a return to national origin, a return whose anthropomorphic representation was the son's return to the womb of the triple goddess (the virgin-mother-whore Pocahontas), he was fleeing desperately from his own mother. In February 1929, Crane wrote to his friends the Rychtariks from Paris, "My mother has made it impossible for me to live in my own country" (*L,* 338).

That Crane understood what was involved psychologically in his mother's obsessive attachment is clear from a letter he wrote to Grace's sister-in-law Zell in the late fall of 1928: Grace "is profoundly attached to me, really loves me, I know. But there are mixtures of elements in this attachment that are neither good for her nor for me. Psychoanalysis reveals many things that it would be well for Grace to know" (Unterecker, p. 565). Crane's mention of psychoanalysis no doubt reflects the knowledge of psychoanalytic theory that he had acquired during the fall of 1928 from his friend Solomon Grunberg, who was part owner of a bookstore Crane frequented and who practiced as a lay analyst at the time Crane knew him. Unterecker reports that though Hart "declined Grunberg's offer to explore his mind ('If I let myself be psychoanalyzed, I'll *never* finish *The Bridge!*'), he did, on long walks, take advantage of Grunberg's listening silences, his offhand leading questions, his summaries of pertinent 'classical' cases" (p. 566). During October and November of 1928, "Hart worried incessantly about his relationship to his mother and father, Grunberg said; and, once, on one of their meanderings, Hart talked about the nightmares he had been having, nightmares that made insomnia preferable to sleep" (Unterecker, p. 566). Unterecker, records two of the dreams that Crane recounted to Grunberg, dreams that not only shed light on Crane's relationship with his parents at this period but also suggest the way in which his differing attitudes toward his father and mother affected his imagining of the primal scene of origin in *The Bridge.*

Before examining these two dreams in some detail, we should note that Crane's knowledge of psychoanalysis, however slight or simplified, tends to give a dual focus to a psychoanalytic reading of his poetry by raising the possibility that Crane consciously introduced psychoanalytic structures into his poem to shape the biographical material. As a result, a psychoanalytic reading of *The Bridge* inevitably becomes an exercise in the history of ideas as well, which is to say, becomes by implication a study of the influence of psychoanalysis on the work of an American poet of the 1920s. In what follows, the psychoanalytic discourse moves back and forth across three

Cranian "texts" that, in their bearing on the poet's relationship with his parents, exhibit a revealing structural continuity—a poetic text (*The Bridge*), a biographical text (Crane's life as reflected in his letters and the biographies of Horton and Unterecker), and a dream text (the two nightmares that Crane recounted to Grunberg which Unterecker includes in hisbiography). Though the poetic and the dream texts both involve the encryption of personal material, the level of encryption (the force of repression) is obviously greater in the poetry than in the dreams, for not only was the poetic text certain to be seen by Crane's parents but, to judge from the letters to his father and mother citing salient passages from the poem, Crane actively called it to their attention as part of what appears to have been an oblique form of self-revelation, a veiled exhibition of his deepest feelings about his parents, his personal origin.

The first of Crane's two nightmares, according to Unterecker,

> seemed to Grunberg clearly about Hart's father and about Hart's own sense of inferiority. Grunberg said he was sure Hart was well aware of its symbolic content. It involved a river, Hart told him. Hart had somehow gotten into a little boat—a rowboat or a canoe—and was floating down the center of the river. He could see the shores on either side and far in the distance he could hear a waterfall. Though his boat floated along very peacefully, he began to worry as the noise of the waterfall got louder. Finally he became frightened. The boat had picked up speed. At it was swept closer and closer to the waterfall, he suddenly saw, standing on the shore just above the falls, an enormous naked Negro. Hart could not keep his eyes off the Negro's huge penis. Even though the noise of the falls was deafening and he was thoroughly frightened, he kept watching. Suddenly he realized that he was naked, too. The boat was at the very brink of the falls now and he felt himself covered with shame. His own penis was tiny, he knew, as tiny as a baby's, and he forced himself to look at it. (pp. 566-67)

The resonances of this dream both in Crane's personal life and in his poetry are far-reaching and complex. Grunberg was undoubtedly correct in thinking that the dream was "about Hart's father and about Hart's own sense of inferiority," yet we should avoid reading the figure of the black man in the dream as simply and solely an image of Crane's father. He is that, but he is a great deal more as well. Keep in mind that it was less than six months prior to this dream that Hart, in describing his boat ride on "the great, magnificent Father of Waters" to the elder Crane, pointed out that he had previously depicted this "tragically beautiful . . . scene" of the Mississippi "pouring itself at last into the oblivion of the Gulf" in the "River section of *The Bridge*." The relevant part of **"The River"**—both to Crane's real boat ride down the Mississippi Delta and to his nightmare boat ride past the naked black man on the bank—is obvious. As the body of the hobo Dan Midland, who has apparently been killed in

a confrontation with the sinister "Sheriff, Brakeman and Authority," is floating down the Mississippi, Crane describes the river's progress in terms that prefigure his dream:

> You will not hear it as the sea; even stone
> Is not more hushed by gravity . . . But slow,
> As loth to take more tribute—sliding prone
> Like one whose eyes were buried long ago
>
> The River, spreading, flows—and spends your
>    dream.
> What are you, lost within this tideless spell?
> You are your father's father, and the stream—
> A liquid theme that floating niggers swell.
>
> Damp tonnage and alluvial march of days—
> Nights turbid, vascular with silted shale
> And roots surrendered down of morraine clays;
> The Mississippi drinks the farthest dale.
>
> O quarrying passion, undertowed sunlight!
> The basalt surface drags a jungle grace
> Ochreous and lynx-barred in lengthening might;
> Patience! and you shall reach the biding place!
>
> Over De Soto's bones the freighted floors
> Throb past the City storied of three thrones.
> Down two more turns the Mississippi pours
> (Anon tall ironsides up from salt lagoons)
>
> And flows within itself, heaps itself free.
> All fades but one thin skyline 'round . . . Ahead
> No embrace opens but the stinging sea;
> The River lifts itself from its long bed,
>
> Poised wholly on its dream, a mustard glow
> Tortured with history, its one will—flow!
> —The Passion spreads in wide tongues, chocked
>    and slow,
> Meeting the Gulf, hosannas silently below.[4]

That passion is the subject of these lines seems certain, indeed they could be said to represent a double dream of passion consistent with a double identification with father and mother. At the climax, the male Father of Waters "lifts itself from its long bed" to pour into the female Gulf. Crane had enclosed an earlier version of these seven stanzas in a letter to his mother dated June 18, 1927, saying that he hoped she would "enjoy the epic sweep of the thing—like a great river of time that takes everything and pours it into a great abyss" (*LF,* 584). But prior to this union of male and female, there is a union of male and male as the poetic quester, imaginatively identified with Dan Midland's corpse, enters the Father of Waters. (This same structure—a union, an imaginative identification, of male and male preceding a union of male and female—governs the quester's subsequent fantasized participation in the sacred marriage of Maquokeeta and Pocahontas, to which **"The River"** leads.)

One of the obvious similarities between Crane's description of the quester's entry into the Father of Waters and his own nightmare of a boat ride down river is that the river in each case is associated with the figure of a black man. In the poem the Mississippi is described as "a liquid theme that floating niggers swell," while in the dream Crane sees on the river bank a naked black man with a "huge penis." Indeed, the image of a huge penis seems to be implicit in the passage from the poem as well: the floating blacks "swell" the paternal stream whose dark "basalt surface drags a jungle grace / Ochreous and lynx-barred in *lengthening might*" [italics mine] as it moves toward the climactic union with the Gulf. The association of the muddy, brown Mississippi with the figure of a powerful black man is easily understood, and Crane would have found a particularly striking example of this association in a popular Broadway musical of the day. *Show Boat* had opened in New York on December 27, 1927, and one of the high points of the musical was the song "Ol' Man River." (The Mississippi had been much in the news during the spring and summer of 1927 when *Show Boat* was being readied for Broadway. Its spring flood had been one of the worst in modern times, making that year memorable in the lore of the river. One recalls the opening of "The Old Man" section of Faulkner's *The Wild Palms,* "Once [it was in Mississippi in May in the flood year 1927]. . . . ") Jerome Kern and Oscar Hammerstein had written "Ol' Man River" with Crane's friend the black singer and actor Paul Robeson in mind. The show's producer, Florenz Ziegfeld, had announced the signing of Robeson for the role of Joe as early as December 1926, but because of delays in getting *Show Boat* into rehearsal, Robeson accepted other engagements and as a result did not appear in the New York production,[5] though he recorded "Ol' Man River" for Victor Records on March 1, 1928, with Paul Whiteman's Concert Orchestra[6] and starred in the London production of *Show Boat* which opened in early May 1928. Charles Morgan, commenting on Robeson's version of "Ol' Man River" in *The New York Times* for May 27, 1928, predicted that his "hymning of the Mississippi" was sure to "become popular."[7] "Ol' Man River" became identified with Robeson, and in turn Robeson's image as the archetypal noble black man of the 1920s struggling against the white man's oppressive paternalism became associated with the song. Crane's nightmare about the enormous naked black man on the river bank occurred in October or November 1928, and on November 30, 1928, Crane's friend Herbert Wise took him to see a performance of *Show Boat* in New York (*L,* 331), though Crane had undoubtedly heard the record of "Ol' Man River" and knew of its dramatic context long before this. In late December, Crane saw *Show Boat* again in London, visited Robeson backstage, and later spent time with Robeson and his wife in their London home (*L,* 333). Crane had first met Robeson in 1924 when the actor starred in Eugene O'Neill's *All God's Chillun Got Wings,* a play "about a negro who marries a white woman," as Crane wrote his mother in March 1924 (*LF,* 287). To judge from another letter to his mother two months later, the black singer had assumed heroic stature for Crane: "Robeson is one of the most superb sort of people. Very black, a deep resonance to his voice and actor eyes, Phi Beta Kappa, half-back on

Walter Camps all-star eleven, and a very fine mind and nature" (*LF,* 315).

Given the popular practice of imaging the Father of Waters as a powerful black man, it requires no great imaginative leap to read the black man by the river in Crane's nightmare as an encrypted image of Crane's father, which is to say, as an image of the threatening aspect of the father. Yet to understand the full significance of the figure of the black man in Crane's dream, we must consider a crucial passage from his life in which he apparently felt that his father had treated him like a Negro. In January 1920, Hart, honoring his father's wish that he enter the family business, went to work for the Crane Chocolate Company in Cleveland and remained in his father's employ for the next fourteen months. Near the end of February 1921, the elder Crane assigned Hart to supervise a basement storeroom in a Cleveland restaurant that the company owned. Unterecker describes the surroundings:

> Across a basement corridor from him were the restaurant kitchens, where Hart delighted in the relaxed, free, good times of the Negro cooks and dishwashers. Grace, when Hart wrote her of his transfer, felt that C. A.'s assigning Hart to this job in this place—particularly because Hart had replaced a discharged Negro handyman—was a deliberate effort to humiliate son and mother; but Hart, lacking Grace's prejudices, managed to thrive on the underground life. For the first time in months he set to work on a poem and in the leisure of his storeroom turned out the first drafts of "Black Tambourine," a study of the store's porter, who, "forlorn in the cellar," seemed caught between two unavailable worlds: lost Africa nothing more than racial memory, and the white, smiling world of the restaurant upstairs barred to him by the world's closed door. (p. 188)

Commenting on the poem in a letter to Gorham Munson, Crane says that "in the popular mind" the Negro has been "sentimentally or brutally 'placed'" in a "midkingdom . . . somewhere between man and beast" (*L,* 58). Crane introduces the figure of Aesop into the poem not only to evoke through Aesop's animal fables this world midway "between man and beast" but also to suggest the way in which the slave Aesop transfigured and thus redeemed the condition of slavery, in which men are treated like animals, by the poetic art of fables in which animals behave like men:

> Aesop, driven to pondering, found
> Heaven with the tortoise and the hare;
> Fox brush and sow ear top his grave
> And mingling incantations on the air.
>
>                                    (p. 4)

On the morning of April 19, 1921, Crane's father paid a surprise visit to the restaurant where his son worked. Hart had left the storeroom and was having a late breakfast with his black friends in the kitchen. As Unterecker recounts it, "their jokes and stories filled the big kitchen with good-natured laughter, and none of them saw Hart's father descend the basement stairs." The elder Crane "reprimanded Hart, ordered him to return to the storeroom, and, as Hart turned to go, added that since Hart was again living with his mother, he could eat his meals with her, too. Hart interpreted the remark as an attack both on himself and on Grace. He whirled to face his father, threw the storeroom keys on the floor, and, in front of the other help, yelled that he was through with C. A. for good. C. A., by now as angry as his son, turned white with rage, shouting that if Hart didn't apologize he would be disinherited. Hart climaxed the scene by screaming curses on his father and his father's money and rushing blindly from the store" (p. 198). The following day Crane wrote to Gorham Munson that he had quit his father's employ for good after having "been treated like a dog now for two years" (*L*, 55). And later he complained that he had "thrown away" two years "at thefeet" of his father performing "peon duties" (Unterecker, p. 200). In view of Crane's evocation of the black's midkingdom "somewhere between man and beast" in **"Black Tambourine,"** it seems clear that Crane felt his father had kept him in economic slavery, had treated the poet (Aesop) "like a dog" by placing him among, and equating him with, the descendants of black slaves who depended on the elder Crane's paternal care.

This early equation of the images of son, poet, slave, and black man in Crane's mind helps explain the later association in **"The River"** of the poetic quester and the blacks as singers. In the passage that immediately precedes the quester's imagined descent into the Father of Waters, Crane evokes the image of the Mississippi in the context of a black spiritual:

> Oh, lean from the window, if the train slows
> 　down,
> As though you touched hands with some ancient
> 　clown,
> —A little while gaze absently below
> And hum *Deep River* with them while they go.
> 　　　　　　　　　　　　　　　(p. 68)

The opening line of "Deep River" ("Deep river, my heart lies over Jordan") is echoed a few lines later in the description of those who, feeding the river timelessly, "win no frontier by their wayward plight, / But drift in stillness, as from Jordan's brow" (p. 68). (The Mississippi and the Jordan are also associated in the verse of "Ol' Man River": the black man says, "Let me go 'way from de Mississippi, / Let me go 'way from de white men boss, / Show me dat stream called de river Jordan, / Dat's de ol' stream dat I long to cross.") It is worth noting that Paul Robeson recorded "Deep River" for Victor Records on May 10, 1927,[8] and that Crane, though he began jotting down lines for **"The River"** as early as July 1926, wrote the bulk of the poem in mid-June 1927 (Unterecker, p. 490). We should also recall that according to an early outline of *The Bridge*, which he included in a letter to Otto Kahn dated March 18, 1926, Crane planned to make the dramatic speaker of one section of the poem a "Negro

porter" on the "Calgary Express . . . singing to himself (a jazz form for this) of his sweetheart and the death of John Brown alternately" (*L*, 241). The section, which was intended to take "in the whole racial history of the Negro in America,"[9] as Crane noted in a synopsis, was never written, but traces of it can perhaps be seen in **"The River"** with its reference to "Pullman breakfasters" (p. 68) and its image of someone leaning from the train to hum "Deep River." At any rate the association of the Mississippi with the song of a black singer is clearly present in the poem even before the crucial stanza in which river, song, and singer merge, as, "lost within this tideless spell," you become "your father's father, and the stream—/ A liquid theme that floating niggers swell." The river is an unending stream of song, a "tideless spell," which is to say, a timeless (magical) spell (incantation, verse, charm [Latin *carmina,* song]) in which the quester immerses himself and to which he joins his own song. And what the river-song is to the black singer, the bridgesong is to the poetic quester, as Crane makes clear when he echoes this passage from **"The River"** in the concluding **"Atlantis"** section: Having addressed the symbolic bridge of the poem as "O River-throated," the quester exhorts his poetic vision: "Atlantis,—hold thy floating singer late!" (p. 116). As the "liquid theme" of the river holds the "floating niggers," so the visionary submerged continent, the mythic land bridge between East and West, is meant to hold the "floating singer." Significantly, the words "niggers" and "singer" are anagrams of one another, an encrypted association that Crane, who describes in "O Carib Isle!" how the temporal erosions of nature "shift, subvert, / And anagrammatize your name" (p. 156), clearly intended. For this anagram, this hidden equation of names, expresses Crane's sense (dating from at least the time of **"Black Tambourine"**) that for white, paternal, commercial America the "singer" (poet) is a "nigger" (slave). The "niggers" and the "singer" are both described as "floating" not only because they expect, in trusting themselves to their songs as a swimmer trusts himself to the water, to be buoyed up and sustained by the creative stream, but also because blacks and poets were considered by commercial America to be economically unstable, to be floaters or drifters. And it is in this regard that the "niggers" and the "singer" are associated with the hoboes in **"The River,"** who are in turnpresented as singers:

> Strange bird-wit, like the elemental gist
> Of unwalled winds they offer, singing low
> *My Old Kentucky Home* and *Casey Jones,*
> *Some Sunny Day.* I heard a road-gang chanting so.
> 　　　　　　　　　　　　　　　(p.64)

What these associations ultimately suggest is the extent to which Crane in his self-embraced role of son-poet-slave identified himself with the Negro and thus the extent to which the figure of the naked black man in his dream is not just an image of Crane's father but of Crane as well. Indeed, I would suggest that the black man in Crane's dream is the son's idealized image of the union of father and son, a figure that combines in one person the powerful Father of Waters and the floating black singer, the paternal master and the filial poet-slave. If the black is a dual figure who represents the son's idealized attempt to assume the father's power and authority without directly combatting the father (a combat that would involve the son's risking either his own destruction or the destruction of the paternal authority to recognize and acknowledge), then we can understand why, in describing the quester's union with the Father of Waters, Crane says that, "lost within this tideless spell," you become not your father but "your father's father"; for if the father is himself a son (as this image of the "father's father" implies), if he is not his own origin but merely a predecessor caught in the same generational series in which the son finds himself, then a paternal authority based on the father's temporal priority to the son is thereby shown to be circumscribed: Father Time is represented as being encompassed (circularized) by the timeless (m)other. It is this timeless mother, the muse, who has the power to circularize time, to confer generational earliness, paternal authority, and originality through the tideless spell of song. Which brings us to the other dream that Crane recounted to Grunberg.

In contrast to the dream in which the father appears in the symbolic form of a black man, the other nightmare of Crane's that Unterecker records is explicitly about Crane's mother. The dream was so vivid, Unterecker notes, that Crane

> had the feeling, long after he was awake, that it was something he had actually experienced. He had gone to bed exhausted, and when he woke up, he was in his old room on 115th Street. He got up, remembering that he had to hunt for something in the attic, and as he stumbled through the dusty attic—half awake—he kept trying to remember what he was looking for. Whatever it was, it was in a trunk. He was sure of that. It was very dark in the attic, but when he found the trunk, there was enough light for him to see that it was full of this mother's clothes. He started rummaging through them, looking for whatever it was he was looking for, pulling out dresses, shoes, stockings, underclothing. But the trunk was so full, it seemed he would never find what he was after. There was so much to look at that when he found the hand, he hardly realized it was a human hand; but when he found another hand and a piece of an arm, he knew there was a body in the trunk. He kept pulling out piece after piece of it, all mixed in with the clothing. The clothing was covered with blood. It was not until he had almost emptied the trunk that he realized he was unpacking the dismembered body of his mother. (p. 567)

I would suggest that this dream expresses, in a series of redundant symbols, the son's desire for a total return to the womb, indeed expresses that desire with a vengeance in its symbolic reduction of the mother's body to a trunk (which is to say, a torso) containing a body that has itself been violently reduced in size in order to fit in this container. Awakening from an exhausted sleep with its sug-

gestion of the amniotic state, Crane finds himself in "his old room" at his maternal grandparents' house on East 115th Street in Cleveland. As an adult, Crane always thought of the house on 115th Street, where he lived from the ages of eight to seventeen, as his family home, and he referred to his bedroom in the north tower of the old Victorian structure as his "ivory tower" (Unterecker, p. 21) and "sanctum de la tour" (Unterecker, photo following p. 48). In a July 1923 letter to Charlotte Rychtarik, Crane reminisced,

> When I think of that room, it is almost to give way to tears, because I shall never find my way back to it. It is not necessary, of course, that I should, but just the same it was the center and beginning of all that I am and ever will be, the center of such pain as would tear me to pieces to tell you about, and equally the center of great joys! *The Bridge* seems to me so beautiful—and it was there that I first thought about it, and it was there that I wrote **"Faustus and Helen."** . . . And all this is, of course, connected very intimately with my Mother, my beautiful mother whom I am so glad you love and speak about (*L,* 140).

This dream of the son's return to the home of his mother's mother resembles the structure we noted in **"The River"** in which the quester, entering the river of time that leads back to the oblivion of the gulf, becomes his father's father. The son attempts to circumvent his parents' generation and its conflicts between mother and father and between parent and child by identifying himself with his grandparents' generation, that prior authority to which his parents were subject, the doting grandparents who are the grandchild's natural ally and his court of higher appeal. In the lyric **"My Grandmother's Love Letters"** (1920), Crane memorialized his maternal grandmother Elizabeth Belden Hart in a scenario that anticipates details of his dream. On a rainy night the poet sits in an attic reading "the letters of my mother's mother, / Elizabeth, / That have been pressed so long / Into a corner of the roof / That they are brown and soft / And liable to melt as snow" (p. 6). (One wonders if the letters had been kept in a trunk in the attic?) As he reads these letters that seem as fragile as the snows of yester-year, the poet attempts to journey back through his grandparents' written memories to the world before his birth. Looking at this intimate exchange of correspondence, this written intercourse between his grandmother and grandfather, the poet seems to be imaginatively present at a scene of origin which is, if not more primal than, certainly prior to that of parental intercourse and clearly more comforting to the poet since these letters attest to a love between his grandparents that Crane had begun to feel was originally absent between his own parents, an original absence that seemed to call into question his personal origin.

In the closing lines of **"My Grandmother's Love Letters"** Crane raises the same question that concerns him in the sections of *The Bridge* that follow the primal scene of origin in **"The Dance":** whether, if one is able to journey back imaginatively to the origin, one can then return to the present with that vision of origin intact. The poet asks himself,

> "Are your fingers long enough to play
> Old keys that are but echoes:
> Is the silence strong enough
> To carry back the music to its source
> And back to you again
> As though to her?"
>
> Yet I would lead my grandmother by the hand
> Through much of what she would not understand;
> And so I stumble. And the rain continues on the
>   roof
> With such a sound of gently pitying laughter.
>
> (p. 6)

The image used to evoke the return to origin—carrying "back the music to its source"—suggests the stream of song flowing to the gulf at the end of **"The River"**—origin and end, source and abyss coinciding in this circular journey.

It is significant that in the months immediately preceding this dream of finding his mother's dismembered body in a trunk Crane was much concerned with establishing a home of his own. His childhood home on 115th Street in Cleveland (the setting of the dream) had been sold in 1925, and his break with his mother three years later seems to have reawakened and intensified his feelings of homelessness. In early July 1928—some two weeks after his letter describing the boat ride on the "great, magnificent Father of Waters"—Crane wrote his fatheragain, asking for a loan to buy a small farmhouse near Patterson, New York, where he was then living, and offering as collateral the $5,000 bequest from his maternal grandfather that was being held in trust for him until his grandmother's death. Clarence Crane replied that business difficulties made it impossible for him to advance Hart the money at that time. By the end of the month Hart wrote his father that he hadn't "enough cash to even get into New York" and that "at present I haven't a place to lay my head": "I've never felt quite as humiliated. I can't ask you for anything more, and I'm not" (*LF*, 626-27). Six weeks later, however, Crane's maternal grandmother died, and suddenly, with his financial worries temporarily at an end, it seemed that he would be able to have a place of his own. But at this point his mother intervened. Trying to coerce Hart into returning to California for a reconciliation, Grace refused to sign the papers needed by the bank to release the $5,000 legacy from his grandfather. In November, Crane sent his mother a telegram threatening her with legal action. Grace replied by telegram that she had signed the papers, but threatened in turn to ask Hart's father "to use his influence with the bank against paying him his inheritance on the grounds of his drinking habits" (Horton, pp. 249-50). Interpreting this as a veiled threat to tell his father about his homosexuality, Hart used his inheritance to leave immediately for Europe, feeling that his mother not only had tried to keep him from having a home of his own but also, as he wrote his friends the Rychtariks, had made it impossible for him to

live in his own country. Crane subsequently memorialized this conflict with Grace over his grandfather's legacy in **"Quaker Hill"** where, faced with the sweeping historical question "Where are my kinsmen and the patriarch race?", the quester has to

> Shoulder the curse of sundered parentage,
> Wait for the postman driving from Birch Hill
> With birthright by blackmail, the arrant page
> That unfolds a new destiny to fill. . . .
>
> (p. 105)

The curse of sundered parentage—in the sense both of his parents' divorce and of his break with his mother and his previous estrangement from his father—was much on Crane's mind during the months he spent writing the final sections of **The Bridge,** for the condition of sundered parentage had come to seem an image of the state of the modern American suffering the effects of a spiritual divorce that had shattered an original union between man and nature in the pre-Columbian "nature-world" of the Indians. Because of that divorce of man and nature, the modern American is a son estranged from the maternal body of the virgin continent, a body which, in his frustration, he violates in search of wealth rather than cultivating and making fruitful. Following immediately on the quester's vision of the nature world of the Indians in **"The Dance,"** **"Indiana"** depicts a characteristic moment in the historical disintegration of that union of man and nature: the deracinating effect that a farmer's abandoning his land to join the Colorado gold rush has on his son who, years later, runs away to sea. The farmer, baffled in his search for gold, died on the way back from Colorado, and the poem's dramatic speaker, the farmer's wife, tells her son the story of his origin as he prepares to leave their Indiana farm.

There can be little doubt that the events of 1928—Crane's break with his mother, his flight and her pursuit through letters, his rapprochement with his father, the battle with his mother over his grandfather's legacy, and his unsuccessful attempt to buy his own home—significantly shaped **"Indiana,"** and these events—along with the nightmares that Unterecker records and what they reveal of Crane's feelings about his father and mother during this period—shed light on Crane's most important alteration of the poem: the reversal that occurred in the roles originally planned for the father and mother in the poem as outlined in the 1927 letter to Kahn. Perhaps the best way to understand the full meaning of this reversal is to recall critics' standard objection to **"Indiana."** From the first reviews of **The Bridge,** **"Indiana"** was singled out as the weakest section of the poem because of what critics felt was its cloying sentimentality. That opinion has generally persisted, supported by the knowledge that **"Indiana"** was one of the last sections completed and the sense that **The Bridge** was finished not out of theforce of its original inspiration but under the pressure of bringing to an end a project that had gone on for seven years. That the tone of **"Indiana"** is sentimental cannot be denied, but what critics have tended to ignore in attributing the poem's tonal lapses either to a momentary failure of Crane's art or to his loss of belief in the project as a whole is that unlike nearly all the other sections of **The Bridge,** "Indiana" is spoken not by Crane's surrogate, the poetic quester, but by another persona. And, to judge from the other major instance of this device in the poem ("**Ave Maria**"), one of the purposes of these sections is to characterize their speakers by the form and quality of the poetry they are given to speak. Thus in "**Ave Maria**" Columbus uses dramatic blank verse of an almost Elizabethan grandeur, while in "**Indiana**" the mother speaks in the mawkish quatrains of a nineteenth-century popular ballad. In each case the verse form evokes a cultural moment personified by its speaker. Crane uses a similar device in "**Virginia**," where, as Susan Jenkins Brown has pointed out, he parodies a popular song of the 1920s "What Do You Do Sunday, Mary?" from the musical *Poppy* to characterize "a little Five-and-Ten salesgirl-virgin letting down her hair from her Cathedral tower [the pseudo-Gothic Woolworth Building on lower Broadway]—but only for her true suitor on her free Saturday."[10] And just as "**Virginia**" alludes to one popular song, so "**Indiana**" evokes another, the 1917 ballad "Indiana" (better known by its first line as "Back Home Again in Indiana"), with its imagery of nostalgic longing for a rural childhood home ("The new mown hay—sends all its fragrance / From the fields I used to roam,—/ When I dream about the moonlight on the Wabash, / Then I long for my Indiana home"), as if the twentieth-century ballad expressed the feelings of the runaway son grown older.

In his 1927 letter to Otto Kahn, Crane said that he planned in "**Indiana**" to allude to the mother "in a way which implies her succession to the nature-symbolism of Pocahontas" (*L,* 307), but this was at the time when he still thought of the poem as "a lyrical summary of the period of conquest" and still planned for its dramatic speaker to be the farmer whose wife had "died on the way back from the gold-rush" (*L,* 307). When the roles of the father and mother were reversed, the mother retained her succession to the nature-symbolism of Pocahontas, but this succession was now presented in what, for American literature, has traditionally been an image of generational decline—the figure of the half-breed. Returning from the gold fields, the mother sees "passing on a stumbling jade / A homeless squaw—/ / Perhaps a halfbreed. On her back / She cradled a babe's body" (p. 78). In a moment of maternal mirroring the white mother holds up her own son for the squaw to see, knowing "that mere words could not have brought us nearer. / She nodded—and that smile across her shoulder / Will still endear her / / As long as Jim, your father's memory, is warm" (p. 78). One senses that the pioneer mother recognizes in the homeless wandering of the squaw the same rootlessness that sent her husband to the gold fields and will send her son to sea.

It seems clear that in imagining the mother in "**Indiana**" Crane was influenced by his feelings about his own mother. The scenario of a mother's self-pitying appeal to

her son to write her from overseas and to return home before it is too late parallels Crane's own situation at the time too closely for us to doubt this. It also seems clear that the major factor in Crane's decision to reverse the roles originally planned for the father and mother in this section was his break with his mother and the reversal in his feelings toward her. Had Crane kept to his original plan for "**Indiana**," it would have been virtually impossible for the father as the poem's speaker to present a negative picture of his dead wife as part of his farewell to his departing son. And if much of the point of "**Indiana**" is the negative characterization of the white mother who symbolizes the degraded maternal landscape of modern America, then the reversal of Crane's earliest feelings about his own mother (which parallels the movement from the mythic dark [m]other in "**The Dance**" to the historical white mother in "**Indiana**") left him with the difficult task of preserving the maternal archetype in its original power and reverence while presenting the white mother as a decadent instance of this archetype. Not uncommonly, this kind of ambivalence is handled by splitting the maternal image into a good and a bad half, each separately embodied, and the final version of "Indiana" shows the traces of such splitting. On the one hand, the structure of the poem, considered in the abstract, suggests an idealized version of the womb fantasy: the father is dead without the son's having to kill him, and the mother pleads with the son to return home. No doubt we are meant to see this structure as completing the epicycle of desire begun by "**Ave Maria**," the poem that leads into "**Powhatan's Daughter**." There, Columbus at mid-ocean prays to the Virgin Mother to grant him safe return home, and in the final poem of "**Powhatan's Daughter**," the mother, as if in reply to that earlier episode, pleads with her son, who is running away to sea, to "come back to Indiana." Yet it is equally clear that the pioneer mother envisions the son's return as occurring entirely on her own terms, not a return that grants the son access to original power but one that keeps him forever subservient. From the first stanza of "**Indiana**," the mother tries to prevent the son's departure or at least to hasten his return by undermining the notion of original power. During the fantasized primal scene of origin in "**The Dance**," the poetic quester had entreated Maquokeeta, "Medicineman, relent, restore—/ Lie to us,—dance us back the tribal morn" (p. 73), but the mother in "**Indiana**" begins her song by evoking the loss of that original earliness:

> The morning glory, climbing the morning long
>   Over the lintel on its wiry vine,
> Closes before the dusk, furls in its song
>   As I close mine . . .
>
>                                          (p. 76)

The mother's story opens with an image of closure that is clearly meant to be experienced by her son as a kind of foreclosure: the glory of the morning has past, here in the dusk there is only the fated repetition of unoriginal action. On that disabling note the mother recounts the son's personal origin, the circumstances that led up to his birth on the trail back from the gold fields. The thrust of this account is to show her son the unoriginality of his leaving the farm to go adventuring, to show "How we, too, Prodigal, once rode off, too—/ Waved Seminary Hill a gay good-bye." In addressing her son as "Prodigal," the mother implies that, like the son in the parable, he will return home one day defeated by his own irresponsibility and seeking parental succor, and in so doing confirm his unoriginality in the repetition of his parents' failure. We should keep in mind that Crane was writing **"Quaker Hill"** with its allusion to the threatened lawsuit against his mother over his grandfather's legacy ("birthright by blackmail") at the same time that he was working on **"Indiana"** in which the mother tries to act as the mediatrix (or perhaps we should say executrix) of her son's birthright by telling him where he comes from, who his people are, and thus where he belongs and what belongs to him:

> You were the first—before Ned and this farm,—
>    First born, remember—
>
> And since then—all that's left to me of Jim
>    Whose folks, like mine, came out of
>       Arrowhead.
> And you're the only one with eyes like him—
>    Kentucky bred!
>
> I'm standing still, I'm old, I'm half of stone!
>    Oh, hold me in those eyes' engaging blue;
> There's where the stubborn years gleam and
>       atone,—
>    Where gold is true!
>
>                         (pp. 78-79)

These lines, filled with an irony unperceived by their speaker, undermine the thing they argue for. The mother tells her son what belongs to him as the "first born," that is, she invokes on his behalf the prerogative of generational earliness, after she has just finished describing the loss of original earliness in the closing of the frontier, the loss of any possibility of being first. The promise of America, of the endless frontier, was the golden promise of an inexhaustible access to the original world. But that was not what the farmer and his wife found in Colorado in 1859 when they arrived at a mining town ("A dreamcalled Eldorado" [The Golden]) that had "no charter but a promised crown / Of claims to stake":

> But we,—too late, too early, howsoever—
>    Won nothing out of fifty-nine—those years—
> But gilded promise, yielded to us never,
>    And barren tears . . .
>
>                         (p. 78)

Though she professes uncertainty as to whether their failure resulted from being too early or too late, everything else in the poem points to her sense of belatedness. And it is consistent with her misunderstanding of her son that she apparently considers this tale of belatedness, of parents' dreams foreclosed by the closing of the frontier, to be in some way an effective argument for the son's remaining on the farm rather than searching for a new frontier on the sea or in some other land. In **"Indiana,"** then,

the mother in mediating a birthright that consists of an absent paternal origin, a lost earliness, functions as a kind of disabling antimuse—neither the origin herself nor the means to a lost original power. And yet it would be a mistake to paint too black a picture of her (particularly since in Crane's color coding the good mother is the dark [m]other). The pioneer woman may be foolish and possessive but she is not intentionally evil, which is to say that Crane's portrait of her, no matter how much it may reflect his personal feelings about Grace Crane at the time, is not intended to discredit the maternal archetype. In terms of Crane's own psychic economy in writing *The Bridge*, **"Indiana"** serves in part to separate the image of his own mother (the white woman of materialist America) from that of the Great Mother, the dark woman of the triple aspect (mother-lover-muse) whom he calls Pocahontas, the poet's true mother. What Crane objects to in the pioneer woman is not the excessive character of maternal love, but rather that this mother offers her love only on her own terms, terms that, because they are ultimately self-pitying and self-regarding, reduce the son to being her mirror.

In a letter Crane wrote to his friend William Wright in November 1930, he confessed to being "considerably jolted at the charge of sentimentality continually leveled" at **"Indiana."** Noting that he "approved of a certain amount of sentiment," he added "Since 'race' is the principal motivation of **'Indiana,'** I can't help thinking that, observed in the proper perspective, and judged in relation to the argument or theme of the Pocahontas section as a whole, the pioneer woman's maternalism isn't excessive" (*L*, 357-58). One suspects that Crane was surprised less by the charge of sentimentality than by the fact that it was leveled at the poet rather than the persona. Yet there is no reason to doubt the sincerity of Crane's remark that the pioneer woman's maternalism was not excessive within the overall context of his fantasized portrait of the muse-mother and the vision of a total return. Indeed, for the poet-son, the more intense and narrowly focused the muse's love is the better, as long as that love is given wholly on the son's terms. It is in light of this split in Crane's feelings about the figure of the mother that we should interpret his puzzling remark about race being "the principal motivation of **'Indiana.'"**

Granting that the poem's implicit comparison of the pioneer woman and Pocahontas as mother figures tends to evoke the maternal difference between them as being in some sense a racial difference, I would argue that in *The Bridge* race functions in regard to the image of the mother in much the same way that it does in relation to the image of the father in Crane's nightmare of the black man on the river bank. Which is to say that since the black and the Indian represented for the white America of Crane's day the world of animal nature as opposed to that of human culture, and since one of the traditional principles of differentiation between nature and culture, between animal and human, is the incest taboo, Crane's symbolic translation of the white father and mother into a black and an Indian respectively circumvents this taboo by placing the objects of desire in an original nature-world where incest does not exist. As the Negro in Crane's dream represents the fantasized incestuous union of father and son, so the Indian maiden Pocahontas in **The Bridge** represents that of mother and son. And since in each case the idealized figure is drawn from a race that isconsidered by white America to be subservient or inferior (a subservience that evokes for Crane the child's subjection to his parents), their use as symbols of the union of father and son and of mother and son, that is, their elevation to the status of ideals, represents the triumph of the son: it marks these fantasized unions as occurring on the son's terms.

Yet obviously Crane is neither black nor an Indian, and so, as one would expect, in the very process of symbolizing his forbidden desires in these dark figures he obliquely reaffirms the prohibition that gives those desires their significance within a differential system. Here one finds perhaps a further, not to say deeper, significance to that reversal in the roles originally planned for the father and mother in **"Indiana."** In 1927, when Crane was close to Grace and at odds with his father, it was his incestuous feelings for his mother that had to be repressed (the estrangement from his father served as a sufficient defense against forbidden desires in that quarter), while at the same period it was the ideal of paternal affection and esteem that had to be reaffirmed. Consequently in the version of **"Indiana"** that he described to Kahn, the mother is absent from the scene (psychically cancelled by death), and the father speaks to the son, presumably to express his love. But in 1929, when Crane was no longer speaking to his mother and had become closer to his father, it was his incestuous feelings for the latter that had now to be repressed (the estrangement from the other parent serving once again as a sufficient defense in that quarter), while it was the ideal of maternal love that had to be reaffirmed. Consequently, in the finished version of the poem the father is absent, and the mother speaks to the son. In this version, however, although Crane projects the son's ideal of maternal love in the abstract form of the poem—that is, in the scenario of a mother pleading with her son to return home in the father's absence—he evokes in the possessiveness of the pioneer woman the real maternal love that he has known.

It may seem that we have spent more time on **"Indiana"** than its poetic merit warrants. Yet both because of its formal importance as the closing section of **"Powhatan's Daughter"** and because of the insight that it provides into Crane's juxtaposition of personal and national history in **The Bridge** as a whole this degree of attention is justified. Indeed, in the latter regard we can see that the autobiographical material which Crane incorporates into the poem is meant to convey his sense of how much this vision, indeed any vision, of a return to national origin depends for its emotional force on the concepts of fatherland and motherland, concepts whose collective force is, in one degree or another, a function of each individual's personal relationship to his parents. That patriotism ultimately derives from the way one feels about one's father,

or that the love of the native land, the physical nature of the nation ("native," "nature," and "nation" are all from the Latin *natus,* "to be born") takes its basic emotional tone from the feeling for one's mother simply means that the most powerful trope for binding individuals to a place and thus to each other has always been the parental image, and that to deal with national feelings about the native land inevitably means dealing with personal feelings about one's parents. For this reason Crane's complex, shifting relationship with his father and mother is part of the very fabric of the poem, both as direct thematic motif and as indirect shaping force. Indeed, inasmuch as Crane had cast himself in the role of the prototypical twentieth-century American poet through his surrogate the poetic quester, he had come to view his successful, overbearing father—the millionaire candy manufacturer who invented the Life Saver and who considered his son's poetic career as a rejection of his own life's work in creating the patrimony of a family business—and his disabling, possessive mother, with her virulent midwestern blend of Christian Science mysticism and Chatauqua artiness, as the prototypical parents of the modern American poet in that they seemed to represent between them virtually every obstacle that the serious practice of poetry would have to confront in this country in this century.

NOTES

[1] Hart Crane, *The Letters of Hart Crane, 1916-1932,* ed. Brom Weber (Berkeley and Los Angeles: University of California Press, 1952), p. 307. All subsequent quotations from this volume will be indicated in the text by the letter *L* and page number.

[2] John Unterecker, *Voyager: A Life of Hart Crane* (New York: Farrar, Straus and Giroux, 1969), p. 534. See also Philip Horton, *Hart Crane: The Life of an American Poet* (New York: The Viking Press, 1957).

[3] *Letters of Hart Crane and His Family,* ed. Thomas S. W. Lewis (New York: Columbia University Press, 1974), pp. 619-20. All subsequent quotations from this volume will be indicated in the text by the letters *LF* and page number.

[4] Hart Crane, *The Complete Poems and Selected Letters and Prose of Hart Crane,* ed. Brom Weber (New York: Liveright, 1966), pp. 68-69.

[5] Gerald Bordman, *Jerome Kern: His Life and Music* (New York: Oxford University Press, 1980), pp. 267-77 and 299.

[6] Brian Rust, *The Complete Entertainment Discography from the Mid-1890s to 1942* (New Rochelle, N.Y.: Arlington House, 1973), p. 552.

[7] *The New York Times,* May 27, 1928, sect. 8, p. 1.

[8] Rust, *Complete Entertainment Discography,* p. 552.

[9] Brom Weber, *Hart Crane* (New York: Bodley Press, 1948), p. 261.

[10] Susan Jenkins Brown, *Robber Rocks: Letters and Memories of Hart Crane, 1923-1932* (Middletown, Conn.: Wesleyan University Press, 1969), p. 111.

## Jared Gardner (essay date 1992)

SOURCE: "'Our Native Clay': Racial and Sexual Identity and the Making of Americans in 'The Bridge'," in *American Quarterly,* Vol. 44, No. 1, March, 1992, pp. 24-50.

[*In the following essay, Gardner discusses Crane's notion of racial and sexual identity in* The Bridge.]

> Being a naïve European, I could not help remarking to my American companion: "I really had no idea there was such an amazing amount of Indian blood in your people."
>
> "What!" said he. "Indian blood? I bet there is not one drop of it in this whole crowd. . . . "
>
> I know the mother nations of North America pretty well, but if I relied solely on the theory of heredity, I should be completely at a loss to explain how the Americans descending from European stock have arrived at their striking peculiarities.
>
> —Carl Jung, "Your Negroid and Indian Behavior" (1930)[1]

In his letters, Hart Crane consistently aligned *The Bridge* (1930) with the cultural project of defining America's identity in the 1920s. From his earliest theorizing on his poem in 1923, Crane imagined its focus in these terms: "The initial impulses of 'our people' will have to be gathered up toward the climax of the bridge, symbol of our constructive future, our unique identity."[2] Although he offered notoriously conflicting assertions about his poem over the next seven years, Crane maintained his motivating interest in the discovery of such an identity. As he told his patron, Otto Khan, he desired "to enunciate a new cultural synthesis of values in terms of our America" (L, 223) out of the "organic and active factors in the experience and perceptions of our common race, time and belief" (L, 261). One of the "startling discoveries" he made during this search for "our common race" was "the currency of the Indian symbolism in whatever is most real in our little native culture, its persistence, despite our really slight contact with that race . . . cropping out in the most unexpected places."[3]

Crane's discovery of the Indian's centrality to American identity was not original to his work. Many writers at the time were attempting to define an American identity with the Indian as a central symbol. America after World War I was now prepared to define a native genealogy distinct from that of Europe. With the nation's creation myths up for grabs, writers such as William Carlos Williams and Waldo Frank created field guides to this incipient culture, pointing away from what seemed to them to be false Old World inheritance and towards the Indian as the potential of the nation. As Frank writes in *The Rediscovery of America* (1929), "our root is in the red men; and our denial of this is a disease within us."[4] Not simply a literary conceit, however, this formulation of the Indian's relation to American identity was one aspect of a social project that sought to claim an inheritance for America that would distinguish it wholly from its European parents.

This version of the making of Americans in the 1920s involved this imagining of a race without blood, defining a people without reference to its biological inheritance, so that, by 1930, it was possible for Jung to conceive of America as a nation of Indians. While lineally the claim is illogical, as Jung's interlocutor argues, it becomes useful in the 1920s precisely *because* no Indian blood was involved. Attempting to theorize this formula, Jung describes the American as unique because of his absorption of primitive behaviors: "the spirit of the Indian gets at the American within and without."[5] As this inheritance was theorized by writers in the 1920s, the cultural embrace of the Indian allows for the rejection of Old World genealogy in favor of a new kind of inheritance, an American self. As we shall see, it is this self-justifying contradiction, divorcing the claim to racial identity from biological inheritance, that makes Crane's myth possible.

Crane's appropriation of the Indian in the formulation of American identity offered by *The Bridge* is unique in what I shall argue is the identification of the nation's Indian inheritance with a myth of homosexual origins. At the time, this identification would have seemed profoundly counterintuitive. Along with the racial and ethnic groups excluded from the model of citizenship in the 1920s, homosexuals were also explicitly proscribed from the construction of citizenship. Crane's *The Bridge,* however, provides a comprehensive allegory of the making of the new American identity, one that, in bridging the theoretical leap that the new formulation of citizenship required, would work to imagine Crane's own sexuality as neither an oppositional nor marginal identity, but as the very definition of the American citizen itself. Although we might today take for granted a certain kind of ideological claim on the Indian by white America, it is important to understand the particular value and demands placed on the 1920s' association. For it is these terms that at once seem to preclude Crane's identification of the homosexual with the Indian, while at the same time empowering the poem's claim for the homosexual as the pure American.[6]

In **"The Dance,"** which Crane referred to as "the basic center and antecedent of all motion" (L, 271) of *The Bridge,* he rewrites one of America's founding myths, the Pocahontas story, editing out aspects of the tale that were troubling to the 1920s' imagination by transforming the miscegenist story into a homosexual myth. Instead of offering herself to the white man, Pocahontas here acts as mediator between white and red man. It is in this union, through the bridge of the female body of Pocahontas, that our America is born. By grounding the identification between Indian chief and white poet in the nonbiological terms that constructions of citizenship in the 1920s made conceivable, the genealogy which Crane reenacts for us in the poem, and through which we are asked to trace our cultural identity, comes to have its inception in the union of two men.

As Crane wrote to Khan in 1927,

> Not only do I describe the conflict between the two races in this dance—I also become identified with the Indian and his world before it is over, which is the only method possible of ever really possessing the Indian and his world as a cultural factor. I think I really succeed in getting under the skin of this glorious and dying animal, in terms of expression, in symbols, which he himself would comprehend. (L, 307)

For Crane, possessing the Indian as a "cultural factor" becomes a homosexual project; as the poem would have it, only the homosexual can claim a genealogy without biology, and only such a genealogy can truly evade all the complications of race. America's identification with the Indian in the 1920s allowed for the formulation of a national self that is at once inherited while also remaining defensible against biological claims to inclusion on the part of immigrant populations. Crane's identification of the Indian with the homosexual, an identity excluded from this inheritance, allows him to rewrite himself as founding father.

The first readers of **The Bridge** overwhelmingly judged it an ambitious "failure," and one of the primary grounds for this critique was the poem's thematic reliance upon extrinsic cultural texts.[7] Much of the later criticism has either followed the New Critics in rejecting the poem's reliance on an external logic, or else has argued that the poem has no interest in history at all.[8] These critical negations of the poem's self-avowed engagement with American culture operate out of the assumption that the poem is a search for poetic identity, relegating concerns central to the poem, such as racial, sexual, and national identity, to extratextual thematic consideration. The criticism has failed to recognize the extremely complex and often troubling levels on which Crane is confronting these issues in his attempt to claim a historical place for the homosexual by inventing a nativist history purified through a marriage between white man and Indian.

The poem's understanding of America demands to be read in relation to specific formulations—literary, political, and popular—of national identity in the 1920s. In order to recover the logic through which **The Bridge** engages American citizenship, two developments that established its terms must first be explored: the energetic recruitment of American Indians and the simultaneous campaign to expel homosexuals from the armed forces in World War I—events focused around two of the poem's central concerns, national and sexual identity, and involving two of its leading actors, the Indian and the sailor. In examining how Crane uses the Indian and the sailor in order to Americanize the homosexual, we shall see how these two apparently opposed identities are brought together (as indeed they also were in Crane's sexual relationships with Indians and sailors) to prove them mutually inextricable in the formulation of an American race.

. . . . .

During World War I, American Indians, most of whom were not yet citizens, were enlisted in unprecedented numbers and "in far greater percentages than their total population warranted."[9] One motivation fueling this drive (one that was not directed to any other ethnic group) was a desire to define Americans returning to Europe as a race apart from the countries from which they were biologically descended. In several important ways, World War I marks the fulcrum in the transition from Progressivist assimilationism to 1920s nativism.[10] And it is at this point that the Indian is transformed from a target of assimilationist policies to a model of an American identity unacquirable through assimilation.[11]

The Indian soldier was an ideological focal point for the battle between proponents of the melting pot and the emerging commitment to a unique American cultural identity. The debate focused on whether these new soldiers should be assimilated into regular troops, as Cato Sells, Commissioner of Indian Affairs insisted, or should be placed instead in segregated units, as Edward Ayer of the Board of Indian Commissioners would have had it.[12] In an article entitled, "The 'First Americans' as Loyal Citizens," Sells imagines the war as a grand Americanization program in which the Indian would fight "side by side with the white man, not as Indians but as Americans . . . gaining by contact an education that will lead them away from the tribal relations, and give them a definite comprehension of the genius of American institutions." The war for Sells is the ultimate civics course, offering "the beginning of the end of the Indian problem."[13]

For those who argued for the unique symbolic function of the all-Indian troop, however, the "vanishing" Indian represented resistance to the melting pot that had failed to produce a unified America. The Indian, brought back to the OldWorld as the unique mark of the American, defined patriotism as the defense against a mixed European identity. The all-Indian troop would encourage the national self-identification that patriotism required. As Dr. Joseph Dixon defended Ayer's plan before Congress:

> The establishment of purely Indian units would . . . have a psychological effect upon the entire country. The enlistment of purely Indian units would fire the enthusiasm and arouse the patriotism of the entire country.[14]

The Indian soldier defined the army in opposition to the nations from which Americans descended, and so would "arouse the patriotism of the entire country" by symbolizing freedom from European inheritance. As a wartime review of a collection of "American Indian Poetry" defines the "real American classic," "none of it has any trace of European influence."[15] And as Coolidge's campaign in Indian head-dress made a spectacle of this process, the donning of the red mask cleanses the American of European racial marks. The Indian enlistment effort imagined that the American was an Indian (not a European), and the legislative process ending in 1924 made certain that the Indian was now an American, closing off access to American identity in the postwar decade. Reviewing the Indian's effort at the war's end, Ayer could write, "Not only were the Indians the first Americans, but they are the first and last Americans as was proved by their record in the World War."[16]

As John Higham and others have demonstrated, by World War I, it was perceived by many in the government and media that the melting pot had failed. The war became, for writers in the twenties, the event which rescued the nation by revealing how fully the ethnic populations had preserved their racial allegiances.[17] Commending the Immigration Act in 1924, Robert DeC. Ward writes,

> During the years of the war various alien racial groups in the country showed clearly enough that their sympathies were not American but European. European antagonisms, bred and nourished through centuries abroad, came to the surface in the United States. Those who had been relying on the Melting Pot to accomplish assimilation realized that they had cherished false hopes. The statistics of the Draft threw a great deal of light upon the whole problem of the foreign-born in the United States . . . [The Johnson Immigration Act] is an emphatic national decision that, to quote President Coolidge, "America must be kept American." It is based on bedrock principles. It marks a turning point in American civilization.[18]

In Lothrop Stoddard's terms, "the late war . . . must bring home the truth that the basic factor in human affairs is not politics, but race."[19] For these writers and the Americans whose anxieties they voiced, the war had shown that a political solution to the preservation of American identity was not adequate; supposedly naturalized immigrants were revealed to be indelibly marked by race as inferior soldiers, cowards, and traitors. And the Indian was now discovered to be the truest patriot; the war revealed that many ethnic groups had maintained strong bonds to Europe while the Indian remained true only to his native land. As the Committee on Public Information lauded the 1918 film, *The American Indian Gets into the War,* because it "shamed the white man into a higher patriotism,"[20] so the Indian soldier, "most forward among the people of America in volunteering for military service,"[21] defined patriotism in an ethnically divided America by offering a native culture which could be claimed without blood descent.

The defining of a national identity to be protected from biology required determining what it was that made the American and identifying those who must be barred from access to that claim. Reading two pieces of legislation of 1924, the Johnson Immigration Act (severely curtailing entrance to America) and the Citizenship Act (making Indians Americans), Walter Benn Michaels has demonstrated how both worked to close off access to and reconstitute citizenship by instituting a notion of culture as that which is held in common by both Indian and American while remaining unattainable to alien populations. The acts defined American citizenship in terms that escaped the necessarily problematic notion of a native identity based wholly on either biology or a technology of instruction; Michaels writes,

> If . . . as an inheritance, culture is unlike the citizenship of the melting-pot because it cannot simply be achieved, it is also unlike race and environment in that it cannot simply be inherited. The distinctive mark of culture is that it must be both achieved and inherited.[22]

Claiming nonbiological inheritance from Indians as the mark of the American allowed for a bulwark against assimilation that retained the force of nativist rhetoric without the complications of a defense grounded wholly on race. Only Americans have claim to the Indian, and this inheritance must be actively protected. Like Coolidge's campaign for the protection of American identity through education in the classics, Indian culture, as America's native "classical" inheritance, comes to function as the nation's unique birthright.

Fighting like Indians, then, not in defense of blood but of cultural inheritance, becomes an alternative to the assimilative process. In his poem, "Our Mother Pocahontas" (1917), Vachel Lindsay describes how the embrace of the nonbiological mother, the Indian, allows those who fought the war to escape their racial inheritances and to become finally and fully American. "John Rolfe is not our ancestor. / We rise from out the soul of her." Through the embrace of Pocahontas, we reject biological descendence from Europe (Rolfe) in favor of a spiritual inheritance ("from out the soul") transmitted through the Indian.

> We here renounce our Saxon blood.
> Tomorrow's hopes, an April flood
> Come roaring in. The newest race
> Is born of her resilient grace.
> We here renounce our Teuton pride:
> Our Norse and Slavic boasts have died:
> Italian dreams are swept away,
> And Celtic feuds are lost today . . .
> She sings of lilacs, maples, wheat,
> Her own soil sings beneath her feet,
> Of springtime
> And Virginia,
> Our Mother, Pocahontas.[23]

Lindsay's poem, entrenched between the rhetoric of the Progressive Era and the anxieties of the 1920s, provides a crucial set of terms for understanding the appropriation of the Indian in the defining of American citizenship during and after the war. In classic Progressivist terms, the war figures as an assimilating institution through which immigrant groups renounce their native cultures for an American identity, but in employing the Indian as the bridge to Americanization, Lindsay moves away from the old formulation of this transmission as fundamentally political and towards an understanding of American identity as a spiritual inheritance. We are born of "our mother" not through biology, but "of her resilient *grace*," "from out the *soul* of her" (emphases added). And the war which grants those who fight access to this non-biological genealogy is also that which closes off access to an American identity to those who follow. In Lindsay's terms, those who fought in the war (and fought like Indians) could now be Americans; those who did not would never escape their "racial marks"[24] and thus could never be Americanized.

. . . . .

The emergence of a national identity defined by the Indian soldier arises concomitantly with the invention and exposure of the homosexual threat to that identity.[25] It was important that an allegedly vanishing population such as the Indians could come, through their recruitment into the army, to function as model citizens who evaded the complications of biology.[26] At the same time, however, another nonprocreative population was in the very process of *appearing* during the war: homosexuals were entering public discourse. And where the Indian could represent a unique native inheritance, the homosexual could stand for Old World decadence, moral degeneracy, and an imagined threat to the heterosexual models upon which Big Business would increasingly depend.[27] As a doubled and inverted model of the Indian's nonbiological relation to American identity, and throughthe same set of terms whereby the Indian became the model for citizenship, the homosexual came to be the model for *decitizenship*.

In the early 1920s, the construction of homosexuality moved beyond the scientific discourse which had invented it. The war was a primary site of the dissemination of consciousness about homosexuality, and contributing dramatically was the scandal surrounding Franklin Delano Roosevelt's vice squad operations at the Newport naval training base, which its historian, Lawrence Murphy, has described as "the most extensive systematic persecution of gays in American history."[28]

As Assistant Secretary of the Navy, responding to complaints of widespread homosexuality at Newport and to Secretary Josephus Daniels's demand for "a wholesome atmosphere for young men training in the navy,"[29] Roosevelt authorized an independent effort to expose and expel the homosexual. His vice squad agents operated by gaining the confidence of suspects and engaging them in sexual acts for the purposes of entrapment. Roosevelt, "eager for the protection of . . . young men from such contaminating influences,"[30] encouraged this internal operation (though he later denied knowledge of its methods), and the squad expanded its focus to civilians. The arrest of a prominent local clergyman brought the scandal into the headlines and before a federal court in 1920, eventuating in a full congressional investigation.

The source of the outrage against the operation was that good sailors were being forced to commit immoral acts by the navy; in the words of one editor, they were "made perverts by official order."[31] As the *New York Times* responded to the release of the committee's report in 1921,

> most of the details of the scandal, as disclosed in the investigation, are of an unprintable nature. The committee finds its basis for its criticism of Mr. Daniels and Mr. Roosevelt in the charge that with their knowledge enlisted men of the navy were used as participants in immoral practices for the purpose of obtaining evidence on which to dismiss offenders from the navy. Such use of enlisted men under orders or suggestions of superior officers, the report declares, "violated the code of the American citizen and ignored the rights of every American boy who enlisted in the Navy to fight for his country.[32]

Roosevelt came to be held responsible for the very thing he had sought to prevent: the homosexualization of the U.S. Navy. The scandal unfolded into Roosevelt's early political career, and as the papers followed investigations into the operation over the next year, many learned for the first time of the existence of a homosexual community in America.[33]

The operation at Newport was part of a widespread effort to expunge homosexuality from the military, and from the terms being used to define the American citizen.[34] Where the Indian comes to define American citizenship through fighting in the war, the exclusion of the homosexual from military service made him the paradigm for decitizenship. But Roosevelt's vice squad served in the public imagination as itself a recruitment device for homosexuality, producing homosexuals where it had sought to eliminate them. The attempt to bracket deviant sexuality from the definition of the American served instead to educate the nation with "the first detailed documentary evidence in America of a distinctive homosexual community."[35]

The recruitment of the Indian provided a model of citizenship which encouraged an understanding of culture based on a genealogical transmission that had to be simultaneously inherited (by Americans) and actively embraced (by fighting to defend that inheritance). At the same time it became necessary to exclude the homosexual who complicated the claims to such an identity by engaging similarly nonprocreative terms of relation and community. As we shall see in discussing the ways in which these two doubled and inverted narratives are negotiated in *The Bridge*, the specter raised by the deviant sailor was the way in which this new model of citizenship, based on a notion of an inheritable culture, described a theory of genealogy that was compatible with homosexuality. In articulating a theoretical correspondence between homosexuality and models of American cultural purity, Crane redefines the homosexual, not as a threat to this new model but as its exemplary citizen.

. . . . .

In his first book of lyrics, *White Buildings* (1926), Crane worked through a highly compacted poetic to discover a new vocabulary for his sexuality, developing what John Irwin calls "progressively more complex names for love."[36] In *The Bridge,* Crane puts this poetic to work in writing a version of America's history and traditions. In doing so, he attempts to inscribe his sexuality as the correct reading of the myths that define American culture, myths whose supposed misinterpretations have led to the degradation of modern society. The Pocahontas myth provides the central site of this effort.

Philip Young writes, "Pocahontas is one of our few, true native myths . . . and [is] offered as a magical and moving explanation of our national origins."[37] This myth has been the hunting ground for projects of national identity from its inception, serving as an advertisement for colonization, as the "first symbol of the United States,"[38] as a subject for nineteenth-century attempts at an indigenous literature, as a genealogical focal point for Virginia's blue blood, as America's "first 'ethnic' woman,"[39] and, most explicitly in Lindsay's terms, as the founding of an American race. But this myth of our national origins has also always been a troubled and contradictory one. Pocahontas has been presented as the Dark Lady and the naked savage; Liberty and Indian Princess; symbol of devotion and promiscuousness; Christian and heathen; childlike and the mother of America.

These racial and sexual contradictions were the focus of the burlesques of the Indian woman that followed Lindsay's embrace of our new mother.[40] In literary parodies, from Philip Moeller's "Pokey—or the Beautiful Legend of the Amorous Indian" (1918) to Christopher Ward's *The Saga of John Smith* (1928), and in the vaudeville halls of New York, the burlesques tell both of a continued obsession with Pocahontas and an increased attention to the aspects of the story that made her a difficult mother for 1920s America. Moeller portrays a Pocahontas motivated entirely by libido, while Ward reveals Pocahontas to be not Indian at all, but instead the best English blood in the New World. Hemingway provides a merciless parody of the obsession with the Indian woman in his novella, *The Torrents of Spring* (1926). In a chapter entitled, "The Passing of a Great Race and the Making and Marring of Americans," the hero, sexually crippled since the war, is miraculously cured by the sight of the last Indian squaw. The hero leaves the town with her, stripping himself naked as he goes, while the Indian men who follow, gathering up the discarded clothes, shake their heads: "White chief going to get pretty cold."[41] All three versions of the joke play on the problems inherent in employing the Indian woman for the making (or, in Hemingway's term, "marring") of Americans, exposing the sexual and racial contradictions in the use of Pocahontas as the source of the American race. As what is essentially a tale of mis-

cegenation, the myth was necessarily troubling to the nativist decade which made popular sensations of the Ku Klux Klan, Lothrop Stoddard, and the Immigration Act.

For Crane, the anxieties these writers read into the story provide the terms and justification for his project of remaking Americans in his own image. Crane retraces the American genealogy in the Pocahontas myth in such a way that the nation is no longer born in an act of miscegenation. Crane's Pocahontas, instead of founding our race with the embrace of the white man, here serves to bring together the two men, Powhatan and Smith. In this union of two men the Jamestown colony is rescued, and the spiritual inheritance that constitutes the unique birthright of the American is begun.

In tracing this native culture to its origins, Crane first presents Columbus worrying over his ability to bring back "the word" he has found: "I bring you back Cathay!"[42] We know that of course he is not bringing back word of Cathay or the "Indian emperies" (48), but the word he *is* bringing back, through this original act of misreading, is Indian. His return mirrors that of America in World War I, bringing back the Indian, and the power of this word has similarly isolated Columbus from the Old World: "I thought of Genoa; and this truth, now proved, / That made me exile in her streets" (48). Columbus is trapped "here between two worlds," for his discovery of the Indian has exiled him from the Old World, while his inability to read the Indian correctly has denied him the New. It is the poet's task to complete this voyage of discovery, "to do a great deal of pioneering myself" (L, 305), in order to establish the correct relation of the Indian to American identity. It is in **"Powhatan's Daughter"** that this pioneering voyage takes place.

The epigraph to **"Powhatan's Daughter,"** from William Strachey's contemporary debunking of Pocahontas, presides over what is to follow by reminding us where the wrong reading of Pocahontas has led:

> "—Pocahuntus, a well-featured but wanton yong girle . . . of the age of eleven or twelve years, get the boyes forth with her into the market place, and make them wheele, falling on their hands, turning their heels upwards, whom she would followe, and wheele so herself, naked as she was, all the fort over." (53)

Where this heterosexual Pocahontas drives the boys "into the market place," the poem's rereading of Pocahontas provides the guide who will lead the poet *away* from the market, "past the din and slogans of the year" (63). Thus, **"Harbor Dawn,"** the first section of **"Powhatan's Daughter,"** introduces the poet waking up to the noises of the Brooklyn waterfront. As in each of the first three poems of **"Powhatan's Daughter,"** a sound produced by the modern commercial society that has severed the poet from his origins doubles as a bridge that will carry him back to a primal memory: "And if they take your sleep away sometimes / They give it back again" (54). Here, lying in the arms of his lover, the harbor's sounds recall him to a timeless encounter, "in a waking dream," with a first love:

> your hands within my hands are deeds;
> my tongue upon your throat—singing
> arms close; eyes wide, undoubtful
> > dark
> > > drink the dawn—
> a forest shudders in your hair!
>
> (56)

And laid out on the page opposite this scene is the motivating question: *"with whom?"* Although the question allows for the assumption that it is to be Pocahontas herself, in this myth she functions not as the lover but as the intercessor, taking the poet back to the site of that original encounter with her own body as the bridge between the sundered pair. As the prose continues:

> Who is the woman with us in the dawn? . . . whose is the flesh our feet have moved upon? . . . Like Memory, she is time's truant, shall take you by the hand. . . .  (57, 59)

"Pocahontas (the continent)," Crane wrote in a letter, "is the common basis of our meeting" (L, 307).

**"Van Winkle"** takes the first step in answering "with whom?" Here the poet's guide, arriving from another American myth, is he who left his wife to join a community of men in the woods. And over the sound bridge of the "hurdy-gurdy," Rip guides the poet through the process of self-recovery:

> The grind-organ says . . . Remember, remember
> The cinder pile at the end of the backyard
> Where we stoned the family of young
> Garter snakes under. . . .
>
> (60)

The poet recalls a childhood suppression of desire, figured in the stoning of the snakes in the backyard:

> the rapid tongues
> That flittered from under the ash heap day
> After day whenever your stick discovered
> Some sunning inch of unsuspecting fibre—
> It flashed back at your thrust, as clean as fire.
>
> (60)

Sundering him from access to the original union, this act had been enforced through corporal punishment by the father ("the whip stripped from the lilac tree / One day in spring my father took to me") and religious hypocrisy by the mother ("the Sabbatical, unconscious smile / My mother almost brought me once from church") (60). The biological family is held accountable for the self-violence which divided the poet from his first love. Through the guidance of Rip, the poet imagines the biological family at the root of this repression, so the renouncement of the family which begins here becomes an act of recovery of sexual identity.

With **"The River,"** another intermediary bridge is constructed, here towards a recovery of racial identity. The roar of commercialism and technology, as embodied in the speeding Twentieth Century Limited, leaves in its tracks three black hobos, modern day stand-ins for Rip, "wifeless or runaway." These men form an intermediate identification for the poet to pass through before he can achieve union with the Indian in the next section, as if he must first put on blackface in order to see red.

The hobos are "born pioneers," innocent possessors of an instinctual knowledge of the land, and Crane juxtaposes these men and their myths to the father who had punished the young poet for his desires. By locating the hobos "Behind / My father's cannery works," they can offer a very different set of lessons from the father's commercialism and the father's whip:

> Rail-squatters ranged in nomad raillery,
> The ancient men—wifeless or runaway
> Hobo-trekkers that forever search
> An empire wilderness of freight and rails.
>
> Each seemed a child, like me, on a loose perch,
> Holding to childhood like some termless play.
>
> (64, 66)

These dispossessed men know the land "without name," they know Pocahontas without knowing "the myths of her fathers." As the missing link between modern America and Native America, the hobos know Pocahontas without the ability to recover the power of that bridge: "They know a body under the wide rain." The poet must first experience the land as they do, learn their myths ("Jesus! Oh I remember watermelon days," "There's no place like Booneville though, Buddy . . . —For early trouting" [64]), hum "Deep River," and walk with them a while to learn all they can teach him of the true Pocahontas.

This section engages blacks as stepping-stones back to the pure race of the Indian. Crane referred to the hobos as "psychological ponies" that would "carry the reader across the country and back to the Mississippi," allowing him to "unlatch the door to the pure Indian world which opens out in 'the Dance' section" (L, 303). Identifying the black men as "Grimed tributaries to an ancient flow" (68), the poet charts his progress through their ancillary knowledge towards the river which will carry him finally to the "pure Indian world" of Maquokeeta and **"The Dance."** Walking on their "backs," the poet empowers his recovery of the Indian for the homosexual American by employing the black as *the* unassimilable minority. Imagined as a dispossessed, drifting, and dying race, the sacrificed black serves as the poet's vehicle back to the Indian in an especially horrific image:

> The River, spreading, flows—and spends your
> > dream.
> What are you, lost within this tideless spell?
> You are your father's father, and the stream—
> A liquid theme that floating niggers swell.
>
> (69)

In his effort to establish a genealogical bond that would evade the biological one of father and mother, the poet seems to authorize racist violence in using the bodies of blacks, a race excluded from *both* Progressivist and nativist constructions of American identity, to propel his course back to the Indian in order that he might truly become his "father's father."

In the first three sections of **"Powhatan's Daughter,"** the poet's "waking dream" (55) of a lost union leads him to travel back over two intermediary bridges: first towards a recovery of sexual identity from the biological family, and then towards a recovery of racial identity through the dispossessed wisdom of an unassimilable race. Having defined his voyage in these terms, the poet is now prepared for the reunion of **"The Dance."**

From the start of **"The Dance,"** we are told that "the swift red flesh" to which the river carries him is not Pocahontas but the "winter king," "her kin, her chieftain lover" (70, 71). Pocahontas has been tamed to appear only as land, river, and bridge—the ground upon which the white man and the Indian are reunited. Crane begins by describing a version of the encounter with the original pioneers that had served to divide the two races:

> Mythical brows we saw retiring—loth,
> Disturbed and destined, into denser green.
> Greeting they sped us, on the arrow's oath:
> Now lie incorrigibly what years between. . . .
>                                                     (70)

But now through the intercession of Pocahontas, to whom the poet prays as Columbus did the Virgin ("O Princess whose brown lap was virgin May"), this distance is negotiated. Through her the poet is able to find the site of the Indian camp, buried deep within the interior of the continent and inaccessible to the traditional pioneer.

> I left the village for dogwood. By the canoe
> Tugging below the mill-race, I could see
> Your hair's keen crescent running. . . .
>                                                     (70)

She guides the poet down the river to its secret core, and she teaches him the Indian's ways: "I learned to catch the trout's moon whisper." After completing his education, Pocahontas leads the poet to that shore which Columbus had earlier vainly bemoaned as the "one shore beyond desire." The acculturated poet can now stride over the landscape like a Whitmanian giant into the hidden interior:

> Over how many bluffs, tarns, streams I sped!
> —And knew myself within some boding shade:—
> Grey tepees tufting the blue knolls ahead,
> Smoke swirling through the yellow chestnut
>        glade. . . .
>
> A distant cloud, a thunder-bud—it grew,
> That blanket of the skies: the padded foot
> Within,—I heard it: 'til its rhythm drew,
> —Siphoned the black pool from the heart's hot
>        root!
>                                                     (72)

Arriving finally at the "pure Indian world," the blackface the poet had assumed in order to undertake this backwards voyage is "siphoned" so that the poet can now become the whitest man of all.

The meeting between the white man and Indian chief is staged at the moment when the Indian is engaged in what is at once his ecstasy and his death-throes in a sacrifice to the earth, Pocahontas. The poet initially positions himself as a' witness to this the dance, exhorting Maquokeeta to die splendidly:

> A cyclone threshes in the turbine crest,
> Swooping in eagle feathers down your back;
> Know, Maquokeeta, greeting; know death's best;
> —Fall, Sachem, strictly as the tamarack!
>
> A birch kneels. All her whistling fingers fly.
> The oak grove circles in a crash of leaves;
> The long moan of a dance is in the sky.
> Dance, Maquokeeta: Pocahontas grieves. . . .
>                                                     (72-73)

But as the poet's commands grow increasingly erotic, the distance remaining between Indian and white man becomes effaced until the poet and Indian can dance as one.

> Dance, Maquokeeta! snake that lives before,
> That casts his pelt, and lives beyond! Sprout,
>        horn!
> Spark, tooth!
>                                                     (73)

The images that describe the dance closely mirror those of the primal union in **"Harbor Dawn,"** identifying the first lover as this Indian man:

> And every tendon scurries toward the twangs
> Of lightning deltaed down your saber hair.
> Now snaps the flint in every tooth; red fangs
> And splay of tongues thinly busy the blue air. . . .
>                                                     (73)

Maquokeeta emerges as the suppressed snake of **"Van Winkle."** As the snake "that casts his pelt, and lives beyond," the Indian chief discards his red skin to live on in the white poet. This image is repeated at the dance's end: "like the lizard in the furious noon, / That drops his legs and colors in the sun, /—And laughs, pure serpent" (74). By casting off his Indian race, sacrificing his identity to the white, he allows the poet to be wholly identified with the Indian dance:

> I, too, was liege
> To rainbows currying each pulsant bone:
> Surpassed the circumstance, danced out the siege!
>
> And buzzard-circled, screamed from the stake;
> I could not pick the arrows from my side.
> Wrapped in that fire, I saw more escorts wake—
> Flickering, sprint up the hill groins like a tide.

In this sacrificial scene, the red man dies that the homosexual poet can be reborn as the true American, and the section ends with Maquokeeta transferring his identity to the poet through a bond of marriage: "We danced, O Brave . . . made our vows." The homosexual poet is sole beneficiary of this identity, he alone returns to tell us, while Pocahontas, the bridge to this reunion, remains "virgin to the last of men" (74).

**"The Dance"** bridges the two nonprocreative models of genealogy that had been polarized as mutually exclusive terms during the war. By rereading Pocahontas in terms of the union of white man and Indian chief, this act becomes the nation's founding moment, originating the nonbiological inheritance that had attempted to proscribe homosexuality from its machinery. The poem redefines American identity in terms that would make this version of the Pocahontas myth the necessarily correct formula for this transmission of cultural identity. And in this way, Crane's seemingly inconsonant statement that "'race' is the principal motivation of **'Indiana'**" (L, 358) begins to make important sense. For the section that follows the ecstatic union of **"The Dance"** reverses the terms it has been defining up to this point in order to follow out the fatal implications of a traditional biological reading of Pocahontas to a conception of an American race.

**"Indiana"** describes a son leaving his mother for the community of men at sea, while she begs him to remain within the family. This mother's significance, according to Crane, lies in "her succession to the nature-symbolism of Pocahontas" (L, 307). But as this heir to Pocahontas asks the son to embrace the reading of the myth that the poem has rejected, we know the succession is to be read as illegitimate. To expose the barrenness of this false genealogy, the poem reveals the mother's arguments for the demands of the family to be self-defeating. Opening with an account of the son's origins, modern capitalism is immediately correlated to biological birth as the mother recounts the family's disastrous search for gold:

> And bison thunder rends my dreams no more
>   As once my womb was torn, my boy, when you
> Yielded your first cry at the prairie's door. . . .
>     Your father knew
>
> Then, though we'd buried him behind us, far
>   Back on the gold trail—then his lost bones
>     stirred. . . .
>                                                          (76)

The violence of biological birth, the destructive drive of greed, and the sundering of the family are all brought together in this account of the son's inception, so that his decision to leave the family for a life at sea becomes a rejection of all these at once.

The mother's tale, told in the attempt to keep her son at home, offers the poem's condemnation of biology:

> The long trail back! I huddled in the shade
>   Of wagon-tenting looked out once and saw
> Bent westward, passing on a stumbling jade
>   A homeless squaw—

> Perhaps a halfbreed. On her slender back
>   She cradled a babe's body, riding without rein.
> Her eyes, strange for an Indian, were not black
>   But sharp with pain
>
> And like twin stars. They seemed to shun the gaze
>   Of all our silent men—the long team line—
> Until she saw me—when their violent haze
>   Lit with love shine. . . .
>
> I held you up—I suddenly the bolder. . . .
>                                                          (78)

The gold rush and son's birth of the same year have yielded nothing but "barren tears" and a broken family. Returning, the mother sees the modern Indian woman, the other successor to Pocahontas, but one who is now (as she indeed must be) a "halfbreed." Dispossessed, aimless, "riding without rein," this modern Pocahontas is, like the pioneer mother, a victim of the violence and greed that Crane portrays as intrinsic to the traditional reading of the myth and to the biological family itself. So when these two sundered aspects of Pocahontas try to find communion on the wasteland, they can only point to the children who define their condition. The condition of pioneer woman and "half-breed" squaw reveals how the wrong reading of Pocahontas has made a notion of a pure race impossible to defend. Crane's statement that **"Indiana"** is all about race turns out to be exactly right: To be a woman, in the terms of this poem, is necessarily to be a halfbreed and to produce halfbreeds; in this way *The Bridge* imagines that only through a homosexual genealogy is a pure race possible.

The family is shattered by the "dream called Eldorado" (78); the Indian is degenerated into a halfbreed; and the progress of the nation is brought to a halt on the barren prairie. Homosexuality becomes the way to have an American race, and biology, as figured by these two mothers, is that which defeats it. The son, rejecting the family to become a sailor, is transformed in the following section, **"Cutty Sark,"** into a Melvillian explorer of the "damned white Arctic" who "can't live on land" (83). And the poet's encounter with this sailor will propel him to cross the Bridge towards the Whitmanian manifesto of **"Cape Hatteras."**

. . . . .

Both the literary search for an American culture and the politicized defenses of American stock worked to invent a fixed national identity and to protect its boundaries; and both spell out anxious scenarios about procreation in which the failure of biology to reproduce American culture results in its extinction. For the nativists and eugenicists, this anxiety surfaces in the belief that immigrant populations are reproducing ever faster and will soon, through sheer number, define what it means to be American. For the literary defenses of America, most graphically in Williams's *In the American Grain* (1925), the enemy is located within the impotence of the Puritan businessman and the barrenness of the modern American woman; defending American culture necessitates the recovery of a native passion in what is imagined to be Indian terms. For both literary and political thinkers, the Indian becomes what will rescue us from our mixed inheritance, defining ours as a race apart precisely because the Indian, no longer a symbol of assimilation, has successfully resisted the melting pot mistake, remaining untainted by European blood. As Waldo Frank valorizes the Indian in *Our America* (1919), he "has preserved his culture admirably. He does not intermarry." This unmixed race reveals in the act of vanishing "the temper of his breeding" as he "withdraws forever farther within himself,"[43] so that his buried culture can now provide the untapped potential of our own.

Working out of the terms established by the war years (the period during which Crane began to define both his poetic project and his sexuality), *The Bridge* seizes upon Pocahontas as a true founding myth of the American culture and, at the same time, a forum for the anxiety over biological reproduction that is evinced by the burlesque, nativist, and modernist texts. Crane employs a burlesque nightmare of Pocahontas in *The Bridge* to portray the natural end of the traditional reading of the myth. His own interest in the burlesques is revealed by a notebook entry, written while composing **"The Dance,"** listing imaginary titles for burlesque songs on Indian themes.[44] The poem makes direct use of this tradition in **"Three Songs,"** the antipode to the climax of **"The Dance,"** in which Pocahontas is exposed in full heterosexual regalia, what R. W. B. Lewis calls "the furthest debasement of the feminine ideal."[45]

The **"Three Songs"** describe the inability of achieving the union of **"The Dance"** with a woman. The first song, **"Southern Cross,"** parades a litany of mythical women from which the poet might choose an object of worship but among which he finds only degenerated versions: "simian Venus, homeless Eve" (98). **"Virginia"** describes the attempt at a worldly object in the form of an office girl, but high atop the Woolworth building she remains inaccessible to the poet, her desires defined entirely by the workaday world: "rain at seven / Pay-check at eleven—/ Keep smiling the boss away" (102).

It is the middle poem in this section, however, which most powerfully enacts the failure of the heterosexual Pocahontas by presenting the barren woman of Williams's nightmare in the artless dance of modern culture. At the **"National Winter Garden,"** the great vaudeville theater for which the poem is named, Crane might well have seen burlesques of Pocahontas, one of the most popular themes of the time.[46] And it is here the poet comes in search of a modern Pocahontas, while finding in the bawdy dancer on stage only "some cheapest echo of them all" (100). He attempts to transform her into an object for his poetic project, by asking: "And shall we call her whiter than the snow?" But simply in raising the question of race through this modern Pocahontas, the quest defeats itself. The poem graphically displays the impossibility of having race through a heterosexual model of genealogy, as the

dancer, artificially tinted "first with ruby, then with emerald sheen," is suddenly exposed by the slide projector which had provided her race: "A caught slide shows her sandstone grey between" (100). And when this raceless, grey Pocahontas removes the veil she had so assiduouslyguarded in **"Powhatan's Daughter,"** exposing her genitalia to the crowd, she reveals something so monstrous that "we flee her spasm through a fleshless door" (100). The poet had come to find a heterosexual model for Pocahontas and discovered only "the burlesque of our lust" (101).

Crane places the heterosexual failures of **"Three Songs"** in opposition to the experience of the previous section, **"Cape Hatteras,"** in which the ideal of male love is enacted through the poet's claim of Walt Whitman as the homosexual father, engaging the spiritual genealogy empowered by **"The Dance."** This bond with a homosexual father holds "us in thrall / To that deep wonderment, our native clay," the "red, eternal flesh of Pocahontas" (88). The founding of this genealogy allows the poet to trace his way back to the true Pocahontas as the mother of this transmission, a mother whose "native clay" can only be defended through the enactment of such an inheritance. Women in Crane's myth are transformed into the land so that men can become men; and **"Cape Hatteras"** goes so far as to sunder the original biological parents:

> Adam and Adam's answer in the forest
> Left Hesperus mirrored in the lucid pool.
>
> (89)

This all-male genealogy, the poem suggests, escapes the fatal narcissism that brought Eve to the pond's edge and evil to the world, for in this Eden the pool in which Milton's Eve revealed her weakness here reflects only the evening star. Whitman embodies this "pure impulse inbred . . . a pact, a new bound / Of living brotherhood!" (93) and the section ends with the engagement of this bond, defying biology (and mortality) to mark a new inheritance: "My hand / in yours, / Walt Whitman—/ so—" (95).

. . . . .

Crane's American myth cannot be fully understood without recasting the logic which defined its terms and made such a project both necessary (by the exclusion of homosexuality from the machinery of citizenship) and conceivable (by theorizing a nonbiological relationship to the Indian) for the homosexual poet in 1920s America. While it was through poetry and the example of Whitman that he began constituting a voice for his sexuality in his early poems, Crane's ambition to be *the* American poet of his generation, defining a "new cultural synthesis" for "our America," must be seen as itself an expression of the model of cultural citizenship emerging from the war.

Working out of the terms whereby the vanishing Indian comes to define American culture, Crane can write himself as the American poet for which the age is calling. The ideal transmission of American culture comes to be reimagined as necessarily a homosexual model of reproduction: the modernist poet as the lover of vanishing Indian men, he who most fully is able to imagine the separation of genealogy from procreation and to trace descendence through nonbiological inheritance, the purest genealogy of all. Thus, homosexuality, actively persecuted during World War I in the process of defining American citizenship in terms of a nonbiological relationship to the Indian, becomes here the perfect example of that relationship. As Werner Sollors identifies Lindsay's Pocahontas as an ancestor "who subverts identification by 'blood' descent,"[47] so Crane, writing in the decade that burned all bridges behind Lindsay's declaration of Americanization, could embrace Pocahontas one last time in order to write a genealogy for America which fully evades the complications of biological descent.

Describing the anxiety of biology as it haunted the 1920s, Michaels writes, "Races, obliged to 'breed' their 'best,' seem required to make do with reproduction, and so the white race, a breeding disaster, seems doomed." In response, American modernists searched out the terms which would "replace reproduction with reincarnation,"[48] substituting a spiritual identification with vanishing American Indians to evade the necessary failure of biology to produce a defensible pure race. And in terms of this concern with the efficacy of reproduction, Crane's poem becomes perhaps the most successful modernist text of all by founding a notion of race that fully bypasses the body in favor of anincorruptible machinery of cultural transmission.

NOTES

[1] Carl G. Jung, "Your Negroid and Indian Behavior," *Forum* 83 (Apr. 1930): 193, 195.

[2] Hart Crane, *The Letters of Hart Crane, 1916-1932,* ed. Brom Weber (New York, 1952), 124. Hereafter, references will be cited in the body of the text as L.

[3] Thomas Parkinson, ed., *Hart Crane and Yvor Winters: Their Literary Correspondence* (Berkeley, 1978), 20.

[4] Waldo Frank, *The Rediscovery of America: An Introduction to a Philosophy of American Life* (1929; reprint, Westport, Conn., 1982), 230.

[5] Jung, "Your Negroid and Indian Behavior," 197.

[6] The best general study by far of the development of the homosexual project central to Crane's poetry is Thomas E. Yingling, *Hart Crane and the Homosexual Text: New Thresholds, New Anatomies* (Chicago, 1990).

[7] As R. P. Blackmur censored the poem, it "requires of the reader that he supply from outside the poem, and with the help of clues only, the important, controlling part of what we may loosely call the meaning." Allen Tate, himself engaged in the founding of the great literary

America, identifies this site "outside the poem" and finds it barren: "If we subtract from Crane's idea its periphery of sensation, we have left only the dead abstraction, the Greatness of America, which is capable of elucidation neither on the logical plane nor in terms of a generally known idea of America . . . Does American culture afford such a subject? It probably does not." (R. P. Blackmur, *Language as Gesture* [New York, 1980], 301; Allen Tate, "Hart Crane," in *Critical Essays on Hart Crane,* ed. David R. Clark [Boston, 1982], 119.)

[8] Where the poem's engagement with American history is taken account of at all, it is often either dismissed as, in William Pritchard's words, "the least attractive and corniest aspect of *The Bridge,"* or is disavowed as being entirely beside the point, as by John Carlos Rowe, who argues that "the poem itself is an extended attack on the very idea of American history." (William Pritchard, *Lives of the Modern Poets* [New York, 1980], 253; John Carlos Rowe, "The 'Super-Historical' Sense of Hart Crane's *The Bridge,"* *Genre* 11 [Winter 1978]: 607.) See also Joseph R. Riddel, "Hart Crane's Poetics of Failure," in *Modern American Poetry: Essays in Criticism,* ed. Jerome Mazzaro (New York, 1970), 273.

[9] "Postwar studies estimated that more than ten thousand Indian men served in the United States and Canadian armies during the war, and fully three-fourths of these were volunteers who did not have to enlist because of their noncitizenship status" (Michael L. Tate, "From Scout to Doughboy: The National Debate over Integrating American Indians into the Military, 1891-1918" *Western Historical Quarterly* 17 [Oct. 1986]: 430). See also, John C. Ewers, "A Crow Chief's Tribute to the Unknown Soldier," *American West* 8 (Nov. 1971): 30-33.

[10] Widespread authorized experiments and tests were performed on enlisted soldiers during World War I by scientists under Robert M. Yerkes in order to prove the existence of inherent racial difference. Coming out of the war, these studies were used by policy makers and racists to give scientific authority to the growing movement towards immigration restriction in the 1920s. In this study I focus on two of the groups, homosexuals and Indians, whose relationship to America was experimented with and redefined during the war. For an excellent account of the broader history and the shift away from assimilationism, see John Higham, *Strangers in the Land: Patterns of American Nativism 1860-1925* (New Brunswick, N.J., 1955); Thomas F. Gossett, *Race: The History of an Idea in America* (New York, 1965); and Stephen Jay Gould, *The Mismeasure of Man* (New York, 1981).

[11] It should be emphasized that what is being described here are ideological appropriations of Indian identity by white America, a history, as Robert Berkhofer has pointed out, that often moves in very different directions from that of Native Americans themselves and the historical appropriations of their lands and rights by white Americans. As Berkhofer writes, "Although the social and cultural attributes of Native Americans influenced the conception

of them by Whites, it is ultimately to the history of White values and ideas that we must turn for the basic conceptual categories, classificatory schema, explanatory frameworks, and moral criteria by which past and present Whites perceived, observed, evaluated, and interpreted Native Americans." Following Berkhofer's history of the "centuries-old White effort to understand themselves through understanding Native Americans," I am using the term "Indian" to refer to white America's image of historical Native Americans (Robert F. Berkhofer, Jr., *The White Man's Indian: Images of the American Indian from Columbus to the Present* [New York, 1978], xvi).

For excellent discussions of the impact of the shift towards anti-assimilationist policies on Native Americans, see Francis Paul Prucha, *The Indians in American Society: From the Revolutionary War to the Present* (Berkeley, 1985); Frederick E. Hoxie, *A Final Promise: The Campaign to Assimilate the Indians, 1880-1920* (Lincoln, Nebr., 1984); Christine Bolt, *American Indian Policy and American Reform: Case Studies of the Campaign to Assimilate the American Indians* (London, 1987).

[12] The best accounts of this debate are found in Tate and in Francis Paul Prucha, *The Great Father: The United States Government and the American Indians* (Lincoln, Nebr., 1984), 771. Interestingly, Tate tells the story from Ayer's point of view, while Prucha's version focuses entirely on Sells's arguments.

[13] Cato Sells, "The 'First Americans' as Loyal Citizens," *American Review of Reviews* 57 (May 1918): 523.

[14] House Committee on Military Affairs, *North American Indian Cavalry: H. R. 3970,* 65th Cong., 25 July 1917, 10.

[15] "American Indian Poetry," *American Review of Reviews* 57 (May 1918): 524.

[16] Frank C. Lockward, *The Life of Edward E. Ayer* (Chicago, 1929), 228.

[17] See note 10. In *The Melting Pot Mistake* (1926), Henry Pratt Fairchild proclaimed, "It seems evident that forces were at work which, if they had not been interrupted by the war, would in a few years have reduced the old immigration almost to zero." (George Harrison Knoles, ed., *The Responsibilities of Power: 1900-1929* [New York, 1967], 387-88.)

[18] Robert DeC. Ward, "Our New Immigration Policy" (1924), in *The Politics of the Nineteen Twenties,* ed. John L. Shover (Waltham, Mass., 1970), 127, 133-34. Nativist writers of the period making similar arguments about the perceived failure of the melting pot include Madison Grant, *The Passing of the Great Race* (New York, 1916); Lothrop Stoddard, *The Rising Tide of Color Against White World-Supremacy* (New York, 1920); Charles Conant Josey, *Race and National Solidarity* (New York,

1923); Gino Speranza, *Race or Nation: A Conflict of Divided Loyalties* (Indianapolis, 1923); Albert Edward Wiggam, *The Fruit of the Family Tree* (Indianapolis, 1924). Most of these works were popular successes.

[19] Lothrop Stoddard, *The Rising Tide of Color Against White World-Supremacy* (New York, 1920), 5.

[20] Larry Wayne Ward, *The Motion Picture Goes to War: The U.S. Government's Film Effort During World War I* (Ann Arbor, Mich., 1981), 103.

[21] Jennings C. Wise, *The Red Man in the New World Drama: A Politico-Legal Study with a Pageantry of American Indian History* (Washington, D.C., 1931), 524.

[22] Walter Benn Michaels, "The Vanishing American," *American Literary History* 2(Summer 1990): 231. My understanding of the 1920s is extremely indebted to Michaels's work in general, and to this essay in particular for its explanation of the use of the Indian in the defining of American citizenship during this period.

[23] Vachel Lindsay, *Selected Poems* (New York, 1963), 117.

[24] John Palmer Gavit, *American By Choice* (New York, 1922), 12.

[25] As with my discussion of the Indian, I wish here to make the similar point that while the events here discussed had very real impact upon historical people, what is central to the argument at hand is the way in which the notion of a "homosexual threat" was constructed during the war based on assumptions and characterizations that had little to do with the experiences of the actual men these policies and theories targeted.

[26] It is important to note that the notion of the vanishing Indian is a white fantasy, and in actuality the Native American population was beginning a period of growth at this time.

[27] Carroll Smith-Rosenberg, *Disorderly Conduct: Visions of Gender in Victorian America* (New York, 1985), 282.

[28] Lawrence R. Murphy, *Perverts by Official Order: The Campaign Against Homosexuals by the United States Navy* (New York, 1988), 299. My account of the Newport scandal is derived primarily from this work, with additional information and insights from Geoffrey C. Ward, *A First-Class Temperament: The Emergence of Franklin Delano Roosevelt* (New York, 1989); Jonathan Katz, *Gay/Lesbian Almanac* (New York, 1983); and George Chauncey, Jr., "Christian Brotherhood or Sexual Perversion?: Homosexual Identities and the Construction of Sexual Boundaries in the World War I Era," in *Hidden From History: Reclaiming the Gay and Lesbian Past,* ed. Martin Bauml Duberman, et al. (New York, 1989), 249-317.

[29] Murphy, *Perverts by Official Order,* 8.

[30] Ibid., 16.

[31] Ibid., 163.

[32] *New York Times,* 20 July 1921, 4.

[33] This dispersal of information helps justify a narrative whereby Roosevelt's vice squad contributes to the homo-sexualization of the American consciousness. Only a few years after the release of the report, the press would find it possible to print many details it here found "unprint-able." As Jonathan Katz writes, it is after the war that the terms of homosexuality move "out of the narrow world of physicians into the larger world reflected in *New York Times* news reports, book, film, and play reviews" (Katz, *Gay/Lesbian Almanac,* 137). There is a sense in which the emergence of the homosexual presence in America was perceived to have been made possible by World War I itself. As the *New York Times* made the connection, "The situation which the committee investigated arose out of the unusual conditions of wartime, when from 15,000 to 20,000 boys and young men who had enlisted in the Navy were sent to Newport for training" (4).

[34] The operation at Newport, while the most widely pro-mulgated campaign, was not an isolated one. In *Psycho-pathology* (1920), Dr. Edward Kempf cites his discovery of the phenomenon of "acute homosexual panic" during the war, "panic due to the pressure of uncontrollable perverse sexual cravings." He presents numerous case histories revealing the widespread and systematic con-finement of soldiers suspected of homosexuality, writing of one characteristic case, "The present psychosis began two years after his first enlistment in the United States Army. His indifference and 'queer, silly' behavior caused him to be confined in the Post Hospital" (Ed-ward J. Kempf, *Psychopathology* [St. Louis, Mo., 1920], 493).

[35] Murphy, *Perverts by Official Order,* 284.

[36] John Irwin, "Naming Names: Hart Crane's 'Logic of Metaphor,'" *Southern Review* 11 (Apr. 1975): 289.

[37] Philip Young, "The Mother of Us All: Pocahontas Reconsidered," *Kenyon Review* 24 (Summer 1962): 391-92.

[38] Leslie Fiedler, *The Return of the Vanishing American* (New York, 1968), 65.

[39] Mary Dearborn, *Pocahontas's Daughters: Gender and Ethnicity in American Culture* (New York, 1986), 5.

[40] For a full account of the history of the Pocahontas burlesque, see Werner Sollors, *Beyond Ethnicity: Con-sent and Descent in American Literature* (New York, 1986), 131-41.

[41] Ernest Hemingway, *The Torrents of Spring: A Roman-tic Novel in Honor of the Passing of a Great Race* (1926; reprint, New York, 1972), 88.

[42] All passages from *The Bridge* are quoted from *The Complete Poems and Selected Letters and Prose of Hart Crane,* ed. Brom Weber (New York, 1966). Hereafter, citations will be given parenthetically in the text by page number.

[43] Waldo Frank, *Our America* (1919; reprint, New York, 1972), 111, 115.

[44] Some examples of Crane's burlesque titles are: "Pipe down, Pocahontas, I'd like to Warm Your Wampum, Who Pokes your Hontas when I'm Gone, Wig Wag-ging in a Wigwam, I'm Happy in your happy Hunting Ground." See Kenneth A. Lohf, "The Prose Manu-scripts of Hart Crane: An Editorial Portfolio," *Proof* 2 (1972): 42-43.

[45] R. W. B. Lewis, *The Poetry of Hart Crane: A Critical Study* (Princeton, N.J., 1967), 343.

[46] Paul Giles, *Hart Crane: The Contexts of "The Bridge"* (Cambridge, 1986), 58.

[47] Sollors, *Beyond Ethnicity,* 79.

[48] Walter Benn Michaels, "The Souls of White Folk," in *Literature and the Body: Essays on Populations and Persons,* ed. Elaine Scarry (Baltimore, 1988), 201, 202.

---

## FURTHER READING

### Criticism

Brunner, Edward. *Splendid Failure: Hart Crane and the Making of "The Bridge."* Urbana and Chicago: University of Illinois Press, 1985, 282 p.
> Comprehensive analysis of *The Bridge*, encompassing the evolution of Crane's writing, an overview of critical response, and an examination of the poem itself.

Buelens, Gert. "The American Poet and His City: Crane, Williams, and Olson; Perceptions of Reality in Amer-ican Poetry (1930-1960)." *English Studies: A Journal of English Language and Literature* 73, No. 3 (June 1992): 248-63.
> Includes Crane's *The Bridge* in a study of "urban poetry" in which the image of the city represents the poet's worldview.

Dembo, L. S. *Hart Crane's Sanskrit Charge: A Study of "The Bridge."* Ithaca, N.Y.: Cornell University Press, 1960, 137 p.

Attempts to analyze *The Bridge* as a poem "out of keeping with the iconoclastic temper of the twenties," in which Crane tries to clarify and delineate his own conflicted feelings about himself and his world.

Franciosi, Robert. "Hart Crane, Lola Ridge, and Charles Reznikoff: A Note on the Early Conception of *The Bridge*." *Essays in Literature* XI, No. 2 (Fall 1984): 305-11.
    Discusses the influence of other poets on Crane's writing of *The Bridge*.

Giles, Paul. *Hart Crane: The Contexts of "The Bridge."* Cambridge: Cambridge University Press, 1986, 275 p.
    Examines the sources and influences that produced the punning and paradoxical elements of *The Bridge*.

Higginbotham, Virginia. "García Lorca and Hart Crane: Two Views from the Bridge." *Neophilologus* LXVI, No. 2 (April 1982): 219-26.
    Comparative study of Lorca's *Poeta en Nueva York* and Crane's *The Bridge*, examining the place of both in American literature and their similar views on the industrial Western world.

Irwin, John T. "The Triple Archetype: The Presence of *Faust* in *The Bridge*." *Arizona Quarterly* 50, No. 1 (Spring 1994): 51-73.
    Discusses the subliminal desire to return to the womb in *The Bridge* as it appears in the Platonic allegory of the cave and later in Goethe's "realm of the Mothers" in *Faust*.

Nilsen, Helge Normann. *Hart Crane's Divided Vision: An Analysis of "The Bridge."* Oslo: Universitetsforlaget, 1980, 202 p.
    Examines *The Bridge* as a distinctly American work informed by "mystic nationalism."

Paul, Sherman. *Hart's Bridge*. Urbana and Chicago: University of Illinois Press, 1972, 315 p.
    Analyzes the personal and historical grounds out of which *The Bridge* arose.

Slote, Bernice. "Transmutation in Crane's Imagery in *The Bridge*." *Modern Language Notes* LXXIII, No. 1 (January 1958): 15-23.
    Notes recurrence of patterns and imagery in *The Bridge* that contribute to the poem's unity.

Sugg, Richard P. *Hart Crane's The Bridge: A Description of Its Life*. University, Ala.: The University of Alabama Press, 1976, 127 p.
    Close reading of *The Bridge* that examines in detail each section of Crane's poem.

——. "Origins and Originality in Hart Crane's American Epic," in *The Origins and Originality of American Culture*, edited by Tibor Frank, pp. 149-56. Budapest: Akadémiai Kiadó, 1984.
    Examines Crane's idea of the individual and the progress toward self-realization in *The Bridge*.

---

**Additional coverage of Crane's life and career is contained in the following sources published by Gale Research:** *Concise Dictionary of American Literary Biography, 1917-1929; Con-temporary Authors*, Vols. 104, 127; *Dictionary of Literary Biography*, Vols. 4, 48; *DISCovering Authors; DISCovering Authors British; DISCovering Authors Canadian; DISC-overing Authors Modules, Most-Studied Authors* **and** *Poets; Major 20th-Century Writers; Poetry Criticism*, Vol. 3; *Twentieth-Century Literary Criticism*, Vols. 2, 5; **and** *World Literature Criticism*.

# W. C. Fields

## 1880-1946

(William Claude Dukenfield) American actor, comedian, and screenwriter.

## INTRODUCTION

Actor and comedian W. C. Fields constituted a singular presence in American entertainment during the 1930s and 1940s. In an era known for its lighthearted and usually wholesome comedies, Fields distinguished himself with his cynical, misanthropic, and hard-drinking persona. He primarily played two roles, either the henpecked husband or the cunning cheat. He portrayed both characters in *The Old-Fashioned Way* (1934); the former in *It's a Gift* (1934), *The Man on the Flying Trapeze* (1935), and *The Bank Dick* (1940); and the latter in *You Can't Cheat an Honest Man* (1939) and *My Little Chickadee* (1940). Whatever the guise, he claimed more or less the same set of dislikes—wives, mothers-in-law, children, pets, bankers, doctors, the law—and the same likes. The latter, a much shorter list than his dislikes, consisted chiefly of alcohol, tobacco, and cards. Like a character from Dickens, whose Mr. Micawber he portrayed in a memorable role for the 1935 production of *David Copperfield*, Fields was well-known for his physical attributes, including a bulbous red nose and a raspy voice that came from a side of his mouth. Fields, who wrote or at least conceived many of his screenplays, created a curmudgeonly persona that closely resembled his real self, according to the accounts of many who knew him. His cynical humor, which often placed him at odds with the attitudes of his era, has made him at least as popular in the decades after his death as he was during his lifetime.

### Biographical Information

Fields was born William Claude Dukenfield in Philadelphia in 1879. The son of a Cockney immigrant, Fields was put to work selling vegetables at an early age. His childhood was by most accounts not an easy one: his trademark nose, which many assumed to be the product of his heavy drinking, in fact took on its shape from being broken in numerous fights during his youth, and his raspy voice may have resulted from the many colds he suffered. At the age of nine, he saw his first vaudeville show, and resolved to become a juggler. In his teens, he began to perform on stage under his newly adopted name of Fields, and by the age of twenty, he was a vaudeville star. Around the turn of the century, he took part in a European tour, during which he performed at Buckingham Palace, and by 1905, he was appearing on Broadway. Greater success followed with a role in the Broadway production of *Watch Your Step* by Irving Ber-

lin in 1914, and with the signing of a seven-year contract with the Ziegfield Follies starting in 1915. By then, Fields had added a comedy routine to his juggling act, and had attracted the attention of the growing film industry. After several experiments with motion pictures during the silent era, Fields began his career as a film actor in 1930—just when sound had replaced silent pictures—with a short called *The Golf Specialist*. Later he would appear in four two-reel movies he wrote himself. *It's a Gift* in 1934 marked the first feature film conceived by and starring Fields. He followed this with a number of acclaimed roles, but a bout of illness in 1936 incapacitated him for some time. During his recovery, Fields began a secondary career as a radio personality, engaging in a celebrated "rivalry" with Charlie McCarthy, the dummy operated by ventriloquist Edgar Bergen. There followed a second series of films written and/or conceived by Fields, who also starred in them: *You Can't Cheat an Honest Man*, which also starred Bergen and McCarthy; *My Little Chickadee*, cowritten with Mae West, his co-star; *The Bank Dick* (1940), and *Never Give a Sucker an Even Break*. Fields died on Christmas Day in 1946.

**Major Works**

"Bill had only one story," recalled director Eddie Sutherland. "It wasn't a story at all, really—there was just an ugly old man, an ugly woman, and a brat of a child." *The Fatal Glass of Beer*, one of four short films Fields wrote during 1932 and 1933, did indeed center around an absurd story involving a father, mother, and their long-lost son; but in *The Dentist*, *The Pharmacist*, and *The Barber Shop*, Fields's character confronted institutions or professions rather than family members. With *It's a Gift*, he began to develop the henpecked persona in the form of a grocer consumed by his dream of starting an orange grove on a worthless plot of land in California. Ambrose Wolfinger in *The Man on the Flying Trapeze* is similarly hapless, as is Fields's character in *The Bank Dick*, a bank security guard who repeatedly escapes his family to drink at the Black Pussy Cat Café. By contrast, Larson E. Whipsnade, the protagonist of *You Can't Cheat an Honest Man*, is typical of Field's other persona, the cynical and conniving rascal. That persona reappeared in *My Little Chickadee*, with Fields and West playing types they had already made famous in their careers. Fields wrote under a variety of unlikely sounding pseudonyms such as "Mahatma Kane Jeeves." The years since Fields's death have seen the appearance of numerous books containing his witticisms, as well as a volume edited by grandson Ronald Fields, entitled *W. C. Fields by Himself: His Intended Autobiography* (1973).

---

## PRINCIPAL WORKS

*The Dentist* (screenplay) 1932
*The Fatal Glass of Beer* (screenplay) 1932
*The Barber Shop* (screenplay) 1933
*The Pharmacist* (screenplay) 1933
*It's a Gift* [as Charles Bogle] (screenplay)* 1934
*The Old-Fashioned Way* [as Charles Bogle] (screenplay)* 1934
*The Man on the Flying Trapeze* [as Charles Bogle, with Sam Hardy] (screenplay)* 1935
*You Can't Cheat an Honest Man* [as Charles Bogle] (screenplay)* 1939
*My Little Chickadee* [with Mae West] (screenplay) 1940
*The Bank Dick* [as Mahatma Kane Jeeves] (screenplay) 1940
*Never Give a Sucker an Even Break* [as Otis Criblecoblis] (screenplay)* 1941
*W. C. Fields by Himself: His Intended Autobiography* [commentary by Ronald Fields] (autobiography) 1973

---

*Fields conceived the story for this work, and other writers received credit for writing the actual screenplay.

## CRITICISM

**Heywood Broun (essay date 1931)**

SOURCE: An essay in *The Nation*, New York, Vol. 132, No. 3419, January 7, 1931, pp. 24-5.

[*In the following essay, Broun offers his appraisal of Fields's performance in the film* Ballyhoo.]

To me this seems a year in which the musical comedies distinctly show the way to so-called legitimate attractions. My quarrel with that word "legitimate" is deep and of long standing. I have never been able to understand why entertainment becomes more important simply because no one sings. In recent years I begin to sense a new point of view among critics. When I held a reviewer's post on a morning paper, it was practically treason not to choose a comedy or a farce if it happened to open on the same night as a musical show. Now there are heretics who abandon the old principle. It would be folly to do otherwise.

For instance, there came a night not so long ago in which the choice lay between W. C. Fields in *Ballyhoo* at Hammerstein's Theater and a comedy drama entitled *Life Is Like That*. Some few of the pundits insisted on being faithful to the memory of Shakespeare and passed up Mr. Fields to witness *Life Is Like That*. The loss was theirs. I found Fields to be at the very top of his glorious best, and I liked the story in which he is set.

A satire on C. C. Pyle, the sporting promoter, has long seemed one of the neglected spaces in the American drama. I will not maintain that the plot runs down all the possibilities of the subject matter. But, at least, the scheme endows Fields with a role in which he is believable as well as amusing.

It is well to remember that a performance in musical comedy is a piece of acting just as a portrayal of Hamlet, the Prince of Denmark, may be. I will grant that there are depths and subtleties in Hamlet not likely to be found in the usual revue. On the other hand, low comedy parts are vastly better played in most instances. I do not see why any sensitive connoiseur of acting should not vastly prefer W. C. Fields to Walter Hampden. A good comic moves in a plane high above the head of an indifferent tragedian. It might be an excellent idea for the American public to pause in its continual program of self-reproach and take a little pride in the fact that we lead the world in the matter of musical comedy.

*Ballyhoo* is not a perfect specimen, but it is amply excellent to provide a hilarious evening. Several of the regular critics found it dull, but I think they are too captious, and to some extent it is the custom to remain slightly aloof and calm while writing about revues.

Much is made of the fact that Mr. Fields does things now which he has shown us previously. This seems to me an ungrateful form of criticism. The fact that he can produce endless fun by capers in an Austin car should not be minimized simply because some seasons ago he did tricks with a Ford. And I feel that one of the high spots in the present theatrical year has been underlined in red because W. C. Fields is juggling again.

I am of the opinion that in this diversion the man falls little short of genius. You may protest that juggling does not belong among the major arts. Such an opinion will be held only by those who have witnessed merely the proficient practitioners. Fields is, as far as I know, the only one who is able to introduce the tragic note in the handling of a dozen cigar boxes. When they are pyramided, only to crash because of a sudden off-stage noise, my heart goes out to the protagonist as it seldom does to Lear or Macbeth.

If one thinks of art in terms of line and movement, then I suggest that there is present in this juggling act as much to please the eye as when Pavlowa dances. Like the best of modern painters, Fields can afford to depart from the orthodox, because he is heretical from choice and not through incapacity. I mean, it is amusing when he muffs a trick because you know that he could easily complete it if he cared to. Certainly, there is something admirable in the ability to emotionalize the task of tossing spheres into the air and catching them in rhythm. Possibly there is even profundity in such a pastime.

Mr. Fields at play among the planets suggests to me an Einsteinian quality. I do not like to rush into symbolism, but if a mortal can personally see to it that these complicated orbits are preserved, each in its entity, then I go home more sure of the safety and sanctity of the universe than before.

And yet, it might be simpler merely to say that *Ballyhoo* is excellent entertainment.

## J. B. Priestley (essay date 1947)

SOURCE: "W.C. Fields," in *The New Statesman and Nation,* Vol. XXXIII, No. 828, January 4, 1947, p. 8.

[*In the following essay, Priestly eulogizes Fields.*]

So now there is another cold gap, for W. C. Fields is dead. I wrote the rough treatment of a film for him once—and kept my family all winter in Arizona on the proceeds (those were the days)—but the film was never made, chiefly, I think, because even then Fields could no longer sustain a leading rôle. It was a story about an itinerant piano tuner wandering round the ranches in the South-West, and had, I think, some good Fieldsian situations in it. In one of them Fields, in despair and after some desperate bragging, decides to get tough and hold up a car, but the car he chooses is full of old Western sharpshooters on their way to a rodeo and delighted to

find a little target practice on the way. If you remember Fields, you can imagine him in that situation.

I saw him long before he found his way to Hollywood, before 1914, when he was touring the halls here with his juggling and trick billiard table act. He was very funny even then, and I seem to remember him balancing a number of cigar boxes and staring with horror at a peculiar box, in the middle of the pile, that wobbled strangely, as if some evil influence were at work. All his confidence, which you guessed from the first to be a desperate bluff, vanished at the sight of this one diabolical box, which began to threaten him with the nightmare of hostile and rebellious things. And this, I fancy, was the secret of his huge and enchanting drollery—though, oddly enough, it seems to have been missed—that he moved, warily in spite of a hastily assumed air of nonchalant confidence, through a world in which even the inanimate objects were hostile, rebellious, menacing, never to be trusted. He had to be able to *juggle* with things, to be infinitely more dexterous than you and I need be, to find it possible to handle them at all. They were not, you see, his things, these commonplace objects of ours. He did not belong to this world, but had arrived from some other and easier planet.

All the truly great clowns—and Fields was undoubtedly one of them—have the same transient look. They are not men of this world being funny. They are serious personages—perhaps musicians like Grock, ambassadors with attendants like the Fratellini, or hopeful inventor-promoters like Fields—who have, through some blunder on the part of a celestial Thomas Cook, landed from the other side of Arcturus on the wrong planet. They make the best of a bad business, but what is easy for us—merely picking up a bag of golf clubs or moving a chair—is horribly difficult for them. Things that give us no trouble offer them obstacles and traps, for nothing here is on their side.

Nobody could suggest the malice of objects better than Fields. At his best moments, an ordinary room, empty of other human beings, could turn itself into a mined mountain pass. He could start a bitter feud with two chairs and a sideboard. When he arrived in places like golf courses or billiards rooms he would be plunged into an Arabian Night of sorcery. Once in a delirious short film he appeared as a dentist, surrounded by gadgets and visited by curious patients, and then there was nothing for it but to go berserk; and as you stared at him you could feel your temperature rising. He wandered through Hollywood films like a hoarse Ally Sloper in Wonderland. Even when he did not care any more, and was only anxious to sail away on a sea of double Martinis and straight Bourbon, and ambled through any kind of supporting part, usually as a broken-down showman, he was still a character in another dimension, still faintly illuminated by the wonder and nonchalant glory of the great clown. In about the last scene I remember him in, he was denounced by the outraged host at a party as "an incorrigible prevaricator" or something of that sort. "Is that good or bad?" the

Fields character demanded, poised between friendship and fury.

Like so many Americans whom we think of with gratitude and affection, he showed what he thought of the American way of life by drinking and thumb-nosing himself clean out of it. Always a ripe character off the stage, he became fruitier and more fantastic in his later years, turning his whole existence into one huge comic character part. He began as a waif and ended as one. The vast pretensions of Hollywood withered away at his glazed look and contemptuous mutter. (Among his entourage he had a man with a tiny head. And with a head like that, Fields announced, "he'll own Hollywood.") He was frequently cast as the boaster whose bluff was called, the inventor who achieved nothing useful, the intriguer who missed success; but one always had an odd feeling, perhaps because one knew that this was not really his world at all, that his failure was better than the other people's triumph. And though he was no Micawber in voice, appearance, manners, somehow he contrived to suggest the indomitable romanticism of Micawber, the spirit that transformed the lower depths of corn and coal agencies into the shining stuff of an epic. He was Micawber's American grandson who had got into show business and had been kicked around.

Fields was a professional droll who defied all conventions and soaked himself in hard liquor. No doubt he had had his day. But his departure, perhaps for his real home where the furniture is quiet and kind and all things behave properly, is a sad loss to America, which could better spare whole rows of hard-faced rich men, glad-handing politicians, obedient editors and raucous commentators, than it could this one rebellious clown. For it is here, among these bitter or uproarious drolls, slapping the custard pie on the faces of solemn prominent citizens, refusing to sign on the dotted line, that American life stays healthy, ripe, still crammed with promise, and not among the brassy patriots and the enquirers into Un-American Activities. Long ago Fields made us laugh by staring in despair at the wobbling cigar boxes. Now the others stare at the wobbling boxes too. But I doubt if they will make anybody laugh.

**Corey Ford (excerpt date 1967)**

SOURCE: "The One and Only," in *The Time of Laughter,* Little, Brown and Company, 1967, pp. 171-95.

[*In the following excerpt, Ford offers his personal recollections of Fields.*]

W. C. Fields is generally acknowledged to be the supreme comic artist of his time, in my own opinion the funniest man who ever lived, and he was even funnier offstage than on. His drawn-out rasping voice was the same, of course, but he had an infectious giggle, a falsetto he-he-he-he-he like the chirp of a cricket, which I never heard him use in his professional work. His everyday speech was extravagantly florid. "Methinks," he would intone, "there's a Nubian in the fuel supply." Due to his zealous reading of the eighteenth-century English romanticists, their stilted phraseology came naturally to his lips—"Betwixt" or "Forsooth" or "Hither and yon"—and he was the only person I've known to start a sentence with the word "Likely."

That occurred one night when Fields and I were having dinner at Chasen's. We were in one of the semicircular booths along the wall, and Bill by preference was facing the rear of the restaurant. Over his shoulder I could see Sabu, the Elephant Boy, making one of his elaborate entrances, clad in Indian robes and followed by two tall Sikh bearers (probably from Central Casting) with white turbans wound on their heads. The *chokras* stood with arms folded while Sabu seated himself in the booth next to ours, back to back with Fields. Bill had become conscious of the commotion behind him, and he swung his head slowly around, his gaze moving like the beam of a revolving harbor light until it fixed on Sabu with a baleful glare. Out of the corner of his mouth, in an aside which could have been heard clear to Santa Barbara, he growled to me, "Likely the little mahout will mistake my nose for a proboscis, and climb on my sho-o-oulder."

We had a weekly date to dine together at Chasen's, joined sometimes by Roland ("Stingy Lips") Young or Billy Grady, Fields's former business manager and vituperative companion, or Dave himself when he had a free moment. Over his eighth or ninth Martini, Bill was wont to lapse into sentimental recollections of his experiences in show business. "Got the theater in my blo-o-ood," he would drawl. "My great uncle Fortescue used to be a Swiss bell-ringer at Elks' smokers. Ah, yaas, poor old Uncle Fortescue. Run over by a horse-car in Scollay Square, Boston, after attending a musi-*cale* at the Parker House." I never knew how much of what he said was factual, for Fields, a true artist, constantly embellished his stories with new imaginative touches. It didn't matter. Bill could have recited the alphabet and had me rolling on the floor.

He had toured the world, under the auspices of Tex Rickard, and loved to boast of his travels to Samoa and Australia. "Once I fell in love with a Melanesian belle," he would reminisce, "a charming little savage with kinky hair that bristled like a barberry hedge. A *Bar-r-rb*'ry hedge, yaas. Had a wooden soup dish in her nether lip, and through her nose was a brass ring from a missionary's hitching post. Prettiest gal on the island." Or: "One day in Melbourne whilst strolling down the street I observed a number of vehicles drawn up before a sumptuous mansion. So I went up to the door, and a butler stuck a silver plate under my nose. I contributed an old laundry slip and a dime, and went in. Most enjoyable soiree, most enjoyable. I had a long talk with the governor's wife."

"What did you talk about?" I asked.

"We discussed the mating habits of the wallaby."

Now and then he would dwell on his early boyhood in Germantown, a suburb of Philadelphia. He was born William Claude Dukenfield, the son of poor but dishonest parents. His mother would lie abed until midday—"besotted with gin," Bill emphasized to me carefully—and when she heard the noon whistle she would leap to her feet, pausing only to tie on an apron and dash some water over her face. Then she would stand on the front steps, mopping the bogus perspiration from her brow with a corner of the apron, and sighing, "Been working all morning over a hot stove" as the neighbors walked by. "Good day to ye, Mrs. Muldoon," she would beam, and add, after the stroller was out of hearing, "Terrible gossip, Mrs. Muldoon. Oh, and how are *you* today, Mrs. Frankel?" Another pause as she passed. "Nasty old bitch, Mrs. Frankel. Ah, there, Mrs. Cudahy, a lovely morning, is it not?" Bill's hypocritical greetings and *sotto voce* asides were clearly patterned on his mother.

His nasal drawl, on the other hand, was a heritage from his father, who owned an elderly nag named White Swan and made a scanty living hawking fresh vegetables from door to door, which he advertised in a hoarse adenoidal voice. Much against his will, young Bill was forced to accompany his father in the grocery wagon and help peddle the produce. He devoted his efforts to mimicking the elder Dukenfield, chanting in the same singsong whine a list of vegetables which he invented because he liked the names: "Pomegranates, rutabagas, calabashes." When housewives hurried out to purchase these exotics, his father would explain that his son was new to the job, and then clout him on the ear when they were out of sight.

Mr. Dukenfield was a firm believer in strict discipline, and whacked his son regularly whether he deserved it or not. He had lost the little finger of his left hand in the Crimean War—or so Bill claimed—and the absence of this digit made his back-hand blow a particularly bruising weapon. Once, at the age of nine, Bill sneaked past the ticket-taker at the local vaudeville house, and spent a fascinated afternoon watching a juggling act. Filled with enthusiasm, he stole some lemons and oranges from his father's cart, and practiced the new art. "By the time I learned to keep two of them in the air at once," he admitted, "I'd ruined several dollars' worth of fruit." His father took stern measures to cure him of this expensive habit, concealing himself in the stable until he caught his son in the act which would one day make him famous, and giving him a parental beating. One afternoon Bill left a small rake in the yard, and when Mr. Dukenfield stepped on it the handle banged his shin. Seeing that Bill was observing him from the doorway with evident amusement, he picked up the rake and bashed it over the boy's head. Bill resolved to square accounts—"I rejected certain measures which might have elicited the attention of the coroner," he said—and settled on the simple solution of hiding on a ledge above the stable door, poising a heavy wooden crate. His father entered, Bill flattened him, and left home at the age of eleven, never to return.

Psychologists have analyzed the humor of W. C. Fields, and concluded that his prejudices and fears were due to a basic hostility toward his father. Mr. Dukenfield was given to singing sentimental ballads around the house, they point out; Bill hated vocal music to his dying day. His cantankerous nature, his never-ending war with producers and directors, indicated a subconscious rebellion against the paternal image. Well, maybe it's all true, and yet I feel with E. B. White that "Humor can be dissected, as a frog can, but the thing dies in the process and the innards are discouraging to any but the pure scientific mind." Personally I prefer to think of Fields as a comic genius who defies analysis, unequaled among America's funnymen, the one and only.

Gene Buck, who hired Fields for the *Follies,* wrote after his death: "He was amazing and unique, the strangest guy I ever knew in my lifetime. He was all by himself. Nobody could be like him, and a great many tried. He was so damn different, original and talented. He never was a happy guy. He couldn't be, but what color and daring in this game of life! He made up a lot of new rules about everything: conduct, people, morals, entertainment, friendship, gals, pals, fate and happiness, and he had the courage to ignore old rules. . . . He had taken a terrible kicking around in life, and he was tough, bitter, and cynical in an odd humorous way. His gifts and talents as an entertainer were born in him, I think. God made him funny. He knew more about comedy and real humor than any other person. . . . When Bill left the other day, something great in the world died, and something very badly needed."

He had the round ruddy face of a dignified and slightly felonious country squire. Its most prominent feature was the celebrated red-veined nose, which would grow redder like a warning light if he felt he was being victimized. When an insurance company doctor examined him and refused to renew his health policy, he protested to Gene Fowler, "The nefarious quack claimed he found urine in my whisky." His very appearance evoked shouts of laughter from an audience: the manorial air that was so obviously false, the too benign smile, the larcenous eye.

"His whole manner suggested fakery in its most flagrant form," Robert Lewis Taylor wrote in a recent biography. "One of the stills from *My Little Chickadee* shows him as Cuthbert J. Twillie, a crooked oil man, in a Western poker game with several desperadoes, all eying him appraisingly. Fields himself is rigged out in a cutaway, striped trousers, and a high gray felt hat with a broad black band; he is wearing formal white gloves, which are turned back delicately, and he has a wilted lily in his buttonhole. His hands, graceful and expressive, are carefully shielding his cards from any possible snooping by the man on his left, while his own furtive, suspicious gaze is plainly directed into the hand of the player on his right. His attitude is so frankly dishonest that the other players seem to sense the inevitability of their financial downfall." Their fears were justified in the ensuing scene in which Fields managed to deal himself four aces and win a thousand-dollar pot without having undergone the inconvenience of putting up any money himself.

Fields's distrust of doctors and lawyers was neurotic. "They're all knaves and thieves," he insisted to Gene Fowler once. "I know a thief when I see one. When I was young I was the biggest thief at large. I'd steal golf balls, piggy banks of dear little kiddies, or the nozzle off the hose on the rectory lawn." He termed the members of the medical profession "dastardly fee-splitters. When doctors and undertakers meet, they always wink at each other." Bankers were even worse, he held. In order to outwit their cunning designs, he deposited small sums of money in banks scattered all over the country, even stepping off a transcontinental train to open an account in a small town while the engine was taking on water. Some of these accounts were under his own name, but most of them were credited to Figley J. Whitesides or Dr. Otis Guelpe or Larson E. Whipsnade, names which he had accumulated in the course of his travels. Gene Fowler told me once that Bill had over seven hundred bank accounts or safe-deposit boxes in such far-flung cities as London, Paris, Sydney, Cape Town, and Suva. "I think he lost at least fifty thousand dollars in the Berlin bombing," he speculated. Since Fields never took anyone into his confidence about his financial arrangements, and no bankbooks showed up after his death, it is probable that a sizable fortune is still stashed away in various banks under assumed names. Bill insisted that his unique deposit system not only insured him against conniving bankers, but also made it difficult for income tax agents to collect revenue for the government, which he likewise mistrusted. "Uncle Whiskers will strike down even a child and take away its marbles," he glowered.

Children were another of Fields's pet phobias. "Of course I like little tots," he would protest righteously, "if they're well cooked." When a group of noisy young autograph seekers surrounded him after John Barrymore's funeral, he bellowed, "Get away from me, you diminutive gamins. For two cents—or even one—I'd kick in your teeth. Back to reform school!" His radio feud with Edgar Bergen's wooden dummy, Charlie McCarthy, was genuine, and he would put real feeling into a snarled threat: "I'll slash you into Venetian blinds." Baby LeRoy, with whom he made several films, was his particular aversion. He was convinced that the infant was deliberately plotting to steal scenes from him, and would eye him with dark suspicion, muttering vague threats under his breath. Once he succeeded in spiking Baby LeRoy's orange juice with a surreptitious shot of gin, and sat back amiably while Norman Taurog, the director, tried in vain to rouse the youngster from his pleasant slumbers. "Walk him around, walk him around," Fields advised professionally from a corner. When Baby LeRoy had to be taken home and the shooting postponed till the next day, Fields was jubilant. "That kid's no trouper," he jeered.

One of the most agreeable moments in his film career occurred while shooting *The Old Fashioned Way,* in the course of which Baby LeRoy dropped Field's watch in the molasses, overturned some soup in his lap, and hit him between the eyes with a spoonful of ice cream. In the following scene, Fields was alone in a room with the obstreperous infant, who was creeping on all four across the carpet. Following the script, his face shining with benevolence, he drew back his foot and lofted his tormentor several feet forward. The cameras recorded some excellent footage, but Fields's conscience evidently troubled him, for the next day he arrived on the set with an armload of toys and gifts for young LeRoy. "One of the gifts was a bowie knife," he chuckled to me malevolently.

Sometimes Bill would lapse into a sentimental mood. "When I was a little tot," he recalled one evening at Chasen's, "I had to earn my way into the circus by lugging water for the elephants. All day long I would trudge back and forth, staggering under the weight of the burdensome receptacles till my arms were numb. Then and there I made a vow that, if I ever succeeded in life, I would donate a sum of money to help some other little tot like myself who had to lug water all day. Waal," and Bill made the gesture of peeling an imaginary glove off his hand and shrugged modestly, "fate proved kind to me, I was blest with more than my share of life's riches, and one day I thought of the money I'd vowed to give that poor little tot lugging water." His eyes narrowed. "And then I had a second thought: f——him."

Strangely his language, though generously larded with obscenities, never seemed off-color or offensive. Today's degenerate jokes and sick humor are, to me, infinitely more filthy than Bill's earthy Anglo-Saxon speech. His drawling voice and squirelike dignity robbed a four-letter word of any suggestion of smut. On stage, of course, he resorted to euphemisms like "Drat!" or "Godfrey Daniel!" to elude the censor; but the truth is that Fields was genuinely embarrassed by dirty stories, particularly when told in the presence of women. If someone started a bawdy anecdote in mixed company, he would make some excuse to leave the room, or wander around uneasily in a pretended search for a match.

Field's attitude toward women was courtly, even a trifle old-fashioned, and he would remove his hat punctiliously in an elevator or rise promptly to his feet if a lady entered the room. One hot afternoon Bill was sitting stark naked behind his desk when Billy Grady and a female companion burst through the door without warning. Ever the gentleman, Bill stood up politely and extended his hand, and then blinked in surprise as the lady gasped and departed in haste. He greeted members of the fair sex with such cavalier terms of endearment as "My little chickadee" or "My glow-worm" or, in a romantic scene with Mae West, "My little brood mare." At the time his residence on Toluca Lake was up for sale, Fields volunteered to show a timid pair of prospective purchasers around the house. "This is the dining room," he explained as they started their tour, "and this is the library, and this is the mah-ster bedroom." He led them across his room, past the rumpled bed where a blonde was lying asleep on her stomach. "How are you, my little turtle-dove?" he inquired, patting her fanny solicitously. "And this," he continued with perfect poise to the speechless couple, "is the sun-porch. . . . "

It was his dislike of birds—still another of Bill's innumerable prejudices—which led him to sell his Toluca Lake home, an imposing mansion with broad green lawns sloping down to an artificial lake, the featured attraction of the real estate development. The shallow lake was populated by numerous ducks and swans, which used to roam over Bill's property and hiss at him, an unforgivable affront to an actor. Whenever Bill spotted one of his web-footed adversaries cropping his grass, he would place a golf ball in position and drive it accurately at the intruder with a number-four iron, whereupon the outraged bird would flap its wings and chase Bill up the lawn and into the house. The battle grew more and more ruthless. Once Bill borrowed a canoe and pursued a large swan all over the lake, until he dozed off after his strenuous efforts, and the swan crept up behind the canoe and nipped him from the rear. "The miscreant fowl broke all the rules of civilized warfare," he complained later.

Norm McLeod, who lived two doors away, was directing him in a picture for Paramount, and was well aware of Bill's reputation for being taken drunk in the middle of the shooting. To make sure that nothing happened, McLeod moved from his own home and spent each watchful night on a cot in Bill's bedroom. One Sunday morning Norm slept late, and awoke with a start to find his roommate missing. As he leaped off the cot, his bare foot collided with an empty Bourbon bottle, and he suspected the worst. Somewhere in the distance he could hear Bill's voice, but he had a little trouble locating it. At last he stepped out onto the sun-porch, which commanded a sweeping view of Toluca Lake and the surrounding estates, their bedroom windows wide open in the early Sabbath stillness. Fields, clad in pajamas and carpet slippers, was wandering around the grass, liberally dotted with unsightly white droppings deposited by the ducks and swans. Grasping a heavy cane by the stick end, he was swinging it right and left at the feathered trespassers, bellowing in a voice which must have penetrated every neighboring boudoir, "If you can't shit green, get off my lawn."

Bill's capacity for alcohol was enormous—his household staff estimated that he consumed two quarts of Martinis a day—but I never saw him show the slightest effect. "I have a system," he confided to me once. "I know I've had enough when my knees bend backward." Although pictured by the public as a lush who indulged in wild drinking sprees, Fields had nothing but contempt for the thick-tongued staggering drunk, and would order a friend from his house if he became tipsy. "Gives drinking a bad name," he growled. His own day started with a modest breakfast of two Martinis (if ravenous, he would take a third), and lunch consisted of another couple of Martinis which he washed down with some heavily reinforced imported beer. He brought a giant foam-rubber ice bucket of

Martinis each day to the studio, the rear of his car was converted into an efficient bar, and he would secrete a dozen miniatures in the pockets of his golf bag before setting out for an afternoon on the links. "I always keep a supply of stimulant handy in case I see a snake," he liked to explain, "which I also keep handy." Generally this would tide him over until the cocktail hour before dinner. "Don't believe in eating on an empty stomach," he maintained.

Alcohol seemed to serve as a sedative for his jangled nerves, and put him in a relaxed mood for a performance. "His timing was better when he was drinking," Mack Sennett claimed. "He was sharp, sure, positive." Every so often, after a hospital siege, he would determine to give up drinking entirely. During one of these periods, we met at Chasen's before going to the opening of the *Ice Follies,* and Bill announced that he was on the wagon. On the wagon, I discovered, meant that he had given up Martinis, and drank only Bourbon and Scotch and beer and brandy. As a result of his abstinence, we did not finish dinner until ten-thirty, and the *Ice Follies* were almost over when we arrived. Even the usual crowd of autograph hunters outside the theater had dispersed, save for one pimply youngster who spotted Fields as he descended from his limousine and ran across the sidewalk, holding out a notebook and pleading, "C'n I have your autograph, Mr. Fields?" "Why, of course, of course, yaas, to be sure," Bill said pleasantly, and inscribed his name with a flourish. The boy stammered his thanks, and Bill patted him fondly on the head. "Quite all right, my nose-picking little bastard," he pronounced in benediction, and entered the theater.

Billy Grady, who had managed Field's business affairs during his early career, assured me one night at dinner that Bill always traveled with two wardrobe trunks, one for clothes and one for gin. "That's a lie," Fields thundered, "I had gin in both trunks." Fields and Grady loved to tell stories of their road trips together, interrupting each other repeatedly with blistering insults. "One night in Homosassa, Florida," Bill began. "It was Ocala, Florida, you feeble-minded moron," Grady broke in. "You call everything Homosassa because you like the name." "Keep your Irish-Catholic mouth shut," Bill roared back, and turned to me. "One night in Homosassa, Florida, we were driving in the rain when I spotted a man with a satchel standing under a street light, signaling for a lift. I requested Grady to halt our vehicle and let the stranger climb aboard—"

"I'm the one who wanted to stop for him, you kindergarten dropout," Grady interrupted. "You were afraid he'd drink some of your gin."

Fields gave him a withering glance. "Out of the goodness of my heart, I proffered the fellow a touch of stimulant to ward off a chill, and he gave me a look of righteous indignation. 'Look not upon the wine when it is red,' he said, 'It stingeth like the adder, and biteth like the serpent. Eschew the curse of the demon rum.'

"I motioned Grady to pull up at the side of the road. 'Who are you, my good man?' I inquired.

"'I am a minister of the gospel,' he said, opening his satchel and taking out some religious tracts, 'and it is my duty to convert you from the evils of drink.'

"'Out, you pious son-of-a-bitch, out!' I said, and placing my foot against his chest I propelled him backward into a drainage ditch, pausing only to toss an empty gin bottle into the ditch beside him before we drove on." Bill shuddered at the recollection. "A most unnerving experience," he sighed, and signaled the waiter to replenish his glass.

Bill had first won fame as "The Tramp Juggler," developing the skill he had acquired with his father's oranges and lemons into a spectacular vaudeville act which he climaxed by juggling twenty-five cigar boxes balanced end on end with a rubber ball on top. He employed no patter, causing *Variety* to observe: "Why Mr. Fields does not speak is quite simple. His comedy speaks for him." As his reputation grew, Gene Buck signed him for the *Ziegfeld Follies of 1915,* part of a glittering cast which included Ann Pennington and George White, Bert Williams, Ina Claire, and Ed Wynn as "Himself." It was in the *Follies* that Fields introduced Broadway to his immortal pool-table act, using an ancient billiard cue warped and twisted into a spiral. He would sight dubiously along the cue, halt his game to shift the chalk a few critical inches right or left because it offended his expert eye, and give the racked balls a single whack. An ingenious system of concealed strings would yank the balls into the pockets like a colony of gophers taking cover. After a heated session, in which he ripped the felt cloth into shreds, he would rear on tiptoes for a final killing shot and drive the cue downward through the splintered table, plunging his arm into the hole up to the shoulder.

Ed Wynn and Fields, as rival comedians, were constantly vying for laughs. During one performance, Wynn concealed himself beneath the pool table and tried to steal the scene by smirking and winking at the audience. Fields became uneasily aware that his laughs were coming at the wrong places, and his eye caught a suspicious movement under the table. He waited patiently until Wynn, on all fours, carelessly stuck his head out too far. With a juggler's perfect timing, Fields swung the butt end of his cue in a half-circle and lowered it onto his rival's skull. Wynn sagged to the floor while Fields continued his game serenely amid boisterous applause. Every time that Wynn struggled back to consciousness and emitted a low moan, the audience laughed louder at what they thought was his clever impersonation. Later Fields suggested that Wynn's bit might be incorporated into the act each night for the duration of the run, but Wynn declined to take advantage of his offer.

During his successive years in the *Follies*—Fields appeared in every edition from 1915 through 1921—he created other comic routines which have become famous: the golf act, in which a stray piece of paper blew across the course and wrapped itself inextricably around his club, defying all his efforts to shake it off; the rear of a three-story tenement, with Fields trying in vain to take a nap in a porch hammock amid the bedlam of neighborhood noises; the subway scene in the 1921 *Follies,* in which he was supported by Fannie Brice, Raymond Hitchcock, and Ray Dooley as a howling infant. Gradually Fields was building the familiar character of a frustrated man, harassed by inanimate objects over which he had no control—much the same beleaguered citizen portrayed, in a different technique, by Robert Benchley. His characterization reached perfection in 1923 with the musical comedy *Poppy,* in which the former Tramp Juggler graduated once and for all into an authentic and expert comedian. Fields played the role of Eustace McGargle, a magnificent fraud who gained his livelihood by fleecing the local yokels at a country fair. The grandiose eloquence and unctuous smile of the unscrupulous mountebank, urging the innocent farmers to participate with him in the shell-game and then commenting in an aside, "Never give a sucker an even break," established the pattern which Fields followed the rest of his life.

*Poppy* was an enormous success, and Bill, in a tender moment, brought his mother from Philadelphia to New York to watch his performance. "Why, Claude, I didn't know you had such a good memory," was Mrs. Dukenfield's cryptic comment. At a midnight supper after the show, Bill regaled her with hair-raising tales of his travels among savage tribes in the South Pacific. "One night some aborigines invited me to dinner," he began, "a tasty repast, starting off with whale—"

"Gracious," Mrs. Dukenfield interrupted, "I should think that would have been a meal in itself."

Fields's film debut occurred in 1925 at the Paramount Studios on Long Island. Paramount had decided to make a silent motion picture of *Poppy*—which was retitled, for obscure reasons, *Sally of the Sawdust*—and, after trying vainly to engage Fatty Arbuckle for the part of Eustace McGargle, reluctantly hired Fields to play his original stage role. Fields, giving the industry a foretaste of what it might expect in future years, usurped the star's dressing room, bullied D. W. Griffith, the director, and generally ran things with a high hand. Since Fields had created the McGargle character and could play it in his sleep, the picture was hailed as a comic masterpiece, and he followed it in 1926 with *So's Your Old Man,* and a year later with *Running Wild,* both directed by Gregory La Cava.

Although they struck sparks from the start—Fields always referred to him as "that dago bastard"—La Cava became a lifelong friend. Out of their intimate association, La Cava formed the theory that Fields's whole life was dedicated to repaying society for his cruel childhood. Robert Lewis Taylor quotes La Cava: "Nearly everything Bill tried to get into his movies was something that lashed out at the world. The peculiar thing is that although he thought he was being pretty mean there wasn't any real sting to it. It was only funny. Bill never really wanted to hurt anybody. He just felt an obligation."

Fields had the divine ability to turn his prejudices to comic advantage. Since acquiring a car, he had developed a persecution complex about road hogs, who he was convinced were out to get him, and would drive with one wary eye on the oncoming lane of traffic, ready for any hostile vehicle to attack him. His sequence in *If I Had a Million* gratified a lifelong thirst for vengeance. With the million dollars which he inherited, he purchased a number of secondhand cars and hired a flock of intrepid drivers, and he and Alison Skipworth set forth at the head of the column, his eye peeled for the first offender to cut across the center line. When he spotted a culprit, he would hold up a hand and signal one of his commandos to wheel out and ram it. Sometimes he and Miss Skipworth would take part in the fray, and Fields would give a bloodcurdling yell of exultation as headlights shattered and wheels came off and fenders crumpled.

His enmity toward children, dating from his own persecuted boyhood, found expression in *Never Give a Sucker an Even Break,* written by Fields himself under the unlikely nom de plume of Otis Criblecoblis. In one gratifying bit with Gloria Jean, as his little niece, Bill lured the child into a saloon and plied her with an opaque fluid which he assured her was goat's milk. "What kind of goat's milk, Uncle Bill?" Gloria asked after a delectable sip.

"Nanny goat's milk, my dear," the doting uncle replied, absently flicking a cigarette lighter as he expelled his breath and sending a long sheet of flame across the bar.

Bill's pictures violated every known moral code, and endorsed such dubious enterprises as swindling, theft, and other degrading aspects of human nature. In *The Bank Dick,* which he wrote under his alternate pen name of Mahatma Kane Jeeves, he not only defied conventions, but reaped all the rewards of dishonesty. The plot, if it could be called that, concerned one Egbert Sousé (Fields insisted on the accent over the *e*) who was trying to acquire five hundred dollars to invest in a beefsteak mine. A couple of robbers, Filthy McNasty and Repulsive Rogan, held up the local bank; but as they fled with the loot McNasty stumbled over a park bench where Sousé was seated and knocked himself out. Sousé modestly explained to the bank president that he had subdued the miscreant at a great personal risk—"He pulled an assagai on me," he claimed—and was rewarded with the job of bank dick. His first official act was to capture a small boy carrying a water pistol.

The plot rambled on with dreamlike nonsequitur through a series of unrelated episodes, including one wildly extraneous sequence in which Fields discovered a movie company on location, and took over the sedan of the director, labeled A. Pismo Clam, to shoot a football sequence. In another episode, he escorted the bank examiner, J. Pinkerton Snoopington (beautifully played by Franklin Pangborn), into the Black Pussy Cat Café and Snack Bar, his favorite saloon, and asked the bartender pointedly, "Have you seen Michael Finn lately?" While the unsuspecting Snoopington was swallowing his Mickey, Fields ordered himself a Scotch with water on the side, downed it, washed his fingers delicately in the water glass, and asked for another Scotch with a fresh chaser. "Never like to bathe in the same water twice," he remarked. Eventually Fields struck a bonanza in the beefsteak mine; and the final scene showed Mr. Sousé, having triumphed over virtue, placing his hat absent-mindedly on his upended cane and setting off in the direction of the saloon, unregenerate to the end.

Bill was fascinated by unusual names, adding new ones to his collection as he came across them. "Every name I use is an actual one I've seen somewhere," he told Norman Taurog. "Posthewhistle & Smunn, Attorneys" was borrowed from a Philadelphia law firm; "Claude Nesselrode" was a local pugilist who took frequent dives at Jeffries' Barn; "Chester Snavely" was an undertaker he had known as a boy in Germantown; "Chester Bogle," the pseudonym he used when writing *You Can't Cheat an Honest Man,* was a bootlegger of his acquaintance. He insisted on authoring his own screen plays, which he would dash off on the back of an old grocery bill and then sell to the studio for twenty-five thousand dollars. Since his contract specified that he had story approval, he would notify the studio that he had rejected the script, and compose a second one for another twenty-five thousand dollars. (Norman McLeod told me that Fields once built up his total take on a single story to eighty-five thousand dollars.) After the script was finally approved and paid for, he would toss it aside and ad-lib on the set as he went along.

His cantankerous attitude toward producers and directors worsened as he became a leading Hollywood star. He refused to sign a lucrative contract with Paramount until he was given complete autonomy in the preparation, direction, and production of his films. When he moved to M-G-M, he was barely prevented from taking over the studio. Directors raved and ranted at his proclivity for altering scenes or inserting new comic routines—when he played the role of Mr. Micawber in *David Copperfield,* he wanted to work in a juggling act, and it took all the studio's efforts to dissuade him—but it must be said that Fields, a consummate craftsman and master of clownery, knew more about his own capabilities than any director. He was equally rebellious during his radio appearances on the "Lucky Strike" program, and kept referring to his son "Chester" for several weeks, until his sponsors belatedly realized that "Chester Fields" might indicate a rival product.

If he failed to have his say, he would stage a one-man strike and sulk until the studio came around to his way of thinking. During the shooting of a picture at M-G-M, he was rebuffed on some minor change (he wanted his name to have top billing above that of the studio) and retired to his residence, leaving orders with his butler to tell any and all callers that he was not at home. As the set lay idle day after day and production costs mounted, a series of executives drove out to see him, but were turned away from his door. At last L. B. Mayer, the head of the studio, decided to make a personal visit. The butler opened the door and recognized the distinguished caller, and left him standing in the hallway while he hurried back to Fields's bedroom for instructions. "It's L.B. himself," he whispered nervously to the master. "What shall I say to him?"

"Give him an eva-a-asive answer," Fields drawled. "Tell him to go f——himself."

Of all the houses that Fields occupied while in Hollywood, his favorite was a run-down Spanish mansion on De Mille Drive, north of Hollywood. He had leased it during the depression for the bargain price of $250 a month, including the services of a Japanese gardener. When conditions improved, the landlord tried in vain to persuade his tenant to change the long-term lease, but Fields gloated over his advantage and refused to yield. The unhappy landlord suggested a compromise, and offered to renovate the old house if his tenant would agree to a financial readjustment. "Not one cent for tribute," Fields bellowed. "Let the joint fall apart."

The situation was a stalemate, and since neither tenant nor owner would invest in repairs, the mansion became more and more down-at-heel in appearance. The wallpaper hung in tatters, the warp of the carpet showed plainly before the three bars which Fields had installed, and chunks of plaster occasionally fell from the sagging ceiling onto the pool table he had set up in the drawing room. The living room was given over to a Ping-Pong table, and high pool-room chairs were arranged along the walls. The dining room featured a barber's chair, complete with towels and aprons, in which Bill used to doze when troubled by insomnia. (In his early days, he had found that getting a haircut in a warm padded barber's chair was one of life's greatest pleasures.) With his native distrust of servants, he had fitted every closet and storeroom door with a special lock to guard his liquor supply, and kept some thirty keys on a chain in his bathrobe pocket. His upstairs bedroom, which he called his "office," contained a combination bar and writing desk and bed, with slats like a crib to keep him from falling out. When his steps grew feeble, he would feel his way from his bed along the desk to the bar, and reinforce his strength with a handy nightcap.

He had an abiding fear of burglars, and his solution, of which he was inordinately proud, was the installation of an intercom system throughout the house, with the master microphone on the desk in his office. Loudspeakers were concealed everywhere, in the pantry, down in the cellar, inside chandeliers, under washbasins, behind pictures, and back of the knocker on the front door, a carved woodpecker which the guest activated by yanking a string. If he heard a suspicious noise during the night, he would grope to the desk and pick up the microphone and bellow into it, "Stand back, I've got you covered!" and then go back to bed, confident that the intruder would remain with arms raised until morning.

During the war, on my way out to the Pacific on Air Force duty, I stopped off in Los Angeles and took a cab out to De Mille Drive. The approach to Bill's house was a red-tiled lane, overhung with flowered trellises, and the velvet lawns, well tended by the Japanese gardener, rolled gently down the contour of the hill to form a bowl with a lily pond in the center. On it was floating a toy sailboat, a gift from one of Fields's friends. I stepped up to the door and reached for the string of the knocker, and the woodpecker yelled, "*Let* go of me, Ford!" in Bill's snarling voice. (He had a telescope in his office, I learned later, with which he could spot any approaching visitor.) He came downstairs, clad in his disreputable white bathrobe and holding a tall glass filled with a yellowish liquid. I had heard that Bill's health was failing, and I assumed that his drinking had been restricted to wine. We adjourned to the outdoor patio, one of Bill's preferred spots, and he bellowed to the butler, "Bring my guest a Scotch highball—and I'll have another Martini." He drank four shakerfuls of Martinis during my visit, and his good humor expanded. I had never seen him in a happier mood. Once the landlord stopped by, to inquire about the month's rent which was overdue, and Bill assured him loftily, "Have no qualms, my good man, your pound of flesh will be forthcoming shortly. *Good* day," and then, in a croaked aside like a honk of a raven, "All landlords should be grilled *en brochette.*" At last it came time to leave, and Bill presented me with an affectionately inscribed photograph of himself, not in clown costume but in street attire with his face turned toward the camera so that his oversized nose did not show. I've never known what impulse prompted him to give me his picture. I made my way carefully up the uneven tile walk, for my knees were beginning to bend backward, and he waved his glass to me gaily as I reached the gate. It was the last time I ever saw him.

I returned to Hollywood shortly before Christmas of 1946, and Dave Chasen told me that Bill had lost the De Mille Drive house, when his lease expired, and had moved to a sanitarium in Los Encinas to sit in a rocking chair and await the Man in the Bright Nightgown. Dave and Billy Grady planned to drive out to see him on Christmas Day, a holiday which Fields always loathed. "I believed in Christmas until I was eight years old," he told Gene Fowler. "I had saved up some money carrying ice in Philadelphia, and I was going to buy my mother a copper-bottom clothes boiler for Christmas. I kept the money hidden in a brown crock in the coalbin. My father found the crock. He did exactly what I would have done in his place. He stole the money. And ever since then I've remembered nobody on Christmas, and I want nobody to remember me either."

Dave promised to take me along to Los Encinas on his next visit. "Bill isn't allowed any callers," he said, "but we'll manage to get in somehow." That was when I realized how seriously ill he was. On Christmas there was a tropical deluge, which flooded the streets with such a boiling torrent that a man stepped out of his car and was swept into a sewer and drowned. ("Rain dampens sidewalks in Los Angeles area," the Los Angeles *Times* admitted grudgingly the next day.) Somehow I kept thinking of Bill all day. It was just the kind of Christmas he would have chosen.

Dave phoned me late that afternoon. He and Billy Grady had arrived at the sanitarium about noon, he said, with a hamper of delicacies from the restaurant and several bottles of whiskey. They made their way through the downpour to Bill's bungalow, and Dave rang the bell and then knelt down, a simple gag designed to startle the party opening the door. A nurse answered the bell, weeping. "Mr. Fields died this morning," she said. Dave climbed to his feet in silence, and they drove back to Hollywood in the gray rain. That night some of Bill's intimates gathered at Chasen's, and phoned a full-page ad to the *Hollywood Reporter:*

> The most prejudiced and honest and beloved figure of our so-called "colony" went away on a day that he pretended to abhor—"Christmas." We loved him, and—peculiarly enough—he loved us. To the most authentic humorist since Mark Twain, to the greatest heart that has beaten since the Middle Ages—W. C. Fields, our friend.

Several weeks after his death, a group of his closest friends met at Chasen's for a wake: Billy Grady, Eddie Sutherland, Ben Hecht, Grantland Rice, Greg La Cava, Gene Fowler, Jack Dempsey, Roland Young, Leo McCarey, Norm McLeod. Dave served us Bill's favorite dinner, accompanied by Bill's usual quota of drinks. None of us could keep up with it, and my recollection of the evening is still hazy. I remember that, by some unexpressed agreement, no one at the table mentioned Bill's name; that wasn't necessary. The only reference to him was when Dave read aloud a telegram he had just received from Frank Sullivan in New York.

I HOPE HE GIVES ST. PETER AN EVASIVE ANSWER, the wire said.

## Hugh Kenner (essay date 1968)

SOURCE: "The Confidence Man," in *National Review*, Vol. XX, No. 16, April 23, 1968, pp. 399-400.

*[In the following essay, Kenner presents Fields as a critic of the society in which he lived.]*

> *"The buyer tries to come back with a lower counteroffer. 'You're crazy!' retorts Fields. 'And you're drunk!' snaps the buyer. 'Yes,' agrees Fields, 'but I'll be sober tomorrow, and you'll be crazy for the rest of your life!'"*

—A detail from *It's a Gift* (1934), and in many ways an epitome of Fields, whose logic could be strangely diffi-

cult to fault. The reader who scents a fallacy will be wiser when he has tried to put a clear statement of what it is into, say, 200 words.

Fields coped in picture after picture with people—a whole population, except maybe an innocent girl or two—who would be crazy the rest of their lives and to lose them in syllogistic thickets was his most benign tactic. They had passed the Volstead Act, a deed as impenetrable to this day as the heart of Nero or the smiles of the Etruscans, and their business in life was to be prim and vigilant and very greedy, pending some mutation that should free the human species from maintaining its body temperature, thus opening to all the paradise of the toad.

They brought forth monstrous children whose affinity for molasses, than which blood is thinner, sent Fields' watch "like a stone in quicksand" to the bottom of a jar of molasses ("The minute hand won't be a bit of use") and flooded Fields' grocery store with molasses ("Closed on Account of Molasses" reads the sign on the door) without winning Fields even the approval of the mother responsible. ("First you try to drown him in molasses," commences one tirade. The name is Mrs. Dunk.)

They affirmed that there were to be no more cakes and ale. Their epicenter was, more or less, the Des Moines YWCA. By the mid-Thirties they had blighted the continent. To transcribe:

> *"That night, Fields has trouble sleeping, and the nagging of his wife, complaining about her years of suffering and hard work, doesn't help. Just as Fields is at the point of falling asleep the phone rings.*
>
> *"'Well, why don't you answer the phone?' demands the tyrant. 'I have no maid, you know; probably never will have!' Sleepily, Fields goes to the phone, but it is a wrong number: somebody calling for the maternity hospital. Mrs. Bissonette mulls this over for a minute, then: 'Funny they should call you from the maternity hospital in the middle of the night.' Fields mumbles an explanation. 'No dear, it was someone trying to get the maternity hospital.' By now Mrs. Bissonette's sarcastic ire is fully aroused: 'Oh, now you change it! Don't make it any worse by lying about it.'"*

Fields, in that blight, was the Obsolescent Man. That was his steady role and his latent pathos. He stood for an older anarchy, which was to such a present as tent shows were to movies. The tent show was his explicit metaphor, and the juggling act, which he sneaked into movie after movie, sometimes by sheer gall *vis-à-vis* the director, was the sign of his incomprehensible *expertise*, a lost freedom asserted.

That the passionate man gives way to the administrative was a truth known to Shakespeare, whose Octavius, minutes after Cleopatra's death-music ("Give me my robe. Put on my crown. I have / Immortal longings in me"), affirms that Fearless Fosdick is his Ideal in asking only

"How died she?" That the passionate man may yet survive and persist, forced into grotesque ritualism of a skill nobody wants (how to juggle balls, pick pockets, raise the ante) was a myth posterior to Shakespeare, affirmed in America, certified by Fields, who made of its affirmation a style of life.

He was a confidence man; his freedom was predatory; hence his redemption from the pathos of Jiggs. It was for no bucolic splendor that he yearned, no *Fête Champêtre*, corned beef and cabbage heaped upon the Spode, nor no lazy drift down-river with Nigger Jim beneath the Missouri stars, but for the Lord God's primal division of mankind into the Fleecers and the Fleeced, in a time before that *tertium quid,* the Respectable, had blurred these satisfying categories. For to be active according to one's nature is a great good, and to be active in the confidence that the primal categories of creation conform to one's appetite, that is a very great good indeed. What is man, that he should presume to give a sucker an even break? Fields was the Ayn Rand of Americana.

Hence *"an episode in which Fields cunningly sells a 'talking dog' to a sucker. After the deal is consummated, the new owner makes a remark at which Fields is quick to take necessary umbrage, and the dog huffily remarks that just for that, he'll never speak again. 'He probably means it, too,' prophesies ventriloquist Fields as he leaves."*

Mankind exists, so Fields thought, to have a talking dog or the Brooklyn Bridge sold to it, or the SST, or a gold brick, or the system that incorporates Fort Knox. So, too, thought Mencken and Barnum; so too, it is difficult not to suppose, thought Poor Richard. As the cube is the flimsy module which multiplied and agglomerated yields the RCA building, a megalomaniac slab, so that transaction with the talking dog is the primary structure which reduplicated and reasserted on a satisfyingly ample scale becomes a W.C. Fields picture: **The Old-Fashioned Way,** or **The Bank Dick.**

The megasucker, when Fields extends himself, is not someone inside the plot but the largest accessible entity outside it, Paramount or Universal, which has been conned into bankrolling a film subversive of its entire corporate message, and has paid Fields not only a high price for savaging mothers and kicking babies on camera, but a high price also for the screen-play, a two-page surrealism which he covertly expanded for his own use with careful prescription of every pause and grimace, all the time letting on that he was barely sober enough to lurch onto the set and rely on his vaudeville reflexes.

The contract typically called for the script to be credited to an Otis Criblecoblis or a Mahatma Kane Jeeves (those were the days of Pandro S. Berman, and Fields himself had been preposterously christened William Claude Dukenfield). The script in turn called for Fields to play himself, thinly disguised as Larson E. Whipsnade or Egbert Sousé. Into at least two motion pictures he in-

serted, like a Bacchic afterthought, a subplot concerning his conning of a motion picture company. Into one he even introduced a movie director named A. Pismo Clam, who is so perpetually drunk that his work has to be taken over by Fields.

These majestic swindles ran, at their best, like the juggling act he brought *in extenso* into **The Old-Fashioned Way,** along with a complete performance of *The Drunkard.* The numerous elements are related by the fact that they are all simultaneously somehow in the air. No useful work is being performed by the juggler; and yet a seeming miracle is occurring, which we may attribute to the hours of practice on which he squandered his youth. If he had been learning a respectable trade there would be nothing for us to see, and here we are, enthralled.

He attempted to work his juggling act into *David Copperfield,* where he played Micawber; it was a transparently relevant piece of business, he argued, which Dickens merely didn't happen to think of. MGM demurred. In **The Bank Dick,** however, his culminating film (1940), he does not visibly juggle yet juggles transcendently, keeping in breathtaking simultaneous motion, up and down and across and past each other, drunks and con men and a movie company, a bank and its president, a bank examiner, two robbers, a nonexistent colored midget with an assegai, a shapeless wife, a brat who heaves rocks, a mother-in-law who rocks and says "Hah!," a paisley shawl and a river of beer and a butler, three careening cars, the Black Pussy Cat Saloon, and the town of Lompoc (Calif.) which existed and exists, and which, like banks and brats and mothers-in-law and the other divertissements of respectability, he hated. I write this thirty miles from Lompoc.

Are they real? Yes, horribly real. Have they moral substance? They have none. The rewards for saving the bank's assets include "a hearty hand-shake" which consists of the president's fingers "barely touching Fields' outstretched palm for a moment—an effect that Fields heightens by going into a split-second freeze-frame," and "a copy of the bank's calendar, illustrated with an inspiring painting of 'Spring in Lompoc.'" Is Fields their moral superior? Only in this, that bumbling through their affairs, and abetted by his *alter ego* the script writer, he can keep them in frenzied motion.

Is he rewarded? He is, and in the only coin creation affords, theirs. He attains to millions, to a butler, to a mansion, to an institutionalized affluence that urges on him of a morning "just one more Baba au Rhum," to the daily opportunity of deciding between a tropical helmet and a top hat, to go with the cutaway and spats. It is supernal Respectability, the apotheosis of Lompoc (a word Fields spoke as though grinding it beneath his heel).

Since the world pays in only one currency, it is easy to assume that he cheated and bamboozled to acquire what Respectability has by birthright. He did not. He bamboozled as an assertion of style, and of what he understood as tradition. Tradition has only common matter in which to assert itself. When the finally affluent Fields failed to make his top hat come to rest on his head because it had landed instead on the tip of his flourished cane, we are not to suppose that he exhibits *nouveau-riche* awkwardness. He is displaying an old vaudevillian's skill, in a bit of business he had performed so often it became his trademark. It attained the same result as might awkwardness, but do not be misled by that.

Do not be misled, similarly, by the nihilism in his premises, or the incoherence in his speeches. It was the ambience he detested that was nihilistic and incoherent, incapable of resolving any issue whatever except by summoning policemen. Black Humor, which he practiced as did Mark Twain, despairs because its capacity to make such distinctions has been forced into the area of style alone, the language, the system of rewards, the entire social idiom, the very basis of appeal to eternal law having been coopted by the adversary.

Hence Fields with his double tongue, persuading a dim-witted protégé, in the interest of ultimate good, to embezzle from the bank, simultaneously addressed his audience and posterity, tonguing and mumbling, never very clearly, an exhortation that welled from the depths of his soul:

*"Don't be a fuddie-duddie, don't be a moon-calf, don't be a jabbernowl—you don't want to be any of those, do you?"* It was nearly all that was left for him to say.

### Raymond Durgnat (excerpt date 1970)

SOURCE: "Suckers and Soaks," in *The Crazy Mirror: Hollywood Comedy and the American Image,* Horizon Press, 1970, pp. 142-9.

[*In the following excerpt, Durgnat compares Fields and Mae West in terms of their careers and of their antipathy to the mores of their time.*]

Mae West and W. C. Fields came to the cinema from the regions where theatre interbreeds with vaudeville, and top the bill among the early 30's influx of vaudeville and radio comedians. Ken Tynan described Wheeler and Wolsey as the only American cross-talk comedians whose films will never have a season at the National Film Theatre, but it would be interesting to see more of the comedies of Joe E. Brown and Jimmy Durante (almost the last of the race comedians, indifferently Jewish, Italian, or East European), which may well possess consistently what they possess in extract: the kind of zany fidelity to grass roots reality which one finds in the corresponding English tradition, of Will Hay, George Formby, Lucan and McShane, Norman Wisdom and the *Carry On* series. Victor Moore, Jack Oakie and others bring to 30's movies something of the brash, down-to-earth, briskly accurate character vignettes which are as vivid as they are

limited, and catch much of the snap-crackle-pop of the American style.

Mae West smilingly acknowledges the applause for her fairground shimmy in *I'm No Angel,* and happily gurgles under her breath: 'Suckers!' The film is directed by Wesley Ruggles, but its credits engagingly proclaim its *politique des auteurs:* 'story, screenplay and all dialogue by Mae West; suggestions by Lowell Bernardo'. The film's plot (pre-Code) is, on paper, ambiguous, but there is so little mistaking its meaning that her films, more than any others, goaded the do-gooders into their successful clean-up campaign.

Yet the film's morality is more complex than opposing the Legions of Decency and the opulent Mae's prime side of high camp. In a climatic courtroom scene, Mae, at bay for her easy virtue, argues that if some men gave her diamonds because of what they thought she was promising, they ought to lose them. The implication that the would-be clients of a supposed prostitute deserved to be bilked is clipjoint morality, and if Mae's male spectators can forgive her for it, it's for a variety of reasons. Certainly her victims are the sort of mean-faced characters who turn up as crooked bankers and sheriffs in B Westerns, and are clearly incapable of matching, even to their nearest and dearest, Mae's conspicuously loyal and generous way with her friends and lovers. Also, however, the film homes in on that challenging old saw which titles a W. C. Fields movie: Never Give a Sucker an Even Break. But as a result of Mae's forensic genius, it is respectability which finds itself in the moral dock. The prostitute's client is not only as immoral as the lady of easy virtue herself, but ten times as ignominious. And when she rounds on her beloved's ex-fiancée and forces her to admit that she wouldn't dream of returning his engagement gifts, she convicts the respectable matriarchy of clipjoint morality in its turn. The comedy's happy end is possible because Cary Grant is generous enough to accept, and to forget, what is, perhaps, most difficult for the proud male: the fact of Mae's close relationship with a man who is clearly a pimp type. Mae clinches her triumph by offering to let any of the jurors 'come up and see her'. But her lover she will ring—any time. . . .

The film manipulates the moral masochism of the mere male as deftly as the more usual blend of puritanism and is, in a sense, a libertarian riposte to it. Mae West is the Statue of Liberties, whose hourglass figure sent Old Father Time into a flat spin, and brought the naughty 90's back to the roaring 20's. Like Westerns, the films are partly exercises in nostalgia, with Edwardian razzamatazz, ragtime pianos trickling notes into the saloon office, music halls with big-voiced tenors and figure-of-8 chorus-girls with high boots and feathered hats. In the streamlined 30's, her sofa contours, her slow-drag way with wisecracks, evoke the epoch of Madams rather than Moms. Indulgent, undulant, monolith, she glides, her hips moving as sweetly as the paddlewheels of a Mississippi pleasure-steamer. Lucky all who sail in her. . . . Her mystery lies in this sumptuosity immingling with a slick, cool, mercenary ruthlessness, a Momist outline with feminine independence, a Nietzschean will to power which has too much humour not to be agreeably self-critical, and a generosity whose tone deliciously blends maternal indulgence and complicity. It's the perpetual possibility of any of these responses which gives tension and wit to lines which, on paper, could hardly seem more mechanical. Her lover asks her what she's thinking of: 'The same as you, honey.' Was ever the need to court a woman more smoothly put aside? 'I'm crazy about you,' he adds. 'Yes . . . I did my best to make you that way.' The wit in that line lies not so much in any revelation of female scheming as in its almost maternal tolerance of manipulable little boys. Baudelaire likened the superior lucidity of one lover *vis-à-vis* the other to the relationship between surgeon and patient or torturer and victim. Mae's view has a worldlier amiability. Mae's celebrated 'Beulah—peel me a grape!' occurs after a row with Cary Grant and suggests that she is soothing herself after a slight heartbreak by a self-indulgence in luxury and power—slightly provocative, perhaps, in the era of *My Man Godfrey*.

Some lines are almost unanalysable, as when she tells Cary Grant that she's come to a decision about their affair. That was very quick, he remarks, to which she replies, 'Oh, I'm very quick, in a slow way,' a line which might mean almost anything, particularly as accompanied by a broadly sensual resettling of her hips. But, whatever it means, it refers to some blend of impulse and scepticism, of impulsive passion and nonchalant reserve, of stalling and pouncing. The sexual innuendo is a magnificent promise.

*I'm No Angel* concludes with Mae adorning herself with a white bridal gown, a defiance of society as outrageous as Groucho's teasing of Margaret Dumont, that anti-Mae West of yearning, lonely, innocent, respectability. One or two lines work on double-entendres of sexual unorthodoxies much to the taste of the kinky sixties. Thus when Cary Grant over-romantically asserts, 'I would be your slave,' she amiably replies, 'That can be arranged. . . . '

The films themselves have aged and creak in every joint, almost giving a curious double nostalgia. One good turn deserves another, and Old Father Time has gallantly rejuvenated the outrageous Mae, for her whole style has a bland, unruffleable cool only enhanced by her archaic opulence.

Disreputable, disillusioned, dissolute and disgruntled, W. C. Fields was Mae West's comrade-in-arms in bawdy comedy's rearguard action against the galloping pasteurization of the 30's. Like Mae West, he wrote most of his own screenplays, under such pseudonyms as Otis T. Criblecoblis and Mahatma Kane Jeeves (and co-stars with her in *My Little Chickadee*). But his bursts of slow-motion slapstick and ethereal fantasy relate him to Harry Langdon, Laurel and Hardy and the Hal Roach tempo. In the vaudeville tradition of pompous fruity rascality, he may recall Will Hay and Wallace Beery, but his cultivation of a lordly Southern drawl irresistibly recalls the

seedier sprigs of decaying gentry, and/or suburban pretensions to such gentility. His sourness at this Hays Code world recalls the Marx Brothers' way with La Dumont, but the butts of his satire are more solidly characterized than theirs. It's no accident that before Sturges, he used Franklin Pangborn and other preferred denizens of the Sturges world. *It's A Gift,* his study of small-town family life, is less hectic, but even more pessimistic, precisely because every humiliation has time to be winced from beforehand, and mused upon afterwards. His world has less warmth, more emptiness; in several films, his nearest approach to human contact is the dour complicity of fellow-topers. In contrast to Mae's all infolding narcissism, he can manage only a mumbling, but obdurate, paranoia.

This grognosed sourpuss is a sort of battered, half-defeated Uncle to the Marx triplets. Where Groucho's frankness is aggressive, Fields mutters to himself in an interminable monologue, compromising between anger and hopelessness. What may have started out with some hope of eventually counterfeiting an elegant Southern drawl has long since decayed, *à la* Tennessee Williams, to an alcohol-grated larynx rasping like a rusty lavatory chain. His extreme suspicion of the world is revealed in his bitter, lopsided lips, narrowed eyes, and the tentative, cagey gestures that give his rolypoly frame the crabbedness of an arthritic teddy-bear. He is a Sir Toby Belch cruelly misplaced in the Prohibition era. Malvolio now is no mere steward, taking orders, but that dread figure, the bank manager, and Olivia's household has become as petty and niggardly as the Bassonets of *It's A Gift* or the Sousés of *The Bank Dick*. Stout, and still as sour as Cassius, he wages a last-bottle-stand against almost everybody, but especially kids, Moms and bluenoses, that is, everything that the American way of life considers sweet and uplifting.

With Mae West, he shared an ultra-slow humour in which part of the joke was what wasn't quite said, but was, as it were, sidled around. He drawls complacently: 'There's been a catastrophe. He's fallen off the parapet. Yes. . . .' Or an enormous blonde waitress tells him: 'There's a something so big about you.' He waits, with misgivings, and in the silence it's as if a shell were whistling over from the enemy lines, where will it land? She says: 'Your nose.' He nurses his ego, and bides his time, while she bends over a table, and then he murmurs, 'There's something so big about you too. . . .' His retort's crudity, its quality of anticlimax, are all part of the defeated mood of the joke. Thus Fields has an odd quality of non-wit, as if wit required a kind of zest that he no longer possesses, because he despairs of mankind. His gags have an eccentric timing, or mistiming, all their own, sometimes loitering on indecisively, sometimes appearing out of nowhere and disappearing almost before one can laugh. Fields himself said that what's really funny is what one doesn't do, and he can almost claim to have developed the shaggy-dog joke to its highest pitch of inanity. (A clerk spends a whole scene wearing a straw hat without a crown, explaining in almost the last line, that he wears it that way because he suffers from hay fever.) His burring-

and-slurring of gags combines a hopeless expectation of audience disapproval, with an ever-frustrated aggression which is nevertheless heroically maintained—as when he stands over an exasperating baby with a chopper in his hand, murmuring by way of excuse, 'Even a worm can turn. . . .'

*It's A Gift,* an unrelenting exposé of small-town life, includes a deliriously cruel episode where Mr. Bassonet (Fields) as the proprietor of a store, has to deal, not only with a baby who releases floods of sticky molasses from a barrel, but, simultaneously, with a customer who knocks over piles of glassware wherever he turns, because he is not only virtually blind but also virtually deaf. (Only Fields could get himself persecuted by creatures so helpless.) All the petty paranoia of the average man is crystallized in a dawn scene where Bassonet, driven out of his bed by his wife's indefatigable nagging, tries to snatch a little sleep on his balcony, only to be disturbed by, successively, the milkman, a coconut bouncing slowly down every tread into the ash-can, a baby in the balcony above bombing him with grapes and screwdrivers, an insurance salesman, his wife, a 'vegetable gentleman', two females being maliciously polite to each other, and his own couch's collapse. In one film he spent eighteen minutes trying to hit a golfball. In a nightmare drive to a maternity hospital he gets his car stuck in a fire-engine ladder, and lifted off the road, but not high enough to spare passing traffic from suicidal swerves. This, a classic episode in the Sennett style, is matched by the automobile's racing up and down and around the corridors, staircases and elevators of the *International House.*

His slapstick homeliness brings him quite near Laurel and Hardy, whose taste he shared for absurd parody-realms. But just as in his 'homely' scenes, he exhibits a far more abrasive hostility to the way of the world (where Stan and Ollie just blunder along), so, these 'absurd' realms have, in Fields's films, a function of derisive liberation that anticipates goonery and its indefinable, but pervasive, affinities with satire. In both *Million Dollar Legs,* written by Joseph L. Mankiewicz, and in ***Never Give a Sucker an Even Break*** (originally released in Britain as *What a Man*), we are introduced to a crazy realm which matches Al Capp's Dogpatch as a parody-opposite of ours.

In the latter film, he falls out of an aeroplane washroom into a strange realm presided over by a Mrs. Haemoglobin (Margaret Dumont), a sort of respectable female Dracula whose ivory tower is equipped with hanging swimming-pools. *Million Dollar Legs* has Fields presiding, like the genially tyrannical Oz, over a Land of Cockayne where all the women are called Angela and all the men are called George (suggesting a happy extreme of democratic equality, and the idyllic community cohesiveness of a South Sea tribe). There's also a vamp called Mata Machri (deliciously played by Lydia Roberti). The million-dollar legs are not, as one might expect, hers, but, of all people's, Andy Clyde's, as an international athlete who, in the old Mack Sennett spirit, keeps in trim by

outrunning express trains, and takes his super-superman speed absolutely for granted.[1] There is also a charmingly erotic scene where Jack Oakie and his girlfriend brush each other down with feathers. Such titillation is rare in Fields films, for, in the presence of women, Fields, though hardly lacking in deep dark desires, seemed in his amorous relationships paralysed by a suspicion that all women, however beautiful, were merely harridans in their butterfly stage. *Million Dollar Legs* isn't simply a Dogpatch: or rather it's a European Dogpatch, it's a last zany image of Ruritania, of the lands from which America's immigrants came. It bristles with secret police, yet everyone is content. According to Aristophanes, Cloud Cuckoo Land was the topsy turvy region where you beat your father and got praised for it. Klopstockia is the land where foreign, fuddy-duddy fathers turn out to be champion weight lifters and supersonic sprinters. Andy Clyde's philosophy is the absolute reverse of American earnestness, he's a deferential, almost feudally modest, messenger boy, and he can hardly be bothered to stir his stumps merely for the sake of winning. 'Have you ever studied astronomy?' he ponders, philosophically. 'Have you ever realized how short a hundred yards is?' Backwoodsmanship is in there too, and Fields's slow, full-blown style, often nearer the anecdote than the gag, sometimes takes on an almost Mark Twain quality, as in *If I Had a Million.* Fields and wife, having at last hit the jackpot, drive round town, followed by a fleet of spare automobiles; after each smash, they climb out and hail the next in line.

The homely and the exotic weirdly coexist. Fields hears a police-car radio describing a wanted man as having 'apple cheeks, cauliflower ears and mutton-chop whiskers' (shades of Arcimboldo); or he buys shares in a beefsteak mine; or, as a bank dick, he dons a disguise which consists mainly of a length of string running from the bridge of his nose to behind his ear. These improbabilities are presented so as to be quietly mulled over, rather than developed, and have a strange halfheartedness which is itself a joke, and rather a sad one. Fields's humour, instead of falling between two stools, of fantasy and satire, wobbles uneasily, and intriguingly, on the edge of both. He seems to be taking a subdued revenge on the real world by substituting for it a fantasy one. Yet he's also too weary to develop the fantasy. It's as if he introduces, into the familiar atmosphere, little 'air-bubbles' of fantasy, which swell, and slowly subside, and at last burst, leaving a sour nostalgia behind.

The passage of time has perhaps enhanced this effect, since his films abound in parodic reference to genres with which later audiences are less familiar. In *Never Give a Sucker an Even Break,* Fields leads an existence weirdly split between a Hollywood director's and a small-town spouse's; he has simply taken, to a *reductio ad absurdum,* Hollywood's picture of homely Hollywood. In *International House,* the Chinese inventor obsessively trying to get a six-day bicycle race on his 'radioscope' (television) is an idiotically Westernized, passified and cretinized Fu Manchu. Fields's flight in an autogyro, out of which he keeps dropping empty beer-bottles, refers at once to the 30's fascination with long-distance solo flights and an outrageous defiance of still vivid Prohibition. (It's easy to forget just how much any reference to any alcoholic beverage, even the presence of a bottle and glass, meant for Prohibition era audiences.) In one of its musical interludes, *International House* also has Cab Calloway singing about 'that funny reefer man', a line whose subversiveness probably strikes more people now than it did then. But the fact that it got there is one of those happy accidents with which a kindly fate blesses those artists who deserve it. It's ironical that *International House* would today have to lose this scene, or be banned.

The one new innocent of the 30's is Eddie Cantor.[2] His *Roman Scandals* (for Goldwyn) started out in Depression America, from which town bum Eddie dreams his way back into the court of Poppeia, finally returning to save the poor from being evicted by the hard-faced businessman. The mixture of comic topicality and wish-fulfilment opulence is evident enough. Less characterful, less rooted in reality than Keaton, Lloyd and Langdon, Cantor had something of their touching intensity, and, in his personality 'aura' seems to have something of each, as if typifying the way in which the various sections, strata and racial groups of America were coalescing into—not the American ideal, for Eddie, like most comedians, was an antihero—but the 'little American'. There's a kind of scuttling nervousness about him which is very much of the period, too, with its hectic pace and its Depression. The stress lies on gags, and bluff-and-cowardice gags, in a way anticipating Bob Hope, a comedian with a slicker, more realistic style. But if *Kid Millions* now seems an awkward anticipation of the Bob Hope style movie, it is saved, like *Roman Scandals*, by the musical numbers of Busby Berkeley, which, in these and other 30's movies, are really little deliriums of the imagination, psychological counterparts of crazy comedy, but, with their lines of milky, healthy, smiling beauties, cosy as well as crazy. As the middle-class tide rises throughout the 30's, Berkeley's Freedonian regiments of lovelies yield, in their turn, the limelight to more intimate and 'cosy' numbers, based on the 'individualistic' couple-of-lovers (Fred Astaire, Ginger Rogers).

NOTES

[1] Are these quick motion effects, one wonders, a parody of King Vidor's was of slowing camera speeds to make his heroes run or work faster (in *Hallelujah*, in *Our Daily Bread*) at inspired moments?

[2] He had made *Kid Boots* with Clara Bow in 1926 but the early 30's are his heyday.

**Leonard Maltin (excerpt date 1972)**

SOURCE: "W. C. Fields," in *Great Movie Shorts*, Crown Publishers, 1972, pp. 81-84.

*[In the following excerpt, Maltin contrasts Fields's popularity with 1970s audiences to the often disapproving response he received in his own day.]*

In the 1920s and 1930s, one of the most interesting parts of several motion-picture trade magazines was a department in which small-town theatre owners across the country sent in brief comments on the films they had played; this was done for short subjects as well as feature films. Today, these comments are invaluable as a barometer of what the mass movie audience really thought of the films that were being made—unaffected by critical reactions, and uncolored by modern reassessments.

Concerning the W. C. Fields comedies, most exhibitors were unanimous. They stank. Of **The Fatal Glass of Beer,** a Michigan theatre owner wrote, "Two reels of film and 20 minutes wasted," and a North Carolina manager added, "This is the worst comedy we have played from any company this season. No story, no acting, and as a whole has nothing."

Moviegoers today are just as unanimous in their opinions of the shorts: they are among the funniest films ever made.

The reasons for this discrepancy are not difficult to discern. Fields went against the grain of what was then popular humor; in an age when audience sympathy was always with the Little Fellow, when love and justice always triumphed, when anti-heroes were unheard of, Fields dared to be different.

He extolled the joys of drinking; he was mean, selfish, and dishonest. He rebelled against many of the silly conventions Americans held near and dear. And, for the most part, Americans were not ready to accept what he did as humorous. Today, some forty years later, the pendulum has swung the other way, and many people share Fields's views. He has become a popular hero.

But Fields had his problems in Hollywood during the 1920s and 1930s. Few people were willing to let him have his head to do the kind of comedy he wanted to do. Far too often, he was made to contend with Hollywoodized story lines and young-lover subplots. Fortunately, he found his niche often enough to create some pure comic masterpieces such as **It's a Gift** and **The Bank Dick,** that show him at his best, unhampered by studio interference.

One of Fields's greatest opportunities came when he went to work for Mack Sennett. Legend has it that Fields signed on with Sennett at a nominal fee to work as a comedy writer, and starred in his own films only as an afterthought. Whatever the background, it is clear that Sennett let Fields do as he pleased; he took screenplay credit for all four shorts and easily dominated the productions. It is probable that he had a hand in casting the films, choosing some excellent players (Elise Cavanna, Grady Sutton, etcetera) who he knew would be good foils.

The first short, **The Dentist,** consists of three major sequences. The first has Fields doing battle with his daughter (Babe Kane) over breakfast when she announces that she's in love with the iceman. The second has him going out for an early round of golf with a perplexed friend (Bud Jamison) who has to put up with Fields's idiosyncrasies. And the third takes place in the dentist's office, where Fields contends with a motley assortment of patients.

On the golf course, it is clear that Fields plays by his own set of rules. Anxious to tee off, he shouts "Fore!" and proceeds to set up his shot before another foursome has left the green. He makes his shot, and we cut to the green, where one gentleman proclaims, "This game is certainly wonderful for your health!" At which point the golf ball knocks him on the head and lays him out flat. After wrestling with the rule book, losing a ball, arguing with his caddy, and being defeated by a water trap, Fields gives up and goes back to his office.

If there is one word to describe the dentist's office sequence, it is "outrageous." So much so, in fact, that it was heavily edited when the film was shown after 1933, when the Production Code took effect. Original uncut prints today bring gasps along with laughter from modern audiences who can't get over what they're seeing. As Fields is talking to a pal in his office, a female patient (Dorothy Granger) is moaning outside. The nurse looks worried, but Fields continues to chat, unconcerned by the squeals from outside. When his nurse tries to call his attention to it, he mutters, "Ah, the hell with her!"

Later, while trying to extract a tooth from the mouth of another woman (Elise Cavanna), he pulls her completely out of the chair, her legs straddling him and resting in his pockets! When he drills her tooth (the machine makes a loud buzz-saw sound), her entire body gyrates with what is apparently excruciating pain. Afterward he asks amiably, "Now that didn't hurt, did it?"

The Fields character in **The Dentist** is completely without redeeming qualities, and it is the shock of realizing this as much as anything else that makes the short unusually funny.

The next Fields short, **The Fatal Glass of Beer,** is undoubtedly the wildest, and at the same time the subtlest, of his four for Sennett. Its humor still eludes some people today, who cannot catch the satire and merely find the action dull. As a spoof of the old-fashioned Yukon melodramas, and the "Dangerous Dan McGrew" type of tales, it is without equal. It was directed by comedy veteran Clyde Bruckman.

The film begins as Fields "sings" to sentimental Mountie Richard Cramer a ballad he has written about his son Chester, who went to the Big City, took the Fatal Glass of Beer, was accused of stealing some bonds, and landed in prison. The song is completely formless and without rhyme, not helped by Fields's off-pitch singing.

A bit later, who should show up at the wintry cabin but Chester (George Chandler), released from prison and come home to make amends with his parents. There are warm greetings all around, and the inane small talk reaches the height of absurdity when Chester, bawling, says, between sniffles, "It's so good to see you both again, and I'm so glad to be back home with you and ma, that I can't talk. I'd like to go to my little bedroom, lay on the bed, and cry like I was a baby again."

"There, there," sobs his mother, "go to your room and have a good cry, dear. I know how you feel."

"I feel so tired," Chester adds pointlessly, "I think I'll go to bed."

"Why don't you lie down and take a little rest first, Chester?" advises Fields.

"Well, good night, pa," says Chester.

"Good night, Chester," he replies.

"Good night, ma," says Chester.

"Good night, Chester," ma answers.

"Sleep well, Chester," says pa.

"Thank you, pa, and you, too," says Chester.

"Thank you, Chester," pa replies.

"Sleep well, Chester," adds ma.

"Thank you, ma, and you sleep well."

"Don't forget to open your window a bit, Chester," says pa.

"Don't forget to open yours a bit, pa."

"I won't, Chester," says pa, as ma adds, "Yes, don't forget to open your window a bit, Chester."

"Open yours a bit, too, ma."

"Good night, Chester," bid both his parents.

"Good night, pa, good night, ma."

"Good night."

"Good night."

"GOOD NIGHT . . . Chester," says pa with finality.

The short is punctuated with Fields's most famous running gag. Whether going in or out of the cabin, or just passing by, he stands at the doorway and says theatrically, "And it ain't a fit night out for man or beast!" as an unseen hand throws a fistful of artificial snow in his face. The gag gets funnier each time he does it, as the pointlessness of it all becomes more and more apparent. At the fade-out, Fields intones the phrase once more, recoiling just slightly as he waits for the snow that does not come.

*The Fatal Glass of Beer* is filled with a hundred little touches that allow the viewer to enjoy the film more each time he sees it, spotting some comic bit that had escaped notice the last time.

Fields's next short, *The Pharmacist,* was really a blueprint for his classic feature *It's a Gift.* In this short Fields has a dual personality; at home with his family, he is his usual nasty self (daughter Babe Kane complains that he doesn't love her. "Of course I love you," he says harshly as he threatens to slap her), but when he goes downstairs and assumes his role a proprietor of a small-town pharmacy, he not only becomes polite and agreeable, but does so to a preposterous extreme. He takes a telephone order for a box of cough drops and obligingly agrees to deliver it, as the customer gives him directions to travel the highway eighteen miles, make a left, etcetera. His biggest business, it seems, is in selling postage stamps at three cents apiece; but even here, success eludes him. A grumpy customer reluctantly agrees to buy one stamp and then insists that Fields give him one from the middle of the sheet. Anxious to please, the proprietor uses a pair of scissors to cut around the middle of the sheet and ruin a dozen others to supply the man with his one stamp, after which the fellow snaps, "Have you got change for a hundred dollar bill?" When Fields tells him no, the customer says he'll pay up the next time he drops in.

And so it goes during a typical day, as Fields nets a total of three cents for his day's work, and manages to give away three gigantic vases as "souvenirs" to each customer—two of whom have dropped in just to use the ladies' room.

Just as *The Dentist* typifies one side of the Fields screen character, the totally unpleasant man, *The Pharmacist* pinpoints the other, the victim, whom Fields was to portray in many of his later feature films—a man who has everything bad happen to him, but who manages to maintain a cheerful visage, even though the audience *knows* exactly what he is thinking and saying under his breath.

The final Fields-Sennett short, *The Barber Shop,* is the weakest, because it is the most conventional of the batch. Its gags for the most part could be carried out by any number of comics, and don't have as strong a tie to the Fields personality as those in the other two-reelers. There are distinctly Fieldsian gags, and a liberal dose of black humor (a dog sits patiently next to the barber chair ever since Fields cut a customer's ear off and the dog got it), but the comedy is decidedly tame when compared to the previous three endeavors.

Nevertheless, these four two-reel shorts present W. C. Fields in his purest form, creating *his* kind of humor, not someone else's filtered through a script. The attention to detail in *The Fatal Glass of Beer,* the variety of gags in *The Pharmacist,* the combination of verbal and visual humor in *The Dentist,* show what care and skill went into their production.

Fields had made shorts before, among them a notable 1930 two-reeler for RKO called *The Golf Specialist,* which stagily reprised his classic golfing routine; but these four Sennett shorts showed him at the height of his powers. They continue to be shown today, and they remain, as ever, a group of true comedy gems.

W. C. FIELDS'S TALKIE SHORTS

W. C. Fields made only five starring two-reel shorts in the sound era; they are indexed below. He appeared in one of Bobby Jones's golf shorts, *Hip Action,* two entries of Paramount's "Hollywood on Parade" series, and one episode of RKO's "Picture People," among other guest appearances. Fields also took screenplay credit for Sennett's 1933 short *The Singing Boxer,* with Donald Novis.

1. *The Golf Specialist.* RKO (8/22/30), Monte Brice. A recreation of Fields's classic vaudeville act in which his attempts to play golf are foiled by a series of minor calamities.

2. *The Dentist.* Paramount-Sennett (12/9/32), Leslie Pearce. Babe Kane, Elise Cavanna, Zedna Farley, Bud Jamison, Dorothy Granger, Billy Bletcher, Bobby Dunn. Dentist Fields goes golfing in the morning, then returns to his office where he contends with an odd group of patients.

3. *The Fatal Glass of Beer.* Paramount-Sennett (3/3/33), Clyde Bruckman. Rosemary Theby, George Chandler, Richard Cramer. Fields's son returns to his home in the North Woods after serving a jail term.

4. *The Pharmacist.* Paramount-Sennett (4/21/33), Arthur Ripley. Babe Kane, Elise Cavanna, Grady Sutton, Lorema Carr. A typical day in Fields's drugstore. Original title: *The Druggist.*

5. *The Barber Shop.* Paramount-Sennett (7/28/33), Arthur Ripley. Elise Cavanna, Harry Watson, Dagmar Oakland, Frank Yaconelli. There is little peace during an afternoon at Cornelius O'Hare's barber shop.

### Donald W. McCaffrey (excerpt date 1973)

SOURCE: "The Latter-Day Falstaff," in *The Golden Age of Sound Comedy: Comic Films and Comedians of the Thirties,* London: The Tantivy Press, No. 1973, pp. 166-72.

[*In the following excerpt, McCaffrey examines Fields's comic technique as displayed in his films.*]

As if he were a gift from some ancient muse, a successful vaudeville juggler underwent a slow but sure metamorphosis to become the outstanding comedian of the sound age. W. C. Fields, like some reincarnation from the past, reminds us of a comic type who has weathered the test of the ages. There is something of the braggart soldier from Roman comedy, a strutting Capitino from the *commedia dell' arte* or Falstaff from Shakespeare's plays. But he has more than these facets. He becomes a bungling husband, harassed by his wife—a comic type that ranges from the classical Greek stage through the medieval tale, the restoration and Eighteenth century comedy, down to modern times. In short, Fields ran the gamut of humour with a multi-faceted character of his own creation—with, of course, some help from his directors. Next to him all other comics of the sound age remain two-dimensional. Appreciated in his day, he now receives praise close to adoration. While this acclaim may seem only a "camp" trend—a temporary fad of those who have recently rediscovered the artistry of this unique comedian—there is enough sober evaluation to establish his status as the comedy king of the Thirties.

Fields's introduction to the sound film proved to be a humble beginning. He had prominent roles in eleven mediocre silent screen comedies. A twenty-minute two-reeler made in 1930, **The Golf Specialist**, merely indicated that he was lifting material from one of his vaudeville routines, a sketch centered on giving golf lessons to a beautiful girl. The full potentiality of Fields's talent did not appear until he made four shorts for Mack Sennett in 1932 and 1933. He scripted the works himself and at least one film, **The Barber Shop**, can be said to contain many of the aspects of the actor's wit. A feature, *Her Majesty Love* (1931), was not a distinguished piece, but it had the virtue of combining the talents of Leon Errol with those of Fields—an interesting combination that was not fully exploited. Obviously, he would not reach the peak of his powers until he was allowed to control the content of his own pictures. Also, he needed experience in a few features before his dramatic talents could be clearly transferred from his vaudeville heritage to the screen.

A much livelier feature than *Her Majesty Love, Million Dollar Legs* (1932) had the advantage of imitating the silent screen tradition. But a copy grafted with voiced gags could not be the real thing, and it now remains a curious bit of nostalgia, almost an ode to the dead art that seemed to be kept alive in its true form by the daring Chaplin who refused to switch to sound until 1940. Unfortunately, *Million Dollar Legs* was not a vehicle for Fields. Had it been so, the work might have been an outstanding comedy. It was more of a "Grand Hotel" of comics, old and new. The new breed, Jack Oakie, Hugh Herbert, and Billy Gilbert had prominent roles. Hank Mann, Ben Turpin, and Andy Clyde played minor parts—almost symbolically indicating the future of the silent screen comedian.

As if to show its loyalty to vintage humour, *Million Dollar Legs* opens with a corny title gag superimposed (with each line appearing one after another) over a view of a mid European town:

> Klopstokia . . . a far away country
> Chief Export . . . Goats and Nuts
> Chief Imports . . . Goats and Nuts
> Chief Inhabitants . . . Goats and Nuts

And this title almost sums up the wacky character of the whole picture.

In the opening scene George Barbier, playing the role of a brash manufacturer declares: "I want to get out of this country. I have a feeling I'm being spied on." Told not to worry because spying could not be possible in Klopstokia, the magnate doesn't see, pressing close behind him, the cross-eyed Ben Turpin with obvious cloak and dagger garb—a large brimmed, black hat and a long cape. In such dress he appears periodically throughout the picture, taking notes on the proceedings—a mute spectre of the silent screen comedy.

Appearing in a carriage, Fields strikes quite a figure as a dictator, even though he is called President. He growls into a dictaphone:

> "My Dear General . . ." No, that's too friendly. "Dear General . . ." Still too friendly. "General Wagonhauls . . ." "Dear Son . . ." Now, why should I be so respectful? I'll demote the pup. "Corporal Wagonhauls . . ." (*He laughs gleefully*) He'll resent that. He'll resent anything I call him. The crud!

The tyrant finally gets so annoyed that he orders the object of his mushrooming wrath completely stripped of rank and placed under arrest. In one, brief monologue Fields establishes the comic potential of his character—an impossible authoritarian who obviously gets his "kicks" by pushing people around. Later we learn that he holds his position because he can best every member of his cabinet in the Indian wrestle. A running gag develops with Hugh Herbert, who plays the role of Secretary of the Treasury. Time after time Herbert is beaten in the contest, and he soothes his injured hand by rubbing it, pulls himself together, and mutters intensely under his breath: "Someday."

As richly as some scenes display Fieldsian humour, the picture doesn't focus enough on the comedian's antics. Jack Oakie, as the comical romantic interest, shares and often dominates a great deal of the footage of the film. In the role of a slick, not very bright, fast-talking salesman, Oakie exhibits a thin, tiny bag of comic tricks. Nevertheless, even with this limited acting vocabulary, his breezy young man has a lot of dash that gives the movie vitality.

Besides the characteristics of a film that seems to be an ode to Mack Sennett, *Million Dollar Legs* retains a hint of the musical comedy influence which develops with the burlesque of the *femme fatale* in the role of Mata Machree. Actress Lyda Roberti dances and sings of her own charms, warning all men who approach her that something drastic will happen to them, as she repeats over and over, " . . . when I get hot." Soon after this, Oakie sings a brief Klopstokian love song which obviously is a type of double-talk. But such musical diversions are confined to these scenes.

Fields's comic tyrant has less influence on the plot as the film progresses. Oakie's character proves to be the plot mover by getting the athletic Klopstokians to enter the international Olympic games. Early in the picture we see Fields juggling medicine clubs, people, and words. But his presence and influence fade half way through the picture.

In his brief stay with Mack Sennett, producing two-reelers, Fields had nearly full control of his material. From 1932 to 1934, he appeared in many pictures—probably too many, for most of his efforts were unrewarding. But all this provided a training ground for the development of some of his best works.

In 1932 *If I Had a Million* was a multi-drama of short tales, with sequences for such personalities as Gary Cooper, George Raft, Charles Laughton, and Wynne Gibson. One of the sequences from the film featured Fields and Alison Skipworth as husband and wife who have their new car demolished by a careless driver. Inheriting a million dollars, they buy a fleet of automobiles and proceed to track down "road hogs" and wreck them with their many vehicles. One by one the cars come in for replacement so that they can run into what they consider to be an offending driver. Actually, this kind of material is more suited to the talents of Harold Lloyd or Buster Keaton. They often handled similar types of situations by developing several comic variations and nuances. Fields seems to lack innovation in this work, and many developments of this situation are repetitious and mechanical.

In 1933 he appeared in three features, *International House, Tillie and Gus,* and *Alice in Wonderland.* The third work, showing Hollywood's emerging, not too successful, bout with the classics, hides W. C.'s face in an egg shell as Humpty Dumpty. In this brief appearance on the screen there is nothing distinctive about his performance. *International House,* in the same manner of the later *Big Broadcast of 1938,* has its roots in stage vaudeville and the radio variety programme of the period. A Chinese inventor, Doctor Wong, uses a "radioscope," an all-seeing but erratic form of television, to bring in various comedy skits and musical shows. Wong's addition of video to audio doesn't fare well with such radio personalities of the time as Rudy Vallee and Colonel Stoopnagle. Fields functions as a character with only part of the plot devoted to him, and the picture seems to have been shot with many of the leading actors seldom meeting each other. Only occasionally does Fields have a chance to lash verbally the scatter-brained Gracie Allen who often engages in weak vaudeville patter with George Burns. One memorable moment develops when the comedian strolls down the hotel hallway and stops to look into a keyhole. He beautifully tosses off the line, "What will they think of next?" in a way that distinguishes his verbal humour from that of Groucho Marx. Similar "off-colour" material was used by Groucho, to be sure, but the execu-

tion would be much different in Marx's hand. He would have rolled his eyes and smirked directly at the camera.

*Tillie and Gus* was the first feature to focus on Fields as the leading character. It was obviously made to exploit the talents of a comedian who had gained fame—both popular and critical acclaim. But the work was not fully in the hands of Bill Fields. Director Francis Martin seemed to favour genteel comedy and didn't let the comedian unleash the complete force of his brand of invective. What might have become one of his masterpieces comes off as second rate. Nevertheless, some of the character facets that he later developed more effectively began to emerge.

Con-man qualities of Fields's screen portrayals were embryonic in this film and would be more fully exploited in **The Old Fashioned Way** (1934), *Poppy* (1936), **You Can't Cheat an Honest Man** (1939), and **My Little Chickadee** (1940). When he is forced to leave an Alaskan town for crooked gambling in *Tillie and Gus,* as Augustus Winterbottom he utters one of his pretentious, garbled statements that would soon grace many of his films: "There comes a tide in the affairs of men, my dear Blubber, when we must take the bull by the tail and face the situation." He meets an ex-wife (played by Alison Skipworth—a cooler version of the Marie Dressler type), calling her "My Little Chickadee" and "My Dove"—labels that he often employed to sweet-talk women, particularly when he had been accused by them of some misdeed. We also see him in the often repeated card game scene. Pretending to be an innocent, he declares he's drawn an ace for a dealer position without showing it to the other players. With mock surprise he discovers he's won the first hand with four aces.

Another facet of his character is less well developed. Fields's dislike for children does not become full-blown because of some of the sentimental touches of the director and scriptwriters. Nevertheless, at one point, when asked if he likes children, he replies, "I do if they're properly cooked." This line, along with variations of it, became one of those statements most often quoted.

One of his staples of later pictures, comedy of frustration—more developed when he plays the harassed husband—evolves when Fields is shown trying to mix paint by listening to directions from a "how to do it" radio programme. Naturally, he gets behind the announcer and ends up throwing paint ingredients encased in cans and bags, plus a pet duck that happens to get in the way.

In the picture also appears Fields's tendency to skirt the rigid censorship of the time by using expletives that are substitutes for a strong oath. "Godfrey Daniel!" for example, appears in a way to create colour in his character. When he describes a paddle-wheel ferry boat, he cleans up a remark men have used to describe a woman with a good figure: "She's solid as a brick telephone booth."

A much tighter work than films that were conceived and authored by the comedian, *Tillie and Gus* does not fully capture the spectrum of Fieldsian wit. Mere clean-cut plot lines do not make a W. C. film and in some ways may be too restrictive to exercise the range of his talents. Most important of all, the touches of anti-sentimental character attitude and situations are too few in number. In fact, there are too many sentimental aspects to the leading figures, Tillie and Gus. They end by helping the niece, her husband, and the offspring (Baby LeRoy) to gain their victory over a villainous lawyer named Phineas Pratt (played by the raspy-voiced, wizened Clarence Wilson). As a Mr. Fixit, Fields also loses one of the essentials of his humour—comic frustration. He becomes funnier when *he* gets into a mess, an altercation, or a minor frustrating task. We also find him funnier when he growls his disdain for anything which the dewy-eyed dote upon. We love him when he declares that he hates a child or dog. Now that we've seen this side of his character, we seem to see a false note at the end of the picture when we spy Uncle Gus crawling on the floor before Baby LeRoy, with the pet duck on his back. When his nephew remarks that the ferryboat race was the "world's greatest gamble," the comedian redeems himself somewhat by replying, "No. Don't forget Lady Godiva put everything she had on a horse."

The year 1934 was Fields's most productive period. While it would seem impossible to create one good picture with an output of five pictures that year, the comedian created three strong works. The two he authored, *The Old-Fashioned Way* and *It's a Gift,* were among the best. He reached a new high in the creation of the con-man in the former picture. The fascinating, self-proclaimed "The Great McGonigle" developed into his most interesting version of this type of character to that date. Leader of an itinerant, seedy, theatrical troupe, McGonigle strikes a pose of fame and fortune and becomes comic to the viewer of the film drama when his false pretensions are realised. At the beginning of the picture his character is established when a process server stands with a summons held behind his back as McGonigle starts to board a train. Unnoticed, the crafty impressario lights the official document. As the paper is quickly thrust into his face, it bursts into flame. With great dignity Fields lights his cigar from the rapidly consumed summons; calmly and politely he says, "thank you very much" and boards the train before the startled town official.

From this opening move McGonigle proceeds to work his con-game on all around him. While he is not always successful, he generally wins by some unusual tactic that might be described as comic ingenuity. His brashness and ability to manipulate become the side of his character that promotes the bulk of the humour in *The Old-Fashioned Way.* But other facets still lie beneath the surface to give the character dimension. While he is often on top, he still remains the pretender and the fake who will be crushed in a forthcoming situation. His dignity will suffer when even his daughter exposes his tricks and gives him a lecture on his behaviour. Even when he plays the ha-

rassed husband in other films, the con-man lurks in the shadows. To a stranger who does not know him as the dominated husband, he will spin tall tales of his accomplishments as a fighter and adventurer.

Uneven as *The Old-Fashioned Way* is, it remains Fields's first solid creation. It is easy to agree with Andre Sennwald, writing in the "New York Times" of July 14, 1934, that the old-fashioned melodrama scenes from *The Drunkard* are laboured. These play-within-a-play scenes are not the comedian's meat, and he fails to handle the burlesque effectively even though he instils a great deal of gusto into the character of the villain. By far the most interesting part of the show-within-a-show part of the film is the actor's revelation of his vaudeville background as a juggler. Strictly a *lazzi* scene in the fashion of the *commedia dell' arte* theatre, it is a portion that has nothing to do with the plot; it merely shows some special skill on the part of the comedian. Seldom did he use the skill except by juggling a cane and hat as a character trait. Full blown in this little scene are his skills in juggling cane, hat, balls, and cigar boxes. In his feats he makes "mistakes" that lead to even greater feats of the art. We see where his comic character was born. A little man with pretensions and a sense of dignity trying to do his best even when he meets frustration. His act goes awry, but he carries on nevertheless.

At the end of the film the "pathos" in the little man who carries on creates not just a vaudeville act, but the last situation in the plot of *The Old-Fashioned Way.* It is the parting of the ways with his daughter, who is also engaged in show business. In a dignified yet pathetic pronouncement he tells her, "If you need me financially or otherwise . . ." indicating that he is off to a greater glory and fame before the footlights. The last scene shows him on a streetcorner reduced to selling a cure-all that prevents hoarseness. He gives an elaborate speech with the climactic moment ending in a loss of his voice—miraculously restored by a quick swallow of the remedy he is selling.

While *You're Telling Me,* a re-make of the 1926 silent feature, *So's Your Old Man,* was not written by Fields, it deserves a rank among the top five pictures in which he starred. Released in the spring just before *The Old-Fashioned Way,* this work revealed the actor in the role of the dominated husband and inventor. The earlier scenes are the strongest in the movie. Unfortunately, the refurbished golf routine for the final scene fizzled. As an inventor he revealed a humorous eccentricity, but his struggles with a nagging wife promoted the loudest laughter. It was a brilliant beginning using the material that would create some of the greatest comedy of the Thirties.

Critics and audiences viewing films by Fields today seem to think they have discovered him, and a myth has developed that he wasn't appreciated in his day. Andre Sennwald realised that a significant clique had developed by 1934. He seemed to be a part of the clan when he used labels of "The magnificent Mr. Fields," and "the great man." By this time, with uneven works being produced, Fields had become one of the leading comedians.

In his screen career the bulb-nosed W. C. appeared in over forty films. Six short works, one- or two-reel films, are extant. About eight of his silent features seem to be lost. The majority of his films, it may be conjectured, were mediocre. But in 1934 he may have produced his best work *It's a Gift* certainly is among the top three features he created. Obviously, he was in control of his material, and director Norman Z. McLeod must have known how to make the best use of the talents of his leading players. *Aficionados* have often thought of Fields's humour centring on the con-man, but while he is still the pretender in this picture, he has many traits of the small town grocery store owner who is badgered by his wife, son, and neighbours. The film is a classic study of comic frustration—a view of the little man struggling against the annoyances produced by a collection of petty people in the average community of the United States.

The comic tone of the family misalliance becomes evident early in the picture as the group gathers for breakfast. Consuming all the sugar without a thought for others, the mouthy, eight-year-old son gets reprimanded by his father. The boy complains: "What's the matter, Pop? Don't you love me anymore?" Ready to strike the brat, Fields as Harold Bissonette harshly declares: "Certainly I love yah." His wife harps, "Don't you touch that child!" Defiantly the reply comes: "He's not goin' to tell me I don't love him."

With his family, however, the hapless father is more often on the receiving end of the abuse. Even in his grocery store he is not king. The most demanding creatures of this town want the impossible from Harold. One of the best scenes in the film shows the comic protagonist pitted against a blind, partly deaf man called Mr. Muckle. Dark humour abounds as the cranky old fellow runs his cane through the front door window of the store, and refusing to stay seated after he comes in, bumps into displays of china and light bulbs. With his attempt to please his patrons regardless of their disposition, Harold Bissonette cries pitifully, "Sit down, Mr. Muckle, please, Dear," as he tries to wrap a package and satisfy another customer, a surly, dignified member of the community named Jasper Fitchmueller, a man bent on obtaining ten pounds of kumquats in a hurry.

In this struggle to please we see Fields in another dimension of his fabulous talent. We laugh at him, but we also feel sorry for him. Maybe a bit of the famed Chaplin pathos develops in this situation. Actually, he becomes a comic hero, with the blind and deaf Mr. Muckle evolving into a comic villain. Only Fields, as it has been noted by critics, could create a scene of this kind.

The little man has a dream. Wishing to escape from it all, he sells his grocery store in order to buy land in California which he believes has a flourishing orchard of orange trees on it. This leads, of course, to a harangue from his wife—forcing him to sleep on the back porch.

The comedian develops a second outstanding sequence by showing Harold's attempt to get to sleep under a barrage of interruptions. Before his exit to the porch the phone rings at 4:30 in the morning. It's a wrong number, but his wife doesn't believe him:

> HAROLD: Somebody called up and wanted to know
> if this is the Maternity Hospital.
> MILDRED: What did you tell them?
> HAROLD: I told them "no."
> MILDRED: Funny thing they should call you up here at this hour of the night from the Maternity Hospital.
> HAROLD: They didn't call me up from the Maternity Hospital. They wanted to know if this *was* the Maternity Hospital.
> MILDRED: Oh! Now you change it.

Too tired to be exasperated, Harold sputters and mumbles, trying to convince the suspicious wife, but she merely declares, "Don't make it any worse," and blames him for keeping her awake. Stumbling sleepily to the back porch of a three story housing complex with a constant stream of chatter fading in the background, the comic protagonist now encounters a series of interruptions to his sleep that develops into a sequence which becomes a humorous ode to frustration—the main ingredient of Fields's best movies:

> 1. Harold lies down on the porch swing only to have it break from its mooring on the ceiling. Just the head end falls, and he is left with head and body slanting downward. His wife complains in the bedroom.

> 2. Enter a milkman with bottles clinking loudly in his wire carrier; this produces mumbled expletives from Harold. "Please stop playing with sleigh bells," he mutters.

> 3. A cocoanut is delivered to the floor above. When the milkman leaves, the harassed soul settles down in his uncomfortable, improvised, broken bed only to have the cocoanut roll step by step down several flights. This Chinese torture produces a series of flinches from Harold and culminates in a banging and clattering as the cocoanut rolls into garbage cans, shattering the morning calm.

> 4. Almost fully awake now, Harold tries to fix the head end of the swing. He's interrupted by a smooth-talking insurance salesman who is searching for a man with the unlikely name of Karl La Fong. Turning his sales pitch to an unwilling subject, he assures Harold he could give him an annuity by which he could retire for life at ninety. His wife enters and yells, "If you and your friend wish to exchange ribald stories, please take it downstairs." Roaring with indignation, "My friend!?" Harold hurries into the house and returns with a meat cleaver in hand. Though he drives the slicker away, he accidentally

receives the final humiliation. Exhausted by the ordeal, he drops the meat cleaver on his foot and emits an agonising whine of pain—a high pitched, inward cry smothered by his injured dignity.

5. Wearily he settles on the porch swing only to have a little boy (played by Baby Le Roy) stuff grapes down a hole in the floor above him and drop them on his head. Sleeping with his mouth open, a grape enters and chokes him. "Shades of Bacchus!" he exclaims. Going up to the third floor to stop the bombardment, he gets accused by the mother of feeding grapes to her offspring.

6. As he nearly goes to sleep again, a girl of about sixteen jumps from step to step with her full weight and hits each landing of the stairs so hard she knocks over garbage cans. From the top floor her mother yells to her about the errand on which the girl's being sent. Loudly they discuss the situation, and Harold mutters that he would like to tell them both where to go. Not only is he accused by these two of disturbing them; his wife berates him for fraternising with women.

7. Lying down, Harold rises to the sound of a squeaky pulley on a clothes line—thinking the sound comes from a rat. He sets a trap for the rodent under his swing. Maddeningly, the sound continues.

8. An Italian vegetable and fruit peddler comes by, hawking his wares. Harold runs into the house and returns with a shot gun. Calling sweetly (but ominously), "Vegetable gentleman?" he keeps his gun levelled to shoot. Not able to locate the offender, he sets the gun down and settles into the swing. The gun explodes, and the whole swing breaks from its mooring and comes crashing down. In a heap and without a pause for reaction, he picks up a fly swatter to strike at some critter that landed with him in the rubble.

Simple as this series of incidents may seem, the comedian makes the most of it. Not only do his utterances of annoyance, his misanthropy to those who plague him, contribute to the humour; there are little, futile gestures of frustration and pained expressions masterfully executed which show the actor at his best. The trials and mock agonies of the little man make this twelve-minute sequence one of the landmarks in film comedy.

Unfortunately, this simple, yet effective, sequence becomes the highlight or climax of the best in the picture. The following complications regarding the trip to California have moments, but they do not surpass what comes before. A comic turn of fortune shows Harold's land to be valuable after all because it is adjacent to the future construction of a race track.

After his first masterpiece of the screen, Fields appeared in two works, *David Copperfield* and *Mississippi,* which added to his stature as a comedian. The latter displayed his talents as the con-man again, with a few notable scenes featuring him as the *braggadocio.* More significant on the ledger, however, was the Dickens film. Though British critics found his accent unacceptable, Americans felt his dialect was suitable to play Micawber. Director George Cukor evidently was able to restrain him from incorporating vaudeville bits into his mannerism, and the comedian created a charming character that was an extension of his con-man. More mellow tones and subtle keying of the comic pretensions built into the character by Dickens gave the performance depth. They proved that at the core of a great comedian lies a "dramatic" actor—that is, one who can interpret a role with serious overtones and nuances. Had he lived into the Fifties and been given the opportunity, Fields might have been able to play a role in a Samuel Beckett drama with the skill similar to that Bert Lahr mustered when he enacted the part of Estragon in *Waiting for Godot.*

With the creation of his third authored picture in 1935, *The Man on the Flying Trapeze,* Fields had his second masterpiece. Like *It's a Gift,* the work was totally controlled by the comedian. The story was developed under the pseudonym of Charles Bogle and had many of the qualities of the 1934 work.

Once more he is pitted against family and relatives. As the harassed husband, Ambrose Wolfinger, he pulls a gun from a drawer to investigate burglars prowling in the basement. When the gun accidentally discharges, his wife screams. In sharp understatement, using half a question with a note of hope he queries: "Oh, I didn't kill you? That's fine." Since he remains the henpecked husband until the end of the film (the inner resentment finally explodes and the sponging relatives are put in their place), much of the best laughter of the picture develops from those situations in which others conspire against his attempts at dignity. This is even more evident than in *It's a Gift.* There are also more mumbled understatements by W. C. than in any of his other films. Many are suppressed, muffled comments on his relatives. But there are other incidents that also use this type of wit. Accused of manufacturing apple jack without a permit, he is placed in a jail cell with a madman who has murdered his wife. In a demented frenzy the bug-eyed lunatic confesses, "I had three wives, but this is the first one I have killed in all my life!" Ambrose, with a slight flicker of terror in his eyes, as coolly as possible, observes: "Oh, that's in your favour, yes."

With more understated humour than his other films, *The Man on the Flying Trapeze* becomes an especially delightful work in the Fields gallery of comic portraits. Furthermore, his character in this film exhibits an odd talent that makes him valuable to the business world. A self-proclaimed "memory expert," he can remember trivial incidents which occurred with his boss and his clients. With a perverseness that is comic, he does little paper work and keeps a roll top desk of cluttered correspondence "filed" in a way that only he can decipher.

While *It's a Gift* and *The Man on the Flying Trapeze* have only recently been lauded by critics, *The Bank*

*Dick* (1940) has long been a favourite of *cinephiles*. In content and quality of execution, it certainly can be rated as one of his top three works. The material is clearly linked to similar substance in his two earlier masterpieces. Once more Fields is an author under an odd name—this time the pseudonym is Mahatma Kane Jeeves. All three films feature him in the role of nagged, bumbling, little man living in a small town. Each of these works, while it has imperfections, is dominated by the leading character.

*You Can't Cheat an Honest Man* (1939), *The Big Broadcast of 1938, My Little Chickadee* (1940), and *Never Give a Sucker an Even Break* (1941), have other comedians whose talents are not as brilliant as Fields's so that the total film meanders in quality of humour and plot. By 1940 reviewers were fully aware of the fact that when W. C. was left to himself as the focus of drama, the work was much better. In the *New York Times* Bosley Crowther held the view that *The Bank Dick* was a superior work because the comedian did not have such "excess baggage as Mae West or even Charlie McCarthy. The picture belongs to him, and his name—or his nom de plume is stamped all over it."

If a person wishes to split hairs, *The Bank Dick* just missed being a product of the Thirties by its release date of 1940. Nevertheless, it was in tone a product of that age that experienced the full range of comedy, and it remains as a masterpiece of its *genre*. Some overlap of the Thirties tradition went into the early Forties. But the World War years were declining years for the comedy, and *The Bank Dick* was the last significant work of the famous comedian.

As in *It's a Gift,* a running gag develops from the last name of the comic protagonist—in *The Bank Dick* the character is called Egbert Sousé. In the former film attempted dignity was stressed through the periodic correcting of people on the French pronunciation of the last name, Bissonette. Built into the name of Sousé is a mispronunciation that reveals a character trait of the protagonist. Naturally, an accent over the "e" becomes necessary to avoid the disparaging label which reveals a comic truth—Egbert practically lives in a bar.

Some of the best scenes of the picture take place in the local saloon and café, the Black Pussy Cat. As the spinner of tales, Egbert explains his exploits in the movies, indicating that he directed Fatty Arbuckle, Chaplin, Keaton, "and the rest of them." [An "in gag" most people in Hollywood would catch. In the silent period these comedians were their own directors.] He drawls, "Can't get the celluloid out of my blood." Later, hired as a bank policeman, he grabs a little boy with a cap pistol and asks, "Is that gun loaded?" Angrily the mother replies, "No. But you are." In this film, more than any other, a weakness for drink becomes one of the essential parts of his character. At the end of the drama he seems to have become a successful executive (through the second accidental capture of a bank robber), and his family see him

as a changed man whom they now respect. But at the fade-out we see him following the town's bartender who evidently is walking to work to open the Black Pussy Cat.

Another interesting feature of *The Bank Dick* lies in the comedian-author's increased use of character names that make some comic comment—either an abstract or explicit view on the nature of these characters' personalities. While Fields often had a revealing title as a leading or supporting figure in his films, he never employed as many wacky names as in *The Bank Dick.* Those associated with the banking business were Mr. Skinner, president of the establishment and J. Pinkerton Snoopington, bank examiner. More abstract is the label for a lush of a movie director, A. Pismo Clam, enacted by a comic bit actor, Jack Norton, who always seemed to be the drunk in films of the Thirties. In a similar vein J. Frothingham Waterbury is the name for a con-man. Most literal are the "handles" for the bank robbers—Filthy McNasty and Repulsive Rogan. Fields, it should be noted, followed a practice used by authors throughout history, but the technique was used particularly by playwrights in the Elizabethan, restoration and Eighteenth century theatre.

The last stand and fade out of Fields came in 1941 with *Never Give a Sucker an Even Break.* The gamut of his humour still exists in this rambling work. Like *The Bank Dick,* it contains a climactic sequence which shows the silent screen heritage still influencing the comic film of the Forties. There is a mad dash to the hospital with a woman Fields believes is about to deliver a baby. More novel than the chase of the bank robber in the former work, this scene includes a tangle with the police and a fire truck. Occasionally, other scenes develop effectively with the support of Franklin Pangborn and Leon Errol, but the work becomes disjointed by the inclusion of musical production numbers featuring Universal's second version (the first, Deanna Durbin) of the sweet, young, light opera soprano, Gloria Jean. These portions of the film, like those in *International House* and *The Big Broadcast of 1938,* seem merely to be tacked on and serve only to slow down the development of a work that would be much better without them.

Some films which need only to be briefly cited are *Poppy* (1936), *The Big Broadcast of 1938, You Can't Cheat an Honest Man* (1939), and *My Little Chickadee* (1940). Fields made only cameo appearances in *Follow the Boys* (1944), *Song of the Open Road* (1944), and *Sensations of 1945.* Some fans of the great comedian may object to the slighting of *My Little Chickadee.* It now achieves much of its recognition from its "camp" qualities. Even though it has many good scenes, it is probably the most overrated work in which the comedian appeared. Since Mae West appears in at least half the footage, doing one of the poorer jobs of her career, the total work suffers. Fields has some good lines, but he has trouble playing with the forceful Miss West. Visually, his uneasiness can be detected. He seems frozen before her and only loosens up when he does a scene with minor players.

The explanation of Fields's genius, I believe, lies a great deal in his ability to combine verbal and visual traits in his comic character. His three masterpieces, *It's a Gift, The Bank Dick, The Man on the Flying Trapeze* (to which might be added the first half of *You're Telling Me*) display this fusion at its best. Along with this evolved a more fully developed comic portrait. And this creation proved to be unique for not only the golden age of sound comedy, the Thirties, but also for the great silent screen comedy of the Twenties. Most prominent in both these ages was the young man with traits of dumbness or *naïveté*. To some extent the fast-talking, stand-up comedians entered the scene to play the young man leading roles in the Thirties, but none of them achieved the stature to make them outstanding artists. As a comic protagonist Bill Fields was the only great actor to play the middle-aged and beyond character with a skill that will place him among the immortals.

When I interviewed Buster Keaton in June, 1965, I asked him if he agreed with my choice of Chaplin, Lloyd, Langdon, and Keaton as the four great comedians of the silent age. In failing health which led to his death on February 1, 1966, he did not understand that my evaluation was confined at that time to the silent age of the Twenties. He protested: "Don't forget Bill Fields." I agreed with him then and I do now, after a thorough examination of his films, that Bill was in the king's row. That is, if the silent and sound eras are combined, Fields certainly ranks above Harry Langdon, whose talent was superior to many others but limited when compared to the master of sound comedy.

Critics today should rate this comedian as the king of the Thirties because of his uniqueness, innovation, and many faceted character. At the core of his personality there is the warmth and charm of a Falstaff even though he snarls and mutters insults. In his weak films the power of his enactment of the role comes through. As with Chaplin, we have begun to associate the man with the character, and when that happens, the artist's works become creations for all seasons—for the ages.

**Wilfrid Sheed (essay date 1974)**

SOURCE: "Toward the Black Pussy Cafe," in *The New York Review of Books,* Vol. 21, October 31, 1974, pp. 23, 26-28.

*[In the following essay, Sheed presents Fields in an unsentimental light, and faults Ronald Fields for his attempts to sanitize his grandfather's autobiography.]*

Of all the subjects that don't need de-mythologizing, one would have thought W. C. Fields was pre-eminent. With comedians in general it seems important that their life and their work be taken as one. "I hear he writes his own lines" is a phrase that echoes from childhood. The lot of the gag-writer is a bitter one: unless he consents to be a

performer himself, like Mel Brooks or Carl Reiner, we don't want to know about him.

Hence, most books about comedians tend to be unsatisfactory. Either they service the myth and give the clown a brain he doesn't deserve ("The trouble with Groucho is he thinks he's Groucho," says one of his old writers) or they tell the truth, as John Lahr did of his father Bert in *Notes on a Cowardly Lion,* leaving us with a somewhat shrunken functionary, barely worth a book, though Lahr got a good one. Comedians are actors, and in dealing with such there is rarely anything between fan magazine falsehood and terrible disillusionment.

Books about W. C. Fields, on the other hand, tend to be satisfactory even when they're bad. For instance, his mistress's book about him, *W. C. Fields and Me*[1] by Carlotta Monti, is hilarious for wholly unintentional reasons. Any book by a chorine that starts out "I can't deny that he was an anomaly" is going to be hilarious. Fields's own voice rumbles like this through every phrase. Because Fields really was a comic genius. There was no question where the lines came from or the style, and some of this had to spill into the private life, leaving a fund of great anecdotes that even a goodhearted starlet couldn't ruin, so long as she followed the master's directions.

Still, we demand more of Fields than even comic genius. We have to believe he meant it. We want certification that such a one existed: a mean, child-hating con man who was so funny about it that he made these things all right. Staged comedy exists partly to resign us to evil, but for this to work we want more than play-acting. As Groucho says of professionals, we want a real old lady crashing downhill into a wall in her wheel chair—only to walk away unharmed.

Robert Lewis Taylor produced a few years back one of the best books ever written about a comedian, *W. C. Fields: His Follies and His Fortunes.*[2] In it Taylor tells just enough truth to qualify as a biographer, including the unfunny horrors of Fields's alcoholism. But his dominant strategy is to accept Fields's own version of Fields, which was a work of art built on a dung heap, like so many artists' lives. He gives us a Fields meaner than any ten men, and yet somehow funny and harmless, where he was probably bitter and brutal. People get hurt and yet they *don't* get hurt. Wife and child are deserted, Fields screams with the DTs. Everyone exits laughing.

Since his early years were the least verifiable, it is here that Fields's remodeling of himself, as transcribed by Taylor, was most thorough. Over the years, Fields spun a version to his cronies, Gene Fowler and the like, that made him sound like a Dickens child: a vagabond, shoplifter, jailbird. This gives his life the convenience of a movie biography in which everything can be explained by filmable incidents: thus, he got his meanness from being swindled by a crooked manager; he got his voice from this and his nose from that. It only needs sketches by Boz to illustrate the turning points. Fields's devotion to Dickens affected not only his art, as we shall see, but his life, and his fans were quite content that this Dickensian version should be the Fields of record. We conspired in accepting it as the real old lady in the wheel chair.

But now his family has come along, in the person of his grandson Ronald, to tidy him up in a book ironically titled *W. C. Fields by Himself:* if only he *were* by himself. But Ronald bounds alongside, keeping a close eye on him at all times, reminding one of the family in *The Bank Dick* who try to make Egbert Souse respectable. It seems he did not hit his old man with a shovel and run away from home; he did not do time in the slam (Taylor has admitted that there is no record of him in the Philadelphia jails, but puts it down lamely to his many aliases; he did not even hate children. Photos are introduced showing him rather gingerly dandling his grandson, which can only dishearten his fans.

In short, like many a doting widow, the family has cruelly stripped Fields of his legends, obviously failing to understand what made him great in the first place. If this were all there were to him, we would not be reading books about him at all, let alone this one. I had almost said Ronald Fields has done the impossible and made him dull; but here, since Fields scholarship grinds on and rational enquiry is thrust upon us, a grudging point must be admitted. It is not as difficult as one had supposed to make Fields dull. Without the subject's face and voice to guide us, we find ourselves staring directly into his subject matter: and the effect is one of a nagging, terrifying boredom.

In fact, I can think of no famous comedian outside of Jack Benny who skirted dullness more perilously than Fields. People who don't worship him tend to be bored even by his best stuff, and to see no point at all. For he is always threatening to sink back into his material—that world of drunken fathers and harridan mothers and squalling brats that is not funny at all, but desperately bleak. Older children may like Fields for what they take to be his congenial anarchy, but smaller ones are apt to be alarmed by this brutal, boozy adult, smelling of Victorian row-houses and failure. The only anarchy allowed in that world was the freedom of a father to strike his children and this W. C.'s father James Dukenfield availed himself of early and often.

In trying to clean his grandfather up, young Fields has linked W. C. once and for all to that gray world—and not as a rebel, but as a sullenly dutiful son who repaid his bullying father with a trip to Paris as soon as he could afford to. W. C.'s early letters are not particularly funny, but are tinged throughout with the sourness of genteel poverty. The flavor is perfectly captured by Ronald when he describes W. C.'s father as "a commission merchant dealing primarily in fruits and vegetables," i.e., a fruit-stand vendor. That this bogus respectability should linger on through three generations suggests how cloying it must have been and how hard for Fields to hold it at

laughing distance. Like Thurber's relatives in Columbus, whom one suspects of being cold and meanly eccentric in real life, Fields's family needed a prodigious swipe of the wand to become funny.

Since one must assume for now that Ronald Fields's documentation is unarguable, the colorful street urchin has to go, and we must look elsewhere for the genius. One startling possibility emerges. Although Ronald shows no mean gift for sniffing out W. C.'s unfunniest material, there is enough of it collected here in sketches and letters to suggest that comedy did not come easily or even naturally to the great man. It is an article of faith among Fields fans that he is always funny: and one remembers the racking chortle of Ed McMahon and the thin strained laughter of the studio audience as a not particularly funny piece of Fields was run on the "Tonight Show." But some of the material Ronald has assembled, e.g., an early sketch in which a scabrous family battles the London underground, or those leaden, one-joke exchanges with Edgar Bergen (vastly overrated), might tax even the susceptible McMahon. To make them work, one has to keep imagining the Fields persona; without it, they would be weaker than the output of any journeyman gag-writer.

The persona itself was the work of genius, and Ronald's book suggests that this was more consciously arrived at than we like to think. Fields's native gifts were industry, physical coordination, and mental retentiveness, plus a downright anal stinginess. The two kinds of retention were possibly connected, and together they account for much of his greatness and misery. Their immediate effect was to make him a master of music hall and vaudeville, where shtiks and bits of business had to be hoarded like miser's gold. I am told it was not unknown for comedians to pull knives on each other when they suspected their acts were being stolen. One's act was all one had, and it had to last a lifetime. Fields was superbly equipped for this cutthroat world: or if not he became so. Very few kindly men can have emerged from vaudeville.

Without detracting from W. C.'s uniqueness, I believe it would be rewarding to study the other comedians of the era for technical similarities. For instance, Fields's habit of throwing up his hands and hunching his shoulders when anyone threatens to touch him might be explained as a reflex flinching from his father's blows. But if memory serves; Leon Errol had a similar style; and before either of them, God knows what forgotten comedian working the London halls in the 1900s when Fields was starting out who may have inspired them both. In payment, Fields's hands fluttering at the throat may have taught young Oliver Hardy a thing or two. And so on. Just as the genius of comics is customarily overrated, so their craft and attention to detail is proportionately ignored. In an allied field, it is often forgotten that Sydney Greenstreet was a D'Oyly Carte veteran and that he played the Fat Man precisely as any Poo Bah would have, while Peter Lorre was a member of Bertolt Brecht's ensemble. Thus *The Maltese Falcon* was a mating of acting traditions, and not just of individual actors.

Fields once called Chaplin "a goddam ballet dancer," but it is no coincidence that they both came out of this London tradition, where techniques in physical comedy had reached a high polish.[3] All commentators agree that Fields had ferocious dedication, spending up to two years learning one juggling trick. And his first approach to comedy was probably similar: a dogged humorless mastering of each movement, until his body work was so good that he could make side-splitting *silent* movies. To this day, there is no actor I would rather see just enter a room and sit down, with the possible exception of Fred Astaire.

The vocal side of his act was carried at first by the physical and has a consequent freedom and experimentation about it, akin to Will Rogers's offhand patter during his rope-twirling. The people had paid to see a juggler, so the commentary was gravy; and Fields used it partly to cover his mistakes and hold the crowd's attention, but partly one suspects, semiconsciously, as a man mutters to himself when engaged on an intricate task—É_suspect Fields would have talked the same with no one around. The result is a dreamlike free-associative quality closer to poetry than to the world of gags.

With both Rogers and Fields it is worth bearing these origins in mind. Rogers's offhand delivery always implies a man doing something else—playing with a rope or looking up from a newspaper. (In those pre-monologue days, a comedian was expected to be usefully occupied.) In Fields's case, the keynote is a narrow concentration on his own concerns at the total expense of everything else. Many of his asides are not heard by the other actors at all and would not be understood if they were. And they have no connection with the needs of the plot. "Either they'll have to move that pole or vaseline the joint," he murmurs as he slides into the Black Pussy Cafe; and we are reminded of the solipsist beginnings of his act.

Buttressing this effect of majestic irrelevance is another quality derived from his stinginess: he would not let any of his old material go, but insisted on inserting it willy-nilly into movies where it had no business. Taylor reports a running dialogue between Fields and Mack Sennett, which would start with Sennett declaiming on the organic nature of comedy, the need for everything to have a reason, and would end with Fields saying, "I think I'll work my golf act into this two-reeler about the dentist." The result is an *oeuvre* of dazzling bits and pieces, but only one great movie (***The Bank Dick***).

If this artistic stinginess was based on artistic insecurity, the instinct was probably sound. Fields had hoarded very well, but when he moved away from those tested routines his comic taste remained uncertain to the end, and he made some uncommonly disappointing films. His most reliable work, to my taste, consists either of his early vaudeville routines—the golf game, the pool game, the fatal glass of beer ("It's not a fit night out for man or beast")—or their offshoots, i.e., sketches of generic similarity, in which the movements are stylized and the tongue is free to ramble. Conversely, his weakest moments come when he tries to let his visual imagination out a notch, as in the airplane sequences in *International House* and ***Never Give a Sucker an Even Break,*** where his urge to let fly, artistically, clashes with his native narrowness and his juggler's affinity for commonplace objects.

When Fields fails, the effect is peculiar: it is not as if a joke hasn't worked, but as if it has not even been made. That is, one wonders why he thought that particular idea was funny to begin with. It is as if his art were trying at times to be something other than comedy. (Those gruesome little scenes between husband and wife—funny?) Comedy was his mode, the thing he had learned so bloodily, but one wonders whether the handsome young chap in the early photos, who looks as if he's posing for the Andover yearbook, wouldn't have liked just a little bit more.

What we do know is that he worked uncommonly hard to educate himself, taking an autodidact's delight in long and unusual words, which later did him a comic favor but may have started out more seriously. Linguistic pretension is a staple of American humor as it is of Cockney, but the taste is not confined to comedians. (A reading by Fields of the later Henry James would about cover the range of cultural aspiration, in an era when even fastidious Americans had to go and overdo it.) Anyway one senses more than once that Fields is sniffing around literature itself with a poor boy's wistfulness. Fields: "That's a triple superlative. Do you think you can handle it?" Mae West: "Yeah, and I can kick it around." Alas, literature in any form other than parody would almost certainly have been beyond him. His early letters are incredibly stilted and ill-phrased, and it is something of a miracle that he wound up such a master of phrasing. But he could only be a master in comedy; and perhaps he used fancy words humorously because he could not get them quite right seriously. His non-comic writing remained as stiff as a schoolboy's to the end: not the least of reasons for hating his family.

Fortunately for everyone he discovered Dickens, and thus found a quasi-literary mode for his gifts, which would have to do. His Mr. Micawber was a masterpiece: and if critics object that he was just being himself—well, that is the whole point. He read Dickens constantly and wanted to play Dick Swiveller next. This he could also have done as himself. For all Dickens's variety, his orotund word-mad wind-bags have a strong family resemblance.

Oddly enough, Carlotta Monti, the fun-loving mistress ("Our respective senses of humor dove-tailed," she says solemnly, as Ann Hathaway might mention her sense of rhythm), does the most justice to the Dickens connection, possibly with a little help from Cy Rice, her collaborator. She notes the similarities between the funny names they both used—though fails to note that this is one further connection with the larger Cockney tradition. Dickens was a great frequenter of London theater, where the humor of quaint names coupled with braggadocio goes back at least to the sixteenth century. Ronald Fields, in one of his brighter moments, observes that "Fields stole as much from Dickens as Dickens took from people like Fields; he plagiarized Shakespeare's Falstaff just as Shakespeare copied an Elizabethan like Larson E. Whipsnade."

Placing this in a Far Western setting, as in *My Little Chickadee,* Fields reproduces the host of English swindlers and con men who ripped off the territories. Yet this is only one aspect of Fields and should not be overstated. I would not dream of claiming this flower of Philadelphia for England, although his grandfather did have a Cockney accent. Fields cannot be reduced to techniques and traditions, even if these have been scandalously overlooked by the trauma-mongers. No technique for instance could account for his nose—though it might account for his voice (has any commentator really told us what he sounded like in real life or when young?). But there is something about the inner Fields that is elusive and bothersome, and holds our attention in a way that mere talent could not. Put it like this. I have always felt that the idea of Fields is funnier than Fields himself; that even the face and voice he has taught us to remember are not quite the real ones. (I am always surprised when I attend a Fields movie by how wrong his imitators are, and by some troubling quality in his face that no cartoonist has captured.) There is something about Fields himself that leaves one staring vacantly after the laughter is over.

"Goddamn the whole friggin' world and everyone in it but you, Carlotta," are the last words Miss Monti records. The same comic techniques can be used for vastly different purposes: when Oliver Hardy fluttered his hands, it expressed embarrassment or foolish pleasure; with Fields, it was naked distaste, a horror of being touched, equal to Twain's and Kaufman's, plus a reaching for his wallet—touched in that sense too. He hated people, all right, although in fits and starts. His bursts of generosity and meanness alternated so violently as to be almost physically painful to watch. No one has properly calibrated this to the rhythms of his drunkenness—e.g., when he calls FDR "Gumlegs, our President," we know it's sanitarium time—but even on his good days, and with friendly biographers like Taylor and Monti on hand, there is a gray bile in the air that must have tormented the good-natured side of him. I tend to shy away from Freudian terminology (Freud on humor being even more undebatably disastrous than Freud on women), but if Ben Jonson was, as Edmund Wilson says, the greatest of anal playwrights, Fields would have been the perfect actor for Jonson, just as he was perfect for the extravagances of Dickens.

To some small extent, his misanthropy, like Groucho's, was a product of stinginess and not just its cause; if you like someone, you may have to give them something. (Also as with Groucho, his misanthropy was profession-

ally necessary, the essence of his comic point of view, so there was every reason to cultivate it and none to restrain it.) In an incredible lifetime of letters to his estranged wife, sunnily explained by Ronald as showing "the strain of trying to maintain a relationship largely by letter," W. C. whines and curses about the money he has to send her and cries poverty, even when he is doing handsomely with the Ziegfeld Follies. The self-pity and sheer hatred of giving come close at times to hysteria. Ronald says, "Only a few people knew of the love he still harbored for [his wife]," so out of deference to the living we'll leave it at that: except to say that publication of these letters will not add to the number.

So loving someone briefly (his wife Hattie became a vaudeville widow almost immediately) had cost him plenty: and the itch was raw until he died, leaving Hattie virtually disinherited. Yet it is worth noting that he did keep the connection with his wife going and that he did not divorce her to marry Miss Monti—and that he left Miss Monti, his loyal mistress of fourteen years, even less money (twenty-five dollars a week to be precise, bequeathing the rest to an orphanage for "white boys and girls, where no religion of any sort is to be preached"). Stinginess was his ultimate weapon against his near ones, a fluttering of the hands against their embrace; yet it was mixed with a punctilious sense of obligation, of hanging on to them even if it cost him. Domesticity had a horrible fascination for Fields, as one might guess from his subject matter, so long as it was kept horrible enough, "with the wedding knot tied around the wife's neck." That was the only kind of home he knew, and he could never quite leave it. He lied about running away as a boy, and he lied about running away as a grown-up. The de-mythologizers win that one. Fields was secretly respectable, during the gaps in his drunken dreamlife.

"On the whole, I'd rather be in Philadelphia" was his chosen epitaph, and one's mind travels back to the Dukenfields' household to see what he meant by Philadelphia, and the first sound one picks up is James Dukenfield's big hand rattling off little Claude's ear. If that was his earliest view of humanity, it can't have appealed to him much. And if he loved his father, he might have decided the returns on loving weren't worth it. A lifetime of parodying and downright imitating his father and his whole wretched family would seem more to the point.

And yet. There is a jaunty confidence and determination in those early photos that argue against any sickroom theory of Fields and his comedy. And he left too many heart-broken friends behind to have been the deformed clown of romantic legend. His humor is not just some neurotic compensation, but a cunning assault on Art, in the limited conditions of his life, and in its way a triumph of character. By his prime in the 1930s he had so welded his act to his life that he could "think he was W. C. Fields" and get away with it—though Ronald's book reminds us that he couldn't always. One must, like Taylor and Monti, follow the master's own selections. Never mind. A man who can slash his Jack roses with his cane, snarling, "Bloom, damn you—bloom for my friends," cannot be tamed by any number of relatives, even the horrific ones of W. C.'s nightmares. The family in *The Bank Dick* stand stiffly on the porch in their Sunday best: Egbert Sousé, Fields's dream of himself, his masterpiece, escapes down the driveway to the Black Pussy Cafe and freedom.

NOTES

[1] Prentice-Hall, 1971; Paperback Library, 1973.

[2] New American Library, 1967.

[3] Since Bob Hope left London as an infant, it is scarcely plausible to connect him with this tradition. Nevertheless this master of the double-take and the hasty retreat would have been physically if not vocally at home in the British music halls.

**Moody E. Prior (essay date 1978)**

SOURCE: "In Search of the Grampian Hills with W.C. Fields," in *The American Scholar,* Vol. 48, No. 1, Winter, 1978/79, pp. 101-5.

*[In the following essay, Prior explores the origins of a line from* You Can't Cheat an Honest Man, *in which Fields refers to "the Grampian Hills."]*

Toward the end of *You Can't Cheat an Honest Man,* W. C. Fields, as Larsen E. Whipsnade, attends a reception for his daughter in the mansion of the Bel-Goodies, where he turns on his charm and succeeds in ruining his daughter's prospective marriage to wealthy young Bel-Goodie, and in consequence his own last hope of saving the insolvent circus of which he is the proprietor and chief con artist. Turned out by his hosts, Fields picks up his top hat and cape with injured dignity, and as he makes his exit he calls out to his son and daughter, "On to the Grampian Hills, children." They flee from failure and rebuff in a Roman chariot that Fields has appropriated from the circus, with the sheriff in hot but futile pursuit. "Where are those Grampian Hills, Dad?" his daughter asks as the chariot careens along a country road. "I wonder, I wonder," says Fields.

No one in the audience would be likely to wonder, and if by remote chance someone in the darkened theater was startled by what sounded like a literary echo, he would have dismissed the thought. The Grampian Hills, along with Whipsnade and Bel-Goodie, had to be just another of Fields's characteristic odd, freakish, and amusing names. After all, popular comedians, especially the products of the old vaudeville circuit, are not supposed to play around with allusions that baffle and are not recognized by their audiences. But the very next film, *My Little Chickadee,* raises a suspicion that this particular name was in a category by itself, for it pops up again at the conclusion. In this film, Mae West outsmarts and exploits Fields, but she saves him from a wild West hanging for cheating at cards, and before leaving town he bids her a courtly farewell: "If you get up around the Grampian Hills, come up and see me sometime." An engaging line, for it combines a phrase made familiar by Mae West and inevitably associated with her, and Fields's own very private allusion.

Fields seems to have had the Grampian Hills on his mind when these films were being made, as we learn from a conversation which Edgar Bergen had with Carlotta Monti, reported in her book *W. C. Fields and Me:* "When we were making *You Can't Cheat an Honest Man,*" Bergen recalled, "we were going somewhere on location, and he said, 'If we get separated, let us all meet at the Grampian Hills.'" Fields claimed that the amusing names he used, although they sounded as if he had made them up, were always names he had come upon somewhere. The Grampian Hills can be found on a map, which is where Edgar Bergen finally discovered them. "I wondered about the name," he explained to Miss Monti, "and years later, while traveling in England, I chanced to scan a map of Scotland, and there, between the Lowlands and the Highlands, were the Grampian Hills." Fields had been to England a number of times in the days of his international travel as a successful juggler, and it would be surprising if some of the odd place-names in the British Isles had failed to appeal to him. What is puzzling about Bergen's explanation is that although Field's mention of the Grampian Hills on location impressed him enough to have stayed in his mind for years, he seemed unaware of the reference to them at the end of the film he had made with Fields. And somehow the geography of Scotland does not quite account for the effect of the final dialogue, especially "I wonder, I wonder."

Only Fields could have revealed the circumstances that brought the name to his attention and gave it its personal meaning, and he seems not to have done so. "The archives of his mind," Bergen told Miss Monti, "are loaded with trivia that amuse him and confound others." The most likely source for the name is literary, and although the tracks are faint, they lead ultimately, if improbably, to an obscure eighteenth-century play, *Douglas,* by John Home. The play was once greatly admired—Walter Scott referred to it as "Home's celebrated tragedy"—and it earned for its author the dubious compliment of being regarded as the Scottish Shakespeare. It had its first performance in Edinburgh in 1756, but its big successes were in London, where the two principal roles were played by the leading actors of the day, including Sarah Siddons and William Macready. In America there are records of performances as early as 1759 and as late as 1853. Even after the play had faded from the stage during the last half of the nineteenth century, its fame survived through one speech, like some outdated opera known only through occasional performances and recordings of one aria. The speech occurs after Lord Randolph brings to his castle a Stranger, apparently of lowly birth, who had just saved Lord Randolph's life by fearlessly attacking four armed assassins. In bearing and conduct the Stranger seems above his station, and Lord and Lady Randolph, admiring him as one "ordained / And stamped a hero by the sovereign hand/ Of Nature," prevail upon him to declare who he is. The Stranger begins:

> My name is Norval: on the Grampian Hills
> My father feeds his flocks, a frugal swain
> Whose constant cares were to increase his store,
> And keep his only son, myself, at home.
> For I had heard of battles, and I longed
> To follow to the field some warlike lord.

And for some thirty lines he recounts how he led an expedition with a few friends against "a band of barbarians" who had made away with their flocks and herds, and how he slew their leader, whose arms and armor he took, and left home to join the king's warriors against the invading Dane. It must follow, of course, that Norval is no ordinary shepherd but the son of the famed Douglas who was killed in battle before "Norval" was born, and that his mother is none other than Lady Randolph. How happily all this might have ended, but for the machinations of the villainous Glenalvon!

It is difficult today to discern beyond the stilted rhetoric and worn sentiments of Norval's speech the qualities that once made it much admired. It acquired a life of its own, independent of the play, and became widely known through public recitations, lessons in speech, school memorizations, and the like (a friend remembers his mother reciting the speech when he was a boy). Books on elocution included it as a set piece. An early instance, published in London in 1774, was William Enfield's *The Speaker; or, Miscellaneous Pieces Selected from the Best English Writers . . . With a View to Facilitate the Improvement of Youth in Reading and Speaking. To which Is Prefixed an Essay on Elocution.* This book was often reprinted, the last edition in 1858. Norval's speech also appears as an exercise in one of the most widely used and frequently reprinted texts in the United States during the nineteenth century, C. P. Bronson's *Elocution; or, Mental and Vocal Philosophy.* The first edition of Bartlett's *Familiar Quotations* (1855) included the opening lines, which have appeared in every subsequent edition. Besides their usefulness as training for the young, recitations had a place in family entertainment. Jane Austen, in *Mansfield Park* (1814), provides a glimpse of how it was. Tom and Edmund Bertram are arguing over whether their absent father would approve of their putting on a contemporary play, and Tom defends the project by reminding Edmund how often they declaimed for the elder Bertram:

> Nobody is fonder of exercise of talent in young people, or promotes it more than my father, and for anything of the acting, spouting, reciting kind, I think he has always a decided taste. I am sure he encouraged it in us as boys. How many a time have we mourned over the dead body of Julius Caesar, and *to be'd* and *not to be'd,* in this very room, for his amusement? And I am sure, *my name was Norval,* every day of my life through one Christmas holidays.

There among the perennial Shakespearian favorites is Norval's speech.

How familiar it had become we can guess from casual allusions and quotations. In *Dombey and Son,* for instance, Dickens says of Captain Cuttle's frugal way with words, "he had better, like young Norval's father, 'increase his store.'" It is not a very illuminating analogy, but for that very reason it attests to the currency of Norval's speech, since it does little more than flatter the reader who catches on as one who shares with the author a common cultural experience. One of the liveliest allusions occurs in Shaw's *You Never Can Tell,* when the irrepressible Clandon twins are being introduced to the family solicitor:

> Philip. I was christened in a comparatively prosaic mood. My name is—
> Dolly [completing his sentence for him declamatorily]. "Norval. On the Grampian Hills—"
> Philip [declaiming gravely]. "My father feeds his flocks a frugal swain—"

in 1897, when this play appeared, a performance of *Douglas* was very unlikely, but Shaw apparently assumed that an appreciable number of his audience would be familiar with Norval's speech, for the full effect of the twins' performance depends on the pleasure of recognition. However, the mocking way in which the twins play with the lines implies that the days when they could be taken seriously were already numbered.

Shaw's stage directions confirm the status of Norval's speech as a recitation piece, but the finest illustration of the flavor and resonance that it once had is preserved in Lionel Barrymore's description—as reported in *Good Night, Sweet Prince,* Gene Fowler's biography of John Barrymore—of his actor-father giving Norval's speech the full treatment:

> It was during our childhood that we first heard from Papa himself concerning the Grampian Hills. Papa used to stride up and down the room in his zebra undershirt, his eyes bright, his long forefinger leveled at some fabulous world unseen by mere mortals, and recite:
>
> "My name is Norval; on the Grampian Hills
> My father feeds his flocks, a frugal swain . . ."

This reminiscence had come about because Fowler asked Lionel to explain the significance of an allusion to the Grampian Hills in a letter John Barrymore had written to Fowler's son in 1937:

> We have found a house [John wrote] which, if we can only get it—as the owner is in Mexico, probably being shot—will have a murderer's room with a concrete base, where you and I, and those cognoscenti of whom we approve (I need scarcely say an excessively attenuated roster!) can cavort and have our being undisturbed. It will also have a swimming pool that will wind tortuously

among overhanging trees. *And* a pool table, at which we will fleece the neighboring bumpkins! Give my best love to your father and mother and the rest of the family. Soon I trust we will all be tending our flocks together on the Grampian Hills—where the cows *really* do come home.

Fowler's attempts to find in Scottish geography and Home's play a clue to the implications of the speech for John were dismissed by Lionel:

> It's news to me what it is or where it comes from. It didn't matter to us then nor would it now; we were not a family for research. Jack never knew what the Grampian Hills actually were; but he knew what they *meant.* What they meant to him. Our father's grand inflections made them appear to us what Utopia must have meant to Sir Thomas More; what the Promised Land, Arcadia, the Elysian Fields, the Garden of the Hesperides, Zion and all the rest rolled together, meant to the groping, dreaming men of all the ages. It was a place where caravans rested; where time itself stood still.

The elder Barrymore's recitations must have been stirring and powerful, but none of the heroic and warlike aspirations of Norval seem to have left an impression on the sons, only the strange place-name and its evocative pastoral associations. Detached from the play and even from its own immediate context of meanings, the speech nevertheless conveyed rich, even magical overtones.

Fields knew the Barrymores well, and in some important respects he and John were compatible. Among random notes that Fields had accumulated for a possible column for the Bell Syndicate there is the following item: "When the Government needed 75,000 more tanks, John Barrymore and W. C. Fields immediately offered their services." Robert Lewis Taylor, in his biography of Fields, tells about one memorable convivial occasion during the war when Gene Fowler, John and Lionel Barrymore, and Fields were moved to enlist and drove to a recruiting station, with Lionel in his wheelchair, to offer their services. ("Who sent you, the enemy?" asked the woman in charge.) In circumstances such as these, Fields may have heard John mention the Grampian Hills with feeling, for Fowler reports that "whenever Jack spoke of those hills a far-away spell would possess him." It is, of course, just as likely that during the years at the turn of the century when Fields was performing in all sorts of theaters in this country and around the world, he might have encountered an old-time actor who, like Maurice Barrymore, would tune up with "My name is Norval." The Barrymore story does not settle the question of the source of the allusions to the Grampian Hills in the two Fields films, but it does provide a significant clue to their meaning, one that points to something basic in his character and his comedy.

Fields played many roles, but they all had an essentially similar central core, and in many respects the character he created was an extension of himself. He was on the way to success even in his teens, but his boyhood was harsh and unhappy, and during his early career he was sometimes cheated by unscrupulous or desperate theatrical managers. Even in the days when he was celebrated and wealthy he never got over the uneasy feeling that he was engaged in a very precarious calling, that success was ephemeral, that banks were untrustworthy, that people were unpredictable and generally unscrupulous, and that every move required his utmost in cunning and sleight of hand. He could be affectionate, friendly, and even generous, but he was chronically suspicious and cranky. Yet he seemed aware of the absurdity of it all. He achieved his initial success as a juggler who dressed as a tramp and who would falter or miss in a routine only to make a desperate recovery that was technically brilliant and funny at the same time. This was his prototype, a metaphor for his comic art and his view of the human condition. In his films his elegant phrases, his fastidious manners, his self-conscious dignity all betray constant vigilance against the imminent possibility of defeat and humiliation, but he seems never lacking in will and resources for a comeback.

The comic character that Fields created is, accordingly, not of the ludicrous kind that is exposed to ridicule for its follies and stupidities and punished for them with laughter. It belongs rather to that more amiable group of comic figures with whom we sympathize, who are masters in the art of survival, employing their talents in a lively gamble to win at the odds, in defiance of nature and the repressions and suspicions of society. It is the kind of comedy that has produced some of the most durable and endearing comic characters of fiction and drama, and includes such familiar comic heroes as Falstaff, Sancho Panza, the Good Soldier Schweik, Groucho, and Chaplin. Even when they find it expedient to employ shady means that we are too respectable to employ, we are on their side because we admire their zest for life, and because they seem to be fighting our battle and enjoying it. Behind their ebullience and bravado there is sometimes a suggestion of gravity, for the game they play must ultimately be lost, although it is not honorable to mention it. "I would it were bed-time, Hal, and all well," says Falstaff just before the battle of Shrewsbury. The prince reminds him, "Why, thou owest God a death." But Falstaff turns aside this intrusive thought: "'Tis not due yet, I would be loath to pay him before his day." The danger of failure is always there, whether immediate or remote, but that only sharpens their wits and seems to justify their outrageous practices and fanciful expedients. And because our sympathies are with them we do not want to see them lose— or, if they do, left without resources to try again. We want to preserve the mood of high spirits and laughter in their company without a turn to pathos at their total defeat.

In some of his films, especially the earlier ones, Fields ends up a success. A fraudulent scheme for selling dry oil wells prospers in an unexpected way when the wells bring in oil; an invention proves its worth after misadventures—the windshield is indeed shatterproof, the tire punctureproof; an orange ranch that turns out to be desert is then profitably sold for a racetrack. But in **You Can't Cheat an Honest Man** and **My Little Chickadee** success completely eludes him. After the usual pattern of brazen effronteries, clever evasions, and dignified yet desperate recoveries, Fields finds himself in a final situation where events are out of his control and there are no more moves left save to accept defeat and go on. But for the comic character that Fields created and the comic effect of which he was the master, there cannot be the implication of a permanent reversal. There must remain the possibility of some recovery, the expectation, at least, of coming upon new territory where the suckers will listen or his luck will turn. Of this ebullience of spirit, this refusal to despair, the Grampian Hills are a sign and a symbol. What makes the allusions to them in these two films especially intriguing is that they are hidden and deceptive. By the time the films appeared (1939 and 1940) Norval's speech had become a cultural fossil from another era, and the kind of recognition that Shaw took for granted could no longer be expected. Fields's references to the Grampian Hills thus amounted to a sly and private game, highly personal since Fields himself was largely responsible for the scripts. Only in the repetition of the allusion in **My Little Chickadee** is there a hint that something beyond the mere oddity of the name is involved—and in the fact that in both films the allusion enters in exactly the same way, as an accompaniment of Fields's departure with the strong suggestion that he is not through.

No matter how Fields came across Norval's speech, it would not have been in character for him to endow it with the romantic inflation of the Barrymores, but the wryly comic air in which he utters the name at the conclusion of the films does not exclude at least a hint of magic. In the landscape through which the chariot passes in the final scene of **You Can't Cheat an Honest Man,** the Grampian Hills can stand for some undetermined place down the road where the irrepressible Fields and his companions can get a fresh start. The conclusion of **My Little Chickadee** is less buoyant and animated. The idea of having Fields and Mae West teamed up in the same film may have sounded great in theory, but although the funniest scenes are those with Fields, Mae West controls the action and Fields is often, uncharacteristically, the victim. At the end his schemes have failed, he has been humiliated, he has barely escaped with his life, and his bravado is deflated. As he stands alone amid these ruins he is as close to down and out as we ever see him. He looks a little wistful as he bids Mae West farewell, but he does not lose his aplomb, and he drops a cryptic hint that he retains in his mind's eye the image of a quirky Utopia which is not shown on any map but which, with the help of some audacity and a little luck, he does not despair of finding.

## Edward L. Galligan (essay date 1985)

SOURCE: "Never Give a Sucker or Yourself an Even Break," in *The Midwest Quarterly,* Vol. XXVI, No. 2, Winter, 1985, pp. 225-237.

[*In the following essay, Galligan examines Fields's psychohistory, with emphasis on ways that Fields overcame the misery of his childhood and the self-pity that might have arisen from it.*]

What a shame that someone can't put a bullet through the Pagliacci myth and bury it once and for all. It tells a lie: that though clowns are laughing on the outside they are crying on the inside; that they are wallowing in self-pity. They do not; they dare not. Clowns and all others who would live by the comic vision are obliged to strive to survive—more accurately, to live as themselves until they actually die—and self-pity, warm and sticky sweet as it is, will do anybody in long before the undertaker comes. So forget Pagliacci and contemplate the life and works of W. C. Fields where you will find a flamboyant, no-holds-barred attack on self-pity.

I doubt that anyone ever felt the temptations of self-pity more strongly than Fields did or ever went to such extravagant lengths to ward them off. As William Claude Dukenfield, born 1879 or 1880 in Philadelphia, he seems to have had the sort of battered, impoverished childhood that sends people to insane asylums; unquestionably he emerged from it with a massive load of grudges against his father, his relatives, and his society. As William C. Fields, born some time in the 1890s when young Dukenfield decided to seek fame and fortune as a comic juggler, he accumulated another load of grudges, these against cheating theater managers and a wife who became not long after he married her pious and fiercely respectable. As W. C. Fields, who passed from being "The World's Greatest Juggler" to being a "Star of Stage, Screen, and Radio," he unloaded all of his grudges and kept himself out of the insane asylum by living as well as acting the part of a man it would be impossible to pity, or even to believe. Two accounts of his life are available: *W. C. Fields, His Follies and His Fortunes* (1949) by Robert Lewis Taylor is a cheerfully mendacious account of the invented character; **W. C. Fields By Himself** (1973), "an intended autobiography" compiled by his grandson, Ronald J. Fields, is a slightly more reliable, much less persuasive attempt to claim the real man for his family.

Had Claude Dukenfield had a miserable childhood? W. C. Fields in movie after movie showed children as blighting the lives of adults, deserving what misery could be visited upon them. In **It's a Gift** a toddler floods his grocery store with molasses, and in **The Bank Dick,** his brat of a daughter (named in honor of two of Dukenfield's siblings, Elsie Mae Adele) hits him on the head first with a ketchup bottle and later with a rock. In private life Fields loved to tell of the time he spiked the orange juice of his co-star Baby Leroy with gin and crowed with triumph, "The kid's no trouper," as he was taken off the set, glassy-eyed. What is more, he may actually have done it. Certainly, he did delight audiences by ending a scene in **The Old-Fashioned Way** by kicking the little tyke (actually, alas, it was only a reasonable facsimile thereof) about six feet through a doorway.

Had he suffered from poverty as a child and been cheated by unscrupulous theater managers in his younger days? As a successful entertainer, he became celebrated for his ability to extort extravagant salaries from producers. The demands that he made on Earl Carroll, who wanted him to appear in a production of his *Vanities,* were so outrageous that his own agent, Billy Grady, quit in disgust; but Carroll paid and Grady remained his friend for life. When he was at Universal Studios near the end of his career he demanded and received an extra $25,000 for writing the stories for his movies—disconnected notes on the back of an envelope. He also demanded and received the credits (an important and much fought over matter in Hollywood) for writing the screen plays—and then took them under such names as Mahatma Kane Jeeves and Otis Criblecoblis. He did something of the same thing with his money, salting the extra salary away in banks spread all over the world, usually under some preposterous name, and never touching it again. Apparently when he died many thousands of dollars worth of bank accounts died with him.

On screen and off he portrayed himself as a man much too fraudulent and unscrupulous ever to be cheated; if there was any cheating to be done he was the man who would do it. He loved the part (which he wrote himself) of the crooked circus man, Larson E. Whipsnade, in *You Can't Cheat an Honest Man;* indeed, he invented a long, malodorous past for himself as a petty confidence man and swindler with a large knowledge of small-town jails. He made life miserable for those who worked for him, as Grady testifies, by paranoid suspiciousness, especially with reference to his liquor supply, and unrelenting efforts to cheat them out of small sums. But he didn't play favorites; he made life just as miserable for those who employed him. He once hounded Flo Ziegfeld for months to get him to pay for $35 worth of tennis balls when he found that he could get a laugh in the *Follies* by knocking them into the audience at the end of his act, an act for which Ziegfeld was already paying several thousand dollars a week.

William Claude Dukenfield must have made the decision to work under the name W. C. Fields casually, simply following the entertainer's custom of using a stage-name for professional purposes, but in May, 1908, he went to the trouble (and expense) of changing his name legally to William C. Fields. When and how his private identity disappeared into his professional one we will never know, but certainly by the time the man went into his first *Follies* in 1915 he was living the part of W. C. Fields. A particularly clear example is the story, which is reasonably well documented, of his relationship with a dwarf named William Blanche and called Shorty. Fields hired Shorty to be his dresser and valet when he learned that Ziegfeld had a superstitious dread of people with malformities. The fellow wasn't bright enough to perform those duties; but he could run very simple errands and stand guard over the steamer trunk full of liquor that Fields kept in his dressing room, and he did annoy Ziegfeld. Fields was ostentatiously ferocious in his treat-

ment of Shorty, checking the levels in the bottles every night, making him walk a chalk line to prove that he hadn't been nipping, cursing him and boxing his ears for his stupidity, firing him once or twice a week, but never letting him go. He even worked him into one of his most successful acts as a caddy to his golfer, mostly, perhaps, to further offend Ziegfeld, but also to get more laughs. It was a perfect symbiotic relationship: Shorty had the pleasure of living a glamorous, show-business life and Fields had the pleasure of demonstrating both on and off the stage that he was mean enough to mistreat a mentally defective dwarf. It lasted until Shorty died.

My theory that Claude Dukenfield saved himself from self-pity and, therefore, from self-destruction by becoming W. C. Fields is borne out by the history of his drinking. It is impossible to say when he passed from being a social to being a serious drinker, but it is certain that he drank prodigiously throughout the thirty or more years that he was a well-known public figure. By anyone's standards he was an alcoholic—what else can you call a man who took to having martinis for breakfast?—and he died, on Christmas Day, 1946, of the classic alcoholic diseases of the liver and heart. Yet he was never a sodden drunk and couldn't stand to be in the company of one. He boasted that in forty-odd years he had never been late for or missed a performance on stage, screen, or radio. He could have added that most of those performances were exceedingly funny, and humor requires the most precise timing known to show business. Where the ordinary alcoholic drinks in order to blot out the memory of his failures and his problems, Fields apparently drank in order to open himself up to the sources of his humor and to rise to the demands that it made upon him.

He had every right, so to speak, to be an ordinary alcoholic. Not only had his childhood been miserable and his one attempt at marriage a failure, his chosen profession was killing. He may have begun by juggling nice, comfortable oranges and lemons stolen from his father's grocery wagon, but he had to go on to harder, more painful objects, billiard balls, cigar boxes, broomsticks and even paring knives. How many hours would a man have to spend learning to juggle cigar boxes or to flip a broomstick on the toe of his shoe? And how many bruises would he acquire in the process of mastering a routine that called for shooting a billiard ball the length of a table, having it bounce back over his head (off a trick cushion), and catching it in his hip pocket? And what sort of fierce concentration would it take to balance a top-hat and a lighted cigar on his foot and then flip them so that the hat landed on his head and the cigar in his mouth several times a day most of the days of a year?

A man who lived a life like that could be expected to learn to look for a little oblivion in the bottom of a bottle, but a W. C. Fields couldn't be so soft on himself. He had to drink, if only to outrage all the pious folk who plunged the country into prohibition, but he had to stay fully conscious, if only to make sure he didn't pass up any chances to mock their other causes and beliefs. His long, well-publicized, ardent love affair with Demon Rum was essentially part of the Fieldsian attack on all of the platitudes associated with the Protestant ethic. He was, or at least made himself out to be, the perfect opposite of a Horatio Alger hero, fraudulent, untrustworthy, cowardly, disreputable. He would kick a man if he were down and a woman if she were too weak to fight back, and he hated children and dogs. He cheated at all games, but especially at pool and golf; he would cheat at anything else, too, but only if it were easy to do so. He was willing to be rich and grasping; he just wasn't willing to work hard and plan ahead. Family life was a hell to be avoided; so was the heaven offered by the churches. Instead of loving his neighbor, he despised the bastard, doing dirt unto him before he could do dirt unto Fields. Theoretically—that is, vocally—he was all for profligacy; actually, he had his mistresses in what was by the standards of Broadway and Hollywood chaste succession, for he had a great fear of venereal disease. He even attempted to arrange for a supply of people who would carry on the fight against the Protestant ethic after he was gone. His will provided that the bulk of his estate was to be used for the establishment of the "W. C. Fields College for Orphan White Boys and Girls, Where No Religion of Any Sort is to be Preached." (An earlier version specified colored orphans, but the insolence, probably imagined, of a colored servant caused him to switch races.) However, his will was overthrown by his wife, who was too good a Catholic ever to divorce him.

But it is the art, not the artist, that matters. No artist ever subscribed more thoroughly to that doctrine than Fields did. He may or may not have been conscious that he was creating a refuge from self-pity when he changed Claude Dukenfield into W. C. Fields, but there is no doubt that he deliberately used his own life as a testing grounds for Fieldsian humor. Nor is there any doubt that a basic theme in nearly all of his work is the superiority of any man at all like W. C. Fields to any kind of pity, from others or from himself. That, I think, is the deep source of his comedy's extraordinarily powerful appeal—for those of us who respond to it, that is. People who can not identify with the Fields character complain of the fearfully ragged, disconnected quality of his films, of the naked hostility of most of the humor, and of the snarling unpleasantness of his speeches. Those of us who can identify with him—who do so eagerly because he displays so many of our own worse faults so openly—are so carried away by even the least of the films that we will attempt to memorize large chunks of the dialogue and to imitate that nasal drawl of his. All great film comedy is potent stuff, leaving clear images on the minds of those who are open to it, but Fields's films are something else again. Their transporting effect is oddly permanent. If one responds to them just once, they will remain alive in one's imagination, always available for use, always close to breaking into full awareness, always likely to color a response to a situation. They create a particularly, perhaps even peculiarly, liberating reality. I would describe it as a reality in which self-pity cannot exist for any length of time.

All of his films capture that reality at least for moments: *The Bank Dick* (1940) holds it from beginning to end. It is so loosely organized and seems to be so sleazily made that it couldn't hold anything for two minutes, yet it is finally a coherent work of art, controlled in almost every single detail by the imagination of a man who was indeed "The World's Greatest Juggler." The central character is one Egbert Sousé, who combines with implausible perfection the qualities of Fields's earlier personas; he is as fraudulent as his circus managers (Eustace McGargle in *Sally of the Sawdust* [1925] and *Poppy* [1936] and Larson E. Whipsnade in *You Can't Cheat an Honest Man* [1939]), as cowardly as his travelling salesman (Cuthbert J. Twillie in *My Little Chickadee* [1939]), and as thoroughly henpecked as his husbands (Harold Bissonette in *It's a Gift* [1934] and Ambrose Wolfinger in *The Man on the Flying Trapeze* [1935]). There are four major pieces—fragments might be a better word—in Sousé's story, involving his family, the Lompoc National Bank, a movie company shooting on location in Lompoc, and the Black Pussy Cat Café.

The family is a loathsome version of the middle-class American family that is drooled over in sentimental novels, plays, and movies. It consists of his wife, a shapeless shrew; his mother-in-law, a woman who is as repulsive as her name, Mrs. Hermisillo Brunch; younger daughter, a prepubescent brat; and older daughter, a late-adolescent idiot. The first three treat Sousé as the enemy; the older daughter is only ashamed of him. However, he gives as good as he gets—his idea of working to support them is to go to "bank nights" at the movie theater.

The bank fragment involves two avowed robbers, Filthy McNasty and Repulsive Rogan; one unavowed robber, the president of the bank; a confidence man who is selling shares in Beefsteak Mines; a teller, Sousé's prospective son-in-law, who is stupid enough to let Sousé talk him into embezzling $500 to invest in Beefsteak Mines; a fabulously prissy bank examiner; and assorted chumps, black and white, male and female. Early on in the film, McNasty and Rogan rob the bank; by the purest accident Sousé captures McNasty and recovers the loot. The bank president rewards our hero with "a hearty handclasp" (a hygienic touching of fingertips shown in a freeze-frame) and a calendar illustrated with a picture of a scantily clad woman entitled "Spring Comes to Lompoc." He also makes him the bank guard, with the convenient provision that the payments on his home mortgage will be deducted from his salary. The confidence man makes a sucker of him by selling him the stock, and the bank examiner threatens to ruin everything by his insanely persistent dedication to duty. But the absence of virtue prevails. The confidence man is thwarted when, according to a headline in the Lompoc *Picayune-Intelligencer*, "Beefsteak Mines Are A Bonanza"; the bank examiner is thwarted when Rogan returns to rob the bank a second time; and Rogan is thwarted when he forces Sousé to drive his getaway car and our hero destroys first the car (bit by accidental bit) and then Rogan.

The movie-making fragment is even more blatantly improbable and insulting than the bank fragment. It involves a frantic producer, a drunken director, a male lead who stands nearly seven feet tall in top hat and tails, and a female lead who stands no more than five feet tall, even in high heels. Sousé is hired to fill in for the director on the basis of his claimed long experience with John Bunny (one of the earliest film comedian), Fatty Arbuckle, and "all that gang." He does very little directing; but he rattles off a story even more incoherent and unbelievable than the one Mahatma Kane Jeeves sold to Universal. The studio head is so dazzled by it that he will pay ten thousand dollars for the rights and wants to hire Sousé to direct it.

In the midst of all this nonsense and fraud The Black Pussy Cat Café stands as the great good place. The bartender, Joe, is Sousé's one true friend, reassuring him that he had spent a twenty-dollar bill in there the night before instead of carelessly losing it, uncomplainingly serving a fresh glass of water (for use as a fingerbowl) with each shot of whiskey, and cheerfully adding a sickening powder to the bank examiner's highball when Sousé inquires if "Michael Finn" has been in. As Sousé tells the bank examiner who wants to pull down the window shade by his booth so that people won't see him drinking, "You can pull anything you want to here, this place is a regular joint."

*The Bank Dick* juggles these various pieces with a healthy contempt for all of the pieties of "family entertainment" and a seemingly total disregard for all of the conventions and skills of "good" film-making. Appearances can be deceiving. Fields assembled a wonderful cast of veteran comic actors and made sure that each had at least one choice moment on camera. There is not a weak performance in the lot, but Grady Sutton as the son-in-law, Cora Witherspoon as the wife, and Russell Hicks as the confidence man were superb. Franklin Pangburn as J. Pinkerton Snoopington, the bank examiner, was even better; if film critics understood the requirements of broad comic acting as well as they should, that performance would have been heaped with honors. Yet otherwise there are no cinematic "values" here—the sets are tacky, the camera work is carefully uninspired, and the transitions, between cuts and between scenes, are artless and abrupt. By the flossy standards of Hollywood's "major productions" it is a shameful affair. That is precisely as it should be, for Fields's theme in *The Bank Dick* is the oppressive puerility of the commercial imagination and ideals of art and behavior which it spawns.

That is why and how the juggled pieces finally do cohere. The bank fragment is the core; the movie-making and the family sequences swing around it. Banks control the movie industry as surely as the sun controls the planets, and the movies, with generous help from the rest of commercial culture, propagate the sentimental images which are wildly burlesqued in the family sequence. (Compare Egbert Sousé throttling his younger daughter and snarling "Don't tell me I don't love you!" with all of the smarmily understanding fathers seen in movies and television.) The Black Pussy Cat Café fragment stands outside and opposite to the other three, testifying to the possibility of a life centered on pleasure rather than on money. Money is worth having but only if you don't have to work to get it.

The final scene of *The Bank Dick* pulls all of this together. (As with other very important things in the film, there is nothing of it in the original screenplay which Simon and Schuster published in 1973 as part of its series of Classic Film Scripts; Fields wouldn't be pinned down by a script, not even one written by Mahatma Kane Jeeves.) Having been made rich by the bonanza in Beefsteak Mines—with $10,000 for his screenplay and $5,000 for capturing Repulsive Rogan thrown in for good measure—Sousé is living in a mansion with his now adoring family. "Won't you have just one more *baba au rhum?*" Preparing to go out for his morning stroll, he graciously permits the butler to persuade him that a silk hat would go better with his striped pants, vest, and morning coat than the pith helmet he is inclined to wear. On the way out the door he does the old vaudeville bit of getting the hat on his cane when he's trying to put it on his head; and strolling down the drive he has the pleasure of kicking a can out of his way with a deft side-wise flick of his right foot while faking a big straight-ahead kick with his left. The scene and the movie end with Sousé cutting across the lawn to catch up with Joe the bartender who is hurrying to start a new day at The Black Pussy Cat Café.

Egbert Sousé is the perfectly blissful man who has subdued all of his enemies, domestic and social, by getting a lot of money without ever having worked for it. He has become a pillar of respectability living the easy life without having changed his fraudulent self one iota. His only skills remain the perfectly useless, self-delighting ones of a juggler of hats and kicker of cans. His one and only virtue is that of a juggler of words—he always has had and always will have something to say for himself. Confronted with a prospective son-in-law who was oddly reluctant to embezzle money from the bank, he crooned, "Don't be a fuddie-duddie, don't be a moon-calf, don't be a jabbernowl—you don't want to be any of those, do you?" Challenged by the bank president who interrupted his account of the robber wielding a huge, double-edged assegai with the question, "Doesn't anybody ever attack you with a small knife?", he promptly told of the time Major Moe, a colored midget, came after him with a small knife—"It wasn't so much a knife as it was a razor, actually." A man who can talk like that never needs to feel sorry for himself, especially because he never believes a word he is saying.

Is it not passing brave to be an Egbert Sousé and walk in triumph through the streets of Lompoc? Is it not better to be a W. C. Fields snarling "Never give a sucker an even break" than a Pagliacci sobbing "Vesti La Giubba"?

All of the great comedies support Fields in his furious rejection of self-pity. Ulysses on the seas separating him from Ithaca, Quixote on the plains of La Mancha, Rosalind in the forest of Arden, Tom Jones on the highways of England, Elizabeth Bennet on her father's entailed estate, Huck Finn on the Mississippi River, Leopold Bloom on the streets of Dublin—all are much too busy being themselves, surviving, to waste time pitying themselves. Of Fields's peers, the handful of other masters of film comedy, only Chaplin opened up to pity, and once he openly asked for it (at the end of *City Lights*) his work went bad. Keaton, Laurel and Hardy, The Marx Brothers, and Jacques Tati act out in their best films a durable idiocy which is as far removed from the possibility of pity, either from themselves or from others, as was Fields's snarling fraudulence. There is not a one of them you would want to cast as Pagliacci, let alone as the great self-pitier of all time, Narcissus.

## Wes D. Gehring (essay date 1985)

SOURCE: "Fields and Falstaff," in *Thalia,* Vol. VIII, No. 2, Fall-Winter, 1985, pp. 36-42.

[*In the following essay, Gehring equates Fields's persona with that of Shakespeare's Falstaff.*]

In writing a book on America's greatest native-born comedian (see *W. C. Fields: A Bio-Bibliography,* Greenwood Press, 1984), the author happened upon occasional fleeting comparisons to Shakespeare's Falstaff. For example, *New Republic* film critic Otis Ferguson, the most poetically articulate of Fields's critical champions, described the comedian as a "natural resource . . . a minor Jack Falstaff on the sawdust of the twentieth century."[1] Fields, a self-taught student of literature, was not beyond comparing himself humorously with Falstaff. Author Gene Fowler, Fields's friend, drinking companion and later biographer, remembers the comedian observing: "If Falstaff had stuck to martinis [Fields's favorite drink], he'd still be with us. Poor soul!"[2]

Unfortunately, no one ever pursued this comparison. Yet today, one argument for the ongoing popularity of W. C. Fields is that he has become a universal symbol as important in today's age of mass communication as the celebrated literary characters of the past.

The most analogous argument is probably film theorist André Bazin's interrelating of Chaplin's Charlie with epic characters of literature: "For hundreds of millions of people on this planet he [Charlie] is a hero like Ulysses or Roland in other civilizations."[3] A character of this type transcends any one story or collection of stories, whether they are printed or cinematic. Such a character has withstood the test of time, and the works in which he is showcased are "read" and "reread" through the years. All of this applies to the art of W. C. Fields.

Fields has been equated with many important literary characters, from Charles Dickens's Micawber (*David Copperfield*) to Mark Twain's Jim Smiley ("The Notorious Jumping Frog of Calaveras County"). This article,

however, will focus upon the parallels between Fields and Falstaff because of the latter's significance as the most important literary comedian in the English language. In fact, according to honored literary critic and historian J. B. Priestley: "With the exception of Hamlet, no character in literature has been more discussed than this Falstaff, who is, like Hamlet, a genius, fastening immediately upon the reader's imagination, living richly in his memory."[4] It seems only fitting that America's foremost film comedian should be compared to English literature's greatest fictional comedian, especially since ties have long been suggested. Therefore, the two will be examined according to the following criteria: (1) celebration of alcohol, (2) bragging and telling of tall tales, (3) quickness of wit and gift for language, (4) physical incongruity of their being men of action, (5) performance of the cowardly act, (6) pathos, and (7) characteristics and general ties between Falstaff's circle of supporting players and Fields's.

Falstaff's and Fields's personae frequently are tall tale-telling revelers who like nothing better than the comradery of male drinking companions, just as Gene Fowler chronicled the real Fields inner circle in *Minutes of the Last Meeting.* Fascination with drink would seem the best starting point for comparison. After all, a beer was even named for Falstaff. And not surprisingly, in the fourth act of Shakespeare's *Henry the IV, Part II,* Falstaff expands at length on the merits of alcohol:

> *A good sherris sack [wine] hath a twofold operation in it. It ascends me into the brain; dries me there all the foolish and dull and crudy vapors which environ it; makes it . . . delectable shapes, which, delivered o'er to the voice, the tongue, which is the birth, becomes excellent wit. The second property of your excellent sherris is the warming of the blood.*[5]

Fields's films represent a nonstop celebration of drinking, but he best articulates the importance of imbibing (in preference to man's best friend, the dog) in the essay **"Alcohol & Me."** Fields cites a number of uncontested facts on why alcohol (in this case, whiskey) is preferable to the pooch: "Whiskey does not need to be periodically wormed, it does not need to be fed, it never requires a special kennel, it has no toenails to be clipped. . . . Whiskey sits quietly in its special nook."[6] Moreover, he appeals to the reader's common sense: "When two kindred souls get together for a friendly session, do they sit there and pet dogs?"[7]

As one might assume of a comedy character so closely associated with drinking, the Fields persona forever approaches his defense of alcohol in mock religious terms, not unlike Falstaff:

> *The responsibility for this crusade has weighed heavily upon my shoulders. Many times I have felt I was a lone voice crying in the wilderness. . . . Then I would let my voice really cry out in all its power and glory. I would cry, "Set 'em up again!"*[8]

Fields's most comic exultation of alcohol, however, is **"The Temperance Lecture,"** the title not-withstanding. Easily the most anthologized of all his radio recordings, it provides a Fieldsian version of the past which makes him a much closer historical neighbor to Falstaff:

> *Throughout the Middle Ages the use of liquor was universal. Drunkenness was so common it was unnoticed. They called it the middle ages because no one was able to walk home unless they were between two other fellows. I was the middle guy.*[9]

Alcohol was just as important in Fields's private life as in his professional one, though he always claimed his red nose was a product of numerous childhood beatings, because his runaway freedom was a source of envy to some boys. Serious drinking came later as a way of coping with the stress of nearly nonstop juggling practice and performing. And while there were few drinks he had not tried, eventually the martini became his staple. His martini intake was massive; during the California years most sources suggest nearly two quarts daily.[10] Fields claimed martinis were best for him because "they work fast, and the sensations are lasting. They prick my mind like the cut of a razor blade. I work better with them inside me."[11] And they seemed to have this positive effect, for he drank continuously, even during film productions, and did not become drunk. (In fact, he strongly disliked drunks.) During film production Fields's only cover-up for his martini cocktail shaker was to claim that it was full of pineapple juice—a hoax generously accepted by all, though pranksters once filled it with real pineapple juice, causing him to boom: "Somebody's been putting pineapple juice in my pineapple juice."[12] And while Falstaff takes a portable bar onto the battlefield in Act V of *Henry the IV, Part I* (Prince Hal discovered Falstaff is carrying a bottle of wine in his pistol case),[13] Fields is equally inventive in his films. Moreover, Fields's real life excursions on his estate, or in his Cadillac, were never complete without his portable bar. (His in-house stock could have doubled for a commercial outlet store.)

Both Falstaff and Fields are also excellent at bragging and telling tall tales. Possibly the most comic example involving Falstaff occurs in the second act of *Henry the IV, Part I,* just after Prince Hal and Poins have robbed Falstaff and several companions—only moments after the latter gang has done some robbing of its own. Falstaff's initial response is to claim the gang was beset by a hundred robbers, though the prankster Prince keeps Falstaff on a braggart's defensive: "if I fought not with fifty of them, I am a bunch of radish! If there were not two or three and fifty upon poor old Jack, then am I no two-legged creature."[14]

Fields, of course, is never far from the tall tale. The antiheroic Ambrose Wolfinger of ***The Man on the Flying Trapeze*** (1935) claims to have a wrestling hold so unique "there isn't a man or boy born in the United States or Canada that could get out of . . . [it]"; the con-man Commodore of *Mississippi* (1935), relating his Indian-

fighting career, is forever describing how he "cut a path through this wall of human flesh."

In real life Fields was also forever spinning tales, which, as he admitted in a 1934 article, were starting to catch up with him.[15] That is, he had been creative with so many facts that when friends and associates requested rehashes of specific stories, he frequently was at a loss. However, there is no denying ties between Fields's public and private yarns. For example, his last mistress Carlotta Monti observed:

> *At dinners Woody [Fields] sometimes grew verbose knowing he had a captive audience, and would grossly exaggerate happenings that supposedly occurred to him in far-off and generally unheard-of spots in the world. The "Rattlesnake" story [about the close friendship of a particular man and his snake] from [his 1939 film]* **You Can't Cheat an Honest Man** *[the mere word "snake" always made the film's stuffy Mrs. Bel-Goodie wail and faint] is a good example.*[16]

While the tales of Falstaff and Fields sometimes got them both in trouble, their quick wit and continued gift for language often came to the rescue. For instance. Prince Hal eventually calls out Falstaff's yarn about bravely fighting a veritable army of robbers on the highway—an army only of the disguised Prince and Poins—by stating, in part: "Falstaff, you carried your guts away as nimbly, with as quick dexterity, and roared for mercy, and still run and roared, as ever I heard bullcalf. . . . What trick . . . canst thou now find out to hide thee from this open and apparent shame?"[17] Falstaff smoothly replies: "By the Lord, I knew ye as well as he that made ye. . . . Was it for me to kill the heir apparent? . . . Why, thou knowest I am as valiant as Hercules, but . . . I was now a coward on instinct."[18]

In a similar manner, the bravery of Fields's former Indian-fighting Commodore is called into question on the point of his character having pulled a revolver during a battle royal years before. Revolvers had not been invented at this time, interjected some skeptic, to which Fields's Commodore coolly replied: "I know that but the Indians didn't know it." (Regarding the verbal magic of Fields's personae, one should not, of course, fail to mention his ability to sell someone a talking dog in *Poppy,* 1936). The private Fields was, if anything, even more determined not to lose a point of debate on any issues. A typical example can be drawn from the comedian's earlier tendency during touring years to open banking accounts all over the world as a safety-valve reflection of both his poor beginnings and the hazards of being stranded on the road. Thus, during a World War II gathering of friends, Fields revealed he had approximately ten thousand dollars in a Berlin bank. David Chasen though he must be kidding, while Gene Fowler volunteered: "Or else you're nuts. With the war on, and the inflation in Germany, how do you expect to get your dough from Hitler?" Fields, never one to underestimate a villain, "put on a superior expression, and the toothpick [in his mouth] stopped moving." (A motionless toothpick meant he was disgruntled. Fowler compared it to a "readied stinger.") The comedian then replied: "Suppose the little bastard wins?"[19]

It should also be noted that the real world frequently echoed (and continues to echo) the words of this performer—words which frequently also represented clever bypasses of difficult situations, such as Fields's use of "Godfrey Daniel" as a substitute for "god damn" in the censorship era, or his often blanket endorsement of both the pretty and the not so pretty with terms of endearment such as "my little chickadee," "my glowworm," and "my dove." Of course, many of Fields's nationally acclaimed statements or catchwords merely turn a traditional observation on its ear, such as his widely quoted **Bank Dick** (1940) comment on bathing. Fields, as Egbert Sousé, is having a scotch and water at a bar. He downs the alcohol, dips his fingers in the small water chaser, and methodically wipes them off on a napkin. Sousé then requests of the bartender: "Make it another one, and another chaser. I don't like to bathe in the same water twice."

While Falstaff and Fields look and feel most natural in taverns and other locations of leisurely debauchery, they often are called upon to be men of action—obviously a visual source of much of their humor. To see the big-bellied, uncourageous Falstaff on a battlefield—despite his position as a soldier—is the most delightful of comic incongruities, probably best captured by Orson Welles (in the title role) in his own outstanding film production *Falstaff* (1967, sometimes titled *Chimes at Midnight*).

Comedian Fields is not unknown to military settings. In *Janice Meredith* (1924) he plays a drunken British sergeant during the American Revolution; in the 1928 remake of *Tillie's Punctured Romance* Fields's circus assists the World War I Allied cause by a slapstick involvement with the German Army. One might say the comedian even improves upon Falstaff's military incongruity, because in both noted cases Fields's greatest involvement is with the losing side. (Fields also co-wrote and copyrighted, with co-author Mortimer M. Newfield, a three-act army farce set on an American base at the time of United States entry into World War I. The farce was entitled **Just Before the Dawn.**[20])

Despite these comedic army involvements of Fields, he is much better known for his civilian skirmishes, all showcasing admirably the comic incongruity of Fields in battle. In **The Man on the Flying Trapeze** (1935), the gun-toting, pajama-clad Ambrose Wolfinger falls down the cellar steps (in the best tradition of the antihero) as he hunts for burglars. Professor McGargle takes it on the lam in *Poppy* when a posse materializes. In **My Little Chickadee**, Cuthbert J. Twillie attempts to fight Indians with a slingshot. And in **The Bank Dick**, Egbert Sousé is at his uniformed-guard best when he attempts to strangle a cowboy-clad child toting a toy pistol.

The real Fields maintained his own private war with the world, a war that sounds as if he were direct from the anti-hero pages of James Thurber. For instance, like Thurber's eccentric collection of relatives in "The Night the Bed Fell," Fields had his own established routine when he was especially aroused by fears of burglars.[21] He would prowl the grounds of his estate, gun in hand, frequently adding a monologue suggesting someone was with him—no doubt intended to further intimidate any crooks in the area, yet also lessening the chances of a direct confrontation.[22] During another period his fears of being kidnapped caused him to multiply his fictitious companion to several equally fictitious bodyguards. And in the middle of the night he would give his crew, who answered to names like "Joe, Bull and Muggsy," directions such as: "I know you boys are former prize fighters and gunmen but I'd rather you didn't shoot to kill. Try to get them in the spinal cord or the pelvis. Ha ha ha ha. . . . "[23]

There was also a comic military air in the daylight manner in which Fields frequently surveyed his estate from the house with a large pair of binoculars. Gene Fowler even went so far as to liken Fields to "an admiral on the bridge of a flagship."[24] In addition, the comedian had a loudspeaker over the main door, and thanks to his binoculars, he was more than prepared for unwanted visitors. For Fields, just about the whole world was the enemy. Thus, he once scared away two nuns collecting for a charity by impersonating

> the violent quarrel of lovers—snarled in his own voice, then answered in falsetto. There were threats by the male voice, piteous entreaties by the artificial voice, such as, "I'll murder you with this baseball bat, you double-crossing tart!" "Don't! Please don't beat me again, Murgatroyd! Think of poor little Chauncey, our idiot child!"[25]

(Fields also played spy, having all his rooms wired so that he could monitor any potentially dangerous conversations from his servants, who were people he rarely trusted.)

Real war did, however, touch Fields's private life. During World War II (at sixty-plus years of age), he and several drinking companions, all of whom were suffering from various physical ailments, appeared at an army center prepared to register for home defense. While they were given forms to fill in (Fields is said to have requested a commando assignment), the woman on duty caught the comic absurdity of the event quite nicely when she inquired: "Gentlemen, who sent you? The enemy?"[26]

Not only are Falstaff's and Fields's personae comically incongruous to "battle," they are very capable of performing the cowardly deed, if it serves their purposes. Thus, in Act IV of *Henry the IV, Part I*, Falstaff first plays dead during battle and later stabs an already-deceased Hotspur, claiming credit for his death.[27] Fields's entertainment alter egos are just as apt to do such deeds, from booting Baby LeRoy in **The Old-Fashioned Way**

(1934) to pushing his rival (Leon Errol) for Margaret Dumont off a mountain in *Never Give a Sucker an Even Break* (1941). But probably the best example of this, and certainly the one in which the on-screen Fields projects the most pride, occurs in **My Little Chickadee** (1940). Twillie, tending bar, tells a customer how he knocked down Chicago Molly. But when someone else claims credit, Fields replies yes—but he was the one who started kicking her. Then he tops the black-comedy effect of this proud admission by going into depth on the kicking experience: "So I starts to kick her in the midriff. Did you ever kick a woman in the midriff that had a pair of corsets on?" The customer replies: "No, I just can't recall any such incident right now." Twillie continues: "Why, I almost broke my great toe. I never had such a painful experience." (Later, however, it is revealed that Twillie and another man were eventually beaten up by the victim and an elderly gray-haired woman with her.)

One would not say the real Fields performed cowardly acts, but his methods could be dangerously eccentric. Probably the most famous case in point is the night he was doing his pool routine in the Ziegfield Follies and found the laughs were not coming at the right times. Eventually he discovered a mugging Ed Wynn under the table. Fields was not amused, and he promised fatal consequences if it happened again. It happened again. This time Fields brained Wynn with his pool stick during the routine, knocking him unconscious. The audience thought it was a set piece and loved it. Fields continued his popular pool routine, which still received additional laughs when Wynn uttered unconscious moans. Fields later offered to incorporate the whole thing into his act, but Wynn declined.[28]

In later Hollywood years, Fields had a muscle-bound butler who worked out on still rings in the garage. The comedian was intimidated by him and eventually sensed disrespect. Thus Fields acted . . . maybe. That is, the next time this live-in Charles Atlas took a swing on his rings, they gave way at the most inopportune of times. "As he lost consciousness, he said later, he heard a kind of hoarse, maniacal laughter from a darkened corner of the building.[29] The two parted company.

Both Fields and Falstaff are comic figures touched by pathos. For Falstaff, this is most poignant when he is banished by a king who was once a fellow reveler—Prince Hal. For Fields, the moments of pathos are smaller but no less moving, such as his character's attempt at suicide in *So's Your Old Man* (1926), which he repeated in his sound era remake, *You're Telling Me* (1934). In either case, additional pathos occurs when Fields thinks he is rescuing a beautiful, young woman from suicide. Appropriately, as if to parallel Falstaff's hobnobbing with royalty, the young beauty is a princess—although Fields does not learn this until later. (Both films are based upon Julian Street's "Mr. Bisbee's Princess," which had won the O. Henry Memorial Award as the best short story of 1925.) While pathos is not something as readily associated with Fields as it is with a Charlie

Chaplin, 1930s film critics not infrequently made reference to Chaplin when describing pivotal moments in Fields.

As has been so often the case in this comparison, the characteristic is also true of Fields himself. The comic foibles of Fields's screen personae did not stop when the cameras did. There is a very real pathos to a master comedian whose on-screen source of humor (the ongoing battle of day-to-day existence) frequently turned to a series of "persecution complexes" in private life, such as the aforementioned example concerning Fields's musclebound butler.[30]

These, then, have been the obvious parallels between Falstaff and Fields. But the comparison does not stop there. Several of Falstaff's supporting players also seem to have similarities or ties with Fields. Most obvious is the case of Bardolph, attendant to Falstaff and possessor of an impressive red nose which invites witty comment. For example, when Bardolph suggests Falstaff is too heavy, the latter directs an attack against the attendant's nose: "Do thou amend thy face, and I'll amend my life. Thou art our admiral [flagship], thou bearest the lantern in the poop—but 'tis in the nose of thee: thou art the knight of the Burning Lamp."[31] Fields, of course, owned quite a "Burning Lamp" too, and references to it are frequent in his comedy, including print, radio, and the movies. For example, in his celebrated radio rivalry with Edgar Bergen's Charlie McCarthy, McCarthy once asked: "Is it true Mr. Fields that when you stood on the corner of Hollywood and Vine forty-three cars waited for your nose to change to green?"[32] (See also Jack Grant's interview/ essay with Fields: "THAT NOSE of W. C. Fields."[33]) With the possible exception of Jimmy "Schnozzola" Durante, no major American comedian probably ever better utilized his proboscis (the term Fields preferred over nose). Strangely enough, however, he was unusually sensitive about his nose in private life and could become easily offended, even when the cracks were from close friends. Once such offending comment was actually reminiscent of Falstaff's aforementioned jab at Bardolph's nose. After John Barrymore's death, his friends had difficulty convincing Fields to serve as a pallbearer, because he felt the time to help pals was when they were alive. But when Fields continued with his "why me" manner, painter-friend John Decker replied: "Well, in case it gets dark, your nose would make an excellent light."[34]

Prince Hal's companion Poins, who devises the comic robbing of the robbers (Falstaff and company), suggests Fields's con-man persona. Pistol, the tavern warrior whose overblown speeches cover a coward, can be like a boastful Fields. Silence, the truly "silent" partner-stooge to country justice Shallow, is like any number of stooges Fields had on stage and in films, as well as in real life. And Dame Quickly, hostess of Boar's-Head Tavern and lender of money to Falstaff, rather anticipates those gullible women whom a conning Fields could manipulate in so many films.

This comparison does not imply that the character of Falstaff directly affected Fields (though it well could have), as seems to have been the case with Micawber. Instead, it puts into perspective the significance of Fields as a modern-day Falstaff, à la Bazin's analogy between Charlie Chaplin and Roland. Moreover, without trying to be sacrilegious in the halls of literature, Fields is now undoubtedly more universally recognizable by the general public than Falstaff, and he has been for some time.

NOTES

[1] Otis Ferguson, "The Great McGonigle," *New Republic,* August 21, 1935, p. 48.

[2] Gene Fowler, *Minutes of the Last Meeting* (New York: Viking Press, 1954), p. 224.

[3] André Bazin, "Charlie Chaplin," in *What Is Cinema?,* vol. 1, selected and trans. by Hugh Gray (1958; rpt. Los Angeles: University of California Press, 1967), p. 144.

[4] J. B. Priestley, *The English Comic Characters* (New York: Dodd, Mead, 1931), p. 69.

[5] *Henry the IV, Part II,* act 4, sc. 3, lines 97-105.

[6] W. C. Fields, "Alcohol & Me," *PIC,* October 13, 1942, p. 32.

[7] "Alcohol & Me," p. 34.

[8] "Alcohol & Me," p. 32.

[9] *The Best of W. C. Fields,* previously released recordings (Columbia, BL 34145), 1976.

[10] Carlotta Monti (with Cy Rice), *W. C. Fields & Me* (1971; rpt. New York: Warner Books, 1973), p. 205.

[11] Monti, p. 206.

[12] Robert Lewis Taylor, *W. C. Fields: His Follies and Fortunes* (Garden City, New York: Doubleday & Company, 1949), p. 242.

[13] *Henry the IV, Part I,* act 5, sc. 4, lines 52-55.

[14] *Henry the IV, Part I,* act 2, sc. 4, lines 185-88.

[15] Sara Hamilton, "A Red-Nosed Romeo," *Photoplay* (December 1934), 33.

[16] Monti, *W. C. Fields & Me,* p. 78.

[17] *Henry the IV, Part I,* act 2, sc. 4, lines 158-61, 263-65.

[18] *Henry the IV, Part I,* lines 268-74.

[19] Fowler, *Minutes of the Last Meeting,* p. 101.

[20] "W. C. Fields Papers," Library of Congress. Manuscript Division (Madison Building), Washington, D.C.

[21] James Thurber, "The Night the Bed Fell," in *My Life and Hard Times* (1933; rpt. New York: Bantam Books, 1947), pp. 19-31.

[22] The domestic private battles of Fields often figure in the biographical literature on the comedian. See especially Taylor's *W. C. Fields: His Follies and Fortunes,* p. 313.

[23] Fowler, *Minutes of the Last Meeting,* p. 257.

[24] Fowler, p. 152.

[25] Fowler, p. 152.

[26] This story also appears frequently in Fields material. See especially Taylor, *W. C. Fields: His Follies and Fortunes,* pp. 264-65; Fowler, *Minutes of the Last Meeting,* pp. 204-5.

[27] *Henry the IV, Part I,* act 4, sc. 4, lines 75, 119, 127-28.

[28] This is another oft-reported incident. See especially Alva Johnston, "Profiles: Legitimate Nonchalance - II," *New Yorker,* February 9, 1935, p. 26; Taylor, *W. C. Fields: His Follies and Fortunes,* pp. 150-51.

[29] Taylor, *W. C. Fields: His Follies and Fortunes,* p. 259.

[30] Taylor, p. 161.

[31] *Henry the IV, Part I,* act 3, sc. 3, lines 25-28.

[32] The sketch "Feathered Friends," from the record album *W. C. Fields on Radio: With Edgar Bergen & Charlie McCarthy* (Columbia CS 9890), n.d.

[33] Jack Grant, "THAT NOSE of W.C. Fields," *Movie Classic* (February 1935), 56, 60.

[34] Fowler, *Minutes of the Last Meeting,* p. 222.

## Wes D. Gehring (essay date 1986)

SOURCE: "W.C. Fields: The Copyrighted Sketches," in *Journal of Popular Film and Televison,* Vol. 14, No. 2, Summer, 1986, pp. 65-75.

[*In the following essay, Gehring provides a review of two dozen short comic sketches written and copyrighted by Fields during a twenty-year period.*]

While doing research on America's greatest native-born comedian (see *W. C. Fields: A Bio-Bibliography,* Greenwood Press, 1984), the author happened upon Fields's seemingly forgotten copyrighted sketches at the Library of Congress.[1]

Between 1918 and late-1930, Fields copyrighted twenty-three separate comedy documents on sixteen subjects (some sketches were copyrighted more than once when changes were made). While generally written for the stage, several of the sketches, or variations of them turned up later in the comedian's films.

Though once housed individually by title in the Copyright Division of the Library of Congress, the documents are now available as one collection, the "W. C. Fields Papers," in the Manuscript Division of the Library (Madison Building).

These sketches, with their frequent variations on a single theme, provide a unique opportunity to examine the misplaced evolution of an American comedy giant. For example, Fields's classic sketch **"An Episode at the Dentist's,"** which was copyrighted three times (February 1919, 12 July and 2 November 1928), was the foundation for the later film *The Dentist* (1932). Much of Fields's most celebrated material had been on the drawing board since the 1910s, enabling him to finely tune his almost clinical dissection of the comic antihero, the frustrated modern man.

**"An Episode on the Links"** (30 August 1918) would later be translated into the short subject *The Golf Specialist* (1930), Fields's first sound film. While golfing material would frequently turn up in the comedian's longer films, the best utilization occurs in *So's Your Old Man* (1926) and its remake, *You're Telling Me* (1934).

**"The Sleeping Porch"** (6 February 1925) would later become possibly his most celebrated film routine. In this sketch, domestic antihero Fields tries to get some early morning rest on a porch swing while the world seems bent only upon both making noise and unleashing dangerous children.

**"The Sleeping Porch"** was possibly inspired by a similar scene in the 1922 publication of Sinclair Lewis' *Babbitt*.[2] Both Lewis and Fields attack Main Street hypocrisy. While Babbitt is more a part of the establishment than Fields's screen antihero will ever be, both suffer from many of the same antiheroic frustrations—including similar trials on the ironically named sleeping porch.

A greater irony was that the sketch was originally part of an unsuccessful comedy stage revue—J. P. McEvoy's *The Comic Supplement,* though the working script for the revue strongly suggests additions by Fields.[3] The best routines from the revue (which closed on the road) eventually reached Broadway in the 1925 spring and summer editions of the Ziegfeld Follies.[4] Variations upon **"The Sleeping Porch"** were the comic highlights of *It's the Old Army Game* (1926) and *It's a Gift* (1934), both of which were loosely based on *The Comic Supplement.*

Fields's copyrighted **"Stolen Bonds"** (12 July 1928) would later be the foundation of his black comedy, short subject *The Fatal Glass of Beer* (1933), a film classic not fully appreciated until years after its initial release. And **"Pullman Sleeper"** (26 February 1921) would later be the premise for a train skit in *The Old-Fashioned Way* (1934) and a plane routine in *Never Give a Sucker an Even Break* (1941).

There were also a number of other key copyrighted sketches that, although not translated as closely as the previous examples, contributed to the spirit of his later films. For instance, there are three copyrighted versions of **"The Family Ford"** (16 October 1919, 3 September and 9 October 1920). The sketch finds a family and friends attempting a motor outing. The occupants of the Ford are George and Mrs. Fliverton, Baby Rose Fliverton, Mrs. Fliverton's father, and friends Elsie May and Adel Smith. Predictably, the car serves as the comedy focus, from engine trouble to a flat tire. And appropriately for a skit that plays upon the victimization of twentieth-century man—frequently at the hands of machines—at one point the "engine starts of its own accord."[5]

The sketch anticipates the attempted exit and eventual travel of the Harold Bissonette (W. C. Fields) family in *It's a Gift.* The routine's use of a blind character is also reminiscent of *It's a Gift's* more famous inclusion of the blind hotel detective who nearly destroys the Bissonette drugstore. And there are small bits in **"The Family Ford"** that appear with only slight variation in later films. For example, Elsie May drops her hat while George (Fields) is pumping up an inner tube. He pushes the hat away, but it makes a complete circle and returns exactly where it started. This is repeated several times; in each case the hat is pushed in a different direction by George. Eventually, he picks up the hat and throws it away. In *Poppy* (1936), Fields suffers from another returning hat, although now is his trying to play a small bass fiddle instead of changing a tire.

Fields also focused on domestic comedy (in a more intensified fashion) in his three later copyrighted versions of **"Off to the Country"** (25 May and 29 June 1921, 3 April 1922). This sketch has Fields trying to get his family on a busy subway train for a trip to the peace of a rural setting. The family is composed of Baby Sammy, "Sap"; daughter Ray, "Tut"; a nagging wife, Mrs. Fliverton; and Emmeline Fliverton, apparently Mr. Fliverton's (Fields's) mother. Besides the difficulty Fields's character has in directing his crew, they are weighed down by a massive collection of vacation items, including a mandolin in a case, a tennis racket, a parrot cage, a suitcase, balloons, an all-day sucker, a can of worms, folding fishing rods, a gun, various bundles, a big doll, a teddy bear, an umbrella, a ukelele in a case, a small phonograph, a baseball mask, a bat, and a hatbox.[6]

**"Off to the Country"** is full of missed trains, troublesome children, a bothersome wife, a surly ticket taker, a sneaky revenue officer ("Pussyfoot Anderson"), and loads of slapstick—largely due to that warehouse of props. The Flivertons never do get their trip; instead, Papa is arrested for violation of the Volstead Act: He is found to have a bottle of brandy, although it was used only "for medicinal purposes."[7] And the family follows in tears as Mr. Fliverton is dragged off to jail.

The surname Fliverton appears frequently in the copyrighted sketches—underlying the antiheroic nature of the Fields family. That is, Fliverton is unquestionably a thinly veiled reference to the most antiheroic of machines, the Model-T Ford, then frequently called the flivver. (Moreover, it must be remembered that one of the sketches in which the Flivertons appear is called **"The Family Ford"**—in three variations.) The Model-T Ford was so associated with comic frustrations that countless jokes circulated on the subject. For example, "The guy who owns a secondhand flivver may not have a quarrelsome disposition, but he's always trying to start something."[8] Several comedy careers are closely identified with the car, including that of Laurel and Hardy. Thus, to name a comedy family (actually, several of them) Fliverton strongly suggests antiheroic tendencies. A reading of the sketches bears this out.

Fields would later, of course, coin the more famous antiheroic character surnames Bissonette (from the aforementioned *It's a Gift*) and Souse (*The Bank Dick*, 1940), both of which call comic attention to themselves by frequently being mispronounced. (The mispronunciation of the latter was also a comic commentary on Fields's alcoholic intake.)

Still more domestic comedy is to be found in the two copyrighted versions of **"10,000 People Killed"** (29 May and 10 October 1922). The sketch finds Mr. and Mrs. Shugg and their baby Oliotha around the radio. They are soon to be shocked with the statement "10,000 killed," but the radio cuts out before the rest of the facts are announced.[9] Eventually they discover it is only a commercial: "10,000 people in San Francisco killed 10,000,000 flies with the Cadula fly swatter last year. Price: 10 cents all fall."[10]

Yet **"10,000 People Killed"** offers more than just a misunderstood radio announcement premise for future Fields film comedy. First, it demonstrates author Fields articulating a nicely comic look at the problems and contradictions of another form of twentieth-century mechanization, the radio, and its greatest comedy victim, the male. Thus Mrs. Shugg says of the radio: "I don't know why they call it wireless. They ought to call it 'nothing but wires' and he [Mr. Shugg] doesn't know how to work it anyhow."[11]

**"10,000 People Killed"** also provides two delightfully bizarre comic bits on domestic middle-class life—both of which will later surface in the short film subject *The Pharmacist* (1933). In the first, a cocktail shaker is affixed to a pogo stick for mixing purposes. In the second, Oliotha, anticipating Sylvester the Cat by years, eats the family canary. Like Tweetie Pie, however, the bird is recovered.

A misunderstood radio broadcast is the basis of an important routine in Fields's *Tillie and Gus* (1933). Augustus Winterbottom (Fields) is mixing paint according to instructions being dictated on the "Handy Andy" radio show, and Baby LeRoy switches the dial to an exercise program.

Other copyrighted material of special interest with relation to Fields's future films include: **"An Episode of Lawn Tennis"** (28 October 1918, a nearly all-pantomime routine that incorporates many of Fields's juggling tricks), **"The Sport Model"** (22 May 1922, examining the difficulties in both packing a small car and keeping it running), **"The Caledonian Express or an American Abroad"** (31 July 1922, an American's refusal to give up a British railroad compartment reserved for a Lord), and **"Midget Car"** (25 November 1930).

**"Midget Car,"** the last of his somewhat familiar copyrighted material, draws from several sources. It utilizes earlier sketches, many of which eventually would be filmed by Fields, if they had not been already. These include traveling with a large number of items, packing everything in a small car, mechanization problems, domestic frustrations, and comic use of a blind character. **"Midget Car"** also introduces a character name that would become very familiar to future students of Fields—Charlie Bogle. (Fields would later use the pseudonym Charles Bogle on several original film stories.)

Besides these sketches, the comedian copyrighted four other properties, none of which is easily discernible as Fields material: **"The Mountain Sweep Stakes"** (21 March 1919, a movie script parody of stage melodrama and silent film stars), **"Just Before Dawn"** (7 April 1919, an army farce in three acts, at the time of U.S. entry into World War I), **"What a Night"** (25 May 1921, a farcical murder mystery sketch with surreal overtones), and **"My School Days Are Over"** (12 July 1928, a short routine of sexual innuendo).

Of the four, **"The Mountain Sweep Stakes"** most merits further attention. It shows Fields to be a much more avid film fan than has been suggested previously, and it reveals very sympathetic feelings toward Chaplin and the Tramp. First, to best demonstrate the script as an example of a product from a 1919 student of cinema, the cast of characters must be presented:

> Jack Cass Fairbanks: An Aviator
> Anna Polly Pickford: A Country Girl
> Lew "Left-foot" Chaplin: A Wag
> Martin Fetlock Keanan: An Adventurer
> [*sic*]
> Molta Zitkrantz Barra: A Vampire
> Bohunk Rogers Hart: A Cowboy
> Rollo Bushman: A Sweet Chap
> Roughneckington Oldfield: An Auto
> Race Driver

Takeitaway Itscold: A Greek Waiter
Blaha Dressler: Still in the Ring.[12]

The plot is a parody of the standard melodrama, anticipating Fields's later parody of the play-within-a-play *The Drunkard* in the film **The Old-Fashioned Way** (1934). In **"The Mountain Sweep Stakes,"** Pickford must marry Keanan or he will take over the mortgage on the farm. Pickford, of course, is in love with Fairbanks ("Dug is my sweet Patootie"), and all will be saved if he can win the prize money for the big car race ("Good luck Dug, win the race Baby").[13] The rest of the cast are integrated according to their stereotyped images, from the picaresque comings and goings of Chaplin to Barra's vamping of him. Fields at all times demonstrated an excellent understanding of these characters.

Second, to find Chaplin the real hero of the script is even more surprising than discovering the film-fan nature of Fields. Fields's view of the creator of Charlie is usually equated with his review of Chaplin's performance in *Easy Street* (1917): "He's the world's greatest ballet dancer, and if I ever meet the son of a bitch I'll murder him!"[14] Even Fields's last mistress observed: "To his [comedy] contemporaries he was fairly charitable, with the one notable exception of Charlie Chaplin. He referred to him as a 'goddamned ballet dancer.' It had to be pure jealousy."[15] Yet in **"The Mountain Sweep Stakes,"** Fields makes the Chaplin character the winner, literally and metaphorically; he wins the big car race (on foot!) and is allowed to maintain more of his screen uniqueness. For example, unlike the other silent film stars parodied in the script, the Chaplin figure maintains the universality of his silence. He does not fall comic victim to lines like "Dug is my sweet Patootie."

Fields also pays Chaplin a rather unusual compliment by including a scene in **"The Mountain Sweep Stakes"** (and thus copyrighting it) that had already appeared in the 1917 Charlie film *The Adventurer*. (One is reminded of the Fields commandment: "Thou shalt not steal—only from other comedians."[16]) The Fields scene in question has ice cream being delivered to Charlie and Barra, with the former spilling some into his trousers. But in trying to shake it down his pant leg without distracting Barra, the ice cream drops through both his pants and the floor grating underneath, ending up on the back of Dressler, who is seated below them.[17] Interestingly enough, in a later interview Fields acknowledges the source of the scene (though not in connection with his script), as well as the uniqueness of Chaplin:

> Chaplin [is] the greatest of all comedians. . . . I think the funniest scene I almost ever saw was in one of Chaplin's old pictures. He is eating some ice-cream and it falls down his trousers. You remember that one [*The Adventurer*].[18]

All in all, Fields's copyrighted material, begun during the Ziegfeld years (1915-21, 1925), offers seven unique insights into the evolution of the comedian's career. First, it documents more fully than ever before the carryover of

Fields material from stage to screen (some of which was repeated more than once on film). Second, it confirms Fields's authorship of a great deal of his key routines. Third, while all the sketch material is strongly visual, the inclusion of dialogue and various supporting players more completely showcases the evolving nature of Fields's comedy during the Ziegfeld years. He moves from juggling, solo pantomimist of the pre-Follies days to the speaking musical comedy star of the Broadway hit show *Poppy* (1923-24), which followed the Ziegfeld period.

Fourth, the copyrighted sketches, though frequently more ambitious than earlier Fields material, still do not neglect the often props-oriented nature (see the aforementioned traveling items included in **"Off to the Country"**) of a comedian who began as, and never completely forgot being, a juggler. Fifth, the very act of copyrighting more than suggests that Fields had come to recognize the growing importance of his work—a foundation he would utilize for the rest of his career.

Sixth, **"The Mountain Sweep Stakes"** revealed Fields to be both a keen student of film and—surprise of surprises—a fan of Chaplin (at least in 1919, the year the script was copyrighted). It also nicely demonstrates, with Fields's theft of Chaplin material, an important sociological analysis of Fields's work by his friend and biographer Alva Johnston. Thus, Johnston draws upon the comedian's youth to make such points as the young Fields survived "because he seized everything he could get away with," a habit the comedian more than continued in his adult life.[19]

Seventh and most important, Fields's sketch concept of the victimized central male—his leisure time usurped by females, machines (especially cars), and the city in general—places Fields's work in the vanguard of the evolution of the comic antihero in American humor.

The Fields sketches do not, however, represent an "open sesame" on the celebrated nature of his 1930s screen persona. The sketch material that he recycled into his sound films, sometimes in blocks but more frequently in bits and pieces, knows little fundamental change. This is true whether it is the finely tuned anti-heroic physical comedy of his golf routine or the verbal gems of his dentist sketch. In the latter case, all the classic lines from the 1932 **The Dentist** adaptation existed in one of the three copyrighted sketches. They include Fields's response to a shapely patient whose doctor says she has a bad leg: "Your doctor is off his nut!" and Fields's question about the extremely short patient: "Is he standing in a hole?" In fact, both the standing-in-a-hole line and another **Dentist** comic observation (on where a tall dog might have bitten Ms Shapely) appear in several other Fields films. (He seldom missed an opportunity to re-use his material.) But to more fully understand how the comic aesthetics of Fields's sketches merged with his delightfully full-blown '30s screen character, three additional factors need to be integrated.

First, the sketches were brief in length (five to ten typed, doublespaced pages)—truly "sketches." While they are funny and contain material frequently recycled verbatim into later films, they focus more on situation than character. Thus, at the risk of being blasphemous to Fields, it is conceivable that another antiheroic comedian might have stepped in and been equally successful. This is not, however, as obvious as it might seem, because one tends to attach the rich image of Fields to the written word. In fact, a similar dilemma confronts the student of Fields's silent films—the viewer tends to supply the Fields voice with the unthinking regularity of a knee-jerk coordination test. What sketch detail there is revolves around the props, the numerous items that comically come between him and his golf game, or the even greater number of props the Fliverton family members drag along for their attempted country outing. Consequently, the first key to understanding the assimilation of the sketches into Fields's later screen world is to underline the significance of their antiheroic, frequently physical comedy nature while recognizing this was not the sum total of the later Fields.

Second, the missing ingredient is the con-man quality of Fields. Although this seems the antithesis of the antihero, the two traits (in varying degrees) later generally graced the same Fields character. For example, the henpecked husband of *It's a Gift* (1934) is forced by his wife to share a sandwich with one of their undeserving children. Before dividing it, however, Fields folds all the meat onto his half of the sandwich.[20] Conversely, his con-man Commodore from *Mississippi* (1935) is forever spinning tall tales about his days as an Indian fighter, when he took down his old Bowie knife and "cut a path through a wall of living flesh." But near the film's close, he is once again heroically rambling when, unbeknownst to Fields, some wooden Indians are being loaded on board. The Commodore mistakes them for the real thing as they are pulled past his porthole. His speech quickly flipflops from boastful courage to imitation compassion, with lines like "some of my best friends are Indians."

Fields's antiheroic nature is the most central characteristic of his comedy success, and therein lies the importance of the copyrighted sketches. But his frequent balancing of this with the huckster creates a more complex comedy than, say, the funny but totally frustrated antiheroic Laurel and Hardy. Frustration is more the tone of Fields's copyrighted sketches. The antiheroic Fields frequently rebels, under his breath, with his patented asides. Thus, film critic Penelope Gilliatt observed, Fields's 1930s comic duality is best described as "fifth-columnist."[21]

The antiheroic Fields who parries with the aside also anticipates the brassier new breed of personality comedians who came out of the World War II era. Best typified by Bob Hope, they fluctuated between the most incompetent of comic antiheroes and the cool, egotistical wise-guy.

Although Fields had labored long to build his repertoire of antihero sketches, the con-man additive can be traced to a single night—the 3 September 1923 Broadway open-ing of Dorothy Donnelly's musical comedy *Poppy*. Fields played Professor Eustace McGargle, a small-time 1870s con-man who attempts to utilize his adopted daughter in a big-time swindle—passing her off as an heir to a fortune. Both Fields and the play were critical and commercial hits. Celebrated contemporary critic Heywood Broun said of Fields's performance: "We can't remember anybody who ever made us laugh more."[22]

Fields would recreate the role twice for film (*Sally of the Sawdust*, 1925, and *Poppy,* 1936) and once for radio (*Lux Radio Theatre,* 7 March 1936), and he frequently would play variations of McGargle for the rest of his career. But Fields's ongoing popularity is more a combination of his antihero foundation (the sketches) with the con-man.

Fields, in fact, immediately began to merge the two personae while appearing on the stage as Professor McGargle. The *New York Times* reviewer was even moved to focus on the antiheroic

> Mr. Fields, veteran of many "Follies," and more cigar boxes [his best-known antiheroic juggling prop] than there are cigars. He has never been quite so amusing as he is in *Poppy*—nor so versatile. His comicalities range from his accustomed juggling to untold difficulties with some bits of tissue paper [comedy business reminiscent of the wayward paper in Fields's sketch **"An Episode on the Links"**].[23]

D. W. Griffith's 1925 film adaptation of *Poppy* (a critical and commercial success) also moved Fields in a more antiheroic direction by softening the McGargle con-man. This helps explain some noticeable differences between the stage and first screen versions of *Poppy,* differences that have been almost totally ignored since the adaptation took place.[24] In addition, it provides an explanation for a frequently asked question: Why did Griffith call the film version *Sally of the Sawdust?* No doubt, as *Variety* would seem to suggest, because "Griffith . . . followed the stage story but sparsely. His picturization is nearly an original other than characters."[25]

The most surprising difference is that Griffith's Fields, as carnival huckster Professor McGargle, is not quite the con-man of the play, in which he manages to install his adopted daughter as the heir to a fortune, *unaware* that she is the rightful descendant. In the film Fields not only knows the girl's true parentage all along, he does not even attempt to use it (misuse it?) until it is necessary to save her from a possible jail term. (Moreover, Fields's on-the-road-with-a-cane physical presence and his caring for a waif figure sometimes seem Chaplinesque—which does not seem that great a departure after Fields's **"The Mountain Sweep Stakes."**)

Another major difference involves time setting: Griffith's version takes place in the present (1925); the stage version is set in 1874. This allows for the inclusion of car chases and bootleggers. Though both items remind one of Griffith, especially the cross-cutting a chase makes possible, they also point to the antiheroic Fields. Fields's comedy had been associated with liquor for years, and since Prohibition he had sometimes included it in his copyrighted sketchs, such as the aforementioned close of **"Off to the Country"** (see footnote 7).

Cars are, of course, even more prevalent in his sketches. And one bit of car comedy from *Sally,* putting his head through the automobile's cloth roof, is included in his last copyrighted sketch—**"Midget Car,"** and still later in *International House.* (Fields's last two starring features, **The Bank Dick,** 1940, and **Never Give a Sucker an Even Break,** 1941, both closed with epic comic car chases.)

Third, Fields maximized the antiheroic nature of his sketches by working with J. P. McEvoy, particularly on *The Comic Supplement.* Whereas Donnelly's *Poppy* had served up a nearly complete comedy type in McGargle, which Fields immediately began to utilize after peppering it with antiheroic traits, *The Comic Supplement* was the proverbial college degree for both McEvoy's and Fields's antiheroic inclinations.

*The Comic Supplement* contained the foundation for two sketches that are now considered pivotal Fields—**"The Drug Store"** and **"The House by the Side of the Road"** (the lawn-destroying picnic). *The Comic Supplement* also gave impetus to Fields's Babbitt-like copyrighted sketch **"The Sleeping Porch,"** which was part of the revised 1925 *Supplement* (see footnote 3). In fact, the latter *Supplement* unquestionably showcases a great number of Fieldsian touches, from a billiard sketch (uncopyrighted by Fields but a standard routine in his vaudeville act for years, as well as the basis for his first nationally distributed film, *Pool Sharks,* 1915), to some patently Fields touches in the picnic sketch, such as opening a can with a hatchet. When the *Supplement* went on the road, more Fields material was added, including the comedian's golf sketch; he then began to share the writing credit with McEvoy.[26] (His copyrighted tale of golfing woe perfectly fit, of course, the antiheroic tone of the *Supplement.*)

To further demonstrate the significance of the antihero to Fields, the last time variations of the *Supplement* were joined in one production, for *It's a Gift* (which would credit both the *Supplement* and an original story by Charles Bogle/Fields), the Fields character would be an even greater milquetoast type. For example, earlier versions of the *Supplement*'s picnic sketch were not so antiheroic as the rest of the revue. Fields and his picnicking family knowingly enter an estate resembling a park, and later do the same to the estate house. Fields's *It's a Gift* revision makes the family's initial trespassing an accident (they mistake the grounds for a park) and eliminates the house scene entirely, keying on the epic-making abilities of a piggish family. Moreover, Fields borrows from two of his own copyrighted sketches, **"Off to the Country"** and **"The Family Ford,"** when he accents both the comic potential of the family car and the million and one items families frequently stuff into them.

In addition to the Fields-McEvoy connection on the *Supplement,* McEvoy's antiheroic hit Broadway play *The Potters* was the basis of Fields's critically praised 1927 film of the same name. McEvoy also provided dialogue for the comedian's excellent though underrated *You're Telling Me* (1934). The kindred antiheroic spirit of both men is best revealed by the fact that *The Potters* is often called Fields's best silent film, while **It's a Gift** frequently wears that distinction among his sound works.

The McEvoy and Donnelly influences were, therefore, more additions to, rather than changes of, Fields's copyrighted sketches. They enriched an already substantial examination of the comic antihero. McEvoy helped broaden it; Donnelly provided a con-man alter ego. Then, when sound film finally allowed Fields's gift for visual comedy to be punctuated with that patented voice, a national audience soon made him one of their comedy favorites. And those forgotten copyrighted sketches became an unacknowledged national legacy.

NOTES

[1] Some sketches, or variations of them—see chronological list which follows notes—are included in *W. C. Fields by Himself: His Intended Autobiography* (1973, an anthology-like collection of Fields's writings edited by his grandson, Ronald J. Fields). But the majority are absent and the Library of Congress collection is not mentioned (the grandson was working from the evidently incomplete, private papers of the comedian). Moreover, the frequent, multiple copyrighting of a single yet changing property is neither included nor alluded to, and specific dates are generally absent.

[2] Sinclair Lewis, *Babbit* (1922; rpt. New York: Signet Classic, 1980), pp. 6-7. The novel first introduces George F. Babbitt as a sleeping porch victim of noise:

> Rumble and bang of the milk-truck.
>
> Babbitt moaned, turned over. . . . The furnace-man slammed the basement door. A dog barked in the next yard . . . the paper-carrier went by whistling, and the rolled-up *Advocate* thumped the front door. Babbitt roused, his stomach constricted with alarm. As he relaxed, he was pierced by the familiar and irritating rattle of some one cranking a Ford. . . . Not till the rising voice of the motor told him that the Ford was moving was he released from the panting tension.

Although the interruptions to sleep encountered by Fields in his "Porch" routine are sometimes more than auditory (his baby nephew hits him over the head with first a mallet and then a milk bottle in the *It's the Old Army Game* adaptation), the same helpless leisure-time frustration is at the center of both. Moreover, Lewis' very description of Babbitt paints a portrait of Fields:

> His large head was pink, his brown hair thin and dry. His face was babyish in slumber. . . . He was

not fat but he was exceedingly well fed; his cheeks were pads, and the unroughened hand which lay helpless upon the khaki colored blanket was slightly puffy. He seemed . . . extremely married and unromantic.

[3] Fields and McEvoy were on similar antihero wavelengths. See the author's *W. C. Fields: A Bio-Bibliography* (Westport, Conn.: Greenwood Press, 1984), pp. 19-21, 97-98, 182. See also J. P. McEvoy's 1924 copyrighted version of *The Comic Supplement*—Library of Congress Copyright Office; and the 1925 rehearsal version of *The Comic Supplement* at the New York Public Library at Lincoln Center—Billy Rose Theatre Collection.

[4] "New Spring Follies Is Rich in Humor" (11 March 1925) and "Ziegfeld Follies Bloom for Summer" (6 July 1925) in *New York Times Theatre Reviews, 1920-1926,* Vol. 1 (New York: New York Times and Arno Press, 1971), n.p.

[5] W. C. Fields, "The Family Ford" ("W. C. Fields Papers," Library of Congress, copyrighted 16 October 1919—first of three versions), p. 6.

[6] W. C. Fields, "Off to the Country" ("W. C. Fields Papers," Library of Congress, copyrighted 25 May 1921—first of three versions), p. 1.

[7] Fields, "Off to the Country," p. 6.

[8] Floyd Clymer, *Those Wonderful Old Machines* (New York: Bonanza Books, 1953), p. 151.

[9] W. C. Fields, "10,000 People Killed" ("W. C. Fields Papers," Library of Congress, copyrighted 29 May 1922—first of two versions), p. 4.

[10] Fields, "10,000 People Killed," p. 5.

[11] Fields, "10,000 People Killed," p. 1.

[12] W. C. Fields, "The Mountain Sweep Stakes" ("W. C. Fields Papers," Library of Congress, copyrighted 21 March 1919), p. 1.

[13] Fields, "The Mountain Sweep Stakes," pp. 2, 10.

[14] Lita Grey Chaplin (with Morton Cooper), *My Life with Chaplin* (New York: Bernard Geis Associates, 1966), p. 143.

[15] Carlotta Monti (with Cy Rice), *W. C. Fields and Me* (1971; rpt. New York: Warner Books, 1973), p. 74.

[16] Monti, *W. C. Fields and Me,* p. 69.

[17] Fields, "The Mountain Sweep Stakes," p. 8.

[18] Sara Redway, "W. C. FIELDS Pleads for Rough HUMOR," *Motion Picture Classic,* September 1925, p. 33.

[19] Alva Johnston, "Who Knows What Is Funny?" *Saturday Evening Post,* 6 August 1938, p. 45. An abridged and slightly revised version of the essay would appear under the same title in the December 1975 issue of the *Saturday Evening Post.*

[20] This action does not occur in *The Comic Supplement.*

[21] Penelope Gilliatt, *Unholy Fools: Wits, Comics, Disturbances of the Peace: Film and Theater* (New York: Viking Press, 1973), pp. 262-263.

[22] Heywood Broun, "The New Play," *New York World Telegraph,* 4 September 1923, p. 9.

[23] "*Poppy* Is Charming," 4 September 1923, in *New York Times Theatre Reviews, 1920-1926,* n.p.

[24] This was no doubt encouraged by the general and continuing unavailability of the play itself. *Poppy* was never published for commercial sales. The Union Catalog of major United States library holdings does not list it, and the Library of Congress has lost its only copyright edition of *Poppy.* In order to note key differences between the original play and Griffith's adaptation, the plot analyses of numerous play reviews of *Poppy* were compared with the film.

[25] *Sally of the Sawdust* review, *Variety,* 5 August 1925, p. 30. Also in this issue is a short but interesting article on the stage prologue for the film.

[26] Ronald J. Fields, *W. C. Fields: A Life on Film* (New York: St. Martin's Press, 1984), p. 25.

W. C. FIELDS COPYRIGHTED SKETCHES

"W. C. Fields Papers," Library of Congress, Washington, D.C. Unpublished copyrighted material by Fields, though some sketches, or variations of them, appeared in *W. C. Fields by Himself: His Intended Autobiography.* The writing is arranged chronologically, though later copyrighted revision dates of the same routine follow the titles. Also, short descriptions are added to material without a self-explanatory title. Though once housed individually by title in the Copyright Division of the Library of Congress, the documents are now available as one collection, the "W. C. Fields Papers," in the Manuscript Division of the Library (Madison Building).

30 Aug. 1918. "An Episode on the Links"—D 50320

28 Oct. 1918. "An Episode of Lawn Tennis"—D 50680

Feb. 1919. "An Episode at the Dentist's"—D 51214 (12 July 1928—84613; 2 Nov. 1928—86848)

21 Mar. 1919. "The Mountain Sweep Stakes"—D 51508 (A film script parodying movies, Fields described it as "A Moving, Talking, Eastern, Western, Society, Dramatic, Spectacular Comedy Motion Stage Picture.")

7 Apr. 1919. "Just Before the Dawn"—D 51558 (coauthored with Moritmer M. Newfield; a three-act military farce)

16 Oct. 1919. "The Family Ford"—D 52882 (3 Sept. 1920—D 54401; 9 Oct. 1920—D 55748)

26 Feb. 1921. "The Pullman Sleeper"—D 56911

25 May 1921. "Off to the Country"—D 57748 (29 June 1921—D 58027; Apr. 1922—D 60419)

25 May 1921. "What a Night"—D 57747 (a parody of the detective-mystery genre, with frequent surreal action)

22 May 1922. "The Sport Model"—D 60861

29 May 1922. "10,000 People Killed"—D 60900 (10 Oct. 1922—D 62425; concerns a radio broadcast misunderstanding)

31 July 1922. "The Caledonian Express"—D 61555 (subtitled heading "Or an American Abroad)

6 Feb. 1925. "The Sleeping Porch"—D 70336

12 July 1928. "Stolen Bonds"—D 84614 (better known under the film title for which it was adapted: *The Fatal Glass of Beer,* 1933)

12 July 1928. "My School Days Are Over"—D 84612

25 Nov. 1930. "Midget Car"—D 8113

---

# FURTHER READING

### Bibliography

Gehring, Wes D. "Bibliographical Checklist of Key Fields Sources." In *W. C. Fields: A Bio-Bibliography*, 192-200. Westport, CT: Greenwood Press, 1984.
    Extensive listing of Fields's work, and of Fields-related writings.

Rocks, David T. *W. C. Fields—An Annotated Guide: Chronology, Bibliographies, Discography, Filmographies, Press Books, Cigarette Cards, Film Clips and Impersonators.* Jefferson, NC: McFarland, 1993, 131 p.
    An exhaustive guide to publications and paraphernalia relating to Fields, along with a twenty-page chronology of his life.

### Biography

Brooks, Louise. "The Other Faces of W. C. Fields." In *Lulu in Hollywood*, 71-84. New York: Knopf, 1982.
    Brooks, who performed with Fields in the Ziegfeld

Follies of 1925, remembers the man behind the curmudgeonly persona.

Edelson, Edward. "Uncle Bill." In *Funny Men of the Movies*, 71-79. New York: Doubleday, 1976.
    Brief and lighthearted chronicle of Fields's life and performances.

Monti, Carlotta with Cy Rice. *W. C. Fields & Me.* Englewood Cliffs, NJ: Prentice-Hall, 1971, 227 p.
    Fields's longtime companion offers an intimate portrait of her fourteen years with him.

Taylor, Robert Lewis. *W. C. Fields: His Follies and Fortunes.* New York: Signet, 1949.
    Taylor wrote this biography, published less than three years after Fields's death, with the help of Gene Fowler and others close to Fields.

### Criticism

Agee, James. From "Time: 1941-1948." In *Agee on Film: Reviews and Comments by James Agee*, 334-35. New York: McDowell, Obolensky, 1958.
    Review of *Never Give a Sucker an Even Break*, which Agee describes as "not a movie [but] 70 minutes of photographed vaudeville by polyp[-]nosed W. C. Fields."

Anobile, Richard J., editor. *A Flask of Fields: Verbal and Visual Gems from the Films of W. C. Fields.* New York: Darien House, 1972, 272 p.
    Anobile brings together actual screen dialogue from ten Fields films, along with 700 frame blow-ups—not stills or publicity shots—to re-create classic scenes at length. Introduction by Judith Crist.

Deschner, Donald. *The Films of W. C. Fields.* New York: Citadel Press, 1966, 192 p.
    Plot summaries and other information on Fields's motion pictures, from *Pool Sharks* to *Sensations of 1945*. Includes two commentaries by Fields, essays by Otis Ferguson and Heywood Broun, and an introduction by Arthur Knight.

Ebert, Roger. "Fields vs. Chaplin." In *The National Society of Film Critics on Movie Comedy*, edited by Stuart Byron and Elizabeth Weis, 53-54. New York: Grossman, 1977.
    Ebert explains the distinction between clowns and comedians, then identifies Charlie Chaplin as film's greatest clown, and Fields as its foremost comedian.

Everson, William K. *The Art of W. C. Fields.* Indianapolis: Bobbs-Merrill, 1967, 232 p.
    Analysis of Fields's on-screen personae and performances, including a chapter on "The Lost Films."

Fields, Ronald J. *W. C. Fields: A Life on Film.* New York: St. Martin's, 1984, 256 p.
    Fields's grandson offers comprehensive profiles of each film, including an unreleased Ziegfeld production and

rare USO footage from World War II; profiles consist of production history, synopsis, Fields's lore, and detailed specifics by filmographer Richard W. Bann.

Gehring, Wes D. *Groucho and W. C. Fields: Huckster Comedians.* Jackson, MS: University Press of Mississippi, 1994, 196 p.
>   Exploration of Fields's work juxtaposed with that of Groucho Marx; includes chapters on "Contrasting Film Huckster Styles" and "Antiheroes and Absurdity" in both men's films.

Gilliatt, Penelope. "Feeling in the Wrong Is Wrong" and "To W. C. Fields, Dyspeptic Mumbler, Who Invented His Way Out." In *Unholy Fools: Wits, Comics, Disturbers of the Peace: Film & Theater*, 253-56, 257-63. New York: Viking, 1973.
>   Brief mention of Fields in a critique of Richard Benjamin's performance in *Goodbye, Columbus*; and a tribute to Fields as "one of the four or five funniest men" of recent history, in a disparaging review of the film *The Maltese Bippy*.

Keough, William. "Round Seven: The Sound and Fury: The Talking Clowns." In *Punchlines: The Violence of American Humor*, 151-69. New York: Paragon House, 1990.
>   Comparison of Fields's work with that of Laurel and Hardy and the Marx Brothers.

Kerr, Walter. From "The Demiclowns." In *The Silent Clowns*, 295-97. New York: Knopf, 1925.
>   Discussion of Fields's silent films.

Maltin, Leonard. "W. C. Fields." In *The Great Movie Comedians: From Charlie Chaplin to Woody Allen*, 142-51. New York: Crown, 1978.
>   Discussion of Fields's film work, with concentration on widely held misconceptions concerning his style—including the notion that he refused to memorize lines in favor of pure ad-libbing.

*Three Films by W. C. Fields.* London: Faber and Faber, 1990, 207 p.
>   Scripts, credits, and cast of *Never Give a Sucker an Even Break*, *Tillie and Gus*, and *The Bank Dick*; with an introduction by Louise Brooks that appeared in her book *Lulu in Hollywood* under the title "The Other Faces of W. C. Fields" (see above).

---

> **Additional coverage of Fields's life and career is contained in the following source published by Gale Research:** *Dictionary of Literary Biography*, **Vol. 44.**

# Sarojini Naidu

## 1879-1949

Indian poet, lecturer, and politician.

## INTRODUCTION

Naidu is remembered as a virtuoso of English metrical forms and romantic imagery in her poetry, which she wrote in English. Her mastery of such difficult poetic constructs as the dactylic prompted the English writers Edmund Gosse and Arthur Symons to praise her work widely and develop friendships with her. Equally concerned with India's freedom movement and women's rights as with writing poetry, Naidu became a close associate of Mahatma Gandhi and lectured on behalf of Indian independence throughout India, Africa, the United States, and Canada. Her political career reached its peak when she was elected the first woman governor of the United Provinces in 1947.

### Biographical Information

Naidu was born into a high-caste Bengali family in 1879. Her father, Aghorenath Chattopadhyaya, became, after obtaining his doctorate from the University of Edinburgh in Scotland, a distinguished scholar and linguist who founded two Indian colleges, one for women. Naidu's mother, Varada Sundari, was a minor poet and noted singer. Naidu began writing poetry as a child and at the age of twelve passed the matriculation examination for the University of Madras. As a teenager, Naidu fell in love with Govindarajulu Naidu, a doctor who was neither Bengali nor of the Brahmin caste. Hoping to prevent their daughter from marrying outside her social group, her parents sent her to England in 1895. There Naidu attended King's College, London, and Girton College, Cambridge, where she further developed her poetic style and became friends with such well-known English critics and writers as Edmund Gosse and Arthur Symons, who helped her to refine her work. In 1898 Naidu returned to India and married Govindarajulu Naidu despite her family's disapproval. Because of her family's high status, Naidu had access to many of the most prominent thinkers, writers, and political figures of India's modern intellectual renaissance. Her first volume of poetry, *The Golden Threshold*, was published in England in 1905; with an introduction by Arthur Symons. The book was well-received, and Naidu was encouraged to continue publishing her work until 1917, when she abruptly stopped. At this point, Naidu became active in Indian politics. She had met Gandhi in 1914 and soon decided to join him in the struggle for Indian independence. Naidu's first cause as a political activist was women's rights; she traveled throughout India lecturing on women's educational needs and promoting suffrage, and

became the first woman to hold several prominent positions in the Indian government. In 1925 she was elected President of the Indian National Congress, and during the 1920s traveled throughout Africa and North America campaigning for Indian independence. Naidu was arrested and imprisoned for revolutionary activities several times during her career. In 1947-when independence was achieved-Naidu was elected acting governor of the United Provinces. She died in 1949.

### Major Works

Naidu's early poetry evidences the strong Western influence of her Brahmin upbringing. Crafting poems in traditional English metrical forms, she concentrated primarily on Western themes and images. Edmund Gosse, upon reading her work when he met her in London, recognized Naidu's potential but encouraged her to incorporate Indian subjects into her work. Naidu followed Gosse's advice, and her first volume, *The Golden Threshold*, combines traditional poetic forms with lush images of India. The book achieved popular and critical success in England, where Edwardian readers admired Naidu's deft handling of the English language as well as the native view of Indian exotica it offered them. Naidu's second collection of poems, *The Bird of Time* (1912), confronted more serious themes such as death and grief as well as containing poems expressing Naidu's patriotism and religious convictions. Gosse provided the forward to this volume, noting Naidu's rich exploration of complex issues in delicate, romantic language. In her third volume, *The Broken Wing* (1917), Naidu included more poems of patriotism and description of Indian culture. More important, *The Broken Wing* contains the work many critics consider Naidu's greatest poetic achievement, "The Temple: A Pilgrimage of Love." A series of twenty-four poems, "The Temple" explores the joys, pain, and vagaries of a mature love relationship in graphic, sometimes violent, imagery, and concludes in a meditation on death. *The Broken Wing* was the last volume of poetry published in Naidu's lifetime. Many critics have wondered about the reason for her apparently sudden departure from literary pursuits to political involvement. Some speculate that her popularity dwindled, particularly in England, when she moved away from the flowery, romantic style of her early poetry to a comparatively morbid and contemplative tone in her later work. Others contend that her preoccupation with patriotic themes caused readers to lose interest. In 1961 Naidu's daughter published a collection of her previously unpublished poems, *The Feather of the Dawn*, but it met with little critical interest. Her poetry has since undergone reevaluation by Indian critics, many of whom regard her as one of India's greatest twentieth-century poets.

# PRINCIPAL WORKS

*Speeches and Writings* (speeches and essays) 1904; revised edition, 1925
*The Golden Threshold* (poetry) 1905
*The Bird of Time: Songs of Life, and Death, and the Spring* (poetry) 1912
*The Broken Wing: Songs of Love, Death, and Destiny, 1915-1916* (poetry) 1917
*The Soul of India* (essays) 1917
*The Sceptered Flute: Songs of India* (poetry) 1928
*Select Poems* [edited by H. G. Dalway Turnbull] (poetry) 1930
*The Feather of the Dawn* (poetry) 1961

# CRITICISM

**Arthur Symons (essay date 1905)**

SOURCE: An introduction to *The Golden Threshold,* by Sarojini Naidu, William Heinemann, 1905, pp. 9-23.

[*In the following introduction of Naidu's* The Golden Threshold, *Symons expresses his strong admiration of Naidu's poetry and relates the friendship he developed with her through letters.*]

It is at my persuasion that these poems are now published. The earliest of them were read to me in London in 1896, when the writer was seventeen; the later ones were sent to me from India in 1904, when she was twenty-five; and they belong, I think, almost wholly to those two periods. As they seemed to me to have an individual beauty of their own, I thought they ought to be published. The writer hesitated. "Your letter made me very proud and very sad," she wrote. "Is it possible that I have written verses that are 'filled with beauty,' and is it possible that you really think them worthy of being given to the world? You know how high my ideal of Art is; and to me my poor casual little poems seem to be less than beautiful I mean with that final enduring beauty that I desire." And, in another letter, she writes: "I am not a poet really. I have the vision and the desire, but not the voice. If I could write just one poem full of beauty and the spirit of greatness, I should be exultantly silent for ever; but I sing just as the birds do, and my songs are as ephemeral." It is for this bird-like quality of song, it seems to me, that they are to be valued. They hint, in a sort of delicately evasive way, at a rare temperament, the temperament of a woman of the East, finding expression through a Western language and under partly Western influences. They do not express the whole of that temperament; but they express, I think, its essence; and there is an Eastern magic in them.

Sarojini Chattopâdhyây was born at Hyderabad on February 13, 1879. Her father, Dr. Aghorenath Chattopâdhyây, is descended from the ancient family of Chattorajes of Bhramangram, who were noted throughout Eastern Bengal as patrons of Sanskrit learning, and for their practice of Yoga. He took his degree of Doctor of Science at the University of Edinburgh in 1877, and afterwards studied brilliantly at Bonn. On his return to India he founded the Nizam College at Hyderabad, and has since laboured incessantly, and at great personal sacrifice, in the cause of education.

Sarojini was the eldest of a large family, all of whom were taught English at an early age. "I," she writes, "was stubborn and refused to speak it. So one day when I was nine years old my father punished me the only time I was ever punished by shutting me in a room alone for a whole day. I came out of it a full-blown linguist. I have never spoken any other language to him, or to my mother, who always speaks to me in Hindustani. I don't think I had any special hankering to write poetry as a little child, though I was of a very fanciful and dreamy nature. My training under my father's eye was of a sternly scientific character. He was determined that I should be a great mathematician or a scientist, but the poetic instinct, which I inherited from him and also from my mother (who wrote some lovely Bengali lyrics in her youth) proved stronger. One day, when I was eleven, I was sighing over a sum in algebra: it *wouldn't* come right; but instead a whole poem came to me suddenly. I wrote it down.

"From that day my 'poetic career' began. At thirteen I wrote a long poem *à la* 'Lady of the Lake' 1300 lines in six days. At thirteen I wrote a drama of 2000 lines, a full-fledged passionate thing that I began on the spur of the moment without forethought, just to spite my doctor who said I was very ill and must not touch a book. My health broke down permanently about this time, and my regular studies being stopped I read voraciously. I suppose the greater part of my reading was done between fourteen and sixteen. I wrote a novel, I wrote fat volumes of journals: I took myself very seriously in those days."

Before she was fifteen the great struggle of her life began. Dr. Govindurajulu Naidu, now her husband, is, though of an old and honourable family, not a Brahmin. The difference of caste roused an equal opposition, not only on the side of her family, but of his; and in 1895 she was sent to England, against her will, with a special scholarship from the Nizam. She remained in England, with an interval of travel in Italy, till 1898, studying first at King's College, London, then, till her health again broke down, at Girton. She returned to Hyderabad in September 1898, and in the December of that year, to the scandal of all India, broke through the bonds of caste, and married Dr. Naidu. "Do you know I have some very beautiful poems floating in the air," she wrote to me in 1904; "and if the gods are kind I shall cast my soul like a net and capture them, this year. If the gods are kind and grant me a little measure of health. It is all I need to make my life perfect, for the very 'Spirit of Delight' that Shelly wrote of dwells in my little home; it is full of the music of birds in the garden and children in the long arched verandah." There are songs about the children in this book; they are called the Lord of Battles, the Sun of Victory, the Lotus-born, and the Jewel of Delight.

"My ancestors for thousands of years," I find written in one of her letters, "have been lovers of the forest and mountain caves, great dreamers, great scholars, great ascetics. My father is a dreamer himself, a great dreamer, a great man whose life has been a magnificent failure. I suppose in the whole of India there are few men whose learning is greater than his, and I don't think there are many men more beloved. He has a great white beard and the profile of Homer, and a laugh that brings the roof down. He has wasted all his money on two great objects: to help others, and on alchemy. He holds huge courts every day in his garden of all the learned men of all religions Rajahs and beggars and saints
and downright villains all delightfully mixed up, and all treated as one. And then his alchemy! Oh dear, night and day the experiments are going on, and every man who brings a new prescription is welcome as a brother. But this alchemy is, you know, only the material counterpart of a poet's craving for Beauty, the eternal Beauty. 'The makers of gold and the makers of verse,' they are the twin creators that sway the world's secret desire for mystery; and what in my father is the genius of curiosity

the very essence of all scientific genius in me is the desire for beauty. Do you remember Pater's phrase about Leonardo da Vinci, 'curiosity and the desire of beauty'?"

It was the desire of beauty that made her a poet; her "nerves of delight" were always quivering at the contact of beauty. To those who knew her in England, all the life of the tiny figure seemed to concentrate itself in the eyes; they turned towards beauty as the
sunflower turns towards the sun, opening wider and wider until one saw nothing but the eyes. She was dressed always in clinging dresses of Eastern silk, and as she was so small, and her long black hair hung straight down her back, you might have taken her for a child. She spoke little, and in a low voice, like gentle music; and she seemed, wherever she was, to be alone.

Through that soul I seemed to touch and take hold upon the East. And first there was the wisdom of the East. I have never known any one who seemed to exist on such "large draughts of intellectual day" as this child of seventeen, to whom one could tell all one's personal troubles and agitations, as to a wise old woman. In the East, maturity comes early; and this child had already lived through all a woman's life. But there was something else, something hardly personal, something which belonged to a consciousness older than the Christian, which I realised, wondered at, and admired, in her passionate tranquillity of mind, before which everything mean and trivial and temporary caught fire and burnt away in smoke. Her body was never without suffering, or her heart without conflict; but neither the body's weakness nor the heart's violence could disturb that fixed contemplation, as of Buddha on his lotus-throne.

And along with this wisdom, as of age or of the age of a race, there was what I can hardly call less than an agony of sensation. Pain or pleasure transported her, and the whole of pain or pleasure might be held in a flower's cup or the imagined frown of a friend. It was never found in those things which to others seemed things of importance. At the age of twelve she passed the Matriculation of the Madras University, and awoke to find herself famous throughout India. "Honestly," she said to me, "I was not pleased; such things did not appeal to me." But here, in a letter from Hyderabad, bidding one "share a March morning" with her, there is, at the mere contact of the sun, this outburst: "Come and share my exquisite March morning with me: this sumptuous blaze of gold and sapphire sky; these scarlet lilies that adore the sunshine; the voluptuous scents of neem and champak and serisha that beat upon the languid air with their implacable sweetness; the thousand little gold and blue and silver breasted birds bursting with the shrill ecstasy of life in nesting time. All is hot and fierce and passionate, ardent and unashamed in its exulting and importunate desire for life and love. And, do you know that the scarlet lilies are woven petal by petal from my heart's blood, these little quivering birds are my soul made incarnate music, these heavy perfumes are my emotions dissolved into aerial essence, this flaming blue and gold sky is the 'very me,' that part of me that incessantly and insolently, yes, and a little deliberately, triumphs over that other part a thing of nerves and tissues that suffers and cries out, and that must die to-morrow perhaps, or twenty years hence."

Then there was her humour, which was part of her strange wisdom, and was always awake and on the watch. In all her letters, written in exquisite English prose, but with an ardent imagery and a vehement sincerity of emotion which make them, like the poems, indeed almost more directly, un-English, Oriental, there was always this intellectual, critical sense of humour, which could laugh at one's own enthusiasm as frankly as that enthusiasm had been set down. And partly the humour, like the delicate reserve of her manner, was a mask or a shelter. "I have taught myself," she writes to me from India, "to be commonplace and like everybody else superficially. Every one thinks I am so nice and cheerful, so 'brave,' all the banal things that are so comfortable to be. My mother knows me only as 'such a tranquil child, but so strong-willed.' A tranquil child!" And she writes again, with deeper significance: "I too have learnt the subtle philosophy of living from moment to moment. Yes, it is a subtle philosophy, though it appears merely an epicurean doctrine: 'Eat, drink, and be merry, for to-morrow we die.' I have gone through so many yesterdays when I strove with Death that I have realised to its full the wisdom of that sentence; and it is to me not merely a figure of speech, but a literal fact. Any to-morrow I might die. It is scarcely two months since I came back from the grave: is it worth while to be anything but radiantly glad? Of all things that life or perhaps my temperament has given me I prize the gift of laughter as beyond price."

Her desire, always, was to be "a wild free thing of the air like the birds, with a song in my heart." A spirit of too much fire in too frail a body, it was rarely that her desire was fully granted. But in Italy she found what she could not find in England, and from Italy her letters are radiant. "This Italy is made of gold," she writes from Florence, "the gold of dawn and daylight, the gold of the stars, and, now dancing in weird enchanting rhythms through this magic month of May, the gold of fireflies in the perfumed darkness 'aerial gold.' I long to catch the subtle music of their fairy dances and make a poem with a rhythm like the quick irregular wild flash of their sudden movements. Would it not be wonderful? One black night I stood in a garden with fireflies in my hair like darting restless stars caught in a mesh of darkness. It gave me a strange sensation, as if I were not human at all, but an elfin spirit. I wonder why these little things move me so deeply? It is because I have a most 'unbalanced intellect,' I suppose." Then, looking out on Florence, she cries, "God! how beautiful it is, and how glad I am that I am alive to-day!" And she tells me that she is drinking in the beauty like wine, "wine, golden and scented, and shining, fit for the gods; and the gods have drunk it, the dead gods of Etruria, two thousand years ago. Did I say dead? No, for the gods are immortal, and one might still find them loitering in some solitary dell on the grey hillsides of Fiesole. Have I seen them? Yes, looking with dreaming eyes, I have found them sitting under the olives, in their grave, strong, antique beauty Etruscan gods!"

In Italy she watches the faces of the monks, and at one moment longs to attain to their peace by renunciation, longs for Nirvana; "then, when one comes out again into the hot sunshine that warms one's blood, and sees the eager hurrying faces of men and women in the street, dramatic faces over which the disturbing experiences of life have passed and left their symbols, one's heart thrills up into one's throat. No, no, no, a thousand times no! how can one deliberately renounce this coloured, unquiet, fiery human life of the earth?" And, all the time, her subtle criticism is alert, and this woman of the East marvels at the women of the West, "the beautiful worldly women of the West," whom she sees walking in the Cascine, "taking the air so consciously attractive in their brilliant toilettes, in the brilliant coquetry of their manner!" She finds them "a little incomprehensible," "profound artists in all the subtle intricacies of fascination," and asks if these "incalculable frivolities and vanities and coquetries and caprices" are, to us, an essential part of their charm? And she watches them with amusement as they flutter about her, petting her as if she were a nice child, a child or a toy, not dreaming that she is saying to herself sorrowfully: "How utterly empty their lives must be of all spiritual beauty *if* they are nothing more than they appear to be."

She sat in our midst, and judged us, and few knew what was passing behind that face "like an awakening soul," to use one of her own epithets. Her eyes were like deep pools, and you seemed to fall through them into depths below depths.

## Edmund Gosse (essay date 1912)

SOURCE: An introduction to *The Bird of Time: Songs of Life, Death & Spring,* by Sarojini Naidu, New York: John Lane Company; London: William Heinemann, 1912, pp. 1-8.

[*In the following introduction to Naidu's* The Bird of Time, *Gosse remembers his early meetings with Naidu in London and how he encouraged her to write poetry.*]

It is only at the request, that is to say at the command, of a dear and valued friend that I consent to write these few sentences. It would seem that an "introduction" can only be needed when the personage to be "introduced" is unknown in a world prepared to welcome her but still ignorant of her qualities. This is certainly not the case with Mrs. Naidu, whose successive volumes, of which this is the third, have been received in Europe with approval, and in India with acclamation. Mrs. Naidu is, I believe, acknowledged to be the most accomplished living poet of India at least, of those who write in English, since what lyric wonders the native languages of that country may be producing I am not competent to say. But I do not think that any one questions the supreme place she holds among those Indians who choose to write in our tongue. Indeed, I am not disinclined to believe that she is the most brilliant, the most original, as well as the most correct, of all the natives of Hindustan who have written in English. And I say this without prejudice to the fame of that delicious Toru Dutt, so exquisite in her fragility, whose life and poems it was my privilege to reveal to the world thirty years ago. For in the case of Toru Dutt, beautiful as her writings were, there was much in them to be excused by her youth, her solitude, the extremely pathetic circumstances of her brief and melancholy career. In the maturer work of Mrs. Naidu I find nothing, or almost nothing, which the severest criticism could call in question.

In a gracious sentence, published seven or eight years ago, Sarojini Naidu declared that it was the writer of this preface "who first showed" her "the way to the golden threshold" of poetry. This is her generous mode of describing certain conditions which I may perhaps be allowed to enlarge upon so far as they throw light on the contents of the volume before us. It is needless for me to repeat those particulars of the Indian poet's early life, so picturesque and so remarkable, which were given by Mr. Arthur Symons in the excellent essay which he prefixed to her volume of 1905. Sufficient for my purpose it is to say that when Sarojini Chattopadhyay as she then was first made her appearance in London, she was a child of sixteen years, but as unlike the usual English maiden of that age as a lotus or a cactus is unlike a lily of the valley. She was already marvellous in mental maturity, amazingly well read, and far beyond a Western child in all her acquaintance with the world.

By some accident now forgotten, but an accident most fortunate for us Sarojini was introduced to our house at an early date after her arrival in London, and she soon became one of the most welcome and intimate of our guests. It was natural that one so impetuous and so sympathetic should not long conceal from her hosts the fact that she was writing copiously in verse in English verse. I entreated to be allowed to see what she had composed, and a bundle of MSS. was slipped into my hand. I hastened to examine it as soon as I was alone, but now there followed a disappointment, and with it an embarrassment, which, in the face of what followed, I make no scruple of revealing. The verses which Sarojini had entrusted to me were skilful in form, correct in grammar and blameless in sentiment, but they had the disadvantage of being totally without individuality. They were Western in feeling and in imagery; they were founded on reminiscences of Tennyson and Shelley; I am not sure that they did not even breathe an atmosphere of Christian resignation. I laid them down in despair; this was but the note of the mocking-bird with a vengeance.

It was not pleasant to daunt the charming and precocious singer by so discouraging a judgment; but I reflected on her youth and her enthusiasm, and I ventured to speak to her sincerely. I advised the consignment of all that she had written, in this falsely English vein, to the wastepaper basket. I implored her to consider that from a

young Indian of extreme sensibility, who had mastered not merely the language but the prosody of the West, what we wished to receive was, not a réchauffé of Anglo-Saxon sentiment in an Anglo-Saxon setting, but some revelation of the heart of India, some sincere penetrating analysis of native passion, of the principles of antique religion and of such mysterious intimations as stirred the soul of the East long before the West had begun to dream that it had a soul. Moreover, I entreated Sarojini to write no more about robins and skylarks, in a landscape of our Midland counties, with the village bells somewhere in the distance calling the parishioners to church, but to describe the flowers, the fruits, the trees, to set her poems firmly among the mountains, the gardens, the temples, to introduce to us the vivid populations of her own voluptuous and unfamiliar province; in other words, to be a genuine Indian poet of the Deccan, not a clever machine-made imitator of the English classics.

With the docility and the rapid appreciation of genius, Sarojini instantly accepted and with as little delay as possible acted upon this suggestion. Since 1895 she has written, I believe, no copy of verses which endeavours to conceal the exclusively Indian source of her inspiration, and she indulges with too enthusiastic gratitude the friend whose only merit was to show her "the way to the golden threshold." It has been in her earlier collections, and it will be found to be in this, the characteristic of Mrs. Naidu's writing that she is in all things and to the fullest extent autochthonous. She springs from the very soil of India; her spirit, although it employs the English language as its vehicle, has no other tie with the West. It addresses itself to the exposition of emotions which are tropical and primitive, and in this respect, as I believe, if the poems of Sarojini Naidu be carefully and delicately studied they will be found as luminous in lighting up the dark places of the East as any contribution of savant or historian. They have the astonishing advantage of approaching the task of interpretation from inside the magic circle, although armed with a technical skill that has been cultivated with devotion outside of it.

Those who have enjoyed the earlier collections of Mrs. Naidu's poems will find that in *The Bird of Time* the note of girlish ecstasy has passed, and that a graver music has taken its place. She has lived and this is another facet of her eminent career in close companionship with sorrow; she has known the joy and also the despair of consolation. The sight of much suffering, it may be, has thinned her jasmine-garlands and darkened the azure of her sky. It is known to the world that her labours for the public weal have not been carried out without deep injury to her private health. But these things have not slackened the lyric energy of Sarojini; they have rather given it intensity. She is supported, as the true poet must be, by a noble ambition. In her childhood she dreamed magnificently; she hoped to be a Goethe or a Keats for India. This desire, like so many others, may prove too heavy a strain for a heart that

s'ouvrit comme une fleur profonde
Dont l'auguste corolle a prédit l'orient.

But the desire for beauty and fame, the magnificent impulse, are still energetic within this burning soul.

These few words I venture to bring to a close with a couple of sentences from one of her own latest letters: "While I live, it will always be the supreme desire of my Soul to write poetry one poem, one line of enduring verse even. Perhaps I shall die without realising that longing which is at once an exquisite joy and an unspeakable anguish to me." The reader of *The Bird of Time* will feel satisfied that this her sad apprehension is needless.

## Poetry (essay date 1917)

SOURCE: A review of 'The Golden Threshold', in *Poetry: A Magazine of Verse*, Vol. X, No. 1, April, 1917, pp. 47-49.

[*In the following review of* The Golden Threshold, *the anonymous critic praises the volume not only for its contribution to Indian literature, but also its contribution to the further development of the English lyric verse.*]

Perhaps because one catches flame from Arthur Symons' beautiful introduction, through which shines the radiantly elusive personality of this young Hindu woman, these poems [in *The Golden Threshold*] are strangely alluring.

They are subtle, delicately-wrought lyrics, self-conscious with the same quiet poise that pervades the Hindu classics, a poise that disregards with mystic certainty the confusing sense of the plurality of the universe which colors so much western thinking, and finds in the simplicity which remains an essense of pure beauty. "We will conquer the sorrow of life with the sorrow of songs," sings the poet triumphantly in one of the most beautiful of these poems, and in the phrase sums up her dream.

The poems are rather unequal in poetic quality, but in the best of them, along with a true lyric cadence, burns an extraordinary vividness of feeling. In the following, called **"Ecstasy,"** this vividness mounts to what Symons happily calls an "agony of sensation":

Cover mine eyes, O my love!
  Mine eyes that are weary of bliss
As of light that is poignant and strong.
  Oh, silence my lips with a kiss,
My lips that are weary of song!

Shelter my soul, O my love!
  My soul is bent low with the pain
And the burden of love, like the grace
  Of a flower that is smitten with rain:
Oh, shelter my soul from thy face!

At times the poems are more strongly nationalistic. This, called **"Leili,"** might almost, in its color and imagery, be an incidental lyric in Kalidasa's *Shakuntala:*

The serpents are asleep among the poppies,
  The fireflies light the soundless panther's way

To tangled paths where shy gazelles are straying,
  And parrot-plumes outshine the dying day.
Oh, soft! the lotus-buds upon the stream
Are stirring like sweet maidens when they dream.

A caste-mark on the azure brows of heaven
  The golden moon burns sacred, solemn. Bright
The winds are dancing in the forest-temple,
  And swooning at the holy feet of Night.
Hush! in the silence mystic voices sing
And make the gods their incense-offering.

Mrs. Naidu has made in *The Golden Threshold* a really valuable contribution, not only to our understanding of the modern Hindu heart, but to the annals of the English lyric.

## James H. Cousins (essay date 1917)

SOURCE: "The Poetry of Saojini Naidu: A Critical Appreciation," in *The Modern Review*, Vol. 22, No. 4, October, 1917, pp. 410-16.

[*In the following essay, Cousins offers an appreciative overview of Naidu's work.*]

The almost simultaneous reception within the pale of English literature of two poets, Indian by ancestry and birth, and acutely Indian in conscious purpose Sarojini Naidu and Rabindranath Tagore is an event that offers a fascinating challenge to the student of literature. The challenge is capable, however, of only a partial acceptance: its full implications and significance remain for the disclosure of the future. One special circumstance in each case makes a complete study at present impossible: the chanting sage of Bengal is probably only *probably* beyond the period of his greatest utterance, but only a portion of his vast work has been put into English: we have, on the other hand, the complete expression of the Deccan songstress, but it is premature to regard it as her utmost. There is, however, a more radical difference between them: the work of Rabindranath, as it appears in English, is a translation, albeit done by the poet himself, and its title of poetry in the accepted technical sense is a courtesy-title given in recognition of an invincible spirit that sifts the essence of poetry through the medium of rhythmic prose: Sarojini's work is English poetry in form and diction, and, as an art, subject to all the laws and ordinances of that particular common instrument for the expression of individual souls.

If, however, we have still to wait for Sarojini's complete expression, there is beneath our hand sufficient work in quantity and kind to justify on a larger scale than a mere book review a study of her development to the point indicated in her new book, *The Broken Wing,* which has recently been published by William Heinemann of London. I have to confess that this book has disappointed me. It does not add, except in quantity, to the poetess' revelation: it goes no deeper and no higher than anything in her two previous books. In one respect, that is, in its preoccupation with love, it appears to go off into a *cul-*

*de-sac;* and in the pursuit of this particular phase of her art, she sometimes achieves something that is perilously like insincerity, and an emotional untidiness that too often knocks her art to pieces. For example, in **"The Time of Roses"**, she cries,

> Put me in a shrine of roses,
> Drown me in a wine of roses. . . . . .
> Bind me on a pyre of roses,
> Burn me in a fire of roses.
> Crown me with the rose of love.

It may be too much to expect sequence in so abandoned a mood, but the mind sees something unworthy of good art, or even of common sense, in burning a person after they are drowned, not to mention the difficulty of crowning a person who has been already reduced to ashes. This is bad enough in the matter of technique, but the emotional fault goes deeper still in a song, "If you were dead," an expression of love so devoted that the singer wishes to die with the object of her affection. Two excellent lines, purely Indian, and in the manner of the earlier Sarojini, are these:

> For life is like a burning veil
> That keeps our yearning souls apart.

They are followed by four lines in similar key, but of less power; but the song falls into the language and thought of the English ballad of the middle and late Victorian era of agnosticism relieved by sentimentality, an attitude foreign to Indian genius, and even in sharp contradiction, as we shall see, to the truer expression, of the poetess' real view of life and death:

> If you were dead I should not weep
> How sweetly would our hearts unite
> In a dim, undivided sleep,
> Locked in death's deep and narrow night.

Much nonsense is written in Western literary criticism about the relationship between art and philosophy; but the fact remains that violence done to a poet's philosophy will show itself in the poet's art. Our poetess has flung herself into an emotional exaggeration that obscures the clear vision of the spirit, and she pays the penalty in positive ugliness in **"The Pilgrim"**, in which slain deer are taken as "love's blood-offering"; and in **"Devotion"**

> Take my flesh and feed your dogs it you choose,
> Water your garden trees with my blood if you will.

Keats truly said that poetry should surprise by a fine excess. But there is a wide difference between an excess that makes itself felt in all phases of the poet's consciousness, and an *excessiveness* that expands one phase at the expense of others. The most indulgent criticism could hardly call such lines as I have quoted "fine" in the Keatsian sense; and it is not improbable that their redundant excessiveness is the complementary cause of such impoverishment of thought and figure as we find in

> Waken, O mother! thy children implore thee,
> Who kneel in thy presence to serve and

> adore thee!
> The night is aflush with a dream of the morrow.
> Why still dost thou sleep in thy bondage
>                     of sorrow?
> Awaken and sever the woes that enthral us,
> And hallow our hands for the triumphs
>                     that call us.
>                     . . . .

> Ne'er shall we fail thee, forsake thee or falter,
> Whose hearts are thy home and thy shield
>                     and thine altar.

There is not an atom of cerebral stuff in the lines: they are exclusively rhetorical, and in the *rumtity tumtity* measure of the poorest English minor poetry. They have the characteristic inconsistency of such verse, in which some kind of sentimental emotion takes the place of the backward and forward vision that links idea to idea; for they call on the mother, (that is, India,) to awaken and set the caller, (that is the people of India) free from their woes, while the caller professes to be the mother's shield. There is something very ineffective in a mother in a "bondage of sorrow" and her children bound in woes that enthral them.

When we place alongside such ill-done work, lines like these **"In Salutation to My Father's Spirit"**

> O splendid dreamer in a dreamless age,
> Whose deep alchemic wisdom reconciled
> Time's changing message with the undefiled
> Calm vision of thy Vedic heritage. . . . . .

and other lines that we shall quote later, we are moved to wish that the poetess would turn her attention deliberately to some theme that would call out her own "Vedic heritage" of wisdom and song. We are pernickety persons, we lovers of poetry, and we are disturbed when the beloved shows herself worse than her best. For our comfort we hang on to poems like **"The Pearl,"** which is as precious as its subject; to **"Ashoka Blossoms"** that defies analysis as the true lyric should; to **"June Sunset"** in its beautiful simplicity:

> A brown quail cries from the tamarisk bushes,
> A bulbul calls from the cassia plume,
> And thro' the wet earth the gentian pushes
> Her spikes of silvery bloom.
> Where'er the foot of the bright shower passes
> Fragrant and fresh delights unfold;
> The wild fawns feed on the scented grasses,
> Wild bees on the cactus gold. . . .

The mind turns also to many an arresting phrase in interpretation of Indian life and nature, such as the temple bells

> Whose urgent voices wreck the sky . . . .

or

> The earth is ashine like a humming bird's wing,
> And the sky like a kingfisher's feather.

To get the full flavour of the last two lines, some acquaintance with Indian atmosphere, with its amazing variety of vivid colours, is necessary: indeed, all through Sorojini's work there are many lines of delicate imaginative beauty that must remain unrifled treasuries to readers unacquainted with the East: for example,

> Were greatness mine, beloved, I would offer
> Such radiant gifts of glory and of fame,
> Like camphor and like curds, to pour and proffer
> Before love's bright and sacrificial flame.

To the untravelled Western reader, "camphor" as a figure of speech will carry queer shades of meaning built up out of clothing and moths; and "curds" will be flavorous only of dining rooms or convalescence. But one who has shared the offering of the substance of life to some Power of the inner worlds, or who has passed his hands through the smoke from camphor, that burns to nothing in token of the participant's desire to be lost in the flame of the Divine, will find through such figures an entrance to the strongest place in the life of India, the place of religious devotion and the perpetual Presence.

It is five years since Mrs. Naidu's previous book was published *The Bird of Time,* 1912. In prefacing the volume, Mr. Edmund Gosse declared that there was nothing, "or almost nothing," in the matured work of the author which the severest criticism could call in question. This is quite true, up to that point, and as we have performed the not very agreeable critical *dharma* of pointing out the subsequent development of the "almost nothing," we can now turn to the full enjoyment of the feast of song which the poetess of the Deccan has given to us in her first two books, *The Golden Threshold,* 1905, and *The Bird of Time.*

In his preface Mr. Gosse recounts how he induced the young Sarojini to scrap all her early imitations of English verse, and urged her to give "some revelation of the heart of India, some sincere and penetrating analysis of native passion, of the principles of antique religion, and of such mysterious intimations as stirred the soul of the East long before the West had begun to dream that it had a soul." So far, however, our poetess has not fulfilled all her counsellors request: she has not given *analyses* of passion or religion; but she has given something that the future may not consider less valuable; passion linked to all life, not merely to one of its phases; religion in action, not merely in theory. Mr. Gosse speaks of her "astonishing advantage of approaching the task of interpretation from inside the magic circle, although armed with a technical skill that has been cultivated with devotion outside of it." Let us consider her work in these two aspects, as Indian, and as literature.

We have already observed the escape of India through phrases and figures of speech. Here are a couple more:

> Why should I wake the jewelled lords
> With offerings or vows,
> Who wear the glory of your love
> Like a jewel on my brows. . . . . .

a reference to the "Festival of Serpents", and to the notion (which may be a fact for aught I know) that the king cobra carries a gem in his forehead. She has another poem directly on the same phase of India's religious life, without the human deflection of the foregoing:

> Swift are ye as streams, and soundless as the dew-
>     fall,
> Subtle as the lightning, and splendid as the sun;
> Seers are ye, and symbols of the ancient silence
> Where life and death and sorrow and ecstasy are one.

The last two lines form a clue to Hindu polytheism, and indicate the grasp of the spiritual unity behind the symbols, lacking which, slavery to the symbol which is the only real idolatry is inevitable. The hissing effect of the sibilants in each line is noticeable.

Besides these and many other, so to say, accidental revelations of India, Mrs. Naidu has given us a series of deliberate presentations of phases of Indian life that have come under her eye and touched her heart, and not the least successful are those that try to do no more than catch the simplest fancies or emotions of familiar scenes. **"Palanquin Bearers,"** for example, rests on no more substantial basis than the likening of a lady in a palanquin to a flower, a bird, a star, a beam of light, and a tear: there is not a thought in it: it is without the slightest suspicion of "literature", yet its charm is instantaneous and complete. **"Dirge"** so vividly expresses the sorrow of bereavement that a recent English critic mistook it as indicating that the poetess was a widow.

Indeed, in this latter respect, that is, in her expression of the feminine side of Indian life, our poetess brings us up at times against a threatened discussion of the problem of sex in poetry. We have to concede to her as much freedom to sing of human love from the woman's side as the poets have from the man's side. But there is a deeper aspect of the matter, an enlargement of consciousness beyond mere sex which strikes *poetry* from the best expressions of love, and without which so-called love-poems are merely poems *about* love. In the case of most masculine love-poetry there is an idealization of the object which, though in ironical contradiction to the facts of the marriage tie, is capable of influencing an adjustment of the facts "nearer to the heart's desire." But this is not the case with much of Mrs. Naidu's love poetry. We have already touched on one aspect of it in **"Devotion"**. Let us take another example, **"The Feast":**

> Being no scented lotus-wreath,
> Moon-awakened, dew-caressed;
> Love, thro' memory's age-long dream
> Sweeter shall my wild heart rest
> With your footprints on my breast.

Were this nothing more than a mood of the poetess we might accept it into memory, as we accept Dante Gabrielle Rosetti's love sonnets, as delightful and impossible. In the case of Mrs. Naidu's poem just quoted, this is not so: it is a reflection of the whole attitude and custom of Hindu Society in relation to its womanhood; and the above stanza, despite its delicate beauty or, rather, perhaps the more insidiously because of its beauty is a menace to the future of India, because of its perpetuation of the "door-mat" attitude of womanhood, which is at the root of India's present state of degeneracy through not only its direct enslavement of womanhood, but through its indirect emasculation of manhood, and the stultification of action for national freedom through the possession of a bad conscience as regards their own womankind.

It is curious to observe that while, in both her private and public life, Mrs. Naidu has broken away from the bonds of custom, by marrying outside her caste, and by appearing on public platforms, she reflects in her poetry the derivative and dependent habit of womanhood that masculine domination has sentimentalised into a virtue: in her life she is plain feminist, but in her poetry she remains incorrigibly feminine: she sings, so far as Indian womanhood is concerned, the India that is, while she herself has passed on into the India that is to be. It is not often in literature that an artist is in front of his or her vision: but it is safest to leave the artistic implications of the circumstance for the fuller illumination of future volumes.

It is in such poems as those just referred to that we find those flaws of structure and expression which suggest a not quite authentic inspiration, a mood worked up till it becomes hectic and unbalanced; but when she touches the great impersonalities she discloses a fine power of phrase, a clear energy of thought, a luminosity and reserve that reach the level of mastery. Such qualities are seen in the verses addressed **"To a Buddha Seated on a Lotus."**

> With futile hands we seek to gain
> Our inaccessible desire,
> Diviner summits to attain,
> With faith that sinks and feet that tire;
> But nought shall conquer or control
> The heavenward hunger of our soul.
> The end, illusive and afar,
> Still lures us with its beckoning flight,
> And all our mortal moments are
> A session of the infinite.

There you have the poetess rejoicing in the Shelleyan stretch of "inaccessible desire" and "heavenward hunger"; and there you have the *Indian* poetess, singing ostensibly of the Buddha, yet throwing the whole philosophy of the Vedanta into the last two lines.

There is another poem of Mrs. Naidu's that here challenges attention as a fitting link between this brief consideration of her work as *Indian* and a glance at her work as *literature*. It is **"Leili",** and it is in ***The Golden Threshold***. The first stanza paints a typically Indian evening, with fireflies, parrots, sunset, and suggestions of the untamed life of nature, all in an atmosphere of stillness. Then she sings:

> A caste-mark on the azure brows of heaven,
> The golden moon burns, sacred, solemn, bright.
> The winds are dancing in the forest temple,
> And swooning at the holy feet of night.
> Hush! in the silence mystic voices sing,
> And make the gods their incense offering.

The immediate parallelism of elements in nature and in Hindu religious observance recalls the similar and yet how temperamentally and racially different method of Francis Thompson in his "Orient Ode", in which the pageant of sunrise and the ritual of Catholic worship appear to be identical:

> Lo! in the sanctuaried East,
> Day, a dedicated priest,
> In all his robes pontifical expressed. . . .

and so on through detail after detail. The symbolism in Mrs. Naidu's poem of the dancing winds as devotees in the temple of nature must surely stand among the fine things of literature; still, good as it is, it is poor in comparison with the splendidly daring piece of anthropomorphosis of the first two lines. The figuring of the moon as a caste-mark on the forehead of heaven is in itself a unique achievement of the imagination in poetry in the English language. It lifts India to the literary heavens: it threatens the throne of Diana of the classics; it releases Luna from the work of asylum-keeper, and gives her instead the office of remembrancer to Earth that the Divine is imprinted on the open face of Nature. And how miraculously the artist makes articulate the seer, and reinforces vision by utterance! State the matter directly and simply, and as a figure of speech: "The moon burns (*like*) a caste-mark on the brow of heaven," and the meaning remains, but it is reduced to thin fancy. Now re-read the original: visualise the images in succession caste-mark, brows of heaven, moon: note the immense conviction that the absence of "like" gives, lifting the lines from cold symbolism to the level of imaginative truth that is the home of the myths of all races; and you have come within hailing distance of the secret of poetry. But that is not quite all. The pattern, of which Stevenson speaks in "The Art of Writing", is there, and is not less remarkable for its inclusion than for its omission; but a detail of the pattern takes us a step nearer the secret. The two words "golden moon" are a perfectly simple statement of the burnished yellow of the rising moon in certain states of the atmosphere. Put it thus: "The moon is the colour of gold," and it is true, but the truth depends on an act of memory; the moon herself is not present to the eye of the mind. But Sarojini's moon, through the very juxtaposition of the big vowels *oh,* and *oo* stands out ardent and palpitant, and makes the word "burn", which is false in fact as the moon only reflects, the one inevitable word to satisfy the imagination. We see the same effect in Thompson's lines which I have quoted, where, in the midst of a congregation of slender vowels, the priest enters in all the rotund importance of *oh, aw, ah* in "robes pontifical." Something is added to the effect of Sarojini's lines by the adverbs "sacred, solemn", ungrammatical though they be, by having their terminations docked but the effect passes, unfortunately, into a pale anticlimax in "bright", a little unnecessary dab of phosphorescence beside the golden burning moon. It is said that Sarojini in her youth had dreams of becoming an Indian Keats. In this particular item she has out-Keatsed her ideal; for while his "gibbous moon" *means* convexity, it has to reach the mind by way of the dictionary: it means, but does not *create* the spherical orb that Sarojini swings on a phrase into the firmament of the imagination.

It will take more evidence than is at present at our disposal, to enable us to decide whether or not we should have a grudge against our poetess for not giving us more of the joy of such a combination of truth, imagination, and art. I do not think her "caste-mark" is accidental: I think it is integral to her genius, and permanent; I think also that the emotional strain of much of her work, and a certain restriction of method, are also integral, but temporary. The passage of years will subdue flame to a steady glow, and bring reserve which is power in place of excessiveness which leads to exhaustion. But in the matter of her restricted method, it is fairly certain that deliberate effort is needed if she is to escape from ruts into which she tends to run. This tendency appeared early. **"Indian Weavers"** in *The Golden Threshold* weave (1) a childs' robe, (2) a marriage veil, (3) a funeral shroud. Corn Grinders tell of (1) a mouse, (2) a deer, (3) a bride, each of whom has lost her "lord". All through her three books we come across this habit of taking three aspects of a subject, and placing them in sequence, mainly without any vital unity, and hardly ever with any imaginative accumulation. Still, despite the mannerism, Mrs. Naidu has given us two haunting lyrics, both in *The Bird of Time.* My first contact with Mrs. Naidu's poetry was through hearing **"The Song of Radha the Milkmaid"** recited by a young Oxford man. I shall never forget the mantric effect of the devotee's repetition of "Govinda" as she carried her curds, her pots, and her gifts to the shrine of Mathura. The other is **"Guerdon,"** with its three refrains, "For me, O my master, the rapture of love!. . . . the rapture of truth!. . . . the rapture of song!" The objective may vary, but the rapture remains. It is not in the poetess to live at a lower degree; and in this particular case her energy has given us a song of the higher *kama* that will take its place among the lyrical classics. The poem justifies the method in its own case, but not for general application. Her metrical skill is capable of great variety. She gives us a specimen of Bengali metre reproduced in English:

> Where the golden, glowing
> Champak buds are blowing
> By the swiftly-flowing streams,
> Now, when day is dying,
> There are fairies flying
> Scattering a cloud of dreams.

Each line, save the last, has two alliteratives, and these with the repeated *O* in the first line, and the inter-linear rhyme of "flowing" in the third line, produce a haunting chime of bells and voices.

These things are, of course, the mere mechanics of poetry; still they contribute a very large element to the total effect, and may have a reflexive influence on the subtler elements for good or ill. In the matter of the thing said, as distinct from *how* it is said, we find the brain and the heart challenged by vibrant utterances from a will and an imagination that must surely triumph over recalcitrant emotion. Take a couple of examples of terse gnomic expression:

> To-day that seems so long, so strange, so bitter,
> Will soon be some forgotten yesterday.

That is an oft-sung truth stated with melodious and memorable newness. It is the passive aspect of

> Let us rise, O my heart, let us gather the dreams
> that remain.
> We shall conquer the sorrow of life with the
> sorrow
> of song.

In these two pairs of lines there is the acute touch of sorrow and struggle. Those who know something of the heroic battle that Mrs. Naidu has waged against physical debility know that she sings of what she has lived. She does not gloss the facts of existence. She gives this message to her children:

> Till ye have battled with great griefs and fears,
> And borne the conflict of dream-shattering years,
> Wounded with fierce desire and worn with strife,
> Children, ye have not lived: for this is life.

At the same time, from the point of view of literature, we have to ask if there is no glimpse of hope or of faith in a poet's work; for life in literature, as in life itself, is positive and joyful: negation and pessimism are rootless and without progeny. We have not far to go in Sarojini's poetry to find the thing of life. Up to the present it has eschewed the reinforcement of the intellect: it is as delicate as

> The hope of a bride or the dream of a maiden
> Watching the petals of gladness unfold,

and looks toward the

> . . . . . . timid future shrinking there alone
> Beneath her marriage-veil of mysteries,

(characteristic Sarojinian imagery); but it is there. We see it the thing of life in **"At Twilight: On the Way to Golconda,"** where the debris of history provokes the question:

> Shall hope prevail where clamorous hate is rife,
> Shall sweet love prosper or high dreams have
> place
> Amid the tumult of reverberant strife
> 'Twixt ancient creeds, 'twixt race and ancient
> race,
> That mars the grave, glad purposes of life,
> Leaving no refuge save thy succouring face?

Her answer is:

> Quick with the sense of joy she hath forgone,
> Returned my soul to beckoning joys that wait,
> Laughter of children and the lyric dawn,
> And love's delight profound and passionate,
> Winged dreams that blow their golden clarion,
> And hope that conquers immemorial hate.

It is further expressed in a spring song entitled **"Ecstasy"**:

> Shall we in the midst of life's exquisite chorus
> Remember our grief,
> O heart, when the rapturous season is o'er us
> Of blossom and leaf?
> Their joy from the birds and the streams let us
>                         borrow,
> O heart! let us sing.
> The years are before us for weeping and sorrow.

>                         . . . .

> To-day it is Spring!

I do not think our poetess has any need to borrow joy. The source of it is within herself in her grip of the fundamental verities that are hers by race and, I believe, realization. It is still as true as when Shelley uttered it, that "Our sweetest songs are those that tell of saddest thought"; but we are entering a new era in literature, at any rate in literature in the English language, in which the accent and joy of the spirit will be heard with increasing assurance and clearness. Certain of the younger poets have felt the first influences of the approach of that era, and their response has been made in attempted revolutions in the machinery of versification; but the real revolution is from within: it is a matter as much of eye as of ear, for poetry is compounded of both vision and utterance, and heretofore the ear of the world has been confused with noises because its eye has wandered from the centre. The "sorrow of song" will be no less, but it will take on a new tone: it will drop the harshness of frustration, the sharpness of regret: its cry will not be the cry of pain inflicted, which comes from uncontrolled nerves; it will be the cry of the intenser but less hurtful agony of bursting bonds; the growing pains of expanding consciousness, as joyfully painful as the spring, as exquisitely pregnant as the sadness evoked by a glorious sunset, which is not sadness, but the call and response of immortal beauty, without and within, across the intervening twilight of mortal mind.

Mrs. Naidu has staked her claim in the new fields of poetry. Her eye is on the centre, and the singing circumference of her sphere will yet adjust itself. All things are possible to one who can sing thus of "solitude" even with the faulty metaphor of gleaning a glimpse

> Or perchance we may glean a far glimpse of the
>                         Infinite Bosom
> In whose glorious shadow all life is unfolded or
>                         furled,
> Through the luminous hours ere the lotus of dawn
>                         shall re-blossom
> In petals of splendour to worship the Lord of the
>                         world.

To anticipate that glimpse is to experience it: to have found the place of reconciliation of beginnings and endings is to have touched the synthesis that is the genius of song.

Sarojini Naidu's poetry belongs to the romantic school, but it is the romance that in its most passionate mood leaves no ashes in the mouth. She has lingered, like "Laurence Hope," in "The Garden of Kama," but with larger eyes and a less heavy chin. She has not become, as Mr. Gosse says she hoped to become, "a Goethe or a Keats for India"; but she has succeeded in becoming a far more vital and compelling entity than a reflection: she has become Sarojini, with her own exquisite qualities, and with the not less interesting defects of those qualities. She has not yet shown signs of the constructive genius of either of her ideals: there is little "elevation" in the technical sense to the edifice of her song: it is an Indian bungalow with rooms opening off one another on the ground floor, not a New York sky-scraper; but she has already added to literature something Keats-like in its frank but perfectly pure sensuousness. Except in the use of a few conventional words, there is hardly any trace of derivative impulse in her work. She wrote to Mr. Arthur Symons long ago, "I am not a poet really. I have the vision and desire, but not the voice." Since then she has found increasing utterance; imagination and emotion interacting, sometimes separately, as in **"Indian Song"**; sometimes, as in **"Street Cries,"** giving life and its emotional accompaniment in a single artistic mould. It is because of the measure of unique accomplishment and optimistic prophecy that emerges from the most searching criticism of Mrs. Naidu's work that one feels a pang of regret to find from the daily newspaper that the flares of the public platform often lure her away from the radiance of her "moon-enchanted estuary of dreams." True, she is out for service to India at a time when it is urgently needed: she has questioned Fate as to whether she would fail ere she achieved her destined deed of song or service for her country's need, but while to those who cannot sing, there may be a distinction between song and service, such song as she has sung, and is capable of singing, is among the greatest and most essential gifts of service which she can render to her country and the world.

### *Poetry* (essay date 1929)

SOURCE: A review of 'The Sceptered Flute: Songs of India', in *Poetry: A Magazine of Verse,* Vol. XXXV, No. III, December, 1929, pp. 169-70.

[*In the following review of* The Sceptered Flute: Songs of India, *the anonymous critic notes that Naidu's poetry needs further development but nonetheless possesses the qualities of "high inspiration."*]

These songs of India [in **The Sceptered Flute: Songs of India**] have been transmuted into the language of the western world, and at first glance the imagery and allusions seem no more genuine than those which we have found in many English imitators of oriental mystery and glamour. But a more careful reading will show that behind these quiet reflective lyrics lies a profound native understanding of India, and a poetic insight which is capable of controlling many subtle aspects of mystical experience. The statements and analogies are always quiet, uneventful, subdued to nostalgic melancholy, and hinting most often of the Victorian style of lyric expression. But Madame Naidu shares with Tagore the power to use invocation and familiar references to love, death, sacrifice, etc., eloquently; while she has not achieved Tagore's broad oratorical massiveness or his fine spontaneity of expression, she strikes the key of real poetry too often to prevent our recognizing in her gentle art qualities of high inspiration.

## Mulk Raj Anand (essay date 1933)

SOURCE: "Sarojini Naidu," in *The Golden Breath: Studies in Five Poets of the New India,* John Murray, 1933, pp. 102-21.

[*In the following essay, Anand surveys Naidu's life and works.*]

Sarojini Naidu is affectionately called by her countrymen "the nightingale of India." A higher compliment than this, implied in the poetess's comparison with the celebrated bird that pervades the whole of Hindustani poetry, could not have been paid, and an apter nickname could hardly be imagined. For Sarojini sings of life as the bulbul of the rose, glorying in all its loveliness, longing to realise its many-coloured forms, and weaving melancholy strains about it when the cold, bare, stark brutality of death has robbed it of its warming glow. And although she has adopted a Western language and a Western technique to express herself, she seems to me to be in the main Hindustani tradition of Ghalib, Zok, Mir, Hali, and Iqbal.

Sarojini Chattopadhyaya was born at Hyderabad on February 13th, 1879, to Dr. Aghore Nath Chattopadhyaya and Shrimati Sundari Devi. Her father was descended from an ancient family of Chattorajes Brahmins well known for their patronage of art and literature throughout Bengal. Dr. Aghore Nath took the degree of Doctor of Science at the University of Edinburgh in 1877 and studied at Bonn. On returning to India he established the Nizam College, Hyderabad.

In her charming letters to Mr. Arthur Symons, the poetess has written about the early influences of her childhood. Here is how she came to write poetry:

"I don't think," she writes, "I had any special hankering to write poetry as a little child, though I was of a very fanciful and dreamy nature. My training under my father's eye was of a sternly scientific character. He was determined that I should be a great mathematician or a scientist, but the poetic instinct, which I inherited from him and also from my mother (who wrote some lovely Bengali lyrics in her youth), proved stronger. One day, when I was eleven, I was sighing over a sum of algebra: it *wouldn't* come right; but instead, a whole poem came to me suddenly. I wrote it down. . . . From that day my poetic career began."

In 1895 she came to England with a scholarship from the Nizam, and studied some time at King's College, London, and at Girton. And for a while she travelled in Italy. Her health broke down in 1898, however, and she returned to India in September to marry Dr. Naidu.

As we have seen from her confession, she had been writing verse ever since she was a child. But the circumstances which determined the character of her first considerable poetry happened during her stay in England. By a very strange coincidence, it was Sir Edmund Gosse, the discoverer of the genius of Toru Dutt, the first poet of the Indian renaissance, who discovered the genius of Sarojini Naidu; he "showed her" the way, as she has gratefully acknowledged, "to the golden threshold" of poetry. Gosse has told the story of his discovery in the memorable words of his preface to the second volume of Sarojini's poems:

> By some accident now forgotten, but an accident most fortunate for us Sarojini was introduced to our house at an early date after her arrival in London, and she soon became one of the most welcome and intimate of our guests. It was natural that one so impetuous and so sympathetic should long conceal from her hosts the facts that she was writing copiously in verse in English verse. I entreated to be allowed to see what she had composed, and a bundle of MSS. was slipped into my hand. I hastened to examine it as soon as I was alone, but now there followed a disappointment, and with it an embarrassment, which, in the light of what followed, I make no scruple of revealing. The verses which Sarojini had entrusted to me were skilful in form, correct in grammar, and blameless in sentiment, but they had the disadvantage of being totally without individuality. They were Western in feeling and in imagery; they were founded on reminiscences of Tennyson and Shelley; I am not sure that they did not even breathe an atmosphere of Christian resignation. I laid them down in despair; this was but the note of the mocking bird with a vengeance.

> It was not pleasant to daunt this charming and precocious singer by so discouraging a judgment; but I reflected on her youth and her enthusiasm, and I ventured to speak to her sincerely. I advised the consignment of all that she had written, in this falsely English vein, to the waste-paper basket. I implored her to consider that from a young Indian of extreme sensibility, who had mastered, not merely the language, but the prosody of the West, what we wished to receive was, not a mere réchauffé of Anglo-Saxon sentiment in an Anglo-Saxon setting, but some revelation of the heart of India, some sincere penetrating analysis of native passion, of the principles of antique religion, and of such mysterious intimations as stirred the soul of the East long before the West had begun to dream that it had a soul.

The result of the advice was wonderful.

> With the docility and the rapid appreciation of genius, Sarojini instantly accepted, and with as little delay as possible acted upon this suggestion. Since 1895 she has written, I believe, no copy of verses which endeavours to conceal the exclusively Indian source of her inspiration, . . . she springs from the very soil of India, her spirit, although it employs the English language as its vehicle, has no other ties with the West. It addresses itself to the expression of emotions which are tropical and primitive, and in this respect, as I believe, if the poems of Sarojini Naidu be carefully and delicately studied, they will be found as luminous in lighting up the dark places of the East as any contribution of savant or historian. They have the astonishing advantage of approaching the task of interpretation from inside the magic circle, although armed with a technical skill that has been cultivated outside of it.

Mr. Arthur Symons, in his beautiful introduction to the first volume of Sarojini's verse, *The Golden Threshold*, has also praised her for her Indianness. "They hint, in a delicately evasive way," he says, "at a rare temperament, the temperament of a woman of the East"; and he has epitomised the whole character of the poetess's life and work in the title of a charming little reminiscence in *Mes Souvenirs* "The Magic of the East."

One has only to open a volume of Sarojini's works to find confirmation for the testimony which the poetic insight of her two most distinguished critics has disclosed to us. I open the first volume, *The Golden Threshold*, and my eye is caught by the very first poem in it "Palanquin Bearers." Sarojini sees a palanquin passing out of the gates of Hyderabad. She does not actually paint a picture of the whole scene as she witnesses it, because she believes a palanquin to be one of those characteristically Indian things which may serve as an "open sesame" to the doors of India. But in order fully to appreciate the song, it should be placed in its proper setting. The splendour of the sun! The fragrance of spring! And the rich lap of earth basking under the glorious canopy of the heavens. And a palanquin passing out of the gates of Hyderabad! Hyderabad! that regal city of gardens and old palaces, where meet men of different religions, castes, and creeds, high and low, where the old-world nobles, in their rich garments of colourful silks set in gold and silver and rubies and sapphires, bend down from their mighty elephants to look kindly at a poor farmer's bullock-cart, or stop awhile to hold converse with a fakir for whom the goods of this world have no meaning, and who sits emaciated, naked, in the heart of the busy throng intent on life's end. Sarojini sees a palanquin passing through such a setting.

A newly wed bride perhaps is being borne away to the house of her lover, or a *houri* from a prince's harem is going visiting. The palanquin bearers burst out in song, to celebrate the poetry implicit in their vocation. They have woven many a song to recite on such occasions, songs which have passed into the inexhaustible store-house of the anonymous national verse of India. Each of them is a poet, and makes verse in his leisure hours to be sung during work-time. Or a new poem is composed during the journey. There are six of them bearing the palanquin. The headman in front sets a verse, the man next to him adds a second line to fit in with the first two, the third supplies another in tune with the first two, the fourth another, and so the fifth; the sixth completes the rhyme as well as the context. Then all of them sing it in a chorus as they run along the dusty road. Their song is caught by the passer-by, who hums it on his way home, and gives it as a gift to his friends on reaching his village or town.

William Morris once said that poetry should be something a man could sing to his fellows as he worked the loom. How truly the **"Palanquin Bearers"** satisfies that ideal of poetry may be obvious if I quote the poem:

> Lightly, O lightly we bear her along,
> She sways like a flower in the wind of one song,
> She skims like a bird on the foam of a stream,
> She floats like a laugh from the lips of a dream,
> Gaily, O gaily we glide and we sing,
> We bear her along like a pearl on a string.
>
> Softly, O softly we bear her along,
> She hangs like a star on the dew of our song,
> She springs like a beam on the brow of the tide,
> She falls like a tear from the eyes of a bride.
> Lightly, O lightly we glide and we sing,
> We bear her along like a pearl on a string.

But though the song incidentally justifies Morris's ideal, it was expressly designed to arrest the spirit of India for us, to catch the poetry and the music of it. If we are to avoid the injustice of an external criticism, therefore, it is in the direction of Sarojini's own ideal of poetry that we must search for a criterion to apply to her. What exactly is her ideal of poetry?

The answer to this question is nowhere specifically laid down by the poetess, but I should think it is possible to glean from the quivering pages of her verse, and from her confidences to Mr. Symons and Sir Edmund Gosse, a coherent enough statement of her views of poetry.

"In her childhood she dreamed magnificently," writes Gosse, recalling one of his conversations with her; "she hoped to be a Goethe or a Keats for India." "This desire, like so many others, may," he comments, "prove too heavy a strain for a heart that

> "S'ouvrit comme une fleur profonde
> Dont l'auguste corolle a prédit l'orient.

"But the desire for beauty and fame, the magnificent impulse, are still energetic within the burning soul."

Gosse's gracious way of putting the ambitious wish of Sarojini's juvenile days does not hide the fact that it was made in an ordinary conversational way without any serious realisation of its precise significance. The richness, the vitality, the exuberance of her lyrics, their burning, palpitating rhythm, passionately throbbing for loveliness, altogether different from Goethe's thoroughly intellectual poetry, may appear to approximate to Keats's early love of "glory and loveliness"; but if we accept the very profound interpretations offered by Mr. Middleton Murry, then the author of

> Beauty is truth, truth beauty that is all
> Ye know on earth and all ye need to know,

is an absolute idealist of the Hegelian sort, or a deep religious romanticist, rather than an hedonist racing for momentary emotion, whereas Sarojini lives on "her nerves of delight," and is stirred into song by the merest feeling certainly.

Her hedonism, however, is not of the ordinary Western kind. It is something more vital. Beginning her poetic career in the England of the nineties, she certainly acquired a taste for the kind of sensation that finds expression in the nice phrases of Mr. Symons and other followers of Swinburne. Suffering from ill-health, the love of ephemeral pleasure was engendered in her rather deeply.

"I too," she writes to Mr. Symons, "have learnt the subtle philosophy of living from moment to moment. Yes, it is a subtle philosophy, though it appears merely as an Epicurean doctrine: 'Eat, drink, and be merry, for to-morrow we may die.' I have gone through so many yesterdays when I strove with death that I have realised to its full the wisdom of that sentence; and it is to me not merely a figure of speech but a literal fact."

But against her "desire to be a wild free thing of the air like the birds with a song in my heart," is the deep-rooted pantheism of her inheritance. On Mr. Symons advising the publication of her first volume of verse she wrote:

"Is it possible that I have written verses that are filled with beauty; is it possible that you really think them worthy of being given to the world? You know how high my ideal of art is; and to me my poor casual little poems seem to be less than beautiful I mean, with that final enduring beauty I desire."

In another letter she writes: "I am not a poet really, I have the vision and the desire but not the voice. If I could write just one poem full of beauty and the spirit of greatness, I should be exultantly silent for ever; but I sing as the birds do, and my songs are as ephemeral."

In the light of this innate idealism which secretly sleeps in her, it would be unfair to call her a mere sensationalist. Omar Khayyámian romanticism seems to me to describe her poetry more aptly. The Oriental poets seem to oscillate between two aspects of the Universe they see around them. Asia is replete with colour and movement. Tints on which the eye never wearies of feasting, sounds that enchant the ear with their weird music, scents that with their luxurious balm ever renew man's zest to breathe life's breath. This loveliness, however, is the superficial aspect of the East. Beneath the surface there is something much deeper. The kaleidoscopic crowds who walk the narrow bazaars of its dream cities seem full of some secret joy; a sweet dignity, a patient resignation reigns about them, and gives to the worldly atmosphere in which they move an other-worldly look.

The Oriental poets sometimes paint the scene in the gayest of colours, at others they seek to arrest the slumbering spiritual numinous that enshrouds it. Living in the fiery emotionalism of an earthly life, the air of heaven hangs upon their words and gestures, waiting to be dragged into light to radiate its bright gleams of deep meaning and overloaded significance. The see-saw between these two dominating currents is seen most conspicuously in Omar Khayyám. In Rumi, in Hafiz, and in Jami, mysticism has got the ascendancy. Sa'adi too emancipates himself towards the end from the shackles of slavery to phenomena, and dedicates himself to the quest for eternal verities. Omar of the *Rubáiyát* lingers somewhere in the middle, inclining now to this side, now to that. Sarojini, who like most of the Hindustani poets is his true child, follows him implicitly. She is always painting lovely little miniatures in Omar's true Persian manner, creating a dream-world of fancy with endless microscopic strokes of the finest of fine brushes, occasionally rising to a conception of the divine, but mostly remaining a mere childlike romanticist.

As miniature paintings then must her poems be enjoyed. They reflect thought in terms of life life coloured and glorious. Seen from this point of view, I think, her lyrics are innocent of a false accent or a false emphasis.

"The people of the East," wrote E. G. Browne, the celebrated historian of Persian literature, "have much of the child's love of the marvellous; they like their kings to be immensely great and powerful, and their queens to be immensely, incomparably beautiful." There come to mind the beautiful panegyrics of the Persian court poets, and of Ghalib and Zok, who both served Bahadur Shah, the last of the Moghuls, whose genius for poetry was more profound than his ability to rule, and whose tragedy is the more poignant because, denied paper and ink, he described it in some of the most passionate verses in Hindustani literature on the walls of his prison house in Burma. Our poetess's ode to H.H. the Nizam of Hyderabad is inspired by the same sentiment, and since it is a definite proof of Persian and Urdu influences, I shall quote a stanza of the poem to illustrate its typically Oriental conceits. She addresses the Nizam:

> Sweet sumptuous fables of Baghdad,
> The splendours of your court recall!
> The torches of a *Thousand nights*
> Blaze through a single festival;
> And Saki-singers down the streets,
> Pour for us, in a stream divine,
> From goblets of your love *ghazals*
> The rapture of your Sufi wine.

If one misses here the absurd flights of fancy of an Hafiz, a Zok, or Ghalib, it is perhaps because Sarojini's enthusiasm for royalty has been partially dulled by her acquisition of Western democratic preferences; but there is enough of the Eastern panegyric in it to make it sound like an echo of those old times when, as the chroniclers tell us, kings would give away whole kingdoms for a song.

To see the poetess's romantic exuberance at its highest pitch of enthusiasm, however, one must turn to her treatment of life and nature in general. That she is a master of landscape painting is suggested by her letters to Mr. Symons. In one of them she writes:

"Come and share my exquisite March morning with me: this sumptuous blaze of gold and sapphire sky; the voluptuous scents of neem and champak and serisha that beat upon the languid air with their implacable sweetness; the thousand little gold and blue and silver-breasted birds bursting with the shrill of life in nesting time. All is hot and fierce and passionate, ardent and unashamed in its exulting and importunate desire for life and love. And do you know that the scarlet lilies are woven petal by petal from my heart's blood, these little quivering birds are my soul made incarnate music, these perfumes are my emotions dissolved into aerial essence, this flaming gold and blue sky is the 'very me,' that part of me which incessantly and insolently, yes, and a little deliberately, triumphs over that other part a thing of nerves and tissues that suffers and cries out, and that must die to-morrow perhaps, or twenty years hence."

Combined with this capacity to ally herself with the very spirit of her surroundings, is, of course, her gift of music, and her desire for beauty. And at their magic touch she is stirred into full-throated melodies about a fairy land in which each fruit, flower, and bird is a golden image of delight.

Sarojini revels in the charms of spring in many a rhyme scattered all over her words. In the volume, *The Bird of Time,* which takes its name from Omar Khayyám's verse:

> The bird of time has but a little way
> To fly . . . and lo! the bird is on the wing, ·

the spring is treated in a section by itself. *"The Golden Cassia," "Asoka Blossom," "The Call of Spring," "June Sunset,"* are perhaps the most beautiful among all her spring songs, and cry out for quotation. A stanza of the last may serve as a specimen:

> A brown koel cries from the tamarisk bushes,
> A bulbul calls from the Cassia plume,
> And through the wet earth the gentien pushes
> Her spikes of silvery bloom
> Whene'er the foot of the bright shower passes
> Fragrant and fresh delights unfold:
> The wild fawns feed on the scented grasses,
> Wild bees on the cactus gold. . . .

The desire for loveliness is inevitably related to love. So love too dominates Sarojini's mind very intensely. The intensity of this feeling in her is, I think, a blessing, for it helps her to steer clear of the pitfalls of sentimentalism into which lack of force may have led her rather dithyrambic voice. As a matter of fact, in her treatment of love she inclines very strongly to the profound idealistic side of her nature, and approaches nearest her ideal of great poetry as objective and impersonal, taking the form of contemplation, as if in prayer, on the very essence of love. The reason for this is perhaps that in regard to love her romantic Urdu and Persian precursors had learnt to be deeply religious. The loves of Laila and Mejnun, Khusrau and Shirin had formed the subject of epic poems by such deep poets as Nizami and Jami, and Maulana Jalal-ud-Din Rumi had used metaphors of ordinary human love to adumbrate the reality of Divine immanence.

In India, apart from the traditional love tales of the epopees, the *Ramayana* and *Mahabharata,* such local legends as Hir and Ranja, Sassi and Punnoo all sought to sanctify the human impulse, so that love of woman and love of God were synonymous. This holy view makes the lover potentially capable of being at the same time an ideal hero of romance, as well as a perfect saint, or endows him with the capacity to rise to the divine from the human without difficulty. In both states, however, whether human or divine, love in the East engrosses the lover's entire being. He has no use for the world, and lives merely for the realisation of his goal; and worldly goods, even food and drink, cease to have any use for him. He pines for union with the beloved, weeps, and spends himself in acquiring the gifts necessary for the achievement of his ideal. His only joy is in his misery, until Oneness with the beloved is realised. The following verses from Sarojini's **"Vision of Love"** reflect the everyday thoughts of Indian lovers:

> O love! my foolish eyes and heart
> Have lost all knowledge save of you,
> And everywhere in blowing skies
> And flowering earth I find anew
> The changing glory of your face,
> The myriad symbols of your grace.

The devotional love which possesses the hundreds and thousands who go to bathe in the Ganges and the Jamuna at Hardwar and Mathura respectively, year by year, finds expression in Sarojini through an ecstatic song put in the mouth of Radha for Krishna:

> I carried my curds to the Mathura fair. . . .
> How softly the heifers were lowing. . . .
> I wanted to cry, "Who will buy, who will buy
> These curds that are white as the clouds in the
>    sky,
> When the breezes of Shrawan are blowing?"
> But my heart was so full of your beauty, Beloved,
> They laughed as I cried without knowing,
>    Govinda! Govinda!
>    Govinda! Govinda!
> How softly the river was flowing!
>
> I carried my pots to the Mathura tide. . . .
> How gaily the rowers were rowing. . . .
> My comrades called, "Ho! let us dance, let us sing

And wear saffron garments to welcome the spring,
And pluck the new buds that are blowing!"
But my heart was so full of your music, Beloved,
They laughed as I cried without knowing,
　　Govinda! Govinda!
　　Govinda! Govinda!
How gaily the river was flowing!

I carried my gifts to the Mathura shrine. . . .
How brightly the torches were glowing. . . .
I folded my hands at the altars to pray,
O shining One guard us by night and by day
And loudly the conch shells were blowing.
But my heart was in your worship, Beloved,
They were wroth when I cried without knowing,
　　Govinda! Govinda!
　　Govinda! Govinda!
How brightly the river was flowing!

Here the poetry of romanticism, of ornate epithets and delicate similes, has become infused with transcendental experience. Sarojini has transformed love as personal desire into divine love, and given it a sense of eternity, of the Universal.

As in her treatment of love, so when she is oppressed by the finite character of life, perhaps because of the gravity of her theme, or perhaps because her enthusiasm for life has paled with the passage of time and given place to speculative interests, the idealist in her seems to dominate the romanticist. The expression too seems in her last two volumes to have become more skilful; there is a perfect fusion of conception and expression, and the philosophy of her race finds adequate utterance. Sarojini was early conscious of the fluctuations of human destiny, and convinced of the fickleness of fate. The Hindus are, one may say, born with such thoughts already in their minds, or they are early taught to think these thoughts as the poetess taught her own children:

Till ye have battled with grief and fears,
And borne the conflict of dream-shattering years,
Wounded with fierce desire and worn with strife,
Children, ye have not lived: for this is life.

So the nature of the goal of salvation to which she points becomes of utmost importance. Happily, Sarojini's inherited race-consciousness can be trusted to steer her course into the embrace of the true ideal:

Perchance we may glean a far glimpse of the
　　Infinite Bosom
In whose glorious shadow all life is unfurled
Through the luminous hours ere the lotus of dawn
　　shall re-blossom,
In petals of splendour to worship, the Lord.

In the following stanza, from the poem in **"Salutation of My Father's Spirit,"** her belief in the ideal of her ancient heritage is more adequately recognised:

Farewell, farewell, O brave and tender sage!
O mystic jester, golden-hearted child!
Selfless, serene, untroubled, unbeguiled

By trivial snares of grief and greed or rage;
O splendid dreamer in a dreamless age!
Whose deep alchemic vision reconciled
Time's changing message with the undefiled
Calm wisdom of thy Vedic heritage.

And in a poem, to the **"Buddha Seated on a Lotus,"** she brings home to us the entire mystery of the Absolute of Hindu thought and aspiration in the following two lines with skill and masterliness:

And all our mortal moments are
A session of the Infinite.

However, the full implications of the Hindu view of life remain yet to be worked out by Sarojini Naidu. The sombreness which pervades her last book is significant of her growth and development, and reflects a period of transition. She dedicated it "to the dream of to-day and the hope of to-morrow." Since that "to-day" (August 1916) there have been many "to-morrows." What beauty, what truth they have produced is not yet known. The cause of Indian nationalism has lain heavy on her heart, and the muses seem to have been out of favour. We shall eagerly await the day when, her political battles finished, she will return to the Infinite of her last-quoted poems: meanwhile we possess, in her **"Dreams of To-day and Yesterday,"** some of the most remarkable emanations of Indian romanticism.

## Jawaharlal Nehru (essay date 1949)

SOURCE: "Sarojini Naidu," in *Independence and After,* The Publications Division: Ministry of Information and Broadcasting, Government of India, 1949, pp. 399-403.

[*In the following essay, which was originally presented as a speech delivered at the Constituent Assembly in New Delhi on March 3, 1949, Nehru eulogizes Naidu, pointing out her social and political achievements.*]

It has been my painful duty, Sir, as Leader of this House, to refer from time to time to the passing away of the illustrious sons and daughters of India. Recently I referred to the passing away of a very eminent son of India, Sir Tej Bahadur Sapru. Then the Governor of a province suddenly died. He was a very distinguished servant of the State. When we refer to these distinguished sons or daughters of the country, we say often enough that it will be difficult to replace them, that they are irreplaceable, which may be true enough in a partial manner. But, to-day, I, with your leave, would like to refer to the passing away early yesterday morning of one about whom it can be said with absolute truth that it is impossible to replace her or to find her like.

She was for the last year and a half or a little more the Governor of a great province with many problems and she acted as Governor with exceeding ability and exceeding success as can be judged from the fact that every one in that province, from the Premier and his Ministers and

Government to the various groups and classes and religious communities down to the worker and the peasant in the field, had been drawn to her and had found a welcome in her heart. She had succeeded very greatly as a Governor and as a great servant of the State in an exalted position. But it is not as a Governor that I should speak much of her, for she was a much greater person than Governors are normally supposed to be. What she was exactly it is a little difficult for me to say, because she had become almost a part of us, a part of our national heritage of today and a part of us individuals who had the great privilege of being associated with her for a multitude of years in our struggle for freedom and in our work.

Sir, it is a little difficult to see persons, with whom you have been so closely associated, in proper perspective, and yet one can feel that to some extent. And thinking of her one sees a person to whom any number of epithets and adjectives might be applied. Here was a person of great brilliance. Here was a person, vital and vivid. Here was a person with so many gifts, but above all with some gifts which made her unique. She began life as a poetess. In later years, when the compulsion of events drew her into the national struggle and she threw herself into it with all the zest and fire that she possessed, she did not write much poetry with pen and paper, but her whole life became a poem and a song. And she did that amazing thing; she infused artistry and poetry to our national struggle. Just as the Father of the Nation had infused moral grandeur and greatness to the struggle, Mrs. Sarojini Naidu gave it artistry and poetry and that zest for life and indomitable spirit which not only faced disaster and catastrophe, but faced them with a light heart and with a song on her lips and smile on her face. Now, I do not think, being myself a politician which most of us are, that hardly any other gift was more valuable to our national life than this lifting it out of the plane of pure politics to a higher artistic sphere, which she succeeded in doing in some measure.

Looking back upon her life, one sees an astonishing combination of gifts. One, here is a life full of vitality; one, here are 50 years of existence not merely existence but a vital, dynamic existence touching many aspects of our life, cultural and political. And whatever she touched, she infused with something of her fire. She was indeed a pillar of fire. And then again, she was like cool running water, soothing and uplifting and bringing down the passion of her politics to the cooler levels of human beings. So it is difficult for one to speak about her except that one realizes that here was a magnificence of spirit and it is gone.

We shall, no doubt, for generations to come remember her, but perhaps those who come after us and those who have not been associated with her so closely will not realize fully the richness of that personality which could not easily be translated into spoken words or records. She worked for India. She knew how to work and she knew how to play. And that was a wonderful combination. She knew how to sacrifice herself for great causes. She knew also to do that so gracefully and so graciously that it appeared an easy thing to do and not anything entailing travail of spirit. If a sensitive person like her must suffer from the tremendous travail of spirit, no doubt she did, but she did it so graciously that it appeared that that too was easy for her. So she lifted our struggle to a higher plane and gave it a certain touch which I cannot think anybody else can give or is likely to give it in future.

Sir, I said she was a curious combination of so many things; she represented in herself a rich culture into which flowed various currents which have made Indian culture as great as it is. She herself was a composite both of various currents of culture in India as well as various currents of culture both in the East and the West. And so she was, while being a very great national figure, also truly an internationalist, and wherever she might go in the wide world she was recognized as such and as one of the great ones of the earth. It is well to remember that, especially today, when through stress of circumstances we may occasionally drift into a narrow nationalism and forget the larger objectives that inspired the great ones who laid the foundations of our national movement.

The great Father of the Nation and this great woman have shaped our national movement so powerfully, not so much on the direct political plane, although she was active there and adequately functioned, but in those invisible planes, which are so very important, because they shape the nation's character; because they mould ultimately its mental and aesthetic and artistic outlook; and without that mental, moral, aesthetic and artistic outlook, any success that we may gain may well be an empty success; because, after all, we seek freedom to gain which is good in itself, but we seek freedom to achieve something else. We seek freedom to achieve a good life for our people. What is a good life? Can you imagine any good life which does not have an artistic and an aesthetic element in it, and a moral element in it? That would not be a good life; it would be some temporary phase of existence, which would be rather dry and harsh, and unfortunately, the world grows drier and harsher and more cruel. In our own experience of the last two years, political life has become a little more harsh, cruel, intolerant and suspicious and in the world today we see suspicion and fear all round, fear of one another. How are we to get over this? It is only through some experience of moral heights that we might overcome it, and that was the way shown to us by the Father of the Nation, or else the other way is to approach it from the human point of view, from the artistic and aesthetic point of view, and the human point of view is the forgiving point of view, is the point of view full of compassion and understanding of humanity and its failings as well as its virtues. And so Sarojini brought that human point of view, full of understanding, full of compassion for all who are in India or outside.

The House knows that she stood more than any single human being in India for the unity of India in all its phases, for the unity of its cultural content, the unity of its geographical areas. It was a passion with her. It was the very texture of her life. It is well to remember, when we sometimes fall into narrower grooves, that greatness has never come from the narrowness of mind, or again, greatness for a nation as for an individual comes from a wide vision, a wide perspective, an inclusive outlook and a human approach to life. So she became an interpreter in India of the various phases of our rich cultural inheritance. She became an interpreter in India of the many great things that the West had produced, and she became an interpreter in other parts of India of India's rich culture. She became the ideal ambassador and the ideal link between the East and the West, and between various parts and groups in India. I do not myself see how we are to find the like of her now or in the future. We shall, no doubt, have great men and women in the future, because India, even when she was low in the political scale, had never failed to produce greatness in her children. And now that India is free, I have no doubt that India will produce great men and women in the future, as she has done in the past and in the present; before our very eyes, we have seen these great figures, and yet I doubt, while India produces great men and women, whether she will or can produce just another like Sarojini. So we think of her as a brightness, as a certain vitality and vividness, as poetry infused into life and activity, as something tremendously important and rich, and yet something which in terms of the material world is rather insubstantial, difficult to grasp and difficult to describe, as something which you can only feel, as you can feel beauty, as you can feel the other higher things of life. Maybe some memory of this will reach other generations who have not seen her and inspire them. I think it will, but I do not think they will ever feel it as we poor mortals have felt who had the privilege of being associated with her.

So, in making this reference to this House, I can only recount various ideas that come into my mind, and perhaps I recount them in a somewhat confused way, because my mind feels afflicted and confused as if an intimate part of it were cut off from it and because it is difficult to speak or to judge people for whom one has a great deal of affection. It was the affection of unity. It was the affection of one who even in his younger days was tremendously inspired by her speech and action and who during the succeeding decades grew more and more to love her and to admire her and to think of her as a rich and rare being. That rich and precious being is no more and that is sorrow for us, inevitably, and yet it is something more than sorrow. It is, if we view it in another light, a joy and triumph for us that the India of our generation produced such rare spirits as have inspired us and as will inspire us in the future.

Sir, it is customary when making such a reference to say that the sympathy and condolence of this House might be conveyed to the relatives of the person who has passed away. I say so and yet really the bond that held Sarojini to all of us here and to thousands and tens of thousands in this country was as close and great as the bond that held her to her own children or to her other relatives and so we send this message of condolence on behalf of this House. All of us really require that message ourselves to soothe our hearts.

## K. R. Srinivasa Iyengar (essay date 1962)

SOURCE: "Sarojini Naidu," in *Indian Writing in English,* Asia Publishing House, 1962, pp. 207-225.

[*In the following essay, Iyengar provides a biographical and critical sketch of Naidu.*]

Like Tagore and Aurobindo, Sarojini Naidu too was more than a poet; she was one of Mother India's most gifted children, readily sharing her burden of pain, fiercely articulating her agonies and hopes, and gallantly striving to redeem the Mother and redeem the time. It was as an English poet Sarojini Naidu first caught the attention of the public, but that was only the beginning. In course of time the patriot exceeded the poet, and Sarojini Naidu came to occupy some of the highest unofficial and official positions in the public life of India.

While it would perhaps be unwise to talk about her poetry without reference to her life, it would be no less unwise to talk at length about her life. Once she wrote to me: "Certainly, you have my blessings for writing about me and for quoting from my letters. But do you know much about me? So few even among those most intimate with me know little more than the bare facts and dates of my life". What really matters to a student of Sarojini Naidu's poetry is her "inner life", and this is largely a closed book to us. The "outer life" is for all to see, and as a last resort one starts guessing, which can be both fascinating and perilous!

Fifty-five years ago, when Sarojini Naidu made a trip to England in search of health, there took place between her and the great nationalist leader, Gopal Krishna Gokhale, this extraordinary conversation:

> Gokhale: Do you know, I feel that an abiding sadness underlies all that unfailing brightness of yours? Is it because you have come so near death that its shadows still cling to you?
>
> Mrs. Naidu: No, I have come so near life that its fires have burnt me.

Indeed, her whole life had been a battle and a struggle: she had to fight without remission the battle of her health, losing and winning and losing again; and she had to struggle long against the bludgeonings of circumstance, neither wincing nor crying aloud. Sunniness and sadness, life and death, victory and defeat early they set up their joint sceptre in her life, in her soul. As she cracked her jokes sparing none, the company invariably exploded in laughter; but how could they guess what was passing in the obscure infinities of her heart?

The girl Sarojini had been almost as tragically and radiantly wedded to pain and ecstasy as the wife and mother of a later day. "All the life of the tiny figure", wrote Mr. Arthur Symons picturing Sarojini at the age of seventeen, "seemed to concentrate itself in the eyes: they turned towards beauty as the sunflower turns towards the sun. . . . Her body was never without suffering, or her head without conflict: but neither the body's weakness nor the heart's violence could disturb that fixed contemplation. . . . " The eldest daughter (she was born on 13 February 1879) of a father who was a scientist-dreamer and a mystic-jester and of a mother who was half-angel half-bird, Sarojini Chattopadhyaya had commenced life at colourful Hyderabad in the most auspicious surroundings. A wide-eyed wonder-drunk childhood had slowly ripened into a girlhood of immeasurable potency and promise. At twelve she had passed the Matriculation, at thirteen she had composed an English narrative poem of about 2000 lines. And at fifteen she had glimpsed the Vision of Love, she had fallen madly in love with the young Dr. Naidu; she *would* marry him, so her trembling lips had affirmed, and would brook no argument. What were the parents to do? Permit the marriage, in defiance of caste and regional prejudices (Sarojini's parents were Bengali Chattopadhyayas, the young man was an Andhra and a Naidu)? It was not to be thought of and, besides, Sarojini was too young to marry, she was hardly more than a child, in fact! And so the distracted unhappy parents promptly shipped her off to England with a scholarship from the Nizam, hoping that the change of scene and the ardours of study would cure her of her violent insane passion. But they had reckoned without Sarojini's fiery-souled stubbornness, her great-hearted adamantine resolution. No wonder she struck Symons in the way she did, no wonder he felt that "this child had already lived through all a woman's life". The Vision of Love that had come so early to her in all its aching magnificence was not to be blotted out; other Visions the Vision of Faith, the Vision of the Mother, the Vision of Patriotism, the Vision of India the Mother might come later in their turn at the appropriate time; but, for the time being, Love filled the horizon of her consciousness. If, however, England did nothing to blur the Vision or displace it by another, it was nevertheless her English interlude her impressionable student days at King's College, London, and Girton College, Cambridge, and her early affiliations with Arthur Symons, Edmund Gosse, and some of the members of the Rhymers' Club that helped her to acquire the verbal and technical accomplishment, the mastery of phrase and rhythm, without which she could not have translated her visions and experiences into melodious poetry.

She had some pertinent counsel, too, from her friend Mr. Gosse. After reading her first poetical effusions, he felt that while she had no doubt a true poet's sensibility, she had been exercising it in a barren unprofitable way: "I implored her to consider that from an Indian of extreme sensibility, who had mastered not merely the language but the prosody of the West, what we wished to receive was, not a rechauffe of Anglo-Saxon sentiment in an Anglo-Saxon setting, but some revelation of the heart of India, some sincere penetrating analysis of native passion, of the principles of antique religion and of such mysterious intimations as stirred the soul of the East long before the West had begun to dream that it had a soul". It is fatally easy to lay too much stress on Gosse's advice. It is not always true that an Indian cannot write sensitively about robins and skylarks or about the English

landscape there is the poetry of Manmohan Ghose, for example, to prove that the feat is not impossible of accomplishment. All that we can ask is that the poet should indent on his own experience, not draw upon hearsay, and preserve a steadiness and intensity of vision without making compromises to mere convention. Besides, as regards the elemental emotions and passions that rock the human heart, they are the same everywhere. Nevertheless, in the given circumstances, there was point and urgency in Gosse's advice, and Sarojini was wise and resourceful enough to profit by it. She decided she would make a fresh start as a poet, and turned her mind inward as well as homeward.

Returning to India in September 1898, Sarojini Chattopadhyaya became, before the year was out, Mrs. Sarojini Naidu enacting (within limits) the role of an Indian Elizabeth Barrett Browning. The girl had become a wife, and she now readily surrendered herself to Love's consuming excess and Motherhood's privileged pains and joys. In quick succession were born Jayasurya, Padmaja, Ranadheera, and Lilamani to whom she addressed bright benedictory verses

> Golden sun of victory, born
> In my life's unclouded morn
> In my lambent sky of love . . .
> Sun of victory, may you be
> Sun of song and liberty.
>
> Lotus-maiden, you who claim
> All the sweetness of your name,
> Lakshmi, fortune's queen, defend you . . .
> Lotus-maiden, may you be
> Fragrant of all ecstasy.
>
> Lord of battle, hail
> In your newly-tempered mail!
> Learn to conquer, learn to fight
> In the foremost flanks of right,
> Like Valmiki's heroes bold,
> Rubies girt in epic gold . . .
>
> Limpid jewel of delight
> Severed from the tender night
> Of your sheltering mother-mine,
> Leap and sparkle, dance and shine,
> Blithely and securely set
> In love's magic coronet . . .

The roses of Dawn presently gave place to the stinging rays of the rising Sun; high-vaulting hopes flamed like rockets, swirled aloft in their dizzy eminence, and suddenly dashed upon the earth. But let Mrs. Naidu tell the story in her own bitter-sweet words

> So the ardent years of her childhood had fled away
> in one swift flame of aspiration; and the lyric child
> had grown into the lyric woman. All the instincts of
> her awakening womanhood for the intoxication of
> love and the joy of life were deeply interfused with
> the more urgent and intimate need of the poet-soul
> for a perfect sympathy with its incommunicable vision,
> its subtle and inexpressible thought . . .

And the dreamer so insatiable for immortality, who
was a woman full of tender mortal wants, wept
bitterly for her unfulfilled inheritance of joy.

Must joy lure one with its soap-bubble brilliance and
crash in its fragility at the very first touch? Must love die
of its own satiety? Must one's soul be

> bent low with the pain
> And the burden of love like the grace
> Of a flower that is smitten with rain?

As Keats moaned, Aye, at the very Temple of Delight
"veiled Melancholy hath her sovran shrine". Life is indeed a shot-silk pattern of tears and laughter, agony and
ecstasy; and so Mrs. Naidu gently insinuated the warning

> Children, ye have not lived, to you it seems
> Life is a lovely stalactite of dreams,
> Or carnival of careless joys . . .
>
> Children, ye have not lived, ye but exist
> Till some resistless hour shall rise and move
> Your hearts to wake and hunger after love
> And thirst with passionate longings for the things
> That burn your brows with blood-red sufferings.
>
> Till ye have battled with great grief and fears,
> And borne the conflict of dream-shattering years,
> Wounded with fierce desire and worn with strife,
> Children, ye have not lived: for this is life.

Mrs. Naidu, however, was not the woman to give way altogether to gnawing regrets or paralysing despair. She was
still largely a creature of emotion and memory who sensed
beauty in colour and odour and song and movement. The
panorama of India's ageless life fascinated her without end.
Hard labour is the lot of the masses in India, but what has
made this life bearable and occasionally even enjoyable is
the stimulus given by songs and jokes and rhythmic movements. In some of her early poems Sarojini Naidu has tried
to catch and reproduce in English the lilt and atmosphere of
some of these folk-songs. Thus the Palanquin-Bearers

> Lightly, O lightly, we bear her along,
> She sways like a flower in the wind of our song;
> She skims like a bird on the foam of a stream,
> She floats like a laugh from the lips of a dream,
> Gaily, O gaily we glide and we sing,
> We bear her along like a pearl on a string . . .

Thus the Wandering-Singers

> Our lays are of cities whose lustre is shed,
> The laughter and beauty of women long dead;
> The sword of old battles, the crown of old kings,
> And happy and simple and sorrowful things . . .

And the Indian Weavers sing that, at break of day, they
weave the robes of a new-born child, at fall of night a
queen's marriage-veils, and, in the moonlight chill, "a dead
man's funeral shroud". How succinctly is human life summarized here! The song of the Coromandel Fishers has a
more sinuous long-drawn quality appropriate to the theme

> Sweet is the shade of the coconut glade, and the
>   scent of the mango grove,
> And sweet are the sands at the full o' the moon
>   with the sound of the voices we love.
> But sweeter, O brothers, the kiss of the spray and
>   the dance of the wild foam's glee:
> Row, brothers, row to the blue of the verge, where
>   the low sky mates with the sea.

The appositeness of the sentiments and imagery and the
perfect management of the rhythm and the internal and ter-
minal rhymes have made this song of three stanzas one of
the most popular of Sarojini Naidu's poems. And so, with
the Snake-Charmer, the Corn-Grinders, the Indian Dancers
and the Bangle-Sellers. No room for obscurity or profundity
here; simplicity and directness are sovereign, and the appeal
is the appeal of the old, the unfading, the undying.

Nature too attracted Sarojini Naidu, and she sang in
praise of Henna

> But, for lily-like fingers and feet,
> The red, the red of the henna-tree

and of harvest-sights and warbling birds and nightfall in
her city, of nasturtiums and lotus lilies and champak blossoms. She also dived into history and legend and rescued
pearls of great price and set them on the glistering foil of
her poetry. **"Humayun to Zobeida",** though an adaptation from the Urdu, is excellent in its kind

> You flaunt your beauty in the rose, your glory in
>   the dawn,
> Your sweetness in the nightingale, your whiteness
>   in the swan.
> You haunt my waking like a dream . . .
> Yet, when I crave of you, my sweet, one tender
>   moment's grace,
> You cry, *"I sit behind the veil; I cannot show my
>   face"* . . .
> What war is this of *Thee* and *Me?* Give o'er the
>   wanton strife,
> You are the heart within my heart, the life within
>   my life.

Or this from the Persian, Princess Zeb-un-nissa singing in
praise of her own beauty, the last of three beautiful stanzas

> And, when I pause, still groves among,
> (Such loveliness is mine) a throng
>   Of nightingales awake and strain
> Their souls into a quivering song.

And always she seemed to sing as birds do, with scarce an
effort; but occasionally she also touched her songs with
something of the "still sad music of humanity, not harsh nor
grating, though of ample power to chasten and subdue".
Fresh-firecoal glints, the light in the shade, the spots on the
Sun, she uncannily sensed them, and not seldom she shot a
revealing light on hidden or half-hidden essences, or, in Mr.
K. D. Sethna's phrase, on "realities not quite of the earth
earthy". She could sum up tragedy in two pitiless lines

> Who shall prevent the subtle years,
> Or shield a woman's eye from tears?

She could galvanize into life with the power of her words the swaying and the heaving, the flush and the fire, of the Indian Dancers

> The scents of red roses and sandalwood flutter and
>     die in the maze of their gem-tangled hair,
> And smiles are entwining like magical serpents
>     the poppies of lips that are opiate sweet . . .
> Now silent, now singing and swaying and
>     swinging like blossoms that bend to the
>     breezes or showers,
> Now wantonly winding, they flash, now they
>     falter, and, lingering, languish in radiant choir;
> Their jewel-girt arms and warm, wavering, lily-
>     long fingers enchant through melodious hours,
> Eyes ravished with rapture, celestially panting,
>     what passionate bosoms aflame with fire?

But the most notable of her early poems was **"To a Buddha Seated on a Lotus",** in which the fever of regret and the fervour of longing fused at last into marble strength and mystic rapture

> For us the travail and the heat,
> The broken secrets of our pride,
> The strenuous lessons of defeat,
> The flower deferred, the fruit denied;
> But not the peace, supremely won,
> Lord Buddha, of thy Lotus-throne.
>
> With futile hands we seek to gain
> Our inaccessible desire,
> Diviner summits to attain,
> With faith that sinks and feet that tire . . .
> How shall we reach the great, unknown
> Nirvana of thy Lotus-throne?

*The Golden Threshold,* Sarojini Naidu's first collection of poems, came out in 1905. The papers were enthusiastic. "This little volume should silence for ever the scoffer who declares that women cannot write poetry", so wrote the *Review of Reviews;* "Her poetry seems to sing itself as if her swift thoughts and strong emotions sprang into lyrics of themselves", cooed *The Times;* and the *Glasgow Herald* made an important point: "The pictures are of the East it is true: but there is something fundamentally human in them that seems to prove that the best song knows nothing of East or West". As a poet, then, Sarojini Naidu had definitely arrived. In India she was hailed as the Nightingale of Indian song, and J. B. Yeats's portrait of her made her a figure of pure romance. She emerged from seclusion, and she appeared on the Congress platform. The times too those were the days of *Bandemataram* were propitious for her entry into politics, and she moved among leaders a leader, lending colour and music and humour and vivacity to their meetings. In 1906, at the Calcutta session of the Indian Social Conference, she adroitly linked up the suppression of women's rights in India with the loss of the country's freedom

> Does one man dare to deprive another of his
> birthright to God's pure air which nourishes his
> body? How then shall a man dare to deprive a
> human soul of its immemorial inheritance of liberty

and life? And yet, my friends, man has so dared in the case of Indian women. That is why you men of India are today what you are: because your fathers, in depriving your mothers of that immemorial birthright, have robbed you, their sons, of your just inheritance. Therefore, I charge you, restore to your women their ancient rights . . .

Gokhale was touched, and he sent this pencilled note to her: "Your speech was more than an intellectual treat of the highest order. It was a perfect piece of art. We all felt for the moment to be lifted to a higher plane". On another occasion he said: "You begin with a ripple and end in eternity". As a general rule, Sarojini's orations seemed thus to soar high above the humdrum, and she herself would often appear, not only to glow with passion, but also literally to rise in stature. A typical Sarojini speech especially in the days of her active participation in the politics of the Gandhian era would be a flood of splendid improvisation, endowed with an oceanic movement, wave upon wave of emotion and sentiment surging and subsiding, each wave immenser and more long-drawn-out than its predecessor, shriller in tone and more overwhelming in effect. Professor Amalendu Bose has thus described in vivid terms one of her great perorations

> For nearly a quarter of an hour, she spoke on the
> glories of poetry, its origin in the primordial spirit
> of man, its infinite variety, its pangs and ecstasies,
> all in a single sentence. And what a sentence! The
> words gushed out of her mouth in a ceaseless flow,
> clause succeeding clause to a richer and richer
> effect. The speaker no longer seemed to be a mortal
> woman; she became transfigured into a resplendent
> personage of a magic world from where the
> astonishing words flowed.

As she warmed up, her eyes acquired a lustre and sparkled more and more; every feather bristled, she was audaciously, imperiously alive. And when she resumed her seat at last, once again she was what Mr. John Gawsworth found her to be "a sigil of honour"; and yet, a random unpredictable moment, and there was the Order and the Star

> In one fast falcon-flash
> Of her vital and vigilant kind eyes.

Sarojini Naidu's second volume of poems, *The Bird of Time,* came out in 1912. In his Foreword to the book, Edmund Gosse remarked that there was discernible in it "a graver music" than in the earlier volume. These are "songs of life and death" life is often brightly painted, but death's shadows creep or linger. The Bird of Time like Galsworthy's Cethru is impartial and sings gay and sad songs alike

> Songs of the glory and gladness of life,
> Of poignant sorrow and passionate strife,
> And the lilting joy of the spring;
> Of hope that sows for the years unborn,
> And faith that dreams of a tarrying morn,
> The fragrant peace of the twilight's breath,
> And the mystic silence that men call death.

There are love-songs, there are also dirges and elegies. Spring inspires her to song, but even as she thrills at the thought of the Festival of Spring, *Vasant Panchami,* her compassionate heart rues the plight of the Hindu widow who has no part in the festive ceremonials

> *Hai!* what have I to do with nesting birds,
> With lotus-honey, corn and ivory curds,
> With plantain blossom and pomegranate fruit,
> Or rose-wreathed lintels and rose-scented lute,
> With lighted shrines and fragrant altar fires,
> Where happy women breathe their hearts' desires?
>
> For my sad life is doomed to be, alas,
> Ruined and sere like sorrow-trodden grass . . .
> Akin to every lone and withered thing
> That hath foregone the kisses of the spring.

Two of the songs are entitled respectively **'Love and Death'** and **'Death and Life';** and the Lord's only assurance is

> *Life is a prism of My light,*
> *And Death the shadow of My face.*

***The Bird of Time*** was greeted by the reviewers as enthusiastically as the earlier volume. "She has more than a profusion of beautiful things", wrote Edward Thomas in the *Daily Chronicle;* "She possesses her qualities in heaped measure", declared *The Bookman;* and the *Yorkshire Post* acknowledged that "Mrs. Naidu has not only enriched our language but has enabled us to grow into intimate relation with the spirit, the emotions, the mysticism and the glamour of the East". The poems comprise the dualities of life and death, joy and pain, and the music is 'graver', but as yet no chord has snapped, and the poet can still claim as her 'guerdon'

> For me, O My Master,
> The rapture of Love! . . .
> The rapture of Truth! . . .
> The rapture of song!

The change in note, however, is sharper in Sarojini Naidu's third and final collection, ***The Broken Wing,*** which was published in 1917. The memorial verses addressed to her father and to Gokhale are nobly articulate. Thus in salutation of her father

> O splendid dreamer in a dreamless age
> Whose deep alchemic vision reconciled
> Time's changing message with the undefiled
> Calm wisdom of thy Vedic heritage!

**'The Flute-Player of Brindaban'** is a jewel of a lyric, comparable only to **'To a Buddha Seated on a Lotus'.** Even as Western poets and artists are for ever trying to picture the face of Jesus or the Madonna, Indian poets and artists have found the Buddha and Lord Krishna a perennial challenge to their imagination. In the caves at Ajanta, the Buddha is the ceaseless inspiration for the artist a challenge as well as an inspiration. How is the artist to convey the whole arc of the Buddha's great com-passion for all? Likewise, how is the artist to convey the power of Krishna's flute-playing to draw all towards him? Like the Hound of Heaven, Krishna's music too gives one no respite, no escape

> Why didst thou play thy matchless flute
>  'Neath the Kadamba tree,
> And wound my idly dreaming heart
>  With poignant melody,
> So where thou goest I must go,
>  My flute-player, with thee? . . .
>
> To Indra's golden-flowering groves
>  Where streams immortal flow,
> Or to sad Yama's silent Courts
>  Engulfed in lampless woe,
> Where'er thy subtle flute I hear
>  Beloved, I must go!

Among the other poems are **'The Lotus',** addressed to M. K. Gandhi, and **'Awake',** addressed to M. A. Jinnah, the Mahatma and the Qaid-e-Azam of the future! But what, in fact, is most characteristic in the volume is the intermittent subterranean rumbling, the pitiless evocation of broken images, the pointed rendering of naked beauty and truth and ferocity in the last section, **"The Temple: A Pilgrimage of Love,"** a trilogy of lyric sequences, each of eight poems. An Indian critic, Mr. R. G. Rajwade, sees in the trilogy "more rhetoric than poetry . . . more violence than strength". On the other hand, Mr. Gawsworth rightly declares that **"The Temple"** is Saro-jini Naidu's "greatest regulated success. . . . Apart from Mrs. Browning's *Sonnets from the Portuguese,* I know of no poetical sequence in English of such sustained passion addressed by a woman to a man". Gokhale himself had once remarked: "It was no doubt a brave and beautiful speech, but you sometimes use harsh, bold phrases"; and in several of the pieces in ***The Broken Wing*** and not alone in the **"Temple"** section she would appear to have conveyed both beauty and boldness, both the bite of anger and the heat of passion. The words 'break', 'broke', and 'broken' recur again and again, and hammer their meaning into our hearts. The vicissitudes of the poet's "pilgrimage of love" petrify us into awed attention. The glow, the surrender, the ecstasy; the recoil, the resentment, the despair; the reaction, the abasement, the acceptance all are here. The flame of the resentment shoots up like mercury as the heat of the frenzy rages, and the instrument itself seems to burst with a bang

> Why did you turn your face away?
>  Was it for love or hate? . . .
> Still for Love's sake I am foredoomed to bear
> A load of passionate silence and despair . . .

The first section of the trilogy describes love's early fulfilment and is named **'The Gate of Delight'.** There is evidently a year's separation between the lovers, and when she comes back to her husband, he turns his face away. For a time, the woman suffers silently. Presently, however, her resentment wells up and **'The Menace of Love',** the third poem in the second section, blazes with almost a Donne-like fury of vindictiveness

The tumult of your own wild heart shall smite you
With strong and sleepless pinions of desire,
The subtle hunger in your veins shall bite you
With swift and unrelenting fangs of fire.

When youth and spring passion shall betray you
And mock your proud rebellion with defeat,
God knows, O Love, if I shall save or slay you
As you lie spent and broken at my feet!

In the fifth poem **'If You were Dead',** she says that his death would seal their difference, and she should therefore welcome his death! In **'Supplication'** she softens and almost invokes his "atoning mercy"

Restore me not the rapture that is gone,
The hope forbidden and the dream denied,
The ruined purpose and the broken pride . . .
Grant in the brief compassion of an hour
A gift of tears to save my stricken soul!

Her pleadings are in vain; he is the "slayer", and denied love, she is already dead

They come, sweet maids and men with shining
   tribute,
Garlands and gifts, cymbals and songs of praise . . .
How can they know I have been dead, Beloved,
  These many mournful days?

He has crushed her soul under his feet, her heart has been flung "to serve wild dogs for meat"; the tragic "secret" of her life is that she is dead, although seemingly alive. The third section, **'The Sanctuary',** attempts a kind of resurrection after the death described in the second section. What is sundered will one day be joined again. Love will transcend present woes and prove triumphant in the long run. In any case, resentment is pointless, and acceptance is the only sane answer to the situation. She will not complain any longer, she will neither cherish hope nor quite give way to despair. She will return to her old adoration, asking nothing and expecting nothing; she is his to do what he likes

Strangle my soul and fling it into the fire!
Why should my true love falter or fear or rebel?
Love, I am yours to lie in your breast like a flower,
Or burn like a weed for your sake in the flame of
   hell.

What are we to make of this group of 24 lyrics? Is it the description of an imaginary situation, or is it in some measure at least the lacerating recordation of a personal experience? The entire collection, *The Broken Wing,* is strewn with suggestions of a sudden distress that has overwhelmed the poet. Even the coming of Spring is no solace

O Sweet! I am not false to you
 Only my weary heart of late
 Has fallen from its high estate
Of laughter and has lost the clue
To all the vernal joy it knew . . .

I buried my heart so deep, so deep,
Under a secret hill of pain,
And said: "O broken pitiful thing,
Even the magic spring
Shall ne'er wake thee to life again . . ."

"Who cares if a woman's heart be broken?" *"O let my Love atone . . . O let my Death atone!"* "Welcome, O fiery Pain!" In a single poem, also entitled **'The Temple',** the Pilgrim answers in reply to the Priest

*O priest! only my broken lute I bring*
*For Love's blood-offering!*

There is no mistaking the agony behind these cries. The poet almost feels like Othello that her "occupation is gone"!

One thing is clear: *The Broken Wing* was Sarojini Naidu's last collection of poems. She lived for another 32 years, but as a poet she ceased to be. It was not because she suddenly realized that one should write only in one's mother tongue hers was Bengali or Urdu and since she hadn't the requisite mastery of it, she gave up the profession of poetry. Neither was it because she realized at last that her poetical language, fashioned in the nineteen nineties under the shadow of the exoticism of Symons, Dowson, Richard la Galliene and the rest, was a mere tinsel, and quite unequal to the demands made upon it by a real poetic inspiration. It was not even because of her entry into politics, for she had been in it for over ten years without damaging her poetic inspiration. We are therefore driven to the conclusion that what had made her poetry possible and indeed inevitable, what had been its main sustenance, the fire that had kindled her words into life had been suddenly extinguished; and, after the final defiant flicker that was *The Broken Wing,* the poet had no desire to live or found no means of living. The woman, the mother, the patriot remained; but the poet was now no more than a memory.

But there was a resurrection all the same. With the arrival of Mahatma Gandhi on the political scene, Sarojini Naidu found a new power to galvanize her to life. It was an age of heroic striving, an age of imperatives and absolutes. She looked into her bruised and broken heart once more and saw there a new Vision the Vision of the chained Mother and vowed to break the bonds. "My woman's intelligence", she once remarked, "cannot grapple with the transcendent details of politics". But love of the Mother was no abstruse science, and therefore for Sarojini Naidu politics was but a form of love, and sedition but a form of poetry. The new lover expressed herself in inspiring oratory and fearless action. She presided over the Congress in 1925; she defied the bureaucracy at Dharasana in 1930, as if she were the Maid of Orleans come back to life; she got her "pension and peerage" and went cheerfully to prison. She had said in 1917: "What though there be no pilot to our boat? Go, tell them we need him not. God is with us, and we need no pilot". Her assurance was all the greater when the nation found in the Mahatma its destined pilot at last. And so through fair weather and foul, in strength and in frailty, Sarojini Naidu kept faith with her leader till the very hour of his martyrdom and beyond! Who can forget her fierce ringing words over the air, those words of terror and pity, those challenging words which seemed to pluck even from the nettle, Disaster, the flower, Hope? Her own death soon followed on 3 March 1949, and Nehru as Prime Minister then paid this fitting tribute to her in the Constituent Assembly:

> She began life as a poetess. In later years, when the compulsion of events drew her into the national struggle and she threw herself into it with all the zest and fire she possessed, she did not write much poetry with pen and paper but her whole life became a poem and a song. . . . Just as the Father of the Nation had infused moral grandeur and greatness into the struggle, Mrs. Sarojini Naidu gave it artistry and poetry and that zest for life and indomitable spirit which, not only faced disaster and catastrophe, but faced them with a light heart and with a song on the lips and a smile on the face.

"Her work has a real beauty", said Sri Aurobindo in 1935 about Sarojini Naidu's poetry; "Some of her lyrical work is likely, I think, to survive among the lasting things in English literature and by these, even if they are fine rather than great, she may take her rank among the immortals". On the other hand, in recent years it has become the fashion to denigrate Sarojini Naidu as no poet at all, or rather as a very bad poet. (Of course, she is in good company; Toru is with her; and so are Tagore and Sri Aurobindo!) So tyrannical is this fashion, so vociferous are the fashion-mongers, that Dr. Shankar Mokashi-Punekar has to begin his recent appreciative essay on a defensive note: "For a practising poet, to write on Sarojini Naidu with an old-world enthusiasm is a business liability". The gravamen of the charge against Sarojini Naidu is that she didn't write like Eliot or Pound; she didn't go on writing even like herself. Her poems are immediately intelligible; they rhyme and they scan; there is no ruggedness in their phrasing; they have a feeling for place, occasion and atmosphere; they have rhythmic variety and melodic richness. But, then, they are not weighted with obscurity, nor knotted with contortions, nor peppered with punctuational or typographical acrobatics. Familiar, traditional, often rhetorical, often sentimental, sometimes obvious; unattractive to the new criticism, unrewarding to Freudian exploration, unresponsive to 'commitment' aesthetics: what's the use of Sarojini's poetry, then?

In the four published volumes, there are about 200 songs and lyrics. Many of them just sing themselves out, thereby gently warding off all attempts at surgical analysis. **'Cradle-Song'** (in *The Golden Threshold*) and **'Child Fancies'** (in the posthumous collection, *The Feather of the Dawn*) are equally poems for children; and children do enjoy them even if adults (oppressed by their sense of mission) cannot:

> From groves of spice
> O'er fields of rice
> Athwart the lotus-stream,
> I bring for you,

Aglint with dew
A little lovely dream . . .

> When the silver sunbeams call,
>   Dragonfly, dragonfly,
> To bumble bees and humming birds,
>   I wonder as you shy
>   In such a crowd to spread
>   Your wings of green and red
> And go gathering lotus honey
>   From the pools, dragonfly?

You don't dissect Keats's 'There was once a naughty boy . . .', and neither should we these songs for children.

Sarojini Naidu loved her native Hyderabad, and she was not afraid to make music out of her fascination for bazaars in the city and the bustling tradesmen and the variegated merchandise:

> What do you weigh, O ye vendors?
> Saffron and lentil and rice.
> What do you grind, O ye maidens?
> Sandalwood, henna, and spice.
> What do you call, O ye pedlars?
> Chessmen and ivory dice.
>
> What do you cry, O ye fruitmen?
> Citron, pomegranate, and plum.
> What do you play, O musicians?
> Sithar, sarangi, and drum.
> What do you chant, O magicians?
> Spells for the aeons to come.

And historic Golconda makes her a little wistful and sad:

> I muse among those silent fanes
> Whose spacious darkness guards your dust . . .

Her description of a tropical night in **'Leili'** is one of her most satisfying Nature poems:

> A caste-mark on the azure brows of Heaven,
> The golden moon burns sacred, solemn, bright.
> The winds are dancing in the forest-temple,
> And swooning at the holy feet of Night.
> Hush! in the silence mystic voices sing
> And make the gods their incense-offering.

She struck the right 'patriotic' note again and again. Love of one's country was an emotion as much as the love of man or Nature, and some of her poems for example, her invocations to the national leaders and her lyrics, **'Awake'**, **'An Anthem of Love'** and **'To India'** are patriotic without the faintest trace of jingoism. Occasionally she could translate her identification with the people's sufferings into a gesture of protest:

> Stay the relentless anger of Thy hand.
> Thine awful war, O Lord, no longer wage
> Against our hapless hearts and heritage . . .

While she usually preferred the calm of mind to the storm, the music of the flute to the tumult of the soul, she has sung of these too the whirling eddies, the raging fe-vers in several of her poems, notably in **The Broken Wing.** She was, above all, sensitive to beauty, the beauty of living things, the beauty of holiness, the beauty of the Buddha's compassion, the beauty of Brindavan's Lord. She didn't specially seek out the bizarre, the exotic, the exceptional, but her poems lack neither variety nor the flavour of actuality. Children's poems, nature poems, patriotic poems, poems of love and death, even poems of mystical transcendence, Sarojini Naidu essayed them all; and with her unfailing verbal felicity and rhythmical dexterity, she generally succeeded as well. Seldom did she venture out of her depth; she wasn't interested in wild experimentation; she didn't cudgel herself towards explosive modernity. But she had genuine poetic talent, and she was a wholesome and authentic singer.

## Rameshwar Gupta (essay date 1975)

SOURCE: "Sarojini's Art," in *Sarojini: The Poetess,* Doaba House Publishers, 1975, pp. 120-135.

[*In the following essay, Gupta discusses the influence of English Romanticism on Naidu's work.*]

INTRODUCTORY REMARKS

One cannot miss in Sarojini's poetry her ease in the English language, her sense of the sounds of English words, and her mastery over the metrical system of English poetry.

Although her life spans across the late Victorian, Decadent, Edwardian and Georgian, and the Hulme-Eliot-Pound, and the Yeatsean, and the Auden-Spender, and the avant garde free verse periods of English poetry, Sarojini, born and brought up in the Romantic tradition, fed on Romantic poetry, tutored by Romantic critics Gosse and Symons , ever remained Romantic, both in her sensibility and art. One could take it as her virtue, or as her defect, according to one's own inclination.

And so, she would never take to free verse; and as to diction, the dry, spare, lean fare of Hulme-Leavis school would not suit her taste; and spontaneous outpouring of feeling rather than an 'intellectual exercise' would continue to be her mode, and sensuous and aesthetic perceptions rather than thought, (generally speaking), the contents of her poetry.

VERSIFICATION

Sarojini has composed in various stanza forms and there is no metrical measure accepted in English tradition which she has not successfully practised iambic, trochaic, anapestic, dactylic, or their permissible combinations. Besides their skilful handling she has also succeeded in setting them to some of the Indian tunes. Repetition it would be, since in our study of some of the poems in the foregoing chapters such things have been pointed out; still let me illustrate, both stanza form and metre. Here is

pure iambic rhythm, a whole stanza; the usual tetrametric quatrain with alternate lines rhyming:

> Lord Buddha, on thy Lotus-throne,
> With praying eyes and hands elate,
> What mystic rapture dost thou own.
> Immutable and ultimate?
>
>                **("To a Buddha")**

And here the sing-song iambic measure fit for a cradle song:

> From groves of spice
> O'er fields of rice
> Athwart the lotus-stream
> I bring for you,
> Aglint with dew
> A little lovely dream.
>
>                **("Cradle Song")**

Then a pure trochaic measure; a rhyming eight-verse stanza in trimetre (the last extra syllable in some lines is stressed, enforcing the trochaic rhythm):

> Golden sun of victory, born
> In my life's unclouded morn,
> In my lambent sky of love,
> May your growing glory prove
> Sacred to your consecration,
> To my art and to my nation
> Sun of victory, may you be
> Sun of song and liberty.
>
>                **("To My Children")**

Here is anapestic measure, lines beginning with an iamb, followed by three anapests:

> Our lays are of cities whose lustre is shed,
> The laughter and beauty of women long dead;
> The sword of old battles, the crown of old kings,
> And happy and simple and sorrowful things.
>
>                **("Wandering Singers")**

Dactylic is a rare measure in English poetry and hard to substain; but Sarojini has it:

> Full are my pitchers and far to carry,
> Lone is way and long,
> Why, O why was I tempted to tarry
> Lured by the boatmen's song?
> Swiftly the shadows of night are falling,
> Hear, O hear, is the white crane calling,
> Is it the wild owl's cry?
>
>                **("Village Songs")**

(Pure dactylic, except trochaic substitutes, which are also in the nature of dactyls). Take another instance. It is from **"Nightfall in the City of Hyderabad"**:

> Round the high Char Minar sounds of gay
>     cavalcades
> Blend with the music of cymbals and serenades.

And look at the wonder of her craftsmanship. Who would easily carry a rhythm flawlessly through long continuously running lines?

Now silent, now singing and swaying and
swinging like blossoms that bend to the
breezes or showers, . . .
Eyes ravished with rapture, celestially
panting, what passionate bosoms
aflaming with fire.

                        **("Indian Dancers")**

a heady rhythmical pattern in which words are relished primarily for sound. Swinburne alone of English poets composed such verses; may be a few others, but not many.

Those of us in India who have ever heard a love duet sung by a lover and his beloved (in the romantic medieval way) should be able to recall the particular native tune the following lines have been written to: She singing:

     How shall I yield to the voice of thy pleading,
        how
          shall I grant thy prayer,
     Or give thee a rose-red silken-tassel, a scented
        leaf
        from my hair?

                        **("An Indian Love Song")**

A prosodic analysis would show that the first verse has as many as seventeen syllables, arranged in six feet, a group of three dactyls followed by a trochee in 'pleading', and this followed by another group of two dactyls; the rhythm in the second verse changes; it is: sixteen syllables arranged again in six feet, beginning and ending with an anapest with four iambs set between.

Besides, some Indian names, and expressions, and cries of birds too have been interwoven to add to the variety of rhythm. We have **"In Praise of Henna"** the kokila crying from a henna-spray: 'Lira! Liree! Lira Liree!'; and in **"Village Songs"** 'Ram re Ram! I shall die', and in **"Song of Radha The Milkmaid"** 'Govinda! Govinda!'; then in **"A Love Song from the North"**:

     Tell me no more of thy love, papeeha,
     Woodest thou recall to my heart, papeeha

the rising tone in the three-syllabled 'papeeha' harmonizing with the rising tone of the preceding anapestic foot in each line.

It is not the various metrical combinations alone that create a verbal rhythm. To do it there are other aural devices too, like rhyme both the end rhyme and the internal rhyme, alliteration, refrain (repetition in the same line not only of words and phrases but of the metrical measure too), consonance (repetition of a pattern of consonants) and assonance (repetition of the same or similar vowel sounds). Sarojini knew these devices and made use of them. We will illustrate:

Sarojini has no blank verse. Her talents did not incline that way. Whatever may be the merits or demerits of rhyme the debate began with the birth of poetry and still continues Sarojini stuck to it. She would not forgo her love for jingle and tinkle: But it has its own fascination.

Sarojini's poems are, of course, all end-rhymed and she frequently made use of internal rhymes too. Here are some illustrations: 'No longer delay, let us hasten away'; 'Sweet is the shade of the coconut glade': 'the sea is our mother, the cloud is our brother' (They are all from **"Coromandel Fishers"**, and they occur within single lines). More could be spotted out.

ALLITERATIONS

Here are some culled haphazardly from her poems: 'fair and frail and fluttering leaves', the alliteration in each stressed syllable beginning with 'f' enhances the effectiveness of the iambic rhythm as well as stresses the intended quality of the leaves; 'fairy-fancies', 'laughter-lighted'; 'tangles of my tresses': 'the dear dreams that are dead'; 'fashion a funeral pyre'; 'the heavenward hunger'; 'glimmering ghosts'; 'the red dawn dances' . They abound. There is no poem without them: Sarojini, as it were, loved to play with words and feel their ring and roll.

RHYTHM CREATED BY A KIND OF A REFRAIN IN THE SAME LINE

For example, 'Through echoing forest and echoing street', 'The voice of the mind is the voice of our fate'; 'no love bids us tarry, no love bids us wait'; etc. Each of these expressions has two parts, marked out in the first case by the conjunction 'and'; in the second the verb 'is'; and in the third by a comma; and each part of an expression is a rhythmic repetition of the other and adds to the rhythmic intensity of the expression as a whole. These examples are from **"Wandering Singers"**: more could be culled.

EXAMPLES OF ASSONANCE AND CONSONANCE

Take two lines from the poem **"Alabaster"**. The heart treasuring rich memories:

     Like odours of cinnamon, sandal and clove,
     Of song and sorrow and life and love.

We have assonance created by the repeated vowel sound 'O'; and again in the line 'with the soul of keora and rose', the 'O' sound is assonant. The repeated combination of 'i' and 'e' sounds and of the consonant 'm' in: 'And weave your mystic measures to the melody of flutes' results in a melody of its own kind. Then in the second stanza of the poem **"To My Fairy Fancies"** a sound pattern is evolved by the repetition of consonant "l" 'longer', 'linger', 'laughter', 'lighted', 'life', 'lonely'; and in the same poem a kind of aural softness is created by the frequency of 's' and 'es' sounds in 'spirit', 'soft', 'fancies', 'caresses', 'tresses',' nesses'. Then the expression 'the blooms that bend to the breezes' (**"Indian Dancers"**) is not only sound consonance, but semantic consonance too, since the sense of the three words 'blossoms', 'bend', and 'breezes' is inter-related. We cannot miss the hissing effect of the sibilants in 'Seers are you and symbols of the ancient silence" (**"The Snake-Charmer"**). It is onomatopoeic. There are other instances too.

Another device, not regarded admirable today, that has been used, not infrequently, by Sarojini to help her rhythm and rhyme is that of "inversion". Here are some examples: 'turn with envy pale' in place of 'turn pale with envy' (in **"The Song of Princess Zeb-un-nissa"**); 'were you' (in **"A Rajput Love Song"**); 'thieving lights of eyes impure' (in **"The Pardah Nashin"**); and 'are we' and 'temple fair' in the lines:

> Bangle-sellers are we who bear
> Our shining loads to the temple fair
>                     (from **"Bangle-Sellers"**)

And yet another device, a product of her own fancy, which she has used to create a kind of rhythm in the total structure or architectonic of a poem, nothing having to do with its versification, is, what has been named 'triplicity' the use of a set of three ideas, or images, or symbols, or states of mind, or idioms in the same poem. For example, **"Corn-Grinders"** sings the sorrows of a little mouse, a little deer, a little bride; **"Bells"** are three Anklet Bells, Cattle Bells, and Temple Bells, and so on. Prof. Viswanathan[1] traces its use to as many as sixteen poems; may be more.

It is enough to show that if Sarojini had genius, it was a genius for verbal rhythm, if for nothing else. The very tissues, nerves and muscles of her body would sometimes go into motion to get the rhythm that rested in her being, and then it would manifest itself in some melodious articulation. English poets who show such variety of rhythmic patterns and tunes are not many. That is Sarojini's contribution to English poetry as a whole. Only prejudice could deny it. An artist of verse patterns that have the lilt and liquidity of song, she would not please Hopkins (the eminent English poet, 1844 1889) and his neo-modernist followers who would cultivate 'jerkiness' for its own sake.

DICTION

A poet's choice of words his diction alone could fairly indicate the kind of world (realistic, surrealistic, religious, mystical, sensuous, romantic, etc.) his imagination moves in or creates. In most cases it could also possiby indicate whether his cadence is going to be sweet or harsh or soft or grating. Here is a typical selection from Sarojins's diction, frequently used by her, almost keywords for her poetry. They have been arranged here in the following order: substantives, verbs, archaic words, epithets, adjective-substantive combinations, and then phrases, fine phrases of which there is an abundance.

SUBSTANTIVES

*Flowers* gulmohurs, champa, champak, tulip, rose, cassia, oleanders, hyacinth, nasturtiums, jasmine, lily, poppy, kimshuk, seemul; and mango, orange, plantain, pomegranate, almond, neem, gourd, and sirisha blossoms.

*Birds* Oriole, lapwig, dhadhikula, koel, bulbul, dove, kingfisher, eagle, hawk, pigeon, papeeha.

*Colours* Opal, gold, amethyst, amber, coral, ivory, pearl, white, blue, azure, yellow, purple, green, red, tawny, crimson, vermillion, golden-red, gold-flecked grey, silver, diaphanous-silver (of the rain).

*Odours* keora, rose, saffron, sandalwood, cinnamon, sandal and clove, heena and spice, the alluring scent of the sirisha plain, odorous breath of heena and neem.

*Jewels* agate, prophery, onyx, jade, opal, peridote, ruby, amber, sapphire, amethyst, pearl.

*Other things* coronet, cavalcade, trellis, stalactite, honey, milk, saffron, citron, plum, pomegranate, mango, garden, rill, hill, leaves, petals, maidens, minstrels, breezes, spring, moonbeams, fairies.

*Abstract things* dream, rapture, perfume, etc.

*Verbs* (words of movement and action): burgeon, travail, dream, languish, scintillate, leap and sparkle, dance and shine, enchant, glide, to lull, fling.

*Archaic words* ye, hath, wert, lithe, lothe, paeon, aeon, fay, tarry, ope, mine, cleaveth.

*Epithets* ardent, elate, radiant, mellifluous, cerulean, limpid, sumptuous, melodious, luminous, tender and clear, shimmering, wildwood (fay), lambent, luscious, fragrant, vernal.

*Epithet-substantive-verb combinations* laughter-bound, sorrow-free, laughter-lighted, jewel-girt, sandal-scented, chamber-threshold, parrot-plume, moonlight-tangled, rose-scented, dawn-uncoloured, thought-worn, wind-blown, wind-inwoven, love-garnered, lotus-throne, hermit-memories, flame-carven.

*Phrases* the sky's unageing dome; a star in the dew of our song; aflaming with fire; life's uncoloured morn; the lilting joy of spring; dance of the wild foam's glee; brows anointed with perpetual weariness; engulfed in lampless woe; faith that sinks and feet that tire; conquer the sorrow of life with the sorrow of death; thieving light of eyes impure; the heavenward hunger of our soul; the radiant promise of renascent morn; joy so frail hope so fugitive; leap and sparkle, dance and shine; the mystic silence that men call death; sky of love; sweet comrades of a lyric spring; sacred and sublime; the burden of human heritage.

These are not the kind of words we hear from a man we accost in the street: It is a diction to which our world of daily round and experience is almost stranger. What kind of world do they then point to? They must, to some, for words do not grow in vacuum. It is some milieu social, political, cultural, which gives them birth and to which they point back. Sarojini's diction most part of it evidently does not belong to our modern writer's world of 'realism' or 'naturalism', to our drab, dingy, 'noisy', 'polluted' industrial or technetronic world. Such diction could point only to some sensuous, rich, glittering, gorgeous world there are so many scents and flowers and jewels and bright epithets and 'silken terms strewn with seeming carelessness' , to some distant world of fancy. The word 'dream' occurs more than several scores of times and we are lifted to where (in Sarojini's own words) champak blossoms give 'rich, voluptuous, magical perfume'; 'sumptuous peacocks dance in rhythmic delight'; koels sing mellifluously and the birds lilt; to where women's bangles twinkle luminous, tender and clear, and where there is 'the delicate silence of love'. It is verily 'the moon-enchanted estuary of dreams', where

> Dreams and delicate fancies
> Dance thro' a poet's mind.

There could be no violence in such a world, pathos might be.

Besides, we shall notice one thing more: It is the *'m'* and *'l'* sounds that predominate in Sarojini's key-diction; sounds that make for liquid melody and softness: qualities that characterize Sarojini's verse cadences. We always hear, if we may say so, 'the nightingale's' sweet song, never the strident song of the cicade.

Everything tells that Sarojini's sensibility and art are romantic, a not very definable term; but it can't be helped. Sarojini, besides, has a number of poems folk songs and lyrics which are simple and plain and which tell of 'happy and simple and sorrowful things'. In fact this is the essential undertone of all her work. Her romantic sensibility and art include it.

FIGURES OF SPEECH

If not all, most of Sarojini's verses are ornate, embellished with one or the other figure of speech, mostly similes, next metaphors and then others. In many cases, almost all, similes and metaphors throw up scintillating images, and poetry becomes revealing. Some select similes, metaphors and other figures of speech occurring in Sarojini's poetry are:

*Similes* The maiden in the palanquin sways like a flower; skims like a bird; floats like a laugh; hangs like a star; springs like a beam on the brow of the tide; falls like a tear from the eyes of a bride (from **"The Palanquin-Bearers"**). The wind lies asleep on the arms of the dawn like a child that has cried all night (from **"Coromandel Fishers"**) The simile is complete: The wind howling all the night is the child crying all the night; the child is lying quietly asleep in the arms of its mother, and the wind at dawn is silent as though lying in the arms of the mother Dawn: It is a simile, a metaphor, a personification, and an image, all in one: It is a scene caught in the flash of a vision. Then a simile and colourful image too: Bright parrots clustering like vermillion flowers on the ripe boughs of many-coloured fruits (**"Indian Love Song"**). Then the sensuous and the subtle mingle in: the beloved's heart hidden in the lover's bosom like the perfume in the petals of a rose; and the beloved haunting the

lover's waking like a dream, his slumber like a moon (the beloved's face: a metaphor too), and pervading him like a musky scent and possessing him like a tune (**"Humayun to Zobeida"**). Then we have sunset hanging on a cloud like a joy on the heart of a sorrow (**"Autumn Song"**), the heart frail as a cassia flower (**"Alabaster"**); and then three at once in a single stanza in **"The Queen's Rival"** seven damsels round queen Gulnaar like seven soft gems on a silken thread, like seven fair lamps in a royal tower, like seven bright petals of Beauty's flower. Then we have in **"The Pardah Nashin"**, the veiled beauty's girdle and fillet gleaming like changing fires on sunset seas, and her raiment like morning mist shot opal, gold and amethyst (both impressionistic images too); and her days guarded and secure like jewels in a turbaned crest, like secrets in a lover's breast; and a host of them. There is no end. Look up any page.

*Metaphors* The day is a 'wild stallion' (**"A Rajput Love Song"**); and the snake (in **"Snake-Charmer"**) the 'subtle bride of my mellifluous wooing', and 'the silver-breasted moonbeam of desire'; and the bangles (in **"Bangle-Sellers"**) are rainbow tainted circles of light. In **"In Praise of Gulmohur Blossoms"** the lovely hue of the gulmohurs is the glimmering red of a bridal robe, and the rich red of a wild bird's wing; and in **"Golden Cassia"**, the golden cassias are fragments of some fallen stars, or golden pitchers for fairy wine, or glimmering tears that some fair bride shed remembering her lost maidenhood; then a string of metaphors, as many as fifteen in the 24-line poem **"A Rajput Love Song"**; and in **"Farewell"** the poet's songs are a 'bright shower of lambent butterflies', and a 'soft cloud of murmuring bees'. The entire poem (an eight-verse one) **"Alabaster"** exists as a fine metaphor for the poet's heart itself: The heart like the alabaster box is carved with delicate dreams and wrought with many a subtle and exquisite thought, and it treasures rich and passionate memories; and the poem **"Past and Present"** turns the past into a 'mountain-cell', where lone, apart, old hermit-memories dwell, and the future into a bride's marriage-veil of mysteries. Like similes, a host.

*Images* Over the city bridge Night comes majestical, borne like a queen to a sumptuous festival (**"Nightfall in the City of Hyderabad"**); but in **"The Indian Gipsy"**, quick Night descends like a black panther from the caves of sleep. In **"The Queen's Rival"** we see the queen laughing like a tremulous rose, and the tissues of her veil glowing with the hues of a lapwing's crest, and the two-spring old baby running to her knee like a wildwood fay; and in **"On Juhu Sands"** the young moonrise falling like a golden rose on the sea's breast. And in **"In Praise of Gulmohur Blossoms"** we see the glimmering red of a bridal rob, the rich red of a wild bird's wing; the mystic blaze of the gem that burns on the brow of serpent king, and also the blood that poured from a thousand breasts to succour a Rajput queen; and in **"Golden Cassia"** the rapturous light that leaps to heaven from a true wife's funeral pyre; and we also see the beloved's heart gliding into the lover's fingers like a serpent to the calling voice of flute. In **"Palanquin-Bearers"** we see a bird skimming on the foam of a stream, a beam springing on the brow of the tide, and a tear falling from the eyes of a bride all vivid visual images executed with gnomic terseness; and then some vague ones, as vague as Pre-Raphaelitic: the maiden floating like a laugh from the lips of a dream, swaying like a flower in the wind of a song; and hanging like a star in the dew of a song. Then we have 'the dance of the wild foam's glee' (in **"Coromandel Fishers"**). Would it not remind us of Wordsworth's 'The waves beside them danced, but they (the daffodils) outdid the sparkling waves in glee'? One could understand how foam could be gleeful. One more from the same poem: 'the blue of the verge, where the low sky mates with the sea, the verb 'mates' does the wonder. We can also see Morning sowing her tents of gold in fields of ivory (**"Indian Love-Song"**); the fire-flies dancing through the fairy neem (**"Cradle-Song"**); and also the gem-like fire of hopes up-leaping like the light of the dawn (**"To the God of Pain"**) an impressionistic image. In **"Indian Weavers"** we come across the expression "the moonlight chill'; the substantive 'moonlight' made to serve as an epithet for 'Chill' turns the expression into a kinesthetic image (an image of felt motion or sensation). And in **"The Joy of the Spring Time"** we see 'the dance of the dew on the wings of a moonbeam' and in **"A Song in Spring"** 'fireflies weaving faerial dances' both kinetic images (images or motion seen). Then, we have a sublime image in **"Leili"**;

> A caste-mark on the azure brows of Heaven
> The golden moon burns sacred, solemn, bright,

and another in **"To India"**: India! Rise

> And, like a bride high-mated with the spheres
> Beget, new glories from thy ageless womb.

We have to gaze afar to feel its sublimity. These alone were sufficient, Sir, to get Sarojini a fellowship in a group of poets.

*Synecdoche* In the poem **"Suttee"**, we have 'Shall the flesh survive when the soul is gone?' Here the substitution of 'flesh' (a part for the whole body) is synecdochic; the word 'body' here will not affect the way 'flesh' does. Then queen Gulenaar's daughter is two Spring times old (spring for the whole, 'year'); the beauty is that 'spring' would convey the freshness and charm of the young baby, which the word 'year' would not. Other examples could be traced.

*Metonymy* Again in **"Suttee"** we have: "Shall the blossom live when the tree is dead?" 'blossom' substituted for 'wife' and 'tree' for 'husband' is metonymic; and **"In the Forest"**, we have, 'till shadows are gray in the west' a whole clause substituted for evening; and then we have 'to clear the sky of thy discontent' sky for mind; very appropriate, serving as a metonymy and besides evoking an image.

*Pathetic Fallacy.* Attributing human traits to non-human objects has been frequent in poetry although regarded morbid by Ruskin. It has been popular with Sarojini too. Her roses turn pale with envy and send forth fragrance like wail from their hearts pierced with pain; her honeyed hyacinths complain and languish in a sweet distress; her winds are wise and her gulmohurs valiant with joy. And when Sarojini characterizes distress as sweet (in **"The Song of Princess Zebu-un-nissa"**) she is making use of a figure we call *Oxymoron* (a flat contradiction); and when her Zebu-un-nissa declares that when she lifts her veil, the roses turn pale with envy of her beauty. She is using *Hyperbole* (exaggeration); and when Sarojini addresses Pain, Death, the Unknown and other such things as if they were persons, she is making use of the figure we call *Personification*. She uses *anti-thesis* too: 'And Death unweaves the web of life' what a juxtaposition of Death and Life, and 'unweaving' and 'web': a pair of antagonistic ideas. Similar juxtapositions can be seen in her expressions: 'the dawn and the dusk go rife'; and 'the flame of hope or the flame of hate.'

*Irony* The very air in the poem **"Ecstasy"** (in *The Golden Threshold*) is ironic. The lover's eyes weary of bliss (the bliss of seeing the beloved), her lips weary of song (song for the beloved), and her request that her soul be sheltered from the sight of the face of the beloved, are all ironic, expressing an attitude quite different from that which is literally expressed. Other instances could be collected.

*Symbolism* Sarojini's **"The Lotus"** is symbolic. It incarnates the Mahatma (Gandhi) with all his sacredness and sublimity, and one can sense the involvement of the poet's whole being in the creative act. We can feel the symbolic touch in her 'slumbering sedges' (of **"Solitude"**) that 'catch from the stars some high tone of their mystical speech'; and also in her gipsy girl (of **"The Indian Gipsy"**) who is twin-born with primal mysteries and drinks of life at Time's forgotten source. The girl remains the gipsy girl all right, but in her we feel something of the primal mysteries and the ancientness of Time. Similarly her serpents (of **"The Festival of Serpents"**) 'who are seers and symbols of the ancient silence, where life and death and sorrow and ecstasy are one' give us an apprehension of some felt mystery, as do 'the mystic voices singing in silence and the winds dancing and swooning at the holy feet of Night' in **"Leili"**. Then we have her Radha chanting 'Govinda! Govinda' (in **"Song of Radha The Milkmaid"**). The chanting of the name reverberates with the ancient experience of fulfilment in 'identity' (identity with or merger into the Beloved), and with the yearning of the eternal feminine for the eternal He.

If we analysed then we could see that these similes and images are drawn mostly from Nature, from legend, from myth, from history, from country scenes (of the days gone by), and from the fairy kingdoms world many removes from our work-a-day world; mostly it is like 'the dance of the dew on the wings of a moonbeam', or 'the veil glowing with the hues of a lapwing's crest'. They confirm what her diction told about Sarojini's sensibility. Besides, they reveal that Sarojini's poetry, as already noted elsewhere is ornate: it is profuse particularly with similes, metaphors and images. There are a few poems like **"Palanquin-Bearers", "The Snake-Charmer", "Humayun to Zobeida", "The Song of Princess Zeb-un-nissa",** each of which is almost nothing else (the involved feeling excepted) but a few similes or metaphors and images put together a kind of a catalogue of similes. It may not please some types of readers, but few would deny that it points to the poetic spontaneity of Sarojini, her gift for the spontaneous perception of the similarity in the dissimilars, and the perceptions flowing to her from so many worlds! She may not make us think but she makes us see the 'scene' realized in colours and in tunes. Everything points to Sarojini's uncommon creative energy: such variety of cadences, such melody in diction, such profuseness of imagery!

A neo-modernist, however, may twitch his nose in disdain and despair at a speech-rhythm which is not the speech-rhythm of the man in the street, at unrealistic diction, and mere fanciful imagery; but nothing else could have created the world of loveliness and melody Sarojini's soul sojourned in. She would have been untrue to herself had she sacrificed her 'swadharma'. How would you like forcing a free singer (a singer by birth and aptitude, not by vocation) to sit down to mould and chisel a 'cool' and 'hard' aluminium spittoon? It was wise Sarojini made and sang songs taking her air from fields and forests, and from bulbuls and koels and dawns and sunsets, and from the coromandel fishers and the corn-grinders, and from Radha, the milkmaid.

RECAPITULATION: CONCLUSION

Sarojini wrote no epic, dramatic, or narrative poetry; nor no blank verse. She had no aptitude or talent for them. Her genius remains confined to short poems lyrics (and songs), not even sonnets, although she wrote ten, three of which **"The Lotus", "In Salutation to My Father's Spirit",** and **"Imperial Delhi",** really good. Essentially she is a lyricist: Not a made poet, she had started warbling at eleven and by thirteen had composed more than 3000 verses. Her heart would tingle and then she must express herself, and she would do it in numbers that came to her naturally. This would happen in happy innocence and there would be no end or purpose in view. And she remains a lyricist throughout without much of a distinct growth of poetic personality, as there was in her brother Harindra.

As a lyricist what most characterizes her work is delicate fancy and haunting melody. She has wrought her poems with material dexterity that is dazzling and rendered them in cadences that are 'mellifluous'. The poems are 'golden' cadences in 'silken' terms, throwing up scintillating images. Her art shows the influence of Keats, Shelley, Tennyson, the Pre-Raphaelites and Swinburne; but it is not derivative. Sarojini had once dreamt that she would be the Keats of India. She couldn't, but she has left behind her certain images, sensuous and mythical, and colourful and perfumed, in which she seems to out-

Keats Keats himself. We have seen them and discussed them elsewhere; still, here is one:

> A caste-mark on the azure brows of heaven
> The golden moon burns, sacred, solemn bright
> ("*Leili*")

and one more:

> . . . moonlight-tangled meshes of perfume,
> Where the clustering *keoras* guard the squirrel's slumber,
> Where the deep woods glimmer with the jasmine's bloom

A western reader not already acquainted with oriental richness in imagery will discover here a new world of similes, metaphors and images.

Her themes mainly are love, nature, and the Indian scene of an age just gone by. We see in her poetry a general aliveness to life its variety, its colour, its beauty, a general sense of the joy of it, and its pathos.

If Sarojini is to be described as belonging to any class or school of poetry, it would be Romantic, aud I would confine her to Elizabethan Romanticism the elemental and simpler kind. That is the impression her poetry as a whole gives. Sarojini is essentially Elizabethan, whatever the influences on her. She even looks like Elizabeth. Had she been born in Elizabethan England she would have been happier, a hundred-fold more: She would have found herself among her likes people enjoying discovering and flaunting new words, new rhythms, new cadences, new expressions; people singing; people wearing 'ear-rings'. As it is, she was 'a dreamer born in a dreamless age.'

Sarojini's poetry, mostly, is ornate. It is in the jewelled, exuberant style; while Toru who preceded her wrote in a simple and transparent style. A thought or a feeling, and even an image sometimes gets blurred, if not altogether lost in a profusion of words, mostly adjectives, and in rhetoric.

Intellectual vigour does not characterize her poetry; and somewhere she betrays sentimentality.

If not all her poems, some of her folk-songs like **"Palanquin-Bearers", "The Snake-Charmer", "Cradle-Song", "Bangle-Sellers", "Song of Radha The Milk Maid",** and **"Village Songs"** (of *The Bird of Time*); and her songs for music like **"Alabaster", "To My Fairy Fancies";** and her poems like **"Leili", "Indian Dancers", "The Queen's Rival", "To a Buddha Seated on a Lotus"; "Raksha Bandhan", "A Song of the Khyber Pass";** and her songs of Life and Death, like, **"The Lotus", "Bells", "The Pearl", "The Flute Player of Brindaban",** and her songs of the springtime like **"Spring", "Champak Blossoms", "June Sunset";** and a few of her love-lyrics in her **"The Temple"** will always go as good poetry and continue to charm perceptive readers.

It can be said that her contribution to English poetry as a whole [it would be hard for the English people and

Indian Anglo-maniacs to digest it] and to Indo-English poetry in particular are two: (1) Her creation of new metrical rhythms and setting some Indian folk-song tunes to them: (2) Re-creation by her of the colour and pageantry of Indian life the country's ethos in English verse. (Be it remembered, however, that it is the sensuous, the lyrical feel of Indian life' rather than the mystic or spiritual that comes up).

Sarojini's poetic canvas is small 'a mere two square inches of ivory like Jane Austen's.'[2] The output is mere 184 short poems; the poetic form only one lyric (including songs and the few sonnets); and the life vision (so far as we find it realized in her poetry) too, limited; limited merely to love-longings, a few romantic fancies and dreams, and a few commom simple joys and sorrows.

The last statement, namely, her vision as realized in her poetry is limited will, however, have to be qualified and explained although it may be a mere rehearse of what has already been said elsewhere in the book. Sarojini does not sort out problems intellectually. Hers are mere romantic feeling, and they relate mostly to love and Vasant (Nature). Her love poems, which are so many, view love in its many aspects and moods; still its canvas though vertically deep touching depths in the realized and realizable experience of devotional surrender and merger , is not horizontally wide: it has nothing of the kind of the moderner's 'realistic vision' of love and its problems: sex, mating, divorce, intellectual companionship, etc. Her nature poems have a still smaller canvas. It is spring, its flowers, fragrances, birds, songs and colours mostly talked of and sung. Nature in its vaster aspects and terrific and mystic moods is absent; only once or twice, say, in **"June Sunset"** or **"Leili"** has she touched different dimensions. Her realm of romance too is limited: Coleridgean supernatural beings spirits, ghosts, and other eerie presences don't inhabit it, fairies once in a while appear, but not as integral part of the human drama; there is nothing like Keatsean magic casements opening on the foam of perilous seas, or a passion for the magic and mystery of the past; nor Shelleyean aspiration for any idealistic future, despite occasional rhetorical lines once or twice, like, "When the terror and tumult of hate shall cease/And life be refashioned on anvils of peace" (**"The Gift of India"**), but nothing like Shelley's "Prometheus Unbound": In fact there could be no comparison. Again and again, when the mood were on, she would only burst out in a lyric and a child of Aghorenath as she was, she would at times, however rare, touch the mystic depths of life. She did it once in **"Leili"**, and then in **"The Lotus"**, and **"Solitude"**, and in **"Salutation to the Eternal Silence"**. When she did so, she had had a certain glimpse into the heart of mystery.

NOTES

[1] Indebted for the idea to Prof. K. Viswanathan. See his article "The Nightingale and the Naughty Gal" in *The Banasthali Patrika.* (January, 1969), pp. 131-133

[2] Prof. K. Vishwanathan's phrase: See *The Banasthali Patrika* (January 1969), p. 128.

## Fritz Blackwell (essay date 1977)

SOURCE: "Krishna Motifs in the Poetry of Sarojini Naidu and Kamala Das," in *Journal of South Asian Literature*, Vol. XIII, No. 1, Fall, 1977, pp. 9-14.

[*In the following essay, Blackwell examines imagery used by Naidu and Kamala Das of "the soul's quest for God (Krishna)."*]

Let us consider four poems, two each by two Indian poets writing in English. The older of the two is Sarojini Naidu (1879-1949), who is the author of three volumes of poetry: *The Golden Threshold* (1905), *The Bird of Time* (1912) and *The Broken Wing* (1915-1916). This first poem is taken from the second volume:

### "Song of Radha the Milkmaid"

I carried my curds to the Mathura fair . . .
How softly the heifers were lowing . . .
I wanted to cry, "Who will buy, who will buy
These curds that are white as the clouds in the sky
When the breezes of *Shrawan* are blowing?"
But my heart was so full of your beauty, Beloved,
They laughed as I cried without knowing:
    *Govinda! Govinda!*
    *Govinda! Govinda! . . .*
How softly the river was flowing!

I carried my pots to the Mathura tide . . .
How gaily the rowers were rowing! . . .
My comrades called, "Ho! let us dance, let us sing
And wear saffron garments to welcome the spring,
And pluck the new buds that are blowing."
But my heart was so full of your music, Beloved,
They mocked me when I cried without knowing:
    *Govinda! Govinda!*
    *Govinda! Govinda! . . .*
How gaily the river was flowing!

I carried my gifts to the Mathura shrine . . .
How brightly the torches were glowing!
I folded my hands at the altar to pray
"O shining ones guard us by night and by day"
And loudly the conch shells were blowing.
But my heart was so lost in your worship,
    Beloved,
They were wroth when I cried without knowing:
    *Govinda! Govinda!*
    *Govinda! Govinda!*
How brightly the river was flowing.

The following poem is taken from the last volume:

### "The Flute-Player of Brindaban"

Why didst thou play thy matchless flute
    Neath the Kadamba tree,
And wound my idly dreaming heart
    With poignant melody,

So where thou goest I must go,
    My flute-player, with thee?

Still must I like a homeless bird
    Wander, forsaking all;
The earthly loves and wordly lures
    That held my life in thrall,
And follow, follow, answering
    Thy magical flute-call.

To Indra's golden-flowering groves
    Where streams immortal flow,
Or to sad Yama's silent Courts
    Engulfed in lampless woe,
Where'er thy subtle flute I hear
    Beloved I must go!

The second poetess is Kamala Das (b. 1934), generally acknowledged as one of the foremost contemporary poets writing in India. These poems are taken from collection *The Descendents* (1967):

"The Maggots"

At sunset, on the river bank, Krishna
Loved her for the last time and left . . .

That night in her husband's arms, Radha felt
So dead that he asked, What is wrong,
Do you mind my kisses, love? and she said,
No, not at all, but thought, What is

It to the corpse if the maggots nip?

"Radha"

The long waiting
Had made their bond so chaste, and all the
    doubting

And the reasoning
So that in his first true embrace, she was girl

And virgin crying
Everything in me
Is melting, even the hardness at the core
O Krishna, I am melting, melting, melting

Nothing remains but
You . . .

A favorite motif of the medieval *bhakti* or devotional poets of India, as well as of the later Himalayan schools of *bhakti* miniatures, was the *abhis_rik_* a woman going to meet her lover, braving the elements, blackness of night, and dangers of the forest including snakes and various categories of ghosts and goblins. She is, of course, Radha, or at least a *gopi,* and the lover she is risking life and social acceptance to seek, is Krishna. And it is all metaphorical of the soul's (Radha) quest for God (Krishna). Very often the poet identified himself with the heroine in the conventional signature line at the end of the poem. Even when not, however, as in Vidyapati, she was usually the sympathetic focus.

Sarojini Naidu and Kamala Das, two twentieth-century Indian poets, have employed this approach in two poems each, with startlingly different attitudes and results. They are about fifty years apart and reflect the difference between two generations of poets, the first of which wrote in a manner which one observer, Prabhakar Machwe, has labeled as "the traditional mystico-romantic idealistic," and the second as the "angry young."[1]

The members of the first came to prominence during the freedom struggle, in which they participated. Naidu is almost a paradigm for this generation. She abandoned poetry for political action shortly after meeting Gandhi, succeeded him as president of the Congress party in 1925, was imprisoned in 1942, and became governor of India's largest state, Uttar Pradesh, in 1947. Her biography, fittingly, has been classified by the Library of Congress call number system with books on history and not with her literary works.[2]

Those of the second generation express dissatisfaction and disenchantment, even disillusionment, with the hopes and ideals that the first nurtured them upon. This has not resulted in a call for action, but rather in, as Machwe puts it, "the quiet acceptance of the fatalistic misery of the silent majority." Das could well be the paradigm. While her poetry is often frankly personal, she does not lead a life in public as did Naidu, and little is known about her private life other than some intriguing rumors and speculation based upon references oblique and direct in her poetry as to her sexual interests and needs (in one, "Composition," she tells us, "Reader, / you may say, / now here is girl with vast / sexual hungers, / a bitch after my own heart. / But, / I am not yours for the asking."). One critic, Subhas Chandra Saha, has suggested that her poetry reflects a "transmuting [of] loneliness into sex-obsession."[3]

With the "sex-obsession" there is a concomitant concern with death both existentially and in terms of use of metaphorical image. Naidu, too, treats of death, and links it with love (especially in the long series of twenty-four poems entitled **"The Temple"** and subtitled "A Pilgrimage of Love" found in *The Broken Wing*); but Naidu's love is not explicitly sexual, and Das's sex is sensual but not devotional. Naidu recognizes suffering and death, but accepts them as a part of life, which is primarily joyous, and as such is celebrated in her poetry, or as she labeled much of it, songs. Das is tormented by, if not obsessed with, death and existential pain, does not find life joyous and does not celebrate it nor does she really find sex joyous, though she does find it necessary and valuable as sensuous experience. Naidu's love or devotion is fulfilling. Das's sex is at best only temporarily so and then not really fulfilling so much as enriching; it is the ultimate, and perhaps only worthwhile, form of human contact and it remains primarily if not entirely human, not ascending to the divine as does Naidu's love, and only transitory, not permanent.

Specifically in regard to the Krishna poems or perhaps more properly, the Radha poems Naidu's are nice little songs, pleasant through their rhythm and sound, and flowing. Those of Das, though much shorter, seem heavier; they are not at all "nice," but intense and arresting, making maximum use of imagery. Curiously, while Naidu's is related in the first person, and Das's in the third, the latter's seem more personal. This is inspite of or perhaps even because of the religious and devotional nature of Naidu's and the literary and psycho-sexual nature of Das's poems.

The poets also reflect the century-old antagonism within Krishna-*bhakti*. Whether the Radha-Krishna relationship is purely spiritual or metaphorical, or whether it is as well physical, does one simply adore Krishna, or does she seek union with him? Do Jayadeva's Krishna and Radha indeed enjoy sexual congress in his *Gita Govinda,* as the Kangra miniatures clearly express, or is such an interpretation a misunderstanding of the nature of the religious metaphor, as the contemporary Hare Krishna people of A. C. Bhaktivedanta Swami Prabhupada maintain?

Das's Krishna and Radha are lovers; the understanding of the metaphor or motif of Krishna and Radha as being lovers seems to be taken for granted by her. On the other hand, there is no suggestion of sexual union as an object of desire on the part of Naidu's Radha or "I." Her poems are not necessarily anti-sexual. It is simply that sex is not a matter of concern in them; it is a non-sexual devotion that is expressed. While in Das's, the sex
implies a deep and intense relationship, it is not devotional. Though both her poems, especially "Radha," might imply a union deeper than the physical one expressed, I feel her concern to be literary and existential, not religious; I think she is using a religious concept for a literary motif and metaphor. The "melting, melting, melting" in "Radha," one critic, Devindra Kohli, has suggested "is the allegorical embrace of the temporal and the eternal, and her sense of dissolution";[4] yet it seems to me reminiscent of a poem of Vidyapati's wherein Radha relates,

> O friend, I cannot tell you
> Whether he was near or far, real or a dream.
> Like a vine of lightning,
> As I chained the dark one,
> I felt a river flooding in my heart.
> Like a shining moon,
> I devoured that liquid face.
> I felt stars shooting around me.
> The sky fell with my dress,
> Leaving my ravished breasts.
> I was rocking like the earth.
> In my storming breath
> I could hear my ankle-bells,
> Sounding like bees.
> Drowned in the last waters of dissolution,
> I knew that this was not the end.

Then the signature line:

> Says Vidy_pati:
> How can I possibly believe such nonsense?[5]

W. G. Archer, in a note to the poem, found the line "I was rocking like the earth" comparable to a passage in Hemingway's *For Whom the Bell Tolls,* "where a lover asks 'Did the earth move?' and the girl replies 'Yes. It moved.'"

Further, while Krishna *bhaktas* or devotees were later to ascribe religious implications to Vidyapati's poems, Archer states that there is "no evidence" that Vidyapati was "a special devotee of Krishna," nor even "a practising member of the Vaishnava cult. Indeed all his later writings," Archer explains, "ignore R_dh_ and Krishna and it is rather on Siva and Durgá that he lavishes attention."[6] It would seem that like Kamala Das six centuries later, he found the Radha-Krishna relationship a good literary focus through which to express the intensity of the human sexual relationship.

But whether there are some sort of religious implications or not, Das's Radha is not a devotee, but a very human lover.

In context with "the burden of darkness" (as Kohli phrased it) in her other poetry, these two poems may be revealing of the almost paranoid concern Das expresses toward death. Naidu only makes one oblique reference to death, toward the end of **"The Flute-Player of Brindaban,"** and that is more in regard to contrasting heaven ("Indra's golden-flowering groves") to hell ("sad Yama's silent Courts") the implication is that her devotion is so complete that she would follow him anywhere, and that even the shadowy underworld would be preferable to separation. In contrast, Das's "The Maggots" uses seven references to finality: sunset, last time, left, night, dead, corpse, maggots.

In summation, the four poems reflect the two differing approaches to Krishna devotee or lover as well as the polarization in twentieth century Indian poetry. Is death a matter of Indra's paradise and "Yama's silent Courts," or of merely a corpse, nipped by maggots? Does worship and adoration of Krishna eternally fill the devotee's heart with his beauty and his music, or does he merely make love to one for a last time and leave? I suppose it would depend upon whether or not one hears the call of his flute.

NOTES

[1] Prabhakar Machwe, "Prominent Women Writers in Indian Literature after Independence," *Journal of South Asian Literature,* XII, Nos. 3-4 (Spring-Summer 1977), 146.

[2] Padmini Sengupta, *Sarojini Naidu: A Biography* (New York: Asia Publishing House, 1966); the call number is DS 481 N25 S4. The call number of the volume of her collected poetry, *The Sceptred Flute: Songs of India* (Allahabad: Kitabistan, 1969; first printed 1943) is PR 6027 A53 S4 1969.

[3] Subhas Chandra Saha, *Modern Indo-Anglian Love Poetry* (Calcutta: Writers Workshop, 1968), p. 24.

[4] Devindra Kohli, *Virgin Whiteness: The Poetry of Kamala Das* (Calcutta: Writers Workshop, 1968), p. 24.

[5] *Love Songs of Vidypati,* trans. Deben Bhattacharya, ed. with intro., noted and comments, W. G. Archer (New York: Grove Press, 1969), p. 44.

[6] *Ibid.,* p. 35. Of course, Archer's opinion is not beyond dispute; e.g., Edward C. Dimock, Jr., refers to Vidyapati as a Vaisnava in his article "Doctrine and Practice among the Vaisnavas of Bengal," in *Krishna: Myths, Rites, and Attitudes,* ed. Milton Singer (Chicago: University of Chicago Press, 1968), p. 43.

## B. S. Mathur (essay date 1977)

SOURCE: "Sarojini Naidu: A Poetess of Sweetness and Light," in *Indo-English Literature: A Collection of Critical Essays,* edited by K. K. Sharma, Vimal Prakashan, 1977, pp. 61-70.

[*In the following essay, Mather discusses the delicacy of Naidu's language and imagery.*]

John Keats has very beautiful lines:

When old age shall this generation waste
Thou shalt remain, in midst of other woe
Than ours, a friend to man, to whom thou say't
"Beauty is truth truth beauty," that is all
Ye know on earth, and all ye need, to know.

These lines are taken from his "Ode on a Grecian Urn". They contain a great philosophy. Many of us think of John Keats as merely sensuous, denied heights of philosophical thoughts. We have been infinitely fascinated by his luxurious line "A thing of beauty is a joy for ever." That line is full of luxury of sensuousness, taken away from the context. But if you fit in the line where it occurs the idea communicated is not of sensuous beauty or emotion. The idea is a truth by itself, which proclaims the intensity of his thought. The same truth we find in the lines above given. The burden is "Beauty is truth, truth beauty." And then you have to remember that that is all that you require to know. Poets have sung of beauty but they seldom refer to truth that must be identical with beauty. Whenever they think of beauty they think in terms of sensuous beauty or emotion. In Keats you find beauty in philosophy of truth or in pursuit of truth. Here you have something like spiritual intensity or consummation, generally associated with sages, living away from the crowd and its pursuits.

What is the idea? Beauty is our goal. We have to be face to face with it, but we have to see in it the great truth. Then alone that beauty is a permanent experience, a thing of constant joy. There is beauty in truth which is a name for harmony. This is the great idea we gather on intense consideration of John Keats' poetry. I have a similar feeling when I think of Sarojini's poetry. To my mind, she is a supreme singer of beautiful songs, songs bathed in melody and thought. A supreme artist that she is, she is capable of creating a new and rich world of ideas fastening herself upon little themes. Remember that all themes are Indian, thoughts are Indian, melody is of India but the language is pure English, delicate and fine and sensuous. A very creditable synthesis, indeed! She is two things, in the main: a supreme artist and a fine melodist with the background of an intense thinker. Her thinking may not be methodical. She is a poet, a being of emotions. And emotions lead her to splendour of thought and beauty. All this is quite in keeping with her profession which is that of a poet and an artist. She cannot begin with ideas. If she does there will be a suggestion that she is not a poet, nor an artist, who has to begin all compositions in supreme forgetfulness to catch the reality and something of perennial preciousness. Emotions first and last. And still when you think of her poems you find plenty of sacred and beautiful thoughts. That is her chief merit. With melody she had wedded mind. In the marriage of mind and melody you have a singer of eternally beautiful songs.

As you think of her themes you might think of meeting trifles in her poems. I have said that she is a great artist, and she has those qualities which transform little things, make them great and dignified, in fact, instruments of great thoughts, powerful enough to transport us with unlimited joy. Actually, she creates. Her descriptive powers are tremendous but more than those powers are her gifts for creation. And the result is this magnificence of beauty and melody in her songs. One thing more. There is an air of romance about what she writes. That is genuine poetry of something that is not entirely of this earth. Poetry has two functions to teach and delight through ideal imitation. These two functions her poetry performs and performs in a characteristic fashion. All the time she seems to sing, seems to be lost in the rapture of beauty, of songs and of words. But think there is thought, think there is nothing that can be crossed out without taking something from the beauty of the song and also something from its meaning. She has words, apt and melodious and delicate. What more do you want? She sings, she delights and she instructs, all the time. And then her poetry is ideal imitation. I call that imitation ideal because she is more than a representative poet, a genuine artist and a creator, who has a mission behind all her romance of words and ideas and images.

Here is an excellent example of her words, images and perpetual music. A little of reflection will point to a long string of ideas behind beautiful images:

Lightly, O lightly we bear her along,
She sways like a flower in the wind of our song;
She skims like a bird on the foam of a stream,
She floats like a laugh from the lips of a dream.
Gaily, O gaily, we glide and we sing,
We bear her along like a pearl on a string.

What a perfection of music? And then to music there you find added wealth of new and captivating images. That is not all. There is a great idea behind. Think of the subject, whose picture here is in words and music. First thing to note is certainly a great delicacy is borne lightly and in the wind of song. It must be beautiful and capable of exciting great intensity of melody and beautiful ideas. It might be associated with something intensely beautiful. What a great touch of lightness? It skims like a bird on the foam of a stream. It floats like a laugh and that too from the lips of a dream. Has a dream lips and can it laugh? Why not think of some beautiful person dreaming and laughing. And laughing why? The person must have got her love. And so this happy laugh. That is about what is inside it. But what is it? It is carried like a pearl on a string. The picture is complete, complete in outlines, emotions and associations. Say that is the song of **"Palanquin-Bearers"**.

Now think of the sensitiveness of the poet. What a little and mundane object! And the reaction is this wealth of images and emotions and associations. This is wealth of the poet herself, who can give meaning and location to little airy things with such a gusto!

> Softly, O softly we hear her along,
> She hangs like a star in the dew of our song;
> She springs like a beam on the brow of the tide,
> She falls like a tear from the eyes of a bride.

Imagination has been used, and used so marvellously. The palanquin is like a tear from the eyes of a bride, who is inside it. Why tears? The bride is going to meet her love. There can be tears, but tears bathed in unlimited joy and also indicative of the joy to follow. Indeed, a great idea behind the palanquin's becoming a tear from the eyes of the bride. All is suggestive of a great hope, hope of happiness. And the song of the palanquin-bearers suggests how happiness must be found in work, and still greater measure of it in the happiness of others.

Why are the palanquin-bearers happy? They are doing their work and carrying some weight. I say "weight" in the physical sense. Else there is no question of weight because the person inside is a great beauty, brimming with love and hope, unspeakable and unheard of. The palanquin-bearers are nevertheless happy because they have found their work. In work they have the blessing of God. Still you have another idea. And that idea can make the entire world happy. Find happiness in the happiness of others. Happiness is personal. We have to agree there. But it is impersonal in the sense that it depends upon the happiness of others. Happiness is catching. You find others happy. You are yourself happy. There is this measure of happiness for the palanquin-bearers because they are aware of the happiness that is to come to the bride they are carrying so gaily and so softly in the wind of their song. Happiness makes their labour, labour of love. And little wonder that they think the palanquin and its load a pearl on a string!

Think of the diction, words and images used to convey her emotions, and why not her ideas, rooted in humanity? There is no indication of efforts. All is spontaneous. One might say that the poet is writing in her mother-tongue. There is no evidence of straining. Such a galaxy of associations and images, communicated (one might say, painted) in beautiful words, is very creditable to an Indian writing in English. Real poetry must be sound and sense both. Lovers of sound, lovers of music, will declare her poetry all music, all emotion, which can soon transport or transform one who gets into it and its rapture. Even those who look invariably to meaning behind sound (I am certainly with them) there is splendour of thought and of idealism, which is highly elevating and compelling. There is something of the other world, dreamy and thrilling. But behind all this, there is life, an entry into the complications of life, which can be imagined upon intense reflection in consequence of her songs.

This is a justification to call her poetry a "criticism of life". It is sensuous as all good poetry has to be; more than that, it is serious as good poetry ought to be a real criticism of life. There is no escape from life, as from emotions, for a genuine poet. Sarojini Naidu is verily a great poet, sensuous and serious both. Else who can think of her entry into active politics, who can think of her becoming Governor of a great province in such a time of crisis?

It is true that as Governor she was like a bird in a cage. But she did her work in an excellent fashion. From her acts and speeches it was clear beyond a doubt that she had enough sense and profundity of thought. This is nothing new in her. Behind her music it is always possible to find great ideas, ideas that might ask us to think of her as a great thinker thinking, it is true, through melodious words, images and emotions. Think of this song:

> Where the voice of the wind calls our wandering
>     feet,
> Through echoing forest and echoing street,
> With lutes in our hands ever-singing we roam,
> All men are kindred, the world is our home.

Here is a song of wandering singers, wandering through forests and streets, endlessly singing their songs. What are these songs about? There is one theme, and that is of the fundamental unity of man throughout the world, from pole to pole. What is that unity? We have come from God and we have the divine essence. The truth is: there is one race all over the world and that is called the human race; there is one blood and that is called the human blood. There is, thus, no occasion for differences. This is the song, put in the mouth of the wandering singers by the poet. Here the poet herself is out in her mission of converting the entire humanity to her way of thinking, the way of thinking that is bound to lead to peace and happiness and brotherhood. Here you have a serious thinker, who has the magic of words, sweet and delicate, and magic of images all familiar and yet captivating. This combination of seriousness with melody is her achievement. Who can think of poets in the presence of such a grandeur of thought as mere idlers, playing in the hands of emotions and sensuousness? Poets, I maintain, can change our course of life. They can be great reformers. A reformer must have the power of feeling intensely and long. This poets possess and they are great reformers. Is it, then, wrong to think of our poet as the poet of the nation, a poet filled with unlimited patriotism that is synonymous with internationalism? Call that love of humanity. That love Sarojini Naidu has in plenty. And the result! Her words, they may be all emotion, are full of meaning and significance, combined with rhythm. Naturally, her poetry instructs, delights and moves. Read it for a necessary preparation for a revolution. I might add she has in this respect the same power which I associate with the poetry of her brother (Harindranath), the power to revolutionise.

Harindranath has rightly sung:

> A poet wields a mighty power,
> The nation cannot lose it:
> Poets, behold your singing hour
> Has come and you must use it.

This is a call to poets. I have a feeling of a similar call made by Sarojini Naidu to poets in her poetry of splendour. In her same song of **"Wandering Singers"** she continues:

> Our lays are of cities whose lustre is shed,
> The laughter and beauty of women long dead;
> The sword of old battles, the crown of old kings,
> And happy and simple and sorrowful things.

Wandering singers, let us remember, are our own poets. They have to wander all the world over. Physically it might be impossible for them. Don't you know they have the great power of vision and imagination, which poets alone possess? Helped by their poetic vision they can cover the entire world. Are they not singers for entire humanity? Whenever we think of a very great poet like Shakespeare or Kalidas or Tagore we have to say that he is a poet for the entire humanity and for all times to come. About poets it has to be noted that they sing melodiously, perennially. In course of their life, their share of rain and sunshine, their extensive journey, physical or mental, they gather some great wisdom and this they communicate with the help of their melody. And so these singers sing of cities whose lustre is shed, of laughter and beauty of women long dead, of the sword of battles and the crown of old kings, and of what not. Is this not entire life with all its complexities? Life today and yesterday and also tomorrow, that life is their theme. And so the wandering singers sing:

> What hope shall we gather, what dreams shall we
>     sow?
> Where the wind calls our wandering footsteps we
>     go.
> No love bids us tarry, no joy bids us wait:
> The voice of the wind is the voice of our fate.

The burden is the voice of fate and that is the voice of the wind. The wind is the hope of the world. That is to indicate the complete picture of conditions of present life.

And so these singers have hope and dreams. Not a bad idea! Here is something which is to assure us success in near future. We canot tarry; we cannot wait. Let us march and soon realise our dreams. Dreams are necessary; they stimulate thinking and thinking is accompanied by action. Ultimately, the voice of fate resolves itself into this voice or call for action. We cannot stop till we have reached the goal. The goal is the revolution itself, a new way of life, full of happiness and comfort.

Sarojini Naidu sings and thinks simultaneously. What is the secret of this unique combination? The great thing about art is that it is consummated in moments of utter forgetfulness. What is this thinking along with singing melodiously for eternity? Sarojini has thought deeply, sensitively and captivatingly. Even when she sings she unfolds her great intensity of thought. But the great thing is that her thoughts appear all emotions and melody as you read them, sing them, or think of their associations. Here is a song of **"Indian Weavers"**:

> Weavers, weaving at break of day,
> Why do you weave a garment so gay?
> Blue as the wing of a halcyon wild,
> We weave the robes of a new-born child.

Read these lines over and over again. You have reinforcement of emotion and music. Words are sweetly arranged. And what of thoughts? You might not think of them at all. But just think. You have a great idea. The idea flashes as you progress through the song:

> Weavers, weaving at fall of night,
> Why do you weave a garment so bright? . . .
> Like the plumes of a peacock, purple and green,
> We weave the marriage-veils of a queen.
>
> Weavers, weaving solemn and still,
> What do you weave in the moonlight chill?
> White as a feather and white as a cloud,
> We weave a dead man's funeral shroud.

A complete picture of life and man's happiness and sorrow on earth is visualised in this beautiful song that captures our attention. The break of day finds one happy. The weaver weaves something gay with a promise for future of brightness. There is the new-born child. Even fall of night finds one still farther in the journey towards happiness. There is the marriage-bell singing; there is the preparation for the marriage-veil. But what happens afterwards? The moonlight is chill; freshness and warmth are gone; the entire drama of man has been enacted and he is found no longer in the kingdom of living beings. He is beyond life and its joys. There is the dead man's white shroud. The race has been run; life's joys have been dried. This is the story communicated by this song of **"Indian Weavers"**.

And this Sarojini's idea is her songs, delightful as perfect emotion and thoughtful like the words of a philosopher, who has passed his life in converse with the world and yet who has not grown this worldly. Her songs have beauty that lives to instruct and delight. This beauty of her songs moves, and that too so magnificently!

> O little mouse, why dost thou cry
> While merry stars laugh in the sky?
> Alas! Alas! my lord is dead!
> Ah, who will ease my bitter pain?
> He went to seek a millet-grain
> In the rich farmer's granary shed;
> They caught him in a baited snare,
> And slew my lover unaware . . .
> Alas! Alas! my lord is dead.

Sing this song. There is an ordinary reference to a mouse whose life is ended because he is caught in a snare, all of a sudden. Now get to the idea. Life is full of accidents. We attach too much importance to life but it comes to an end quite suddenly, and what is left behind is a feeling of sadness. But that feeling of sadness must soon be over. Else there is none to console the sorrow-stricken. Consolation must come from within. Life without this consolation will be in vain. You might weep for some moments but soon this weeping and wailing should be over. Weeping is necessary as an outlet for grief but that has not to be practised long lest it should pass into our character and nature. That passing into our character and nature will be the end of our life and work on earth. This is not to be our aim. And this cannot be the aim of a reformer and a revolutionary in poetry. And so let us sing, think and move. And thus we should go onwards. Take life as it is. There is sadness in it. Feel it, experience it, and then come to its end. Let us then sing. And so this divine singer sings on, and singing goes on instructing delightfully for all time to come:

> Cover mine eyes, O my love!
> Mine eyes that are weary of bliss
>     As of light that is poignant and strong,
> O silence my lips with a kiss,
>     My lips that are weary of song!
> Shelter my soul, O my love!
> My soul is bent low with the pain
>     And the burden of love like the grace
> Of a flower that is smitten with rain:
>     O shelter my soul from thy face!

There is ecstasy, excessive joy and bliss. And yet more of it. And so the course of life runs in hope and still more of hope. Here you have a profound message. The message is of insatiable desires. Also the hint is for ceaseless efforts. And if that message is taken there is a promise of all-round beauty on earth. That is also the message of Sarojini Naidu, a singer of beautiful songs and sweet thoughts.

There is a poem **"Coromandel Fishers"** by Sarojini Naidu. The idea behind the poem is life's reality and its continued success.

She sings:

> The sea is our mother, the cloud is our brother,
>     the waves are our comrades all.
> What though we toss at the fall of the sun,

> where the hand of the sea-god drives?
> He who holds the storm by the hair,
>     will hide in his breast our lives.

Here is a message of fellowship, of real brotherhood, indeed, of working together for our emergence and of manifestation of our divinity in our visions, thoughts and deeds. We have to take it up.

We have complications in life. We have to take them as our mother or friend or comrade. There has to be nothing but love and this love has to consummate in real fulfilment of man.

She merrily continues to sing:

> But sweeter, O brother, the kiss of the spray
>     and the dance of the wild foam's glee:
> Row, brothers, row to the blue of the verge,
>     where the low sky mates with the sea.

How concrete and penetrating the poet in her expression! We just marvel. But that is not the end.

Let us go ahead. That is eternal music for us and we have to hear it and pass it into our life, into the world we live in.

### Asloob Ahmad Ansari (essay date 1977)

SOURCE: "The Poetry of Sarojini Naidu," in *Indo-English Literature: A Collection of Critical Essays,* edited by K. K. Sharma, Vimal Prakashan, 1977, pp. 61-70.

[*In the following essay, Ansari presents an overview of Naidu's poetry.*]

"I am not a poet really. I have the vision and the desire, but not the voice. If I could write just one poem full of beauty and the spirit of greatness, I should be exultantly silent for ever, but I sing just as the birds do, and my songs are as ephemeral". This statement of Sarojini Naidu should be examined carefully before it is accepted as a judicious judgment on her poetry. No critical criterion can pronounce any one of her poems as "full of beauty and the spirit of greatness" if we use these words in the same sense in which they are applicable to the poetry of Keats and Shelley, let alone the poetry of such supreme masters as Shakespeare and Goethe. But that her poems are possessed of an individual beauty and are the product of a fine sensibility acutely responsive to the material of art is not only the impression of a casual reader but the verdict of such fastidious and discriminating critics as Sir Edmund Gosse and Arthur Symons. Again, there does not seem to be much scope for dispute on the point that she had complete mastery over that physical medium that is indispensable for communicating the vision to the audience, and which she designates as "voice".

Naidu had the instinct of a poet. Brought up in a fruitfully stimulating atmosphere, her inborn poetic impulse drew its sustenance from her immediate environment. Her father, though an eminent scientist and passionately devoted to the pursuit of philosophy, had the temperament of a poet. He was a dreamer of enchanting dreams, and in him the curiosity of the scientist had been coalesced with the imaginings of a poet. Her mother had written some Bengali lyrics in her youth. These influences unconsciously reacted upon the malleable substance of her poetic self, and she was forced, by a sort of inner prompting, to utter herself in the form of song.

Whether Naidu's poetry will survive for long, it is only for posterity to decide. But with a quick feminine perception she has apprehended the fact, and makes us apprehend it, too, that she sings as the birds do. Whatever other qualities her poems may possess, and we shall have occasion to point them out in the course of an analysis of different poems, they are pre-eminently characterised by spontaneity, warmth and exuberance. They possess the same light-hearted ease, the same expanding movement, the same heedless freedom, and the same exhilarating gusto as is possessed by the melodies of birds. Their very contact is refreshing and delightful. The "frail, serene, indomitable" soul of the poet seems to be full of a subconscious urge. She sings her mellifluous songs with the "full-throated" abundance of a bird of Spring.

Naidu started composing poems at the early age of thirteen. When she visited England in 1895, her hands were already full of songs. These outpourings of a raw imagination she candidly laid before Sir Edmund Gosse for scrutiny and approval. The limpid flame in her soul kept on burning all this time till *The Golden Threshold* was published in 1905. The very title of the book suggests the presence of undistinguished emotion conveyed in colourful and gorgeous imagery.

In these early poems she indulges in exquisite romantic fancies, and tries to weave all sorts of delicate patterns, sometimes by the mere skilful and effective juxtaposition of dazzling phrases, and sometimes by describing or representing some unusual situation or deeply touching mood. In one of the folk-songs, called **"Indian Weavers"**, she tries to throw glamour around a commonplace craft by establishing a kind of correspondence between the emotional suggestiveness of different hours of time and the texture of the garments woven at them.

Naidu's delight in the various manifestations of Nature, as revealed at this stage and as it was intensified later on, is primal and instinctive. She is possessed of keen sensations, and can enter into sensuous proximity with the objects of Nature. The senses of sight and taste and smell not only afford a fleeting, physical pleasure, but they have been used by the lyric poets as means to build up their specific symbolism. The sense of freedom and expansiveness that we feel in the bare bosom of the sea and the limitless spaces that lie between the sea and the sky, fill Naidu's heart with a perennial joy. The visual and tactile images get blended with one another when she unburdens herself thus in **"Coromandel Fishers"**:

> Sweet is the shade of the cocoanut glade, and the
> 　scent of the mango grove,
> And sweet are the sands at the full o' the moon
> 　with the sound of the voices we love.
> But sweeter, O brothers, the kiss of the spray and
> 　the dance of the wild foam's glee:
> Row, brothers, row to the blue of the verge, where
> 　the low sky mates with sea.

Nature offers her a kind of escape, and deepens her romantic predilections. The over-sophisticated life that is full of trivial luxuries seems to be clogging to the life of the spirit. The glimpse of an idealised life of peace and security in the underworld, attended by the glories of Nature we unmistakably catch in one of the earlier poems, **"Village Song"**. This strong craving for a mythological existence is expressed through the undertones of a child. It seems as if Naidu is not singing an ordinary song, but all the rapture of her soul has been concentrated in this fantasy:

> Mother mine, to the wild forest I am going,
> Where upon the champa boughs the champa buds
> 　are blooming;
> To the köil-haunted river-isles where lotus lilies
> 　glisten,
> The voices of the fairy-folk are calling me, O
> 　listen!

The lines seem strangely reminiscent, in a different setting, of some verses in "The Forsaken Merman" where the picture of an idyllic world has been so attractively drawn by Matthew Arnold, though it must be confessed that Arnold's poem, in its sober simplicity and meaningfulness, emerges out of a deeper life experience:

> Sandstrewn caverns, cool and deep,
> Where the winds are all asleep;
> Where the spent lights quiver and gleam,
> Where the salt weed sways in the stream,

But the bond of intimacy with Nature always remains inviolate with her. The presence of fertility manifested by Nature dawns upon her with a quickened sense of surprise. In the **"Harvest Hymn"**, the tributes paid to the different deities form one complex symphony. Man's voices pay a glowing homage to Surya for the mellow fruitfulness which he brings to the whole vegetable kingdom. When we read the lines:

> We bring thee our songs and our garlands for
> 　tribute,
> The gold of our fields and the gold of our fruit;
> 　O giver of mellowing radiance, we hail thee,
> 　We praise thee, O Surya, with cymbal and
> flute.

we are at once reminded of the Maturing Sun of Keats's "Ode to Autumn" that contributes its own share to the ripening and blossoming of different kinds of fruits and flowers. But it is self-evident that Keats's poem, on account of its periodic movement, its clear and luminous objectivity and its opulent serenity of mood is altogether superior not only to the **"Harvest Hymn"** but to so many other poems written on such a subject and against a similar background.

But this delight in Nature and this desire for escape never blinded Sarojini Naidu to the active interests of human life and the delineation of human emotions. For, to her, nature and man, in spite of their individuality and distinction, are components of a single whole. She is also possessed of a wide, dramatic sympathy with the pursuits and passions of human beings. In **"Indian Love Song"**, the imagery in which the emotion of love shared by both the man and the woman is steeped has an Indian colour. Moreover, she seems to be fully aware of the nice distinction in the shades of feeling as experienced by both owing to the fact of their having a separate psychophysical constitution. The similes used by the woman reflect abandon, concentration and continuity, while those employed by the man imply freedom, expansiveness and transience. The poem opens with these lines uttered by the woman:

> Like a serpent to the calling voice of flutes,
> Glides my heart into thy fingers, O my Love!

and they are paralleled by an identical effusion by the man in the second section of the same poem:

> Like the perfume in the petals of a rose,
> Hides thy heart within my bosom, O my Love!

Even though most of the poems in *The Golden Threshold* are full of a fragile and ephemeral kind of music, but before the period of early romantic poetry is quite over, notes of a graver intonation begin to be audible. It seems as if the inefficacy of the merely decorative poetry is becoming more and more apparent to her, and the urgent issues of life are clamouring for statement, if not solution. The youthful freshness and the virginal delicacy is not quite gone, yet the poet has moved some way towards the thorny paths of life. In the midst of the graceful and scintillating intermingling of threads, woven by her fancies, we occasionally come across lines which compel us to pause and ponder:

> No, no longer ye may linger
>     With your laughter-lighted faces,
> Now I am a thoughtworn singer
>     In life's high and lonely places,
> Fairy fancies, fly away,
>     To bright wind in woven spaces,
>         Fly away.

And it is only when she has forsaken her "lovely stalactite of dreams" that the difference between life, with all its fascination and dangers, its colour, mystery and turbulence, its misfortunes, pains and sufferings, and existence that has a merely physical and biological connotation, becomes transparently clear to her. This awareness of distinction between "being" and "existence" has been given a poetic expression in these lines:

> Till ye have battled with great grief and feats
> And borne the conflict of dream-shattering years,

> Wounded with fierce desire and worn with strife,
> Children, ye have not lived: for this life.

Yet the poetry of the senses was not wholly superseded by the poetry of reflection, and so the zest for life on its purely physical side continued. In **"Indian Dancers"** the serpentine, subtle movements of the arms and the body, the passionate bosoms heaving with fire, and the eyes ravished with the ecstasy of emotion are described with intensity and vigour. It seems as if the poet has, during the moment of creation, imaginatively identified herself with the dancers in order to feel the vital rhythm of life herself. The free and languishing movement of the concluding verses are a measure of the fullness and strength of her feeling:

> Now silent, now singing and swaying and
>     swinging like blossoms that bend to the
>     breezes or showers,
> Now wantonly winding, they flash, now they
>     falter, and lingering, languish in radiant choir;
> Their jewel-girt arms and warm, wavering, lily-
>     long fingers enchant through melodious hours,
> Eyes ravished with rapture, celestially panting,
>     what passionate bosoms aflaming with fire.

Naidu is capable of drawing in a few richly expressive words an effective picture of persons and situations that is riveted in the mind for ever. She focuses light on features that are really striking and significant, and through the choice of apposite words makes the picture stand out brilliantly as when she describes an Indian Gipsy:

> Behold her, daughter of a wandering race,
> Tameless, with the bold falcon's agile grace,
> And the lithe tiger's sinuous majesty.

And then with a dexterous stroke of her pen, she exalts her identity by making her co-existent with primal mysteries. She represents a class which has been roaming upon the earth since times immemorial. Naidu combines pathos and a care for minute details in the poem. The tattered clothes of the gipsy girl, her simple wants which she satisfies somehow or other and the unsteady, uncertain mode of her life leads the poet to think of the river of time, with its shoals and torrents, its changing, swift, irrevocable course ending in unfathomable seas, and she surmises as if the river of gipsy's life and the river of Time have had some inscrutable origin:

> Time's river winds in foaming centuries
> Its changing, swift, irrevocable course
> To far-off and incalculate seas;
> She is twin-born with primal mysteries,
> And drinks of life at Time's forgotten source.

These lines, beautiful in their own way, suggest a comparison with the description of the majestic river Oxus "A foil'd circuitous wanderer" in Matthew Arnold's *Sohrab and Rustum.*

Even while her imagination was not completely mature, she could visualise the continuity of the past with the present. Kings and generals may come and go, kingdoms and empires may flourish or decay, but the achievements of one historic age in the form of architecture, sculpture, literature and philosophy become a portion of the heritage of humanity and all these diverse expressions of human intellect and intuition confer a kind of immortality upon their creators. The Royal Tombs of Golconda preserve the memories of these human agents beyond the encroachment of oblivion.

The poem **"To Buddha Seated on a Lotus"** marks the culminating point of Naidu's first poetic period. The attainment of peace through renunciation is its *motif*. This craving for fixity of purpose in the whirlpool of life, this inaccessible desire for unlocking its mystery, this hunger of the soul for a verified experience heralds a new beginning. All this implies an intuitive effort on the part of the poet to comprehend the enigma of life and to hush the insistent and painful agonising of doubts in the certainty of knowledge:

> For us the travail and the heat,
> The broken secrets of our pride,
> The strenuous lessons of defeat,
> The flower deferred, the fruit denied;
>
> With futile hands we seek to gain
> Our inaccessible desire,
> Diviner summits to attain,
> With faith that sinks and feet that tire;
>
> The end, delusive and afar,
> Still lures us with its beckoning flight,
> And all our mortal moments are
> A session of the Infinite.

These stanzas curiously reverberate some very significant lines of Matthew Arnold's two famous poems "Thyrsis" and "The Scholar Gipsy", that are regarded as a superb expression of the contemporary mood of religious and philosophical scepticism engendered by the disintegration of one set of well-establishod values of life and the vague and boubtful emergence of an alternative set.

But the "shades of the prison-house" that seem to close upon Naidu at the end of *The Golden Threshold* did not obliterate her vivacity and bloom permanently. For some of the themes of this book recur in the *Bird of Time* which appeared in 1912, with the difference that they are now treated with a more neutralised emotionality. Her warm and quick imagination can follow the curves of the dance and penetrate to the inner joy of the spirit of which the dance is but an external manifestation. In **"The Indian Dancers"**, the emphasis is laid upon the overflowing passion and supreme ecstasy which is hidden behind the dance; in **"The Dance of Life"**, the poet is fascinated by grace and symmetry of the limbs, and by the formal, aesthetic aspect of this most dynamic art. Instead of romantic fervour we sense the presence of a sort of classical restraint when we read lines like these:

> Like bright and wind-bloom lilies,
> The dancers sway and shine,

> Swift in a rhythmic circle,
> Soft in a rhythmic line;
> Their little limbs gleam like amber
> Thro' their veils of golden gauze,
> As they glide and bend and beckon,
> As they wheel and wind and pause.

This susceptibility to the seduction of the senses is part of a wider, impulsive response to life. Every fibre of her personality is tingling with the pain and misery of life, and sympathy with suffering individuals is genuine and unfeigned. But she is not an ascetic. The magic of this colourful, variegated and disquieting pageant is irresistible. Out of the depths of despondence and gloom well up confidence, courage and hope. After being moved by a scene of the burning of pyre in **"On the Way to Golconda"**, she instinctively turns to the joys of life, and thus sings with all the inherent exuberance of her spirits:

> Quick with the sense of joys she hath foregone,
> Returned my soul to beckoning joys that wait,
> Laughter of children and the lyric dawn,
> And love's delight, profound and passionate,
> Winged dreams that blow their golden clarion,
> And hope that conquers immemorial hate.

Her intent gaze can pierce through the veil of darkness and she can be inspired by "new hopes, new dreams, new faces," for she is confident that tomorrow will lighten the load of that misery which had been weighing upon yesterday:

> Nay, do not grieve tho' life be full of sadness,
> Nay, do not pine tho' life be dark with trouble,
> Time will not pause or tarry on his way;
> To-day that seems so long, so strange, so bitter,
> Will soon be forgotten yesterday.

In *The Bird of Time,* Sarojini Naidu's art seems to have acquired a kind of technical perfection. There are occasional lines of fine description in which, by the choice of a few suitable epithets and method of severe selection, the poet lends vividness to her picture as when she speaks of fireflies in **"A Song in Spring"**:

> Fireflies weaving aerial dances
> In fragile rhythms of flickering gold

Or, as in **"The Festival of Serpents"**, she describes the serpents in a few apt similes:

> Swift are ye as streams and soundless as the
>     dewfall,
> Subtle as the lightning and splendid as the sun;
> Seers are ye and symbols of the ancient silence,
> Where life and death and sorrow and ecstasy are
>     one.

The note of patriotic feeling is struck when in reply to Death's offering of redemption from the vicissitudes of mortal existence and subsequent reincarnation into some beautiful form of plant or animal life, the poet reveals a hidden desire to fulfil the destiny of her life through song or service:

O Death, am I so purposeless a thing,
Shall my soul falter or my body fear
Its poignant hour of bitter suffering,
Or fail ere I achieve my destined deed
Of song or service for my country's need?

And it is on account of the same love for action and resolve to minimize human follies and sufferings through the message of love and faith and truth that she bids a farewell to **"The Faery Isle of Janjira"**.

The feeling of patriotism is an important thematic strand running through *The Broken Wing* which was printed in 1917. The idea of her own intended sacrifice not unnaturally leads her mind to the offerings in men and money made by India in World War I. Her tender and feeling soul leaps forward to sympathise with that flower of Indian manhood who displayed feats of valour on the different battle-fronts in favour of the Allies. These brave sons of India met the cold hand of Death in strange climes and foreign lands, and their bodies were consigned to the limb of oblivion without any one casting tears of pity upon them. The poet pays a glowing and worthy homage to these heroes in **"The Gift of India"**:

Gathered like pearls in their alien graves,
Silent they sleep by the Persian waves,
Scattered like shells on Egyptian sands,
They lie with pale brows and brave, broken hands,
They are strewn like blossoms mown down by
    chance
On the blood-brown meadows of Flanders and
    France.

The sentiment of love and reverence for the motherland is always surging in her heart, and she stands firm and inflexible in the defence of her honour. The prayer to Lakshmi on behalf of the motherland is a measure of Mrs. Naidu's devout affection and sincere attachment to the land of her ancestors.

And the Imperial Delhi evokes from her a similar tribute. That which is the essence of the artistic and historic sublimity of Delhi is immune to the spells of Death, and is a symbol of the greatness of the past:

Thy changing kings and kingdoms pass away
The gorgeous legends of a bygone day,
But thou dost still immutably remain
Unbroken symbol of proud histories,
Unaging priestess of old mysteries
Before whose shrine the spells of Death are vain.

The fusion of political element in lyric poetry carries our mind back to the tradition of Urdu Ghazal. While they expressed themselves invariably through certain public symbols, the Ghazals of the most conspicious among these Urdu poets were not only impregnated with rich and diversified personal experiences, but also reflected the social and political conditions of their times. Among contemporary poets, the Ghazals of Maulana Hasrat Mauhani that poet, patriot and politician, who has been a staunch and reckless fighter in the freedom movement of India for over half a century or so, and who, at the same time, occupies an immortal place in the domain of Urdu poetry are a continuation of the old tradition.

Unfortunately, Sarojini Naidu's poetry, unlike Shelley's, not only lacks revolutionary ardour, but is also deficient in that core of political experience which can be assimilated with the spirit of lyrical poetry provided the poet possesses the necessary command over the linguistic resources. One explanation which is not quite plausible is this. Mrs. Naidu, although she had responded to the clarion call of renascent India much earlier, as is evident from the poem with which her last slender poetical volume opens, she entered the arena of political strife only in 1919. It is rather surprising that after that date she practically wrote no poems of enough literary merit. Perhaps her political activities dried the springs of her creative energy.

But in spite of feeling the keen joy and zest for life, and being chained to the tyranny of time, Sarojini Naidu sometimes feels the mystic longing to escape from the mutations of worldly existence. An intense craving for wider horizons, for unexplored and unfamiliar regions, for supra-mundane experiences, for the deep tranquillity lying beyond the earthly shackles constitutes the distinctive traits of a romantic temperament. In **"The Flute-Player of Brindabun"**, Naidu's heart is thrilled to the unfathomable mysteries of the Infinite:

Still must I like a homeless bird
    Wander, forsaking all;
The earthly loves and worldly lures
    That held my life in thrall,
And follow, follow, answering
    The magical flute-call.

Some of the finest pieces of descriptive realism are found in poems in which Mrs. Naidu describes the glories of the Spring season. In one of the pieces in **"The Flowering Year"**; while addressing her two daughters, she succumbs to the magic of Spring and thus describes the bounties of Nature:

I know where the ivory lilies unfold
In brooklets half-hidden in sedges,
And the air is aglow with the blossoming gold
Of thickets and hollows and hedges.

But some sad, inner disturbance has snatched away from her heart its spirit of primal joy and she feels herself unable to respond to the call of spring with as much enthusiasm and spontaneity as she used to:

O Sweet I am not false to you
Only my weary heart of late
Has fallen from its high estate
Of laughter and has lost the clue
To all the vernal joy it knew.

The same note of despair and the same desire for escape is sustained for some time, for in **"Summer Woods"** we hear the poet craving for freedom from "the toil and weariness, the praise and prayers of men":

> O let us fling all care away, and lie alone and
>     dream
> 'Neath tangled boughs of tamarind and molsari
>     and neem.

The agony of soul goads her to merge herself in the calm of Nature. She offers the poet a kind of refuge from her prolonged, inner disquietude. Naidu had, perhaps, according to Edmund Gosse, lived in close companionship with sorrow and the experience of much suffering had "darkened the azure of her sky". Whenever she feels herself to be overwhelmed in her unequal struggle with pain and evil, she turns to the solace offered her by Nature. In **"June Sunset",** this search for consolation in the lap of Nature has been given a consummate expression:

> Here shall my heart find its haven of calm,
> By rush-fringed rivers and rain-fed streams
> That glimmer thro' meadows of lily and palm.
> Here shall my soul find its true repose
>     Under a sunset sky of dreams
>     Diaphanous, amber and rose.

This restlessness naturally gives birth to a sense of solitude. Amid the crowded atmosphere of life the stricken soul of the poet experiences a vast vacuum. For her "the joy has taken a flight", and everything in the universe seems to bear an alien, frigid and cold look. The old verve and spark of life have disappeared, and her heart does not beat in tune with the poetry of the earth for everything seems to have an antagonistic attitude towards her:

> But amid the gleaming pageant
> Of life's gay and dancing crowd
> Glides my cold heart like a spectre
> In a rose-encircled shroud.

This wistful melancholy of Sarojini Naidu does not seem to have an intellectual genesis. It appears to be rooted in a purely emotional experience. The poem from which we have just quoted a few lines is followed by **"The Festival of Memory"** in which the poet states the paradox of love. She feels the rapture and agony of love alternately, but is unable to attain to a state of inward bliss. This is something inherent in the very nature of love, for it is a creative process. Just as the created work is always an inadequate representation of the idea lying behind it, in the same way the feeling of love is never satiated; it is an everlasting craving in search of its own completeness through the intended and achieved existential union of two personalities. Love is a cognitive act in which the lover tries to comprehend the soul of the beloved by the sacrifice of his egoism. The separateness of the two should be changed into a pure togetherness. Only then does the extension of human personality take place and the potentialities of life are liberated to construct a paradise upon the face of this earth.

**"The Festival of Memory"** leads on to that series of remarkable love-poems in which the best of Sarojini Naidu is revealed. They are saturated with all the poignant passion of her tremulous soul. Whether she had actual, direct, first-hand experience of all the delicate shades of this most powerful of human emotions, and whether she had undergone all the phases of its tyrannous sway, may well be dubious. But her thorough, imaginative understanding, and her spontaneous, forceful presentation of them bespeak her keenness of vision and sincerity of feeling. The genuine poet always looks into his heart and writes but the great poet so closely identifies himself with the experiences of others that the impersonal is changed into the personal. And if his gift of utterance is unique and inevitable, it is difficult to isolate the different elements.

However, the taste and distinction with which Mrs. Naidu has delineated the different moods and vagaries of love defy all critical commentary:

> But I have naught save my heart's deathless
>     passion
> That craves no recompense divinely sweet,
> Content to wait in proud and lovely fashion,
> And kiss the shadow of love's passing feet.
>                                     **"The Gate of Delight"**

> Let spring unlock the melodies of fountain and of
>     flood,
> And teach the winged word of man to mock the
>     wild bird's art
> But wilder music thrilled me when the rivers of
>     your blood
> Swept o'er the flood-gates of my life to drown
>     my waiting heart.
>                                     **"Ecstasy"**

> To my enraptured sight you are
> Sovereign and sweet reality,
> The splendour of the morning star,
> The might and music of the sea,
> Rich fruit of all Time's harvesting.
>                                     **"The Vision of Love"**

> Quenched are the fervent words I yearn to speak
> And tho' I die how shall I claim or seek
> From your full rivers one reviving shower,
> From your resplendent years one single hour?
> Still for Love's sake I am foredoomed to bear
> A load of passionate silence and despair.
>                                     **"The Silence of Love"**

> When youth and spring and passion shall betray
>     you
> And mock your proud rebellion with defeat,
> God knows, O Love, if I shall save or slay you
> As you lie spent and broken at my feet!
>                                     **"The Menace of Love"**

> Restore me not the rapture that is gone,
> The hope forbidden and the dream denied,
> The ruined purpose and the broken pride,
> Lost kinship with the starlight and the dawn.
> But you whose proud, predestined hands control
> My springs of sorrow, ecstasy and power,
> Grant in the brief compassion of an hour

A gift of tears to save my stricken soul!

                              **"Supplication"**

Burn me, O Love, as in a flowing censer
Dies the rich substance of a sandal grain,
Let my soul die till nought but an intenser
Fragrance of my deep worship doth remain
And praise thee for my death!

                       **"The Worship of Love"**

O Love, is there aught I should fear to fulfil at
    your word?
Your will my weak hands with such dauntless
    delight
      would endow
To capture and tame the wild tempest to sing like
    a bird,
And bend the swift lightning to fashion a crown
    for your brow,
Unfurl the sealed triumph of Time like a foot-
    cloth outspread,
And rend the cold silence that conquers the lips of
    the dead.

                         **"Love Omnipotent"**

      O be thou still,
A radiant and relentless flame,
      A crucible
To shatter and to shape anew
      My heart and will.
Still be thy grief the bitter crown
      That bows my head,
Thy stern, arraigning silences
      My daily bread!
So shall my yearning love at last
      Grow sanctified,
Thro' sorrow find deliverence
      From mortal pride,
So shall my soul, redeemed, reborn,
      Attain thy side.

                              *"Invocation"*

Naidu's poetical output is scanty, and she has not written on a large variety of themes. We relish her poetry not because of its metaphysical conceits, its devotional fervour or its moral bearings. We are fascinated by it because she seems to be speaking to us in familiar tones on subjects with which we are thoroughly acquainted. She is a lyrical poet who expresses the fluctuating fortunes of love in snatches of poetry. Her vision is comprehensive and catholic and her interests wide-ranging. She not only sympathizes with her fellow human beings but falls in love with all that belongs to the soil. In her love poetry, something seems to be precipitated out of the depths of her being which she is unable to suppress or resist. It is the quality of downright sincerity and deep warmth that marks them out from poems written on commonplace topics. When the precise and appropriate emotion is wanting, she degenerates into mere rhetoric that fails to create any abiding impression. She has reached the acme of excellence in her love poetry.

Sarojini Naidu is also a flawless craftsman. Through the magic of her words, she always succeeds in creating a definite atmosphere in the course of the evolution of her thought-process. The ordinary, innocuous words acquire expressiveness under her hands and play an important part in clarifying the emotion that she wants to communicate in a certain poem. Apart from these two purposes that they serve, she is attracted by their formal qualities their tone and rhythm, richness and colour, muscle and fibre and chooses them to enhance the beauty of expression with loving care.

But the most characteristic quality of Sarojini Naidu's poetry, besides its lyrical wealth, is its purely Indian character. For one thing, her poems are drenched in Indian myths and legends. Their atmosphere, too, is always Indian. Her splendid phraseology sometimes betrays the mixture of an exotic element, but it is more in conformity to the practice of Persian poets rather than to that of English or French. Owing to the Western influences in her early equipment she developed the art of expressing herself in a foreign linguistic medium, but the spirit of her poetry is always indigenous. Mrs. Naidu is the first poetess who has been able to synthesise these two disparate elements in the form of an art so complex and subtle, and with such superb success.

### R. K. Das Gupta (essay date 1980)

SOURCE: "Sarojini Naidu: The Poet as a Politician," in *Indian and Foreign Review,* Vol. 17, No. 6, January 1-15, 1980, pp. 13-15.

[*In the following essay, Das Gupta discusses ways in which Naidu's poetic sensibilities affected her political career and actions.*]

When John Stuart Mill drew up an antithesis between eloquence and poetry and said that while the one was heard the other was over-heard, he did not add that one could not at once be an orator and a poet. Mill, however, did not know of any fine public speaker who was also a fine poet. The combination of the two in Sarojini Naidu is unique in the history of letters even in the language she used in speech and song.

When the lofty eloquence of Sarojini Naidu's presidential address at the fortieth session of the Indian National Congress held in Kanpur in 1925 drew the applause of the entire audience, Motilal Nehru gently remarked: 'but what did she say?' Today, a century after her birth and more than twenty-five years after her death we seem to ask ourselves the same question what did she say in politics and in poetry? The author of the Nehru Report had his own reason to be suspicious of rhetoric, however noble, but he certainly had a fine ear for a fine English sentence and knew that to move a large assembly of Indian listeners to tears by turning out extempore, rolling Ciceronian periods needed a genius of whom any country could be proud. But the art of politics is no longer dependent on the art of expression. Sarojini Naidu's voice does not now ring the ears accustomed to listen to a different political idiom.

GANDHI'S ADMIRATION

Sarojini Naidu's poetry too appears to the average reader of English verse in his country as an Indian echo of the late Victorian English Muse, something which has nothing to offer to those who are fed on Eliot, Auden and Spender. And here too the question is what does she say in her verse? And even if we can find some message in her poetry how important is it today when the language in which she wrote that poetry is understood by less than two per cent of our people. Her poetry like her oratory is an achievement in a language that is foreign to our soil.

But fifty years ago Sarojini's oratory was valued as much as her poetry and they were valued by one who was a confirmed apologist of Hindi and the other vernaculars of our country and who placed action above rhetoric in politics. To Motilal's ironic comment on Sarojini Naidu's eloquence we can mention Mahatma Gandhi's admiration for it in the *Navajivan* of 3 January 1926: 'The president's speech is poetic. What need to praise the beauty of its English. It was not Sarojini Devi's part to outline a strategy. That was for Pandit Motilal to do'. In a great political movement noble words passionately delivered may be as important as bugles that sing to battle: they are the breath and finer spirit of the shrewdest of strategies. Sarojini's finest speeches are the poetry of Indian politics of the days of Gandhi and Nehru: that we hear no echoes of that poetry in these latter days is due to the changes in world's political style after the second world war.

Mahatma Gandhi was no less admirer of Sarojini's poetry. On the eve of her return to India from South Africa he wrote in *Young India* (3.7.1924) 'to remind Bombay of its duty when India's nightingale returns to delight the Indian ear with her sweet music'. Perhaps none of us can say if Mahatma Gandhi chose for his metaphor song-bird which was also a night-bird to express response to the poems in her **The Broken Wing.** But that Mahatma Gandhi called her poetry 'great music' is good criticism though it is so simple and the two words have value when they come from the pen of one who was a master of the English language.

But Mahatma Gandhi did not admire Sarojini Naidu for her oratory and her poetry only. He extols her for what he called her two outstanding achievements. 'I propose Sarojini Devi for the highest honour in the power of the country to bestow on her, for though a woman she has achieved in Africa what no man could have ever achieved and also because she is an ambassador of Hindu-Muslim unity'. This was excellent work at home and abroad, an earnest for her brave acts during the Civil Disobedience and Quit India movements.

RARE PERSONALITY

But when we consider Sarojini Naidu at this distance of time it may seem useless to speak of her politics when there is something far more striking to speak of, her poems and the poem behind her poems, a most charming personality in our national history. While her poetry can be fairly ably introduced to us by those who enjoy reading poetry it requires an Andre Maurois to present her rare personality. There was in her nature such a mixture of strength and tenderness, of a fine sense of humour and high seriousness, of shrewdness and simplicity which only a master of the art of biography can delineate. Margarita Barns gives a portrait of this great woman in her *India Today and Tomorrow* (1937) which a master artist should now enlarge in more vivid colours and sharper lines. Poetess politician walking encyclopaedia on every one's affairs she says, 'Sarojini Naidu combines the shrewdness of her years with the vivacity of a young girl. While she can laugh at others, she can also convulse an audience with jokes against herself'. And her jokes were not just clever sallies: they would illuminate the situation which occasioned them. Looking for Mahatma Gandhi at the second Round Table Conference she asked 'Where is our little Mickey Mouse?' and at the same Conference she told a delegate pressing for a second chamber 'why not a third, and a lethal one for certain politicians'. Each anecdote of her life is crowned with a neat epigram like the one she threw at Mahatma Gandhi when it was quite a problem to get a third class railway compartment for his travel. 'Bapu it is so expensive to keep you poor', she told her master who reciprocated this token of deep affection with a disarming smile.

The modern reader's interest in Sarojini Naidu's poetry is declining mostly because he is used to kind of imported modernity which has become fashionable in this country since the publication of T.S. Eliot's *The Waste Land in 1922.* An intelligible, beautiful lyrical line like Sarojini's 'The earth is ashine like a humming bird's wing' now seems to be a kind of Tennysonian frippery. The best of Sarojini's verse has an authentic lyricism which is now suspect on the very ground of the authenticity. Sarojini was too sensible a poet to fancy that good poetry must necessarily be odd verse and she was too deeply emotional to be afraid of appearing sentimental.

FINEST VERSE

But in the first three decades of this century Sarojini Naidu's poetry was judged as the finest English verse written by an Indian and the judgement was confirmed by men of taste both in this country and in England. Edmund Gosse said in his introduction to her second book of verse **The Golden Threshold** (1905) that 'she is the most brilliant, the most original, as well as the most correct of all the natives of Hindustan who have written in English'. Arthur Symons said about her that 'her eyes turned towards beauty as the sunflower turns towards the sun'. The *London Times* said that 'her poetry seems to sing itself, as if her swift thoughts and strong emotions sprang into lyrics of themselves'; The *Manchester Guardian* said that 'her simplicity suggests Blake' and *The Review of Reviews* wrote that her poetry 'should silence forever the scoffer who declares that women cannot write poetry'. . .

Soon after the publication of Sarojini Naidu's **The Broken Wing** (1917) appeared an interesting anthology called *The Bengali Book of English Verse* (1918) edited by T.O.D. Dunn and with a foreword by Rabindranath Tagore. In his introductory essay Dunn remarks that 'it is significant that the task of wedding the rich vocabulary of England's poetry to purely oriental subjects has been accomplished by two Indian women, Toru Dutt and Sarojini Naidu'. Five years later Margaret Macnicol stressed this oriental spirit of her poems in her introduction to *Poems by An Indian Woman* (1923).

In this country one of the most distinguished admirers of Sarojini Naidu's poetry was Sri Aurobindo who says in one of his letters (24.1.1935): 'Some of her lyrical work is likely to survive among the lasting things in English literature and by these she may take her rank among the immortals'. The judgement was sustained about twenty years later by H.G. Rawinson who said that she 'stands in the front rank of English lyrical writers'. Perhaps we need to recall these appreciations of her poetry at an hour when it is being slighted as but a feeble Indian echo of late Victorian English voice. It is, however, a pity that the finest criticism of her poetry is included in a book which is now extremely rare and which should be used as a general introduction to her *Complete Works,* if at all such a volume is published to mark her birth-centenary.

NO IMPORTED REVOLUTION

The 28-page essay on '*The Poetry* of *Sarojini Naidu,* by James H. Cousins (1873-1956), the Irish poet and critic, included in his title *The Renaissance in India* (1918) is finely critical of some of the weaknesses in her poetry and it is equally finely appreciative of its excellences. 'She has not become', Cousins says, 'as Mr Gosse says she hoped to become, a Goethe or a Keats for India; but she has succeeded in becoming a far more vital and compelling entity: she has become Sarojini, with her own exquisite qualities and with the not less interesting defects of those qualities. She has already added to literature something Keats-like in its frank but perfectly pure sensuousness. Except in the use of a few conventional words, there is hardly any trace of derivative impulse in her work'. Cousins regretted that 'the flares of the public platform often lure her away from the radiance of her "moon-enchanted" estuary of dreams'. But at the end of the essay he affirms that 'with such song as she' has sung and is capable of singing she is among the greatest and her most essential gifts of service made a great contribution 'to the incarnating Spirit of Renaissance, and the world in the hour of its crying need for pure and healing utterance'. If we have lost the ear for such 'pure and healing utterance' it is because we have no notion of this second coming of the Spirit of Renaissance and our taste of those who write cleverly on Sarojini's 'saccharine-sweetness' is under the influence of what they call the 'literary revolution of the twenties'. Sarojini Naidu saved her soul and her poetry by keeping herself away from that 'revolution'. She was involved in another revolution, a revolution nearer home and she knew that the revolution

in poetry brought about by T.S. Eliot's *The Waste Land* had little meaning for an Indian poet. She did not believe in imported revolution in poetry or in politics.

A year before the publication of Cousins' book D.H.S. Nicholson and A.H.E. Lee included three poems of Sarojini Naidu in their *The Oxford Book of English Mystical Verse* (1917) **'The Soul's Prayer', 'In Salutation to the Eternal Peace'** and **'To a Buddha Seated on a Lotus'.** To be counted amongst the hundred and sixty-four poets who wrote mystical verse in the English language was a distinction for one not born to the language. It is a distinction that is irrelevant to a generation which has rejected mysticism as a form medievalism.

Perhaps what makes the modern man turn away from the poetry of Sarojini Naidu, more than anything else, is its rhyme which strikes him as something too fine and too precise for ears used to different rhythms. But we cannot reject neat rhymes without rejecting a great deal of good poetry. And Sarojini Naidu can produce what Cousins has called "a haunting chime of bells and voices" by her mastery of rhyme as in

> Where the golden, glowing
>   Champak buds are blowing
> By the swiftly-flowing streams,
>   Now, when day is dying,
> There are fairies flying
>   Scattering a cloud of dreams.

In her more powerful poems in which she expresses her deepest thoughts there is yet another kind of mastery of diction and metre which gives them a permanent place in English poetry. One of such poems is her **'To a Buddha Seated on a Lotus':**

> With futile hands we seek to gain
> Our inaccessible desire,
> Diviner summits to attain,
> With faith that sinks and feet that tire;
> But nought shall conquer or control
> The heavenward hunger of our soul.
> The end illusive and afar,
> Still lures us with its beckoning flight,
> And all our mortal moments are
> A session of the infinite.

Words such as these may not strike the ears of the sophisticated readers of today as words of great meaning: but they are words which survive 'revolution in literature and taste' as the true voice of poetry. And as we repeat them we may also hear the gentle flutterings of 'a homing bird that bears a broken wing' and wonder at the height to which she soared when her wing was whole.

To criticise that the orator in Sarojini Naidu killed the poet may be a misreading of her career as a whole. She brought to her national work the soul of a poet and not a few of her great public speeches were soliloquies spoken in company.

**A. N. Dwivedi (essay date 1981)**

SOURCE: "The Muse's Bower: Sarojini's Poetic Achievement," in *Sarojini Naidu and Her Poetry,* Kitab Mahal, 1981, pp. 121-144.

[*In the following essay, Dwivedi presents an overview of Naidu's career.*]

Sarojini's poetic output has been meagre but qualitative. Her early verses were entirely English in form and content, but a timely advice of Sir Gosse turned her to her native land for themes and raw materials. Exquisitely did she sing about the beauty of the Indian landscape, about the common man and woman, about the Hindu-Muslim unity, and about the country's subjection under the Britishers. With a stroke of good luck, she came in touch with such distinguished literary personalities of the day as Edmund Gosse and Arthur Symons, who showed her, as she has confessed, the path to the Golden Threshold of Poetry, the path from which she never swerved. Later, she thrived on her own poetic merits, and not on anyone's recommendations.

Poetry came to Sarojini, as we know, as a natural gift, and she could not help writing it when the mood overpowered her. She had received it by way of inheritance: her parents were also composers of charming verses. The romantic surroundings of Hyderabad and the short stay in England unquestionably quickened Sarojini's poetic perception, and whatever she wrote thereafter reflects the maturity of her mind and the fullness of her heart.

I. THE POETIC CREED

It was the desire of beauty that made Sarojini a poetess; her "nerves of delight" were always quivering at the contact of beauty. Her eyes turned towards beauty as the sunflower turns towards the sun, opening wider and wider until one saw nothing but the eyes. Like Keats, she was an adorer of Beauty. In one of her letters to Arthur Symons, she wrote: "Your letter made me very proud and very sad. Is it possible that I have written verses that are 'filled with beauty', and is it possible that you really think them worthy of being given to the world? You know how high my ideal of Art is; and to me my poor casual little poems seem to be less than beautiful I mean with that final enduring beauty that I desire".[1] In another letter, she noted down: "I am not a poet really. I have the vision and the desire but not the voice. If I could write just one poem full of beauty and the spirit of greatness, I should be exultantly silent for ever; but I sing just as the birds do, and my songs are as ephemeral".[2] Out of the beautiful, Sarojini used to derive "a strange sensation"[3] which lifted her up and transformed her into an elfin spirit.

Sarojini wanted to give to the world something of lasting value, something wrought with fine artistry. In one of her letters to Edmund Gosse, she wrote: "While I live, it will always be the supreme desire of my soul to write poetry one poem, one line of enduring verse even. Perhaps I shall die without realising that longing which is at once an exquisite joy and an unspeakable anguish to me."[4] Sarojini, who aimed at perfection and excellence in art, did realise "that longing" by composing enduring verses, and has shown that her early sad apprehension was "needless". One of her enduring poems is **"Palanquin-Bearers"**, which is partly quoted here for the delight and judgment of the reader:

> Lightly, O lightly, we bear her along,
> She sways like a flower in the wind of our song;
> She skims like a bird on the foam of a stream,
> She floats like a laugh from the lips of a dream.
> Gaily, O gaily we glide and we sing,
> We bear her along like a pearl on a string.
>
> (p. 3).

It is a poem of great artistic beauty and has a rhythmic swing in it which is well in accord with the soft onward movement of the palanquin-bearers.

II. THE BIRD-LIKE QUALITY OF SONG

Sarojini was primarily "a singer of songs" and "a song-bird". She has been called "the Nightingale of India". The first thing that strikes us in reading her poetry is her exquisite melody and fine delicacy of feeling and expression blended with freshness and
exuberance of spirit. Arthur Symons valued her poetry for "this bird-like quality of song.'[5]. Prof. Vishwanathan has rightly pointed out that it would be a closed mind to think that she was not a song-bird.[6] Sarojini did not seek to grapple with life's intricate problems as does a philosopher. For her there were only situations that made her nerves tingle and stirred her into quivering songs. Life for her was not a riddle to be solved, but a miracle to be sung and celebrated. Its endless variety excited her, its colours dazzled her, its beauty intoxicated her. Her spontaneous response to it may be interpreted by some people as her weakness, but in this lies also her strength the secret of her perennial youthfulness. Prof B. S. Mathur thinks that Sarojini was "a supreme singer of beautiful songs, songs bathed in melody and thoughts",[8] especially so in her Indian folk-songs, one of which is **"Song of Radha, the Milkmaid"**:

> I carried my curds to the Mathura fair . . .
> How softly the heifers were lowing . . .
> I wanted to cry, "Who will buy
> These curds that are white as the clouds in the sky
> When the breezes of *Shrawan* are blowing?"
> But my heart was so full of your beauty, Beloved,
> They laughed as I cried without knowing:
>
> > *Govinda! Govinda!*
> > *Govinda! Govinda! . . .*
> How softly the river was flowing! (p. 112).

This is the first stanza of the poem which is sung to Indian tunes, and which nicely evokes the image of a soft, rhythmic flow not only in the river Yamuna but also in the heart of the singer. The "mantric effect"[9] produced by it in the repetition of "Govinda" is really unforgettable.

### III. THE LYRICAL IMPULSE

There can be no two opinions about the predominance of lyrical impulse in Sarojini's poetry. Her poems are mostly short swallow flights of fancy. Some are effusions of the rapture of Spring, some others transport us into a world of inner ecstasy and spiritual elation, and many others quiver with the passion of love. There are some poems which enable us to peer into India's luminous past. In Sarojini's poetry the lyric appeal is "various and wonderful and full of the magic of melody".[10] Among her notable lyrics, one may mention **"The Festival of Memory"**, **"Palanquin-Bearers"**, **"To a Buddha Seated on a Lotus"**, **"Wandering Singers"**, **"Guerdon"**, etc. As a matter of fact, the poetess, when inspired, cannot live at a lower level, this is clearly borne out by the poem **"Guerdon"**, which will inevitably "take its place among the lyrical classics".[11] A critic has even suggested that Sarojini's metrical accomplishment is part of her lyricism.[12]

### IV. WIDE SYMPATHIES

It is somewhat difficult to conceive of a true lyric poet with narrow sympathies. As regards Sarojini, she has very aptly kept her antipathies, if any, out of her poetry. Her sympathetic interpretation of life has covered a wide range of subjects, and the poems like **"Corn-Grinders"** and **"The Pardah Nashin"** are evidently inspired by her sympathy for the sufferer and downtrodden. The opening stanza of **"Corn-Grinders"**, quoted below, is an illustration of this:

> *O little mouse, why dost thou cry*
> *While merry stars laugh in the sky?*
> Alas! Alas! my lord is dead!
> Ah, who will ease my bitter pain?
> He went to seek a millet-grain
> In the rich farmer's granary shed;
> They caught him in a baited snare,
> And slew my lover unaware . . .
> Alas! alas! my lord is dead.
>
> (p. 9).

Sarojini sympathized not only with human beings but also with birds, flowers, animals and insects. Surrounded by all forms of natural beauty and innocent joy, she felt herself one with the vital rhythm of the world and became almost a part of the expanding life of birds and flowers, animals and insects. Her sympathetic attitude towards the different religions of the world is well reflected in **"The Call to Evening Prayer"**. She depicted the Hindu and Muslim ways of life with equal zeal and devotion. In fact, she was "at home everywhere and at all kinds of gatherings",[13] and this evidently speaks of "the greatness and richness of her personality".[14]

### V. THE ROMANTIC FERVOUR

Sarojini's poetry belongs to the Romantic school, but it is the romance that in its most passionate mood leaves no

ashes in the mouth. She has lingered in the Garden of Kama, but with larger eyes and a less heavy chin. She has not become, as Edmund Gosse says she hoped to, "a Goethe or a Keats for India", but she has certainly become a far more living entity than a mere reflection of either: she has become Sarojini Naidu, with her own distinctive qualities. Keats and Shelley were undoubtedly her early models; in her impassioned lyrical outpourings she is very close to Shelley, and in her perfectly sensuous apprehension of thought and feeling she is near the heart of Keats. But there is hardly any trace of derivative impulse in her work except for the use of a few conventional words and phrases.

### VI. THE PHILOSOPHICAL STRAIN

There is a grain of truth in the assertion that poetry, especially lyrical, expresses a philosophy of life. Poetry attempts the emotional appreciation of the universe, while science tries to understand it through the intellect. As philosophy is no other than an explanation of life, every lyrical poet unconsciously expounds it.[15]

In Sarojini's case, an undercurrent of serious thought runs in some of her poems.[16] **"Indian Weavers"** is a glaring example of it:

> Weavers, weaving at break of day,
> Why do you weave a garment so gay? . . .
> Blue as the wing of a halcyon wild,
> We weave the robes of a new-born child.
> Weavers, weaving at fall of night,
> Why do you weave a garment so bright? . . .
> Like the plumes of a peacock, purple and green,
> We weave the marriage-veils of a queen.
> Weavers, weaving solemn and still,
> What do you weave in the moonlight chill? . . .
> White as a feather and white as a cloud,
> We weave a dead man's funeral shroud.
>
> (p. 5).

This poem is reflective in nature, and its flow and melody should not blur its thought.

Sarojini's poetry has a message to deliver to mankind. It is the message of a self-surrendering life of love in the midst of Nature or of an indomitable struggle of love on behalf of the poor, the lowly, and the suffering. Sarojini's is "a philosophy of giving away one's love and energy in the cause of good in the living present, supremely hopeful of the ultimate destiny and supremely happy in the privilege of giving".[17] The poetess had acutely experienced the blows and buffets of life and identified herself with the sorrow-stricken people:

> O Fate, betwixt the grinding-stones of Pain,
> Tho' you have crushed my life like broken grain,
> Lo! I will leaven it with my tears and knead
> The bread of Hope to comfort and to feed
> The myriad hearts for whom no harvests blow
>     Save bitter herbs of woe.
>
> (p. 174).

These lines from the poem **"Invincible"** speak of Sarojini's disillusionment and grasp of reality. In them emotion is blended with talent, art with thought. Sarojini was actually two things in one: a supreme artist and a fine melodist with the background of an intense thinker.[18] It is a different question whether her thought is methodical or not. The obvious fact is that she is basically a creature of emotions who is momentarily touched by the splendour of thought.

Sarojini wrote some mystic verses in her hours of thoughtful exaltation. Her appreciation of Truth led her to a consideration of Man, God, the Universe, their inter-relationship, Life and Death. Her three poems found a place in *The Oxford Book of English Mystical Verse*. In one of these, she says:

> I, bending from my sevenfold height,
> Will teach thee of quickening grace,
> Life is a prism of My light,
> And Death the shadow of My face.
> ("**The Soul's Prayer**", p. 124).

In another, she seems to be in a challenging mood:

> Say, shall I heed dull presages of doom,
> Or dread the rumoured loneliness and gloom,
> The mute and mystic terror of the tomb?
>
> For my glad heart is drunk and drenched with
>     Thee,
> O inmost Wine of living ecstasy!
> O intimate essence of eternity!
> ("**In Salutation to the Eternal Peace**", p. 137).

The mystical note is well-pronounced in the two poems partly reproduced here. The third one is addressed to Lord Buddha seated on a Lotus. In it the poetess expresses her desire to attain *Nirvana*:

> The end, elusive and after,
> Still lures us with its beckoning flight,
> And all our mortal moments are
> A session of the Infinite.
> How shall we reach the great, unknown
> Nirvana of thy Lotus-throne?
> ("**To a Buddha Seated on a Lotus**", p. 62).

These three poems are not the only mystic verses which Sarojini wrote; her four slender volumes are rather sprinkled with a philosophy of life and other-worldly vision. She did not, however, strive to formulate a systematic sequence of poetic thought, and when she did it at all, as in **"The Temple"** in *The Broken Wing*, she was not convincing to the reader.[19]

### VII. IMAGERY

Sarojini wove a rich tapestry of images in her poetry. Her images are usually impressive and impressionistic; they are also varied and sublime. They are mostly drawn from nature, myth, legend, country-scenes and the fairy kingdoms, which are far removed from our work-a-day world.

They are like the dance of the dew on the wings of a moon-beam, or the veil glowing with the hues of a lapwing's crest. They tend to confirm the fact that Sarojini was a woman of high poetic sensibility and delicate imagination, and give us an idea of her ornate poetry abounding in a luxuriant feast of similes and metaphors. Her **"Palanquin-Bearers"**, **"The Snake-Charmer"**, and **"Humayun to Zobeida"** are nothing but a kind of catalogue of images put together.

It has been pointed out that Omar Khayyam influenced Sarojini with his images, and that she was a scholar in Persian and Urdu and so repeatedly brought in images of the Islamic world.[20] An unfailing resourcefulness of appropriate epithets, metaphors and similes rendered her imagery graphically graspable. Thus, in **"Leili"**, the poetess compares the moon to a caste-mark:

> A caste-mark on the azure brows of Heaven,
> The golden moon burns sacred, solems, bright . . .
> (p. 31).

Another instance of brilliant imagery is **"Nightfall in the City of Hyderabad"**, in which she gives us:

> See how the speckled sky burns like a pigeon's
>     throat,
> Jewelled with embers of opal and peridote.
> (p. 55).

And again:

> Over the city bridge Night comes majestical,
> Borne like a queen to a sumptuous festival.
> (p. 56).

Some other poems having natural images are: **"On Juhu Sands"**, **"In Praise of Gulmohur Blossom"**, **"Golden Cassia"** and **"Coromandel Fishers"**. In the last-named poem, one finds the image of the dance of the wild foam's glee which is reminiscent of Wordsworth's golden daffodils "The waves beside them danced, but they/Out-did the sparkling waves in glee". Another apt yet startling image in the same poem is to be found in:

> Row, brothers, row to the blue of the verge, where
>     the low sky mates with the sea.
> (p. 7).

Sarojini introduced impressionistic images in **"Indian Love-Song"**, wherein the morning sows her "tents of gold on fields of ivory", in **"Cradle-Song"**, wherein the wild fire-flies dance "through the fairy *neem*", and in **"To the God of Pain"**, wherein the flower-like dreams and the gem-like fire of hopes upleap "like the light of dawn".

### VIII. SYMBOLISM

Some of Sarojini's poems have symbolistic overtones. As a symbolist, she was influenced by Arthur Symons, whose *The Symbolist Movement in Literature* (1899) proved to be epoch-making. The symbols employed by her are both traditional and personal. Traditional symbols, as we know, are stock symbols used in literature since immemorial days, but personal symbols being new and arbitrary pose some difficulty for the reader.

In **"The Indian Gipsy"**, the gipsy girl, who is twin-born with primal mysteries and drinks of life at Time's forgotten source, is a symbolic representation of the obscurity and oldness of Time. The serpents of **"The Festival of Serpents"** fill us with a sense of awe and apprehension of some felt mystery when we read following lines:

> Swift are ye as streams and soundless as the
>    dewfall,
> Subtle as the lightning and splendid as the sun;
> Seers are ye and symbols of the ancient silence,
> Where life and death and sorrow and ecstasy are
>    one.
>
> (p. 111).

The last two lines are significant from the viewpoint of our discussion. **"Song of Radha, the Milkmaid"**, has the repeated chanting of the name "Govinda" which reverberates with the ancient experience of fulfilment in identity (identity or merger with the Beloved and with the yearning of the Eternal Feminine for the Eternal Masculine). Similarly, the "slumbering sedges" that "catch from the stars some high tone of their mystical speech" in the poem **"Solitude"**, and the "mystic Lotus" in the poem **"The Lotus"** are full of symbolic connotations.

### IX. A SENSE OF HUMOUR

Sarojini had a remarkable sense of humour, and this was actually an integral part of her sharp mind. This unique quality made her a welcome person in any kind of gatherings. Her lively intelligence, her maddening interest in the good things of life, her jokes and jibes endeared her to everyone. She was quite responsive to the funny side of life. Sahib Singh Ahuja maintains that "She was a fount of bubbling humour wherever she was in a conference or committee room, in a circle of friends or even in jail."[21] In dealing with Gandhiji, she never scrupled from making fun, and would call him "Mickey Mouse", and even said in his presence that he looked exactly like a bat.[22] She was certainly a licensed jester in Gandhiji's little court. Her humour found its best expression in her letters and speeches. In one of her letters to Arthur Symons, she wrote: "Of all things that life or perhaps my temperament has given me I prize the gift of laughter as beyond price."[23] Sympathy and a sense of humour were natural gifts to her. Her humour, like the dedicate reserve of her manner, became a mask or a shelter for her. It supported or protected her in all favourable or unfavourable circumstances.

### X. POWER OF DESCRIPTION

Sarojini was endowed with an immense descriptive power. She always described a scene or situation in accurate detail. Her method of description was natural, with or without comments or reflections according to the requirement. Instances of purely descriptive poems are: **"Indian Dancers"** and **"Nightfall in the City of Hyderabad"**. In **"The Indian Gipsy"** and **"June Sunset"** we have good examples of description mingled with reflection. The poems in which reflection predominates over description are: **"The Royal Tombs of Golconda"** and **"To a Buddha Seated on a Lotus"**. Here it may be noted that the reflections are such as are appropriate to poetry; they make no pretence to great depth, but give us at any rate genuine poetry.[24]

### XI. OTHER METHODS OF COMPOSITION

Apart from the descriptive method considered earlier, Sarojini employed various other methods of composition too.[25] The method of direct expression of the poetess's own personal feelings can be seen at work in **"Love and Death"**, **"Caprice"**, and **"The Soul's Prayer"**. The love poems are direct utterances of her feelings, moods and ecstasies. The sole justification for revealing one's private feelings to the world is that they should have something of a universal quality about them and that they should be expressed more aptly and powerfully than the reader would usually do for himself. At times Sarojini spoke dramatically through the mouth of another person, either in monologue or dialogue. Most of the Indian Folk-Songs in *The Golden Threshold* are examples of the dramatic method. At other times the poetess adopted the method of direct address, such as in the Memorial Verses on **"Ya Mahbub"** and **"Gokhale"**, in **"In Salutation to My Father's Spirit"**, and in **"Ode to H. H. the Nizam of Hyderabad"**.

### XII. "AUTOCHTHONOUSNESS"

It was Sir Edmund Gosse who remarked that Sarojini was "in all things and to the fullest extent autochthonous."[26] What the noted critic meant thereby was that she sprang from the very soil of India; her spirit, though it employed the English language as its vehicle, had no other tie with the West, and addressed itself to the exposition of tropical and primitive emotions. The poetess employed purely Indian themes in her poetry. With the eager sensibility, she was always ready to receive impressions from all corners of the richly coloured Indian life throbbing around her. The commonest of sights and sounds, the shrillest of street cries, the humblest of her fellowmen: all had for her some peculiar intimation, some mysterious meaning. Out of the simple chants and homely joys of her people, she "fashioned a subtle, melodious measure, capable of an astonishing range of notes and rhythms."[27] The bazaars of Hyderabad, the palanquin-bearers, the weavers, the snake-charmers, the wandering beggar-minstrels: all inspired in the poetess a strange, rich mood, and she portrayed different walks of Indian life in the glittering pages of her poetry.

### XIII. THEMES

The themes of Sarojini's poetry are usually drawn from Indian sources. In this respect, she was indebted to Edmund Gosse, who advised her to turn away from robins, skylarks and English landscapes and concentrate on "some revelation of the heart of India, some sincere penetrating analysis of Native passion, of the principles of antique religion and of such mysterious intimations as stirred the soul of the East, long before the West had begum to dream that it had a soul".[28]

From the thematic point of view, Sarojini's poems fall into five heads: (1) nature poems, (2) love poems, (3) patriotic poems, (4) poems of life and death, and (5) poems of the Indian scene. We shall briefly consider these heads hereafter.

Nature was to Sarojini, as also to Wordsworth, a perennial source of inspiration. She wrote many lovely lyrics on natural scenes and sights. Her nature poetry is glutted with soft, delicate, hundred-hued blossoms, with honey sweetness, and with a hundred-toned music of the birds. That is what one comes across in her Spring poems which form a major portion of her nature poetry. A keen sense of beauty never missed her. There are striking similes, metaphors, images and rhythmic phrases in her poems. Not only soft aspects of Nature attracted her, but her terrific and cruel aspects, such as tempestuous oceans and volcanic eruptions and stormy winds, had their impact on her. The poetess often lent her personal moods to Nature, and hence her poems are only rarely realistic portrayals. Nature was to her what it was to Tennyson a background for the portraiture of human emotions.[29] Mrs. Sengupta, however, does not agree with this view.[30] Some of Sarojini's best-known nature poems are: **"Leili"**, **"Songs of the Springtime"** (ten poems describing Spring in all its splendour), and **"The Flowering Year"** (six poems, of which **"June Sunset"** is the most charming), **"Spring in Kashmir"**, **"The Gloriosa Lily"**, **"The Water Hyacinth"**, etc. Mark the following lines from **"Spring in Kashmir"**:

> Heart O my heart, hear the Springtime is calling
>     With her laugher, her music, her beauty
>     enthralling.
>
> Thro' glade and thro' glen her winged feet let us
>     follow,
>     In the wake of the oriole, the sunbird and
>     swallow.
>             (*The Feather of the Dawn,* p. 14).

They reveal the very heart of the poetess that is now wholly taken up with the Springtime.

There are many delightful love songs in the four books of poetry by Sarojini Naidu. One may sort out such poems in this connection as **"Indian Love-Song"**, **"Humayun**

to Zobeida"**, **"Ecstasy"**, **"The Poet's Love-Song"**, **"An Indian Love Song from the North"**, **"A Rajput Love-Song"**, **"Song of Radha, the Milkmaid"**, **"The Temple"**, **"The Flute-Player of Brindaban"**, **"Perplext"**, **"The Gift"**, **"The Amulet"**, **"Immutable"**,** and **"Songs of Radha"**. From the last-mentioned poem the following lines are being quoted for the enjoyment of the reader:

> Krishna Murari, my radiant lover
> Cometh. O sisters spread
> Buds and ripe blossoms his couch to cover,
> Silver and vermeil red.
> With flowering branches the doorways darken,
> Is that his flute call? Sisters hearken!
> Why tarrieth he so long?
> O like a leaf doth my shy heart shiver,
> O like a wave do my faint limbs quiver.
> Softly, softly, Jamuna river,
> Sing thou our bridal song.
>             (*The Feather of the Dawn,* pp. 41-2).

The beloved lies in an anxious wait for the lover and all the preparations are ready to receive him, but he does not turn up immediately and this sends a shiver through her heart.

Obviously, about one third of Sarojini's poetry has love for its theme. Her love poetry traverses Love's almost whole expanse, with the possible exception of the neo-modernist's display of naked sex and the Freudian subtle anatomization. It may also afford us little of intellectual companionship; it does possess sensuousness though not shameless sex. The kind of love we discover in Sarojini is actually inspired by the lofty ideals of self-sacrifice. There is much that is personal and conventional in it. Sarojini's love poetry reveals a variety of moods irony, hope, despair, challenge and ecstasy. Both aspects of love union and separation have been beautifully depicted. Sarojini drew inspiration from the medieval devotional poets, especially the Vaishnavites, and, like theirs, her poetry is usually colourful and romantic.

Sarojini's poetry throbs with the passionate love for the Motherland. There are some poems which express the poetess's devotion to her hopes of India's glorious renaissance. In this connection, one may remember poems such as **"To India"**, **"The Gift of India"**, and **"The Lotus"**. The poem, **"To India"**, is given below in full:

> O young through all thy immemorial years!
> Rise, Mother, rise, regenerate from thy gloom
> And, like a bride high-mated with the spheres,
> Beget new glories from thine ageless womb!
> The nations that in fettered darkness weep
> Crave thee to lead them where great mornings
>
>     break. . . .
>
> Mother, O Mother, wherefore dost thou sleep?
> Arise and answer for thy children's sake!
>
> Thy Future calls thee with a manifold sound
> To crescent honours, splendours, victories vast;

Waken, O slumbering Mother, and be crowned,
Who once wert empress of the sovereign Past.

(p. 58).

For some of her poems Sarojini went to national leaders like Gokhale, Tilak, Gandhi, and Umar, who are immortalized in the opening pages of *The Feather of the Dawn.* "The Lotus" is reminiscent of Mahatma Gandhi, his sacredness and sublimity.

Sarojini wrote many poems dealing with the problems of life and death. **"Life", "To the God of Pain", "Damayanti to Nala in the Hour of Exile", "The Poet to Death", "To a Buddha Seated on a Lotus", "Dirge", "Love and Death", "Death and Life", "The Soul's Prayer", "A Challenge to Fate", "In Salutation to the Eternal Peace",** and **"Invincible"** are the poems of life and death. The poetess had been through the varied experiences of life, and would long to get at the secret of life and death. This is her soul's prayer to God:

In childhood's pride I said to Thee:
"O Thou, who mad'st me of Thy breath,
Speak, Master, and reveal to me
Thine inmost laws of life and death. . . . "

(p. 123).

All aspects of life carried a peculiar fascination for the poetess, and she sang gaily and spontaneously of them. But she was sometimes seized with fear, pain, and she uttered aloud of them too. Thus, in **"To the God of Pain"**, she cried in a mood of agony:

I have no more to give, all that was mine
Is laid, a wrested tribute, at thy shrine;
Let me depart, for my whole soul is wrung,
And all my cheerless orisons are sung;
Let me depart, with faint limbs let me creep
To some dim shade and sink me down to sleep.

(p. 37).

Sarojini was, however, not cowed by pain or death and its attendant horrors. On the contrary, she occasionally hurled challenges to it, as also to fate, with all courage at her command.

In Sarojini's poetry we have many poems centred round the Indian scene. **"Palanquin-Bearers", "Wandering Singers", "Indian Weavers", "Coromandel Fishers", "The Snake-Charmer", "Corn-Grinders", "Village-Song", "Harvest", "The Indian Gipsy", "Nightfall in the City of Hyderabad", "Street Cries", "Bangle-Sellers", "The Festival of Serpents", "Hymn to Indra, Lord of Rain", "Wandering Beggars", "Lakshmi, the Lotus-Born", "Kali the Mother", "Raksha Bandhan". "The Festival of the Sea",** and **"Kanhaya":** all are taken from the Indian sources. Sarojini rarely touched modern industrialized life. Like W. B. Yeats, she was of an old-type aristocratic temperament that would love the gentle nobility of things and never feel at home with the drab of industrial life. The slum, the street arab, and the chimney smoke; the motorhorn, the locomotive or the pylon; the labourer and the labour-leader are all absent

from her poetry.[31] What appealed to her most was the varied pageantry of Indian life. Her poems of the Indian scene tend to be mostly objective and impersonal. The folk-songs charmed her as much as the picturesque scenes. She often painted the general impressions of the common life, but these impressions wanted in particularity as to the occurrence of place and time. Sarojini's scenes, therefore, remain generalized and conventional, and the principal reason of their appeal to us is that they almost invariably have a human context.

### XIV. STYLE

Sarojini's style is her own and gives us an impression of her individuality. Arthur Symons saw in her poems "an individual beauty of their own".[32] Sarojini did not imitate any particular English poet, or belonged to the school of any one master, or followed the formula of any particular group. She was, in fact, a *sui generis.*

There is a sense of refinement in Sarojini's style. Although all kinds of style suited her, she showed a propensity for the ornate style with the choicest jewels of language. She was a polished artist who never sacrificed her art to dreams and visions. It would, however, be wrong to think that she invariably resorted to the ornate or sophisticated style. Sarojini could be simple as well; poetic passages of extreme simplicity exist side by side with exuberant and luxuriant images and metaphors. The last stanza of **"The Time of Roses"** is an exemplification of the simplicity of her poetic style amidst madness of spring-festivity and love-loyalty:

Hide me in a shrine of roses,
Drown me in a wine of roses
Drawn from every fragrant grove!
Bind me on a pyre of roses,
Burn me in a fire of roses,
Crown me with the rose of Love!

(pp. 194-5).

In the same poem, the second and the third stanzas are composed in a high-strung style. It may, therefore, be safely deduced that the poetess was an adept in the use of different styles well in accord with different themes and situations.

### XV. DICTION

Sarojini earned tributes from critics for her masterly poetic diction. The native idioms have not been spared. Sarojini's diction tends to be fluent and fiery, and follows the pattern of the Decadents. The poetess exploited all the poetical resources of the English language. Her lyrics usually have a refrain, which constitutes the soul of the poems. In some poems the idea is carried on to a number of stanzas. The device of contrast or comparison lends variety and strength to her poetic art. The device of repetition of ideas is made most by Sarojini in **"The Poet to Death"**:

Tarry a while, O Death, I cannot die

While yet my sweet life burgeons with its spring;
Fair is my youth, and rich the echoing boughs
Where *dhadikulas sing.*
Tarry a while, O Death, I cannot die
with all my blossoming hopes unharvested,
My joys ungarnered, all my songs unsung,
And all my tears unshed.
Tarry a while, till I am satisfied
Of love and grief, of earth and altering sky;
Till all my human hungers are fulfilled,
O Death, I cannot die!

(p. 49).

Sarojini sometimes used uncommon words and phrases, and this generates an air of artificiality in her diction. The vocabulary is greatly influenced by the Romantic poets of the early 19th century.[33] Like Keats and Shelley, she employed a high-browed diction, which is steeped in passion, pulse, and power. Her sonorous and unusual words add to the subtlety of expression of ideas and display a keen perception of beauty.

### XVI. FIGURES OF SPEECH

Sarojini's verses are ornate and embellished and abound in various figures of speech. Her similes, metaphors, and other figures of speech throw up scintillating images and make her poetry revealing.[34] Several striking similes are to be seen in **"Palanquin-Bearers"**: the maiden in the palanquin sways like a flower, skims like a bird, floats like a laugh, hangs like a star, springs like a beam on the brow of the tide, falls like a tear from the eyes of a bride. **"Coromandel Fishers"** gives us the wind lying asleep on the arms of the dawn like a child that has cried all night. **"Indian Love-Song"** presents bright parrots clustering like vermilion flowers on the ripe boughs of many-coloured fruits. In **"Humayun to Zobeida"**, we have the beloved's heart hidden in the lover's bosom like the perfume in the petals of a rose, and the beloved haunting the lover's waking like a dream, his slumber like a moon; in **"Autumn Song"**, the sunset hanging on a cloud like a joy on the heart of a sorrow; in **"Alabastor"**, the heart frail as a cassia flower; in **"The Queen's Rival"**, seven damsels round Queen Gulnaar like seven soft gems on a silken thread, like seven fair lamps in a royal town, like seven bright petals of Beauty's flower; in **"The Pardah Nashin"**, the veiled beauty's girdle and fillet gleaming like changing fires on sunset seas, and her raiment like morning mist shot opal, gold and amethyst, and her days guarded and secure like jewels in a turbaned crest, like secrets in a lover's breast; and in **"The Water Hyacinth"**, the hyacinth's loveliness displayed like a fatal labyrinth.

Metaphors have been abundantly used by Sarojini. Thus in **"The Snake-Charmer"**, the snake is the subtle bride of the charmer's mellifluous wooing; in **"Bangle-Sellers"**, the bangles are the bright rainbow-tinted circles of light in **"In Praise of Gulmohur Blossoms"**, the lovely hue of the gulmohurs is the glimmering red of a bridal robe, and the rich red of a wild bird's wing; in **"Golden Cassia"**, the golden cassias are the fragments of some new-fallen star or the golden lamps for a fairy shrine, or the golden pitchers for fairy wine, or the bright anklet-bells from the wild spring's feet, or the gleaming tears that some fair bride shed remembering her lost maidenhead, or the glimmering ghosts of a bygone dream; in **"A Rajput Love Song"**, the day is a wild stallion, and the beloved wishes her lover to be a basil-wreath to twine among her tresses, a jewelled clasp of shining gold to bind around her sleeve, the *keora's* soul that haunts her silken raiment, a bright, vermilion tassel in the girdles that she weaves, the scented fan that lies upon her pillow, a sandal lute, or silver lamp that burns before her; in **"Farewell"**, the poetess's songs are a bright shower of lambent butterflies, and a soft cloud of murmuring bees; in **"Past and Future"** the past is turned into a mountain-cell, where lone, apart, old hermit-memories dwell, and the future into a bride's marriage-veil of mysteries; and in **"A Song of the Khyber Pass"**, the Pakhtoons are called the wolves of the mountains and the hawks of the hills.

Apart from similes and metaphors, Sarojini has employed other figures of speech too. In the poem **"Suttee"**, the line "Shall the flesh survive when the soul is gone?" offers a fine example of synecdoche; here "flesh" (a part) is substituted for "body" (the whole). Another example of this figure of speech is to be found in **"The Queen's Rival"**, where Queen Gulnaar's daughter is said to be "two spring times old" (spring being used for the whole year). **"Suttee"** also provides a pointed instance of metonymy "Shall the blossom live when the tree is dead?" In this case, "blossom" is substituted for "wife" and "tree" for "husband" by way of association. The clause "till the shadows are gray in the west" in the poem **"In the Forest"** is a substitution for evening and is metonymic. The Song of Princess Zeb-Un-Nissa in **"Praise of Her Own Beauty"** makes a nice use of oxymoron in the phrase "sweet distress". The same poem demonstrates hyperbole in the declaration of Zeb-Un-Nissa that when she lifts her veil, the roses become pale with envy of her beauty. Some other poems have direct addresses to Death, Life, Pain, Love, and the Unknown as though they were persons, and in them we have a beautiful application of personification.

### XVII. PROSODY

Sarojini followed, in the main, the great English poetical tradition in matters of prosody. Her poems have "a prosodical correctness and regularity which seldom if ever becomes merely mechanical".[35] Sarojini was a great metrical artist with a delicate ear. She used a number of metres effectively, though one may find a few faults in scansion. She experimented with various stanza forms and matrical measures (iambic, trochaic, anapestic, dactylic, and their permissible combinations). Besides their skilful handling, she also succeeded in setting them to some of the Indian tunes. She never wrote blank verse. To create a verbal rhythm, she employed several aural devices like alliteration, refrain, consonance, and assonance. She introduced anapestic feet in the middle of iambic measures and seldom erred in her melodic cadences. She had a remarkable command of her epithets. In her writings we have "a jewelled beauty of phrase, and her subtle magic of imaginative temperament that makes her illuminate by a single flash of epithet a world of new ideas and feelings".[36] Her metrical inventiveness is best seen in those poems where she wove vernacular cries and phrases for Indian colour:

> From the threshold of the Dawn
> On we wander, always on
> Till the friendly light be gone
>     *Y' Allah! Y' Allah!*
> We are free-born sons of Fate,
> What care we for wealth or state
> Or the glory of the great?
>     *Y' Allah! Y' Allah!*
>         (**"Wandering Beggars"**, p. 165).

The fakirs are a common sight in India, and the above poem is a living reproduction of their wandering songs.

### XVIII. ORATORY

Sarojini was an acknowledged orator and a fine conversationalist. Her speeches used to be a rare combination of oration and poetry. As Sarojini became involved in the political movement of the country, she was more and more in demand on public platforms and grew into an impressive orator. It has been pointed out that, through her speeches, she "certainly received louder and more widespread applause than she ever could have received through her poetry. . . . "[37] The passionate rhythmic flow of her appeals to her countrymen's patriotic conscience, her highly charged language, and the perfect modulation of her voice: these put Indians under a spell, and they fully appreciated the ennobling words falling from her mouth. Her oratory became all the more forceful because to noble language she set "a peerless regality and sincerity of spirit."[38] Some of her poems are rich in rhetorical effects.

### XIX. SAROJINI NAIDU AND TORU DUTT

It is interesting to compare and contrast the two great Indo-Anglian poetesses Sarojini Naidu and Toru Dutt. Both chose English as the medium of their expression, and both wrote verses with beauty, ease and command. The tragedy of Toru Dutt lies in the fact of "what might have been" had she lived longer, and of Sarojini of calling a halt to her own writing at a time of maturity and immersing herself in public affairs and politics. Both the poetesses had received their education and training, at least in part, in the West, and both were polyglots, with the scale swinging in favour of Toru Dutt.

Curiously enough, both the poetesses were introduced to the literary world by Edmund Gosse. Sarojini has admitted that Gosse "first showed her the way to the Golden Threshold" of poetry. The noted English critic deserves congratulations of all Indians for his sympathetic treatment of India's poetic genius. Of Toru Dutt, Gosse said:

"When the history of literature of our country comes to be written, there is sure to be a page in it dedicated to this fragile, exotic blossom of songs".[39] The prominent qualities of Toru's verse are its simplicity, its directness, and its sincerity. In Sarojini's poetry, however, one should not look for the artless simplicity of Toru Dutt. The fact is that Sarojini's poetry is more complex and subtle than that of Toru's.

Sarojini is more personal in her verse than Toru. The latter never strove to tell the world of her personal pains and pleasures, whereas the former did so vociferously. In the poem, "Our Casuarina Tree", Toru did pour out her inner feelings, but elsewhere she seldom mentioned the plight and tragedy of her own short life.

The attitude of the two poetesses towards Nature was also different. Toru's observation of Nature was more minute and deep than that of Sarojini's. To Toru the trees she described happened to be Indian, but to Sarojini they must be described with an oriental background. A study of Toru's "Sonnet Baugmaree" and Sarojini's **"Champak Blossoms"** will bear out the contrast. Sarojini never quite excelled in understanding or revealing human nature too.[40] But Toru's *Ancient Ballads and Legends of Hindustan* contains many living human characters, both male and female.

A critic thinks that Sarojini's genius as contrasted with that of Toru, is "wholly native".[41] It is entirely dedicated to the service of the Motherland and deeply attuned to the immemorial harmonies of the country's age-long story. Toru's genius is also native, though not wholly. Her *Ancient Ballads* is steeped in old Indian myths and legends and noble Hindu ideals.

In points of metrical skill and command of suggestive and melodious verse, Sarojini must be placed above Toru Dutt.[42] Sarojini wielded a wonderful command of many and varied metrical forms. The melody and the rhythmic graces of her poetry hold us spellbound. According to a critic, "The genius of Toru Dutt is to that of Mrs Sarojini what the jasmine is to the rose the jasmine that finds its most congenial home in the East, that has got a charming simplicity and beauty of appearance, that wears the artless grace of budding maidenhood in the realm of flowers, that is full of a delicate though sweet fragrance to the rose that finds a happy home in the West as well as the East, that has a queenly pomp and pageantry of colour and beauty, that has the mellow sweetness and charm of perfect womanhood in the realm of flowers, that commands homage by its regal loveliness, that has a pervasive and powerful perfume that bears our fancies away to a world of mystic inner happiness."[43]

### XX. SAROJINI'S WEAKNESSES

Critics have pointed out certain weaknesses in Sarojini's poetry. That she should have chosen English as the language of her poetry has been regretted in certain quarters. But what she might have been, had she written in a language other than English, is simply a matter of speculation and hence a futile exercise.

A charge has been levelled against the poetess that she offered us no high thought or philosophy. If we accept the definition that poetry is musical thought, we must admit that Sarojini was only a "music-maker and a dreamer of dreams". But what we require of a poet is truth to imagination, and Sarojini fulfilled this essential requirement.[44] She could also rise to the heights of contemplation in the song **"To a Buddha Seated on a Lotus"**. This beautiful poem gives expression to "the heavenward hunger of her soul" and her wistful longing "diviner summits to attain". It shines out of a great calm, the calm which rises superior to the weariness, the fever, and the fret of frail humanity. But this restraint is least characteristic of our poetess who, in her normal moods, remains the "hectic flamelike rose of our verse, All colour and all odour and all bloom."

Most of Sarojini's poems, opines a critic, have "a highly strung diction which sometimes smacks of artificiality." The same critic further observes: "The vocabulary used in most cases is uncommon and is greatly influenced by the Romantic Vocabulary of the early 19th century poets of England."[45] Her images and similes are usually drawn from a dream-world, and her poetry sometimes leaves the impression of being rhetorical and wordy. Her style tends to be extremely ornate and chiselled. Her faint sighs in exquisite numbers wring only temporary tears. There is an unacceptable nostalgia in her poetry, and under no conditions the poetess may be called "modern". She virtually ceased writing verses when the modernistic trends set in. She unquestionably knew some of the modernists personally and read their work with a sense of appreciation, but herself practised otherwise.[46] A close textual scrutiny of her poems is sure to reveal her vulnerability, and it is not difficult to get "a superfluous word, an inversion, an archaism, in every single poem of Sarojini' . . ."[47]

### XXI. CONCLUDING REMARKS

The weaknesses mentioned above should not lead readers to construe that Sarojini's poetry is mere trash; there is rather much to soothe and console them. Her love poetry is of special charm to youthful hearts. Her metrical felicity adds an additional feather to her cap. In matters of rhyme, Sarojini surpassed even some of the modern English poets. In the opinion of a critic, "Her poems have rhythms of life, as they come out direct from a vital personality." He says further: "Actualities, imagination, feeling and music are sweetly blended into an artistic form aglow with life and fire of real passion. She is a supreme artist in words, imagery and patterns, and her canvas is a whole nation. What is more, she knows the art of being artless. It is a pity that she did not give us many more of those fine-cut jewels of beauty."[48] In Sarojini's poetry one comes across yearning and dream, action and suffering, laughter and song. Rarely has the world perhaps seen women who have combined in themselves such diverse

qualities: an intense poetic temperament, sensitive to beauty in all forms; a gift of language overwhelming in its richness; and vivacity and wit and oratorical eloquence.[49] Sarojini was not only an aesthete wallowing in sensation, but one who showed a certain sanity and balance and a purpose in her poetry. The range of her poetry is surely limited, but she, like Jane Austen, moved within that range with grace and skill. Her flawless and varied art has prompted a critic to remark that "no Indian woman has written so many and such perfect songs of India as Mrs Naidu".[50] Though her poetry lacks serious thought, its artistic perfection can hardly be questioned, and even Edmund Gosse has admitted that "she is the most brilliant, the most original, as well as the most correct, of all the natives of Hindustan who have written in English."[51] Through her poetry, Sarojini articulated the dream of a rising nation against the imperialistic forces. In it one may witness a beautiful marriage of Western culture with Eastern idealism.[52] One may also witness in it that widespread upheaval of thought and feeling which is likely to affect the future of mankind. It was perhaps this in Pt. Nehru's mind when he remarked that "Mrs Naidu was a great nationalist and mighty internationalist."[53] Like Tagore and Aurobindo, Sarojini projected an aspect of Indian sensitivity at that level of creative synthesis where tradition and individuality respond to the human predicament without any sense of hiatus. Whether about love or nature, death or dreams, life or loss, temples or dancers, festivals or fishermen, her poems reveal her own awareness of the distinct connection between the self and the world. Whatever the theme and mood of her poem, Sarojini remains mainly a "songbird" twittering melodiously in the Muse's bower.

### NOTES

[1] Symons, "Introduction," *The Golden Threshold*, pp. 9-10.

[2] *Ibid.*, p. 10.

[3] *Ibid.*, p. 21.

[4] Gosse, "Introduction," *The Bird of Time*, p. 8.

[5] Symons, "Introduction," p. 10.

[6] K. Vishwanathan, "The Nightingale and the Naughty Gal," *The Banasthali Patrika*, No. 12 (January 1969), p. 127.

[7] Dustoor, *Sarojini Naidu*, p. 47.

[8] B.S. Mathur, "Sarojini Naidu: A Singer of Beautiful Songs," *The Calcutta Review* (August 1949), pp. 115-116.

[9] Cousins, "The Poetry of Sarojini Naidu: A Critical Appreciation," *The Modern Review*, p. 414.

[10] *Mrs Sarojini Naidu*, 2nd ed. (Madras, 1917), p. 21.

[11] Cousins, "The Poetry of Sarojini Naidu: A Critical Appreciation," *The Modern Review,* p. 414.

[12] Punekar, "A Note on Sarojini Naidu," *Critical Essays on Indian Writing in English,* p. 77.

[13] Diwan Chand Sharma, "Sarojini Naidu," *The Modern Review* (December 1949), p. 479.

[14] *Ibid.,* p. 481.

[15] S. Sivaraman, "The Philosophy of Mrs. Sarojini Naidu's Poetry," *The Calcutta Review* (November-December 1932), p. 261.

[16] Jha, "The Poetry of Sarojini Naidu," *The Hindustan Review,* p. 208.

[17] Sivaraman, "The Philosophy of Mrs Sarojini Naidu's Poetry," *The Calcutta Review,* p. 270.

[18] Mathur, "Sarojini Naidu: A Singer of Beautiful Songs," *The Calcutta Review,* p. 116.

[19] Sengupta, *Sarojini Naidu,* p. 85.

[20] *Ibid.,* p. 89.

[21] Sahib Singh Ahuja, "The Humour of Mrs Sarojini Naidu," *The Modern Review* (February 1962), p. 151. A Similar observation has also been made by Prof. K.K. Bhattacharya "She had a great fund of wit and humour and sparkled with repartees and sallies. Dullness and Sarojini were strangers. She would shine wherever she would be, and magnetize the men and women she came across and make them her friends." See his article "Sarojini Naidu, the Greatest Woman of Our Time." *The Modern Review* (April 1949), p. 290.

[22] Brailsford, "Mrs Naidu: A Great Human Being," *The Hindustan Review,* p. 212.

[23] Quoted from Symons, "Introduction," *The Golden Threshold,* p. 20.

[24] Turnbull, "Introduction," *Sarojini Naidu: Select Poems,* p. 23.

[25] *Ibid.,* pp. 22-23.

[26] Gosse, "Introduction," *The Bird of Time,* p. 6.

[27] S.V. Mukerjea," "The Art of Sarojini Naidu, *Disjecta Membra: Studies in Literature and Life* (Bangalore, 1959), p. 23.

[28] Gosse, "Introduction," *The Bird of Time,* p. 5.

[29] *Mrs Sarojini Naidu,* p. 27.

[30] Sengupta, *Sarojini Naidu,* p. 96.

[31] Gupta, *Sarojini: The Poetess,* p. 94.

[32] Symons, "Introduction," *The Golden Threshold,* p. 9.

[33] A.N. Gupta and Satish Gupta, *Sarojini Naidu: Select Poems* (Bareilly, 1976), p. 52.

[34] Gupta, *Sarojini: The Poetess,* p. 127.

[35] Turnbull, "Introduction," *Sarojini Naidu: Select Poems,* p. 30.

[36] *Speeches and Writings of Sarojini Naidu,* p. XVIII.

[37] A. Bose, "Sarojini Naidu," *The Literary Criterion,* II. No. 3 (Winter 1955), 7. In an exaggerated tone, Prof. K.K. Bhattacharya says: "As an orator she has perhaps no equals in any land. Words danced out of her lips in perfect rhythm . . . investing the theme she would speak on with sanctity and nobility breathing intense patriotism." "Sarojini Naidu, the Greatest Woman of Our Time," *The Modern Review* (April 1949), pp. 249-250.

[38] Bose, "Sarojini Naidu," *The Literary Criterion,* p. 8.

[39] Edmund Gosse, "Introductory Memoir," *Ancient Ballads and Legends of Hindustan* (London, 1882), p. XXVII.

[40] Sengupta, *Sarojini Naidu,* p. 96.

[41] Mukerjea, "The Art of Sarojini Naidu", *Disjecta Membra,* p. 22.

[42] *Mrs. Sarojini Naidu,* p. 19.

[43] *Ibid.,* pp. 19-20.

[44] S. Narayanan, "Some Sarojini Naidu's Poems", *The Hindustan Review* LXXXII (April 1949), 215.

[45] R. Bhatnagar, *Sarojini Naidu: The Poet of a Nation,* p. 50.

[46] H. H. Anniah Gowda, "Toru Dutt and Sarojini Naidu as Poets", *The Literary Half-Yearly,* IX, No. 1, 30.

[47] Punekar, "A Note on Sarojini Naidu", *Critical Essays on Indian Writing in English,* p. 81.

[48] Bhatnagar, *Sarojini Naidu: The Poet of a Nation,* pp. 55-56

[49] K. K. Mehrotra, "The Poetry of Sarojini Naidu", *Essays and Studies* (Allahabad, 1970), p. 76.

[50] *Ibid.,* p. 88.

[51] Gosse, "Introduction," *The Bird of Time,* p. 2.

[52] Mukerjea, "The Art of Sarojini Naidu", *Disjecta Membra,* p. 38.

53 Nehru, "Sarojini Naidu: A Tribute in India's Parliament," *The Hindustan Review*, p. 205.

## Izzat Yar Khan (essay date 1983)

SOURCE: "The Poetic Outlook," in *Sarojini Naidu: The Poet,* S. Chand & Company Ltd., 1983, pp. 26-55.

[*In the following essay, Khan examines major themes and images in Naidu's work.*]

Sarojini was once a name to conjure with. She magnetised and attracted the young.[1] The quantity of her verse is not large, but her verse, in her own words, is a treasure "of song and sorrow and life and love."[2]

### VARIETY OF SUBJECTS

Sarojini's poems tell us of her fancies and longings, her moments of ecstasy and moments of loneliness. In her thought-provoking poems she speculated on the transitoriness of life and the caprice of fortune, the purpose of life and the mystery of death. She is attracted to the great religions of the world Buddhism and Hinduism, Christianity and Islam. Mythology interests her and she sings of the gods and goddesses of her own ancient land Krishna and Lakshmi and Kali and others. She writes on the distinguished persons of her own day Mahatma Gandhi, Gopal Krishna Gokhale, the Nizam of Hyderabad. In the humblest professions she sees the beauty of life and she writes poems on palanquin-bearers and bangle-sellers, singers and dancers, corn-grinders and weavers, gipsies and snake-charmers, fishermen and beggars. When she deals with some social customs of India *sati* and *pardah* she gives us a penetrating criticism of life which is artistic, not argumentative.

Sarojini chooses fascinating subjects from the history of her own land and reproduces the love of Humayun for Zobeida and the beauty of Aurangzeb's daughter Princess Zeb-un-Nissa. She writes on the kings and queens who lie asleep beneath the tombs of Golconda. She sings of the Rajput hero Amar Singh and his lady-love Parvati. She is moved by the vicissitudes in the history of Delhi, the capital of successive kings and emperors. The legends of the past provide her with themes for poems and she writes on Damayanti addressing Nala in the hour of his exile. Her poetical works include poems on Indian festivals Vasant Panchami, Nag Panchami, and Moharrum and poems on Indian flowers the red *gulmohur,* the fragrant nasturtium, the golden cassia, the rich *champak,* the lovely *ashoka.* She sings of the seasons of her land autumn and its sadness, spring and its joy. She recaptures the scenery around her dawn over fields full of harvest, blossoming woods in summer, sunset in June, twilight over hills, nightfall in the city of Hyderabad.

### NOTE OF IDEALISM

The prominent note of Sarojini's poetry is a pure and intense aspiration. The hatred of tyranny, the overthrow of the tyrant, the love of liberty, the regeneration of her country these are the recurring notes of her idealistic poetry. A passion for a glorious age when India will be free, when love will reign and tyranny disappear, is manifest, in many of her poems. She believes that she cannot die as long as her youth is fair and her life burgeons with its spring. She wants to fulfil all her human hungers; she is convinced that she cannot die

> With all my blossoming hopes unharvested,
> My joys ungarnered, all my songs unsung.[3]

She wants to participate in the

> Laughter of children and the lyric dawn,
> And love's delight, profound and passionate,
> Winged dreams that blow their golden clarion,
> And hope that conquers immemorial hate.[4]

Her insatiate soul insists on draining "earth's utmost bitter, utmost sweet". She prays to God,

> Spare me no bliss, no pang of strife,
> Withhold no gift or grief I crave,
> The intricate lore of love and life
> And mystic knowledge of the grave.[5]

Sarojini wants to be "a thought-worn singer in life's high and lonely places".[6] She wants to sing "songs of the glory and gladness of life, of poignant sorrow and passionate strife, and the lilting joys of the spring". The songs she wants to sing are songs

> Of hope that sows for the years unborn,
> And faith that dreams of a tarrying morn,
> The fragrant peace of the twilight's breath,
> And the mystic silence that men call death.[7]

She is convinced that neither will her soul falter nor her body fear "its poignant hour of bitter suffering", and that she will not fail

> ere I achieve my destined creed
> Of song or service for my country's need.[8]

She feels that it is her poetic mission to go "where the loud world beckons and the urgent drum-beat of destiny calls",

> Into the strife of the throng and the tumult,
> The war of sweet against folly and wrong;
> Where brave hearts carry the sword of battle,
> 'Tis mine to carry the banner of song.[9]

She wanted to fashion and forge "a deathless sword to serve my stricken land".[10] With deep faith in her poetical powers, she declares:

> Love, my dreaming heart would wake,
> And its joyous fancies break

Into lyric bloom
To enchant the passing world
And their wild perfume.[11]

The ideal of Sarojini is to see the land of her birth free, independent, and regenerated. To her India is young, in spite of immemorial years, and fertile enough to "beget new glories from thine ageless womb". To her India is fit for the leadership of "nations that in fettered darkness weep". India was once the "empress of the sovereign past," and now her future calls her

To crescent honours, splendours, victories vast.[12] But the idealism of the poet suffers a setback at the sight of the contemporary Indian scene, and she feels despondent for a while:

Shall hope prevail where clamorous hate is rife,
Shall sweet love prosper or high dreams find place
Amid the tumult of reverberant strife
'Twixt ancient creed, 'twixt race and ancient race,
That mars the grave, glad purposes of life.[13]

The song-bird finds her wing to be broken, but this neither daunts nor tires her because of her abiding faith in her country's ultimate destiny. She says,

Behold: I rise to meet the destined spring
And scale the stars upon my broken wing.[14]

She determines to knead the bread of hope to comfort and to feed "the myriad hearts for whom no harvests blow save bitter herbs of woe." She makes up her mind to shelter, under the boughs of her love.

The myriad soul for whom no gardens bloom
Save bitter buds of doom.[15]

Union being strength, she strives to bring about unity among the people of India. The common tie of patriotism binds the people together and they unanimously declare:

One heart are we to love thee, O our Mother,
One undivided, indivisible soul
Bound by one hope, one purpose, one devotion
Towards a great, divinely-destined goal.[16]
Lo! we would thrill the high stars with thy story.
And set thee again in the forefront of glory.[17]

Sarojini and her fellow patriots see visions of a great dawn. The mournful night is over and her country wakes at last from her deep age-long sleep. Sweet and long-slumbering buds of gladness open fresh lips to the returning winds of hope; and

Our eager hearts renew their radiant flight
Towards the glorious renascent light,
Life and our land await their destined spring.[18]

It is the coming generation that will enjoy the fruits of the labours of Sarojini and her fellow fighters for freedom. Addressing children, she says:

Yours are the hands that will reap

Dreams that we sow while you sleep,
Fed with our hope and our sorrow,
Rich with the tears that we weep.[19]

The hands of these patriots, says Sarojini, were weak, but their service was tender. In darkness they dreamed of the dawn of the splendour of the coming generation. In silence they strove for the joys of the future,

And watered your seeds from the wells of our
                    sorrow,
We toiled to enrich the glad hour of your waking,
Our vigil is done, lo! the daylight is breaking.[20]

NOTE OF LIBERALISM

The poems reveal her noble-mindedness and candour, a liberal voice in politics and in religion. Nowhere is to be found a critical attack upon persons and politics. Her wandering singers have great fellow-feeling: they say,

All men are our kindred, the world is our home.[21] It pains her to see hate rife in her country: in an atmosphere of hate neither love can prosper not dreams be realised. In a land where people of one ancient religion are at strife with people of another ancient religion, life loses all purpose.[22] It pleases her to see people of diverse creeds living in brotherhood:

The votaries of the Prophet's faith

                    . . . . .

And they who bear on Vedic brows
Their mystic symbols of belief;
And they who, worshipping the sun,
Fled o'er the old Iranian sea;
And they who bow to Him who trod
The midnight waves of Galilee.[23]

Sarojini thinks of man as man; she has sympathy for the poor and the oppressed. Her liberalism is always ready to receive the new. Her keen heart hastens to forget "old longings in fulfilling new desires."[24] In her broad-mindedness she does not want to treat the widow in the conventional manner. Her heart feels the pain of the widow's unfulfilled desires. She appreciates the moonless vigils of the widow's lonely nights. She understands the anguish of the widow's tears.[25] She pleads for toleration and love. She condemns those of her countrymen who, remembering the feud of old faiths and the blood of old battles, do not want to forge a new unity. To them her message is the message of love, for

Love recks not of feuds and bitter follies, of
                    stranger, comrade or kin,
Alike in his ear sound the temple bells and the cry
                    of the muezzin.
For Love shall cancel the ancient wrong and
                    conquer the ancient rage,
Redeem with his tears the memoried sorrow that
                    sullied a bygone age.[26]

Sarojini advocates perfect religious freedom. She is delighted when she sees people of different religions worshipping in perfect peace. It is an ennobling sight for her to see from mosque and *minar* the *muezzins* calling the faithful to prayer, the worshippers of the Son of the Virgin kneeling at their prayers, those who make obeisance to flame and light bending low in prayer, the children of Brahma lifting their voices in adoration.[27] And she is happy to see the love of Hindus and Parsees, Muslims and Christians, for their joint motherland: the Hindus crowning her with the flowers of their worship, the Parsees surrounding her with the flame of their hope, the Muslims defending her with the sword of their love, the Christians attending her with the song of their faith.[28] We can address this champion of liberalism in her own so apposite words:

> Thy life was love and liberty thy law,
> And truth thy pure imperishable goal.[29]

## NOTE OF REVOLT

In many of her poems Sarojini sounds a note of revolt. She revolts against the prevailing attitude of fatalism, against stale social customs, and against her own occasional feeling of despondency. Sarojini is insurgent, as a caged song-bird beating itself against the bars of its cage. She revolts against the accepted convention of woman's place in the routine of life. She revolts against the formalism and hypocrisy, the harshness and cruelty, that she saw around her. She does not want that the widow should at all times be made to feel and look like a widow: she disapproves of the social convention that divests her of fine clothes and jewellery. She raises her hand to stop this harshness and cruelty:

> Nay, let her be! . . . what comfort can we give
> For joy so frail, for hope so fugitive?
> The yearning of unfulfilled delight,
> The moonless vigils of her lonely night,
> For the abysmal anguish of her tears,
> And flowering springs that mock her empty
> years?[30]

The harsh treatment meted out to her makes the widow indignant: she rises in revolt against the state of affairs in which she is singled out for needless victimisation.

> My soul burns with the quenchless fire
> That lit my lover's funeral pyre.[31]

At times, under stress of emotion, the revolt of the widow is against life itself. When death has "rent us in twain who are but one," says she,

> Shall the blossom live when the tree is dead . . .
> Shall the flesh survive when the soul is gone?[32]

Sarojini's whole nature rises up against the tame-bird view of life. She asks her third child Ranadheera to be lord of love and chivalry, inspiring him in these words:

> Learn to conquer, learn to fight
> In the foremost flanks of right.[33]

She revolts against the attitude that makes her downcast and down-hearted:

> But soon we must rise, O my heart, we must
>                    wander again
> Into the war of the world and the strife of the
>                    throng;
> Let us rise, O my heart, let us gather the dreams
>                    that remain,
> We will conquer the sorrow of life with the
> sorrow of song.[34]

She challenges Fate. Fate may strike her blind, enfeeble her memory, render her short of hearing, rob her of her power of speech, but, she asks,

> Say, shall my heart lack its familiar language
> While earth has nests for her mellifluous birds?
> Shall my impassioned heart forget to sing
> With the ten thousand voices of the spring?
>
> . . . . .
>
> How will you tether my triumphant mind,
> Rival and fearless comrade of the wind?[35]

Yet for all her revolutionary ardour Sarojini has nothing of the satirist in her nature. Her tolerant sympathy prevents her from turning her pen into a lash.

## NOTE OF MYSTICISM

Some poems of Sarojini reveal her to be inclined at times to mysticism. To her spiritual insight is necessary in order to have a knowledge of divine things. The natural is scarcely distinguishable from the supernatural. She believes in the mystical philosophy of "the one in two and the two in one." She loves to dwell on the love of the human soul for the divine. Occasionally she shows traits of Platonic idealism, according to which the mundane and the mortal is a reflection of its immortal idea in some supersensible world. Sometimes she sees visions and hears mystical voices. She feels, however, that direct and immediate communion with God cannot be attained by ordinary people.

Time and future are hidden from the eyes of the ordinary man: they are revealed only to a spiritually enlightened mind. Sarojini reproduces mental images of the reality called time and the reality called future:

> Time is like a wind that blows,
> The future is a folded rose,
> Who shall pluck it no man knows.[36]

The faith of a worshipper hardly makes a distinction between the natural and the divine: addressing the serpents, their worshipper says,

> Seers are ye and symbols of the ancient silence
> Where life and death and sorrow and ecstasy

are one.[37]

In the following lines the eternal is presented as the natural. Sarojini reproduces the mental image of the Mahatma (the Great Soul) by the symbol of the lotus that has attained "ageless beauty born of Brahma's breath" and is

> Coevai with the Lords of Life and Death.[38]

To the mystic there is hardly any distinction between the loved and the lower: the two are one. Passionate mutual love breaks down the hard walls of the ego, producing a new being composed of two in one:

> Hourly this subtle mystery flowers anew,
> O Love, I know not why . . .
> Unless it be, perchance, that I am you,
> Dear Love, that you are I.[39]

The quest of the human soul for the Infinite takes the form of human love. Radha's love for Krishna points out that the relation of the human soul to the Ultimate Reality is one of subjection and surrender.[40] The nectar of Krishna's flute is turned to spiritual account by the God-intoxicated mystic-poet. The symbolic nectar washes clean the weather-stains of cares, stimulates the torpid heart, and fills the recipient with sudden greatness:

> Still must I like a homeless bird
>     Wander, forsaking all;
> The earthly loves and worldly lures
>     That held my life in thrall,
> And follow, follow, answering
>     Thy magical flute-call.[41]

Plato believed that every impression received through the eye or the ear is assimilated direct from the embodiments of beauty, and this imperceptibly leads one from earliest childhood into a harmony with the Spirit of Truth, and into a love for that Spirit. This Platonic idea is conveyed by Sarojini in the following lines:

> Our shrines, our sacred streams, our sumptuous
>                art,
> Old hills that scale the sky's unaging dome,
> Recalled some long-lost rapture to your heart,
> Some far-off memory of your spirit's home.[42]

The doctrine of the Platonic system of philosophy[43] that what seem to be realities on earth are but appearances of the Divine appears in the following lines:

> We are the shadows of Thy light,
> We are the secrets of Thy might,
> The visions of Thy primal dream.[44]

There are traces of Platonism when Sarojini prepares her mind for spiritual enlightenment:

> Or perchance we may glean a fair glimpse of the
>           Infinite Bosom
> In whose glorious shadow all life is unfolded
>           or furled.[45]
> Open, O vast Unknown,

> Thy sealed mysterious portal:
> I go to seek my own
> Vision of Love Immortal.[46]

Visions and voices, not authority and the process of reasoning, are the media through which the mystic attains spiritual insight and experience. Under stress of elevated spiritual feelings, the birds that sing are the spirits of truth, the stars that shine become the spirits of love, and the streams that flow are transformed into the spirits of peace, and in such a state of ecstasy

> I felt the stars of the spirits of Love
> Gather and gleam round my delicate youth,
> And I heard the song of the spirits of Truth;
> To quench my longing I bent me low
> By the streams of the spirits of Peace.[47]

The Buddhist doctrine of Nirvana, the return of every individual soul to its eternal peace, is regarded as beyond the attainment of the common people. It is not everybody that can overcome desire and conquer the self to obtain the serenity of soul, the highest good:

> The end, elusive and afar,
> Still lures us with its beckoning flight,
> And all our mortal moments are
> A session of the Infinite.
> How shall we reach the great, unknown
> Nirvana of thy Lotus-throne?[48]

NOTE OF MEDIEVALISM

Sarojini has a disposition to seek the romance that is coloured by distance and strangeness. The mysterious East, perfumed like a flower, never fails to inspire her. The medieval element in Sarojini is her love for sensuousness and mystical suggestion. Many of her poems show us a spirit intoxicated with the romance of the past and striving after a perfect transmission of beauty. She loves the past for its romance and chivalry, its fabulous glamour and spectacle. She recreates the beauty and glamour and love-making in the imperial palaces of Mughal India. Humayun sees the beauty of Zobeida in the rose, her glory in the dawn, her sweetness in the nightingale, her whiteness in the swan. When he is awake, he thinks of Zobeida; when he is asleep, he dreams of Zobeida. When he declares his passion for her, he makes a reference to the vanished culture when women sat behind the veil:

> Yet when I crave of you, my sweet, one tender
>           moment's grace,
> You cry, "I sit behind the veil, I cannot show
>           my face."[49]

She loves the Baghdad of fables for its vanished splendours, its Saki-singers, its love-ghazals, its Sufi wine. The spectacular durbar of one of the wealthiest Indian princes provides her with an opportunity of recreating the old-world romance of the Middle East:

Sweet, sumptuous fables of Baghdad
The splendours of your court recall,
The torches of a *Thousand Nights*
Blaze through a single festival;
And Saki-singers down the streets,
Pour for us, in a stream divine,
From goblets of your love-*ghazals*
The rapture of your Sufi wine.[50]

The sensuous beauty of the Mughal Emperor Aurangzeb's daughter fascinates Sarojini. When Princess Zeb-un-Nissa lifts the veil from her cheek, the roses turn pale with envy. If by chance one perfumed lock of the Princess is loosened to the caress of the wind, the hyacinths complain and languish in distress. The Princess is so lovely that, when she pauses among groves,

> a throng
> Of nightingales awake and strain
> Their souls into a quivering song.[51]

Sarojini is attracted to the Persian King Firoz and his beautiful Queen Gulnaar for the beauty and romance of their lives. The reader feels vicarious pleasure in the description of the splendours of the Queen's chamber. Queen Gulnaar has an ivory bed to sit on. Her chamber walls are richly inlaid with precious stones agate, porphyry, onyx, and jade. King Firoz sits on his ebony seat. The Queen decks her exquisite head with jewels. Her two-year old daughter is dressed in blue robes having tassels of gold. All the pomp, wealth, and luxury of the East is laid bare by Sarojini.[52] The spectacular element is also provided by her own city of Hyderabad at night, where languid and luminous faces gleam from trellised balconies, and

> Leisurely elephants wind through the winding
>                                         lanes,
> Swinging their silver bells hung from their silver
>                                         chains.
> Round the high Char Minar sounds of gay
>                                         cavalcades
> Blend with the music of cymbals and serenades.[53]

Sarojini's passion for medievalism is charged with a nostalgia for its departed greatness and glory. Kings and Queens have returned to dust in the royal tombs of Golconda, but in the ruins of their fort there is a tragic grandeur. The Queens had flower-like bodies and their beauty was like the beauty of pomegranate groves in spring.[54] In medieval Rajputana Sarojini finds romance and chivalry. In the conversation between Parvati at her lattice and Amar Singh in the saddle, Sarojini reproduces a whole culture of a vanished age. Ladies of noble rank twined a basil-wreath among their tresses. They fastened a jewelled clasp of shining gold around their sleeve. They wore silken raiment perfumed with the scent of the *keora*. Their girdles had a bright vermilion tassel. Scented fans lay upon their pillow. Silver lamps burned before their shrine. Men of noble rank rode with a hooded hawk upon their hand. The collar-band of their hawk had gleaming bells. A radiant sword swung at their side. They wore an amulet of jade against the perils of the way.[55]

The bazaars of Hyderabad, abounding in wealth and luxury, recall to mind the capital city of an Oriental prince in a leisurely age. The rich wares displayed by merchants consist of turbans of crimson and silver, tunics of purple brocade, mirrors with panels of amber. The vendors weigh saffron and lentil. The maidens grind sandalwood and henna. The pedlars sell chessmen and dice. The goldsmiths make bells for the feet of blue pigeons, girdles of gold for the dancers, and scabbards of gold for the king. The fruitmen sell citron, pomegranate, and plum. The musicians play sitar and sarangi. The flower-girls make crowns for the brow of a bridegroom and chaplets to garland his bed.[56] When the Nizam died, Sarojini's memorial verses on him contain references to the fabulous galmour of old Baghdad and its heroes of romantic legends:

> O hands that succoured a people's need
> With the splendour of Haroun-al-Rasheed:
> O heart that solaced a world's cry
> With the sumptuous bounty of Hatim Tai:
> Where are the days that were winged and clad
> In the fabulous glamour of old Baghdad.[57]

NOTE OF REALISM

The great charm of Sarojini is that she remains a true Indian in her thoughts and imagery. She gives us Indian pictures in English verse which have the ring of originality. The India of Sarojini is not the India of the god-like Sahibs and abject natives, but the India in which she lived and died. She looks at things straight with her eyes and sets down faithfully what she has seen, with perfect fidelity to details. She is quick in appraising the value of local colour. She has wide knowledge of Indian birds and animals, flowers and fruits, articles of dress and decoration, kings and queens, precious stones and musical instruments. Even when she describes feelings and colours we find realistic touches. The note of realism in her poetry adds to it a freshness, a living interest, a power to grip, without making it a medium of social propaganda.

There is truth in Sarojini's artistic treatment of the facts of nature and life. Birds of a large variety appear in her poems birds with gay brilliant plumage like the peacock and the parrot; song-birds like the *koil*, the *bulbul*, the *dhadhikula*; birds of peculiar cries like the lapwing; water-birds like the swan, the heron, the halcyon, the gull; birds of prey like the falcon; and such peaceful birds as the pigeon and the dove. The animals that find a place in her verse are such herbivorous quadrupeds as the elephant, the deer, the gazelle, the heifer, the sheep; carnivorous quadrupeds like the tiger and the panther; rodents like the squirrel and the mouse; and reptiles like the serpent. The flowers that bloom in her poems are the *ashoka*, the cassia, the *champa*, the *gulmohur*, the hyacinth, the jasmine, the *Keora*, the lily, the lotus, the nasturtium, the oleander, the poppy, the rose, the *sirisha*, the tulip. Sarojini is very fond of mentioning such fruits as the mango and the coconut, the peach and the pomegranate.

Sarojini accepts and represents things as they really are in India. The women of Sarojini wear such things as the fillet, the girdle, or the veil; the bride wears the marriage-veil and has a tilak on her forehead. Her kings and queens have splendid regalia crowns or turbans, an ivory bed or an ebony seat, jewelled sceptre, canopies, armies, armour, forts, heralds, vassals. She mentions a number of precious stones agate, amber, amethyst, gem, jade, jewel, onyx, opal, peridot, porphyry, sapphire, ruby. She writes of various musical instruments string instruments like the lute and the *sitar,* wind instruments like the flute and the pipe, percussion instruments like the cymbal, and re-sounding instruments like the drum. The colours that occur frequently are blue, green, purple, red, saffron.[58] Her weavers are real persons: they earn their honest bread by waving all kinds of clothing the robes of a new-born child, the marriage-veils of a queen, the funeral shroud of a dead man.[59]

There is truth in Sarojini's artistic treatment of the customs of Indian society. The maidens in her poem send their pitchers afloat on the tide and hasten away to gather the leaves of the henna-tree: in their opinion, the red of the *tilak* looks beautiful on the brow of a bride, the red of the betel-nut looks lovely on lips that are sweet, but for lily-like fingers and feet there is nothing like the red of the henna tree.[60] There is realism in the attitude of an Indian who sees the moon as

> A caste-mark on the azure brows of heaven.[61]

In the following lines there is no idealisation of life, but an intense awareness of the distinction between "being" and "existence":

> Till ye have battled with great grief and fears,
> And borne the conflict of dream-shattering years,
> Wounded with fierce desire and worn with strife,
> Children, ye have not lived: for this is life.[62]

Sarojini is a realist: she writes faithfully not only of princes but also of beggars. She sings not only of canopies and forts but of the wind and the rain, not only of gems and jewels but of poverty and hunger. Her beggar woman is an old creature, bent and blind, sitting under a banyan three, holding a battered begging bowl in her hand

> In hope of your succour, how often in vain,
> So patient she sits at my gates,
>
> In the face of the sun and the wind and the rain,
> Holding converse with poverty, hunger, and pain,
> And the ultimate sleep that awaits.[63]

In the following lines there is a faithful representation of an evening scene in an Indian village:

> An ox-cart stumbles upon the rocks,
> And a wistful music pursues the breeze

> From a shepherd's pipe as he gathers his flocks
> Under the *pipal*-tree.
> And a young *Banjaran* driving her cattle
> Lifts up her voice. . . . [64]

NOTE OF EROTICISM

Love is the breath of life to Sarojini, the be-all and end-all of human life. Other writers may write on love for varied reasons, but Sarojini wrote on love simply because love was a necessary condition of her existence. In some of her love poems, she establishes a confidential relationship between the writer and the reader and unburdens the soul, not of a particular woman, but of every woman. Her stark sincerity would put to shame the average sentimental writer of today: she writes

> Of sobbing breath and broken speech,
> Sweet anguish of rose-scented nights
> And wild mouths calling each to each
> Or mute with yearning ecstasy.[65]

Love is a relation which is psycho-physical involving considerable emotion:

> How would the drum-beats of the dawn divide me
>                     from your bosom,
> Or the union of the midnight be ended with the
>                     day?
>
>             . . . . .
>
> Come, O tranquil night, with your soft, consent-
>                     ing darkness,
> And bear me to the fragrance of my beloved's
>                     breast.[66]

The poet has written of lonely, repressed womanhood with passion and sincerity. She writes on love from the woman's point of view, revealing the woman as a human being:

> Cover mine eyes, O my Love!
>     Mine eyes that are weary of bliss
> As of light that is poignant and strong,
>     O silence my lips with a kiss.[67]

The poet feels keenly the tragedy of an unloved woman, yet there is no breath of lawlessness in her passion. The agonies of a woman yearning for affection are exhibited specially in the following lines:

> I hear the bright peacock in glimmering
>     woodlands
> Cry to its mate in the dawn;
> I hear the black *Koel's* slow, tremulous wooing,
> And sweet in the gardens the calling and cooing
> Of passionate *bulbul* and dove.[68]

Love is the principal means of escape from the loneliness which afflicts most men and women throughout the greater part of their lives:

All pain is compassed by your frown;
All joy is centred in your kiss.[69]

Sarojini is a woman of a strong, passionate temperament. She is keenly sensitive to the sensuous side of life. She believes that the bodily impulse of sex and the spiritual impulse of ideal love cannot be separated from each other. If the animal and the spiritual natures are at war, neither can reach its full fruition:

Shall any foolish veil divide my longing from
my bliss?
Shall any fragile curtain hide your beauty from
my kiss?
What war is this of Thee and Me? Give o'er the
wanton strife,
You are the heart within my heart, the life within
my life.[70]

The love of man and woman at its best is free and fearless, compounded of body and mind in equal proportions, not dreading to idealise because there is a physical basis, and not dreading the physical basis lest it should interfere with the idealisation:

Lift up the veils that darken the delicate moon
of thy glory and grace,
Withhold not, O Love, from the night of my longing the joy of thy luminous face.

. . . . .

Faint grows my soul with thy tresses' perfume
and the song of thy anklets' caprice,
Revive me, I pray, with the magical nectar that
dwells in the flower of thy kiss.[71]

NOTE OF JOY

Sarojini finds joy in love and in nature. The shade of the coconut glade, the scent of the mango grove, the sands at the full of the moon, the sound of the voices she loves, the kiss of the spray, the dance of the wild foam, the blue of the verge where the sky mates with the sea all these are sweet to her.[72] She hears the hollows murmuring and sees the oleanders scatter their ambrosial fire.[73] She loves to go

Where upon the *champa*-boughs the *champa*-
buds are blowing;
To the *koil*-haunted river-isles where lotus lilies
glisten.[74]

When temple-bells ring, she sees Kamala lingering in the grove,

And Krishna plays on his bamboo flute
An idyll of love and spring.[75]

The scenic effects are highly coloured, but they show real joy, and appreciation of the sublime in nature:

The dawn and the dusk grow rife
With scent and song and tremulous mirth;

The winds are drunk with the odorous breath
Of henna, *sirisha,* and *neem.*[76]

When springtime wakes in meadow and grove, Sarojini is filled with ecstasy. The mellifluous *koels* sing paeons of love, the flow of rivers and rills is melodious, the peacocks dance in rhythmic delight: in the season of blossom and leaf the mystic hears "life's exquisite chorus". In her mysticism there is a radiant clarity and a serenity which spring from her conviction that there is in spring a joy of which man's life is a part:

Their joy from the birds and the streams let us
borrow.
O hear! let us sing,
The years are before us for weeping and
sorrow . . .
Today it is spring![77]

The lilt of a *bulbul,* the laugh of a rose, the dance of the dew on the wings of a moonbeam, the voice of the zephyr that sings as he goes all these are manifestations of the joy of springtime.[78] The *bulbul,* the *maina,* and the dove welcome the spring in their songs. There is some suggestion of Wordsworth in the following lines:

I know where the ivory lilies unfold
In brooklets half-hidden in sedges,
And the air is aglow with the blossoming gold
Of thickets and hollows and hedges.[79]

NOTE OF MELANCHOLY

In some poems there is a load of anguish and agonising grandeur, a wistful longing, the desire to speak of tears and shattered dreams. She is the poet of the moment, of its splendour and transience, its burden and its grief. She complains that her heart is weary and sad and alone, for its dreams like the fluttering leaves have gone.[80] She complains of the heavy burden of dreams that are dead and she wants to scatter their ashes away.[81] She asks the fireflies,

What do you know in your blithe, brief season
Of dreams deferred and a heart grown old?[82]

She likens her heart to the fallen flower and the faded leaf, plucked by the wind of sorrow, and "to every lone and withered thing that hath foregone the kisses of the spring."[83] She writes,

Pain-weary and dream-worn I lie awake,
Counting like beads the blazing stars o'erhead.[84]

She complains that her weary heart of late has fallen from its high estate of laughter and has lost all the vernal joy it knew.[85]

In many of her sombre poems the greys are flecked here and there with gold. Her wandering singers point to the message of the past and, by implication, contrast its large

vitality and freshness with the jaded commercial restlessness of today:

> Our lays are of cities whose lustre is shed,
> The laughter and beauty of women long dead;
> The sword of old battles, the crown of old kings,
> And happy and simple and sorrowful things.[86]

The exquisite poem **"To the God of Pain"** is profoundly
melancholic, yet there is nothing maudlin, nothing cowardly about it:

> Let me depart, for my whole soul is wrung,
> And all my cheerless orisons are sung;
> Let me depart, with faint limbs let me creep
> To some dim shade and sink me down to sleep.[87]

She gives us greyness to counterbalance the glut of rose-
pink:

> O glowing hearts of youth, how shall I sing to you
> Life's glorious message from a broken lyre?[88]

She portrays the victory of sorrow long endured:

> Nay, do not pine, tho' life be dark with trouble,
> Time will not pause or tarry on his way;
> Today that seems so long, so strange, so bitter,
> Will soon become forgotten yesterday.[89]

There is no whining, no luxury of grief, no sentimental
pessimism. Neither is there any joy, any real peace, but
there is the serenity of a brave and troubled spirit:

> The wind of change for ever blows
> Across the tumult of our way,
> Tomorrow's unborn griefs depose
> The sorrows of yesterday,
> Dream yields to dream, strife follows strife,
> And Death unweaves the webs of Life.
>
> . . . . .
>
> With futile hands we seek to gain
> Our inaccessible desire,
> Diviner summits to attain,
> With faith that sinks and feet that tire;
> But nought shall conquer or control
> The heavenward hunger of our soul.[90]

The suavity of Sarojini's method, the wistfulness of her
Muse; and the serenity of her outlook are peculiarly individual:

> Time lifts the curtain unawares,
> And sorrow looks into her face . . .
> Who shall prevent the subtle years,
> Or shield a woman's eyes from ears?[91]

The pessimistic note is by no means dominant in Sarojini
and cheerfulness breaks through at times:

> O I am tired of strife and song and festivals and
>                                 fame,
> And long to fly where cassia-woods are breaking

> into flame.
> Love, come with me where Koels call from
>                 flowering glade and glen,
> Far from the toil and weariness, the praise and
>                 prayers of men.[92]

But there is more cloud than sunshine:

> Men say the world is full of fear and hate,
> And all life's ripening harvest-fields await
> The restless sickle of relentless fate.[93]

Some of her poems are of wistful melancholy, which
crystallises into a more or less pessimistic criticism of
life:

> The bridal-songs and cradle-songs have cadences
>                     of sorrow,
> The laughter of the sun today, the wind of death
>                     tomorrow.[94]
>
> . . . . .
>
> Earth's glories flee of human eyes unseen,
> Earth's kingdoms fade to a remembered dream.[95]

The mature poet leaves us with a larger charity and with
a deeper faith in humanity:

> Yet will I slake my individual sorrow
> At the deep source of universal joy. . . .
> O Fate, in vain you hanker to control
> My frail, serene, indomitable soul.[96]

ATTENTION TO MUSIC AND METER

Among Indo-Anglian poets Sarojini is a subtle artist and
metrist. She is the poet of the choice word and the fine
phrase. She is learned in her art and uses artistic devices
deliberately and consciously. She concentrates as much
on form and style as on thought and meaning. Her rhythm
is at no place unpleasant and her rhymes are never grotesque. To convey her sense-impressions accurately she
has recourse to varied imagery and compound expressions and epithets which are both pictures and ideas she
writes of "lily-like fingers" and "flower-like bodies," of
"rose-scented nights" and "rose-pastured kine," of "Koil-
haunted river-isles" and "laughter-lighted faces," of
"slumber-soft feet" and "sorrow-trodden grass," of "gold-
flecked grey" and "moonlight-tangled meshes of perfume."

Sarojini pays a good deal of attention to vowel music, to
artistic meters, and to the choice of musical words. In
many of her poems we come across triumphs of word-
music, and at no place has the vowel music been carried
to an extreme. Skilled in meter and versification, Sarojini
does not sacrifice sense for the sake of sound. Inferior
Indo-Anglian poets have expressed their ideas in halting
verse, Sarojini gave her ideas music and colour: her
dancers look like wind-blown lilies

As they glide and bend and beckon,
As they wheel and wind and pause.[97]

The seductive alliterative music of her verse reminds one of Swinburne:

I know where the dragon-flies glimmer and glide,
And the plumes or wild peacocks are gleaming,
Where the fox and the squirrel and timid fawn
      hide
And the hawk and the heron lie dreaming.[98]

The following difficult verse of eight measures shows her wealth of expression and abundant ideas on Indian dancers:

Their jewel-girt arms and warm, wavering, lily-
      long
    fingers enchant through melodious hours,
Eyes ravished with rapture, celestially panting,
    what passionate bosoms aflaming with fire![99]

In order to appreciate the rhythms and harmonies of Sarojini properly, it is necessary that her poems should be read aloud:

A brown quail cries from the tamarisk bushes,
A *bulbul* calls from the cassia-plume,
And thro' the wet earth the gentian pushes
Her spikes of silvery bloom.[100]

### LIMITATIONS

Sarojini was not inspired by the stirring episodes of her own day. She ignored the tragic perplexities of the actual situation. She did not depart from the purely aesthetic standard of art for art's sake. She was not influenced by the literary revolution taking place in English poetry in the twenties and earlier. Her poetry, in general, taught no lesson, had no moral, called for no reform. She was not actuated by any definite moral purpose to uplift and instruct. She did not point out what life ought to be. She did not attempt to show moral and physical diseases as they are, and so her realism was highly selective.

In a few of her poems passages of singular beauty and power are mingled with others that are commonplace and high-flown. Her feelings sometimes get out of her control and, instead of a logical sequence, we have a conglomeration as the following:

Hide me in a shrine of roses,
Drown me in a wine of roses,
Drawn from every fragrant grove:
Bind me on a pyre of roses,
Burn me in a fire of roses,
Crown me with the rose of love.[101]

It is not impossible to burn her in a pyre of roses after she has been drowned in a wine of roses, but it is impossible to revivify her to crown her with the rose of love. Again, the following lines are repelling in their excess:

Take my flesh to feed your dogs if you choose,
Water your garden-trees with my blood if you
      will.[102]

The later poems of Sarojini, particularly those in the sections entitled "The Flowering Year" and "The Peacock Lute," are intellectual exercises rather than creations. A few of her poems **"To a Buddha Seated on a Lotus," "The Flute-Player of Brindaban," "June Sunset," "Imperial Delhi,"** and one or two others should survive when the other poems have been buried in oblivion.

All her work exhibits a marked strain of the sensuous and the mystic, a sense of the flesh and a sense of the spirit. Whatever her shortcomings as a poet, she has few peers in Indo-Anglian poetry. Her maturer work is marked by a sense of disenchantment, almost frustration, but her greatest merit is that she helped to keep hope alive in an age of despair.

### NOTES

[1] "I can recall Somerset Maugham," Baig writes, "sitting in our flat in Bombay, entranced and enthralled, and thanking us most profusely afterwards for giving him the privilege of meeting such a wonderful person". (M.R.A. Baig: *In Different Saddles,* Asia Publishing House, Bombay, 1967, p. 46).

[2] "Alabaster", *The Sceptred Flute,* Kitabistan, Allahabad, 1943, p. 4.

[3] "The Poet to Death", *S.F.,* p. 49.

[4] "At Twilight", *S.F.,* p. 78.

[5] "The Soul's Prayer", *S.F.* . p. 123.

[6] "To My Fairy Fancies", *S.F.,* p. 26.

[7] "The Bird of Time", *S.F.,* p. 65.

[8] "Death and Life", *S.F.,* p. 119.

[9] "The Faery Isle of Janjira", *S.F.,* p. 122.

[10] "Three Sorrows", *S.F.,* p. 176.

[11] "Ashoka Blossom", *S.F.* ., p. 22.

[12] "To India", *S.F.,* p. 58.

[13] "At Twilight", *S.F.,* p. 77.

[14] "The Broken Wing", *S.F.,* p. 145.

[15] "Invincible", *S.F.,* p. 174.

[16] "An Anthem of Love", *S.F.,* p. 131.

[17] "Awake", *S.F.,* p. 180.

[18] "The Broken Wing", *S.F.*, p. 145.

[19] "In the Night", *S.F.*, p. 128.

[20] "At Dawn", *S.F.*, p. 129.

[21] "Wandering Singers", *S.F.*, p. 4.

[22] "At Twilight", *S.F.*, p. 77.

[23] "Ode to H.H. the Nizam of Hyderabad", *S.F.*, p. 29.

[24] "Past and Future", *S.F.*, p. 34.

[25] "Dirge", *S.F.*, p. 67.

[26] "An Indian Love Song", *S.F.*, p. 67.

[27] "The Call to Evening Prayer", *S.F.*, p. 136.

[28] "Awake", *S.F.*, p. 181.

[29] "In Salutation to my Father's Spirit", *S.F.*, p. 160.

[30] "Dirge", *S.F.*, p. 67.

[31] "Corn-Grinders", *S.F.*, p. 10.

[32] "Suttee", *S.F.*, p. 18.

[33] "To my Children", *S.F.*, p. 52.

[34] "In the Forest", *S.F.*, p. 33.

[35] "A Challenge to Fate", *S.F.*, p. 135.

[36] "Wandering Beggars", *S.F.*, p. 165.

[37] "The Festival of Serpents", *S.F.*, p 111.

[38] "The Lotus", *S.F.*, p. 167.

[39] "A Persian Love Song", *S.F.*, p. 82.

[40] "Song of Radha", *S.F.*, pp. 112, 113.

[41] "The Flute-Player of Brindaban", *S.F.*, p. 161, 162.

[42] "In Remembrance", *S.F.*, p. 70.

[43] It may be argued that seeing the material as embodying the spiritual is not exclusively a Platonic approach and that it is originally an ancient Indian approach. However, we have still to examine whether Plato himself did not come under Indian influence as far as this approach is concerned.

[44] "The Prayer of Islam", *S.F.*, p. 168, 169.

[45] "Solitude", *S.F.*, p. 133.

[46] "Welcome", *S.F.*, p. 205.

[47] "Song of Dream", *S.F.*, p. 21.

[48] "To a Buddha seated on a Lotus", *S.F.*, p. 62.

[49] "Humayun to Zobeida", *S.F.*, p. 22.

[50] "Ode to H.H. the Nizam of Hyderabad," *S.F.*, p. 29, 30.

[51] "The Song of Princess Zeb-un-Nissa," *S.F.*, p. 38.

[52] "The Queen's Rival", *S.F.*, pp. 45 48.

[53] "Nightfall in the City of Hyderabad", *S.F.*, pp. 55, 56.

[54] "The Royal Tombs of Golconda", *S.F.*, pp. 59, 60.

[55] "A Rajput Love Song", *S.F.*, pp. 80, 81.

[56] "In the Bazaars of Hyderabad", *S.F.*, pp. 106, 107.

[57] "Memorial Verses", *S.F.*, p. 157.

[58] "Sarojini adored beautiful jewels and clothes as much as any other woman", Tara Ali Baig writes. "In fact, colour permeates all she wrote, but she was herself an equal devotee of colour, loving rich silks and golden chains, shoulder brooch and bangles, so favoured in Bengal. Later, twin tiger claws mounted on a gold pendant and chain were a permanent feature of her jewellery, and in a photograph taken of her in sick bed in 1918 she is decked with ear-rings, necklace and bangles. There is also a picture of her as a girl in bustled dress with long frilly sleeves, her brothers in velvet suits and white stockings and boots and her mother in a dainty *sari* with Chinese embroidered, border and ivory bangles." ("Sarojini Naidu," Publications Division, New Delhi, 1975, p. 29).

[59] "Indian Weavers", *S.F.*, p. 5.

[60] "In Praise of Henna", *S.F.*, p. 13.

[61] "Leili", *S.F.*, p. 31.

[62] "Life", *S.F.*, p. 35.

[63] "The Old Woman", *S.F.*, p. 126.

[64] "June Sunset" *S.F.*, pp. 192, 193.

[65] "Bells", *S.F.*, p. 170.

[66] "A Rajput Love Song", *S.F.*, p. 81.

[67] "A Love Song from the North". *S.F.*, pp. 75, 76.

[68] "A Love Song from the North", *S.F.*, pp. 75, 76.

[69] "The Vision of Love", *S.F.*, p. 227.

[70] "Humayun to Zobeida", *S.F.*, p. 22.

[71] "An Indian Love Song", *S.F.*, p. 68.

[72] "Coromandel Fishers", *S.F.*, p. 6.

[73] "The Snake-Charmer", *S.F.*, p. 8.

[74] "Village-Song", *S.F.*, p. 11.

[75] "Spring", *S.F.*, p. 87.

[76] "In a Time of Flowers", *S.F.*, p. 92.

[77] "Ecstasy", *S.F.*, p. 99.

[78] "The Joy of the Springtime", *S.F.*, p. 89.

[79] "The Call of Spring", *S.F.*, p. 185.

[80] "Autumn Song", *S.F.*, p. 23.

[81] "In the Forest", *S.F.*, p. 32.

[82] "A Song in Spring", *S.F.*, p. 88.

[83] "Vasant Panchami", *S.F.*, p. 91.

[84] "The Garden Vigil", *S.F.*, p. 172.

[85] "The Coming of Spring", *S.F.*, p. 187.

[86] "Wandering Singers", *S.F.*, p. 4.

[87] "To the God of Pain", *S.F.*, p. 37.

[88] "Farewell", *S.F.*, p. 163.

[89] "Transience", *S.F.*, p. 125.

[90] "To a Buddha Seated on a Lotus," *S.F.*, pp. 61, 62.

[91] "The Pardah Nashin", *S.F.*, p. 53.

[92] "Summer Woods", *S.F.*, p. 190.

[93] "In Salutation to the Eternal Peace", *S.F.*, p. 137.

[94] "Village Song", *S.F.*, p. 12.

[95] "Damayanti to Nala", *S.F.*, p. 43.

[96] "A Challenge to Fate", *S.F.*, p. 135.

[97] "The Dance of Love", *S.F.*, p. 73.

[98] "The Call of Spring", *S.F.*, p. 185.

[99] "Indian Dancers", *S.F.*, p. 38.

[100] "June Sunset", *S.F.*, p. 192.

[101] "The Time of Roses", *S.F.*, p. 194.

[102] "Devotion", *S.F.*, p. 231.

## Meena Alexander (essay date 1986)

SOURCE: "Sarojini Naidu: Romanticism and Resistance," in *Ariel: A Review of International English Literature*, Vol. 17, No. 4, October, 1986, pp. 49-61.

[*In the following essay, Alexander examines feminism in Naidu's life and works, noting in particular the conflict between the turn-of-the-century English poetry and lifestyle she absorbed while studying in London and the tumultuous social and political atmosphere of India prior to the country's independence.*]

I

What follows is a brief inquiry into the complex feminism of a woman who lived at the interface of two cultures, that of the Hyderabad she was born into and the colonial culture of British India. She passed through the diction and manners of the latter into a poetry and politics forged, at least in her later years, within the very tumult of Nationalist politics. Yet there are questions to be asked of her life and letters. There seems to be a radical cleft between the intense if imprisoning passions of her poetry and the political life she espoused. Did the female self she discovered in political action successfully subvert the passive if anguished images she picked up from turn-of-the-century English poetry? Or is there a dichotomy between poet and politician scarcely to be explained, pointing towards complicated, covert procedures of creativity? Further, how did the English language, which she was greatly dependent on, work for her, first colonizing and then releasing her into the ferment of India?

II

Her first meeting with Gandhi helped to set the tone of her political life. It's London 1914. Gandhi is there after South Africa, after the success of his *satyagraha* protest against the British imposition of taxes on Indians, and against the law that all Indians should be fingerprinted and forced to carry passes. Naidu calls on him. She climbs the stairs and comes on an open door

> . . . framing a living picture of a little man with a shaven head, seated on the floor on a black prison blanket and eating a messy meal of squashed tomatoes and olive oil out of a wooden prison bowl. Around him were ranged some battered tins of parched ground nuts and tasteless biscuits of dried plantain. I burst in instinctively into happy laughter . . .

Gandhi invites her to share his meal, remarking, "'Ah, you must be Mrs. Naidu! Who else dare be so irreverent?'" "'An abominable mess,'" she replies, "'no thanks!'" Looking back Sarojini Naidu comments: "In this way and at that instant commenced our friendship . . . which never wavered for a single hour . . ."[1]

The vivid adherence to detail and the refusal to romanticize, both disclosed in this small encounter, were to characterize Naidu's political career. In 1930, five years after she was elected President of the Indian National Congress, she was powerfully involved in Gandhi's Salt March. At the crack of dawn on 6 April 1930, Gandhi and his company went down to the sea to bathe; he then gathered up in his palm a few grains of the salt that had dried on the beach. In symbolic defiance of the British salt law, which held a monopoly on the production of salt, thousands followed after Gandhi. Countless women participated, bearing earthern ware and metal pots in which they carried away salt water. The salt, once dried, was auctioned off quite publicly, nature itself harnessed in the struggle for national freedom. On 5 May Gandhi was arrested and the leadership of the non-violent movement fell to Sarojini Naidu. With 25,000 volunteers she approached Darshana determined to enter the salt works there as Gandhi had planned. It was hot and dry, and the volunteers suffered from terrible thirst. The police were ranged to meet them and beat them violently, often over the head. Naidu never flinched. She addressed the volunteers, prayed with them, and at times, to keep her strength going, sat in a small deckchair writing or spinning *khadi*.[2] As the Gandhian volunteers who courted arrest fell to the police blows, Naidu sat calm, keeping watch. By mid-month she herself was arrested and carted off to jail.

She suffered frequent imprisonment, the most lengthy and painful in 1942 after the Quit India Resolution when she, together with Gandhi and his wife Kasturba, was incarcerated in the Aga Khan palace. Sickness and inaction haunted them all. In February of the following year, while still imprisoned, Gandhi started a fast unto death. It was a tragic blow when Kasturba, who had been suffering from a slow, prolonged fever, died; after her death Gandhi was released. Naidu herself, the victim of malarial fever, was set free on 21 March 1943, aged 64.

### III

Despite her great political prominence, Sarojini Naidu first entered the public realm as a poet, and was celebrated as such. She espoused a mellifluous if dated English diction: her images of private, pained women suffering emotional deprivation, even psychic imprisonment, stand as a direct foil to the public life she so fearlessly took to. In the cause of National freedom, she travelled countless miles, often in hardship, courting arrest, campaigning in her strong orator's voice all over India from as early as 1903. Was she indeed able to cauterize her private pain through her poems and then move outwards into the public sphere? Or did the poems with their sometimes cloying diction, their female figures trapped in an unredeemed sexuality, force her to leave them behind, the writer herself consumed more and more by the political struggle so that by 1917 she effectively stopped writing?

Naidu inherited something of the complex linguistic situation of India. Born in 1879 of Bengali parents in the city of Hyderabad, she spoke not Bengali but Urdu, the Islamic language of culture in Hyderabad. Living at the edge of Bengali and espousing Urdu, Naidu added to these English, the language of colonization. She used English both in her poetry and in her powerful orations.

Her first book of poetry, *The Golden Threshold,* was published in London in 1905. Its frontispiece was a pen and ink drawing by J. B. Yeats: "June 1896" appears under the clearly legible signature. Her image is instructive. The face of the young woman, her posture upright though not stiff, is grave, composed. Her eyes are dark, etched firmly under the straight brows. Her hair is tied back. The hands clasped above her chest form a graceful line to the chin. The shoulders are erect. It is clear from this line drawing that both the gravity and the innocence of this adolescent were visible. Sarojini was only fifteen when she was sent off to England on a scholarship from the Nizam of Hyderabad. She had indiscreetly fallen in love with a Dr. Naidu, far older than she and of the wrong caste; she had to be got out of the country. The portrait was made at the end of her sojourn abroad.

*The Golden Threshold* was published with an introduction by Arthur Symons, an established man of letters by the time the volume appeared. He tells us that the volume is being published at his "persuasion."[3] His English turn-of-the-century awe at the "mystic" Orient and decadent concern with the exotic in this young woman emerge in his lengthy description of her eyes, which he says concentrate all her beauty, and in his glowing descriptions of her "clinging dresses of Eastern silk" and her "long black hair" (p. 16).

Interwoven with Symons's praise for the "agony of sensation" (p. 17) in this young woman are extracts from her letters from Hyderabad, in which she reveals just how she came to use the English language with all the fluency, even euphony, that Symons and others so admired. Sarojini tells of how she was "stubborn and refused to speak" English. Her father, a famous chemist whose obsession was alchemy, locked up his daughter alone in a room for a whole day. She was a child of nine, and the letter written years later conveys the shock of this first punishment: "I came out of it a full-blown linguist. I have never spoken any other language to him or to my mother who always speaks to me in Hindustani" (p. 11).

It would seem crucial that the young girl acquired the language of colonization, English, via the closed room, forerunner of the prisons she was forced to inhabit as an activist in the National movement. Nor was it merely an accident that she chose to speak English to both parents, mother and father severed from her through that deliberate choice of the language of both punishment and accomplishment.

Indeed, Naidu's early poetry (and all her poetry was composed in English) establishes a theme never overcome in her career as a writer. The work is haunted by a voice telling of other female selves, resonances of subjectivity, that endure mutilation and are imprisoned psychically. The search for "the blind ultimate silence of the dead" that overtakes the speaker on the way to Golconda finds its emotive counterpart in the lives of the women in a poem like **"Pardah Nashin"**: their days behind the veil are described as "a revolving dream / Of languid and sequestered ease. . . . " Their clothing, idealized and unreal, caught within the walls of a segregated dwelling, becomes "morning mist / Shot opal, gold and amethyst."[4] The stasis Naidu evokes is not so far from that of a Dowson or Symons enthralled by the deathly passivity in which a woman must be fixed. In his poem "Morbidezza," for instance, Symons in full flourish as a decadent celebrates a "White girl," her "flesh as lilies" now "Grown, 'neath a frozen moon. . . . " In "Maquillage" he describes in detail the artifice of a woman, her "rouge on fragile cheeks, / Pearl-powder, and about the eyes / The dark and lustrous Eastern dyes."[5] Both poems appeared in *Silhouettes,* a volume whose second edition appeared in 1896, when Sarojini was still in England. The young Sarojini learnt her lesson all too well, embracing for herself the world-weary sensations, the stasis, the unmistakable agony of women who have nowhere to go. The irony is that she should learn from Symons or Dowson, carrying their diction back to India, using in her poetry images of exhausted women, hermetically sealed, a double colonization that the interchange of cultures drew her to.

In **"Suttee,"** Naidu goes a step further. The voice is that of a woman mourning the death of her beloved husband: he was the "lamp of my life"; without him she is condemned to live in the dark. He was the "Tree of my life," now crushed by death's cruel foot. How should she, a mere blossom, survive without trunk, root, or stalk? In the culminating stanza, the mellifluous language highlighting the terrible self-destruction the woman is ready to embrace, the voice asks:

> Life of my life, Death's bitter sword
> Hath rent us like a broken word,
> Rent us in twain who are but one . . .
> Shall the flesh survive when the soul is gone?
>                                                     (*Poems,* p. 18)

Self and other are united as substance and sense in a word that is now "broken." The language of dualism rises up to buttress the division of gender, the woman likened in this trope, not unfamiliar to readers of Romantic poetry, to the flesh in all its weakness, and the man linked to the powerful soul, the immortal spirit. The question is merely rhetorical; there is no question of the woman's survival without her beloved husband. Lacking the soul, the flesh is dross, fit merely to be consigned to the fire. From stasis and the enclosure of a woman's life we move to the immolation of the female body once it has been cleft from its male counterpart. Romanticism imposed by colonial British education allies Naidu's **"Pardah Nashin"** and **"Suttee"** with Wordsworth's *Ruined Cotage,* where Margaret, abandoned by Robert, can only wait within the decay of domestic walls or roam abroad in madness, and with Tennyson's *Lady of Shallott.*

IV

When *The Golden Threshold* appeared in 1905, Naidu was a young woman of twenty-six, married, with four young children. But far from being content to remain within the walls of the home she shared with her husband, she moved outwards, into the political realm. It was as if the immobilization portrayed in her female images cauterized her own pain, permitting her self an entry into the public realm. In December 1904 at the eighteenth session of the Indian National Congress a large portion of which was devoted to issues of women's rights like education, purdah, child marriage, and polygamy Naidu met some of the great reformers of her day, including the powerful Ramabai Ranade, who presided over the women's sessions. For her part, Naidu recited the patriotic **"Ode to India,"** which was much appreciated at this first public reading.[6] At the centre of the poem lies the image of India as a "slumbering Mother" who must be awoken by the daughter's cry. If in **"Suttee"** the bond to the male lover (husband) renders the woman helpless, here the longing to awaken the mother quickens a desire for empowerment, political myth intersecting with subjective need. The ancient Indian earth is still able to "Beget new glories." The idealization of the past is drawn into the voice in the quest for a future, equally idealized:

> Mother, O Mother, wherefore doest thou sleep?
> Arise and answer for thy children's sake!
>
>                     . . . . .
>
> Waken O slumbering Mother and be crowned,
> Who once wert empress of the sovereign past.
>                                                     (*Poems,* p. 58)

It is as if the daughter imprisoned by passion is striking free of her own bondage in the act of awakening the mother.

Indeed, the image of India as mother struck a deep vein in the culture. *Punya bhumi* (blessed earth) and *bharat mata* (mother India) were linked together for both poet and audience. The mother was sacred, potent, terrible to her foes when awoken. In a later poem, Naidu celebrates "Kali the mother," the fierce, passionate goddess of both life and destruction: "O terrible and tender and divine! / O mystic mother of all sacrifice" opens the poem, which ends with an invocation: *"Kali! Maheshwari!"* Mindful of her foreign readers, Naidu has added a note: "These are some of the many names of the Eternal Mother of Hindu Worship" (*Poems,* pp. 177-79).

India's association with British colonialism provides a telling twist to the pervasive femaleness of the Indian earth. Citations from Keshub Chunder Sen, one of the great figures of the Bengal Renaissance, reveal how the trope acquires symbolic power for anti-colonial activity. Sen, who had visited England in 1870, was immensely taken with English culture and longed to unite Britain and India, Christianity and Hinduism. In his extended figure India becomes the bride and England the groom:

Let India, beloved India be dressed in all her jewellery those sparkling orient gems for which this land is so famous. . . . The bridegroom is coming. . . . Let India be ready in due season.[7]

But by 1883 the image turns; in Sen's "Asia's Message to Europe," the mother country is a woman raped, a prisoner of England, violated, bleeding. The artifice of diction opens up the pain of an earth violated:

Behold the sweet angel of the East into whose beauty the very colours of heaven seem to have been woven the fair East . . . lies prostrate, a bleeding prisoner . . . The rivers that run eastward and the rivers that run westward are crimson with Asiatic gore . . .

(Iyengar, pp. 44-45)

If Keshub Chunder Sen's tragic realization provides a momentary insight into the symbolic femaleness of India, Naidu carried that symbolism into her growing sense of feminist commitment. By 1906, when she spoke to the Indian Social Conference in Calcutta, there is a causal connection between the deprivation of civil rights that Indian women suffer and the success of the British colonizers. Her language is fierce and direct. Whereas in **"Suttee"** the man had been invoked as the woman's soul, here the woman is given full autonomy, a "human soul" and with it the inalienable birthright of "liberty and life." Now the liberation of India is held to be inseparable from the liberation of its women. The soul, when evoked, is firmly placed in female flesh, and linked to the radical powers of maternity:

Does one man dare to deprive another of his birthright to God's pure air which nourishes his body? How then shall a man dare to deprive a human soul of its immemorial inheritance of liberty and life? And yet my friends, man has so dared in the case of Indian women. That is why you men of India are today what you are: because your fathers in depriving your mothers of that immemorial birthright have robbed you, their sons, of your just inheritance. Therefore I charge you, restore to your women their ancient rights . . . [8]

As in **"Ode to India,"** the idealized Vedic past stands as a golden age. Naidu was famed as an orator throughout India and in many of her speeches the deprivation suffered by the women around her, and by her own self in its most private portions, comes to figure as the ground of change. Restoration of women's rights becomes a necessary condition for National freedom.

Often in the poems, however, a woman's pain is conveyed as a portion of things as they are, without reference to possible change; the telling seems to suffice. In **"Nasturtiums"** for instance, the speaker evokes both the bitter fragrance of the bloom and the sensations elicited by the sight of the petals, then moves on to a recitation of the names of women from Hindu mythology. Each of the women, Savitri or Sita, Draupadi, Damayanti or Shakuntala, has suffered pain or betrayal at the hands of a man. The poet's footnote points them out as "immortal women of Sanskrit legend and song"; their grief and virtue still "inspire" the lives of Indian women (*Poems,* p. 95). The tale of Sita in particular haunted Naidu, especially the portion of her life set forth in the disputed Uttar Rama Kanda of the *Ramayana.* There King Rama, still dubious about her virtue after the years of exile he has forced upon her, requires Sita to undergo a test by fire. Sita, white haired now and the mother of grown twins, their faces the spitting image of Rama's own, utterly blameless still, is humiliated. She cries out to the mother earth and earth, quite literally her mother, splits open to save her. Sita is swallowed back into the earth from which she had emerged (King Janaka, her 'father,' discovered her while a field was being ploughed). Naidu puts this myth, with its ontological base in the maternity of the earth, to startling political use. In her activities with Gandhi and C. F. Andrews to prevent the abuse of indentured women labourers who were taken from India to South Africa and Fiji, Naidu makes covert use of the fate of Sita. The godly figure of Rama, in his role as cruel husband, is elided and the British rulers take his place: "I . . . raise my voice" cries Naidu in a speech of 1917, "not for the men, but for women, for those women whose proudest memory it is that Sita would not stand the challenge to her honour but called upon the mother earth to avenge her and the earth opened up to avenge her" (*Speeches,* p. 92).

v

1917 saw the publication of Naidu's last volume of poetry, *The Broken Wing.* She was 38. After it, though she might have scribbled a few lines from time to time, she never seriously wrote poetry. Her life was consumed by the rigours of public campaigning, her years punctuated by imprisonment. Politically, she was known throughout India. This last volume culminates in a long poem called **"The Temple,"** a poem of undeniable eroticism that the epigram from Tagore ("My passion shall burn as the flame of Salvation") cannot quite mask. One gathers that the poem caused quite a stir when the volume first appeared. There were rumours of illicit love or a sexual passion the poet could not wholly fulfil in her life. The poem itself is divided into three main sections, each in turn broken up into short poems, three or four stanzas in length. The tight stanzaic form Naidu chooses is heightened in formality by the use of a title for each short poem, "The offering," "The feast," and so forth. In each case the symbolism is sexual, the religious sense subservient to the erotic delight or suffering received at the hands of the beloved. In the third section the tone intensifies. The voice is fierce with the energy of having broken through the frozen stasis "My cold heart like a spectre / In a rose encircled shroud" required of female beauty. "But I have plucked you, O miraculous Flower of my desire," writes the poet, "And crushed between my lips the burning petals of your mouth" (*Poems,* pp. 204, 212).

The petals, a figure for the beloved lips, dissolve into the literal and fiercely desired mouth. Yet in the following poem, **"The Lute Song,"** sexuality, grasped so avidly, eats into the core of the self. Almost like Oothoon in Blake's *Vision of the Daughters of Albion,* the voice in Naidu's poem cries to be wiped out, nullified, so that the self might reflect the purity of a male lover. Oothoon's position was starker: raped by Bromion she must cry out to Theotormon's eagle to tear her breast. In the bloody place left in her body she longs to reflect the "image of Theotormon."⁹ The woman raped, instead of turning out-wards in anger at her assailant, first turns in shame to herself, wounding herself, seeking to cross out her own existence or to mirror, in her doubly wounded flesh, the image of the beloved. In Naidu's poem the violence against the self is incipient. First the self must mirror the beloved. Her eyes "shadowless wells of desire" almost a carry over of Symons's image for Sarojini's own eyes must bear the beloved's face to perfection. The self is effectively nullified. But the ferocity of passion, having taken this first step, now abates. The voice asks forgive-ness. Desire overwhelms the speaker; she has trespassed her own bounds: "Forgive me the sin of my eyes" begins the sixth poem, which then flows into a list of wrongs. The speaker has "assailed," "encircled," "oppress'd," even "ravished" the beloved. Now comes the time for atonement. She will brew her own soul into wine to make him strong; through the strength of love, she will "fashion" him into a god. There is no irony in the voice; the sentiment, unflawed by desperation, is lifted straight out of a tradition that advocates worship of the husband as if he were a god. Eroticism, once powerful, is again covert as the poet writes in the cloying lan-guage of mysticism: "You are the substance of my breath / And you the mystic pang of Death" (***Poems,*** p. 217).

The speaker's true state, with her desire so severely re-pressed, sublimated into a pseudo-mysticism, becomes clear in a painful poem called **"The Secret."** Here (the poem is a portion of **"The Temple"**) the speaker is *already dead.* Passion unrequited has killed her. People come forward to her bearing tribute, powerless to tell of the death within her. In a perfect masking of her posthumous condition, she is visible to them, as if completely alive. The cruelty of desire has killed her. Her throbbing heart was flung "to serve wild dogs for meat." Now she must fend off, as best she can, "the ravening fire / Of my own heart's desire." Terror at the impasse she has reached breaks the voice open, and it turns yet again, now to celebrate the "passionate sin" for which punishment must be craved, a punishment which paradoxically serves to affirm a trespassing pas-sion. In a poem called **"The Sanctuary"** the poet writes:

> My proud soul shall be unforgiven
> For a passionate sin it will ne'er repent,
> And I shall be doomed, O Love and driven
> And hurled from Heaven's high battlement,
>
> Down through the deep ages, alone, unfrightened,
> Flung like a pebble thro' burning space;

> But the speed of my fall shall be sweet and
> brightened
> By the memoried joy of your radiant face!
> (***Poems,*** p. 229)

What a fall the woman suffers for her passion, dropping through the gulf of time; yet her self coheres to her pas-sion and its burning space, heat reinforcing the "passion-ate sin" the stanzas celebrate. Desire, outlawed by the world, defines the speaker, yet the last stanza of the poem reveals a curious change. While the self falls through the immense gulf, the male beloved is held secure in "God's mystic garden." He must be preserved blameless, as a "saint even." His lack of sexual response, his chilling neutrality, now come to stand as virtue while she, fierce and tender, must be thrust out. Yet one line stands in relief: "My outlawed spirit shall crave no pardon" (***Po-ems,*** p. 230). Standing outside the laws of the world, she gathers strength through defiance, the very strength the political woman needs to work against colonial will. Her romantic torment then would seem to create a shock of resistance that the political self can draw on.

Yet **"The Temple"** does not end there. Gender works its strange corrosions. In the very last stanza of the long poem we discover a poem entitled **"Devotion"** where the previous image of female flesh thrown to the dogs returns with a vengeance. There is masochism here, a total rejec-tion by the voice of the outlawed self. All her defiance dissolved, she throws herself at the beloved: she is his; he may do what he will. The heroic drop through space has lapsed into this all-too-earthly desecration:

> Take my flesh to feed your dogs if you choose,
> Water your garden trees with my blood if you
> will,
> Turn my heart into ashes, my dreams into dust
> Am I not yours, O love to cherish or to kill?
> (***Poems,*** p. 231)

The poetic self is in the grip of a sexuality so atavistic that desire equals destruction. Effectively, there were no more poems.

Naidu's political self, however, flourished. In 1925 she reached the height of her fame when she was the first Indian woman elected President of the National Con-gress. At her inauguration, she was led to the podium in a great procession that included Mahatma Gandhi and both Motilal and Jawaharlal Nehru. With the eyes of the nation on her she acknowledged the honour done to her as a "generous tribute to Indian womanhood." Indeed, as a woman, she wanted nothing more than to propose a "most modest domestic programme." It was one she was willing to die for: "to restore to India her true position as the supreme mistress in her own home. . . . It will be my [l]ovely though difficult task, through the coming year, to set my mother's house in order . . ."¹⁰

What could be a more fitting desire for a feminist and Nationalist? The image of the maternal home, the locus of earliest nurturing, consoles and releases, inspiring confidence in the future. Not that this feminine image should be misinterpreted as quiescent, for Naidu goes on in her speech to argue for resolute, even war-like measures to combat the British, measures that were in conflict with Gandhi's posture of total *ahimsa*. She wanted compulsory military training for all children, remobilization of the villages, and the organization of urban workers so that both women and men could arm themselves. This arming of the nation against colonialism seemed to her a "natural and indispensable auxiliary of political emancipation." It seemed to her that there was no other way of overthrowing the enemy that lay both within and without: those "deadly forces of repression that challenge our human rights of liberty."[11] Now the passage of her resistance seems clear. The confrontation with the sometimes tragic bonds of her own culture empowered her psyche, permitting it to attack the public bonds laid down by a colonizing power. If there is regret that her poetry did not keep pace with her life, it is equally possible to sense that her private and at times agonizing conflicts, as recorded in poetry, were crucial to the integrity of her living voice.

### NOTES

[1] H. S. L. Polak, H. N. Brailsford, and Lord Pethick-Lawrence, *Mahatma Gandhi,* fwd. and appreciation by H. E. Sarojini Naidu, Governor of the United Provinces (London: Odhams Press, 1949), p. 7.

[2] Eleanor Morton, *Women behind Mahatma Gandhi* (London: Max Reinhardt, 1954), p. 158.

[3] Sarojini Naidu, *The Golden Threshold,* int. Arthur Symons (London: William Heinemann, 1909), p. 9.

[4] Sarojini Naidu, *The Sceptered Flute; Songs of India,* The Collected Poems of Sarojini Naidu (New York: Dodd, Mead, 1928), p. 53; hereafter cited parenthetically as *Poems.*

[5] Arthur Symons, *Silhouettes,* 2nd ed. (London: Leonard Smithers, 1896), p. 13 ("Morbidezza"). "Maquillage" is included in *Poetry of the Nineties,* ed. R. K. R. Thornton (Penguin: Harmondsworth, 1970), pp. 44-45.

[6] See Padmini Sengupta, *Sarojini Naidu: A Biography* (Bombay: Asia Publishing House, 1966), pp. 48-49.

[7] Quoted in Srinivasa Iyengar, *Indian Writing in English,* 2nd ed. (New York: Asia Publishing House, 1973), p. 44.

[8] Sarojini Naidu, *Speeches and Writings* (Madras: Natesan, 1918), p. 16.

[9] William Blake, *The Complete Poems,* ed. Alicia Ostriker (Harmondsworth: Penguin, 1977), p. 198: "Rend away this defiled bosom that I may reflect / The image of Theotormon on my pure transparent breast."

[10] Pattabhi Sitaramayya, ed., *The History of the Indian National Congress, 1: 1885-1935* (Bombay: Padma Publications, 1946), p. 290; from the message published by the President-Elect in October 1925.

[11] A. M. Zaidi and S. G. Zaidi, eds., *The Encyclopedia of the Indian National Congress, 9: 1925-1929* (New Delhi: S. Chand, 1980), pp. 30, 31.

## Harish Raizada (essay date 1989)

SOURCE: "Indian Ethos in Sarojini Naidu's Poetry," in *Perspectives on Sarojini Naidu,* edited by K.K. Sharma, Vimal Prakashan, 1989, pp. 78-113.

[*In the following essay, Raizada discusses Naidu as an Indian poet—rather than an Indian writing English poetry—and reassesses her work in those terms.*]

### I

With the change in literary fashions, critical attitudes and critical values also change. The canons of criticism which are highly esteemed in one age are discarded in favour of new ones in another. In the changed perspective, the great writers of the preceding age wane into mediocrity in the succeeding one, and old idols become new abhorrences. The new aesthetics which evolved in the wake of modernism in the European literature during the inter-war years, depedastalized many literary demi-gods who were looked upon with awe and inviolable reverence by the earlier generations. Even the greatness of Shakespeare for whom Arnold has asserted: "Others abide our question Thou are free!"[1] has to be vindicated by a Wilson Knight on the basis of modern aesthetics.

It is not surprising therefore that now when *The Golden Threshold* is judged by the touchstone of *The Wasteland,* "the gifted poetess," the Nightingale of India of yester years, on whom Arthur Symons and Edmund Gosse showered unreserved encomium and about whom that "profound judge of life and literature"[2] Sri Aurobindo said that she had "qualities which make her best work exquisite, unique and unchallenged in its own kind",[3] is now relegated to mediocrity, unworthy of any attention as a poet. Sisir Kumar Ghose avows nonchalantly: "Her period piece juvenilia had been, we now see, praised out of proportion, if not for the wrong reasons",[4] and then lapses into unpardonable heresy: "Most of her polite, meaningless words, stylised product of a 'delicate, dreaming soul', have been blown away by age. There hangs a mild, musty museum air about most of the poems. Nothing will bring back the glory departed. . . . The Muses have become menacingly cerebral".[5] Nissim Ezekiel condescends to remark: "It was Sarojini's ill luck that she wrote at a time when English poetry had touched rock-bottom of sentimentality and technical poverty. By the time it recovered its health she had entered politics, abandoning the possibility of poetic development and maturity."[6] R. Parthasarathy praises her for her versification but discards her as a poet: "Prosodically, her verse is excellent; as poetry, it disappoints. In spite of her having pumped enough feeling into them, the poems invariable have trouble getting started."[7] The modesty of the poetess who said: "I am not a poet really. I have the vision and the desire, but not the voice. If I could write just one poem full of beauty and the spirit of greatness, I shall be exultantly silent for ever; but I sing just as the birds do, and my songs are as ephemeral",[8] is treated as a confession and enthusiatic ignoramuses credit her for it with honest assessment of her place as poet.

It is not only Sarojini Naidu who is pilloried so mercilessly, Toru Dutt, Manmohan Ghosh, Aurobindo Ghosh, Joseph Furtado, Harindranath Chattopadhyaya are all condemned as "colonialitis"[9] by this T. S. Eliot sycophancy. They are questioned for "their outsize reputations"[10] and are considered worthy "today only of historical interest".[11] Manmohan Ghose is described as "an extreme case of 'Colonialitis' and Laurence Binyon is chided for praising him instead of asking him "to stop composing pastiches of the English poets".[12] Binyon's commendation of Ghose is called damaging to the poet: "More than one Indian English poet has been ruined by such adulation."[13] The greatest Indian English epic of Sri Aurobindo, *Savitri,* is dubbed as "embarrassingly bad: dated in language, emotionally inflated to the point of grotesqueness and confused in ideas".[14] The literary heresy does not spare even the great Rabindranath Tagore about whom the following judgment is passed by David Cevet:

> . . . the old man himself lived out a certain contradiction since his concern with the eternal had manifested itself in an eternal garrulousness. And since it is arguable that Rabindranath never did write more than half a dozen good poems it might be said that his concern for moral purity had ended in his emasculation of the vocabulary as well as repression of the instinct.[15]

In their enthusiasm the new Indian English poets assert: "Indian poetry in English doesn't seriously begin to exist till after independence. . . . The unacknowledged birth of this poetry took place in the 1950s".[16] R. Parthaswamy writing in the vein of Adil Jussawalla remarks: "It is true that Indian English verse has a past that is best forgotten. There are far too many skeletons in the cupboard for the poet to feel comfortable or secure today."[17]

It is forgotten that to fall in line with the Romantics or Later Romantics (Pre-Raphaelites and Aesthetes) and not in line with Hulme-Pound-Eliot school of poetry, is not to be devoid of poetic sensibility and creative urge. If the subjectivity, exotic imagination and profound emotional rapture are not conducive to the health of poetry, objectivity, wit, irony and arid intellectualism too do not necessarily contribute to great poetry. The vogue of Eliot is, however, on the wane now and even his most zealot admirer F. R. Leavis has gradually moved on the road of rejection of his great master in his last years. Eliot's "Tradition and the Individual Talent" is condemned and the doctrine of impersonality so crucial to Eliot's aesthet-

ics and poetry firmly dismissed by Leavis when he remarks: "The relevant truth, the clear essential truth, is stated when one reverses the dictum and says that between the man who suffers and the mind which creates there can never be a separation."[18] "The whirligig of literary taste is about to come full circle", and hence a re-revaluation of old masters, including "the foremost of Indian English poetesses is timely".[19]

II

Sarojini Naidu was in reality a born poet, one eminently endowed with the temperament and nature of true artist. Except for Keats there are very few poets who had such an overpowering passion for poetry as she. To her it was poetry that charged her every moment, to which she directed her best efforts and in which she burned. This keen poetic sensibility did not desert her even after she had stopped writing verses and entered politics. It expressed itself through her conversations, letters and speeches. According to Jawaharlal Nehru she gave to politics an artistic touch. Speaking on her death he said: "she did that amazing thing, she infused artistry and poetry into the national struggle, just as the Father of the Nation had infused moral grandeur to it." Sardar Vallabhbhai Patel called her and a great politician remarked that thoughts came to her like verses and she wove them into a pattern which bore the immutable mark of her gifts of poetry. The famous Singhalese journalist, D. B. Dhanapala, said about her: "She talks politics but in the words of a poet".[20] Kamaladevi Chattopadhyaya made a very significant observation when she wrote: "Those who are poets first and last, continue to be poets, whether they be lying in the trenches or in the enemy's dungeons. . . . If Sarojini has stopped composing verses, she has certainly not ceased being a poetess. That same spirit comes out in all her movements and forms of expression."[21]

Sarojini Naidu's poetic sensibility is reflected in her profound passion for delight in beauty. In this respect too she comes very close to Keats who prefixed to the first volume of his poems the motto from Spenser:

> What more felicity can fall to creature
> Than to enjoy delight with liberty?

Arthur Symons writes about Sarojini: "Her desire, always, was to be 'a wild free thing of the air like the birds, with a song in my heart'. A spirit of too much firm in too frail a body. . . . " What Sidney Colvin said of Keats, "the spirit which animates him is essentially the spirit of delight: delight in the beauty of nature and the vividness of sensation, delight in the charm of fable and romance, in the thoughts of friendship and affection, in anticipations of the future, and in the exercise of the art itself which expresses and communicates all these joys", is equally true of Sarojini. She believes in "a poet's craving for beauty, the eternal beauty" and in a letter to Arthur Symons writes: "What in my father is the genius of curiosity the very essence of all scientific genius in me is the desire for beauty. Do you remember Pater's phrase about Leonardo da Vinci, 'curiosity and the desire of beauty'".[22] Elaborating her remark Arthur Symons writes: "It was the desire of beauty that made her a poet; her 'nerves of delight' were always quivering at the contact of beauty. To those who knew her in England, all the life of the tiny figure seemed to concentrate itself in the eyes; they turned towards beauty as the sunflower turns towards the sun, opening wider and wider until one saw nothing but the eyes."[23]

Sarojini's love for beauty was strengthened by the seductive Persian and Urdu poetry on which she was nourished at Hyderabad. While in England she met the aesthetic poets of the nineties, who were averse to the dross and drab of mundane life which had entered the English landscape with the growth of industrialism and struck at the very roots of man's aesthetic sensibility. They were also full of deep passion for delight in beauty. Sarojini Naidu found an echo of her own aesthetic temperament in their works. She was introduced by Edmund Gosse to these poets of the Rhymers' Club Arthur Symons, William Watson, John Davidson, Earnest Dowson, Oscar Wilde, George Moore, Henley and others which was founded in the 1880's by William Butler Yeats and Earnest Rhys. She learnt from these members of the Rhymers' Club "the verbal and technical accomplishment, the mastery of the phrase and rhythm" of English verse and like them stuck to the verbal felicity, metrical discipline, and musical texture.

Sarojini's intense love for beauty, her natural bent of mind and her happy life, both with her parents and husband, led her to experience profound delight in life. She once wrote to Symons: "the very 'Spirit of Delight' that Shelley wrote of dwells in my little home". She had drunk from the sweet fountain of life to her fill. When Gopal Krishna Gokhale once asked her, "'Do you know, I feel that an abiding sadness underlies all that unfailing brightness of yours? Is it because you have come so near death that its shadows still cling to you?', she replied, 'No, I have come so near life that its fires have burnt me.'"[24]

Sarojini's delight in life was further intensified by the age in which she lived. It was the age of cultural renaissance and national upsurge in India. Earlier Keshub Chunder Sen, Dayanand Saraswati, Mahadev Govind Ranade, Sir Syed Ahmad Khan, Surendranath Banerjee and later Mrs. Annie Besant, Dadabhai Naoroji, Balgangadhar Tilak, Gopal Krishna Gokhale, Aurobindo Ghosh, Rabindranath Tagore and Mahatma Gandhi had infused new life and boundless enthusiasm in the country. Sarojini too like Keats could sing: "Great spirits now on earth are sojourning",[25] or like Wordsworth could reminisce:

> Bliss was in that dawn to be alive,
> But to be young was very heaven[26]

Sarojini's temperament and conditions of her life and age, all combined to make her a lyricist of joy in life.

Those who criticize her for drawing a blank over sordid and coarse aspects of Indian life, demand from her what she being a genuine person and poet, could not have given them without sounding unnatural and unauthentic.

### III

Sarojini Naidu has written large number of love lyrics full of profound feelings and saturated with soul-slumbering sensuousness which a critic calls the "latticed window view of nuptial aspiration".[27] Some of these songs are subjective in nature and represent her soulful attachment to her husband. Her love for her husband is also symbolized in the songs woven round the popular Radha-Krishna legend. These love poems of Sarojini express her deep emotions of yearning, aspiration, fulfilment, and ecstasy.

The most important of Sarojini Naidu's poems are, however, those which reflect the colourful pageant of Indian life in all its picturesque variety. "The panorama of India's ageless life", writes K. R. Srinivasa Iyengar, "fascinates her without end."[28] It is not surprising that she won her early renown in the West because of her representation of the soul of the East and the ethos of India. Edmund Gosse wrote admiringly:

> It has been . . . the characteristic of Mrs. Naidu's writing that she is in all things and to the fullest extent autochthonous. She springs from the very soil of India; her spirit, although it employs the English language as its vehicle, has no other tie with the West. It addresses itself to the exposition of emotions which are tropical and primitive, and in this respect, as I believe, if the poems of Sarojini Naidu be carefully and delicately studied they will be found as luminous in lighting up the dark places of the East as any contribution of savant or historian. They have the astonishing advantage of approaching the task of interpretation from inside the magic circle, although armed with a technical skill that has been cultivated with devotion outside of it.[29]

The credit for discouraging Sarojini from providing in her verses "a réchauffé of Anglo-Saxon sentiment in an Anglo-Saxon setting", and awakening her to the need of "some revelation of the heart of India, some sincere penetrating analysis of native passion, of the principles of antique religion and of such mysterious intimations as stirred the soul of the East long before the West had begun to dream that it had a soul",[30] goes to Edmund Gosse. He writes how after discarding her early poems, he entreated her "to write no more about robins and skylarks, in a landscape of our Midland counties, with the village bells somewhere in the distance calling the parishioners to church, but to describe the flowers, the fruits, the trees, to set her poems firmly among the mountains, the gardens, the temples, to introduce to us the vivid populations of her own voluptuous and unfamiliar province; in other words, to be genuine Indian poet of the Deccan, not a clever machine-made imitator of the English classics".[31] After this encounter with Gosse,

Sarojini's extraordinary creative imagination has tried to capture the visions of Indian ethos in all its entirety. It is, however, the vision of a poet who glows with passion for delight in beauty. The realities that she portrays are therefore "not quite of the earthy".[32] She herself says, "I am of a tribe of beauty". She enshrines in her verses beautiful images of Indian life and ethos.

Living in the age of national upsurge Sarojini is led to dream of the beautiful vision of the glorious India "that is to be", and put in her heart and soul to make it a reality. Answering the querry of the veteran national leader Gopal Krishna Gokhale, "Why should a song-bird like you have a broken wing"? she replies:

> Shall spring that wakes mine ancient land again
> Call to my wild and suffering heart in vain?
>
> . . . . .
>
> Behold! I rise to meet the destined spring
> And scale the stars upon my broken wing![33]

Sarojini projects an impressive image of the resurgent India in this poem:

> The great dawn breaks, the mournful night is past,
> From her deep age-long sleep she wakes at last!
> Sweet and long-slumbering buds of gladness open
> Fresh lips to the returning winds of hope,
> Our eager hearts renew their radiant flight
> Towards the glory renascent light,
> (*The Broken Wing*, p. 145)

The call of the awakened motherland is so powerful that she is unable to luxuriate in the beautiful fairy island of Janjira "where life glides by to a delicate measure, with the glamour and grace of a far-off time". She is compelled to join her countrymen in their struggle for freedom:

> Yet must I go where the loud world beckons,
> And the urgent drum-beat of destiny calls,
> Far from your white dome's luminous slumber,
> For from the dream of your fortress walls,
>
> Into the strife of the throng and the tumult,
> The war of sweet Love against folly and wrong;
> Where brave hearts carry the sword of battle,
> 'Tis mine to carry the banner of song,
>
> The solace of faith to the lips that falter,
> The succour of hope to the hands that fail,
> The tidings of joy when Peace shall triumph,
> When truth shall conquer and love prevail.
> (**"The Faery Isle of Janjira"**, pp. 121-22)

In the poem **"Awake",** which Sarojini dedicated to her friend Mohamed Ali Jinnah and recited at the Indian National Congress Session of 1915, she exhorts the motherland to wake up and shake off the shackles of slavery:

> Waken, O mother thy children implore thee,

> Who kneal in thy presence to serve and adore
>      thee!
> The night is aflush with a dream of the morrow,
> Why still dost thou sleep in thy bondage of
>      sorrow!

India's children of all communities and creeds Hindus, Parsees, Mussulmans, Christians pledge to restore to it its pristine glory:

> Lo we would thrill the high stars with thy story,
> And set thee again in the forefront of glory.
> (**"Awake"**, p. 180)

All these children are united as one soul by the strong ties of love for their country:

> One heart are we to love thee, O our Mother,
> One undivided, indivisible soul,
> Bound by one hope, one purpose, one devotion
> Towards a great, divinely destined goal.
> (**"The Anthem of Love"**, p. 131)

Sarojini pays a tribute to her brave compatriots who sacrificed their lives for peace in the First World War:

> Gathered like pearls in their alien graves
> silent they sleep by the Persian waves,
> Scattered like shells on Egyptian sands,
> They lie with pale brows and brave, broken hands,
> They are strewn like blossoms mown down by
>      chance
> On the blood-brown meadows of Flanders and
>      France.
> (**"The Gift of India"**, p. 146)

and asks Britain not to forget them when it pays memorial thanks to its own countrymen:

> When the terror and tumult of hate shall cease
> And life be refashioned on anvils of peace,
> And your love shall offer memorial thanks
> To the comrades who fought in your dauntless
>      ranks,
> And you honour the deeds of the deathless ones,
> Remember the blood of my martyred sons!
> (**"The Gift of India"**, p. 147)

When owing to her deeper involvement in political life, she is unable to perform her wifely duties and is physically separated from her husband, she exhorts him:

> Give not to me, but to the world, winged words
> Of Vision, Valour, faith-like carrier words
> Bearing your message O'er all lands and seas,
> Scatter the lustre of resplendent deeds
> O'er journeying world words like immortal seeds
> Of sheaves enriching freedom's granaries.[34]

Whenever there was any calamity in any part of the country, Sarojini was deeply pained by it as if it were her own personal loss. At the time of the disastrous flood in 1927 in Gujerat, she addresses a moving poem to angry God:

> Stay the relentless anger of thy hand

Thine aweful war, O Lord, no longer wage
Against our hopeless hearts and heritage,
Nor rend with ravening doom our ancient land.

Cease lest thy maddened creatures turn from thee
And in the midnight of deep wild travail
Mock thee with mouths of bitter blasphemy.
("Gujerat", *The Feather of the Dawn*, p. 5.)


IV

During active participation in the national struggle for
independence, Sarojini Naidu came in close contact with
the great political leaders of her age Bal Gangadhar
Tilak, Gopal Krishna Gokhale, M. A. Jinnah, Mahatma
Gandhi, Sardar Patel, Jawaharlal Nehru and others. Tara
Ali Beg refers to four great men her father, Gokhale,
Jinnah and Gandhi who really shaped her life and influ-
enced her.

The most powerful of these influences was, however, of
Gokhale who remained her political mentor from 1907 to
1914. He advised her, "consecrate your life, your
thought, your song, your charm to the Motherland". She
in a letter to Gokhale (November 28, 1917) called him "a
beacon light, and a symbol of national service". Paying a
tribute to him on his death she addressed her second
**"Memorial Verse"**, 'Gokhale,' to him:

Heroic heart lost hope of all our days
Need'st thou the homage of our love or praise?
Lo, let the mournful millions round thy pyre
Kindle their souls with consecrated fire
Caught from the brave torch fallen from thy hand,
To succour and to serve our suffering land,
And in a daily worship taught by thee
Upbuild the temple of her unity.
(p. 159)

In another poem, **"In Gokhale's Garden"**, she symbolizes him as life-giving showers of rain. Like the rain
which revives and infuses life in meadows, barren rocks
and plants, Gokhale infused life in the dead hearts of
Indians and awakened them to free their motherland from
alien yoke. Describing his great qualities of head and
heart, she writes:

Steadfast, serene, dauntless, supremely wise,
In earth's renascent bloom with prescient eyes
You sought hope's symbol and you strove to teach
My heart with patient, high prophetic speech
The parable of Beauty's brave emprise.
(*The Feather of the Dawn*, p. 1)

Though dead, he lives in the hearts of his countrymen for
ever and inspires them to brave deads to accomplish the
liberty of the country:

Your ashes lie in old Prayag, but we,
Heirs of your spirit's immortality,
Find in your vision Love's perpetual flame
Of adoration lit in freedom's name,

Rekindling all our dream of liberty.
(*The Feather of the Dawn*, p. 2)

Equally inspiring is his poem addressed to Bal
Gangadhar Tilak "who taught our nation freedom's
Gayatri," i.e. "freedom is my birth-right and I will attain
it":

How shall our mortal love commemorate
Your sovereign grandeur, O victorious heart?
Changeless, austere, your fame is counterpart
Of your own storied hills inviolate.
The darkness of our land, and star-like dart
The lustre of your wisdom, valour, art,
Transfiguring sorrow and transcending fate.
("Lokmanya Tilak", *The Feather of the Dawn*,
p. 3)

Sarojini Naidu pays a glowing tribute to Umar Sohani
(died on 6 July, 1926), a millionaire philanthropist of
Bombay, who was one of the first Muslim nationalists to
join Mahatma Gandhi when he launched his Civil Disobedience Movement.

You were not of my kindred or my creed,
O kingly heart, but closer still you stood
In gracious bond of tender brotherhood
Than they who blossomed from my father's seed.
("Uman", *The Feather of the Dawn*, p. 4)

Sarojini's father Dr. Aghorenath Chattopadhyaya, descended from the ancient family of Chatterjees who were
noted throughout Eastern Bengal as patrons of Sanskrit
learning, and for their practice of Yoga. He took his
degree of Doctor of Science at the University of Edinburgh
in 1877, and afterwards studied brilliantly at Bonn. On his
return to India he founded the Nizam College at Hyderabad,
and devoted himself to the cause of education till his death.
He exercised deep influence on Sarojini and her brother,
Harindranath. The elegy Sarojini wrote on his death epitomizes his nature and qualities beautifully:

Farewell, farewell, O brave and tender age.
O mystic jester, golden-hearted child
Selfless, serene, untroubled, unbeguiled
By trivial snares of grief and greed or rage;
O splendid dream in a dreamless age
Whose deep alchemic vision reconciled
Time's changing message with the undefiled
Calm wisdom of thy vedic heritage.
("In Salutation to My Father's Spirit", p.
160)

Sarojini Naidu has dedicated her poem of national integration, **"Awake"**, to M.A. Jinnah who was her close
friend and whom she considered a great man of India.
After Gokhale she was more attached to Mahatma
Gandhi than to any other Indian leader. Gandhiji in
*Young India* compared her with Mirabai in terms of her
devotion to the cause of freedom and lyricism. She on her
turn said: "Gandhi is my Kanhaya; I am his humble
flute". In the poem. **"The Lotus"**, which she has dedicated to him, the symbolizes him as lotus, the national
flower of India:

But who could win thy secret, who attain
Thine ageless beauty born of Brahma's breath,
Or pluck thine immortality, who art
Coeval with the Lords of Life and Death?
                                        (**"The Lotus"**, p. 167)


V

Born in Hyderabad, a city in which Hindu and Muslim cultures fused and flowered, Sarojini imbibed its cosmopolitan spirit and strived for Hindu-Muslim and national unity with greater fervour than other Indian leaders. She expresses her deep concern at the strifes and differences among the people of different creeds and communities in her country, when she writes:

Shall hope prevail where clamorous hate is rife,
Shall sweet love prosper or high dreams find place
Amid the tumult of reverberant strife
'Twixt ancient creeds, 'twixt race and ancient
        race,
That mars the grave, glad purposes of life,
Leaving no refuse save thy succouring face?
                                        (**"Twilight"**, p. 77)

She is, however, hopeful that these discordant notes will disappear and there will usher in the happy times of love's delight:

Quick with the sense of joys she hath foregone,
Returned my soul to beckoning joys that wait,
Laughter of children and the lyric dawn,
And love's delight, profound and passionate,
Winged dreams that blow their golden clarion,
And hope that conquers immemorial hate.
                                        (**"Twilight"** p. 78)

In her famous poem **"The Call to Evening Prayer"**, Sarojini Naidu projects an impressive image of the secular India where all religious faiths flourish freely:

*Allah ho Akbar! Allah ho Akbar!*
From mosque and minar the Muezzins are calling;

*Ave Maria! Ave Maria!*
Devoutly the priests at the altars are singing,

*Ahura Mazda! Ahura Mazda!*
How the sonorous Avesta is flowing

*Naray'yana! Naray'yana!*
Hear to the ageless, divine invocation!
                                                (p. 136)

Sarojini Naidu has inculcated from Hyderabad not only her love for Urdu and Persian but also a deep acquaintance with and regard for Muslim life and culture. She has written touching verses about Muslim heroes and heroines **"A Song from Shiraz"**, **"Humayun to Zubeida"**, **"Ode to H. H. The Nizam of Hyderabad"**, **"The Song of Princess Zeb-un-Nissa and Muslim Religion"**, **"The Prayer of Islam"**, **"The Night of Mar-**

**tyrdom"**, etc. **"A Song from Shiraz"** captures the oriental spirit of Shiraz and brings forth in immemorial lines the loving soul of Islam:

The singers of Shiraz are fasting afar
To great the Nauraz with sarang and cithar . . .
But what is their music that calleth to me,
From glimmering garden and glowing minar?

*The stars shall be scattered like jewels of glass,*
*And beauty betossed like a shell in the sea,*
*Ere the lutes of their magical laughter surpass,*
*The lute, of thy tears, O Mohamed Ali!*

Sarojini has eulogized the loving and gracious nature of the late Nizam of Hyderabad, Mir Mahbub Ali Khan, the well-beloved of people, and the glamour of his princely state in two of her poems. In **"Ode to H. H. The Nizam of Hyderabad"** she describes how the people of different religious faiths flourish in his cosmopolitan state and do obeisance to him:

The votaries of the Prophet's faith,
Of whom you are the crown and chief
And they, who bear on vedic brows
Their mystic symbols of belief;
And they, who worshipping the sun,
Fled O'er the old Iranian sea;
And they, who bow to him who trod
The midnight waves of Galilee.
                                                (p. 29)

She prays to God to give him strength and grace to stand for truth and virtue:

God give you joy, God give you grace,
To shield the truth and smite the wrong,
To honour virtue, valour, worth,
To cherish faith and foster song
So may the lustre of your days
Outshine the deeds Firdausi sung,
Your name within a nation's prayer,
Your music on a nation's tongue.
                                                (p. 30)

In one of the memorial verses, **"Ya Mahbub"** she mourns the death of the Nizam and pays a glowing tribute to him. The title of the poem is derived from the device, 'Ya Mahbub' (Beloved) designed on the state banner of the Nizam.

O hands that succoured a people's need
With the splendour of Haroun-al-Rasheed
O heart that solaced a sad world's cry
With the sumptuous bounty of Hatim Tai
Where are the days that were winged and clad
In the fabulous glamour of old Baghdad.
And the bird of glory used to sing
In your magic kingdom . . . when you were king?
                                                (pp. 157-58)

**"The Prayer of Islam"** composed on Id-ul-Zoha in 1915 is soaked with the memorable spirit of the great humanistic religion of Muslims. Each stanza ends with some of the ninety-nine beautiful Arabic names of God as used by followers of Islam 'Hameed', 'Hafeez', 'Ghaffar', 'Wahab', 'Waheed', 'Quadeer', 'Quari', 'Rahman', 'Raheem'. The poem ends with the inspiring lines:

> We are the shadows of Thy light,
> We are the secrets of Thy might,
> The visions of Thy primad dream,
> *Ya Rahman! Ya Raheem.*
>
> (p. 169)

With remarkable ingenuity she weaves the refrain, "Y' Allah! Y' Allah!" used as the burden in the prayers chanted by wandering Muslim beggars:

> Time is like a wind that blows,
> The future is a folded rose,
> Who shall pluck it no man knows.
> *Y' Allah! Y' Allah!*
>
> ("Wandering Beggars", p. 165)

Equally touching is the prayer of the old beggar woman sitting in the street under a banyan tree:

> In her weary old age, O dear God is there none
> To bless her tired eyelids to rest? . . .
> Tho' the world may not tarry to help her or heed,
> More clear than the cry of her sorrow and need,
> Is the faith that doth solace her breast:
> *"Lailah illa-l-Allah*
> *La ilaha illa-l-Allah,*
> *Muhammad-ar-Rasul-Allah"*

In the poem about the Imam Bara of Lucknow, which is a chapel of lamentation where Muslims of the Shia community celebrate the tragic martyrdom of Ali, Hassan, and Hussain during the mourning month of Muharram, Sarojini gives a vivid account of the passion-play that takes place to the accompaniment of the refrain, "Ali! Hassan! Hussain!"

> Out of the sombre shadows,
> Over the sunlit grass
> Slow in a sad procession
> The shadowy pageants pass
> Mournful, majestic, and solemn,
> Stricken and pale and dumb,
> Crowned in their peerless anguish
> The sacred martyrs come.
> Hark, from the brooding silence
> Breaks the wild cry of pain
> Wrung from the heart of the ages
> *Ali! Hassan! Hussian!*
>
> ("The Imam Bara", p. 152)

Still more graphic is the description of the mourning procession given in **"The Night of Martyrdom"**:

> Blackrobed, barefooted, with dim eyes that rain
> Wild tears in memory of thy woeful plight,
> And hands that in blind, rhythmic anguish smite
> Their bloodstained bosoms to a sad refrain
> From the old haunting legend of thy pain,
> The votaries mourn thee through the tragic night,
> With mystic dirge and melancholy rite,
> Crying aloud on thee Hussain! Hussain!

The poem ends with a subtle irony on the celebration:

> Why do thy myriad lovers so lament?
> Sweet saint, is not thy matchless martyrhord
> The living banner and brave covenant
> Of the high creed thy Prophet did proclaim,
> Bequeathing for the world's beautitude
> Th' enduring loveliness of Allah's name?
>
> ("The Night of Martyrdom",
> *The Feather of the Dawn,* p. 6)

VI

Sarojini Naidu has pictured in several of her poems the Hindu religious ethos in all its variety by the treatment of Radha-Krishna legend, hymns of gods and goddesses, and different festivals. The myth of the temporal love of Radha, the milkmaid and Krishna, the cowherd, symbolizes the yearning of human soul for the infinite. It is very popular among Indians and many renowned poets like Jayadeva, Vidyapati and Surdas have woven their memorable verses round it. Krishna, the Divine flute-player of Brindaban, plays the tune of the Infinite that lures every human heart away from mortal griefs and attachments. The sweet music enchants Radha, the beautiful village belle and spell-bound by it she is drawn towards Krishna irresistibly. Krishna responds to her love but the consummation eludes her. She is unable to get the fulfilment of her soul's yearning. Sarojini has enshrined this eternal love in her poems, **"Song of Radha, the Milkmaid"**, **"The Flute-player of Brindaban"**, **"Poems of Krishna"**, and **"Songs of Radha"**. **"Song of Radha, the Milkmaid"** reveals how Radha is so much lost in the thought of her lover that she is unable to utter anything except his name:

> I carried my curds to the Mathura fair . . .
> How softly the heifers were lowing . . .
> I wanted to cry, "Who will buy
> These curds that are white as the clouds in the sky
> When the breezes of *Shrawan* are blowing?"
> But my heart was so full of your beauty, beloved,
> They laughed as I cried without knowing:
>
> *Govinda! Govinda!*
> *Govinda! Govinda!*
>
> How swiftly the river was flowing.
>
> (p. 112)

Drawn by the sweet music played by Krishna, the flute-player of Brindaban, Radha follows him undauntedly and forsaking all earthly ties:

> Still must I like a homeless bird
> Wander, forsaking all;
> The earthly loves and wordly lures
> That held my life in thrall,
> And follow, follow, answering
> Thy magic flute call.
>
> ("The Flute Player of Brindaban", p. 161)

Two songs of **"Poems of Krishna"** are entitled as 'Kanhaya' and 'Ghanashyam'. In the former is shown how mother Yashoda tries to punish Kanhaya on listening from village men and women the complaints of his mischief:

> Boastful One! Boastful One! Yashoda took a rod
> And hushed the peccant lips of him who was a
> laughing God.

The latter, **'Ghanashyam'**, is in the form of the poet's prayer to the divine deity who gifts his glory, healing breath, joy, mercy to the elements of nature and transcendental calm to sages and mystics:

> Let me be lost, a lamp of adoration,
> In thine unfathomed waves of ecstasy.
> *(The Feather of the Dawn,* p. 39)

**"Songs of Radha"** contain three poems 'At Dawn', 'At Dusk' and 'The Quest'. 'At Dawn' pictures the yearning of Radha for Ghanashyam at dawn after she has kept a vigil for him at night. **'At Dusk'** depicts the eagerness of Radha to adorn and prepare herself to receive Krishna Murari in the night. **'The Quest'** describes Radha's search for her lover Kanhaya at dawn, at dusk, and at moonrise in the forest, glade and woods. On meeting her, Krishna chides her:

> Thou saidst O Faithless one, self-slain with doubt,
> Why seekest thou my loveliness without
>
> . . . . .
>
> And askest wind or wave, or flowering dell
> The secret that within thyself doth dewell?
>
> . . . . .
>
> I am of thee, as thou of me, a part
> Look for me in the mirror of thy heart.
> *(The Feather of the Dawn,* pp. 42-3)

**"Hymn to Indra, Lord of Rain"** is the prayer of Indian peasantsmen and women to the God of Rain to favour them by his bounty for their very existence depends on his mercy:

> O Thou, who rousest the voice of the thunder,
> And biddest the storms to awake from their sleep,
>
> . . . . .
>
> Thou who art mighty to succour and cherish,
> Who savest from sorrow and shieldest from pain,
> Withhold not thy merciful love, or we perish,
> Hearken, O Lord of Rain!
> (p. 116)

In **"Lakshmi, The Lotus-Born"**, Indians invoke the Goddess of fortune to shower her gifts on their country:

> For our dear land do we offer oblation,
> O keep thou her glory unsullied, unshorn

> And guard the invincible hope of our nation,
> Hearken, O Lotus-born!
> (p. 150)

In **"Kali The Mother"**, the eternal Mother of Hindu worship is referred by its various mythical names 'Uma Haimavati', 'Ambika', 'Parvati', 'Girija', 'Shambhavi', 'Kali', and 'Maheshwari'. Her worshippers make their offerings to her and seek her blessings:

> O Terrible and tender and divine
> O mystic mother of all sacrifice,
> We deck the sombre altars of thy shrine
> With sacred basil leaves and saffron rice;
> All gifts of life and death we bring to thee,
> *Uma Himavati!*
> (p. 177)

Sarojini Naidu's songs of Hindu festivals not only project the spirit and occasion of these festivals, but also reveal the faith and enthusiasm of those who celebrate them. The Vasant Panchami is the spring festival when Hindu girls and married women carry gifts of lighted lamps and new-grown corn as offerings to the goddess of the spring and set them afloat on the face of the waters. Hindu-widows are denied the pleasure to take part in any festive ceremonials, for they are treated as unfortunate ones and have to lead the life of sorrow and austerity. The poem, **"Vasant Panchami"**, describes the lament of a Hindu widow at the festival of spring:

> O joyous girls who rise at break of morn
> With sandal soil your thresholds to adorn,
>
> Ye brides who streamward bear on jewelled feet
> Your gifts of silver lamps and new-blown wheat,
>
> I pray you dim your voices when you sing
> Your radiant salutations to the spring.
> (pp. 90-91)

On the festival of serpents, "Nag Panchami", celebrated three days before the festival of the birth of Lord Krishna, Hindu women offer milk, maize, wild figs and golden honey to serpents and pray to them to protect their lives from dangers:

> Guard our helpless lives and guide our patient
> labours,
> And cherish our dear vision like the jewels in your
> crests;
> **("The Festival of Serpents"**, p. 110)

Sarojini Naidu gives a vivid account of the festival of the sea, i.e. "Narieli Purnima" or Coconut Day which is celebrated by the people of the Western India, who live by sea and prosper by it. On this day, which marks the end of the monsoon and beginning of the fishing season, fishermen, traders, pilgrims and their women folk all pay homage to the sea the repository of treasure for their prosperity and safety by offering the auspicious coconuts to it. Women of sea-faring folk pray to the ocean by chanting:

> We worship thee with chaplets of devotion,

Cherish our dear desire,
And guard the lives we yield thee, sacred ocean,
Lower and son and sire.
       **("The Festival of the Sea",**
       ***The Feather of the Dawn,*** p. 8)

'Raksha Bandhan' is one of the most popular and colourful festivals of the Hindus in North India. On this day following an ancient Rajput custom, Hindu women tie bracelets of gold-twined silk on the wrists of their brothers. The silken thread is a symbol both of the deep love of sisters for their brothers and of the pledge of brothers to protect their sisters:

  A garland how frail of design,
  Our spirits to clasp and entwine
  In devotion unstained and unbroken,
  How slender a circle and sign
  Of secret deep pledges unspoken
     **("Raksha Bandhan",** *The Feather of the*
       ***Dawn,*** p. 10)

## VIII

Sarojini Naidu has revealed through her poems emotional and mental make-up of Indian men and women, their particular regional traits, their fancies and changing moods, their reactions to happiness and frustration in personal love and marital relations, their attitude to children and their agelong customs. Some of their instincts and qualities are of universal nature for being human beings they resemble men and women of all ages and countries. But in certain respects they are different from others owing to their peculiar habits and traditions. Muslim tribes of North West Frontier prize nothing more than a maiden to love and a battle to fight:

  Wolves of the mountains
  Hawks of the hills,
  We live or perish
  As Allah wills.

  Two gifts for our portion
  We ask thee, O Fate,
  A maiden to cherish,
  A kinsman to hate.

  Children of danger,
  Comrades of death,
  The wild scene of battle
  Is breath of our breath.
     **("A Song of the Khyber Pass"**
     ***The Feather of the Dawn,*** p. 12)

The Indian gipsy girl though poor, loves free and daring life:

  In tattered robes that hoard a glittering trace
  Of by gone colours, broidered to the knee,
  Behold her, daughter of a wandering race,
  Tameless, with the bold falcon's agile grace,
  And the little tiger's sinuous majesty.
     **("The Indian Gipsy",** p. 50)

While a city woman anoints her fingers and feet with the paste of henna leaves:

  The tilka's red for the brow of a bride,
  And betel-nut's red for lips that are sweet,
  But, for lily-like fingers and feet,
  The red, the red of henna tree.
     **("In Praise of Henna",** p. 13)

and hide herself in a veil:

  From thieving light of eyes impure,
  From coveting sun or wind's caress,
  Her days are guarded and secure
  Behind her carven laltices,
  Like jewels in a turbaned crest,
  Like secrets in a lover's breast.
     **("The Pardah Nashin",** p. 53)

A Rajput wife yearns for her warrior husband gone to the battle field,

  Haste, O wild-bee hours, to the gardens of the
    sunset!
  Fly, wild-parrot day, to the orchards of the west!
  Come, O tender night, with your sweet, consoling
    darkness,
  And bring me my beloved to the shelter of my
    breast!
     **("A Rajput Love Song",** p. 80)

and a Muslim one feels happy or sad according to the changing moods of her lover:

  O Love I know not why, when you are glad
  Gaily my glad heart leaps.
  O love I know not why, when you are sad,
  Wildly my sad heart weeps.
     **("A Persian Long Song",** p. 82)

or plays on the lute eagerly waiting for her husband to return (**"A Persian Lute Song"** in *F.D.*).

An Indian woman surrenders her all for the love of her husband:

  O love of all the riches that are mine
  What gifts have I withheld before thy shrine?
     **("To Love",** p. 83)

and when forsaken by her lover feels the panges of void in her heart:

  I hear the black *koel's* slow, tremulous wooing,
  And sweet in the gardens the calling and cooing
  Of passionate bulbul and dove. . . .
  But what is their music to me, *papeeha*
  Songs of their laughter and love, *papeeha,*
  To me, forsaken of love?
     **("A Love Song from the North",** pp. 75-76)

The death of her husband deprives her of all pleasures of life:

  Shatter her shining bracelets, break the string

Threading the mystic marriage-breads that cling
Loth the desert a sobbing throat so sweat,
Unbind the golden anklets on her feet,
Divest her of her azure veils and cloud
Her living beauty in a living shroud.

**("Dirge", p. 66)**

or drives her to death with her husband:

Life of my life, Death's bitter sword
Hath severed us like a broken word,
Rent us in twain who are but one. . . .
Shall the flesh survive when the soul is gone?

**("Suttee", p. 18)**

The folk songs of Sarojini Naidu open before us the vistas of variegated and bizaree life in India and enchant us by their lilting, rhythmic music. These songs project feelings, aspirations and wishes of the wide range of Indian people coming from the lower strata of life, The poet has cast them in different metres and verse forms, which bring out their spirit most effectively. **"Village Songs"** and **"Harvest Hymn"** describe the concerns and joys of rural people. A village maiden, who goes to the river Jamuna to fill her pitchers, feels worried as she gets late to return to her house:

Full are my pitchers and far to carry,
Lone is the way and long,
Why, O why was I tempted to tarry
Lured by the boatmen's song?

. . . . .

If in the darkness a serpent should bite me,
Or if an evil spirit should smite me,
R_m re R_m I shall die.

**("Village Songs", p. 103)**

**"Harvest Hymn"** is the song of farmers who rejoice at the sight of their ripe corn and express their gratitude to the gods 'Surya', 'Varuna', 'Prithvi', 'Brahma' who bless their fields with rich bounty:

Lord of the rainbow, lord of the harvest,
Great and beneficent lord of the main!
Thine is the mercy that cherished our furrows,
Thine is the mercy that fostered our grain.

(p. 14)

The song **"Indian Weavers"** (p. 5) succinctly summarizes human life as it passes through the stages of birth, marriage and death. The time of the day when weavers weave dresses suitable to these occasions robes of a new born child "at break of day", the wedding dress for a queen "at the fall of night" and shroud for dead man "in the chill of moonlight" is in harmony with the mood of the occasion. Imagery and rhythm used in **"Coromandel Fishers"** are appropriate to the sentiments of enthusiasm and robust spirits of the fishermen who go deep in the sea "to capture the leaping wealth of the tide":

No longer delay, let us hasten away in the track
of the sea-gull's call,

The sea is our mother, the cloud is our brother,
the waves are our comrades all.
What though we toes at the fall of the sun where
the hand of the sea-god drives?
He who holds the storm by the hair, will hide in
his breast our lives.

(p. 6)

The colourful scenes pictured in the poems, **"Palanquin-Bearers"**, **"Wandering Singers"**, **"The Snake Charmer"**, **"Indian Dancers"**, **"Bangle-Sellers"**, and **"Wandering Beggars"**, are the common sights in the towns of India. Sarojini Naidu has tried to galvanize into life with the use of apposite diction, power of words, and picturesque imagery the sentiments, rhythmic movements, and the flush and the fire of these folk singers and dances. Slow, careful and tender are the swaying and heaving of palanquin-bearers as they carry a beautiful maiden in their palanquin:

Softly, O softly we bear her along,
She hangs like a star in the dew of her song;
She springs like a beam on the brow of the tide,
She falls like a tear from the eyes of a bride
Lightly, O lightly we glide and we sing,
We bear her along like a pearl on a string.

**("Palanquin-Bearers", p. 3)**

Cosmopolitan by temperament wandering singers roam about singing and playing on their flute:

Where the voice of the wind calls our wandering
feet,
Through echoing forest and echoing street,
With lutes in our hands ever-singing we roam,
All men are our kindred, the world is our home.

**("Wandering Singers", p. 4)**

**"The Snake-Charmer"** is characterized by picturesque imagery and keenness of desire of the snake-charmer who woos snakes by the magic of his flute-call in fragrant bushes and flower-beds:

Come, thou subtle bride of my mellifluous
wooing,
Come, thou silver-breasted moonbeam of desire.

(p. 8)

With the help of onomatopoeic effects and rich use of alliterative diction, Sarojini portrays vividly the rhythm and felicity of accomplished Kathak dancers:

Now silent, now singing and swaying and
swinging, like blossoms that bend to the
breezes or showers,
Now wantonly winding, they flash, now they
falter, and, lingering, languish in radiant choir;
Their jewel-girt arms and warm, wavering lily-
long fingers enchant through melodious hours,
Eyes ravished with rapture, celestially panting,
what passionate bosoms aflaming with fire!

**("Indian Dancers", pp. 37-40)**

The rich feast of charming colours is displayed in the song of bangle-sellers roaming about in streets of a town:

Bangle-sellers are we who bear
Our shining loads to the temple fair. . . .
Who will buy these delicate, bright
Rainbow-tinted circles of light?
Lustrous tokens of radiant lives,
For happy daughters and happy wives.
                    (**"Bangle-Sellers"**, p. 108)

## VIII

Sarojini Naidu has captured colourful life of towns in several of her poems. Even the pictures of natural landscape, Indian flora and fauna, projected by her in her poems, are such as she has come across in the towns, particularly in her native town Hyderabad to which she was deeply attached. The picturesque scenes of Hyderabad figure prominently in her poems like **"Nightfall in the City of Hyderabad"**, **"Street Cries"**, **"Songs of My City"**, **"In a Latticed Balcony"** and **"In the Bazars of Hyderabad"**. How vividly and beautifully she images the verious sights of Hyderabad at nightfall:

Hark, from the minaret how the muezzin's call
Floats like a battle-flag over the city wall.

From trellised balconies, languid and luminous
Faces gleam, veiled in a splendour voluminous.

Leisurely elephants wind through the winding lanes,
Swinging their silver bells hung from their silver chains.

Round the high Char Minar sounds of gay cavalcades
Blend with the music of cymbals and serenades.

Over the city bridge Night comes majestical,
Borne like a queen to a sumptuous festival.
            (**"Night fall in the City of Hyderabad"**, pp. 55-6)

In the poem **"Street Cries"**, Sarojini describes how hawkers cry to sell their 'breads' in the morning,

When dawn's first cymbals beat upon the sky,
Rousing the world to labour's various cry.

their 'fruits' in the noon,

When the earth falters and the waters swoon
with the implacable radiance of noon;

and their 'flowers' at the nightfall,

When twilight twinkling o'er the gay bazars,
Unfurls a sudden canopy of stars,

**"In the Bazars of Hyderabed"** written to a tune of the Bazars, are given the pictorial scenes of merchants, vendors, pedlars, goldsmiths, fruitmen and flower-girls selling their articles, musicians playing on their instruments and magicians diverting crowds by their magic games and tricks:

What do you sell, O ye merchants?

Richly your wares are displayed.
*Turbans of crimson and silver,*
*Tunics of purple brocade,*
*Mirrors with panels of amber,*
*Daggers with handles of jade.*

                                    (p. 106)

The scene of Juhu in Bombay figures in the poem **"On Juhu Sands"** (*The Feather of the Dawn*) and the famous Imam Bara of Lucknow, a chapel of lamentation where the Muslims of Shia community celebrate Moharram, is envisioned in the poem, **"The Imam Bara"**.

Paying a tribute to the imperial city of Delhi which has witnessed the hanging fortunes of a long line of Indian kings and emperors from times immemorial, Sarojini writes:

The changing kings and kingdoms pass away
The gorgeous legends of a by gone day,
But thou dost still immutably remain
Unbroken symbol of proud histories,
Unageing priestess of old mysteries
Before whose shrine the spells of death are vain.
                    (**"Imperial Delhi"**, p. 156)

## IX

Some of the best lyrics of Sarojini Naidu are about beautiful and charming aspects of Nature changing moods of day and seasons, the sun, the moon, stars, clouds, birds, flowers, rivers, lakes and seas. They are in the best traditions of English romantic nature poetry and are characterized by Keatsian ecstasy and sensuousness. The season of Spring the time of gaudy, riotous colours, winged glory, and fragrance of eye-catching loveliness is the most favourite of her seasons. She has written several poems **"Spring"**, **"A Song in Spring"**, **"The Joy of Spring Time"**, **"Vasant Panchami"**, **"In a Time of Flowers"**, **"Ecstasy"**, **"The Call of Spring"**, **"The Coming of Spring"**, **"The Magic of Spring"**, **"Spring in Kashmir"** in praise of its luscious and lustrous beauty. In **"Spring in Kashmir"** she gives beautiful images of rapturous songs of birds:

Thro' glade and thro' glen her winged feet let us follow,
In the wake of oriole, the sunbird and swallow.

sweet fragrance of colourful flowers:

Lo! how she bends on the emerald grasses,
To scatter sweet iris in dim, purple, masses.

warbling and sparkling mountain streams:

And hearken at noon to the jubilant paean,
The mountain streams chant from gay aeon to aeon.
                    (*The Feather of the Dawn*, p. 14)

and shining moon and twinkling stars. Like an epicurean she sings,

If spring grant us but one rich tulip for token,

Shall we fear if on Fortune's blind wheel we are
  broken.
                    (*The Feather of the Dawn*, p. 15)

With the coming of spring the whole nature burgeons
with new life, the plants and trees turn green, the blossoming rich-coloured flowers scatter sweet fragrance,
and shining birds burst into melodious singing:

> Young leaves grow green on the banyan twigs,
> And red on the peepal tree,
> The honey birds pipe to the budding figs,
> And honey blooms call the bee.
>
> Poppies squander their fragile gold
> In the silvery aloe-brake,
> Coral and ivery lilies unfold
> Their delicate lives on the lake.
>
> Kingfishers ruffle the feathery sedge,
> And all the vivid air thrills
> With butterfly-wings in the wild-rose hedge,
> And the luminous blue of the hills.
>                    ("Spring", p. 87)

The whole atmosphere is enlivened by music and mirth.
Thrilled with joy the beloved tells her lover:

> O Love! do you know the spring is here
> With the lure of her magic flute?
> The old earth breaks into passionate bloom
> At the kiss of her fleet, gay foot,
> The burgeoning leaves on the almond boughs,
> And the leaves on the blue wave's breast
> Are crowned with the limpid and delicate light
> Of the gems in your turban crest.
> The bright pomegranate buds unfold,
> The frail wild lilies appear,
> Like the blood red jewels you used to fling
> O'er the maidens that danced at the feast of spring
> To welcome the new-born year.
>                    ("In A Time of Flowers", p. 92)

or sings with rapture:

> Heart, O my heart! lo, the spring time is waking
>     In meadow and grove
> Lo, the mellifluous *koels* are making
>     Their paens of love.
> Behold the bright rivers and rills in their glancing,
>     Melodious flight,
> Behold how the sumptuous peacock are dancing,
>     In rhythmic delight.
>                    ("Ecstasy", p. 99)

As the spring wakes anew, the poet calls her children to
come out and play with her:

> I know where the dragon-flies glimmer and glide,
> And the plumes of wild peacocks are gleaming,
> Where the fox and the squirrel and timid fawn
>     hide
> And the hawk and the heron lie dreaming.
>
> The earth is ashine like a humming bird's wing,
> And the sky like a kingfisher's feather,

O come, let us go and play with the spring,
Like glad-hearted children together.
                    (**"The Call of Spring"**, pp. 185-86)

As the poet grows old she like Wordsworth is unable to respond
to the beauty of nature "apparelled in celestial light",[35] with the
same enthusiasm as she did in her young age:

> O Spring I cannot run to greet
> Your coming as I did of old,
> Clad in shining veil of gold,
> With champa-buds and blowing wheat
> And silver anklets on my feet.
>                    (**"The Coming of Spring"**, p. 187)

The blossoming flowers and chirping birds remind her
only faintly that the spring has come:

> The kimshuks burst into dazzling flower,
> The seemuls burgeoned in crimson pride,
> The palm-groves shone with the oriole's wing,
> The koels began to sing,
> The soft clouds broke in a twinkling tide . . .
> My heart leapt up in its grave and cried,
> *Is it the spring, the spring?*
>                    (**"The Magic of Spring"**, p. 189)

Indian summer is the season of "low-voiced silences and
gleaming solitudes". In this season one likes to rest under
the shade of trees or walk in the evening along the river
bank or cool oneself by bathing in pools:

> O let us fling all care away, and lie alone and
>     dream
> 'Neath tangled boughs of tamarind, *molsari* and
>     *neem!*
>
> And bind our brows with jasmine sprays and play
>     on carven flutes,
> To wake the slumbering serpent kings among the
>     banyan roots,
> And roam at fall of eventide along the river's
>     brink,
> And bathe in water-lily pools where golden
>     panthers drink!
>                    (**"Summer Woods"**, pp. 190-91)

In rainy season, the "necromantic rain" with its "crystal
rods" touches dead loveliness to life again and "revives
on withered meads and barren rocks" (*F. D.*, p. 1). During
this season the lovelorn maiden pines for her lover as she
listens to the cry of *papeeha:*

> I see the soft wings of the clouds on the river,
> And jewelled with rain drops the mango-leaves
>     quiver,
> And tender boughs flower on the plain . . .
> But what is their beauty to me, *papeeha,*
> Beauty of blossom and shower, *papeeha,*
> That brings not my lover again.
>                    (**"A Love Song for the North"**, p. 75)

very impressive is Sarojini's pictorial description of the
sunset in the autumn season, with clouds hanging, fallen
leaves fluttering and wild wind blowing:

> Like a joy on the heart of a sorrow,

The sunset hangs on a cloud;
A golden storm of glittering sheaves,
Of fair and frail and fluttering leaves,
The wild wind blows in a cloud.

("Autumn Song", p. 23)

Wistful music, queer movements and gleaming light create an aerie effect of the sunset in summer season:

An ox-cart stumbles upon the rocks,
And a wistful music pursues the breeze,
From a shepherd's pipe as he gathers his flocks
Under the *peepal* trees.
And a young *Banjara* driving her cattle
Lifts up her voice as she glitters by
In an ancient ballad of love and battle
Set to the best of a mystic tune,
And the faint stars gleam in the eastern sky
To herald a rising moon.

Apposite visual images make the description of a tropical night in **"Leili"** very satisfying:

The serpents are asleep among the poppies,
The fireflies light the soundless panther's way
To tangled paths where shy gazelles are straying,
And parrot-plumes outshine the dying day.
O soft! the lotus-buds upon the stream
Are stirring like sweet maidens when they dream.

The silent solemness of night is conveyed impressively by religious imagery used in the second stanza:

A cast-mark on the azure brows of Heaven
The golden moon burns sacred, solemn, bright.
The winds are dancing in the forest-temple,
And swooning at the holy feet of Night,
Hush! in the silence mystic voices sing
And make the gods their incense offering.

(p. 31)

The inter-communion between nature and man is conveyed by linking nature images with feelings of human heart in **"Medley"**, a Kashmiri song:

The poppy grows on the roof-top
The iris flowers on the grave;
Hope in the heart of a lover,
And fear in the heart of a slave
The opul lies in the river,
The pearl in the ocean's breast,
Doubt in a grieving bosom,
And faith in a heart at rest.

(p. 138)

The variety of emotions that goad the bird in the poem **"The Bird of Time"** to burst in spontaneous music make it a typical Indian bird and the poem about it more convincing than Robert Bridges' "Nightingales":

O Bird of Time, say where did you learn
The changing measures you sing? . . .
In blowing forests and breaking tides,
In the happy laughter of new-made brides,

And the nests of the new-born spring,
In the dawn that thrills to a mother's prayer,
And the night that shelters a heart's despair,
In the sigh of pity, the sob of hate,
And the pride of a soul that has conquered fate.

The beautiful visual and aural images woven round Indian birds 'bulbul', 'oriole', 'honey bird', 'sh_ma', 'hoopoe', 'kingfisher', gray pigeons', 'jade-green gipsy parrots' give an impressive description of their colourful features and sweet songs:

In your quiet garden wakes a magic tumult
Of winged choristers that keep the Festival of
      dawn,
Blithely rise the carols in richly cadenced rapture,
From lyric throats of amber, of ebony and fawn.
      (**"The Bird Sanctuary"**, *The Feather of the
                              Dawn,* p. 19)

Sarojini Naidu's overwhelming predilection for sensuousness is in evidence in her poems about Indian flowers 'silver jasmine', 'golden champak', 'bakul', 'gloriosa lily', 'water hyacinth', 'golden cassia', 'gulmohur', 'nasturtimus', 'lotus', 'red roses', 'poppy bole', 'ashoka blossom', and fragrant cinammon, sandal and clove. All of her poems of Indian flowers **"The Gloriosa Lily"**, **"The Water Hyacinth"**, **"In Praise of Gulmohur Blossoms"**, **"Nasturtimus"**, **"Golden Cassia"**, **"Champak Blossoms"**, **"The Lotus"**, **"The Garden Vigil"**, **"Ashoka Blossom"** provide a rich, sensuous feast of colours and scents. Amazed by the beauty of lily flower the poet exclaims:

Who lit your clustering lanterns, all
All in firnged fire to make
Rosered and amber carnival
In woodland bower and brake,
And lure the purple moth to search
Her rich wings at your blossoming torch.
                  (**"The Gloriosa Lily"**
            *The Feather of the Dawn,* p. 16)

Describing water hyacinth, she writes:

Magical, mist purple, pale,
In alluring splendour spread,
Snaring pool and riverhead
In your perilous and frail
Farflung, subtly painted veil.
                  (**"The Water Hyacinth"**,
            *The Feather of the Dawn,* p. 17)

Gulmohur blossoms appear unexcelled to her in their lovely hues:

What can rival your lovely hue
O gorgeous boon of the spring?
The glimmering red of a bridal robe,
Rich red of wild bird's wing?
Or the mystic blaze of the gem that burns
On the brow of a serpent king?
            (**"The Praise of Gulmohur Blossoms"**
            *The Feather of the Dawn,* p. 94)

There is a remarkable novelty in Sarojini's description of the beauty of nasturtiums by the use of mythopoetic images of immortal heroines of Indian myths:

> Your leaves interwoven of fragrance and fire
> Are Savitri's sorrow and Sita's desire,
> Draupadi's longing, Damayanti's fears,
> And sweetest Sakuntala's magical tears.
>                                   (**"Nasturtiums"**, p. 95)

Beautiful cassia flowers appear to her creations of a fairy land and not of earth:

> But, I sometimes think that perchance you are
> Fragments of some new-fallen star,
> Or golden lamps for a fairy shrine,
> Or golden pitchers for fairy wine.
>                                   (**"Golden Cassia"**, p. 96)

Champak blossoms flood the poet's senses by their 'ambrosial sweetness' and 'voluptuous' perfume:

> Yet, 'tis of you thro' the moolit ages
> That maidens and minstrels sing,
> And lay your buds on the great god's altair,
> O radiant blossoms that fling
> Your rich, voluptuous, magical perfume,
> To ravish the winds of spring.
>                                   (**"Champak Blossoms"**, pp. 97-8)

Praising the mystic beauty of lotus flower, she writes:

> O mystic lotus, sacred and sublime,
> In myriad-petalled grace inviolate,
> Supreme O'er transient storms of tragic fate,
> Deep-rooted in the waters of all time.
>                                   (**"The Lotus"**, p. 167)

Relying upon the transforming power of Ashoka leaves, described in legends, the poet wishes:

> If your glowing foot be prest
> O'er the secrets of my breast,
> Love, my dreaming heart would wake,
> And its joyous fancies break
> Into lyric bloom
> To enchant the passing world
> With melodious leaves unfurl'd
> And their wild perfume.
>                                   (**"Ashoka Blossom"**, p. 202)

X

Sarojini Naidu's poetry is overtly Indian in spirit. No other Indian English poet has unfolded Indian milieu and ethos in such wide variety and with such ardent passion as Sarojini Naidu has done. From the very beginning of her poetic career she has been admired for the lyrical intensity and the vivid treatment of Indian ethos in her poems. In the Introduction of **The Bird of Time,** Edmund Gosse described her as "The most brilliant, the most original, as well as the most correct, of all the natives of Hindustan who have written in English".[36] The very first

of her anthologies, **The Golden Threshold,** was welcomed with highly laudatory comments by English reviewers. *The Times* wrote: "Her poetry seems to sing itself as if her swift thoughts and strong emotions sprang into lyrics of themselves", and the *Glasgow Herald* commented: "Delicacy and subtlety of expression are all at her command. . . . Her thought's crowning delight is to find radiant utterance . . . The pictures are of the East it is true? But there is something fundamentally human in them that seems to prove that the best song knows nothing of East or West." *Manchester Guardian* described her lyrics as "genuine poetry" and remarked: "It is always musical, its Eastern colour is fresh, and its firm touch is quick and delicate".

The changing vagaries of critical canons cannot obliterate the enduring charm of such imaginative creative power, metrical virtuosity and authentic emotional intensity as found in Sarojini's poetry. Sri Aurobindo has truly remarked: "Her work has a real beauty. Some of her lyrical work is likely, I think, to survive among the lasting things in English literature and by these, even if they are fine rather than great, she may take her rank among the immortals".[37]

NOTES

[1] Matthew Arnold's sonnet, "Shakespeare".

[2] Sisir Kumar Ghose, "Sarojini Naidu: Towards Revaluation", *Osmania Journal of English Studies,* Sarojini Naidu Special Number, p. 28.

[3] *Ibid.*

[4] *Ibid.*

[5] *Ibid.,* p. 33.

[6] *Ibid.,* p. 28.

[7] R. Parthasarathy, "Introduction", *Ten Twentieth Century Indian Poets* (Delhi: Oxford University Press, 1979), p. 3.

[8] Arthur Symons, "Introduction", *The Golden Threshold* (London: William Heinemann, 1916), p. 10.

[9] R. Parthasarathy, "Indian English Verse: The Making of a Tradition", Avadhesh K. Srivastava, ed. *Alien Voice* (Lucknow: Print-House, 1981), p. 41.

[10] *Ten Twentieth Century Indian Poets,* p. 2.

[11] *Ibid.,* p. 1.

[12] *Alien Voice,* p. 41.

[13] *Ibid.*

[14] *The Times of India* (Sunday: July 23, 1972), p. 9.

[15] Quoted by S. C. Harrex, "Small-Scale Reflections on Indian English-Language Poetry", *The Journal of Indian Writing in English,* Vol. 8 (January-July, 1980), p. 145.

[16] Adil Jussawalla, "The New Poetry", *The Journal of Commonwealth Literature,* No. 5 (July, 1968), p. 65.

[17] *Alien Voice,* p. 40.

[18] F. R. Leavis, *Lectures in America* (London, 1969), p. 33.

[19] Shankar Mokashi Punekar, "A Note on Sarojini Naidu", M. K. Naik *et al* ed. *Critical Essays on Indian Writers in English* (Delhi: The Macmillan Co. of India Ltd., 1977), p. 70.

[20] D. B. Dhanapala, *Eminent Indians* (Bombay, 1947), p. 58.

[21] Kamaladevi Chattopadhyaya, "Introduction", *Sarojini Naidu: The Poet of Nation,* R. Bhatnagar ed. (Allahabad, n.d.), p. x.

[22] Arthur Symons, "Introduction", Sarojini Naidu, *The Golden Threshold* (London: William Heinemann, 1916), p. 15.

[23] *Ibid.*

[24] Quoted by K. R. Srinivasa Iyengar, *Indian Writing in English* (New Delhi: Sterling Publishers Pvt. Ltd., 1985), p. 207.

[25] "Sonnet Addressed to Haydon", *Keats' Poetical Works* (London: Collins Clear-Type Press, 1923), p. 51.

[26] Wordsworth, *The Prelude,* Book XI. pp. 108-109.

[27] P. V. Rajyalakshmi, *The Lyric Spring: A Song of the Poetry of Sarojini Naidu* (New Delhi: Abhinav Publications, 1977), p. 25.

[28] Iyengar, p. 211.

[29] Edmund Gosse, "Introduction", Sarojini Naidu, *The Bird of Time: Songs of Life, Death and Spring* (London: William Heinemann, 1917), p. 6.

[30] *Ibid.,* pp. 4-5.

[31] *Ibid.,* p. 5.

[32] Iyengar, p. 213.

[33] "The Broken Wing", *The Sceptred Flute: Songs of India* (Allahabad: Kitabistan, 1979), p. 145. Most of the extracts-quoted from Sarojini Naidu's poems are from this anthology of her poems till otherwise mentioned.

[34] Sarojini Naidu, "Renunciation", *The Feather of the Dawn* (Bombay: Asia Publishing House, 1961).

[35] Wordsworth, "Ode on Intimations of Immortality".

[36] Gosse, p. 2.

[37] Iyengar, quoted in "Sarojini Naidu", pp. 222-23.

## N. K. Sharma (essay date 1989)

SOURCE: "The Evolution of the Poetic Persona in Sarojini's Poetry," in *Perspectives on Sarojini Naidu,* edited by K.K. Sharma, Vimal Prakashan, 1989, pp. 114-128.

[*In the following essay, Sharma discusses Naidu's poetic persona, which is assessed as "invariably objective, impersonal, or universal."*]

Sarojini Naidu is a powerful exponent of the poetic Persona in her poetic explorations. Undoubtedly, the Persona is the poetic nucleus from which her poetry originates and constitutes its chief motivating force. She (the Persona) is the light of Sarojini's life and is the centre of her existence and vision. The "I" and "Me" are not always personal and can stand for any exploring Self. The egoism of Sarojini is invariably objective, impersonal or universal. She loves to celebrate universal qualities through the seemingly personal ones. The use of the Persona helps Sarojini in the realization of the desired aesthetic distance in her poems. The object of this investigation is to trace the "evolution" of the poetic Persona in Sarojini's four major works, namely, *The Golden Threshold* (1905), *The Bird of Time* (1912), *The Broken Wing* (1917) and *The Feather of the Dawn* (1961).

The Persona in the poetry of Sarojini Naidu is neither passive nor inert. Her chief beauty lies in resenting detention in any form. As a mobile observer, she has no pre-planned destination before her. So she loves to explore life freely and strives to dramatise its "real" reality. The Persona has no fixed shape, form or voice in Sarojini's poetry and she undergoes definite "evolution" during the progress of her material-cum-spiritual voyage. She loves to meet and identify with others for the satisfaction of her poetic urge and self-expansion. The quest of the Persona betrays no impression of self-projection. The Persona does not follow any stereotyped way of observing life. She resorts to realistic, romantic, socio-political and spiritual ways to see life in its totality. The basic premise of the Persona is to interpret life without prejudice.

The poetic Persona in Sarojini's poetry is deeply involved in Nature. The dramatic interplay of the Persona with the external world constitutes its potential strength. It is difficult to accept Rajyalakshmi's erroneous contention that Sarojini's "response to nature is radical, elemental and total".[1] Sarojini's approach to Nature is neither "radical" nor "total". Her response to Nature has a typical traditional bias. The Persona does not respond to Nature as a whole. She loves to capture the beauty of Nature at the spring or summer times only. She rarely displays the same depth of feelings in depicting the winter scenes. She loves spring as the symbol of her basic faith in the joys of life. Sarojini's poetics of Nature is romantic in a limited sense only.

The Persona's romantic orientation of mind finds its clearest expression in *The Golden Threshold* (1905). She is intensely fascinated by the enchanting world of beauty, glamour, romance, fancies and dreams. She is completely identified with the object of her contemplation and looks quite satisfied in its realization. It looks as if the two exist for each other. The Persona is one with Nature and is completely involved in it. According to Prof. A. A. Ansari, her poetic sensibility displays "keen sensations, and can enter into sensuous proximity with the objects of Nature".[2] The Persona observes Nature as an "insider" and reveals its real beauty in its various manifestations. Whatever is being visualized, has a touch of authenticity about it in its presentation. The beauty of Sarojini's poetry is that it never fails to click or to impart its real "feel". The Persona's rapport with Nature is very intimate: "Hark to a voice that is called/To my heart in the voice of the wind".[3] The poetic personality is perfectly at home in the natural set-up and discovers startling kinship with it: "The sea is our mother, the cloud is our brother, the waves are our comrades".[4] The Persona's sensuous nature is best demonstrated in her quest for beauty. She loves to shadow a young bride being carried along in her palanquin "like a pearl in a string".[5] Her romantic search may take her to luxurious chambers whose walls are "richly inlaid/With a gate, porphory, onyx and jade".[6] **"Alabaster"** finds the Self (Persona) "carven with delicate dreams and wrought/With many subtle and exquisite thought".[7] **"Cradle Song"** is a "little lovely dream"[8] song.

The poetic personality has undergone a definite change in her perception of Nature in *The Bird of Time* (1912). She is no more confined to the surface-depiction of beauty but to discover the intrinsic one. The main thrust of the new quest is to unearth "the roots of delight in the heart of the earth".[9] The Persona begins to evaluate beauty in a comparative focus. She is convinced that the beauty of gulmohars has no equal: "What can rival your lovely hue/O gorgeous boon of the spring?"[10] and is particularly impressed by their "frail, victorious fire".[11] She is all intoxicated by the "Exquisite, luminous, passionate bloom"[12] of Nasturtiums. She has also discovered "purposeless beauty/To serve or profit the world"[13] of the Champak blossoms. She welcomes spring because "Coral and ivory lilies unfold/Their delicate lives on the late".[14] The Persona begins to nourish the dream of having the glimpse of the creator in this romantic exploration: "Or perchance, we may glean a far glimpse of the Infinite Bosom/In whose glorious shadow all life is unfolded or furled".[15]

The Persona's romantic evolution suffers from a strange tension in *The Broken Wing* (1917). The Persona is no more enthusiastic about the onset of Spring: "My heart leapt up in its grave and cried,/Is it the spring?"[16] She is

no more hypnotised in its pressure: "O Spring! I cannot run to greet/You coming as I did of old".[19] The tone of voice is no more respectful: it has become ironical and teasing. The Persona is aware of the fact that she has "lost the clue/To all the vernal joy it knew".[18] The interest of the Persona in Spring is, no doubt, diminished but is not completely lost in *The Broken Wing*. She invites everyone to make the most of the Spring season: "O come, let us go and play with the spring/Like gladhearted children together".[19] She is glad to have discovered a "haven of calm"[20] in Spring. She realizes spiritual happiness in it: "Like Krishan and like Radhika, encompassed with delight".[21] The very sight of roses sends her in rapture: "Burn in a fire of roses,/Crown me with the rose of Love".[22]

The Persona's poetic sensibility is tremendously enlarged in *The Feather of the Dawn* (1961) a collection of poems written in July-August 1927 by Sarojini Naidu. The Persona's range of observation has grown manifold. She has realized that rain can transform "dead loveliness to life again"[23] and "sows wet fields with red and ivory grain".[24] She is overwhelmed by Spring "With her laughter, her music, her beauty enthralling".[25] Nature's balming impact is always experienced by the lovers of Nature. In Armando Menezes's "The Train", it puts the speaker in mood of ecstasy: "I hear a far-off rapture sweep/Me as I pass!"[26] The intoxicating voice of G. K. Cheltur's "Chochee" sends the poet in a mood of jubilations: "But my heart leaps exultantly/For love of you, Chochee, Chochee".[27] Likewise, the Persona in Sarojini's **"The Bird Sanctury"** is thrilled by "the carols in richly cadenced rapture".[28] She can request the silver star for the favour of kissing her "in the black night when I cry".[29] The sea-wares can inspire and put her in a mood of poetic frenzy: "The sea-waves fashion for my ear/Translucent melodies",[30] The Persona, sometimes, feels disturbed in its presence: "O Spring how you grieve me!"[31]

The Persona in Sarojini's poetry is more than a romantic explorer. She is not an escapist in the romantic sense of the term: she can never operate in vacuum. She is like the speaker in Frost's "Birches" who has finally realized that "Earth's the right place for love:/I don't know where it's likely to go better".[32] She may be compared to the Self in S. N. Purohit's "Inconstant Wishes" who must "think of others"[33] and "disdains to injure/Feeling of others".[34] Sarojini's poetry is a study in realism and displays a remarkable social consciousness. Sunanda P. Chavan has misjudged the dimensions of Sarojini's social awareness when she says that the "poetic sensibility rarely communicates her social consciousness".[35] Sarojini responds to social realities with alertness. Her commitment to life is beyond question. The Persona's response to life is steadily increased and deepened as she moves from *The Golden Threshold* (1905) to *The Feather of the Dawn* (1961).

The poetic personality involved in *The Golden Threshold* (1905) is in touch with her times and lends credibility to the scenes depicted by her. She finds herself engaged in the socio-political scene in India before independence. She keeps herself busy in the "war of the world and strife of the throng".[36] Her resentment against the Purdah system is implied in **"The Purdah Nashin":** "Time lifts the curtain unawares,/And sorrow looks into her face . . ."[37] The pathetic flight of an Indian woman is graphically presented in "Suttee" where she is made to "dwell in living dark"[38] and has to count every minute of her life. She shares the fate of the pavement dwellers in Margaret Chatterjee's "The Pablo Neruda" who are seen "Sprawling on pavement, Awaiting death".[39] The life of the Indian weavers in Sarojini's **"The Indian Weaver"** is gradually consumed in preparing "the robes of a new-born-child", "the marriage-veils of a queen" and "a dead man's funeral shroud".[40] The same story is repeated in Baldoon Dhingra's "Factories are Eye-Sores" where a "Man works beneath, until he drops/Out of the wheels one day".[41] A. K. Ramanujan's "Another View of Grace" captures the same mood when he shudders "to the bone at hungers that roam the street".[42] The Persona in Sarojini's poetry shows how the fisherman spend their time in possessing "the leaping wealth of the tide"[43] from birth to death. There is nothing to arrest the onward march of the singers in **"The Wandering Singers":** "No love bids us tarry, no joy bids us wait;/The voice of the wind is the voice of our own fate".[44] The Indian Gipsy has been aptly described as the "daughter of wandering race".[45] The Persona's political involvement in politics is stepped up in *The Golden Threshold.* Like a true patriot, she imbibes the spirit of Rabindranath Tagore who wants India to rise "Into that heaven of Freedom, my father, let my country awake".[46] She reminds Mother India for her glorious past and calls upon her to be prepared for the "crescent honour, splendours, victories vast".[47] She pleads with her to assume the leadership of the "nations that in fettered darkness weep".[48]

*The Bird of Time* (1912) shows a much deeper involvement of the Persona in the social transformation of the society. "From then on the poet", observes P. E. Dustoor, "in her receded and the active patriot and fighter for freedom came to the fore".[49] She is like Harindranath Chattopadhyaya her younger brother who has realizcd that "only by giving/That life becomes the gateway of true living".[50] She is now almost identified with "the strife of the throng and tumult".[51] She begins to talk in terms of Peace and Love: "The tidings of joy when Peace shall triumph,/when Truth shall conquer and Love prevail".[52] She is quite optimistic about India's final victory in her struggle for liberation: "Bound by one hope, one purpose, one devotion/Towards a great, divinely destined goal".[53] The Persona is also in touch with the social life of her times. She is happy to observe the bangle-sellers carrying bangles to the temple fair "Lustrous tokens of radiant lives,/For happy daughters and happy wives".[54] **"The Festival of Serpents"** dramatizes the anxiety of the devotees to please the serpents and get their future secured: "O bless our lowly offerings and hearken to our prayer".[55]

The Person's political evolution is nearing its vortex in *The Broken Wing* (1917). She pledges full support to the struggle for the independence of India: "Ne'er shall we fail thee, forsake or falter".[56] She invokes Lakshmi to "guard the invisible hope of our nation".[57] The Persona assures continuous support to her allies: "And yield the sons of my striken womb/To the drum-beats of duty, the sabres of doom".[58] She accepts Gandhiji as a political guru who symbolizes moral courage for her: "But who could win thy secret, who attain/Thine ageless beauty born of Brahama's breath".[59]

*The Feather of the Dawn* (1961) marks the climax of the Persona's political evolution. She is all plunged into India's struggle for independence and her watchwards are freedom and national unity. She is like the speaker in V. N. Bhusan's "Ninth August 1942" who has gladly opted for championing "the country's cause of freedom and peace!"[60] The tone of the Persona is no more submissive: it calls for fearless action. She idealizes Gokhale who is "Steadfast, serene, dauntless, supremely wise"[61] and an eternal source of "love's perpetual flame."[62] She admires that dauntless soldier whose "Freedom's Gayatri"[63] has inspired every heart. She calls for vision, valour and faith for "enriching freedom's granaries".[64]

The Persona's involvement in love undergoes steady evolution from *The Golden Threshold* (1905) to *The Feather of the Dawn* (1961). Sarojini's poetry is devoid of sentimentalism or crude depiction of sexual acts. There is nothing obscene or trivial about her handling of love-ties. Sarojini's approach to sex is both refined and thought-provoking. Unlike Walt Whitman, Sarojini's aim is never limited to the blunt glorification of the human flesh. She has always regarded man's sexual impulses as clean and healthy.

Separation in love occupies a central situation in all love poetry. According to Harindranath Chattopadhyaya separation in love is implied in love-realationships and it determines the genuineness of love. It can point to "The depth of his love".[65] It is a "Farewell to discover its ultimate bridal state in separation."[66] Separation in Sarojini's *The Golden Threshold* is looked upon as a natural corollary of any love-experience. It is a painful experience and ought to add to the sufferings of the love-lorn lovers. The Persona can be seen pleading with her lover to "Kiss me who hold thine image in my heart."[67] She is eager to communicate with her departed lover in absentia: Love, like the magic of wild melodies/Let thy soul answer mine across the sea."[68] Separation can produce a conflict in the mind of the lover: "What war is this of *Thee* and *Me?*"[69] A beloved may not allow anyone to "unking thee, husband of a queen"[70] in his separation from her. The Persona's spiritual evolution is noticed in her search for the divine through love in this opening phase of her quest. The Persona craves for the divine protection: "O shelter my soul from thy face."[71] She begins to define the body-soul real relationship in a critical manner: "Shall the flesh survive when the soul is gone?"[72]

*The Bird of Time* shows a significant advance in the Persona's evolution in spiritual (or vertical) direction. Unlike Walt Whitman, she does not think that physical love is the gateway to the spiritual love. She discussed love at greater length in terms of the spiritual or mystical context only. The Persona feels that love can change hearts and "shall cancel the ancient wrong and conquer the ancient sage."[73] There is nothing secretive about love; it is priceless: "Love! Of all the treasures that I own/ What gift I withheld before thy throne?"[74] She is convinced that by reciting "Govinda! Govinda! Govinda! Govinda!"[75] Self can be merged with God. *The Bird of Time* also shows that separation in love makes one snap one's ties with Nature: "But what is then beauty to me *papeeha*,/Beauty of blossom and shower, *papeeha*/That brings not my lover again!"[76]

*The Broken Wing* shows the Persona's curiosity to know the dimensions of love in depth. It is realized that sorrow in love cannot risk-off "the passionate bondage of memory."[77] Separation in love is very common but it should not dampen the spirit of the lovers: "And on some deep tide of slumber/Reach the comfort of your heart."[78] The lover is happy "to wait in proud and lovely fashion,/ And kiss the shadow of love's passing feet."[79] True lovers can make any sacrifice to save each other: "If you call me, I will come/Fearless what befalls."[80] And: "Strangle my soul and fling it into the fire!/Why should my true love falter or fear or rebel?"[81] Like Sarojini Naidu, Harindranath Chattopadhyaya also believes that "sweet love yet survives."[82] A genuine lover can release his beloved from the "sore decree of Fate."[83] Lalita Venkateswaran's "Fired" shows that love can ensure invincibility: "Your love gives beauty back to me,/With you I am invincible."[84] Like, Lalitha, Sarojini's **"Love Omnipresent"** also reveals that person in love can "rend the cold silence that conquers the lips of the dead."[85] Sarojini's Persona is different from Sylvia Plath for whom "Love is a shadow"[86] only. Love is its own reward in Sarojini's "The Silence of Love": "Still for Love's sake I am foredoomed to bear/A load of passionate silence and despair."[87]

Love is a sublime relationship and should not be governed by selfish motives and their realization. Like Sarojini Naidu, S. N. Purohit's "Reciprocal Give and Take" shows that "Love knows no obligations, right,/ privileges, bounden-duties,/It's a matter of spontaneity."[88] The lover in Sarojini's **"Supplication"** is more than satisfied by a tear or two: "A gift of tears to save my stricken soul".[89] The Persona's hatred for lust is also continued in *The Broken Wing*. She finds false love as a case of mere cheating or exploitation of the worst form". "Who cares if a woman's heart be broken?"[90] It is all fun: "Idly you tore its crimson leaves apart . . . /Alas! it was my heart".[91] The Persona also realizes that Death paves the way for ultimate unity: "All anger fled, all sorrow past,/O love, at last!"[92] Sunita Jain discovers "liquid joy"[93] in love: Saroji Naidu finds her "soul, redeemed, reborn"[94] in it. The Persona's final epiphany is that love can give man "The very vision of God's dwelling-place".[95]

*The Feather of the Dawn* marks the culmination of the Persona's spiritual nature of love. The Persona realizes that there is no return in love: "I ask thee no reward".[96] A genuine lover is a "chosen instrument"[97] of God. A true lover can put his life in danger to protect his partner in love: "My eyes shall burn like beacon fires/To guard your battle camps".[98] It, finally, dawns upon the Persona's mind that Death cannot break spiritual marriages: "Shall even Death set free/My soul such intricate unity?"[99] Unlike Sarojini Naidu, Sylvia Plath rejects the cementing value of love in uniting love-lorn hearts in any meaningful relationship. She concludes that no unity is possible if "There is nothing between us".[100] Sarojini's Persona finds that love can merge the lover with the beloved: "O are you not/The very text and title of my thought/The very pattern of my joy and pain".[101] She can go to the extent of releasing the lover from the custody of Death: "Hourly redeem from the sharp toll of death/ Thy fragile human breath".[102] Like Sarojini Naidu, Toru Dutt also believes that love can ensure immortality: "My love defend thee from oblivision curse".[103] Armand Meneze's "To-Night" gives the lover a glimpse of immortality: "And let me once forget that man is dust;/To-night I'm heir to immortality".[104] Nissim Ezekiel's, "Marriage" pin-points to the realization of Eternity through love: "Lovers, when they marry face/Eternity with touching grace".[105]

The Persona in Sarojini's poetry undergoes steady evolution in her historic quest from *The Golden Threshold* (1905) to *The Feather of the Dawn* (1961). She accepts the reality of Death and is often seen in dialogue with it. *The Golden Threshold* presents the Persona a little in love with Death. She does not mind surrendering before Death but not "till all my human hungers are fulfilled".[106] This shows the Persona's guts to resist it till she has accomplished her material goal. She is like the speaker in S. N. Purohit's "Pleasure of Surrender" who "won't give up for the reason/To oblige someone or avert the crash".[107] Sylvia Plath's "Lady Lazarus" can live perpetually: "Out of the ash/I rise with my hair".[108] Similarly the Persona in Sarojini's poetry in convinced that Death is not the end but the beginning of life: "Death is in truth the vital seed/Of your imperishable bloom".[109] She is, unlike the Self in S. P. Ranchan's "Swan Song", who has abondoned the very will to live: "Our day is dying: let it."[110] Sarojini's Persona is opposed to this type of abject surrender in life.

*The Bird of Time* marks a definite shift in the Persona's response to death. Her new epiphany is that Death cannot ensure the "rich and joyous immortality".[111] There is nothing to overlook or violate "the swift decrees of Death".[112] Death's invincibility is clearly established in this phase of the Persona's spiritual expansion: "To the blind, ultimate silence of the dead . . ."[113] The Persona's helplessness may be compared to the speaker in Sylvia Plath's "Totem" who finds himself "Roped in at the end by one/Death with its many sticks".[114] Death in *The Bird of Time* is opposed to all that stands for beauty. It cannot relish anyone blossoming: "Till Death unsurped your vivid loveliness/In wanton envy of its radiant bloom".[115] Death is not opposed to life. The Self in S. N. Purohit's "Devotion is Death" wants "to die so that I may live".[116] Harindranath Chattopadhyaya's "Beside a Death Bed" reinforces the opinion that "life is the cradle of death".[117] Life and Death are also closely connected with each other in Sarojini's **"The Soul's Prayer"**: *Life is a Prism of my light/And Death the show of my life".*[118] The Persona finds death as "the mystic silence".[119] She realizes that one can discover "peace in the hands of Death".[120]

The Persona begins to free death in a spirited manner in *The Broken Wing.* She has gained a new insight in death. The Persona is not inclined to shed tears at the time of death: "If you were dead I should not weep".[121] Death is a blessing in disguise. It can unite the isolated lovers in "a dim, undivided sleep".[122] The Persona faces death in a very courageous manner: "Welcome, O tranquil Death!/Thou hast no ills to grieve me".[123] But the final evolution of the Persona shows her inability to deal with death in *The Feather of the Dawn.* She seems helpless and can be seen standing "beside your narrow resting place".[124] She has, finally, reposed all her faith in God: "We live or perish/As Allah Wills".[125]

The Persona's divine quest is continued from the beginning to the end of her career. *The Golden Threshold* marks the start of her quest of God. The Persona is all set for the "Diviner summits to attain."[126] She may be seen invoking God for "the bounty that prospered our sowing"[127] or the "plentiful bosom that feeds us".[128] She is like the poetic Self in P. Lal's "A Song for Beauty" who remembers God for supplicating "with sweet gifts my heart your worshipper"[129]. The speaker in Voegeli-Arya's "In the Beginning there was Light" implores God to "Lend thine ears into our supplication/And bless us".[130] Similarly the Self in S. N. Purohit's "Form of Speech" shows unshakable faith in God: "I humbly repeat/*Tamaso ma Jyotirgamaya*' ".[131]

The Persona's religions-cum-spiritual evolution is continued in *The Bird of Time* (1912). The Persona's secular nature is graphically revealed in this phase of her development. She emerges a liberated being in her response to religions. She is opposed to any religions interference in the matter of love: "What are the sins of my race, Beloved, what are my people to thee,/And what are thy shrine,.... What are thy Gods to me?"[132] Man's faith in God can equip him to face ordeals of life: "Lailaha illa-l-Allah,/La ilaha illa-Allah, Muhammad-ar-Rasul-Allah".[133] God is being approached for His Mercy and Grace: "Withhold not Thy merciful love, or we perish,/Heaven, O Lord of Kain!"[134] He may be invoked for tackling the "inmost laws of life and death".[135] The Persona discovers God in His two basic *akaras:* "Life is a prison of my light,/And Death the shadow of my face".[136] She is eager to be united with God by reciting "Govinda! Govinda! Govinda! Govinda! Govinda!"[137] She knows that her absorption in God can lead to joy and peace: "For my glad heart is drunk and drenched with Thee,/O inmost wine of living ecstasy/O intimate essence of eternity".[138]

The speaker in Nishikanto's "Three-fold-Flower" comes face-to-face with God in a flash: "In a second flight/I gain my beloved the Infinite".[139] The Persona in Sarojini's **"Solitude"** is quite hopeful of having the "glimpse of the Infinite Bosom/In whose glorious shadow all life is unfolded or furled."[140]

*The Broken Wing* shows the Persona's deeper involvement in God and His functioning. She finds in Him a unique combination of the "terrible and tender and divine".[141] She has come to accept God as the "Master of Life and Time and Fate".[142] She knows that He is "the goal for which we long".[143] The Persona will follow God like a shadow: "So where thou goest I must go".[144] She is ready to sacrifice all "The earthly loves and world lure"[145] for her merger with God. She implores God to grant "peace for suffering hearts that die"[146]. The wandering beggars feel that they can temporarily forget their poverty by repeating "Y'Allah! Y'Allah!"[147] Nothing is left to win God's favour: "All glory and all grace we bring to thee,/Kali! Maheshwari!"[148] The Persona is convinced that God can help us in the realization of the "invincible hope of our nation".[149]

*The Feather of the Dawn* marks the culmination of the Persona's spiritual evolution. The Persona requests God "Not rend with ravening doom our ancient land."[150] God is the perpetual source of life: "Life of all myriad lives that dwell in thee".[151] Like Sarojini's Persona, the speaker in Swami Rama Tirtha's "Love Consecration" is ready to possess God at any cost: "Take my eyes and then be intoxicated, God, with Thee".[152] The Self in J. Krishnamurti's "The Immortal Friend" is very happy at the end of his spiritual voyage: "My search is at an end./In Thee I behold all things".[153] Similarly, the Persona in Sarojini's **"Ghanashyam"** would like to have no other identity apart from God: "Let me be lost, a lamp of adoration,/In thine unfathomed waves of ecstasy".[154] She can never bear her separation from Him: "Come back, come back from thy wild wandering./Sweet Ghanashyam, my King".[155]

In sum, Sarojini's utilization of the Persona has added a new dimension to her poetry. It helps in maintaining the much-needed but rarely discussed aesthetic distance in it. The Persona has a clear-cut feminine sensibility and appraches life from the woman's point-of-view. But the Persona is not the photostat copy of the writer herself. The Persona is the figment of the poet's creative imagination and has no bearing on her life. She is a distinct personality and loves to retain it at all cost. The Persona's romantic nature is beautifully revealed in her confrontation with Nature. She has responded sensitively and passionately to the beauty of Nature and is lucky to have discovered happiness and peace in its sanctuary. The social evolution of her thought shows that she is dead against the philosophy of escapism. The Persona's main anxiety has been the social transformation of the poverty-ridden society. She is opposed to every type of exploitation and emerges as an apostle of love, peace and freedom. The religious evolution of the poetic sensibility reveals her characteristic secular character and its affinity with God. She has all along been pleading with Him for His Grace and Mercy. Her evolution about Death moves from the denial to its final acceptance. The Persona accepts life with all its plus minus points and has no where shown her desire to give up the will to live.

### NOTES AND REFERENCES

[1] P. V. Rajyalakshmi, *The Lyric Spring: A Study of the Poetry of Saroiini Naidu* (New Delhi: Abhinav Publication, 1977), p. 74.

[2] K. K. Sharma, ed., *Indo-English Literature* (Ghaziabad: Vimal Prakashan, 1977), p. 73.

[3] Sarojini Naidu, "Autumn", *The Sceptred Flute* (Allahabad: Kitabistan, 1979), p. 23.

[4] *Ibid.,* "Coromandal Fishers", p. 6,

[5] *Ibid.,* "Palanquin-Bearers", p. 3.

[6] *Ibid.,* "The Queen's Rival", p. 45.

[7] *Ibid.,* "Alabaster", p. 24.

[8] *Ibid.,* "Cradle Song", p. 17.

[9] *Ibid.,* "The Joy of the Spring-time", p. 89.

[10] *Ibid.,* "In Praise of Gulmohur Blossoms", p. 94.

[11] *Ibid.,* p. 94.

[12] *Ibid.,* "Nasturtiums", p. 95.

[13] *Ibid.,* "Champak Blossoms", p. 97.

[14] *Ibid,* "Spring", p. 87.

[15] *Ibid.,* "Solitude", p. 133.

[16] *Ibid.,* "The Magic of Spring", p. 189.

[17] *Ibid.,* "The Coming of the Spring", p. 187.

[18] *Ibid.,* p. 187.

[19] *Ibid.,* "The Call of Spring", p. 185.

[20] *Ibid.,* "June Sunset", p. 192.

[21] *Ibid.,* "Summer Woods", p. 191.

[22] *Ibid.,* "The Time of Roses", p. 195.

[23] Sarojini Naidu, "The Gokhale's Garden", *The Feather of the Dawn* (Bombay: Asia Publishing House, 1961), p. 1.

[24] *Ibid.,* p. 1.

[25] *Ibid.,* p. 14.

[26] V. K. Gokak, ed., *The Golden Treasury of Indo-Anglian Poetry: 1828-1965* (New Delhi: Sahitya Akademi, 1970), p. 170.

[27] *Ibid.,* p. 165.

[28] Sarojini Naidu, "The Bird Sanctuary", *The Feather of the Dawn*, p. 19.

[29] *Ibid.,* "The Lovely Child", p. 20.

[30] *Ibid.,* "On Juhu Sands", p. 23.

[31] *Ibid.,* "Mimicry", p. 22.

[32] Robert Frost, "Birches", from E. S. Oliver's *American Literature: 1890-1965: An Anthology* (New Delhi: Eurasia Publishing House (Pvt.) Ltd., 1967), p. 402.

[33] S. N. Purohit, *Delicate Dawn* (Jaipur: Printwell Publishers, 1983), p. 34.

[34] *Ibid.,* p. 27.

[35] Sunanda P. Chavan, *The Fairy Voice: A Study of Indian Women Poets in English* (New Delhi: Sterling Publishers Private Ltd., 1984), p. 26.

[36] Sarojini Naidu, "In the Forest", *The Sceptred Flute*, p. 32.

[37] *Ibid.,* "The Pardah Nashin", p. 53.

[38] *Ibid.,* "Suttee", p. 18.

[39] Margret Chatterjee, *The Sound of Wings* (New Delhi: Arnold-Heinamann, 1978), p. 28.

[40] Sarojini Naidu, "The Indian Weavers", *The Sceptred Flute*, p. 5.

[41] V. K. Gokak, ed., *The Golden Treasury of Indo-Anglian Poetry*, p. 215.

[42] *Ibid.,* p. 248.

[43] Sarojini Naidu, "Coromandal Fishers", p. 6.

[44] *The Sceptred Flute*, p. 4.

[45] *Ibid.,* p. 53.

[46] Rabindranath Tagore, "Heaven of Freed", from Gokak's *The Golden Treasure of Indo-Anglian Poetry*, p. 56.

[47] Sarojini Naidu, "To India", *The Sceptred Flute*, p. 58.

[48] *Ibid.,* p. 58.

[49] P. E. Dustoor, *Sarojini Naidu* (Mysore: Rao and Raghvan, 1961), p. 4.

[50] Harindranath Chattopadhyaya, *Masks and Farewells* (Bombay: Asia Publishing House, 1961), p. 21.

[51] Sarojini Naidu, "The Faery Isle of Janjura", *The Sceptred Flute,* p. 121.

[52] *Ibid.,* p. 122.

[53] *Ibid.,* "An Autumn of Love", p. 131.

[54] *Ibid.,* "Bangle-Sellers", p. 108.

[55] *The Sceptred Flute,* p. 110.

[56] *Ibid.,* "Awake", p. 180.

[57] *Ibid.,* 'Lakshmi, The Lotus-Born", 150.

[58] *Ibid.,* "The Gift of India", p. 146.

[59] *Ibid.,* "The Lotus", p. 167.

[60] Gokak, ed., *The Golden Treasury of Indo-Anglian Poetry,* p. 203.

[61] Sarojini Naidu, "In Gokhale's Garden", *The Feather of the Dawn,* p. 1.

[62] *Ibid.,* p. 2.

[63] *Ibid.,* "Lokmanya Tilak", p. 3.

[64] *Ibid.,* "Renunciation", p. 157.

[65] Gokak, ed., p. 157.

[66] Harindranath Chattopadhayaya, "Love's Irony", *Masks and Farewells,* p. 8.

[67] Sarojini Naidu, "Youth", *The Sceptred Flute",* p. 54.

[68] *Ibid.,* "The Poet's Love", p. 36.

[69] *Ibid.,* "Humayun to Zubeida", p. 22.

[70] *Ibid.,* "Damayante to Nala in the Hour of Exile", p. 43.

[71] *Ibid.,* "Ecstasy", p. 25.

[72] *Ibid.,* "Suttee", p. 18.

[73] *Ibid.,* "An Indian Love Song", p. 69.

[74] *Ibid.,* "To Love", p. 83.

[75] *Ibid.,* "Song of Radha, The Milkmaid", p. 112.

[76] *The Sceptred Flute,* p. 75.

[77] *Ibid.,* "The Sorrows of Love", p. 218.

[78] *Ibid.,* "Longing", p. 204.

[79] *Ibid.,* "The Offering", p. 211.

[80] *Ibid.,* "If You Call Me", p. 214.

[81] *Ibid.,* "Devotion", p. 231.

[82] Harindranath Chattopadhayaya, "Estrangement", *Masks and Farewells,* p. 23.

[83] Sarojini Naidu, "Love Triumphant", *The Sceptred Flute,* p. 16.

[84] Lalitha Venkateswaran, *Tree-Bird* (Calcutta: Writers Workshop, 1975), p. 16.

[85] Sarojini Naidu, "Love Omnipresent", *The Sceptred Flute,* p. 229.

[86] Sylvia Plath, "ELM", *Ariel* (London: Faber & Faber, 1965), p. 25.

[87] *The Sceptred Flute,* p. 219.

[88] S. N. Purohit, *Delicate Dawn,* p. 34.

[89] *The Sceptred Flute,* p. 222.

[90] *Ibid.,* "Destiny", p. 201.

[91] *Ibid.,* "Caprice", p. 200.

[92] *Ibid.,* "If You Were Dead", p. 221.

[93] Sunita Jain, "In Love Time", *Love Time* (New Delhi: Arnold-Heinnemann, 1980), p. 11.

[94] *The Sceptred Flute,* "Invocation", p. 231.

[95] *Ibid.,* "The Illusion of Love", p. 226.

[96] *The Feather of the Dawn,* "Devotion", p. 28.

[97] *Ibid.,* "Conquest", p. 32.

[98] *Ibid.,* "Immutable", p. 34.

[99] *Ibid.,* "Unity", p. 29.

[100] Sylvia Plath, "Medusa", *Ariel,* p. 46.

[101] *The Feather of the Dawn,* "Unity", p. 29.

[102] *Ibid.,* "Devotion", p. 28.

[103] Gokak, ed., "Our Castuaria Tree", p. 51.

[104] *Ibid.*, p. 171.

[105] *Ibid.*, p. 34.

[106] *The Sceptred Flute*, "The Poet to Death", p. 49.

[107] S. N. Purohit, *Delicate Dawn*, p. 1.

[108] Sylvia Plath, *Ariel*, p. 17.

[109] *The Sceptred Flute*, "To Royal Tombs of Golconda", p. 57.

[110] Gokak, ed., p. 249.

[111] *The Sceptred Flute*, "Love and Death", p. 72.

[112] *Ibid.*

[113] *Ibid.*, "At Twilight", p. 77.

[114] Sylvia Plath, *Ariel*, p. 77.

[115] *The Sceptred Flute*, "In Remembrance", p. 71.

[116] S. N. Purohit, *Delicate Dawn*, p. 38.

[117] Gokak.

[118] *The Sceptred Flute*, "The Soul's Prayer", p. 124.

[119] *Ibid.*, "The Bird of Time", p. 65.

[120] *Ibid.*, "Medley", 138.

[121] *Ibid.*, "If You Were Dead", p. 221.

[122] *Ibid.*

[123] *Ibid.*, "Welcome", p. 205.

[124] *The Feather of the Dawn*, p. 4.

[125] *Ibid.*, "A Song of the Khyber Pass", p. 12.

[126] *Ibid.*, p. 62.

[127] *Ibid.*, "Harvest Hymn", p. 14.

[128] *Ibid.*

[129] Gokak, ed., p. 250.

[130] *Ibid.*, p. 129.

[131] S. N. Purohit, *Delicate Dawn*, p. 14.

[132] *The Sceptred Flute*, p. 69.

[133] *Ibid.*, "The Old Woman", p. 127.

[134] *Ibid.*, "Hymn to Indira, Lord of Rain", p. 116.

[135] *Ibid.*, "The Soul's Prayer", p. 123.

[136] *Ibid.*, p. 124.

[137] *Ibid.*, "Song of Radha, The Milkmaid", p. 132.

[138] *Ibid.*, "In Salutation to the Eternal Peace", p. 137.

[139] Gokak, ed., p. 212.

[140] *The Sceptred Flute*, p. 133.

[141] *Ibid.*, "Kali the Mother", p. 177.

[142] *Ibid.*, "The Prayer of Islam", p. 168.

[143] *Ibid.*, p. 168.

[144] *Ibid.*, "The Flute-player of Brindaban", p. 161.

[145] *Ibid.*, p. 161.

[146] *Ibid.*, "Bells", p. 171.

[147] *Ibid*, "Wandering Beggars", p. 165.

[148] *Ibid.*, "Kali the Mother", p. 179.

[149] *Ibid.*, "Lakshmi, The Lotus-Born". p. 110.

[150] *The Feather of the Dawn*, "Gujerat". p. 5.

[151] *Ibid.*, "Ghanashyam", p. 39.

[152] Gokak, ed., p. 130.

[153] *Ibid.*, p. 148.

[154] *The Feather of the Dawn*, "Ghanashyam", p. 39.

[155] *Ibid.*, "Song of Radha", p. 41.

---

# FURTHER READING

## Biography

Baig, Tara Ali. *Sarojini Naidu*. Bombay: Publications Division, Ministry of Information and Broadcasting, Government of India, 1974, 175 p.
Focuses on Naidu's political career.

Dustoor, P. E. *Sarojini Naidu*. Mysore: Rao and Raghavan, 1961, 54 p.
Brief overview of Naidu's life and works that provides a bibliography and critical assessment.

Sengupta, Padmini. *Sarojini Naidu: A Biography*. Bombay:

Asia Publishing House, 1966, 359 p.
  Biography focusing on Naidu's work as a writer and
  a social activist.

**Criticism**

Prasad, Deobrata. *Sarojini Naidu and Her Art of Poetry*.
Delhi: Capital Publishing House, 1988, 216 p.
  Analyzes major themes and imagery in Naidu's poetry.

Nageswara Rao, G. *Hidden Eternity: A Study of the Poetry
of Sarojini Naidu*. Tirupati: Sri Venkateswara University,
1986, 67 p.
  Brief overview of Naidu's poetry; includes a
  bibliography of selected sources.

# Yone Noguchi

## 1875-1947

Japanese poet, critic, essayist, and autobiographer.

## INTRODUCTION

Yone Noguchi was a Japanese poet best known for his writing in English. This included not only his poetry itself, which appeared in works such as *Seen and Unseen or, Monologues of a Homeless Snail* (1897), but also his critical works on both poetry and art. Noguchi's poetic style in English was characterized by a halting quality which, given his proficiency with the language, appears to have been conscious. His words and the way he used them writing nostalgically of Japan in *From the Eastern Sea* (1903), for instance serve to indicate his abiding awareness that he was operating in a world far removed from that of his upbringing. In *The Spirit of Japanese Poetry* (1914), Noguchi presented forms of Japanese literature, including haiku or hokku, in a manner comprehensible to western readers; according to Yoshinobu Hakutani, a leading authority on Noguchi, it in part was through such works that Noguchi influenced Ezra Pound's later Imagist experiments.

### Biographical Information

Noguchi was born in a village near the city of Nagoya, southwest of Tokyo, in 1875. Japanese society, which a generation before had been closed to western ideas, had in recent times become increasingly open to the influence of the West, and Noguchi took a great interest in the English language. As a preparatory school student in Tokyo in the 1890s, he read the works of historian Thomas Macauley and other British writers. These Anglophile tendencies found greater expression when he enrolled at Keio University, also in the Japanese capital. There he expanded his readings of British writers to include the poet Thomas Gray, the philosopher Herbert Spencer, the critic and historian Thomas Carlyle, the humorist Oliver Goldsmith, and others. In addition, he also began reading the American short-story writer Washington Irving, and after finishing high school, he left Japan for America. In December of 1893, an eighteen-year-old Noguchi arrived in San Francisco, beginning a two-year period in which he worked at a series of odd jobs. He continued to study the works of American writers including Edgar Allan Poe, and in 1896 met poet Joaquin Miller. Miller took an interest in the young man, who lived with him for three years. During this time, Noguchi published his first books of poetry, *Seen and Unseen or, Monologues of a Homeless Snail* and *The Voice of the Valley* (1897). Noguchi travelled to the eastern United States and later to England, where in 1903 he published *From the Eastern Sea*. During his London sojourn, as he would later record, he had the idea of using the Japanese form of haiku to write in English, thus avoiding "the impossibility in translation... [of] a *hokku* feeling" from Japanese. Around this time, Noguchi married an American, Leonie Gilmour, and they had a son named Isamu, who would later attain international fame as a sculptor. Relations between father and son, however, would be strained throughout their lives: in 1904, the year of Isamu's birth, Noguchi returned to Japan for good, leaving his family behind in America. Back in Tokyo, he returned to Keio University, where he would serve as a professor of English for several decades. During these years, he published dozens of books in Japanese, as well as a number of notable English-language works, including books of criticism and an autobiography. He traveled to the West occasionally, and corresponded with at least two of the era's literary principals, Pound and William Butler Yeats. With the coming of World War II, Noguchi supported the Japanese government; thus like Pound, who sided with the Fascists in Italy, he found himself ideologically cut off from friends in England and America. Amid the devastation that was postwar Japan, Noguchi died in 1947.

### Major Works

Noguchi published some half-dozen books of poetry, the first three during his decade-long tenure in the West as a young man. The most well-known of these is the first, *Seen and Unseen*, which won the praise of Willa Cather. In this and other volumes, Noguchi showed the naturalistic influence of Walt Whitman, and of his friend Miller. Around the time he published *From the Eastern Sea* in London, he began experimenting with the use of Japanese forms, particularly haiku, which he explored in *The Pilgrimage* (1908). *The Spirit of Japanese Poetry* established Noguchi as not only a poet, but as an authority on Japanese literary forms, including haiku and Noh theatre. He also published a number of volumes of art criticism, beginning with *The Spirit of Japanese Art* in 1915. The period around the beginning of World War I was a particularly fruitful one in Noguchi's career: during this time, in addition to his two principal books of criticism, he also published *Through the Torii* (1914), a collection of essays that presented comparative views of the East and West; and an autobiography, *The Story of Yone Noguchi Told by Himself* (1914).

---

## PRINCIPAL WORKS

*Seen and Unseen or, Monologues of a Homeless Snail* (poetry) 1897

*The Voice of the Valley* (poetry) 1897
*From the Eastern Sea* (poetry) 1903
*The Pilgrimage* (poetry) 1908
*The Spirit of Japanese Poetry* (criticism) 1914
*The Story of Yone Noguchi Told by Himself* (autobiography) 1914
*Through the Torii* (essays) 1914
*The Spirit of Japanese Art* (criticism) 1915

---

# CRITICISM

### The Bookman (essay date 1913)

SOURCE: A review of 'The American Diary of a Japanese Girl', in *The Bookman,* January, 1913, p. 240.

[*In the following essay, a review of* The American Diary of a Japanese Girl, *a critic observes that the book's supposedly naive narrator possesses a knowledge of western culture on a level with Noguchi's own.*]

Mr. Noguchi, the poet, we have long admired; he is one of the two Japanese authors who have captivated us in the net of their imperfect, very skilfully imperfect, English. He seemed to us before to be a Japanese butterfly which had strayed somehow into a Hebridean sunset and had grown deliciously intoxicated. At the same time he strayed no more out of himself than did Shelley, and we apprehended that in attempting to depict a Japanese girl on whose untutored mind America thrusts itself [in *The American Diary of a Japanese Girl*], Mr. Noguchi would bring too much of himself into the sketch. He is indeed far too profound for his heroine, and in some places he goes so far in the direction of naïvité that we look askance at the performance. In other words, it seems to us that the requisite sense of European humour there is no humour worth dignifying with the title American is not easily to be acquired, even by a most gifted Japanese. As an example of observation not unworthy of Tolstoi we have this:

> "It is astonishing to notice what a condescending manner the white gentlemen display towards ladies. They take off their hats in the elevator some showing such a great bald head, like a funny O Binzuru, that is as common as spectacled children if any woman is present. They stand humbly as Japs to the august 'Son of Heaven.' They crawl out like lambs after the woman steps away. It puzzles me to solve how women can be deserving of such honour.

> "What a goody-goody act!

> "But I wonder how they behave themselves before God!"

Again, is it not rather Noguchi than this Miss Morning Glory, the book's heroine, who says:

> "Snake, one of my greatest foes! (The others being cheese and mathematics.) I turned pale. But I bravely faced it, hoping that it would speak a word or two, as one did to Eve. I placed my eyes on it, though in fear. Perhaps it wasn't as intelligent as the one in the Garden of Eden. Maybe it thought it nothing but a waste of time to address a Jap poorly stored in English. It crept away. I ran down the hill."

And, on second thoughts, even if Mr. Noguchi does not give us surely he does not! the simple soul of this Miss Morning Glory, yet we have reason to be thankful for what he does give.

### Yoshinobu Hakutani (essay date 1985)

SOURCE: "Yone Noguchi's Poetry: From Whitman to Zen," in *Comparative Literature Studies,* Vol. 22, No. 1, Spring, 1985, pp. 67-79.

[*In the following essay, Hakutani examines critical influences, both eastern and western, on Noguchi's poetry.*]

I

Despite recent interest in American ethnic poetry, particularly that of black poets such as Paul Laurence Dunbar and Langston Hughes, very little has been said about Yone Noguchi, perhaps the most gifted Japanese American poet. It is not difficult to find some of the reasons for this neglect. He was not a native American writer; born in Japan in 1875, he came to America as a young immigrant. With little money in his pocket he struggled to live among the early Japanese immigrants in California for two years, but with some prior knowledge of English he swiftly learned the language. Already an aspiring poet, the young Noguchi paid homage to the Western poet Joaquin Miller by leading a hermit's life for three years.

In 1896 he published some of his earliest poems in three ephemeral journals of the day, the *Lark,* the *Chap Book,* and the *Philistine.* These poems attracted attention from some critics, and he brought out in the following year his first collections of poetry, *Seen and Unseen or, Monologues of a Homeless Snail* and *The Voice of the Valley.*[1] Although he received praise from established writers,[2] his literary production became erratic and his fragile reputation was not sustained for long. Like the wandering bard traditional in Japan, the young Noguchi spent his energy walking around and reading in the countryside.[3] He also traveled to Chicago, Boston, and New York, and after the turn of the century he journeyed to England, where he published his third volume of poetry, *From the Eastern Sea.*[4] This collection stirred some interest among the English readers, especially Thomas Hardy and George Meredith. "Your poems," Meredith wrote to Noguchi, "are another instance of the energy, mysteriousness, and poetical feeling of the Japanese, from whom we are receiving much instruction."[5]

Noguchi's wandering journey came to an end when he returned to Japan in 1904 and became a professor of English at Keio University in Tokyo. Among his some fifty books, in both English and Japanese, only two are genuine collections of poetry: *The Summer Cloud: Prose Poems* and *The Pilgrimage.*[6] The rest of them range from books of literary and art criticism to travelogues.[7] In the midst of his burgeoning literary career in Japan, he often came back to America, and once visited England to deliver a lecture at Oxford's Magdalen College. His poetic reputation grew in the West through the early thirties, but World War II severed his ties to the West. In 1947, without quite accomplishing his mission as a poet and interpreter of the divergent cultures of the East and the West, he died in Japan.

II

Like his famous sculptor son, Isamu Noguchi, he evolved his own distinct style, which drew upon both Western and Eastern traditions. Noguchi's first book, **Seen and Unseen,** shows that he was initially inspired by Walt Whitman and Joaquin Miller. The poet's affinity with nature, as reflected in these poems, is clearly derived from Japanese traditions, but the sweeping lines and his romanticized self, which abound in his poetry, are reminiscent of Whitman:

> The flat-boarded earth, nailed down at night,
>   rusting under the darkness:
> The Universe grows smaller,
>   palpitating against its destiny:
> My chilly soul center of the world gives seat
>   to audible tears the songs of the cricket.
> I drink the darkness of a corner of the Universe,
>
>         . . . . .
>
> I am as a lost wind among the countless atoms
>   of high Heaven![8]

What unites the two men with different backgrounds is not only their style but their world vision. In "Song of Myself" Whitman includes under the name of Self body and soul, good and evil, man and woman. The conclusion of this section in the poem, where he introduces the concept of balance, is a lyrical passage which celebrates the ecstasy of love. Whitman writes: "Prodigal, you have given me love therefore I to you give love! / O unspeakable passionate love."[9] After this lyrical outburst he declares: "I am not the poet of goodness only, I do not decline to be the poet of wickedness also . . . / I moisten the roots of all that has grown."[10] As the poet of balance, Whitman accepts both good and evil; because he moistens the roots of all that has grown, he can call himself "a kosmos."[11] Noguchi's kosmos in "My Universe" has similar manifestations:

> The world is round; no-headed, no-footed,
>   having no left side, no right side!
> And to say *Goodness* is to say *Badness:*
> And to say *Badness* is to say *Goodness.*
>
>         . . . . .

> The greatest robber seems like saint:
> The cunning man seems like nothing-wanted
>     beast!
> Who is the real man in the face of God?
> One who has fame not known,
> One who has Wisdom not applauded,
> One who has Goodness not respected:
> One who has n't loved Wisdom dearly!
> One who has n't hated Foolishness strongly![12]

Like Whitman, Noguchi believes in monism, and his ultimate goal in writing poetry is to achieve the ecstasies of the self in nature. Many of his early poems thus abound in the image in which life flows in upon the self and others in nature. While Whitman in "Song of Myself" reincarnates himself into a sensitive quahaug on the beach, Noguchi identifies himself with a lone quail:

> Underneath the void-colored shade of the trees,
>   my 'self' passed as a drowsy cloud into
>     Somewhere.
> I see my soul floating upon the face of the deep,
>   nay the faceless face of the deepless deep
>
>         . . . . .
>
> Alas, I, without wisdom, without foolishness,
>   without goodness, without badness, am
>   like god, a negative god, at least!
> Is that a quail? One voice out of the back-hill
>   jumped into the ocean of loneliness.[13]

Though he became a different kind of nature poet after he returned to Japan, his later poems still bear out Whitman's influence. The last stanza of Noguchi's religious poem **"By a Buddha Temple"** reads:

> Ah, through the mountains and rivers,
>   Let thy vastness thrill like that of air;
> I read thy word in the flash of a leaf,
>   Thy mystery in the whisper of a grass.[14]

Grass, which both poets love, is perhaps the most common and universal image in nature poetry. Such a technique, however, not only reveals the poet's sincere admiration of nature, but betrays his abhorrence of civilization. In "Song of Myself" Whitman declares his independence of "civilization," which is represented by "houses and rooms."[15] He detests the perfumes that envelop the domestic atmosphere because the fragrance is artificially distilled; the outdoor atmosphere, he argues, "is not a perfume, it has no taste of the distillation, it is odorless."[16] One of the disappointments Noguchi felt upon his return to Japan was the rise of commercialism he witnessed. The beauty of the seashores near Tokyo was often marred by "the bathing crowd." But after summer, "with the autumn mellow and kind, the season of the clearest sky and softest breeze,"[17] he was able to recapture what Whitman called "Nature without check with original energy":[18]

> Into the homelessness of the sea I awoke:
>   Oh, my heart of the wind and spray!
> I am glad to be no-man to-day
>   With the laughter and dance of the sea-soul.[19]

Noguchi's aversion to people, and to materialism in particular, originated from his mentor, Joaquin Miller, "the Poet of the Sierras," as he called him. It was Miller who urged the fledgling poet to live "amid the roses, quite high above the cities and people." Noguchi pays Miller this compliment: "Never did I think Miller was particularly eccentric, never even once during my long stay with him; he was the most natural man; and his picturesqueness certainly was not a crime." Once Miller brought him a bunch of poppies ("The golden poppy is God's gold" is Miller's song), saying that they were the state flower.[20] Then, he recalls, Miller's lecture followed:

> "The sweetest flowers grow closest to the ground; you must not measure Nature by its size: if there is any measure, it will be that of beauty; and where is beauty there is truth. First of all, you must know Nature by yourself, not through the book. It would be ten thousand times better to know by your own knowledge the colour, the perfume and the beauty of a single tiny creeping vine in the valley than to know all the Rocky Mountains through a book; books are nothing. Read the history written on the brows of stars!"[21]

Such an attitude Miller inspired in him led to the art of poetry Noguchi practiced in his early work. Remembering Miller's often repeated statement, "My life is like the life of a bird," he tried to relive the life of a creature, or merge himself into the existence of a natural element:

> "Good-bye my beloved family" I am to-night
>   buried under the sheeted coldness:
> The dark weights of loneliness make me
>   immovable!
> Hark! the pine-wind blows, blows!
> Lo, the feeble, obedient leaves flee down to the
>   ground
>   fearing the stern-lipped wind voices!
> Alas, the crickets' flutes to-night, are broken!
> The homeless snail climbing up the pillow,
>   stares upon the silvered star-tears on my eyes!
> The fish-like night-fogs flowering with mystery
>   on the Bare-limbed branches:
> The stars above put their love-beamed fires out,
>   one by one
> Oh, I am alone! Who knows my to-night's feeling![22]

Far from being sentimentalized, man's harsh plight in nature is underscored by the images of coldness: the frozen ground, the blowing pine-wind, the falling leaves, the crying crickets, the slowly climbing snail, the silvered stars above, the mysterious night-fogs. This transformation of man into nature enables Noguchi to pose the following question: "When I am lost in the deep body of the mist on the hill, / The world seems built with me as its pillar! / Am I the god upon the face of the deep, deepless deepness in the Beginning?"[23] In both poems Noguchi is speculating about the spiritual and transcendental power of man; conceptually at least he is uniting the will of man with the spirit of nature.

What Noguchi learned at the "Heights of the Sierras" was not only Miller's habit "to loaf and invite his own soul"

in the presence of nature, a way of seeing nature, but also a way of experiencing love. For Noguchi, Miller was "the singer of 'a brother soul in some sweet bird, a sister spirit in a rose,' not the maker of loud-voiced ballads like the tide of a prairie fire or the marches of the Sierra mountains, but the dove-meek poet of love and humanity which . . . grow best and sweetest in silence."[24] Interestingly enough, Noguchi's autobiography, written in Japan years later, reprints Miller's favorite poem on silence:

> Aye, Silence seems some maid at prayer,
> God's arm about her when she prays
> And where she prays and everywhere,
> Or storm-strewn days or sundown days
> What ill to Silence can befall
> Since Silence knows no ill at all?
>
> Vast Silence seems some twilight sky
> That leans as with her weight of stars
> To rest, to rest, no more to roam,
> But rest and rest eternally.
> She loosens and lets down the bars,
> She brings the kind-eyed cattle home,
> She breathes the fragrant field of hay
> and heaven is not far away.[25]

Many of Noguchi's poems, written both under the tutelage of Miller and later in Japan, echo Miller's ideas and methods of writing. In **"My Poetry"** (1897) Noguchi writes:

> My Poetry begins with the tireless songs of the
>   cricket,
>   on the lean gray haired hill, in sober-faced
>   evening.
> And the next page is Stillness
> And what then, about the next to that?
> Alas, the god puts his universe-covering hand
>   over its sheets!
> *"Master, take off your hand for the humble*
>   *servant!"*
> Asked in vain:
> How long for my meditation?[26]

**"Bird of Silence"** (1909) deals with the same theme:

> Lonely ghost away from laughter and life,
> Wing down, I welcome thee,
> From the skies of thoughts and stars,
> Bird of Silence, mystery's brother, as white
> And aloof as is mystery,
> Tired of humanity and of voice,
> With thee, bird of Silence, I long to sail
> Beyond the seas where Time and sorrows die,
>
>   . . . . .
>
> I lost the voice as a willow spray
> To whom a thrill is its golden song,
> As a lotus whose break of cup
> Is the sudden cry after aerial dance.[27]

In this piece the poet is preoccupied with the idea of silence, because silence is "whole and perfect." Silence in nature provides man with rest and happiness, creating a sense of eternity. Through silence, the poet implies, you are able to establish "your true friendship with the ghosts and the beautiful. . . . You have to abandon yourself to the beautiful only to create the absolute beauty and grandeur that makes this our human world look trifling." Through imagination, then, you can achieve "true love, when the reality of the external world ceases to be a standard, and you yourself will be a revelation, therefore a great art itself, of hope and passion which will never fail."[28]

The theme of silence in Noguchi's poetry is, furthermore, related to that of death and eternity. In **"Eternal Death"** (1897), death is treated as if it were alive: "a thief . . . with long and dusty beard," "the poetry-planted garden of silence," "the pearl-fruited orchard of meditation," "the song of my heart strings." To Noguchi, life and death are but two phases of the human soul; death is as much "a triumph to me" as life.[29] In **"Moon Night"** (1909), written at a Buddhist temple, he concludes the poem with this stanza:

> Down the tide of the sweet night
> (O the ecstasy's gentle rise!)
> The birds, flowers and trees
> Are glad at once to fall
> Into Oblivion's ruin white.[30]

"The real poetry," Noguchi once stated, "should be accidental and also absolute."[31] Such a poem as **"Moon Night"** captures the exact circumstances where the natural phenomena reveal both meanings of the accidental and the absolute. His method is, indeed, akin to that of great Japanese poets who write only of isolated aspects of nature but sing mainly of infinity from their accidental revelation.

## III

Although Noguchi owes his poetry to Whitman and Miller, one cannot overlook the Japanese poetics that underlie much of his work. The most obvious tie can be found in its subject matter. Just as Japanese haiku do not treat such subjects as physical love, sex, war, beasts, earthquakes, and floods, Noguchi's poems shun eroticism, ugliness, hate, evil, and untruth. Unlike some poets in the West, Japanese poets abhor sentimentalism, romance, and vulgarity. "The Japanese poetry," Noguchi cautions, "is that of the moon, stars, and flowers, that of a bird and waterfall for the noisiest."[32] Japanese poets' way of avoiding the negative aspects of life, such as illness, is best illustrated by the poem Basho, the most celebrated haiku poet, wrote at his deathbed:

> Lying ill on journey
> Ah, my dreams
> Run about the ruins of fields.[33]

Thus Japanese poetry is focused on nature because, as Noguchi says, "we human beings are not merely a part of Nature, but Nature itself."[34] To be sure, this is pantheism; he is accepting man and nature as a whole and leaving them as they are. But more importantly, he is suggesting that Japanese poets always go to nature to make man's life meaningful, to make "humanity more intensive." They share an artistic susceptibility where, as Noguchi says, "the sunlight falls on the laughter of woods and waters, where the birds sing by the flowers."[35] This mystical affinity between man and nature, between the beauty of love and the beauty of natural phenomena, is best stated in this verse by Noguchi:

> It's accident to exist as a flower or a poet;
> A mere twist of evolution but from the same force:
> I see no form in them but only beauty in evidence;
> It's the single touch of their imagination to get the
>     embodiment of a poet or a flower:
> To be a poet is to be a flower,
> To be the dancer is to make the singer sing.[36]

The fusion of man and nature, and the intensity of love and beauty with which it occurs, can be amply seen in haiku. Noguchi regards Kikaku's haiku on the autumn moon as exemplary:

> Autumn's full moon:
> Lo, the shadows of a pine tree
> Upon the mats![37]

The beauty of the moonlight here is not only humanized but intensified by the shadows of a pine tree that fall upon the mats. "The beauty of the shadow," Noguchi observes, "is far more luminous than the light itself, with such a decorativeness, particularly when it stamps the dustless mats as a dragon-shaped ageless pine tree."[38] Noguchi, too, seems to unify the image of man and the image of nature in his own work. **"Lines"** (1909) begins with this verse:

> The sun I worship,
> Not for the light, but for the shadows of the trees
>     he draws:
> Oh shadows welcome like an angel's bower,
> Where I build Summer-day dreams!
> Not for her love, but for the love's memory,

The poem ends on another suggestion of paradox:

> To a bird's song I listen,
> Not for the voice, but for the silence following
>     after the song:
> O Silence fresh from the bosom of voice!
> Melody from the Death-Land whither my face
>     does ever turn![39]

As Kikaku unifies the images of the moonlight and the mats, Noguchi unifies those of the sun and the love, the bird and the poet. Through the paradox of union both poets express the affinity of man and nature while at the same time maintaining one's separate identity.

The most important tradition by which Noguchi's poetry is influenced is that of Zen. Zen practice calls for the austerity of the human mind; one should not allow his individuality to control his actions. "Drink tea when you are thirsty," says Noguchi, "eat food in your hunger. Rise with dawn, and sleep when the sun sets. But your trouble will begin when you let desire act freely; you have to soar above all personal desire."[40] Zen does not recognize human reality, the existence of good and evil, because it is but the creation of man's will rather than the spirit of nature. The aim of the Zen poet, therefore, is to understand the spirit of nature. Observing the silent rites of a Zen priest, Noguchi once wrote: "Let the pine tree be green, and the roses red. We have to observe the mystery of every existence. . . . The language of silence cannot be understood by the way of reason, but by the power of impulse, which is abstraction."[41]

To demonstrate a state of Zen, he composed the following poem when he visited the Engakuji Temple:

> Through the breath of perfume,
> (O music of musics!)
> Down creeps the moon
> To fill my cup of song
> With memory's wine
>
> Across the song of night and moon,
> (O perfume of perfumes!)
> My soul, as a wind
> Whose heart's too full to sing,
> Only roams astray . . . [42]

The poet's motivation for the union with nature, represented by the fragrance of the atmosphere and the moonlight, does not stem from his knowledge or desire. It is not the poet who is filling his "cup of song," but the moon that is creeping down. In the second stanza the poet accomplishes a state of Zen where, giving himself, he enters wholly into his actions "the song of night and moon." That his soul is roaming astray suggests that he is giving up the ego. The loss of individuality within the union with nature is a condition of what R. H. Blyth calls "absolute spiritual poverty in which, having nothing, we possess all."[43]

Noguchi himself tried his hand at haiku in Japanese as well as in English. How successful a haiku poet he was is debatable, but he certainly tried to adhere to the basic tenets of the genre. One of his English haiku reads:

> My Love's lengthened hair
> Swings o'er me from Heaven's gate:
> Lo, Evening's shadow![44]

In an autobiographical essay he tells us that he came to this sensation when he walked in Hyde Park, "my mind being filled with the thought of the long hair of Rossetti's woman as I perhaps had visited Tate's Gallery that afternoon."[45] While the poem gives a precise impression of the union between the image of the London dusk descending from the sky and the image of the woman's lengthened hair, it also conveys the sensation of each separate object perceived. As a result, the poet is not trying to personify a natural phenomenon; the evening is seen as an evening, the woman's hair is seen as a woman's hair, and there is no artificial attempt to bring them together.

In haiku, there is little division between the perceiver and the perceived, spirit and matter, man and nature. "In the realm of poetry," Noguchi maintains, "there is no strict boundary between the domains generally called subjective and objective; while some _Hokku_ poems appear to be objective, those poems are again by turns quite subjective through the great virtue of the writers having the fullest identification with the matter written on."[46] Noguchi's poem **"The Passing of Summer"** reads:

> An empty cup whence the light of passion is
>     drunk!
> To-day a sad rumour passes through the trees,
> A chill wind is borne by the stream,
> The waves shiver in pain;
> Where now the cicada's song long and hot?[47]

Such images as the chilly wind and the shivering waves are not used to signal the passing of summer. Rather the chilly wind and the shivering waves themselves constitute the passing of summer. Similarly, such phrases as "the light of passion" and "the cicada's song long and hot" are not metonymies of summer, thereby expressing nostalgia or some sort of sentiment about summer; rather they are the summer itself. In Noguchi's poetry, then, as in traditional haiku, poetry and sensation are spontaneously joined in one and the same, so that there is scarcely any room left for rationalism or moralism.

IV

Not all of Noguchi's English poems, however, adhere to Japanese traditions. Most of his early poems, collected in _Seen and Unseen_ and _The Voice of the Valley,_ are beautiful expressions of the young poet's delight in his dreams, reveries, and mysteries about nature, the high Sierras, where he actually spent the life of a recluse. But the relationship of man to nature he creates in his early work is quite different from that of his later work. The ecstasies of the self in nature he describes in his early poetry are sometimes overindulgent, and this dependency of the self on nature results in a loss of equilibrium between them. Speaking of the same experience, Whitman cautions his own senses: "You villain touch! . . . / Unclench your floodgates, you are too much for me."[48] Unlike Whitman, however, the young Noguchi is at times unable to resist an urge toward overstatement and crude symbolism. In his poem **"In the Valley,"** for example, the reveries of nature are most appropriately presented in terms of "the Sierra-rock, a tavern for the clouds" and "the Genii in the Valley-cavern." Man's will and desire, on the other hand, are alluded to by such prosaic expressions as "Fame" and "Gold"; "Heaven" and "mortals" are merely equated with "Glory" and "Decay."[49]

Such a poem as **"In the Valley"** smacks of didacticism and moralism. It is not these qualities in his early poetry that attracted critics' attention. It is, to use his editor's phrase, "this unconventional child of nature . . . whose heart and soul lie naked and bare. . . . If he is sometimes obscure, it is because he has flown into cloud-land, where obscurity is a virtue."[50] Noguchi himself believed in the virtue of obscurity and indefiniteness in poetry. To demonstrate this he quotes the following haiku by a Japanese poet:

> "Thought I, the fallen flowers
> Are returning to their branch;
> But lo! they are butterflies."

Noguchi says that if this poem "means anything, it is the writer's ingenuity perhaps in finding a simile; but I wonder where is its poetical charm when it is expressed thus definitely."[51]

What Noguchi strove to accomplish in his poetry, particularly in his later career, was to perceive a harmonious relationship between man and nature. For him the aim of poetry is not only to achieve the union between man and nature, but to maintain the identity of each within that union. The poet's chief function is not to express the feelings of man by the spirits of nature. This is analogous to what Noguchi saw in the print "Autumnal Moon at Tamagawa" by Hiroshige, a nineteenth-century Japanese landscape painter, in which the moon over the river, the low mountain ranges in the background, and the fishermen engaged in night work are all harmoniously blended into a whole picture. Hiroshige in this painting, as Noguchi realized, is not attempting to imitate nature or to make a copy whereby "the artist may become a soft-voiced servant to nature . . . not a real lover who truly understands her inner soul."[52] In providing expression for nature, the artist must not convey his own thought and logic. When Wordsworth sings, "I wandered, lonely as a cloud," he is simply feeling akin to the cloud rather than imposing the human will upon the will of nature. Similarly, in Noguchi's successful poems man's position in nature becomes neither subordinate nor obtrusive, and both worlds can maintain a great sense of dignity and autonomy.

NOTES

[1] *Seen and Unseen or, Monologues of a Homeless Snail* (San Francisco: Burgess and Garnett, 1897); *The Voice of the Valley* (San Francisco: The Doxey Press, 1897).

[2] See Willa Cather, "Two Poets: Yone Noguchi and Bliss Carman," *The World and the Parish: Willa Cather's Articles and Reviews, 1893-1902* (Lincoln: Univ. of Nebraska Press, 1970), II, pp. 579-81. Cather writes: "While Noguchi is by no means a great poet in the large, complicated modern sense of the word, he has more true inspiration, more melody from within than many a greater man" (II, p. 579).

[3] On this experience Noguchi wrote in his journal: "I thank the rain, the most gentle rain of the Californian May, that drove me into a barn at San Miguel for two days and made me study 'Hamlet' line after line; whatever I know about it to-day is from my reading in that haystack." See Yone Noguchi, *Japan and America* (Tokyo: Keio Univ. Press, 1921), preface.

[4] Yone Noguchi, *From the Eastern Sea* (London: Elkin Mathews, 1903)

[5] *Japan and America,* p. 111.

[6] *The Summer Cloud: Prose Poems* (Tokyo: The Shunyodo, 1906); *The Pilgrimage,* 2 vols. (Tokyo: The Kyobunkan Press, 1909).

[7] Among the books he wrote in Japan, *The Story of Yone Noguchi* (London: Chatto and Windus, 1914) is the most informative account of his life in the United States, as well as his experiences in England and his impressions of Japan after an eleven year absence.

[8] Yone Noguchi, "The Invisible Night," *Seen and Unseen,* p. 21. The poem first appeared in the *Lark.*

[9] Walt Whitman, "Song of Myself" in *Complete Poetry and Selected Prose,* ed. James E. Miller, Jr. (Boston: Houghton Mifflin, 1959), p. 39.

[10] Whitman, p. 40.

[11] Whitman, p. 41.

[12] Yone Noguchi, "My Universe," *Seen and Unseen,* p. 50.

[13] Yone Noguchi, "Seas of Loneliness," *Seen and Unseen,* p. 32.

[14] Yone Noguchi, *Kamakura* (Kamakura: The Valley Press, 1910), p. 35.

[15] Whitman, p. 25.

[16] Whitman, p. 25.

[17] See *Kamakura,* p. 38.

[18] Whitman, p. 25.

[19] Yone Noguchi, "At the Yuigahama Shore by Kamakura," *The Pilgrimage,* I, 34. The poem is reprinted in Noguchi's travelogue *Kamakura,* pp. 38-39.

[20] See *The Story of Yone Noguchi,* pp. 55-63.

[21] *The Story of Yone Noguchi,* p. 63.

[22] Yone Noguchi, "Alone in the Canyon," *Seen and Unseen,* p. 25.

[23] Yone Noguchi, "To an Unknown Poet," *Seen and Unseen,* p. 9.

[24] *The Story of Yone Noguchi,* pp. 67-68.

[25] *The Story of Yone Noguchi,* p. 68.

[26] Yone Noguchi, "My Poetry," *Seen and Unseen,* p. 22.

27 Yone Noguchi, "Bird of Silence," *The Pilgrimage*, I, 53-54.

28 *The Story of Yone Noguchi*, pp. 223-24. Noguchi discusses elsewhere the true meaning of realism: "While I admit the art of some artist which has the detail of beauty, I must tell him that reality, even when true, is not the whole thing; he should learn the art of escaping from it. That art is, in my opinion, the greatest of all arts; without it, art will never bring us the eternal and the mysterious." See *The Spirit of Japanese Art* (London: John Murray, 1915), p. 103.

29 Yone Noguchi, "Eternal Death," *Seen and Unseen*, p. 43.

30 *The Pilgrimage*, I, 5-6.

31 *Japan and America*, p. 98.

32 Yone Noguchi, *The Spirit of Japanese Poetry* (New York: E. P. Dutton, 1914), pp. 18-19.

33 Quoted in *The Spirit of Japanese Poetry*, p. 38.

34 *The Spirit of Japanese Poetry*, p. 19.

35 *The Spirit of Japanese Poetry*, p. 34.

36 Quoted in *The Spirit of Japanese Poetry*, p. 37.

37 Quoted in Yone Noguchi, *Through the Torii* (Boston: The Four Seas, 1922), p. 132.

38 *Through the Torii*, p. 132.

39 *The Pilgrimage*, II, 79.

40 *The Story of Yone Noguchi*, p. 242.

41 *The Story of Yone Noguchi*, pp. 231-32.

42 Yone Noguchi, "By the Engakuji Temple: Moon Night," *The Pilgrimage*, I, p. 5. The Engakuji Temple, located in Kamakura, an ancient capital of Japan, was founded in the thirteenth century by Tokimune Hojo, hero of the feudal government, who was a great believer in Zen Buddhism.

43 R. H. Blyth, *Haiku* (Tokyo: The Hokuseido Press, 1949), I. p. 172.

44 *The Pilgrimage*, II, 140.

45 *Through the Torii*, p. 146.

46 *The Spirit of Japanese Poetry*, pp. 43-44.

47 Yone Noguchi, "The Passing of Summer," *The Pilgrimage*, I, 68.

48 Whitman, p. 46.

49 Yone Noguchi, "In the Valley," *The Voice of the Valley*, p. 29.

50 See Chas. Warren Stoddard, "Introduction," *The Voice of the Valley*, pp. 10-11.

51 *Through the Torii*, p. 51.

52 Yone Noguchi, *Hiroshige and Japanese Landscapes* (Tokyo: Maruzen, 1936), p. 25.

## Yoshinobu Hakutani (essay date 1990)

SOURCE: "Father and Son: A Conversation with Isamu Noguchi," in *Journal of Modern Literature*, Vol. 17, No. 1, Summer, 1990, pp. 13-33.

[*In the following essay, Hakutani outlines the careers of both Yone Noguchi and his son, sculptor Isamu Noguchi (1904-88), with whom Hakutani conducted an interview in December of 1986.*]

"Isamu Noguchi and the airplane," Buckminster Fuller writes, "were both born in the United States of America in the first decade of the twentieth century."[1] Noguchi* was born in Los Angeles to the Japanese immigrant poet Yone Noguchi and the American literary enthusiast Leonie Gilmour, a Bryn Mawr graduate, but the place where the future sculptor spent his early years, curiously enough, was a small town in northern Indiana. By 1918, when Noguchi was taken to Indiana, it was a notable center of literary production that had reared many popular as well as serious writers, including Lew Wallace of *Ben Hur*, James Whitcomb Riley, George Ade, Booth Tarkington, Edward Eggleston, and Theodore Dreiser (son of a German immigrant).

Few would question Isamu Noguchi's artistic accomplishments over half a century. The collection of his work at his Long Island studio-museum, only part of his life work, presents an awesome sight. Some critics say that he is one of a small group of artists who have shaped the course of modern American sculpture. Yet while his work is well known the world over, his fascinating background is much less familiar. Equally intriguing is his relationship to his father, whose life and work both in America and in Japan, despite their significance, remain unheralded.

Yone Noguchi was born in a small town near Nagoya in 1875. In the late 1880s, the young Noguchi, taking great interest in English texts used in a public school, read Samuel Smiles's writings on self-help. Perhaps inspired by Smiles, but in any case dissatisfied with his public school instruction, he withdrew from a middle school in Nagoya and went to Tokyo in 1890. A year of preparatory school enabled him to enter Keio University, one of the oldest colleges in Japan, at which he studied Spenser and Carlyle and devoured works by Washington Irving, Oliver Goldsmith, and Thomas Gray. He even tried his hand at translating into Japanese such poems as "The Deserted Village" and "An Elegy Written in a Country Churchyard."

Although two years of college provided him with substantial reading in English, the young aspiring poet was not content with his education, for he had been dreaming of living and writing in an English-speaking country. In December 1893, with little money in his pocket, he arrived in San Francisco. For the next two years, he lived mainly among the Japanese immigrants in California and, for almost a year, was employed by a Japanese-language newspaper in San Francisco primarily translating news of the Sino-Japanese War sent from Japan. However, his industry and interests led him to walk from San Francisco as far as Palo Alto, and for several months he lived near Stanford University, reading, among other writings, Edgar Allan Poe's poems.[2] His re-reading of *The Sketch Book,* particularly Irving's portrayal of England, inspired him to plan to travel some day across the Atlantic.

The turning point of Noguchi's life in America came in 1896, when he paid homage to the Western poet Joaquin Miller. Miller, in turn, admired Noguchi's youth and enthusiasm. Except for a few occasions when Noguchi had to travel to Los Angeles, partly on foot, or to walk down the hills to see his publishers in San Francisco, he led a hermit's life for three years, living in Miller's mountain hut in Oakland. Through Miller, he became acquainted with Edwin Markham, Charles Warren Stoddard, Gelett Burgess (a noted humorist), and Porter Garnett, Burgess's publisher associate.

Within a year after meeting Miller, Noguchi published his earliest poems in *The Lark, The Chap Book,* and *The Philistine.* These poems attracted critical attention, and in the following year Burgess and Garnett brought out his first collections of poetry, **Seen and Unseen** and **The Voice of the Valley.** These, too, received praise. Willa Cather, for example, wrote, "While Noguchi is by no means a great poet in the large, complicated modern sense of the word, he has more true inspiration, more melody from within than many a greater man."[3] But his literary production became erratic, and his fragile reputation was not sustained for long.

Like the wandering bard traditional in Japan, the young Noguchi spent much of his time walking and reading in the high mountains and in the fields. Of one of these experiences he wrote in his journal: "I thank the rain, the most gentle rain of the Californian May, that drove me into a barn at San Miguel for two days and made me study 'Hamlet' line after line; whatever I know about it today is from my reading in that haystack."[4]

Later he travelled to Chicago, Boston, and New York, where he published a novella about a Japanese parlormaid. After the start of the century, he journeyed to England, where he published his third volume of poetry in English, **From the Eastern Sea.** This collection cre-

ated some interest among English readers, especially Thomas Hardy and George Meredith. "Your poems," Meredith wrote, "are another instance of the energy, mysteriousness, and poetical feeling of the Japanese, from whom we are receiving much instruction."[5]

Yone Noguchi's wanderings came to an end when he returned to Japan in 1904, shortly before Isamu Noguchi was born and left behind in America with his mother. The elder Noguchi became a professor of English at Keio University in Tokyo, the same college from which he had withdrawn eleven years earlier. Among the well over ninety books which he wrote in Japan, many of them in English, only two are genuine collections of English poetry. The rest range from books of literary and art criticism to travelogues. In the midst of his burgeoning literary career in Japan, he occasionally returned to America, and once he visited England to deliver a lecture at Oxford's Magdalen College.

His role in East-West literary relations can scarcely be overestimated.[6] Although the standard explanation for the influences of Japanese poetry, especially haiku, on T.E. Hulme and Ezra Pound is that they studied Japanese poetics through Ernest Fenollosa, the Harvard Sinologist had a poor command of the Japanese language; and since Noguchi's later poetry collected in **The Pilgrimage** and his literary criticism, **The Spirit of Japanese Poetry** in particular, were widely circulated, the standard explanation seems questionable. It is much more likely that the Imagists responded directly to their fellow poet Noguchi's example. Pound, for instance, wrote to Noguchi:

> c/o Elkin Mathews
>
> Vigo St. London
>
> Sep. 2, 1911
>
> Dear Yone Noguchi:
>
> I want to thank you very much for your lovely books & for your kindness in sending them to me.
>
> I had, of course, known of you, but I am much occupied with my mediaeval studies & had neglected to read your books altho' they lie with my own in Mathews shop & I am very familiar with the appearance of their covers.
>
> I am reading those you sent me but I do not yet know what to say of them except that they have delighted me. . . . You are giving us the spirit of Japan, is it not? very much as I am trying to deliver from obscurity certain forgotten odours of Provence & Tuscany. . . .
>
> You ask about my "criticism." There is some criticism in the "Spirit of Romance" & there will be some in the prefaces to the "Guido" and the "Arnaut." But I might be more to the point if we who are artists should discuss the matters of technique & motive between ourselves. Also if you

should write about these matters I would discuss your letters with Mr. Yeats and likewise my answers.

I have not answered before because your letter & your books have followed me through America, France, Italy, Germany and have reached me but lately.

Let me thank you again for sending them, and believe me,

Yours very sincerely

Ezra Pound[7]

In the 1920s and 1930s Noguchi was also the most well-known interpreter of Japanese visual arts in the West, especially in England. Beginning with *The Spirit of Japanese Art,* he published, in English, ten volumes with colorful illustrations dealing with traditionally celebrated painters such as Hiroshige, Korin, Utamoro, Hokusai, and Harunobu. Yeats, whose interest in the Noh play is well known, wrote to Noguchi[8]:

4 Broad St., Oxford

June 27 [1921?]

Dear Noguchi:

Though I have been so long in writing, your **"Hiroshige"** has given me the greatest pleasure. I take more and more pleasure from oriental art; find more and more that it accords with what I aim at in my own work. The European painter of the last two or three hundred years grows strange to me as I grow older, begins to speak as if in a foreign tongue. When a Japanese, or Mogul, or Chinese painter seems to say, "Have I not drawn a beautiful scene," one agrees at once, but when a modern European painter says so one does not agree so quickly, if at all. All your painters are simple, like the writers of Scottish ballads or the inventors of Irish stories, but one feels that Orpen and John have relatives in the patent office who are conscious of being at the fore-front of time. The old French poets were simple as the modern are not, & I find in François Villon the same thoughts, with more intellectual power, that I find in the Gaelic poet Raftery. I would be simple myself but I do not know how. I am always turning over pages like those you have sent me, hoping that in my old age I may discover how. . . . It might make it more easy to understand their simplicity. A form of beauty scarcely lasts a generation with us, but it lasts with you for centuries. You no more want to change it than a pious man wants to change the Lord's Prayer, or the Crucifix on the wall [words blurred] at least not unless we have infected you with our egotism. . . .

Yours sincerely

W.B. Yeats[9]

Noguchi's reputation as poet and critic grew in the West through the early 1930s, but World War II severed his ties to the West just as his relationship to his son, Isamu, had been strained ever since the latter's birth. "I am getting old," Yone Noguchi wrote to his son after the war, "and feel so sad and awful with what happened in Japan."[10] In 1947, in the midst of the chaos and devastation brought about by the war, without quite accomplishing his mission as a poet and interpreter of the divergent cultures of the East and the West as he had wished, Yone Noguchi died in Japan.

The only published memoir discussing his son at any length appears in his autobiography, *The Story of Yone Noguchi Told by Himself,* which relates a story from 1906 when Isamu Noguchi was barely two years old, and father and son met by the cabin door of the steamer that had carried Noguchi's American wife and child across the Pacific:

> This Mr. Courageous landed in Yokohama on a certain Sunday afternoon of early March. . . . Now and then he opened a pair of large brown eyes. "See papa"; Léonie tried to make Isamu's face turn to me; however, he shut his eyes immediately without looking at me, as if he were born with no thought of a father. . . . I felt in my heart a secret pride in being his father; but a moment later, I was really despising myself, thinking that I had no right whatever to claim him, when I did not pay any attention to him at all for the last three years. "Man is selfish," I said in my heart; and again I despised myself.[11]

The childhood which Isamu Noguchi spent in Japan until he returned to America at thirteen was understandably unhappy. Not only was his father married to an American woman, but the young Noguchi, a child of mixed blood growing up in a race-conscious society, was considered a stranger. His piece of sculptural landscape called *Play Mountain* (1933) betrays the child's yearning to belong to America, his motherland. He created such a work, he seems to tell us, out of his genuine sympathy for all the lonely childhoods represented by his own. His youth in Japan had, indeed, made an indelible mark upon his personality and work.

By the mid 1920s, Isamu Noguchi had immersed himself in New York's art world. He often visited Alfred Stieglitz's gallery and began attending various exhibitions of modern art, including the Brancusi exhibit at the Brummer Gallery, which attracted him powerfully. It was about the same time that Harry Guggenheim, seeing one of Noguchi's earliest pieces shown at the Roman Bronze Exhibit, suggested that Noguchi apply for the newly founded Guggenheim Fellowship. One of the recommenders was his friend, Stieglitz, and Noguchi won the award, which enabled him to study in Paris eventually under Brancusi's tutelage although his original plans had included travel and work in India, China, and Japan.

By 1930 he already had to his credit several exhibits both in America and in Europe, and about this time he made long-lasting friendships with Martha Graham and

Buckminster Fuller, the latter whom he called "a great teacher." Because of these friendships, perhaps, Noguchi became known not only as a sculptor but as a stage designer and landscapist. He designed stage sets for the Balanchine-Stravinsky ballet *Orpheus* (1948) and for John Gielgud's *King Lear* (1955) with success.[12] But he achieved greater fame with such works as the *2 Peace Bridges* (1951-52) for Hiroshima, the *Gardens for Unesco* in Paris (1956-58), the *Sculpture Gardens for the National Museum* of Israel (1960-65), the *Playground in Piedmont Park* in Atlanta (1975-76), and the *Philip A. Hart Plaza* in Detroit (1973-78). As a sculptor, the 1960s were Noguchi's most productive period. His reputation soared, as the celebrated sculptural gardens he created for Yale's Beinecke Rare Book and Manuscript Library and the Chase Manhattan Bank Plaza in New York attest.

Back in 1930, however, his illustrious career had barely begun, as his Guggenheim application indicates:

I have selected the Orient as the location for my productive activities for the reason that I feel a great attachment for it, having spent half my life there. My father, Yone Noguchi, is Japanese and has long been known as an interpreter of the East to the West, through poetry. I wish to do the same with sculpture.

May I, therefore, request your assistance in enabling me to fulfill my heritage?[13]

Noguchi's journey into the Orient as a young artist led to self-discovery but also generated in him great enthusiasm for America. In the early 1930s, many museums in New York and Chicago were eager to exhibit the terra cottas and drawings that he had done in the Far East. His new work was shown even in England, and yet these times were as hard for artists as for everyone else. What was worse, art critics often catered to city administrators and politicians, who were not likely to see beyond traditional modes of artistic expression, and Noguchi's lifelong zeal for new horizons and self-identity often ran counter to his economic well-being. After his proposed design for a city park, *Play Mountain* [1933], was rejected by the New York Park commissioner, Noguchi fled to Mexico, a country more congenial to his work. There he no longer felt estranged as an artist and considered himself useful to the community, completing his first major work, a high relief mural in colored cement on carved bricks for the Rodriguez market, called *History Mexico,* in 1936.

After Mexico, Noguchi found America depressing, despite his successful exhibits. Then came Pearl Harbor, an unmitigated shock to him, suspending his work entirely. Even though he was only half-Japanese, he was considered a *Nisei.* To counteract the racial hysteria that soon appeared in the press, he organized an association, the Nisei Writers and Artists for Democracy, but to no avail. Unlike the Japanese-Americans living on the West Coast who had no choice, Noguchi a New Yorker voluntarily entered an internment camp in Arizona, where he gained a feeling of identity with the internees. At first, the fan-tastic landscape of the desert and the blessings of the administrator in charge inspired him to create designs for parks and recreation areas, work that often led him deep into the desert to collect ironwood roots for sculpting. But then the War Relocation Authority, at odds with the camp administrator, forced Noguchi to abandon such activities. Fortunately, he was released on a temporary basis after seven months of internment, and he never returned to the camp. Fortunately as well, such influential individuals as Frank Lloyd Wright and Langdon Warner helped to rescue him, and he was able to resume his work.

By the time the war ended, Noguchi had achieved the kind of recognition few other young sculptors could equal. And yet for all those years he was considered a Japanese artist in America, while in Japan he was regarded as an American, a foreigner. He became victimized by such prejudice in Japan when he was not given the authority to design the *Memorial to the Dead* (1952), a sequel to his own *2 Peace Bridges* in Hiroshima. After rejecting Noguchi's proposed design, a Japanese architect forced Kenzo Tange, the architect's disciple, to take over the project in place of Noguchi and to redesign the *Memorial.*

However, this prejudice was not universal. When he had returned to Japan in the spring of 1950, Noguchi had been welcomed by his relatives and friends as a native son. The war seemed to have changed the attitudes of some of the Japanese people toward Western things in general and American in particular. He was asked to design the faculty building *Shin Banraisha* (1951-52) on the Keio University campus, at which his father had taught; he did so not only as a memorial but as his own act or reconciliation with his father and the Japanese people. In the garden adjacent to the building, he placed two sculptures: one, an iron welding, called *Student,* and the other, in stone, *Mu,* the Zen term meaning "nothingness."

"It is my desire," Noguchi stated at the beginning of his career, "to view nature through nature's eyes, and to ignore man as an object for special veneration." This intention reveals not only Noguchi's attitude toward nature but also the profound influence which Zen had upon him as an artist. To him, man has extended the horizon of knowledge through science but has overlooked the unthinkable heights of beauty that sculpture can reach. Only by denying one's self-consciousness can one enter the world of natural beauty. "Trees grow in vigor," he still says forty years later, "flowers hang evanescent, and mountains lie somnolent with meaning."[14] His aim in sculpture was to bring home the spirit of nature rather than impose the will of man upon her. Zen teaches one to annihilate the illusion of mind so that one can achieve nirvana, the extinction of all that is called self. The Zen metaphysician would argue that self is blindness, that it must be destroyed, and that reality will be revealed as infinite vision and infinite peace.

The genuine interest which Noguchi acquired in the Zen garden when he returned to Japan after the war bears out his unique vision of earth and space. It can scarcely be coincidental that many of his father's early poems, written on the high Sierras in the 1890s, or in Japan well into the twentieth century, contain a characteristic mark of Zen Buddhism. In 1908, two years after Isamu Noguchi's arrival in Japan, the elder Noguchi maintained a study on the premises of the Engakuji Temple in Kamakura. In order to demonstrate a state of Zen, Yone Noguchi composed a poem:

> Through the breath of perfume,
> (O music of musics!)
> Down creeps the moon
> To fill my cup of song
> With memory's wine
>
> Across the song of night and moon,
> (O perfume of perfumes!)
> My soul, as a wind
> whose heart's too full to sing,
> Only roams astray . . . [15]

The poet's motivation for the union with nature, represented by the fragrance of the atmosphere and the moonlight, stems not from his knowledge or desire. It is not the poet who is filling his "cup of song" but the moon that is creeping down. He accomplishes a state of Zen in which, giving of himself, he enters wholly into his actions "the song of night and moon." Zen calls for the austerity of the human mind; one must not allow one's individuality to control one's actions. Observing the silent rites of a Zen priest, Yone Noguchi once wrote: "Let the pine tree be green, and the roses red. . . . The language of silence can not be understood by the way of reason, but by the power of impulse, which is abstraction."[16]

To call Isamu Noguchi a Zen sculptor, however, tells only part of his story. His work is enlightened by his affinity for nature, and as Isamu Noguchi tells us, he returns recurrently to the earth in search of the meaning of sculpture. Wood and stone, the primeval elements of the earth that existed long before man, have the greater capacity to comfort man. And yet what Noguchi contributes to the relationship of man and nature is man's participation in it. Noguchi would chide the traditional Japanese gardener whose sole interest is in finding natural stones, ready-made sculptures, that satisfy the eyes of connoisseurs. "This," says Isamu Noguchi, "is not quite correct; it is the point of view that sanctifies; it is selection and placement that will make of anything a sculpture, even an old shoe." Sculpture is a means by which one can participate in the creation and make one's own life more meaningful. Sculpture is equated with what Noguchi calls "the definition of form in space, visible to the mobile spectator as participant. Sculptures move because we move."[17]

Such participation in sculpture is reminiscent of Kikaku, one of the innovative Japanese poets of the seventeenth century, whose haiku Yone Noguchi discusses at length in *Through the Torii*. Yone Noguchi regards Kikaku's haiku on the autumn moon as a slight departure from Zen doctrine:

> Autumn's full moon;
> Lo, the shadows of a pine tree
> Upon the mats!

This poem expresses the fusion of man and nature, and the intensity of love and beauty with which it occurs. The beauty of the moonlight is not only humanized but intensified by the shadows of a pine tree that fall upon the *tatami* mats. "The beauty of the shadow," Yone Noguchi observes, [is] "far more luminous than the light itself, with such decorativeness, particularly when it stamp[s] the dustless mats as a dragon-shaped ageless pine tree."[18]

"If we insist on his Eastern identity," a recent art critic has written about Isamu Noguchi, "he grows abstract and Western before our eyes; his rationalism in the use of modern materials and constructivist design only conceals an equally convincing irrational and playful invention."[19] The 1986 Venice Biennale exhibited Isamu Noguchi's new work, *Slide Mantra,* as a representative sculpture from the United States. Isamu Noguchi is regarded today as an American artist, and his influence has felicitously synthesized Modernist sculptural forms with Zen notions of form and space. It is more than coincidence that his father was as much a Zen poet as he was an American poet. If Isamu Noguchi is a Zen artist, he is also a Modernist in the tradition of Western art. His father as a poet attempted to bridge the East and West in his time; Isamu Noguchi as a sculptor has amply fulfilled his mission in ours.

AN INTERVIEW WITH ISAMU NOGUCHI

The streets outside his residence near Central Park are bustling with cars and pedestrians. Having just come out of a literary conference, I meet Michiko Hakutani for a quick lunch, and we hurry to Isamu Noguchi's address for a two o'clock appointment. Inside the small building in which he has an apartment, it is comfortably quiet. We arrive a few minutes late, and the two attendants at the door swiftly direct us to his modest penthouse apartment. The door is ajar. At once he invites us inside and introduces us to Shoji Sadao, an architect and associate who is leaving momentarily after a visit. "*Dozo kochirae* [Please, this way]," Noguchi says in Japanese, very politely, but warmly. He is in his eighty-second year, but his voice is firm; he speaks like a middle-aged man.

In one corner of a room decidedly not his living room, we face one another across a small round table.[20] Would he mind our recording the conversation? Not in the least. By way of introducing myself, I present him with two of my books, both on Dreiser.

*Noguchi:* I used to know Dreiser very well when he was in New York in his later years.[21]

*Hakutani:* In the late 1890s, before he wrote *Sister Carrie,* Dreiser made a living by writing many magazine articles, some about artists such as Alfred Stieglitz.

*Noguchi:* Stieglitz was my friend. It was when I was sixteen that I first read Dreiser's writing, The *"Genius,"* in Indiana. I would like to read the novel again. My mother, who was teaching English in Yokohama, read in a maga-

zine something about a prep school in Indiana. She bought a ticket for me to travel to a small town in northern Indiana and attend a private school called Interlaken. But by the time fall came around it failed to open, and I was stuck there. There was no other place to go; I didn't have money to go back to Japan. Two caretakers were also there. I spent nearly a year at the school and in Rolling Prairie, the village
nearby.

*Hakutani:* Where was your father then?

*Noguchi:* He was in Japan, but I had nothing to do with him. Actually I had little to do with my mother either. All these relationships I had difficulty understanding at that time. You would perhaps understand them better. My father and I never corresponded with each other. My mother wrote me from time to time, however. Dr. Edward A. Rumley, founder of the Interlaken School, heard about my plight and came to my rescue. He put me to board with the minister of the New Church in La Porte, Indiana, which follows the teachings of Swedenborg. I stayed with his family for three years and got through high school, doing all kinds of things to pay for part of my expenses.[22] (It's easier for me to speak in English.) Anyway, it was Dr. Rumley who thought it wiser for me to study medicine as he himself had done. He knew people like Henry Ford and former President Teddy Roosevelt; he was instrumental in building factories in northern Indiana to make tractors. I told him I wanted to become an artist. It was then, when I was fifteen or sixteen, that he, a great admirer of Dreiser, gave me *The "Genius"* to read. He said it would be foolish for me to survive as an artist, but agreed to send me as an apprentice to his friend, the sculptor Gutzon Borglum, who was carving Presidents' faces in South Dakota. Mr. Borglum asked me to tutor his son. So I really grew up in the Midwest, though I am a mixture of the extreme differences in heritage. Please don't forget I am a real product of Midwestern America. [Noguchi rises from his chair for a few minutes to leaf through a heap of memorabilia on certain Midwestern personages.] See, this is a bust of Buckminster Fuller.

*Hakutani:* Many a distinguished American writer in our times came from the Midwest, like Dreiser and Hemingway. Dreiser came from a poor family, while Hemingway was from a well-to-do family his father was a physician. I might say your father was a distinguished poet and art critic.

*Noguchi:* That was incidental. So, you see, my growing up in this country had nothing to do with art; it had to do with the Middle West and the American idealism that flourished in the twenties and thirties. What was interesting about my father is that he was not an immigrant but a person eager to know this energy of the American frontier; the image of the frontier space, you see energized him.

*Hakutani:* Earlier in his career as a poet, Yone Noguchi, as you know, was very much influenced by Walt Whitman, who was perhaps in the same spirit.

*Noguchi:* Yes, Whitman was energized by the same spirit. So was my own upbringing. As you can see, I was under the influence of people like Dr. Rumley and Buckminster Fuller. Those were my friends. Through them I saw something that was totally unknown in the art world an American phenomenon. I saw this in Dreiser and also in Ezra Pound. Pound was an interesting man. When I went to Europe on a Guggenheim grant in 1927, I had a letter of introduction from Michio Itoh, a Japanese dancer, for me to meet Pound.[23] Itoh came to this country around 1925, perhaps earlier; he had been well acquainted with Pound and Yeats. A year before I went to Europe, I had made masks for Itoh to do Yeats's Noh drama, *At the Hawk's Well*. In any event, I met Pound in Europe, but not till much later by which time he was not speaking to anybody but I came to see him a good deal. Pound, I felt, also had this quality of the American frontier and kept it in all his poetry. I've felt that my father in his early years in America had tapped the same energy, the energy which motivated many of the American writers.

*Hakutani:* Literary historians generally believe that the so-called Imagism advocated by Ezra Pound and T.E. Hulme derived from Japanese poetics through the Harvard Sinologist and Japanologist Ernest Fenollosa. But Fenollosa did not know the Japanese language well enough to inform them of Japanese poetry, and of haiku in particular. Your father's poetry and literary and art criticism were widely circulated in English-speaking countries in the mid-1910s. Don't you think it was your father rather than academicians like Fenollosa who made a greater contribution to the Imagist movement?

*Noguchi:* Of course, you know, the influence of Japanese art was prior to all that. I mean van Gogh, Monet, and all those French artists were deeply influenced by Japanese art. In the case of Pound, I don't know. I'm not contradicting you. It may be, may be, may be. I would say that certainly my father's influence was an additional one. The influences of Japanese art and literature on Yeats go back earlier than that on Pound. My father's influence on Yeats in the earlier 1910s was, as a matter of fact, even earlier than that on Pound. My relationship with Yeats began in 1925, when I designed masks for his *At the Hawk's Well*, through Michio Itoh, as I have mentioned. The Japanese influence on Yeats, I think, was before he wrote *At the Hawk's Well*. You know *The Iris*, a quarterly magazine my father edited in Japan in the mid-1900s, published poems by Yeats among other English and American writers.[24] I'm merely saying these were many, perhaps simultaneous, streams of influence.

*Hakutani:* Isn't it true that scholars such as Fenollosa are often cited but that Yone Noguchi, his work notwithstanding, is virtually unknown today?

*Noguchi:* That's the reason why I gave to the Keio University Library those letters Yeats, Pound, and other intellectuals in England had written to my father. Those show a great impact he made upon many of the British intellectuals at the time. He made a great success in

England. The English had more earnest appreciation of Japanese art and literature than the Americans. The curators of the British Museum, for instance, took great interest in Japanese art. In the month of January, 1927-28, I was studying Japanese prints there, and I saw Laurence Binyon, the curator of prints at the British Museum quite often. Although I doubt that Pound actually knew my father, but still because of my father he was kind and warm to me over the years. I have books of his around here, which were dedicated to me. [Noguchi rises from his chair and leans toward the shelf.] If they aren't here, they must be in my studio. He had sent me all sorts of books; they must be at the studio. Do you know that couplet Pound wrote which reads something like "Yone Noguchi . . ."?

*Hakutani:* Do you own any of your father's letters other than those you donated to the Keio University Library?

*Noguchi:* Yes, I have some. I gave many of them to the Bancroft Library at Berkeley. It has a whole section of California writers, among whom is my father. You might take a look at the collection and see the man in charge of the rare book collection, a very nice man. Please give him my regards when you see him.

*Hakutani:* Does the Bancroft Library own your writings or work as well?

*Noguchi:* No. I haven't yet had many opportunities to give things. I also have many letters between Frank Putnam and my father.[25] Putnam was apparently a very radical publisher then, but later he became very conservative. You may come to my studio to look at those letters by Pound and Putnam.

*Hakutani:* Nobody doubts Yone Noguchi was your father because you resemble him very much.

*Noguchi:* Well, he resembles me! [We all laugh.]

*Hakutani:* Last December we went to the Art Institute of Chicago to look for your father's head done by Alfeo Faggi in 1920.[26] How well-known a sculptor is he?

*Noguchi:* He was well-known then, sure.

*Hakutani:* The relationship between you and your father has been regarded as less than harmonious. How would you respond to such a statement?

*Noguchi:* Oh, not actually. Well, let me relate something that happened after World War II. The *Japan Times* asked me to comment about the war, and my comments were published on the front page. When my father read them, he wrote me that he had made a terrible mistake in supporting his country during the war. An interesting letter. My papers have to be looked into; they are interesting, historically. I wish someone knowledgeable about such matters would examine them. My father apparently felt guilty about the role he had played in the rise of Japanese nationalism. That was his first contact with me after the war.

*Hakutani:* When did you see him for the last time before the war?

*Noguchi:* I only saw him in 1931; I didn't see him after that. I went back to Japan in the spring of 1950 and visited his tomb at a temple in Fujisawa whose priest was his brother.[27] So the temple was run by the priest's adopted son, also named Noguchi, when I visited there. The priest, my father's brother, was very, very friendly to my mother. As a matter of fact, all my father's relatives were very fond of my mother. They were all against my father; they were very critical of him.

*Hakutani:* I wonder what caused all this, and the disharmony between you and your father in particular.

*Noguchi:* Something to do with my mother. I did not think he treated her fairly. That was all. When I became a bit older, in 1931 or so, I came to know him better and was less sort of bitter about it.

*Hakutani:* What was your first impression of him when you were young, say when you were six, seven, or eight?

*Noguchi:* I didn't know him then. I saw him when I left Japan in the spring of 1918; I was thirteen years old then. He came to the boat. I was then living with my mother. I used her name Gilmour and only changed it to Noguchi when I was nineteen years old and decided to be a sculptor, for I thought Gilmour was not an appropriate name. When my father came into the boat to see me, he was of course a stranger to me in the sense that I hadn't seen him for a long while. I remember seeing him when I was about eight years old.

*Hakutani:* Did you feel any affinity for him when you were a boy, an eight-year old or a thirteen-year old? Did you regret that your father was not close to you?

*Noguchi:* My mother was very pleased when he came to visit when I was eight years old. I had the measles, had to stay home, and he came to visit me and my mother. I felt happy at the time. When he came to see me on the bridge to the *America* and tried to say, "You are to stay in Japan," I didn't know what to say. My mother said, "No," so I said, "No." I was on my way outside to a tremendous adventure. Did I grow to regret this? Who knows? I don't know. It was very difficult to know in the past what was right or wrong. My mother stayed on in Japan, and I didn't see her until 1924, when she returned to New York, her home. In 1930, I waited for three months to get a transit visa to travel across Russia. I finally headed toward Japan by way of Siberia, but before I left Paris I had received a letter from my father which said, "Don't come. Don't use the name Noguchi." So I went to Peking. I stayed there for eight months. After that I thought I'd better go and see Japan, and that I wouldn't use my name; I'd just go see it. On the boat there was a man I was talking to. I didn't know he was a newspaper reporter, so that when I got to Japan his article about me appeared in the *Asahi Newspaper.*[28]

*Hakutani:* What was your father's reaction?

*Noguchi:* He didn't say anything when I did see him. My contact with him after all those years was not exactly pleasant; however, I had no quarrels with him at all. When I saw him in 1931, I understood him; before I didn't. He was a hen-pecked man. So he said to me. *Nazeka to yu* [The reason why]. *Saigo no kodomo ga dekiru koto ni nattetan de* [As his last child was to be born], his wife told him that I could not come, using his name, because I'm the oldest, you see.

*Hakutani:* You did not meet your stepmother?

*Noguchi:* Oh, yes, years later, not then. At that time I didn't. When I went back in 1950, I stayed there with her and her children. She was very nice then. She was the mother of Hifumi, Michio, and others.[29]

*Hakutani:* Did your father marry twice, then, your mother and then . . . ?

*Noguchi:* Maybe he didn't marry either of them; I don't know. Anyway, 1931 was the last time I saw him. . . . (I forgot to make you some tea. Good idea!)[30]

*Hakutani:* As you know, Yone Noguchi wrote a great deal about Japanese art Hiroshige, Harunobu, and other eminent painters. Did your father as an art critic have any influence upon you? Do you have any affinity for Japanese art?

*Noguchi:* Not consciously. For instance, the Japanese dancer Michio Itoh, whom I've mentioned earlier, got interested in the frontier spirit in America and finally became a kind of choreographer for Hollywood. He always urged me to do the impossible. He came from a family of artists; one of his brothers also was here. I learned a great deal from them.

*Hakutani:* Your father came here as a young poet, and, as you say, he became enchanted with the free spirit of America. But upon his return to Japan, he rediscovered Japanese art and Zen in particular. He was keenly interested in Zen art, as indicated by his essays on haiku and on Japanese art. From time to time, I wonder whether you yourself have been influenced by Zen art.

*Noguchi:* Anybody is. Anyone who goes to Japan is fascinated by Zen.

*Hakutani:* I'd also like to know your assessment of your father's poetry and his art and literary criticism. He wrote a great deal in Japanese as well as in English about the Japanese tradition and Japanese art. What do you think of his writings?

*Noguchi:* I don't know his Japanese writings; I don't read Japanese, unfortunately. I've read some of his writings in English. I've found it difficult to read his books, for instance, on *ukiyoye* because he tries to be a poet or literary man discussing something else.[31] I'm, therefore, not much interested in his writing on art in the descriptive sense. So I don't think I have any influence from my father in my view of Japanese art. In fact, I do not try to be a Japanese artist, although I am very fond of Japanese art. I find my own way; I don't need somebody else to tell me.

*Hakutani:* What about Brancusi, or any other European artist?

*Noguchi:* Brancusi had some influence on me, I'm sure, but I didn't want even that kind of influence. We always want to find our own way. As a matter of fact, I would say that my father also wanted to find his own way. Only when he returned to Japan and tried to become Japanese, did he fail, for he was no longer Japanese. He had become a pioneer Westerner. It is a misconception that he was regarded as a Japanese poet while he was in America. To say Japanese or something else becomes shorthand; it's not a real thing. In the imaginary sense, a Japanese can become a Westerner, or a Westerner can become a Japanese. In the case of my father, I think, he became a pioneer American in a sense with the eyes of an Oriental. Take Pound, for instance; he was a Midwesterner who went to Europe and saw Europe with the eyes of a Midwesterner. He tried to transform the English language from this radical point of view. Unfortunately, my father's viewpoint is not understood in Japan because, first of all, they don't understand how historically important it was that he was here at such a time. They don't understand that he became somebody like all these people whose eyes were open to the ideal of the American frontier from Whitman and Joaquin Miller down to Pound, Dreiser, and so on. I have the attitude of the Midwest certainly as strongly as I have emotionally that of Japan, though you can say I am interested in the ideas of Japan. But I'm strongly interested in the ideas of the West, as well.

*Hakutani:* Did this idea of the West which you see in you, your father, Pound, Dreiser, and others occur to them because they had grown up in the soil?

*Noguchi:* Not necessarily. Anybody can be like that. My father did not grow up in that soil, but he became like that. He and others like him were attracted to the openness and freedom of the West, which may not be the classical view of the aesthetics. It's not, in a way; it's beyond aesthetics. It's a kind of nonaesthetic openness. And I have that kind of feeling myself.

*Hakutani:* Every artist has a desire to be different from any other. Critics used to say that Dreiser, for instance, was influenced by such and such writers, say Zola and Balzac, but if you had read all his work, you would realize he just wanted to be unique and always wanted to create something new.

*Noguchi:* That's right. Already there was something in this Midwestern journalist, a kind of ambition which is not quite ordinary. I knew Dreiser in the last years of his life. I used to see him. I used to go to the cafe run by a woman named Belle Livingston, who was a type of Mae West. She opened the cafe on Park Avenue, and I used to go there and Dreiser would go there, right here near the Racquet Club.

*Hakutani:* Did you happen to meet Helen Richardson, his second wife?

*Noguchi:* No, I didn't. He didn't have any woman around him at the time, as you know. Maybe he did.

*Michiko Hakutani:* May I ask a personal question, if you don't mind? I'm curious about something as a student of art. You were married once, but you haven't been married since.[32] Why is that?

*Noguchi:* I'm too old. [He and I laugh.]

*Michiko Hakutani:* Is it because of what happened to your father and mother?

*Noguchi:* Well, marriage and art don't mix, I don't think. The idea of freedom that the artist needs is not congenial to marriage. I don't know whether or not I could be a good husband, and by now, I think, I've found it too late for me to attempt to be a husband.

*Hakutani:* As you know, your former wife has been very active as a Representative in the Japanese Parliament.

*Noguchi:* Yes, she has.

*Michiko Hakutani:* Was your decision not to marry again partly influenced by your view of your parents?

*Noguchi:* It may very well have been. I may not have approved of what my father did. I decided that I was not inclined to make similar mistakes.

*Michiko Hakutani:* I have one more question, if I may. Why did you change your name from Isamu Gilmour to Isamu Noguchi? I'm curious because when I make something and put my name to it, critics often say my work has a Japanese influence.

*Noguchi:* Your name doesn't mean much; their discussion of you does. You change. You are different if you get married and call yourself, say, Kazuo Jones instead of Kazuo Itoh.

*Michiko Hakutani:* Did you think about it when you changed your name?

*Noguchi:* At that time all I wanted to do was to become an artist. If I had let my imagination dictate to me, I would have taken some other name, but I couldn't think of anything better. For one thing, I spent my childhood in Japan from when I was two until when I was thirteen. And I associated in some way the life of art closer to Japan than to America. The man who made me into a sculptor was an Italian named Onorio Ruotolo. Mr. Borglum was no good, but Mr. Ruotolo was my kind. He was the one who said I should be a sculptor. Well, in those days, to be an Italian was also to be a foreigner here. America was composed of many foreigners Italians, Germans. . . . I used to know a German sympathizer who was put into jail although he was not a German.

*Hakutani:* But your mother was an American. Noguchi is such a common name in Japan as you know. The most famous Noguchi in Japan is Dr. Hideyo Noguchi.[33]

*Noguchi:* He was very kind to me. He was the one who said, "Don't be a doctor." He was the one who said, "If you have to be a doctor, come to my place and I'll help you." He was with the Rockefeller Institute. He had a sort of fix for me to become a doctor if I wanted to, but he said, "Don't give up art." So I probably listened to him.

*Hakutani:* The relationship between you and your father is fascinating, but his views about you are unknown.

*Noguchi:* There is very little to draw on. It would be more interesting to see the relationship between my father and my mother. It was almost like a business relationship. She was an excellent editor for him. When he got back to Japan, he didn't have the services of a severe editor that she no doubt was.

*Hakutani:* I'm also interested in your views about your mother, but since you're such a well-known figure, I thought your views about your father would be fascinating.

*Noguchi:* It would be more interesting, however, to examine myself in relation to America and myself in relation to Japan. The problem is that I don't think I fit in. I'm not understood either way; over here I am Japanese, and over there I am American, a peculiar sort of thing.

*Hakutani:* Your father was regarded in the same way.

*Noguchi:* Yes, his problem was that because he had written good poems in English, he was considered to be an English poet, not a Japanese poet. My brother Michio, who was recently reading my father's poems in Japanese, told me that my father had tried to translate his English poems into Japanese, but that they are terrible in Japanese. He says my father did not understand the Japanese language.

*Hakutani:* But his critical writings in English and in Japanese are both impeccable, for his ideas are identical in both languages.

*Noguchi:* I'm merely quoting my brother Michio, who can read English sufficiently well to note the difference. I really don't know why he says they are terrible in Japanese; it's possible that my father couldn't translate them. Perhaps somebody else can. I know he was an excellent creative writer; he was occupied with the essence of creation no disturbances as you might say. When he went back to Japan, he ran into all kinds of disturbances.

*Hakutani:* He had a big family to support, and now I can see from his writings in Japan that he might have wasted some of his talent there.

*Noguchi:* Now you see why I don't get married.

*Hakutani:* Recently a friend and colleague of mine has sent me an article about you in Japan, which appeared in the *Asahi Newspaper.*

*Noguchi:* Actually there have been an awful lot of things about me in the press in Japan recently, [it's been] full of them, because I got a prize, a Kyoto prize.

*Hakutani:* So they're trying to reclaim you.

*Noguchi:* Oh, yes, I'm suddenly popular there.

*Hakutani:* You have also been frequently talked about in the Japanese-American press. They say that, with Henry Moore dead, you are one of the two or three eminent living sculptors of our times. Do you go back to Europe sometimes? How often do you go back to Japan?

*Noguchi:* Yes, sometimes I go to Europe. I have a studio in Shikoku Island and go there twice a year. I like it there very much. If you ask me if I go there because of my father, I doubt it very much. I would say no, but maybe yes, if it is because of my mother. I think, probably, I find myself closer to Japan nowadays than to America.

*Hakutani:* Because you're older now?

*Noguchi:* I find things more congenial over there than in America food, people, and so forth, as you know. It's curious, I mean, considering my mother she was also very fond of Japan so that maybe I was influenced by her in that sense, too. I think I'm more influenced by my mother than by my father.

*Hakutani:* Do people in Shikoku know that you have a studio there and work there? I don't mean politicians.

*Noguchi:* I don't know any politicians, but I know some people there. Sometimes letters from the United States are addressed, "Isamu Noguchi, Shikoku, Japan," and I get them. I can be very at home in Japan, and I don't know why I come here.

*Hakutani:* You have a studio in Long Island.

*Noguchi:* Yes, I know, I know, but I'm trying to establish something separate from me. I'm making a museum in that place so I don't have to be here.

*Hakutani:* Are you going to do the same with the Shikoku Studio?

*Noguchi:* Maybe.

It is time to leave, but he seems tireless and could carry on our conversation into the evening. I thank him for the opportunity to interview him. He reminds us of lunch together at the Long Island studio the next day, the address, and the way to get there. He sounds like a veteran New Yorker. He may be thinking of a busy schedule to follow at the studio, his work, his visitors, and all, but he is poised and relaxed. Like a courteous but warm Japanese gentleman, he slowly comes to the door, bidding us goodbye only till the next day. We are bound for our hotel to attend more conference activities in the evening. As we hurriedly walk back through the busy streets, we keep thinking of him and his father and of all those events that had a hand in the making of an extraordinary relationship between father and son.

Isamu Noguchi died of heart failure at 84 on December 30, 1988, in New York. It is my great regret that he died before the publication of this article.

NOTES

[1] R. Buckminster Fuller, "Foreword" in Isamu Noguchi, *A Sculptor's World* (Harper & Row, 1968), p. 7.

[2] That Poe's poems made a great impact upon the aspiring poet from Japan is indicated by a close similarity in a certain part of "Lines" [*The Pilgrimage* (Kamakura: Valley Press, 1909), II, p. 79], one of Noguchi's early poems in English, and Poe's "Eulalie." When Noguchi's poems, including "Lines," appeared in *The Lark, The Chap Book,* and *The Philistine,* in 1896, he was accused of plagiarism by some critics while he was defended by his friends. Noguchi later refuted the charge in his autobiography, *The Story of Yone Noguchi Told by Himself* (London: Chatto & Windus, 1914), pp. 18-19). Hereafter cited as *Story.* About this controversy, see Don B. Graham, "Yone Noguchi's 'Poe Mania,'" *Markham Review,* 4 (1974), 58-60.

[3] See Willa Cather, *The World and the Parish: Willa Cather's Articles and Reviews, 1893-1902* (University of Nebraska Press, 1970), II, p. 579.

[4] Yone Noguchi, Preface, *Japan and America* (Tokyo: Keio University Press, 1921]).

[5] *Japan and America,* p. 111.

[6] While it is well known that Noguchi's work had a considerable impact upon such major poets in Japan as Toson Shimazaki (1872-1943). Sakutaro Hagiwara (1886-1942), and Kotaro Takamura (1883-1956), it is quite possible that Noguchi also had noteworthy influence upon such poets as Yeats, Pound, and Tagore, and above all upon the Imagist poets of the day.

[7] Yone Noguchi, *Collected English Letters,* ed. Ikuko Atsumi (Tokyo: Yone Noguchi Society, 1975), pp. 210-211. Hereafter cited as *English Letters.*

[8] Yone Noguchi had earlier met Yeats in London, where *From the Eastern Sea* was published in 1903. In a letter of February 24, 1903, to his wife Leonie Gilmour he wrote: "I made many a nice young, lovely, kind friend among literary *geniuses* (attention!). W. B. Yeats or Laurence Binyon, Moore and Bridges. They are so good; they invite me almost everyday. They are jolly companions. Their hairs are not long, I tell you" (*English Letters,* p. 106).

[9] *English Letters,* pp. 220-221.

[10] *A Sculptor's World,* p. 31.

[11] *Story,* pp. 185-187.

[12] His project goes back to 1926, when Isamu Noguchi designed (in England) papier-mâché masks for the Japanese dancer, Michio Itoh, in the production of Yeats's Noh drama entitled *At the Hawk's Well.* At that time, Isamu Noguchi was virtually unknown in England except as the son of Yone Noguchi, the most well-known living Japanese poet and critic among English writers.

[13] *A Sculptor's World,* p. 17.

[14] *A Sculptor's World,* pp. 16, 40.

[15] Yone Noguchi, "By the Engakuji Temple: Moon Night," *The Pilgrimage,* I, p. 5. The Engakuji Temple in Kamakura, an ancient capital of Japan, was founded in the thirteenth century by Tokimune Hojo, hero of the feudal government, who was a great believer in Zen Buddhism.

[16] *Story,* pp. 231-32.

[17] *A Sculptor's World,* p. 39.

[18] Yone Noguchi, *Through the Torii* (Four Seas, 1922), p. 132.

[19] Sam Hunter, Preface, *Isamu Noguchi,* (Andre Emmerich Gallery & Pace Gallery, 1980).

[20] It occurred to us later that his apartment has only this one room; thus the living room is also his bedroom. The furnishings consist of a self-made bed on a tatami mattress with very few pieces of furniture around as in a Japanese room, and there were two or three sculptures placed nearby.

[21] The initial conversation, which was conducted in Japanese, I have translated into English.

[22] This is the last statement Noguchi made in Japanese.

[23] Two of Itoh's younger brothers, Kinsaku Itoh and Koreya Senda (who also distinghished themselves in the theater in Japan after World War II) are both famous for their work as stage designers and as dancers.

[24] *The Iris,* entitled *Ayame-gusa* in Japanese, was discontinued after the second issue, December 1906. The first, issue, June 1906, had a twenty-one page introduction in Japanese and contained ninety-two pages of poems by Arthur Symons, Joaquin Miller, Josephine Reston Peabody, W.B. Yeats, and John B. Tabbs, besides Yone Noguchi. *The Iris,* No. 2, entitled *Toyohata-gumo* in Japanese, published in its English section poems by Arthur Symons, Madison Cowein, Laurence Housman, Mary MacNeil Fenollosa, Richard Hovey, Edith M. Thomas, Frank Putnam, and Duchess Sutherland, besides Yone Noguchi.

[25] More than twenty letters between Frank Putnam and Yone Noguchi from 1901 to 1920 survive. Isamu Noguchi obtained them from Putnam's daughter, who lives in Houston, Texas; a xerox copy of these letters is available in the Keio University Library Rare Book and Manuscript Room.

[26] This sculpture, in bronze (size 18 1/4 inches, base 4 3/4 by 4 1/4 inches) is a gift (dated 1921) of the Arts Club of Chicago to the Art Institute of Chicago.

[27] Yone Noguchi visited other Zen temples in the Kamakura-Fujisawa area during his writing career in Japan. One of his best poems is entitled "By the Engakuji Temple: Moon Night" (*The Pilgrimage,* I, p. 5).

[28] The *Asahi Newspaper* has been one of the most influential dailies in Japan, much like the *New York Times* in the United States and the *London Times* in England.

[29] Hifumi (1908-86), Yone Noguchi's oldest daughter by his Japanese wife, was married to Usaburo Toyama, a Japanese art historian and the editor of the three-volume collection, *Essays on Yone Noguchi.* Michio Noguchi is a photographer who has been working for Isamu Noguchi over the years.

[30] Noguchi stepped into the kitchen for a few minutes, brought a pot of green tea, and poured it into three cups, which he said, were made by Rosanjin, one of the most celebrated Japanese potters in modern times.

[31] *Ukiyoye,* "pictures of the floating world," is a style of genre painting that flourished in seventeenth-century Japan. Its main theme, man's transient, fleeting life on earth, resembles in some aspects the *carpe diem* theme in the West.

[32] In the early 1950s, Isamu Noguchi was married to the famous Japanese actress and singer Yoshiko (Shirley) Yamaguchi. Like Arthur Miller's marriage to Marilyn Monroe, Noguchi's also ended in divorce.

[33] Like Yone Noguchi, Hideyo Noguchi (1876-1928) came to the United States as a young man. It has become

a legend in modern Japanese history that he was an eminent bacteriologist in the West and that while conducting research in Africa, he died of typhoid fever, having discovered the cause of the disease.

## Yoshinobu Hakutani (excerpt date 1990)

SOURCE: An introduction to *Selected Writings of Yone Noguchi: An East-West Literary Assimilation,* Volume 1, Associated University Presses, 1990, pp. 13-29.

[*In the following excerpt, Hakutani provides a short biography of his subject, and discusses the primary influences, both eastern and western, on Noguchi's poetry.*]

1

Yone Noguchi was born in a small town near Nagoya in 1875. In the late 1880s the young Noguchi, taking great interest in English texts used in a public school, read Samuel Smiles's writings on self-help. Perhaps inspired by Smiles, but in any case dissatisfied with his public school instruction, he withdrew from a middle school in Nagoya and went up to Tokyo in 1890. At a prep school there he diligently read such Victorian writings as Thomas Macauley's, exactly the type of reading many a literary aspirant was doing on the other side of the Pacific.

A year later, detesting the national university that an ambitious young man of his circumstance would be expected to attend, Noguchi entered Keio University, one of the oldest private colleges in Japan, where he studied Herbert Spencer and Thomas Carlyle, whose hero worship, in particular, made an impact on him. At the same time he devoured such works as Washington Irving's *Sketch Book,* Oliver Goldsmith's "The Deserted Village," and Thomas Gray's "Elegy Written in a Country Churchyard." He even tried his hand at translating these eighteenth-century English poems into Japanese. On the other hand, he did not ignore his native culture. His lifelong interest in haiku and Zen dates from this period, and the frequent visits he made to Zen temples while in college established a practice he continued later in his career in Japan.[1]

Although two years of college provided him with omnivorous reading in English, the young aspiring poet was not content with his education, for he had been dreaming of living and writing in an English-speaking country. In the last decade of the nineteenth century, Japanese immigration to the United States was at a beginning stage, so it was not difficult for a young man without technical skills to obtain a passport and visa. His initial plans were to look for some sort of employment near San Francisco, where he arrived in December 1893 with little money in his pocket, and to continue his studies.

For the next two years he lived mainly among the Japanese immigrants in California. For almost a year he was employed by a Japanese language newspaper in San Francisco and spent a great deal of time translating news sent from Japan of the Sino-Japanese War. As a Japanese patriot, he was delighted to learn about the triumphant military campaign in China. In late 1894 his industry and interests led him to walk from San Francisco to Palo Alto, where he was able to live for several months at a prep school near the campus of Stanford University and to read Edgar Allan Poe's poems.[2] His continued reading of *Sketch Book,* particularly Irving's portrayal of life in England, inspired him to plan travels some day across the Atlantic.

The turning point of Noguchi's life in America came in 1896, when, twenty-one years old and already an aspiring poet in English, he paid homage to the Western poet Joaquin Miller. Miller in turn admired Noguchi's youth and enthusiam. Except for a few occasions when Noguchi had to travel to Los Angeles, partly on foot, or to walk down the hills to see his publishers in San Francisco, he led a hermit's life for three years in Miller's mountain hut in Oakland. Through Miller he became acquainted with Edwin Markham, Dr. Charles Warren Stoddard, and the publishers Gelett Burgess and Porter Garnett.

Within a year of meeting Miller, Noguchi published some of his earliest poems in three ephemeral journals of the day, *The Lark, The Chap Book,* and *The Philistine.* These poems attracted critical attention, and in the following year he brought out his first collections of poetry, ***Seen and Unseen or, Monologues of a Homeless Snail*** and ***The Voice of the Valley.***[3] These, too, received praise. Willa Cather, for instance, commenting on Yone Noguchi and Bliss Carman, the Canadian poet, wrote, "While Noguchi is by no means a great poet in the large, complicated modern sense of the word, he has more true inspiration, more melody from within than many a greater man."[4] Despite initial success, however, his literary production became erratic, and his fragile reputation was not sustained for long. Like the wandering bard traditional in Japan, the young Noguchi spent his energy walking and reading in the high mountains and in the fields. Of this experience he wrote in his journal: "I thank the rain, the most gentle rain of the Californian May, that drove me into a barn at San Miguel for two days and made me study 'Hamlet' line after line; whatever I know about it today is from my reading in that haystack."[5]

Later he traveled to Chicago, Boston, and New York, where he published, under the pseudonym Miss Morning Glory, a novella about a Japanese parlormaid.[6] After the turn of the century he journeyed to England, where he published his third volume of poetry in English, ***From the Eastern Sea.***[7] This collection stirred some interest among the English readers, especially Thomas Hardy and George Meredith. "Your poems," Meredith wrote to Noguchi, "are another instance of the energy, mysteriousness, and poetical feeling of the Japanese, from whom we are receiving much instruction" (***Japan and America,*** p. 111).

Yone Noguchi's wandering journey came to an end when he returned to Japan in 1904, the year Isamu Noguchi was born and left behind in America with his mother. The elder Noguchi became a professor of English at Keio University in Tokyo, the same college from which he had withdrawn eleven years earlier. Among the well over ninety books he wrote in Japan, many of them in English, four are genuine collections of English poetry.[8] The rest ranges from books of literary and art criticism to travelogues. In the midst of his burgeoning literary career in Japan, he revisited England in 1913 to deliver a lecture at Oxford's Magdalen College, and once came back to America in 1919.

His role in East-West literary relations can scarcely be overestimated. The significance of his work should become even more evident when one tries to determine the nature of his influences on such major poets in Japan as Toson Shimazaki (1872-1943), Sakutaro Hagiwara (1886-1942), and Kotaro Takamura (1883-1956), as well as on some of the poets abroad, for example, W. B. Yeats, Ezra Pound, and Rabindranath Tagore, but above all on the imagist poets of the day.

The standard explanation for the influences of Japanese poetry, especially haiku, on T. E. Hulme and Ezra Pound is that they studied Japanese poetics through the Harvard sinologist Ernest Fenollosa, who had a poor command of the Japanese language; but since Noguchi's later poetry, collected in *The Pilgrimage,* and his literary criticism, *The Spirit of Japanese Poetry*[9] in particular, were widely circulated, the standard explanation seems questionable. (A detailed discussion of the influences Noguchi's writings might have had upon imagism will be given in the introduction to the second volume of this edition.) Much more likely is the possibility that the imagists responded directly to the example of their fellow poet Noguchi. Pound, for instance, wrote Noguchi the following letter:

c/o Elkin Mathews

Vigo St. London

Sep. 2, 1911

Dear Yone Noguchi:

I want to thank you very much for your lovely books & for your kindness in sending them to me.

I had, of course, known of you, but I am much occupied with my mediaeval studies & had neglected to read your books altho' they lie with my own in Mathews shop & I am very familiar with the appearance of their covers.

I am reading those you sent me but I do not yet know what to say of them except that they have delighted me. Besides it is very hard to write to you until I know more about you, you are older than I am I gather from the dates of the poems you have been to New York. You are giving us the spirit of Japan, is it not? very much as I am trying to deliver from obscurity certain forgotten odours of Provence & Tuscany. . . .

. . . . .

Of your country I know almost nothing surely if the east and the west are ever to understand each other that understanding must come slowly & come first through the arts.

You ask about my "criticism". There is some criticism in the "Spirit of Romance" & there will be some in the prefaces to the "Guido" and the "Arnaut". But I might be more to the point if we who are artists should discuss the matters of technique & motive between ourselves. Also if you should write about these matters I would discuss your letters with Mr. Yeats and likewise my answers.

I have not answered before because your letter & your books have followed me through America, France, Italy, Germany and have reached me but lately.

Let me thank you again for sending them, and believe me

Yours very sincerely

Ezra Pound[10]

In the 1920s and 1930s Noguchi was also the most well-known interpreter of Japanese visual arts in the West, especially in England. Beginning with *The Spirit of Japanese Art,*[11] he published, in English, ten volumes with colorful illustrations dealing with traditionally celebrated painters, such as Hiroshige, Korin, Utamaro, Hokusai, and Harunobu. Yeats, whose interest in the noh play is well known, wrote this letter to Noguchi:[12]

4 Broad St., Oxford

June 27, [1921?]

Dear Noguchi:

Though I have been so long in writing, your **"Hiroshige"** has given me the greatest pleasure. I take more and more pleasure from oriental art; find more and more that it accords with what I aim at in my own work. The European painter of the last two or three hundred years grows strange to me as I grow older, begins to speak as if in a foreign tongue. When a Japanese, or Mogul, or Chinese painter seems to say, "Have I not drawn a beautiful scene", one agrees at once, but when a modern European painter says so one does not agree so quickly, if at all. All your painters are simple, like the writers of Scottish ballads or the inventors of Irish stories, but one feels that Orpen and John have relatives in the patent office who are conscious of being at the fore-front of time. The old French poets were simple as the modern are not, & I find in François Villon the same thoughts, with more intellectual power, that I find in the Gaelic poet [Raftery]. I would be simple myself but I do not know how. I am always turning over pages like those you have sent me, hoping that in my old age I may discover how. I wish somehow Japanese would tell us all about the lives . . . their talk, their loves, their religion, their friends . . . of these painters. I would like to know these things minutely and to know too what their houses looked like, and if they still stand, to know all those things that are known about Blake, and about Turner, and about Rossetti. It might make it more easy to understand their simplicity. A form of beauty scarcely lasts a generation with us, but it lasts with you for centuries. You no more want to change it than a pious man wants to change the Lord's Prayer, or the Crucifix on the wall [words blurred] at least not unless we have infected you with our egotism.

I wish I had found my way to your country a year ago & were still there, for my own remains un[words blurred] as I dreaded that it would. I have not seen Galway for a long time now for I am warned that it is no place for wife and child.

Yours sincerely

W. B. Yeats

(*English Letters*, pp. 220-21)

Noguchi's reputation as a poet and a critic grew in the West through the early thirties, but World War II severed his ties to the West just as his relationship to his son Isamu had been strained ever since his birth. "I am getting old," Yone Noguchi wrote his son after the war, "and feel so sad and awful with what happened in Japan."[13] In 1947, in the midst of the chaos and devastation brought about by the war, without quite accomplishing his mission as he had wished, he died in Japan. Literary history, however, would amply justify that Yone Noguchi had played the most important role in modern times as a poet and interpreter of the divergent cultures of the East and the West.

2

Like his famous sculptor son, Isamu Noguchi, Yone Noguchi evolved his own distinct style, which drew upon both Western and Eastern traditions. Noguchi's first book, *Seen and Unseen,* shows that he was initially inspired by Walt Whitman and Joaquin Miller. The affinity with nature, as reflected in these poems, is clearly derived from Japanese traditions, but the sweeping lines and his romanticized self, which abound in his poetry, are reminiscent of Whitman:

> The flat-boarded earth, nailed down at night,
>     rusting under the darkness:
> The Universe grows smaller,
>     palpitating against its destiny:
> My chilly soul center of the world gives seat
>     to audible tears the songs of the cricket.
> I drink the darkness of a corner of the Universe,
>
>                 . . . . .
>
> I am as a lost wind among the countless atoms
>     of high Heaven![14]

What unites the two men with different backgrounds is not only their style but their world vision. In "Song of

Myself" Whitman includes, under the name of Self, body and soul, good and evil, man and woman. The conclusion of this section in the poem, where he introduces the concept of balance, is a lyrical passage that celebrates the ecstasy of love. Whitman writes: "Prodigal, you have given me love therefore I to you give love!/ O unspeakable passionate love."[15] After this lyrical outburst he declares: "I am not the poet of goodness only, I do not decline to be the poet of wickedness also . . . / I moisten the roots of all that has grown." As the poet of balance, Whitman accepts both good and evil; because he moistens the roots of all that has grown, he can call himself "a kosmos" (*Complete Poetry,* pp. 40 41). Noguchi's kosmos in **"My Universe"** has similar manifestations:

> The world is round; no-headed, no-footed,
>     having no left side, no right side!
> And to say *Goodness* is to say *Badness:*
> And to say *Badness* is to say *Goodness.*
>
>                 . . . . .
>
> The greatest robber seems like saint:
> The cunning man seems like nothing-wanted
>     beast!
> Who is the real man in the face of God?
> One who has fame not known,
> One who has Wisdom not applauded,
> One who has Goodness not respected:
> One who hasn't loved Wisdom dearly!
> One who hasn't hated Foolishness strongly!
>                         (*Seen and Unseen,* p. 50)

Like Whitman, Noguchi believed in monism, and his ultimate goal in writing poetry was to achieve the ecstasies of the self in nature. Many of his early poems thus abound in the image in which life flows in upon the self and others in nature. While Whitman, in "Song of Myself," reincarnates himself into a sensitive quahaug on the beach, Noguchi, in **"Seas of Loneliness,"** identifies himself with a lone quail:

> Underneath the void-colored shade of the trees,
>     my 'self' passed as a drowsy cloud into
>     Somewhere.
> I see my soul floating upon the face of the deep,
>     nay the faceless face of the deepless deep
>
>                 . . . . .
>
> Alas, I, without wisdom, without foolishness,
>     without goodness, without badness, am
>     like god, a negative god, at least!
> Is that a quail? One voice out of the back-hill
>     jumped into the ocean of loneliness.
>                         (*Seen and Unseen,* p. 32)

Although he became a different kind of nature poet after he returned to Japan, his later poems still bear out Whitman's influence. The last stanza of Noguchi's religious poem **"By a Buddha Temple"** reads:

> Ah, through the mountains and rivers,
>     Let thy vastness thrill like that of air;

I read thy word in the flash of a leaf,
    Thy mystery in the whisper of a grass.[16]

Grass, which both poets loved, is perhaps the most common and universal image in nature poetry. Such a technique, however, not only reveals the poet's sincere admiration of nature, but betrays his abhorrence of civilization. In "Song of Myself" Whitman declares his independence of "civilization," which is represented by "houses and rooms." He detests the perfumes that envelop the domestic atmosphere because the fragrance is artificially distilled; the outdoor atmosphere, he argues, "is not a perfume, it has no taste of the distillation, it is odorless" (*Complete Poetry,* p. 25). One of the disappointments Noguchi felt upon his return to Japan was the rise of commercialism he witnessed. The beauty of the seashores near Tokyo was often marred by "the bathing crowd." But after summer, "with the autumn mellow and kind, the season of the clearest sky and softest breeze" (*Kamakura,* p. 38), he was able to recapture what Whitman called "Nature without check with original energy" (*Complete Poetry,* p. 25):

Into the homelessness of the sea I awoke:
    Oh, my heart of the wind and spray!
I am glad to be no-man to-day
    With the laughter and dance of the sea-soul.[17]

Noguchi's aversion to people, and to materialism in particular, originated from his mentor Joaquin Miller, "the Poet of the Sierras," as he called him. It was Miller who urged the fledgling poet to live "amid the roses, quite high above the cities and people." Noguchi pays Miller this compliment: "Never did I think Miller was particularly eccentric, never even once during my long stay with him; he was the most natural man; and his picturesqueness certainly was not a crime." Once Miller brought him a bunch of poppies ("The golden poppy is God's gold" is Miller's song), saying that they were the state flower. Then, he recalls, Miller's lecture followed:

"The sweetest flowers grow closest to the ground; you must not measure Nature by its size: if there is any measure, it will be that of beauty; and where is beauty there is truth. First of all, you must know Nature by yourself, not through the book. It would be ten thousand times better to know by your own knowledge the colour, the perfume and the beauty of a single tiny creeping vine in the valley than to know all the Rocky Mountains through a book; books are nothing. Read the history written on the brows of stars!" (*Story of Noguchi,* pp. 55-63)

Such an attitude Miller inspired in him led to the art of poetry Noguchi practiced in his early work. Remembering Miller's often repeated statement, "My life is like the life of a bird," he, in **"Alone in the Canyon,"** tried to relive the life of a creature, or merge himself into the existence of a natural element:

"Good-bye my beloved family" I am to-night
    buried under the sheeted coldness:
The dark weights of loneliness make me immovable!
Hark! the pine-wind blows, blows!

Lo, the feeble, obedient leaves flee down to the
    ground
    fearing the stern-lipped wind voices!
Alas, the crickets' flutes to-night, are broken!
The homeless snail climbing up the pillow,
    stares upon the silvered star-tears on my eyes!
The fish-like night-fogs flowering with mystery
    on the Bare-limbed branches:
The stars above put their love-beamed fires out,
    one by one
Oh, I am alone! Who knows my to-night's feeling!
                    (*Seen and Unseen,* p. 25)

Far from being sentimentalized, man's harsh plight in nature is underscored by the images of coldness: the frozen ground, the blowing pine-wind, the falling leaves, the crying crickets, the slowly climbing snail, the silvered stars above, the mysterious night-fogs. This transformation of man into nature enables Noguchi, in **"To an Unknown Poet,"** to pose the following question: "When I am lost in the deep body of the mist on the hill, / The world seems built with me as its pillar! / Am I the god upon the face of the deep, deepless deepness in the Beginning?" (*Seen and Unseen,* p. 9). In both poems Noguchi is speculating about the spiritual and transcendental power of man; conceptually, at least, he is uniting the will of man with the spirit of nature.

What Noguchi learned at the "Heights of the Sierras" was not only Miller's habit "to loaf and invite his own soul" in the presence of nature, a way of seeing nature, but also a way of experiencing love. For Noguchi, Miller was "the singer of 'a brother soul in some sweet bird, a sister spirit in a rose,' not the maker of loud-voiced ballads like the tide of a prairie fire or the marches of the Sierra mountains, but the dove-meek poet of love and humanity which . . . grow best and sweetest in silence." Interestingly enough, Noguchi's autobiography, written in Japan years later, reprints Miller's favorite poem on silence:

Aye, Silence seems some maid at prayer,
God's arm about her when she prays
And where she prays and everywhere,
Or storm-strewn days or sundown days
What ill to Silence can befall
Since Silence knows no ill at all?

Vast silence seems some twilight sky
That learns as with her weight of stars
To rest, to rest, no more to roam,
But rest and rest eternally.
She loosens and lets down the bars,
She brings the kind-eyed cattle home,
She breathes the fragrant field of hay
and heaven is not far away.
                    (*Story of Noguchi,* pp. 67-68)

Many of Noguchi's poems, written both under the tutelage of Miller and later in Japan, echo Miller's ideas and methods of writing. In **"My Poetry"** (1897) Noguchi writes:

My Poetry begins with the tireless songs of the
    cricket,

on the lean gray haired hill, in sober-faced
    evening.
And the next page is Stillness
And what then, about the next to that?
Alas, the god puts his universe-covering hand
    over its sheets!
*"Master, take off your hand for the humble
    servant!"*
Asked in vain:
How long for my meditation?

                    **(*Seen and Unseen,* p. 22)**

**"Bird of Silence"** (1909) deals with the same theme:

Lonely ghost away from laughter and life,
Wing down, I welcome thee,
From the skies of thoughts and stars,
Bird of Silence, mystery's brother, as white
And aloof as is mystery,
Tired of humanity and of voice,
With thee, bird of Silence, I long to sail
Beyond the seas where Time and sorrows die,

       . . . . .

I lost the voice as a willow spray
To whom a thrill is its golden song,
As a lotus whose break of cup
Is the sudden cry after aerial dance.

                    **(*Pilgrimage* 1:53-54)**

In this piece the poet is preoccupied with the idea of silence, because silence is "whole and perfect." Silence in nature provides man with rest and happiness, creating a sense of eternity. Through silence, the poet implies, you are able to establish "your true friendship with the ghosts and the beautiful. . . . You have to abandon yourself to the beautiful only to create the absolute beauty and grandeur that makes this our human world look trifling." Through imagination, then, you can achieve "true love, when the reality of the external world ceases to be a standard, and you yourself will be a revelation, therefore a great art itself, of hope and passion which will never fail."[18]

The theme of silence in Noguchi's poetry is, furthermore, related to that of death and eternity. In **"Eternal Death"** (1897), death is treated as if it were alive: "a thief . . . with long and dusty beard," "the poetry-planted garden of silence," "the pearl-fruited orchard of meditation," "the song of my heart strings." To Noguchi, life and death are but two phases of the human soul; death is as much "a triumph to me" as life (**Seen and Unseen,** p. 43). In **"Moon Night"** (1909), written at a Buddhist temple, he concludes the poem with this stanza:

Down the tide of the sweet night
(O the ecstasy's gentle rise!)
The birds, flowers and trees
Are glad at once to fall
Into Oblivion's ruin white.

                  **(*Pilgrimage* 1:5-6)**

"The real poetry," Noguchi once stated, "should be accidental and also absolute" (**Japan and America,** p. 98).

Such a poem as **"Moon Night"** captures the exact circumstances where the natural phenomena reveal both meanings of the accidental and the absolute. His method is, indeed, akin to that of great Japanese poets who write only of isolated aspects of nature but sing mainly of infinity from their accidental revelation.

3

Although Noguchi owes his poetry to Whitman and Miller, one cannot overlook the Japanese poetics that underlies much of his work. The most obvious tie can be found in its subject matter. Just as Japanese haiku do not treat such subjects as physical love, sex, war, beasts, earthquakes, and floods, Noguchi's poems shun eroticism, ugliness, hate, evil, and untruth. Unlike some poets in the West, Japanese poets abhor sentimentalism, romance, and vulgarity. "The Japanese poetry," Noguchi cautions, "is that of the moon, stars, and flowers, that of a bird and waterfall for the noisiest" (**Spirit of Japanese Poetry,** pp. 18-19). Japanese poets' way of avoiding the negative aspects of life, such as illness, is best illustrated by the poem that Basho, the most celebrated haiku poet, wrote at his deathbed:

Lying ill on journey
Ah, my dreams
Run about the ruins of fields.[19]

Japanese poetry is focused on nature because, as Noguchi says, "We human beings are not merely a part of Nature, but Nature itself" (**Spirit of Japanese Poetry,** p. 19). To be sure, this is pantheism; he is accepting man and nature as a whole and leaving them as they are. But, more importantly, he is suggesting that Japanese poets always go to nature to make man's life meaningful, to make "humanity more intensive." They share an artistic susceptibility where, as Noguchi writes, "the sunlight falls on the laughter of woods and waters, where the birds sing by the flowers" (**Spirit of Japanese Poetry,** p. 34). This mystical affinity between man and nature, between the beauty of love and the beauty of natural phenomena, is best stated in this verse by Noguchi:

It's accident to exist as a flower or a poet;
A mere twist of evolution but from the same force:
I see no form in them but only beauty in evidence;
It's the single touch of their imagination to get the
    embodiment of a poet or a flower:
To be a poet is to be a flower,
To be the dancer is to make the singer sing.[20]

The fusion of man and nature, and the intensity of love and beauty with which it occurs, can be amply seen in haiku. Noguchi regards Kikaku's haiku on the autumn moon as exemplary:

Autumn's full moon:
Lo, the shadows of a pine tree
Upon the mats![21]

The beauty of the moonlight in Kikaku's poem is not only humanized but intensified by the shadows of a pine tree that fall upon the mats. "The beauty of the shadow," Noguchi observes, "is far more luminous than the light itself, with such a decorativeness, particularly when it stamps the dustless mats as a dragon-shaped ageless pine tree" (***Through the Torii,*** p. 132). Noguchi himself unifies the image of man and the image of nature in his own work. **"Lines"** (1909) begins with this verse:

> The sun I worship,
> Not for the light, but for the shadows of the trees
>  he draws:
> Oh shadows welcome like an angel's bower,
> Where I build Summer-day dreams!
> Not for her love, but for the love's memory,

The poem ends on another suggestion of paradox:

> To a bird's song I listen,
> Not for the voice, but for the silence following
>  after the song:
> O Silence fresh from the bosom of voice!
> Melody from the Death-Land whither my face
>  does ever turn!
>
>                (***Pilgrimage*** 2:79)

As Kikaku unifies the images of the moonlight and the mats, Noguchi unifies those of the sun and the love, the bird and the poet. Through the paradox of union both poets express the affinity of man and nature while at the same time maintaining man's separate identity and autonomy.

The most important tradition by which Noguchi's poetry is influenced is that of Zen. Zen practice calls for the austerity of the human mind; one should not allow his individuality to control his actions. "Drink tea when you are thirsty," says Noguchi, "eat food in your hunger. Rise with dawn, and sleep when the sun sets. But your trouble will begin when you let desire act freely; you have to soar above all personal desire" (***Story of Nougchi,*** p. 242). Zen does not recognize human reality, the existence of good and evil, because it is but the creation of man's will rather than the spirit of nature. The aim of the Zen poet, therefore, is to understand the spirit of nature. Observing the silent rites of a Zen priest, Noguchi once wrote: "Let the pine tree be green, and the roses red. We have to observe the mystery of every existence. . . . The language of silence cannot be understood by the way of reason, but by the power of impulse, which is abstraction" (***Story of Noguchi,*** pp. 231-32).

To demonstrate a state of Zen, he composed the following poem when he visited the Engakuji Temple:

> Through the breath of perfume,
> (O music of musics)
> Down creeps the moon
> To fill my cup of song
> With memory's wine
>
> Across the song of night and moon,
> (O perfume of perfumes!)
> My soul, as wind
> Only roams astray . . . [22]

The poet's motivation for the union with nature, represented by the fragrance of the atmosphere and the moonlight, does not stem from his knowledge or desire. It is not the poet who is filling his "cup of song," but the moon that is creeping down. In the second stanza the poet accomplishes a state of Zen where, giving himself, he enters wholly into his actions "the song of night and moon." That his soul is roaming astray suggests that he is giving up the ego. The loss of individuality within the union with nature is a condition of what R. H. Blyth calls "absolute spiritual poverty in which, having nothing, we possess all."[23]

Noguchi himself tried his hand at haiku in Japanese as well as in English. How successful a haiku poet he was is debatable, but he certainly tried to adhere to the basic tenets of the genre. One of his English haiku reads:

> My Love's lengthened hair
> Swings o'er me from Heaven's gate:
> Lo, Evening's shadow!
>
>                (***Pilgrimage*** 2:140)

In an autobiographical essay he tells us that he came to this sensation when he visited Hyde Park in London around 1914: "I walked slowly, my mind being filled with the thought of the long hair of Rossetti's woman as I perhaps had visited Tate's Gallery that afternoon" (***Through the Torii,*** p. 146). While the poem gives a precise impression of the union between the image of the London dusk descending from the sky and the image of the woman's lengthened hair, it also conveys the sensation of each separate object perceived. The poet is not trying to personify a natural phenomenon; the evening is seen as an evening, the woman's hair is seen as woman's hair, and there is no artificial attempt to bring them together.

In haiku, there is little division between the perceiver and the perceived, spirit and matter, man and nature. "In the realm of poetry," Noguchi maintains, "there is no strict boundary between the domains generally called subjective and objective; while some *Hokku* poems appear to be objective, those poems are again by turns quite subjective through the great virtue of the writers having the fullest identification with the matter written on" (***Spirit of Japanese Poetry,*** pp. 43-44). Noguchi's poem **"The Passing of Summer"** (1909) reads:

> An empty cup whence the light of passion is
>  drunk!
> To-day a sad rumour passes through the trees,
> A chill wind is borne by the stream,
> The waves shiver in pain;
> Where now the cicada's song long and hot?
>
>                (***Pilgrimage*** 1:68)

Such images as the chilly wind and the shivering waves are not used to signal the passing of summer. Rather, the chilly wind and the shivering waves themselves constitute the passing of summer. Similarly, such phrases as "the light of passion" and "the cicada's song long and hot" are not metonymies of summer, thereby expressing nostalgia or some sort of sentiment about summer; instead they are the summer itself. In Noguchi's poetry, then, as in traditional haiku, poetry and sensation are spontaneously joined in one and the same, so that there is scarcely any room left for rationalism or moralism.

Not all of Noguchi's English poems, of course, adhere to Japanese traditions. Most of his early poems, collected in *Seen and Unseen* and *The Voice of the Valley,* are beautiful expressions of the young poet's delight in his dreams, reveries, and mysteries about nature, the high Sierras, where he actually spent the life of a recluse. But the relationship of man to nature he creates in his early work is quite different from that of his later work. The ecstasies of the self in nature he describes in his early poetry are sometimes overindulgent, and this dependency of the self on nature results in a loss of equilibrium between them. Speaking of the same experience, Whitman cautions his own senses: "You villain touch! . . . / Unclench your floodgates, you are too much for me" (*Complete Poetry,* p. 46). Unlike Whitman, however, the young Noguchi is at times unable to resist an urge toward overstatement and crude symbolism. In his poem **"In the Valley,"** for example, the reveries of nature are most appropriately presented in terms of "the Sierra-rock, a tavern for the clouds" and "the Genii in the Valley-cavern." Man's will and desire, on the other hand, are alluded to by such prosaic expressions as "Fame" and "Gold"; "Heaven" and "mortals" are merely equated with "Glory" and "Decay" (*Voice of Valley,* p. 29).

Such a poem as **"In the Valley"** smacks of didacticism and moralism. It is not these qualities in his early poetry that attracted critics' attention. It is, to use his editor's phrase, "this unconventional child of nature . . . whose heart and soul lie naked and bare. . . . If he is sometimes obscure, it is because he had flown into cloud-land, where obscurity is a virtue."[24] Noguchi himself believed in the virtue of obscurity and indefiniteness in poetry and in art. To show this he quotes the English translation of a haiku by Moritake:

> "Thought I, the fallen flowers
>   Are returning to their branch
> But lo! they are butterflies."

Noguchi can only say that if this poem "means anything, it is the writer's ingenuity perhaps in finding a simile; but I wonder where is its poetical charm when it is expressed thus definitely" (*Through the Torii,* p. 51).

What Noguchi strove to accomplish in his poetry, particularly in his later career, was to perceive a harmonious relationship between man and nature. For him the aim of poetry was not only to achieve the union between man and nature, but to maintain the identity of each within that union. The poet's chief function was not to express the feelings of man by the spirits of nature. This is analogous to what Noguchi saw in the print "Autumnal Moon at Tamagawa" by Hiroshige, an eminent nineteenth-century Japanese landscape painter, in which the moon over the river, the low mountain ranges in the background, and the fishermen engaged in night work are all harmoniously blended into a whole picture. Hiroshige, in this painting, as Noguchi realized, was not attempting to imitate nature or to make a copy whereby "the artist may become a soft-voiced servant to nature . . . not a real lover who truly understands her inner soul."[25] In providing expression for nature, the artist must not convey his own thought and logic. When Wordsworth sings, "I wandered, lonely as a cloud," he is simply feeling akin to the cloud rather than imposing the human will upon the will of nature. Similarly, in Noguchi's successful poems, man's position in nature becomes neither subordinate nor obtrusive, and both worlds can maintain a great sense of dignity and autonomy.

NOTES

[1] Much of Yone Noguchi's biographical information is found in the autobiographical essays written in English and in Japanese. The most useful is a collection of such essays entitled *The Story of Yone Noguchi Told by Himself* (London: Chatto & Windus, 1914). Later page references to this edition are indicated in parentheses.

[2] That Poe's poems made a great impact upon the aspiring poet from Japan is indicated by the close similarity in a certain part of "Lines," one of Noguchi's early poems in English, and Poe's "Eulalie." See "Lines," in *The Pilgrimage* (Kamakura: The Valley Press; Yokohama: Kelly & Walsh, 1909), 2:79; and "Eulalie," *Complete Works of Poe,* ed. James A. Harrison (New York: Crowell, 1902), 1:121-22. When Noguchi's poems, including "Lines," appeared in *The Lark, The Chap Book,* and *The Philistine,* in 1896, he was accused of plagiarism by some critics, while he was defended by his friends. Noguchi later refuted it in *The Story of Yone Noguchi* (p. 18). About this controversy, see Don B. Graham, "Yone Noguchi's 'Poe Mania,'" *Markham Review* 4 (1974): 58-60. Later references to *The Pilgrimage* are to the edition indicated above.

[3] *Seen and Unseen or, Monologues of a Homeless Snail* (San Francisco: Gelett Burgess & Porter Garnett, 1897); *The Voice of the Valley* (San Francisco: The Doxey Press, 1897). Subsequent textual references are to these editions.

[4] See Willa Cather, "Two Poets: Yone Noguchi and Bliss Carman," in *The World and the Parish: Willa Cather's Articles and Reviews, 1893-1902* (Lincoln: University of Nebraska Press, 1970), 2:579.

[5] See *Japan and America* (Tokyo: Keio University Press, 1921), preface. Subsequent references are to this edition.

[6] *The American Diary of a Japanese Girl* was published by Frank Leslie Publishing House, New York, in 1901, and also by Frederick A. Stokes Company, New York, in 1902. Both editions are illustrated in color and black and white by Genjiro Yeto. This book was later expanded

into a full novel under the same title. Cf. *The American Diary of a Japanese Girl* (Tokyo: Fuzanbo; London: Elkin Mathews, 1902).

[7] *From the Eastern Sea* (London: Unicorn Press, 1903). Subsequent references are to this edition.

[8] The most comprehensive, although often inaccurate, bibliography of Yone Noguchi's writings in Japanese and in English is included in Usaburo Toyama, ed., *Essays on Yone Noguchi* (Tokyo: Zokei Bijutsu Kyokai, 1963), vol. 1.

[9] *The Spirit of Japanese Poetry* (New York: E. P. Dutton, 1914). Subsequent page references are to this edition.

[10] See *Yone Noguchi: Collected English Letters*, ed. Ikuko Atsumi (Tokyo: The Yone Noguchi Society, 1975), pp. 210-11.

[11] *The Spirit of Japanese Art* (London: John Murray, 1915). Subsequent references are to this edition.

[12] Yone Noguchi had earlier met Yeats in London, where *From the Eastern Sea* was published in 1903. In a 24 February 1903 letter to his wife Leonie Gilmour, he wrote: "I made many a nice young, lovely, kind friend among literary *geniuses* (attention!). W. B. Yeats or Laurence Binyon, Moore and Bridges. They are so good; they invite me almost everyday. They are jolly companions. Their hairs are not long, I tell you" (*English Letters*, p. 106).

[13] See Isamu Noguchi, *A Sculptor's World* (New York: Harper & Row, 1968), p. 31.

[14] Yone Noguchi, "The Invisible Night," in *Seen and Unseen*, p. 21. The poem first appeared in *The Lark*.

[15] Walt Whitman, "Song of Myself," in *Complete Poetry and Selected Prose*, ed. James E. Miller, Jr. (Boston: Houghton Mifflin, 1959), p. 39. Subsequent references are to this edition.

[16] Yone Noguchi, *Kamakura* (Kamakura: The Valley Press, 1910), p. 35. Subsequent references are to this edition.

[17] Yone Noguchi, "At the Yuigahama Shore by Kamakura," in *The Pilgrimage*, 1:34. The poem is reprinted in Noguchi's travelogue *Kamakura*, pp. 38-39.

[18] *The Story of Yone Noguchi*, pp. 223-24. Noguchi discusses elsewhere what is to him the true meaning of realism: "While I admit the art of some artist which has the detail of beauty, I must tell him that reality, even when true, is not the whole thing; he should learn the art of escaping from it. That art is, in my opinion, the greatest of all arts; without it, art will never bring us the eternal and the mysterious" (*Spirit of Japanese Art,* p. 103).

[19] Quoted, in Noguchi's translation, in *The Spirit of Japanese Poetry*, p. 38.

[20] Quoted in *The Spirit of Japanese Poetry*, p. 37. This particular poem, however, cannot be found in any of Noguchi's poetry collections.

[21] Quoted, in Noguchi's translation, in Yone Noguchi, *Through the Torii* (Boston: The Four Seas, 1922), p. 132. Subsequent references are to this edition.

[22] Yone Noguchi, "By the Engakuji Temple: Moon Night," in *The Pilgrimage*, 1:5. The Engakuji Temple, located in Kamakura, an ancient capital of Japan, was founded in the thirteenth century by Tokimune Hojo, hero of the feudal government, who was a great believer in Zen Buddhism.

[23] R. H. Blyth, *Haiku* (Tokyo: The Hokuseido Press, 1949), 1:172.

[24] See Chas. Warren Stoddard, "Introduction," in *The Voice of the Valley*, pp. 10-11.

[25] Yone Noguchi, *Hiroshige and Japanese Landscapes* (Tokyo: Maruzen, 1936), p. 25.

### Yoshinobu Hakutani (essay date 1992)

SOURCE: "Ezra Pound, Yone Noguchi, and Imagism," in *Modern Philology*, Vol. 90, No. 1, August, 1992, pp. 46-69.

[*In the following essay, Hakutani discusses the impact of Noguchi's work on Ezra Pound, with whom Noguchi corresponded on several occasions.*]

It is commonplace to say that imagism played a crucial role in poetic modernism and that Ezra Pound, more than anyone else, put this poetics to practice in the 1910s. Yet imagism still remains a somewhat cloudy topic. Many discussions content themselves with restatements of Pound's celebrated essay on vorticism, published in September 1914.[1] Even Hugh Kenner, the most eminent critic of Pound, says, "The history of the Imagist Movement is a red herring." He admonishes one "to keep one's eyes on Pound's texts, and avoid generalities about Imagism."[2]

In that "Vorticism" essay, Pound acknowledged for the first time in his career his indebtedness to the spirit of Japanese poetry in general and the technique of hokku in particular. Among the Poundians, and there have been many in the East and in the West, who have tried to reconstruct the historical set of circumstances in which Pound moved, Earl Miner gives the best account of the profound influences Japanese poetry had upon the early Pound. It is Miner who offers the best annotated evidence that the sources for Pound's interest in Japanese poetics were partly provided by Pound's fellow imagists such as T. E. Hulme, F. S. Flint, and Richard Aldington.[3]

It is Miner as well who most frequently comments on the role Yone Noguchi played in the introduction and interpretation of Japanese poetry to an English audience during the early decades of the twentieth century.[4] Noguchi was indeed a well-known bilingual Japanese and American poet, who by 1915 had published not only books of criticism widely read in England and America (*The Spirit of Japanese Poetry* and *The Spirit of Japanese Art*), but also several collections of his own English poems. By this date, moreover, his poems had been praised by Willa Cather, Joaquin Miller, and Gelett Burgess in America, by Bliss Carman in Canada, and by George Meredith, William Rossetti, Thomas Hardy, and others in England. What is surprising, therefore, is Miner's dismissive treatment of Noguchi's English writings as having had little to do with the imagist movement and with Pound in particular.

## II

As Pound explained in his essay, the image is not a static, rational idea: "It is a radiant node or cluster; it is what I can, and must perforce, call a VORTEX, from which, and through which, and into which, ideas are constantly rushing. In decency one can only call it a VORTEX. And from this necessity came the name 'vorticism'" ("Vorticism," pp. 469-70). A year later Pound defined the form of an image by stating that the image "may be a sketch, a vignette, a criticism, an epigram or anything else you like. It may be impressionism, it may even be very good prose." An image, he argued, does not constitute simply a picture of something. As a vortex, the image must be "endowed with energy."[5] Imagism, in turn, is likened to the painter's use of pigment. "The painter," Pound wrote, "should use his colour because he sees it or feels it. I don't much care whether he is representative or non-representative. . . . It is the same in writing poems, the author must use his *image . . . not* because he thinks he can use it to back up some creed or some system of ethics or economics" ("Vorticism," p. 464).

To demonstrate his poetic theory, Pound thought of an image not as a decorative emblem or symbol but as a seed capable of germinating and developing into another organism. As an illustration he presented what he called "a *hokku*-like sentence" he had written:

> The apparition of these faces in the crowd:
>    Petals, on a wet, black bough.

"In a poem of this sort," he explained, "one is trying to record the precise instant when a thing outward and objective transforms itself, or darts into a thing inward and subjective" ("Vorticism," p. 467). The image of the faces in the crowd is based in immediate experience at a metro station in Paris; it was "a thing outward and objective." Not only did Pound actually see the "thing," but it generated such a sensation that he could not shake it out of his mind. This image, he emphasizes, "transforms itself, or darts into a thing inward and subjective," that is, the image of the "Petals, on a wet, black bough." Imagism is further contrasted to symbolism: "The symbolist's *symbols* have a fixed value, like numbers in arithmetic, like 1, 2, and 7. The imagiste's images have a variable sig-

nificance, like the signs *a, b,* and *x* in algebra" ("Vorticism," p. 463).

Although Pound's definition is clear enough, the sources for his ideas are hard to determine. Most discussions about the genesis of the imagist movement are speculative at best. Pound's insistence that an image in poetry must be active rather than passive suggests that a poem is not a description of something, but, as Aristotle had said of tragedy, an action. Pound approaches Aristotelianism in his insistence that the image of the faces in the crowd in his metro poem was not simply a description of his sensation at the station but an active entity capable of dynamic development. According to his experience, this particular image instantly transformed itself into another image, the image of the petals on a wet, black bough. To Pound the success of this poem resulted from his instantaneous perception of the relatedness between the two entirely different objects.

But Pound's note on the genesis of "In a Station of the Metro" in the "Vorticism" essay makes it clear that there was nothing instantaneous about the composition of this poem. It was in 1911 that Pound, having seen those "beautiful faces" at La Concorde, wrote a thirty-line poem "and destroyed it because it was what we call work 'of second intensity'" ("Vorticism," p. 467). Six months later he reduced the longer text to a poem half the length, and still a year later he wrote the final version, a two-line poem. Pound's insistence on the instantaneous perception of the metro images drove him to repeated attempts at recreating the instantaneous images he had perceived a year-and-a-half earlier. Traditionally, the principles of instantaneity and spontaneity are as fundamental for the composition of hokku as when applied to Zen-inspired painting and calligraphy. In any event, his discovery of hokku in 1913-14 was, as he says, "useful in getting out of the impasse in which I had been left by my metro emotion" ("Vorticism," p. 467). To Pound, the most important thing he learned about hokku was "this particular sort of consciousness," which he was unable to identify with any version of impressionist art.[6]

Another equally important tenet of imagism calls for directness in expression. The immediate model for this principle was nineteenth-century French prose. Pound did not mention specific English poets but seemed adamantly opposed to Victorian poetry, which he characterized as wordy and rhetorical. Instead he urged his fellow poets "to bring poetry up to the level of prose." "Flaubert and De Maupassant," he believed, "lifted prose to the rank of a finer art, and one has no patience with contemporary poets who escape from all the difficulties of the infinitely difficult art of good prose by pouring themselves into loose verses" ("Vorticism," p. 462).

If Pound's ideal poetry has the directness and clarity of good prose as opposed to the suggestiveness and vagueness of symbolist poetry, then his sources certainly did not include W. B. Yeats. Even though Yeats dedicated the noh play *At the Hawk's Well* to Pound, Yeats was not enthusiastic about Pound's poetics. "My own theory of poetical or legendary drama," Yeats wrote to Fiona Macleod, "is that it should have no realistic, or elaborate, but only a symbolic and decorative setting. A forest, for instance, should be represented by a forest pattern and not by a forest painting."[7] The difference between Pound and Yeats reveals itself in the two poets' differing views of the Japanese noh play. A symbolist and spiritualist poet, Yeats was fascinated by the noh play. By contrast, Pound was interested not in particular images and symbols but in the unifying effect a noh play produces on the stage.

This disagreement between Pound and Yeats over whether poetic images should be suggestive or active also involves what Noguchi, a poet and critic well acquainted with both poets, felt compelled to write in **"What Is a Hokku Poem?"** published in London.[8] In that essay, Noguchi first defined hokku as an expression of Japanese poets' "understanding of Nature" or, better put, as a song or chant of "their longing or wonder or adoration toward Mother Nature" that is "never mystified by any cloud or mist like Truth or Beauty of Keats' understanding." Noguchi differentiated between the "suggestive" and subjective coloration of English poetry and the Japanese hokku, "distinctly clear-cut like a diamond or star." "I say," he argued, "that the star itself has almost no share in the creation of a condition even when your dream or vision is gained through its beauty. . . . I value the 'hokku' poem, at least some of them, because of its own truth and humanity simple and plain." Noguchi then analyzed the aim of hokku: the hokku poet expresses the spirit of nature rather than the will of man or woman. Noguchi would agree that hokku is "suggestive" only if the word 'suggestive' means that "truth and humanity are suggestive." He added, "But I can say myself as a poet . . . that your poem would certainly end in artificiality if you start out to be suggestive from the beginning."[9]

Finally, Noguchi based his definition and analysis of aim in Zen philosophy, understood as discipline of the mind: one should not allow one's individuality to control action. Zen does not, indeed, recognize human reality, the existence of good and evil, because this reality is but the creation of man's will rather than the spirit of nature. Noguchi thus observed that "there is no word in so common use by Western critics as suggestive, which makes more mischief than enlightenment." Although Western critics "mean it quite simply . . . to be a new force of salvation, . . . I say that no critic is necessary for this world of poetry."[10]

By 1918 Pound's vorticist theory had extended to his discussion of Chinese characters. As the correspondence between Pound and Mary Fenollosa, widow of Ernest Fenollosa, indicates, Pound began to receive Fenollosa's manuscripts as early as 1913.[11] Fenollosa's essay "The Chinese Written Character as a Medium of Poetry," posthumously published by Pound in *The Little Review* in 1918, attempted to show that Chinese characters, which Pound called ideograms, derive from visual rather than aural experiences. A Chinese character, Fenollosa noted, signifies an observable action instead of an abstract notion. Unlike a Western word, a phonetic sign, it denotes a concrete, natural phenomenon. The Chinese character, Fenollosa wrote, "is based upon a vivid shorthand picture of the operations of nature. In the algebraic figure and in the spoken word there is no natural connection between thing and sign: all depends upon sheer convention. But the Chinese method follows natural suggestion."[12]

Pound's attempt to verify Fenollosa's theory involved not only his contemporaries, poets and critics living in London in the 1910s, but his own effort to search for ideas in other sources. One of these sources was the Japanese noh play, in which Pound became interested through Fenollosa's notes. It is generally understood that Pound's interest in Japanese poetry, especially hokku, grew partly through his acquaintance with Fenollosa's writings. None of Fenollosa's writings, however, directly concerns Japanese poetry, let alone hokku. Having lived many years in Japan as an art critic, Fenollosa became well versed in Japanese art and literature, but his actual knowledge of the Japanese language was not profound.[13] It is, therefore, inconceivable that Pound became well acquainted with hokku through Fenollosa. It is also unlikely that English contemporaries such as T. E. Hulme and F. S. Flint, who are said to have introduced hokku to Pound, served his purpose. Pound would not have been able to learn from them the subtle elements of Japanese poetry because they had no firsthand knowledge of the Japanese language.[14]

## III

Pound's most likely source of information was Noguchi. He first corresponded with Pound and then met Pound, along with Yeats, when he gave a series of lectures on Japanese poetry in England in early 1914. The relationship between Pound and Noguchi began in 1911, when Noguchi sent his fifth collection of English poems, *The Pilgrimage* (1908 and 1909) in two volumes, to Pound with a note: "As I am not yet acquainted with your work, I wish you [would] send your books or books which you like to have me read. This little note may sound quite businesslike, but I can promise you that I can do better in my next letter to you." Noguchi also wrote as a postscript: "I am anxious to read not only your poetical work but also your criticism."[15] Pound acknowledged receipt of the books and note in a letter postmarked September 2, 1911.

c/o Elkin Mathews

Vigo St. London.

Dear Yone Noguchi:

I want to thank you very much for your lovely books & for your kindness in sending them to me.

I had, of course, known of you, but I am much occupied with my mediaeval studies & had neglected to read your books altho' they lie with my own in Mathews Shop & I am very familiar with the appearance of their covers.

I am reading those you sent me but I do not yet know what to say of them except that they have delighted me. Besides it is very hard to write to you until I know more about you, you are older than I am I gather from the dates of the poems you have been to New York. You are giving us the spirit of Japan, is it not? very much as I am trying to deliver from obscurity certain forgotten odours of Provence & Tuscany (my works on Guido Cavalcanti, & Arnaut Daniel, are, the one in press, the other ready to be printed.)

I have sent you two volumes of poems. I do not know whether to send you "The Spirit of Romance" or not: It treats of mediaeval poetry in southern Europe but has many flaws of workmanship. . . .

Of your country I know almost nothing surely if the east & the west are ever to understand each other that understanding must come slowly & come first through the arts.

You ask about my "criticism". There is some criticism in the "Spirit of Romance" & there will be some in the prefaces to the "Guido" & the "Arnaut". But I might be more to the point if we who are artists should discuss the matters of technique & motive between ourselves. Also if you should write about these matters I would discuss your letters with Mr. Yeats & likewise my answers. . . .

Yours very sincerely

Ezra Pound[16]

Although Noguchi did not write again as Pound had suggested, Noguchi published his essay **"What Is a Hokku Poem?"** in London in January 1913, as noted earlier. In the meantime three books of criticism by Noguchi appeared during this period: *The Spirit of Japanese Poetry* (London, 1914; cited hereafter in the text), *Through the Torii* (London, 1914), and *The Spirit of Japanese Art* (London, 1915). Noguchi was also invited to contribute **"The Everlasting Sorrow: A Japanese Noh Play"** in 1917 and an article, **"The Japanese Noh Play,"** in 1918 to *The Egoist*.[17] Pound's encouragement was perhaps responsible for the publication of some of Noguchi's own hokku poems in *The Egoist* and in *Poetry*.[18]

Because his essays and lectures during this period also dealt with Japanese art, Yeats, who was interested in Japanese painting and the noh play, became interested in Noguchi's work as well.[19] As Pound's and Yeats's letters to Noguchi indicate, Pound and Yeats not only were close associates themselves but also were both well acquainted with Noguchi. Despite the active dialogues that occurred between Pound and Noguchi, critics have not seriously considered their relationship. The only critic who has mentioned Noguchi in discussing the imagist movement regarded him not as a poet and critic from whose ideas Pound might have benefited but as one of the poets whom Pound himself influenced.[20] Such a preposterous connection is undermined by the simple fact that most of Noguchi's English poems, as Pound noted in

his letter to Noguchi, had been published in America and England long before the early 1910s, when Pound and his fellow poets began to discuss imagism among themselves. It is more accurate historically to say that Noguchi influenced Pound rather than the other way around.

Pound had apparently known little about Japanese poetry before he attended the April 1909 meeting of the Poets' Club. This group, headed by T. E. Hulme, was succeeded by another group called "Les Imagistes," or "Des Imagistes," which Pound led from 1912 to 1914.[21] Although Pound in fact joined the Poets' Club, its sessions did not prove of much inspiration to him. Richard Aldington, who joined in 1911, was more interested in the color prints of Utamaro, Hokusai, and others found in the British Museum than in Japanese poetry.[22] The fact that Pound was more seriously interested than Aldington was in Japanese poetry is indicated by Aldington's parody of Pound's metro poem that appeared in the January 1915 issue of *The Egoist*.[23] Allen Upward, another member of "Les Imagistes" whom Pound had met in 1911, had some importance for Pound because Upward used the term "whirl-swirl" in his book *The New Word* (New York, 1908). Upward, a self-styled intellectual and a poet, had "a powerful and original mind clearly and trenchantly concerned with matters that bear directly on what Pound meant by 'vortex.'"[24] But Upward, who was well read in Confucius and perhaps familiar with Chinese poetry, did not have sufficient knowledge of Japanese poetry, let alone of hokku, to influence Pound.[25]

The degree of Pound's initial interest in hokku, therefore, was not entirely clear, for he was much occupied with Provençal poetry and criticism, as his letter to Noguchi indicates. It is quite possible that Pound learned about hokku from T. E. Hulme and F. S. Flint, who were experimenting with hokku and tanka, the thirty-one-syllable Japanese poetic form.[26] The difficulty with this assumption, however, is that Hulme and Flint studied hokku through French translators and critics who used the terms 'haiku' and 'haikai', more modern words, rather than 'hokku'. Most strikingly, neither Pound nor Noguchi referred to the Japanese poem as 'haiku' or 'haikai'; both consistently called it 'hokku' in their writings.

However coincidental this might have been, there are two more pieces of evidence suggesting that Pound might have learned about hokku in Noguchi's work. First, as I have already observed, the essay **"What Is a Hokku Poem?"** in which Noguchi declared that poetic images must be active instead of suggestive, direct instead of symbolic, and that the aim of a hokku is to understand the spirit of nature rather than to express the will of man was published in *Rhythm* (London) in January 1913, almost two years before Pound's essay "Vorticism." Even Pound's essay "A Few Don'ts," the earliest manifesto on imagism, appeared in the March 1913 issue of *Poetry* (Chicago) two months after Noguchi's essay. Second, Noguchi's book of criticism, *The Spirit of Japanese Poetry,* was published in London by John Murray in March 1914, half a year before Pound's "Vorticism" essay.[27]

Moreover, the key chapter of Noguchi's book, entitled **"The Japanese Hokku Poetry,"** was a lecture delivered in the Hall of Magdalen College, Oxford, on January 28, 1914, at the invitation of Robert Bridges, the poet laureate, and T. H. Warren, president of the college and professor of poetry in the university. The first chapter, "Japanese Poetry," was also based on a lecture Noguchi gave at the Japan Society of London on January 14. The rest of the book had been presented as other lectures to such audiences as the Royal Asiatic Society and the Quest Society in England before April 1914, when Noguchi left London for Tokyo by way of Paris, Berlin, and Moscow. It is altogether possible that Pound heard Noguchi lecture at the Quest Society since Pound, Wyndham Lewis, and T. E. Hulme all lectured there in 1914.[28] During this stay in England, **Through the Torii,** another collection of essays that included a variety of commentary on William Rossetti, James Whistler, W. B. Yeats, and Oscar Wilde, and his autobiography, *The Story of Yone Noguchi Told by Himself,* also appeared in print.

Interestingly enough, Pound's "Vorticism" essay quoted a famous hokku by Moritake (1452-1540) just before discussing the often-quoted metro poem:

> The fallen blossom flies back to its branch:
>     A butterfly.
>                              ["Vorticism," p. 467]

This hokku in Japanese has three lines:

> Rak-ka eda ni
> Kaeru to mireba
> Kocho-o kana

Noguchi translated this poem in three lines:

> I thought I saw the fallen leaves
> Returning to their branches:
> Alas, butterflies were they.
>              [*Spirit of Japanese Poetry,* p. 50]

Pound must have reconstructed the hokku in two lines simply because he had in mind "a form of super-position" in which his metro poem was to be composed. The similarities between Pound's and Noguchi's versions of the poem in question do not seem coincidental, because the superpository division is indicated by a colon in both constructions. Both translations have identical key words: "fallen," "branch," and "butterfly." The only difference in diction is between Pound's "blossom" (*ka* in Japanese) and Noguchi's "leaves." In syntax, however, these translations are different: Noguchi's version is subjective from the start and ends objectively; the reverse is true in Pound's rendering. Syntactically, Noguchi's version is closer to the Japanese original than Pound's. A literal translation of Moritake's first two lines, "Rak-ka eda ni / Kaeru to mireba," would read: "The fallen blossom appears to come back to its branch."

What appealed to Pound was the terseness and intensity of imagery in a hokku. Irked by the decorative and super-fluous style of much Victorian poetry, he urged his fellow poets to eliminate words that do not contribute to the central meaning of the poem. "All poetic language," Pound insisted, "is the language of exploration. Since the beginning of bad writing, writers have used images as ornaments" ("Vorticism," p. 466). By saying, "Great literature is simply language charged with meaning to the utmost possible degree," he meant to elaborate the imagist principle that using fewer words maximizes and intensifies meaning.[29] In **"What Is a Hokku Poem?"** Noguchi wrote, "I always thought that the most beautiful flowers grow close to the ground, and they need no hundred petals for expressing their own beauty; how can you call it real poetry if you cannot tell it by a few words?"[30]

Pound, furthermore, applied the principle of terseness and intensity to the construction of a single image in his poetry. "The 'one image poem,'" Pound noted, "is a form of super-position, that is to say it is one idea set on top of another. I found it useful in getting out of the impasse in which I had been left by my metro emotion" ("Vorticism," p. 467). Noguchi pointed out the same technique: "*Hokku* means literally a single utterance or the utterance of a single verse; that utterance should be like a 'moth light playing on reality's dusk,' or 'an art hung, as a web, in the air of perfume,' swinging soft in music of a moment" (*Spirit of Japanese Poetry,* p. 39). To illustrate his point, Noguchi quoted a hokku by Buson:

> The night of the Spring,
> Oh, between the eve
> And the dawn.

This hokku was placed against the opening passage of *Makura Zoshi (Pillow Sketches)* by Sei Shonagon, a celebrated prose writer in medieval Japan: "I love to watch the dawn grow gradually white and whiter, till a faint rosy tinge crowns the mountain's crest, while slender streaks of purple cloud extend themselves above." Noguchi considered Buson's image far more vivid and intensive than Sei Shonagon's, remarking, "Buson is pleased to introduce the night of the Spring which should be beautiful without questioning, since it lies between those two beautiful things, the eve and the dawn" (*Spirit of Japanese Poetry,* pp. 48-49).

IV

Not only was Noguchi an interpreter of hokku poems for the English reader, but he tried his hand at writing hokku poems in English as well. He later collected them in the volume **Japanese Hokkus** (Boston, 1920), which he dedicated to Yeats.[31] One of Noguchi's earliest hokku is reminiscent of Buson's, quoted above:

> Tell me the street to Heaven.
> This? Or that? Oh, which?
> What webs of streets!

He wrote this hokku in England, he says, "when I most abruptly awoke in 1902 to the noise of Charing Cross. . . .

And it was by West-minster Bridge where I heard the evening chime that I wrote again in 'hokku' which appears, when translated, as follows":

> Is it, Oh, list:
> The great voice of Judgment Day?
> So runs Thames and my Life.[32]

Noguchi wrote many such hokku-like poems in imitation of the Japanese hokku, as did Pound. The superpositiory technique, which Pound said he had discovered in Japanese hokku, resembles that of Noguchi. For instance, Pound's "Alba," typical of his many hokku-like poems, reads:

> As cool as the pale wet leaves
>                 of lily-of-the-valley
> She lay beside me in the dawn.[33]

Most of Noguchi's hokku, as the two poems quoted above show, do have a form of superposition. Like Pound's, Noguchi's hokku constitutes one image poem which has two separate ideas set on top of one another. In the first poem by Noguchi, an idea of "the street to Heaven" is set on top of an idea of "webs," despite a close similarity between the two images. In the second, an idea of the flow of the Thames is set on top of an idea of the course of "my Life."

But there are some differences between Noguchi's and Pound's hokku. Noguchi does not as closely adhere to the well-established Japanese syllabic measure of five or seven as does Pound. Noguchi's two hokku above have 7-5-4 and 4-7-6 measures; Pound's "Alba," "Fan-Piece, for Her Imperial Lord," and "Ts'ai Chi'h" have those of 7-7-8, 7-5-7, and 8-7-7, respectively. If the first line of Pound's metro poem had been reconstructed as two lines, the poem would have had a measure of 5-7-7 (The apparition / Of these faces in the crowd: / Petals, on a wet, black bough) much like a Japanese hokku. Noguchi, moreover, tends to ignore the long-established poetic tradition in which a Japanese hokku has an explicit reference to a season. Pound, on the other hand, consciously adheres to this tradition as seen in many of his hokku-like poems and somewhat longer pieces such as "Heather" and "Society."[34]

What a Japanese hokku and Pound's image share besides their brevity and intensity is the poet's ability to escape the confinement of the poem. The sense of liberation in hokku is usually accomplished through references to time and space. A Japanese hokku contains not only a reference to a season, an indication of time, but also an image of nature, that of space. Pound's hokku-like poems, such as "In a Station of the Metro" and "Alba," indeed have references to time and space. Pound called the metro emotion, which came from the image of the faces in the crowd, "a thing outward and objective" and the image of the "petals, on a wet, black bough" "a thing inward and subjective." The image of the petals, nevertheless, is a natural object in contrast to that of the faces in the crowded station, a human object.

In Pound's mind in the realm of subjective perception the image of the faces, an objective image, transforms into the image of the petals, a subjective image. This perception also means that the image of the faces, an image of man, transforms into that of the petals, an image of nature. The shifting of objective and subjective images in Pound's poem is depicted in terms of a vortex, in which an image is not only active in itself but capable of merging into another image that appears in its wake. Because Pound's image has this tendency, it is often as difficult to separate the mental vision from the external as it is to separate mind from matter, the perceiver from the perceived, in Japanese hokku.

In *The Spirit of Japanese Poetry,* Noguchi is as critical as Pound of the Western poet's tendency to wordiness. Noguchi's emphasis on the Japanese hokku as "the real poetry of action" entails that a hokku aim to narrow the distance between man and nature, the perceiver and the perceived. The narrower the distance, the better the hokku becomes. Based upon "Lao Tze's canon of spiritual anarchism" and Zen's principle of controlling the mind, Noguchi declares:

> To attach too closely to the subject matter in literary expression is never a way to complete the real saturation; the real infinite significance will only be accomplished at such a consummate moment when the end and means are least noticeable, and the subject and expression never fluctuate from each other, being in perfect collocation; it is the partial loss of the birthright of each that gains an artistic triumph. . . . I do never mean that the *Hokku* poems are lyrical poetry in the general Western understanding; but the Japanese mind gets the effect before perceiving the fact of their brevity, its sensibility resounding to their single note, as if the calm bosom of river water to the song of a bird. [*Spirit of Japanese Poetry,* p. 34]

To illustrate what he calls "the sense of mystical affinity between the life of Nature and the life of man, between the beauty of flowers and the beauty of love," he quotes his own poem:

> It's accident to exist as a flower or a poet;
> A mere twist of evolution but from the same force:
> I see no form in them but only beauty in evidence;
> It's the single touch of their imagination to get the
>     embodiment of a poet or a flower:
> To be a poet is to be a flower,
> To be the dancer is to make the singer sing.
>                 [*Spirit of Japanese Poetry,* p. 37]

Pound, on the other hand, views the affinity between man and nature differently. What Pound calls "a thing inward and subjective" does not necessarily correspond to a vision of man; nor is "a thing outward and objective" the same thing as a vision of nature.

To explain the transformation of images between man and nature, the perceiver and the perceived, in Japanese hokku, Noguchi quoted Basho's "The Old Pond," perhaps the most celebrated hokku ever written:

The old pond!
A frog leapt into
List, the water sound!

One may think a frog an absurd poetic subject, but Basho focused his vision on a scene of autumnal desolation, an image of nature. The pond was perhaps situated on the premises of an ancient temple whose silence was suddenly broken by a frog plunging into the deep water. As Noguchi conceived the experience, Basho, a Zen Buddhist, was "supposed to awaken into enlightenment now when he heard the voice bursting out of voicelessness, and the conception that life and death were mere change of condition was deepened into faith" (*Spirit of Japanese Poetry*, pp. 45-46). Basho was not suggesting that the tranquility of the pond meant death or that the frog symbolized life. Just as Pound had the sensation of seeing the beautiful faces in the metro station, Basho here had the sensation of hearing the sound bursting out of soundlessness. A hokku is not a representation of goodness, truth, or beauty; there is nothing particularly good, true, or beautiful about a frog's jumping into the water.

It seems as though Basho, in writing the poem, carried nature within him and brought himself to the deepest level of nature where all sounds lapse into the world of silence and infinity. Though his vision is based upon reality, it transcends time and space. What a Zen poet like Basho is showing is that man can do enough naturally, enjoy doing it, and achieve his peace of mind. This fusion of man and nature is called spontaneity in Zen. The best hokku poems, because of their linguistic limitations, are inwardly extensive and outwardly infinite. A severe constraint imposed on one aspect of hokku must be balanced by a spontaneous, boundless freedom on the other.

From a Zen point of view, such a vision is devoid of thought and emotion. Since Zen is the most important philosophical tradition influencing Japanese hokku, the hokku poet aims at understanding the spirit of nature. Basho thus recognizes little division between man and nature, the subjective and the objective; he is never concerned with the problems of good and evil. Placed against this tradition, Pound's poetics in its philosophical aspect considerably differs from Basho's. Pound cannot be called a Zen poet because he declared: "An 'Image' is that which presents an intellectual and emotional complex in an instant of time."[35] A Zen poet seeks satori, an enlightenment that transcends time and place, and even the consciousness of self. This enlightenment is defined as a state of mu, nothingness, which is absolutely free of any thought or emotion; it is so completely free that such a state corresponds to that of nature. For a Zen-inspired poet, nature is a mirror of the enlightened self; one must see and hear things as they really are by making one's consciousness pure and clear. Pound seems to be able to appreciate this state of mind, but obviously he does not necessarily try to seek it in his own work.

In fact, Japanese hokku seldom take physical love, war, beasts, earthquakes, floods, and the like for their subjects. And while Pound's poetry does express good and evil, love and hatred, individual feeling and collective myth, Basho's shuns such sentiments and emotions altogether. Pound and a Zen poet, however, do agree that their poetic vision is spontaneous and capable of attaining enlightenment. Pound maintained, "It is the presentation of such a 'complex' instantaneously which gives that sense of sudden liberation; that sense of freedom from time and space limits; that sense of sudden growth, which we experience in the presence of the greatest works of art."[36] Pound's observation, however, is very much a Western formulation of an experience familiar to Zen-inspired artists.

This sense of liberation suggests an impersonal conception of poetry, for it focuses attention not upon the poet but upon the image. T. S. Eliot, whom most observers agree Pound influenced, held the same view.[37] Japanese poets such as Basho and Buson held the same principle. Their poetry seldom dealt with dreams, fantasies, or concepts of heaven and hell; it was strictly concerned with the portrayal of nature mountains, trees, birds, waterfalls, nights, days, seasons. For the Japanese hokku poet, nature is a mirror of the enlightened self; the poet must see and hear things as they really are by making his or her consciousness pure, natural, and unemotional. "Japanese poets," Noguchi wrote, "go to Nature to make life more meaningful, sing of flowers and birds to make humanity more intensive" (*Spirit of Japanese Poetry*, p. 37).

As opposed to his later poetry, Pound's early poetry, and his hokku-like poems in particular, have little to do with his personal emotion or thought. In such poetry, Pound is not really concerned with thought and emotion. If Pound's hokku sounded intellectual or emotional, it did so only to an English reader who was still Arnoldian in his or her taste and unfamiliar with the imagist movement of the 1910s, not to mention with "the spirit of Japanese poetry" Noguchi tried to introduce to the English audience. Japanese poetry shuns symbols and metaphors because figurative language might lessen the intensity and spontaneity of a newly experienced sensation. Such expressions would not only undermine originality in the poet's sensibility but resort to intellectualization as well as what Noguchi, perhaps echoing Matthew Arnold, called "a criticism of life," which traditionally Japanese poetry was not.[38]

The hokku poet may not only aim at expressing sensation but also at generalizing and hence depersonalizing it. This characteristic can be shown even by one of Basho's lesser-known hokku:

How cool it is,
Putting the feet on the wall:
An afternoon nap.[39]

Basho was interested in expressing how his feet, anyone's feet, would feel when placed on a wall inside a house on a warm summer afternoon. His subject was none other than this direct sensation. He did not want to convey any emotion, any thought, any beauty; there remained only poetry, only nature.

In "Alba" what Pound expressed was not the personal feeling he had about the woman lying beside him at dawn but his spontaneous sensation of the coolness of "the pale wet leaves / of lily-of-the-valley." Likewise, the sensation of slowly cooling hot water was Pound's subject in "The Bath Tub," as the title suggests, rather than his feelings about the woman.[40] The image of a "fan of white silk, / clear as frost on the grass-blade" is central in "Fan-Piece, for Her Imperial Lord," where a minimal image of the lord's concubine is evoked by a one-word reference to her: "You also are laid aside."[41] Such subtleties could not have been learned from Pound's fellow imagists like Flint and Aldington, who remained labored, superficial imitators of Japanese hokku. Pound and Noguchi, by contrast, showed themselves far more capable of understanding the spirit of Japanese poetry.

V

As partly suggested in the remarks on superposition quoted above, the hokku also provided a structural model for Pound's version of imagism. Acknowledging that the Japanese had evolved this short form of poetry, Pound seized upon the unique form of "super-position" which, he observed, constitutes a hokku. To him, the hokku often consists of two disparate images in juxtaposition, and yet it appears as a single image. Lacking the copula 'is' or the preposition 'like', the image cannot be metaphoric or analogical. As Pound's account of the composition of the metro poem shows, he had no intention of likening the image of the beautiful faces in the crowd to the image of petals on a wet, black bough or of making one image suggestive or representative of the other.[42] If one image is used to suggest another or to represent another, both images would be weakened. But if one image is used to generate or intensify another, and the other image, in turn, intensifies the first one, then the whole poem as one image would be intensified.

The key to the superpository structure of Pound's image is a coalescence of two unlike images. Such an image must be generated "in an instant of time," as Pound cautions in his essay "A Few Don'ts."[43] Creating such an image needs no preparations, no explanations, no qualifications; Pound calls "the 'natural course of events' the exalted moment, the vision unsought or at least the vision gained without machination."[44] In *The Spirit of Japanese Poetry* and *The Spirit of Romance* Noguchi and Pound respectively emphasized this revelatory moment when high poetry must be written. But such a parallel in their poetics does not necessitate that one's ideas came from the other's. Pound's observations might have been made independently.

It is quite possible that Pound became acquainted through other sources with many of the superpository hokku which Noguchi cited as examples in *The Spirit of Japanese Poetry*. In addition to Moritake's "I Thought I Saw the Fallen Leaves" and Basho's "The Old Pond," quoted earlier, Noguchi translated the following in *The Spirit of Japanese Poetry:* Buson's "Oh, How Cool " (p. 47) and "Prince Young, Gallant" (p. 36), Basho's "Lying Ill on Journey" (p. 38), and Hokushi's "It Has Burned Down" (p. 27). It may be significant, however, that in another collection of critical essays Noguchi cited several of his own numerous hokku in English along with those by ancient masters. Many of Noguchi's English hokku, moreover, had been published in *The Pilgrimage* (1908, 1909). Pound might have acquainted himself with Noguchi's published hokku before he experimented with his version.

As Pound would account for the circumstances of his metro poem in Paris in 1912, Noguchi also narrated the experience he had had in London in 1903:

> I myself was a *hokku* student since I was fifteen or sixteen years old; during many years of my Western life, now amid the California forest, then by the skyscrapers of New York, again in the London 'bus, I often tried to translate the *hokku* of our old masters but I gave up my hope when I had written the following in English:
>
> My Love's lengthened hair
> Swings o'er me from Heaven's gate:
> Lo, Evening's shadow!

It was in London, to say more particularly, Hyde Park, that I wrote the above *hokku* in English, where I walked slowly, my mind being filled with the thought of the long hair of Rossetti's woman as I perhaps had visited Tate's Gallery that afternoon. . . . I exclaimed then: "What use to try the impossibility in translation, when I have a moment to feel a *hokku* feeling and write about it in English?"[45]

Structurally, Pound's metro poem resembles Noguchi's Hyde Park hokku. As in Pound's poem where the outward image of the faces in the crowd is set on top of the inward image of petals on a wet, black bough, so the actual vision of an evening shadow in Noguchi's poem is juxtaposed to an envisioning of a woman's long hair. In each poem a pair of images, similar in form but different in content, coalesces into another autonomous image, which generates different meaning. The superposition of the paired images transforms into a different image in form and content, what Pound calls "the 'one image' poem" ("Vorticism," p. 467). This transformation of images retains the sensation of each separate object perceived, but it also conveys a greater sensation by uniting the two experiences.[46] For both poets, such a transformation is optimal, for they believe that images in poetry cannot and should not be divided as external and internal, physical and mental, objective and subjective.[47]

To illustrate the energy latent in this transformation of images, Pound provided an anecdote: "I once saw a small child go to an electric light switch and say, 'Mamma, can I *open* the light?' She was using the age-old language of exploration, the language of art" ("Vorticism," p. 466). Although he later became interested in Fenollsa's explanation that written Chinese characters denote action, he was first attracted to the poetics of the hokku, what he called "the sense of exploration . . . the beauty of this sort of knowing" ("Vorticism," pp. 466-67). Noguchi expounded this poetics in terms of an intensive art by referring to Kikaku's celebrated hokku:

> Autumn's full moon:
> Lo, the shadows of a pine-tree
> Upon the mats!

The beauty of the harvest moon is not only humanized but intensified by the shadow of a tree Kikaku saw on the tatami mats. "Really," Noguchi wrote, "it was my first opportunity to observe the full beauty of the light and shadow, more the beauty of the shadow in fact, far more luminous than the light itself, with such a decorativeness, particularly when it stamped the dustless mats as a dragon-shaped ageless pine-tree."[48] The situation here, shared by Pound and Noguchi, is one of finding, discovering, and hence of inventing the new.

As if to bear out Pound's vorticist thinking in poetry, Noguchi made a modest proposal for English poets. "I think," he wrote, "it is time for them to live more of the passive side of Life and Nature, so as to make the meaning of the whole of them perfect and clear, to value the beauty of inaction so as to emphasise action, to think of Death so as to make Life more attractive." To the Japanese mind, an intensive art can be created not from action but from inaction. Noguchi thus argued that the larger part of life "is builded upon the unreality by the strength of which the reality becomes intensified; when we sing of the beauty of night,
that is to glorify, through the attitude of reverse, in the way of silence, the vigour and wonder of the day" (*Spirit of Japanese Poetry*, pp. 24-25). Noguchi's paradox was echoed in Pound's statement about vorticism. To Pound, an intensive art is not an emphatic art. By an intensive art, Pound meant "one . . . concerned with the relative intensity, or relative significance, of different sorts of expression. . . . They are more dynamic. I do not mean they are more emphatic, or that they are yelled louder" ("Vorticism," p. 468).

Pound illustrated this intensive art with a hokku-like sentence in his essay "Affirmations," first published in the *New Age* in 1915:

> The pine-tree in mist upon the far hill looks like
> a fragment of Japanese armour.

The images appear in simile form, but Pound has no intention of intensifying the beauty of either image by comparison to the other. "In either case," he points out, "the beauty, in so far as it is beauty of form, is the result of 'planes in relation.' . . . The tree and the armour are beautiful because their diverse planes overlie in a certain manner." Unlike the sculptor or the painter, the poet, who must use words to intensify his art, Pound says, "may cast

on the reader's mind a more vivid image of either the armour or the pine by mentioning them close together . . . for the works not with planes or with colours but with the names of objects and of properties. It is his business so to use, so to arrange, these names as to cast a more definite image than the layman can cast."[49]

Critics have shown over the years that Pound's idea of vorticism underlies not only his short imagistic poems but also his longer pieces such as the *Cantos, Cathay*, and his translations of noh plays. Noguchi, on the other hand, attempted to intensify an image in a poem longer than the hokku by endowing it with action and autonomy. **"The Passing of Summer"** (1909), for instance, reads:

> An empty cup whence the light of passion is
> drunk!
> To-day a sad rumour passes through the trees,
> A chill wind is borne by the stream,
> The waves shiver in pain;
> Where now the cicada's song long and hot?[50]

Such visual images as an empty cup, the chilly wind blowing over the stream, and the shivering waves do not simply denote the passing of summer; they constitute its action. Similarly, experiences or memories of experiences like drinking "the light of passion" and hearing "the cicada's song long and hot" do not merely express the poet's nostalgia or sentiment about the summer; these images, rather than being metonymies, recreate the actions of the summer.[51] In Noguchi's poetry, as in the hokku, poetry and sensation are spontaneously conjoined and intensified, to leave no room for rationalism or moralism.

## VI

Numerous parallels between Pound's poetics and Noguchi's do not entail the conclusion that both poets held the same principles throughout their respective careers. Much of Noguchi's art and literary criticism shows great enthusiasm at times for Yeats's mysticism and Whitman's transcendentalism.[52] Noguchi had a taste for certain styles of poetry that Pound obviously did not. But their writings as a whole suggest that both writers, as poets and critics, agreed on the ideas of imagism during the period between 1908 when *The Pilgrimage*, Noguchi's fifth collection of English poems, appeared in Tokyo and London and 1914, when Noguchi's *The Spirit of Japanese Poetry* was published in London. For Noguchi, this period came in the middle of his career as it coincided with Pound's early career and interest in imagism. This agreement on imagism constituted an interpenetrating relationship of Japanese poetics and Western intentions in early modernism. Pound's launching of "Imagism" in London in 1912 and 1913 with the support of T. E. Hulme, F. S. Flint, H. D., Richard Aldington, and others has become a legend of sorts. And much of the imagist work by various hands began to appear in Chicago in *Poetry* and in London in *Des Imagistes* and *The Freewoman* (later *The Egoist*). But the sources that Noguchi brought to Western attention as early as 1903, when *From the Eastern Sea,* the third collection of his English poems, was published in London, have become not only obscure but neglected.

In March 1913 Pound and his associates collectively drew up and published the three principles of their "faith." The first was "direct treatment of the 'thing,' whether subjective or objective." Noguchi would whole-heartedly have endorsed the formulation. The second principle called for using "absolutely no word that does not contribute to the presentation," and Noguchi had documented the practice of this tenet in the hokku by Japanese masters as well as in his own work. The third principle was "to compose in sequence of the musical phrase, not in sequence of the metronome" ("Vorticism," p. 462). Because the Japanese language radically differs from a Western language in rhythm, rhyme, stress, or tone, Noguchi would readily have assented to the proposal.

Much of Pound's early work and Noguchi's clearly reflects this accord between the imagists and Noguchi. It is true that while Pound was fascinated by Japanese poetics, he was also interested in vorticism as applied to visual arts, as his commentary on such artists as Gaudier-Brzeska, Brancusi, and Picasso indicates. Through the Poets' Club, Pound was also closely associated with Hulme, Flint, Aldington, Upward, and others, some of whom were initially attracted to Japanese color prints by such painters as Utamaro and Hokusai exhibited in the British Museum. There is clear evidence that Pound's associates also tried their hand at hokku with various degrees of seriousness and success. By the mid 1910s, imagism had indeed become the literary zeitgeist, and any poet living in London would have received some influence from the Japanese sources.

To sum up, then, Noguchi's English poems had been widely circulated in London well before September 1914, when Pound's "Vorticism" essay appeared, and Noguchi's essay on hokku in *Rhythm* and his book *The Spirit of Japanese Poetry* were published in January 1913 and March 1914, respectively. The material in the essay and the book was delivered as a series of lectures during his stay in England from December 1913 to April 1914. In these circumstances, it is hardly conceivable that the imagists did not acquaint themselves with Noguchi's ideas. Even though Pound's modernist theory might partly have derived from other sources, one can scarcely overlook the direct link between Japanese poetics and Pound's imagism through Noguchi.

NOTES

[1] Ezra Pound, "Vorticism," *Fortnightly Review,* n.s., no. 573 (September 1, 1914): 461-71; hereafter cited as "Vorticism."

[2] Hugh Kenner, *The Poetry of Ezra Pound* (Millwood, N.Y., 1947), p. 58.

[3] Earl Miner, "Pound, *Haiku* and the Image," *Hudson Review* 9 (Winter 1957): 570-84, and *The Japanese Tra-*

*dition in British and American Literature* (Princeton, N.J., 1958). There is some ambiguity in Miner's chronology since, in his article, the date of Pound's joining the Poets' Club is said to be "just before the first World War," which means perhaps between 1913 and 1914 (Miner, "Pound," p. 572). There is also another ambiguity with respect to the time and circumstance of Pound's learning about "the usefulness of Japanese poetry from Flint." Flint's interest in Japanese poetry is indicated in his own account of the matter, published in *The Egoist* for May 1, 1915: "I had been advocating in the course of a series of articles on recent books of verse a poetry in *vers libre,* akin in spirit to the Japanese" (Miner, *Japanese Tradition,* p. 100).

[4] For Noguchi's life and work, see Yoshinobu Hakutani, ed., *Selected English Writings of Yone Noguchi: An East-West Literary Assimilation,* vol. 1, *Poetry* (Cranbury, N.J., 1990), and vol. 2, *Prose* (Cranbury, N.J., 1992). For the most recent study of Noguchi's life, including an interview with his son, the late American sculptor Isamu Noguchi, see Hakutani, "Father and Son: A Conversation with Isamu Noguchi," *Journal of Modern Literature* (in press). For a discussion of Noguchi's English poetry and literary criticism, see Hakutani, "Yone Noguchi's Poetry: From Whitman to Zen," *Comparative Literature Studies* 22 (Spring 1985): 67-79.

[5] Ezra Pound, "As for Imagisme," *New Age* 14 (1915): 349.

[6] The impact of hokku on Pound was apparently greater and more beneficial than that on his fellow imagists. Regarding the form of superposition as ideal for expressing instantaneous perception, Pound wrote in a footnote: "Mr. Flint and Mr. Rodker have made longer poems depending on a similar presentation of matter. So also have Richard Aldington, in his *In Via Sestina,* and 'H. D.' in her *Oread,* which latter poems express much stronger emotions than that in my lines here given" ("Vorticism," p. 467). Pound's argument here suggests that hokku and Pound's hokku-like poems can express instantaneous and spontaneous perception better than can the longer poems and the poems with stronger emotions.

[7] E. A. Sharp, *William Sharp* [Fiona Macleod]: *A Memoir* (London, 1910), pp. 280-81.

[8] Yone Noguchi, "What Is a Hokku Poem?" *Rhythm* 11 (1913): 354-59. The essay was reprinted in Noguchi's *Through the Torii* (London, 1914; Boston, 1922), pp. 126-39. The page numbers cited hereafter refer to the *Rhythm* version.

[9] Noguchi, "What Is a Hokku Poem?" p. 355.

[10] Ibid.

[11] In a November 24, 1913, letter to Pound, Mary Fenollosa wrote: "I am beginning with [*sic*] right now, to send you material." On the following day she wrote

again: "Please don't get discouraged at the ragged way this manuscript is coming to you. As I said yesterday, it will all get there in time, which is the most important thing." See *Ezra Pound and Japan: Letters and Essays*, ed. Sanehide Kodama (Redding Ridge, Conn., 1987), p. 6.

[12] Ernest Fenollosa, *The Chinese Written Character as a Medium for Poetry*, ed. Ezra Pound (New York, 1936), p. 8.

[13] One of Pound's critics who acknowledge this fact, Roy E. Teele, demonstrates Fenollosa's failure to understand the Japanese language, particularly the essential rhythm of the noh text Fenollosa translated. See Roy E. Teele, "The Japanese Translations," *Texas Quarterly* 10 (1967): 61-66.

[14] Earl Miner, who states that Pound knew nothing about Japanese poetry before 1913 or 1914, believes that Pound later learned about hokku in the writings of the French translators (Miner, "Pound," pp. 572-73).

[15] *Ezra Pound and Japan*, p. 4.

[16] Yone Noguchi, *Collected English Letters*, ed. Ikuko Atsumi (Tokyo, 1975), pp. 210-11.

[17] See Yone Noguchi, "The Everlasting Sorrow: A Japanese Noh Play," *The Egoist* 4 (October 1917): 141-43, and "The Japanese Noh Play," *The Egoist* 5 (August 1918): 99.

[18] See K. L. Goodwin, *The Influence of Ezra Pound* (London, 1966), p. 32.

[19] Noguchi first met Yeats in 1903 as indicated in a letter Noguchi wrote to Leonie Gilmour, his first wife: "I made many a nice young, lovely, kind friend among literary *genius* (attention!) W. B. Yeats or Laurence Binyon, Moore and Bridges. They are so good; they invite me almost every day" (Noguchi, *Collected English Letters*, p. 106). In 1921, Yeats in Oxford wrote to Noguchi in Tokyo: "Though I have been so long in writing[,] your 'Hiroshige' has given me the greatest pleasure. I take more and more pleasure from oriental art; find more and more that it accords with what I aim at in my own work. The European painter of the last two or three hundred years grows strange to me as I grow older, begins to speak as with a foreign tongue. . . . The old French poets were simple as the modern are not, & I find in Francois Villon the same thoughts, with more intellectual power, that I find in the Gaelic poet [Raftery]. I would be simple myself but I do not know how. I am always turning over pages like those you have sent me, hoping that in my old age I may discover how. . . . A form of beauty scarcely lasts a generation with us, but it lasts with you for centuries. You no more want to change it than a pious man wants to change the Lord's Prayer, or the Crucifix on the wall [blurred] at least not unless we have infected you with our egotism" (Noguchi, *Collected English Letters*, pp. 220-21).

[20] Goodwin, p. 32.

[21] See William Pratt, *The Imagist Poem* (New York, 1963), pp. 14-15; J. B. Harmer, *Victory in Limbo: Imagism 1908-1917* (New York, 1975), p. 17; Humphrey Carpenter, *A Serious Character: The Life of Ezra Pound* (Boston, 1988), p. 115.

[22] It is speculative, of course, but quite possible that Aldington, fascinated by Japanese visual arts, might have read the three articles Noguchi published about the subject in this period: "Utamaro," *Rhythm* 11, no. 10 (1912): 257-60, "Koyetsu," *Rhythm* 11, no. 11 (1912): 302-5, "The Last Master [Yoshitoshi] of the Ukiyoye School," *Transactions of the Japan Society of London* 12 (1914): 144-56. Moreover, Yone Noguchi, *The Spirit of Japanese Art* (London, 1915) includes chapters on major Japanese painters such as Koyetsu, Kenzan, Kyosai, and Busho Hara, besides Utamaro and Hiroshige. If Aldington had read these essays, he would very well have been acquainted with Noguchi's writings about Japanese poetics.

[23] Aldington's poem reads:

> The apparition of these poems in a crowd:
> White faces in a black dead faint.

See Aldington, "Penultimate Poetry," *The Egoist* (January 15, 1915). This poem sounds more like senryu, a humorous haiku, than the hokku Pound was advocating.

[24] Donald Davie, *Ezra Pound* (New York, 1975), p. 42; Carpenter, p. 247.

[25] Compare Harmer, p. 38.

[26] Miner, "Pound" (n. 3 above), p. 572.

[27] See Usaburo Toyama, ed., *Essays on Yone Noguchi* (Tokyo, 1975), 1:327. (The text is mostly in Japanese.) Toyama, an art historian, was married to Noguchi's daughter Hifumi.

[28] A. R. Jones, *The Life and Opinions of Thomas Ernest Hulme* (Boston, 1960), p. 122. Neither Noel Stock, in *Poet in Exile: Ezra Pound* (Manchester, 1964), nor Humphrey Carpenter in *A Serious Character* mentions Pound's activities at the Quest Society, let alone Pound's possible interactions with Noguchi.

[29] See T. S. Eliot, ed. and introduction, *Literary Essays of Ezra Pound* (Norfolk, Conn., 1954), p. 23.

[30] Noguchi, "What Is a Hokku Poem?" (n. 8 above), p. 355.

[31] About this time Noguchi also wrote an essay entitled "A Japanese Note on Yeats," included in *Through the Torii* (n. 8 above), pp. 110-17.

[32] Noguchi's "Tell Me the Street to Heaven" was first published in his essay, "What Is a Hokku Poem?" (p.

358) and reprinted in *Through the Torii.* "Is It, Oh, List" was also included in the same issue and reprinted in *Through the Torii* with a change in the third line: "So runs Thames, so runs my Life" (p. 136).

[33] Ezra Pound, *Personae* (New York, 1926), p. 109.

[34] Ibid., pp. 109-11.

[35] Eliot, ed., p. 4.

[36] Ibid.

[37] See T. S. Eliot, *Selected Essays, 1917-1932* (New York, 1932), pp. 8-10.

[38] Noguchi, *Through the Torii,* p. 159.

[39] The original in Japanese reads "Hiya hiya to / Kabe wo fumaete / Hirune kana." See Harold G. Henderson, *An Introduction to Haiku* (Garden City, N.Y., 1958), p. 49. The English translation of this hokku is mine.

[40] Pound, *Personae,* p. 100.

[41] Ibid., p. 108.

[42] Alan Durant tries to show that Pound's metro poem contains a number of metaphors and associations, and that it is not as imagistic as critics say. While Durant's interpretation holds insofar as the various elements in the poem appear to the reader as metaphors and associations, Pound's intention does differ from the emphases of such an interpretation. The same thing may occur in the interpretation of a Japanese hokku, but traditionally the language of the hokku, as Noguchi demonstrates throughout *The Spirit of Japanese Poetry* (London, 1914), shuns metaphor and symbolism. See Alan Durant, "Pound, Modernism and Literary Criticism: A Reply to Donald Davie," *Critical Quarterly* 28 (1986): 154-66.

[43] Eliot, ed. (n. 29 above), p. 4.

[44] Ezra Pound, *The Spirit of Romance* (London, 1910; reprint, New York, 1968), p. 97.

[45] Noguchi, "Again on *Hokku,*" in *Through the Torii* (n. 8 above), pp. 140-46. A verbatim account is given in the introduction to his *Japanese Hokkus* (Boston, 1920), pp. 22-23. For Noguchi's London experiences, see "My First London Experience (1903)," and "Again in London (1913-14)," in *The Story of Yone Noguchi Told by Himself* (London, 1914), pp. 119-65.

[46] The union of different experiences is reminiscent of T. S. Eliot's statement about an amalgamation. In reference to John Donne's poetry, Eliot writes, "When a poet's mind is perfectly equipped for its work, it is constantly amalgamating disparate experience; the ordinary man's experience is chaotic, irregular, fragmentary. The latter falls in love, or reads Spinoza, and these two experiences have nothing to do with each other, or with the noise of the typewriter or the smell of cooking; in the mind of the poet these experiences are always forming new wholes" (*Selected Essays,* p. 247).

[47] In *The Spirit of Japanese Poetry,* Noguchi wrote, "As the so-called literary expression is a secondary matter in the realm of poetry, there is no strict boundary between the domains generally called subjective and objective; while some *Hokku* poems appear to be objective, those poems are again by turns quite subjective through the great virtue of the writers having the fullest identification with the matter written on. You might call such collation poetical trespassing; but it is the very point whence the Japanese poetry gains unusual freedom; that freedom makes us join at once with the soul of Nature" (pp. 43-44).

[48] Noguchi, "What Is a Hokku Poem?" p. 357.

[49] Ezra Pound, *Gaudier-Brzeska: A Memoir* (London, 1916; reprint, New York, 1970), pp. 120-21.

[50] Yone Noguchi, *The Pilgrimage* (London, 1908), 1:68.

[51] To the Japanese, such expressions as "the light of passion" and "the cicada's song" immediately evoke images of hot summer. These phrases in Japanese are attributed to or closely associated with summer.

[52] For Whitman's influence on Noguchi, see Hakutani, "Yone Noguchi's Poetry: From Whitman to Zen" (n. 4 above): "Like Whitman, Noguchi believes in monism, and his ultimate goal in writing poetry is to achieve the ecstasies of the self in nature. . . . Though he became a different kind of nature poet after he returned to Japan, his later poems still bear out Whitman's influence" (p. 69).

## Yoshinobu Hakutani (excerpt date 1992)

SOURCE: An introduction to *Selected Writings of Yone Noguchi: An East-West Literary Assimilation,* Volume 2, Associated University Presses, 1992, pp. 13-51.

[*In the following excerpt, Hakutani explores the influence of Noguchi's work on that of William Butler Yeats and—in a fuller elucidation of topics discussed by Hakutani earlier—Ezra Pound.*]

1

Since childhood, W. B. Yeats felt in his heart that "only ancient things and the stuff of dreams were beautiful."[1] It was the rise of science and realism in the Victorian age that directed his attention to the Middle Ages and the world of myths and legends. As he read *Certain Noble Plays of Japan,* translated by Ezra Pound and Ernest Fenollosa in 1916, he found in them what he would emulate in reshaping his own poetic drama. "In fact," he wrote, "with the help of these plays . . . I have invented a form of drama, distinguished, indirect and symbolic, and having no need of mob or press to pay its way an aristocratic form."[2] Although there is no controversy over who introduced Yeats to the noh play, critics have overlooked other sources on which he might have relied.[3]

Having lived many years in Japan as an art historian, Fenollosa became well versed in Japanese art and literature, but his actual knowledge of the language was not profound.[4] Pound, on the other hand, who edited Fenollosa's notes, had no knowledge of Japanese. Since he did not visit Japan, he was unable to see the actual performance of a noh play in Japanese. Nor did he have firsthand knowledge of the drama and its cultural background. The most likely source of information available to Yeats, besides Fenollosa and Pound, was a bilingual poet and critic named Yone Noguchi, who had by the mid 1910s published not only such widely read books of criticism in England and America as *The Spirit of Japanese Poetry* (1914) and *The Spirit of Japanese Art* (1915), but several collections of his own poems in English.[5] In *The Spirit of Japanese Poetry,* in particular, Noguchi included a long discussion of noh entitled "*No:* The Japanese Play of Silence" with his own composition of a noh play in English, **"The Morning-Glory (A Dramatic Fragment)"** (54-70). Noguchi was also invited to contribute another English noh play, **"The Everlasting Sorrow: A Japanese Noh Play"** (1917), and an article, **"The Japanese Noh Play"** (1918), to *The Egoist.*[6]

Not only through Noguchi's writings did Yeats learn about Japanese art and literature, and the noh play in particular, but he made much of his acquaintance with Noguchi in person. Noguchi, in fact, delivered in England several lectures on Japanese art and literature. Among them, **"The Japanese *Hokku* Poetry"** was a lecture given at Oxford's Magdalen College in January 1914 at the invitation of Robert Bridges, the Poet Laureate, and Dr. T. H. Warren, President of the college.[7] In the same month Noguchi gave another lecture, "Japanese Poetry" at the Japan Society of London.[8] It seems as though Yeats's interest in Japanese painting and noh coincided with the publication of Noguchi's essays and lectures on these subjects during this period.

But Yeats's personal acquaintance with Noguchi goes back a decade earlier. Yeats first met Noguchi in 1903 as indicated in a letter Noguchi wrote to Leonie Gilmour, Noguchi's first wife: "I made many a nice young, lovely, kind friend among literary *genius* (attention!) W. B. Yeats or Laurence Binyon, Moore and Bridges. They are so good; they invite me almost everyday."[9] Many years later Yeats wrote to Noguchi, who was in Japan:

4 Broad St., Oxford

June 27 [1921?]

Dear Noguchi:

Though I have been so long in writing your "Hiroshige" has given me the greatest pleasure. I take more and more pleasure from oriental art; find more and more that it accords with what I aim at in my own work. The European painter of the last two or three hundred years grows strange to me as I grow older, begins to speak as with a foreign tongue. When a Japanese, or Mogul, or Chinese painter seems to say, "Have I not drawn a beautiful scene", one agrees at once, but when a modern European painter says so one does not agree so quickly, if at all. All your painters are simple, like the writers of Scottish ballads or the inventors of Irish stories, but one feels that Orpen and John have relatives in the patent office who are conscious of being at the fore-front of time. The old French poets were simple as the modern are not, & I find in François Villon the same thoughts, with more intellectual power, that I find in the Gaelic poet [Raftery]. I would be simple myself but I do not know how. I am always turning over pages like those you have sent me, hoping that in my old age I may discover how. I wish [now] some Japanese would tell us all about the lives [blurred] their talk, their loves, their religion, their friends [blurred] of these painters. I would like to know these things minutely and to know too what their houses looked like, and if they still stand, to know all those things that are known about Blake, and about Turner and about Rossetti. It might make it more easy to understand their simplicity. A form of beauty scarcely last a generation with us, but it lasts with you for centuries. You no more want to change it than a pious man wants to change the Lord's Prayer, or the Crucifix on the wall [blurred] at least not unless we have infected you with our egotism.

I wish I had found my way to your country a year ago & were still there, for my own remains un[blurred] as I dreaded that it would. I have not seen Galway for a long time now for I am warned that it is no place for wife and child.

Yours sincerely

W. B. Yeats

(*English Letters*, 220-21)

As this letter suggests, Yeats's introduction to the noh came after his fascination with the oriental paintings he had seen in England. His interest in Japanese visual arts was intensified by Noguchi's *The Spirit of Japanese Art* (1915) and later by his *Hiroshige* (1921), which was produced with numerous collotype illustrations and a colored frontispiece.[10] What seemed to have inspired Yeats was the "simplicity" of the artists, a century-old form of beauty that transcends time and place. Irked by modern ingenuity and science, he was adamantly opposed to realism in art and literature. For him realism failed to uncover the deeply ingrained human spirit and character. He later discovered that noble spirits and profound emotions are expressed with simplicity in the noh play. His statement about the simple beauty of Japanese arts is reminiscent of Noguchi's characterization of noh drama. "It was the time," Noguchi writes, "when nobody asked who wrote them, if the plays themselves were worthy.

What a difference from this day of advertisement and personal ambition! . . . I mean that they are not the creation of one time or one age; it is not far wrong to say that they wrote themselves, as if flowers or trees rising from the rich soil of tradition and Buddhistic faith" (*Spirit of Japanese Poetry,* 63).

Yeats and Noguchi thus shared the notion that simplicity and naturalness in Japanese arts came from the cultural backgrounds of the arts rathern than the individual emotions of artists. Yeats clearly implied in his letter to Noguchi that contemporary arts in the West were "infected with egotism" while classical works of art in Japan, as Noguchi observed, were created as if anonymously. "The names of the authors, alas," Noguchi writes, "are forgotten, or they hid their own names by choice. Even when some of their names, Seami and Otoami for instance, are given, it is said by an authority that they are, in fact, only responsible for the music, the dance, and the general stage management" (*Spirit of Japanese Poetry,* 63).

Among the classic arts in Japan, noh drama had the strongest appeal to Yeats because it was buttressed by a spiritual and philosophical foundation. Initially he was attracted to noh, which had developed from religious rites practiced in the festivals of the Shinto gods, as Fenollosa notes in *The Classic Noh Theatre of Japan.* Although Yeats was introduced to noh through Fenollosa's historical accounts of the genre, first published in 1916, he quite likely acquired further knowledge from Noguchi's *The Spirit of Japanese Poetry* (1914). In it Noguchi reminds the reader that as the Japanese tea-ceremony grew out of Zen, the noh drama had an intimate connection with Buddhism. Among the three hundred existing noh plays, he points out, there is no play in which a priest does not appear to offer prayers so that the ghost of a warrior, a lady, a flower, or a tree may attain Nirvana. The purpose of a noh play is to recount "the human tragedy rather than comedy of the old stories and legends seen through the Buddhistic flash of understanding" (63). To Yeats, such a form of beauty as seen in the classic art of Japan, which lasts for centuries, changes no more than the Lord's Prayer or the Crucifix on the wall portrayed in the classic art of Europe changes.

The spiritual foundation of noh drama also has a corollary to the abhorrence both Yeats and Noguchi felt about realism and sensationalism in contemporary arts. In place of surface realism a great dramatist would employ rituals and masks. When Yeats was introduced to the noh theatre, he was at once impressed with such devices. In the performance of *At the Hawk's Well,* he used masks to present intensified, time-honored expressions as the Roman theatre "abandoned 'make-up' and used the mask instead." He thought the use of the mask is "to create once more heroic or grotesque types that, keeping always an appropriate distance from life." The images created by the mask can convey "those profound emotions that exist only in solitude and in silence" rather than in actual scenes and personages.[11] His idea about the mask, in fact,

repeats Noguchi's: "the mask," Noguchi argues, "is made to reserve its feeling, and the actors wonderfully well protect themselves from falling into the bathos of the so-called realism through the virtue of poetry and prayer" (*Spirit of Japanese Poetry,* 60).

The comments Yeats made after the performance of *At the Hawk's Well* in 1917 are foreshadowed in a passage written in the previous year:

A mask never seems but a dirty face, and no matter how close you go is still a work of art; nor shall we lose by staying the movement of the features, for deep feeling is expressed by a movement of the whole body. In poetical painting and in sculpture the face seems the nobler for lacking curiosity, alert attention, all that we sum up under the famous word of the realists 'vitality.' It is even possible that being is only possessed completely by the dead, and that it is some knowledge of this that makes us gaze with so much emotion upon the face of the Sphinx or Buddha. . . .

Let us press the popular arts on to a more complete realism, for that would be their honesty; and the commercial arts demoralise by their compromise, their incompleteness, their idealism without sincerity or elegance, their pretence that ignorance can understand beauty. In the studio and in the drawing-room we can found a true theatre of beauty. (*Classic Noh Theatre,* 155-56)

In *The Spirit of Japanese Poetry,* published a few years earlier than Yeats's essay, Noguchi, as if to call for Yeats's response, had written:

When the Japanese poetry joined its hand with the stage, we have the *No* drama, in which the characters sway in music, soft but vivid, as if a web in the air of perfume; we Japanese find our joy and sorrow in it. Oh, what a tragedy and beauty in the *No* stage! I always think that it would be certainly a great thing if the *No* drama could be properly introduced into the West; the result would be no small protest against the Western stage, it would mean a real revelation for those people who are well tired of their own plays with a certain pantomimic spirit underneath. (*Spirit of Japanese Poetry,* 11)

The salient feature of noh that must have held a strong appeal for Yeats is the structure of a noh play. Unlike a realistic, mimetic play in the West, the noh play thrives on its unity and concentration. It was Pound again who called Yeats's attention to this play as a concentrated image. In "Vorticism," an essay on imagism published in *The Fortnightly Review* in 1914, Pound included a note: "I am often asked whether there can be a long imagiste or vorticist poem. The Japanese, who evolved the hokku, evolved also the Noh plays. In the best 'Noh' the whole play may consist of one image. I mean it is gathered about one image. Its unity consists in one image, enforced by movement and music."[12] Pound's statement, however, was derived from Fenollosa, who wrote:

The beauty and power of Noh lie in the concentration. All elements costume, motion, verse, and music unite to produce a single clarified impression. Each drama embodies some primary human relation or emotion; and the poetic sweetness or poignancy of this is carried to its highest degree by carefully excluding all such obtrusive elements as a mimetic realism or vulgar sensation might demand. The emotion is always fixed upon idea, not upon personality. (*Classic Noh Theatre,* 69)

Fenollosa's notes, moreover, made Pound realize that a series of different noh plays presents "a complete service of life" (11). Visions of life portrayed on the noh stage are not segmented; they are continuous and unified. "We do not find," Pound reminds the reader, "as we find in Hamlet, a certain situation or problem set out and analysed. The Noh service presents, or symbolizes a complete diagram of life and recurrence" (11-12). In some ways noh resembles the Greek play, for the individual plays deal with well-known legends and myths. As an Oedipus play treats the character of Oedipus in a known predicament, *Suma Genji,* for example, features Shite, an old wood-cutter, who appears as the ghost of the hero Genji at the seashore of Suma.

To present a cycle of life and death, the noh play often employs spirits and ghosts. Such a structural device, obviously different from the Western convention of plot, accounts for a different philosophy of life that underlies noh. As if to explain this difference, Noguchi made a modest proposal for Western writers. "I think," he urged, "it is time for them to live more of the passive side of Life and Nature, so as to make the meaning of the whole of them perfect and clear, to value the beauty of inaction so as to emphasise action, to think of Death so as to make Life more attractive" (*Spirit of Japanese Poetry,* 24). The concept of unity and continuity expressed in Japanese literature primarily stemmed from Zen Buddhism, which teaches its believers to transcend the dualism of life and death. Zen master Dogen (1200-54), whose work *Shobogenzo* is known in Japan for its practical application rather than his theory of Zen doctrine, said that there is no need to avoid death because it is beyond man's control.[13] Dogen's teaching is a refutation of the assumption that life and death are entirely separate entities as are seasons.

Among the fifteen noh plays translated by Fenollosa and Pound, seven of them present characters that appear as spirits and ghosts to interact with living persons. In *Nishikigi,* the priest has a dream in which the unrequited love of a dead man for a living woman is consummated through the priest's prayer. Yeats's *The Dreaming of the Bones* (1919) has a plot structure strikingly similar to that of *Nishikigi:* the lovers Diarmuid and Dervorgilla as spirits brought the Norman invaders into Ireland after seven centuries to consummate their love by an Irish revolutionary taking the role of a noh priest. Yeats's attempt to reconcile life and death also extends to other opposites in human life: body and soul, man and spirit, man and woman, good and evil, and so on. The image of man and spirit, life and death, recurs frequently in Yeats's later poem, "Byzantium" (1930):

> Before me floats an image, man or shade,
> Shade more than man, more image than a shade;
> For Hades' bobbin bound in mummy-cloth
> May unwind the winding path;
> A mouth that has no moisture and no breath
> Breathless mouths may summon;
> I hail the superhuman;
> I call it death-in-life and life-in-death.[14]

There is nothing new in the West, however, about the poet's bringing the rich opposites into a unified vision. Whitman seeks a reconciliation between life and death, man and God, and other oppositions. He turns the bereavement in "When Lilacs Last with the Dooryard Bloom'd" into a celebration of death. In "A Sight in Camp in the Daybreak Gray and Dim," the poet, after seeing two of his comrades lying dead, one old and another young, comes upon a third "a face nor child nor old, very calm, as of beautiful yellow white ivory." The third dead soldier is identified with "the Christ himself, / Dead and divine and brother of all, and here again he lies."[15] But the problem with Western poetry and drama, Yeats felt, was the lack of intensity and artistry in presenting the image of unity and continuity.

Pound's and Fenollosa's notes about symbolism on the noh stage, therefore, were of great use to Yeats, who was eager to adapt an image that unifies the play or an action that foreshadows the outcome. The well in *At the Hawk's Well,* the birds in *Calvary,* and Cuchulain lying on his death bed in *The Only Jealousy of Emer* were all consciously modeled on the noh play. In 1920 Arthur Waley, who translated with success the monumental *Tale of Genji,* also published *The No Plays of Japan,* a translation of over twenty well-known plays, with lengthy notes, but his writings were of no particular interest to Yeats. Waley's introduction is primarily a historical survey of the genre with well-detailed biographical and textual notes on Zeami, the most celebrated noh dramatist. Waley thus in no significant way helped Yeats understand symbolism in the noh play. The only native scholar writing in English was Yone Noguchi, who not only wrote about noh but even tried his hand at composing noh plays in English.

Yeats's interest in the symbolism used on the noh stage came from a desire to condense and simplify the action of his plays. This means that action must be reduced to its essentials and that the characters involved in it must be freed from anything that may distract the viewer's attention from the meaning of the play. The stage does not show any elaborate scenery, nor do subsidiary persons appear on the scene. The stage for the well-known *Takasago,* for instance, contains a painted old pine-tree which, Noguchi describes, "looms as if a symbol of eternity out of the mist." The word *pine-tree,* signaling "the hosts of pine-trees in the shapes of an old man and woman singing death-lessness and peace," is repeated throughout the performance. On the gallery connected with the stage, Noguchi says, "*No* actors move as spectres and make the performance complete, the passage of a beginning and ending, I might say Life and Death" (*Spirit of Japanese Poetry,* 58).

Simplicity and concentration are so essential to the performance of a noh play that the stage itself must be physically small and confined. "There is no other stage like this *No* stage," Noguchi emphasizes, "the actors and audience go straight into the heart of prayer in creating the most intense atmosphere of grayness, the most suggestive colour in all Japanese art, which is the twilight soared out of time and place." As Yeats would wholeheartedly have agreed, "it is a divine sanctuary where the vexation of the outer world and the realism of modern life" are left behind (*Spirit of Japanese Poetry,* 55-58). Anything that gets in the way of concentration, such as scenery, is eliminated. In the notes to *At the Hawk's Well,* Yeats writes:

> I do not think of my discovery as mere economy, for it has been a great gain to get rid of scenery, to substitute for a crude landscape painted upon canvas three performers who, sitting before the wall or a patterned screen, describe landscape or event, and accompany movement with drum and gong, or deepen the emotion of the words with zither or flute. Painted scenery, after all, is unnecessary to my friends and to myself, for our imagination kept living by the arts can imagine a mountain covered with thorn-trees in a drawing-room without any trouble, and we have many quarrels with even good scene-painting. (*Plays of Yeats,* 415-16)

Equally effective is the use of the mask that enables the actors and audience alike to concentrate on the meaning of the play. "*No,*" as Noguchi reminds the English reader, "is the mask play to speak directly, although that is not an exact translation." Noguchi further points out that the noh mask is able "to differentiate the most delicate shades of human sensibility; we should thank our own imagination which turns the wood to a spirit more alive than you or I, when neither the actors nor the mask-carvers can satisfactorily express their secret" (*Spirit of Japanese Poetry,* 59-60). The mask, a permanent work of art, is made to preserve its feeling so that the actors, uninfluenced by the superficial actuality, protect themselves from falling into what Noguchi calls "the bathos of reality which would, in nine cases out of ten, alienate them from the rhythmical creation of beauty."[16] Yeats was convinced of the notion that the mask can convey legendary emotions far more artistically than the actual face of an actor. For his Cuchulain, a legendary figure, can show with the mask "a face, not made before the looking-glass by some leading player . . . but moulded by some distinguished artist." For Yeats, the device of the mask is a culmination of the joint effort by a poet and an artist to keep "an appropriate distance from life" (*Plays of Yeats,* 416).

Another structural device is the dance performed at the climax. Dance in noh is not choreographic movement as

in the ballet, but, as Yeats cautions, "a series of positions and movements which may represent a battle, or a marriage, or the pain of a ghost in the Buddhist purgatory." While the Western dance often presents mimetic movements of arms or body to express physical beauty, dancers in noh, always keeping the upper part of their body still, "associate with every gesture or pose some definite thought." The focus of attention in the noh dance is not on the human form, but on the rhythm to which it moves. "The triumph of their art," Yeats recognizes, "is to express the rhythm in its intensity." The aim of such dance is to intensify the deep meaning of the play, and the deeper the meaning is the fewer and simpler the gesture of the dance is. As Yeats observed, dancers in the noh stage "pause at moments of muscular tension." The dancers walk on the stage "with a sliding movement, and one gets the impression not of undulation but of continuous straight lines" (*Classic Noh Theatre,* 158).

The function of dance in noh was later adapted to Yeats's poetry. In "Among School Children," for example, Yeats uses the metaphor of the dance to suggest a unity of oppositions in human life:

> Labour in blossoming or dancing where
> The body is not bruised to pleasure soul,
> Nor beauty born out of its own despair,
> Nor blear-eyed wisdom out of midnight oil.
> O chestnut tree, great rooted blossomer,
> Are you the leaf, the blossom or the bole?
> O body swayed to music, O brightening glance,
> How can we know the dancer from the dance?
>                                         (*Poems of Yeats,* 217)

In Yeats's vision the body and the soul become indistinguishable because of the unifying image of the dance.[17] In a similar vein, Noguchi as a Japanese poet goes to nature to make life more meaningful; he, too, tries to bring the opposition of man and nature into a unified vision:

> It's accident to exist as a flower or a poet;
> A mere twist of evolution but from the same force:
> I see no form in them but only beauty in evidence;
> It's the single touch of their imagination to get the
>         embodiment of a poet or a flower:
>
> To be a poet is to be a flower,
> To be the dancer is to make the singer sing.
>                                 (*Spirit of Japanese Poetry,* 37)

The reconciliation of oppositions also occurs with the image of a flower in Noguchi's noh play, **"The Morning-Glory,"** as is the consummation of love between the estranged lovers symbolized by the climactic dance of the Rainbow Skirt and Feather Jacket in his other noh play, **"The Everlasting Sorrow."**[18] In **"The Morning-Glory,"** the Priest at the end of the play speaks to the Lady, the personification of a flower:

> "Poor child, there is no life where is no death:
> Death is nothing but the turn or change of note.
> The shortest life is the sweetest, as is the shortest
>         song:
> How to die well means how to live well.

Life is no quest of longevity and days:
Where are the flowers a hundred years old?
Oh, live in death and Nirvana, live in dissolution
    and rest,
Make a life out of death and darkness;
Lady or flower, be content, be finished as a song
    that is sung!"
                                (*Spirit of Japanese Poetry*, 70)

Yeats's adaptation from the noh play is not only in structure and technique, but in style. His borrowing of the conventions and devices from noh are apparent in his stage directions included in the text as well in the notes written separately, but the stylistic influences of the Japanese poetics upon Yeats's writing are subtle. To define Japanese characteristics in his style would be to find fine distinctions between his earlier style and that of his later period as a result of his familiarity with noh drama.

His *Autobiography* (1938) makes it clear that his early poetry was aesthetic. His poetical style was the product of the emotionalism associated with the *fin de siècle*, as well as of late nineteenth-century impressionism. Because he was not altogether content with the conventional refinement and gentility of English aestheticism, he was eager to vitalize his style as he was introduced to the noh play. The language of noh is consistently devoid of embellishment and tautology; the aim of a great noh dramatist like Zeami is to seek the profound beauty in expression influenced neither by the wishful thinking of the writer nor by the fashion of the day. Yeats recognized this mode of expression when he studied certain of the noh dances with Japanese players.[19] What he noticed was "their ideal of beauty, unlike that of Greece and like that of pictures from Japan and China" (*Classic Noh Theatre*, 158).

In writing *At the Hawk's Well* Yeats attempted to adapt a style of tension and intensity which is characteristic of the noh structure and of the noh dance in particular. The dramatic power of this play lies in the opening lines sung by the musicians while they unfold a piece of cloth symbolizing the well. The verse is direct and taut, the image clear, and the song rhythmic:

I call to the eye of the mind
A well long choked up and dry
And boughs long stripped by the wind,
And I call to the mind's eye
Pallor of an ivory face,
A man climbing up to a place
The salt sea wind has swept bare.
                                (*Plays of Yeats*, 399)

The vividness and intensity of imagery can also be seen in Yeats's later poetry. In "Byzantium," for example, passion and violence coalesce into the unified and intensified image of a dance:

Where blood-begotten spirits come
And all complexities of fury leave,
Dying into a dance,
An agony of trance,
An agony of flame that cannot singe a sleeve.
                                (*Poems of Yeats*, 248)

The symbolic use of a dance also occurs in Noguchi's English poem **"Hagoromo,"** a summary translation of the well-known noh *Hagoromo*.[20] Pound made a poetic translation of the play into English, based on Fenollosa's notes, and incorporated into his *Cantos*.[21] Noguchi, on the other hand, renders the scene of the dance in a prose poem:

The fisherman blushed hugely from shame, and restored the robe to the angel. The angel in her waving robe, with every secret and charm of clouds and sky, with Spring and beauty, began to dance: the fisherman cried in rapturous delight, "Behold! Behold!" The angel sung: "And then in the Heavens of melody and peace, a place of glory and Love was built by magic hands: it bears the name of Moon. . . . I now stray from the golden sphere, and show the heavenly dance to Mankind. . . ."

The air overflowed with dreams: the Heavens and earth joined their arms and hearts. O angel, dance on through the purple hours: Oh, dance on, fair maiden, while the heavenly flowers crown thy tresses in odorous breeze: O beauteous angel, dance on in Life and Love![22]

The metaphor of dance used by Yeats and Noguchi, an increased dramatic intensity in poems of dialogue, is thus adapted from the noh play.

The element of style most pervasive in the language of noh is called in Japanese *yugen,* an aesthetic principle originated in Zen metaphysics. *Yugen* designates the mysterious and dark, what underlies the surface. The mode of expression is subtle as opposed to obvious, suggestive rather than declarative. In reference to the *Works* by Zeami, the author of many of the extant noh plays, Arthur Waley expounds this difficult term *yugen:*

It is applied to the natural graces of a boy's movements, to the gentle restraint of a nobleman's speech and bearing. "When notes fall sweetly and flutter delicately to the ear," that is the *yugen* of music. The symbol of *yugen* is "a white bird with a flower in its beak." "To watch the sun sink behind a flower-clad hill, to wander on and on in a huge forest with no thought of return, to stand upon the shore and gaze after a boat that goes hid by far-off islands, to ponder on the journey of wild geese seen and lost among the clouds" such are the gates to *yugen.*[23]

The fisherman in Noguchi's **"Hagoromo,"** watching the complete performance of a dance as promised by the angel, is left with the feeling of *yugen:*

The angel abruptly stopped, and looked on the fisherman, and with a pretty little bow (like that of a drowsy rose) said: "'Tis the time I have to return home: farewell, dear man!" She soon caught the zephyr from paradise: her feather robe winged Heavenward. What a strangely splendid sight! And she vanished beyond the clouds and mortal reach. The fisherman stupidly looked round over the empty sea. The singing wind passed amid the pines of the dreamy shore. (*Summer Cloud*, 4-5)

Such a scene conveys a feeling of satisfaction and release as does the catharsis of a Greek play, but *yugen* differs from catharsis because it has little to do with the emotional stress caused by tragedy. *Yugen* functions in art as a means by which man can comprehend the course of nature. Although *yugen* seems allied with a sense of resignation, it has a far different effect upon the human psyche. A certain type of noh play like *Takasago* celebrates the order of the universe ruled by heaven. The mode of perception in the play may be compared to that of a pine tree with its evergreen needles, the predominant symbol presented on the stage. The style of *yugen* can express either happiness or sorrow. Cherry blossoms, however beautiful they may be, must fade away; love between man and woman is inevitably followed by sorrow.

This mystery and elusion, which surrounds the order of the universe, had a strong appeal to Yeats. The hawk at the climax of Yeats's noh play performs an enigmatic dance, luring away the young man and inducing the old man to sleep. The dance is a symbol of the mysterious and elusive forces of the universe that thwart man's desire for immortality and knowledge. When Cuchulain hears the cry of the hawk for the first time, he utters: "It sounded like the sudden cry of a hawk, / but there's no wing in sight." During the dance, while he is mesmerized by the hawk's demeanor, the chorus sings in his behalf: "O god, protect me / From a horrible deathless body / Sliding through the veins of a sudden" (*Plays of Yeats,* 406-10). As Noguchi's dancer in "Hagoromo" "vanished beyond the clouds and mortal reach," Yeats's bird "seemed to vanish away" whenever Cuchulain approached her.

Noguchi attributes the principle of *yugen* to the ghostliness of Buddhism. "The *No,*" he says, "is the creation of the age when, by virtue of sutra or the Buddha's holy name, any straying ghosts or spirits in Hades were enabled to enter Nirvana" (*Spirit of Japanese Poetry,* 66). As an illustration he cites a Japanese noh play called *Yama Uba* or *Mountain Elf,* in which the author, a learned Buddhist priest, portrays how mortals are confused in "a maze of transmigration."[24] Noguchi describes the ending of the play "after making her prayer to the Elf, the dancer disappears over mountains and mountains, as her life's cloud of perplexity is now cleared away, and the dusts of transmigration are well swept," and adds, "This little play would certainly make a splendid subject for a modern interpretation" (*Spirit of Japanese Poetry,* 66-67).

Although Yeats's noh play at times carries religious overtones as does the Japanese noh, his mode of perception seldom reflects the religious belief. In *Calvary,* where the two principal dialogues of Christ with Lazarus and of Christ with Judas are presented, the focus of the play is upon the story of man. In the notes, Yeats writes: "I have used my bird-symbolism in these songs to increase the objective loneliness of Christ by contrasting it with a loneliness, opposite in kind, that unlike His can be, whether joyous or sorrowful, sufficient to itself." Yeats's emphasis is not on Christ but on "the images of those He cannot save"; the birds thus signify "Lazarus and Judas

and the Roman soldiers for whom He has died in vain." Departing from the Scripture, Yeats deliberately uses birds as symbols of subjective life:

> Certain birds, especially as I see things, such lonely birds as the heron, hawk, eagle, and swan, are the natural symbols of subjectivity, especially when floating upon the wind alone or alighting upon some pool or river, while the beasts that run upon the ground, especially those that run in packs, are the natural symbols of objective man. (*Plays of Yeats,* 789-90)

For Yeats, then, *yugen* is a purely aesthetic principle with which the natural symbols of subjectivity are presented. "Subjective men," Yeats further comments, "are the more lonely the more they are true to type, seeking always that which is unique or personal" (789). This manner of perception about the lonely flight of the bird exactly corresponds to the style of expression reminiscent of noh, a kind of veiled, melancholic beauty full of mystery and depth. In Yeats's *The Dreaming of the Bones,* which in its structure closely resembles the noh play *Nishikigi,* a young man describes the dance performed by the lovers Diarmuid and Dervorgilla at the climax:

> So strangely and so sweetly. All the ruin,
> All, all their handiwork is blown away
> As though the mountain air had blown it away
> Because their eyes have met. They cannot hear,
> Being folded up and hidden in their dance.
>
>          . . . . .
>
> They have drifted in the dance from rock to rock.
> They have raised their hands as though to snatch
>     the sleep
> That lingers always in the abyss of the sky
> Though they can never reach it. A cloud floats up
> And covers all the mountain-head in a moment;
> And now it lifts and they are swept away.
>                           (*Plays of Yeats,* 774-75)

The consummation of love celebrated in this play epitomizes the poetics of *yugen,* for "the aim of the Noh play," Noguchi asserts in *The Egoist,* "is to express a desire of yearning, not for beauty, but for the beauty we dream" ("**Japanese Noh Play,**" 99). The success of the noh play, therefore, depends not so much upon the truth of history or humanity as upon the attainment of what Edgar Allan Poe called "a portion of that Loveliness whose very elements, perhaps, appertain to eternity alone."[25]

This concept of beauty was instrumental in drawing Yeats's interest to Japanese poetics. Historically, the influence of noh on Yeats's style was inevitable. Yeats was deeply impressed with noh drama because he found himself in the age of realism. "I am bored and wretched, a limitation I greatly regret," he complained, when the artist seemed to him "no longer a human being but an invention of science" (*Classic Noh Theatre,* 152). Yeats did not merely attempt to imitate noh plays, but succeeded in adapting the form to his own purposes. His aim was to restore the Irish legends as Zeami yearned for the lost world of the Heian period when Japanese literature achieved its elegance.

Yeats, however, was not the earliest writer in modern times who came in close contact with Japanese literature. Lafcadio Hearn, disheartened by the onslaught of modern civilization, was inspired by the mysticism of Japanese Buddhism. Ernest Fenollosa, originally interested in Japanese visual arts, was the first to interpret the noh play for the West. And Ezra Pound, strongly influenced by Japanese poetry and by haiku, or *hokku,* in particular, launched the movement of imagism. These predecessors of Yeats, whose writings had undoubtedly a significant role in Yeats's introduction to Japanese art and literature, were, as was Yeats himself, all looking in from outside. But, more than anyone else, Noguchi, the only writer deeply ingrained in both Eastern and Western traditions, inspired Yeats's interest in Japanese culture in general and noh drama in particular.

2

It is commonplace to say that imagism played a crucial role in poetic modernism, and that Ezra Pound, more than anyone else, put this poetics to practice in the 1910s. Yet imagism still remains a somewhat cloudy topic. Many discussions content themselves with restatements of Pound's celebrated essay on vorticism, published in *The Fortnightly Review* in September 1914.[26] Even Hugh Kenner, the most eminent critic of Pound, says, "The history of the Imagist Movement is a red herring." He admonishes one "to keep one's eyes on Pound's texts, and avoid generalities about Imagism."[27]

In that "Vorticism" essay, Pound acknowledged for the first time in his career his indebtedness to the spirit of Japanese poetry in general and the technique of *hokku* in particular. Among the Poundians, and there have been many in the East and in the West, who have tried to reconstruct the historical set of circumstances in which Pound moved, Earl Miner gives the best account of the profound influences Japanese poetry had upon the early Pound. It is Miner who offers the best annotated evidence that the sources for Pound's interest in Japanese poetics were partly provided by Pound's fellow imagists such as T. E. Hulme, F. S. Flint, and Richard Aldington.[28]

It is Miner as well who most frequently comments on the role Yone Noguchi played in the introduction and interpretation of Japanese poetry to the English audience during the early decades of the twentieth century.[29] As noted earlier, Noguchi was indeed a well-known bilingual Japanese and American poet, who by 1915 had published not only books of criticism widely read in England and America (*The Spirit of Japanese Poetry* and *The Spirit of Japanese Art*), but also several collections of his own English poems. By this date, moreover, his poems had been praised by Willa Cather, Joaquin Miller, and Gelett Burgess in America, by Bliss Carman in Canada, and by George Meredith, William Rossetti, Thomas Hardy, and others in England. What is surprising, therefore, is Miner's dismissive treatment of Noguchi's English writings as having had little to do with the imagist movement and with Pound in particular.

As Pound explained in his essay, the image is not a static, rational idea:

> It is a radiant node or cluster; it is what I can, and must perforce, call a VORTEX, from which, and through which, and into which, ideas are constantly rushing. In decency one can only call it a VORTEX. And from this necessity came the name "vorticism." (469-70)

A year later Pound defined the form of an image by stating that the image "may be a sketch, a vignette, a criticism, an epigram of anything else you like. It may be impressionism, it may even be very good prose."[30] An image, he argued, does not constitute simply a picture of something. As a vortex, the image must be "endowed with energy" ("As for Imagisme," 349). Imagism, in turn, is likened to the painter's use of pigment. "The painter," Pound wrote, "should use his colour because he sees it or feels it. I don't much care whether he is representative or non-representative. . . . It is the same in writing poems, the author must use his *image* . . . not because he thinks he can use it to back up some creed or some system of ethics or economics" ("Vorticism," 464).

To demonstrate his poetic theory, Pound thought of an image not as a decorative emblem or symbol but as a seed capable of germinating and developing into another organism. As an illustration he presented what he called a "*hokku*-like sentence" he had written:

> The apparition of these faces in the crowd:
>     Petals, on a wet, black bough.

"In a poem of this sort," he explained, "one is trying to record the precise instant when a thing outward and objective transforms itself, or darts into a thing inward and subjective" ("Vorticism," 467). The image of the faces in the crowd is based in immediate experience at a metro station in Paris; it was "a thing outward and objective." Not only did Pound actually see the "thing," but it generated such a sensation that he could not shake it out of his mind. This image, he emphasizes, "transforms itself, or darts into a thing inward and subjective," that is, the image of the "Petals, on a wet, black bough." Imagism is further contrasted to symbolism: "The symbolist's *symbols* have a fixed value, like numbers in arithmetic, like 1, 2, and 7. The imagiste's images have a variable significance, like the signs *a, b,* and *x* in algebra" ("Vorticism," 463).

Although Pound's definition is clear enough, the sources for his ideas are hard to determine. Most discussions about the genesis of the imagist movement are speculative at best. Pound's insistence that an image in poetry must be active rather than passive suggests that a poem is not a description of something, but, as Aristotle said of tragedy, an action. Pound might have had Aristotle in mind when he thought that the image of the faces in the crowd in his metro poem was not simply a description of his sensation at the station, but an active entity capable of dynamic development. According to his experience, this particular image instantly transformed itself into another image, the image of the petals on a wet, black bough. To Pound the success of this poem resulted from his instantaneous perception of the relatedness between the two entirely different objects.

But Pound's note on the genesis of "In a Station of the Metro" in the vorticism essay makes it clear that there was nothing *instantaneous* about the composition of this poem. It was in 1911 that Pound, having seen those "beautiful faces" at La Concorde, wrote a thirty-line poem, "and destroyed it because it was what we call work 'of second intensity'" (467). Six months later he reduced the longer text to a poem half the length, and still a year later he wrote the final version, a two-line poem. Pound's insistence on the instantaneous perception of the metro images drove him to repeated attempts at recreating the instantaneous images he had perceived a year-and-a-half earlier. Traditionally, the principle of instantaneity and spontaneity is as fundamental for the composition of *hokku* as the same principle is when applied to Zen-inspired painting and calligraphy. In any event, his discovery of *hokku* in 1913-14 was, as he says, "useful in getting out of the impasse in which I had been left by my metro emotion" (467). To Pound, the most important thing he learned about *hokku* was "this particular sort of consciousness," which he was unable to identify with any version of impressionist art.[31]

Another equally important tenet of imagism calls for directness in expression. The immediate model for this principle was nineteenth-century French prose. Pound did not mention specific English poets, but seemed adamantly opposed to Victorian poetry, which he would characterize as wordy and rhetorical. Instead he urged his fellow poets "to bring poetry up to the level of prose." "Flaubert and De Maupassant," he believed, "lifted prose to the rank of a finer art, and one has no patience with contemporary poets who escape from all the difficulties of the infinitely difficult art of good prose by pouring themselves into loose verses" ("Vorticism," 462).

If Pound's ideal poetry has the directness and clarity of good prose as opposed to the suggestiveness and vagueness of symbolist poetry, then Pound's sources certainly did not include W. B. Yeats. Even though Yeats dedicated the noh play *At the Hawk's Well* to Pound, Yeats was not enthusiastic about Pound's poetics. "My own theory of poetical or legendary drama," Yeats wrote to Fiona Macleod, "is that it should have no realistic, or elaborate, but only a symbolic and decorative setting. A forest, for instance, should be represented by a forest pattern and not by a forest painting."[32] The difference between Pound and Yeats reveals itself in the two poets' differing views of the Japanese noh play. A symbolist and spiritualist poet, Yeats was fascinated by the noh play. By contrast, Pound was interested not in particular images and symbols, but in the unifying effect a noh play produces on the stage.

This disagreement between Pound and Yeats over whether poetic images should be "suggestive" or "active" also involves what Noguchi, a poet and critic well acquainted with both poets, felt compelled to write in his essay "What Is a Hokku Poem?" published in London in the January 1913 issue of *Rhythm*.[33] Noguchi first defined *hokku* as an expression of Japanese poets' "understanding of Nature," or, better put, as a song or chant of "their longing or wonder or adoration toward Mother Nature" that is "never mystified by any cloud or mist like Truth or Beauty of Keats' understanding." Noguchi differentiated between the "suggestive" and subjective coloration of English poetry and the Japanese *hokku,* "distinctly clear-cut like a diamond or star." "I say," he argued, "that the star itself has almost no share in the creation of a condition even when your dream or vision is gained through its beauty. . . . I value the 'hokku' poem, at least some of them, because of its own truth and humanity simple and plain." Noguchi then analyzed the aim of *hokku:* the *hokku* poet expresses the spirit of nature rather than the will of man or woman. Noguchi would agree that *hokku* is "suggestive" only if the word *suggestive* meant that "truth and humanity are suggestive." He added: "But I can say myself as a poet . . . that your poem would certainly end in artificiality if you start out to be suggestive from the beginning" (355).

Finally, Noguchi based his definition and analysis of aim in Zen philosophy, which is to be understood as discipline of the mind: one should not allow one's individuality to control action. Zen does not, indeed, recognize human reality, the existence of good and evil, because this reality is but the creation of man's will rather than the spirit of nature. Noguchi thus observed that "there is no word in so common use by Western critics as suggestive, which makes more mischief than enlightenment." Although Western critics "mean it quite simply . . . to be a new force of salvation . . . I say that no critic is necessary for this world of poetry" (355).

By 1918 Pound's vorticist theory had extended to his discussion of Chinese characters. As the correspondence between Pound and Mary Fenollosa, widow of Ernest Fenollosa, indicates, Pound began to receive Fenollosa's manuscripts as early as 1913.[34] Fenollosa's essay "The Chinese Written Characters as a Medium of Poetry," posthumously published by Pound in *The Little Review* in 1918, attempted to show that Chinese characters, which Pound called ideograms, derive from visual rather than aural experiences. A Chinese character, Fenollosa noted, signifies an observable action instead of an abstract notion. Unlike a Western word, a phonetic sign, it denotes a concrete, natural phenomenon. The Chinese character, Fenollosa wrote, "is based upon a vivid shorthand picture of the operations of nature. In the algebraic figure and in the spoken word there is no natural connection between thing and sign: all depends upon sheer convention. But the Chinese method follows natural suggestion."[35]

Pound's attempt to verify his theory involved not only his contemporaries, poets and critics living in London in the 1910s, but his own effort to search for ideas in other sources. One of these sources was the Japanese noh play, in which Pound became interested through Fenollosa's notes. It is generally understood that Pound's interest in Japanese poetry, especially *hokku,* grew partly through his acquaintance with Fenollosa's writings. None of Fenollosa's writings, however, directly concerns Japanese poetry, let alone *hokku.* Having lived many years in Japan as an art critic, Fenollosa became well versed in Japanese art and literature, but, as noted earlier, his knowledge of the language was not profound.[36] It is, therefore, inconceivable that Pound became well acquainted with *hokku* through Fenollosa. It is also unlikely that English contemporaries, such as T. E. Hulme and F. S. Flint, who are said to have introduced *hokku* to Pound, served his purpose. For Pound would not have been able to learn from them the subtle elements of Japanese poetry because they did not have firsthand knowledge of the language.[37]

Pound's most likely source of information was Noguchi. He first corresponded with Pound and then met Pound, along with Yeats, when he gave a series of lectures on Japanese poetry in England in early 1914. The relationship between Pound and Noguchi began in 1911, when Noguchi sent his fifth collection of English poems, *The Pilgrimage* (1908 and 1909) in two volumes, to Pound with a note: "As I am not yet acquainted with your work, I wish you [would] send your books or books which you like to have me read. This little note may sound quite businesslike, but I can promise you that I can do better in my next letter to you." Noguchi also wrote as a postscript: "I am anxious to read not only your poetical work but also your criticism" (*Pound and Japan,* 4). Pound acknowledged receipt of the books and note in a letter postmarked September 2, 1911:

c/o Elkin Mathews

Vigo St. London

Dear Yone Noguchi:

I want to thank you very much for your lovely books & for your kindness in sending them to me.

I had, of course, known of you, but I am much occupied with my mediaeval studies & had neglected to read your books altho' they lie with my own in Mathews shop & I am very familiar with the appearance of their covers.

I am reading those you sent me but I do not yet know what to say of them except that they have delighted me. Besides it is very hard to write to you until I know more about you, you are older than I am I gather from the dates of the poems you have been to New York. You are giving us the spirit of Japan, is it not? very much as I am trying to deliver from obscurity certain forgotten odours of Provence & Tuscany (my works on Guido

Cavalcanti, & Arnaut Daniel, are, the one in press, the other ready to be printed.)

I have sent you two volumes of poems. I do not know whether to send you "The Spirit of Romance" or not: It treats of mediaeval poetry in southern Europe but has many flaws of workmanship. . . .

Of your country I know almost nothing surely if the east & the west are ever to understand each other that understanding must come slowly & come first through the arts.

You ask about my "criticism". There is some criticism in the "Spirit of Romance" & there will be some in the prefaces to the "Guido" & the "Arnaut". But I might be more to the point if we who are artists should discuss the matters of technique & motive between ourselves. Also if you should write about these matters I would discuss your letters with Mr. Yeats & likewise my answers. . . .

Yours very sincerely

Ezra Pound[38]

Although Noguchi did not write again as Pound had suggested, Noguchi published his essay **"What Is a Hokku Poem?"** in London in January 1913, as noted earlier. In the meantime three books of criticism by Noguchi appeared during this period: *The Spirit of Japanese Poetry* (1914), *Through the Torii* (1914), and *The Spirit of Japanese Art* (1915).[39] As mentioned earlier in connection with Yeats, Noguchi was also invited to contribute **"The Everlasting Sorrow: A Japanese Noh Play"** in 1917 and an article, **"The Japanese Noh Play,"** in 1918 to *The Egoist.*[40] Pound's encouragement was perhaps responsible for the publication of some of Noguchi's own *hokku* poems in *The Egoist* and in *Poetry.*[41]

Because his essays and lectures during this period also dealt with Japanese art, Yeats, who was interested in Japanese painting and the noh play, as noted earlier, became interested in Noguchi's work as well. As Pound's and Yeats's letters to Noguchi indicate, Pound and Yeats not only were close associates themselves but were both well acquainted with Noguchi. Despite the active dialogues that occurred between Pound and Noguchi, critics have not seriously considered their relationship. The only critic who has mentioned Noguchi in discussing the imagist movement regarded Noguchi not as a poet and critic from whose ideas Pound might have benefited, but as one of the poets whom Pound himself influenced (Goodwin, 32). Such a preposterous connection is undermined by the simple fact that most of Noguchi's English poems, as Pound noted in his letter to Noguchi, had been published in America and England long before the early 1910s, when Pound and his fellow poets began to discuss imagism among themselves. It is more accurate historically to say that Noguchi influenced Pound rather than the other way around.

Pound had apparently known little about Japanese poetry before he attended the April 1909 meeting of the Poets'

Club. This group, headed by T. E. Hulme, was succeeded by another group called "Les Imagistes," or "Des Imagistes," in which Pound was the leader from 1912 to 1914.[42] Even after Pound joined the club, its sessions were not of much inspiration to him. Richard Aldington, who joined in 1911, was more interested in the color prints by Utamaro, Hokusai, and others found in the British Museum than in Japanese poetry.[43] The fact that Pound was more seriously interested than Aldington was in Japanese poetry is indicated by a parody of Pound's metro poem that Aldington published in the January 1915 issue of *The Egoist*.[44] Allen Upward, another member of "Les Imagistes" group, whom Pound had met in 1911, had some importance for Pound because Upward used the term "whirl-swirl" in his book *The New World* (1908). As Donald Davie has shown, Upward, a self-styled intellectual and a poet, had "a powerful and original mind clearly and trenchantly concerned with matters that bear directly on what Pound meant by 'vortex.'"[45] But Upward, who was well read in Confucius and perhaps familiar with Chinese poetry, did not have sufficient knowledge of Japanese poetry, let alone of *hokku,* to influence Pound.[46]

The degree of Pound's initial interest in *hokku,* therefore, was not entirely clear, for he was much occupied with Provençal poetry and criticism, as his letter to Noguchi indicates. It is quite possible, as Miner says, that Pound learned about *hokku* from T. E. Hulme and F. S. Flint, who were experimenting with *hokku* and *tanka,* the thirty-one-syllable Japanese poetic form ("Pound," 572). The difficulty with this assumption, however, is that Hulme and Flint studied *hokku* through French translators and critics who used the terms *haiku* and *haikai,* more modern words, rather than *hokku.* Most strikingly, neither Pound nor Noguchi referred to the Japanese poem as *haiku* or *haikai;* both consistently called it *hokku* in their writings.

However coincidental this might have been, there are still two more pieces of evidence suggesting that Pound might have learned about *hokku* in Noguchi's work. First, as I have already pointed out, the essay **"What Is a Hokku Poem?"** in which Noguchi declared that poetic images must be active instead of suggestive, direct instead of symbolic, and that the aim of a *hokku* is to understand the spirit of nature rather than to express the will of man was published in *Rhythm* (London) for January 1913, almost two years before Pound's essay "Vorticism." Even Pound's essay "A Few Don'ts," the earliest manifesto on imagism, appeared in the March 1913 issue of *Poetry* (Chicago) two months after Noguchi's essay. Second, Noguchi's book of criticism, ***The Spirit of Japanese Poetry,*** was published in London as well by John Murray in March 1914, still half a year before Pound's "Vorticism" essay.[47]

Moreover, the key chapter of the book, entitled **"The Japanese Hokku Poetry,"** was a lecture delivered in the Hall of Magdalen College, Oxford, on 28 January 1914, at the invitation of Robert Bridges, the Poet Laureate, and T. H. Warren, President of the college and Professor of poetry in the university. The first chapter, **"Japanese Poetry,"** was also based on a lecture Noguchi gave at the Japan Society of London on 14 January. The rest of the book had similarly been presented as lectures to such audiences as the Royal Asiatic Society and the Quest Society in England before April 1914, when Noguchi left London for Tokyo by way of Paris, Berlin, and Moscow. It is altogether possible that Pound heard Noguchi lecture at the Quest Society since Pound, Wyndham Lewis, and T. E. Hulme all lectured there in 1914.[48] During this stay in England, ***Through the Torii,*** another collection of essays that included a variety of commentary on Dante Gabriel Rossetti, James Whistler, W. B. Yeats, and Oscar Wilde, and his autobiography, ***The Story of Yone Noguchi Told by Himself*** also appeared in print.

Interestingly enough, Pound's vorticism essay quoted a famous *hokku* by Moritake (1452-1540) just before discussing the oft-quoted metro poem:

> The fallen blossom flies back to its branch:
> A butterfly.
> ("Vorticism," 467)

This *hokku* in Japanese has three lines:

> Rak-ka eda ni
> Kaeru to mireba
> Kocho-o kana

Noguchi translated this poem in three lines:

> I thought I saw the fallen leaves
> Returning to their branches:
> Alas, butterflies were they.
> (***Spirit of Japanese Poetry,*** 50)

Pound must have reconstructed the *hokku* in two lines simply because he had in mind "a form of super-position," in which his metro poem was to be composed. The similarities between Pound's and Noguchi's versions of the poem in question do not seem coincidental, because the super-pository division is indicated by a colon in both constructions. Both translations have identical key words: "Fallen," "branch," and "butterfly." The only difference in diction is between Pound's "blossom" ("ka" in Japanese) and Noguchi's "leaves." In syntax, however, these translations are different: Noguchi's version is subjective from the start and ends objectively; the reverse is true in Pound's rendering. Syntactically, Noguchi's version is closer to the Japanese original than Pound's. A literal translation of Moritake's first two lines, "Rak-ka eda ni / Kaeru to mireba," would read: "The fallen blossom appears to come back to its branch."

What appealed to Pound was the terseness and intensity of imagery in a *hokku.* Irked by the decorative and superfluous style of much Victorian poetry, he urged his fellow poets to eliminate words that do not contribute to the central meaning of the poem. "All poetic language," Pound insisted, "is the language of exploration. Since the beginning of bad writing, writers have used images as ornaments" ("Vorticism," 466). By saying, "Great literature is simply language charged with meaning to the utmost possible degree," he meant to elaborate the imagist principle that using fewer words maximizes and intensifies meaning.[49] In **"What Is a Hokku Poem?"** Noguchi wrote: "I always thought that the most beautiful flowers grow close to the ground, and they need no hundred petals for expressing their own beauty; how can you call it real poetry if you cannot tell it by a few words?" (355).

Pound, furthermore, applied the principle of terseness and intensity to the construction of a single image in his poetry. "The 'one image poem,'" Pound noted, "is a form of super-position, that is to say it is one idea set on top of another. I found it useful in getting out of the impasse in which I had been left by my metro emotion" ("Vorticism," 467). Noguchi pointed out the same technique: "*Hokku* means literally a single utterance or the utterance of a single verse; that utterance should be like a 'moth light playing on reality's dusk,' or 'an art hung, as a web, in the air of perfume,' swinging soft in music of a moment" (*Spirit of Japanese Poetry*, 39). To illustrate his point, Noguchi quoted a *hokku* by Buson:

> The night of the Spring,
> Oh, between the eve
> And the dawn.

This *hokku* was placed against the opening passage of *Makura Zoshi (Pillow Sketches)* by Sei Shonagon, a celebrated prose writer in medieval Japan:

> I love to watch the dawn grow gradually white and whiter, till a faint rosy tinge crowns the mountain's crest, while slender streaks of purple cloud extend themselves above.

Noguchi considered Buson's image far more vivid and intensive than Sei Shonagon's, for "Buson is pleased to introduce the night of the Spring which should be beautiful without questioning, since it lies between those two beautiful things, the eve and the dawn" (*Spirit of Japanese Poetry,* 48-49).

Not only was Noguchi an interpreter of *hokku* poems for the English reader, but he tried his hand at writing *hokku* poems in English. He later collected them in the volume *Japanese Hokkus* (1920), which he dedicated to Yeats.[50] One of Noguchi's earliest *hokku* is reminiscent of Buson's, quoted above:

> Tell me the street to Heaven.
> This? Or that? Oh, which?
> What webs of streets!
> 　　　　("What Is a Hokku Poem?," 358)

He wrote this *hokku* in England, he says, "when I most abruptly awoke in 1902 to the noise of Charing Cross. . . . And it was by Westminster Bridge where I heard the evening chime that I wrote again in 'hokku' which appears, when translated, as follows" (358):

> Is it, Oh, list:
> The great voice of Judgment Day?
> So runs Thames and my Life.[51]

Noguchi wrote many *hokku*-like poems like these in imitation of the Japanese *hokku*, as did Pound. The superpository technique, which Pound said he had discovered in Japanese *hokku*, resembles that of Noguchi. For instance, Pound's "Alba," typical of his many *hokku*-like poems, reads:

> As cool as the pale wet leaves
> 　　　　of lily-of-the-valley
> She lay beside me in the dawn.[52]

Most of Noguchi's *hokku*, as the two poems quoted above show, do have a form of super-position. Like Pound's, Noguchi's *hokku* constitutes one image poem which has two separate ideas set on top of one another. In the first poem by Noguchi, an idea of "the street to Heaven" is set on top of an idea of "webs," despite a close similarity between the two images. In the second, an idea of the flow of the Thames is set on top of an idea of the course of "my Life."

But there are some differences between Noguchi's and Pound's *hokku*. Noguchi does not as closely adhere to the well-established Japanese syllabic measure of 5 or 7 as does Pound. Noguchi's two *hokku* above have 7-5-4 and 4-7-6 measures; Pound's "Alba," "Fan-Piece, for Her Imperial Lord," and "Ts'ai Chi'h" have those of 7-7-8, 7-5-7, and 8-7-7, respectively. If the first line of Pound's metro poem had been reconstructed as two lines, the poem would have had a measure of 5-7-7 (The apparition / Of these faces in the crowd / Petals on a wet, black bough) much like a Japanese *hokku*. Noguchi, moreover, tends to ignore the long-established poetic tradition in which a Japanese *hokku* has an explicit reference to a season. Pound, on the other hand, consciously adheres to this tradition as seen in many of his *hokku*-like poems and somewhat longer pieces such as "Heather" and "Society" (*Personae*, 109-11).

What a Japanese *hokku* and Pound's image share besides their brevity and intensity is the poet's ability to escape the confinement of the poem. The sense of liberation in *hokku* is usually accomplished through references to time and space. A Japanese *hokku* contains not only a reference to a season, an indication of time, but an image of nature, that of space. Pound's *hokku*-like poems, such as "In a Station of the Metro" and "Alba," indeed have references to time and space. Pound called the metro emotion, which came from the image of the faces in the crowd, "a thing outward and objective," and the image of the "petals, on a wet, black bough" "a thing inward and subjective." The image of the petals, nevertheless, is a natural object in contrast to that of the faces in the crowded station, a human object.

In Pound's mind in the realm of subjective perception the image of the faces, an objective image, transforms into the image of the petals, a subjective image. This perception also means that the image of the faces, an image of man, transforms into that of the petals, an image of nature. The shifting of objective and subjective images in Pound's poem is depicted in terms of a vortex, in which an image is not only active in itself but capable of merging into another image that appears in its wake. Because Pound's image has this tendency, it is often as difficult to separate the mental vision from the external as it is to separate mind from matter, the perceiver from the perceived, in Japanese *hokku.*

In *The Spirit of Japanese Poetry,* Noguchi is as critical as Pound of the Western poet's tendency to wordiness. Noguchi's emphasis on the Japanese *hokku* as "the real poetry of action" entails that a *hokku* aims to narrow the distance between man and nature, the perceiver and the perceived. The narrower the distance the better the *hokku* becomes. Based upon "Lao Tze's canon of spiritual anarchism" and Zen's principle of controlling the mind, Noguchi declares:

> To attach too closely to the subject matter in literary expression is never a way to complete the real saturation; the real infinite significance will only be accomplished at such a consummate moment when the end and means are least noticeable, and the subject and expression never fluctuate from each other, being in perfect collocation; it is the partial loss of the birth-right of each that gains an artistic triumph. . . . I do never mean that the *Hokku* poems are lyrical poetry in the general Western understanding; but the Japanese mind gets the effect before perceiving the fact of their brevity, its sensibility resounding to their single note, as if the calm bosom of river water to the song of a bird. (34)

To illustrate what he calls "the sense of mystical affinity between the life of Nature and the life of man, between the beauty of flowers and the beauty of love," he quotes his own poem, cited earlier in connection with Yeats:

> It's accident to exist as a flower or a poet;
> A mere twist of evolution but from the same force:
> I see no form in them but only beauty in evidence;
> It's the single touch of their imagination to get the
>     embodiment of a poet or a flower:
> To be a poet is to be a flower,
> To be the dancer is to make the singer sing.
>
> (37)

Pound, on the other hand, views the affinity between man and nature differently. What Pound calls "a thing inward and subjective" does not necessarily correspond to a vision of man; nor is "a thing outward and objective" the same thing as a vision of nature.

To explain the transformation of images between man and nature, the perceiver and the perceived, in Japanese *hokku,* Noguchi quoted Basho's "The Old Pond," perhaps the most celebrated *hokku* ever written:

> The old pond!
> A frog leapt into
> List, the water sound!

One may think a frog an absurd poetic subject, but Basho focused his vision on a scene of autumnal desolation, an image of nature. The pond was perhaps situated on the premises of an ancient temple whose silence was suddenly broken by a frog plunging into the deep water. As Noguchi conceived the experience, Basho, a Zen Buddhist, was "supposed to awaken into enlightenment now when he heard the voice bursting out of voicelessness, and the conception that life and death were mere change of condition was deepened into faith" (*Spirit of Japanese Poetry,* 45-46). Basho was not suggesting that the tranquillity of the pond meant death or that the frog symbolized life. Just as Pound had the sensation of seeing the beautiful faces in the metro station, Basho here had the sensation of hearing the sound bursting out of soundlessness. A *hokku* is not a representation of goodness, truth, or beauty; there is nothing particularly good, true, or beautiful about a frog's jumping into the water.

It seems as though Basho, in writing the poem, carried nature within him and brought himself to the deepest level of nature where all sounds lapsed into the world of silence and infinity. Though his vision was based upon reality, it transcended time and space. What a Zen poet like Basho is showing is that man can do enough naturally, enjoy doing it, and achieve his peace of mind. This fusion of man and nature is called spontaneity in Zen. The best *hokku* poems, because of their linguistic limitations, are inwardly extensive and outwardly infinite. A severe constraint imposed on one aspect of *hokku* must be balanced by a spontaneous, boundless freedom on the other.

From a Zen point of view, such a vision is devoid of thought and emotion. Since Zen is the most important philosophical tradition influencing Japanese *hokku,* the *hokku* poet aims at understanding the spirit of nature. Basho thus recognizes little division between man and nature, the subjective and the objective; he is never concerned with the problems of good and evil. Placed against this tradition, Pound's poetics in its philosophical aspect considerably differs from Basho's. Pound cannot be called a Zen poet, because he declared: "An 'Image' is that which presents an intellectual and emotional complex in an instant of time." A Zen poet seeks *satori,* an enlightenment that transcends time and place, and even the consciousness of self. This enlightenment is defined as a state of *mu,* nothingness, which is absolutely free of any thought or emotion; it is so completely free that such a state corresponds to that of nature. For a Zen-inspired poet, nature is a mirror of the enlightened self; one must see and hear things as they really are by making one's consciousness pure and clear. Pound seems to be able to appreciate this state of mind, but obviously he does not necessarily try to seek it in his own work.

In fact, Japanese *hokku* seldom take physical love, war, beasts, earthquakes, floods, and the like for their subjects. And while Pound's poetry does express good and evil, love and hatred, individual feeling and collective myth, Basho's shuns such sentiments and emotions altogether. Pound and a Zen poet, however, do agree that their poetic vision is spontaneous and capable of attaining enlightenment. Pound maintained: "It is the presentation of such a 'complex' instantaneously which gives that sense of sudden liberation; that sense of freedom from time and space limits; that sense of sudden growth, which we experience in the presence of the greatest works of art" (*Literary Essays,* 4). Pound's observation, however, is very much a Western formulation of an experience familiar to Zen-inspired artists.

This sense of liberation suggests an impersonal conception of poetry, for it focuses attention not upon the poet but upon the image. T. S. Eliot, whom most observers agree Pound influenced, held the same view.[53] Japanese poets such as Basho and Buson held the same principle. Their poetry seldom dealt with dreams, fantasies, or concepts of heaven and hell; it was strictly concerned with the portrayal of nature mountains, trees, birds, waterfalls, nights, days, seasons. For the Japanese *hokku* poet, nature is a mirror of the enlightened self; the poet must see and hear things as they really are by making his or her consciousness pure, natural, and unemotional. "Japanese poets," Noguchi wrote, "go to Nature to make life more meaningful, sing of flowers and birds to make humanity more intensive" (*Spirit of Japanese Poetry,* 37).

As opposed to his later poetry, Pound's early poetry, and his *hokku*-like poems in particular, have little to do with his personal emotion or thought. In such poetry, Pound is not really concerned with thought and emotion. If Pound's *hokku* sounded intellectual or emotional, it did so only to an English reader who was still Arnoldian in his or her taste and unfamiliar with the imagist movement of the 1910s, let alone with "the spirit of Japanese poetry" Noguchi tried to introduce to the English audience. Japanese poetry shuns symbols and metaphors because figurative language might lessen the intensity and spontaneity of a newly experienced sensation. Such expressions would not only undermine originality in the poet's sensibility, but resort to intellectualization and what Noguchi, perhaps echoing Matthew Arnold, called "a criticism of life," which traditionally Japanese poetry was not (*Through the Torii,* 159).

The *hokku* poet may not only aim at expressing sensation but also at generalizing and hence depersonalizing it. This characteristic can be shown even by one of Basho's lesser-known *hokku:*

> How cool it is,
> Putting the feet on the wall:
> An afternoon nap.[54]

Basho was interested in expressing how his feet, anyone's feet, would feel when placed on the wall in the house on a warm summer afternoon. His subject was none other than this direct sensation. He did not want to convey any emotion, any thought, any beauty; there remained only poetry, only nature.

In "Alba," what Pound expressed was not the personal feeling he had about the woman lying beside him at dawn, but his spontaneous sensation of the coolness of "the pale wet leaves / of lily-of-the-valley." Likewise, the sensation of slowly cooling hot water was Pound's subject in "The Bath Tub," as the title suggests, rather than his feelings about the woman (*Personae,* 100). The image of a "fan of white silk, / clear as frost on the grass-blade" is central in "Fan-Piece, for Her Imperial Lord," where a minimal image of the lord's concubine is evoked by a one-word reference to her: "You also are laid aside" (*Personae,* 108). Such subtleties could not have been learned from Pound's fellow imagists like Flint and Aldington. These imagists remained the labored, superficial imitators of Japanese *hokku* rather than the English poets, like Pound and Noguchi, who were truly capable of understanding the spirit of Japanese poetry.

The *hokku* also served as a structural model for Pound's version of imagism. Acknowledging that the Japanese had evolved this short form of poetry, Pound seized upon the unique form of "super-position," which, he observed, constitutes a *hokku.* To him, the *hokku* often consists of two disparate images in juxtaposition, and yet it appears as a single image. Lacking the copula *is* or the preposition *like,* the image cannot be metaphoric or symbolic. As Pound's account of the composition of the metro poem shows, there was no intention on his part to liken the image of the beautiful faces in the crowd to the image of petals on a wet, black bough, or make one image suggestive or representative of the other.[55] If one image is used to suggest another or to represent another, both images would be weakened. But if one image is used to generate or intensify another, and the other image, in turn, intensifies the first one, then the whole poem as one image would be intensified.

The key to the super-positary structure of Pound's image is a coalescence of two unlike images. Such an image must be generated "in an instant of time," as Pound cautions in his essay "A Few Don'ts" (*Literary Essays,* 4). Creating such an image needs no preparations, no explanations, no qualifications; Pound calls "the 'natural course of events' the exalted moment, the vision unsought or at least the vision gained without machination."[56] In *The Spirit of Japanese Poetry* and *The Spirit of Romance* Noguchi and Pound respectively emphasized this revelatory moment when high poetry must be written. But such a parallel in their poetics does not necessitate that one's ideas came from the other's. Pound's observations might have been made independently.

It is quite possible that Pound became acquainted through other sources with many of the super-positary *hokku* which Noguchi cited as examples in *The Spirit of Japanese Poetry.* In addition to Moritake's "I Thought I Saw the Fallen Leaves" and Basho's "The Old Pond," quoted earlier, Noguchi translated the following: Buson's "Oh, How Cool " (47) and "Prince Young, Gallant" (36), Basho's "Lying Ill on Journey" (38), and Hokushi's "It Has Burned Down" (27). It may be significant, however, that in another collection of critical essays Noguchi cited several of his own numerous *hokku* in English along with those of ancient masters. Many of Noguchi's English *hokku,* moreover, had been published in *The Pilgrimage* (1908 and 1909). Pound might have acquainted himself with Noguchi's published *hokku* before he experimented with his version.

As Pound accounted for the circumstances of his metro poem in Paris in 1912, Noguchi also narrated the experience he had had in London in 1903:

> I myself was a *hokku* student since I was fifteen or sixteen years old; during many years of my Western life, now amid the California forest, then by the skyscrapers of New York, again in the London 'bus, I often tried to translate the *hokkus* of our old masters but I gave up my hope when I had written the following in English:
>
> My Love's lengthened hair
> Swings o'er me from Heaven's gate:
> Lo, Evening's shadow!

It was in London, to say more particularly, Hyde Park, that I wrote the above *hokku* in English, where I walked slowly, my mind being filled with the thought of the long hair of Rossetti's woman as I perhaps had visited Tate's Gallery that afternoon. . . . I exclaimed then: "What use to try the impossibility in translation, when I have a moment to feel a *hokku* feeling and write about it in English?"[57]

Structurally, Pound's metro poem resembles Noguchi's Hyde Park *hokku.* As in Pound's poem where the outward image of the faces in the crowd is set on top of the inward image of petals on a wet, black bough, so the actual vision of an evening shadow in Noguchi's poem is juxtaposed to an envisioning of a woman's long hair. In each poem, a pair of images, similar in form but different in content, coalesces into another autonomous image, which generates different meaning. The super-position of the paired images transforms into a different image in form and content, what Pound calls "the 'one image' poem" ("Vorticism," 467). This transformation of images retains the sensation of each separate object perceived, but it also conveys a greater sensation by uniting the two experiences.[58] For both poets, such a transformation is optimal, for they believe that images in poetry cannot and should not be divided as external and internal, physical and mental, objective and subjective.[59]

To illustrate the energy latent in this transformation of images, Pound provided an anecdote: "I once saw a small child go to an electric light switch and say, 'Mamma, can I *open* the light?' She was using the age-old language of exploration, the language of art." Although he later became interested in Fenollosa's explanation that written Chinese characters denote action, he was first attracted to the poetics of the *hokku,* what he called "the sense of exploration . . . the beauty of this sort of knowing" ("Vorticism," 466-67). Noguchi expounded this poetics in terms of an intensive art by referring to Kikaku's celebrated *hokku:*

> Autumn's full moon:
> Lo, the shadows of a pine-tree
> Upon the mats!

The beauty of the harvest moon is not only humanized but intensified by the shadow of a tree Kikaku saw on the *tatami* mats. "Really," Noguchi wrote, "it was my first opportunity to observe the full beauty of the light and shadow, more the beauty of the shadow in fact, far more luminous than the light itself, with such a decorativeness, particularly when it stamped the dustless mats as a dragon-shaped ageless pine-tree" (**"What Is a Hokku Poem?,"** 357). The situation here, shared by Pound and Noguchi, is one of finding, discovering, and hence of inventing the new.

As if to bear out Pound's vorticist thinking in poetry, Noguchi made a modest proposal for English poets. "I think," he wrote, "it is time for them to live more of the passive side of Life and Nature, so as to make the meaning of the whole of them perfect and clear, to value the beauty of inaction so as to emphasise action, to think of Death so as to make Life more attractive." To the Japanese mind, an intensive art can be created not from action, but from inaction. Noguchi thus argued that the larger part of life "is builded upon the unreality by the strength of which the reality becomes intensified; when we sing of the beauty of night, that is to glorify, through the attitude of reverse, in the way of silence, the vigour and wonder of the day" (*Spirit of Japanese Poetry,* 24-25). Noguchi's paradox was echoed in Pound's statement about vorticism. To Pound, an intensive art is not an emphatic art. By an intensive art, Pound meant that "one is concerned with the relative intensity, or relative significance, of different sorts of expression. . . . They are more dynamic. I do not mean they are more emphatic, or that they are yelled louder" ("Vorticism," 468).

Pound illustrated this intensive art with a *hokku*-like sentence in his essay "Affirmations," first published in the *New Age* in 1915:

> The pine-tree in mist upon the far hill looks like a fragment of Japanese armour.

The images appear in simile form, but Pound has no intention of intensifying the beauty of either image by comparing it to that of the other. "In either case," he points out, "the beauty, in so far as it is beauty of form, is the result of 'planes in relation.' The tree and the armour are beautiful because their diverse planes overlie in a certain manner." Unlike the sculptor or the painter, the poet, who must use words to intensify his art, Pound says, "may cast on the reader's mind a more vivid image of either the armour or the pine by mentioning them close together . . . for he works not with planes or with colours but with the names of objects and of properties. It is his business so to use, so to arrange, these names as to cast a more definite image than the layman can cast."[60]

Critics have shown over the years that Pound's idea of vorticism underlies not only his short imagistic poems, but also his longer pieces such as the *Cantos, Cathay,* and his translation of noh plays. Noguchi, on the other hand, attempted to intensify an image in a poem longer than the *hokku* by endowing it with action and autonomy. **"The Passing of Summer"** (1909), for instance, reads:

> An empty cup whence the light of passion is
>     drunk!
> To-day a sad rumour passes through the trees,
> A chill wind is borne by the stream,
> The waves shiver in pain;
> Where now the cicada's song long and hot?
>                              (*Pilgrimage* I, 68)

Such visual images as an empty cup, the chilly wind blowing over the stream, and the shivering waves do not simply denote the passing of summer; they constitute its action. Similarly, experiences or memories of experiences like drinking "the light of passion" and hearing "the cicada's song long and hot" do not merely express the poet's nostalgia or sentiment about the summer; these images, rather than being metonymies, recreate the actions of the summer.[61] In Noguchi's poetry, as in the *hokku,* poetry and sensation are spontaneously conjoined and intensified, to leave no room for rationalism or moralism.

Numerous parallels between Pound's poetics and Noguchi's do not entail the conclusion that both poets held the same principles throughout their respective careers. Much of Noguchi's art and literary criticism shows great enthusiasm at times for Yeats's mysticism and Whitman's transcendentalism.[62] Noguchi had a taste for certain styles of poetry that Pound obviously did not. But what their writings as a whole suggest is that both writers, as poets and critics, agreed on the ideas of imagism during the period between 1908, when *The Pilgrimage,* Noguchi's fifth collection of English poems, appeared in Tokyo and London, and 1914, when Noguchi's *The Spirit of Japanese Poetry* was published in London. For Noguchi, this period came in the middle of his career as it coincided with Pound's early career and interest in imagism. This agreement on imagism constituted an interpenetrating relationship of Japanese poetics and Western intentions in early modernism. Pound's launching of "Imagism" in London in 1912 and 1913 with the support of T. E. Hulme, F. S. Flint, H. D., Richard Aldington, and others has become a legend of sorts. And much of the imagist work by various hands began to appear in Chicago in *Poetry* and in London in *Des Imagistes* and *The Freewoman* (later *The Egoist*). But the sources that Noguchi brought to Western attention as early as 1903, when *From the Eastern Sea,* the third collection of his English poems, was published in London, have become not only obscure but neglected.

In March 1913 Pound and his associates collectively drew up and published the three principles of their "faith." The first was "direct treatment of the 'thing,' whether subjective or objective." Noguchi would wholeheartedly have endorsed the formulation. The second principle called for using "absolutely no word that does not contribute to the presentation," and Noguchi had

documented the practice of this tenet in the *hokku* by Japanese masters as well as in his own work. The third principle was "to compose in sequence of the musical phrase, not in sequence of the metronome" ("Vorticism," 462). Because the Japanese language radically differs from a Western language in rhythm, rhyme, stress, or tone, Noguchi would readily have assented to the proposal.

Much of Pound's early work and Noguchi's clearly reflects this accord between the imagists and Noguchi. It is true that while Pound was fascinated by Japanese poetics, he was also interested in vorticism as applied to visual arts, as his commentary on such artists as Gaudier-Brzeska, Brancusi, and Picasso indicates. Through the Poets' Club, Pound was also closely associated with Hulme, Flint, Aldington, Upward, and others, some of whom were initially attracted to Japanese color prints by such painters as Utamaro and Hokusai exhibited in the British Museum. There is clear evidence that Pound's associates also tried their hand at *hokku* with various degrees of seriousness and success. By the mid 1910s, imagism had indeed become the literary zeitgeist, and any poet living in London would have received some influence from the Japanese sources.

To sum up, then, Noguchi's English poems had been widely circulated in London well before September 1914, when Pound's vorticism essay appeared, and Noguchi's essay on *hokku* in *Rhythm* and his book *The Spirit of Japanese Poetry* were published in January 1913 and March 1914, respectively. The material in the essay and the book was delivered as a series of lectures during his stay in England from December 1913 to April 1914. In these circumstances, it is hardly conceivable that the imagists did not acquaint themselves with Noguchi's ideas. Even though Pound's modernist theory might partly have derived from other sources, one can scarcely overlook the direct link between Japanese poetics and Pound's imagism through Noguchi.

NOTES

[1] W. B. Yeats, *Reveries Over Childhood and Youth* (Dublin: Cuala Press, 1916), p. 82.

[2] W. B. Yeats, "Introduction to *Certain Noble Plays of Japan,*" *The Classic Noh Theatre of Japan,* eds. Ezra Pound and Ernest Fenollosa (New York: New Directions, 1959), p. 151.

[3] Earl Miner, in *The Japanese Tradition in British and American Literature* (Princeton: Princeton University Press, 1958), closely examines Yeats's relationship to the noh play and also discusses Yeats's association with Ezra Pound with respect to East-West literary relations. But Miner does not consider Yone Noguchi in this context. Makoto Ueda's *Zeami, Basho, Yeats, Pound* (The Hague: Mouton, 1965) does not mention Noguchi. Nor does Liam Miller's *Noble Drama of Yeats* (Dublin: Dolmen Press, 1977), which includes well-annotated analyses of

Yeats's noh plays in comparison with the Japanese model, mention Noguchi.

[4] Among the East-West comparative critics, Roy E. Teele is the one who demonstrates Fenollosa's failure to understand the Japanese language, particularly the essential rhythm of the noh text Fenollosa translated. See Teele's "The Japanese Translations," *Texas Quarterly,* 10 (1967), 61-66.

[5] Noguchi, born in Japan in 1875, came to America in 1893 and studied poetry under the tutelage of Joaquin Miller. During the earlier period in his career, he published four of his collections of English poetry: *Seen and Unseen* (1897), *The Voice of the Valley* (1897), *From the Eastern Sea* (1903), and *The Pilgrimage,* 2 vols. (1909). He also published three books of criticism: *The Spirit of Japanese Poetry* (1914), *The Spirit of Japanese Art* (1915), and *Through the Torii* (1914 and 1922).

[6] *The Egoist* was one of the influential literary magazines published in London in the 1910s. When Noguchi contributed two of his articles to the magazine, its assistant editor was T. S. Eliot.

[7] This lecture was published as "Chapter II: The Japanese Hokku Poetry" in Noguchi's *The Spirit of Japanese Poetry,* pp. 33-53.

[8] This lecture was published as "Japanese Poetry" in *Transactions of the Japan Society of London,* 12 (1914), 86-109.

[9] Yone Noguchi, *Collected English Letters,* ed. Ikuko Atsumi (Tokyo: Yone Noguchi Society, 1975), p. 106.

[10] See Yone Noguchi, *Hiroshige.* This book was followed by other books on Japanese painting: *Korin, Utamoro, Hokusai, Harunobu,* and *The Ukiyoye Primitives.*

[11] W. B. Yeats, *The Variorum Edition of the Plays of W. B. Yeats,* ed. Russell K. Alspach (New York: Macmillan, 1966), p. 416. Later textual references to this edition are indicated in parentheses.

[12] Ezra Pound, "Vorticism," *Fortnightly Review,* No. 573, n.s. (1914), 471.

[13] Kodo Kurebayashi, *Introduction to Dogen Zen* [in Japanese] (Tokyo: Daihorinkaku, 1983), pp. 121-29.

[14] W. B. Yeats, *The Poems of W. B. Yeats,* ed. Richard J. Finneran (New York: Macmillan, 1983), p. 248.

[15] Walt Whitman, *Leaves of Grass,* eds. Sculley Bradley, *et al.* (New York: New York University Press, 1980), II, 496.

[16] Yone Noguchi, "The Japanese Noh Play," *Egoist,* 5 (1918), 99.

[17] A unifying image or action appears frequently in Yeats's noh plays as it does in Japanese noh plays. The well choked up with leaves in *At the Hawk's Well* is represented by a piece of cloth that remains throughout the performance just as the bed-ridden lady Aoi no Ue, the heroine of the noh play *Aoi no Ue,* is symbolized by a sleeve laid on the stage during the performance. In Yeats's *The Dreaming of the Bones* the young girl's spirit speaks impersonally of herself as the old man and the old woman in the noh play *Nishikigi,* in Pound's version, speak in unison. The climactic dance of the Rainbow Skirt and Feather Jacket performed in Noguchi's noh play "The Everlasting Sorrow" is also a unified image since it symbolizes the flight of two birds with one wing.

[18] See Noguchi's "Everlasting Sorrow: A Japanese Noh Play," *Egoist* 4 (1917), 141-43, in which the Sovereign Ming Huang longs for the earthly return of his mistress Yang Kuei-fei, who has long departed for Heaven. A Taoist priest is commanded by the Sovereign to find the lady Yang's lost soul. Upon finding her the priest asks her to give a token as proof of his meeting with her. Though she offers her hairpin to take back with him, he declines it as too common and asks her to present something special that Ming Huang would remember as belonging to her alone. "Indeed," Yang Kuei-fei responds, "I now happen to recall to my mind how on the seventh day of the seventh moon, in the Hall of Immortality, at midnight when no one was anear, " Then the chorus sings: " the Sovereign whispered in my ears, after pledging the two stars in the sky:

> In heaven we will ever fly like one-winged birds;
> On earth grow joined like a tree with branches
>     twining tight.

At the climax of the play, Yang Kuei-fei performs for the priest a dance of the Rainbow Skirt and Feather Jacket to convey Ming Huang "the dancer's heart." Noguchi adds a note: "Each bird must fly with a mate, since it has only one wing."

[19] One of the players who made an indispensable contribution to Yeats's understanding of noh performance was a Japanese dancer, Michio Itoh. He came from a distinguished family of theatre artists. Two of his brothers, Kensaku Itoh and Koreya Senda, who also distinguished themselves in the theatre in Japan as late as after World War II, are both famous for their work as stage designers and as dancers. The papier-mâché mask Itoh wore for the performance in 1926 of *At the Hawk's Well* was made by Isamu Noguchi, the son of Yone Noguchi and his American wife Leonie Gilmour. See Isamu Noguchi, *A Sculptor's World* (New York: Harper & Row, 1968), p. 123. The performance of the play demanded in its music, movement, and visual effect, first-hand knowledge of the noh theatre. It was Pound who introduced Itoh to Yeats, who thought Itoh's "minute intensity of movement in the dance of the hawk so well suited our small room and private art" (*Plays of Yeats,* 417).

[20] In the play a fisherman finds on a pine tree a feather robe that belongs to a fair angel. She begs him to return

the robe and offers to dance for him in return. He insists on keeping the robe with him until she completes her dance. She assures him that angels never break promises, saying that falsehood exists only among mortals. The fisherman, deeply ashamed, hands back the robe to her. The angel, completing her performance, vanishes into the air.

[21] For Pound's and Fenollosa's version, see Pound and Fenollosa, *Classic Noh Theatre,* pp. 98-104.

[22] Yone Noguchi, *The Summer Cloud: Prose Poems* (Tokyo: The Shunyodo, 1906), pp. 1-4.

[23] Arthur Waley, *The No Plays of Japan* (New York: Grove Press, 1920), pp. 21-22.

[24] In the play, the Mountain Elf during the night circles round the mountain, a symbol of life. At the climax a famous dancer, another elf, who has lost her way in the Hill of Shadow on her way to the Holy Buddhist Temple, appears and inquires the right road of the Mountain Elf "with large star-like eyes and fearful snow-white hair." The Mountain Elf then shows the dancer how to encircle the mountain (*Spirit of Japanese Poetry,* 66-67).

[25] Edgar Allan Poe, *Selected Writings of Edgar Allan Poe,* ed. Edward H. Davidson (Boston: Houghton Mifflin, 1956), p. 470.

[26] See Ezra Pound, "Vorticism," *Fortnightly Review,* No. 573, n. s. (September 1, 1914), 461-71.

[27] See Hugh Kenner, *The Poetry of Ezra Pound* (Millwood, NY: Kraus, 1947), p. 58.

[28] See Earl Miner, "Pound, *Haiku* and the Image," *Hudson Review,* 9 (Winter 1957), 570-84; and *The Japanese Tradition in British and American Literature.* There is some ambiguity in Miner's chronology since, in his article, the date of Pound's joining the Poet's Club is said to be "just before the first World War," which means perhaps between 1913 and 1914 ("Pound," 572). There is also another ambiguity with respect to the time and circumstance of Pound's learning about "the usefulness of Japanese poetry from Flint." Flint's interest in Japanese poetry is indicated in his own account of the matter, published in *The Egoist* for May 1, 1915: "I had been advocating in the course of a series of articles on recent books of verse a poetry in *vers libre,* akin in spirit to the Japanese" (*Japanese Tradition,* 100).

[29] For a discussion of Noguchi's English poetry and literary criticism, see Hakutani, "Yone Noguchi's Poetry: From Whitman to Zen," *Comparative Literature Studies,* 22 (Spring 1985), 67-79.

[30] Ezra Pound, "As for Imagisme," *New Age,* 14 (1915), 349.

[31] The impact of *hokku* on Pound was apparently greater and more beneficial than that on his fellow imagists. Regarding the form of super-position as ideal for ex-

pressing instantaneous perception, Pound wrote in a footnote: "Mr. Flint and Mr. Rodker have made longer poems depending on a similar presentation of matter. So also have Richard Aldington, in his *In Via Sestina,* and 'H. D.' in her *Oread,* which latter poems express much stronger emotions than that in my lines here given" ("Vorticism," 467). Pound's argument here suggests that *hokku* and Pound's *hokku*-like poems can express instantaneous and spontaneous perception better than can the longer poems and the poems with stronger emotions.

[32] Printed in E. A. Sharp, *William Sharp* [Fiona Macleod]: *A Memoir* (London: Heinemann, 1910), pp. 280-81.

[33] See Yone Noguchi, "What Is a Hokku Poem?" *Rhythm,* 11 (January 1913), 354-59. The page number in parentheses refers to the *Rhythm* version.

[34] In a letter of 24 November 1913 to Pound, Mary Fenollosa wrote: "I am beginning with right now, to send you material." On the following day she wrote again: "Please don't get discouraged at the ragged way this manuscript is coming to you. As I said yesterday, it will all get there in time, which is the most important thing." See *Ezra Pound and Japan: Letters and Essays,* ed. Sanehide Kodama (Redding Ridge, CT: Black Swan Books, 1987), p. 6.

[35] Ernest Fenollosa, *The Chinese Written Character as a Medium for Poetry,* ed. Ezra Pound (New York: Arrow, 1936), p. 8.

[36] See note 4 above.

[37] Earl Miner, who states that Pound knew nothing about Japanese poetry before 1913 or 1914, believes that Pound later learned about *hokku* in the writings of the French translators ("Pound," 572-73).

[38] Yone Noguchi, *Collected English Letters,* pp. 210-11.

[39] *The Spirit of Japanese Poetry* (London: John Murray, 1914); *Through the Torii* (Boston: The Four Seas, 1914 and 1922); *The Spirit of Japanese Art* (London: John Murray, 1915).

[40] See *Egoist,* 4 (October 1917), 141-43; *Egoist,* 5 (August 1918), 99.

[41] See K. L. Goodwin, *The Influence of Ezra Pound* (London: Oxford University Press, 1966), p. 32.

[42] See William Pratt, *The Imagist Poem* (New York: E. P. Dutton, 1963), pp. 14-15; J. B. Harmer, *Victory in Limbo: Imagism 1908-1917* (New York: St. Martin's Press, 1975), p. 17; Humphrey Carpenter, *A Serious Character: The Life of Ezra Pound* (Boston: Houghton Mifflin, 1988), p. 115.

[43] It is speculative, of course, but quite possible that Aldington, fascinated by Japanese visual arts, might have

read the three articles about the subject Noguchi published in this period: "Utamaro," *Rhythm,* 11, No. 10 (November 1912), 257-60; "Koyetsu," *Rhythm,* 11, No. 11 (December 1912), 302-5; "The Last Master [Yoshitoshi] of the Ukiyoye School," *The Transactions of the Japan Society of London,* 12 (April 1914), 144-56. Moreover, *The Spirit of Japanese Art* (1915) includes chapters on major Japanese painters such as Koyetsu, Kenzan, Kyosai, Busho Hara, besides Utamaro and Hiroshige. If Aldington had read these essays, he would very well have been acquainted with Noguchi's writings about Japanese poetics.

[44] Aldington's poem reads:

> The apparition     of these poems     in a crowd:
> White faces    in a black     dead faint.

See Aldington, "Penultimate Poetry," *Egoist* (January 15, 1915). This poem sounds more like *senryu,* a humorous haiku, than the *hokku* Pound was advocating.

[45] See Donald Davie, *Ezra Pound* (New York: Viking, 1975), p. 42; Carpenter, p. 247.

[46] Cf. Harmer, p. 38.

[47] See Usaburo Toyama, ed., *Essays on Yone Noguchi* [mostly in Japanese], I (Tokyo: The Yone Noguchi Society, 1975), p. 327. Toyama, an art historian, was married to Noguchi's daughter Hifumi.

[48] A. R. Jones, *The Life and Opinions of Thomas Ernest Hulme* (Boston: Beacon, 1960), p. 122. Neither Noel Stock in *Poet in Exile: Ezra Pound* (Manchester: Manchester University Press, 1964) nor Humphrey Carpenter in *A Serious Character* mentions Pound's activities at the Quest Society, let alone Pound's possible interactions with Noguchi.

[49] See T. S. Eliot, ed., and introd., *Literary Essays of Ezra Pound* (Norfolk: New Directions, 1954), p. 23.

[50] About this time Noguchi also wrote an essay entitled "A Japanese Note on Yeats," included in his book of essays, *Through the Torii,* pp. 110-17.

[51] Noguchi's "Tell Me the Street to Heaven" was first published in *Rhythm,* 11 (January 1913), 358, as indicated earlier, and reprinted in *Through the Torii* (1914 and 1922). The other *hokku,* "Is It, Oh, List:" also included in the same issue, is reprinted, in *Through the Torii,* with a change in the third line: "So runs Thames, so runs my Life" (136).

[52] Ezra Pound, *Personae* (New York: New Directions, 1926), p. 109.

[53] See T. S. Eliot, *Selected Essays, 1917-1932* (New York: Harcourt, 1932), pp. 8-10.

[54] The original in Japanese reads "Hiya hiya to / Kabe wo fumaete / Hirune kana." The English translation of this *hokku* is mine.

[55] Alan Durant tries to show that Pound's metro poem linguistically contains a number of metaphors and associations, and that it is not as imagistic as critics say. While Durant's interpretation is valid as far as the various elements in the poem appear to the reader as metaphors and associations, Pound's intention does differ from the reader's interpretation. The same thing may occur in the interpretation of a Japanese *hokku,* but traditionally the language of the *hokku,* as Noguchi demonstrates throughout *The Spirit of Japanese Poetry,* shuns metaphor and symbolism. See Alan Durant, "Pound, Modernism and Literary Criticism: A Reply to Donald Davie," *Critical Quarterly,* 28 (Spring-Summer 1986), 154-66.

[56] Ezra Pound, *The Spirit of Romance* (New York: New Directions, 1968 [1910]), p. 97.

[57] This passage is quoted from "Again on *Hokku,*" included in *Through the Torii,* pp. 140-46. A *verbatism* account is given in the introduction to his *Japanese Hokkus,* pp. 22-23. For Noguchi's London experiences, see "My First London Experience (1903)" and "Again in London (1913-14)" in *The Story of Yone Noguchi Told by Himself* (London: Chatto & Windus, 1914), pp. 119-65.

[58] The union of different experiences is reminiscent of T. S. Eliot's statement about an amalgamation. In reference to John Donne's poetry, Eliot writes: "When a poet's mind is perfectly equipped for its work, it is constantly amalgamating disparate experience; the ordinary man's experience is chaotic, irregular, fragmentary. The latter falls in love, or reads Spinoza, and these two experiences have nothing to do with each other, or with the noise of the typewriter or the smell of cooking; in the mind of the poet these expriences are always forming new wholes" (*Selected Essays,* 247).

[59] In *The Spirit of Japanese Poetry* Noguchi wrote: "As the so-called literary expression is a secondary matter in the realm of poetry, there is no strict boundary between the domains generally called subjective and objective; while some *Hokku* poems appear to be objective, those poems are again by turns quite subjective through the great virtue of the writers having the fullest identification with the matter written on. You might call such collation poetical trespassing; but it is the very point whence the Japanese poetry gains unusual freedom; that freedom makes us join at once with the soul of Nature" (43-44).

[60] Ezra Pound, *Gaudier-Brzeska: A Memoir* (New York: New Directions, 1970 [1916]), pp. 120-21.

[61] To the Japanese, such expressions as "the light of passion" and "the cicada's song" immediately evoke images of hot summer. These phrases in Japanese are attributed to or closely associated with summer.

[62] For Whitman's influence on Noguchi, see Hakutani, "Yone Noguchi's Poetry: From Whitman to Zen": "Like Whitman, Noguchi believes in monism, and his ultimate

goal in writing poetry is to achieve the ecstasies of the
self in nature. . . . Though he became a different kind of
nature poet after he returned to Japan, his later poems
still bear out Whitman's influence" (69).

# Jacob Riis

## 1849-1914

(Jacob August Riis) American social reformer, journalist, autobiographer, and biographer.

## INTRODUCTION

Through such works as *How the Other Half Lives* (1890), journalist Riis exposed Americans to the miseries endured by New York City's slum residents. His was not the first writing on the living conditions of the urban underclass, but among that literature it was original in its use of the relatively new photographic medium to illuminate its text. Even more significant was the fact that Riis did not merely draw national attention to tenement conditions: he offered recommendations for their remedy. Principal among his solutions was housing reform, not just the making of laws to limit the number of people who could be crammed into a given living space, but also the destruction or renovation of old buildings. Individually, and as a leader in a larger social reform movement that included such pivotal figures as Jane Addams, Riis would have an enormous impact on urban life in America. During his time, he saw the passing of numerous zoning laws and initiatives such as New York state's Tenement House Law of 1901, as well as the demolishing of thousands of tenements and other run-down areas, and the building of new structures. In part because of Riis, a century later the cities of the United States would have more parks, more safe and well-lit buildings, and more space per person than they did in the late 1800s.

### Biographical Information

Riis was born the son of a schoolteacher in the town of Ribe, Denmark, about which he would later reminisce in *The Old Town* (1909). At the age of twenty-one, in 1870, he emigrated to the United States and spent the next seven years wandering the northeastern part of the country. He barely made a living during that time, and his career as such did not begin until 1877, when he obtained a job as a police reporter for the New York *Tribune*. In 1888, he took a position with the *Evening Sun*. Through his newspaper work, Riis became closely acquainted with New York's poorest and most dangerous neighborhoods. This became the impetus for his first and most famous book, *How the Other Half Lives*, a landmark in the history of slum reform. On the popularity of his book and his own growing reputation, Riis became a well-known lecturer and activist who called for child-labor reform, creation of school playgrounds, improvements in the city water supply, and new housing. His activities brought him into contact with the city police commissioner, Theodore Roosevelt, and the two became lifelong friends. Throughout the 1890s, Riis continued to

publish books, conduct lectures, and engage in reform activities that included a position as secretary of the New York City Small Parks Commission. In 1899 he retired from newspaper work, though he continued his other activities up to the time of his death in 1914.

### Major Works

By far the most significant of Riis's books was his first, *How the Other Half Lives*. In it he presented what would become familiar themes and images, most notably that of the dark, dirty, and dangerous tenement house. Such dwelling spaces produced children deprived of typical childhood pleasures through overwork, neglect, and other forms of abuse, and these unfortunate children assumed almost as much significance in Riis's studies of the urban underbelly of the Gilded Age. Thus his second major work was *The Children of the Poor* (1892). In *A Ten Years' War* (1900) and *The Battle with the Slum* (1902), Riis presented a record of his own activities to combat the disastrous conditions of the poor neighborhoods. With *The Making of an American* (1901), he took the autobiographical approach a step further, in a presentation of his whole career as an American success story and an example of a European immigrant's assimilation into the larger culture of the New World. His last major work, *The Old Town,* focused on one aspect of his biography in its portrayal of his Danishhome. With *Theodore Roosevelt, The Citizen* (1904), Riis offered a largely uncritical portrayal of his well-known friend.

# PRINCIPAL WORKS

*How the Other Half Lives: Studies among the Tenements
   of New York* (journalism) 1890
*The Children of the Poor* (journalism) 1892
*A Ten Years' War* (journalism) 1900
*The Making of an American* (autobiography) 1901
*The Battle with the Slum* (journalism) 1902
*Theodore Roosevelt, The Citizen* (biography) 1904
*The Old Town* (memoirs) 1909

# CRITICISM

## Jacob Riis (essay date 1888)

SOURCE: "Flashes from the Slums: Pictures in Dark Places by the Lighting Process," in *Photography: Essays & Images,* edited by Beaumont Newhall, The Museum of Modern Art, 1980, pp. 154-57.

[*In the following essay, which originally appeared in the New York Sun, Riis comments on some of his photographs.*]

With their way illuminated by spasmodic flashes, as bright and sharp and brief as those of the lightning itself, a mysterious party has lately been startling the town o' nights. Somnolent policemen on the street, denizens of the dives in their dens, tramps and bummers in their so-called lodgings, and all the people of the wild and wonderful variety of New York night life have in their turn marvelled at and been frightened by the phenomenon. What they saw was three or four figures in the gloom, a ghostly tripod, some weird and uncanny movements, the blinding flash, and then they heard the patter of retreating footsteps, and the mysterious visitors were gone before they could collect their scattered thoughts and try to find out what it was all about. Of course all this fuss speedily became known to THE SUN reporters, and equally as a matter of course they speedily found out the meaning of the seeming mystery. But at the request of the parties interested the publication of the facts was delayed until the purpose of the expedition was accomplished. That has now been done, and its history may now be written.

The party consisted of members of the Society of Amateur Photographers of New York experimenting with the process of taking instantaneous pictures by an artifical flash light, and their guide and conductor, an energetic gentleman, who combines in his person, though not in practice, the two dignities of deacon in a Long Island church and a police reporter in New York. His object in the matter, besides the interest in the taking of the pictures, was the collection of a series of views for magic lantern slides, showing, as no mere description could, the misery and vice that he had noticed in his ten years of experience. Aside from its strong human interest, he thought that this treatment of the topic would call attention to the needs of the situation, and suggest the direction in which much good might be done. The nature of this feature of the deacon-reporter's idea is indicated by the way he has succeeded in interesting the children in his Sunday school on Long Island in the work of helping the destitute children of the metropolis. The ground about the little church edifice is turned into a garden, in which the Sunday school children work at spading, hoeing, planting, and weeding, and the potatoes and other vegetables thus raised are contributed to a children's home in this city. In furtherance of just such aims the deacon-reporter threw himself with tireless energy into the pursuit of pictures of Gotham's crime and misery by night and day to make a foundation for a lecture called **"The Other Half; How it Lives and Dies in New York,"** to give at church and Sunday school exhibitions, and the like.

The entire composition of the night rousing party was: Dr. Henry G. Piffard and Richard Hoe Lawrence, two accomplished and progressive amateur photographers; Dr. John T. Nagle of the Health Board, who is strongly interested in the same direction, and Jacob A. Riis, the deacon-reporter.

The first picture in this report gives a view of life among the white slaves, as the needle-women of New York are truthfully and pathetically designated since THE SUN has disclosed so much of the misery and oppression they suffer. The women are mother and daughter, both widows. As they are both able to work, and have no children or any one depending on them, they are exceptionally well off among the class to which they belong. But it is only by unremitting work, early and late, that they are able to keep over themselves the poor shelter of a tenement house roof and provide the actual necessaries of life.

The adventures of the picture-taking party in other directions were interesting and sometimes amusing. Their night pictures were faithful and characteristic, being mostly snap shots and surprises. In the daytime they could not altogether avoid having their object known, and, struggle as they might against it, they could not altogether prevent the natural instinct of fixing up for a picture from being followed. When a view was of interest and value as they found it, they were sometimes unable to stop the preparation and posing from almost destroying the interest in it. Mr. Riis has kindly furnished a number of his photographs to the *Sun*'s artist, and they are given here. An example of the flash-light pictures is this from the lodging room of the Thirtieth street police station. The three women caught in the flash are three different types of the station house lodger. One is shown in sodden or brazen indifference, one in retiring modesty and averted face, and the third in angry defiance of camera and visitors.

Another flash-light picture, though showing only still life, is eloquent of the misery and destitution of those with whom imagination can people it, as each recurring night does people it, with the wrecks of humanity that form its clientage. It is a Pell street seven-cent lodging house, whose cots or beds or bunks or hammocks, partaking as they do of the characteristics of all three, are simply strips of canvas stretched between beams, six feet apart. Mr. Riis has other views of this place at night which are a revelation to those who were never there.

The pictures secured of some of the notorious courts and alleys of the lowest tenement districts of the Fourth and Sixth wards are very interesting, and are especially relied upon by Mr. Riis to make his points in favor of the Children's Aid Society and other children helpers, because they are always swarming with children. The court at 22 Baxter street, long of an unsavory reputation, and with a still more unsavory name, is now almost wholly given up to Italian occupancy. It is still dirty and distressed, and its picture, as given here, is not without interest. It is a typical tenement house yard, the clothes lines, the hydrant, the push cart, and the children being always to be found.

At 59 Baxter street is a similar place, an alley leading in from the sidewalk, with tenements on either side crowding so close as to almost shut out the light of day. On one side they are brick and on the other wood, but there is little difference in their ricketiness and squalor. This is also an Italian colony, and the bags of rags and bones and paper shown are gathered by these people, despite the laws and ordinances and the 8,000 police.

At 59 Mulberry street, in the famous Bend, is another alley of this sort, except it is as much worse in character as its name, "Bandits' Roost," is worse than the designations of most of these alleys. It has borne this name these many years, and though there have been many entire changes in the occupants in that time, each succeeding batch seems to be calculated in appearance and character to keep up the appropriateness of the name. There are no bags of rags to indicate even that low form of industry here. Many Italians live here, but they are devoted to the stale beer industry. On each side of the alley are stale beer dives in room after room, where the stuff is sold for two or three cents a quart. After buying a round the customer is entitled to a seat on the floor, otherwise known as a "lodging," for the night.

Another outcropping of the benevolent purpose of Mr. Riis in behalf of the boys is his showing of a touching picture of street Arabs in sleeping quarters, which it must

have taken a hunt to discover. These youngsters have evidently spent their lodging money for gallery seats at the show, and have found shelter on the back stoop of an old tenement house.

The researches into the manner of life of the "other half" continually brought the investigators face to face with "the growler," which is the highly suggestive name of the can or pitcher in which beer is brought by the pint or quart from the corner saloon. The bright youngster here pictured as the Growler Ganymede has thousands of prototypes in this city. He serves both the families in the tenements and the gangs that congregate on the corners or in stables or some other shelter to work the growler. In many cases yet younger children are pressed into this service, and girls, as well as boys, of tender years are sent into saloons of bad character for this purpose.

A "growler gang" that is the exemplification of all that is degrading and disreputable in the whole range of the practice is the one whose headquarters is under the Jackson street dump. The surroundings of these drinkers are dirt, flying ashes, and refuse of all kinds, the tin-can carpeted floor, and the stench-laden air, and there are no attractions except the one of beer guzzling. Decent people are not expected here, and interruptions are not to be feared. So these fellows, who, though young and sturdy, never work, can assemble here and "rush the growler" until the last eight cents is gone.

A similar gang on the west side in the greater freedom they enjoy around the stables and slaughter houses up town, indulge in all the beer they can get while assembled in the open air. They have, nevertheless, means of getting under cover when, as is frequently the case, that becomes necessary.

A feature of growler gang life is the proceeding known as "wrastling for the price." That means getting money with which to buy beer. And when these young toughs talk about getting money, it simply means getting it, and there is no restriction expressed or implied regarding the means to be employed. At these times the advent of a drunken man into the district patrolled by the gang is a piece of good luck for the boys—not for him. The interesting process of robbing a "lush" as here shown is deftly and quickly gone through with.

The degradation pictured in this view of a Thompson street dive is, perhaps, as low as any that the picture takers came across. The dive is one of the places known as "Black and Tans," because its frequenters are colored men and white women of the most degraded sort. The man who is lounging on the barrel is an ignorant, worthless black of a capacity equal to work as a day laborer were it not that the energy for such occupation can only be supplied by the pressure of the most dire necessity. The woman shown is white as to complexion, but a dissolute life and the effects of drink have dragged her down to the level of the man, if, indeed, she is not beneath it.

## Edith Kellogg Dunton (essay date 1902)

SOURCE: A review of *The Making of an American,* in *The Dial,* Vol. 32, January 1, 1902, pp. 8-10.

[*In the following essay, Dunton presents a review of Riis's autobiography.*]

Jacob Riis, reporter, philanthropist, reformer, author of ***How the Other Half Lives,*** needs no introduction to the nation whose ideals he could scarce honor more highly than he has done in calling his autobiography ***The Making of an American.***

The most striking quality of his book is undoubtedly its artless frankness, which is at first in equal measure appalling and delightful. But before one has read far, he agrees unqualifiedly with that wise friend of Mr. Riis's who told him, when he was hesitating over the first chapters of his reminiscences, "to take the short cut and put it all in." She evidently knew her man, understood the absolute unity of purpose that ran through every act of his life, and felt how fatal it would be should his readers miss seeing that here is a man whose house of life has no back doors and no alley windows. The whole of Mr. Riis is in his book, then, and the real Mr. Riis. He is "speaking right on" in words that have no fictitious limelight glare about them, and little of the grace of artful manipulation; but they are plain-speaking words, whose charm is that they are instinct with the thrill and throb of life, with the joy of labor and the pathos of joy. *The Making of an American* is the work of a man who deals not with words *per se,* but with the things behind the words. It is the work of a man, too, who never forgets his past in his present, nor loses sight of his defeat because, he has turned it into a victory. So the second remarkable thing about Mr. Riis's book is that every page of it is alive.

And why did the son of a Danish schoolmaster in the sleepy little old town of Ribe, want to become an American? Because Elisabeth, now his "silver bride," had jilted him, out of respect to her father's very natural scruples about his eligibility as a son-in-law. Here was a boy who seemed to have no sense of the fitness of things, who preferred carpentry to schooling, and who during the short time he had spent at his books had been interested in no study but English, and that only in order to read Charles Dickens's paper, "All the Year Round." In view of what followed it was very fortunate that the Riis family subscribed to "All the Year Round." The boy Jacob's first years in America were difficult enough without the additional hardship that absolute ignorance of the "American language" would have involved.

He landed in New York at the age of twenty-one, with the vaguest notion of what he meant to do next, but with plenty of youthful assurance that Providence would provide for him somehow, if he only gave her a fair chance.

"Of course I had my trade to fall back on, but I am afraid that is all the use I thought of putting it to.

The love of change belongs to youth, and I meant to take a hand in things as they came along. I had a pair of strong hands, and stubbornness enough to do for two; also a strong belief that in a free country, free from the dominion of custom, of caste, as well as of men, things would somehow come right in the end, and a man get shaken into the corner where he belonged if he took a hand in the game. I think I was right in that."

The confirmatory sentence comes easily now, but his trust in the ultimate justice of a democracy must have been strained well-nigh to breaking in the six years' struggle that followed. The first two years were spent literally in taking "a hand in things as they came along,"—in putting up miners' huts on the Allegheny, working in clay-bank and brick-yard, as wood-chopper, trapper, hired man, carpenter, ship-builder, and peddler. Between jobs the young Dane was a homeless, often penniless, wanderer, a tramp except at heart. But he never lost hope; instead he faced life with a smile and bided his time for setting right the injustices done him and others like him. He tells of one awful night spent in a station house in New York City, when he was robbed, and the only friend he had in America, a little black-and-tan terrier, was maliciously killed before his eyes.

"The outrage of that night became, in the providence of God, the means of putting an end to one of the foulest abuses that ever disgraced a Christian city, and a mainspring in the battle with the slum as far as my share in it is concerned."

Thus Mr. Riis made acquaintance with Mulberry Street and the Five Points, in a fashion that was later to give sting and poignancy to the police-reporter's attitude toward them. To these years also can be traced his ambition to be a reporter. Writing of his second winter in America, he says:

"It was about this time that I made up my mind to go into the newspaper business. It seemed to me that a reporter's was the highest of all callings; no one could sift wrong from right as he, and punish the wrong. In that I was right. I have not changed my opinion on that point one whit, and I am sure I never shall. The power of fact is the mightiest lever of this or of any day. The reporter has his hand upon it, and it is his grievous fault if he does not use it well."

Jacob Riis has apparently wasted very little time changing his mind. It would take too long to tell how he won Elisabeth through sheer conviction that he could not do without her, and how for a precisely similar reason, by the hard road of under-pay and over-work, he finally got a staff appointment at Police Headquarters, on the New York "Tribune."

Now began the real work of his life, for which everything hitherto had been a sort of preparation. Mulberry Street was his chance both from a professional and a philanthropic point of view. There were hostile police to circumvent and rival reporters to beat; there were all the woes of the Other Half to be reported in the big sense—which is always Mr. Riis's sense—of the word. He prayed that he might do his work well and then he "dived in," bent on exploiting the facts in which he trusted, determined to tell each story of shame and crime so that beneath the "foulness and the reek of blood" his readers might "see its meaning, or at all events catch the human drift of it."

In this spirit he began his career as police-reporter. On its professional side it immediately resolved itself into "a ten years' war," out of which the despised "Dutchman" came with what he tells us is the only renown he ever coveted, "that of being the 'boss reporter' in Mulberry Street." The "battlesome account" of those stirring days is full of good stories of the ups and downs, the set-backs and triumphs, of the fray. The one perhaps which best proves Mr. Riis's oft-repeated assertion that the true reporter is a man of power, having absolutely nothing in common with the ubiquitous, sensation-loving nuisance who sometimes bears the name, is the story of his famous trip up the Croton water-shed. The printed report of what he saw, confirmed by photographs, made a sensation, but it was not sensational. It was fact, and the result was an unpolluted water-supply for New York City. Incidentally the disclosure of the imminent possibility of a cholera epidemic was one of the biggest "beats" on record.

"Beats" alone, however, did not satisfy Mr. Riis; he remembered his dog and he wanted to settle with Mulberry Bend, through which he walked home between one and four o'clock every morning.

> "There were cars on the Bowery, but I liked to walk, for so I saw the slum when off its guard. The instinct to pose is as strong there as on Fifth Avenue. It is a human impulse, I suppose. . . . But at 3 A. M. the veneering is off and you see the true grain of a thing. So, also, I got a picture of the Bend upon my mind which so soon as I should be able to transfer it to that of the community would help settle with that pig-sty according to its deserts. It was not fit for Christian men and women, let alone innocent children, to live in, and therefore it had to go. So with the police lodging-rooms, some of the worst of which were right there. . . . The way of it never gave me any concern that I remember. That would open as soon as the truth was told. The trouble was that people did not know and had no means of finding out for themselves. But I had."

Delightfully Platonic, this trust in the power of truth to make men free; but it is not advanced as a general proposition, and it was justified. There were those who had ears to hear—the Charity Organization Society, the City Health Department, the King's Daughters, the various social settlements and tenement commissions, above all President Roosevelt of the Police Board and the rest of the Strong administration,—and they put themselves at the other end of the line, the organized, administrative end, whose value Mr. Riis fully appreciated, though he never meddled with it much.

> "To represent is not my business. To write is; I can do it much better and back up the other, so we are two for one. . . . I value the good opinion of my fellow-men, for with it comes increased power to do things. But I would reserve the honors for those who have fairly earned them, and on whom they set easy. They don't on me. I am not ornamental by nature."

Nor did he care to be ornamental. Always a worker, he wished to be known as one who worked well; after that to avenge the death of a little black-and-tan dog. This, it seemed to him, could best be done by letting light and air into the slums whose spiritual darkness and foulness had killed his dog,—by bringing to them the flowers of the fields, by planting small parks there to be bits of God's country in a godless place, by establishing decent schools and pleasant play-grounds, which are the children's rights. How he "sat up with his club," the fact, until these reforms were achieved, is the story that makes up the last half of his autobiography.

"I would not have missed being in it all for anything." That sentence strikes the keynote of the impression which Mr. Riis's book leaves with the reader. If its frankness and virility are singular, no less so is its unassuming optimism, its keen sense of the joy of combat, of the infinite interest and inestimable value of a life lived honestly and with purpose. Every journalist who is weighted with a sense of the futility of newspaper work, passing, as it does, into innocuous desuetude with the next "extra," should read this book. He can scarcely fail to get from it an inspiration that will make him view his responsibilities in their largeness and take up his "club," the fact, with new purpose to wield it well. But the thesis has a wider application. To "hitch your wagon to a star," to make cosmic connections, to see each little day as an important item in a big account, is a philosophy that will ennoble every worker. And Mr. Riis's contribution to its literature is of special value because he shows its practical bearing, freights it with no isms nor ologies, combines it with a very human sense of the importance, not of martyrdom, but of success; and best of all, perhaps, tinges it with a delightful sense of humor. His quality as a humorist and a charming *raconteur,* with a full fund of racy anecdotes about himself and his friends, each reader must enjoy for himself. It has been the purpose of this review to show the motives which made his game of life seem worth while to him, and, from his point of view, gave his autobiography its excuse for being.

## Mary Mills West (essay date 1903)

SOURCE: A review of *The Battle with the Slum,* in *The Journal of Political Economy,* Vol. 11, March, 1903, pp. 334-35.

[*In the following essay, West reviews* The Battle with the Slum.]

This latest work of Mr. Riis [*The Battle with the Slum*] supplements his *How the Other Half Lives* and *A Ten*

*Years' War,* and completes the history of a struggle to improve conditions in the tenement-house districts of New York city. The book describes the work of the Tenement-House Commissions of 1894 and 1900, and the voluntary citizens' committee of 1898, which led up to the creation of the present Tenement-House Department; but it is far from being a statistical report. It is rather an intimately personal account of the awful conditions which prevailed in the tenement-house districts, with their population of over two millions, and of what has been done, and against what odds, to purge the city. Such triumphs as the razing of Mulberry Bend, the opening of various small parks and playgrounds, the model tenements, the Mills hotels, the vacation schools—all these make a story not often exceeded in interest. *The Battle with the Slum* illustrates many important civic truths, not the least of which is that sometimes a *made* American may be worth a great many of the indigenous variety.

The book is enlivened with anecdotes, and contains many telling reproductions from photographs.

### The Nation (essay date 1903)

SOURCE: A review of *The Battle with the Slum,* in *The Nation,* Vol. 76, No. 1973, April 23, 1903, pp. 338-39.

[*In the following essay, a reviewer for* The Nation *offers a critique of* The Battle with the Slum.]

This book [*The Battle with the Slum*] would have attracted more attention than it has, but for the fact that most, if not all, of it is a republication. After writing *How the Other Half Lives,* the author published, three years ago, *A Ten Years' War,* a series of papers intended to account for the progress of "the battle with the slum" since the first volume appeared. Since that time, as he hints in his preface, a good many things have happened, and he has been occupied, not only in the conflict itself, but incidentally in writing about it. In the present volume he has passed the later stages of the conflict in review, "retaining all that still applied of the old volume and adding as much more." The "stories" are reprinted from the *Century,* and these, he adds, are fact, not fiction. The volume is copiously illustrated, and has plenty of real interest without the pictures.

This interest centres about two points: first, the author, and, secondly, what it is the fashion to call the "point of view" of the cause he advocates. Mr. Riis is, of course, an enthusiast, and in his enthusiasm fails to see that a much more restrained way of writing would be more effective for his purposes than that which he employs. But his enthusiasm is genuine, and carries conviction. He is so evidently honest in his sympathy for human suffering and ignorance, and even for human perversity—his character shines so transparently through what he says—that the most critical (or, as he would say, most pessimistic) nature is forced first to attend and then to follow. "What the Fight is About," the first half-dozen pages of the book, sums up its whole theory. This theory, to put it in our own words, is that the slum is the

measure of civilization. So far from its being tolerable, as those who went before thought, that squalor and filth and vice and crime should exist in great masses and plague-spots, side by side with wealth and education and order and happiness, the new theory is that, in a civilized community, the slum has no business to exist at all; that it can be extirpated, and that if it is not extirpated, the crime lies at the door of the prosperous classes who suffer it to go on. Now when we look at the slums of New York, we look at the worst case in point in the world, for here the slums have been permitted not only to fester and breed their kind, but to give a government to the city. Tammany, which thirty years ago meant only robbery, came in a generation to mean a government devoted to the propagation of vice and crime for private gain—probably the nearest approach to a "hell on earth" yet seen. Even Tammany never quite attained its ideal, but it came near enough to show us that it would have included, when perfect, a police dedicated to the work of deriving a revenue from the licensing not merely of bawds and pimps, but robbers and murderers; a fire department conniving in the work of the police by the spread of fires; a health board propagating disease; a building department aiding the main purpose of the government by selling licenses to violate the laws designed to secure life and limb and prevent the spread of pestilence—all directed to pouring a stream of money into the pocket of the man who managed the ingenious machinery by which he enslaved, plundered, and debauched his principality.

This system it is which has produced the New York pessimist for whom Mr. Riis has so little sympathy; fortunate for us if it has produced enthusiasts like Mr. Riis, who, seeing, as he says, that "we win or we perish," is ready for the battle. His battle with the slum is really only another side of the struggle for good government in which even "pessimists" now know they must take part or perish. Everybody cannot be an enthusiast; but everybody feels the force of inspiration, and Mr. Riis is inspired by that sympathy for the poor and weak and unsuccessful which drives men, not to alms-giving or psalm-singing, but to daily action against evil and its causes. The motive to which he appeals is in the end religious:

> "We shall win, for we are not letting things be, the way our fathers did. But it will be a running fight, and it is not going to be won in two years, or in ten, or in twenty. For all that, we must keep on fighting, content if in our time we avert the punishment that waits upon the third and the fourth generation of those who forget the brotherhood. As a man does in dealing with his brother, so it is the way of God that his children shall reap, that through toil and tears we may make out the lesson which sums up all the commandments and alone can make the earth fit for the kingdom that is to come."

### Thomas Arthur Gullason (essay date 1959)

SOURCE: "Brief Articles and Notes: The Sources of Stephen Crane's *Maggie,*" in *Philological Quarterly,* Vol. XXXVIII, No. IV, October, 1959, pp. 497-502.

*[In the following essay, Gullason identifies writers—among them Riis—who influenced Stephen Crane's novel* Maggie.*]*

For over a half-century, Stephen Crane's *Maggie* (1893) has been linked with European naturalism, particularly with Zola's *L'Assomoir*.[1] A single recent critic, Marcus Cunliffe, admits that while one can draw parallels between *Maggie* and *L'Assomoir* the most obvious place to search for possible sources "is not Europe but America: not Zola's Paris but Crane's New York." He points to such things as the social consciousness of *The Arena* (to which Crane contributed two propagandistic tales, "The Men in the Strom," and "An Ominous Baby"); Charles Loring Brace's *The Dangerous Classes of New York;* and Thomas DeWitt Talmage's sermons. With no definite proof that any of the above-mentioned are influences, Cunliffe concludes: "So, when young Crane writes with would-be savage candor of the slums, the preachers have been there before him. He cannot help borrowing some of their material."[2]

I suggest that much of Stephen Crane's materials for *Maggie* did come from two never-mentioned sources: his father, the minister Jonathan Townley Crane; and the famed social reformer, Jacob Riis. Though he died in 1880 when Stephen was only eight, Jonathan Crane left behind a number of works, mostly theological, which his favorite son always cherished.[3] As late as 1900 in England, young Crane kept a "shelf of books, for the most part the pious and theological works of various antecedent Stephen Cranes. He had been at some pains to gather together these alien products of his kin."[4]

There was more than enough in Jonathan Crane's writings to inspire his son to deal with the manifold problems presented in *Maggie*. In *The Annual Sermon,* for example, the minister reveals his awareness of the city slum and its effect on children:

> And while in our great cities the missionary finds no difficulty in collecting crowds of children into his school, in the worst localities, the vilest dens of murder and pollution, the Church of God ought to be very slow to give up any child as hopeless and utterly beyond the reach of good.[5]

The theme of alcoholism in *Maggie,* also central to *L'Assomoir,* could have easily been suggested by Jonathan Crane's *Arts of Intoxication* (1870). In one place, the minister notes: "The great problem of the times is, 'What shall be done to stay the ravages of intoxication?'"[6] In Chapter X of the book, he discusses the psychological effects of alcoholism on the individual: "When he is so far gone [in drinking] as to stammer in his speech and totter in his gait, and be helpless in mind and body, his sense of his wisdom, his strength, his greatness, and his goodness is at its highest point."[7] In Chapter XI, he adds: "Anger, malice, revenge, every destructive passion rages, because the palsied mind feels only the evil impulse, and cares nothing for consequences."[8]

Jonathan Crane even deals with the hereditary effects of alcoholism. There is no reference to the word "heredity"

in *Maggie,* yet Stephen Crane does show how Jimmie acquires the characteristics of his inebriate parents.[9] The minister says of this aspect: "When one parent is an inebriate, the child is, in a certain degree, liable to inherit constitutional peculiarities which increase the danger of his becoming a prey to the same remorseless destroyer. Where both parents are intemperate, the danger is still greater."[10] Further:

> . . . the saddest fact of all is that his [the parent's] innocent children may inherit his scars, and feel the sharp teeth of the devourer. They may be born not only with the dangerous susceptibility of alcoholic influence, but with organizations perverted and depraved by the vice of the parent, so thatthey too have their paroxysms of morbid restlessness and undefinable longing, when no employment contents them, no pleasures already known to them attract, no healthful food or drink satisfies, but when the first casual taste of the intoxicant thrills them with insane rapture, and marks them for a mad career and a doom from which all human tenderness and pity toil in vain to save them.[11]

Still other materials of his father's, as important as those on the slums and alcoholism, aided young Crane. In *Popular Amusements* (1870), Jonathan Crane probably suggested one of the key themes of his son's first novel: Maggie's romantic-realistic conflict. Though she is not a novel reader, Maggie attends a play and continually acts like the dreamy working girl, "the Countess of Moonshine," whom Jonathan Crane describes as follows:

> But as things are, novel-readers spend many a precious hour in dreaming out clumsy little romances of their own, in which they themselves are the beautiful ladies and the gallant gentlemen who achieve impossibilities, suffer unutterable woe for a season, and at last anchor in a boundless ocean of connubial bliss. . . . In fact, the Cinderella of the old nursery story is the true type of thousands of our novel-readers. They live a sort of double life—one in their own proper persons, and in their real homes; the other as ideal lords and ladies in dream-land.[12]

His father's works, then, besides suggesting themes, characters, and psychology could have also given Stephen Crane enough incentive to do further research on city slum conditions. For on July 10, 1892, he was in New York studying his materials firsthand. He wrote a news report which hints at the Bowery dialect and at the crude first sketches of Maggie and Jimmie:

> A sixteen-year-old girl without any hat and with a roll of half-finished vests under her arm crossed the front platform of the green car. As she stepped up on to the sidewalk a barber from a ten-cent shop said "Ah! there!" and she answered "smarty!" with withering scorn and went down a side street. . . . At the door he [a van driver] almost stepped on a small boy with a pitcher of beer so big that he had to set it down every half block.[13]

A second important influence on Stephen Crane's *Maggie* was Jacob Riis. The twenty-year-old Crane, as a shore correspondent at Asbury Park, heard Riis's lecture on July 24, 1892. He wrote:

> The two thousands of summer visitors who have fled from the hot, stifling air of the cities to enjoy the cool sea breezes are not entirely forgetful of the unfortunates who have to stay in their crowded tenements. Jacob Riis, the author of *How the Other Half Lives*, gave an illustrated lecture on the same subject in the Beach Auditorium on Wednesday.[14]

Crane must have been impressed by Riis's comments from *How the Other Half Lives* (1891), for they met on other occasions. Hamlin Garland recalled one meeting: "On arrival at the cafe I found that he [Theodore Roosevelt] had three other guests, William Chanler (a big-game hunter), Jacob Riis, the social worker, and Stephen Crane."[15] Theodore Roosevelt wrote to Anna Cowles on July 26, 1896: "I spent three nights in town, and the others out here; a Professor Smith, a friend of Bob's turned up, and dined with me—also Jacob Riis & Stephen Crane. . . . "[16]

It is known that Stephen Crane started writing *Maggie* in 1891 while a student at Syracuse University.[17] No one knows how much of the novel had been completed at that time, nor how many revisions were made before it was published in 1893. There is a strong possibility that Crane got some valuable details, not only from Riis's lecture and later conversations with him, but also from his clinical study of the New York slums, *How the Other Half Lives.*

*How the Other Half Lives* and *Maggie* show striking parallels.[18] Both contrast effectively the pathetic conditions of the slum folk and the world of the well-to-do. Both indicate that the complete disregard of the plight of the poor by the rich could lead to class war. In Riis's book, a pauper slashes his knife in the air as a feeble sign of protest against the rich; he "represented one solution of the problem of ignorant poverty versus ignorant wealth that has come down to us unsolved, the danger-cry of which we have lately heard in the shout that never should have been raised on American Soil—the shout of the 'masses against the classes'—the solution of violence" (p. 264). In *Maggie*, Jimmie "maintained a belligerent attitude toward all well-dressed men. To him fine raiment was allied to weakness, and all good coats covered faint hearts. . . . Above all things he despised obvious Christians and ciphers with the chrysanthemums of aristocracy in their buttonholes" (pp. 17-18).

Both books deal mainly with the youth of the slum world. Riis observes the gangs of hoodlums and their "stores of broken bricks." He adds: "The gang is the ripe fruit of tenement house growth. It was born there, endowed with a heritage of instinctive hostility to restraint by a generation that sacrificed home to freedom, or left its country for its country's good" (p. 218). The opening of *Maggie* has a gang war:

> A very little boy [Jimmie] stood upon a heap of gravel for the honour of Rum Alley. He was throwing stones at howling urchins from Devil's Row, who were circling madly about the heap and pelting him. His infantile countenance was livid with the fury of battle. His small body was writhing in the delivery of oaths (p. 3).

Both writers see in gang warfare an essential cowardice. Riis says: "From all this it might be inferred that the New York tough is a very fierce individual, of indomitable courage and naturally as blood-thirsty as a tiger. On the contrary he is an arrant coward" (p. 220). In *Maggie*, Jimmie's gang returns to war only when the enemy has retreated:

> Then the Rum Alley contingent turned slowly in the direction of their home street. They began to give, each to each, distorted versions of the fight. Causes of retreat in particular cases were magnified. Blows dealt in the fight were enlarged to catapultian power, and stones thrown were alleged to have hurtled with infinite accuracy. Valour grew strong again, and the little boys began to brag with great spirit (p. 5).

Riis analyzes the evil forces that help to destroy the young children of the slums. He complains of youths who carry pitchers of beer to their elders: "I once followed a little boy, who shivered in bare feet on a cold November night so that he seemed in danger of smashing his pitcher [for carrying beer] on the icy pavement, into a Mulberry Street saloon . . . and forbade the barkeeper to serve the boy" (p. 215). In *Maggie*, Jimmie goes on a similar errand: "He passed into the side door of a saloon and went to the bar. Straining up on his toes he raised the pail and pennies as high as his arms would let him. He saw two hands thrust down to take them. Directly the same hands let down the filled pail, and he left" (p. 13).

To both writers, the young working girls are the greatest sufferers in the slums. Riis describes in detail the sweat-shops of the shirt-makers where they labor. If one of these girls does not want to deprive herself of the real necessities of life (for her salary is too small), she "must in many instances resort to evil [prostitution]" (p. 234). Maggie also works in a collar-and-cuff factory (p. 21), and after having been rejected by her lover Pete, she turns to prostitution (p. 72). Still, Riis and Crane see clear evidences of untainted goodness amidst this degradation. Riis confesses that "it is not uncommon to find sweet and innocent girls, singularly untouched by the evil around them"; they are "like jewels in a swine's snout" (p. 161). Crane says virtually the same thing about the younger Maggie; he calls her a "flower in a mud-puddle" (p. 21).

Native American sources, such as these works by Jonathan Crane and Jacob Riis, served Stephen Crane well; they gave him his pessimistic bias as well as hints for characters, setting, themes, and psychology. He did not need further inspiration or other materials, like Zola's *L'Assomoir.*

NOTES

[1] For discussions of Zola's so-called influence on *Maggie*, see Lars Ahnebrink, *The Beginnings of Natural-*

*ism in American Fiction* (Upsala: American Institute, 1950), pp. 231-276; John Berryman, *Stephen Crane* (New York, 1950), p. 63; Oscar Cargill, *Intellectual America* (New York, 1941), pp. 85-86; and H. S. Canby *et al.*, *Literary History of the United States* (New York, 1948), II, 1022. Yet Crane "disliked most of Zola's work"; see Thomas Beer, *Stephen Crane: A Study in American Letters* (New York, 1923), p. 147.

[2] "Stephen Crane and the American Background of *Maggie*," *American Quarterly*, VII (1955), 35-36, 43.

[3] See *Dictionary of American Biography*, IV, 506.

[4] Edmund Wilson, ed., *The Shock of Recognition* (New York, 1943), p. 671.

[5] *The Annual Sermon* (New York, 1858), p. 22.

[6] *Arts of Intoxication* (New York, 1870), p. 3.

[7] *Ibid.*, p. 145.

[8] *Ibid.*, p. 165. This sentence suggests the character of the drunken Swede in "The Blue Hotel."

[9] Crane seemed to be interested only in environment and its effect on character. In an inscription on a copy of *Maggie*, he said: "It is inevitable that you [Dr. Lucius L. Button] will be greatly shocked by the book but continue, please, with all possible courage, to the end. For it tries to show that environment is a tremendous thing in the world and frequently shapes lives regardless." (See Robert W. Stallman, ed., *Stephen Crane: An Omnibus* [New York, 1952], p. 594.) Yet his treatment of Jimmie suggests that Crane was also deeply interested in the question of heredity.

[10] *Arts of Intoxication,* p. 177.

[11] *Ibid.*, p. 184.

[12] *Popular Amusements* (New York, 1870), pp. 136-138. For references to Maggie's similar romantic yearnings, see Carl Van Doren, ed., *Stephen Crane: Twenty Stories* (New York, 1940), pp. 24, 36-37. All later references to *Maggie* are to this edition.

[13] "Travels in New York," New York *Tribune*, July 10, 1892, p. 8. In the novel, Maggie works in a collar-and-cuff factory while Jimmie carries beer to one of the tenants.

[14] "On The New Jersey Coast," New York *Tribune*, July 24, 1892, p. 22.

[15] *Roadside Meetings* (New York, 1931), p. 329.

[16] Elting E. Morison *et al., The Letters of Theodore Roosevelt* (Cambridge, Mass., 1951), I, 550.

[17] Stallman, pp. 5-7.

[18] Crane may have gotten the name of Maggie's neighborhood, Rum Alley, from the title of Chapter XVIII in Riis's book, "The Reign of Rum." See *How the Other Half Lives* (New York, 1932), p. 215. All later references to Riis's book are to this edition.

**Sam Bass Warner, Jr. (essay date 1970)**

SOURCE: An introduction to *How the Other Half Lives*, by Jacob Riis, edited by Sam Bass Warner, Jr., Cambridge, Mass.: The Belknap Press of HarvardUniversity Press, 1970, pp. vii-xix.

[*In the following essay, the editor's introduction of* How the Other Half Lives, *Warner discusses Riis's classic work.*]

This is one of the great books of American journalism. Published in 1890, early in the era of muckraking, ***How the Other Half Lives*** stands with Lincoln Steffens' *Shame of the Cities* (1904) and John Steinbeck's *The Grapes of Wrath* (1939) for its impact on its own generation and for its lasting ability to secure a reader's emotional assent to the vision of the author. Today the book is in continuous use by historians seeking evidence of our urban past and by all students of America's reform tradition.

With this book Riis succeeded in doing what every newspaperman dreams of. At just the right moment in our history—when the tide of immigration was reaching its flood, and many Americans had grown fearful of foreigners; when the new rings of growth of the American metropolis first fully separated city dwellers into a core of poverty and suburbs of success; when a generation of health and charity studies of poverty filled a bookshelf with neglected expertise; and when American cities themselves had grown huge and ominous—Jacob Riis fashioned a portrait of our largest city's largest slum that captured the public imagination.

The portrait was at once a confirmation of popular belief and a call to action. Riis affirmed the humanity of the poor immigrant; he assured middle-class Americans that most slum dwellers sought the same kind of life that the mainstream possessed; he painted a colorful landscape of the Lower East Side, so that poverty became an interesting subject for social tourism; and, finally, he presented the slum as a social problem for which there were specific public remedies.

Before Riis there was no broad popular understanding of urban poverty that could lead to political action. A long tradition of charitable writing existed, a line stemming from John Woolman's *A Plea for the Poor* (1793) and Mathew Carey's pamphlet of the same name (1837) to Charles Loring Brace's *The Dangerous Classes of New York and Twenty Years' Work Among Them* (1872), but such works were merely calls for more private charitable effort. They did not urge public action of a magnitude that could give the public confidence in the city's ability to cope with the tide of immigrant poor. Sweeping reforms had been proposed in the years just previous to the appearance of Riis's book. Henry George (*Progress and Poverty,* 1877) and Edward Bellamy (*Looking Backward,* 1888) had published popular attacks on the capitalist system, a system which was in part responsible for American poverty, but few Americans wanted to abandon or radically alter capitalism. Riis's work entered the space between these two lines of thought. It proposed remedies which could permanently improve the everday life of the poor, and it followed the general American tradition by staying well to the right of any call for socialism.

Armed with the muckraker's confidence that publicity can solve problems by creating an intelligent public opinion,[1] Riis set out to fuse his personal experiences into a generalized statement and a call for reform. For his evidence he used his own daily experience as a police reporter stationed for twelve years in the Lower East Side. To this he added the reports of health and charity workers. His synthesis was an ecological definition of the slum. The slum was a special environment which bore in special ways upon the men, women, and children dwelling within it.

In the subtitle of the book Riis called his study "Life Among the Tenements," thereby suggesting his frequent use of the physical objects, the decaying old homes, the back alleys, and the tall tenement barracks as symbols for the patterns of human life in the slum. By his definition—and his definition has persisted in the popular mind and official government mind at least until Michael Harrington's *The Other America* (1963)—the slum is a poor immigrant quarter of overcrowded rooms, sweatshop manufacturing, poverty-stricken churches, broken-down schools, cheap retail shops, saloons, vice, and political corruption. Here the strong prey upon the weak; the ordinary man or woman trying to make adecent living and trying to lead a normal family life is continually harassed. Many are totally defeated.

Having defined the slum as an ecology of injustice, Riis proposed a multiple program for coping with it. He gathered up all the sentiments and ideas current at the moment of his writing. To satisfy the longing for the country, felt by immigrant and Americans alike, he proposed parks, fresh air funds, and flower campaigns; to assuage the homesickness for the small town or village he proposed clubs, settlement houses, and better schools; to meet the demand for decent living conditions he proposed general policing of the slum, enforcement of the housing laws against greedy landlords, and the building of model tenements by limited-dividend corporations; and to help the down-and-out he proposed municipal lodging houses and compulsory work. Above all he appealed to the middle class of New York to come, to take an interest, to lend a hand in municipal politics and in charity work, to see that every New Yorker got a chance to work and live according to the American standards which Riis himself ardently believed in. Put most simply, he appealed to his fellow citizens to help give the poor a decent break.

In his reminiscences[2] Riis wrote that his perception of the slum and his prescription for it grew naturally out of his personal experience—his experience as a child growing up in a small country mill town in Denmark, and his experience as a young immigrant drifting about for six years in New York and Pennsylvania seeking to find himself and his place in America.

Born on May 3, 1849, in Ribe, Denmark, Jacob was the third of fourteen children.[3] While he was growing up there were twelve children in the house, two elder brothers, two younger sisters, four younger brothers (one of whom drowned when Jacob was eleven years old), and three infants who died in their first years. These deaths, and the relentless struggle of his schoolteacher father against the pains of genteel poverty, were etched in black in Riis's memory. In contrast he recalled the bright cheerfulness and easy companionship of his large family and the freedom of his small-town childhood. The tension between these opposing sets of memories formed Riis's deep sense of family. He believed the family to be the heart of life; it was both a group of people struggling together for life and a place where the most intense emotions of existence were experienced. In this commitment to the family lay the lines of Riis's later perception of the slum as a poisonous environment for the poor family and his vigorous demands for decent housing, decent schools, and neighborhood action. Such a reform focus allied him with the settlement house workers, who were also family and community oriented, as opposed to contemporary writers like William Dean Howells (*Hazard of New Fortunes,* 1890) or socialists and unionists who saw the city in terms of the "industrial question"—that is, who saw the city as a conflict of an army of toilers against greedy business organizations. Riis never saw industrial armies and masses; he saw individuals and families.

After grammar school, despite his father's hopes, Jacob refused professional training and chose instead to become a carpenter. In the mid-nineteenth century, Denmark, like all European countries, was urbanizing rapidly, so there were plenty of openings for skilled men in the building trades. Accordingly, Jacob was apprenticed to a Copenhagen builder and spent the next four years living and working in the metropolis. Although he always enjoyed outdoor life and working with his hands, carpentry did not satisfy him. Loneliness also spoiled his apprentice years. The moment the carpenter's guild admitted him, therefore, Jacob abandoned his tools and returned to Ribe. But Ribe, a stagnant town of three thousand, whose main employment was a single textile mill, had no room for a young carpenter. When his childhood sweetheart, the millowner's daughter, refused him, Riis embarked for America.

Riis landed in New York in 1870 to begin, at the age of twenty-one, three years of wandering and of searching for a place for himself in America. Over the weeks and months of 1870-1873 he acted out what must have been a common experience of nineteenth-century American boys and what became for American writers in the early twentieth century almost a ritual passage from youth to manhood.

Uncertain of everything, determined in some vague way to be a success, restless, independent, aggressive, self-righteous, unwilling to assume the harness of the craft for which he had been trained, Jacob wandered for three years over New York, New Jersey, and Pennsylvania. He took the first job offered him, building workers' shacks for an Allegheny iron mill; he tried to enlist in the French army to avenge the German conquest of his homeland; he got into a fight with the French consul in New York. He went broke, bummed in New York City, begged rolls and bones from Delmonico's restaurant, spent a night in a police lodging house with other down-and-outs, was robbed and expelled for complaining of his treatment, spent a day in the rain staring at the oily waters of the East River, worked with a drunken crew of brickmakers in New Jersey, and was nursed back to health by the Danish consul in Philadelphia. He became a hired hand for a country doctor, did some lumbering, ran a line of muskrat traps in upstate New York, built ships on Lake Erie, worked in Buffalo lumberyards and a planing mill, tried lecturing and failed, took up selling furniture for a Danish furniture co-operative—it also failed, but selling was righter than odd jobs and carpentry. Jacob was a talker and a hustler. He made a small bankroll as a drummer in flatirons, selling up and down the smoky oil, mill, and mining towns of western Pennsylvania. He was cleaned out when he tried the Chicago flatiron agency, was defrauded by his fellow salesmen in Pittsburgh, and went on the road again back into the small towns. He took sick and spent weeks holed up in a lonely boarding-house, recovered and spent a summer selling his way back to New York city, studied to be a telegrapher, peddled books part-time without success, and finally secured a job as a reporter with a free-lance news service.

Out of the experience of these three years came Riis's strong confidence in himself and his conviction of the rightness of American ways. Despite greed, meanness, and fraud, all of which he had fought and suffered, Riis believed a man had a chance in America; it was a free country, and any man with guts who was willing to work hard could make a decent living for himself and his family. This personal self-confidence and faith in American individualism permeated Riis's writing. In *How the Other Half Lives* it appeared in his harsh attacks on loafers, bums, grafting politicians, petty criminals, greedy landlords, and chiseling employers: all those who refused to try or who preyed upon the honest men who were trying. The same convictions also blinded Riis's vision. He never saw the slum as part of a metropolitan and national economy; he never absorbed the growing contemporary criticism of capitalism into his understanding of what he saw on the Lower East Side. For Riis the slum was the product of individual greed, immigrant ignorance, political corruption, and the slipshod habits of previous generations.

After his first entry into the newspaper business in 1873, it took five years for Riis to establish himself permanently in New York. He ran a weekly in Brooklyn for some local politicians, then purchased it and successfully managed it himself. He sold the paper and with the proceeds returned to Ribe to marry the millowner's daughter. Upon his return to New York he tried lantern slide shows and then finally settled down as a police reporter for the *New York Tribune*. In this job he mastered his basic stylistic technique: the short vignette.[4] He wrote hundreds of human interest stories about the people he met at the station, in the courts, or while following up leads from the police blotter. In these little stories Riis learned to make his vision reach people. The Riis method was to begin with a quick dramatic statement of a person's plight, then to reveal the tension between the relentless struggle for survival and the quick emotions of love, anger, greed, and friendship, which Riis portrayed as heightened in intensity by the slum environment, and to close with an appeal to the common reader's sense of justice.

Steadily his career led him from slum vignettes to more systematic observation of the life around him. The offices of the city's Health Department were then around the block from the *Tribune* reporters' office; Riis could stop in regularly. He first became acquainted with the department on a smallpox story, then took to making regular calls in search of material. In time, as he formed friendships with the staff, he began going out on inspection rounds through the slums. The night rounds, especially, when inspectors checked against overcrowding of rooms, revealed the Lower East Side at its worst—the ragpickers' cellar nest, the flophouses, the all-night dives. Riis's shock and anger at these night scenes gave him the motive to take up the new invention of flash photography to portray to the public what the health inspectors were teaching him. The health officers also taught him to look beyond the single case toward a view of the entire environment. This experience is mirrored in the contents of *How the Other Half Lives,* in which Riis builds the whole concept of a slum out of dozens of individual cases. Presumably the health officers also informed him of the literature of the sanitary movement, which by the 1880's consisted of a long shelf of investigations and calls for reform. Riis later frequently cited these works.

In his autobiography Riis recounted the specific steps which led to the writing and publication of *How the Other Half Lives.*[5] The first step was his experience in reporting the hearings of the 1884 Tenement-House Commission. The failure of the laws of 1879 and previous years to improve markedly the sanitary condition of New York tenements and the menacing spread of the new large five-story double house (the "dumbbell tenement") through the city led to the creation of still another state commission. Felix Adler (1851-1933), founder of the Ethical Culture Society, is generally credited with getting the investigation authorized and driving it forward.[6] The commission employed tenement inspectors of its own for a survey of one thousand dwelling units and during the summer and fall of 1884 conducted hearings and heard its inspectors' reports. As Riis listened to the parade of landlords, tenants, inspectors, charity workers, and reformers he became especially impressed at the way in which Adler led their testimony to bring out the basic issues of everyday life in the slum. In later years, when Riis had become a full-time reform journalist, he and Adler were associated on a number of projects. They shared a belief that children, child development, and education were society's most important tasks, and they shared a personal approach to life which was captured in Adler's slogan, "deed not creed."

For Riis the immediate outcome of this reporting experience was the confirmation of his personal view that the slum dwellers were better than their environment. The public confirmation was, he said, "a big white milestone on a dreary road."[7] The people didn't make the slums; the slum environment made the slum dweller.

The next step toward the writing of *How the Other Half Lives* came four winters later, in 1888. This time Riis was reporting at a meeting of Protestant ministers and laymen who were deploring the failure of the church to reach the slum residents. Alfred T. White (1846-1921), by then a well-known builder of philanthropic tenements and President of the Brooklyn Bureau of Charities, stood up in the hall and cried out, "How are these men and women to understand the love of God you speak of, when they see only the greed of men?"[8] Riis often quoted White's statement. He recalled that the whole concept of the book, built around the theme of the title, *How the Other Half Lives,* began to grow upon him immediately upon hearing White's statement.

That fall and winter he had been seeking a platform for illustrated lectures on conditions in the Lower East Side. He resigned the diaconate of his Brooklyn church when his minister refused to let him lecture to the congregation on the subject, and other ministers also turned him down. On February 12, 1888, the *New York Sun* published some of his slum photographs. Two weeks later he opened his career as a reformer-journalist with a slide lecture at the Broadway Tabernacle in behalf of the City Mission Society. The lecture was a success, and, thanks to the patronage of Rev. Josiah Strong (1847-1916), he began to lecture in other New York churches.

With every month his personal commitment to a campaign of some kind became a little deeper. In June 1888 he published his appeal to the *Tribune*'s readers, asking them to send flowers to his office for distribution to slum residents. "There are too many sad little eyes in the crowded tenements, where the sunshine means disease and death, not play and vacation, that will close without ever having looked upon a field of daisies," he wrote.[9] His office was soon flooded with flowers, and he needed all the police reporters and some volunteers from the force to give them out.

As he went about lecturing, a *Scribner's Magazine* editor heard him speak and urged him to write a piece for the magazine. The December 1889 *Scribner's* carried a capsule version of what later became the book, a nineteen-page illustrated article entitled **"How the Other Half Lives."**[10]

Finally, a letter he received from another journalist encouraging him to expand the article into a book-length treatment of the slum led him to the task of writing the book. During the winter and spring of 1890 he wrote the manuscript at night at home, after his day's work as a police reporter. In November 1890 Scribner's published it, incorporating some of the illustrations from the magazine article and making engravings and halftones from many of Riis's photographs.

The book was well received by critics and welcomed by the general reader. It stated clearly and dramatically what middle-class Americans feared slum conditions were like. In the years before the first World War, *How the Other Half Lives* was read by all settlement house workers, all social workers, and all Progressive reformers. From the summer of 1890 on, Riis abandoned his regular newspaper work and became a free-lance journalist and active reformer. He went about lecturing on the slum, calling for city parks and playgrounds, urging better tenement regulations and the building of model tenements, working to support a settlement house that bore his name, and writing numerous books and articles. His most famous pupil was Theodore Roosevelt, whom he guided through the slums of New York when the latter became Police Commissioner. Roosevelt later wrote, *"How the Other Half Lives* had been to me both an enlightenment and an inspiration for which I felt I never could be too grateful."[11] Jacob Riis died at his summer farm in Massachusetts on May 25, 1914.

There are some antique habits of thought and style which today's reader must understand and overcome if he is to be able to evaluate Riis's descriptions and to appreciate the significance of Riis's appeal for reform. The use of ethnic and racial stereotypes shocks the modern, war-weary, and riot-torn sensibility: the greedy, dirty, quarrelsome Jews; the happy-go-lucky, long-suffering Negroes; the home-loving, orderly Germans; the stealthy and secretive Chinese; the exuberant, lighthearted Italians; the somber Bohemians; the dirty Arabs; the thrifty Swiss; the saloon-loving, political Irish. The entire list of phrases rings unpleasant echoes of European nationalism, American nativism, and white racism.[12] These were the stereotypes created by Riis's newspaper audience, the working-class and middle-class native Americans of the late nineteenth century. Because the degree of opprobrium assigned to each group is directly proportional to the distance from Denmark we may assume that Riis, the Danish immigrant, found these American attitudes congenial. Fear of and prejudice against the incoming waves of foreigners are an old American habit, as old as immigration itself, and the political and cultural consequences of this fear have been dealt with by our scholars.[13] All that needs to be said here is that the modern reader must accommodate himself to the unpleasant fact that in 1890 an open-hearted, fair-minded appeal for justice for the poor could be couched in terms of racial and ethnic prejudice as well as individual compassion and understanding.

In addition to stereotyping there is a stylistic device of seeking picturesque you-were-there detail which may distract the modern reader. Riis, like most journalists of his day, imitated the style of Charles Dickens. Both in his vignettes of individuals and in his more general street scenes Riis piles up detail of sight, smell, and touch to give the reader the sensation that he might be there, standing beside the narrator.

For instance, Charles Dickens climbed the stairs of the old brewery in the Five Points on his visit to New York in 1841. "Ascend these pitch-dark stairs," he wrote, "heedful of the false footing on the trembling boards, and grope your way with me into this wolfish den, where neither ray of light nor breath of air, appears to come."[14] Half a century later Jacob Riis leads his reader up the stairs of an old house on Cherry Street, a mere five blocks downtown from the Five Points. "Be a little careful, please! The hall is dark and you might stumble over the children pitching pennies back there. Not that it would hurt them; kicks and cuffs are their daily diet. They have little else. Here where the hall turnsand dives into utter darkness is a step, and another, another. A flight of stairs. You can feel your way if you cannot see it. Close? Yes!"[15] At the top of the stairs there is a family with a dying baby.

The modern sensibility may also be offended by Riis's role as a tour guide, a journalist driving a literary bus full of middle-class American attitudes through the narrow and crowded streets of the ethnic slums of New York. "Down the street comes a file of women carrying enormous bundles of firewood on their heads, loads of decaying vegetables from the market wagons in their aprons, and each a baby at the breast supported by a sort of sling that prevents it from tumbling down. The women do all the carrying, all the work one sees going on in 'the Bend.' The men sit or stand in the streets, on trucks, or in the open doors of the saloons smoking black clay pipes, talking and gesticulating as if forever on the point of coming to blows. Near a particularly boisterous group, a really pretty girl with a string of amber beads twisted artlessly in the knot of her raven hair has been bargaining long and earnestly with an old granny, who presides over a wheel-barrow load of second-hand stockings and faded cotton yarn, industriously darning the biggest holes while she extols the virtues of her stock."[16]

This straining for the picturesque was the style of the age. Today it seems but a partial discount against Riis's wide sympathy for the men, women, and children of New York's slums. His basic account was "A story of thousands of devoted lives, laboring earnestly to make the most of their scant opportunities for good; of heroic men and women striving patiently against fearful odds and by their very courage coming off the victors in the battle with the tenement. . . . "[17] And for the poor of New York, all of whom he saw in this light of a struggle for decency, he had one goal and one remedy: to help their family life by decent housing, decent schools, and decent working conditions.

Finally, the modern reader should be forewarned about the historical uniqueness of the place Riis described.

Because New York has been for so long the literary center of the nation, and because Riis's book became such a popular text, the Lower East Side in general and Riis's portrayal of it in 1890 in particular have often been taken as representative of American urban poverty. They were not. Riis's slum population was young, its housing was unusually dense, and its centrality gave it a very untypical concentration of crime.

Although Riis stressed the bad sanitation, the high incidence of disease, and the generally lethal quality of the Lower East Side tenements, they were by no means America's worst urban death trap. Other slums levied a higher death toll. The inner wards of Newark, downtown St. Louis, New Orleans, Jane Addams' Chicago Ward 19—all had higher death rates. The mortality of the Lower East Side stood low in relation to these other cities in part because the quarter was inhabited by so many young immigrants and in part because the quarter had so few Negroes, a group whose death rate was always very much higher than that of whites.[18]

During Riis's years the Lower East Side was becoming a high-walled city of tenements, but in 1890 it had not yet been rebuilt in that form. As the pictures in this book reveal, physically it did not resemble today's Harlem. Its appalling crowding of the land—densities of 522, 429, and 386 persons per acre in the most crowded wards[19]— was achieved by a mixture of new five- and six-story tenements, conversions of old houses, and the filling of every backyard and alley with shacks and shanties. Most city slums in America were not and never have been filled so densely with structures. Jane Addams' Ward 19 in Chicago had a density of 83.5 persons per acre in 1895. Its housing consisted of adaptations of wooden farm structures, small houses of one and a half, two, or three stories placed often several to a narrow lot, one behind the other. Hers was the typical American city or mill town slum ecology. DuBois's Philadelphia Ward 7 had a density of 118 persons per acre in 1890. Its crowding took the English form of three- and four-story row houses on the main streets and tiny two-story rows in the alleys behind. Robert Woods's slum in Boston's South End in 1898 had the densest housing in that city, but only 157 persons per acre. In other words, Riis's Lower East Side was a unique physical setting and therefore a unique ecology of poverty.[20]

Riis's slum was also a special urban place in that it was a core city slum where the criminals dwelt in large numbers among the poor. This mixture of crime and poverty in *How the Other Half Lives* joined literary tradition with special urban spatial patterns. Frightening the middle class with the specter of the depravity of the slum was already by Riis's time a much-used style. George Lippard and other popular writers of fiction had portrayed the slum as a terrifying haunt of criminals in order to sell books, while reformers like the New York Council of Hygiene and Charles Loring Brace threatened revolution, riot, and constant criminal harassment in order to encourage people to support their programs.[21] Riis was, after all, a police reporter, and he did not fail to make the conventional links between the slum, revolution, and criminality. It seems likely that this technique more confirmed the conservative reader in his belief that the poor were depraved and beyond redemption than it galvanized the fearful middle class into action, but American reform has long remained committed to the formula.

The criminals of New York concentrated in the Lower East Side and neighboring areas because this slum was next to the metropolitan shopping, transport, and business core. Here were prey for pickpockets, customers for prostitutes, gamblers, dope peddlers, and all-night joints; here were the stores, shops, trains, and warehouses to be robbed, and here were the offices and factories to be broken into. Moreover, in Manhattan, the police and political bosses, like the police and political bosses of other American cities in the nineties, segregated the criminals, endeavoring to keep them out of the "better" neighborhoods and to concentrate them in certain quarters where they could be controlled and milked for revenue. Although no Jacob Riis wrote of the outer areas of poverty in the American metropolis of the late nineteenth century, there is no reason to believe that residents of these districts or indeed that most of the urban poor lived in criminal-infested areas.

The denomination of the criminal slum as the symbol of all urban poverty had, and still has, unfortunate consequences. In Riis's day it led to Progressive campaigns against crime, vice, and political corruption to the neglect of remedies for poverty. The persistence of this wrongful use of Riis's criminal slum has had the result of encouraging reformers and their audiences to spend their energy on the demeaning philanthropic task of distinguishing between the deserving and undeserving poor.

But Jacob Riis, despite his concentration on criminal elements, his anger at bums and loafers, his racial and ethnic stereotypes, and his use of what is now an antique style of picturesque detail, did manage to convey in his book the central theme that every man, woman, and child of the slum deserved a decent house, a decent job, a decent school, fresh air, clean water, and safety against fire, epidemics, and crime. He never lost sight of these basic urban rights of being human. It is this universal and still unanswered appeal which saves *How the Other Half Lives* from misinterpretation by its readers and accounts for its unending popularity.

NOTES

[1] "It seemed to me that a reporter's was the highest and noblest of all callings; no one could sift wrong from right as he, and punish the wrong. In that I was right. I have not changed my opinion on that point one whit, and I am sure I never shall. The power of the fact is the mightiest lever of this or any day." Jacob A. Riis, *The Making of an American,* ed. Roy Lubove (New York, 1966), p. 99.

[2] Riis, *Making of an American,* pp. 1-100; *idem., The Old Town* (New York, 1909).

[3] There is a very good biography of Riis: Louise Ware, *Jacob A. Riis, Police Reporter, Reformer, Useful Citizen* (New York, 1938), and Riis's papers are now at the New York Public Library.

[4] Ware, *Jacob Riis,* pp. 40-46.

[5] Riis, *Making of an American,* pp. 245-248.

[6] Lawrence Veiller, *Tenement House Reform in New York, 1834-1900, Prepared for the Tenement House Commission of 1900* (New York, 1900), pp. 25-30.

[7] Riis, *Making of an American,* p. 246.

[8] *Ibid.,* p. 248.

[9] *Ibid.,* p. 288.

[10] *Scribner's Magazine,* 6 (December 1889), 643-662.

[11] Theodore Roosevelt, *An Autobiography* (New York, 1916), p. 174.

[12] These stereotypes and the harshness of tone toward the down-and-outs did not go unnoticed by reviewers when the book appeared. Ware, *Jacob Riis,* pp. 74-75.

[13] John Higham, *Strangers in the Land* (New Brunswick, 1955).

[14] Charles Dickens, *American Notes and Pictures from Italy* (London, 1857), p. 89.

[15] Riis, *How the Other Half Lives,* p. 32.

[16] *Ibid.,* pp. 42-43.

[17] *Ibid.,* p. 106.

[18] See Bureau of the Census, U.S., *Eleventh Census, 1890,* vol. XXI: *Report on Vital and Social Statistics,* part 2, *Vital Statistics* (Washington, 1896).

[19] Riis, *How the Other Half Lives,* Appendix, Wards 10, 13, 11.

[20] See Residents of Hull House, *Hull House Maps and Papers* (New York, 1895), pp. 3-19; W. E. Burghardt DuBois, *The Philadelphia Negro: A Social Study* (Philadelphia, 1899), p. 58; Robert A. Woods, ed., *The City Wilderness: A Settlement Study* (Boston, 1898), p. 61.

[21] George Lippard, *The Quaker City* (Philadelphia, 1845) and *New York: Its Upper Ten and Lower Million* (Cincinnati, 1853); Citizens' Association of New York, *Report of the Council of Hygiene and Public Health upon the Sanitary Condition of the City* (New York, 1865); Charles Loring Brace, *The Dangerous Classes of New York, and Twenty Years' Work among Them* (New York, 1872).

**Park Dixon Goist (essay date 1977)**

SOURCE: "Social Workers, Reformers, and the City, Jane Addams and Jacob Riis," in *From Main Street to State Street; Town, City, and Community in America*, Kennikat Press, 1977, pp. 80-93.

[*In the following excerpt, Goist compares and contrasts Riis's formative experiences with those of another social reformer, Jane Addams.*]

The emphasis of the urban novels written by Hamlin Garland, Theodore Dreiser, and Henry Blake Fuller was essentially on the consequences of city living for individuals. In Garland there is some notice taken of a limited social network in which Rose Dutcher attempts to find her place. In Fuller's novel the Marshall family, though badly weakened by events, still plays some role. But the real concern of these novelists is with the individual. This is even more noticeable, of course, in Dreiser's work. Here the focal point is entirely on the unattached individual; no sustained social group ties or family bonds are enjoyed by the lonely characters in *Sister Carrie*. The perspective of the early urban novelists focused, then, on the impact upon the indivudal of the urban milieu.

Contemporaneous with this emphasis on the individual was a growing consciousness among middle class reformers of the important role played in cities by groups.Theodore Brower's proposed justice center for the poor, the settlement work of Isabel Herrick's university friends, even Jane Marshall's lunchroom for working girls and Mrs. Granger Bates's camp for needy children, were fictional counterparts of efforts actually being made by social workers to understand and cope with changing urban conditions in terms of group needs. In Chicago the work of Jane Addams (1860-1935) at Hull-House is the best-known of such endeavors. In her work one notices a shift from individual to group concerns in dealing with the industrial city. Also, her life provides an opportunity to trace the relationship between a particular kind of nonurban upbringing and the social work approach to urban society. A similar perspective, which also offers some interesting contrasts to Addams, can be seen in the work of the famous New York newspaperman and reformer Jacob Riis (1849-1914). An immigrant himself, Riis personally experienced the awful poverty and lonely isolation which was the fate of many in late nineteenth-century American cities. But he was fortunate enough to survive and eventually achieve success as a police reporter in New York. These experiences shaped his view of the city which he tried so hard to change. Addams and Riis were two of the outstanding reform figures of their day, and they provide an insight into an important middle class response to the rapidly changing turn-of-the-century American city.

Jane Addams was born in the northern Illinois village of Cedarville. This settlement (founded in the 1830s) is just south of the Wisconsin border, and a few miles north of the small city of Freeport. Addams's parents had settled here on the Cedar River in 1844. By the time of Jane's birth her father, John, who had previously been a miller in Pennsylvania, was the most prominent man in the area. He owned a flour mill and a sawmill, was president of an insurance company and of a Freeport bank, which he had helped organize, and had invested money in railroads and land. A self-made man, he was also a community builder. He helped organize the first school, the first church, and the first library in Cedarville, and was instrumental in bringing a railroad into the Cedar River region. John Addams was also an Illinois state senator for sixteen years (1854-70) and one of the organizers of the Republican Party, to which he remained loyal throughout his life. He died in 1881 at the age of fifty-nine, leaving an estate worth a quarter of a million dollars.[1]

Jane was two years old when her mother died at the age of forty-nine. Sarah Addams had given birth to nine children, five of whom lived. Jane was the youngest; she had three sisters and a brother. She was eight when her father married Anna Haldeman, the attractive widow of a prominent Freeport man. Anna brought a son with her to live in the Addams household, and he became a close companion and playmate of his stepsister Jane. The second Mrs. Addams had intellectual and cultural aspirations, and was a talented musician. She provided her new home not only with a piano but also with an insistence upon the daily use of linen table cloths, good china, and silver. The emphasis upon culture and taste meant for young Jane drawing and music lessons in Freeport, stylish clothes, and, following college, a grand tour of Europe. It also meant the lectures, concerts, and fashionable parties of Baltimore, where Mrs. Addams moved after her second husband's death.

Jane Addams's recent biographer Allen Davis points out that, despite her rather complex family structure and early illnesses (the most serious of which left her with a slight curvature of the spine), she had a happy childhood. Davis also maintains that in spite of her father's prominent position and the cultural aspirations her second mother had for Jane, she attended the one-room village school and played with the children of millhands. These were not the sons and daughters of immigrants, however, and nearly all were Protestants. Davis finds further evidence of the "natural equality" of the small town in the fact that the Addamses' "hired girls" were not treated as servants. They agreed to work for a year or two in order to learn to cook and sew, and were included in the Addams family circle. Davis's point here is that the rather aristocratic tendencies of her stepmother conflicted with the easy equality of village life, thus producing some of the ambivalence and contradictions in Addams's character.

At seventeen Jane entered Rockford Female Seminary, where she was an undergraduate from 1877 to 1881. Although nearby Rockford did not yet haveofficial college ranking, those attending were self-conscious of being college women. They were in fact among the first generation of full-fledged college educated women. The purpose of this "Mount Holyoke of the West" was to combine domestic training with religious and cultural instruction. Addams was somewhat formal and aloof as a student, but entered fully into the life of the school. She was president of the literary society and an editor of the school magazine, she read widely and debated, struggled with religious questions, became interested in science, did well in class work, and developed the habits of a writer. In her essays she broke with Rockford tradition and argued for the special role of women in world affairs. Upon graduation she planned to go on to Smith College for a Bachelor of Arts.

But for the next eight years, until the opening of Hull-House, Addams was buffeted by family tragedy and responsibility, physical disability, and severe mental depression. For convenience, this time in her life can be divided into four periods. During the two years following graduation from Rockford, Addams was generally ill and despondent. She gave up hopes of going to Smith for a B.A., was forced to leave the Women's Medical College in Philadelphia because of her health, spent a good deal of time as an invalid, and had major surgery on her back. She also faced family tragedy, including the sudden death of her adored father and the mental breakdown of her brother. With other members of the family scattered, Jane took on the burden of managing family business affairs. Between August, 1883, and June, 1885, she and her step-mother and a small party of friends lived and traveled in Europe. Returning to the United States in the summer of 1885, for the next two and a half years she spent the winters with her stepmother in Baltimore, the rest of the time in Cedarville. It was during the winter months of 1885 and 1886 in Baltimore when, according to her recollections some twenty-five years later, "I seemed to have reached the nadir of my nervous depression and sense of maladjustment."[2] In December, 1887, she departed again for Europe, in a party which included her close friend Ellen Starr. During this trip the scheme which resulted in the founding of Hull-House apparently took shape. Addams and Starr returned to America in October, 1888, moved to a Chicago boarding house in January of the next year, raised money for their scheme, and took up residence in the old Charles Hull mansion the following September.

The question remains: Why did Jane Addams turn to social work and become a leader of the social settlement movement at the turn of the century? The two most interesting recent efforts to answer this question have been put forward by Christopher Lasch in 1965, and Allen Davis in 1973.

Lasch discusses Jane Addams and the founding of Hull-House within the framework of his analysis of *The New Radicalism in America (1889-1963): The Intellectual as a Social Type* (1965). Indeed, the key date in locating this phenomenon is the very year Addams and Starr moved to the house on Halsted Street. According to Lasch, the growth of a new radicalism coincides with the emergence of intellectuals as a "status group" alienated from the general life of society. This, in turn, is an aspect of a more general cultural fragmentation, characteristic of industrial and postindustrial societies.

> The decline of a sense of community, the tendency of the mass society to break down into its component parts, each having its own autonomous culture and maintaining only the most tenuous connections with the general life of the society—which as a consequence has almost ceased to exist. . . . (Introduction, p. x)

The new radicals, in rebelling against culture, conventional family standards, and values of the middle class, acquired a "radical reversal of perspective." They identified with what Jacob Riis called the "other half" of humanity, thus seeing society from the bottom up.

Within this context Addams's involvement in the settlement is seen as a resolution of certain debilitating personal tensions caused by the effect of those general cultural and domestic crises. In the first place, the social settlement was an outlet for the combined moral piety and intellectual energies which she could not satisfy by religious missionary work or by a purely secular career like medicine. According to Lasch, tension was created by the persistence of the old moral urge in face of the failure of religious theology to provide an adequate medium for intellectual speculation. Jane Addams needed an outlet for both urges. Social work was a successful resolution because "it combined good works with the analysis not only of the conditions underlying urban poverty but also of one's own relation to the poor" (p. 12). The settlement combined good works and intellectual excitement.

Equally important for Lasch's understanding of Addams is the tension caused by her resistance to and final rejection of "the life her [step] mother was trying to get her to lead" (p. 35). She came to realize that the educational and cultural advantages of the first generation of college women often acted as a barrier to understanding and responding to the "real," changing world around them. In comparing her generation to that of her grandmother's, she wondered during the first European trip if the younger women "had taken their learning too quickly" and "departed too suddenly from the active emotional life led by their grandmothers and great-grandmothers." Education for her generation had been all taking and no giving, merely "acquiring knowledge" and "receiving impressions." Thus, she remarked in *Twenty Years at Hull-House* (1910), " . . . somewhere in the process of 'being educated,' they had lost that simple and almost automatic response to the human appeal, that old healthful reaction resulting in activity from the mere presence of suffering or of helplessness . . ." (p. 64). Addams and many of her intellectual and cultivated friends, ironically like plodding and inarticulate Hugh McVey, had great difficulty "making real connection with the life about them." The smothering advantages enforced "the assumption that the sheltered, educated girl has nothing to do with the bitter poverty and the social maladjustment which is all about her" (p. 65).

But reality can break through the cultural barrier. In Addams's case that breakthrough was symbolized in her own mind by an experience at a Madrid bullfight during the second European trip in April, 1888. She was initially fascinated by the spectacle, "rendered in the most magnificent Spanish style," during which five bulls and a number of horses were killed. Seeing the scene through historic Christian imagery, where the ring became an amphitheater, the riders knights, and the matador a gladiator, she outlasted the rest of her party as an enthralled witness of the bullfight. That evening revulsion at her endurance set in, and she generalized the scene to include "the entire moral situation which it revealed." Prior to this event Addams claims she had begun to think about the plan which eventually led to the establishment of Hull-House.

> It may have been even before I went to Europe for the second time, but I generally became convinced that it would be a good thing to rent a house in a part of the city where many primitive and actual needs are found, in which young women who had been given over too exclusively to study might restore a balance of activity along traditional lines and learn of life from life itself. . . . (p. 72)

Then, with the bullfight scene freshly in mind, she realized that her "dreamer's scheme" was a mere paper reform which "had become a defense for continued idleness" and a rationale for indefinitely continued study and travel. The moral reaction to the bullfight experience revealed that she had become "the dupe of a deferred purpose," that she was caught in "the snare of preparation." But no longer: she soon revealed her plan to Ellen Starr, visited Toynbee Hall (a university settlement in East London) in June, and six months later moved to Chicago to carry out her plan.

Lasch accepts the importance which Addams attached to the bullfight. But he interprets it within the context of his discussion of the new radicalism:

> The bullfight was more than a reminder of her self-deception, her endlessly deferred plans and projects. It was the embodiment of the aesthetic principle toward which she was appalled to find herself so strongly drawn. Nothing could have made more clear to her what was wrong with a life devoted to beauty alone, the kind of life represented by her stepmother; for here was beauty intertwined with and depending upon the most outrageous cruelty—beauty boughtwith blood. . . . Henceforth not only the pursuit of beauty for its own sake but all those intellectual pursuits which had so long confused and misled her, those tangled theological speculations which she could neither resolve nor put aside, were to give way before her conviction that the only god she could worship was a god of love—a god, that is, of doing rather than of knowing. (pp. 27-29)

In his recent study *American Heroine: The Life and Legend of Jane Addams* (1973), Allen Davis rejects Lasch's interpretation. Davis dismisses the importance of the

bullfight scene and places less emphasis than Lasch on Addams's rebellion against an upper class Victorian family. Instead, he argues for a more multifaceted explanation of motivation. Davis stresses the influence of various reform movements which Addams came across in London, and the warm support of Ellen Starr. Davis asserts that in letters written at the time of the event there is no indication that the bullfight experience caused any change in Addams's plans or thinking. But she did respond to the reform spirit and new awareness of the poor which was widespread in London during the late 1880s. She found Toynbee Hall "so free from 'professional doing good,' so unaffectedly sincere and so productive of good results in its classes and libraries . . . that it seems perfectly ideal."[3] During those June weeks in London Addams visited the People's Palace, a philanthropic institute for workers. She also read the settlement-oriented novels of Walter Besant. "The mission side of London is the most interesting side it has," she wrote to her sister. From such evidence Davis concludes it was probably during these two weeks in London that she decided to move to a working class neighborhood in Chicago.

> Her decision to establish a settlement in a poor section of Chicago was essentially a religious commitment, but the kind of Christianity she witnessed at Toynbee Hall and the People's Palace was a religion of social action, a version of religion that solved her doctrinal difficulties and doubts, which demanded also a desire to serve. (p. 51)

Ellen Starr's enthusiasm and her eager willingness to aid in every way possible are seen by Davis as the needed incentive for Addams's pursuit of the project.

When one turns to Jane Addams's own reflections on the motives behind social settlements, the combination of elements emphasized by both Lasch and Davis is striking. Less than three years after moving into Hull-House, she gave a lecture entitled "The Subjective Necessity for Social Settlements," at a summer school sponsored by the Ethical Cultural Societies. Reflecting in *Twenty Years at Hull-House* on the group of settlement workers who attended that summer session, she remarked that they seemed convinced that in the settlement "they had found a clue by which the conditions in crowded cities might be understood and the agencies for social betterment developed" (p. 91). She noted further that those who were most enthusiastic about the movement in the early 1890s had continued active for some twenty years because they had found "the Settlement was too valuable as a method, as a way of approach to the social question to be abandoned . . ." (p. 91). Thus, as a method for understanding cities the settlement satisfied her intellectual needs, and as an agency for social betterment it answered her desire for action.

In her 1892 speech Addams posited three trends which she felt had led to the founding of Hull-House. She defined them as (1) an urge to socialize democracy, (2) the progressive thrust to better the conditions of mankind, and (3) a regenerated Christian humanitarian impulse to share the lives of the poor. Taken together, these felt needs constituted the subjective necessity behind the settlement movement. In light of her own experience, it follows that she found a growing desire on the part of educated young people to overcome the burden of their cultural backgrounds which had shut them "off from the common labor by which they live." Such young people, she argued, sought to socialize democracy and develop a fuller civic life by making universal the cultural advantages they enjoyed. Addams was sure that more and more people like herself had a strong desire to make contact with those who were engaged in "the starvation struggle." The settlement was a means of achieving this contact. It provided communication where alienation had existed previously, the kind of alienation which she described in the following passage:

> You may remember the forlorn feeling which occasionally seizes you when you arrive early in the morning a stranger in a great city: the stream of laboring people goes past you as you gaze through the plate-glass window of your hotel; you see hard workingmen lifting great burdens; you hear the driving and jostling of huge carts and your heart sinks with a sudden sense of futility. The door opens behind you and you turn to the man who brings you in your breakfast with a quick sense of human fellowship. . . . You turn helplessly to the waiter and feel that it would be grotesque to claim from him the sympathy you crave because civilization has placed you apart, but you resent your position with a sudden sense of snobbery. (P. 93)

In this striking passage Addams has connected her own class sense of guilt to the feeling of an entire generation of educated upper and upper middle class men and women.

The settlement, continued Addams, provides these young people an opportunity to break away from "elaborate preparation" and to satisfy their need for action and involvement in life. Now the young girl returning from college who wants to fulfill her feeling of social obligation to the "submerged tenth" need not let the family claim be so strenuously asserted. No longer need educated and informed young people suffer, as Addams herself had, from a "sense of uselessness" and inaction, for the settlement offers them something definite to do. "Our young people feel nervously the need of putting theory into action, and respond quickly to the Settlement form of activity" (p. 95). Addams felt the settlement was also related to a "renaissance of the early Christian humanitarianism" which saw Christ's ideas best expressed in the social life of the community. Thus, the settlement aims "to develop whatever of social life its neighborhood may afford, to focus and give form to that life, to bring to bear upon it the results of cultivation and training . . ." (p. 97). The function of the settlement, then, was to focus on the neighborhood as a basis for urban community, and as a basis for bridging the gap between social classes in the city.

Addams concluded her essay by asserting that the settlement sought to relieve destitution at one end of society and the sense of uselessness at the other. "The Settle-

ment, then, is an experimental effort to aid in the solution of the social industrial problems which are engendered by the modern conditions of life in a great city" (p. 98). The key figure in this effort was the settlement resident. She/he must be flexible, tolerant, hospitable, patient, committed to the idea of the solidarity of the human race, humble, and respectful of the differences of neighborhood residents. The settlement resident must be ready to arouse and interpret neighborhood opinion, to understand the needs of neighbors, and to furnish data for needed legislation. "In short [settlement] residents are pledged to devote themselves to the duties of good citizenship and to the arousing of the social energies which too largely lie dormant in every neighborhood given over to industrialization" (p. 100).

The work of Jane Addams was aimed at creating an atmosphere conducive to community in the urban environment. In the first place, she hoped the settlement would be a place where the growing disparity between classes could be checked, and where greater harmony between upper class natives and lower class immigrants could be achieved. In other words, she sought to encourage and maintain social interaction among immigrants and native Americans. Second, she envisioned the settlement house as a bridge between European peasant patterns and the urban industrial environment of America. It was a difficult task, but she sought to encourage pride in certain ethnic practices while also instilling respect for American values and institutions. Among the various groups she worked with at Hull-House, Addams tried to foster a sense of sharing both in ethnic accomplishments and in the advantages of local life in Chicago. The locale in which she sought to facilitate interaction and sharing was the city neighborhood. To a large extent, then, the social settlement efforts of Jane Addams were aimed at creating and sustaining community in the same sense that recent sociologists have defined that phenomenon.

Jacob Riis, journalist and reformer, was among those many people from nonurban backgrounds who sought to come to terms with the late nineteenth- and early twentieth-century American city. Unlike any of the other figures looked at so far in this study, Riis was an immigrant who had also to adjust to a new culture. Born in the small Danish town of Ribe (population 3,000), he migrated to this country at the age of twenty-one in 1870. After years of struggle and privation he became a nationally known newspaper reporter and writer, active campaigner for numerous reform movements, and close personal advisor to President Theodore Roosevelt.

Hamlin Garland started his literary career as a spokesman for the downtrodden middle western farmer but lived the majority of his life in cities. Jacob Riis became a publicist for the city tenement dweller, but like Garland always felt deep ambiguity toward the city. He lived in New York City until about a year before his death. Of his move to a farm in Massachusetts, Riis's biographer has remarked, "Riis's personal move to Pine Brook Farm and his continuing interest in urban reform represented in microcosm his ambivalence about the city." Indeed, one of the main themes in James Lane's biography of Jacob Riis is the interesting dynamic between Riis's rural background and inclinations on the one hand, and his involvement in city life and reform on the other.[4]

Riis experienced hard times and near-starvation upon his arrival in the United States. He knocked about the country from one job to another until he landed a position with the *New York Tribune* in 1877. But he was from a well-placed and educated, though not wealthy, family (his father was a schoolmaster). Thus, even when reduced to accepting handouts from understanding cooks and bakers he "did not consider himself of the lower class." On the contrary, he "considered himself a young man of culture rather than a common laborer."[5] His background and his experience in America thus confirmed Riis in a belief that coincided perfectly with one of his adopted land's major credos, individualism. He firmly believed that "nothing is more certain, humanly speaking, than this, that what a man wills himself to be, that he will be." While some immigrants and native radicals were socialists critical of capitalism, Riis was an avid advocate of individualism and privatism. When he wrote his autobiography, he portrayed himself as a prime example of the fulfillment of the American dream of success—an individual who by hard work and will power had risen from humble origins to the position of counselor to presidents.[6]

Riis established his reputation as a police reporter, first for the *Tribune* and then with the *Evening Sun*. He wrote articles about people in the slum areas of New York's East Side. Here he set up shop on Mulberry Street, across from police headquarters. He gathered much of his information by accompanying inspectors from the city's health department on their nightly rounds in the area of Mulberry Bend. As a result of this work, his social consciousness was raised. Using a new flash lighting technique which allowed cameras to photograph dark interiors, he started to record in graphic pictures the slum living conditions in the Bend area. In 1888 he began presenting illustrated lectures on conditions in the tenements and writing magazine articles about what he saw. Two years later, encouraged by the fascinated response of audiences to his vivid portrayal of urban misery, he turned his work into a book.

*How the Other Half Lives* (1890) is a classic of American reform journalism. It was an exposé of urban conditions largely unfamiliar to the middle class reading public. In this sense it was in the same genre as such earlier books as Charles Loring Brace's *The Dangerous Classes of New York and Twenty Years among Them* (1872) and Benjamin O. Flower's contemporaneous *Civilization's Inferno, or, Studies in the Social Cellar* (1893). Brace argued for the need of greater organization among charitable institutions devoted to the poor, supplemented by state aid, in order to prevent "an explosion from this class which might leave this city in ashes and blood" (p. 29). Flower, who found "deplorable conditions existing at our very door which are a crying reproach to the Re-

public" (p. 99), was both fascinated and shocked by what he discovered. Causes and cures, however, escaped him.

Riis's perspective was somewhat different from that of Brace or Flower. To some extent Riis was attempting to make sense of his own experiences, first as a threadbare drifter and then as a police reporter. In this important sense, he "had been there," the others hadn't. It should be emphasized that such experiences do not automatically guarantee greater understanding, but in Riis's case they did provide an alternative perspective for viewing "the other half" in the city. What Riis concluded about the other half is that they were largely a product of the conditions under which they lived, and those conditions were summed up in one word, "tenements." Thus, beyond providing vivid descriptions of slum life, the focal point of his inquiry was the impact that living in New York's 37,316 tenements had on their estimated 1,230,000 occupants in 1890. The impact was potentially explosive, and Riis concluded *How the Other Half Lives* by expressing a fear similar to that of his friend Charles Brace: "The sea of a mighty population, held in galling fetters, heaves uneasily in the tenements. . . . If it rise . . . no human power may avail to check it" (p. 226). But he was generally optimistic that the challenge could be met, and met within the boundaries of the American system of free enterprise.

Riis's suggestions for improving the condition of the tenement districts included providing more open space by replacing the worst tenements with parks and playgrounds; encouraging neighborhood clubs, settlement houses, and better schools; establishing clean municipal lodging houses; building model tenements under the aegis of limited-dividend companies; enacting and enforcing tenement house laws (including state-enforced ceilings on rents); and the remodeling of certain tenements. While Riis had progressed beyond the emphasis on the organized charity and Christian voluntarism of a Josiah Strong (in *The Challenge of the City*, 1907) to solve the problem of urban poverty, he remained committed to the principles of private enterprise as the best way of providing improved housing for the city's poor immigrants.

Riis argued that while it is easy to convince a man that he should not harbor a thief, it is more difficult to make the same man understand that he has no right to kill tenants by allowing his property to become a death trap. It is, he continued, a matter of education, and there were "men and women who have mended and built with an eye to the real welfare of their tenants as well as to their own pockets" (p. 205). He was insistent that these two, the general welfare and individual profit, were inseparable. Workingmen had a just claim to a decent home—"at a reasonable price." "The business of housing the poor, if it is to amount to anything, must be business, as it was business with our fathers to put them where they are" (p. 205). In listing the three effective ways of dealing with the tenements in New York—housing laws, remodeling older tenements, and building model tenements—Riis was sure that "private enterprise—conscience, to put it in the category of duties where it belongs—must do the lion's share under the last two heads" (p. 216).

In writing of Riis such students of urban history as Sam Bass Warner, Jr., James Lane, and Roy Lubove have noted the close connection between his reform proposals and his commitment to nature, family, the local neighborhood, and individualism.[7] Lubove maintains of Riis that "he could not literally recreate New York in the image of Ribe, but he wanted an environment compatible with stable family life, neighborhood cohesiveness, and not least, the rejuvenating contact with nature he had known as a youth."[8] According to Lane, Riis "sought to apply to his urban surroundings the values which he had acquired in a traditional rural environment" (p. 4). Thus, the values of individual effort and hard work, love of nature, and a concept of community based on family, local place, and religion were translated under urban conditions into an advocacy of improved housing, neighborhood social centers, settlement houses, and better schools, parks, and playgrounds. Riis did not advocate a radical alteration of the economic system, but rather a gradual change in the environment to be brought about by educating the public to the needs of the other half.

What the slum and tenement were doing, Riis told his largely middle class audience, was destroying individual initiative and undermining the traditional family and primary group foundations of community. Housing and neighborhoods must be improved because they make up the environment in which community either flourishes or decays. "Where home goes, go family, manhood, citizenship, patriotism."[9] Essentially the slum was a ruinous environment because it destroyed family life and the home.

The neighborhood was of equal importance with the family. Lane quotes Riis as saying his main purpose in urban reconstruction was "to arouse neighborhood interest and neighborhood pride, to link the neighbors to one spot that will hold them long enough to take root and stop them from moving" (p. 91). For Riis, then, an important element in community was the rooted continuity over time which he had known as a child in the Danish village of his birth. In a book entitled *The Old Town* (1909), written three years before his death, Riis paid tribute to the continuity and community which Ribe and villages like it always symbolized for him. In his ambivalence toward American culture, Hamlin Garland had sought stability and continuity in Europe; in his devotion to American values Riis sought social stability and control in improved housing and neighborhood conditions.

Riis's response to the city is interesting because in it we are provided an example of a certain kind of ambiguity. He sought to meet the challenge of changing urban conditions primarily on the basis of values frequently equated with nonurban areas. His passionate conviction regarding individual worth and responsibility led him to condemn the tramp (whose rootlessness undermined the stability of society). It also led him to speak out against those landlords whose greed was seen as the cause of the slum tenement. If individual landlord greed and immigrant ignorance produced dangerous tenements, then the education of the individual toward fair play and giving the other guy an even break was essential. But the hand of the law would also have to be asserted on occasion. Thus, the need for certain restrictive, minimum-standard housing legislation. More frequently, however, he looked to limited-dividend model tenements, and the "fair-play between tenant and landlord" exhibited by a handful of paternalistic managers and owners.

Both Jane Addams and Jacob Riis were moderate, middle class reformers. They were committed to the idea of the importance of the localized community as a basis for individual worth. In their emphasis upon the urban neighborhood, both assumed that a specific geographic place was essential as an arena for the social interaction and sharing of common ties which are today taken to be basic characteristics of community life. In this sense, they were the early twentieth-century antecedents of those in the 1960s and 1970s who are advocates of the "resurgent neighborhood," and participants in neighborhood improvement organizations.[10] On this issue they were thus closer to recent neighborhood organizers than to such of their own contemporaries as Theodore Dreiser and Henry Blake Fuller, who held out little or no hope for community in the city.

The significant point of difference between a Dreiser and an Addams on the issue of the possibilities of community in the urban setting was that Addams assumed that there had to be a group basis for the realization of individual significance. Groups that fulfilled that function in the city included families, ethnic clusters, and settlement houses. Such groups operated within a given locale, the neighborhood. Dreiser, on the other hand, saw the city individual as bereft of any meaningful family or group ties, alone and adrift amidst forces over which he/she had no control. The impact of the city upon the individual was, then, to impose its own kind of lonely isolation. The isolation that Addams perceived was an isolation of groups. Her efforts were aimed at using ethnic group solidarity first as a means of encouraging individual worth, and then at employing the settlement as a cultural bridge between ethnic group isolation and the larger system of the city. Her assumption and that of Riis was, in contrast to Dreiser and Fuller, that community based on locale, interaction, and sharing was as natural in the city as in the small town.

NOTES

[1] Except where indicated, biographical material on Addams is based on Allen F. Davis, *American Heroine.*

[2] Jane Addams, *Twenty Years at Hull-House,* p. 67. All page references are to the New American Library edition.

[3] Letter cited by Davis, p. 40.

[4] James Lane, *Jacob Riis and the American City* p. 216. Except where indicated, the biographical material on Riis in this chapter is based on Lane.

[5] Ibid., p. 20.

[6] Jacob Riis, *The Making of an American* (New York, 1901).

[7] Sam Bass Warner, Jr., introduction, Jacob Riis, *How the Other Half Lives* (Cambridge, Mass., 1970); Roy Lubove, *The Progressives and the Slums: Tenement House Reform in New York City, 1890-1917;* Lane.

[8] Roy Lubove, introduction, Jacob Riis, *The Making of an American,* pp. xi-xii.

[9] Cited by Lane, p. 205.

[10] For example, James V. Cunningham, *The Resurgent Neighborhood,* and Marshall Kaplan, *Urban Planning in the 1960s.*

## Louis Fried (essay date 1979)

SOURCE: "Jacob Riis and the Jews: The Ambivalent Quest for Community," in *American Studies,* Vol. 20, No. 1, Spring, 1979, pp. 5-24.

*[In the following essay, Fried examines Riis's interest in, and study of, eastern European Jews.]*

There have been few figures in American immigrant history who more tirelessly expounded upon the nature of Americanization than Jacob Riis. Against the steady growth of a disenchanting critical realism assessing the costs of estrangement in American life, Riis continually pointed out how the immigrant's past could comport well with his present. Riis' very achievements—and they surely were no mean ones—led him as well as such differing figures as Theodore Roosevelt, Lincoln Steffens, and Jane Robbins to see his life invested with a culturally significant form, one worthy of emulation.[1] As James Lane, Riis' most recent and astute biographer, has suggested, his importance can be traced to his bridging "the gap between the two Americas that he confronted as an immigrant";[2] he had hoped that a divided America, one rich and one poor, could "evolve into an organic unity."[3]

Riis' works can be read to indicate that such a hope was not delusive. His studies of the slums (*How the Other Half Lives,* 1890; *A Ten Years' War,* 1900; *The Battle with the Slum,* 1902), his portrayal of and tales about tenement youth (*The Children of the Poor,* 1892; *Out of Mulberry Street,* 1898), his exhortation about the family (*The Peril and Preservation of the Home,* 1903), his memoirs (*The Making of an American,* 1901; *The Old Town,* 1909), and his venture in campaign biography (*Theodore Roosevelt, the Citizen,* 1903) are all of a kind. As a whole, they confirm his belief that American promises of civil liberties and social freedom would erode the narrow sectarianism of the European past if they could be nurtured.

But despite this faith, his prejudice, while deeply suppressed as his prominence grew, makes the body of his social thought problematic. His use of often unsettling racial stereotypes in his writing has, at best, been dismissed as a sign that he was not unaffected by the controversial hatreds of his time.[4] But his attitudes about race, ethnicity, an immigrant group's cultural autonomy, were not merely off-the-cuff responses. Instead, they were genuine expressions of the unresolved elements that composed his thought and marked his life. In many ways they illuminate his place within a larger American response concerned with defining the acceptable norms of a culture. The American Home Missionary Society, a Congregationalist association; theologians such as Josiah Strong in *Our Country* (1885) and *The New Era* (1893); and literary realists and naturalists such as William Dean Howells and Frank Norris in their fiction all addressed themselves to what they felt were the unassimilable aspects of immigrant and urban life that challenged the nature of acculturation. The swelling of cities by hordes of non Anglo-Saxon immigrants, the inability of the Protestant clergy to make contact with the tenement masses, the clinging to European mores and, at times, attraction to socialism, anarchism and communism by the foreign born wrought changes in the day-to-day texture of American urban life. It is Riis' impassioned sketches of the foreign-born poor that call into doubt our acceptance of his program for a desirable community. A study of this aspect of his work may well provide us with a different understanding of not only the man, but also the fears and hopes of his contemporaries. In particular Riis' depiction of "downtown" or Eastern European Jewry in New York's lower East Side throws his aspirations for a democratic culture of promise into relief.

Modern social criticism has pointed out that the Jews played a central role, somewhat emblematic, in the testing of an American ethos.[5] The image of the Jew in American letters and urban discourse was protean, reflecting on the one hand social and economic frustration, produced by a maturing, industrial capitalism, expressing on the other hand the redemptive mission of Christianity. Whether seen as the predatory animal of unchecked capitalism (a phrase taken up in Riis' lifetime in the New York guide books of G. G. Foster, a mid-nineteenth-century reporter for the New York *Tribune,* as well as by Henry Adams, Frank Norris, and Ignatius Donnelly) or the creature of a debased religion, hostile to promises of salvation (dramatized by such novelists as Joseph Ingraham and Florence Kingsley),[6] the Jew evoked responses that pointed out the disparity between American promises of egalitarianism and American social realities.

Riis' thought expressed such tensions. He wished to aid the growth of what best can be called an historically relevant Christian culture, one receptive to and appreciative of, the industrial achievements and values of his time. The elements of a Social Gospel (cooperation, an individualism based upon and held in check by shared religious assumptions, a devotion to Christ through strenuous service to man) were ironically wed to the most robust features of an American secularism (rugged individualism, a bold entrepreneurial spirit, a powerful chauvinism). His espousal of such a self-devouring ideology that exalted notions of both universalism and particularism, one that was committed to two differing interpretations of human nature and rational endeavor, invariably reflected paradox and contradiction—often the actual expression of the very terms of analysis and assumption. For the notion of a Christian capitalist society could only be deployed to check the excesses—but not the very nature—of the competitive market: witness the slogan "Philanthropy and five per cent," an exhortation to make a modest, humane profit from tenement construction; such an interpretation seizes upon one out of many versions of democratic civil life and identifies it as the acceptable norm of a national culture. In fact, Riis was given to speak of Americanization as the triumph of homogenous *mores* and aspirations that subdued undesirable folkways, competing allegiances and radical politics. Acculturation, for Riis, could be measured by its success in eradicating a group's unique, informing past by sloughing off inappropriate, though often felt ties, to European loyalties which fostered, for example, the *padrone* and ward boss in New York and politics such as socialism and anarchism. Ironically, many of these were the avenues so often sought by and invariably denied to the European emigre before he made his journey into the modern world of America.

While Riis rarely devoted himself to studying the ways and neighborhoods of northern European immigrants who found New York a convenient, attractive *entrepot,* the Eastern European Jews caught his attention. From his early newspaper days, through his mature years, he took an interest in charting, at times instructing, and occasionally complaining about such immigrants in their quest for community. For Riis, the downtown Jew proved a perplexing figure. Riis saw him as rapacious and somewhat unassimilable, yet highly responsive to American promises of freedom and opportunity by the mere fact of his having emigrated to the United States; he could be stiffnecked in his own spiritual blindness, yet an indication of the spiritual decay of American Christianity; he preserved a valued familial cohesiveness, yet fractured it through sweat-shop labor; he could be an ardent patriot, but not one uncritical of American society.

Possibly, his fascination with Eastern European Jews was one way Riis had of strategically distancing himself from his own process of Americanization, for his life can be interpreted as paradoxical, in fact suggestive of an American duality, as he himself tried to mediate the heady distractions of materialism and the steady tug of Christian piety. His own past was becoming but a memory (he had written to a relative that he was losing his fluency in Danish, and that he was writing for the Danish press to regain, in part, his native tongue; years later, he would sadly admit that his recollection of Ribe, the town of his birth, had been swept away by the present). His success was hard won, and he could never rest on his income (his finances were often depleted by his children's brushes with misfortune, and in the last years of his life, he undertook grueling lecture tours—in order to have money for his farm—that surely hastened his death). His aspirations for a harmonious family life were shattered (one son was berated as a scapegrace; another made an unfortunate marriage; one daughter married a ne'er-do-well by Riis' own accounts). He could be an embarrassingly fervent chauvinist, but would remain uneasy with the rich diversity and extreme ends of American social life.[7]

He was not beset by feelings about the political thinness of the chauvinism of his day which provoked, in many instances, the strident aesthetic and political manifestoes of his times. Unlike Hutchins Hapgood, who was bedazzled by Jewish life, anarchist politics and bohemian ways, or Jane Addams, who encouraged ethnic diversity as a legitimate part of settlement work, or Vida Scudder, who was not at all reluctant to admit she carried a "red card," or Florence Kelley, who was versed in the theory and nature of alienation, Riis was discomfited with the pressures that immigrants applied to resist the practice of a homogenous American life. I suspect that his divided loyalties made such alternative ways of dealing with diversity and ethnicity personally uncomfortable and potentially disruptive to his own notion of himself: an American in the making.

Whether Riis described the foreign born with a humane sympathy or was unable to respond emphatically with their plight raises a question, often asked by his readers who are responsive to these affective, opposing elements of his writing. Possessing a Dickensian eye for quickly vivifying a milieu, a group, a character, Riis was both adulatory and condescending—tactically measuring the immigrant's potential for Americanization at the expense of an often enriching past. Describing what he felt to be the major traits of Orientals, Italians, and Jews, he was quick to limn those features that hindered the growth of a uniform culture. His revulsion for Orientals never diminished. In his early days of fame, he declaimed that the "Chinese must go."[8] Twenty years later, he pronounced, with no qualm, that "For . . . many years now we have been discussing the immigrants. . . . Only as regards the Asiatic we have made a flat verdict of exclusion."[9] The ferocious energies of Russian Jews astonished him, but he reminded his reader that "Money is their God."[10] The vibrancy of Italian life proved attractive, but he argued that this group "promptly reproduces conditions of destitution and disorder which, set in the framework of Mediterranean exuberance, are the delight of the artist but in a matter-of-fact American community become its danger and reproach."[11]

His studies, then, have a cautionary timbre. *How the Other Half Lives* warned its public of the "sea of a mighty population held in galling fetters, [heaving] uneasily in the tenements."[12] *The Battle With the Slum* (a somewhat revised version of *A Ten Years' War*) admonished its audience that the "children are our tomorrow, and as we mould them to-day so will they deal with us then."[13] *The Children of the Poor* claimed that there was good reason "for the sharp attention given at last to the life and doings of the other half, too long unconsidered. Philanthropy we call it sometimes with patronizing airs. Better call it self-defence."[14]

His lectures also conveyed a persistent sense of urgency. Delivering an address entitled **"Changing the Slums,"** he argued that "any sacrifice" in aiding the children of the poor,

> will be *cheap insurance:* We hear much of socialism in our days. There are two brands of socialism and one we shall have to *let* in. One says: *What is mine* is thine—that is service. The other says: *What is Thine is mine*—that is vengeance of which let us beware lest, sowing the storm we reap the whirlwind.[15]

Or, as he remarked in his speech **"On the Boy Scout Movement,"** if a youth "is left to the *opportunities of the street,* of the gutter, he will take them, and they do not lead to respect for property."[16] Or, as he pointed out about the poor who felt that justice in America could only be bought, *"There is but one step from that to the torch and the bomb. Property in the eyes of such a maddened man becomes a crime."*[17]

Riis was aware of his strident rhetoric and once mentioned how consciously it was crafted. Discussing the writing of *How the Other Half Lives,* he reflected, "My aim was to arouse conscience and excite sympathy. In a crowd of a hundred the one who limps excites attention & sympathy—those who go on sound legs go unnoticed. Therefore I 'limped' purposely, I was presenting wrongs to be redressed."[18] While there can be no doubt that Riis was deeply shaken by the plight of the immigrant poor, and described in eloquent terms the nature of their life, his very language expressed both his own ambivalence about the value of an ethnic group's enduring mores and the fears of a nativist audience uneasy with the rapid changes wrought in American life by massive waves of immigrants. As Henry Cabot Lodge declaimed, one only has to turn to *How the Other Half Lives* for a "vivid picture" of "the degrading effect of this constant importation of the lowest forms of labor."[19] Eradicating the slum, replacing ethnic diversity with a felicitous norm and restricting immigration were, ultimately, ways to fend off radical politics and fear of the mob. Riis' remarks can easily be placed alongside William Dean Howells' temporizing sketches and comments of lower East Side life, Henry James' uneasiness with a transnational Manhattan, and Hamlin Garland's snide distaste for polyglot New York. As Riis himself put it, in *How the Other Half Lives,*

> The one thing you shall vainly ask for in the chief city of America is a distinctly American community. There is none; certainly not among the tenements. Where have they gone to, the old inhabitants? . . . They are not here. In their place has come this queer conglomerate mass of heterogenous elements, ever

striving and working like whiskey and water in one glass, and with the like result: final union and a prevailing taint of whiskey.[20]

Yet to raise this question in these terms and not to see American history as the register of immigration and acculturation would stress the palliative notion that the American character was essentially a homogenous one formed by the uniform influence of environment, whether it be the prairie, the forests, or the city. (Such was Edward Saveth's brilliant interpretation of such nineteenth-century historians as Francis Parkman, Theodore Roosevelt, Frederick Jackson Turner, and Henry Cabot Lodge.)[21] This reading of the American persona, this invention of that persona, would lend itself to misconceptions about ethnic particularism; for this could be seen as something easily stripped away from a pure or undifferentiated self and replaced by more compelling allegiances and mores.[22]

In fact, Riis bleached the wildly contrasting colors of downtown Jewry. He often portrayed it as monochromatic, and his most well-known portrait of it in *How the Other Half Lives* reduced its spectrum to an easily graspable eidetic norm: the rapacious figure of an antique faith. Yet the downtown community was a teeming one; its inhabitants were as various as its organizations were variable. Amidst socialist, Zionist, religious, agnostic, atheistic, and linguistic circles, East Side Jewish life exhibited underlying characteristics, albeit with paradoxical qualities.[23] While Jewish life had its traditional center in the notion of an autonomous history and community, one ringed by exile and embraced by promised redemption, it was, nonetheless, a highly porous group, whose members often adjusted themselves to larger social demands and modern claims. The promise of life in the *goldene medinah,* for many, was that of a civil freedom that permittedand protected diversity; varieties of Jewish life, expressive of whatever mode of identification, would be valid within the context of modern political democracy. Who can forget Cahan's wealthy Levinsky, arguing that his authentic self was the Talmud student named David? Or Lewisohn's argument that Americanization may subdue, but not pacify, the search for an authentic, comforting Jewish life? Or for that matter, the gradual displacement in American-Jewish fiction of American opportunities by the wistful image of Zion?

I

The quest for a desirable community was of such import to Riis that he could never free himself from the remembered image of his early years and the place of his birth—Ribe, Denmark, of the 1850s. His sense of Christian stewardship, of man's moral obligation to others, of nature as a category of modern urban life, and of an abiding sense of purposeful endeavor was rooted in his village past and would be celebrated in his later years when he would stand aghast at the sordidness and chaos of New York's tenement districts. *How the Other Half Lives, The Peril and Preservation of the Home,* and *A*

*Ten Years' War* emphasized the need for the restoration of traditional agents of social control—the church, the school, the loving family. He would come to support almost any enterprise that encouraged the growth of face-to-face contact, social intimacy and concern. Whether encouraging the work of the Small Parks Committee (he served as its secretary in 1897), or supporting a pedagogical movement to restore "play" to children's lives, or fighting for schools to attach parks and playgrounds to their buildings or starting a campaign to bring flowers into the slums and gardens into the schools, he was engaged in sharing with the children of the slums the significant values of his youth.

His recollections of his childhood, poignantly expressed in *The Making of an American* and *The Old Town,* belong to a substantial body of American letters that praised the cohesive, intimate nature of village life. During Riis' American years, 1870 through 1914, the United States became a nation of cities; depictions of rural life and childhood recollections on the part of natives and immigrants alike were often redefinitions of communal virtues that seemed to be eroded by an urban milieu. The lament for the village, the longing for what Ferdinand Tönnies defined for a generation of social thinkers as *gemeinschaft* or community, runs like a leitmotif through the fiction of Booth Tarkington, the poetry of James Whitcomb Riley, the memoirs of William Dean Howells and the social philosophies of Jane Addams, Josiah Royce, and John Dewey.[24]

While a psychoanalytic reading of Riis' public memoirs might suggest how fragile and attenuated his visions of the past really were, what emerges from his recollections are childhood scenes of wide vistas, open horizons, a vast terrain for an aesthetic education. Ribe, with its apparently intimate life, gave him a scale to measure the integrity and health of American neighborhoods. It also gave him much more: he was led to emphasize—as did Friedrich Froebel, the German nineteenth-century educator, whose writings Riis seemed to have known—that an aesthetic of order was consonant with moral experience (playgrounds, he pointed out, echoing Froebel, would help slum children perceive "moral relations").[25] Moreover, Ribe's somewhat placid life suggested to him that the emphatic values of community could resist the avaricious spirit of the market. For the town, as he recalled it, stood distractedly between two epochs: one, characterized by amity, cooperation, a common heritage and face-to-face trade; the other, marked by the impersonal, calculating values of a nascent capitalism. In *The Old Town,* Riis traced the moral heritage of this transitory period:

> Varde was the next town, a little way up the coast. The symbol of that justice was an iron hand over the town gate which, tradition said, warned any who might be disposed to buy up grain and foodstuffs to their own gain, that for "cornering" the means of living, in Ribe a man had his right hand cut off. Good that the hand was never nailed on Trinity Church or on the Chicago Board of Trade, else what a one-handed lot of men we should have there and in Wall Street![26]

As he recalled, Ribe had little diversity; economic conflict, social polarization and extreme poverty were not present. As he put it, "there were no very rich people, but the poor were not poor either in the sense in which one thinks of poverty in a great city. They had always enough to eat and were comfortably housed. There were no beggars. . . . "[27] Cultural homogeneity was so powerful a feature of the town's life (its citizens were still shocked by the power of the Prussian military) that amidst praise of the indomitable folk-spirit of the Danes, Riis jestingly recounted how the spirit of community could hold in check authentic differences. He spoke of Ribe's Jews:

> Across the main street from the Quedens home one of the two Jewish families in Ribe kept shop. They were quiet good people, popular with their neighbors, who took little account of the fact that they were Jews. The Old Town was not given to religious discussions, for good cause: with this exception it was all one way. There was not a Roman Catholic in the country, I think. . . . We were all Lutherans, and that as such we had a monopoly of the way of salvation followed, of course.
>
> So perhaps it was not so strange after all that Mrs. Tacchau should fall out with her life-long friend, Mrs. Kerst, who was as stubbornly zealous in her churchmanship as she was good and generous in her life. The Jewess had always known how to steer clear of the dangerous reef, but at last they struck it fair.
>
> "Well, well, dear friend," said she, trying to desperately back away, "don't let us talk about it. Some day when we meet in heaven we shall know much better."
>
> It was too much. Her friend absolutely bristled.
>
> "What! *Our* heaven? Indeed, no! Here we can be friends, Mrs. Tacchau. But there—really, excuse *me!*
>
> It has helped me over many a stile since to remember that she really was a good woman. She was that. I have seldom known a better.[28]

Elsewhere, Riis repeated this anecdote with minor variation; yet the point remained the same—that of good fellowship and the fine triumph of the refusal to breach seeming notions of universality and convention. The spirit of public life was not to reflect private difference. Clearly, such Jewish families were likable because they would not permit their religious beliefs to affect their civic life.

The impulse for cultural unity, for common values beneath different practices, was one measure Riis found serviceable to judge a religious or ethnic group's potential for assimilation. The other was a firm, abiding affirmation of Christian endeavor in the midst of the market. In his early American days, his father had cautioned him against confusing spiritual interests with "those things that rust and moths can destroy. . . . " Jacob was admonished to resist the "restless search for money"[29] that characterized American business life. Amidst penniless times and jobs that sorely tested his character, his experience in a police lodging house (he was robbed; a pet dog was clubbed to death by a policeman) confirmed the gravity of his father's advice. "The outrage of that night became, in the providence of God, the means of putting an end to one of the foulest abuses that ever disgraced a Christian city, and a mainspring in the battle with the slum as far as my share in it is concerned."[30] Years later, he would have another and no less powerful "conversion" through which he came to see his civic life and personal endeavor as consecrated. In his **"The Methodist Spirit: A Tribute,"** he recalled that

> It was in the old Eighteenth Street Methodist Church in Brooklyn, where I was editing a newspaper in the days long gone by, that I made the beginning. I was young, hot-headed, alone in the world, when Brother Ichabod Simmons came there and preached, and brought me to my knees in no time. In deep contrition for the past, and joy in the life I had found, I would have thrown away pen and pencil and begun over again, but Brother Simmons' hand stayed me. With the zeal of the convert, I would have gone preaching; nothing else would do.
>
> "No, not that," said he, "we need consecrated pens more than we need preaching."[31]

Riis cast his life into mythic form: exile from Ribe, the material temptations of American life, confirmation of purpose, the winning of his childhood sweetheart and sanctified battle. His America, far distant from the unsettling cries found, for example, in the *Jewish Daily Forward,* was the geography of value and the life of fable; it was one's horizon for willful development of the struggling self. (In fact, it is tempting to see his hatred of the slum and visible chaos as that of a religious devotee who would wish to destroy encrusting, barbaric matter that enshackled the soul.)

His public autobiographical statements interpret the dislocation of immigrant life as a confirmation of American idealism and a promise of equality and upward mobility. Disenchantment, failure and sorrow are reduced to symbolic and unambiguous issues. Analysis of self becomes confused with formulae for success: a characteristic facelessness ensues in spite of all the recounting of personal struggle. Yet such strategies of rhetoric and myth could hardly be deployed by the characters he so vividly studied. The various forms of community that immigrants either brought with them or developed as protective defenses against the distractions of American life were tactics not demanded by the imagination but by rational judgment in its desire to accommodate tradition to American novelty. They were attempts, and on the whole rather successful ones, to participate in selected aspects of American culture while maintaining parallel institutions that bespoke of political and religious allegiances often alien to Riis.

Yet such activities were perplexing and at times abrasive responses to the spirit of fraternalism, as Riis saw them. In one of his earliest and least muted pieces, he described his impressions of Hamburg. Datelined Ribe, 1876, the article details his trip home. Passing through Hamburg, his eye rested upon the Jews. For Riis,

> Hamburg, much as we had longed for it, did not hold us long, nor interest us much. It is an old city and had never had any other importance than that which its commerce gave it. . . . On the whole everything in Hamburg appeared to us to bear a stamp of Jewish avarice that was extremely repulsive; from the brokers at the Boerse [sic], of whom the majority were unquestionably Jews, to the servant girls who with their badges of servitude, a sort of white pad on the head, paraded the streets. We were glad to leave, and when we paid our bowing and smiling Jew waiter at the hotel his "Trinkgeld," it was with the mental resolution that the city should not be honored by our presence oftener and longer than unavoidably necessary.[32]

This is as representative a display of the anti-Semitic temper as one can find, and it would be unfair to suggest that Riis never repudiated this view—which he did, many times. Yet the image of Jews as an alien, exotic, unassimilable race, as a group expressing the destructive spirit of capitalism unchecked, as a people resistant to the promises of Christian universalism was never entirely absent from his writings.

II

As Riis gradually advanced from editor of a small Brooklyn paper to a major figure as a police reporter, his journalism reflected his maturing concerns over the anguishing conditions of urban life. For him, exploring the city and coming upon deserted graveyards, traveling on police launches and watching the dead hauled out of the East River, studying the reports about child abandonment and describing the boom in foundlings, the restoration of community—in its religious and social aspects—became an imperative. Riis was captivated by the urban spectacle; in his newspaper columns, as in his later attacks upon a social science given to quantification, he could not lose sight of human misery in all its trappings.

The Eastern European Jew became part of an unusual dialectic: whereas Jewish life emphasized the loss of a commanding center in Christian society, the orthodox Jewish community's application of law to everyday life pointed out to Riis how much more the Christian community would have to commit itself to redressing the social inequities of the age. Amidst the dizzying opportunities urban life offered the immigrant for advancement and mobility, the "downtown" Jew seemed to maintain a valued, and valuable, cohesiveness. In one of his most poignant columns, one that appeared in the New York *World,* Riis described his having chanced upon a deserted spot in the middle of "swarming east-side tenements." Speaking of himself in the third person, he explained how he was confronted suddenly and rather awkwardly by an opening in the rear fence, through which he fell prone on his face while endeavoring to gain an idea of the locality. . . . It was a wide inclosure [sic] many times larger than an ordinary yard and rather like a school play-ground, devoid apparently of all traces of vegetation. . . . Inquiry developed the fact that the graveyard had belonged to Methodists who built a church two generations ago where the school now stands. . . . His interest having been strongly excited, the reporter found a number of like spots scattered through the city— old burial grounds—the names and original owners of which have been forgotten by the busy world that lives and moves around them. . . . Sometimes survivors are not willing to have the rest of their dead disturbed. Notably this is the case with Hebrews with whom it amounts to an article of faith. However sharply a Jew may trade with living men, he will not bargain about his father's dust or his grave. Hence there are many Jewish graveyards in odd places in New York.[33]

As an emigre whose ties to his mother country were strong, he had such a distinct wish for communal preservation that towards the end of his life he pointed out to a Chautauqua audience that such preservation had wide moral and philanthropic values. In his lecture, given in the summer of 1908, he reflected that it was

> not so long since I came across on the East side [sic], in the densest crowd, a Jewish Loan Ass'n, *started for the poor by the very poor,* whose unusual plan was to lend money to those in need *without pledge and without interest.* And though they were orthodox Jews, they did not ask whether those *who applied were Jews,* or Christians or pagans. It was enough *that they were in need.*
>
> So they understand the duty of man to man, of neighbor to neighbor, *all God's children.*
>
> Find me such a Xian [sic] Loan Ass'n.[34]

For Riis, numerous Talmud-Torah academies and the application of Jewish law to the problems of everyday life became vital signs of a group's capacity to weather a competitive, capitalistic climate. Whether puzzled over the sudden rise of Jewish adolescent criminality ("**The Making of Thieves in New York**"[35]) or praising experiments like the Woodbine Colony that rescued Jews from the tenements, Riis made it clear that the willingness of Jews to respond in a positive manner to the enervating opportunities of an American secularism reminded the Christian community of its own lack of similar enterprise.

On the broadest social level, the vibrant spirit of Talmudics pointed the way for a morally imperative civic rehabilitation. In an article entitled **"Playgrounds for City Schools,"** Riis remembered that

> I was told once by an ex-superintendent of school buildings in a great city that he had no end of trouble trying to make his school-board understand the relation between the number of their scholars

and the cubic air-space of the class-rooms. They paid no attention to him until one day he brought a copy of the Talmud to the chief among them, who was a Jew, and showed him that it was all down in the Mosaic law ages and ages ago. That settled it. After that he had his way. We in New York can get up a fine frenzy at short notice over the question of keeping the Bible in our public schools. By all means let it stay, and hoist the flag on the school, too, if it is worthy of it, but until our schools have been made places for which no Christian needs to blush, as he must for many that are crowded every day in this city, this zeal for the Bible is sheer mockery and humbug. It were better to put the Talmud on the principal's desk, and upon the desk of every School Commissioner as well, until they have learned its lesson.[36]

On the most subjective level, the willingness to answer and be answerable to, the spirit and letter of religion bore witness to Riis's own fervor. As he put it, speaking to an audience in 1907 at Harlan, Iowa:

> It was a little Jewish lad who taught me my duty as a Christian and a churchman. I had been sitting discontented and rebellious in my own church, because it happened that the ceremonial did not appeal to me—I am not naturally of high church tendencies, but rather a Free Methodist by disposition when a *twelve-years* [sic] *old* lad whose people were orthodox, and who was to be a Rabbi in the family scheme, made a panic in the tenement by announcing that he would not—*that he would rather be a tailor like his father.* When they got the reason out of him, he said: "I don't want to be a Rabbi when I grow up because I should never be able to find words beautiful enough to speak to God in." And I saw a great light, and ever after have sat content in my pew—a loyal Churchman.[37]

Yet these very qualities served to emphasize the uneasy relationship between the Jews' desire for *kehillah* (community) and Riis' wish for a homogenous culture. He was uneasy with a self-nurturing impulse for sectarian cultural autonomy, and his early writings temporized about the legitimate nature of Jewish life in a predominantly Christian culture. For example, the very framework of *How the Other Half Lives,* with its stress upon the tenements as bearing the mark of Cain and, by implication, upon their dwellers as part of a fragmented though formerly harmonious family, came to place the Jew within the context of an imperious recalcitrance, one deliberately opposed to the promises of universalism and a reconstituted community. Writing about a Christian missionary who aroused the Tenth Ward's ire, Riis argued that

> As at Jerusalem, the Chief Captain was happily at hand with his centurions, in the person of a sergeant and three policemen, and the preacher was rescued. So, in all matters pertaining to their [Jewish] religious life that tinges all their customs, they stand, these East Side Jews, where the new day that dawned on Calvary left them standing, stubbornly refusing to see the light.[38]

According to Riis, the East Side Jew clung to an anti-quated, outworn history, while satisfying an instinctual avarice made possible by the modern age. Stressing the sheer mystery of Jewish life, he described the noise of "Jewtown" as a "Babel of confusion." The suspender pedlar was "omnipresent and unfathomable" and a visit to a house of mourning spanned "the gap of two thousand years." Just as Judaism would remain stranded on the road to Calvary, the hard struggle for making a living would have its own secular retribution, for "An avenging Nemesis pursues this headlong hunt for wealth. . . . "[39] In lines that echo his earlier description of Hamburg's Jewish population, Riis proclaimed that "Thrift is the watchword of Jewtown, as of its people the world over."[40] (It is important to note that the imperatives for ceaseless struggle, when bleached of their Jewish context, would later evoke praise when Riis in ***Theodore Roosevelt the Citizen*** would exhort, "'In life, as in a football game, the principle to follow is: Hit the line hard; don't foul and don't shirk, but hit the line hard!'"[41] No less revealingly, he would urge his son John to practice thrift and be careful of prodigal spending.)

As Riis became a national figure, he moderated his public statements about the repugnant—as he saw them—features of Jewish life. He began to see Jewish history as a fearful response to the deteriorating philanthropic spirit of Christian obligation. In **"The Tenant"** (1899), Riis pointed out that if the slum census-taker had crossed the Bowery,

> he would have come upon the refugee Jew, the other economic marplot of whom complaint is made with just reason. . . . In fourteen years more than 400,000 Jewish immigrants have landed in New York. They had to have work and food, and they got both as they could. In the strife they developed qualities that were anything but pleasing. They herded like cattle. They had been so herded by Christian rulers, a despised and persecuted race, through the centuries. Their very coming was to escape from their last inhuman captivity in a Christian state. They lied, they were greedy, they were charged with bad faith. They brought nothing—neither money nor artisan skill—nothing but their consuming energy, to our land, and their one gift was their greatest offence. One might have pointed out that they had been trained to lie, for their safety; had been forbidden to work at trades, to own land; and been taught for a thousand years, with the scourge and the stake, that only gold would buy them freedom from torture. But what was the use? The charges were true. The Jew was—he still is—a problem of our slum.[42]

Riis' program for Americanizing the Eastern European Jew depended upon the notion of a dismissible past; the claims of the present would cut the bonds that tied the Jew to an earlier time and place. The modern world could be entered through the door of fraternal, homogenous American life. In the same essay, Riis claimed that

> if ever there was material for citizenship, the Jew is such material. Alone of all our immigrants he

comes to us without a past. He has no country to renounce, no ties to forget. Within him there burns a passionate longing for a home to call his, a country which will own him, that waits only for the spark of such another love to spring into flame which nothing can quench.[43]

Riis had met Rabbi Stephen Wise, a member of the Reform wing of Judaism, in Portland, Oregon, and in New York, and I suspect that as their friendship deepened, Riis would come to see the figures of Jewish history related to those of American nationalism. While Wise rejected the spiritually regenerative message of Ahad Ha'am and stressed the compatibility of Jewish ethics and American social democracy,[44] Riis would see the nationalism of the Old Testament as easily transplanted to American shores. Speaking of the Jewish immigrant in 1908, Riis suggested, "Let *us make Americans of them, and of their children.* Let us tell them of Washington, of Lincoln, of Grant, and set them beside the *heroes of their own lands.* . . . And to go back to the days when Jews had a nation and a history of their own, where will you find leaders *to set beside Moses, Joshua, and the Maccabees?*"[45] Riis stripped these figures of their redemptive, specifically Zionist prophecies and transformed them into figures bearing universal tidings.

As he grew older, a nostalgic agrarianism pressed its claims more strongly upon him. In his most active years, he had settled in Richmond Hills, Queens—far away from the Five Points and the Bend. In his last years, he bought a farm at Barre, Massachusetts, and proclaimed that "Just now that mission [of the Danish nation] is to teach the world in this *city-mad day* that husbandry, farming, is both patriotic and profitable, as indeed it must be since upon it rests all prosperity of man."[46] He had found a tactical solution for recovering his past within the context of a salutary enterprise. Earlier, he had been in favor of transplanting the urban poor and laboring classes to abandoned farms: an attractive way of fostering rugged individualism while hacking away at unbridled commerce. He became fascinated with experiments such as Woodbine, run under the auspices of the de Hirsch Fund, which aided immigrants, especially those from Russia and Roumania, by teaching them trades and agricultural skills. Riis believed that the Jew could regain his inherent dignity and ancient past through a solution similar to his own: he wanted to transform the downtrodden East Side Jew into a figure reminiscent of the Danish farmer.

Recalling a visit to a "struggling Jewish colony" in New Jersey, he remembered walking along a country road at sunset and seeing alongside a horse-drawn cart,

> a sunburned, bearded man, with an axe on his shoulder, talking earnestly with his boy, a strapping young fellow in overalls. The man walked as one who is tired after a hard day's work, but his back was straight and he held his head high. He greeted us with a frank nod, as one who meets an equal. . . . This was the Jew of my dream, no longer despised,

driven as a beast under impossible burdens, in the Ghetto of men's contempt, but free and his own Master. . . . The Jew redeemed to the soil, to his ancient heritage, a prince among his fellows, a man among men.[47]

No matter how charming the image, it proved unacceptable to the masses of urban Jewry who paid scant attention to the attractions proffered by socialist communes and agricultural cooperatives. Their future was committed to the opportunities of petit-capitalism, the promises of social mobility and educational advantage. They had few illusions, remembering *shtetl* life, about the joy of working the soil.

In private, Riis could be angered by the Jewish community's efforts to prevent civic life's taking on Christian color. His comments were at times petty ("The jews [sic] have long memories," he wrote—speaking of New York elections—to Jane Robbins[48]), at other times defensive and caustic. While it would be rare for him to lapse into the genteel revulsion of his Hamburg sketch, its sentiments could infect his thought. In Alameda, California, he realized he was being underpaid for a tour by his agents and complained to his second wife, "I hate anything that smacks of . . . crookedness. My sub-agents here are Jews."[49] Responding to the pressures brought to bear in order to halt Christmas celebrations in New York public schools, Riis informed Jane Robbins of his plans, by noting that

> . . . I have just written to Mr. Schiff (between you and me) asking him to call off the jews [sic] who are meddling with Xmas festivals in the schools—warning him that *that* thing is loaded. I didn't know they had any Xmas festivals in the schools but since they have, *the Jews* must not question it. If they do they will precipitate trouble they will be sorry for. The reply will come in an inquiry as to how many Jewish teachers there are in those same schools, and what may be *their* influence upon the children, *if that* is their spirit. It is not, but once that dog is loosed, we shall have trouble as they have had abroad, and of peace and good will there will be an end. I for one will not stand it for a moment when it comes to Christmas.[50]

In fact, Riis was familiar with such protests. Though he would staunchly support the right to have such practices continued, he was genuinely unable to understand the Jewish community's fear of enforced conversion and insinuated dogma. By dismissing the Jew's attachment to a past that had taught the need for wariness and skepticism over the promises of political enlightenment, Riis was able to argue sincerely that Christian observance could offend few, even if it took the form of an enlightened Social Gospel. Responding to charges made as early as 1903 that Riis House, as one complaint stated, was "conducted in a spirit not commendable to our [Jewish] people,"[51] Riis argued, "Ours is a Christian settlement. I do not mean by that a sectarian settlement, or a mission. But we wish it understood that we are Christians, and that

is why we are there, to bind up the wounds, to help the sick brother, pay his rent for him if need be."[52]

Yet he was clear about the import of such work, raising if not justifiable concern, legitimate questions about his understanding of religious diversity. He wrote, for example:

> We are Christians, but we are not there to proselyte Jewish children or break up homes. We would help build up the home, not break it. We are there to show them, Jews and Gentiles, what Christianity means in dealing with the brother, and if they like it, we shall be glad. So the world is going to be brought to Him who is the Source of all love.[53]

Riis, of course, was well within his rights. After all, the house had been initially a project of the King's Daughters. Nonetheless, the charges which suggest the uneasiness of the surrounding community did not abate, and Riis' later remarks, though not unsympathetic, indicated his concern about being misunderstood. In 1908, Riis asked his daughter Kate, living in Minneapolis, if she had

> heard anything out there of the war that has raged over our settlement here. The Catholic priest and the Jewish rabbi in the neighborhood have jumped on me with all their eight feet, all through Holy Week, declaring me a proselyter and a grafter. I will send you my reply in the *Outlook*. It is all in the day's work, and shows that we are making headway.[54]

In his essay, Riis explained the dispassionate nature of settlement work, a labor that he had seen as an important step in the assimilative process; yet his essay revealed the conflicts between universality and religious particularism that so bedeviled his thought. As he put it, "Once a year, at Christmas, if I am at home, I claim it as my privilege, which nothing can make me surrender, to talk to the people, young and old, of the peace and good will which He came to bring whose birthday we keep, and those who might not wish to come, are then warned to stay away."[55] He continued by telling his readers that once during Christmas he was in Portland, Oregon, helping a poor family. He had to leave, "so it was left to a friend there to light the Christmas tree, to hang it with toys and clothing for the children, and to make the father and mother happy. And he did. That friend was the Rabbi Stephen S. Wise, now back in New York, who comes to talk to our children when he can."[56] What could the Jewish orthodox, or even labor Zionists, make of that?

Riis' emphasis on Christian love, not only as a value shared by rational men but also as an act common to all religions, would distort the awesome intrusion of the sacred into the secular and erode the fearful solemnity of a religious engagement of being. Yet love, for Riis, was the center of gravity for the truly religious, and it invariably energized his work and counsel. He spoke of it many times, most eloquently when he charged Riis House's Board of Advisors to keep the settlement "always faithful to the seal and spirit of our Christian faith, that 'Thou shalt love thy neighbor as thyself' Be he Christian, Jew, or pagan,"[57] and most simply when he advised his son, John, that "you will realize what Jesus meant when he constantly put love of neighbor beside love of God. They are essentially the same thing. You can not love God whom you can not grasp, by Himself alone; but you can love Him through his [sic] children who bear his [sic] image in them. So, all theology becomes simple to me . . . love one another."[58] Riis was hard put, though, to accept the consequences. His fervid chauvinism would not rest easily within this creed, and late in life he would be unwilling to distinguish his political values from Christian piety. He would raise, all too easily, the politics of redemption and suggest, by intimation, the backsliding of the Jews—issues that had earlier marked *How the Other Half Lives.* In a draft entitled **"On Christianity,"** written at Barre, his final home, Riis thrust election issues into sacred history. As he declared,

> We can not compromise—"he looks like Him"—"He might be"—Those Jews didn't want to be unpopular. They knew well enough that the young man was he who was born blind, but they were willing to sneer behind a *coward's screen to avoid trouble.*

> The cowards are not all dead 1900 years ago—how many waited in the last election to make up their minds till *they knew they would win.* They were the moral cowards of our day. They are of no use to the Republic and of none in God's kingdom, for they would carry the same spirit into that fight. God has no use for cowards. Even the devil has only contempt for them. *No use for trimmers either.* You can not step into the Kingdom of heaven without the pass-word: *Jesus Christ, our Lord.*[59]

The circle had come fully closed: Mrs. Tacchau, the subject of Riis' anecdote about Jewish life in Ribe, was wrong.

### III

What, then, are we to make of this paradoxical figure Jacob Riis—an immigrant anguished at the wasted lives the tenements spawned, yet a reporter who argued for severe exclusion at European ports; a devoutly religious man, more temperamentally inclined to the charismatic than formal, yet one who would find little sympathy for the embracing religious character—mystic and hylic—of the orthodox Jew; a writer who would cling to the image of rural Denmark, yet a journalist somewhat contemptuous of a history more exotic than his own; a reporter who would devote his life to writing about and working for a democratic community, yet someone blind to its manifold varieties?

These questions neither belittle Riis's achievements nor make them less variable. They do provide, however, more than a tentative clue to the perplexities faced by Riis as he not only tried to accommodate immigrants to American life, but also strained to acclimatize himself to aspects of immigrant life. His legacy—that beyond his he-

roic battle with the slums, his work to ensure children the rights to and facilities for a decent education—is the attempt to find the conserving stable traditions of an American nationality (as in his hagiography of Roosevelt) that would splinter what he saw as the abrasive, sectarian features of immigrant characters. Yet the pathos of such an endeavor was that such features had hardened for him into myth; while he eloquently pleaded for a restoration of the human subject within the enterprise of a growing, quantifying sociology, he remained unfortunately blind to desires and hopes other than his own.

NOTES

[1] See Theodore Roosevelt, "Jacob Riis," *Outlook,* 107 (6 June 1914), 284; Lincoln Steffens, "Jacob A. Riis: Reporter, Reformer, American Citizen" *McClure's,* 21 (August 1903), 419-425; Jane E. Robbins, "A Maker of Americans," *Survey,* 32 (6 June 1914), 285-286.

[2] James B. Lane, *Jacob A. Riis and the American City* (Port Washington, New York, 1974), 222.

[3] *Ibid.,* x.

[4] I say "at best" with good reason, for this problem has received cursory treatment—or none—by Riis' major biographers: Louise Ware, in *Jacob A. Riis; Police Reporter, Reformer, Useful Citizen* (New York, 1938); James Lane, in his previously cited work, and Alexander Alland, in his study emphasizing Riis's photojournalism, *Jacob A. Riis: Photographer & Citizen* (Millerton, N.Y., 1974). The issue has received minor attention in Donald Bigelow's "Introduction" to *How the Other Half Lives* (New York, 1957); Francesco Cordasco's "Introduction" to *Jacob Riis Revisited; Poverty and the Slum in Another Era* (Garden City, 1968); Roy Lubove's now classic study, *The Progressives and the Slums* (Pittsburgh, 1968), and Louis Harap's massive *The Image of the Jew in American Literature* (Philadelphia, 1968). Sam Bass Warner, Jr.'s insightful "Editor's Introduction" to *How the Other Half Lives* (Cambridge, Mass., 1970) is, of necessity, limited to a brief discussion of the problem; nonetheless, his prolegomena is intellectually capacious.

[5] See Michael N. Dobkowski, "American Anti-Semitism: A Reinterpretation," *American Quarterly,* 39 (Summer, 1977), 166-181; Louis Harap, *The Image of the Jew in American Literature;* John Higham, *Send These to Me* (New York, 1975), *Strangers in the Land* (New York, 1963); and Richard Hofstadter, *The Age of Reform: From Bryan to F.D.R.* (New York, 1956).

[6] See G. G. Foster's *New York by Gas-Light* (1850), and *New York in Slices* (1852); Henry Adams' *Letters of Henry Adams,* ed. W. C. Ford (Boston, 1930 and 1938), 2 vols; Ignatius Donnelly's *Caesar's Column* (1890); Frank Norris' *McTeague* (1899), *Vandover and the Brute* (1914); Joseph H. Ingraham's *The Prince of the House of David* (1855), *The Pillar of Fire* (1859), and *The Throne of David* (1860); Florence M. Kingsley's *Stephen* (1896),

*Paul* (1897), and *The Cross Triumphant* (1898). Dobkowski's above-cited article is especially good at calling attention to Ingraham's and Kingsley's works, as well as to a host of other popular nineteenth-century American novelists who focused upon the Jews as a theologically unassimilable people.

[7] James Lane is especially good at bringing to light these problems in *Jacob A. Riis and the American City*. Also, see the following letters: from Niels Riis to Jacob Riis, 28 March 1873; from Jacob Riis to Emma, 10 July 1895; from Jacob Riis to Elizabeth Riis, 21 December 1904 (these are in container 1, Riis papers, Library of Congress); from Jacob Riis to Mary Riis, 1 December 1910; from Jacob Riis to John Riis, 28 July 1911; Jacob Riis to Emma, 5 March 1913 (these are in container 2, Riis papers, Library of Congress). Also, see fugitive letters in Riis papers at Newspaper Division, Forty-Second Street Library, New York, for information about his farm expenses.

[8] Anon., "Shadows of a Great City," *Jamestown Journal*, 22 July 1891, Riis papers, Library of Congress.

[9] Jacob Riis, "The Man Who Is an Immigrant," *Survey*, 27 (18 February 1911), 868-869.

[10] Jacob Riis, *How the Other Half Lives* (New York, 1957), 79.

[11] *Ibid.*, 37.

[12] *Ibid.*, 226.

[13] Jacob Riis, *The Battle With the Slum* (New York, 1902), 7.

[14] Jacob Riis, *The Children of the Poor* (New York, 1892), 1-2.

[15] Jacob A. Riis, Holograph manuscript, "Changing the Slums," 1912, Riis papers, Library of Congress.

[16] Jacob A. Riis, Holograph manuscript, "On the Boy Scout Movement," Undated lecture, Riis papers, Library of Congress.

[17] Jacob A. Riis, Holograph manuscript, "On Anarchism," approximately 1908, Riis papers, Library of Congress.

[18] Jacob A. Riis, undated letter, no addressee given, Riis papers, Cohen Library, City College of New York.

[19] Henry Cabot Lodge, "The Restriction of Immigration," *North American Review* (January 1891), 27-36.

[20] *How the Other Half Lives*, 16.

[21] Edward Saveth, *American Historians and European Immigrants, 1875-1925* (New York, 1948).

[22] See Jacob Riis, "The Jews of New York," *The American Monthly Review of Reviews,* 13 (January 1896), 58-62.

[23] See, for example, Samuel Joseph, *Jewish Immigration to the United States* (New York, 1914); Ronald Sanders, *The Downtown Jews* (New York, 1969); Jules Chametzky, *From the Ghetto* (Amherst, 1977); Irving Howe, *World of Our Fathers* (New York, 1976), Moses Rischen, *The Promised City* (Cambridge, Mass., 1962).

[24] There is a great deal of commentary about the American transition from community to society. At present, the most recent works are Paul Boyer's *Urban Masses and Moral Order in America, 1820-1920* (Cambridge, Mass., 1978), Thomas Bender's *Community and Social Change in America* (Rutgers, 1978), Park Dixon Goists's *From Main Street to State Street* (Port Washington, 1977); I'm also indebted to such works as Jean Quandt's *From the Small Town to the Great Community* (Rutgers, 1970), R. Jackson Wilson's *In Quest of Community* (New York, 1968), Anselm Strauss' *Images of the American City* (Glencoe, 1961), and, of course, Roy Wiebe's *The Search for Order, 1877-1920* (New York, 1967).

[25] Anon., "Children of the Tenements," New York *Mail and Express* (29 March 1895), Riis papers, Library of Congress.

[26] Jacob Riis, *The Old Town* (New York, 1909), 32-33.

[27] *Ibid.*, 128.

[28] *Ibid.*, 56-57.

[29] Letter from Niels Riis to Jacob Riis, 18 March 1873, Riis papers, Library of Congress.

[30] Jacob Riis, *The Making of an American* (New York, 1925), 46.

[31] Jacob Riis, *The Methodist Spirit: A Tribute* (no date given, no pagination given), Riis papers, Library of Congress.

[32] Jacob A. Riis, "Across the Ocean: Leaves from the Journal of a Traveler," *South Brooklyn News,* 4 March 1876, Riis papers, Library of Congress.

[33] Jacob A. Riis, "Are We So Soon Forgot," New York *World,* 2 October 1883, Riis papers, Library of Congress.

[34] Jacob A. Riis, ms. "Chautauqua Lecture," (Summer, 1908), n.p., Riis papers, Library of Congress.

[35] Jacob A. Riis, "The Making of Thieves in New York," *Century,* 27 (November 1894), 109-116.

[36] Jacob Riis, "Playgrounds for City Schools," *Century,* 26 (September 1894), 666.

[37] Jacob A. Riis, "Speech," Harlan, Iowa, 1907, Riis papers, Library of Congress.

[38] *How the Other Half Lives,* 82-83. Three years later, Josiah Strong, in *The New Era or the Coming Kingdom,* would echo these lines, by declaiming that "The first city was built by the first murderer, and crime and vice have festered in it ever since" (New York, 1893), 202.

[39] *How the Other Half Lives,* 79.

[40] *Ibid.,* 78.

[41] Jacob Riis, *Theodore Roosevelt, the Citizen* (New York, 1903), 21.

[42] Jacob Riis, "The Tenant," *Atlantic,* 84 (August 1899), 157.

[43] *Ibid.,* 157.

[44] Melvin Urofsky, *American Zionism from Herzl to the Holocaust* (New York, 1976), 128.

[45] "Chautauqua Lecture," (Summer, 1908).

[46] Jacob Riis, "Commencement Address, Barre, Massachusetts High School," (no date given, no page given), Riis papers, Library of Congress.

[47] Speech, "On Jews," (no date), Riis papers, Library of Congress.

[48] Jacob Riis to Jane Robbins, 27 October 1906, Riis papers, Library of Congress.

[49] Jacob Riis to Mary Riis, 11 February 1907, Riis papers, Library of Congress.

[50] Jacob Riis to Jane Robbins, 26 December 1906, Riis papers, Library of Congress.

[51] Mr. A. Lucas to Jacob A. Riis, 1903, Riis papers, Library of Congress.

[52] Jacob Riis, "Jacob A. Riis on the New York City Election," *The Churchman,* 190 (21 November 1903), 646.

[53] *Ibid.*

[54] Jacob A. Riis to Kate Riis, 24 April 1908, Riis papers, Library of Congress.

[55] Jacob Riis, "What Settlements Stand For," *Outlook,* 89 (9 May 1908), 70.

[56] *Ibid.,* 71.

[57] Jacob Riis, "Will," 7 November 1911, Riis papers, Library of Congress.

[58] Jacob Riis to John Riis, 9 October 1905, Riis papers, Library of Congress.

[59] Jacob Riis, Ms., "On Christianity," (no date), Riis papers, Library of Congress.

## Jeffrey S. Gurock (essay date 1981)

SOURCE: "Jacob A. Riis: Christian Friend or Missonary Foe? Two Jewish Views," in *American Jewish History,* Vol. 71, No. 1, September, 1981, pp. 29-47.

[*In the following essay, Gurock takes a close look at Riis's relationships with Jews.*]

I. JACOB RIIS ATTACKED AND DEFENDED

A. *The Lucas-Riis Letters*

On August 14, 1903, the *American Hebrew* excitedly reported that "a particular settlement house on the lower East Side. . . . that has attracted much attention in the past few years, mainly owing to the fact that one of its patrons is a gentleman of international repute as an advocate and friend of the poor" was not living up to its announced "high and commendable purpose." Its work, they declared, "has not been of a strictly non-sectarian character, as has always been supposed. Children have gone to their homes singing religious hymns in honor of the Christ and the Virgin" taught to them by "Christians carrying on proselytizing work under our noses." They did not identify the patron or his mission by name but did record his following "passion(ate)" response to a reporter's query:

> Yes, the house is a Christian settlement . . . We have nailed the Cross to the door and it is going to remain there. If your Jewish mothers don't know where they are sending their children, it is about time that Christian influence stepped in and took care of these children.[1]

Two weeks later, the ghetto-based *Yiddishes Tageblatt* expanded upon its uptown contemporary's exposé and identified both the missionary and his institution. Under the headline, "Mothers Beware," downtown readers were informed that the "raison d'être for the existence of the King's Daughters (the settlement's original name) is to come to Christ and bring others to Christ." Immigrants were warned that "it is a Christian Settlement and our children must be kept away." The patron in whose honor the Settlement had been renamed several years earlier was once again quoted as arrogantly suggesting: "Let the Jewish women find out the nature of the house before they send their children there."[2]

These revelations may well have shocked many within the New York Jewish community, for until then muckraker and social reformer Jacob A. Riis had been publicly counted as one of the most knowledgeable and supportive friends of these new immigrants. The *American Hebrew* had described him just two years earlier as "a close observer in whom the philanthropic impulse has been ingrained by his journalistic experience." One month later, the same journal had praised him as "one whose judgment carries weight because of the fulness [sic] of his knowledge of existing conditions as well as the difficulties surrounding the solution of the problems involved."[3] That might well explain that newspaper's initial reticence to identify the New Yorker as an opponent by name. Indeed, respect for Riis' good works was so ingrained within local Jewry that, even after the exposés, some Jewish observers found it difficult to believe that Riis himself could be active in the missionizing seemingly going on in Henry Street. The *Hebrew Standard,* a vehicle which consistently spearheaded anti-conversionist drives, suggested that the reformer be given the benefit of the doubt by the Jewish community.

> As a sign of the times, we choose to take the most optimistic view of thesituation. Having done this we may well ask, has not the impartial reviewer of the situation in which misery and degradation play so great a part permitted himself to become an agent of the soul savers whose personal Christianity resolves itself into a supreme effort to make conversions of children of Jewish parents.[4]

Riis, for his part, was quickly afforded the opportunity to refute newspaper allegations and to publicly disassociate himself from downtown conversionists. On August 26, 1903, just 12 days after the first charges appeared, Albert Lucas, secretary of the Union of Orthodox Jewish Congregations of America, wrote to Riis officially requesting that he issue a statement to the Jewish community explaining "the religious influence and work (if any) that is carried on at the Jacob Riis Home." But Riis' reply, which talked of "love for a young Jew in (whose) name the work at Henry Street began . . . and has been carried on all these many years" and which asserted that the "Gospel of Love shall be preached in that spot at least as long as we live," did little to allay Jewish suspicions. If anything, his failure to explicitly deny missionary objectives convinced Lucas, a grizzled veteran of many anti-conversionist fights, that in Riis, Jews were encountering the most pernicious type of anti-Jewish foe. Here was a widely-respected social servant—seemingly above public reproach—who secreted his soul-saving goals beneath the rhetoric of Christian love.[5]

Lucas was soon troubled further by Riis' unexpected publication of their correspondence in the New York *Evening Post* in mid-September. Now it seemed that Riis was intent on publicly obscuring his anti-Jewish stance. And when the same exchange of letters appeared sometime later both in the *American Hebrew* and in the *Churchman,* a missionary publication, Lucas was undeniably persuaded that Riis was at one and the same time seeking to confound the Jewish community while truthfully appealing to his real clients, supporters of missionary societies.[6]

These private and public exchanges convinced Lucas and other ghetto spokesmen that from then on Riis' activities

would have to be closely monitored and downtowners frequently reminded that the well-known reformer was no friend of theirs. Accordingly, when a *Hebrew Standard* reader later inquired whether "the Jacob Riis Settlement . . . is one of the places where Christianity is forced upon Jewish children," the newspaper replied: "The Jacob Riis Settlement is one of the worst offenders among the proselytizing influences on the lower East Side." And when Riis subsequently publicly supported the opening of 30 Federation of Churches Summer Vacation schools in the ghetto, the downtown journal reacted predictably: "That Jacob A. Riis gives his endorsement is only what is to be expected from him. His view of Christianity is that it should be forced into the lives of all the 'lower half' whether it wants it or not." Lucas publicly defined Riis' motives in establishing "proselytizing missions" as "in exactly the same spirit as the missionaries . . . sent abroad for converting the savage heathens." And by 1906 the Riis Settlement—one of many so-described "proselytizing missions"—had become the primary focus of Lucas-led anti-missionary activities. In March of that year, for example, the Jewish Center movement was created on the lower East Side "to provide as many suitable centers as possible where Jewish children and youths shall receive under Jewish influence—religious, physical and moral training." They planned to establish their first refuge "in the immediate vicinity of the Jacob Riis Home." It also followed that Lucas and his stalwarts would be quick to support a neighboring Catholic priest in his own attack against Riis' sectarian settlement efforts in Spring, 1908.[7] Only then they were to find that the problem of opposing Jacob Riis had become somewhat more complicated. Now when attacked, the reformer piously denied any Christianizing motives whatsoever. More significantly, there were now Jewish spokesmen—most notably Rabbi Stephen S. Wise—who were prepared to testify to Riis' non-sectarian sincerity.

*B. The Curry Incident*

On Easter Sunday, 1908, Father James B. Curry, Rector of the St. James Roman Catholic Church on the Lower East Side denounced Riis and his settlement workers for allegedly "pauperizing the children and making grafters of their parents." He blasted them for "misleading the public and exaggerating conditions . . . to obtain money little of which reaches the poor." Most significantly, he pointedly accused Riis of seeking converts among Roman Catholic as well as Jewish children. In his remarks, which received front page coverage in the *New York Times,* Curry explained that Riis' original intention had been to proselytize only among Jews. But when, "several of the rich patrons of the Settlement House went there and found a number of young Jews, they made a protest against having the money used exclusively for Jews." From then on "the settlement folks decided to draw in a few St. James boys."[8]

These new revelations certainly came as no surprise to Lucas. Riis had now been proved an enemy of all poor immigrants. Still, the Curry protest was an important outsider's reminder to downtown Jews that the missionary threat continued. Lucas' letter of support for Curry published in the *Times* predictably reiterated his long standing perception: "Mr. Riis' settlement societies are proselytizing societies to the fullest extent and . . . endeavor to attract children from Roman Catholic and Jewish congregations." This time, however, Lucas closed with a word of advice for Riis. Speaking on behalf of both downtown's Catholics and Jews, Lucas suggested that the reformer "transfer his activities to Hell's Kitchen . . . We feel we are able to take care of ourselves."[9]

Riis had no intention of moving to midtown Manhattan. His Easter repose—or "The Peace of Quiet Week" as he called it—shattered by these new allegations, Riis was in no mood to take travel or other instructions from the "perennial Mr. Lucas." Angered and hurt by this renewed impugning of his reputation, Riis now staunchly and explicitly denied that "proselytizing" or "sectarianism" played a role in Henry Street activities. And also unlike five years earlier, Riis set out to publicly remove all doubt about the sincerity of his labors.[10]

Riis opened his defense by questioning the reliability of his critics. Riis countercharged that Curry was a liar and "the greatest hardship . . . the poor of the tenements have . . . to endure." And Lucas, he declared, was motivated by crass materialistic designs. Recalling his first encounter with downtown anti-missionary forces, Riis wrote:

> We invited a body of Jewish rabbis . . . to see if they could find any trace of religious instruction there. The upshot of that was a proposition to 'sell' our house to the Jews. One does not traffic in settlement houses as in stocks and bonds.[11]

Privately, Riis was even more vitriolic and racist when he identified Curry and Lucas as sub-humans. He wrote to his daughter ten days after the new controversy broke:

> Have you heard anything . . . about the war that has raged over our settlement house? The Catholic priest and Jewish rabbi in the neighborhood have jumped as one *with all their eight feet* (emphasis mine) . . . declaring me a grafter and a proselytizer.[12]

Riis' unqualified denial and his strident counterattack were heard and accepted most warmly within Protestant "non-sectarian" social reform circles. *The Charities and the Commons,* an organ of the Charity Organization Society, declared: "We hold no brief for settlements when they are fairly criticized, but unless the newspapers have done him grievously wrong, Father Curry has borne false witness." The priest was advised to "emulate the settlement in their practical concern for . . . the young people of his parish rather than fulminate against his neighbors."[13]

Their sentiments were echoed, surprisingly, by a number of Jewish settlements house workers. David Blaustein, director of the Educational Alliance, led the rally to the defense of the Christian activist when he characterized

the new charges "as a rule not justifiable." While admitting that some individuals did enter the welfare field to make human and other capital out of it, in this instance it clearly was not the case. Lucas' five year campaign to discredit Riis within his community also had seemingly made little impact on Henry Moskowitz, a Jewish leader of the downtown Ethical Culture Society who now responded that in his 16 years of service he had never witnessed "any attempt at direct or 'insidious' proselytizing." And Charles Bernheimer, assistant headworker at the University Settlement, reported in Riis' defense that committed workers placed great importance upon the immigrant maintaining his ancestral faith. All settlements, he emphasized, "transmute . . . the morality of the fathers and mothers in Israel in (making) for the genteel, decent and honorable young man and woman."[14]

Such support did not satisfy Riis. Lucas and Curry could be discredited, but future liars and opportunists would arise unless the public understood exactly where he stood on the settlement/missionary issue. He searched for a vehicle which would "clear the air for good." *The Outlook,* a Progressive periodical, published his definitive rejoinder in May 1908.[15]

The purpose of settlement house work, Riis there admitted, was undeniably "religious," but only in the sense that it sprang "from the impulse to help the brother . . . to quicken . . . the rebirth of faith in an all-loving Father whose children we are, call Him what we will." Proselytizing, on the other hand, was totally foreign to his thought and action. Indeed, he argued, one of the House's goals was to work with and not against existing local immigrant religious institutions to better serve "the Jews and Catholics . . . who are the real settlement."

Christianity, he acknowledged, did play a role in the House's life, but only once a year, at Christmas. Then Riis claimed the privilege "which nothing could make (him) surrender, to talk . . . of the peace and good will which He came to bring whose birthday we celebrate." And to graphically underscore the non-denominational nature of this ceremony Riis pointed out that once he had invited Rabbi Stephen S. Wise to participate in the Yuletide ceremony. There he had instructed his youthful listeners that "every Jew and every Christian in our house should be as big as Rabbi Wise, to come up to his ideal." These actions, Riis believed, were in no wise offensive to downtown clients. Rather, they contributed to "bettering spiritually the condition of Jews and Roman Catholics alike."[16]

Rabbi Wise, Riis' co-celebrant in the Christmas ceremony, was one Jewish leader who heartily endorsed Riis' multi-faceted apologia. Opposed to Lucas' allegations and apparently untroubled by Riis' published anti-Semitic opinions, Wise now redoubled his efforts to convince his co-religionists that Riis was no missionary but a thoughtful and sensitive friend of the Jews. Accordingly, Wise agreed to participate in an inaugural "Maccabean Festival" which was held at the Riis House that following December. It was there that Wise report-edly declared that Riis' "unselfish desire to do good to grown persons and children regardless of creed and with-out attempt at proselytizing, had given him a new con-ception of Christianity."[17]

Several years later, Wise recounted the sincere plea which brought him to Henry Street for the 1908 Hanukah observance:

> Soon after I came to New York, Riis came to me saying "I must have your help." He put it in all earnestness and simplicity, saying: "You know I have no wish to proselytize among your people. I want them to be the best of Jews and I want you to come down to the Riis Settlement and tell them so." And then his was the plan of having me come down to the Jewish boys and girls who foregathered at the Settlement and point out to them the heroic story of the Maccabees. Riis' eyes glistened as he himself spoke to me of the Maccabees. He could not have spoken with deeper admiration if he had been thinking of his Danish forebears . . . and we had the . . . celebration . . . This was Riis' way of answering those who protested against what they conceived to be his attempt to wean children from Judaism and win them to his own faith.[18]

The debate over Riis and his House within the New York Jewish community would continue for at least one more year. In December 1909 the *Hebrew Standard* angrily reported that the Lilies of the Valley Circle of Young Judea, a Zionist organization led by such luminaries as Professor Israel Friedlaender, Henrietta Szold and Rabbi Mordecai M. Kaplan, was holding its meetings at the RiisSettlement. Were these Zionists unaware, the periodi-cal wondered out loud, that the Henry Street center was "persistent and nefarious in its proselytizing activities?" And didn't they understand that their presence in the House would be used by missionaries "to show that Jews were in favor of the work done at the Riis Settlement?"[19]

The Young Judeans responded that as an organization which exists "to counter missionary influence and to en-courage Jewish programs" they had no fear either of the impact of meeting in non-Jewish surroundings nor of in-sidious cooptation by conversionists. But that was not even the case. Riis, they asserted, encouraged their ef-forts and "never interfered in the slightest way with the strictly Jewish programming of the circle. Their patron placed but one restriction on their efforts. "The study of Hebrew was denied," they calmly reported, "as the study of all foreign languages has never been permitted in the House." For them, as for Wise, Riis was no foe of Jews or Judaism.[20]

## II. EXPLORING THE TWO JEWISH VIEWS

Albert Lucas perceived Jacob Riis as an insidious mis-sionary foe. He was supported by newspaper editorials and joined in his struggle by a seemingly unlikely ally, a neighboring Catholic priest. Stephen S. Wise, on the other hand, saw the downtown reformer as a warm Chris-tian friend. Jewish settlement workers and to a lesser extent Young Judeans echoed his words. How could a man so consistently reviled by one segment of New York Jewry retain the admiration and support of others within the same community?

Albert Lucas probably would have answered that the key was trickery. Riis, he would have said, was a missionary unchanged from 1903-1909 who through differing means of subterfuge convinced Wise and other gullible Jewish spokesmen that he was no soul saver. But to prove that a conspiracy was afoot, Lucas would have to first estab-lish that Riis was a missionary. And such evidence was not then, and is not now, easily forthcoming. Since Riis never explicitly admitted, publicly or privately, that he was proselytizing, proof of his conversionist designs can and could be only inferred from statements and activities.[21]

Consider Riis' publication of the Lucas letters in the *Churchman,* the action which clinched the Jewish leader's suspicions. The downtowner undoubtedly would have argued that the choice of this publication reflected Riis' desire to have those who ordinarily followed and supported missionary groups understand that he was one of them. And had Lucas known of Riis' contemporaneous correspondence with other settlement house leaders, he would have further suggested that the Henry Street work-ers wanted financial more than moral support. The Lucas controversy had begun at the height of the institution's fund-raising season. And Riis was concerned that *Churchman* readers "who wish to contribute to our fund" be made aware of his good work downtown. Lucas would have sadly observed that for Riis the newspaper allega-tions could have not come at a more opportune moment. He was able to adroitly coopt Jewish complaints both to publicize the Christian work at his home and to raise funds from missionary sources to continue his nefarious labors.[22]

But does an appeal to Christians who support conversionists conclusively prove that the settlement workers making the pitch are themselves missionaries? Is it not possible that the acute exigencies of fund raising convinced a clever Riis to publish a most ambiguous let-ter in a conversionist journal permitting many potential backers to believe that his settlement was a missionary center. More convincing evidence would have to be of-fered to prove that Riis was precisely what Lucas said he was.

A document from the Riis family unpublished papers which suggests that cooptation motivated the settlement's invitation to Wise to participate in the 1908 Maccabean Festival might provide just such evidence. Consider this undated letter which was obviously composed in Decem-ber 1908, written by Riis' wife to the Settlement's headworker:

> Don't be worried about the Jewish festival. Charles McDowell [a settlement trustee] thinks it is a fine idea and he is a good Christian and no one is a

better Christian, if being a lover of Christ makes a Christian . . . [23]

Was Mrs. Riis reassuring Henry Street workers that the celebration of Hanukah constituted no deviation from their longstanding promotion of Christian policies? Was the Jewish festival to be used ultimately as a way of bringing Jews to Christianity? Unfortunately, once again, bits of inferential evidence do not unquestionably substantiate the anti-missionary's understanding of Riis' motivations and tactics.

. . . . .

A change in Riis' approach to settlement house work might better explain the basis of the Jewish split over the downtown reformer. If the uncorroborated 1903 newspaper allegations were in fact correct, if Riis was then a missionary, it is possible that by 1908 and due specifically to fundraising considerations, he had been forced to back-track and could no longer impose his religious views upon his youthful charges. It might then follow that each Jewish group knew a "different" Jacob Riis. Wise et al knew, mistakenly revered, and vocally supported a man who had grudgingly abandoned his Christianizing goals. Lucas and his supporters, on the other hand, were either unaware of or were unmoved by any changes in their long-standing opponent.

This supposition would offer as evidence of Riis' change the tenor of his reaction to Jewish attacks in 1903 as compared with his response to the Curry-Lucas renewal five years later. In the former instance, the settlement patron was seemingly pleasantly surprised by the furor created and calmly planned the exploitation of this publicity. He took the initiative in publishing the Lucas letters and was apparently troubled only when the *Evening Post* buried his correspondence on the back page.[24] In 1908, Riis was publicly angered by the Curry-Lucas statements. And privately he and his associates appeared very concerned over the conceivable negative impact of the affair. Contributors were writing in, bothered that Christianizing, graft and/or pauperization could be rife in the House. Here, quite unlike his first encounter with public criticism, Riis was seemingly compelled by outside pressure to defend his work and to widely disavow proselytism both to the public and to his supporters.[25]

This pronounced shift in public demeanor and private behavior, it is suggested, reflected the settlement's changed financial/ideological profile. In 1903, Riis was a missionary reaching out to a limited—albeit substantial—parochial Christian constituency. Over the next five years, the settlement's needs required that Riis broaden its charity base. Riis realized that new contributors might include affluent Jews and others who would never support a Christian mission.[26] Placing practicalities ahead of theology, he abandoned the proselytizing once regnant in his House. Having changed his orientation and squarely facing a $500 budget deficit, he was being unfairly accused; hence his anger and concern.[27]

But to prove that Wise et al met and came to know a "new" Riis requires more than just the extant inferential evidence here available. Riis was certainly in 1908 more troubled than before. But the roots of his discontent cannot be determined. Riis' settlement records are significantly almost silent on any supposed change of tactics or approaches. There is but one reference, early in 1908, to a policy shift; a suggestion that consideration be given to the hiring of a "Jewish assistant."[28] But it cannot be determined whether that unrealized move was designed to meet Jewish and supporter needs and requests or to simply mislead Jewish opponents. Indeed, this same inferential evidence can be used to argue, with the same measure of uncertainty, that Riis was in 1908—to use Lucas' favorite term—as "disingenuous" as before. But now he was out to trick not only Jewish clients but Gentile supporters as well. He had broadened his charity base since 1903 with private assurances of non-sectarianism and consequently was obligated to publicly reassure potential critics both from within and without. Public apologias, private letters and most dramatically the cooperation of an unwitting Wise was the answer.

. . . . .

Neither trickery nor change can conclusively explain the roots of the split Jewish view of the reformer. The more convincing argument is that the two groups of Jews who witnessed the same consistent pronouncements and activities defined Riis' sincere, if poorly conceived and communicated, ideas differently. But only Wise et al correctly understood and accented Riis' ideas and intentions. For Riis never perceived himself as an active missionary with conscious designs upon Jewish souls. He was rather a committed believing Christian who felt strongly that universal Christian teachings were basic to settlement work and could contribute much towards the immigrants' Americanization and cultural upbringing.

A close reading of some of Riis' unpublished papers and less-publicized statements make evident just this commitment to Christianity within the settlement, short of proselytism. In an undated draft speech to settlement workers, written in a tone highly reminiscent of his 1908 public apologia, Riis observed: "Settlement work, Christian work . . . not sectarian not preaching but Christian. It is because you are a Christian that you are there searching for your brothers."[29]

To Riis, settlement Americanization goals could be reached only under Christian auspices. Discounting completely the "non-sectarian approach towards Americanization of the immigrants," Riis once declared at a settlement meeting that "social work . . . could not have developed except in a Christian country." But he was also quick to assert that a Christian environment did not necessitate making all clients Christians. "It is not to proselytize Hebrew children," he wrote, "but to teach Hebrew and Gentile children what Christianity means." And Christianity as expressed here meant the universal teachings of peace, good will and brotherhood as well as the essential American values of loyalty and patriotism, all exemplified by Jesus and transmitted through universalized Christian traditions.[30]

Riis sincerely believed that this devoutly Christian approach to settlement house work should not have pricked Jewish sensibilities. Were they all not engaged in the search for the best means of changing the newcomers? Dr. Wise and others had no trouble with his methods. Riis' social theology did, however, greatly disturb Lucas and his constituency who generally had little patience for Christian good works and who saw the missionary's subtle undermining of the immigrant's faith in the methods he used.[31]

This interpretation effectively clarifies the mystery of Riis' changed demeanor in response to Jewish attacks between 1903 and 1908. In the earlier instance, Riis did not feel threatened because he was simply asked to explain the nature of the religious activities at the settlement. And he thought that his references to "Gospel of Love" or to "his love for a young Jew" in no way implied that proselytism was the settlement's goal. Riis, in this view, sincerely believed his parting words to Lucas in 1903: "If there is anything in that [Christian settlement] spirit not commendable to your people, I am very sorry for you. I think you are wrong." Riis' publication of the Lucas letters may well have reflected fund-raising priorities, but not as a missionary center. That many downtown Jews misunderstood his statement was, for Riis, either a separate issue or unimportant.[32]

In 1908, the encounter with immigrant criticism was quite different. Riis was now publicly and explicitly attacked as a missionary. He was startled and angered that his message of Christian concern had been misconstrued. But more importantly, he was also accused of misusing funds designated for the poor and of breaking the spirit of dependent families. This latter attack, coming at a time when settlements were being widely criticized for their alleged insensitivity to client needs, constituted a most serious challenge both to his and his institution's basic integrity. The proselytism charge was now one of several pressing allegations which required concerted public and private defense.[33]

This interpretation helps us understand the motivation which led the several professional Jewish social workers to actively support Riis' apologia. For them, the Curry-Lucas attacks undeniably represented the expansion of an on-going crisis of confidence between them and their fellow Jewish immigrant clients. Lucas must have long been a thorn in their side too. He was a most vocal critic of the lack of Jewishness in German-run philanthropic efforts on the lower East Side.[34]

Rabbi Wise's own affinity for Riis' cause also grew out of a long-standing commitment to the settlement house movement. But it was strengthened greatly by his close personal relationship with the reformer and clinched by his belief that the mixture of universal Christian and American social values in settlement work in no way threatened to undermine the Jewishness of ghetto clients.[35] From that vantage point, Wise could participate in a Yuletide-Christmas celebration without apprehensions. The rabbi may have well seen this joyful mixture of Christian and Jewish holidays as a major statement by his Gentile colleagues that Judaism too possessed universal and American values worthy of exhortation to immigrant clients.[36]

Rabbi Wise was not alone in his belief that Christianity's universal messages as taught to downtowners posed no real barrier to Jewish continuity. Consider, for example, the reaction of two other well-known Americanized, religiously liberal Jews to downtown protests over Christmas celebrations in the public schools. While downtown leaders feared that "missionaries find the task made much easier when the minds of our children are impregnated with a sympathy for Christianity through the celebration of Christmas," uptown spokesmen like Rabbi Maurice Harris of Harlem's Temple Israel declared that he was "sorry to see a week usually associated with peace and good will made one of discord." He protested against "the well-meaning but indiscreet people who rushed into print with grievances . . . which made the judicious grieve."[37]

Similarly, at the height of the 1906 controversy over Christmas pageants in the New York schools, Rabbi Judah Magnes of Temple Emanu-El preached that "the true Hebrew, the real Hebrew resents the activity of those Hebrews who would strip Christmas of all its beauty." Turning to what Jews could derive from another's religious observance, he declared:

> Peace on earth. Good will to men; glory to God in the highest. Shall not the day come when, we, too, shall be able to sing this? Sing it as Jews, as men and women who have something to give to this world.[38]

When taken to task by downtown journalists for seemingly advocating that Jews actually celebrate the birth of the Christian messiah, Magnes denied that that was his intention. Although he would never suggest that Jews accept the "god-like life" of Jesus as the truth, he reiterated that "peace on earth, good will to men, this is a universal thought in which we as Jews could join."[39]

Albert Lucas would have nothing of his liberal Jewish colleagues' distinctions between the offensive parochial and acceptable universal teachings of Christianity. For him, Christianizing influences of any sort constituted the most pressing external threat to Jewish continuity in America. Lucas best expressed his position in response to a 1905 *New York Sun* editorial which criticized his attacks against Christian-run settlements and which saw nothing wrong in clubs "carried on in the love of Christ," if they "make a larger and truer life possible" for their Jewish clients.[40]

"The violence of my attacks upon the settlements," Lucas declared, "has grown with each new recruit to their number until today I look upon all assertions of 'unsectarianism,' 'undenominationalism' and 'altruism' with suspicion." Lucas further argued that "it is not from a genuine altruistic love of mankind, unmixed with proselytizing intentions that these Christians seek . . . the lives of our children." In all events, he concluded "no believer in . . . constitutional American institutions will ask . . . that our boys and girls shall forswear their own faith."[41]

Accordingly, although Lucas unquestionably believed that Riis was a missionary, the issue of the reformer's hidden motives was, ultimately, of secondary importance. Even if Riis and his fellows were sincerely committed only to theadvocacy of universal Christian values in Americanization work, they would have still constituted a major threat to the immigrant community. As he saw it, Christian workers inculcated a disrespect for the Jewish heritage and paved the way both for individual conversions and mass disaffection from ancestral faith. For Lucas, downtown Jews were faced with a threefold agenda: overt missionaries had to be stopped, subtle conversionists identified and undermined, and immigrant Jews convinced that Americanized Jewish institutions—like his Jewish Center—could teach universal and national virtues as well if not better than Christian settlements. Thus committed, he opposed all of Jacob Riis' efforts.[42]

CONCLUSION

Wise and his fellows may have well been correct in their understanding that Riis was no missionary foe. But were they also right in their depiction of him as a warm Christian friend? A review of his variegated reactions to his encounters with Jewish criticism suggests that they too may not have truly understood the reformer's propensities and attitudes.

Insensitivity towards the needs and fears of immigrant clients marked Riis' responses to Jewish indictments. He was either unaware or unconcerned that East European Jews, coming from a world where the Cross meant only conversion, if not deprivations and pogroms, could not differentiate between Christian methods and Christianizing goals. He made no attempt to acknowledge and dispel downtown apprehensions over the significance of crucifixes on the door, New Testament bible stores and/or Christian holiday commemorations. He certainly never entertained the thought that good Americanization work could be done in a truly non-sectarian or Jewish environment. And he never explicitly placed distance between himself and self-declared missionaries operating downtown.[43]

This uncompromising attitude was first manifest at the very beginning of the controversy when he brusquely informed reporters that the Cross on the settlement door would never be removed. It reappeared soon thereafter, when he published the Lucas letters without comment in both the general press and in Christian and Jewish journals, leaving the documents open to a variety of interpre-

tations or misconceptions. It was seen again, when he accused an advocate of Jewish social work and education of the crassest of materialistic designs. And it culminated in a published comprehensive apologia which spoke to fears of contributors, Progressives, Christian colleagues and Americanized Jews. Not a word was addressed to downtown clients or immigrant leaders. The Maccabee celebration may have been a step in the right direction. But a more sensitive patron would have met with his critics and attempted to explain away nagging misperceptions.

But that was not Riis' style. He could see no validity in immigrant protests over Christian teachings in the ghetto. If anything, he was moved more than once to anger and to expressions of anti-Semitism by Jewish activists. Consider his troubled and threatening response to Lucas' 1906 efforts to eliminate Christmas celebrations from the public schools:

> I have just written to Mr. Schiff . . . asking him to call off the Jews who are meddling with Xmas [sic] in the public schools warning them that *that* [emphasis his] was bad. I did not know they had any festivals in the schools but since they have, *the Jews* [emphasis his] must not question it. If they do, they will precipitate trouble they will be sorry for. The reply will come in an inquiry as to how many Jewish teachers there are in those same schools and what may be their influence upon the children if *that* [emphasis his] is their spirit. It is not, but once that dog is loosed, we shall have trouble as they had abroad and of peace and good will there will be an end. I for one will not stand it for a moment.[44]

Years of living among the immigrants and of reporting on the difficulties of their adjustment to America had not sensitized him to their fears of Christianity nor convinced him of the legitimacy of their conceptions of Americanization.[45]

It may be that Wise et al were personally too close to the reformer to see thesefundamental faults in his attitudes towards their fellow Jews. It is also possible that these same Americanized Jews engaged in social reform work suffered from the same myopia to immigrant sensibilities. But for us it is clear, whether his contemporary supporters acknowledged it or not, Jacob Riis though probably no missionary, was certainly no friend of those he was pledged to serve.[46]

NOTES

* Research for this article was undertaken under a grant from the Memorial Foundation for Jewish Culture.

The following abbreviations are used:

*AH American Hebrew*

AJA American Jewish Archives

*HS Hebrew Standard*

JARNSP-NYPL Jacob A. Riis Neighborhood Settlement Papers-New York Public Library

JARP-LC Jacob A. Riis Papers-Library of Congress

JARP-NYPL Jacob A. Riis Papers-New York Public Library

JHSP-AJA Jacob H. Schiff Papers-American Jewish Archives

LMP-AJA Louis Marshall Papers-American Jewish Archives, Permission of James Marshall

*YT Yiddishes Tageblatt*

[1] *AH,* August 14, 1903, pp. 407-408.

[2] *YT,* August 26, 1903, p. 8.

[3] *AH,* July 17, 1901, p. 284; August 2, 1901, p. 387.

[4] *HS,* November 9, 1903, p. 6.

[5] New York *Evening Post,* September 16, 1903, p. 16. Soon after receiving Riis' reply, a concerned Lucas wrote to Louis Marshall, another long-time opponent of missionaries, and characterized Riis' response as "about as disingenuous a communication as could have been written." Lucas argued that Jews would have to offer "bribe for bribe" to stop conversionists. Albert Lucas to Louis Marshall, September 3, 1903, LMP-AJA.

[6] *AH,* September 25, 1903, p. 614; *The Churchman,* September 26, 1903, p. 351; Albert Lucas to Louis Marshall, September 17, 103, LMP-AJA. Riis may have unclouded ever so slightly Jewish knowledge of what exactly was going on in the Settlement when he spoke with uptown Rabbis H. P. Mendes and Joseph Ascher and granted their request to be told the names of Jewish children attending his home and whether they came with their parents' consent. There was no reported discussion of the curriculum taught on Henry Street. There is also no indication either in the Jewish press or in the Riis Neighborhood House Papers whether such a visit ever took place. The Mendes papers (AJA) are totally silent on this incident. See, Minutes and Reports, Executive Committee, Jacob A. Riis Neighborhood Settlement, Executive Committee Meeting, November 13, 1903. JARNSP-NYPL. One should also note that despite the negative publicity generated by the exposés, Jewish children seem to have continued to attend the Riis Home in significant numbers. See, Minutes and Reports, Boys' Department, Jacob A. Riis Neighborhood Settlement, Report of F. W. Maaloe, Director of Boys and Men's Work, January 1904, JARNSP-NYPL.

[7] *HS,* April 20, 1906, p. 8; May 25, 1906, p. 8; *AH,* August 5, 1905, p. 266; March30, 1906, p. 578. Although Riis was now frequently seen as no friend of the Jews, when he succeeded in clearly non-sectarian work (e.g. pleading for children's playgrounds in Chicago), he was praised by the Jewish press. See, *YT,* June 3, 1905, p. 8.

[8] *New York Times,* April 13, 1980, p. 1; see also New York *Sun,* April 13, 1908, p. 4; April 15, 1908, p. 4.

[9] *New York Times,* April 14, 1908, p. 1.

[10] *New York Times,* April 15, 1908, p. 5; *The Outlook,* May 9, 1908, p. 69.

[11] New York *Sun,* April 15, 1908, p. 4; *New York Times,* April 15, 1908, p. 5.

[12] Jacob Riis to Kate, April 24, 1903, JARP-NYPL. The 1908 attack on Riis seems to have disturbed greatly many members of Riis' family. One of them could not fathom "that a man who gives himself as he does should be hated by anyone." See Marietta to Kate, April, 1908, JARP-NYPL.

[13] *The Charities and the Commons,* April 18, 1908, pp. 89-90.

[14] Blaustein quoted from New York *Sun,* April 16, 1908, in *The Charities and the Commons,* April 25, 1908, pp. 140-141; see also *AH,* May 9, 1908, p. 566.

[15] Jacob Riis to Miss Charlotte A. Waterbury, April 28, 1908, JARP-NYPL.

[16] *The Outlook,* May 9, 1908, pp. 69-71. This full-length apologia was followed one month later by a shorter open letter "To our Supporters" detailing the course of the 1908 controversy. Lucas and Curry were described as having "not the remotest idea of what we are trying to do here, though they are our near neighbors." It also noted Wise's appearance at the House a year earlier. This document was to be reproduced in the thousands of copies to be used if they were ever again attacked. See, Jacob A. Riis to Miss Waterbury, June 18, 1908, JARP-NYPL. See also "To Our Supporters," June 1908, JARP-NYPL.

[17] *New York Times,* December 21, 1908, p. 2.

[18] Stephen S. Wise to Rev. Newell Dwight Hollis, D.D., June 12, 1914, JARP-NYPL.

[19] *HS,* December 24, 1909, p. 8.

[20] *HS,* December 31, 1909, p. 8. In spite of the protests the Riis Settlement House continued to serve and was appreciated in its service by its Jewish clients. Controversy and condemnations never placed the House as out of bounds for Jewish youths. A Souvenir Journal commemorating the 28th anniversary of the Settlement lists the alumni of each of the young men's clubs housed at the Settlement. Among them are the Riis and Wingate Clubs organized in 1907—after the first exposé—and

which numbered 12 and 13 boys with Jewish-sounding names as former members. The Seminole and Spartan Clubs, established in 1913, boasted of 12 and 19 Jewish former members, respectively. See *Souvenir Journal, Jacob A. Riis House* (New York: 1920), JARP-NYPL. Indeed, one Jewish former client Elias A. Cohen was destined to be a leader in Jewish religious communal affairs. See Elias A. Cohen letter to Roger Williams Riis, undated, 1938, JARP-NYPL.

[21] There is unfortunately no recorded public reaction from Lucas to the statements made by Wise, Blaustein, et. al at the time of the Curry controversy or to the 1909 debate. The Lucas papers are not extant and the Wise papers contain no correspondence with Lucas.

[22] Riis to Mrs. Julian Heath, September 24, 1903, JARP-NYPL.

[23] Mary Riis to Miss Charlotte A. Waterbury, undated, JARP-NYPL.

[24] Jacob A. Riis to Mrs. Julian Heath, September 21, 1903, JARP-NYPL.

[25] Charlotte A. Waterbury to C. E. Halberstadt, April 20, 1908, JARP-NYPL; H. S. Braucher to Clara Field, April 22, 1908, JARP-NYPL; see also Riis' letter circulated "To Our Supporters" (June, 1908) JARP-NYPL, which reviewed the entire Curry affair with a decidedly apologetic tone.

[26] Jacob Schiff, Felix Warburg and a Mr. Seligman were all important Jewish benefactors of the Settlement in 1908. Indeed two years earlier the three had raised $2,100 to build a gymnasium designated for use by Jewish clients. See Jacob A. Riis to Jacob Schiff, November 20, 1906, JHSP-AJA. Nathan Bijur, Nathan Straus and Miriam K. Wildberg of the Columbian Council of the Council of Jewish Women were also either Jewish friends or associates of the settlement leader. Each penned a warm letter of condolence to Riis in May, 1905 at the death of Riis' first wife, Elizabeth. See Nathan Bijur to Jacob A. Riis, May 19, 1905; Nathan Straus to Jacob A. Riis, May 18, 1905; Miriam K. Wildberg to Jacob A. Riis, June 11, 1905, JARP-NYPL. Riis' relationship with Schiff needs further elucidation, for although Schiff never expressed himself on the Settlement's ideological position, not in 1903 nor in 1908, it is clear that he was a financial supporter of Riis' Home as early as 1902. See Jacob A. Riis to Mrs. Julian Heath, December 18, 1902, JARP-NYPL, which discusses a Schiff contribution to the Riis building fund. Could it be that as Schiff's influence grew in the Settlement Riis became more sensitive to Jewish concerns? Unfortunately, the few extant Schiff papers from that period note just one instance of the Jewish patron reacting to activities in the Riis House—fund raising in 1906. There was no discussion of the ideology then taught in the House. See Jacob H. Schiff to Jacob A. Riis, undated, 1906, JHSP-AJA. As previously noted, Schiff never entered the public debate over Riis' settlement activities.

[27] *The Outlook,* May 9, 1908, p. 88. This issue which contains Riis' complete public response to Curry-Lucas also includes a plea for funds to offset a $500 deficit.

[28] Mary Riis to Miss Charlotte Waterbury, undated, 1908, JARNSP-NYPL.

[29] Jacob A. Riis, "To Settlement Workers," (n.d.), JARP-NYPL. See also Riis, "Pamphlet," (n.d.), JARP-NYPL.

[30] *YT,* July 1, 1904, p. 8.; *The Outlook,* May 29, 1909, p. 8.

[31] Riis' crucial definitions of narrow sectarianism, non-sectarianism and Christian non-sectarianism in settlement work is seen clearly in a specific provision of his will. Fearful that the House not "fall into narrow sectarian ways," he appointed a 17-member board of advisors to insure that upon his death the settlement ideology remain Christian non-sectarian, to wit, "that they keep it faithful to the zeal and spirit of our Christian faith, that Thou love they neighbor as thyself be he Christian, Jew or pagan." Interestingly no Jews were included as projected advisory board members, although Schiff was a trustee of the will. See Jacob A. Riis, "Will," November 7, 1911, JARP-LC.

[32] New York *Evening Post,* September 16, 1903, p. 16.

[33] From 1902 on there were yearly criticisms of the settlements, Jewish and non-Jewish, published in the Yiddish and Anglo-Jewish press. Settlements were accused of undermining the religious faith of Jews, of alienating children from their parents, of failing to check criminality, of encouraging criminality by restricting the natural exuberance of youths and, of course, of promoting proselytizing. See, as examples of discussions of this subject, *HS,* April 11, 1902, p. 6; July 6, 1903, p. 8; October 18, 1907, p. 8; *YT,* July 15, 1903, p. 5; July 22, 1903, p. 8; *AH,* May 27, 1904, p. 507; June 3, 1904, p. 75; December 7, 1906, p. 108.

[34] For discussions of the origins and purposes of the Albert Lucas Religious Classes, the forerunner of the Jewish Center, established downtown both to counter missionaries and to promote more intensively Jewish programming for children than then offered by existing German-run settlements, see *HS,* June 26, 1903, p. 8; July 21, 1905, p. 8; May 13, 1905, p. 8; *AH,* April 14, 1905, p. 645.

[35] Rabbi Wise learned first hand of Riis' deep social commitment based on religious faith from an earlier Christmas time incident in Portland, Oregon, where he was a rabbi in 1904. Arriving in town on a lecture tour, Riis was "getting a little troubled about where to get in a little kindness to someone in need before Xmas [sic]." Riis subsequently found a woman suffering from rheumatism and with Wise's assistance raised monies from local philanthropists to cover expensive medical treatments. Riis himself donated one-third of his honorarium from

his lecture at Wise's synagogue to this good cause and joyously recorded this event in a letter to his wife back in New York. Undoubtedly impressed by this sincere act of piety, Wise agreed to help that poor woman's family celebrate their Christmas. See Jacob A. Riis to My Sweet Darling Lamb, December 18, 1904, JARP-NYPL. For the rabbi, participation in that seasonal observance certainly did not reflect a belief in a parochial Christian faith. It was rather a natural outgrowth of his support for good social work done in the name of another man's faith.

Wise's ongoing support for Christian social activism in the New York ghetto is reflected in the appearance of such well known social gospelers as Walter Rauschenbusch, Edward Everett Hale and John Haynes Holmes in the Free Synagogue pulpit. Riis himself spoke there in 1907 and 1912. Indeed, the activities of the Free Synagogue paralleled and were influenced by those of these Christian activists. One might also suggest that Wise's apparent serenity towards the issue of Christian teachings—universal or not—within the immigrant community had something to do with his own contemporaneous belief that the message of Jesus, as opposed to the teachings of Christianity, had something to teach both Jews and Christians. Wise first expressed this view in 1900 when he suggested that Jewish Sunday School instruction include Jesus as a Jewish prophet. He reiterated this idea in several sermons in Portland in 1905. And later on in his career, his sermon "A Jew's View of Jesus" caused a major stir within American Jewish ranks. Stephen S. Wise, "Is it Possible to Have a Fellowship of the Churches," *Beth Israel Pulpit,* March, 1905, pp. 31-45; Melvin I. Urofsky, "Stephen S. Wise and the 'Jesus Controversy,'" *Midstream,* June/July 1980, pp. 36-40.

[36] In the early years of his career, Wise frequently preached on Judaism's ability to teach the ideals of morality, ethics and social justice as well as Christianity. See, for example, Stephen S. Wise, "The National Church Federation," *Beth Israel Pulpit,* November, 1905, pp. 108-118. And Riis, to be sure, made a point at the Chanukah celebration of noting what Christians could learn about brotherhood, loyalty and patriotism from the Maccabees. See *The Outlook,* May 29, 1909, p. 8.

[37] *HS,* December 15, 1905, p. 5; *AH,* January 11, 1907, p. 256.

[38] *AH,* December 28, 1906, p. 201; *HS,* December 28, 1906, p. 4.

[39] *HS,* December 28, 1906, p. 8.

[40] New York *Sun,* August 2, 1905, reprinted in *HS,* August 4, 1905, p. 8.

[41] *HS,* August 4, 1905, p. 5.

[42] One of the major problems which Lucas faced—apart from the identification of who his foes actually were—was the question of fund raising to continue his struggle. Could it be that Lucas really knew that Riis was not a missionary, but used his well-known figure as a focus for his own pecuniary purposes? Unfortunately, the total absence of Lucas' papers makes the determination of this conceivable hidden agenda the most problematic of all. See on his fund raising problems, *HS,* July 8, 1904, p. 10; July 21, 1905, p. 8. For a critique of Lucas' zealousness by one contemporary downtowner see, *AH,* July 28, 1905, p. 235.

[43] In his frequent attempt to rouse downtown Jews from their complacency about Christian work downtown, Lucas often evoked the imagery of what the Cross meant to Jews in Eastern Europe. He would remark that at a time when Jews still in Russia were suffering martyrdom, New York Jews were oblivious to Christian incursions within this free country. See, for example, *HS,* December 15, 1905, p.5.

[44] Jacob A. Riis to Jane Robbins, December 26, 1906, JARP-LC.

[45] This interpretation of Riis' attitudes towards immigrant Jews tends to contradict Richard Tuerk's recent article which argues that as Riis got to know the immigrants better!he grew in sensitivity to their problems. Tuerk characterizes Riis as having been "blatantly anti-Semitic" when he wrote *How the Other Half Lives* in 1890. However, "as the American public became increasingly antagonistic towards the immigrants . . . Riis became more compassionate and even militant in his defense of immigrants in general and Jews in particular." This growth argument is based almost exclusively upon Riis' published writings and pays little attention to Riis' private papers. See Richard Tuerk, "Jacob Riis and the Jews," *New-York Historical Society Quarterly,* 63, 3 (July, 1979), 179-199. Our work follows the older historiographical view of Riis as concerned with the poverty of Jews but unaware of client ideas and social needs. See, for examples of this interpretation, Isidore S. Meyer's review of Hutchins Hapgood, *The Spirit of the Ghetto, American Jewish Historical Quarterly,* 60, 4 (June, 1970), 545; Irving Howe, *World of Our Fathers* (New York: 1976), pp. 396-397; and Lewis Fried, "Jacob Riis and the Jews . . . ," *American Studies,* 20, 1 (Spring, 1979), 5-25. This latter work delves into much of Riis' private papers and views in understanding Riis' Christian view of social work and his insensitivity to different views of how to approach immigrants. He only notes in passing Jewish response to Riis.

[46] Riis' anti-Semitic references were clearly restricted to un-Americanized, immigrant Jews and may have reflected his frustration at the slowness of their assimilation. As noted previously he had nothing but the highest regard for Jacob Schiff, Wise and other Jewish uptown notables.

---

# FURTHER READING

### Bibliography

Fried, Lewis and John Fierst. *Jacob A. Riis: A Reference*

*Guide.* Boston: G. K. Hall, 1977, 168 p.
A comprehensive listing of writings about Riis from 1899 to 1975, with extensive reference to his collected papers housed in the Library of Congress.

## Biography

Goist, Park Dixon. "Social Workers, Reformers and the City: Jane Addams and Jacob Riis." In *From Main Street to State Street: Town, City, and Community in America,* pp. 80-93. Port Washington, N.Y.: Kennikat Press, 1977.
Presents Riis's career alongside that of his contemporary and fellow social reformer Jane Addams of Chicago, with a portrayal of both similarities and differences in their activities.

Madison, Charles A. "Preface to the Dove Edition." In *How the Other Half Lives: Studies among the Tenements of New York,* by Jacob Riis, pp. v-viii. New York: Dover Publications, 1971.
The story of the means by which Riis came to write *How the Other Half Lives,* along with brief comments on the photography and other aspects of his most well-known book.

Owre, J. Riis. "An Epilogue by J. Riis Owre." In *The Making of an American,* by Jacob A. Riis, pp. 285-237. London: MacMillan, 1970.
Riis's grandson offers his own, and other family members', very personal recollections of Riis's last years.

## Criticism

Bigelow, Donald N. "Introduction." In *How the Other Half Lives: Studies among the Tenements of New York,* by Jacob A. Riis, pp. vii-xiv. New York: Sagamore Press, 1957.
A brief portrayal of Riis as a vigorous reformer, with a discussion of the strengths and weaknesses of his most famous book.

Cordasco, Francisco. "Introduction." In *Jacob Riis Revisited: Poverty and the Slum in Another Era,* edited by Francisco Cordasco, pp. xiii-xxii. New York: Anchor Books, 1968.
Places Riis's work within a historical context defined both by the tradition of reform that preceded it, and by the "War on Poverty" of the 1960s.

Stange, Maren. "Jacob Riis and Urban Visual Culture: The Lantern Slide Exhibition as Entertainment and Ideology." *Journal of Urban History* 15, No. 3 (May 1989): 274-303.
Examines Riis's photographic work in its historical and social context, and in the context of its actual presentation—not as printed pictures, but as slide shows with an accompanying lecture. Ten reproductions of his photos are included.

Twigg, Reginald. "The Performance Dimension of Surveillance: Jacob Riis' *How the Other Half Lives.*" *Text and Performance Quarterly* 12, No. 4 (October 1992): 305-328.
With reference to concepts introduced by Michel Foucault, Twigg presents Riis's photographic and journalistic work as an act of surveillance and objectification of the lower classes on behalf of the bourgeoisie.

The following sources published by Gale contain additional coverage of Riis's life and career: *Contemporary Authors,* Vol. 113, *Dictionary of Literary Biography,* 23.

# Xavier Villaurrutia

## 1903-1950

Mexican poet, dramatist, essayist, critic, and novelist.

## INTRODUCTION

Xavier Villaurrutia was among the most significant figures in Mexican literature during the first half of the twentieth century. As co-founder and editor of the journals *Ulises* and *Los Contemporáneos*, and as a leading figure of the literary groups associated with each, he was a powerful force in Mexican letters during the 1920s and 1930s. Villaurrutia's published only three collections and a fourth volume of previously uncollected poetry; nonetheless his verse, particularly that found in *Nostalgia de la muerte* (1938; *Nostalgia of Death*), is highly acclaimed. Villaurrutia's output as a playwright was larger, and of his plays *Invitación a la muerte* (1943; *Invitation to Death*) is the most notable. As is evident from the titles of both works, death was a subject of interest to Villaurrutia, and much of his poetry likewise revolves around imagery of nighttime and darkness; however, his later work shows increasing attention to themes of love and rebirth.

### Biographical Information

Villaurrutia was born in Mexico City in 1903, the son of a commissions agent and the nephew of Jésus Valenzuela, a figure of minor stature in the Modernist movement within Mexican literature. Villaurrutia attended the French High School of Mexico, and later the Escuela Preparatoria Nacional, where he met other future literary notables such as Salvador Novo, Jaime Torres Bodet, and Jorge Cuesta. Following a short stint in law school, he left his studies to write full-time. Villaurrutia's first poems appeared in 1919, and at this point his work showed the influence of French Symbolists including Francis Jammes, as well as Mexican Modernists including González Martinez and Juan Ramón Jiménez. With Bodet and Bernardo Ortiz de Montellano, he founded the journal *La Falange* in 1922. During the next years, he published his poems in several literary magazines, and after *La Falange* ceased operation in 1923, he and Novo founded another magazine, *Ulises*, in 1927. Short-lived but highly influential, *Ulises* was followed by yet another publication, *Contemporáneos*. These journals, through the circles of writers that they spawned, set the tone of the Mexican avant-garde for decades to come, though their universalism would invoke the ire of nationalists such as the left-wing painter Diego Rivera, who created a mural depicting the "Contemporáneos" (as Villaurrutia's circle was called) as traitors to their people. Villaurrutia had meanwhile published his first volume of poetry, *Reflejos* (1926; *Reflections*), and through his association with the Contemporáneos, became involved in drama.

The latter put on plays in the home of a wealthy patron, presenting works by Eugene O'Neill, Lord Edward Dunsany, Jean Cocteau, and others. This, too, was an affront to the prevailing mood in Mexican letters, which favored imitations of Spanish plays. During this period of the early 1930s, Villaurrutia began to write plays in earnest, and he further expanded his knowledge of drama when, in 1935 and 1936, he attended Yale University on a Rockefeller scholarship. Returning to his homeland, he accepted a teaching position at the Universidad Nacional Autónoma de Mexico (UNAM) and became involved in productions by the Instituto Nacional de Bellas Artes (INBA). As such he continued to present plays by foreign writers, helping to bring about a revolution in the Mexican theatre. At some point Villaurrutia, a homosexual, became involved with the painter Agustín Lazo. The two would later collaborate in the writing of *La mulata de Córdoba* (1939; *The Mulatto Woman from Cordoba*). The late 1930s and 1940s saw the production of numerous plays by Villaurrutia, including *Invitation to Death* and the critically acclaimed *Autos profanos* (1943; *Popular Allegories*). In 1943, he formed another magazine, *El Hijo Pródigo*, with Octavio Barreda, and during the 1940s wrote a string of successful plays. Villaurrutia died in 1950, and after his death a Xavier Villaurrutia Prize for literary excellence was established.

### Major Works

Villaurrutia's first significant publication was *Reflections* in 1926, a book of poems in which he first developed his signature themes of solitude, quiet, and loneliness—conveyed in part through the physical imagery of night and darkness. The book was also marked by a strong use of metaphor, perhaps a product of his past interest in the Symbolists. His next volume of poetry came twelve years later, in 1938, with *Nostalgia of Death*. In this, considered by many critics to be his finest work, Villaurrutia pursues the death theme with even greater intensity than he had in *Reflections*, and explores the idea of an inner reality that is more firmly rooted in his persona's consciousness than is the external world. With *Canto a la primavera* (1948; *Song to Spring*), his third and last major poetic work, he made a sharp departure from earlier thematic preoccupations: the principal concerns of *Spring* are sensuality and beauty. In the area of drama, Villaurrutia's *Popular Allegories* are notable for their experimental quality. Far removed from reality, these five short plays present a negatively idealized world in which human beings are mere automatons or puppets. *Invitation to Death* attempted a Mexican interpretation of *Hamlet*, with a troubled character whose existence is rooted in contemporary Mexico. Villaurrutia, who began his career as a playwright with one-act dramas intended only for a very small audience, later wrote a string of popular three-act plays in which he developed his ideas about theatre within a highly accessible format. He also wrote, early in his career, a single novel, *Dama de corazones* (1928; *Queen of Hearts*.)

# PRINCIPAL WORKS

*Reflejos* [*Reflections*] (poetry) 1926
*Dama de corazones* [*Queen of Hearts*] (novel) 1928
*Nocturnos* [*Nocturnes*] (poetry) 1933
*Parece mentira* [*It Seems Untrue*] (drama) 1934
*¿En qué piensas?* [*What Are You Thinking About?*] (drama) 1938
*Nostalgia de la muerte* [*Nostalgia of Death*] (poetry) 1938
*La mulata de Córdoba* [*The Mulatto Woman from Cordoba*] [with Agustín Lazo] (drama) 1939
*Textos y pretextos* [*Texts and Pretexts*] (essays) 1940
*Décima muerte y otros poemas no coleccionados* [*Death in Tenths and Other Uncollected Poems*] (poetry) 1941
*Autos profanos* [*Popular Allegories*] (drama) 1943
*Invitación a la muerte* [*Invitation to Death*] (drama) 1943
*La mujer legítima* [*The Legitimate Wife*] (drama) 1943
*Canto a la primavera y otros poemas* [*Song to Spring and Other Poems*] (poetry) 1948

# CRITICISM

## Ruth S. Lamb (essay date 1954)

SOURCE: "Xavier Villaurrutia and The Modern Mexican Theatre," in *Modern Language Forum,* Vol. XXXIX, No. 2, December, 1954, pp. 108-14.

[*In the following essay, Lamb offers a brief overview of Villaurrutia's career, with emphasis on his dramatic work.*]

Xavier Villaurrutia appears in Mexican letters among the young men who formed the group known as "Contemporáneos," which soon became by its own efforts a literary generation.[1] A poet above all, Xavier Villaurrutia has not failed to utilize the other disciplines of letters, and he has demonstrated his ability and his technical strength in the theatre and in critical writing.[2]

According to Villaurrutia himself the most important mission of the "Contemporáneos" group was to put Mexico in touch with the universal. "We tried to make known the contemporary manifestations of art, to open the way for a knowledge of foreign literatures . . . It can be said that the most important group of modern painters

was formed with us. On the other hand, we are the only ones who have occupied ourselves seriously with the most authentic modern theatre and with its diffusion and expression in Mexico."[3] He goes on to say, "Some time ago we made attempts to make it known in the theatrical groups of Ulysses and Orientation, and we have also been occupied with the study of theatricaltechnique in the centers where it is best understood."[4]

Without realizing the potential dramatist within him, Villaurrutia had an irresistible affection for the theatre, in which he found one of his most intimate intellectual pleasures. He is the first Mexican translator of Luigi Pirandello, André Gide, Jean Giraudoux, writers more atune to his character among the modern playwrights, whom he has followed with avid curiosity.[5] Writing in 1933, Villaurrutia considered Elmer L. Rice and Eugene O'Neill the best North American dramatists.

> They are not the only ones, but they are already dedicated (to the theatre). Their plays are given in Europe and they are included with the best among the moderns. They are masters of a style because they have obtained, each in his own way, the exact and imperceptible accommodation of his own inner vision to the scenes, pictures and acts, in which lucidly and consciously, their poetical intentions, their intuition, and their ideas are objectified.[6]

Speaking of the theatre in Mexico, Villaurrutia says, "No literary form should be accepted in Mexico with greater attention than the drama. The theatre is not our strong point, and never has been." But he continues,

> To write plays in a country such as ours, whose theatre and whose public only occasionally support works of good quality—is like constructing a building for the public, in one's bedroom. A classic spirit cannot accept this. If he has no public, he must work to form it. And what else were the experimental theatres of Ulysses and Orientation, but efforts to create a public, a new curiosity?[7]

According to Villaurrutia the bad habits and outmoded customs of the Spanish theatrical tradition of the nineteenth century weigh upon the companies who habitually perform in the Mexican theatres. "Old age seems to be its necessary atmosphere, improvisation, its only method, lack of culture, its content. Old age, improvisation, and lack of culture work together to enclose the theatre in a dark and stuffy corner, in order to free it from the temptation that might return it to the health it has lost."[8]

Villaurrutia decries the lack of adequate theatre buildings and the lack of competent actors. "Too big or too uncomfortable, the legitimate theatres do not fit any of the needs of the show nor of the modern public."[9] As for the actors, "Where are the actors, masters of a new or classical criterion toward their art that permits them to give more than superficial versions of the personage which they are playing?"[10] He goes on to say that if it has any, the remedy for the theatre in Mexico is in creating a new atmosphere for it, in making it breathe a pure air, "untying it from a false tradition, renewing its human material, its useful materials, and creating young, living friendships to form its new public."[11]

Xavier Villaurrutia believes it would be wrong to take into account the state of the theatre in Mexico, and not extend it a hand that would perhaps help save it. He cites as an example the Ulysses experiment:

> Take for instance that theatre of Ulysses, formed exclusively by artists or apprentices in which we were everything, actors, translators, directors, scenographers. The modern critics of the Mexican theatre speak of this as an exotic attempt. Discounting the irony which they wish to give to their definition they are right. The Ulysses experiment was exotic, because its triumphs came from outside: new works, a new sense of interpretation, and attempts at new staging, could not come from where they did not exist. A curious fear this, of foreign influence. Fear of losing a personality it did not have.[12]

When Villaurrutia and José Gorostiza were in the Department of Fine Arts of the Ministry of Education they organized an informal experiment called the "Theatre of Orientation." Based on the same ideas of universality and modernity as the Ulysses group, the plans were outlined, the repertoire decided upon and activities begun in 1932. Celestino Gorostiza undertook the directing of the players. "With great care he trained new actors, introduced new techniques. He directed ten plays in one year, always obtaining correct versions, and at times, definite successes.[13]

The repertoire of the "Theatre of Orientation" in 1932, chosen from the best classical and modern works, ranged from the *Antigone* of Sophocles, modernized by Jean Cocteau, to the recent play, *Intimacy,* of Jean Victor Pellerin. A short play of Cervantes, *The Jealous Old Man,* and a comedy of Shakespeare were among the classical works; Chekhov, Romains, O'Neill, Shaw, Synge, among the modern writers. Except for the work of Shakespeare, adapted by Jacinto Benavente, the rest were translated especially for these presentations by Xavier Villaurrutia and Augustín Lazo. The impetus acquired by the "Theatre of Orientation" in the same year, made it possible to present certain other works: *Marriage* by Gogol, *Macbeth* by Shakespeare, in an excellent simplification and adaptation for little theatre by Agustín Lazo, and a comedy by Jules Romains, *Amadeus or Knights in a Row.* Of the work of this group, Villaurrutia says, "If the Theatre of Orientation has not given the truth, if it is not theatre, it is a good conception of the theatre."[14]

As a young man, Xavier Villaurrutia was an actor in the Fábregas theatre, and in the Orpheus theatre at the time of the Ulysses theatrical experiment. Later he limited his theatrical activities to directing, teaching dramatics, and writing plays. He was cautious in the initiation of his career as a dramatist. Even though he had attained fame young as a poet, he started his dramatic writing with a series of one-act dramatic pieces, only after he was well grounded in the continental theatre. In these sketches he turned briefly to the impressionistic and expressionistic models he found there. They were studies in the art of learning the technique of the theatre, which Villaurrutia later came to dominate.

When he edited these in one volume, he called them *Popular Allegories.*[15] The influence of Oscar Wilde and Luigi Pirandello is perceptible in these first plays of Villaurrutia: **"It Seems a Lie," "The Moment Has Come," "What Are You Thinking About?" "Be Brief," "The Absent One."**[16] They are witty, dramatic riddles, with no sentimental material in them, full of play on words and clever conversations. The spectator is obliged to do mental gymnastics to follow them and to appreciate them.

After these small works were presented, Villaurrutia felt himself ready to write longer, more complete plays, such as ***The Ivy, The Legitimate Wife, Invitation to Death, The Great Mistake, Poor Blue Beard, Dangerous Game.***[17] Enrique Díez Canedo says:

> The days are past in which Villaurrutia, preoccupied with the desire 'to be modern,' gave his farces a juvenile subtleness, difficult to be captured by the public in general. Now without being less modern, rather on the contrary, presenting modern works, he succeeds in interesting and moving the public of Mexico, taking advantage of elements which are capable of winning the entire public, not only today's, but tomorrow's.[18]

In these later plays, Xavier Villaurrutia has preferred to give up many of his experimental ideas, substituting for them works of psychological analysis and moral conflict.[19] Love and death, the great themes of his poetry, born from the testimony of his own feelings, appear in his plays, and here too, they become anguished and tragic when pierced by his intelligence.

Against the generally held doctrines of the perfectibility of the human race and of the unceasing march of progress, Xavier Villaurrutia finds himself in dissent. He believes neither in the fetish of progress nor in the power of men in groups to raise themselves above the level of the individuals who make up the group. Villaurrutia is at heart a pessimist. Inexorability, changelessness, are the laws of life as he sees it, for example, in **Invitation to Death.** Behind man is the calm will of nature.

It is this fatalistic point of view that gives a humorous and pathetic cast to Villaurrutia's profound interest in personality in all its guises and variations. **Poor Blue Beard** presents the problem of the man who feigned love for several women to regain the love of his wife, and was successful in doing so. **The Legitimate Wife** brings us the psychological conflict involved when the second wife is introduced into the home where grown children are already present. Both plays reveal the incommensurable power generated by those who are held to be the weakest among us.

The dramatic efforts of Xavier Villaurrutia extended to the cinema, where in addition to his talents as a critic, he exercised his gifts as a dialogist and dramatic writer. One of his original movies was the **"Mulatto Woman of Cordoba"**; and under the same title he wrote the libretto for an opera in one act, in collaboration with Agustín Lazo. The opera, with music by Pablo Moncayo, was presented in the Palace of Fine Arts in 1948.[20] The picture, directed by Adolfo Fernández Bustamante had been filmed previously.

Especially for Virginia Fábregas, Villaurrutia wrote the dialogue for **"The House of the Fox,"** and included scenes from other works which the actress had performed with success in her career. The director, Juan J. Ortega, directed a film version of *The Legitimate Wife,* with Anita Blanch, and María Antioneta Pons in the leading roles.[21] Villaurrutia collaborated closely with Julio Bracho in some of his best pictures; to Villaurrutia is due the difficult film version of Luís Fernández Ardavín's work in verse, "The White Monk." He also supervised the adaptation and dialogue of "Another Dawn," and other pictures by this same director.

At the time of his death[22] Villaurrutia was working on a drama concerning the short-lived empire of Iturbide, he had just finished a new picture for Julio Bracho, and he was preparing for a trip to Italy. In reality, Villaurrutia had traveled very little; he had made only one trip to the United States in 1939 to study dramatics in New Haven, under a grant from the Rockefeller Foundation. In the Institute of Fine Arts, he held the chair of dramatic arts; he helped start such actors as Beatriz Aguirre, Orazio Fontanot, and Raúl Dantés.

Just when Xavier Villaurrutia had attained control of his medium, when he had in hand the instrument that was to permit him to write his own masterpiece, he died. We can say that he realized himself fully as a poet, but not as a dramatist. His plays were but steps, studies, preparatory works for something which death did not permit him to complete.

Only those who knew him in his works and dealt with him personally, only those who have enjoyed his brilliant conversation, witty, ingenuous, and wise, and have followed the studious and solid career of this true man of literature, can realize, at this time, what the death of Xavier Villaurrutia means to Mexican letters, where he is recognized as one of the outstanding values.[23]

NOTES

[1] "Contemporáneos" included such writers as Carlos Pellicer, Jaime Torres Bodet, Bernardo Ortiz de Montellano, Enrique González Rojo, Octavio G. Barreda, José Gorostiza, Xavier Villaurrutia, Salvador Novo. Their aims were purely literary; they were influenced by the modern French writers, and to some extent, by the later English and North American authors. Their magazine was also known as *Contemporáneos,* and was published in Mexico from 1928 to 1931. José Luis Martínez in his *Literatura mexicana siglo XX, primera parte*

(Robredo, Mexico, 1949), p. 30, says of these men: "Les caracteriza su preocupacion exclusivamente literaria y los límites que imponen a su formación cultural. En ella privan las letras francesas más modernas, con predilección las del grupo de la *Nouvelle Revue Française* y, en menor grado, la poesía española posterior a Juan Ramón Jiménez y la estética de los nuevos prosistas y pensadores de la *Revista de Occidente*. Junto a estos elementos de la formación de los "contemporáneos" debe añadirse, aunque no sea común a todos, la frecuentación de los nuevos autores ingleses, norteamericanos, italianos y, ocasionalmente, hispanoamericanos."

[2] Villaurrutia's poetry: *Reflejos,* Ed. Cultura, Mexico, 1926; *Dos nocturnos,*Supplement of Barandal, Mexico, 1931; *Nocturnos,* Ed. Fábula, Mexico, 1933; *Nocturno de los ángeles,* Ed. Hipocampo, Mexico, 1936; *Nocturno mar,* Ed. Hipocampo, Mexico, 1937; *Nostalgia de la muerte,* Ed. Sur, Buenos Aires, 1938; *Décima muerte y otros poemas no coleccionados* Ed. Nueva Voz, Mexico, 1941; *Nostalgia de la muerte,* Ed. Mictlán, Mexico, 1946 (enlarged edition); *Canto a la primavera y otros poemas,* Ed. Nueva Floresta, Mexico, 1948. His theatre: *Parece mentira,* Imprenta Mundial, Mexico, 1934; *¿En qué piensas?* Ed. Letras de Mexico, Mexico, 1938; *Sea Vd. breve,* Ed. Cuadernos de Mexico Nuevo, Mexico, 1938; *La hiedra,* Ed. Nueva Cultura, Mexico, 1941; *La mujer legítima,* Ed. Rafael Loera y Chávez, Mexico, 1943; *Autos profanos,* Ed. Letras de Mexico, Mexico, 1943; *Invitación a la muerte,* Ed. Letras de Mexico, Mexico, 1944; *El yerro candente,* Ed. Letras de Mexico, Mexico, 1945; *El pobre Barba Azul,* Ed. Teatro Mexicano Contemporáneo, Mexico, 1948; *La mulate de Córdoba,* opera in one act, Mexico, 1948 (in collaboration with Augustín Lazo); *Juego peligroso,* Mexico, 1950; *La tragedia de las equivocaciones,* a monologue, Mexico, 1950. His essays and criticism: *La poesía de los jóvenes en Mexico,* Ed. Revista Antena, Mexico, 1924; *Textos y pretextos,* Ed. La Case de España en México, Mexico, 1940; critical prologues, and articles in *El Hijo Pródigo,* Letras de México, *Romance, Contemporáneos, Ulises, Tierra Nueva, Hoy.*

[3] José Luis Martínez, "Entrevista con Xavier Villaurrutia," *Novedades,* January 14, 1951, p. 1.

[4] Martínez, *op. cit.,* p. 1.

[5] *Cf.* Celestino Gorostiza, "El teatro de Xavier Villaurrutia," *Letras de México,* April 1, 1938, #26, pp. 1-2.

[6] *Textos y pretextos,* p. 171.

[7] *Textos y pretextos,* p. 179.

[8] *Ibid.,* p. 184.

[9] *Ibid.,* p. 184.

[10] *Textos y pretextos,* p. 184.

[11] *Ibid.,* p. 187.

[12] *Ibid.,* p. 187.

[13] *Textos y pretextos,* p. 188.

[14] *Ibid.,* p. 190.

[15] *Autos profanos.*

[16]"Parece mentira," "Ha Ilegado el momento," "En qué piensas?" "Sea usted breve," "El ausente." *Cf.,* also Rafael Solana, "Villaurrutia: comediógrafo," *Hoy,* January 27, 1951, p. 38.

[17]*La hiedra, La mujer legítima, Invitación a la muerte, El yerro candente, El pobre Barba Azul, Juego peligroso.*

[18]Introduction to *La mujer legitima,* pp. 9-10.

[19]José Luís Martínez feels that Villaurrutia betrays the cause of the experimental theatre in these later plays. *Cf.* his *Literatura mexicana siglo XX,* p. 135.

[20]*Cf.,* Rafael Solana, *op. cit.,* p. 38.

[21]*Ibid.*

[22]Xavier Villarrutia was born in the city of Mexico, December 3, 1903; he died there suddenly, the 25th of December, 1950.

[23]His friends and contemporary writers dedicated to him the January 14, 1951 issue of *Novedades* and entitled it "Homenaje a Xavier Villaurrutia."

## Frank Dauster (essay date 1955)

SOURCE: "A Commentary on Villaurrutia's 'Décima Muerte'," in *Kentucky Foreign Language Quarterly,* Vol. II, No. 4, 1955, pp. 160-5.

[*In the following essay, Dauster closely examines the ten verses that make up* "Décima muerte."]

Although the poetic production of Xavier Villaurrutia is comparatively restricted, consisting of three brief volumes—*Reflejos* (1926), *Nostalgia de la Muerte* (second and definitive edition, 1946), and *Canto a la Primavera y Otros Poemas* (1948)—it represents one of the major achievements of contemporary Latin American poetry. His phantasmagoric world of specters and dream-fantasy, expressed in a taut, opaque style classical in its economy and concision, is a remarkable esthetic achievement.

His work illustrates a major tendency in modern poetry: the preoccupation with the problem of death. **"Décima Muerte,"** his finest single poem, investigates this problem in its relation to his personal situation: a personality which was unable to burst through the confines of solip-

sism, and the knowledge that he suffered from a cardiac condition which could end his life at any moment.

**"Décima Muerte"** is rooted in the Renaissance tradition of the Petrarchan love poem. On this framework of the poet and his beloved, Villaurrutia constructed a double symbolism: his own imminent end, and his concept of a personalized death. These two levels are implicit throughout, so that each of the ten *décimas* of which the poem is composed represents a double intellectual-emotional complex of attitudes. It is the poet's reaction to his own impending death, and at the same time an allegory of death as the Beloved.

The first *décima* presents the poet in the guise of lover, as he meditates on the arrival of his beloved:

> ¡ Qué prueba de la existencia
> habrá mayor que la suerte
> de estar viviendo sin verte
> y muriendo en tu presencia!
> Esta lúcida conciencia
> de amar a lo munca visto
> y de esperar lo imprevisto;
> este caer sin llegar
> es la angustia de pensar
> que puesto que muero existo.

This is no ordinary beloved, this never-seen mistress. She is the personification of death. No longer an intellectual concept or a mere physical fact, Death has here become an individual.

At the same time Villaurrutia is parodying Descartes' *Cogito; ergo sum. Cogito* is equated with *muero,* thought with death, and death with existence. This type of conceptual play is a constant in Villaurrutia's poetry, and serves as the point of departure for the theme of **"Décima Muerte."**

In the second *décima* this equivalence is developed further:

> Si en todas partes estás,
> en el agua y en la tierra,
> en el aire que me encierra
> y en el incendio voraz;
> y si a todas partes vas
> conmigo en el pensamiento,
> en el soplo de mi aliento
> y en mi sangre confundida,
> ¿ no serás, Muerte, en mi vida,
> agua, fuego, polvo y viento?

Death is identical with Empedocles' four principles of existence. She is, therefore, the single principle surpassing all the others: life equals death, and living is a process of dying.

In both form and content, this stanza recalls a multitude of poems in the style of the *Petrarquistas.* The four elements mentioned singly—water, air, fire, and earth—are then collected in the final line. This is the technique which Dámaso Alonso has called "dispersion and recollection," and here it recalls two of the great lines of the Baroque era, Gongora's " . . . en tierra, en polvo, en humo, en sombra, en nada," and Sor Juana's " . . . es cadáver, es polvo, es sombra, es nada." This is no coincidence. Both these poems express a profound knowledge of the role of death in existence, and **"Décima Muerte"** is of the same family. It is a song to Death, to the finality which has become the "Coy Mistress" to be courted in haste.

The third *décima* continues the mode of allusion which has been used to set the theme. The source is the famous *copla* employed by Lope and Santa Teresa de Jesús:

> Ven, muerte, tan escondida,
> que no te sienta venir,
> porque el placer de morir
> no me vuelva a dar la vida.

Within the framework of the love poem, the poet awaits the arrival of the beloved. On the level of symbolic meaning, he hopes only that Death come quietly and without warning:

> Si tienes manos, oue sean
> de un tacto sutil y blando,
> apenas sensible cuando
> anestesiado me crean;
> y que tus ojos me vean
> sin mirarme, de tal suerte
> que nada me desconcierte
> ni tu vista ni tu roce,
> para no sentir ni un goce
> ni un dolor contigo, Muerte.

In the fourth *décima,* this allusional mode is abandoned. He awaits the arrival of the beloved, in order that her coming resolve the opaque world of shadows in which he dwell:

> Por caminos ignorados,
> por hendiduras secretas,
> por las misteriosas vetas
> de troncos recién cortados,
> te ven mis ojos cerrados
> entrar en mi alcoba oscura
> a convertir mi envoltura
> opaca, febril, cambiante,
> en materia de diamante
> luminosa, eterna y pura.

The dominion of Death extends to all things. She is at once the beloved and the principle of life, and through each opening of existence she comes to the dreaming lover.

The Petrarchan lover eagerly anticipates the arrival of the beloved in order that he may savor completely the experience of her arrival. In **"Décima Muerte,"** the poet dares not sleep, that he may remain master of himself even in Death, that he may die awake and aware:

> No duermo para que al verte
> llegar lenta y apagada,
> para que al oír pausada

> tu voz que silencios vierte,
> para que al tocar la nada
> que envuelve tu cuerpo yerto,
> para que a tu olor desierto
> pueda, sin sombra de sueño,
> saber que de ti me adueño,
> sentir que muero despierto.

This is the lover anxious to possess his mistress, but in a possession whose meaning is a desperate attempt to retain self control in the most harrowing moment of each man's existence—the moment when that existence ceases.

In these first five *décimas,* the internal structure of each stanza has been largely conceptual, based on the contrast and comparison of terms. Thus the baroque antithesis of the fourth *décima:*

> . . . opaca, febril, cambiante . . .
> . . . luminosa, eterna y pura.

This is also the source of the conceptual play of these lines of the first stanza:

> . . . estar viviendo sin verte
> y muriendo en tu presencia!

> . . . puesto que muero existo.

This antithetical procedure is also used in the creation of some startling images. The beloved is described in terms diametrically opposed to the usual amorous terminology: "tu cuerpo yerto," "tu olor desierto." This imagery is carried to the extreme: the Deadly Mistress, while retaining her corporeal aspect, becomes the incarnation of the principle of Death:

> . . . al verte/ . . . lenta y apagada . . .
> . . . al oír . . . /tu voz que silencios vierte
> . . . al tocar la nada . . .

The sixth *décima* describes this final embrace, beyond space and time, so far beyond all previous experience that it may even transcend its own limits to create a new zone of existence:

> La aguja del instantero
> recorrerá su cuadrante,
> todo cabrá en un instante
> del espacio verdadero
> que, ancho, profundo y señero,
> será elástico a tu paso
> de modo que el tiempo cierto
> prolongará nuestro abrazo
> y será posible, acaso,
> vivir después de haber muerto.

*Décima* VII is a remarkable inversion of the technique known as *poesía a lo divino,* in which erotic imagery is used to express the mystical union with God, the Ultimate Reality. Villaurrutia, while apparently writing of the emotional impact of the sexual act, is describing the moment of death. In this parallel, his attitude toward the fact of death becomes completely clear. The almost play-ful intellectual response of the first stanza, with only the single word *angustia* to indicate an emotional reaction, has become an emotional and intellectual longing to ex-perience the ultimate union:

> En el roce, en el contacto,
> en la inefable delioia
> de la suprema caricia
> que desemboca en el acto,
> hay el misterioso pacto
> del espasmo delirante
> en que un cielo aluoinante
> y un infierno de agonía
> se funden cuando eres mía
> y soy tuyo en un instante.

The eighth *décima* expresses most completely the extent to which Death has become an individual. In itself, it could serve as a love poem to a younger and more allur-ing mistress. It is precisely this which enhances the actual significance: Death *is* an enticing mistress. There is no horror as the poet speaks of the extent to which she has permeated his consciousness; he has passed beyond such facile reactions to a more complex understanding:

> ¡Hasta en la ausencia estás viva!
> Porque te encuentro en el hueco
> de una forma y en el eco
> de una nota fugitiva;
> porque en mi propia saliva
> fundes tu sabor sombrío,
> y a cambio de lo que es mío
> me dejas sólo el temor
> de hallar hasta en el sabor
> la presencia del vacío.

A new note is injected in the ninth *décima*. If Death is personal and unique, what will become of her after the poet's death?

> Si te llevo en mí prendida
> y te acaricio y escondo;
> si te alimento en el fondo
> de mi más secreta herida;
> si mi muerte te da vida
> y goce mi frenesí,
> ¿qué será, Muerte, de ti
> cuando al salir yo del mundo,
> deshecho el nudo profundo,
> tengas que salir de mí?

This mocking challenge introduces the tenth and final *décima:*

> En vano amenazas, Muerte,
> cerrar la boca a mi herida
> y poner fin a mi vida
> con una palabra inerte.
> ¡Qué puedo pensar al verte,
> si en mi angustia verdadera
> tuve que violar la espera;
> si en vista de tu tardanza
> para llenar mi esperanza
> no hay hora en que yo no muera!

The poet does not fear the coming of Death; she may threaten him in vain. In a concentration of bitter irony, he points out his victory over her, for in his life of constant anticipation, he has already violated the hour of their meeting. In this existence whose Ultimate Reality is Death, there is no hour in which he does not die.

## Robert Nugent (essay date 1960)

SOURCE: "Villaurrutia and Baudelaire," in *Hispania,* Vol. XLIII, No. 2, May, 1960, pp. 205-8.

[*In the following essay, Nugent draws parallels between the poetry of Villaurrutia and that of Charles Baudelaire, and points out areas of divergence as well.*]

The influence of various French authors on Villaurrutia has already been noted: Alí Chumacero in his introduc-tion to the complete works of Villaurrutia[1] has pointed out (p. xxii) the importance of Proust, Cocteau, Supervielle, Giraudoux, the surrealists, the intellectual example of Gide, for the Mexican poet. Behind them all, however, stands the figure of Baudelaire, whose work forms the beginning of modern French poetic theory and attitudes. The present paper is an attempt to indicate some relationships between the author of the *Fleurs du mal* and the Mexican *contemporáneo,* not so much in the way of direct imitation but more in the way of compari-sons which seem significant. These relationships center about those themes of death, night, and dream, usually present in a discussion of Villaurrutia's poetry.

The theme of death is an important one for both Baudelaire and Villaurrutia. The *Fleurs du mal* has a section of six poems entitled "La Mort." In the first of these poems, "La Mort des amants,"[2] we find a note of a certain exaltation, the angel who "entre 'ouvrant les portes,/Viendra ranimer, fidèle et joyeux,/Les miroirs ternis et les flammes mortes." Thus life is associated, in Baudelaire, with memory, remembrance of things past. There is also an essential association with death and its necessary opposite, or complement, life. This parallel is basic in Villaurrutia. In the poem, **"Canto a la primavera,"** it is the poet who poses this question which is the beginning of all poetic activity, the origin of love and its end, or a repetition of the love-death motif which can be found in the Baudelaire poem. Inherent in the Baudelaire piece is the idea of regeneration or rebirth: there is in the figure of the Angel the possible announcer of the final judgment, which is to be the beginning of another life. In Villaurrutia there is a similar innate im-pulse towards regeneration, but with the modification that it counts less in a moral or intellectual decision on the poet's part and is more natural in origin, somewhat com-parable to Bergson's *élan vital.* With this association of the quest for an answer the poem follows a series of possibilities. First, from the earth characterized as *sumisa, dormida, fatigada, herida,* and which includes the past *(olvidado)* and death, emerges the dream of re-birth, of renascence:

desde la muerte misma,
germina o se despierta
y regresa a la vida.

(p. 60)

And for Villaurrutia it is through poetry that the poet, like the star, will continue, even though there has been a death of the body. For both Baudelaire and Villaurrutia the symbol is that of a guiding light or star; for the French poet, "C'est la clarté vibrante à notre horizon noir. . . ." ("La Mort des pauvres") In Villaurrutia the conceit is similarly that of the star, dead for centuries, which continues to give off light, as the poet—dead through the abandonment by love—continues to live.

Estrella que te asomas, temblorosa y despierta,
tímida aparición en el cielo impasible,
tú, como yo—hace siglos—, estás helada y muerta,
más por tu propria luz sigues siendo visible.
("**Estancias nocturnas**," p. 51)

So that the eventual *primavera* is possible:

Dicen que he muerto.
No moriré jamás:
¡estoy despierto!

("**Epitafios**," p. 75)

In *Nostaligia de la muerte* the first part reproduces an earlier volume, *Nocturnos*. The title associates night and death. In Baudelaire's "La Fin de la journée" there is the comfort of death, an association with death and the finality of a certain cessation of troubles, of the need for an end to the difficulties, the struggle for existence, that called forth the "héroisme de la vie moderne": "La nuit volupteusement monte, Apaisant tout. . . ." In Villaurrutia there is a longing for death for a similar reason. The "Nocturno" is a category type, listing all the emotions—*placer, vicio, deseo, sueño*—which arise in a sensual pattern during the night. At the end of the poem, as does Baudelaire, he subsumes all in one word *todo:* the complete emotional pattern, all his love, his actions, which

circula en cada rama
del árbol de mis venas,
acaricia mis muslos,
inunda mis oídos. . . .

("**Nocturno**," p. 32)

The secret vitality of this emotional response lies in the contrast between life and death; or rather, in that the means of expression are limited by the eyes *(vive en mis ojos muertos)* and the lips *(en mis labios duros)*. In "**Nocturno Grito**" a parallel Baudelairean spleen or acedia, an emotional impotence, is noticed: when the poet wishes to enquire of his heart what it contains, his hands will be "duros/pulsos de mármol helado." ("**Nocturno Grito**," p. 33)

Villaurrutia could probably have had in mind these words from Baudelaire: "Who among us is not a *homo duplex?* I mean those whose minds since infancy have been *touched with pensiveness;* always double, action and in-

tention, dream and reality; one always harming the other."[3] The modern poet is a person who is trying to find out what sort of person he is; the problem is one of solitude, as for example when he hears "el grito de la estatua desdoblando la esquina." ("**Nocturno de la Estatua**," p. 33) He wonders what is to be his response, In Baudelairean terms this type of inquiry or self-interrogation illustrates the difference between "action and intention, dream and reality." The essence of this division can be stated in phrases reminiscent of Baudelaire: *ennui* (moral) and *spleen* (physical) of a constant frustration:

querer tocar el grito y sólo hallar el eco,
querer asir el eco y encontrar sólo el muro
y correr hacia el muro y tocar un espejo.
("**Nocturno de la Estatua**," p. 34)

Furthermore, as Baudelaire has pointed out in the *Journaux intimes,* there are two "sentiments contradictoires: l'horreur de la vie et l'ectase de la vie."[4] These feelings are most poignantly expressed in a time of solitude, "en esta soledad sin paredes." For Baudelaire there is a conflict when the contrasting emotions are struggling with one another and which the French poet describes as "simultanées." The resulting mood is one of despair:

en un interminable descenso
sin brazos que tender
sin dedos para alcanzar. . . .
("**Nocturno en que nada se oye**," p. 34)

For Baudelaire, moreover, there is a further pair of opposing elements, *volupté* and *extase*. The former is more physical, felt by the senses. The latter is more intellectual, or, at times, more deeply aware of, say, religious values. They are, for Baudelaire, as for Villaurrutia, fleeting states, not the inherited part of man's nature, but more those states which tend to come and go, depending on the moment. They are related to love and death.

These themes of love and death are inextricably intertwined in both Baudelaire and Villaurrutia. If the Mexican poet lacks the sardonic humor, the bitterness, of the French poet, he is close to the feeling of the nearness of death in any poetic mood. For Baudelaire in "Le Rêve d'un curieux":

—J'allais mourir. C'était dans mon âme amoureuse,
Désir mêlé d'horreur, un mal particulier. . . .

For Villaurrutia there is the same attraction of love and death. In "**Amor condusse noi ad una morte**," the theme is that of the dark night of the soul transposed to a secular and more sensuous plane. The fear is not only that of knowledge, but also of the non-fulfillment of love, the lack of the total giving of oneself to love, "acaso en otros brazos te abandonas." (p. 63) And eventually what Freudians have termed the death-wish, and what certain critics have called the morbidity of Baudelaire, takes place: the act of love which is a kind of death:

y morir otra vez la misma muerte
provisional, desgarradora, oscura.

**("Amor condusse noi ad una morte,"** p. 63)

The paradox is carried out to its ultimate conclusions: that of hope and not hoping; of hoping that something will happen, and when it does happen, of hoping for the death of hope:

> la sola posesión de lo que espero,
> es porque cuando llega mi esperanza
> es cuando ya sin esperenza muero.
>> **("Soneto de la esperanza,"** p. 65)

For Baudelaire, in "Le Goût du néant":

> Morne esprit, autrefois amoureux de la lutte,
> L'Espoir, dont l'éperon attisait ton ardeur,
> Ne veut plus t'enfourcher!

The ultimate result of this paradox is the corresponding reaction on the part of the woman, who also fears the end of love, the abnegation of the individual personality, the incomplete giving of oneself. For Villaurrutia the problem is similar:

> de tal suerte
> que si no me dejas verte
> es por no ver en la mía
> la imagen de tu agonía
> porque mi muerte es tu muerte.
>> **("Décimas de nuestro amor,"** III, p. 66)

The basic theme is that of *sueño, souvenir,* dream. Dream, with all that is implied in the dream act: the re-organization of the past, the search for significance and meaning to one's actions, the adjustment to one's surroundings. For Baudelaire there is the implication of nostalgia:

> Ainsi dans la forêt où mon esprit s'exile
> Un vieux Souvenir sonne à plein souffle du cor!
>> ("Le Cygne," II)

For Villaurrutia the poem, **"Canto a la primavera,"** represents a posing of the problem of the dream in relation to its origins and to its rôle as a means of identification with *primavera;* additionally, the essentials of mystic rites are explored. In Villaurrutia the function of verse has this prophetic note, a Mallarmean ritualism, which is close to a kind of earth-worship, an almost Blake-like pantheism. For earth is the romantic repository of mystery, *elmisterioso sueño,* to which the poet must go for an answer. In the *Fleurs du mal, le souvenir* (or the remembrance of the past) is necessary to complete the past, to give to the past the fullest possible identity. It comes near to Proust's *mémoire involontaire. Sueño* is similarly a principal theme; it recalls Hamlet's line, *and in that sleep what dreams may come,* and the whole tradition of Hamletism so important in nineteenth-century French poetic outlook and in Baudelaire. In Villaurrutia sleep (a type of death) and death are inevitably joined, *estoy muerto de sueño.* The central difficulty in his discussion of death is one of definition, both of himself and what has happened to him, during a period of silence of

a night: "en medio de un silencio . . . sin respirar siquiera para que nada turbe mi muerte . . ." (**"Nocturno en que nada es oye,"** p. 34) As Reyes Nevares has indicated: "Esta carecia de motivos, que es tal carecia para el amante, quien no puede en un momento dado decifrar la conducta del otro, es verdaderamente la muerte en el amor. La muerte que aflora en la superficie del episodio erótico."[5] The image is reciprocal, the lover and the loved one; it is a means whereby the poet keeps alive his love, even though he has no hope of finding it:

> Mi amor por ti. ¡no murió!
> Sigue viviendo en la fría,
> ignorada galería
> que en mi corazón cavó.
>> (**"Décimos,"** X, p. 68)

Thus Baudelaire fights against time:

> Noir assassin de la Vie et de l'Art.
> Tu ne tueras jamais dans ma mémoire
> Celle qui fut mon plaisir et ma gloire!
>> ("Un fantôme," IV, "Le portarait")

This deeply personal type of experience might be described as characteristic of one point of view. The problem is further heightened by the fact that each experience is an individual one, but one in which some one else is affected. Who can afford to give up his identity; is it possible to share what is usually referred to as the death-wish. The modern individual, and especially Baudelaire, is torn by the belief that without individualization there is no generalization possible; that in the love-death relationship the individual emotion and the individual death must remain, with the parallel notion of love and life. As a Mexican critic has written: "La muerte y la vida caminan juntas; así, al descubrir la muerte, se ve la vida."[6]

The essential difference between Baudelaire and Villaurrutia lies in the rôle the intellect plays. For both poets fatalism is evident. For Baudelaire, however, because of the Catholic tradition within which he worked, the notion of love was linked with sin, that of death with pride. The dream motive in Baudelaire is an escape motive, even in the sense of an ideal world where an ideal Beauty can be attained, whatever its origins. This dualism is the source of much of Baudelaire's spleen and ideal:

> Trois mille six cents fois par heure, la Seconde
> Chichote: *Souviens-toi!*—Rapide, avec sa voix
> D'insecte, Maintenant dit: Je suis Autrefois,
> Et j'ai pompé ta vie avec ma trompe immonde.
>> ("L'Horloge")

And even though Villaurrutia has little concern for this Christian world-view, there is still an intellectual inquiry which relates him to the French poet. As an American scholar has said concerning *Nostalgia de la muerte:* " . . . la melancolia se ha hecho angustia y la soledad es amenaza. En este libro una afirmación de las realidades filosóicas que persiguen al poeta en la lucidez desesperada de la noche."[7] The moments of anguish remind the reader of twentieth-century philosophy of crisis, of Existentialist *Angst*.

> Si nuestro amor no fuera
> en el sueño doloroso
> en que vives, sin mí,
> dentro de mí una vida
> que me llena de espanto. . . .
>
>                      (**"Nuestro amor,"** p. 69)

In summary: there is little evidence of a direct imitation of Baudelaire by Villaurrutia. As is generally true in France, Baudelaire's influence is indirect, through a similarity of approach to problems of love, death, dream. These themes are interrelated in the poetry of Baudelaire and Villaurrutia in a similar outlook: that the poet is truly only alive and functioning in these moments of extreme anguish, or even fear; that eventually there is an affirmation of poetic vitality and purpose, which affords a reason or a kind of explanation for the suffering and the doubts experienced. Can we not say that there is in poetry, as in science, a common basis of thought in which one poet is indebted to another?

NOTES

[1] Xavier Villaurrutia, *Poesía y teatro completos* (México, Fondo de Cultura Económica, 1953). Titles of poems and page numbers after citations refer to this edition.

[2] Charles Baudelaire, *Oeuvres complètes* (Paris: Editions de la Pléiade, 1951). Titles of poems in text refer to this edition.

[3] Ibid., p. 1008. In a review of *La Double Vie* by Charles Asselineau; the English phrase appears in English in the French text.

[4] Ibid., p. 1220. Section LXXIII of *Mon coeur mis à nu.*

[5] Salvador Reyes Nevares, *El amor y la amistad en México* (México: Porrúa y Obregon, 1952), p. 53.

[6] Albert R. Lopes, "La Poesía de Xavier Villaurrutia," in *Memoria del segundo congreso internacional de catedráticos de literatura iberoamericana* (Berkeley and Los Angeles: University of California Press, 1941), p. 255.

[7] Frank Dauster, "La poesía de Xavier Villaurrutia," *Revista Iberoamericana,* XVIII (enero-sept., 1953), p. 346.

## Antonio Moreno (essay date 1960)

SOURCE: "Xavier Villaurrutia: The Development of His Theater," in *Hispania,* Vol. XLIII, No. 4, December, 1960, pp. 508-14.

[*In the following essay, Moreno chronicles Villaurrutia's career as a playwright, and examines some of his principal themes.*]

Rafael Solana, an outstanding contemporary Mexican dramatist and critic, remarked shortly after Villaurrutia's death that the *Sociedad de Autores* and whoever else loved the man should do something to perpetuate his name. As one who admired him, I wish to contribute this appraisal of his dramatic works to that end.

According to the surviving members of his family, Villaurrutia was a precocious child, who learned to read at the age of three, and at an early age entertained his brothers and sisters with puppet shows for which he himself wrote the scripts, handled the marionettes, and painted the scenery.[1] During his very active membership in the group known as the *Contemporáneous* he contributed endless hours to the publication of a periodical which was issued regularly under the same name as that of the organization. Then, because of his conscientious dedication to writing, and a display of outstanding talents in several fields of literature, he was rewarded with a scholarship by the Rockefeller Foundation which enabled him to spend one year in the United States for the study of dramatic technique. Immediately after his return to Mexico from the Yale School of Drama, Villaurrutia organized the *Grupo teatral del sindicato de electricistas,* with the specific purpose of applying, through the presentation of one-act plays, the knowledge of theater technique that he had gained at Yale. He hoped thereby to arrive eventually at a technique suitable to his spirit. This group presented eight one-act plays in a room of the Department of Education. Of these plays three were by himself, and others were translations of Chekhov, Romains, and Schnitzler. As the director of this group and others, Villaurrutia displayed characteristics that were entirely consistent with his nature: discretion, restraint, simplicity, among others, characteristics that produced an overall subjugation of gestures and movement. Although a busy man, Villaurrutia found time to write a substantial amount of poetry with the themes ". . la muerte y la angustia . . la angustia del hombre ante la nada."[2] He not only invited death to come to him throughout a major portion of his poetry but treated it humorously in his first long play, ***Invitación a la muerte,*** and looked forward to it without bitterness or fear in his only prose work, ***Dama de corazones.*** In this connection his epitaph is worth studying.

> Duerme aquí silencioso e ignorado
> El que en vida vivió mil y una muertes.
> Nada quieres saber de mi pasado.
> Despertar es morir; no me despiertes.[3]

With respect to the previously mentioned prose work, a series of sketches autobiographical in form, journalistic in style, and written in his early twenties, Villaurrutia preferred to say nothing; nevertheless, it was good enough to have had one outstanding Mexican critic remark that Villaurrutia was one of three who had mastered the art of prose writing at a very tender age.[4]

Because of his pertinacity Villaurrutia is credited with having begun the experimental theater in Mexico during the year 1928, when he assembled a group of men at a

". . . salón de Mesones 42" and called the school "Teatro Ulises."[5] Villaurrutia served as its director and as one of its actors during the four years of its activity. This school attempted to create a theater audience that appreciated a universal literature, and which would serve as a type of counterstimulant to the commercial theater of Mexico, whose entire organization was suffering from its imitation and almost worship of the decadent Spanish theater. It was during this time that Villaurrutia started his long list of translations of French, English, and Italian dramatists, sometimes alone, and at other times in collaboration with Augustín Lazo. Luigi Pirandello was apparently his favorite among the foreign playwrights, for he translated more of his plays than those of the others.

In 1953, three years after his death, "El Instituto Nacional de la Juventud Mexicana" sponsored a movement in Mexico City to invite the youth between the ages of fourteen and twenty-one interested in the theater to form groups with the purpose of presenting the prize-winning plays of the year. Among these was one called "El Grupo Xavier Villaurrutia." Moreover, "El Pequeño Teatro" of Venezuela, and the "Little Theater" of Middlebury College[6] among others have also presented his plays. Radio station XEW of Mexico City presented in serial form his *Tú eres mi secreto*, and the movie industry filmed his *La mujer legítima* and *La mulata de Córdoba*. The latter was also offered to the public as an operetta. Also, in addition to the reading public, further evidence of Villaurrutia's popularity was registered shortly after his death when an "In Memoriam" appeared in *Cuaderni iberoamericani* of Turin, Italy,[7] and when Willis K. Jones included one of Villaurrutia's plays in his *Anthology of Latin American Drama* with the remark that the latter was one of the "grandes dramaturgos mexicanos" of all times.

His first one-act play, *Parece mentira*, written in 1933 and presented shortly afterwards in the "Teatro Hidalgo", was followed in quick succession by four more, all of which were later collected in 1943 in one volume titled *Autos profanos*. The latter apparently attracted only the intelligentsia; for, to be sure, these ingenious games of dramatic rhetoric are really gymnastics by the characters who, in turn, are manipulated as marionettes by the author with the sole purpose of conveying to his audience a rich ideology. This conduct on his part is comprehensible if we bear in mind that it was Villaurrutia's sincere feeling that " . . . si existe goce sentimental o emotivo, ¿por qué no puede haber un goce de la idea?"[8] The leitmotif or common denominator that characterizes these five plays is sex, but a sex treated a la Villaurrutia and not vulgarly.

The conflicts involving this element are diversified in the *Autos profanos;* they originate and are nurtured in the minds of individuals, and cross the footlights, as it were, only to resolve themselves ambiguously in the mind of each member of the audience. A reader of this group of plays is alerted immediately that they cannot be digested in the easy chair of his living room, but rather must be examined at the desk in his study, where, in the proper atmosphere, the intellectualism of Villaurrutia becomes crystal clear. There are found here no sentimental matter and no characters with personality. Nor does anyone of the plays contain more than one situation. It is somewhat of a " . . . torneo de ingenio, como esgrima ditirámbica de los personajes . . . lleno el diálogo de sutilezas, de gracia . . . (and in which) no se trata solamente de agilidad en las palabras, sino que se dicen cosas de fondo."[9] The conflicts are so intellectually controlled that their solutions are reached without the use of a melodramatic pyrotechnics peculiar to the plays in which the problem involves characters pitted against each other rather than a character and an event in his life. Villaurrutia appears to be working in a high ivory tower far from life, which is full of the problems, the strife, the frustrated yearnings of millions of people, far from the real Mexico indeed. In such a solitude his astute mind receives its nourishment from the emptiness or void about him, where, of course, his intellectual concepts are uninfluenced by the experiences of human contacts; and in such an environment, to be sure, he felt at home; it was his element, his life. To have come down from that perch of isolation would have been tantamount to the life of a fish out of water.

Because of this hermetic life, his characters are never made to feel directly the problems of the world, but rather must imagine or experience them vicariously and must hope to find solutions to their problems not in the materialistic world but in the nebulous atmosphere of the unknown. They become evasive and reticent, possess no conception whatsoever of the art of conversation, and interrupt each other repeatedly; moreover, they have difficulty understanding the other person, and when rapport is established, the conversations become more like a case in court between two shrewd lawyers parrying each other's brief, or between those on the one hand probing for information and those on the other hand avoiding the giving of said information. Since their vicarious experiences have been so complete, so intense, they can always imagine what others feel when confronted with difficulties, and consider themselves capable of offering advice to whoever solicits it. Moreover, their lack of association with other people makes them want to avoid them, or if they should be forced into the presence of others, then the characters behave as misanthropes and seek out the less conspicuous places. They have a phobia of the truth and consequently every possible attempt is made to avoid hearing it. Then too, although they know each other well enough to be able to reveal their secrets to each other in their nebulous world, they prefer, nevertheless, not to do so; they confide rather in people with whom they have no ties, for to them a friend is someone to whom they tell their victories but from whom they keep their defeats.

Villaurrutia manipulates the strings of his puppet-characters so well that they obey him slavishly and thus lose almost completely the individualism of a human being with the ability to think, feel, and do things for himself; and become rather, emissaries or figureheads presenting his ideology, which is treated implicitly in their ratiocination with each other. Yet, there were moments when these mouthpieces longed to mutiny against their master, and charge headlong into the world to meet and wrestle with life's problems physically rather than mentally, directly rather than imagined. But because of the strong attachment between themselves and the master manipulator their bonds had to wait to be severed until a later phase of writing. So they continued in their ratiocination with one another to give free rein to puns in an effort to spar and thereby evade direct revelation of their inclinations toward the various problems confronting them.

It is not uncommon for the characters in these plays to find themselves in many situations involving ambivalent impulses. Two examples follow. When any one of the characters had knowledge of his dual personality, which knowledge was not the possession of every character, he behaved coldly and evasively in the face of such a realization, preferring to go through life not wanting to accept this fact, in whose knowledge lay the possibility of finding an explanation for his mental anguish which could result in happiness. A husband in *Parece mentira* receives the opportunity for the first time to debate with himself whether to continue his monotonously uneventful life, or whether to deal directly and not vicariously with the living situation before him, the situation being that, according to information received, his wife has just had an escapade with another man. He may, if he wishes, become so disturbed by his wife's adultery as to allow it to affect the complacency and routine of his life and reawaken his love for her. Such a decision, it must be stated, will not be reached with a demonstration of frenzied emotion involving any desire for revenge, but rather with control and after intelligent calculation.

Let us consider several of the concepts of his ideology. Villaurrutia's norm for the concept of love has nothing whatsoever to do with the physical, sexual desire. It is never the surrender of one individual to the physical attractions of a member of the other sex. One can easily assume that the husband in *Parece mentira* condoned the unfaithfulness of his wife simply because it interrupted an otherwise uneventful, stagnant life, and gave them another lease, such as it was. Antonio and Mercedes of *Ha llegado el momento* have reached a similar state of stagnation in their life together, and so, the former searches for a reason to be jealous of his wife, or for a reason for her to be jealous of him; without either reason, all love is gone. Love is not a prerequisite for marriage according to these characters; they rather prefer disputes whose words cut deeply, for they are already imagining how sweet will be the nectar when they kiss and make up, as it were. So long as these people continue to try to feel emotions with the mind, so long as they call upon the mind to dictate their every move with the opposite sex, just so long will their love remain cold and confused.

Another concept that Villaurrutia treats implicitly in his ideology is time. In *Parece mentira* the husband receives an anonymous letter informing him of his wife's infidel-

ity with an attorney. He hurries to the office of the latter and becomes engaged in conversation with the male secretary there. Meanwhile three veiled women of identical appearance, or is it one woman, enter or enters the private office at separate times. After a while the same three veiled women, or is it one woman, leave or leaves the office at separate times. Since only one card is seen on the secretary's desk, it is supposed that only one woman left the office on this Monday in question. However, according to the secretary, she has been there twice before, but he isn't certain whether it was on succeeding Mondays, three consecutive days, or even three times in one day. In this successive series of mental affectations, it seems that only the last visit was present to consciousness; the antecedent visits were not equally present; in fact, they were not present at all. They were represented only as reproductions of themselves. The mind of the husband was in the past and endured; therefore, it was able to think of the past in the present; or it had the inexplicable power of attaching to a present feeling the belief of the past.

A different aspect of time is seen in *¿En qué piensas?* María Luisa loves three men, not each one in turn, nor one after the other. If this were the case, then Carlos, whom she had loved in the past, would not exist for her in the present, since he loved her no more. Víctor was her present lover and Ramón, who as yet was not in love with her, would eventually; so the mere knowledge of this made her love him at the time that she was loving the other. All of time is fused in her manifestation of love so that she could live simultaneously with three men, each of whom represented one of the times.

Still another treatment of time is shown in his *Autos profanos* when one of the characters expresses concern over the precious time lost because of the interruptions of an idea, the continuity of a monologue, or the deep concentration on a beautiful memory. Villaurrutia feels that time lost from mental interruptions is of greater significance than that lost from interruptions of specific physical activities, for the latter can be started and terminated at will.

Time in a lighter vein is presented in his *Sea Vd. breve*. Here two characters, each representing a different generation, have difficulty understanding each other because the older one is patient, slow, and deliberate with his lengthy speeches, and the younger one is typical of the fast moving youth.

Villaurrutia continues with his ideology. His solution for two people who lack a reason for existence is death. There is no such thing as divorce or separation. Since love is the reason for existence, then, conversely, there can be no existence without love. Death is the natural ending for such a state of being, and the characters speak of it casually.

The most notable feature of these early plays of Villaurrutia is their immobility, whether we speak of the physical movements of the few characters and their internal feelings, or of their plots, such as they are. These spineless characters are definitely puppets placed in situations which are not natural to life, and instilled with a slavish obedience to conduct themselves consistent with the nebulous world in which they live. The plots involve a character and some circumstance of life, yet they are always devoid of action. Villaurrutia defends his writing of such poetic-like plays which resemble philosophical treatises with his belief that " . . . si existe un goce sentimental o emotivo, ¿por qué no puede haber un goce de la idea?"[10] The full import of these words strikes immediately the reader or viewer of his *Auto profanos* in which the mental activity is sufficiently dramatic as to engage the participation of one or the other. His brilliant dialogue in no way offered inspiration to one's emotions, but certainly to the thought mechanism. He was convinced that the individual discourses of the characters had to be spoken, hence their rapid-fire repartee composed of short speeches. Yet, because his ideology was sufficiently complex, the dialogue was perforce highly selective, and lacked therefore the casualness and indirection of most conversations.

In going from these early works to a second phase of his writing Villaurrutia behaves just as he is expected to do. There is no sudden change, no immediate veering off the beaten path, nothing that is abnormal. These are the characteristics of one who is capricious, and Villaurrutia, to be sure, was not that. To him the welfare of the Mexican theater was of prime importance, and if it meant changing his style to one treating the real issues of the people in order to help create a larger theater-going public, then that's exactly what he would do, and did, but not in any headlong fashion. This is not to say, however, that there is not a discernible break.

*Invitación a la muerte,* his first long play written during the last years of the first period, serves as a natural bridge between the two phases of his theater in that it contains a fair proportion of the ingredients of each. Alberto, the leading character of this play, is as though reincarnated from the first period. While the earlier character was naturally misanthropically evasive, Alberto understands his condition and explains his evasiveness at various times throughout the play. We detect also a consistency with the earlier works in certain avowed ideas of his such as, the routine existence of one's life; the confusion of youth; man's ignorance of his ambivalent self; his constant search for an answer to everything; his constant search for the truth, which, when known, is avoided by some and accepted by others. These, and the other characteristics already covered earlier in our discussion, recur throughout all the second period. The dialogue of both phases of his writing contains similarities such as the fear of the characters that their words were not reaching the audience comprehensibly, the frequent use of these words and their derivatives: "amor, angustia, comprender, existir, ignorar, imaginar, muerte, razón, sorprender, verdad, etc.," his wit in playing around with words, and a good helping of oxymorons.

While there exist these consistencies between the two periods, there exist also many dissimilarities, without which, of course, there would be no development in his theater. We observe immediately a concentration on dramatic structure and content in the second phase of his writing. All but three plays contain three acts; however, although short in form, the three do not return to the earlier style; they conform, rather, to the later mold prescribed by Villaurrutia. Suspense is sufficiently created so that the interest is held to the culmination of the play. Conflicting forces are introduced immediately to make the arguments more convincing. It becomes immediately obvious that Villaurrutia is catering to an audience wider than to the intelligentsia who had attended his *Autos profanos.* His first play of the second period, *Invitación a la muerte,* foreshadows a theater in which the characters, unlike their predecessors, are not mechanical people saturated with eloquent literary gems and maneuvered according to the dictates of the author, but people who move about freely and naturally in situations that appear created by themselves. Naturally then, instead of the cold, passionless, intellectual conflicts of the earlier "rompecabezas" that were controlled by Villaurrutia until fruition, and reached their solutions without the characters' being affected, the later vintage presents more characters with feeling and, of necessity, more situations involving the characters with each other, as if they were permitted to leave the ivory tower to experience life face to face. Now provision is made for ample action, emotion, real characterization, and unaffected dialogue.

Unlike the principal character of old, upon Alberto, principal character of *Invitación a la muerte,* are dependent the life of his girl friend, the future of his mother, and the welfare of both El Viejo and El Joven. In *La hiedra* the love between Hipólito and Teresa, not an Oedipus complex as some suggest, creates incidents that are warm, incidents that reach across the footlights to the hearts of the audience; Sara of *La mujer legítima* fills one with great emotion as she attempts to defend herself before her husband and stepchildren. Another of many dialogues full of interest and true to life in the same play, involves Rafael as he tries to be calm and firm while informing his grown children that he expects them to show respect to his second wife, who is soon to come to live in their home. Moreover, in *El yerro candente,* one can never forget the touching scenes between Román, the father who can't reveal who he is, and Antonia, his daughter, who is ignorant of their relationship. Other real problems such as, the "mordida" (greasing the palm), which is as much a part of the Mexican politics as hot dogs are a part of any baseball game; other facets of politics; adultery as a growing problem of Mexico; and medicine as a necessary evil, all bring into play the emotions that had lain dormant in the *Autos profanos* and now permeate the entire second phase of writing.

In addition, Villaurrutia includes an abundance of local color that adds immeasurably to the development of his theater, which grew from a cerebral-type drama for a particularly choice audience of literati to a drama that increased in physical proportion and loosened considerably the latchstrings of its heart in order that more people could partake of its enjoyment. In studying the two periods, a trend is discernible to cement completely the breach between his brain grappling with ideas and his heart grappling with situations, a breach which seems to have occurred at too early an age in his life, and to have caused him to seek nourishment where each person had his own world of time and space readily comprehensible to him alone. One of several events contributing to the cementing of this breach was his acceptance of a position with the movie industry. Since nothing was nearer the heart of Villaurrutia than to educate the movie-conscious Mexican public to become theater-conscious as well, it was not surprising that he, the movie-industry's severest and most constructive critic, should have accepted the position, or should we say tribute, of being named one of its outstanding editors of dialogue. This undoubtedly would have added considerably to strengthen the trend of his later phase of writing by giving him an even broader outlook on how and what to write than that which he had at the time of his death. Thus, had more time been granted him, he might have arrived at " . . . una reunión equilibrada de valores técnicos, de valores poéticos, y de valoresdramáticos. . . ,"[11] a workable equilibrium of ideas and emotions in juxtaposition.

NOTES

[1] Rafael Solana, "Villaurrutia, comediógrafo," *Hoy,* No. 727 (México, 1951), p. 38.

[2] José Luis Martínez, "Con Xavier Villaurrutia," *Tierra Nueva,* (México, 1950), I, p. 78.

[3] Fernando Benítez, "In Memoriam," *Novedades,* No. 102 (México, 1951), p. 5.

[4] Rafael Solana, *Hoy,* No. 725, p. 46.

[5] Antonio Magaña Esquivel, "Imagen del teatro," *Letras de México,* (México, 1940), p. 85.

[6] A personal interview with Ermilo Abreu Gómez, a close friend of Villaurrutia, revealed this information.

[7] According to a letter received from Pedro Frank de Andrea of Mexico City, dated April 10, 1958.

[8] José Luis Martínez, "Xavier Villaurrutia," *Novedades,* (México, 1951), No. 102, p. 5.

[9] Julio Sapietsa, "El teatro en acción," in *Las Crónicas de las Obras Teatrales de Xavier Villaurrutia* (México, 1950).

[10] See Note 8.

[11] Rodolfo Usigli, "Noticias Gráficas," in Section on *La hiedra in Las Crónicas de las Obras Teatrales de Xavier Villaurrutia,* (México, 1950).

## Anthony W. Moreno (essay date 1962)

SOURCE: "The Contemporary Cultural Revolution in Latin America as Reflected in the Theater of Xavier Villaurrutia," in *Topic,* Vol. II, No. 4, Fall, 1962, pp. 30-38.

[*In the following essay, Moreno posits the coming of a social and cultural revolution in Latin America, and notes evidence of this shift in Villaurrutia's work.*]

The political and economic development of the Latin American republics from their independence to the twentieth century had been so gradual as to be scarcely discernible. The masses had been contained in a strait jacket of paternalism and had not been permitted to plan or direct their own lives, to participate in the affairs of their villages, or even to think for themselves. The precedent for such a wretched lot had been established during the wars of independence in which their role had been as inactive as it has been in the political upheavals since. The *leitmotif* or common denominator of all these revolutions has been simply a change of personnel in the upper echelons with no real concern for the broad base or mass. The twentieth century, however, has been nourishing a political and economic emergence which has been moving at a very active pace, and which has been accompanied by mounting revolutionary changes in the cultural atmosphere.

There has been a rapid broadening of the audience resulting from the increasing participation of the masses in the moulding of the cultural patterns south of the Rio Grande. No longer are the common people in this region indifferent or docile, unquestioning or passive; they have become more assertive, if not fully articulate. Faced with this larger and more diversified audience in an era of burgeoning national self-consciousness, and in a continent where artists and menof letters frequently guide national destinies, writers have been adapting their themes and characters to the interests of the wider clientele. In fact, since politicians as a rule double also as authors and literary critics, literature easily takes on a social or political flavor designed for the palate of this larger group. In addition, the more traditional forms of artistic and literary expression have been challenged by new methods of communication, especially the movies, the radio, and the mobile cultural units, which from the beginning have directed their efforts toward the masses. The cinema, radio, and television as communication media (the latter understandably not having the prominence of the other two as yet) continue to receive increasing attention in this era of social ferment. They are able to reach the more fortunate citizens individually and the large urban masses collectively; but, more particularly, they also reach the hitherto forgotten souls in the rural areas, since all three forms of communication require minimal standards of literacy.

These media are rapidly destroying the iniquitous foundations of absolutism, obscurantism, bigotry, and individualism, which dealt with the masses as an insignificant entity whose role on the stage of the New World was simply that of marionettes to be manipulated by their directors, the militarists, dictators, and despots—benevolent or otherwise—of Latin America. Today there is an interplay of influence as new political, economic, social, and cultural institutions emerge. And in this emergence the hitherto-ignored common people are making themselves heard as never before in an effort to create a public opinion or ideology of their own and thereby to become nationals in the sense that the country can be a nation. Consequently, the natural reaction to these changes by men of letters has been a decline and eclipse of literature and art directed to the social elite and a widespread surge to " . . . American self-expression . . . in exploring New World themes, backgrounds, and man; [such as] the tragedy of the rubber workers [by Eustasio Rivera], . . . humans tossed about by . . . revolution [by Mariano Azuela], . . . the enormous Venezuelan plain and its primitive untamed beauty which devour man and will not let him escape [by Rómulo Gallegos], . . . the Andean mountainside which is indissolubly linked to the hopes and fears of the peasants [by Ciro Alegría]."[1] There is apparent a distinct effort to arrive at the whole man, body and soul, who will recognize the meaning of human relationships, indeed the meaning of life itself. "There are being reflected in our works the institution of large landed estates, political corruption, religious fanaticism, economic misery, gambling, prostitution, alcoholism, illiteracy, the appearance of sociological theories . . . , imperialism, immigration, etc."[2] Literature has become " . . . the mirror of our life . . . the control stick of action, and a moral force of fundamental importance."[3] The story of *The Underdogs*, a Mexican novel by Mariano Azuela, is being told today through every media available and to the largest audience ever.

This increasing concern with real people living under readily recognizable circumstances, facing familiar trials and tribulations, and reacting in true-to-life fashion is the most noticeable change in the contemporary literature of the Latin American republics. It reflects a sudden awareness of the continent's natural setting and of the "varied human mosaic" inhabiting it. Such a literature attuning the elemental violence of human emotions to the natural setting spans the length and breadth of Latin American territory. The literary output of the new writers makes full use of the vernacular language and does not deviate from its realism in order to provide happy endings or complete answers to the vexing problems of life. The inevitable consequence of this preoccupation with realism has been a narrowing of cultural horizons coinciding with the upsurge of national consciousness in the political, economic, and social spheres. The average Latin American is not yet concerned with the conditions of his fellow-men in the distant lands of Asia, Africa, or elsewhere. He is only now showing progress in being weaned from a sense of impractical individualism which had given him that quality of refractoriness conducive to a profound provincial loyalty to his own *patria chica*, his village. The decline of aristocratically-oriented literature has meant the disappearance of themes and treatment which

are supra-national in appeal. It is not surprising that this anti-aristocratic nationalist tendency in literature has been paralleled by a weakening of the influence of the church on the masses. For centuries the church had played its role so well that it imposed an absolute spiritual domination over the souls of the masses. The resultant religious preoccupation of the common people infiltrated fanatically into every phase of their lives until there grew to be no distinction between a religious and a patriotic fervor. With the departure of Spain from the New World and the independence of the colonies, there began a deterioration of the social and educational welfare of the people, two responsibilities carried on almost exclusively by the church under Spanish rule. As a result, the church has now renounced any right to influence politics or to maintain exclusive control of public education.

The general tendencies in the literature of Latin America as a whole can be discerned in the writings of authors in the individual countries. Themes and characters may differ in Mexico, Peru, or Argentina, according to varying local conditions, but the trends toward secularism, realism, nationalism, and the use of the vernacular are to be found virtually everywhere. It would be superfluous and indeed somewhat ridiculous to attempt to name all the works illustrating the shift from literary narcissism to the fulfillment of the demand for realism, especially since such a list would be as exhausting as it would be imposing. At times the transition from the old to the new orientation can be seen in the works of a single writer. Such a metamorphosis is most dramatically illustrated in the tragically short career of Xavier Villaurrutia (d. 1950), Mexican author and scholar of the 1930's and 1940's. His plays, which were his principal means of expression, fall into two sharply defined periods. In the earlier phase (the old orientation) his efforts were directed primarily at a small aristocratic audience much like those "Gallic admirers of the swan, whose pens rarely dip . . . into the founts of national life. . . ."[4] In his later dramas (the new orientation) he abruptly shifted his style and themes to appeal to the broader audience whose existence was being demonstrated by the cinema and the radio.[5]

Villaurrutia's dramatic interest was apparently brought to the fore by his translations of Pirandello, Schnitzler, and Lenormand. We should not assume, however, that any one man was a sole influence on Villaurrutia, especially when we remember that he was very actively absorbed by necessity in constant reading because of his varied occupations in life, such as professor of literature, critic, dramatist, director, actor. One is more likely to feel that a man of Villaurrutia's ability, who spent a considerable portion of his life striving to bring a universal theater to Mexico, would have been influenced generally rather than specifically. From Lenormand, whose plays tend toward the elucidation of the mystery of the inner life, toward a solution of the enigma that man presents to himself in the form of a conflict between the conscious and the unconscious, Villaurrutia borrowed a common concept of the time:[6]

     . . . it is our minds that have moved across an

unmoving dream. Yesterday, today, tomorrow are only words . . . words which correspond to no reality except within our narrow brains, for beyond our brains there is neither past or future; nothing but one vast present . . . the past, the present and the future are co-existent.

Schnitzler's *Death of a Bachelor* gave him the idea of the posthumous joke or diversion, which he employed in two of his plays *El solterón* and *Juego peligroso.* From Pirandello he borrowed one of the principal ideas in the theaters of both writers, the concept that in order to exist, an individual had to grapple directly, not vicariously with the problems of life, that he could not remain a separate entity in this modern world and be happy. Finally, Pirandello could not have known that when "[he had] established the proposition that the dramatic crises of the mind are as vivid and absorbing as those of the emotion,"[7] Villaurrutia was to reiterate that very sentiment in his *Autos profanos;* for in his earlier orientation, he felt that " . . . if there is such a thing as a sentimental or emotional enjoyment, then why can't there be an enjoyment of an idea?"[8]

After many successful translations of foreign writers, Villaurrutia tried his hand at one-act plays, such as the *Autos profanos,* which apparently attracted only the intelligentsia since they were written in a high ivory tower and wereof such a nature that they couldn't be digested in the easy chair of one's living room but rather must be studied at the desk in one's study where, in an appropriate atmosphere, the intellectualism of Villaurrutia became crystal clear. No sentimental matter was to be found in this early theater, no characters with personality. There were rather ingenious games of dramatic rhetoric in which the characters were manipulated as marionettes by the author with the sole purpose of conveying to the audience a rich ideology by means of repartee, much like two good lawyers parrying each other's thrusts. From this period, his plays have been judged to be intellectually cold, lacking in reality, mobility, warmth, and comprehension, and failing to inspire. The appearance of *Invitación a la muerte* holds a position between the two periods somewhat analogous to that of Calderón, who is considered by some as the last of the Golden Age writers and by others as the first of the Romanticists. That is to say, this play serves as a natural bridge between the two parts of his theater in that it contains a fair proportion of the ingredients of each.

Of course, there are inevitably some characteristics shared in common by both periods of his writing. There is the misanthropic evasiveness of the characters, and we detect also a consistency in certain avowed ideas of his, such as the routine existence of a person's life and the continuing confusion of youth. In both periods there is an expressed desire to want to break out of one's stifling hermetic world. Villaurrutia appeared to have felt deeply man's ignorance of himself and his life, for in the knowledge of these lay one's happiness. Ambivalence which he had expressed in *Parece mentira,* the play with which he had made his debut in the theater, recurs in *La hiedra*

and *El yerro candente.* The anguish and suffering of mankind in his constant search for an answer to everything are represented in both periods. Then, once he had his answer, the truth that he had been seeking he is quick to say in imitation of any of the puppets of the *Autos profanos:*[9]

> But it isn't truth that I am seeking because I already have it or think I have it, at least, here like an endless emptiness in my heart; it isn't truth but the search for truth . . . outside of me, in a word, in a gesture, in a situation that my senses can feel.

Moreover, once he has arrived at some definite knowledge of his problem, the individual, like Maria Luisa in *¿En qué piensas?,* Antonia in *El yerro candente,* and the husband in *Parece mentira,* finds himself in the enviable position of being able to say:[10]

> Without my knowing it that's what was growing inside of me like a material pain. That's what was making me grope in the dark, inside and outside of me blind with anguish and indecision. That's what it was! My Lord! But now I no longer doubt! Now I know it and I am rid of indecisions. Now I am a free man.

Villaurrutia's concept of love in both periods was based on a foundation of quarrels and difficulties of all types. The lack of understanding between the older and younger generations is another recurrent theme. Finally, a study of the language of the two periods reveal common and frequent usage of many concepts, such as reason, anguish, the unknown, existence, imagination, ambivalence, love, time, death, etc.

But it is the differences in his writings which reflect the changing literary outlook of his age. It is fitting that we should return to the *Invitación a la muerte* with its seasoning of atmospheres of mystery, evasiveness, and death, all distinguishing characteristics of the *Autos profanos,* and reveal the other portion of its dual personality which is characteristic of the later writing. We observe immediately a concentration on dramatic structure and content in this latter period. All the later plays, excepting three, contain three acts. However, even the shorter plays do not return to the earlier style; they conform rather, to the mould prescribed by Villaurrutia in every other respect.

In reading the plays of the second period it becomes obvious that Villaurrutia now began to cater to a wider audience than merely to the intelligentsia who hadattended his *Autos profanos.* To Villaurrutia the welfare of the Mexican theater was of prime importance, and if it meant changing his style from that of the *Autos profanos,* written in an ivory tower and presented before a limited audience, to one treating the real issues of the people in order to help create a large theater-going public, then that's exactly what he would do, and did in his first play *Invitación a la muerte,* and to a much greater degree in his subsequent plays.

The *Invitación* foreshadows a theater in which the characters unlike their predecessors, are not mechanical people saturated with eloquent literary gems and usurped by the dictates of the author, but people who move about freely and naturally in situations that appear to be created by themselves. Naturally then, instead of the cold, passionless, intellectual conflicts that were controlled by Villaurrutia until fruition and reached their solutions without the participation of the persons affected, we see now more characters with feeling, and, of necessity, more situations involving the characters with each other, and a warmth that reaches across the footlights to the hearts of the audience. Since each character is what he is, it is obvious that they will be involved in many situations, which in turn will provide ample action and sufficient opportunity for real characterization, emotion, and excellent dialogue, as is the case throughout this second period. Real problems that bring into play the emotions that had lain dormant in the *Autos profanos* permeate the entire second period of writing. How interesting that Villaurrutia could begin to show a reversal of technique after approximately one decade of playwriting! It was as if he set aside the pen from which flowed nothing but intellectualism for the *Autos profanos,* and picked up the one that wrote down only what was human, passionate, true-to-life, and, of course, comprehensible.

Throughout this period of writing Villaurrutia presents and discusses many of the problems of Mexico. Since politics is a vital part of Mexican life, it is only natural that Villaurrutia would allude to it often, especially the "mordaza" or graft which is as much a part of Mexican politics as hot dogs are of a baseball game. Another growing problem in Mexico, touched upon by Villaurrutia, is that of adultery.

As has happened to many of us, and most assuredly to Villaurrutia, who was a great believer in blue-printing everything, plans do not always materialize consistent with one's desires: "I committed the error in believing that between a perfectly calculated plan and its execution there was no doubt."[11] But sure of the course that he was taking now, Villaurrutia frequently admonished his audience in his plays: "and do you think that difficulties end merely by keeping them inside? What a price we have had to pay for hypocrisy, pretense, and false pride."[12] He could have been thinking of his younger days in expressing himself thus—days when he tried to put himself above the crowd and project his ideology to the select few. For, at times, he seems almost to reprove his audience for not having dressed him down a little during that earlier period.

In addition to revealing himself as a crusader for a Mexican theater, Villaurrutia includes in his plays an abundance of local color which added immeasurably to the development of his theater since its inception.

In reflection, we are conscious of the metamorphosis that the theater of Villaurrutia underwent. Its development from an intellectual drama that reached across the foot- lights and catered primarily to the intelligentsia, to a drama that grew in physical proportion and loosened somewhat the latchstrings of its heart so that more people could partake of its enjoyment is, indeed, an accomplishment. It becomes more so, when one realizes that this change drew no adverse criticism from his original few select and faithful followers.

His *Autos profanos* were so highly intellectual that the limited audience surely must have caused him disappointment. Thereupon his intimate friends must have volunteered counsel to combat this. It can be supposed that their advice to him to endeavor to be more comprehensible to a wider audience began to prey on his mind and reached the proportion of a mania during the writing of his second groupof plays. For, can anybody be convinced that it is an accident that one character asks another several times on one page whether the meaning is clear and then continues only after receiving a "yes" or "no" to his inquiry? Each succeeding play was received with tremendous success and critical acclaim.

In view of this reception Villaurrutia could not help but be impressed, and encouraged to try even more strongly to reach the majority of the people. It was becoming gradually easier for Villaurrutia to do this, in direct proportion to the wisdom that he was gaining as he matured. Indeed, the older he became, the more remote seemed the brash ideas or convictions of a youth whose brain had severed relations at too early an age with his heart, and had gone to seek its nourishment where each person had his own world of time and space, and each had a reality that was comprehensible to him alone. Here he had learned to grapple with ideas rather than with situations.

There was then an obvious connection between the trend of the writing of Villaurrutia and the very warm reception being accorded each succeeding play. Nothing was nearer the heart of this writer than to educate the movie-conscious Mexican public to become theater-conscious as well.

NOTES

[1] Kurt L. Levy, "Some Cultural Influences," in *The Latin Americas,* 29th Couchiching Conference (Toronto, 1960), pp. 84, 85.

[2] Arturo Torres Rioseco, *La novela en la América hispana* (Berkeley and Los Angeles, 1949), p. 171.

[3] *Ibid.*

[4] Mariano Azuela, "Introduction" of *Los de abajo* (New York, 1939), p. XIV.

[5] Radio station XEW of Mexico City presented in serial form his "Tú eres mi secreto," and the movie industry filmed his *La mujer legitima* and *La mulata de Córdoba.*

[6] Henri-Rene Lenormand, "Time is a Dream," in *Modern Continental Dramas* (New York, 1941), p. 600.

[7] William Drake, *Contemporary European Writers* (New York, 1928), p. 339. My translation.

[8] José L. Martinez, "Xavier Villaurrutia," in *Novedades*, No. 102 (Mexico City, 1951), p. 5. My translation.

[9] Xavier Villaurrutia, *Invitación a la muerte* (Mexico City, 1947), p. 41. My translation.

[10] Xavier Villaurrutia, *El yerro candente* (Mexico City, 1945), p. 99. My translation.

[11] *Ibid.*, p. 27.

[12] *Ibid.*, p. 37.

## Sandra M. Cypess (essay date 1969)

SOURCE: "The Influence of the French Theatre in the Plays of Xavier Villaurrutia," in *Latin American Theatre Review*, Vol. 3, No. 1, Fall, 1969, pp. 9-15.

[*In the following essay, Cypess closely examines the influence of French playwrights, particularly Henri-René Lenormand, on Villaurrutia's dramatic work.*]

Before Xavier Villaurrutia became involved with the Mexican theatre, he had already gained fame as a poet and was associated with the avant-garde literary group Los Contemporáneos. Before he produced his first play in 1933, he had been intimately connected with a new trend in the Mexican theatre, the experimental movement. For Villaurrutia the experimental theatres provided first a learning experience and then a testing ground for his theatrical ideas. Villaurrutia acknowledges the importance of this experience, admitting, "I . . . would very likely never have written plays without the *Ulises* experience."[1] His apprenticeship as a playwright took him through the roles of actor, director, and translator of many of the contemporary foreign plays admired by the avant-garde. Thus, when critics refer to the influences which played a role in the formation of the theatre of Xavier Villaurrutia, the most common procedure has been to link Villaurrutia's name with the dramatists whose works he translated and leave it at that. For example, Rafael Solana, in discussing "Villaurrutia, comediógrafo," says, "Este trato estrecho con dramaturgos de primer orden contribuyó a enriquecer el talento dramático de Xavier y le permitió adquirir un conocimiento a fondo de la técnica de algunos autores bien escogidos para maestros. . . ."[2] One cannot disagree with this statement. However, it would be of value in understanding the originality of Villaurrutia's theatre if we could determine more specifically what lessons he had learned from the dramatists he had chosen as his teachers.

In treating the critical problem of influences, especially in the case of an artist already established, as Villaurrutia was established as a poet, we should be aware of the contrasts between the concepts of tradition and polygenesis.[3] That is, we should inquire whether the element which is similar in the works of two artists is a result of the example set by the first artist, the tradition that he has established, or whether the similarity is purely fortuitous, the result of an independent act of creativity reached unknowingly by different people at different times. Clearly there are many examples of both phenomena in the annals of literary history. Our problem here is to determine how we should consider some of the similarities which link Villaurrutia's work with the dramatists whose plays he translated. Because this discussion is necessarily limited by space, I have chosen examples from the works of playwrights who were important not only to the experimental movement in Mexico, but who were important innovators and renovators of the theatre during the period of Villaurrutia's formation as a dramatist; they are Henri-René Lenormand, Jean Cocteau, and Jean Giraudoux.

Through the plays of Lenormand, Freudian subjects and outlook were first given dramatic expression in the French theatre.[4] Today Lenormand is generally remembered for his treatment of the abnormal personality; it is in relation to this subject that Professor Dauster has linked his name to Villaurrutia's theatre.[5] At the time Villaurrutia was writing his early one-act plays, he was also engaged in translating Lenormand's *A L'Ombre du mal*, an analysis of evil and superstition. Translated as *A la sombra del mal*, this play was presented as part of the repertoire of *Teatro de Orientación* in 1934, the same year the second of Villaurrutia's one-act plays was produced. In this play, *¿En qué piensas?*, and in *Parece mentira*, which had been given the previous year, we can see the direct influence of one of Lenormand's works. Before translating *A L'Ombre du mal*, Villaurrutia had already become familiar with Lenormand's *Le Temps est un songe*, translated by Celestino Gorostiza as *El tiempo es sueño* and presented in 1929 under the auspices of *Teatro Ulises*. This play associates Lenormand's name with innovations in the dramatic treatment of time.[6] The play revolves around the idea of the relativity of time. Relativity of time is not a unique concept introduced by Lenormand; rather, it is Lenormand's treatment of time on stage that inspired Villaurrutia when he also dramatized this concept.

In tableau two of Lenormand's play, Romée, one of the three principal characters, witnesses an accident which appears to be occurring at some distance from where she stands. As the play progresses, this distance is revealed to be a remoteness of time rather than of space. The explanation for this phenomenon is expressed by another character, Niko. He describes to Romée a new concept of time that he has learned from the wise men of Java. They believe that all time is coexistent. Thus, the past, present, and future are on one plane. The events of the future exist in a different spatial position, for example, but occur simultaneously with the events normally designated as present time. Depending on one's perspective, the aspects of time can be seen as a whole or only in part.

Villaurrutia also dramatizes this concept of time. In *Parece mentira* the three women of identical appearance who are seen in the lawyer's office are either three women who enter at different times on that same day, or are the same woman who makes her appearance on three different occasions. In the latter explanation, the three visits of the one woman, like the event of the future which Romée had seen as an occurrence in the present, are perceived as existing at the same time although they do take place in different chronological periods.

In *¿En qué piensas?* we meet María Luisa who loves three men, each one representing a different aspect of time—past, present, and future. When she declares her love for all of them, one of the men remarks that it is impossible for her to love them all "a un tiempo." María Luisa responds, "a un tiempo, no; en el tiempo." For her, the words past, present, and future do not convey the meaning of separation of time, but as Niko expressed it in *Le Temps est un songe*, "le passé, le présent et l'avenir coexistent." Villaurrutia has María Luisa express the coexistence of time to her three lovers: "Pero qué son, en este caso, pasado, presente y porvenir, sino palabras: Si yo no he muerto, el pasado está como el presente, y del mismo modo que el futuro, en mí, dentro de mí, en mis recuerdos, en mi satisfacción, en mis deseos, que no pueden morir mientras yo tenga vida" (Scene VII). María Luisa, a sensuous creature, has expressed the coexistence of time in terms of her own internal feelings. The three men whom she equally considers to be her lovers are the physical manifestation similar to the three women in *Parece mentira* and the accident in Lenormand's play.

Although Villaurrutia's later plays do not continue the dramatization of this interesting concept of time, he does use a technique which is reminiscent of this early experiment. In *La hiedra* (1942) and *Invitación a la muerte* (1947) he effectively restages later in the play scenes which occur early in the action, just as the accident occurs twice in *Le Temps est un songe*. The repeated scenes in Villaurrutia's later plays, however, do not suggest the coexistence of time, but rather act as premonitions of what is to come in the future. In *La hiedra* one of the reasons the living room scene has been kept static, unchanged in all the years of Hipólito's absence, is to enable Teresa to go back to that past time and try to recapture Hipólito's love. Her failure can be predicted by the enactment of their final encounter in the same setting which saw her failures so many times before. In *Invitación a la muerte* we also see the presentation early in the play of a scene which is to be repeated in the future. In the last scene of Act I, Alberto sits alone, waiting for his father. When this scene is again reproduced at the end of the play, the earlier scene is recalled as the prefiguration of the future event.

In this example of Lenormand's influence we have seen that Villaurrutia was able to accept the model presented before him with two results: in his early plays he incorporated the element into his works without much change. But as he gained greater experience as a playwright, it seems that he no longer merely accepted the model, but developed the acquired technique until it became refash-

ioned in a unique Villaurrutian way. This same kind of refashioning of an already established technique can be seen in Villaurrutia's dramatic use of objects. It is Jean Cocteau, whose *Orfée* (1926) was among the first plays produced by the Teatro de Ulises, who revitalized for the experimental theatre the trend towards the use of objects, not for their realistic value, but as a means to elaborate the dramatic action.[7] Although more work still needs to be done concerning the relationship between Cocteau and Villaurrutia, let us consider now the use of objects by the two dramatists.[8]

In the preface to *Les Maries de la Tour Eiffel,* Cocteau alluded to a special kind of "poetic language" for the stage which would reveal the hidden meaning of objects. The presence of objects on stage, used in new and unusual ways, remained a part of Cocteau's theatre. For example, in *La Machine infernale,* one of Cocteau's reworkings of the Oedipus myth, dramatic irony is present—as always in the enactment of a myth—because the situations are known beforehand by the audience but not by the actors. More significantly, Cocteau also creates dramatic irony by the use of certain objects which he endows with dramatic existence by associating their actions with actions in the plot. Jocasta's blood-red scarf, for example, leaves threatening imprints of fingers on her throat; it is with this very scarf that she later hangs herself. Her brooch, which she innocently describes as "cette broche que crève l'oeil de tout le monde" later becomes the instrument with which Oedipus literally scratches his eyes out. An extension of this technique of focusing on objects and creating a dramatic existence for them can be seen in Villaurrutia's use of the shawl in *La hiedra,* the picture of the mother in *La mujer legítima,* and the oversized coffin in *Invitación a la muerte.* As a representative example of this technique, let us consider the use of Teresa's shawl.

The shawl, which surrounds Teresa and gives her protection, is a reminder of her adherence to the past. She is given the shawl in a conspicuous manner just before Hipólito's entrance in Act I. As he embraces her for the first time, the shawl falls away from her as his arms replace it. Teresa recaptures the shawl as she expresses her feeling of distance towards him. At the end of Act I the shawl falls again from her shoulders. In his stage directions, Villaurrutia comments on the importance of this action: "El movimiento hace que el chal resbale de los hombros de Teresa hasta el suelo. Toda la belleza, toda la audacia, toda la madurez vital de Teresa resplandece en ese momento. Hipólito la contempla atónito." When Teresa is without her shawl, she appears to be moving away from the past towards a future with Hipólito. Whenever he leaves her, the shawl surrounds her once again, replacing him as the protective force and situating her again in the past. The article of clothing thus becomes a dramatic entity whose actions reveal the state of the relationships in the play.

Our discussion up to this point has uncovered the role which tradition has played in the formulation of

Villaurrutia's dramatic techniques. We have been able to identify some of the links between Villaurrutia and Lenormand and Cocteau which would justify the statement that he was influenced by the works of these two Frenchmen. When we come to analyze the reasons for the association of Villaurrutia's name with Jean Giraudoux's, the task becomes more complex. A superficial comparison does lead to the conclusion that the similarities are plentiful, and that, perhaps, Villaurrutia was, after all, the attentive pupil of Giraudoux, as Ángel Estivel has designated him.[9] But we cannot necessarily interpret these similarities as the result of the influence of Giraudoux.

Villaurrutia, like Giraudoux, utilizes the Electra figure. Giraudoux's *Electre* was presented in 1937; Villaurrutian characters who recall the Electra figure are Marta in *La mujer legítima* (1942) and Antonia of *El yerro candente* (1945). But while justice and uncompromising conscience are the themes of Giraudoux's work, Villaurrutia is more interested in exploring the psychological relationships among the characters. Another similarity in relation to characters is that both dramatists have created plays in which women are the chief protagonists and the forceful figures. In Giraudoux we find Judith, Electre, Alcmène, Lucile. Some of the outstanding female roles created by Villaurrutia are María Luisa, Teresa, Antonia, Carmen, and Irene. Yet, except for the Electra figures, the women do not resemble each other; we can attribute this similarity to the phenomenon of polygenesis.

The subject of the couple is also a recurring preoccupation in the works of both writers. The happy couple of Giraudoux's *Amphitryon trente-huit* (1929) and the adulterous pair of *Sodomme et Gommorrhe* (1943) represent the extremes with which Giraudoux envisioned the couple. In Villaurrutia we see the subject of the couple beginning with his first play, *Parece mentira,* and reappearing throughout his work until his last plays, *Juego peligroso* (1950) and *El solterón* (1954). Always, the couple is connected with the problem of adultery. More than Giraudoux, however, Villaurrutia presents the complication of the children involved in the problems of the couple, as we see in *El yerro candente, La mujer legítima,* and *Invitación a la muerte.* However, the presence of these subjects in the plays of both writers reflects their link to the larger literary context and cannot beconsidered as an example of influence.

A striking parallel between the two artists can be noted in their use of language. Most noticeable are the many examples of word play which are common to both. They reveal their wit not through situations but through a nimble juggling of the literal and figurative meanings of words.[10] In relation to this question of language, we should remember that before turning to drama, Villaurrutia had already revealed his literary style in his poetry. Villaurrutia's predilection for word play is characteristic of his poetry. Thus, we would say that as for style, the similarities between Giraudoux and Villaurrutia can be attributed to polygenesis. It would seem, then, that from the evidence available at this time,

Villaurrutia was attracted to the theatre of Giraudoux because they shared some of the same interests, but that Giraudoux did not exercise any direct influence. Perhaps we can say that Villaurrutia in Mexico was trying to follow the same path that Giraudoux paved in France: to create plays which were not mere after-dinner spectacles but were worthy of being considered literature and thus, to revitalize the state of the theatre. These were the aims of Jean Giraudoux and Xavier Villaurrutia.

In conclusion, these examples reveal that in relation to dramatic technique, Villaurrutia did enrich his work with the lessons he learned from his association with the avant-garde movement. His presentation of time and his dramatic use of objects link his name to Lenormand and Cocteau. While he apparently was not openly influenced by Giraudoux, that great renovator of the French theatre was perhaps a stimulus for Villaurrutia to continue his own important contribution to the Mexican theatre. For although Villaurrutia was an apt student of these dramatists, he was not only capable of absorbing their lessons but was able through his creative genius to produce an original theatre.

NOTES

[1] "Experimental Theatre: as a source," *Theatre Arts Monthly,* XXLL (August 1938), 607.

[2] *Hoy,* No. 727 (Jan. 27, 1951), p. 38.

[3] See Dámaso Alonso, "Tradition or Polygenesis," *M.H.R.A.,* No. 32 (November 1960), 17-34. Professor Alonso discusses the critical problem of influences with specific references to Spanish poetry, as well as offering important comments on the problem in general.

[4] Thomas Bishop, *Pirandello and the French Theater* (New York, 1960), p. 66. Henri-René Lenormand has been called one of the most important playwrights of the years 1919-1930 by Jacques Guicharnaud in *Modern French Theatre, from Giraudoux to Beckett* (New Haven, 1961), p. 6.

[5] "The Literary Art of Xavier Villaurrutia" (Ph.D. Dissertation, Yale University, 1953), p. 171.

[6] See Serge Radine, *Anouilh, Lenormand, Salacrou* (Geneva, 1951), p. 84; Paul Blanchart, *Le Théatre de Henri-René Lenormand* (Paris, 1947), p. 42.

[7] David Grossvogel, *The Self-Conscious Stage in Modern French Drama* (New York, 1958), p. 59, refers to Cocteau's "poetry of objects."

[8] The influence of Cocteau on the poetry of Villaurrutia has been noted by Alí Chumacero, "Prólogo," *Obras de Xavier Villaurrutia,* 2ª ed. (México, 1966), xix, and Elías Nandino, "La poesía de Xavier Villaurrutia," *Estaciones,* I, Núm. 4 (January 1956), 462.

9 "Opiniones escritas ex-profesamente para esta edición por los críticos teatrales de México," in *El solterón* by Xavier Villaurrutia (México, 1954), p. 41.

10 For an analysis of the style of Giraudoux, refer to Laurent LeSage, "Thecliché basis for some of the metaphors of Jean Giraudoux," *Modern Language Notes,* LVI (June 1941), 435-439; *Jean Giraudoux, His Life and Works* (Pennsylvania State College, 1959); *Jean Giraudoux's Use of Metaphor* (Urbana, 1940). Merlin Forster in *Los contemporáneos: 1920-1932* (México, 1964), refers to the frequent word play by Villaurrutia (see p. 87). Antonio Moreno in "Xavier Villaurrutia: the Development of his Theatre," *Hispania,* 43 (1960), mentions Villaurrutia's wit and his use of oxymorons (p. 513).

## Frank Dauster (essay date 1971)

SOURCE: "The Poetry," in *Xavier Villaurrutia,* Twayne Publishers, 1971, pp. 31-68.

[*In the following excerpt, Dauster chronicles the development of Villaurrutia's poetic style from* Reflections *and his earliest work to* Song to Spring *and the later poems.*]

Xavier Villaurrutia's poetic production was quantitatively slight: the "early poems" included in the collected works, **Reflections** (1926), the definitive edition of **Nostalgia of Death** (1946), and **Song to Spring** (1948). This restricted production was due to the fact that Villaurrutia was not, in spite of the verbal facility which characterizes much of his work, a facile poet. Writing was, for Villaurrutia, a long process of maturation of his thought until the moment of actual creation over which he had little control; he wrote, as he himself said, inevitably:

> It is not possible for me to tell myself: I am going to start writing!, it is necessary to abandon myself for a long time during which I go on maturing, crystallizing . . . an idea, until a moment arrives over which I have no control and I can say to myself: Now I *know* that I am going to write. That is, I write *inevitably,* that is the exact word!1

This is perfectly consistent with Villaurrutia's intellectual concept of poetry, a concept which has been radically misunderstood by critics who have seized upon Villaurrutia's 1927 definition of poetry as a "difficult game, of irony and intelligence."2 The error of interpreting this comment to mean that Villaurrutia regarded poetry exclusively as a passionless pastime (an error difficult to understand in anyone who has read the poems) is manifest when we consider Villaurrutia's further remarks in the interview quoted above.

> For me, poetry which is pure external game or delight of the senses has no meaning. The musicality of a verse, the beauty of certain words, do not speak to me at all when they are sought as the intent of poetry.3

The function of poetry, he goes on, is the expression of man's drama, and this drama must be, above all, authentic. Writing was, for Villaurrutia, a conscious intellectual act after a previous process of slow preparation, and the appeal of the finished poem was also intellectual: "if there exists a sentimental or emotional enjoyment, why can there not be any enjoyment of the idea?"4 "Poetry can be built with ideas, just as long as these appear as a function of authentic life and preoccupation."5

This intellectual concept of the nature of poetry clarifies much of what has been mistakenly considered Villaurrutia's excessive addiction to verbal trickery and, as we shall see later, is closely akin to his idea of the proper matter of poetry. It does not appear fully developed in the earliest work; rather, there is a process of development which falls naturally into three periods, corresponding to **Reflections** and the other early poems, the period which culminates in the definitive version of **Nostalgia of Death,** and the works written between 1946 and the poet's death. Chumacero has described these periods as being characterized respectively by an excessive reliance on trickery, by a progressive restriction of themes and a strict vigilance of the intellectual faculties, and, in the late work, by the dominance of the emotions over the intellect.6 While this last is perhaps an extreme statement and the earlier poems are much lesstricks than this would lead us to believe, there is a clear developmental progression through **Nostalgia of Death,** followed by a distinct shift in theme marked by a lessening of quality.

However, in stressing this intellectual theory of poetry and the role of the intellect in Villaurrutia's esthetic theory and actual creativity, we run the risk of ignoring an equally important element: his clear and direct debt to the Surrealists, Baudelaire, Nerval and, in general, the line of tortured solitary introspection which runs throughout these figures. Despite his intellectualism, his rigorous effort at control of subject matter, and his technical mastery, Villaurrutia is, in the best sense, a Romantic. His clear affinities with Heidegger, his thoughtful essay on Nerval, and his own words as he describes the moment of creation itself, testify to this relationship. Villaurrutia's demon may not have been orthodox, but demon it was.

### I REFLECTIONS AND THE EARLY POEMS

Villaurrutia's first published poems appeared in periodicals; the earliest known are from 1919. They betray a clear influence of González Martínez, whose influence is also visible, mixed with echoes of López Velarde, in works such as **"With a Humble Glance . . ."** (**"Con la mirada humilde . . . ,"** 1921). Generally, they are orthodox in style and content, with little indication of the highly original development which was to characterize the mature work. Their melancholy was probably rather more due to Villaurrutia's admitted reading of Samain, Jammes and other Symbolists, as well as López Velarde, whose vocabulary is clearly visible in several, than to any real personal commitment. **"Tarde"** (Evening), **"La**

**bondad de la vida"** (The Goodness of Life), **"Antes"** (Before), **"Bajo el sigilo de la luna"** (Beneath the Reserve of the Moon), **"En el agua dormida"** (In the Sleeping Water) have in common the humble pleasures of life, with lines such as "There is sweetness in the soul, and youth, and life, and perfume in the evening . . ."[7] or "A humble truth as rest,/ a peaceful silence, a loved book. . . ."[8] The same mood is expressed in amorous terms in **"Canción apasionada,"** (Passionate Song), which is far more nostalgic than passionate, or **"Lamentación de primavera"** (Spring Lament). This melancholy achieves greater profundity in poems such as **"Más que lento,"** (More Than Slow), in which the pressure of the beloved's hand confers tranquillity, but at the same time the young poet feels as though he is "in the aged chiaroscuro/ of a melancholy portrait. . . ."[9]

These poems are clearly more learned than profoundly felt; their melancholy wears the words of other poets. There are several, however, which are of greater importance. The two best are **"Ya mi súplica es llanto"** (Now My Plea Is Tears) and **"Ni la leve zozobra"** (Not the Slight Suffering), both of which bear the clear imprint of López Velarde's vocabulary, but are considerably less bookish and more tightly constructed than the others. The last stanza of the latter, particularly, achieves a tense, crabbed expression not unworthy of the model. Both poems express in religious terms a growing sense of estrangement, and it is significant that the plea for faith of the first and the grateful acceptance of this gift of the second, are the last specifically religious formulations of the poet's alienation for more than twenty-five years. Whatever personal religious beliefs he may have held, Villaurrutia's mature poetry demonstrates the opposite pole from this peace and acceptance. There is in few of these early works any real hint of the anguish and the concentration on death of the later poems, and the occasional appearance of such key later terms as "bedroom," the suggestion of the *Reflections* in **"Midnight,"** the conventional references to death, which are often remarked as antecedents, are hardly more than coincidental. Only in **"Presentimiento"** (Presentment), **"Canción"** (Song) or **"La visión de la Lluvia"** (The Vision of the Rain) do we find a suggestion of the anguish of *Nostalgia of Death.*

*Reflections* (1926) is a product of the vogue of "pure" poetry, and particularly Juan Ramón Jiménez' persistent efforts to arrive at a quintessential poetry, with the elimination of narrative, anecdote, and other supposedly nonpoetic factors. The volume consists of a series of brief lyrics, and as the title suggests, they are reflections of the external world, sensory impressions elevated to an abstract plane, in the poet's effort to create an objective portrait, withoutbeing personally involved in his creation. Eduardo Colín has pointed out how appropriate is the title to this fusion of painting and literature, in which life is "focused as in a picture . . . ,"[10] and Alberto R. Lopes calls the *Reflections* still lives in the style of Cezanne.[11] There is a good deal of truth in these observations; **"Aire"** (Air) is in large measure an objective portrait of the atmosphere and the tricks it plays on human perceptions of color, sound, and distance. **"Jardín"** (Garden) is a reflection of a spring garden, and **"Pueblo"** (Village) a portrait of a village left desolate when its inhabitants went off to fight. Indeed, three of the poems are entitled **"Cuadro"** (Portrait), **"Interior"** and **"Cezanne."** But the parallel should not be pushed too far, since the seeming objectivity of many of the poems does not hide a strong note of melancholy. In **"Sueño"** (Dream), the poet wonders whether the lovers will be joined in life as they were in the dream, and in **"Noche"** (Night), they are so stricken by the approaching separation that the moment of passion becomes a simple "Let us love, if you wish . . ." ("Gocemos, si quieres . . ."). At times, this melancholy becomes an overwhelming ennui; the world seen from a hilltop is a **"Puzzle"** not worth arranging. Or it is a colorless nothingness, a total lack of affirmation **"Incolor"** (Colorless). The melancholy becomes sharper as the sense of solitude grows, a solitude which overpowers as it follows from the eyes of the woman in the portrait **"Soledad"** (Solitude). The poet would flee the village "so that Sunday/ would come behind the train/ pursuing me . . ." (**"Sunday"**),[12] flee the silence which "has crumpled us,/ useless, in the corners" (**"Phonographs"**).[13] Just as these lines are a clear anticipation of the hallucinated flight of the nocturnes, in **"Amplificaciones"** (Amplifications) the silence becomes a living menace which predicts the horror of the later poems.

> And the silence moves
> and vibrates
> about the soft flame,
> like the wing—of what omen?
> of what insect?—which caresses,
> which cools, which diminishes.[14]

And the solitude grows about him.

> The solitude grows
> like the shadows
> on the sheet of the wall,
> like the faces of yesterday . . . [15]

The increasing importance of this theme even at this early stage is shown by Chumacero's affirmation that Villaurrutia's favorites from *Reflections* were **"Calles"** (Streets), **"Solitude," "Portrait,"** and **"Amplifications,"**[16] which are among those poems which most clearly foreshadow the steady emergence of the major themes of solitude and death.

Among the best of the *Reflections* are the eight brief lyrics of the **"Suite del insomnio"** (Insomniac's Suite), a group of haiku. Originally a Japanese verse form which appeared in the seventeenth century, the haiku are normally composed of three lines of five, seven, and five syllables, whose principal esthetic concentration is the effort to capture a momentary perception of significance or beauty. There have been at least two distinct waves of interest in the haiku in Mexico, among the Modernists and in the poetry of Tablada, and Villaurrutia's interest probably stems from the latter's use of the form, although

Juan Ramón Jiménez, who influenced virtually every member of Villaurrutia's generation during their formative years, cultivated forms which sometimes resemble the haiku closely. In any event, the rigid structure of the model was relaxed in Spanish to include two, three, or four lines of seven to nine syllables, although the insistence on pure imagery is retained.

**"Insomniac's Suite"** includes several poems which are haiku in almost the purest sense, such as **"Eco"** (Echo)— "Night plays with the noises/ copying them in her mirrors/ of sounds"[17] and **"Alba"** (Dawn)—"Slow and violet/ she puts rings under the glasses/ and the glance."[18] There is, however, in several, a furtheranticipation of the themes and techniques of *Nostalgia of Death*. The **"Tranvías"** (Streetcars) which "run mad/ with fire, fleeing/ from themselves,/ among the skeletons of the others/ immobile . . ."[19] are very nearly the germ of a nocturne, and there are technical devices which later play an important role, such as the transposition of terms in **"Lugares. I"** (Places. I):

> Let us go, unmoving, on a trip
> to see the evening of always
> with another glance,
> to see the glance of always
> with a different evening.
>
> Let us go, unmoving.[20]

This is not simple playing with words; it is not only the same old afternoon, it is the same old look. Both externally and internally, the poet finds the same lack of meaning; it is not accident that the word "empty" should occur so frequently throughout. Another typical note is the use in **"Phonographs"** of the following figure:

> And the heart,
> the heart of mica
> —without diastole or sistole—
> goes mad beneath the needle
> and bleeds its past in cries.[21]

Villaurrutia's frequent references to the heart have been referred to in the previous chapter, but here we have the first clear use of medical terminology, and the suffering evoked by the playing of the record is at least suggested to be equivalent to the suffering of a surgical operation.

The imagery of *Reflections* presents a remarkable insistence on concretion and depersonalization. The personality of others is "the metal of reflections . . .";[22] time is " . . . the metal of the instants. . . ."[23] Memory becomes a mirror of silence in which to survey the past (Air), and nude bodies take on the sheen of fine wood (Night). Moonlight is " . . . this white dust . . . ,"[24] the atmosphere a glass barrier between eyes and landscape (Air). Further, this process is reflected in the poet himself; his ear is the " . . . . shell of hearing . . . ,"[25] filled with " . . . silver echoes of water . . ."[26] (Air). His heart is mica (Phonographs), his voice a hidden record (Streets), and the memory of the departing lover is caught on " . . . the plate of my retina."[27]

There is also considerable use of inversion and antithesis. The nude bodies of **"Night"** take on the sheen of fine wood, but they also become opaque, and in the same poem, dawn is a bottomless pit, not of darkness but of light. The air which returns from a voyage " . . . full of golden heat/freezes . . . ,"[28] and of water the poet asks no more taste "than that it have no taste. . . ."[29]

These techniques, like the insistence on echoes, walls, mirrors, streets and other recurrent terms, are sometimes only hinted in *Reflections,* but they crystallize in the later volumes. The preoccupation with concrete materials and attributes as symbols of the poet's state of mind is a manifestation, or perhaps we should say an inversion, of his growing concern with questions which were to become the focus of *Nostalgia of Death*. An increasing sense of solitude led him to grope for symbols which demonstrated his union with external reality; at the same time, walls and mirrors began to reflect his alienation. The human beings become depersonalized, and the poet seems to communicate best with inanimate beings. As Jorge Cuesta pointed out, in Villaurrutia's preoccupation with external form in his search for identification, he became a mirror reflecting outward all that he perceived.[30]

Perhaps the most important poem of this period is **"Poesía"** (Poetry), written in 1927 just after the publication of *Reflections;* Villaurrutia has said that had it been completed in time, it should have appeared as the first poem in thevolume.[31] He called it the ars poetica of *Reflections,* and it is the only poem of its sort he wrote. In **"Poetry,"** Villaurrutia speaks to his art directly in terms which are startlingly close to those which he would later use to speak to his inseparable companion, Death. "You are the company with whom I speak/ suddenly, alone."[32] This is a poetry formed of "the words which emerge from silence . . . ,"[33] an introspective poetry formed more and more of the poet's internal world, a poetry which surges from the "tank of sleep in which I drown/ free until I awake."[34] It is obvious that despite the poet's statements, **"Poetry"** demonstrates a clear tendency away from the semiobjective poems of *Reflections* and toward the obsessive themes of *Nostalgia of Death*. Further, if Villaurrutia indeed felt that it represented his creative process during the period of the *Reflections,* it demonstrated the coherence of his esthetic, since it clearly represents the same approach as that expressed in the interview with José Luis Martínez some years later. In both instances, the poet quite clearly has no control over the act of creation; in **"Poetry,"** the poem gradually appears to him, even in sleep, until it is fully formed. Even admitting Villaurrutia's repeated stress on the role of the intellect in poetry and his undeniable control of the finished form, this is very close indeed to the Surrealists, and there is more than a hint of their automatic writing in the second verse.

> Your metallic hand
> hardens my hand's hurry
> and leads the pen
> which traces on the paper its shore.[35]

Curiously, the identical notion is applied to Death in one of the best of the later poems, **"Nocturno en que habla la muerte"** (Nocturne in Which Death Speaks). The similarity is heightened by the use in **"Poetry"** of a technical trick which characterizes many of the later works, and which is all but nonexistent in *Reflections*. This is paronomasia, or similarity of sounds, here exemplified by the repeated *oz* in "Tu voz, hoz de eco" ("Your voice, sickle of echo"), by the play between "por mil Argos" ("through a thousand Argos") and "por mí largos" ("long for me"). Another example is the repetition "sin más cara,/ sin máscara . . ." ("with no more face,/ without a mask"). To what extent this word play is a momentary surrender to automatic writing is impossible to determine, but that it is much more is undeniable, in spite of somewhat less than careful critics who have seen in these usages simple games, verbal and aural trickery. The extent to which they were in error in this and the extent to which such verbal deftness enriches some of Villaurrutia's finest work will be seen later, but even here it is obvious that he is not simply playing games. The function of paronomasia is to establish an illogical, rather than a logical, association. The voice of poetry is a sickle of echoes in that it resumes past experience, allusion and suggestion, all the multiple echoes which produce the poetic word. The "mil Argos—mí largos" paronyms have an obvious function; the reference is clearly to the Argonauts and their encounter with the one-eyed giant, Cyclops. The allusion to a personage whose chief identification is through his single staring eye reinforces the preceding "I am watching myself watch me" ("me estoy mirando mirarme"); the poet becomes transfixed by his own stare, and the seconds, understandably, become very long indeed. The same function is visible in "más cara—máscara"; he is left without pulse or voice or face, that is, without individuality, since this is conferred by the act of poetic creation. The poet exists as poet in function of his poem. But when this transpires, he is left too without his mask, reduced to the defenseless self.

**"Poetry"** is, then, remarkably close in both theme and technique to the later work. To what extent Villaurrutia consciously identified his fundamental theme with poetry and art, to what extent **"Nocturne in which death speaks"** may have been modeled on **"Poetry,"** we cannot say. It is clear, however, that they were somehow related for him, and **"Poetry"** proves for us that as early as 1927, when he had just published a volume which is usually considered to be totally different from his mature work, this identification of form and substance was already developed.

II QUEEN OF HEARTS

In 1928, Villaurrutia published **Queen of Hearts,** a brief prose narrative which is included here because its values are not those of the novel or novelette as we know them. Although he appears to have written others,[36] this is the only complete prose work extant. **Queen of Hearts** is a minor work, within a genre abandoned thereafter by the author, but it is of interest largely because of a number of lyrical passages which are virtually poetry arranged in prose form, and for its anticipation in embryonic form of themes which were not fully developed until the mature poetry and plays. Villaurrutia has clarified his purpose in an article published only recently. "The text of **Queen of Hearts** does not attempt to be that of a novel nor achieve anything more than what I proposed that it be; an interior monologue in which I followed the consciousness of a character during a precise real time and during a psychic time conditioned by the conscious reflections, by the emotions and by the real or invented dreams of the protagonist who, in spite of expressing himself in the first person, is not necessarily I. . . . At the same time, **Queen of Hearts** attempted to be an exercise in dynamic prose, prickly with metaphors, agile and light, like that which Giraudoux or, more modestly, Pierre Girard cultivated, like an image of the time in which it was written."[37]

**Queen of Hearts** is one of a series of experimental short novels written by the "Contemporáneos" during the late 1920's and early 1930's under the influence of Giraudoux, Proust, and possibly Joyce. These experimental works were a reaction to the mediocrity and vulgarity of the usual novel, sheer action and anecdote, to the flight toward Spain visible in the work of Alfonso Reyes, to the mannered interest in the colonial period which occupied many novelists.[38] It shows the same preoccupation with material substance which we have seen in *Reflections* and which is to become a constant technique in *Nostalgia of Death*. In description, there is a constant emphasis on specific detail, on exact shadings of color and exact properties of fabrics.

> . . . I look at the study draped in somber green.[39]
>
> The light . . . is tinted softly in the glass and in the curtains of light cretonne.[40]

There is the same concretion in the image.

> . . . a splendid day which you are to slice and enjoy like a ripe fruit. . . . [41]
>
> . . . that watery tunnel of the years, which can at last drown you. . . . [42]
>
> The sound of my steps comes out to meet me rejected by the walls.[43]

The plot of **Queen of Hearts** is so simple as to be tenuous. Julio, a Mexican student in the United States, has returned to Mexico for a holiday to visit his aunt and his barely remembered cousins Aurora and Susana. During the visit the aunt dies, and Julio leaves. This nearly transparent narrative is simply a frame for the themes, the virtual identity of Aurora and Susana. Although initially they are indistinguishable for him, he soon recognizes differences of personality which intrigue him greatly; where Aurora is reserved, Susana is highly emotional. Aurora is engaged to a man whom she does not love, and

Julio begins to fall in love with Susana, whether from preference or simply opportunity is not clear. His departure leaves the reader with only rapid impressions of two nearly identical personalities who perhaps hide beneath their similarities very different natures. Or perhaps these differences are the superficial level, and beneath they are indeed identical. This theme returns in *The Tragedy of Errors* in which Villaurrutia toys with the concept of identical twins of very different natures, and the sometimes crippling, sometimes ribald confusion to which their identical appearance leads.

Another antecedent of a later play is the scene in which Julio ventures into a funeral agency; the entire scene is an obvious early version of the setting for the play *Invitation to Death.* More important, however, is the death theme which is here more fully developed than in *Reflections.* Although not yet the seductively fatal mistress of *Death in Tenths,* death is present.

> It is not difficult to die. I had already died, in life, a few times. Everything depends on not making a single movement, on not saying a single word, on fixing one's eyes on a point, near, far. Above all, on not being distracted by a thousand things.[44]

This astonishing passage is part of a dream sequence which occupies more than a tenth of the story. In itself, it is a fascinating incursion into a region where perspectives are changed and familiar objects strangely altered. It may destroy what little narrative exists, and the limits of the dream are not entirely defined; the reader is never completely a part of the dream because he is left suspended between dream and reality. Nevertheless, in the passage quoted we find a clear anticipation of the major themes of the later work, and the closing of the passage is very close to being a poem in itself.

> Dying is equivalent to being nude, on a divan of ice, on a hot day, with one's thoughts directed to a single target which does not spin like the target of the ingenuous marksmen who lose their fortune at the fair. Dying is being happily out of communication with people and things, and looking at them as the lens of a camera must look, with exactitude and coldness. Dying is no more than becoming a perfect eye which looks without becoming emotional.[45]

III NOSTALGIA OF DEATH

Villaurrutia's highest poetic achievement was published in definitive form in 1946; it is a radical intensification of themes hinted at in the earlier work. The relatively objective reproduction of the external world has disappeared entirely, and the nostalgic loneliness is here a livid nightmare of anguished solitude. In the desperate lucidity of the night, the poet faces the horror of existence, a horror compounded of absolute isolation and the inevitable presence of death. Octavio Paz has described this work in a review of the 1938 edition as "his own death, which he cultivates like a terrible personal plot of land with the same passion and fever with which others construct their long ruinous lives . . . and on cultivating his death, his

like his love, like his solitary desire, he has cultivated his life, creating it there where his death dwells. . . . "[46]

The 1946 edition includes the three sections **"Nocturnos"** (Nocturnes), **"Otros nocturnos"** (Other Nocturnes), to which Chumacero has added the poem **"When the Evening"** ("Cuando la trade"), and a section entitled **"Nostalgias."** The first two are substantially alike and may logically be treated as the major portion of the work, while the last includes several poems rather different in spirit and the splendid sequence, **"Décima muerte"** (Death in Tenths). **"Nocturnes"** is preceded by a line from the sonnet sequence "Idea" of the Elizabethan poet, Michael Drayton (1563-1631): "Burned in a sea of ice, and drowned amidst a fire." It is significant that Villaurrutia chose such a baroque antithetical line, since, aside from his own predilection for such verses, this frustration raised to a metaphysical level, the despairing effort to express the inexpressible, is precisely what he here attempts. The world of *Nostalgia of Death* is a nocturnal world in which all that is real has vanished, and we are besieged by shadows, menacing figures, distorted shapes, in a universe gone mad. In this desperate solitude, the poet asks repeatedly who and what he is. Unable to establish meaningful contact with anyone, he doubts his own existence.

> And who among the shadows of a deserted street,
> in the wall, livid mirror of solitude,
> has not seen himself pass or come to meet
> and has not felt fear, anguish, mortal doubt?
>
> The fear of being only an empty body
> which someone, I myself or any other, can occupy,
> and the anguish of seeing oneself outside, living,
> and the doubt of being or not being reality.[47]
>                                                ("Fear Nocturne")

In the mystery of the night, the poet has become a disembodied intellect, unable to find one who might say to him, "I see you, ergo, you exist." Wherever he looks, he sees only himself reflected in walls, in the faces of passersby, until he doubts his own being. This theme is obsessive; in **"Nocturno grito"** (Cry Nocturne), he asks:

> Can that be my shadow
> disembodied, which passes?
> And mine the lost voice
> which goes setting fire to the street?[48]

Existence is, for Villaurrutia, this search for identification; even in his theater, as we shall see, a hallucinated flight through empty streets in search of meaning. **"Nocturno solo"** (Nocturne Alone) is almost a definition of this void.

> Solitude, boredom,
> vain profound silence,
> liquid shadow in which I sink,
> vacuum of the thought.[49]

In the last line, he completes the definition: "this invisible shipwreck."[50] The same theme is developed at greater length in **"Nocturno eterno"** (Eternal Nocturne), a description of the utter desolation of this life without life. When men shrug their shoulders and pass by, when a dust finer even than smoke adheres to the crystal of the voice, when the eyes close their windows which look into the rays of the prodigal sun (!) and prefer blindness to pardon and silence to the sob, it is the time when life. "or what we call thus uselessly . . ."[51] chooses death by drowning in alcohol or by fire in the snow. It is the moment when man makes the inevitable choice between a desperate hedonism and an even more desperate intellectualism. It is the moment when life longs to cease, when forgotten stars shine in a dead sky, when a sudden cry leaves behind a blinding silence which is more silent for having been broken. It is the moment when all has died, so slowly that one is afraid to make a sound for fear of hearing no answer. Man is afraid to answer the mute question lest he learn that he no longer exists, that the voice is only a memory in the throat, and night the eternal blindness of a living death.

> . . . because life silence skin and mouth
> and solitude memory sky and smoke
> are nothing but shadows of words
> which come to meet us in the night.[52]

The uninterrupted, unpunctuated series emphasizes the opaque, almost solid darkness through which the poet struggles.

The "Other Nocturnes" are in the same vein. **"Nocturno"** (Nocturne) describes the moment before sleep, the long awaited and yet feared moment before the dream becomes real and reality disappears.

> At last the night arrived to waken words
> alien, unused, one's own, vanished. . . . [53]

And becomes silent, and the senses are heightened.

> The slightest sound grows suddenly and, then,
> dies without agony.[54]

The poet sleeps and is drawn into the shadow of the dream.

> And it is useless to light a lamp at my side:
> the light makes deeper the mine of silence
> and through it I descend, unmoving, from
> myself.[55]

He sinks into the ancient ocean,

> . . . sea of an ancient dream,
> of a dream hollow and cold in which nothing now
> remains
> of the sea except the remains of a shipwreck of
> oblivions.[56]

This is the true significance of the dreams, for in them all the torment of the day lives a doubly hideous and yet compellingly attractive reality.

> Because the night drags on its low tide
> anguished memories, congealed fears,

> the thirst for something which, trembling, we
> drank one day,
> and the bitterness of what we no longer
> remember.[57]

Again, the repetition of symbol: the night is a pit into which the poet descends or a low tide choked with half-forgotten memories. These symbols and the constant disassociation of natural phenomena from the senses which normally perceive them are essential techniques in Villaurrutia's attempt to express the nightmare quality of his vision.

In **"Nocturno mar"** (Sea Nocturne), Villaurrutia uses the sea-motif to develop further his preoccupation with solipsism, the eternal and absolute solitude of the individual. The sea here is the poet's inability to break through the restrictions of his own personality, "the sea ancient Oedipus. . . ."[58] This curious and, given the basic themes of Villaurrutia's plays, certainly conscious equation of the Oedipus complex with the attempt to establish some kind of human relationship, is one of the few references to external, objective myth in the poems, although the plays are in their majority reassessments or reinterpretations of mythological or archetypal forms. In **"Sea Nocturne,"** at least in the womb, there is total identification with another, even though it requires complete submersion of the individual personality. The sea, thus, is simultaneously the whole ebb tide of detritus which seals us within our own psyches—the level on which it functions throughout the poem—and the only solution to the problem, abandonment of self—a secondary level of significance.

There is an unusual amount of alliteration in **"Sea Nocturne,"** frequently concentrated on harsher consonants; there is also a considerable use of paronomasia. Perhaps the most arresting portion of the poem, however, is the last verse, whose understatement underlines the despair of the previous verses. Recognizing the impossibility of any satisfactory resolution, the poet speaks of his agony almost tenderly.

> I carry it within me like remorse,
> alien sin and mysterious dream,
> and I soothe it and I lull it
> and I hide it and I care for it and I keep its
> secret.[59]

This solipsistic anguish is given a further dimension in **"Nocturno amor"** (Love Nocturne), the impossibility of maintaining more than momentary communication. The moment of passion over, the lovers lie quietly, each deep within the rigid confines of his own personality: "next to your body deader than dead/ which is your body no longer but only its void. . . ."[60] This is the form which love takes, after the spasmodic moment is irretrievably lost, in nearly all Villaurrutia's poetry. There is no longer any contact, and the lover's body is *hueco,* empty space, the hollow left behind, devoid of meaning. At the same time, reinforcing the dreadful realization of their inability to break down the walls between them, it is an *eco,* a memory of what can never be more than a fragmentary relief. Each is doomed, locked forever within his own mind, forever "the statue which wakes/ in the alcove of a world which has died."[61]

**"Nocturno de la alcoba"** (Nocturne of the Bedroom) fuses this solipsistic despair with the presence of death. Death is inherent in the form of the objects in theroom and raises a cold, crystalline wall between them; it is the hollow left by her body when she rises, another of Villaurrutia's obsessive metaphors of the double agony of the realization that for an instant they have almost broken the barrier. This love is not so much a physical or spiritual mating as a mutual desire to establish contact or at least to find that the other understands. It is *this* need which is unfulfilled, and they are left "more than alone and shipwrecked, /still more, and more each time, still."[62]

The only bitter possibility of identification is expressed in **"Estancias nocturnas"** (Nocturnal Stanzas). The poet wanders the streets of the "submerged city,"[63] awake and yet dreaming: "And I doubt! And I do not dare to wonder if the awakening from a dream or the dream is my life."[64] The echoes of his footsteps are perhaps only the echoes of other steps; perhaps his steps have no sound. Perhaps, even, there are no steps; perhaps he does not even exist.

> The fear of being only a shred of the dream
> of someone—of God?—who dreams of this bitter
>     world.
> The fear he may awaken, this someone—God?—
>     the lord
> of a dream forever longer and more profound.[65]

The fear is heightened by the double nature of the Spanish *sueño*, which may mean either sleep or dream, so that while the first line clearly expresses the poet's fear that he may be only the fragment of another's dream, in the last line this dream is simultaneously a deeper and even longer sleep, thus dooming the poet to an even deeper and unending anguish.

The stars, like the poet, are cold and dead, but they, at least, have the consolation that their light is visible still, while he can be only "dust in the dust and oblivion in the oblivion!"[66] Despairing, he grasps for the only shred of identification with another, in a direct allusion to González Martínez' *"Mañana los poetas"* (Tomorrow the Poets), completing the circle by identifying himself with the man he once called an impossible master.

> But someone, in the anguish of an empty night,
> without knowing it, he or I, someone not yet born
> will speak with my words his nocturnal agony.[67]

This is no Romantic search for immortality in the afterlife or in the consolation of the eternal cycle of matter. The poet can only hope for the anonymous immortality of the community of suffering.

These are intellectual preoccupations, a conscious investigation of a philosophical dilemma which distresses contemporary thinkers and creative artists. This interest has frequently caused Villaurrutia to be labeled an Existentialist. As we shall see, there is some community of interest, but such labeling fails to take into account certain vital differences. For Villaurrutia, this dilemma is an absorbing passion which blurs the distinction between modes of existence and which finds perhaps its higher expression in the area between sleeping and waking. Not only does he wander in a nightmarish nocturnal world; he becomes part of this world and exists in a realm where such distinctions have no meaning, where the normal guidelines of reality disappear. In **"Nocturno de la estatua"** (Nocturne of the Statue), one of his best poems, he dreams of a screaming statue which flees his approach. As he rounds a corner after it, he finds only the cry; when he attempts to capture the cry, he finds only the echo, and the effort to seize the echo results only in touching a wall, which in turn becomes an opaque mirror in which he sees only himself. This progression of decreasing concreteness and the confusion of sensory perceptions represent again the ceaseless failure to communicate, the utter isolation into which he has been led by reason and which, at the same time, bursts from his psyche as soon as logical controls are withdrawn. Waking or sleeping, each thing to which he turns disappears, and he finds only himself, the eternal and unique companion. When, at last, he finds the statue-assassinated-and gives it life by closing his eyes (for only in dreams can he hope to achieve his goal), she says to him, "I am dead tired."[68] This deliberate use of a popular cliché underlines the grotesque failure; even this dream companion is dying of the fatal malady, sleep. Theentire poem is represented in terms of a nightmare, of a voyage to hell, and sleep becomes both the medium of the search and the irremissible moment of total failure. It is for this reason that Villaurrutia called sleep "a daily provisional death . . .",[69] as we shall see, it is also closely linked with the second of the obsessive themes, the constant presence of death.

But these poems are not merely the record of a repeated nightmare; in wakefulness and sleep, and even in that timeless moment before sleeping, the moment which is neither sleep nor waking, the restless intellect sought the answers to the unanswerable questions. In **"Nocturno en que nada se oye"** (Nocturne in Which Nothing Is Heard), pure intellect, disembodied, records its thoughts in that instant when consciousness has abandoned the body, that "bloodless statue,"[70] to descend interminably, into the water which does not moisten, into the vitreous air, into the livid fire: metaphors of the movement of the mind through that realm where all its frighteningly familiar, yet terribly changed.

In this hallucinated world unspeakable terror lurks at every corner. **"Nocturno sueño"** (Dream Nocturne), suddenly, horribly, but only indirectly, the disembodied intellect meets its own body. In this tangential quality of the encounter resides the greatest horror, for whatever the consequences of coming face to face with one's self, it is at least a direct confrontation. Even this is forbidden: the poet hears the sounds of his own steps as they pass.

Suddenly, inexplicably, after the fashion of dreams, he holds a dagger.

> Without a drop of blood
> without sound or weight
> at my frozen feet
> my body fell.
>
> I took it in my arms
> I bore it to my bed.
>
> Sleep closed
> its profound wings.[71]

Physical and intellectual have met again, and once more the search has ended, temporarily, to be renewed in an incessant cycle.

Thus far, we have been concerned primarily with the first of Villaurrutia's obsessive themes, the anguish of absolute personal uniqueness and all that this uniqueness implies. The second major theme, which we encounter first in **"Dream Nocturne"** and which plays an increasingly important role thereafter, is the implacable presence of death.

In **"Nocturno muerto"** (Dead Nocturne), Villaurrutia describes with almost affectionate care each detail of the death which haunts him, from the first slow, tepid breath which will cling to him like the bandage to the wound to the final opaque solitude and ashen shadow. Although the emphasis here lies rather on the moment of death itself than on its previous presence, this is almost a hymn to death, which is awaited, if not with rejoicing, certainly with trembling and expectation. In this sense, it is clearly in the vein of **"Death in Tenths." "Nocturno en que habla la muerte"** (Nocturne in Which Death Speaks), written in 1935 while Villaurrutia was studying at the Yale Drama School, is the first clear statement of the concept of individual death which haunts the later poems, although, as we have seen, it has a direct antecedent in **"Poetry,"** written eight years earlier. Death is not here an abstract concept, nor is it the physical fact presented in **"Dead Nocturne";** instead, it is an almost concrete entity, which is the poet's alone. The first stanza, of thirty-five lines, really consists of two parts. The first is the voice of the poet as he reflects on the possibility of a *personal* death having accompanied him, not mentally or spiritually, but like a stowaway, "hidden in an empty spot of my clothing in the suitcase,/ in the pocket of one of my suits,/ between the pages of a book. . . ."[72] In the second part, he imagines the words of the personalized Death as she might speak to him:

> . . . Here I am.
> I have followed you like the shadow
> which it is impossible to leave behind at home;
> like a bit of air, calid and invisible
> mixed with the hard cold air you breathe;
> like the memory of what you most love. . . . [73]

Death is strangely near to being the beloved here, "what you most love. . . ." But this beloved is far more persis-

tent than any mortal woman, for the sea across which he fled is nothing, nor is the "dream in which you would like to believe you live/ without me, when I myself sketch it and erase it. . . ."[74] Almost tenderly, she concludes: "Here I am, don't you feel me?/ Open your eyes; close them, if you wish."[75] And in the last two brief verses, the poet is suddenly certain that she has come; a door closes in an empty room; a paper falls with no breeze to move it; there is a strange pulsation in his pen, and the words which are written are not his own.

This highly personal concept of Death as the inseparable companion, with its ambiguous love-fear attitude, is far from simple fear of the physical fact of dying or the Romantic despair before the extinguishing of the unique individual. Elías Nandino has suggested that death signified for Villaurrutia a return to the essence of the cosmos;[76] such a concept, however, seems much more true of Nandino's own work than of his friend. Rodolfo Usigli feels that it was rather the only stable reality in a world which was rapidly losing its sanity: "the return to death as to a piece of land, the only nontransferable, untouchable, inalienable. . . ."[77] Villaurrutia himself commented directly on his attitude toward death on several occasions, and these remarks underline both the immediacy and the ambiguity of his attitude.

> Modern man dies and attends—at least I attend—his own death. And . . . that of the rest. The *memento mori* and the *art of dying* are for me of an anguished immediacy.[78]

> Death is, for me, neither an end nor a bridge stretching toward another life, but a constant presence, a living and touching it second by second . . . a presence which surprises in pleasure and in pain.[79]

> Death is not, for me, only the end of life. Living to prepare for dying well or simply dying seem to me truths from which one more profound truth remains justifiably absent. Neither am I satisfied to consider life as a prison which we leave, at last, thanks to death. My poetry is the presence of death throughout all of life, since man lives his own death.[80]

> . . . At moments like those we now live, death is the only thing which cannot be taken from man; they can take away time, life, illusion, but death, who will take it from me? We carry death, as a poet said, within, as the fruit bears the seed. It accompanies us always, from birth, and our death grows with us. Death is also a fatherland to which one returns; that is why it is possible to have a book of verses called *Nostalgia of Death*. Nostalgia of what is already known. Death is something already known by man.[81]

These flat rejections of death as the end, whether from the religious or the nihilistic points of view, place Villaurrutia directly in the context of his clearly existential attitude. This in no way implies that he was a disciple of any particular existentialist philosopher—indeed, as we shall see, there are rather good grounds to believe that such is not at all the case—or that he received this concept of death from any one source. The search for influences on Villaurrutia's development of his theme has been badly overdone, and later we will attempt to show that he is well within his own national poetic tradition. He was an existentialist in the same sense that Antonio Machado, Quevedo, and many others are existentialists: they are preoccupied by the relationship of life to death as an organic part of the existential process in its fundamental sense, the process of existence.

*Nostalgia of Death* concludes with five poems grouped under the heading,"Nostalgias"; of these, all with the exception of **"Death in Tenths"** appeared in final form in the 1938 edition. **"North Carolina Blues"** seems strangely out of place; dedicated to Langston Hughes, it is an unfruitful effort to assimilate Hughes's jazz-influenced rhythms and is interesting only because of several unusually sensual images and Villaurrutia's concise comment on Jim Crowism.

> In different waiting rooms
> awaiting the same death
> the passengers of color
> and the whites, first-class.[82]

In the three **"Nostalgias"** properly speaking, Villaurrutia makes use of the explicit symbol, equating winter and snow directly to his own spiritual climate. **"Nostalgia de la nieve"** (Nostalgia of the Snow) is for Villaurrutia, a rare example of the emotional refusal to face the logical consequences of his poetic single-mindedness. There is a passionate yearning to return to a time when sleep did not mean a descent into a very personal hell, a heightening of the very faculties which make the day torture.

> . . . something of sweet sleep,
> of sleep without anguish,
> childlike, tender, light
> joy unremembered. . . . [83]

**"Cementerio en la nieve"** (Cemetery in the Snow) presents the comparison of a snow-covered cemetery with a corpse, even a corpse twice dead; the falling of the snow upon the cemetery is like the "fall of one silence upon another and of the white persistence of forgetfulness . . . ,"[84] like the silence of death falling upon the death-in-life which is the fate of man, condemned to think. However, the best of these poems by far is **"Muerte en el frio"** (Death in the Cold), which closely resembles the first of the nocturnes with its four parallel introductory lines;[85]

> When I have lost all faith in miracle . . .

> . . . when the winter sky is no more than the ash
> of something which burned many, many centuries
>     ago . . .

> . . . when I find myself so alone, so alone . . .

> . . . when I close my eyes thinking uselessly . . . [86]

The torture he suffers is "the cold hell . . . the eternal winter,"[87] another effective use of paronomasia in the yoking of hell-winter (*infierno-invierno*). In this bitter climate of the soul, the poet traces his inevitable fate in a spare style which progresses from setting of mood through despair to an almost stoic contemplation. The heightened perception of this moment of esthetic and intellectual concentration is reflected in a striking series of images:

> . . . I find myself so alone, so alone,
> that I search for myself in my room,
> as one searches, at times, for a lost object,
> a letter crumpled in the corner. . . .  [85]

In a stanza strikingly similar to some of the best of Neruda and Quevedo, perhaps the two greatest poets of death in Spanish, he sums up his anguish before the ineluctable fact.

> I feel that I am living here my death,
> my only present death,
> my death which I cannot share or weep,
> my death of which I shall never be consoled.[89]

In the last stanza, this intensely personal sense of loss gives way before an almost detached contemplation of the army of infinitesimal workers ceaselessly hammering on the "trembling lymph and flesh. . . ."[90]

> . . . how the water and the blood
> are once more the same marine water,
> and how first it freezes
> and then becomes glass
> and then hard marble
> until I am immobilized in the most anguished,
>     slowest time
> with the secret life, mute and imperceptible
> of the mineral, of the trunk, of the statue.[91]

Here, perhaps, is the true key to Villaurrutia's concrete imagery, to his use of adjectives which denote opaqueness and hardness, in this final moment when the body returns to the mineral of the earth.

**"Death in Tenths"** is an intense and ironic summing up, as though death and anguish had become such familiar figures that there was no longer any need for formality. It appeared in the 1938 edition of *Nostalgia of Death* as a sequence of five *décimas,* a verse form composed of ten lines of eight syllables each, with a normal rhyme scheme of *abbaaccddc;* the five in the 1938 edition appear as numbers 3, 4, 5, 6, and 10 of the definitive version, first published in 1941. Villaurrutia said of them, "I wrote the five remaining after a long and involuntary pause."[92] Formally, it is a sequence patterned on the sonnet sequence familiar to the Elizabethans and uses many of the conventions common to the sequence; the theme is again that of the personal and private death, expressed here on the double level of death the fact, and Death personalized. Thus, the ten *décimas* present a double emotional-intellectual complex, the poet's reaction to his own imminent and inevitable death and simultaneously, an allegory of Death as the Beloved.

The first stanza is a baroque meditation on the nature of his love in a series of linked antithetical constructions. This beloved, however, is no mere woman stooping to momentary folly, but the personification of death, not merely an intellectual concept or a physical fact, but an individual being who awakens in the poet a deep emotional reaction. At the same time, the obsession with solipsism returns in a brilliant parody of Descartes' *Cogito ergo sum;* the constant opposition between life and death is resolved in the substitution of *muero,* I die, for *cogito,* I think. The only proof of our existence is that it must cease to exist, and death, then, is our very being. In an ambivalence which lies behind much of Villaurrutia's poetry, he awaits death not without fear, but expectantly, even eagerly.

The second stanza is again parodic, this time of the Baroque technique which has been called "dispersion and recollection," the summary in the final verse of related elements scattered throughout the poem.[93] Here, this technique and the specific vocabulary of the stanza deliberately recall a number of Baroque sonnets, particularly Góngora's *"Mientras por competir con tu cabello"* (While to Rival Your Hair), with its final verse, "in earth, in dust, in smoke, in shadow, in nothing,"[94] and Sor Juana's *"Este que ves, engaño colorido"* (This You See, Colorful Deceit), with its summary, "is corpse, is dust, is shadow, is nothing."[95] This is hardly coincidental; these two magnificent poems are akin in their profound understanding of the relationship between life and death, and **"Death in Tenths"** is of the same family. At the same time, Villaurrutia's use of the four elements water-fire-dust-wind recalls Empedocles' four vital principles. They are equivalent to death, which is, then, the sovereign principle. Life is death, and to live is to die.

The third *décima* continues this semiparodic allusive mode; here, the source is the popular verse used by Lope de Vega and Saint Teresa, the famous "Come death so hidden/ that I do not feel you come."[96] The poet hopes that when Death arrives she will do so silently; he is willing and perhaps even eager to see her, but he would prefer the visit to be quiet and without advance notice. This is, of course, also a stock technique of the Elizabethan sonneteer, who often hoped for the same surprise visit in order to savor more fully the joy of the moment, and we see again Villaurrutia's significant use of what is essentially an erotic form to express his attitude toward death. The fourth stanza is again allusive in that it employs erotic imagery to express the union with death, just as Renaissance mystical poetry employed the same sort of imagery to express the union with God. This inversion of "poesía a lo divino" reflects the shift from the ironic, intellectual mode of the first verse to the total desire to take part in the final consummation, which is, in its own way, as much a mystical experience as the union with God, since for both Villaurrutia and the mystics, this union signified the ultimate experience, the perception of the final significance.

In the fifth stanza, Villaurrutia makes extended use of synesthesia, one of the most effective devices in the cre-

ation of this highly personalized phantomworld, to contrast strikingly the attributes of this fair lady without mercy, to those of the less striking, if less fatal, charms of the more orthodox mistress. Just as the Baroque structure is striking in its unexpectedness, so the reader is startled to find the mistress referred to as "your rigid body."[97] She becomes the incarnation of the principle of death, the principle before which love and life are erased. In the following stanza, Villaurrutia explores the temporal significance of this encounter, this fatal embrace beyond space and time, so far beyond all previous experience that it may even transcend its own limitations and, paradoxically, create a new zone of existence in which "it will be possible, perhaps,/ to live after having died."[98] This contrasts sharply with the return to erotic imagery in the seventh *décima,* which, while apparently describing the emotional impact of the sexual act, is actually anticipating the moment of death. In this parallel, the role of death becomes clear once more; from the cold dread induced by the first thought of her, through the agonized metaphysical speculation, to the longing which her constant presence has finally produced, she has emerged, not as abstraction, but as Death. She is no longer a metaphor; she is an enticing mistress. Thus, the eighth verse is a love poem to an absent mistress, that is to Death, *the* ultimate beloved. There is no nocturnal horror as the poet speaks of the extent to which she permeates his consciousness; he has abandoned such facile reactions for a more complex understanding. They are linked so indissolubly that even in her absence "I find you in the hollow/ of a form. . . ."[99]

But if Death is this personal and unique,

> what will be of you, Death
> when, as I leave the world,
> with the profound knot untied,
> you must abandon me?[100]

With this mocking challenge, Villaurrutia arrives at the final stanza. There is no fear of the beloved's arrival; in vain Death may menace him, for he has triumphed. In a concentration of bitter irony, he shows us again the true nature of this beloved and taunts her with the knowledge that he has already violated the hour of their meeting. In an existence whose only reality is death, "there is no hour in which I do not die!"[101]

**"Death in Tenths"** is one of Villaurrutia's finest poetic achievements in its purification of technique and the reduction of nonessentials in this very personal mode of expression. His rendezvous with Death and his willingness to recognize the need to abandon any thought of love as a mode of escape are a tribute to the personal and poetic integrity which he brought to the expression of his anguish.

IV STYLE AND TECHNIQUE IN NOSTALGIA OF DEATH

A number of critics have commented on Villaurrutia's predilection for visual and particularly tactual metaphors, to the point that Jorge Cuesta stated "The plasticity of his poetry is best adjusted to the equilibrium of forms, to the outline of objects, to the quality of the material employed, to the static nature of attitudes";[102] and, "poetry constructed in function of touch and sight."[103] The reader will recognize the truth of these statements; Villaurrutia's poetic vocabulary is composed predominantly of visual and tactual expressions. Further, certain key words are employed repeatedly: night, shadow, solitude, cold. What is perhaps unusual about *Nostalgia of Death* is the insistence with which the metaphoric vocabulary and the poetic technique are subordinated to this same insistence on the immediate, the concrete, or, to use one of Villaurrutia's favorite adjectives, the opaque nature of reality, as though the poet were almost able to glimpse the truth beyond the forms which pursued him.

There are two major aspects of this emphasis which deserve further comment: personification of the inanimate or abstract, and use of adjectives whose primary characteristic is their denotation of hardness. The former is almost constant: night "sketches with her hand/ of shadow . . . ,"[104] statues flee constantly through streets peopled by the harsh sound of silence, and so on. Death is a person who is able to secrete herself "in an empty spot of my clothing in the suitcase,/ in the pocket of one of my suits,/ between the pages of a book. . . ."[105] Silence and solitude are repeatedly referred to as "hard," *duro,* and even the lover's silence becomes "your silence hard crystal of hard rock. . . ."[106] Repeatedly, the poet's body becomes a frozen statue, alien to him, encountered at random or turning a corner. The function of these techniques seems clear; within the hallucinated world of his nocturnal search, the poet is besieged by the menace of death, not an abstract death but a specific and concrete threat. At the same time, his flight is persistently obstructed by objects, which prevent the human communication which is the only hope for escape. The progressive decorporalization in **"Nocturne of the Statue"** represents the fleeting nature of human contact, which ends, fatally and irrevocably, in the wall-mirror, the limits of human personality which prevent any meaningful human relationships. Totally enclosed by the hermetic oneness, besieged by death, the poet stumbles from one object to another, groping hopelessly for the touch of another hand in the "submerged city"[107] in a night which is "the sea of an ancient dream,/ of a cold and empty dream in which there now remains/ of the sea only the remains of a shipwreck of forgetfulness" (**"Nocturne"**).[108]

One of Villaurrutia's favorite technical devices has awakened frequent criticism because it has been misunderstood as simple playing with words, verbal and aural trickery. César Rodríguez Chicharro has carefully examined it in his "Disemia y paronomasia en la poesía de Xavier Villaurrutia"[109] and finds that the commonest forms of this device are disemia, double meaning of the same sound pattern, and paronomasia, use of words containing similar and different phonemes, or, more simply, the similarity of sounds between the words. It is curious that this device in Villaurrutia should awaken such an-

tipathy, since it is really one of the commonest manifestations of the baroque school of conceptism, the yoking of opposites to achieve paradoxical expression. Given Villaurrutia's well-known preference for Sor Juana Inés de la Cruz, who used such expressions extensively, and the use of the equally baroque quotation from Drayton, there seems no cause for surprise. Villaurrutia is, as Rodríguez Chicharro has pointed out, essentially a neobaroque poet. In addition to the systematic use of such ironic twists in **"Death in Tenths,"** Villaurrutia's poetry abounds in typically baroque antithetical expressions; curiously, these do not seem to have awakened any serious objection, although Arturo Torres Ríoseco refers to marble coldness and affirms that "a pallid smile of death plays on the poet's lips."[110] This seems a misunderstanding of the poet's attitude, and certainly Tomás Segovia is closer to the truth when he affirms that Villaurrutia is the most emotional of the "Contemporáneos" in his poetry.[111] There is no question of coldness, but rather of the need for a restrained ironic mode to control the volcanic theme which strained constantly against form.

In any case, it is not the baroque antithesis but rather the equally baroque use of identical or similar sound patterns with different meanings which has awakened opposition. The harshest criticism is reserved for lines such as the following, from **"Nocturne in Which Nothing Is Heard"**:

> . . . y mi voz que madura
> y mi voz quemadura
> y mi bosque madura
> y mi voz quema dura. . . .

These four lines are pronounced identically, although they mean four quite distinct things: "And my voice which matures,/ and my burning voice,/ and my mature forest,/ and my voice burns hard. . . ." Nor is this the only poem in which such phonetic trickery plays a major part; others are **"Eternal Nocturne"** and even the early **"Poetry."** In his *Ensayos sobre literatura latino-americana,* Torres Ríoseco refers to these lines as "exercises which, although ingenious, deprive the poem of intensity. . . ."[112] To represent these lines as simple word juggling is a serious misreading. Villaurrutia himself has commented on this: "I would never put in my poetry a single word without an exact sense or which was purely decorative. If I have used 'word games' it is because they have been necessary to express an idea. Furthermore, the 'word game' appears in Spanish poetry—in Lope, for example— although not with the frequency with which it exists in French poetry, and in English, where it is entirely common."[113] José Luis Martínez has explained their significance in a brilliant elucidation. He refers back to a previous line, "And in the anguished play of one mirror before another/ my voice falls . . . ,"[114] and calls this "a graphic and subtle means for representing the anguished rebounding of a voice fallen between the mutual and infinite reflection of two mirrors face to face, reproduced again and again, in their surface, in different tints represented by the play of the words which preserve identical phonemes."[115] These verses seem clearly to be an effort to reproduce the illusion of hearing one's own voice echo and re-echo precisely at the moment of losing consciousness, a phenomenon known to those who have been anesthetized. The same technique is employed a few lines later; the pertinent words are underlined:

> . . . here in the ear's shell
> the beating of a sea in which *I know nothing*
> in which *one does not swim. . . .*[116]

The poet hears the beating of his blood, a reference, of course, to the well-known children's game of listening to the sea in a seashell, which has the same general shape as the human ear. He interprets it as the beating of the sea, of which he knows nothing, for it is produced at the exact moment of losing consciousness, and is, furthermore, the very essence of his existence, the problem which he is attempting to solve. It is a sea in which one dare not swim, for it is a deadly sea which will be heard again when this daily provisional death is exchanged for the final and unique annihilation of consciousness. It has not, perhaps, been widely noted that the title of the poem is exactly the same sort of double meaning. Nothing is heard in both senses; all is silent, but the *nada*, ultimate nothingness personified, speaks clearly.

V SONG TO SPRING: THE LAST POEMS

Villaurrutia's last collection, *Song to Spring and Other Poems,* was published in 1948; it includes the title poem, which won first prize at the Mexico City Spring Festival in 1948, and nine others, several of which had previously appeared elsewhere. This last volume differs considerably from the poet's earlier work; most of the poems are love lyrics, although they are far from the conventional. The beloved is no longer death, but a mortal being, and the anguish of approaching annihilation is replaced by the despair of the disappointed lover. The change of emphasis is not quite crystallized, as though the poet's death had truncated the development of this new tendency. Just as **"Death in Tenths"** first appeared in unfinished form, **"Décimas of Our Love,"** the best poem in *Song to Spring,* was later published in a revised and incomparably better version. This would indicate that the period represented by the volume may never have attained its final expression.

All this hardly means that the volume is a failure. If it is less successful than *Nostalgia of Death,* the latter sustains a poetic tension not often achieved. The title poem is, despite its name, a hymn to despair. There are reminiscences of the adjectivization of the nocturnes, but there is considerably less of the striking imagery associated with the earlier poems. The first six stanzas represent the arrival of spring; it is a wave, a cloud appearing in the sky, the dream of earth. The second section is composed of four verses which present mankind's reaction. These two sections are particularly atypical in manner and content; they are also rather undistinguished. Even allowing for the possibility of deliberately pedes-

trian language for purpose of later contrast, such lines as "Because Spring Is a Cloud!" are a distinct shock in a poet whose detestation of stock imagery was well known.

The third section reveals the falsity of this ideal of regeneration, and we see spring in its true nature.

> The smile of the child
> who does not understand the world
> and finds it beautiful:
> of the child who does not yet know![117]

Spring is the whispered promise which awakens eyes and lips, the trembling hope which displaces anguish. What matter if the promise go unfulfilled, if the hope only postpone the inevitable disillusionment, for spring, *primavera,* is above all the first truth, the *primera verdad,* the transitory nature of man's happiness, which seems that it will endure forever and vanishes suddenly, "leaving no more trace/ than that left by the wing/ of a bird on the wind."[118] This last section of the poem is both more typical of the author and considerably better poetry. Villaurrutia does not succeed in making the first portion plausible; the bitter twist of his conception of spring's true meaning is more sincere and more convincing as poetry, but it lacks the compressed agony, the concentrated expression which raises *Nostalgia of Death* to such unusual poetic heights.

"Amor condusse noi ad una morte," which Chumacero has called the end of Villaurrutia's most intense period of poetic creativity,[119] was first published in the review *Taller* in 1939 and later included in *Death in Tenths and Other Poems* (1941). Rather than the end of the period of greatest intensity, it would seem rather to mark the beginning of a period of transition during which Villaurrutia was beginning the series of love poems represented by his last volume of poetry, while completing **"Death in Tenths"** and perfecting the final version of *Nostalgia of Death.* Chumacero also indicates the similarity in theme and tone between "Amor condusse noi ad una morte" and Salvador Novo's *"Amor"* (Love), from his collection *"Espejo"* (Mirror). Whatever influence Novo's poem may have exercised on Villaurrutia, the source of the title is verse 103 of Canto V of Dante's *Inferno;* the speakers are the ill-fated lovers Francesca and Paolo, killed by Francesca's husband and Paolo's brother Gianciotto when he surprised them in an adulterous affair. Dante's verse refers, of course, to both a physical and a spiritual death, their murder and subsequent damnation, while Villaurrutia's poem refers to the spiritual death of erotic despair, the mood of doubt about the beloved's faithfulness which sets the tone for most of the book. This beloved is not Death, but a living human who maintains the poet in a state of tormented suspense. The expression of this suspense is far more felicitous than the preceding poem; his love is "an anguish, a question,/ a suspenseful and luminous doubt."[120] He is totally absorbed by the beloved, anxious to learn every detail, and yet fearful of knowing.

> Love is the reconstruction, when you are far,
> of your steps, your silences, your words,

and trying to follow your thought
when at my side, at last immobile, you are
    silent.[121]

The mood and imagery are familiar, but the difference is unmistakable. What had been the effort to establish contact, to penetrate the shell of individuality, is now a lover's anxious effort to possess the beloved completely, mentally and spiritually as well as physically. And even here, he fails.

Love is not sleeping when in my bed
you dream between my arms which gird you,
and hating the dream in which, beneath your
    forehead,
perhaps in other arms you are abandoned.[122]

The cast of characters is the same, but the tragedy is now on a poetically lower level, if a more human one. Excellent poetry indeed, but it pales beside the hallucinated agony of the **"Nocturnes."**

This thirst for total possession of the beloved reappears in **"Soneto de la granada"** (Sonnet of the Pomegranate), with a note of desperate hope that he may find another to share this thirst and, in sharing, to slake it. This is almost a return to the despairing solipsism of the earlier poems; less anguished, perhaps, but equally powerful in its half-believed hope. The imagery marks an almost complete return; his flesh is again hard and cold in its isolation. **"Soneto de la esperanza"** (Sonnet of Hope) is in the same vein, analyzing love in terms of the lover's suffering as he awaits the beloved. His uncertainty drives him to the wish that he might change the nature of their love, captivating her with his thought alone.

The high point of this stage of Villaurrutia's poetry is found in the two poems **"Nuestro amor"** (Our Love) and **"Décimas de nuestro amor"** *(Décimas of Our Love)*. The former is an effort to express the physical and psychological bases of love, but this is hardly an idyll. Love, for Villaurrutia, was a total absorption, including every instant, every mental and physical phenomenon. Where in *Nostalgia of Death* love had been more a means of human contact than a state in itself, it is here of immediate significance, based not on happiness or even, apparently, a profound mutual attraction, but on a mutual anguish, as though at last, Villaurrutia had found one person capable of comprehending; it is almost a mutual effort at self-preservation.

    . . . if our love were not
like a tight thread
on which we go, we two
without a net above the abyss. . . . [123]

By its nature, this love is far more important than an ordinary affair; the lovers are united much more closely by their mutual agony than they could be by a mutual attraction. If their love were not this, if it were not a total fusion of this mutual despair, it could not be.

The three *décimas* included in *Song to Spring* are actually stanzas 2, 3, and 10 of **"Décimas of Our Love,"** which was published posthumously; it is one of the high points of this period and indicates a return to the manner of the **"Nocturnes."** Here is the same opaque compression of language, the same rigorous economy which is one of Villaurrutia's most effective qualities, but applied to the new theme. The anguish of these *décimas* springs not from contemplation of a death which, however personal, is not the here and now, but from a profound sentiment of bitter loss. The imagery has not changed; there is the same insistence on concrete metaphor.

    . . . the somber
cavern of my agony. . . . [124]

    . . . and when alone I invoke you,
in the dark stone I touch
your impassible company.[125]

My love for you did not die,
it goes on living in the cold,
unknown gallery
which it dug in my heart.[126]

There are the same baroque reminiscences of contrast and antithesis.

For the fear of loving me
as much as I love you,
you have preferred, rather,
to save yourself, losing me.[127]

There is a return to the despair of *Nostalgia of Death,* a return to the desolation of the knowledge of the utter vacuity of existence.

    . . . why do we not break
this painful and withered anguish
to leave this nothingness?[128]

    . . . I hear your voice in the echo
and I find your form in the emptiness
which you have left in the vacuum.[129]

These verses, identical in tone and style with the best of the nocturnes, can only cause us to ask whether Villaurrutia would not perhaps have returned to the spirit of his earlier work, or whether he would have gone on in the new direction indicated in the bulk of *Song to Spring*.

The remaining poems are of minor importance. **"Inventar la verdad"** (To Invent the Truth) is a conventional love lyric, interesting only because of the transformation of conventional diction by Villaurrutian imagery. **"Madrigal sombrío"** (Somber Madrigal) might almost be another stanza of **"Our Love,"** although lacking some of the latter's impact.

Included in this section in the complete works are several poems which did not appear in the 1948 edition. **"Deseo"** (Desire) and **"Palabra"** (Word) were written at some point before 1938 but were first published in 1953.[130] Curiously, **"Desire"** is a love poem close to the idiom of

"Our Love" and demonstrates that even as early as the first edition of *Nostalgia of Death,* Villaurrutia was experimenting in the new direction, while "Word" is a brief four-line stanza of no real significance. "Mar" (Sea) was published at the same time, but in the second edition of the works is included among the early poems, although in tone it is far closer to later works. It treats the sea as though it were human, a lover to be held tightly lest it, too, escape. This is an unusual poem in that it is one of the rare instances in which water retains for Villaurrutia its traditional symbolic significance of love and regeneration even here, and expectedly,

> . . . although I was yours, cold between your arms,
> your heat and your breath were in vain:
> I feel you ever less mine.[131]

The **"Soneto del temor a Dios"** (Sonnet of the Fear of God) was first published in 1950; it is a highly unusual work for Villaurrutia. If it were not for the title, the sonnet could well be another in the sequence of desolate love poems which preoccupied him at the time of his death, with an echo of the ambiguous attitude toward the beloved seen in **"Death in Tenths."** It is, however, possible to interpret the unnamed "you" of the poem as God, in view of the title, which would then cause us to read the sonnet as an effort to find some religious understanding and the failure of this attempt. It is also conceivable that the "Fear of God" of the title refers ironically to the poet's frustration at his inability to snare the beloved in his net of words. Whether God or the beloved—and, given Villaurrutia's motion of love, there is no real reason to discard the double intention—he is helpless.

> My fever to reach you is useless,
> while you who can do all
> do not come to be ensnared in my net.[132]

**"Epigramas de Boston"** (Boston Epigrams), published in 1949 in the review *Prometeus,* is a series of light ironic comments on a Boston which is both traditional and stylized, the Boston of George Apley, the Lowells, and the cod. Neither intent nor import is substantial.

Three further poems not included in the original edition (and in two cases, unpublished in book form) deserve rather more extended comment. **"Cuando la tarde . . ."** (When the Evening . . . ) was found among Villaurrutia's papers at hisdeath and was included by Chumacero in the section *Nostalgia of Death* of the collected works. The poem bears substantial similarities of style and vocabulary to the poems of this book, but its theme makes this attribution dubious. The basic metaphor of the poem is that of the dusty, ashen city from whose every cranny night creeps. However, it ends startlingly (for Villaurrutia) in that this lurking night brings, not the livid nightmare of always, but, simply, desire. The development of the poem is such that the reader anticipates the fatal slip into the renewed nightly small death, and the final climactic word is both unexpected and jarring. Given the return toward the end of Villaurrutia's life to the idiom of *Nostalgia of Death* for the expression of a theme which, if not precisely erotic, is rather closely allied, **"When the Evening . . ."** would seem rather to belong to the sequence represented by *Song of Spring* than to the earlier poems.

**"Estatua"** (Statue) was first published in the review *Los Sesenta* in 1963; its date of composition appears to be unknown. The poem is curious in that it describes a supposed statue, or more likely, an unnamed person who has succeeded in forging an impenetrable wall about himself, such that he is isolated from all others, finally and perfectly. The vocabulary is certainly that of the best nocturnes, but the sense of final acceptance, of resignation before the ultimate knowledge of absolute and irredeemable solitude, suggest that **"Statue"** may well have been a late poem, a step—perhaps the last?—in the swing back to the themes of *Nostalgia of Death.* This possibility is reinforced by Villaurrutia's last poem, **"Volver"** (Return), written just a few hours before his death and given to his close friend and physician, Elías Nandino; it was unpublished until 1960. **"Return"** is a compact expression of what must surely have preoccupied the poet during his last hours, particularly in view of Nandino's statement to this writer that he had shortly before warned Villaurrutia that he had a cardiac disturbance and that he should exercise caution. Instead, the poet attended a party at which he was his typical witty self, enjoyed himself enormously, danced extensively, and returned home to die. The poem is quite brief.

> Return to a distant fatherland,
> return to a forgotten fatherland,
> obscurely deformed
> by the exile in this land.
> To leave the air which encloses me!
> And anchor once again in the nothing.
> The night is my mother and my sister,
> the nothing is my distant land,
> the nothing full of silence,
> the nothing full of emptiness,
> the nothing without time or cold,
> the nothing in which nothing happens.[133]

This is certainly an extraordinary poem to have been written at that particular time under those particular conditions, although its significance in the poet's final hours can be only conjectured. In any case, the theme, the vocabulary, and even the totally typical verbal play between *destierro-tierra* (exile-land) and the two meanings of *nada,* "nothing," in the last line, place this poem squarely in the line of *Nostalgia of Death.* Even further, this is virtually a poetic statement of the theme of Villaurrutia's adaptation of *Hamlet,* **Invitation to Death,** written a number of years earlier, and it clearly suggests that the phase of *Song to Spring* was transitory and that the last few years of creation mark a gradual return to the expression of the obsessive themes of solitude and death.

*Song to Spring* concludes with two brief **"Epitaphs,"** the first of which is dedicated to J. C., almost certainly Jorge Cuesta, since it is virtually a definition of Cuesta's life and death. The second bears no identifying initials. It is perhaps not overly romantic a temptation to see in it Villaurrutia's own farewell.

> Here sleeps, silent and unknown,
> one who in life lived a thousand and one deaths.
> Do not wish to know of my past.
> Awakening is dying. Do not wake me![134]

NOTES

[1] "A mí no me es posible decir: ¡Voy a ponerme a escribir!, es preciso abandonarme por largo tiempo en el que voy madurando, cristalizando . . . una idea, hasta que llega un momento sobre el que no tengo ningún mandato y puedo decirme: ¡Ahora *sé* que voy a escribir! Es decir, escribo *inevitablemente,* ¡esa es la palabra exacta!" Quoted by José Luis Martínez, "Con Xavier Villaurrutia," *Tierra Nueva* (marzo-abril, 1940), 77.

[2] "Juego difícil, de ironía y de inteligencia." Quoted by Chumacero, *Obras,* p. xi.

[3] "Para mí no tiene sentido alguno la poesía que es puro juego exterior o encanto de los sentidos. La musicalidad de una estrofa, la belleza de ciertas palabras, no me llama en lo absoluto cuando se busca como intención de la poesía." Martínez, "Con Xavier Villaurrutia," p. 76.

[4] " . . . si existe un goce sentimental o emotivo, ¿por qué no puede haber un goce de la idea?" *Ibid.,* pp. 76-77.

[5] " . . . puede construirse con ideas la poesía, siempre que éstas se den en función de vida y preocupación auténticas." *Ibid.,* p. 80.

[6] *Obras,* xiv.

[7] "Dulzura hay en el alma, y juventud, y vida,/ y perfume en la tarde . . . ," "Tarde."

[8] "Una humilde verdad como descanso,/ un silencio apacible, un libro amado . . . ," "La bondad de la vida."

[9] " . . . en el claroscuro envejecido/ de un melancólico retrato. . . . "

[10] *Rasgos,* México, 1943, p. 130.

[11] "La poesía de Xavier Villaurrutia," *Memoria del Segundo Congreso Internacional de Catedráticos de Literatura Iberoamericana,* Los Angeles, 1940.

[12] " . . . para que el domingo/ fuera detrás del tren/ persiguiéndome . . . ," "Domingo."

[13] " . . . nos ha estrujado,/ inútiles, en los rincones," "Fonógrafos."

[14] Y el silencio se mueve
y vibra
en torno de la llama blanda,
como el ala—¿de qué presagio?,

¿de qué insecto?—que acaricia,
que enfría, que empequeñece.

[15] La soledad se agranda
como las sombras
en la sábana del muro,
como las caras de ayer. . . .

[16] *Obras,* xviii.

[17] "La noche juega con los ruidos/ copiándolos en sus espejos/ de sonidos."

[18] "Lenta y morada/ pone ojeras en los cristales/ y en la mirada."

[19] " . . . Corren locas/ de incendio, huyendo/ de sí mismas,/ entre losesqueletos de las otras/ inmóviles. . . ."

[20] Vámonos inmóviles de viaje
para ver la tarde de siempre
con otra mirada,
para ver la mirada de siempre
con distinta tarde.
Vámonos, inmóviles.

[21] Y el corazón,
el corazón de mica
—sin diástole ni sístole—
enloquece bajo la aguja
y sangra en gritos su pasado.

[22] " . . . el metal de los reflejos . . . ," "Reflejos."

[23] " . . . el metal de los instantes . . . ," "Reloj."

[24] " . . . este polvo blanco . . . ," "Noche."

[25] " . . . caracol de los oídos. . . ."

[26] " . . . ecos de plata de agua. . . ."

[27] " . . . la placa de mi retina," "Lugares-III."

[28] " . . . lleno de dorado calor/ se hiela . . . ," "Interior."

[29] " . . . que no tenga sabor . . . ," "Interior."

[30] *Antología de la poesía mexicana,* México, 1928, p. 20.

[31] Introductory note to *Décima muerte y otros poemas no coleccionados.*

[32] "Eres la compañía con quien hablo/ de pronto, a solas."

[33] "Las palabras que salen del silencio. . . ."

[34] "Tanque de sueño en que me ahogo/ libre hasta despertar."

[35] Tu mano metálica

endurece la prisa de mi mano
y conduce la pluma
que traza en el papel su litoral.

[36] See Enrique González Rojo, "Dama de Corazones," *Contemporáneos*, I, 3 (agosto 1928), 320.

[37] "El texto de *Dama de corazones* no pretende ser el de una novela ni alcanzar nada más de lo que me propuse que fuera: un monólogo interior en que seguía la consciencia de un personaje durante un tiempo real preciso, y durante un tiempo psíquico condicionado por las reflexiones conscientes, por las emociones y por los sueños reales o inventados del protagonista que, a pesar de expresarse en primera persona, no es necesariamente yo mismo. . . . *Dama de corazones* pretendía, a la vez, ser un ejercicio de prosa dinámica, erizada de metáforas, ágil y ligera, como la que, como una imagen del tiempo en que fue escrita, cultivaban Giraudoux o, más modestamente, Pierre Girard." "El relato. *Dama de corazones*. La novela," *Revista de Bellas Artes*, 7 (enero-febrero 1966), 19-20.

[38] See Rafael Solana, "Villaurrutia, prosista," *Hoy*, 725 (13 enero 1951), 46-47.

[39] . . . miro el cuarto de estudio tapizado de un verde sombrío. *Obras*, p. 573.

[40] La luz . . . se tamiza suavemente en los cristales y en las cortinas de ligeracretona. *Obras*, p. 574.

[41] . . . un día espléndido que habrás de partir y gustar como el fruto maduro. . . . *Obras*, p. 579.

[42] . . . ese túnel de agua de los años, que puede al fin ahogarte. . . . *Obras*, p. 582.

[43] El ruido de mis pasos me sale al encuentro rechazado por los muros. *Obras*, p. 591.

[44] No es difícil morir. Yo había muerto ya, en vida, algunas veces. Todo estriba en no hacer un solo movimiento, en no decir una sola palabra, en fijar los ojos en un punto, cerca, lejos. Sobre todo, en no distraerse en mil cosas. *Obras*, pp. 585-86.

[45] Morir equivale a estar desnudo, sobre un diván de hielo, en un día de calor, con los pensamientos dirigidos a un solo blanco que no gira como el blanco de los tiradores ingenuos que pierden su fortuna en las ferias. Morir es estar incomunicado felizmente de las personas y las cosas, y mirarlas como la lente de la cámara debe mirar, con exactitud y frialdad. Morir no es otra cosa que convertirse en un ojo perfecto que mira sin emocionarse. *Obras*, p. 586.

[46] "Cultura de la muerte," *Sur*, año VIII, 47 (agosto 1938), 82.

[47] ¿Y quién entre las sombras de una calle desierta

en el muro, lívido espejo de soledad,
no se ha visto pasar o venir a su encuentro
y no ha sentido miedo, angustia, duda mortal?
El miedo de no ser sino un cuerpo vacío
que alguien, yo mismo o cualquier otro, puede ocupar,
y la angustia de verse fuera de sí, viviendo,
y la duda de ser o no ser realidad.
(Nocturno miedo.)

[48] ¿Será mía aquella sombra
sin cuerpo que va pasando?
¿Y mía la voz perdida
que va la calle incendiando?

[49] Soledad, aburrimiento,
vano silencio profundo,
líquida sombra en que me hundo,
vacío del pensamiento.

[50] " . . . este naufragio invisible."

[51] " . . . o la que así llamamos inútilmente. . . ."

[52] . . . porque vida silencio piel y boca
y soledad recuerdo cielo y humo
nada son sino sombras de palabras
que nos salen al paso de la noche.

[53] Al fin llegó la noche a despertar palabras
ajenas, desusadas, propias, desvanecidas. . . .

[54] El más ligero ruido crece de pronto y, luego, muere sin agonía.

[55] Y es inútil que encienda a mi lado una lámpara:
la luz hace más honda la mina del silencio
y por ella desciendo, inmóvil, de mi mismo.

[56] . . . . mar de un sueño antiguo,
de un sueño hueco y frío en el que ya no queda
del mar sino los restos de un naufragio de olvidos.

[57] Porque la noche arrastra en su baja marea
memorias angustiosas, temores congelados,
la sed de algo que, trémulos, apuramos un día,
y la amargura de lo que ya no recordamos.

[58] " . . . el mar antiguo edipo. . . ."

[59] Lo llevo en mí como un remordimiento,
pecado ajeno y sueño misterioso,
y lo arrullo y lo duermo
y lo escondo y lo cuido y le guardo el secreto.

[60] . . . junto a tu cuerpo más muerto que muerto
que no es tu cuerpo ya sino su hueco. . . .

[61] " . . . la estatua que despierta/ en la alcoba de un mundo que ha muerto."

[62] " . . . más que solos y náufragos,/ todavía más, y cada vez más, todavía."

[63] "Ciudad sumergida. . . ."

[64] ¡Y dudo! Y no me atrevo a preguntarme si es
el despertar de un sueño o es un sueño mi vida.

[65] Miedo de no ser nada más que un jirón del sueño
de alguien—¿de Dios?—que sueña en este mundo
amargo.
Miedo de que despierte ese alguien—¿Dios?—el dueño
de un sueño cada vez más profundo y más largo.

[66] "¡ . . . polvo en el polvo y olvido en el olvido!"

[67] Pero alguien, en la angustia de una noche vacía,
sin saberlo él, ni yo, alguien que no ha nacido
dirá con mis palabras su nocturna agonía.

[68] "Estoy muerta de sueño."

[69] " . . . cotidiana muerte provisional . . . ," *Obras*, p. 684.

[70] "Estatua sin sangre. . . ."

[71] Sin gota de sangre
sin ruido ni peso
a mis pies clavados
vino a dar mi cuerpo.
Lo tomé en los brazos
lo llevé a mi lecho.
Cerraba las alas
profundas el sueño.

[72] " . . . escondida en un hueco de mi ropa en la maleta,/
en el bolsillo de uno de mis trajes,/ entre las páginas de
un libro. . . ."

[73] . . . Aquí estoy.
Te he seguido como la sombra
que no es posible dejar así no más en casa;
como un poco de aire cálido e invisible
mezclado al aire duro y frío que respiras;
como el recuerdo de lo que más quieres. . . .

[74] " . . . sueño en que quisieras creer que vives/ sin mí,
cuando yo misma lo dibujo y lo borro. . . ."

[75] "Aquí estoy, ¿no me sientes?/ Abre los ojos; ciérralos,
si quieres."

[76] "La poesía de Xavier Villaurrutia," *Estaciones,* Invierno
1956, p. 26.

[77] "Estética de la muerte," *El Universal* (3 nov. 1938), 3.

[78] "El hombre actual muere y asiste-al menos yo asisto-a
su propia muerte. Y . . . a la de los demás. El *memento
mori* y el *arte de morir* son para mí de una angustiosa
actualidad." "Contestación a la encuesta de *Romance*,"
*Romance,* I, 4 (15 marzo 1940), 2.

[79] "La muerte no es, para mí, ni fin, ni un puente tendido
hacia otra vida, sino una constante presencia, un vivirla

y palparla segundo a segundo . . . presencia que
sorprende en el placer y en el dolor." Martínez, "Con
Xavier Villaurrutia," 77.

[80] "La muerte no es, para mí, sólo el término de la vida.
El vivir para disponerse a bien morir o simplemente
morir me parecen verdades de las que una verdad más
profunda queda justificadamente ausente. Tampoco me
satisface considerar la vida como una prisión de la que
salimos, al fin, gracias a la muerte. Mi poesía es la
presencia de la muerte durante toda la vida, ya que el
hombre vive su propia muerte." Letter to Alfredo
Cardona Peña, quoted in *Semblanzas mexicanas*, México,
1955, p. 150.

[81] " . . . en momentos como los que ahora vivimos, la
muerte es lo único que no le pueden quitar al hombre; le
pueden quitar la fortuna, la vida, la ilusion, pero la
muerte, ¿quién me la a quitar? Si la muerte la llevamos,
como decía un poeta, dentro, como el fruto lleva la
semilla. Nos acompaña siempre, desde el nacimiento, y
nuestra muerte crece con nosotros. La muerte es también
una patria a la que se vuelve; por eso es posible que haya
un libro de versos que se llama *Nostalgia de la muerte.*
Nostalgia de lo ya conocido. La muerte es algo ya
conocido por el hombre." "La poesía," *Revista de Bellas
Artes,* 7 (enero-feb. 1966), 18.

[82] En diversas salas de espera
aguardan la misma muerte
los pasajeros de color
y los blancos, de primera.

[83] . . . algo de dulce sueño,
de sueño sin angustia,
infantil, tierno, leve
goce no recordado. . . .

[84] " . . . caída de un silencio sobre otro/ y de la blanca
persistencia del olvido. . . ."

[85] Villaurrutia's use of the term "nocturne" for many of
his poems does not correspond to any particular formal
structure or thematic mode; many of his poems which
bear other titles could just as well have been called nocturnes. Why he chose to call this particular section
"Nostalgias" is difficult to determine, except that all but
"Death in Tenths" are marked by a non-Mexican geographical setting: North Carolina, snow.

[86] Cuando he perdido toda fe en el milagro . . .
. . . cuando el cielo de invierno no es más que la ceniza
de algo que ardió hace muchos siglos . . .
. . . cuando me encuentro tan solo, tan solo . . .
. . . cuando cierro los ojos pensando inútilmente . . .

[87] " . . . el infierno frío, . . . el eterno invierno. . . ."

[88] . . . me encuentro tan sólo, tan sólo,
que me busco en mi cuarto
como se busca, a veces, un objeto perdido,

una carta estrujada en los rincones. . . .

[89] Siento que estoy viviendo aquí mi muerte,
mi sola muerte presente,
mi muerte que no puedo compartir ni llorar,
mi muerte de que no me consolaré jamás.

[90] " . . . mi linfa y mi carne estremecidas. . . ."

[91] . . . cómo el agua y la sangre
son otra vez la misma agua marina,
y cómo se hiela primero
y luego se vuelve cristal
y luego duro mármol,
hasta inmovilizarme en el tiempo más angustioso y lento,
con la vida secreta, muda e imperceptible
del mineral, del tronco, de la estatua.

[92] "Escribí las cinco restantes después de una involuntaria y larga pausa," *Décima muerte y otros poemas no coleccionados,* note.

[93] Recently a number of critics have examined the use and scope of this and related techniques. See, for example, Dámaso Alonso, *Poesía española. Ensayo de métodos y límites estilísticos,* especially his chapter "Lope de Vega, símbolo del barroco."

[94] " . . . en tierra, en polvo, en humo, en sombra, en nada."

[95] " . . . es cadáver, es polvo, es sombra, es nada."

[96] "Ven muerte tan escondida/ que no te sienta venir."

[97] "tu cuerpo yerto."

[98] " . . . será posible, acaso,/ vivir después de haber muerto."

[99] " . . . te encuentro en el hueco/ de una forma. . . ."

[100] ¿qué será, Muerte, de ti
cuando al salir yo del mundo,
deshecho el nudo profundo,
tengas que salir de mí?

[101] " . . . no hay hora en que yo no muera!"

[102] "Lo plástico de su poesía se ajusta mejor al equilibrio de las formas, al dibujo de los objetos, a la calidad de la materia empleada, a la estática de las actitudes." *Antología de la poesía mexicana moderna,* p. 203.

[103] " . . . poesía construida en función del tacto y la vista." *Ibid.*

[104] " . . . dibuja con su mano/ de sombra . . . ," "Noche."

[105] " . . . en un hueco de mi ropa en la maleta,/ en el bolsillo de uno de mis trajes,/ entre las páginas de un libro . . . ," "Nocturno en que habla la muerte."

[106] " . . . tu silencio duro cristal de dura roca . . . ," "Nocturno mar."

[107] " . . . ciudad sumergida . . . ," "Estancias nocturnas."

[108] " . . . el mar de un sueño antiguo,/ de un sueño hueco y frío en el que ya no queda/ del mar sino los restos de un naufragio de olvidos," "Nocturno."

[109] *La Palabra y el Hombre,* abril-junio, 1964. See also his "Correlación yparalelismo en la poesía de Xavier Villaurrutia," *La Palabra y el Hombre* (enero-marzo 1966), 81-90.

[110] " . . . una pálida sonrisa de muerte juguetea en los labios del poeta." "Tres poetas mexicanos," *Revista Iberoamericana,* I, 1 (mayo 1939), 86.

[111] "Villaurrutia desde aquí," *Nivel,* 36, 25 dic. 1961.

[112] " . . . ejercicios que aunque ingeniosos, restan intensidad al poema . . . ," Berkeley-Los Angeles, 1953, p. 205.

[113] "Nunca pondría en mi poesía una sola palabra sin un sentido exacto o bien que fuera puramente decorativa. Si he usado de los 'juegos de palabras' es porque han sido precisos para expresar con ellos alguna idea. Por otra parte, el 'juego de palabras' aparece ya en la poesía española—en Lope, por ejemplo—aunque no con la frecuencia con que existe en la poesía francesa y en la inglesa, donde es enteramente común." "La poesía," *Revista de Bellas Artes,* 7 (enero-febrero 1966), 18.

[114] "Y en el juego angustioso de un espejo frente a otro/ cae mi voz. . . ."

[115] " . . . un medio gráfico y sutil para representar el rebote angustioso de una voz caída entre el mutuo e infinito reflejo de un espejo frente a otro, reproducido una vez y otra vez, en su superficie, en diferentes matices representados por el juego de las palabras que conservan idénticos fonemas." "Con Xavier Villaurrutia," 79.

[116] . . . aquí en el caracol de la oreja
el latido de un mar en el que *no sé nada*
en el que *no se nada.* . . .

[117] La sonrisa del niño
que no comprende al mundo
y que lo encuentra hermoso:
¡del niño que no sabe todavía!

[118] " . . . sin dejar otra huella/ que la que deja el ala/ de un pájaro en el viento."

[119] *Obras,* p. xx.

[120] " . . . una angustia, una pregunta,/ una suspensa y luminosa duda."

[121] Amar es reconstruir, cuando te alejas,

tus pasos, tus silencios, tus palabras,
y pretender seguir tu pensamiento
cuando a mi lado, al fin inmóvil, callas.

122 Amar es no dormir cuando en mi lecho
sueñas entre mis brazos que te ciñen,
y odiar el sueño en que, bajo tu frente,
acaso en otros brazos te abandonas.

123 . . . si nuestro amor no fuera
como un hilo tendido
en que vamos los dos
sin red sobre el vacío. . . .

124 . . . la sombría
caverna de mi agonía . . .

125 . . . y cuando a solas te invoco
en la oscura piedra toco
tu impasible compañía.

126 Mi amor por ti, ¡no murió!
sigue viviendo en la fría,
ignorada galería
que en mi corazón cavó.

127 Por el temor de quereme
tanto como yo te quiero,
has preferido, primero,
para salvarte, perderme.

128 . . . ¿por qué, dolorosa y mustia,
no rompemos la angustia
para salir de la nada?

129 . . . oigo tu voz en el eco
y hallo tu forma en el hueco
que has dejado en el vacío.

130 *Summa,* no. 1, julio 1953.

131 . . . aunque fui tuyo, entre tus brazos frío,
tu calor y tu aliento fueron vanos:
cada vez más te siento menos mío.

132 Es inútil mi fiebre de alcanzarte,
mientras tú mismo que todo lo puedes
no vengas en mis redes a enredarte.

133 Volver a una patria lejana,
volver a una patria olvidada,
oscuramente deformada
por el destierro en esta tierra.
¡Salir del aire que me encierra!
Y anclar otra vez en la nada.
La noche es mi madre y mi hermana,
la nada es mi patria lejana,
la nada llena de silencio,
la nada llena de vacío,
la nada sin tiempo ni frío,
la nada en que no pasa nada.

134 Duerme aquí, silencioso e ignorado,
el que en vida vivió mil y una muertes.
Nada quieras saber de mi pasado.
Despertar es morir. ¡No me despiertes!

### Sandra M. Cypess (essay date 1972)

SOURCE: "The Function of Myth in the Plays of Xavier Villaurrutia," in *Hispania,* Vol. 55, No. 2, May, 1972, pp. 256-63.

[*In the following essay, Cypess explores the classical roots of the imagery employed by Villaurrutia in his dramatic works.*]

As a dramatist, Xavier Villaurrutia has been classified *universalista* and *afrancesado* but rarely *mexicano,* despite the fact that his efforts were directed toward the creation of a Mexican theatrical tradition.[1] It is true that in the plays of his first period—one-acters all given as part of the experimental theater movements of the thirties—he made no attempt to represent scenes from contemporary or historical Mexico. These plays did not allude to historical or literary figures or typical Mexican characters with whom the audience could identify. Instead, Villaurrutia was involved in making general statements on the themes of love, truth, illusion and reality, and in practicing the techniques he had learned from the dramatists of the avant-garde movements outside Mexico.[2]

The Villaurrutia of this first period was not a popular playwright; his works were not attuned to the preferences of the commercial theater.[3] Also, there were those who criticized his plays for their "anti-nationalist" flavor. In his second period—the plays of the forties which were three-act works—Villaurrutia appeared to have answered some of this criticism. All these plays specify a temporal and physical setting of contemporary Mexico and are peopled with middle-class Mexicans with family or amorous problems.

In commenting on this change, Antonio Moreno has said of Villaurrutia: "To him the welfare of the Mexican theater was of prime importance, and if it meant changing his style to one treating the real issues of the people in order to help create a larger theater-going public, then that's exactly what he would do."[4] While it is true that in these three-act plays Villaurrutia appears to have forsaken the avant-garde techniques and the attempts at universality, it will be seen that he has not forgotten the lessons learned in association with the experimental theater. In five of the six plays of this period Villaurrutia uses literary or Greek mythological references. An examination of these plays will reveal that Villaurrutia has transcended a national environment by introducing these allusions to classical theater. His desire to create a Mexican theatrical tradition was not forgotten in this second period despite the more realistic and commercial nature of these plays.

The use of ancient myths and legends among twentieth century dramatists has been a widespread device and one that has gained critical attention. Yet, in Mexico, Villaurrutia alone of the young men involved in the avant-garde movement, seems to have successfully applied the use of classical myth to his dramaturgy.[5] In the four plays under discussion here, the characters are products of contemporary Mexico at the same time they recall figures from the classical theater.[6] This pattern is a conscious and deliberate esthetic decision whose function is the purpose of this inquiry.

Critics have been quick to point out the allusions, for they are not obscure. In the first play, *Invitación a la muerte,* the characterization of Alberto and his family circumstances recalls the situation of Orestes. *La hiedra* is based on the Phaedra-Hippolytus myth. The female protagonists of both *La mujer legítima* and *El yerro candente* have been called Electra figures. These plays, however, are not thinly disguised parallels of the myths in which these classical figures appear, in the manner of O'Neill's *Mourning Becomes Electra* or even Cocteau's *Orphée*. Rather, descriptions of the plays reveal that Villaurrutia adapted certain features of characterization or situation to form the nucleus of his own individual works.

In *Invitación a la muerte,* Villaurrutia creates a variation of what is to become a recurrent family situation in his plays. Because one parent is absent, a conflict exists among a child, the remaining parent, and an intruder who attempts to replace the missing parent, a conflict with marked similarities to the legend of Orestes and Electra. In this first play, Villaurrutia focuses on the absence of the father and the son's reaction to this loss, thereby equating Alberto with Orestes. It should be noted also that Frank Dauster has already considered the many similarities between Alberto and Hamlet and the two plays in which these characters appear.[7] In this present discussion of classical references, I have taken this comparison one step further, to the Orestes figure, following Gilbert Murray who identified Hamlet with Orestes in his essay "Hamlet and Orestes," in *The Classical Tradition* (Cambridge: Harvard University Press, 1927), pp. 205-40. Alberto, however, is not a prince of noble blood as Orestes (or Hamlet), but the son of a businessman. Villaurrutia has thus made his hero a middle-class "prince"—the heir to a funeral home founded by his father. Alberto's father has not been murdered like Agamemnon (or Hamlet the King), but instead has mysteriously disappeared. In the ten-year absence of her husband, Alberto's mother, like Clytemnestra, has maintained a liaison with her lover, a man Alberto hates. Alberto, however, cannot definitely blame his mother and her lover for provoking his father's disappearance. Alberto's motivation throughout the play is not to seek revenge for his father's death, but to try to understand his father's disappearance and, in turn, to understand himself. The blow to his psyche caused by his father's inexplicable absence is as devastating as the discovery by Orestes (or Hamlet) of the unjust and evil circumstances of his father's death.

The adolescent years of Alberto are disturbed, like those of Orestes, because of his father's absence. Alberto is characterized as a solitary, unsociable figure, who indulges freely in soliloquies. He is also on the verge of madness. He becomes unbalanced after seeing, or believing to see, the return of his father. While Orestes' father returns as a vision or in dreams (and Hamlet sees his father's ghost), Alberto at the end of act one appears to have also seen a vision of his father. While Orestes becomes mad as a result of the murders he has to commit (and Hamlet feigns madness), Alberto immediately undergoes a severe physical and mental crisis. He acts like a man possessed: "por un momento la razón parecía huir para siempre de Alberto."[8]

In addition to being under the shadow of madness, Alberto is characterized as suffering from another fault. If we were to consider the *hamartia* of Alberto's character, we would see that he is subject to paralyzing doubts and hesitations. His doctor describes him as "un joven complicado, moderno, comido por preocupaciones y por interrogaciones" (p. 371). This aspect of his character is dramatized fully in the scene where Alberto finally meets his father, not as a vision, but in the flesh. Alberto hesitates to reach out and recognize the man as his father. Their scene together, the penultimate in the play, is the climax of their ten-year search. Alberto had been longing all that time to reunite with his father, just as his father had never been able to forget the thought of the son he had left behind. This scene of constrained passion, of ignored anagnorisis, is the climax of the play. It reveals Alberto's inability to act positively as he retreats back into the shadows of non-action. Although he is finally convinced, with the help of his friend Horacio, that he should recognize his father, he acts too late to find him. This scene recalls Euripides' *Electra,* where Orestes hesitates before he is convinced by Electra to murder his mother. Orestes finally kills his mother. Alberto emotionally cripples both his father and himself by not finding his father in time. Alberto, left in isolation in the funeral home, is surrounded by elements of death. Although no one has been physically killed in the play, Alberto has forfeited a role in life and answered instead the invitation to death: "estoy aquí en este ambiente, dentro de estas paredes, rodeado por estos muebles y por estos objetos que son la imagen o la compañía de la muerte, porque la muerte es mi elemento, como el agua al pez . . ." (p. 402).

In the second play the title both alludes to the mythic source and conditions the audience to this frame of reference. *La hiedra,* is also the image used to characterize the Phaedra figure, Teresa. In addition, her step-son is called Hipólito, his girl friend, Alicia.[9] Dauster has commented that Villaurrutia probably changed the name of his Phaedra to Teresa because Phaedra is not a common Spanish name.[10] While this may be true about the name, that reason did not inhibit another Spanish interpreter of this myth. Miguel de Unamuno called his play *Fedra,* retaining only the names of Fedra and Hipólito from the traditional persons associated with the story.[11] Perhaps it was because of Unamuno's work that Villaurrutia did not wish to use the name Fedra and call to mind this Spanish play at a time when he was attempting to dissociate the Mexican theater from the Spanish tradition. There is, however, an additional reason to justify why Villaurrutia called his chief protagonist Teresa. The literary reason for the name, to be explained in the course of this discussion, is as meaningful as his choice of title. Dauster has explained the importance of the title: "Lo importante aquí es que la obra se llama *La hiedra,* que aconsonanta con Fedra. Y nada de juegos vacíos. La hiedra encuentra tanto apoyo como nutrición en otras plantas: es, pues, símbolo del personaje central. A la vez, la hiedra es flor de la fidelidad eterna. Asi, el autor quiso señalar, en el título de la obra, el tema, y el carácter de la protagonista mientras añade un comentario irónico."[12]

The next allusion to the myth is presented in the first scene. The housekeeper and a female servant, performing as a Greek chorus in their expository function, are discussing the expected return of Hipólito, now a young man of twenty-five. Hipólito has been away from his home since he was twelve, and has returned now as a result of his father's death. The conversation between the two women revealsthat Teresa is not Hipólito's mother, but his step-mother. Teresa, unlike the Phaedra of Euripides or Racine, is sterile, without hopes of having a child of her own.[13] Therefore, it appears that to Teresa, at least, Hipólito is a fulfillment of her own desire for a child. The young maid says, for example, "La señora habla como si el niño Hipólito fuera su hijo" (p. 256). Villaurrutia, then, while causing his audience to remember the mythic tradition of Hippolytus and Phaedra, creates his own relationships among the characters.

The major problem for Teresa does not involve a conflict between her love for Hipólito contrasted with her responsibility towards her husband; Teresa's husband is dead, and not just missing as in Racine's *Phaedra.* Rather, the conflict within her involves her changing attitude towards Hipólito. She had always wanted his love, as a mother wants the love of her child. Hipólito, however, had always considered her an intruder in the family. Ironically he does begin to love her now, not as a mother, but as a woman he wants to marry. When Alicia, who wants to marry Hipólito, refers to Teresa as his mother, he emphatically declares, "Teresa no es mi madre. . . . No puedo pensar en ella de ese modo" (p. 282).

Hipólito is caught in a triangle of his own making. He previously inferred that he would marry Alicia before realizing his love for Teresa. Teresa does momentarily reach out to accept the love he offers her. It is in her nature, like the *hiedra,* to search for someone to cling to. The conflict between the two loves—the maternal and the sexual—reaches its culmination when Teresa discovers that Alicia is expecting a child fathered by Hipólito. With the help of Ernesto, who has been said to fulfill the function of the chorus,[14] Teresa realizes her true responsibilities. She cannot leave her dead husband's house, for she is rooted to all that it represents. Instead of escaping with Hipólito, she tells him to leave without her: "Tu vida está fuera de aquí. No la mía. No puedo pensarme siquiera fuera de aquí, de estos muros, de estos objetos, de estas alfombras donde he echado raíces, ya para siempre. Para ti, aún es tiempo. ¡Vete!" (p. 313). There is the implication that if Hipólito were to remain with her, he would be creating an Oedipus situation.[15]

It is interesting to note, too, that Teresa, like Racine's Theseus, has been betrayed by Hipólito in his relationship with Alicia. Racine's Hippolytus tells Theseus that his true offense is his love for Aricia, the sister of Theseus' worst enemy. For Villaurrutia, Phaedra also takes on the role of Theseus in this relation to Hippolytus. Alicia, like Aricia to Theseus, has been one of Teresa's enemies, plotting with her mother to alienate Hipólito from Teresa. Hipólito's interest in Alicia, then, is a betrayal of his love for Teresa. Fathering Alicia's illegitimate child is perhaps his greatest betrayal for he has given to Alicia a child that he is denying to Teresa by refusing to accept the latter's maternal love. It is in order to imply this dual role, as both a Phaedra and a Theseus, which may explain why Villaurrutia has chosen to call his protagonist Teresa.

The ironic handling of the triangle of Alicia-Hipólito-Teresa reveals Villaurrutia at his most original in reworking the myth. It is his Hipólito, and not Teresa-Phaedra who is guilty of a sin of passion. The chaste Hippolytus of the mythic tradition has become in Villaurrutia's treatment a representative of sexual love. Villaurrutia has evoked the myth only to reject its basic plot and characterizations. Instead, he has presented an ironic interpretation, remodeling the values and motives of the characters. Unlike the tragedies of Euripides, Racine, and Unamuno, no one has committed suicide or died a violent death. Yet Teresa, like Phaedra, has been deprived of the love she sought. And Hipólito is once again an exile from his father's house.

In the next two plays, Villaurrutia's references to the myths are not as sustained as in the earlier plays. In *La mujer legítima* there is not the ironic interpretation of *La hiedra* nor the parallel characterization of the protagonist of *Invitación a la muerte.* The family situation of the play, however, can be interpreted as an echo of the relationships between Electra and the members of her family. It is not the father who is the missing parent, but the mother who has died. Again, as in the other plays, her death is not the result of murder, but is caused by her mental and physical breakdown. The play begins when Rafael,a widower, wants to bring his former mistress Sara into the house as his legitimate wife now that his first wife has died. His daughter Marta, the Electra figure, considers this proposed marriage an unforgivable reproach to her own mother. Her paramount obsession is to avenge the memory of her mother by ousting the mistress from the house. To prevent Sara from ever becoming the "mujer legítima" she misuses other people to achieve her end. Like Euripides' Electra, she is also deranged by her sorrow and feels that any means is justified to achieve the justice she seeks. In her monomania, she goes so far as to write a compromising letter to her own fiancé allegedly coming from Sara. The letter comes to the attention of Rafael with the unwitting help of Cristina (Chrysotemis?). Ángel, Marta's brother, is at first conditioned to believe that Sara has had an adulterous relationship with Marta's fiancé Luis. Unlike Orestes, however, Ángel does not follow all Marta's plans. Ángel succeeds in discovering Marta's role in slandering Sara. Marta's plan, nevertheless, does achieve its aim when Sara leaves the house without taking the place of the mother. Marta has dedicated all her efforts, like an insane Electra, to avenge the wrong she believes was committed against her parent. Ángel remains with Marta, like Orestes with Electra, to face the consequences of their interference in their parent's life.

Another variation of the Electra figure has been found in Antonia of *El yerro candente.* Magaña Esquivel has directed attention to this mythic reference: "aquí, en esta pieza, es el conflicto filial y la conciencia de su destrucción como lazo de amor, que acerca a Antonia, su personaje femenino, al ejemplo de Electra."[16] Antonia, like Electra, expresses devoted attachment to her father, Eduardo. Villaurrutia, however, has once again added an ironic cast to the classical story. Antonia learns through the course of action that Eduardo is not her real father. The antagonist, Román, fathered her in a brief affair he had with her mother. Antonia, nevertheless, rejects Román when she is given the choice between him and Eduardo. With the exception of Antonia's faithfulness to her chosen father and her antagonism toward her mother and lover, there are no other elements in the play which convey an impression of Electra or her situation.

*El yerro candente,* then, is more than a play with an Electra figure. The interest for the audience is not in seeing how cleverly Villaurrutia has manipulated the classical theme. Even in the earlier plays where the mythic references are more sustained, the modification of the myth is not in itself the interest of the play, as it has been in other uses of myth by contemporary playwrights. One recalls Sartre's *Les Mouches* in which "it is Orestes' refusal of guilt, Sartre's modification of the legend, which is the main interest."[17] Just as Villaurrutia's recourse to myth does not function in this Sartrean fashion, neither can it be said to compare with the presence of myth in Cocteau's *Orphée* or Anouilh's *Eurydice.* Although both plays, like Villaurrutia's works, have been created with contemporary scenes and characters, the French plays would be "almost unintelligible without knowledge of the myth."[18] But Teresa or Alberto, Martha or Antonia, the plays themselves, can be dissociated from the myths and still retain significance as dramatic creations.

In *La hiedra,* for example, the distinctive feature of Teresa's characterization does not rest on the comparison of her differences from Phaedra. Teresa surpasses the confines of her association with Phaedra and represents as well a particular thematic preoccupation of Villaurrutia's. In an article which does not consider mythic allusions, Donald Shaw has explained the meaning of Teresa's conflicts in relation to the whole of Villaurrutia's work: "Sobre todo en el personaje de Teresa . . . el tema de la soledad contrapuesto al del amor muestra cómo confluyen en la obra dramática de Villaurrutia estas dos tendencias de su sensibilidad: goce de pasión por una parte, y por otra, mediata pero ineluctable visión del aislamiento individual."[19] Alberto also personifies this same thwarted search for passion in life. Although he is presented with opportunities to express his love for Aurelia and his filial affection for his father, his incapacity to act results in his final state of isolation. The funeral home as his ambiance is a salient element in the play, not because its name, "Agencia de Inhumaciones Dinamarca," is an allusion to the prince of Denmark, but because it is a fitting symbol of Alberto's psychological reality. Thus at the same time he was incorporating in each play a reference to classical theater, Villaurrutia wascreating characters true to his own artistic vision.

What led Villaurrutia to express his dramatic needs on two levels, one within the play and the second, evoking the broader mythic tradition? Why has Villaurrutia purposely included these allusions to a tradition he has contradicted, as in *La hiedra,* or suggested in passing, as in *El yerro candente*? He has successfully created an ironic mood with his counterpoint in *La hiedra,* but it would also seem that irony is not his only justification. It is also evident that by placing his own characters, Mexicans all, in situations which echo the examples of the mythic figures, Villaurrutia has attributed a universality to the Mexican situation. The allusion to myth in order to cast the light of universality upon a particular moment is not a new nor even unusual use of myth. There is, however, still another function to be performed by Villaurrutia's deliberate references to the myths.

I refer now to his preoccupation with creating a theatrical tradition in Mexico. By recalling the mythic pattern as an undercurrent in his contemporary plays, Villaurrutia in a sense has linked his work to a broader theatrical tradition. He has attached his theater to its origins in ancient Greece and recalled along the way the works of Shakespeare and Racine. We can appreciate Villaurrutia's efforts to connect the Mexican theatrical experience with the classical tradition by remembering the historical context in which these plays were written.

At the time Villaurrutia first became associated with the Mexican theater, the state of theatrical productions had deteriorated to such a level that to Villaurrutia and his friends it was an embarrassment: "sucios locales, viejos actores, anacrónicas decoraciones e imposibles repertorios . . . he aquí los síntomas de la enfermedad que no es lo bastante fuerte para acabar con el teatro, pero sí lo bastante aguda para hacerlo arrastrar una existencia abierta de llagas . . ." These words were written in an article in which Villaurrutia explains his criticisms of the theater in Mexico and the way to bring the sick one back to health.[20] "Si tiene alguno, el remedio del teatro en México está en crearle un ambiente nuevo, hacerlo respirar un aire puro, desatarlo de una falsa tradición, hacerlo correr un camino de orden clásico, renovar su material humano, sus útiles materiales, y crearle amistades jóvenes, vivientes que formen su nuevo público." The remedy proposed by Villaurrutia involved throwing out what was on the boards and starting anew. Up to this point the theater had been dominated artistically and economically by Spaniards—Spanish companies, Spanish actors, the peninsular accent and gesture were norms.[21] In order to replace this false tradition, Villaurrutia and Salvador Novo, his co-editor in the literary journal *Ulises,* began the Teatro de Ulises in 1928. This first modern experimental theater was followed by Grupo de Orientación in 1932 and other small theater groups in the thirties and forties, all attempts to create a valid and authentic Mexican theatrical tradition.

The experimental movements were criticized because their repertoires were not Mexican but instead consisted of the classical masterpieces and controversial plays by new and exciting foreign authors: from Sophocles to Shakespeare, Molière, Synge, O'Neill, Romains, Cocteau.[22] Villaurrutia answered such anti-nationalistic criticism with a straightforward statement emphasizing the emptiness of the current Mexican theatrical climate and intimating the need for foreign influences: "Exótico fue el Teatro de Ulises, porque sus aciertos venían de fuera: obras nuevas, sentido nuevo de la interpretación y ensayos de nueva decoración, no podían venir de donde no los hay. Curioso temor éste de las influencias extranjeras. Miedo a perder una personalidad que no se tiene" (p. 738). Villaurrutia himself did not hesitate to accept the examples presented by the foreign playwrights.[23] Villaurrutia implies that the Mexicans had no recourse but to look beyond their borders as a means to establish their own tradition. His commentary on the efforts of a contemporary avant garde dramatist is enlightening in regard to his own preoccupations with achieving this connection with universal theater. In discussing the importance of Celestino Gorostiza's *Ser o no ser* and *La escuela de amor,* Villaurrutia says, "Ambas parten de una tradición dramática que el autor no pudo obtener regalada, como la obtienen los autores europeos, pero a la que Celestino Gorostiza ha logrado ligarse por medios más intelectuales pero no por ellos menos sino más precisos. Porque no es una hipérbole afirmar quecon estas obras, como con muy pocas más, el teatro mexicano contemporáneo logra, de pronto, colocarse en un plano de universalidad sin perder por ello el contenido que la personalidad de su autor, mexicano selecto, ha sabido vaciar en un continente que tiene validez en cualquier latitud espiritual" (p. 738). These words of praise are even more appropriate when applied to Villaurrutia's plays. For Villaurrutia expressed a conscious effort in his plays to present both a Mexican and a universal theater. The surface level of his plays reveals contemporary Mexico, with references to current events for those who want to see their familiar world reflected in the play.[24] But below the surface, Villaurrutia has incorporated the elements intended to associate his theater with the broader tradition he wished to see flourish in Mexico. Myths have been defined as a means to testify to the living reality of communal inheritance,[25] and through mythic references, Villaurrutia has linked his theater to the universal theatrical tradition.

NOTES

[1] Carlos Solórzano labels Villaurrutia *universalista* while he classifies the works of other writers of this period of innovation—Agustín Lazo, Celestino Gorostiza and Rodolfo Usigli—in the category of *teatro nacionalista.* See his *Teatro latinoamericano del siglo XX* (Buenos Aires, 1961). For a discussion of these labels as they apply to Villaurrutia's poetry, see Frank Dauster, *Ensayos sobre poesía Mexicana* (Mexico: Ediciones de Andrea, 1963) pp. 27-28.

[2] For further discussion of this topic see my paper "The Influence of the French Theatre in the Plays of Xavier Villaurrutia," *Latin American Theatre Review,* 3, No. 1 (1969), 9-15.

[3] See Vera Beck, "Xavier Villaurrutia, dramaturgo moderno," *Revista Iberoamericana,* 18, 35 (1952), 27.

[4] "Xavier Villaurrutia: The Development of His Theater," *Hispania* 43 (1960), 512.

[5] Although the trend toward the use of mythological allusions was not in evidence in Mexico until the late forties, Alfonso Reyes did produce one play which was a reinterpretation of the myth of Iphigenia in Tauris. His *Ifigenia cruel,* written in 1923, opened in 1934 in the same season as Villaurrutia's *¿En que piensas?*

[6] My discussion concerns four plays because the fifth work is not based on classical mythology but deals instead with the figure of a Blue Beard—*El pobre Barba Azul* (1947). For complete bibliographic information concerning the dates of publication and production for Villaurrutia's plays, see his *Obras,* 2ª edicion aumentada (México, 1966), xxxi-xxxii.

[7] For a more detailed discussion of the similarities between *Invitación a la muerte* and *Hamlet,* see "El teatro de Xavier Villaurrutia," *Estaciones* 1 (núm. 4, invierno de 1956), 484.

[8] "Invitación a la muerte," *Obras,* 2ª edicion, aumentada (Mexico, 1966), p. 369. Further quotations from Villaurrutia's plays are from this edition.

[9] By including Alicia, Villaurrutia has followed the myth as it has been interpreted by Racine. See Dauster, p. 485.

[10] Dauster, p. 485.

[11] *Fedra* was written in 1911 and produced in 1918. For details on the play's composition, see Miguel de Unamuno, *Obras completas,* XII (Madrid, 1958), 86-103.

[12] Dauster, p. 485.

[13] It is interesting to note that Unamuno's Fedra is also sterile.

[14] Antonio Magaña Esquivel, *Sueño y realidad del teatro* (México, 1949), p. 134.

[15] References to the semi-incestuous nature of their romance are found in Dauster, p. 483 and in an anonymous article, "Xavier Villaurrutia y el teatro clásico," *Romance,* año 11 núm. 22 (15 marzo 1941), 18.

[16] Magaña Esquivel, p. 137.

[17] Raymond Williams, *Drama from Ibsen to Eliot* (London, 1952), p. 200.

[18] Although Gilbert Highet said this in reference to Anouilh's work alone, the opinion also applies to Cocteau's *Orphée.* See his article, "The Reinterpretation of the Myths," *The Virginia Quarterly Review,* 25 (Winter 1949), 200.

[19] "Pasión y verdad en el teatro de Villaurrutia," *Revista iberoamericana,* 28, 54 (julio-diciembre 1962), 344.

[20] "El teatro es así," Imagen, núm. 4 (21 julio 1933). Reprinted in *Obras,* pp. 737-38.

[21] See Salvador Novo, "Chaos and Horizons of Mexican Drama," *Theatre Arts,* 25, no. 5 (May 1941); Celestino Gorostiza, "Apuntes para una historia del teatro experimental," *México en el arte,* num. 10-11 (1950), 24.

[22] The repertoires of the experimental movements can be found in Antonio Magaña Esquivel *Imagen del teatro* (México, 1940), pp. 96-101.

[23] See note 2 above.

[24] Villaurrutia is always explicit in his stage directions concerning the scenery, specifying that the furnishings reflect a typical Mexican home of the middle-class. In addition he refers to current events, such as the construction of the Palacio de Bellas Artes in *Invitación a la muerte* (p. 389). See also *El yerro candente,* pp. 415, 430.

[25] Harry Slochower, "Andre Gide's *Theseus* and the French Myth," *Yale French Studies* 2, no. 2, 34.

## Merlin H. Foster (essay date 1976)

SOURCE: "Themes," in *Fire and Ice: The Poetry of Xavier Villaurrutia,* U.N.C. Dept. of Romance Languages, 1976, pp. 105-54.

[*In the following excerpt, Foster provides an overview of major and minor themes—including solitude, love, death, and others—in Villaurrutia's poetry.*]

GENERAL

Villaurrutia's poetry turns on three obsessions which find expression as the three principal themes: 1) human beings live separated one from another in inevitable and anguished solitude; 2) love, when it exists, is incomplete, secret, impossible, and at times illicit; 3) death is a constant presence in an empty and solitary existence. In the first section of this chapter, I shall examine these three thematic groupings as exemplified in a number of important poems.

In addition to the three main themes, there are several smaller complexes of meaning which will be discussed in the second part: poetry and the poetic muse, nature and the peaceful life, religious experience, and recollection of childhood.

MAJOR THEMES

*Solitude*

An essential awareness of separation and solitude is developed with increasingintensity in the poet's four collections. In *Primeros poemas,* for example, solitude is implied in the scenes of silent nature found in many of the poems, and anguished separation is sharply underscored in the pronominal separation of **"Ellos y yo":** *"Ellos* saben vivir / y reír / y besar . . . / *Yo:* sólo sé llorar . . ." (p. 7). Even the hot rays of the summer sun make visible a shadowy process of fragmentation and isolation:

> El viento, alto, en los árboles
> sonaba a río
> ¡río en el azul!
> Yo dejé ir mi corazón
> 5   al frío,
> al viento,
> al río, no sé . . .
> "Vámonos sin amor y sin deseo:
> sin dolor.
> 10  Ahora que el corazón se va
> en el frío,
> en el viento,
> en el río, vámonos . . ."
>
> La sombra, azul, aliviaba
> 15  la frente,
> ¡la frente bajo el sol!
> Yo dejé ir mi corazón
> al frío,
> a la sombra,
> 20  al azul . . .
>
> "Vámonos sin amor y sin deseo:
> sin dolor.
> Ahora que el corazón se queda
> en el frío,
> 25  en la sombra,
> en el azul, vámonos
> va-
> mo-
> nos . . ."
>
> ("**Estío,**" pp. 15-16).

In spite of the title, which suggests the description of a brilliant summer day, the poem moves thematically in the opposite direction. In the first stanza, for example, the wind in the trees becomes a frigid stream which carries away the heart (the consciousness?) of the poet. The second stanza, set off by quotation marks as if it were spoken to another person (perhaps even to the speaker himself), repeats in more uneven metrical terms some of the same elements, and with a first person plural command form recommends emotionless movement in the same stream. The third stanza, equally uneven from a metrical point of view, underscores with many of the same elements the shadowy movement away from the rays of the sun. The final stanza, again with quotation marks, represents the heart and being of the poet in the precise moment of surrender to the shadowy flow. Here the verb "quedarse" is used in place of "irse", and the command form is repeated with a final fragmentation. Thus the poet moves away from the brilliance of the external world lighted by sunshine into the somber, and in a way comforting, depths of contemplative solitude.

In *Reflejos,* the theme is considerably expanded and runs the gamut from objective to subjective treatment. For example, the description of the solitude and isolation of a small Mexican town has little to do with the psychic reality of the poet:

> Aquel pueblo se quedó soltero,
> conforme con su iglesia,
> embozado en su silencio,
> bajo la paja—oro, mediodía—
> de su sombrero ancho,
> sin nada más:
> en las fichas del cementerio
> los + son—.
>
> Aquel pueblo cerró los ojos
> para no ver la cinta de cielo
> que se lleva el río,
> y la carrera de los rieles
> delante del tren.
> El cielo y el agua,
> la vía, la vía
> —vidas paralelas—,
> piensan, ¡ay! encontrarse
> en la ciudad.
>
> Se le fue la gente
> con todo y ganado.
> Se le fue la luna novia,
> ¡la noche le dice
> que allá en la ciudad
> se ha casado!
> Le dejaron, vacías, las casas
> ¡a él que no sabe jugar
> a los dados!
>
> ("Pueblo," pp. 34-35).

A personification of the town is the central device for carrying out the theme of isolation. In the first stanza, for example, it is represented as remaining in perpetual bachelorhood, sleeping in the golden silence between the church and the cemetery. Perhaps the most Mexican detail, and one of the few in all of Villaurrutia's verses, is the broadbrimmed Mexican hat (perhaps suggested by the rays of the midday sun) under which the personified town

finds shade and protection. In the second strophe the person-town closes his eyes so as not to see those pathways which lead away from isolation. The river against the sky and the parallel rails of the railroad right-of-way suggest a coming together only at some distant point, here suggested as the city. The personification continues into the third stanza as well, and the town becomes a lonely person who has been deserted by all others and has been left to gaze aimlessly at the empty shapes around him. The city has attracted the inhabitants of the town, and even the moon is a girl who has left to find marriage in the city. The empty houses are like parts of a pointless game of dice, a figure which is important both as a part of the visual representation of the poem and for the thematic development of solitude.

In **"Cinematógrafo,"** the poet wanders along a lonely street which takes on the elongated shape and darkness of a movie theater:

> En la calle, la plancha gris del cielo,
> más baja cada vez,
> nos empareda vivos . . .
> El corazón, sin frío de invierno,
> quiere llorar su juventud
> a oscuras.
>
> En este túnel el hollín
> unta las caras,
> y sólo así mi corazón se atreve.
>
> En este túnel sopla
> la música delgada,
> y es tan largo que tardaré en salir
>
> por aquella puerta con luz
> donde lloran dos hombres
> que quisieran estar a oscuras.
>
> ¿Por qué no pagarán la entrada?
>
> (p. 41).

The first stanza establishes the visual limits of the scene. The street is darkened and oppressed by the heavy grayness of the night sky, and the absence of wintry cold suggested in line 4 releases emotions rather than inhibiting them. In the short second stanza the walled-in street is a tunnel in which faces are blackened by the shadows and the anonymity necessary for a release of emotions is maintained. The longer third stanza continues the same figure, but now music is heard as if in a movie house and an illuminated exit (the lighted door of the theater?) is made a part of the description. The reference to the two men who stand crying at the door is a puzzling one. It is possible to see them as two people who have not paid for a ticket into the theater, and therefore must remain outside (this would also explain in part the final line of the poem). Perhaps they have even been inside the theater and have been moved to emotion by what they have seen. However, if the tunnel of the poem is really a street which has many of the characteristics of a movie theater, then the two men would have to be seen as being unwilling or unable to enter the dark solitude of the street, perhaps without the power to pay the emotional price necessary. At any rate, the poet sees himself as separated by considerable distance from those two figures and shrouded in the blackening which is provided by the scene which he develops.

In **"Soledad,"** the poet gazes at a painting and sees his feeling of solitude reflected in the eyes of one of the figures:

> Soledad, soledad
> !cómo me miras desde los ojos
> de la mujer de ese cuadro!
>
> Cada día, cada día,
> todos los días . . .
> Cómo me miras con sus ojos hondos.
>
> Si me quejo, parece que sus ojos
> me quisieran decir que no estoy solo.
> Y cuando espero lo que nunca llega,
> me quisieran decir: aquí me tienes.
>
> Y cuando lloro—algunas veces lloro—
> también sus ojos se humedecen,
> o será que los miro con los míos.
>
> (pp. 28-29).

Solitude is personified through the development of the poem, and is the presence which gives some kind of life to the figure in the painting. The first two stanzas, for example, develop this basic distinction by careful use of second and third person forms, particularly in line 6. The final three stanzas represent a contradictory view of the theme based on that duality already established. The eyes of the painting seem to tell him that he is not alone, but the only presence which accompanies him is that of the personified figure of solitude speaking through those eyes. They also seem to be wet with tears, but as the poet observes, this is probably due to his own tears, which come perhaps from the realization of an inescapable solitude which follows his every motion.

The most internalized treatment of the theme is found in **"Amplificaciones,"** in which candlelight throws flickering shadows on the wall and the poet looks within himself for some kind of meaning:

> En el cuarto del pueblo,
> fantástico y desnudo,
> amarillo de luz de vela,
> sobrecogido,
> mis sienes dan la hora
> en no sé qué reloj
> puntual y eterno.
>
> La soledad se agranda
> como las sombras
> en la sábana del muro,
> como las caras de ayer
> asomadas para adentro
> en el marco de sus ventanas.
>
> Y el silencio se mueve
> y vibra

> en torno de la llama blanda,
> como el ala—¿de qué presagio?,
> ¿de qué insecto?—que acaricia,
> que enfría, que empequeñece.
>
> (pp. 36-37).

The first stanza develops the basic figure of the poem, a room in which the world is reduced to two things: the sputtering yellow light of a candle and the inexorable temporal flow of the poet's life as seen in the pulse of his temples. In the second stanza solitude is represented in two similes which are interconnected by the flickering light of the candle. Solitude resembles, the poet says, the moving shadows which are thrown on the whiteness of the wall or the remembered faces of yesterday which are captured within the frame of a window. In another extended simile, the third strophe develops silence as something which is visible and circles the flame of the candle as if it were a moth attracted by its light. This silence caresses but at the same time reduces the size of things and creates a sensation of coldness. Through the careful imagery of the poem, the poet turns his awareness inward and finds there the hazy figures of solitude and silence.

In *Nostalgia de la muerte* the descriptive aspect of the theme disappears and solitude becomes limitless and internalized. Perhaps the best example of this view of solitude is **"Nocturno en que nada se oye,"** in which the consciousness of the poet descends into an endless aquatic world:

> En medio de un silencio desierto como la calle
>      antes del crimen
> sin respirar siquiera para que nada turbe mi
>      muerte
> en esta soledad sin paredes
> al tiempo que huyeron los angulos
> 5   en la tumba del lecho dejo mi estatua sin
>      sangre
> para salir en un momento tan lento
> en un interminable descenso
> sin brazos que tender
> sin dedos para alcanzar la escala que cae de un
>      piano invisible
> 10  sin más que una mirada y una voz
> que no recuerdan haber salido de ojos y labios
> ¿qué son labios? ¿qué son miradas que son
>      labios?
> y mi voz ya no es mía
> dentro del agua que no moja
> 15  dentro del aire de vidrio
> dentro del fuego lívido que corta como el grito
> Y en el juego angustioso de un espejo frente a
>      otro
> cae mi voz
> y mi voz que madura
> 20  y mi voz quemadura
> y mi bosque madura
> y mi voz quema dura
> como el hielo de vidrio
> como el grito de hielo
> 25  aquí en el caracol de la oreja
> el latido de un mar en el que no sé nada
> en el que no se nada
> porque he dejado pies y brazos en la orilla

siento caer fuera de mí la red de mis nervios
30  mas huye todo como el pez que se da cuenta
hasta siento en el pulso de mis sienes
muda telegrafía a la que nadie responde
porque el sueño y la muerte nada tienen ya que
decirse.

                      (pp. 47-48).

From the point of view of metrics and structure, this is one of the poems which comes closest to the reproduction of a free-flowing mental stream. There are no stanzas, the line lengths vary widely and have no particular pattern, and there is only scattered assonance. Even the punctuation is greatly reduced, and the impression of continuous movement from one line to another is enhanced. Nevertheless, it is possible to divide the poem into four structural elements which are in keeping with the thematic development as well.

The first of these divisions includes the first twelve lines of the poem, in which the general thematic lines of the poem are established. The silence and solitude are limitless (lines 1-4), and in a death-like descent the consciousness of the poet leaves behind the totality of his physical body. The descent is momentary, but at the same time interminable, and the poet retains only the powers of sight and speech. As the descent becomes deeper (lines 8-12) this reduction becomes more pronounced but also is expressed more chaotically (the interrogative utterances of line 12 are exemplary of this pattern).

The second segment is made up of lines 13-16, in which the descent into solitude has become so deep that the poet's voice no longer belongs to him, and certain elemental relationships no longer operate: water does not make things wet, air is as hard and brilliant as glass, and livid fire cuts and penetrates only as a remembered shout.

The third element is made up of lines 17-24, and continues the representation of deepened dream-like solitude. The series of reflecting mirrors which produces the endless echoing and changing of the poet's voice is an anguished and sterile reverberation which is finally expressed in the intense thermic contrasts of heat and ice (lines 22-24).

In the final segment (lines 25-33), the state of solitude is represented as a profound sea in which the poet is unable to swim or move himself. This is the moment of deepest descent, and the poet feels that even the impulses of his nervous and circulatory systems fall into silence. The verbal plays of this last segment emphasize strongly the difficulty or impossibility of communication of any sort, and the silence and anguished solitude of the dream foreshadow the immobility and the muteness of death.

The same sense of anguished separation and silence is expressed strongly in the five compositions grouped under the title **"Estancias nocturnas"**:

Sonámbulo, dormido y despierto a la vez,
en silencio recorro la ciudad sumergida.

¡Y dudo! Y no me atrevo a preguntarme si es
el despertar de un sueño o es un sueño mi vida.

En la noche resuena, como en un mundo hueco,
el ruido de mis pasos prolongados, distantes.
Siento miedo de que no sea sino el eco
de otros pasos ajenos, que pasaron mucho antes.

Miedo de no ser nada más que un jirón del sueño
de alguien—¿de Dios?—que sueña en este mundo
    amargo.
Miedo de que despierte ese alguien—¿Dios?—, el
    dueño
de un sueño cada vez más profundo y más largo.

Estrella que te asomas, temblorosa y despierta,
tímida aparición en el cielo impasible,
tú, como yo—hace siglos—, estás helada y
    muerta,
mas por tu propia luz sigues siendo visible.

¡Seré polvo en el polvo y olvido en el olvido!
Pero alguien, en la angustia de una noche vacía,
sin saberlo él, ni yo, alguien que no ha nacido
dirá con mis palabras su nocturna agonía.

                      (pp. 62-63).

The *estancias* are careful quatrain stanzas using Alexandrine lines and a constant ABAB rhyme scheme. The only metrical complication is that of a frequent series of run-on lines which alter somewhat the measured flow of the conventional metrics. In spite of an evident desire on the part of the poet (or the editors of the edition) to separate into five distinct compositions, the *estancias* should be read as a single poem on the meaning of existence from the point of view of anguished solitude. If seen in that fashion, there are three divisions which need to be considered. The first *estancia* sets the scene, in which the poet wanders in silence through a dream-like city. It is against that background that the persistent question comes as to dream or reality, meaning or lack of meaning. *Estancias* 2 and 3 form a second structural element in the poem. The poet hears his own footsteps resounding in the hollow world of the city, and fears that they are but the echo of other footsteps from times past. This fear carries him to the more profound concern that perhaps his entire existence is nothing more than the dream of someone else, perhaps of God himself, who has powers superior to his own. *Estancias* 4 and 5 make up the final structural element of the poem. The poet raises his eyes to the night sky and likens himself to the early star that he sees there; he, as the star, is able to give an impression of life and light in spite of the reality of coldness and death. In the same way that the star expresses to him both existence and death, his words will help some person as yet unborn to express the same kind of anguish.

Along the deserted streets of a phantasmal world the solitary figure of the poet searches for himself and some kind of meaning:

Tengo miedo de mi voz
y busco mi sombra en vano.

¿Será mía aquella sombra
sin cuerpo que va pasando?
¿Y mía la voz perdida
que va la calle incendiando?

¿Qué voz, qué sombra, qué sueño
despierto que no he soñado
serán la voz y la sombra
y el sueño que me han robado?

Para oír brotar la sangre
de mi corazón cerrado,
¿pondré la oreja en mi pecho
como en el pulso la mano?

Mi pecho estará vacío
y yo descorazonado
y serán mis manos duros
pulsos de mármol helado.

("**Nocturno grito,**" p. 46).

The poem is presented in octosyllabic quatrains with conventional rhyme scheme. The only variation from that pattern is the unrhymed couplet which serves as the first stanza. The theme is isolation and an internalized searching for meaning, and is developed in three segments. The first is the two-line introductory stanza which presents the poet's sense of fear and his search for shadowy form. This is an ambiguous search, and it is interesting to note that these two lines are the only declarative elements in the whole poem. The second structural element is made up of the following two stanzas. Three interrogations built on verbs in the future of probability underscore sharply the tentativeness of the inquiry by the poet as to the identity of the formless shadow and the lost voice which move along the street. These have stolen from the poet, and identification is now probably impossible. The third structural segment of the poem is made up of the final two stanzas. The poet turns to an examination of himself, but one which is almost as tentative as the questions about his disembodied shadow and voice. In order to be sure that his heart is beating, it is necessary for the poet to put figuratively his ear to his own chest as he would his hand on the pulse in his wrist. In so doing, the poet will undoubtedly find that he is but an empty shell and as cold as marble (one should note the poet's pun on "descorazonado", with a double meaning as "disheartened" and "de-hearted"). Here again the direction of the poem is from a background of silence and isolation toward emptiness and death.

At times the search for self and meaning in anguished isolation reaches frenetic proportions, as can be seen in "**Nocturno de la estatua**":

Soñar, soñar la noche, la calle, la escalera
y el grito de la estatua desdoblando la esquina.

Correr hacia la estatua y encontrar sólo el grito,
querer tocar el grito y sólo hallar el eco,
querer asir el eco y encontrar sólo el muro
y correr hacia el muro y tocar un espejo.
Hallar en el espejo la estatua asesinada,
sacarla de la sangre de su sombra,

vestirla en un cerrar de ojos,
acariciarla como a una hermana imprevista
y jugar con las fichas de sus dedos
y contar a su oreja cien veces cien cien veces
hasta oírla decir: "estoy muerta de sueño."

(pp. 46-47).

The poem is structured in two stanzas of unequal length. The first of these is an unrhymed couplet which presents the thematic problem of the poem: the dream of the night street and of the statue, another shadowy human figure. These elements are represented as if in a dream, without precise time or person. The second and longer stanza continues the same imprecision, as well as making use of the elements already introduced in the brief beginning stanza. There is a sense of constant movement in pursuit of the shadowy figure of the statue, a movement which is rewarded only by partial perception. First the statue, then the scream, then the echo, then the wall, and finally the mirror are illusive, and escape the grasp of the pursuer. Only in the mirror can the form of the statue finally be touched, and here only because of violent death. The successively connected images, the careful impersonality and nontemporality of the tenses, and the feverish, almost insane, movement of the poem all seem to suggest a symbolic search for self along the deserted streets of the subconscious, a search which ends, as most of the other poems using the same theme, in incompleteness and death.

The theme of solitude does not figure strongly in *Canto a la primavera,* but there is one late poem which shows that the theme was not entirely forgotten. The short poem "**Volver . . . ,**" which in spite of its placement in the second edition of Villaurrutia's works was probably one of the poet's last compositions,[1] is a consideration in rather contemplative terms of the state of solitude which had been one of the essences of the poet's existence:

Volver a una patria lejana,
volver a una patria olvidada,
oscuramente deformada
por el destierro en esta tierra.
¡Salir del aire que me encierra!
Y anclar otra vez en la nada.
La noche es mi madre y mi hermana,
la nada es mi patria lejana,
la nada llena de silencio,
la nada llena de vacío,
la nada sin tiempo ni frío,
la nada en que no pasa nada.

(pp. 69-70).

"La nada," empty, silent, inactive, and dark, is represented as the distant homeland toward which the poet desires to travel, leaving behind the elements and distortions of life on earth. The poem is a fitting climax to the development of this particular theme. Gone are the frantic and anguished wanderings of the earlier poems, and only the desire for silence and solitude remains, a desire purified and refined by the fires of previous emotions. The poet no longer seems to dread but rather to be resigned and even desirous of such a state.

*Love*

This theme appears abundantly in all of the collections of the poet, though perhaps more importantly in the early poems with a somewhat conventional turn and in the last collection with a strong sense of anguish and unfulfillment. Some examples from the various collections will make these distinctions and developments clear.

In **Primeros poemas** love is usually represented in positive emotional terms with just a suggestion of bitterness or uncertainty. **"Canción apasionada"** is an appropriate example:

> Como la primavera, ponía
> en cada espíritu un azoro;
> en su sonrisa desleía
> la miel del ansia que encendía
> en un relíampago sonoro.
>
> Y como la noche, callaba,
> y en el silencio azul y fuerte
> de sus pupilas, concentraba
> un temblor mayor que la muerte . . .
>
> Su voz era mansa y cercana;
> tenía brillos de manzana.
> Y mi fervor asiduo ardía
> en su carne como una llama
> que ningún soplo inclinaría.
>
> ¡Qué fiel el zumo que su boca
> exprimió en la mía temblorosa!
> Su calor en mi alma coloca
> reminiscente y roja rosa.
>
> ¡Qué firme apego el de sus brazos!
> Lo siente ahora el desamor
> en que se inundan mis ribazos
> y en que se calla mi clamor . . .
>
> (p. 17).

The poem is presented in careful eneasyllabic lines with a simple ABAB scheme of consonantal rhyme. The two stanzas which depart from the quatrain pattern vary the system somewhat, but in general the impression is one of order and control.

The theme of remembered love is developed lineally along the five stanzas of the poem. The first three depend on a series of interconnected descriptive similes comparing the remembered figure of the beloved to spring, night, and the polished brilliance of an apple. The poet's emotion is also compared to a flame which cannot be extinguished or even moved from its position. The last two stanzas begin with exclamatory utterances and with a more contemplative idea. In stanza4 the poet remembers the touch of his beloved and the warmth which that presence, or even remembered presence, leaves with him. In stanza 5 an embrace is recalled, and the final three lines contrast the bitter present to the remembered passions of the past. The lack of love at the present moment overflows all and silences the poet's bitter outcries. This poem characterizes, then, the early development of the theme: remembered emotion contrasted with an unfulfilled present.

The composition **"Más que lento,"** is which the experience of love is the present and unfulfilled desire of the past, is a contrasting example:

> Ya se alivia el alma mía
> trémula y amarilla;
> y recibe la unción apasionada
> de tu mano . . . Y la fría
> rigidez de mi frente,
> dulcemente entibiada,
> ya se siente . . .
>
> Yo no sé si mi mal indefinido
> se decolora o se desviste,
> pero ya no hace ruido.
>
> Yo no sé si la luz que todo anega,
> o el latido leal que te apresura
> en mis sienes, o el ansia prematura,
> inunda las pupilas y las ciega.
>
> Qué conmovida está mi boca,
> e inconforme.
> Y distinto mi cuerpo
> a la distinta llama de tu sangre.
> Y mi sed ulterior acaso es poca.
>
> Siento una languidez, y un desvaído
> cansancio, casi de relato
> pueril . . . Me siento como
> en el claroscuro envejecido
> de un melancólico retrato . . .
>
> (pp. 23-24).

Here the metrical form of the poem is a good deal less regular than is the composition just discussed. Line lengths vary widely in some of the strophes, consonantal rhyme exists but with less of an impression of established scheme, and the patterns of the strophe range from seven to three lines in length. The development of the theme, also, seems to be less linear, and can be divided into four segments. The first of these is the first stanza of the poem, in which the basic relationships are established. The soul of the poet receives the comforting touch of his beloved's hand, and the hardness and cold of his being are reduced. The adjective "amarilla" suggest, however, that the soul's jaundice is not entirely removed. The second segment is made up of the two following stanzas, which begin with a parallel negative declaration. The warmth of the present is recognized, but the discoloration and the anxieties are reduced only for the moment. The strong present emotion obstructs or blinds temporarily, and without doubt the past state will return again. The fourth stanza, with its suggestion of exclamation, constitutes the third segment of the poem. Again certain corporeal elements of the poet's being (mouth, body, blood) recognize the distinctness of the present moment, but at the same time the thirst of the past is only reduced, not entirely removed. The final stanza forms the fourth thematic segment of the poem, and though the present view is maintained the impression is one of tiredness and flaccidity rather than joy and passion. Instead of feeling the joy of fulfillment which might be expected from the experience of the present moment, the poet feels that his past weighs as heavily upon him as if he were a figure in the faded colors of an old painting. In this poem, then, present love is expressed, but with a strong coloration of melancholy from the past.

The theme of love appears less frequently in *Reflejos* and *Nostalgia de la muerte,* but there are nonetheless several poems from those two collections that should be considered. For example, the composition **"Noche"** from *Reflejos* is a typically sensorial representation of a present intimate moment of sexual love, in which boredom and pain are also to be found:

> ¡Qué tic-tac en tu pecho
> alarga la noche sin sueño!
>
> La media sombra viste,
> móvil, nuestros cuerpos desnudos
> y ya les da brillos de finas maderas
> o, avara, los confunde opacos.
>
> —Gocemos, si quieres,
> provocando el segundo de muerte
> para luego caer—¿en qué cansancio?,
> ¿en qué dolor?—como en un pozo
> sin fin de luz de aurora . . .
>
> Callemos en la noche última;
> aguardemos sin despedida:
> este polvo blanco
> —de luna ¡claro!—
> nos vuelve románticos.
>
>                                              (p. 28).

The first two stanzas of this poem develop in sensorial terms the main point of the poem: the night is measured in the endless ticking of the beloved's heart, and the darkness of the night gives a contradictory sense of mobility and of carefully sculptured beauty to the nude bodies of the lovers. The third stanza deals with the sensations of love itself, first as a moment of death-like orgasm and then as a contrary all-consuming *ennui* and even pain. In the fourth stanza there is no need to speak; the lovers know well all of the limits of this experience and live it as if it were their last night together. The handling of the theme here is much more frankly sensual than in the previous poems, but continues the same bittersweet quality which has already been commented on. Love exists and can be experienced, but is essentially physical and inevitably transitory.

In *Nostalgia de la muerte* there are two compositions which should be commented on in this discussion of the theme of love. The first is the rather long **"Nocturno amor":**

> El que nada se oye en esta alberca de sombra
> no sé cómo mis brazos no se hieren
> en tu respiración sigo la angustia del crimen
> y caes en la red que tiende el sueño
> 5   Guardas el nombre de tu cómplice en los ojos

> pero encuentro tus párpados más duros que el
>         silencio
> y antes que compartirlo matarías el goce
> de entregarte en el sueño con los ojos cerrados
> sufro al sentir la dicha con que tu cuerpo busca
> 10   el cuerpo que te vence más que el sueño
> y comparo la fiebre de tus manos
> con mis manos de hielo
> y el temblor de tus sienes con mi pulso perdido
> y el yeso de mis muslos con la piel de los tuyos
> 15   que la sombra corroe con su lepra incurable
> Ya sé cuál es el sexo de tu boca
> y lo que guarda la avaricia de tu axila
> y maldigo el rumor que inunda el laberinto de
>         tu oreja
> sobre la almohada de espuma
> 20   sobre la dura página de nieve
> No la sangre que huyó de mí como del arco
>         huye la flecha
> sino la cólera circula por mis arterias
> amarilla de incendio en mitad de la noche
> y todas las palabras en la prisión de la boca
> 25   y una sed que en el agua del espejo
> sacia su sed con una sed idéntica
> De qué noche despierto a esta desnuda
> noche larga y cruel noche que ya no es noche
> junto a tu cuerpo más muerto que muerto
> 30   que no es tu cuerpo ya sino su hueco
> porque la ausencia de tu sueño ha matado a la
>         muerte
> y es tan grande mi frío que con un calor nuevo
> abre mis ojos donde la sombra es más dura
> y más clara y más luz que la luz misma
> 35   y resucita en mí lo que no ha sido
> y es un dolor inesperado y aún más frío y más
>         fuego
> no ser sino la estatua que despierta
> en la alcoba de un mundo en el que todo ha
>         muerto.
>
>                                       (pp. 49-50).

Here again, as was the case with **"Nocturno en que nada se oye,"** there is an evident attempt to approximate incoherent mental flow. There is almost no punctuation, no stanza divisions at all, line length varies widely and with no pattern, and while there is some scattered assonance, there is no system of end rhyme. In addition, there is an overriding sense of disconnection between contiguous grammatical elements of the poem, and it is difficult to suggest any lineal development.

As the title suggests, the poem has to do with the theme of love and the principal vehicle is a *yo—tú* relationship. As developed throughout the poem, however, it is not a relationship of passionate fulfillment but rather the opposite: a secretive, jealous love which finds expression in emptiness and death.

Although the poet marks no stanza at all, it is possible to separate the poem into five structural segments. The first of these (lines 1-4) presents the basic elements of the poem: a shadowy dreamstate, the presence of both *yo* and *tú,* and the sense of wrong-doing. A characteristic nonsequentiality is also seen clearly; none of the lines is related grammatically or conceptually to the contiguous ones but instead each line stands alone as a separate figure. The second segment (lines 5-15) develops several of these basic ideas further. The *yo—tú* relationship is continued, with the *yo* very much awake in the world of dreams and the *tú* asleep and therefore incommunicative. The sense of something criminal is reflected in several of the words ("cómplice," "matarías"), but the beloved person continues to sleep and the poet finds no response to his jealous searchings. The differences between the two people are striking and serve as the final element in this segment: heat versus cold, obvious indication of heartbeat and circulation versus imperceptible pulse, the softness of the beloved's skin as opposed to the hardness ("yeso") of that of the poet. Lines 16-20 form the third structural element of the poem, and intensify the corporeal sensuality with which the poet regards his beloved. He looks upon various parts of the body as having almost a life or passion of their own, and again feels jealousy for even those involuntary processes which are beyond his control. The fourth element is formed by lines 21-26, in which the poet, almost as in a nightmare, is consumed by an intense anger as if it were the life-giving substance which circulates through his body. The images of light, sound, and reflection all support this anguished circulation. The final segment (lines 27-38) is the longest of the five, and probably the most complex. The continued silence of the beloved, submerged in the pleasures of a distant dream, has deepened the sense of anguish on the part of the poet and caused him to see everything around him as cold and dead, even the body of the beloved person which is near to him. The deep frigidness which the poet feels is so intense that it is perceived at times with a contradictory sense of heat and light, a sensation which only intensifies the feeling of isolation and death which consumes him. With intense pain, represented in these contradictory terms, the poet sees himself as a petrified figure ("estatua") who struggles to uncertain wakefulness surrounded only by death.

Another important example of this theme in *Nostalgia de la muerte* is **"Nocturno de los ángeles"**:

> Se diría que las calles fluyen dulcemente en la
> noche.
> Las luces no son tan vivas que logren desvelar
> el secreto,
> el secreto que los hombres que van y vienen
> conocen,
> porque todos están en el secreto
> 5   y nada se ganaría con partirlo en mil pedazos
> si, por el contrario, es tan dulce guardarlo
> y compartirlo sólo con la persona elegida.
>
> Si cada uno dijera en un momento dado,
> en sólo una palabra, lo que piensa,
> 10   las cinco letras del DESEO formarían una
> enorme cicatriz luminosa,
> una constelación más antigua, más viva aún
> que las otras.
> Y esa constelación sería como un ardiente sexo
> en el profundo cuerpo de la noche,
> o, mejor, como los Gemelos que por vez
> primera en la vida

15   se miraran de frente, a los ojos, y se abrazaran
ya para siempre.

> De pronto el río de la calle se puebla de
> sedientos seres,
> caminan, se detienen, prosiguen.
> Cambian miradas, atreven sonrisas
> forman imprevistas parejas . . .
>
> 20   Hay recodos y bancos de sombra,
> orillas de indefinibles formas profundas
> y súbitos huecos de luz que ciega
> y puertas que ceden a la presión más leve.
>
> El río de la calle queda desierto un instante.
> 25   Luego parece remontar de sí mismo
> deseoso de volver a empezar.
> Queda un momento paralizado, mudo,
> anhelante
> como el corazón entre dos espasmos.
> Pero una nueva pulsación, un nuevo latido
> 30   arroja al río de la calle nuevos sedientos
> seres.
> Se cruzan, se entrecruzan y suben.
> Vuelan a ras de tierra.
> Nadan de pie, tan milagrosamente
> que nadie se atrevería a decir que no caminan.
>
> 35   ¡Son los ángeles!
> Han bajado a la tierra
> por invisibles escalas.
> Vienen del mar, que es el espejo del cielo,
> en barcos de humo y sombra,
> 40   a fundirse y confundirse con los mortales,
> a rendir sus frentes en los muslos de las
> mujeres,
> a dejar que otras manos palpen sus cuerpos
> febrilmente,
> y que otros cuerpos busquen los suyos hasta
> encontrarlos
> como se encuentran al cerrarse los labios de
> una misma boca,
> 45   a fatigar su boca tanto tiempo inactiva,
> a poner en libertad sus lenguas de fuego,
> a decir las canciones, los juramentos, las malas
> palabras
> en que los hombres concentran el antiguo
> misterio
> de la carne, la sangre y el deseo.
>
> 50   Tienen nombres supuestos, divinamente
> sencillos.
> Se llaman Dick o John, o Marvin o Louis.
> En nada sino en la belleza se distinguen de los
> mortales.
> Caminan, se detienen, prosiguen.
> Cambian miradas, atreven sonrisas.
> 55   Forman imprevistas parejas.
>
> Sonríen maliciosamente al subir en los
> ascensores de los hoteles
> donde aún se practica el vuelo lento y vertical.
> En sus cuerpos desnudos hay huellas
> celestiales;
> signos, estrellas y letras azules.
> 60   Se dejan caer en las camas, se hunden en las
> almohadas
> que los hacen pensar todavía un momento en

las nubes.
Pero cierran los ojos para entregarse mejor a
los goces de su encarnación misteriosa,
y, cuando duermen, sueñan no con los ángeles
sino con los mortales.
　　　　—Los Angeles, California. (pp. 55-57).

Tomás Segovia finds this poem to be unique among the *nocturnos* in that it is, as he puts it, "un poco sonriente."[2] The poet's obvious pun on the name of the city of Los Angeles (the poem was at least conceived during the time that Villaurrutia was traveling and studying in the United States) might lead one to agree in part with that opinion, though for me the tone is not one of levity. This is a poem on homosexual love, incomplete, unrealized, and represented in terms of physical desire.

Though the poet divides the composition into stanzas, there is no fixed length or arrangement for those divisions. Line length varies very widely and again with no visible patterning, and aside from scattered assonance there is no rhyme at all. The development of the theme is built on the contrast "ángeles—mortales" and the ten stanzas of the poem can be divided into three developmental segments.

The first of these elements (lines 1-15) develops the setting for the entire poem and also the first element of the contrast. The scene is a nocturnal one, in which the streets seem to flow as rivers and people on them move as silent shadows. The attention seems focused here on "mortales" or "hombres", though beneath the surface of each man lies a secret desire which is revealed only during the night. The use of sexual imagery in the second stanza underlines sharply an element of physical sensuality which persists throughout the poem. The second segment (lines 16-34) depicts, on the flowing rivers of nocturnal streets, the movement of two series of "sedientos seres" who walk about, gaze at each other, form couples, and then enter suddenly into lighted doors which open up along the street. These beings are obviously not mortals as were those described in the previous stanzas, but often transport themselves as if they were flying or even swimming in a standing position.

The final structural segment of the poem (lines 35-64) begins by affirming that these mysterious figurations are "los ángeles," who have come to the earth to find some sort of relationship with mortals. They come from the sea, as some kind of mysterious seafarers,[3] and in the same way that the sky finds its reflection in the sea these beings have come to reflect and release with tongues of fire the expression of the sensuality and desire which lies immediately beneath the surface of mortal beings. Again, the imagery is highly sexual, and physical desire is represented strongly in repeated tactile sense impressions. They are more beautiful than the mortal beings with whom they desire to associate, and although they carry celestial markings on their bodies (perhaps a reference to a sailor's tattoo?) they have taken on mortal form and when they sleep dream not of angels but of mortals.

The final meaning of this very complex poem depends on the successful interpretation of the "ángeles—mortales" contrast. On a most elementary level, it is possible to see the mortals as the usual inhabitants of a port city, and the angels to be strangers who mingle with them, as sailors on liberty from their assignments. However, the highly sensual imagery and the nocturnal backdrop for the poem makes this interpretation hardly satisfactory. A better approach is to suggest that the contrast is symbolic of a dual expression of desire. The mortal, or conscious, represses a somewhat secret and shameful awareness of this desire, and only in the completely unfettered existence of the angels does all that which is hidden and repressed find expression. Every man, this interpretation wouldsuggest, has both aspects in his personality, and only in the shadowy galleries of the night can his repressed desires be expressed. A third interpretation is to see the "ángeles—mortales" contrast as representing homosexual love and desire. The poet makes use of a mythical—astronomical reference to the Twins to suggest an all-consuming emotion. Mortals and angels have the same form, but nonetheless desire each other and can find expression for this desire only in the mysterious coupling which is possible in the limitless shadows of the night.

In **Canto a la primavera** the theme of love is primary, and can be found in almost every composition in the entire collection. Here again the emotional response depicted is not one of joy and fulfillment, but rather of incompleteness and despair.

**"Décimas de nuestro amor,"** is probably the most imposing and carefully organized expression of the theme. This composition is made up of ten carefully worked *décimas* which develop the opposing multiple facets of an anguished and unrealized love.

The first *décima* serves as a prologue to those that follow:

I

A mí mismo me prohibo
revelar nuestro secreto,
decir tu nombre completo
o escribirlo cuando escribo.
Prisionero de ti, vivo
buscándote en la sombría
caverna de mi agonía.
Y cuando a solas te invoco,
en la oscura piedra toco
tu impasible compañía.

　　　　　　　　　　(p. 79).

In this *décima* the essential qualities of the entire poem are presented. The central relationship is that of a *yo* who is present and in a state of anguish and a *tú* who is distant and indifferent. The search for love does not exist face to face with the beloved person, but rather in the hidden and darkened caverns of the lover's own consciousness. It is here that he realizes that their relationship is secret and even prohibited, and that the beloved exists only as an impassive, indifferent presence.

The following two *décimas* make up the second thematic segment of the poem:

II

> Si nuestro amor está hecho
> de silencios prolongados
> que nuestros labios cerrados
> maduran dentro del pecho;
> y si el corazón deshecho
> sangra como la granada
> en su sombra congelada,
> ¿por qué, dolorosa y mustia,
> no rompemos esta angustia
> para salir de la nada?

III

> Por le temor de quererme
> tanto como yo te quiero,
> has preferido, primero,
> para salverte, perderme.
> Pero está mudo e inerme
> tu corazón, de tal suerte
> que si no me dejas verte
> es por no ver en la mía
> la imagen de tu agonía:
> porque mi muerte es tu muerte.

(p. 79).

These two stanzas pursue further the essence of hidden love, and represent two of its aspects. This love is unexpressed and imprisoned, as the figure of the pomegranate again suggests. The anguished interrogation at the end of II seeks to break through these limitations and to soften the silence which exists. In III love is seen again as unexpressed, here by the refusal of the beloved person to infuse the relationship with life and communication. The poet sees himself as dead and finds the same death in the lack of expressed love.

The third segment of the poem is composed of the following four *décimas,* all of which revolve around the interplay of the contradictory absence and presence of the beloved:

IV

> Te alejas de mí pensando
> que me hiere tu presencia,
> y no sabes que tu ausencia
> es más dolorosa cuando
> la soledad se va ahondando,
> y en el silencio sombrío,
> sin quererlo, a pesar mío,
> oigo tu voz en el eco
> y hallo tu forma en el hueco
> que has dejado en el vacío.

V

> ¿Por qué dejas entrever
> una remota esperanza,
> si el deseo no te alcanza,
> si nada volverá a set?

> Y si no habrá amanecer
> en mi noche interminable
> ¿de qué sirve que yo hable
> en el desierto, y que pida,
> para reanimar mi vida,
> remedio a lo irremediable?

VI

> Esta incertidumbre oscura
> que sube en mi cuerpo y que
> deja en mi boca no sé
> qué desolada amargura;
> este sabor que perdura
> y, como el recuerdo, insiste,
> y, como tu olor, persiste
> con su penetrante esencia,
> es la sola y cruel presencia
> tuya, desde que partiste.

VII

> Apenas has vuelto, y ya
> en todo mi ser avanza,
> verde y turbia, la esperanza
> para decirme: "¡Aquí está!"
> Pero su voz se oirá
> rodar sin eco en la oscura
> soledad de mi clausura
> y yo seguiré pensando
> que no hay esperanza cuando
> la esperanza es la tortura.

(pp. 80-81).

In each stanza the figure of the beloved is distant from the poet; in each there is contradictory mitigation and agitation of the anguish brought about by that absence. In IV, for example, the beloved has gone but the poet finds indication of reality in the empty forms which have been left behind. In V the separation is an emotional one, in which the poet laments the mere presence of a remote hope that the distance between can be overcome. In VI, the poet has a bitter sense of desolation and solitude, and in VII the merest suggestion of a return causes a painful and turbulent flourishing of hope.

Décimas VIII and IX make up the fourth structural segment of the poem:

VIII

> Ayer to soñé. Temblando
> los dos en el goce impuro
> y estéril de un sueño oscuro.
> Y sobre tu cuerpo blando
> mis labios iban dejando
> huellas, señales, heridas . . .
> Y tus palabras transidas
> y las mías delirantes
> de aquellos breves instantes
> prolongaban nuestras vidas.

IX

> Si nada espero, pues nada
> tembló en ti cuando me viste

y ante mis ojos pusiste
la verdad más desolada;
si no brilló en tu mirada
un destello de emoción,
la sola oscura razón,
la fuerza que a ti me lanza,
perdida toda esperanza,
es . . . ¡la desesperación!

(p. 81).

These two *décimas* represent the dark and sterile dream of a desperate love. In VIII the poet brings his beloved to life in the figuration of a dream, and in the very act of expressing love leaves only wounds which have a symbolic quality. The delirious emotion on the part of the poet and the brief utterances on the part of the beloved seem to prolong this existence, but still in the unreality of the dream. In IX the situation is continued, and the poet realizes that there is no responding emotion in the eyes nor the being of his beloved, and he feels impelled only by the same desperate search for love and communication.

The fifth segment is composed of the final *décima* of the poem, which is a counterbalance to the first and introductory stanza:

X

Mi amor por ti ¡no murió!
Sigue viviendo en la fría,
ignorada galería
que en mi corazón cavó.
Por ella desciendo y no
encontraré la salida,
pues será toda mi vida
esta angustia de buscarte
a ciegas, con la escondida
certidumbre de no hallarte.

(p. 82).

This final segment is an affirmation of continuing love, in spite of its impossible condition and the irrevocable absence of the beloved. The poet's emotion is alive in the cold expanse of his being, and he continues to search for the pathway which leads him toward life and a communication of his love. At the same time, however, he realizes with a sense of blind anguish that he will never be able to realize this possibility, and is condemned to search eternally without recompense.

The careful structuring of the thematic development of the poem, as well as the equally balanced and exact syntactical and metrical development of each of the individual *décimas,* makes this poem a successful representation of the peculiar love theme in Villaurrutia's poems.

A somewhat different aspect of the theme is presented by the composition **"Amor condusse noi ad una morte"**:[4]

Amar es una angustia, una pregunta
una suspensa y luminosa duda;
es un querer saber todo lo tuyo
y a la vez un temor de al fin saberlo.

5  Amar es reconstruir, cuando te alejas,
tus pasos, tus silencios, tus palabras,
y pretender seguir tu pensamiento
cuando a mi lado, al fin inmóvil, callas.

    Amar es una cólera secreta,
10  una helada y diabólica soberbia.

    Amar es no dormir cuando en mi lecho
sueñas entre mis brazos que te ciñen,
y odiar el sueño en que, bajo tu frente,
acaso en otros brazos te abandonas.

15  Amar es escuchar sobre tu pecho,
hasta colmar la oreja codiciosa,
el rumor de tu sangre y la marea
de tu respiración acompasada.

    Amar es absorber tu joven savia
20  y juntar nuestras bocas en un cauce
hasta que de la brisa de tu aliento
se impregnen para siempre mis entrañas.

    Amar es una envidia verde y muda,
una sutil y lúcida avaricia.

25  Amar es provocar el dulce instante
en que tu piel busca mi piel despierta;
saciar a un tiempo la avidez nocturna
y morir otra vez la misma muerte
provisional, desgarradora, oscura.

30  Amar es una sed, la de la llaga
que arde sin consumirse ni cerrarse,
y el hambre de una boca atormentada
que pide más y más y no se sacia.

    Amar es una insólita lujuria
35  y una gula voraz, siempre desierta.

    Pero amar es también cerrar los ojos,
dejar que el sueño invada nuestro cuerpo
como un río de olvido y de tinieblas,
y navegar sin rumbo, a la deriva:
40  porque amar es, al fin, una indolencia.

(pp. 76-77).

This is not one of the poems in which there is a considerable amount of metrical or syntactical freedom, but rather a sense of connection and organization. There is a systematic strophe pattern and a relationship of quatrain to couplet, and as well the line length is hendecasyllabic. Perhaps the greatest sense of connection, however, comes from the anaphoric use of the verb "amar" in each of the stanzas in succession.

The central theme of the poem is a consideration of the nature of love, suggested by the repetition of the infinitive form, and is developed in four segments. Each of the segments has the same structure: a specific statement of various aspects of the yo—tú love relationship, followed by an abstract statement related to one or more of the capital sins. For example, the first segment (lines 1-10) is composed of two quatrains which make up the specific statement and a closing couplet which is the abstraction.

Love is, this segment suggests, anguish, questioning, doubting, and the reconstructing, both in the absence and presence of the beloved, of those small things which go to make up the reality of a person. The couplet, without any direct mention of the beloved, suggests that the act of loving is both passionate anger and cold and calculating pride.

The same alternating pattern between quatrain and couplet is to be seen in the following two structural segments. The second (lines 11-24) is made up of three quatrains which suggest a very close physical relationship between the two lovers. The poet keeps watch over his sleeping beloved, and is aware of life and movement which only he can see. The poet also feels the effects of his awareness in those moments in which intimate physical contact is made. The closing couplet again reduces these particularized stanzas to an abstraction. The act of loving is an envy which flourishes as a silent plant and an avarice which is sharp and clear. Segment three (lines 25-35) differs slightly in metrical form in that the first stanza has five lines rather than the four which have been the pattern up to this point. However, the thematic development is the same. Love is represented here as reaching an emotional climax, but never really being fulfilled. The couplet again makes the abstraction: the act of loving is a lust which is never satisfied.

The final segment of the poem (lines 36-40) is made up of the final five lines of the poem. There is no closing couplet here, but the structural pattern is the same. The first four lines of the stanza represent the act of loving as dreaming, as floating down a shadowy river of forgetfulness, without direction or particular purpose, and the final line is the abstraction: the act of loving is after all else indolence.

In this poem the relationship between lover and beloved is not one of absence or distance, but rather one of contact and emotional climax. The act of loving, together with the need for love and communication, is repeatedly made the axis of the poem. However, the recurring abstraction toward the capital sins creates an overriding sensation of guilt in the relationship between the two beings, and love is filled with a sense of anguish and doubt.

Still another example of the theme of love can be seen in the **"Soneto del temor a Dios"**:

> Este miedo de verte cara a cara,
> de oír el timbre de tu voz radiante
> y de aspirar la emanación fragante
> de tu cuerpo intangible, nos separa.
>
> ¡Cómo dejaste que desembarcara
> en otra orilla, de tu amor distante!
> Atado estoy, inmóvil navegante,
> ¡y el río de la angustia no se para!
>
> Y no sé para qué tendiendo redes
> con palabras pretendo aprisionarte,
> si, a medida que avanzan, retrocedes.
> Es inútil mi fiebre de alcanzarte,
> mientras tú mismo, que todo lo puedes,
> no vengas en mis redes a enredarte.
>
> (p. 85).

The careful hendecasyllables and the *abrazado* rhyme scheme make this a perfect classical sonnet in form, and the equally careful oppositions developed throughout are very reminiscent of Sor Juana Inés de la Cruz and other earlier figures of the Spanish baroque period.

Tomás Segovia suggests that this poem is indicative of a return to religious themes which the poet had not used since his earliest works.[5] The title suggests immediately a love poem "a lo divino," and the strong *yo—tú* relationship in the sonnet can be seen as the gulf between suffering man and distant deity. The first quatrain suggests an unbridgeable chasm between the two, in which the features, voice, and fragrance of the divine being can only be imagined. The second quatrain laments this separation, questions the reason for man's separation from God, and recognizes the difficulties and anguishes of man's existence. The two tercets develop, in succeedingly intricate oppositions, the desire on the part of man to reach out toward divinity, and the inevitable impossibilities of such an attempt. The image of the net is suggestive in this context of similar imagery recorded in the New Testament in some of the parables of Christ and actions of some of his disciples.

As is usually the case with poetry "a lo divino," an interpretation in terms of worldly love is just as acceptable. The forces and uncertainties of "amor mundano" can just as well be the motivating impulse behind the anguished and impassioned *yo—tú* relationship. The poet is separated from his beloved and must imagine a face, the sound of a voice, and the fragrance of an untouchable and distant person. The poet laments the action of the beloved, which has forced him to live in complete separation, inextricably bound and immobilized in a flow of anguish. The verbal nets which he throws out to imprison anew his beloved are useless, because the beloved continues to withdraw from him. Only by an impossible act of love will the poet finally be able to encompass his beloved as he so ardently desires.

*Death*

The theme of death differs from the other two major themes already considered in this chapter, in that its development is confined mainly to *Nostalgia de la muerte*. The consideration of the theme, therefore, will take up only compositions from that collection.

The theme of death is not always developed in the same fashion, but is represented in some poems as a presence which pervades the surroundings, in others as a process which affects the poet inevitably in his circumstance, and in others as a personification which also has an intimate relationship with the poet. Perhaps the best example of the first of these facets is the composition **"Nocturno de la alcoba,"** in which death takes on the multiple forms which the poet sees in the room in which he finds himself:

> La muerte toma siempre la forma de la alcoba
> que nos contiene.

Es cóncava y oscura y tibia y silenciosa,
se pliega en las cortinas en que anida la
          sombra,
5   es dura en el espejo y tensa y congelada,
y profunda en las almohadas y, en las sábanas,
          blanca.

Los dos sabemos que la muerte toma
la forma de la alcoba, y que en la alcoba
es el espacio frío que levanta
10   entre los dos un muro, un cristal, un silencio.

Entonces sólo yo sé que la muerte
es el hueco que dejas en el lecho
cuando de pronto y sin razón alguna
te incorporas o te pones de pie.

15   Y es el ruido de hojas calcinadas
que hacen tus pies desnudos al hundirse en la
          alfombra.

Y es el sudor que moja nuestros muslos
que se abrazan y luchan y que, luego, se
          rinden.

20   Y es la frase que dejas caer, interrumpida.
Y la pregunta mía que no oyes,
que no comprendes o que no respondes.

Y el silencio que cae y te sepulta
cuando velo tu sueño y lo interrogo.
25   Y solo, sólo yo sé que la muerte
es tu palabra trunca, tus gemidos ajenos
y tus involuntarios movimientos oscuros
cuando en el sueño luchas con el ángel del
          sueño.

La muerte es todo esto y más que nos circunda,
30   y nos une y separa alternativamente,
que nos deja confusos, atónitos, suspensos,
con una herida que no mana sangre.

Entonces, sólo entonces, los dos solos,
          sabemos
que no el amor sino la oscura muerte
35   nos precipita a vernos cara a cara a los ojos,
y a unirnos y a estrecharnos, más que solos y
          náufragos,
todavía más, y cada vez más, todavía.
                                    (pp. 60-61).

The form of the poem is generally free, with no specific pattern of line length, stanza, or rhyme. There is a very definite division into stanzas, however, and there is a considerable amount of non-systematic assonance throughout the poem. The central theme of the poem is the omnipresence of death and its ability to take on the shapes and essences of things which surround the poet. There is a consistent *yo—tú* relationship which is reminiscent of the love poems already commented on, but used here to provide a kind of double reflection for the pervasive presence of death.

The poem can be divided into three developmental segments. The first of these segments is composed of the first three stanzas (lines 1-10), and develops the basic relationships and direction of the entire composition. Death takes the form of the bedroom in which the poet and his beloved find themselves, and conforms itself to the shapes and sounds of the room. It has curvature, color, warmth, reflection, and hardness, as the situation demands. Both the poet and his beloved recognize this multiplicity of forms, and know that death erects between them a silent and crystalline wall which separates them from each other.

The second segment includes the following six stanzas (lines 11-28). Here the point of view shifts from the duality of the *yo—tú* to the singleness of the *yo*. The poet realizes also that many of the things which he associates with the presence of his beloved also speak of death: a hollow which indicates the previous presence of the beloved, the sound of bare feet on the floor, the warmth of a sexual embrace, and the interrupted phrases and questions which remain unanswered. This segment of the poem is very highly connected by a series of verbs and conjunctions which operate in an anaphoric fashion to suggest themeanderings of the poet's mind as he considers these matters.

The final two stanzas of the poem (lines 29-37) make up the third major segment of the poem, and serve as a kind of recapitulation of those elements which have gone before. Death is all the many things which the poet passes before his consciousness, and this all-encompassing presence separates and unifies the poet and his beloved at the same time. The realization of this presence leaves them confused and expectant, as well as deeply wounded. The two at that moment, together but alone at the same time, realize that their experience is not one of love entirely but rather of a common tasting of the presence of death which throws them more closely together. The contradictory ambiguousness of the final lines, with the impossible interfacing of intimacy and shipwreck, heighten the anguish and ambiguity of this all-encompassing presence.

In other poems of the collection death is seen as an inevitable process. **"Muerte en el frío"** is probably the best example:

Cuando he perdido toda fe en el milagro,
cuando ya la esperanza dejó caer la última nota
y resuena un silencio sin fin, cóncavo y duro;

cuando el cielo de invierno no es más que la
          ceniza
5   de algo que ardió hace muchos, muchos
          siglos;

cuando me encuentro tan solo, tan solo,
que me busco en mi cuarto
como se busca, a veces, un objeto perdido,
una carta estrujada, en los rincones;

10   cuando cierro los ojos pensando inútilmente
que así estaré más lejos
de aquí, de mí, de todo
aquello que me acusa de no ser más que un
          muerto,

siento que estoy en el infierno frío,
15 en el invierno eterno
que congela la sangre en las arterias,
que seca las palabras amarillas,
que paraliza el sueño,
que pone una mordaza de hielo a nuestra boca
20 y dibuja las cosas con una línea dura.

Siento que estoy viviendo aquí mi muerte,
mi sola muerte presente,
mi muerte que no puedo compartir ni llorar,
mi muerte de que no me consolaré jamás.

25 Y comprendo de una vez para nunca
el clima del silencio
donde se nutre y perfecciona la muerte.
Y también la eficacia del frío
que preserva y purifica sin consumir como el
    fuego.

30 Y en el silencio escucho dentro de mí el
    trabajo
de un minucioso ejército de obreros que
    golpean
con diminutos martillos mi linfa y mi carne
    estremecidas;

siento cómo se besan
y juntan para siempre sus orillas
35 las islas que flotaban en mi cuerpo;

cómo el agua y la sangre
son otra vez la misma agua marina,
y cómo se hiela primero
y luego se vuelve cristal

40 y luego duro mármol,
hasta inmovilizarme en el tiempo más
angustioso y lento,
con la vida secreta, muda e imperceptible
del mineral, del tronco, de la estatua.
                                    (pp. 66-68).

It can be seen at once that although there is clear division into strophes and consistent punctuation that the poem has considerable freedom in its form. The lines are largely conventional (predominantly heptasyllables, hendecasyllables, and Alexandrines), but there is no consistent arrangement into strophes. There is no fixed rhyme scheme, although there is scattered assonance throughout the poem, in particular in *á-o* in the second half.

The principal theme of the composition is that of inevitable death as a process, and this theme is developed in three principal structural parts. The first of these is made up of the first five strophes (lines 1-20). The first strophe is an extensive dependent clause in which an auditory image suggests the sensation of desperateness and resounding silence, a sense impression which is augmented by aspects of hardness and visual form. A second suspended clause follows the first, and the winter sky, now gray and ashen, is added to the previous silence and lack of hope. The two following strophes (lines 6-14), each in the same syntactical form, relate a state of solitude to the silent wintry panorama. The poet has no identity, and he must close his eyes in order to escape from himself and from the silence of his own existence. Three run-on lines (10-13) produce two extensive syntactic periods arranged around the particle "de mí," and underline the anonymity and solitude of the poet's internal state. A fifth strophe (lines 14-20) is the syntactical resolution of the previous strophes, and is at the same time a summary and a thematic extension. The first two lines make apparent, principally by means of thermic images, the frigid inferno of the poet. The word play "invierno—infierno" (lines 14-15) suggests intensity and amplitude. The four following verses (16-19) describe in parallel constructions the effects of this icy desolation: the processes of the physical body are suspended and the means of communication is closed off. The final line of the strophe shows that the spectral images of silence and solitude are to be seen everywhere.

Strophes 6 and 7 (lines 21-29) constitute the second structural part of the poem. Here the silent and desperate isolation of winter becomes the environment in which life is changed into solitary and unlamented death. The thermic images continue to function: cold and silence do not consume as do fire and passion, but rather preserve the superficial appearance of life.

The final three strophes (lines 30-43) form the third structural division of the composition, and here the process which takes life toward death is represented and experienced. In the eighth strophe the poet realizes that he is living material, shaped by a host of diminutive workers who possibly can represent the numerous small actions of life which determine the reality of our existence. In the ninth strophe the circulation of the blood is suspended and in the tenth strophe the transformation is completed. The body fluids congeal, then crystallize, and finally become marble. The poet thus is left immobile, silent and mineral-like in a suspended and anguished temporal dimension. The thermic images are combined here with auditory impressions of silence and noisy hammering as well as tactile and lapidary suggestions in order to communicate the anguished thematic resolution of the whole poem.

In other poems of the collection death is personified, at times as nothing more than a shadowy figure ("Para darme muerte/la muerte esperaba", p. 48) and at other times as a woman with whom one has had a long and familiar relationship. **"Nocturno en que habla la muerte"** is probably the best example of this view of death:

Si la muerte hubiera venido aquí, a New Haven,
escondida en un hueco de mi ropa en la maleta,
en el bolsillo de uno de mis trajes,
entre las páginas de un libro
5 como la señal que ya no me recuerda nada;
si mi muerte particular estuviera esperando
una fecha, un instante que sólo ella conoce
para decirme: "Aquí estoy.
Te he seguido como la sombra
10 que no es posible dejar así nomás en casa;

como un poco de aire cálido e invisible
mezclado al aire duro y frío que respiras;
como el recuerdo de lo que más quieres;
como el olvido, sí, como el olvido
15  que has dejado caer sobre las cosas
que no quisieras recordar ahora.
Y es inútil que vuelvas la cabeza en mi busca:
estoy tan cerca que no puedes verme,
estoy fuera de ti y a un tiempo dentro.
20  Nada es el mar que como un dios quisiste
poner entre los dos;
nada es la tierra que los hombres miden
y por la que matan y mueren;
ni el sueño en que quisieras creer que vives
25  sin mí, cuando yo misma lo dibujo y lo borro;
ni los días que cuentas
una vez y otra vez a todas horas,
ni las horas que matas con orgullo
sin pensar que renacen fuera de ti.
30  Nada son estas cosas ni los innumerables
lazos que me tendiste,
ni las infantiles argucias con que has querido
dejarme engañada, olvidada.
Aquí estoy, ¿no me sientes?
35  Abre los ojos; ciérralos, si quieres."

Y me pregunto ahora,
si nadie entró en la pieza contigua,
¿quién cerró cautelosamente la puerta?
¿Qué misteriosa fuerza de gravedad
40  hizo caer la hoja de papel que estaba en la
      mesa?
¿Por qué se instala aquí, de pronto, y sin que
      yo la invite,
la voz de una mujer que habla en la calle?

Y al oprimir la pluma,
algo como la sangre late y circula en ella,
45  y siento que las letras desiguales
que escribo ahora,
más pequeñas, más trémulas, más débiles,
ya no son de mi mano solamente.

                    (pp. 54-55).

The poem is divided into three stanzas of unequal length in which there is also no pattern of metrical length or of end rhyme. There is however some scattered assonance, as in a number of other poems of this collection, and notably frequent run-on lines.

The theme of the poem is the omnipresence of death, and the impossibility of escaping it no matter how far the poet may travel. The reference to New Haven in line 1 suggests that here again the poem was at least conceived during the time the poet was in the United States and thus removed from his customary surroundings. It is possible to see the development of the central theme in two segments. The first of these is made up entirely by the first long stanza, which represents an imaginary confrontation between the poet and a personified death. A series of verbs in the imperfect subjunctive prepare for the utterance of personified death. "If my own private figure of death were here with me, waiting for the proper moment to reveal herself", muses the poet and then constructs for himself the words she might say. Even though she cannot

be seen or touched, death observes that it is impossible for the poet to leave her behind or to erase her from his consciousness. Death continues to surround him and at the same time be deeply within him.

The second part of the poem is made up of the final two strophes (lines 36-48), and brings the poet back to reality. Yet, certain things seem to happen which are beyond his control, and which suggest an unknown presence. A door closes, a paper falls to the floor, a woman's voice is heard within the room, and as the poet writes a mysterious power affects the letters which flow from his pen. Here the actions are expressed in present and past indicative; the poet no longer has to suppose the presence of accompanying death: she is with him, revealing herself through many small circumstances.

Another and more complex example is to be found in **"Décima muerte,"** one of the poet's best known compositions. Here again, as in the previously discussed **"Décimas de nuestro amor,"** the poet chooses the carefully worked *décima* form in ten stanzas.

The *yo—tú* relationship which has been seen in many of the other poems is here also the principal vehicle for the development of the theme. There is a constant exchange between the poet's anguished awareness of himself as the *yo* and the shadowy and overwhelming presence of death as the *tú*. This contradictory relationship, developed through the careful *décima* stanzas, can be seen in four developmental segments. The first of these, made up of the first three *décimas,* can be seen as an attempt to describe this relationship:

     I

¡Qué prueba de la existencia
habrá mayor que la suerte
de estar viviendo sin verte
y muriendo en tu presencia!
Esta lúcida conciencia
de amar a lo nunca visto
y de esperar lo imprevisto;
este caer sin llegar
es la angustia de pensar
que puesto que muero existo.

     II

Si en todas partes estás,
en el agua y en la tierra,
en el aire que me encierra
y en el incendio voraz;
y si a todas partes vas
conmigo en el pensamiento,
en el soplo de mi aliento
y en mi sangre confundida,
¿no serás, Muerte, en mi vida,
agua, fuego, polvo y viento?

     III

Si tienes manos, que sean
de un tacto sutil y blando,

apenas sensible cuando
anestesiado me crean;
y que tus ojos me vean
sin mirarme, de tal suerte
que nada me desconcierte
ni tu vista ni tu roce,
para no sentir un goce
ni un dolor contigo, Muerte.

(pp. 70-71).

In the first stanza, life and existence can be explained by the unrealizedsearch for death which the poet insists upon. The awareness of loving something which has not been seen yet and expecting the unexpected, causes the poet to reflect in anguish that the only proof of his existence is the process toward death. The second *décima,* which is very reminiscent of both Góngora and Sor Juana Inés de la Cruz, sees death as an elemental part of life. Death is so much a part of him and the things around him that he must reflect, in the final two lines of the stanza, that death or personified death is for him as important as the four principal elements were for ancient man.

*Décima* III exists in the form of a request, expressed in a series of subjunctive verbs. The poet, in view of the intimate relationship between himself and personified death, requests that her touch be barely felt, as if he were anaesthetized or unaware of other sense impressions.

The following two *décimas* change the focus of the poem slightly:

IV

Por caminos ignorados,
por hendiduras secretas,
por las misteriosas vetas
de troncos recién cortados,
te ven mis ojos cerrados
entrar en mi alcoba oscura
a convertir mi envoltura
opaca, febril, cambiante,
en materia de diamante
luminosa, eterna y pura.

V

No duermo para que al verte
llegar lenta y apagada,
para que al oír pausada
tu voz que silencios vierte,
para que al tocar la nada
que envuelve tu cuerpo yerto,
para que a tu olor desierto
pueda, sin sombra de sueño,
saber que de ti me adueño,
sentir que muero despierto.

(p. 71).

In both of these stanzas the figure of death enters the bedroom of the poet, and in a dream-like sequence he sees that certain things will occur at that particular moment. In IV, for example, death enters his room in a number of small and secret ways, perhaps again indica-

tive of the almost imperceptible progress of death in life, and is able to convert his existence into something resembling the hardness and luminosity of a diamond. In V the poet lies awake in order to watch the slow and silent arrival of death, and by reaching out to the contradictory silences and emptinesses of death, is able to be more deeply aware of that process.

The third segment is made up of *décimas* VI-VIII, which depend on a physical relationship between the *yo* of the poet and the personified death figure:

VI

La aguja del instantero
recorrerá su cuadrante,
todo cabrá en un instante
del espacio verdadero
que, ancho, profundo y señero,
será elástico a tu paso
de modo que el tiempo cierto
prolongará nuestro abrazo
y será posible, acaso,
vivir después de haber muerto.

VII

En el roce, en el contacto,
en la inefable delicia
de la suprema caricia
que desemboca en el acto,
hay un misterioso pacto
del espasmo delirante
en que un cielo alucinante
y un infierno de agonía
se funden cuando eres mía
y soy tuyo en un instante.

VIII

¡Hasta en la ausencia estás viva!
Porque te encuentro en el hueco
de una forma y en el eco
de una nota fugitiva;
porque en mi propia saliva
fundes tu sabor sombrío,
y a cambio de lo que es mío
me dejas sólo el temor
de hallar hasta en el sabor
la presencia del vacío.

(p. 72).

In VI the moment of death is likened to a lover's embrace, and the poet contemplates the extension of this embrace in his obsessive musings on death. Perhaps in this way, the poet indicates, he will be able to achieve death in life and thereby a kind of life after death. VII continues the figure of a lover's embrace in more intensity and detail, and contemplates death as something which can be represented in the caresses and even the spasms of physical love. However, this love and awareness are momentary, and therefore extremely hallucinatory and anguished. In stanza VIII the physical relationship is only suggested, here as absence and echo and emptiness, but nonetheless physical in the suggestion of the image of saliva. The poet fears that in return for his surrender of himself in the lover's embrace with the figure of death that he will find only the same emptiness which has characterized his life.

The fourth part is one of summation, and is made up of the last two *décimas* of the poem:

IX

> Si te llevo en mí prendida
> y te acaricio y escondo;
> si te alimento en el fondo
> de mi más secreta herida;
> si mi muerte te da vida
> y goce mi frenesí,
> ¿qué será, Muerte, de ti
> cuando al salir yo del mundo,
> deshecho el nudo profundo,
> tengas que salir de mí?

X

> En vano amenazas, Muerte,
> cerrar la boca a mi herida
> y poner fin a mi vida
> con una palabra inerte.
> ¡Qué puedo pensar al verte,
> si en mi angustia verdadera
> tuve que violar la espera;
> si en vista de tu tardanza
> para llenar mi esperanza
> no hay hora en que yo no muera!

(p. 73).

*Décima* IX is a summarized recognition of the intimacy and anguish of the *yo—tú* relationship which has been developed. The poet carries with him at all times the figure of death, and continues to nourish it within the most intimate part of his being. At the same time, however, he questions Death directly as to what will happen at that moment when he really dies. Since his anguish gives pleasure and his death will give life in the sense of being freed from his embrace, the poet then wonders about the continued existence of this particular and peculiar figuration which he has contrived.

*Décima* X exists as a challenge to the personified death figure. Her silence, the poet says, does not frighten him nor can it really put an end to his existence. If death approaches, as he sees that it does, his intense anguish in life gives him at least one satisfaction: death has no real power over him since there has not been a time in which his life has not been a living death. He no longer fears death because he has met her, embraced her, and becomes one with her many times before.

The development of **"Décima muerte,"** with its careful metrical patterns, its neo-baroque plays of precise counterposition, and its insistent development of a personified death, lead to one final example which is a fitting close to the consideration of this theme in Villaurrutia's poems. This composition, with the title of **"Epitafio,"**[6] expresses with finality the idea of multiple experiences of death in a contradictory state of life:

II

> Duerme aquí, silencioso e ignorado,
> el que en vida vivió mil y una muertes.
> Nada quieras saber de mi pasado.
> Despertar es morir. ¡No me despiertes!

(p. 90).

*Minor Themes*

In addition to the main themes already discussed in this chapter, there are several minor thematic threads which appear intermittently throughout Villaurrutia's poems, and need to be considered separately here. Poetry and poetic creation, nature and the peaceful life, and religious experience are all themes which appear in some poems, particularly in the very early and the last collections, and there are some compositions which are related thematically to Villaurrutia's travel in the United States. None of these is insistent enough to warrant discussion as a primary focal point of the poet's verses, but each should be considered briefly.

The theme of poetic creation is first used by Villaurrutia in a very early poem, **"Le pregunté al poeta . . . ,"** which is very reminiscent of some early Modernist verses:

> Le pregunté al poeta su secreto
> una tarde de lloro,
> de lluvia y de canción,
> y me dijo el poeta: "Mi secreto
> no lo dictan los sabios en decreto.
> En la orilla del Nilo y en la aurora
> interroga a Memnón . . ."
>
> Le pregunté al poeta su secreto
> una noche de luna,
> una noche de augurios y de mal.
> El poeta me contestó con una
> mirada que era un reto
> y me dijo: "Interroga
> a la estatua de sal . . ."
>
> Yo descansé la frente entre las manos
> (un grupo de aves emprendió la huida).
> Mis preguntas y anhelos eran vanos,
> el poeta callaba su secreto
> porque era ese secreto el de su vida.

(pp. 4-5).

The poem takes the form of an imagined dialogue between the young and inexperienced *yo* and "el poeta," who already knows the secret of life. On several occasions the voice of inexperience questions, but instead of receiving answers is commanded to turn to Memnon or the Biblical statue of salt. The questions and concerns are all in vain, since the poet can no more explain the process of poetry than he can explain the reasons for his own existence.

In **"Poesía,"** the composition which now opens *Reflejos,* the poet finds himself immersed in the mystery of the words and the processes of poetry. The words which spring from the deep well of his being form a personification, whose hand takes control of the creative process ("Tu mano metálica . . . conduce la pluma/que traza en el papel su litoral.", p. 26) and whose external form is as a mirror in which the poet can view himself ("y en tu piel de espejo/me estoy mirando mirarme . . .", p. 26). However, these structures are so fragile that the slightest sound will destroy them, and the poet again finds himself deserted ("y me dejas/sin más pulso mi voz y sin más cara,/sin máscara como un hombre desnudo/en medio de una calle de miradas.", p. 26). In this composition the poet seems to emphasize, rather than the mystery and secret of poetry, its essential impossibility and fragileness.

In **"Palabra,"** a composition that appeared posthumously, the poet personifies the poetic word and assigns to her regal qualities of pride and mystery:

Palabra que no sabes lo que nombras.
Palabra, ¡reina altiva!
Llamas nube a la sombra fugitiva
de un mundo en que las nubes son las sombras.
(p. 85).

Here the word itself, rather than the poet or poetry as indicated in the previous two compositions, is the focus for the mystery of poetic creation. The word in its personified regal form can express in a single figure the complex and subterranean reality which stands behind it, in this case the relationship being nube = sombra = mundo fugitivo (nubes = sombras).

The poet's' development of this theme is not extensive, as can be seen from these examples, but there is enough of a development to underscore sharply the poet's interest in the expressiveness of language and the mystery of poetic creation.

Villaurrutia cannot in any way be characterized as a religious poet; his principal themes lead strongly in the direction of immediate physical experience. However, there are several poems in which religious experience becomes the dominant thematic focus. Most of these are to be found in **Primeros poemas** ("Plegaria," "Breviario," "Ya mi súplica es llanto"), and probably the best example is **"Ni la leve zozobra":**

Mi corazón, Señor, que contiene el sollozo,
que palidece y deja sin rumbo su latir,
mi corazón huraño y misericordioso
se te da como un fruto maduro de sufrir.

Mi corazón, Señor, hermética granada
de un resignado huerto donde no llega el
luminar de cielo de la casta mirada,
ni la antorcha perenne de la palabra fiel.

Se abandona al saber que tu milagro quedo
enterrará el afán, el presagio y el miedo,
y el más íntimo engaño ahogará desde hoy.

Porque el dolor tenaz sustituirá un aroma,
y desde la oblación que a tu quietud se asoma,
ni la leve zozobra temblará en lo que soy . . .
(p. 20).

This composition, a sonnet which differs slightly from the classical metrical pattern, takes the form of a lament in which the poet recognizes the depths of his suffering and at the same time the miracle which will remove pain and fear. The quatrains of the sonnet express the suffering felt by the poet, and use the figure of the pomegranate to symbolize the heart hidden from any of the mitigating effects of divine power. The tercets take the opposite aspect, and in spite of the suffering already expressed, there is a recognition of a quiet miraculous power which will touch the most distant part of the poet's being. This poem uses many of the same symbols which become familiar in the later works of the poet, but here the emphasis is on a release from pain and suffering, rather than on the anguish which becomes apparent in later compositions.

The poet does not continue with this theme in **Reflejos** or in **Nostalgia de la muerte,** and it is only taken up momentarily again in the posthumous composition **"Soneto del temor a Dios."** This sonnet has been discussed in detail already in this chapter, and needs be mentioned here only as a closing point for this minor theme.

A third minor theme which appears from time to time in the two earlier collections but which disappears entirely in **Nostalgia de la muerte** and **Canto a la primavera,** is that of a peaceful life in bucolic surroundings. For example, **"En el agua dormida"** from **Primeros poemas** develops in careful Alexandrine quatrains a peaceful scene in which the poet exists without anxiousness or anguish at any time:

En el agua dormida mi caricia más leve
se tiende como el perro humilde de la granja;
la soledad en un impalpable oro llueve,
y se aclara el ambiente oloroso a naranja.

Las pupilas, alertas al horizonte puro,
interrogan sin rumbo, sin anhelo ni angustia,
cada sombra cobija un cansancio futuro
que doblega la frente en una flexión mustia.

En tanto, un inefable candor que nada implora
es descanso a los ojos . . . Escucho un trino
    huraño,
y pienso inversamente que a una nube viadora
guía el pastor biblico conduciendo el rebaño.

En un temblor de seda se deshoja la hora,
ni un súbito reflejo turba el agua dormida,
ni un cansancio impaciente en mi alma se
    desflora,
ni la vida me siente, ni yo siento la vida . . .
(p. 21).

The scene developed in the poem is that of a peaceful summer's afternoon in which all of the senses find joy and comfort: the gold of the sunlight, the sound of a bird, the smell of orange blossoms, and the calm surface of the water. The striking image of the first stanza, in which the poet's caress (perhaps hisglance) on the still water is compared to the reclining shape of the farmyard dog, adds to the visual quality of the poem. Also, the pastoral suggestion made in the third stanza increases the sense of bucolic peace, and heightens as well the visual impression of clouds tumbling one on top of another. Amidst all these elements of calm and peace, the poet finds himself in the same state of emotion: he does not feel upset or hurried and is satisfied with simply being.

An example from *Reflejos* is the composition **"Domingo,"** in which the poet imagines a Sunday's journey into the country:

> Me fugaría al pueblo
> para que el domingo
> fuera detrás del tren
> persiguiéndome . . .
>
> Y llegaría en la tarde
> cuando, ya cansado
> el domingo, se sentara
> a mi lado,
> frente al paisaje
> quieto,
> bajo los montes
> que tampoco se habrían rasurado.
>
> Así podría yo tenderme
> sin hastío.
> Oír sólo el silencio,
> y mirar el aire incoloro
> y poroso.
>
> Muy abajo, muy pequeño,
> junto al domingo
> fatigado,
> siguiendo la sola nube:
> ¡Dios fuma tras de la montaña!
>
> (p. 34).

The composition takes the form of an imagined journey away from the town, a journey which is conditioned by a series of verb tenses in the imperfect subjunctive and conditional and as well by a curious personification of Sunday. The poet longs to flee and would have the personified Sunday follow behind him. Upon their arrival, both tired, they would be able to sit quietly and contemplate the scenery before them. They would both sit underneath trees made shaggy by leaves and vegetation, or as the image of the second stanza suggests, still "unshaven". In that way the poet would simply be able to exist, to listen to the silence and be aware of the transparent atmosphere. His contemplations make him feel small, and as he watches the movements of the clouds he wonders if they are not produced by some superhuman being (God is the word the poet uses but seemingly without any religious reference) who is smoking behind the mountain. Here again the development of theme and imagery seems to reduce any sense of anguish to nothingness and to increase the feeling of pleasurable existence within peaceful surroundings.

The compositions in which Villaurrutia uses situations from his trip to the United States represent a separate thematic grouping. In other poems already discussed, there have been occasional references to place names and situations, but in two compositions this becomes a primary thematic focus. The first of these, **"North Carolina Blues,"** is a take-off on the jazz music of the time and is dedicated to Langston Hughes, the American Negro poet. The poem has an unusual structure, in that it is made up of eight segments of varying length, each of which is followed by the refrain line "En North Carolina." These elements all have to do with Villaurrutia's reaction to the situation of the black man in North Carolina and the United States. For example, the first strophe captures the tragedy in a drop of sweat:

> En North Carolina
> el aire nocturno
> es de piel humana.
> Cuando lo acaricio
> me deja, de pronto,
> en los dedos,
> el sudor de una gota de agua.
>
> *En North Carolina* (p. 65).

Stanza 6 reveals in separate waiting rooms the absurdity of this kind of separation:

> En diversas salas de espera
> aguardan la misma muerte
> los pasajeros de color
> y los blancos, de primera.
>
> *En North Carolina* (p. 66).

Stanza 7 is the culmination of the poem. Here Villaurrutia perceives the entire situation as nightmarish, a nocturnal hotel in which things move by themselves and into which invisible couples (invisible because they are dark) enter. A disembodied hand, as if it were the hotel attendant receiving guests, writes and erases black names on the blackboard, which again suggests invisibility and even insanity:

> Nocturnos hoteles:
> llegan parejas invisibles,
> las escaleras suben solas,
> fluyen los corredores,
> retroceden las puertas,
> cierran los ojos las ventanas.
> Una mano sin cuerpo
> escribe y borra negros
> nombres en la pizarra.
>
> *En North Carolina* (p. 66).

The second composition in which this same thematic organization functions is the gathering of short satiric verses on Boston which are entitled **"Epigramas de Boston."** There are eight numbered sections of widely varying length and organization, but all with the purpose of poking fun at the puritanism and conventionality of Bostonians. In strophe 1, for example, Bostonians dress so much alike that they might as well be nudists:

> I
>
> El puritanismo
> ha creado
> un nuevo pecado:

el exceso de vestido,
que, bien mirado
y por ser tan distinguido,
en nada se distingue del nudismo.

(pp. 87-88).

Even architecture is acceptable only when it is traditional:

IV

Como los rascacielos
no son tradicionales,
aquí los ponen por los suelos,
horizontales.

(p. 88).

The desire for superficial morality is so strong, the poet affirms, thatmen and women must have separate exits from hotels and elevators and at the same time must find secret ways to meet far from the public gaze:

VI

En hoteles y ascensores
la moral consabida
exige diferente salida
a las damas y a los señores.

De modo que los maridos,
los amantes, los pretendientes
y los recién casados
tienen que estar pendientes
para reunirse, de manera
subrepticia y privada,
con la esposa, la amada,
la novia o la niñera.

(p. 89).

The puritanical condemnation of passion is so great that even the poet is reluctant to mention certain fallen women, and must create a verbal play in order to express himself:

VIII

En Boston es grave falta
hablar de ciertas mujeres,
por eso aunque nieva nieve
mi boca no se atreve
a decir en voz alta:
ni Eva ni Hebe.

(p. 89).

NOTES

[1] This composition was found in the poet's coat pocket at the time of his death, but was not published until 1960 when it appeared in *Cuadernos de Bellas Artes*, Núm. 5 (dic. de 1960). For some reason the editors of the second edition chose to include this poem with *Nostalgia de la muerte.*

[2] "Xavier Villaurrutia," *Revista Mexicana de Literature,* Núm. 16-18 (oct.-dic. de 1960), 60.

[3] It is interesting to note that in the autographed manuscript of the poem there are a number of characteristic line drawings by the poet which indicate that at one point at least he conceived of these figures as sailors dressed in traditional mariners' garb.

[4] The title is a line from Dante's *Inferno* (Canto V, line 106) in which Francesca laments her physical and spiritual death. In an unpublished study, Donald Bevelander has considered the possible significance of the title for Villaurrutia and the dantesque structuring of this poem in terms of the capital sins, in particular anger, envy, avarice, and lust.

[5] Segovia, "Xavier Villaurrutia," *op. cit.,* p. 62.

[6] There is some indication that Villaurrutia intended this as a real epitaph, but it curious to realize that at the time of his death his family and his friends had inscribed on his tomb another epitaph, also included in his poetic works, which was evidently dedicated to Jorge Cuesta.

## Gwen Kirkpatrick (review date 1994)

SOURCE: A review of *Nostalgia for Death and Hieroglyphs of Desire,* by Xavier Villaurrutia and Octavio Paz, in *Latin American Literary Review,* Vol. 22, No. 44, July-December, 1994, pp. 90-92.

[*In the following review of* Nostalgia for Death and Hieroglyphs of Desire, *Kirkpatrick offers an assessment of Villaurrutia's work nearly fifty years after his death.*]

The publication of Xavier Villaurrutia's **Nostalgia for Death** is an important contribution to the English-speaking world's knowledge of Mexican literature and of poetry in Spanish. It is, in a sense, a curiously belated translation, both of Villaurrutia's poetry, here beautifully translated by Eliot Weinberger, and of Octavio Paz's accompanying essay, "Hieroglyphs of Desire" (1978), translated by Esther Allen. Villaurrutia began publishing these poems in the late 1920s and published the definitive collected edition in 1946. Villaurrutia's poetry occupies a strong place in the canons of Mexican poetry; he was also a dramatist and critic. He and his work, however, have been difficult to place within an overall vision of Latin American literature. Ahistorical, not quite in step with the most recognized vanguard poets of his time, Villaurrutia belonged to that literary group known as the "Contemporáneos," important in the thirties and forties, whose history stands somewhat apart from the currents we most associate often with post-revolutionary Mexican culture.

Acknowledged as a major poet in Mexico, Villaurrutia (1903-1950) along with José Gorostiza, Carlos Pellicer, Salvador Novo, Jorge Cuesta, among others of the "Contemporáneos," was one of the founders of the literary magazine of the same name. Paz, while acknowledging several of this group as his literary mentors, is somewhat ambivalent in his evaluations of them. Of their poetry he says, "A poetry with wings but without the weight—the nightmare—of history" (105). For Paz, it is a poetry devoid of people: "In the poems of Gorostiza, Villaurrutia, and Ortiz de Montellano no one is there: everyone and everything has become a reflection, a ghost" (105). He characterizes their stance as that of "inner exile," and develops a group portrait which, though handy for classification, perhaps characterizes them as more similar than they were.

With Paz's evocations and evaluations in this fascinating essay, there is quite clearly an anxiety of literary paternity. Paz traces for us a personal as well as literary history in Mexico, touching on other topics such as the representation of death and the erotic in several cultures and times. His history, luckily for its readers, is somewhat idiosyncratic, mixing personal reminiscence with cultural and political history. He tells us that Villaurrutia, like most of his literary brotherhood, held posts in the Mexican government. Yet in Mexico's post-revolutionary years, especially during the presidency of Lázaro Cárdenas, those who did not adhere to the nationalist revolutionary ideology were sometimes isolated, censored, or worse. Complicating matters even further, Villaurrutia, like several members of the Contemporaries, was openly homosexual in a society dominated by machismo. It is this fact which perhaps accounts for the makings of the "inner exile" to which Paz refers, and which has moved Weinberger to bring us these translations.

In his preface, Eliot Weinberger tells us that his outrage at the censorship and homophobia directed at the National Endowment of the Arts in 1990 prompted these translations, a project he had planned for many years. Thus another context for Villaurrutia's poetry is created, that of the homosexual poet writing erotic poetry in repressive societies. As Weinberger states, "he was one of the great poets of desire: one whose beloved, finally, is not another man but Death itself, Death himself" (2).

Even without the contexts given by Paz and Weinberger, Villaurrutia's poetry speaks for itself. Not a prolific poet—almost all his poetry is included here—he was nevertheless a major one. Paz underlines the visual nature of Villaurrutia's poetry, a plasticity noted by most readers. But there is also a sonorous universe here, that of a poet in love with language, its traditions and its sounds. In these impeccable translations, this sound quality, the echoes of other poets—Sor Juana Inés de la Cruz, Rubén Darío and Ramón López Velarde, among others—andverse forms associated with them, must be sacrificed to another language. What the translator does capture, however, is the poet's playfulness with language, his love of antitheses, the familiarization of oxymorons.

While Villaurrutia's themes are largely somber ones—death, nostalgia, shadow, dream, doubt, anguish—the palpable presence of his language relieves their shadows. His is a very physical, yet not earthy or colloquial language that makes the antitheses he draws—sleep and wakefulness, life and death, desire and nothingness, take on a life of their own. A dream wishes to escape from the body (**"Nocturne: Imprisoned"**), parts of the body fall apart like syllables in word games (**"Nocturne: Nothing is Heard"**), the body descends through the sky in sleep (**"Nocturne: Dream"**), death hides in the folds of a suitcase taken to New Haven (**"Nocturne: Death Speaks"**), hidden erotic thoughts are transformed into billboards or constellations that light up the sky (**"L.A. Nocturne: Los Angeles"**). Word play is not the dominant element of these poems, but the sense of continuity between the contours of language and the subterranean corridors of nocturnal worlds form a seamless universe, where sound becomes light and desire writes on the sky, and the sea is the mirror of the sky. In the well-known poem **"Death in Décimas"** we can sense the presence of Sor Juana in its form and language and in its questioning of consciousness and wakefulness:

> Down the unknown pathways,
> through the hidden fissures,
> through the mysterious veins
> of trunks newly sawn apart,
> my closed eyes are watching you
> come into my dark bedroom
> to change this earthly trapping,
> opaque, restless and unfixed,
> into a stuff of diamonds,
> shining, eternal and pure.
>
> (87)

This is the dreamlike quality of *Nostalgia for Death.* It is not a diaphanous, free-floating dream state or a mesh of undefined symbols. The dream is in the articulation of very distinct elements, the magic performed on objects as desire transforms the body and the mind.

Villaurrutia's poems are tantalizing. Because they focus on a limited repertoire of images, we hope to decipher a secret. What is the nostalgia for death? Where is the secret link between shadow and light, the sea and desire, sleep and wakefulness? Have we tasted death before and now dimly recognize its constant presence? While we puzzle for answers, Villaurrutia reminds us always of limits—the limits of the body, the mystery of snow, and a "nocturnal angerless sea, content/to lap the walls that hold it prisoner" (55). The pull of the mysteries of death, life and identity are often brought down to earth:

> when I find myself alone, so alone,
> that I look for myself in my room
> the way one looks for some misplaced thing,
> a crumpled letter in some corner.
>
> (75)

As Paz reminds us, Villaurrutia makes almost no concession to local color or to a specifically Mexican reality. His territory is the space of paradox and of searching. In Villaurrutia's poetry, death mocks the realities which console us:

> " . . . These things are nothing, like the countless
> traps you set for me,
> like the childish sophistries with which you tried
> to trick me, forget me.
> Here I am, can't you feel me?
> Open your eyes; or close them if you prefer."
>
> (43)

This carefully crafted translated edition will give wider access to a poet whose words can still speak to us. In a time when publications of poetic translations are extremely limited, this book gives new hope for a wider world of poetry.

---

## FURTHER READING

### Criticism

Bedoya, Roberta. "To Speak of Desire." *Hungry Mind Review*, No. 27 (Fall 1993): 28-29.
> Review of Villaurrutia's and Octavio Paz's *Nostalgia for Death/Hieroglyphs of Desire: A Critical Study of Villaurrutia* which treats Villaurrutia's work as a positive embodiment of a gay social agenda.

Merrill, Christopher. "Streets That Flow Sweetly through the L.A. Night." *Los Angeles Times Book Review* (June 13, 1993): 10.
> Positive review of *Nostalgia for Death/Hieroglyphs of Desire* as part of a long tradition of night or sleep literature.

Mojica, Rafael H. Review of *Nostalgia for Death/Hieroglyphs of Desire: A Critical Study of Villaurrutia*, edited and translated by Eliot Weinberger and Esther Allen. *World Literature Today* 69, No. 1 (Winter 1995): 111.
> Provides historical background regarding Villaurrutia's friendship with Paz, and faults Weinberger's attempt to enlist Villaurrutia in "today's culture wars" simply because he was gay.

> **The following source published by Gale contains further coverage of Villaurrutia's life and career:** *Hispanic Writers*.

# Twentieth-Century Literary Criticism

Cumulative Indexes
Volumes 1-80

# How to Use This Index

## The main references

Calvino, Italo
1923–1985 ....... CLC 5, 8, 11, 22, 33, 39,
73; SSC 3

list all author entries in the following Gale Literary Criticism series:

*BLC* = *Black Literature Criticism*
*CLC* = *Contemporary Literary Criticism*
*CLR* = *Children's Literature Review*
*CMLC* = *Classical and Medieval Literature Criticism*
*DA* = *DISCovering Authors*
*DAB* = *DISCovering Authors: British*
*DAC* = *DISCovering Authors: Canadian*
*DAM* = *DISCovering Authors: Modules*
    *DRAM*: *Dramatists Module;* *MST*: *Most-Studied Authors Module;*
    *MULT*: *Multicultural Authors Module;* *NOV*: *Novelists Module;*
    *POET*: *Poets Module;* *POP*: *Popular Fiction and Genre Authors Module*
*DC* = *Drama Criticism*
*HLC* = *Hispanic Literature Criticism*
*LC* = *Literature Criticism from 1400 to 1800*
*NCLC* = *Nineteenth-Century Literature Criticism*
*PC* = *Poetry Criticism*
*SSC* = *Short Story Criticism*
*TCLC* = *Twentieth-Century Literary Criticism*
*WLC* = *World Literature Criticism, 1500 to the Present*

## The cross-references

See also CANR 23; CA 85-88;
obituary CA116

list all author entries in the following Gale biographical and literary sources:

*AAYA* = *Authors & Artists for Young Adults*
*AITN* = *Authors in the News*
*BEST* = *Bestsellers*
*BW* = *Black Writers*
*CA* = *Contemporary Authors*
*CAAS* = *Contemporary Authors Autobiography Series*
*CABS* = *Contemporary Authors Bibliographical Series*
*CANR* = *Contemporary Authors New Revision Series*
*CAP* = *Contemporary Authors Permanent Series*
*CDALB* = *Concise Dictionary of American Literary Biography*
*CDBLB* = *Concise Dictionary of British Literary Biography*
*DLB* = *Dictionary of Literary Biography*
*DLBD* = *Dictionary of Literary Biography Documentary Series*
*DLBY* = *Dictionary of Literary Biography Yearbook*
*HW* = *Hispanic Writers*
*JRDA* = *Junior DISCovering Authors*
*MAICYA* = *Major Authors and Illustrators for Children and Young Adults*
*MTCW* = *Major 20th-Century Writers*
*NNAL* = *Native North American Literature*
*SAAS* = *Something about the Author Autobiography Series*
*SATA* = *Something about the Author*
*YABC* = *Yesterday's Authors of Books for Children*

# Literary Criticism Series
# Cumulative Author Index

Aldanov, M. A.
    See Aldanov, Mark (Alexandrovich)
Aldanov, Mark (Alexandrovich) [1886(?)-1957]
    TCLC 23
    See also CA 118
Aldington, Richard [1892-1962] ....... CLC 49
    See also CA 85-88; CANR 45; DLB 20, 36, 100,
    149
Aldiss, Brian W(ilson) [1925-]CLC 5, 14, 40;
    DAM NOV
    See also CA 5-8R; CAAS 2; CANR 5, 28, 64;
    DLB 14; MTCW; SATA 34
Alegria, Claribel [1924-] ........ CLC 75; DAM
    MULT
    See also CA 131; CAAS 15; CANR 66; DLB
    145; HW
Alegria, Fernando [1918-] ................. CLC 57
    See also CA 9-12R; CANR 5, 32; HW
Aleichem, Sholom ........................ TCLC 1, 35
    See also Rabinovitch, Sholem
Aleixandre, Vicente [1898-1984] CLC 9, 36;
    DAM POET; PC 15
    See also CA 85-88; 114; CANR 26; DLB 108;
    HW; MTCW
Alepoudelis, Odysseus
    See Elytis, Odysseus
Aleshkovsky, Joseph [1929-]
    See Aleshkovsky, Yuz
    See also CA 121; 128
Aleshkovsky, Yuz ........................... CLC 44
    See also Aleshkovsky, Joseph
Alexander, Lloyd (Chudley) [1924-] CLC 35
    See also AAYA 1; CA 1-4R; CANR 1, 24, 38,
    55; CLR 1, 5, 48; DLB 52; JRDA; MAICYA;
    MTCW; SAAS 19; SATA 3, 49, 81
Alexander, Samuel [1859-1938] ..... TCLC 77
Alexie, Sherman (Joseph, Jr.) [1966-]CLC 96;
    DAM MULT
    See also CA 138; CANR 65; DLB 175; NNAL
Alfau, Felipe [1902-] .......................... CLC 66
    See also CA 137
Alger, Horatio, Jr. [1832-1899] ........ NCLC 8
    See also DLB 42; SATA 16
Algren, Nelson [1909-1981] .... CLC 4, 10, 33
    See also CA 13-16R; 103; CANR 20, 61;
    CDALB 1941-1968; DLB 9; DLBY 81, 82;
    MTCW
Ali, Ahmed [1910-] ........................... CLC 69
    See also CA 25-28R; CANR 15, 34
Alighieri, Dante
    See Dante
Allan, John B.
    See Westlake, Donald E(dwin)
Allan, Sidney
    See Hartmann, Sadakichi
Allan, Sydney
    See Hartmann, Sadakichi
Allen, Edward [1948-] ...................... CLC 59
Allen, Paula Gunn [1939-] ..... CLC 84; DAM
    MULT
    See also CA 112; 143; CANR 63; DLB 175;
    NNAL
Allen, Roland
    See Ayckbourn, Alan
Allen, Sarah A.
    See Hopkins, Pauline Elizabeth
Allen, Sidney H.
    See Hartmann, Sadakichi
Allen, Woody [1935-]CLC 16, 52; DAM POP
    See also AAYA 10; CA 33-36R; CANR 27, 38,
    63; DLB 44; MTCW
Allende, Isabel [1942-]CLC 39, 57, 97; DAM
    MULT, NOV; HLC; WLCS
    See also AAYA 18; CA 125; 130; CANR 51;
    DLB 145; HW; INT 130; MTCW
Alleyn, Ellen

See Rossetti, Christina (Georgina)
Allingham, Margery (Louise) [1904-1966]
    CLC 19
    See also CA 5-8R; 25-28R; CANR 4, 58; DLB
    77; MTCW
Allingham, William [1824-1889] ... NCLC 25
    See also DLB 35
Allison, Dorothy E. [1949-] ............... CLC 78
    See also CA 140; CANR 66
Allston, Washington [1779-1843] .... NCLC 2
    See also DLB 1
Almedingen, E. M. ............................ CLC 12
    See also Almedingen, Martha Edith von
    See also SATA 3
Almedingen, Martha Edith von [1898-1971]
    See Almedingen, E. M.
    See also CA 1-4R; CANR 1
Almqvist, Carl Jonas Love [1793-1866]NCLC
    42
Alonso, Damaso [1898-1990] ............. CLC 14
    See also CA 110; 131; 130; DLB 108; HW
Alov
    See Gogol, Nikolai (Vasilyevich)
Alta [1942-] ...................................... CLC 19
    See also CA 57-60
Alter, Robert B(ernard) [1935-] ....... CLC 34
    See also CA 49-52; CANR 1, 47
Alther, Lisa [1944-] ......................CLC 7, 41
    See also CA 65-68; CANR 12, 30, 51; MTCW
Althusser, L.
    See Althusser, Louis
Althusser, Louis [1918-1990] ........... CLC 106
    See also CA 131; 132
Altman, Robert [1925-] ...................... CLC 16
    See also CA 73-76; CANR 43
Alvarez, A(lfred) [1929-] ............... CLC 5, 13
    See also CA 1-4R; CANR 3, 33, 63; DLB 14,
    40
Alvarez, Alejandro Rodriguez [1903-1965]
    See Casona, Alejandro
    See also CA 131; 93-96; HW
Alvarez, Julia [1950-] ....................... CLC 93
    See also AAYA 25; CA 147; CANR 69
Alvaro, Corrado [1896-1956] ......... TCLC 60
    See also CA 163
Amado, Jorge [1912-]CLC 13, 40, 106; DAM
    MULT, NOV; HLC
    See also CA 77-80; CANR 35; DLB 113;
    MTCW
Ambler, Eric [1909-] .................... CLC 4, 6, 9
    See also CA 9-12R; CANR 7, 38; DLB 77;
    MTCW
Amichai, Yehuda [1924-] ........ CLC 9, 22, 57
    See also CA 85-88; CANR 46, 60; MTCW
Amichai, Yehudah
    See Amichai, Yehuda
Amiel, Henri Frederic [1821-1881] . NCLC 4
Amis, Kingsley (William) [1922-1995]CLC 1,
    2, 3, 5, 8, 13, 40, 44; DA; DAB; DAC; DAM
    MST, NOV
    See also AITN 2; CA 9-12R; 150; CANR 8, 28,
    54; CDBLB 1945-1960; DLB 15, 27, 100,
    139; DLBY 96; INT CANR-8; MTCW
Amis, Martin (Louis) [1949-]CLC 4, 9, 38, 62,
    101
    See also BEST 90:3; CA 65-68; CANR 8, 27,
    54; DLB 14, 194; INT CANR-27
Ammons, A(rchie) R(andolph) [1926-]CLC 2,
    3, 5, 8, 9, 25, 57, 108; DAM POET; PC 16
    See also AITN 1; CA 9-12R; CANR 6, 36, 51;
    DLB 5, 165; MTCW
Amo, Tauraatua i
    See Adams, Henry (Brooks)
Anand, Mulk Raj [1905-] CLC 23, 93; DAM
    NOV
    See also CA 65-68; CANR 32, 64; MTCW
Anatol

See Schnitzler, Arthur
Anaximander [c. 610B.C.-c. 546B.C.] C M L C
    22
Anaya, Rudolfo A(lfonso) [1937-] .. CLC 23;
    DAM MULT, NOV; HLC
    See also AAYA 20; CA 45-48; CAAS 4; CANR
    1, 32, 51; DLB 82; HW 1; MTCW
Andersen, Hans Christian [1805-1875]NCLC
    7; DA; DAB; DAC; DAM MST, POP; SSC
    6; WLC
    See also CLR 6; MAICYA; YABC 1
Anderson, C. Farley
    See Mencken, H(enry) L(ouis); Nathan, George
    Jean
Anderson, Jessica (Margaret) Queale [1916-]
    CLC 37
    See also CA 9-12R; CANR 4, 62
Anderson, Jon (Victor) [1940-]CLC 9; DAM
    POET
    See also CA 25-28R; CANR 20
Anderson, Lindsay (Gordon) [1923-1994]
    CLC 20
    See also CA 125; 128; 146
Anderson, Maxwell [1888-1959] ..... TCLC 2;
    DAM DRAM
    See also CA 105; 152; DLB 7
Anderson, Poul (William) [1926-] .... CLC 15
    See also AAYA 5; CA 1-4R; CAAS 2; CANR
    2, 15, 34, 64; DLB 8; INT CANR-15;
    MTCW; SATA 90; SATA-Brief 39
Anderson, Robert (Woodruff) [1917-] .. C L C
    23; DAM DRAM
    See also AITN 1; CA 21-24R; CANR 32; DLB
    7
Anderson, Sherwood [1876-1941]TCLC 1, 10,
    24; DA; DAB; DAC; DAM MST, NOV;
    SSC 1; WLC
    See also CA 104; 121; CANR 61; CDALB
    1917-1929; DLB 4, 9, 86; DLBD 1; MTCW
Andier, Pierre
    See Desnos, Robert
Andouard
    See Giraudoux, (Hippolyte) Jean
Andrade, Carlos Drummond de ........ CLC 18
    See also Drummond de Andrade, Carlos
Andrade, Mario de [1893-1945] .... TCLC 43
Andreae, Johann V(alentin) [1586-1654] L C
    32
    See also DLB 164
Andreas-Salome, Lou [1861-1937] TCLC 56
    See also DLB 66
Andress, Lesley
    See Sanders, Lawrence
Andrewes, Lancelot [1555-1626] ........... LC 5
    See also DLB 151, 172
Andrews, Cicily Fairfield
    See West, Rebecca
Andrews, Elton V.
    See Pohl, Frederik
Andreyev, Leonid (Nikolaevich) [1871-1919]
    TCLC 3
    See also CA 104
Andric, Ivo [1892-1975] ...................... CLC 8
    See also CA 81-84; 57-60; CANR 43, 60; DLB
    147; MTCW
Androvar
    See Prado (Calvo), Pedro
Angelique, Pierre
    See Bataille, Georges
Angell, Roger [1920-] ....................... CLC 26
    See also CA 57-60; CANR 13, 44; DLB 171,
    185
Angelou, Maya [1928-] . CLC 12, 35, 64, 77;
    BLC 1; DA; DAB; DAC; DAM MST,
    MULT, POET, POP; WLCS
    See also AAYA 7, 20; BW 2; CA 65-68; CANR
    19, 42, 65; DLB 38; MTCW; SATA 49

Anna Comnena [1083-1153] .......... **CMLC 25**
Annensky, Innokenty (Fyodorovich) [1856-
    1909] ....................................... **TCLC 14**
    See also CA 110; 155
Annunzio, Gabriele d'
    See D'Annunzio, Gabriele
Anodos
    See Coleridge, Mary E(lizabeth)
Anon, Charles Robert
    See Pessoa, Fernando (Antonio Nogueira)
Anouilh, Jean (Marie Lucien Pierre) [1910-
    1987] ........................................................
**CLC 1, 3, 8, 13, 40, 50; DAM DRAM; DC 8**
    See also CA 17-20R; 123; CANR 32; MTCW
Anthony, Florence
    See Ai
Anthony, John
    See Ciardi, John (Anthony)
Anthony, Peter
    See Shaffer, Anthony (Joshua); Shaffer, Peter
    (Levin)
Anthony, Piers [1934-] . **CLC 35; DAM POP**
    See also AAYA 11; CA 21-24R; CANR 28, 56;
    DLB 8; MTCW; SAAS 22; SATA 84
Antoine, Marc
    See Proust, (Valentin-Louis-George-Eugene-)
    Marcel
Antoninus, Brother
    See Everson, William (Oliver)
Antonioni, Michelangelo [1912-] ...... **CLC 20**
    See also CA 73-76; CANR 45
Antschel, Paul [1920-1970]
    See Celan, Paul
    See also CA 85-88; CANR 33, 61; MTCW
Anwar, Chairil [1922-1949] ........... **TCLC 22**
    See also CA 121
Apollinaire, Guillaume [1880-1918]**TCLC 3,
    8, 51; DAM POET; PC 7**
    See also Kostrowitzki, Wilhelm Apollinaris de
    See also CA 152
Appelfeld, Aharon [1932-] .......... **CLC 23, 47**
    See also CA 112; 133
Apple, Max (Isaac) [1941-] ............ **CLC 9, 33**
    See also CA 81-84; CANR 19, 54; DLB 130
Appleman, Philip (Dean) [1926-] ...... **CLC 51**
    See also CA 13-16R; CAAS 18; CANR 6, 29,
    56
Appleton, Lawrence
    See Lovecraft, H(oward) P(hillips)
Apteryx
    See Eliot, T(homas) S(tearns)
Apuleius, (Lucius Madaurensis) [125(?)-175(?)]
    **CMLC 1**
Aquin, Hubert [1929-1977] .............. **CLC 15**
    See also CA 105; DLB 53
Aragon, Louis [1897-1982] **CLC 3, 22; DAM
    NOV, POET**
    See also CA 69-72; 108; CANR 28; DLB 72;
    MTCW
Arany, Janos [1817-1882] ............... **NCLC 34**
Arbuthnot, John [1667-1735]................ **LC 1**
    See also DLB 101
Archer, Herbert Winslow
    See Mencken, H(enry) L(ouis)
Archer, Jeffrey (Howard) [1940-] .. **CLC 28;
    DAM POP**
    See also AAYA 16; BEST 89:3; CA 77-80;
    CANR 22, 52; INT CANR-22
Archer, Jules [1915-] ......................... **CLC 12**
    See also CA 9-12R; CANR 6, 69; SAAS 5;
    SATA 4, 85
Archer, Lee
    See Ellison, Harlan (Jay)
Arden, John [1930-] .... **CLC 6, 13, 15; DAM
    DRAM**
    See also CA 13-16R; CAAS 4; CANR 31, 65,
    67; DLB 13; MTCW

Arenas, Reinaldo [1943-1990]**CLC 41; DAM
    MULT; HLC**
    See also CA 124; 128; 133; DLB 145; HW
Arendt, Hannah [1906-1975] ..... **CLC 66, 98**
    See also CA 17-20R; 61-64; CANR 26, 60;
    MTCW
Aretino, Pietro [1492-1556] ................**LC 12**
Arghezi, Tudor .................................... **CLC 80**
    See also Theodorescu, Ion N.
Arguedas, Jose Maria [1911-1969]**CLC 10, 18**
    See also CA 89-92; DLB 113; HW
Argueta, Manlio [1936-] ................... **CLC 31**
    See also CA 131; DLB 145; HW
Ariosto, Ludovico [1474-1533] ............. **LC 6**
Aristides
    See Epstein, Joseph
Aristophanes [450B.C.-385B.C.]**CMLC 4; DA;
    DAB; DAC; DAM DRAM, MST; DC 2;
    WLCS**
    See also DLB 176
Arlt, Roberto (Godofredo Christophersen)
    [1900-1942]**TCLC 29; DAM MULT; HLC**
    See also CA 123; 131; CANR 67; HW
Armah, Ayi Kwei [1939-] **CLC 5, 33; BLC 1;
    DAM MULT, POET**
    See also BW 1; CA 61-64; CANR 21, 64; DLB
    117; MTCW
Armatrading, Joan [1950-] ............... **CLC 17**
    See also CA 114
Arnette, Robert
    See Silverberg, Robert
Arnim, Achim von (Ludwig Joachim von
    Arnim) [1781-1831] ... **NCLC 5; SSC 29**
    See also DLB 90
Arnim, Bettina von [1785-1859] .... **NCLC 38**
    See also DLB 90
Arnold, Matthew [1822-1888].. **NCLC 6, 29;
    DA; DAB; DAC; DAM MST, POET; PC
    5; WLC**
    See also CDBLB 1832-1890; DLB 32, 57
Arnold, Thomas [1795-1842] ......... **NCLC 18**
    See also DLB 55
Arnow, Harriette (Louisa) Simpson [1908-
    1986] ................................. **CLC 2, 7, 18**
    See also CA 9-12R; 118; CANR 14; DLB 6;
    MTCW; SATA 42; SATA-Obit 47
Arp, Hans
    See Arp, Jean
Arp, Jean [1887-1966] ......................... **CLC 5**
    See also CA 81-84; 25-28R; CANR 42
Arrabal
    See Arrabal, Fernando
Arrabal, Fernando [1932-] . **CLC 2, 9, 18, 58**
    See also CA 9-12R; CANR 15
Arrick, Fran ...................................... **CLC 30**
    See also Gaberman, Judie Angell
Artaud, Antonin (Marie Joseph) [1896-1948]
    **TCLC 3, 36; DAM DRAM**
    See also CA 104; 149
Arthur, Ruth M(abel) [1905-1979] ... **CLC 12**
    See also CA 9-12R; 85-88; CANR 4; SATA 7,
    26
Artsybashev, Mikhail (Petrovich) [1878-1927]
    **TCLC 31**
Arundel, Honor (Morfydd) [1919-1973]**C L C
    17**
    See also CA 21-22; 41-44R; CAP 2; CLR 35;
    SATA 4; SATA-Obit 24
Arzner, Dorothy [1897-1979] ........... **CLC 98**
Asch, Sholem [1880-1957] ................ **TCLC 3**
    See also CA 105
Ash, Shalom
    See Asch, Sholem
Ashbery, John (Lawrence) [1927-]**CLC 2, 3, 4,
    6, 9, 13, 15, 25, 41, 77; DAM POET**
    See also CA 5-8R; CANR 9, 37, 66; DLB 5,
    165; DLBY 81; INT CANR-9; MTCW

Ashdown, Clifford
    See Freeman, R(ichard) Austin
Ashe, Gordon
    See Creasey, John
Ashton-Warner, Sylvia (Constance) [1908-
    1984] ........................................... **CLC 19**
    See also CA 69-72; 112; CANR 29; MTCW
Asimov, Isaac [1920-1992]**CLC 1, 3, 9, 19, 26,
    76, 92; DAM POP**
    See also AAYA 13; BEST 90:2; CA 1-4R; 137;
    CANR 2, 19, 36, 60; CLR 12; DLB 8; DLBY
    92; INT CANR-19; JRDA; MAICYA;
    MTCW; SATA 1, 26, 74
Assis, Joaquim Maria Machado de
    See Machado de Assis, Joaquim Maria
Astley, Thea (Beatrice May) [1925-] **CLC 41**
    See also CA 65-68; CANR 11, 43
Aston, James
    See White, T(erence) H(anbury)
Asturias, Miguel Angel [1899-1974]**CLC 3, 8,
    13; DAM MULT, NOV; HLC**
    See also CA 25-28; 49-52; CANR 32; CAP 2;
    DLB 113; HW; MTCW
Atares, Carlos Saura
    See Saura (Atares), Carlos
Atheling, William
    See Pound, Ezra (Weston Loomis)
Atheling, William, Jr.
    See Blish, James (Benjamin)
Atherton, Gertrude (Franklin Horn) [1857-
    1948] ............................................. **TCLC 2**
    See also CA 104; 155; DLB 9, 78, 186
Atherton, Lucius
    See Masters, Edgar Lee
Atkins, Jack
    See Harris, Mark
Atkinson, Kate ..................................... **CLC 99**
    See also CA 166
Attaway, William (Alexander) [1911-1986]
    **CLC 92; BLC 1; DAM MULT**
    See also BW 2; CA 143; DLB 76
Atticus
    See Fleming, Ian (Lancaster); Wilson, (Thomas)
    Woodrow
Atwood, Margaret (Eleanor) [1939-]**CLC 2, 3,
    4, 8, 13, 15, 25, 44, 84; DA; DAB; DAC;
    DAM MST, NOV, POET; PC 8; SSC 2;
    WLC**
    See also AAYA 12; BEST 89:2; CA 49-52;
    CANR 3, 24, 33, 59; DLB 53; INT CANR-
    24; MTCW; SATA 50
Aubigny, Pierre d'
    See Mencken, H(enry) L(ouis)
Aubin, Penelope [1685-1731(?)] ............. **LC 9**
    See also DLB 39
Auchincloss, Louis (Stanton) [1917-]**CLC 4, 6,
    9, 18, 45; DAM NOV; SSC 22**
    See also CA 1-4R; CANR 6, 29, 55; DLB 2;
    DLBY 80; INT CANR-29; MTCW
Auden, W(ystan) H(ugh) [1907-1973]**CLC 1,
    2, 3, 4, 6, 9, 11, 14, 43; DA; DAB; DAC;
    DAM DRAM, MST, POET; PC 1; WLC**
    See also AAYA 18; CA 9-12R; 45-48; CANR
    5, 61; CDBLB 1914-1945; DLB 10, 20;
    MTCW
Audiberti, Jacques [1900-1965]**CLC 38; DAM
    DRAM**
    See also CA 25-28R
Audubon, John James [1785-1851]**NCLC 47**
Auel, Jean M(arie) [1936-]**CLC 31, 107; DAM
    POP**
    See also AAYA 7; BEST 90:4; CA 103; CANR
    21, 64; INT CANR-21; SATA 91
Auerbach, Erich [1892-1957] ......... **TCLC 43**
    See also CA 118; 155
Augier, Emile [1820-1889] .............. **NCLC 31**
    See also DLB 192

**August, John**
  See De Voto, Bernard (Augustine)
**Augustine, St.** [354-430] ........ **CMLC 6; DAB**
**Aurelius**
  See Bourne, Randolph S(illiman)
**Aurobindo, Sri**
  See Ghose, Aurabinda
**Austen, Jane** [1775-1817] **NCLC 1, 13, 19, 33,**
    **51; DA; DAB; DAC; DAM MST, NOV;**
    **WLC**
  See also AAYA 19; CDBLB 1789-1832; DLB
    116
**Auster, Paul** [1947-] ........................... **CLC 47**
  See also CA 69-72; CANR 23, 52
**Austin, Frank**
  See Faust, Frederick (Schiller)
**Austin, Mary (Hunter)** [1868-1934] **TCLC 25**
  See also CA 109; DLB 9, 78
**Autran Dourado, Waldomiro**
  See Dourado, (Waldomiro Freitas) Autran
**Averroes** [1126-1198] ........................ **CMLC 7**
  See also DLB 115
**Avicenna** [980-1037] ........................ **CMLC 16**
  See also DLB 115
**Avison, Margaret** [1918-] **CLC 2, 4, 97; DAC;**
    **DAM POET**
  See also CA 17-20R; DLB 53; MTCW
**Axton, David**
  See Koontz, Dean R(ay)
**Ayckbourn, Alan** [1939-] **CLC 5, 8, 18, 33, 74;**
    **DAB; DAM DRAM**
  See also CA 21-24R; CANR 31, 59; DLB 13;
    MTCW
**Aydy, Catherine**
  See Tennant, Emma (Christina)
**Ayme, Marcel (Andre)** [1902-1967] .. **CLC 11**
  See also CA 89-92; CANR 67; CLR 25; DLB
    72; SATA 91
**Ayrton, Michael** [1921-1975] .............. **CLC 7**
  See also CA 5-8R; 61-64; CANR 9, 21
**Azorin** .................................................... **CLC 11**
  See also Martinez Ruiz, Jose
**Azuela, Mariano** [1873-1952] **TCLC 3; DAM**
    **MULT; HLC**
  See also CA 104; 131; HW; MTCW
**Baastad, Babbis Friis**
  See Friis-Baastad, Babbis Ellinor
**Bab**
  See Gilbert, W(illiam) S(chwenck)
**Babbis, Eleanor**
  See Friis-Baastad, Babbis Ellinor
**Babel, Isaac**
  See Babel, Isaak (Emmanuilovich)
**Babel, Isaak (Emmanuilovich)** [1894-1941(?)]
    **TCLC 2, 13; SSC 16**
  See also CA 104; 155
**Babits, Mihaly** [1883-1941] ........... **TCLC 14**
  See also CA 114
**Babur** [1483-1530] ................................. **LC 18**
**Bacchelli, Riccardo** [1891-1985] ....... **CLC 19**
  See also CA 29-32R; 117
**Bach, Richard (David)** [1936-] **CLC 14; DAM**
    **NOV, POP**
  See also AITN 1; BEST 89:2; CA 9-12R; CANR
    18; MTCW; SATA 13
**Bachman, Richard**
  See King, Stephen (Edwin)
**Bachmann, Ingeborg** [1926-1973] .... **CLC 69**
  See also CA 93-96; 45-48; CANR 69; DLB 85
**Bacon, Francis** [1561-1626] ........... **LC 18, 32**
  See also CDBLB Before 1660; DLB 151
**Bacon, Roger** [1214(?)-1292] ........ **CMLC 14**
  See also DLB 115
**Bacovia, George** .............................. **TCLC 24**
  See also Vasiliu, Gheorghe
**Badanes, Jerome** [1937-] ................. **CLC 59**
**Bagehot, Walter** [1826-1877] ......... **NCLC 10**

  See also DLB 55
**Bagnold, Enid** [1889-1981] .... **CLC 25; DAM**
    **DRAM**
  See also CA 5-8R; 103; CANR 5, 40; DLB 13,
    160, 191; MAICYA; SATA 1, 25
**Bagritsky, Eduard** [1895-1934] ...... **TCLC 60**
**Bagrjana, Elisaveta**
  See Belcheva, Elisaveta
**Bagryana, Elisaveta** ........................... **CLC 10**
  See also Belcheva, Elisaveta
  See also DLB 147
**Bailey, Paul** [1937-] ........................... **CLC 45**
  See also CA 21-24R; CANR 16, 62; DLB 14
**Baillie, Joanna** [1762-1851] ........... **NCLC 71**
  See also DLB 93
**Bainbridge, Beryl (Margaret)** [1933-] **CLC 4,**
    **5, 8, 10, 14, 18, 22, 62; DAM NOV**
  See also CA 21-24R; CANR 24, 55; DLB 14;
    MTCW
**Baker, Elliott** [1922-] ........................... **CLC 8**
  See also CA 45-48; CANR 2, 63
**Baker, Jean H.** .............................. **TCLC 3, 10**
  See also Russell, George William
**Baker, Nicholson** [1957-] **CLC 61; DAM POP**
  See also CA 135; CANR 63
**Baker, Ray Stannard** [1870-1946] . **TCLC 47**
  See also CA 118
**Baker, Russell (Wayne)** [1925-] ......... **CLC 31**
  See also BEST 89:4; CA 57-60; CANR 11, 41,
    59; MTCW
**Bakhtin, M.**
  See Bakhtin, Mikhail Mikhailovich
**Bakhtin, M. M.**
  See Bakhtin, Mikhail Mikhailovich
**Bakhtin, Mikhail**
  See Bakhtin, Mikhail Mikhailovich
**Bakhtin, Mikhail Mikhailovich** [1895-1975]
    **CLC 83**
  See also CA 128; 113
**Bakshi, Ralph** [1938(?)-] ................... **CLC 26**
  See also CA 112; 138
**Bakunin, Mikhail (Alexandrovich)** [1814-1876]
    **NCLC 25, 58**
**Baldwin, James (Arthur)** [1924-1987] **CLC 1,**
    **2, 3, 4, 5, 8, 13, 15, 17, 42, 50, 67, 90; BLC**
    **1; DA; DAB; DAC; DAM MST, MULT,**
    **NOV, POP; DC 1; SSC 10; WLC**
  See also AAYA 4; BW 1; CA 1-4R; 124; CABS
    1; CANR 3, 24; CDALB 1941-1968; DLB
    2, 7, 33; DLBY 87; MTCW; SATA 9; SATA-
    Obit 54
**Ballard, J(ames) G(raham)** [1930-] **CLC 3, 6,**
    **14, 36; DAM NOV, POP; SSC 1**
  See also AAYA 3; CA 5-8R; CANR 15, 39, 65;
    DLB 14; MTCW; SATA 93
**Balmont, Konstantin (Dmitriyevich)** [1867-
    1943] .................................... **TCLC 11**
  See also CA 109; 155
**Balzac, Honore de** [1799-1850] . **NCLC 5, 35,**
    **53; DA; DAB; DAC; DAM MST, NOV;**
    **SSC 5; WLC**
  See also DLB 119
**Bambara, Toni Cade** [1939-1995] **CLC 19, 88;**
    **BLC 1; DA; DAC; DAM MST, MULT;**
    **WLCS**
  See also AAYA 5; BW 2; CA 29-32R; 150;
    CANR 24, 49; DLB 38; MTCW
**Bamdad, A.**
  See Shamlu, Ahmad
**Banat, D. R.**
  See Bradbury, Ray (Douglas)
**Bancroft, Laura**
  See Baum, L(yman) Frank
**Banim, John** [1798-1842] ............... **NCLC 13**
  See also DLB 116, 158, 159
**Banim, Michael** [1796-1874] ......... **NCLC 13**
  See also DLB 158, 159

**Banjo, The**
  See Paterson, A(ndrew) B(arton)
**Banks, Iain**
  See Banks, Iain M(enzies)
**Banks, Iain M(enzies)** [1954-] .......... **CLC 34**
  See also CA 123; 128; CANR 61; DLB 194;
    INT 128
**Banks, Lynne Reid** ............................. **CLC 23**
  See also Reid Banks, Lynne
  See also AAYA 6
**Banks, Russell** [1940-] ................. **CLC 37, 72**
  See also CA 65-68; CAAS 15; CANR 19, 52;
    DLB 130
**Banville, John** [1945-] ....................... **CLC 46**
  See also CA 117; 128; DLB 14; INT 128
**Banville, Theodore (Faullain) de** [1832-1891]
    **NCLC 9**
**Baraka, Amiri** [1934-] **CLC 1, 2, 3, 5, 10, 14,**
    **33; BLC 1; DA; DAC; DAM MST, MULT,**
    **POET, POP; DC 6; PC 4; WLCS**
  See also Jones, LeRoi
  See also BW 2; CA 21-24R; CABS 3; CANR
    27, 38, 61; CDALB 1941-1968; DLB 5, 7,
    16, 38; DLBD 8; MTCW
**Barbauld, Anna Laetitia** [1743-1825] **N C L C**
    **50**
  See also DLB 107, 109, 142, 158
**Barbellion, W. N. P.** ........................ **TCLC 24**
  See also Cummings, Bruce F(rederick)
**Barbera, Jack (Vincent)** [1945-] ....... **CLC 44**
  See also CA 110; CANR 45
**Barbey d'Aurevilly, Jules Amedee** [1808-1889]
    **NCLC 1; SSC 17**
  See also DLB 119
**Barbusse, Henri** [1873-1935] ........... **TCLC 5**
  See also CA 105; 154; DLB 65
**Barclay, Bill**
  See Moorcock, Michael (John)
**Barclay, William Ewert**
  See Moorcock, Michael (John)
**Barea, Arturo** [1897-1957] ............. **TCLC 14**
  See also CA 111
**Barfoot, Joan** [1946-] ........................ **CLC 18**
  See also CA 105
**Baring, Maurice** [1874-1945] ........... **TCLC 8**
  See also CA 105; DLB 34
**Barker, Clive** [1952-] .... **CLC 52; DAM POP**
  See also AAYA 10; BEST 90:3; CA 121; 129;
    INT 129; MTCW
**Barker, George Granville** [1913-1991] **CLC 8,**
    **48; DAM POET**
  See also CA 9-12R; 135; CANR 7, 38; DLB
    20; MTCW
**Barker, Harley Granville**
  See Granville-Barker, Harley
  See also DLB 10
**Barker, Howard** [1946-] .................... **CLC 37**
  See also CA 102; DLB 13
**Barker, Pat(ricia)** [1943-] ........... **CLC 32, 94**
  See also CA 117; 122; CANR 50; INT 122
**Barlow, Joel** [1754-1812] ............... **NCLC 23**
  See also DLB 37
**Barnard, Mary (Ethel)** [1909-] ......... **CLC 48**
  See also CA 21-22; CAP 2
**Barnes, Djuna** [1892-1982] **CLC 3, 4, 8, 11, 29;**
    **SSC 3**
  See also CA 9-12R; 107; CANR 16, 55; DLB
    4, 9, 45; MTCW
**Barnes, Julian (Patrick)** [1946-] **CLC 42; DAB**
  See also CA 102; CANR 19, 54; DLB 194;
    DLBY 93
**Barnes, Peter** [1931-] ..................... **CLC 5, 56**
  See also CA 65-68; CAAS 12; CANR 33, 34,
    64; DLB 13; MTCW
**Baroja (y Nessi), Pio** [1872-1956] ... **TCLC 8;**
    **HLC**
  See also CA 104

**Baron, David**
    See Pinter, Harold
**Baron Corvo**
    See Rolfe, Frederick (William Serafino Austin Lewis Mary)
**Barondess, Sue K(aufman)** [1926-1977]**CLC 8**
    See also Kaufman, Sue
    See also CA 1-4R; 69-72; CANR 1
**Baron de Teive**
    See Pessoa, Fernando (Antonio Nogueira)
**Barres, (Auguste-) Maurice** [1862-1923] **TCLC 47**
    See also CA 164; DLB 123
**Barreto, Afonso Henrique de Lima**
    See Lima Barreto, Afonso Henrique de
**Barrett, (Roger) Syd** [1946-] ............. **CLC 35**
**Barrett, William (Christopher)** [1913-1992] **CLC 27**
    See also CA 13-16R; 139; CANR 11, 67; INT CANR-11
**Barrie, J(ames) M(atthew)** [1860-1937]**TCLC 2; DAB; DAM DRAM**
    See also CA 104; 136; CDBLB 1890-1914; CLR 16; DLB 10, 141, 156; MAICYA; YABC 1
**Barrington, Michael**
    See Moorcock, Michael (John)
**Barrol, Grady**
    See Bograd, Larry
**Barry, Mike**
    See Malzberg, Barry N(athaniel)
**Barry, Philip** [1896-1949] ............... **TCLC 11**
    See also CA 109; DLB 7
**Bart, Andre Schwarz**
    See Schwarz-Bart, Andre
**Barth, John (Simmons)** [1930-]**CLC 1, 2, 3, 5, 7, 9, 10, 14, 27, 51, 89; DAM NOV; SSC 10**
    See also AITN 1, 2; CA 1-4R; CABS 1; CANR 5, 23, 49, 64; DLB 2; MTCW
**Barthelme, Donald** [1931-1989]**CLC 1, 2, 3, 5, 6, 8, 13, 23, 46, 59; DAM NOV; SSC 2**
    See also CA 21-24R; 129; CANR 20, 58; DLB 2; DLBY 80, 89; MTCW; SATA 7; SATA-Obit 62
**Barthelme, Frederick** [1943-] ............ **CLC 36**
    See also CA 114; 122; DLBY 85; INT 122
**Barthes, Roland (Gerard)** [1915-1980]. **C L C 24, 83**
    See also CA 130; 97-100; CANR 66; MTCW
**Barzun, Jacques (Martin)** [1907-] .... **CLC 51**
    See also CA 61-64; CANR 22
**Bashevis, Isaac**
    See Singer, Isaac Bashevis
**Bashkirtseff, Marie** [1859-1884] .... **NCLC 27**
**Basho**
    See Matsuo Basho
**Bass, Kingsley B., Jr.**
    See Bullins, Ed
**Bass, Rick** [1958-] ............................... **CLC 79**
    See also CA 126; CANR 53
**Bassani, Giorgio** [1916-] ...................... **CLC 9**
    See also CA 65-68; CANR 33; DLB 128, 177; MTCW
**Bastos, Augusto (Antonio) Roa**
    See Roa Bastos, Augusto (Antonio)
**Bataille, Georges** [1897-1962] .......... **CLC 29**
    See also CA 101; 89-92
**Bates, H(erbert) E(rnest)** [1905-1974] .. **C L C 46; DAB; DAM POP; SSC 10**
    See also CA 93-96; 45-48; CANR 34; DLB 162, 191; MTCW
**Bauchart**
    See Camus, Albert
**Baudelaire, Charles** [1821-1867]**NCLC 6, 29, 55; DA; DAB; DAC; DAM MST, POET; PC 1; SSC 18; WLC**
**Baudrillard, Jean** [1929-] .................. **CLC 60**

**Baum, L(yman) Frank** [1856-1919] **TCLC 7**
    See also CA 108; 133; CLR 15; DLB 22; JRDA; MAICYA; MTCW; SATA 18
**Baum, Louis F.**
    See Baum, L(yman) Frank
**Baumbach, Jonathan** [1933-] ........**CLC 6, 23**
    See also CA 13-16R; CAAS 5; CANR 12, 66; DLBY 80; INT CANR-12; MTCW
**Bausch, Richard (Carl)** [1945-] ........ **CLC 51**
    See also CA 101; CAAS 14; CANR 43, 61; DLB 130
**Baxter, Charles (Morley)** [1947-]**CLC 45, 78; DAM POP**
    See also CA 57-60; CANR 40, 64; DLB 130
**Baxter, George Owen**
    See Faust, Frederick (Schiller)
**Baxter, James K(eir)** [1926-1972] ..... **CLC 14**
    See also CA 77-80
**Baxter, John**
    See Hunt, E(verette) Howard, (Jr.)
**Bayer, Sylvia**
    See Glassco, John
**Baynton, Barbara** [1857-1929] ...... **TCLC 57**
**Beagle, Peter S(oyer)** [1939-] ..... **CLC 7, 104**
    See also CA 9-12R; CANR 4, 51; DLBY 80; INT CANR-4; SATA 60
**Bean, Normal**
    See Burroughs, Edgar Rice
**Beard, Charles A(ustin)** [1874-1948]**TCLC 15**
    See also CA 115; DLB 17; SATA 18
**Beardsley, Aubrey** [1872-1898] ....... **NCLC 6**
**Beattie, Ann** [1947-] .. **CLC 8, 13, 18, 40, 63; DAM NOV, POP; SSC 11**
    See also BEST 90:2; CA 81-84; CANR 53; DLBY 82; MTCW
**Beattie, James** [1735-1803] ............. **NCLC 25**
    See also DLB 109
**Beauchamp, Kathleen Mansfield** [1888-1923]
    See Mansfield, Katherine
    See also CA 104; 134; DA; DAC; DAM MST
**Beaumarchais, Pierre-Augustin Caron de** [1732-1799] ................................... **DC 4**
    See also DAM DRAM
**Beaumont, Francis** [1584(?)-1616]**LC 33; DC 6**
    See also CDBLB Before 1660; DLB 58, 121
**Beauvoir, Simone (Lucie Ernestine Marie Bertrand) de** [1908-1986]**CLC 1, 2, 4, 8, 14, 31, 44, 50, 71; DA; DAB; DAC; DAM MST, NOV; WLC**
    See also CA 9-12R; 118; CANR 28, 61; DLB 72; DLBY 86; MTCW
**Becker, Carl (Lotus)** [1873-1945] .. **TCLC 63**
    See also CA 157; DLB 17
**Becker, Jurek** [1937-1997] ............. **CLC 7, 19**
    See also CA 85-88; 157; CANR 60; DLB 75
**Becker, Walter** [1950-] ...................... **CLC 26**
**Beckett, Samuel (Barclay)** [1906-1989]**CLC 1, 2, 3, 4, 6, 9, 10, 11, 14, 18, 29, 57, 59, 83; DA; DAB; DAC; DAM DRAM, MST, NOV; SSC 16; WLC**
    See also CA 5-8R; 130; CANR 33, 61; CDBLB 1945-1960; DLB 13, 15; DLBY 90; MTCW
**Beckford, William** [1760-1844] ...... **NCLC 16**
    See also DLB 39
**Beckman, Gunnel** [1910-] .................. **CLC 26**
    See also CA 33-36R; CANR 15; CLR 25; MAICYA; SAAS 9; SATA 6
**Becque, Henri** [1837-1899] ............... **NCLC 3**
    See also DLB 192
**Beddoes, Thomas Lovell** [1803-1849]**NCLC 3**
    See also DLB 96
**Bede** [c. 673-735] ............................ **CMLC 20**
    See also DLB 146
**Bedford, Donald F.**
    See Fearing, Kenneth (Flexner)
**Beecher, Catharine Esther** [1800-1878]**NCLC**

**30**
    See also DLB 1
**Beecher, John** [1904-1980] ................. **CLC 6**
    See also AITN 1; CA 5-8R; 105; CANR 8
**Beer, Johann** [1655-1700] ...................... **LC 5**
    See also DLB 168
**Beer, Patricia** [1924-] ......................... **CLC 58**
    See also CA 61-64; CANR 13, 46; DLB 40
**Beerbohm, Max**
    See Beerbohm, (Henry) Max(imilian)
**Beerbohm, (Henry) Max(imilian)** [1872-1956] **TCLC 1, 24**
    See also CA 104; 154; DLB 34, 100
**Beer-Hofmann, Richard** [1866-1945] **T C L C 60**
    See also CA 160; DLB 81
**Begiebing, Robert J(ohn)** [1946-] ..... **CLC 70**
    See also CA 122; CANR 40
**Behan, Brendan** [1923-1964]**CLC 1, 8, 11, 15, 79; DAM DRAM**
    See also CA 73-76; CANR 33; CDBLB 1945-1960; DLB 13; MTCW
**Behn, Aphra** [1640(?)-1689] ... **LC 1, 30; DA; DAB; DAC; DAM DRAM, MST, NOV, POET; DC 4; PC 13; WLC**
    See also DLB 39, 80, 131
**Behrman, S(amuel) N(athaniel)** [1893-1973] **CLC 40**
    See also CA 13-16; 45-48; CAP 1; DLB 7, 44
**Belasco, David** [1853-1931] ............. **TCLC 3**
    See also CA 104; DLB 7
**Belcheva, Elisaveta** [1893-] ............... **CLC 10**
    See also Bagryana, Elisaveta
**Beldone, Phil "Cheech"**
    See Ellison, Harlan (Jay)
**Beleno**
    See Azuela, Mariano
**Belinski, Vissarion Grigoryevich** [1811-1848] **NCLC 5**
    See also DLB 198
**Belitt, Ben** [1911-] ............................. **CLC 22**
    See also CA 13-16R; CAAS 4; CANR 7; DLB 5
**Bell, Gertrude (Margaret Lowthian)** [1868-1926] ............................................ **TCLC 67**
    See also DLB 174
**Bell, James Madison** [1826-1902]. **TCLC 43; BLC 1; DAM MULT**
    See also BW 1; CA 122; 124; DLB 50
**Bell, Madison Smartt** [1957-] ... **CLC 41, 102**
    See also CA 111; CANR 28, 54
**Bell, Marvin (Hartley)** [1937-] .... **CLC 8, 31; DAM POET**
    See also CA 21-24R; CAAS 14; CANR 59; DLB 5; MTCW
**Bell, W. L. D.**
    See Mencken, H(enry) L(ouis)
**Bellamy, Atwood C.**
    See Mencken, H(enry) L(ouis)
**Bellamy, Edward** [1850-1898] ......... **NCLC 4**
    See also DLB 12
**Bellin, Edward J.**
    See Kuttner, Henry
**Belloc, (Joseph) Hilaire (Pierre Sebastien Rene Swanton)** [1870-1953]**TCLC 7, 18; DAM POET**
    See also CA 106; 152; DLB 19, 100, 141, 174; YABC 1
**Belloc, Joseph Peter Rene Hilaire**
    See Belloc, (Joseph) Hilaire (Pierre Sebastien Rene Swanton)
**Belloc, Joseph Pierre Hilaire**
    See Belloc, (Joseph) Hilaire (Pierre Sebastien Rene Swanton)
**Belloc, M. A.**
    See Lowndes, Marie Adelaide (Belloc)
**Bellow, Saul** [1915-] **CLC 1, 2, 3, 6, 8, 10, 13,**

15, 25, 33, 34, 63, 79; DA; DAB; DAC;
DAM MST, NOV, POP; SSC 14; WLC
See also AITN 2; BEST 89:3; CA 5-8R; CABS
1; CANR 29, 53; CDALB 1941-1968; DLB
2, 28; DLBD 3; DLBY 82; MTCW

Belser, Reimond Karel Maria de [1929-]
See Ruyslinck, Ward
See also CA 152

Bely, Andrey ...................... TCLC 7; PC 11
See also Bugayev, Boris Nikolayevich

Belyi, Andrei
See Bugayev, Boris Nikolayevich

Benary, Margot
See Benary-Isbert, Margot

Benary-Isbert, Margot [1889-1979] . CLC 12
See also CA 5-8R; 89-92; CANR 4; CLR 12;
MAICYA; SATA 2; SATA-Obit 21

Benavente (y Martinez), Jacinto [1866-1954]
TCLC 3; DAM DRAM, MULT
See also CA 106; 131; HW; MTCW

Benchley, Peter (Bradford) [1940-]CLC 4, 8;
DAM NOV, POP
See also AAYA 14; AITN 2; CA 17-20R; CANR
12, 35, 66; MTCW; SATA 3, 89

Benchley, Robert (Charles) [1889-1945]
TCLC 1, 55
See also CA 105; 153; DLB 11

Benda, Julien [1867-1956] .............. TCLC 60
See also CA 120; 154

Benedict, Ruth (Fulton) [1887-1948]TCLC 60
See also CA 158

Benedict, Saint [c. 480-c. 547] ....... CMLC 29

Benedikt, Michael [1935-] ............. CLC 4, 14
See also CA 13-16R; CANR 7; DLB 5

Benet, Juan [1927-] ........................... CLC 28
See also CA 143

Benet, Stephen Vincent [1898-1943]TCLC 7;
DAM POET; SSC 10
See also CA 104; 152; DLB 4, 48, 102; DLBY
97; YABC 1

Benet, William Rose [1886-1950] . TCLC 28;
DAM POET
See also CA 118; 152; DLB 45

Benford, Gregory (Albert) [1941-] ... CLC 52
See also CA 69-72; CAAS 27; CANR 12, 24,
49; DLBY 82

Bengtsson, Frans (Gunnar) [1894-1954]
TCLC 48

Benjamin, David
See Slavitt, David R(ytman)

Benjamin, Lois
See Gould, Lois

Benjamin, Walter [1892-1940] ....... TCLC 39
See also CA 164

Benn, Gottfried [1886-1956] ............ TCLC 3
See also CA 106; 153; DLB 56

Bennett, Alan [1934-]CLC 45, 77; DAB; DAM
MST
See also CA 103; CANR 35, 55; MTCW

Bennett, (Enoch) Arnold [1867-1931]TCLC 5,
20
See also CA 106; 155; CDBLB 1890-1914;
DLB 10, 34, 98, 135

Bennett, Elizabeth
See Mitchell, Margaret (Munnerlyn)

Bennett, George Harold [1930-]
See Bennett, Hal
See also BW 1; CA 97-100

Bennett, Hal ........................................... CLC 5
See also Bennett, George Harold
See also DLB 33

Bennett, Jay [1912-] ........................... CLC 35
See also AAYA 10; CA 69-72; CANR 11, 42;
JRDA; SAAS 4; SATA 41, 87; SATA-Brief
27

Bennett, Louise (Simone) [1919-] ... CLC 28;
BLC 1; DAM MULT

See also BW 2; CA 151; DLB 117

Benson, E(dward) F(rederic) [1867-1940]
TCLC 27
See also CA 114; 157; DLB 135, 153

Benson, Jackson J. [1930-] ............... CLC 34
See also CA 25-28R; DLB 111

Benson, Sally [1900-1972] ................. CLC 17
See also CA 19-20; 37-40R; CAP 1; SATA 1,
35; SATA-Obit 27

Benson, Stella [1892-1933] ............. TCLC 17
See also CA 117; 155; DLB 36, 162

Bentham, Jeremy [1748-1832] ....... NCLC 38
See also DLB 107, 158

Bentley, E(dmund) C(lerihew) [1875-1956]
TCLC 12
See also CA 108; DLB 70

Bentley, Eric (Russell) [1916-] .......... CLC 24
See also CA 5-8R; CANR 6, 67; INT CANR-6

Beranger, Pierre Jean de [1780-1857] N C L C
34

Berdyaev, Nicolas
See Berdyaev, Nikolai (Aleksandrovich)

Berdyaev, Nikolai (Aleksandrovich) [1874-
1948] ......................................... TCLC 67
See also CA 120; 157

Berdyayev, Nikolai (Aleksandrovich)
See Berdyaev, Nikolai (Aleksandrovich)

Berendt, John (Lawrence) [1939-] ... CLC 86
See also CA 146

Beresford, J(ohn) D(avys) [1873-1947]T C L C
81
See also CA 112; 155; DLB 162, 178, 197

Bergelson, David [1884-1952] ........ TCLC 81

Berger, Colonel
See Malraux, (Georges-)Andre

Berger, John (Peter) [1926-]..........CLC 2, 19
See also CA 81-84; CANR 51; DLB 14

Berger, Melvin H. [1927-] ................. CLC 12
See also CA 5-8R; CANR 4; CLR 32; SAAS 2;
SATA 5, 88

Berger, Thomas (Louis) [1924-] CLC 3, 5, 8,
11, 18, 38; DAM NOV
See also CA 1-4R; CANR 5, 28, 51; DLB 2;
DLBY 80; INT CANR-28; MTCW

Bergman, (Ernst) Ingmar [1918-]CLC 16, 72
See also CA 81-84; CANR 33

Bergson, Henri(-Louis) [1859-1941]TCLC 32
See also CA 164

Bergstein, Eleanor [1938-] ................. CLC 4
See also CA 53-56; CANR 5

Berkoff, Steven [1937-] ..................... CLC 56
See also CA 104

Bermant, Chaim (Icyk) [1929-] ......... CLC 40
See also CA 57-60; CANR 6, 31, 57

Bern, Victoria
See Fisher, M(ary) F(rances) K(ennedy)

Bernanos, (Paul Louis) Georges [1888-1948]
TCLC 3
See also CA 104; 130; DLB 72

Bernard, April [1956-] ....................... CLC 59
See also CA 131

Berne, Victoria
See Fisher, M(ary) F(rances) K(ennedy)

Bernhard, Thomas [1931-1989]CLC 3, 32, 61
See also CA 85-88; 127; CANR 32, 57; DLB
85, 124; MTCW

Bernhardt, Sarah (Henriette Rosine) [1844-
1923] ..............................................

TCLC 75
See also CA 157

Berriault, Gina [1926-]CLC 54, 109; SSC 30
See also CA 116; 129; CANR 66; DLB 130

Berrigan, Daniel [1921-] ..................... CLC 4
See also CA 33-36R; CAAS 1; CANR 11, 43;
DLB 5

Berrigan, Edmund Joseph Michael, Jr. [1934-
1983]

See Berrigan, Ted
See also CA 61-64; 110; CANR 14

Berrigan, Ted ..................................... CLC 37
See also Berrigan, Edmund Joseph Michael, Jr.
See also DLB 5, 169

Berry, Charles Edward Anderson [1931-]
See Berry, Chuck
See also CA 115

Berry, Chuck ..................................... CLC 17
See also Berry, Charles Edward Anderson

Berry, Jonas
See Ashbery, John (Lawrence)

Berry, Wendell (Erdman) [1934-]CLC 4, 6, 8,
27, 46; DAM POET
See also AITN 1; CA 73-76; CANR 50; DLB 5,
6

Berryman, John [1914-1972]CLC 1, 2, 3, 4, 6,
8, 10, 13, 25, 62; DAM POET
See also CA 13-16; 33-36R; CABS 2; CANR
35; CAP 1; CDALB 1941-1968; DLB 48;
MTCW

Bertolucci, Bernardo [1940-] ........... CLC 16
See also CA 106

Berton, Pierre (Francis De Marigny) [1920-]
CLC 104
See also CA 1-4R; CANR 2, 56; DLB 68

Bertrand, Aloysius [1807-1841] ..... NCLC 31

Bertran de Born [c. 1140-1215] ...... CMLC 5

Beruni, al [973-1048(?)] ................. CMLC 28

Besant, Annie (Wood) [1847-1933] .. TCLC 9
See also CA 105

Bessie, Alvah [1904-1985] ................. CLC 23
See also CA 5-8R; 116; CANR 2; DLB 26

Bethlen, T. D.
See Silverberg, Robert

Beti, Mongo ... CLC 27; BLC 1; DAM MULT
See also Biyidi, Alexandre

Betjeman, John [1906-1984]CLC 2, 6, 10, 34,
43; DAB; DAM MST, POET
See also CA 9-12R; 112; CANR 33, 56; CDBLB
1945-1960; DLB 20; DLBY 84; MTCW

Bettelheim, Bruno [1903-1990] ......... CLC 79
See also CA 81-84; 131; CANR 23, 61; MTCW

Betti, Ugo [1892-1953] ....................... TCLC 5
See also CA 104; 155

Betts, Doris (Waugh) [1932-] ... CLC 3, 6, 28
See also CA 13-16R; CANR 9, 66; DLBY 82;
INT CANR-9

Bevan, Alistair
See Roberts, Keith (John Kingston)

Bey, Pilaff
See Douglas, (George) Norman

Bialik, Chaim Nachman [1873-1934]TCLC 25

Bickerstaff, Isaac
See Swift, Jonathan

Bidart, Frank [1939-] ......................... CLC 33
See also CA 140

Bienek, Horst [1930-] ..................... CLC 7, 11
See also CA 73-76; DLB 75

Bierce, Ambrose (Gwinett) [1842-1914(?)]
TCLC 1, 7, 44; DA; DAC; DAM MST; SSC
9; WLC
See also CA 104; 139; CDALB 1865-1917;
DLB 11, 12, 23, 71, 74, 186

Biggers, Earl Derr [1884-1933] ..... TCLC 65
See also CA 108; 153

Billings, Josh
See Shaw, Henry Wheeler

Billington, (Lady) Rachel (Mary) [1942-]
CLC 43
See also AITN 2; CA 33-36R; CANR 44

Binyon, T(imothy) J(ohn) [1936-] .... CLC 34
See also CA 111; CANR 28

Bioy Casares, Adolfo [1914-1984] .CLC 4, 8,
13, 88; DAM MULT; HLC; SSC 17
See also CA 29-32R; CANR 19, 43, 66; DLB
113; HW; MTCW

See also CDBLB 1660-1789; DLB 104, 142

**Bottoms, David** [1949-] ...................... CLC 53
See also CA 105; CANR 22; DLB 120; DLBY 83

**Boucicault, Dion** [1820-1890] ......... NCLC 41

**Boucolon, Maryse** [1937(?)-]
See Conde, Maryse
See also CA 110; CANR 30, 53

**Bourget, Paul (Charles Joseph)** [1852-1935]
TCLC 12
See also CA 107; DLB 123

**Bourjaily, Vance (Nye)** [1922-] ..... CLC 8, 62
See also CA 1-4R; CAAS 1; CANR 2; DLB 2, 143

**Bourne, Randolph S(illiman)** [1886-1918]
TCLC 16
See also CA 117; 155; DLB 63

**Bova, Ben(jamin William)** [1932-] ... CLC 45
See also AAYA 16; CA 5-8R; CAAS 18; CANR 11, 56; CLR 3; DLBY 81; INT CANR-11; MAICYA; MTCW; SATA 6, 68

**Bowen, Elizabeth (Dorothea Cole)** [1899-1973]
CLC 1, 3, 6, 11, 15, 22; DAM NOV; SSC 3, 28
See also CA 17-18; 41-44R; CANR 35; CAP 2; CDBLB 1945-1960; DLB 15, 162; MTCW

**Bowering, George** [1935-] ......... CLC 15, 47
See also CA 21-24R; CAAS 16; CANR 10; DLB 53

**Bowering, Marilyn R(uthe)** [1949-] . CLC 32
See also CA 101; CANR 49

**Bowers, Edgar** [1924-] ...................... CLC 9
See also CA 5-8R; CANR 24; DLB 5

**Bowie, David** .................................. CLC 17
See also Jones, David Robert

**Bowles, Jane (Sydney)** [1917-1973]CLC 3, 68
See also CA 19-20; 41-44R; CAP 2

**Bowles, Paul (Frederick)** [1910-1986]CLC 1, 2, 19, 53; SSC 3
See also CA 1-4R; CAAS 1; CANR 1, 19, 50; DLB 5, 6; MTCW

**Box, Edgar**
See Vidal, Gore

**Boyd, Nancy**
See Millay, Edna St. Vincent

**Boyd, William** [1952-] .......... CLC 28, 53, 70
See also CA 114; 120; CANR 51

**Boyle, Kay** [1902-1992]CLC 1, 5, 19, 58; SSC 5
See also CA 13-16R; 140; CAAS 1; CANR 29, 61; DLB 4, 9, 48, 86; DLBY 93; MTCW

**Boyle, Mark**
See Kienzle, William X(avier)

**Boyle, Patrick** [1905-1982] ................ CLC 19
See also CA 127

**Boyle, T. C.** [1948-]
See Boyle, T(homas) Coraghessan

**Boyle, T(homas) Coraghessan** [1948-] .. C L C 36, 55, 90; DAM POP; SSC 16
See also BEST 90:4; CA 120; CANR 44; DLBY 86

**Boz**
See Dickens, Charles (John Huffam)

**Brackenridge, Hugh Henry** [1748-1816]
NCLC 7
See also DLB 11, 37

**Bradbury, Edward P.**
See Moorcock, Michael (John)

**Bradbury, Malcolm (Stanley)** [1932-]CLC 32, 61; DAM NOV
See also CA 1-4R; CANR 1, 33; DLB 14; MTCW

**Bradbury, Ray (Douglas)** [1920-]CLC 1, 3, 10, 15, 42, 98; DA; DAB; DAC; DAM MST, NOV, POP; SSC 29; WLC
See also AAYA 15; AITN 1, 2; CA 1-4R; CANR 2, 30; CDALB 1968-1988; DLB 2, 8;

MTCW; SATA 11, 64

**Bradford, Gamaliel** [1863-1932] ... TCLC 36
See also CA 160; DLB 17

**Bradley, David (Henry, Jr.)** [1950-] CLC 23;
BLC 1; DAM MULT
See also BW 1; CA 104; CANR 26; DLB 33

**Bradley, John Ed(mund, Jr.)** [1958-] CLC 55
See also CA 139

**Bradley, Marion Zimmer** [1930-] ... CLC 30;
DAM POP
See also AAYA 9; CA 57-60; CAAS 10; CANR 7, 31, 51; DLB 8; MTCW; SATA 90

**Bradstreet, Anne** [1612(?)-1672]LC 4, 30; DA;
DAC; DAM MST, POET; PC 10
See also CDALB 1640-1865; DLB 24

**Brady, Joan** [1939-] ........................... CLC 86
See also CA 141

**Bragg, Melvyn** [1939-] ...................... CLC 10
See also BEST 89:3; CA 57-60; CANR 10, 48;
DLB 14

**Brahe, Tycho** [1546-1601] .................... LC 45

**Braine, John (Gerard)** [1922-1986]CLC 1, 3, 41
See also CA 1-4R; 120; CANR 1, 33; CDBLB 1945-1960; DLB 15; DLBY 86; MTCW

**Bramah, Ernest** [1868-1942] .......... TCLC 72
See also CA 156; DLB 70

**Brammer, William** [1930(?)-1978] .... CLC 31
See also CA 77-80

**Brancati, Vitaliano** [1907-1954] .... TCLC 12
See also CA 109

**Brancato, Robin F(idler)** [1936-] ...... CLC 35
See also AAYA 9; CA 69-72; CANR 11, 45;
CLR 32; JRDA; SAAS 9; SATA 97

**Brand, Max**
See Faust, Frederick (Schiller)

**Brand, Millen** [1906-1980] ................. CLC 7
See also CA 21-24R; 97-100

**Branden, Barbara** .............................. CLC 44
See also CA 148

**Brandes, Georg (Morris Cohen)** [1842-1927]
TCLC 10
See also CA 105

**Brandys, Kazimierz** [1916-] .............. CLC 62

**Branley, Franklyn M(ansfield)** [1915-]. C L C 21
See also CA 33-36R; CANR 14, 39; CLR 13;
MAICYA; SAAS 16; SATA 4, 68

**Brathwaite, Edward Kamau** [1930-]CLC 11;
BLCS; DAM POET
See also BW 2; CA 25-28R; CANR 11, 26, 47;
DLB 125

**Brautigan, Richard (Gary)** [1935-1984]C L C 1, 3, 5, 9, 12, 34, 42; DAM NOV
See also CA 53-56; 113; CANR 34; DLB 2, 5;
DLBY 80, 84; MTCW; SATA 56

**Brave Bird, Mary** [1953-]
See Crow Dog, Mary (Ellen)
See also NNAL

**Braverman, Kate** [1950-] ................... CLC 67
See also CA 89-92

**Brecht, (Eugen) Bertolt (Friedrich)** [1898-1956]

TCLC 1, 6, 13, 35; DA; DAB; DAC; DAM DRAM, MST; DC 3; WLC
See also CA 104; 133; CANR 62; DLB 56, 124;
MTCW

**Brecht, Eugen Berthold Friedrich**
See Brecht, (Eugen) Bertolt (Friedrich)

**Bremer, Fredrika** [1801-1865] ....... NCLC 11

**Brennan, Christopher John** [1870-1932]
TCLC 17
See also CA 117

**Brennan, Maeve** [1917-] .................... CLC 5
See also CA 81-84

**Brent, Linda**
See Jacobs, Harriet A(nn)

**Brentano, Clemens (Maria)** [1778-1842]
NCLC 1
See also DLB 90

**Brent of Bin Bin**
See Franklin, (Stella Maria Sarah) Miles (Lampe)

**Brenton, Howard** [1942-] .................. CLC 31
See also CA 69-72; CANR 33, 67; DLB 13;
MTCW

**Breslin, James** [1930-1996]
See Breslin, Jimmy
See also CA 73-76; CANR 31; DAM NOV;
MTCW

**Breslin, Jimmy** ................................CLC 4, 43
See also Breslin, James
See also AITN 1; DLB 185

**Bresson, Robert** [1901-] .................... CLC 16
See also CA 110; CANR 49

**Breton, Andre** [1896-1966] CLC 2, 9, 15, 54;
PC 15
See also CA 19-20; 25-28R; CANR 40, 60; CAP 2; DLB 65; MTCW

**Breytenbach, Breyten** [1939(?)-]CLC 23, 37;
DAM POET
See also CA 113; 129; CANR 61

**Bridgers, Sue Ellen** [1942-] ............... CLC 26
See also AAYA 8; CA 65-68; CANR 11, 36;
CLR 18; DLB 52; JRDA; MAICYA; SAAS 1; SATA 22, 90

**Bridges, Robert (Seymour)** [1844-1930]
TCLC 1; DAM POET
See also CA 104; 152; CDBLB 1890-1914;
DLB 19, 98

**Bridie, James** ................................... TCLC 3
See also Mavor, Osborne Henry
See also DLB 10

**Brin, David** [1950-] ........................... CLC 34
See also AAYA 21; CA 102; CANR 24; INT CANR-24; SATA 65

**Brink, Andre (Philippus)** [1935-]CLC 18, 36, 106
See also CA 104; CANR 39, 62; INT 103;
MTCW

**Brinsmead, H(esba) F(ay)** [1922-] .... CLC 21
See also CA 21-24R; CANR 10; CLR 47;
MAICYA; SAAS 5; SATA 18, 78

**Brittain, Vera (Mary)** [1893(?)-1970]CLC 23
See also CA 13-16; 25-28R; CANR 58; CAP 1;
DLB 191; MTCW

**Broch, Hermann** [1886-1951] ........ TCLC 20
See also CA 117; DLB 85, 124

**Brock, Rose**
See Hansen, Joseph

**Brodkey, Harold (Roy)** [1930-1996] . CLC 56
See also CA 111; 151; DLB 130

**Brodsky, Iosif Alexandrovich** [1940-1996]
See Brodsky, Joseph
See also AITN 1; CA 41-44R; 151; CANR 37;
DAM POET; MTCW

**Brodsky, Joseph** [1940-1996]CLC 4, 6, 13, 36, 100; PC 9
See also Brodsky, Iosif Alexandrovich

**Brodsky, Michael (Mark)** [1948-] ..... CLC 19
See also CA 102; CANR 18, 41, 58

**Bromell, Henry** [1947-] ...................... CLC 5
See also CA 53-56; CANR 9

**Bromfield, Louis (Brucker)** [1896-1956]
TCLC 11
See also CA 107; 155; DLB 4, 9, 86

**Broner, E(sther) M(asserman)** [1930-]CLC 19
See also CA 17-20R; CANR 8, 25; DLB 28

**Bronk, William** [1918-] ..................... CLC 10
See also CA 89-92; CANR 23; DLB 165

**Bronstein, Lev Davidovich**
See Trotsky, Leon

**Bronte, Anne** [1820-1849] ............... NCLC 71
See also DLB 21, 199

TCLC 41
See also CA 165
**Chandler, Raymond (Thornton)** [1888-1959]
**TCLC 1, 7; SSC 23**
See also AAYA 25; CA 104; 129; CANR 60;
CDALB 1929-1941; DLBD 6; MTCW
**Chang, Eileen** [1920-1995] ................ **SSC 28**
See also CA 166
**Chang, Jung** [1952-] ......................... **CLC 71**
See also CA 142
**Chang Ai-Ling**
See Chang, Eileen
**Channing, William Ellery** [1780-1842]**N C L C
17**
See also DLB 1, 59
**Chaplin, Charles Spencer** [1889-1977] . **C L C
16**
See also Chaplin, Charlie
See also CA 81-84; 73-76
**Chaplin, Charlie**
See Chaplin, Charles Spencer
See also DLB 44
**Chapman, George** [1559(?)-1634] ..... **LC 22;
DAM DRAM**
See also DLB 62, 121
**Chapman, Graham** [1941-1989] ....... **CLC 21**
See also Monty Python
See also CA 116; 129; CANR 35
**Chapman, John Jay** [1862-1933] ..... **TCLC 7**
See also CA 104
**Chapman, Lee**
See Bradley, Marion Zimmer
**Chapman, Walker**
See Silverberg, Robert
**Chappell, Fred (Davis)** [1936-] .. **CLC 40, 78**
See also CA 5-8R; CAAS 4; CANR 8, 33, 67;
DLB 6, 105
**Char, Rene(-Emile)** [1907-1988]**CLC 9, 11, 14,
55; DAM POET**
See also CA 13-16R; 124; CANR 32; MTCW
**Charby, Jay**
See Ellison, Harlan (Jay)
**Chardin, Pierre Teilhard de**
See Teilhard de Chardin, (Marie Joseph) Pierre
**Charles I** [1600-1649] ........................... **LC 13**
**Charriere, Isabelle de** [1740-1805] **NCLC 66**
**Charyn, Jerome** [1937-] ............ **CLC 5, 8, 18**
See also CA 5-8R; CAAS 1; CANR 7, 61;
DLBY 83; MTCW
**Chase, Mary (Coyle)** [1907-1981] .........**DC 1**
See also CA 77-80; 105; SATA 17; SATA-Obit
29
**Chase, Mary Ellen** [1887-1973] ......... **CLC 2**
See also CA 13-16; 41-44R; CAP 1; SATA 10
**Chase, Nicholas**
See Hyde, Anthony
**Chateaubriand, Francois Rene de** [1768-1848]
**NCLC 3**
See also DLB 119
**Chatterje, Sarat Chandra** [1876-1936(?)]
See Chatterji, Saratchandra
See also CA 109
**Chatterji, Bankim Chandra** [1838-1894]
**NCLC 19**
**Chatterji, Saratchandra** ................. **TCLC 13**
See also Chatterje, Sarat Chandra
**Chatterton, Thomas** [1752-1770]**LC 3; DAM
POET**
See also DLB 109
**Chatwin, (Charles) Bruce** [1940-1989] . **C L C
28, 57, 59; DAM POP**
See also AAYA 4; BEST 90:1; CA 85-88; 127;
DLB 194
**Chaucer, Daniel**
See Ford, Ford Madox
**Chaucer, Geoffrey** [1340(?)-1400]**LC 17; DA;
DAB; DAC; DAM MST, POET; PC 19;**

WLCS
See also CDBLB Before 1660; DLB 146
**Chaviaras, Strates** [1935-]
See Haviaras, Stratis
See also CA 105
**Chayefsky, Paddy** ............................... **CLC 23**
See also Chayefsky, Sidney
See also DLB 7, 44; DLBY 81
**Chayefsky, Sidney** [1923-1981]
See Chayefsky, Paddy
See also CA 9-12R; 104; CANR 18; DAM
DRAM
**Chedid, Andree** [1920-] ..................... **CLC 47**
See also CA 145
**Cheever, John** [1912-1982]**CLC 3, 7, 8, 11, 15,
25, 64; DA; DAB; DAC; DAM MST, NOV,
POP; SSC 1; WLC**
See also CA 5-8R; 106; CABS 1; CANR 5, 27;
CDALB 1941-1968; DLB 2, 102; DLBY 80,
82; INT CANR-5; MTCW
**Cheever, Susan** [1943-] ................ **CLC 18, 48**
See also CA 103; CANR 27, 51; DLBY 82; INT
CANR-27
**Chekhonte, Antosha**
See Chekhov, Anton (Pavlovich)
**Chekhov, Anton (Pavlovich)** [1860-1904]
**TCLC 3, 10, 31, 55; DA; DAB; DAC; DAM
DRAM, MST; DC 9; SSC 2, 28; WLC**
See also CA 104; 124; SATA 90
**Chernyshevsky, Nikolay Gavrilovich** [1828-
1889] ......................................... **NCLC 1**
**Cherry, Carolyn Janice** [1942-]
See Cherryh, C. J.
See also CA 65-68; CANR 10
**Cherryh, C. J.** ..................................... **CLC 35**
See also Cherry, Carolyn Janice
See also AAYA 24; DLBY 80; SATA 93
**Chesnutt, Charles W(addell)** [1858-1932]
**TCLC 5, 39; BLC 1; DAM MULT; SSC 7**
See also BW 1; CA 106; 125; DLB 12, 50, 78;
MTCW
**Chester, Alfred** [1929(?)-1971] .......... **CLC 49**
See also CA 33-36R; DLB 130
**Chesterton, G(ilbert) K(eith)** [1874-1936]
**TCLC 1, 6, 64; DAM NOV, POET; SSC 1**
See also CA 104; 132; CDBLB 1914-1945;
DLB 10, 19, 34, 70, 98, 149, 178; MTCW;
SATA 27
**Chiang, Pin-chin** [1904-1986]
See Ding Ling
See also CA 118
**Ch'ien Chung-shu** [1910-] ................ **CLC 22**
See also CA 130; MTCW
**Child, L. Maria**
See Child, Lydia Maria
**Child, Lydia Maria** [1802-1880] ...... **NCLC 6**
See also DLB 1, 74; SATA 67
**Child, Mrs.**
See Child, Lydia Maria
**Child, Philip** [1898-1978] .......... **CLC 19, 68**
See also CA 13-14; CAP 1; SATA 47
**Childers, (Robert) Erskine** [1870-1922]**TCLC
65**
See also CA 113; 153; DLB 70
**Childress, Alice** [1920-1994] **CLC 12, 15, 86,
96; BLC 1; DAM DRAM, MULT, NOV;
DC 4**
See also AAYA 8; BW 2; CA 45-48; 146; CANR
3, 27, 50; CLR 14; DLB 7, 38; JRDA;
MAICYA; MTCW; SATA 7, 48, 81
**Chin, Frank (Chew, Jr.)** [1940-] ............**DC 7**
See also CA 33-36R; DAM MULT
**Chislett, (Margaret) Anne** [1943-].... **CLC 34**
See also CA 151
**Chitty, Thomas Willes** [1926-] ......... **CLC 11**
See also Hinde, Thomas
See also CA 5-8R

**Chivers, Thomas Holley** [1809-1858] . **N C L C
49**
See also DLB 3
**Chomette, Rene Lucien** [1898-1981]
See Clair, Rene
See also CA 103
**Chopin, Kate TCLC 5, 14; DA; DAB; SSC 8;
WLCS**
See also Chopin, Katherine
See also CDALB 1865-1917; DLB 12, 78
**Chopin, Katherine** [1851-1904]
See Chopin, Kate
See also CA 104; 122; DAC; DAM MST, NOV
**Chretien de Troyes** [c. 12th cent. -] **CMLC 10**
**Christie**
See Ichikawa, Kon
**Christie, Agatha (Mary Clarissa)** [1890-1976]
**CLC 1, 6, 8, 12, 39, 48, 110; DAB; DAC;
DAM NOV**
See also AAYA 9; AITN 1, 2; CA 17-20R; 61-
64; CANR 10, 37; CDBLB 1914-1945; DLB
13, 77; MTCW; SATA 36
**Christie, (Ann) Philippa**
See Pearce, Philippa
See also CA 5-8R; CANR 4
**Christine de Pizan** [1365(?)-1431(?)] .... **LC 9**
**Chubb, Elmer**
See Masters, Edgar Lee
**Chulkov, Mikhail Dmitrievich** [1743-1792]**LC
2**
See also DLB 150
**Churchill, Caryl** [1938-] .. **CLC 31, 55; DC 5**
See also CA 102; CANR 22, 46; DLB 13;
MTCW
**Churchill, Charles** [1731-1764] ............ **LC 3**
See also DLB 109
**Chute, Carolyn** [1947-] ..................... **CLC 39**
See also CA 123
**Ciardi, John (Anthony)** [1916-1986]**CLC 10,
40, 44; DAM POET**
See also CA 5-8R; 118; CAAS 2; CANR 5, 33;
CLR 19; DLB 5; DLBY 86; INT CANR-5;
MAICYA; MTCW; SAAS 26; SATA 1, 65;
SATA-Obit 46
**Cicero, Marcus Tullius** [106B.C.-43B.C.]
**CMLC 3**
**Cimino, Michael** [1943-] ................... **CLC 16**
See also CA 105
**Cioran, E(mil) M.** [1911-1995] .......... **CLC 64**
See also CA 25-28R; 149
**Cisneros, Sandra** [1954-] ....... **CLC 69; DAM
MULT; HLC**
See also AAYA 9; CA 131; CANR 64; DLB 122,
152; HW
**Cixous, Helene** [1937-] ...................... **CLC 92**
See also CA 126; CANR 55; DLB 83; MTCW
**Clair, Rene** ......................................... **CLC 20**
See also Chomette, Rene Lucien
**Clampitt, Amy** [1920-1994] .. **CLC 32; PC 19**
See also CA 110; 146; CANR 29; DLB 105
**Clancy, Thomas L., Jr.** [1947-]
See Clancy, Tom
See also CA 125; 131; CANR 62; INT 131;
MTCW
**Clancy, Tom** .. **CLC 45, 112; DAM NOV, POP**
See also Clancy, Thomas L., Jr.
See also AAYA 9; BEST 89:1, 90:1
**Clare, John** [1793-1864]**NCLC 9; DAB; DAM
POET; PC 23**
See also DLB 55, 96
**Clarin**
See Alas (y Urena), Leopoldo (Enrique Garcia)
**Clark, Al C.**
See Goines, Donald
**Clark, (Robert) Brian** [1932-] .......... **CLC 29**
See also CA 41-44R; CANR 67
**Clark, Curt**

DAB; DAC; DAM DRAM, MST, POET; DC 2; WLC
See also CDBLB 1660-1789; DLB 39, 84

**Connell, Evan S(helby), Jr.** [1924-] **CLC 4, 6, 45; DAM NOV**
See also AAYA 7; CA 1-4R; CAAS 2; CANR 2, 39; DLB 2; DLBY 81; MTCW

**Connelly, Marc(us Cook)** [1890-1980] **CLC 7**
See also CA 85-88; 102; CANR 30; DLB 7; DLBY 80; SATA-Obit 25

**Connor, Ralph** ........................ **TCLC 31**
See also Gordon, Charles William
See also DLB 92

**Conrad, Joseph** [1857-1924] **TCLC 1, 6, 13, 25, 43, 57; DA; DAB; DAC; DAM MST, NOV; SSC 9; WLC**
See also CA 104; 131; CANR 60; CDBLB 1890-1914; DLB 10, 34, 98, 156; MTCW; SATA 27

**Conrad, Robert Arnold**
See Hart, Moss

**Conroy, Donald Pat(rick)** [1945-] **CLC 30, 74; DAM NOV, POP**
See also AAYA 8; AITN 1; CA 85-88; CANR 24, 53; DLB 6; MTCW

**Conroy, Pat**
See Conroy, Donald Pat(rick)

**Constant (de Rebecque), (Henri) Benjamin** [1767-1830] ........................ **NCLC 6**
See also DLB 119

**Conybeare, Charles Augustus**
See Eliot, T(homas) S(tearns)

**Cook, Michael** [1933-] ........................ **CLC 58**
See also CA 93-96; CANR 68; DLB 53

**Cook, Robin** [1940-] ..... **CLC 14; DAM POP**
See also BEST 90:2; CA 108; 111; CANR 41; INT 111

**Cook, Roy**
See Silverberg, Robert

**Cooke, Elizabeth** [1948-] ........................ **CLC 55**
See also CA 129

**Cooke, John Esten** [1830-1886] ....... **NCLC 5**
See also DLB 3

**Cooke, John Estes**
See Baum, L(yman) Frank

**Cooke, M. E.**
See Creasey, John

**Cooke, Margaret**
See Creasey, John

**Cook-Lynn, Elizabeth** [1930-] **CLC 93; DAM MULT**
See also CA 133; DLB 175; NNAL

**Cooney, Ray** ........................ **CLC 62**

**Cooper, Douglas** [1960-] ........................ **CLC 86**

**Cooper, Henry St. John**
See Creasey, John

**Cooper, J(oan) California** ....... **CLC 56; DAM MULT**
See also AAYA 12; BW 1; CA 125; CANR 55

**Cooper, James Fenimore** [1789-1851] **NCLC 1, 27, 54**
See also AAYA 22; CDALB 1640-1865; DLB 3; SATA 19

**Coover, Robert (Lowell)** [1932-] **CLC 3, 7, 15, 32, 46, 87; DAM NOV; SSC 15**
See also CA 45-48; CANR 3, 37, 58; DLB 2; DLBY 81; MTCW

**Copeland, Stewart (Armstrong)** [1952-] **CLC 26**

**Copernicus, Nicolaus** [1473-1543] ....... **LC 45**

**Coppard, A(lfred) E(dgar)** [1878-1957] **TCLC 5; SSC 21**
See also CA 114; DLB 162; YABC 1

**Coppee, Francois** [1842-1908] ....... **TCLC 25**

**Coppola, Francis Ford** [1939-] ......... **CLC 16**
See also CA 77-80; CANR 40; DLB 44

**Corbiere, Tristan** [1845-1875] ....... **NCLC 43**

**Corcoran, Barbara** [1911-] ........................ **CLC 17**
See also AAYA 14; CA 21-24R; CAAS 2; CANR 11, 28, 48; CLR 50; DLB 52; JRDA; SAAS 20; SATA 3, 77

**Cordelier, Maurice**
See Giraudoux, (Hippolyte) Jean

**Corelli, Marie** [1855-1924] ............ **TCLC 51**
See also Mackay, Mary
See also DLB 34, 156

**Corman, Cid** [1924-] ........................ **CLC 9**
See also Corman, Sidney
See also CAAS 2; DLB 5, 193

**Corman, Sidney** [1924-]
See Corman, Cid
See also CA 85-88; CANR 44; DAM POET

**Cormier, Robert (Edmund)** [1925-] **CLC 12, 30; DA; DAB; DAC; DAM MST, NOV**
See also AAYA 3, 19; CA 1-4R; CANR 5, 23; CDALB 1968-1988; CLR 12; DLB 52; INT CANR-23; JRDA; MAICYA; MTCW; SATA 10, 45, 83

**Corn, Alfred (DeWitt III)** [1943-] ..... **CLC 33**
See also CA 104; CAAS 25; CANR 44; DLB 120; DLBY 80

**Corneille, Pierre** [1606-1684] .. **LC 28; DAB; DAM MST**

**Cornwell, David (John Moore)** [1931-] **CLC 9, 15; DAM POP**
See also le Carre, John
See also CA 5-8R; CANR 13, 33, 59; MTCW

**Corso, (Nunzio) Gregory** [1930-] . **CLC 1, 11**
See also CA 5-8R; CANR 41; DLB 5, 16; MTCW

**Cortazar, Julio** [1914-1984] **CLC 2, 3, 5, 10, 13, 15, 33, 34, 92; DAM MULT, NOV; HLC; SSC 7**
See also CA 21-24R; CANR 12, 32; DLB 113; HW; MTCW

**Cortes, Hernan** [1484-1547] ................ **LC 31**

**Corwin, Cecil**
See Kornbluth, C(yril) M.

**Cosic, Dobrica** [1921-] ........................ **CLC 14**
See also CA 122; 138; DLB 181

**Costain, Thomas B(ertram)** [1885-1965] **CLC 30**
See also CA 5-8R; 25-28R; DLB 9

**Costantini, Humberto** [1924(?)-1987] **CLC 49**
See also CA 131; 122; HW

**Costello, Elvis** [1955-] ........................ **CLC 21**

**Cotes, Cecil V.**
See Duncan, Sara Jeannette

**Cotter, Joseph Seamon Sr.** [1861-1949] **TCLC 28; BLC 1; DAM MULT**
See also BW 1; CA 124; DLB 50

**Couch, Arthur Thomas Quiller**
See Quiller-Couch, Sir Arthur (Thomas)

**Coulton, James**
See Hansen, Joseph

**Couperus, Louis (Marie Anne)** [1863-1923] **TCLC 15**
See also CA 115

**Coupland, Douglas** [1961-] ... **CLC 85; DAC; DAM POP**
See also CA 142; CANR 57

**Court, Wesli**
See Turco, Lewis (Putnam)

**Courtenay, Bryce** [1933-] ................ **CLC 59**
See also CA 138

**Courtney, Robert**
See Ellison, Harlan (Jay)

**Cousteau, Jacques-Yves** [1910-1997] **CLC 30**
See also CA 65-68; 159; CANR 15, 67; MTCW; SATA 38, 98

**Cowan, Peter (Walkinshaw)** [1914-] . **SSC 28**
See also CA 21-24R; CANR 9, 25, 50

**Coward, Noel (Peirce)** [1899-1973] **CLC 1, 9, 29, 51; DAM DRAM**

See also AITN 1; CA 17-18; 41-44R; CANR 35; CAP 2; CDBLB 1914-1945; DLB 10; MTCW

**Cowley, Abraham** [1618-1667] ............ **LC 43**
See also DLB 131, 151

**Cowley, Malcolm** [1898-1989] .......... **CLC 39**
See also CA 5-8R; 128; CANR 3, 55; DLB 4, 48; DLBY 81, 89; MTCW

**Cowper, William** [1731-1800] **NCLC 8; DAM POET**
See also DLB 104, 109

**Cox, William Trevor** [1928-] . **CLC 9, 14, 71; DAM NOV**
See also Trevor, William
See also CA 9-12R; CANR 4, 37, 55; DLB 14; INT CANR-37; MTCW

**Coyne, P. J.**
See Masters, Hilary

**Cozzens, James Gould** [1903-1978] **CLC 1, 4, 11, 92**
See also CA 9-12R; 81-84; CANR 19; CDALB 1941-1968; DLB 9; DLBD 2; DLBY 84, 97; MTCW

**Crabbe, George** [1754-1832] .......... **NCLC 26**
See also DLB 93

**Craddock, Charles Egbert**
See Murfree, Mary Noailles

**Craig, A. A.**
See Anderson, Poul (William)

**Craik, Dinah Maria (Mulock)** [1826-1887] **NCLC 38**
See also DLB 35, 163; MAICYA; SATA 34

**Cram, Ralph Adams** [1863-1942] .. **TCLC 45**
See also CA 160

**Crane, (Harold) Hart** [1899-1932] **TCLC 2, 5, 80; DA; DAB; DAC; DAM MST, POET; PC 3; WLC**
See also CA 104; 127; CDALB 1917-1929; DLB 4, 48; MTCW

**Crane, R(onald) S(almon)** [1886-1967] **CLC 27**
See also CA 85-88; DLB 63

**Crane, Stephen (Townley)** [1871-1900] **TCLC 11, 17, 32; DA; DAB; DAC; DAM MST, NOV, POET; SSC 7; WLC**
See also AAYA 21; CA 109; 140; CDALB 1865-1917; DLB 12, 54, 78; YABC 2

**Crase, Douglas** [1944-] ........................ **CLC 58**
See also CA 106

**Crashaw, Richard** [1612(?)-1649] ....... **LC 24**
See also DLB 126

**Craven, Margaret** [1901-1980] **CLC 17; DAC**
See also CA 103

**Crawford, F(rancis) Marion** [1854-1909] **TCLC 10**
See also CA 107; DLB 71

**Crawford, Isabella Valancy** [1850-1887] **NCLC 12**
See also DLB 92

**Crayon, Geoffrey**
See Irving, Washington

**Creasey, John** [1908-1973] ................ **CLC 11**
See also CA 5-8R; 41-44R; CANR 8, 59; DLB 77; MTCW

**Crebillon, Claude Prosper Jolyot de (fils)** [1707-1777] ........................ **LC 28**

**Credo**
See Creasey, John

**Credo, Alvaro J. de**
See Prado (Calvo), Pedro

**Creeley, Robert (White)** [1926-] **CLC 1, 2, 4, 8, 11, 15, 36, 78; DAM POET**
See also CA 1-4R; CAAS 10; CANR 23, 43; DLB 5, 16, 169; MTCW

**Crews, Harry (Eugene)** [1935-] **CLC 6, 23, 49**
See also AITN 1; CA 25-28R; CANR 20, 57; DLB 6, 143, 185; MTCW

**Crichton, (John) Michael** [1942-]**CLC 2, 6, 54, 90; DAM NOV, POP**
See also AAYA 10; AITN 2; CA 25-28R; CANR 13, 40, 54; DLBY 81; INT CANR-13; JRDA; MTCW; SATA 9, 88
**Crispin, Edmund** ............................. **CLC 22**
See also Montgomery, (Robert) Bruce
See also DLB 87
**Cristofer, Michael** [1945(?)-] . **CLC 28; DAM DRAM**
See also CA 110; 152; DLB 7
**Croce, Benedetto** [1866-1952] ........ **TCLC 37**
See also CA 120; 155
**Crockett, David** [1786-1836] ............ **NCLC 8**
See also DLB 3, 11
**Crockett, Davy**
See Crockett, David
**Crofts, Freeman Wills** [1879-1957] **TCLC 55**
See also CA 115; DLB 77
**Croker, John Wilson** [1780-1857] .. **NCLC 10**
See also DLB 110
**Crommelynck, Fernand** [1885-1970] **CLC 75**
See also CA 89-92
**Cromwell, Oliver** [1599-1658] ............ **LC 43**
**Cronin, A(rchibald) J(oseph)** [1896-1981] **CLC 32**
See also CA 1-4R; 102; CANR 5; DLB 191; SATA 47; SATA-Obit 25
**Cross, Amanda**
See Heilbrun, Carolyn G(old)
**Crothers, Rachel** [1878(?)-1958] .... **TCLC 19**
See also CA 113; DLB 7
**Croves, Hal**
See Traven, B.
**Crow Dog, Mary (Ellen)** [(?)-] .......... **CLC 93**
See also Brave Bird, Mary
See also CA 154
**Crowfield, Christopher**
See Stowe, Harriet (Elizabeth) Beecher
**Crowley, Aleister** ............................... **TCLC 7**
See also Crowley, Edward Alexander
**Crowley, Edward Alexander** [1875-1947]
See Crowley, Aleister
See also CA 104
**Crowley, John** [1942-] ....................... **CLC 57**
See also CA 61-64; CANR 43; DLBY 82; SATA 65
**Crud**
See Crumb, R(obert)
**Crumarums**
See Crumb, R(obert)
**Crumb, R(obert)** [1943-] .................... **CLC 17**
See also CA 106
**Crumbum**
See Crumb, R(obert)
**Crumski**
See Crumb, R(obert)
**Crum the Bum**
See Crumb, R(obert)
**Crunk**
See Crumb, R(obert)
**Crustt**
See Crumb, R(obert)
**Cryer, Gretchen (Kiger)** [1935-] ....... **CLC 21**
See also CA 114; 123
**Csath, Geza** [1887-1919] ................. **TCLC 13**
See also CA 111
**Cudlip, David** [1933-] ........................ **CLC 34**
**Cullen, Countee** [1903-1946]**TCLC 4, 37; BLC 1; DA; DAC; DAM MST, MULT, POET; PC 20; WLCS**
See also BW 1; CA 108; 124; CDALB 1917-1929; DLB 4, 48, 51; MTCW; SATA 18
**Cum, R.**
See Crumb, R(obert)
**Cummings, Bruce F(rederick)** [1889-1919]
See Barbellion, W. N. P.

See also CA 123
**Cummings, E(dward) E(stlin)** [1894-1962] **CLC 1, 3, 8, 12, 15, 68; DA; DAB; DAC; DAM MST, POET; PC 5; WLC 2**
See also CA 73-76; CANR 31; CDALB 1929-1941; DLB 4, 48; MTCW
**Cunha, Euclides (Rodrigues Pimenta) da** [1866-1909] .........................................................
**TCLC 24**
See also CA 123
**Cunningham, E. V.**
See Fast, Howard (Melvin)
**Cunningham, J(ames) V(incent)** [1911-1985] **CLC 3, 31**
See also CA 1-4R; 115; CANR 1; DLB 5
**Cunningham, Julia (Woolfolk)** [1916-]. **C L C 12**
See also CA 9-12R; CANR 4, 19, 36; JRDA; MAICYA; SAAS 2; SATA 1, 26
**Cunningham, Michael** [1952-] .......... **CLC 34**
See also CA 136
**Cunninghame Graham, R(obert) B(ontine)** [1852-1936] .................................................
**TCLC 19**
See also Graham, R(obert) B(ontine) Cunninghame
See also CA 119; DLB 98
**Currie, Ellen** [19(?)-] ......................... **CLC 44**
**Curtin, Philip**
See Lowndes, Marie Adelaide (Belloc)
**Curtis, Price**
See Ellison, Harlan (Jay)
**Cutrate, Joe**
See Spiegelman, Art
**Cynewulf** [c. 770-c. 840] ................ **CMLC 23**
**Czaczkes, Shmuel Yosef**
See Agnon, S(hmuel) Y(osef Halevi)
**Dabrowska, Maria (Szumska)** [1889-1965] **CLC 15**
See also CA 106
**Dabydeen, David** [1955-] ................... **CLC 34**
See also BW 1; CA 125; CANR 56
**Dacey, Philip** [1939-] ......................... **CLC 51**
See also CA 37-40R; CAAS 17; CANR 14, 32, 64; DLB 105
**Dagerman, Stig (Halvard)** [1923-1954]**T C L C 17**
See also CA 117; 155
**Dahl, Roald** [1916-1990] .... **CLC 1, 6, 18, 79; DAB; DAC; DAM MST, NOV, POP**
See also AAYA 15; CA 1-4R; 133; CANR 6, 32, 37, 62; CLR 1, 7, 41; DLB 139; JRDA; MAICYA; MTCW; SATA 1, 26, 73; SATA-Obit 65
**Dahlberg, Edward** [1900-1977] **CLC 1, 7, 14**
See also CA 9-12R; 69-72; CANR 31, 62; DLB 48; MTCW
**Daitch, Susan** [1954-] ....................... **CLC 103**
See also CA 161
**Dale, Colin** ...................................... **TCLC 18**
See also Lawrence, T(homas) E(dward)
**Dale, George E.**
See Asimov, Isaac
**Daly, Elizabeth** [1878-1967] .............. **CLC 52**
See also CA 23-24; 25-28R; CANR 60; CAP 2
**Daly, Maureen** [1921-] ....................... **CLC 17**
See also AAYA 5; CANR 37; JRDA; MAICYA; SAAS 1; SATA 2
**Damas, Leon-Gontran** [1912-1978] .. **CLC 84**
See also BW 1; CA 125; 73-76
**Dana, Richard Henry Sr.** [1787-1879] **N C L C 53**
**Daniel, Samuel** [1562(?)-1619] ............ **LC 24**
See also DLB 62
**Daniels, Brett**
See Adler, Renata
**Dannay, Frederic** [1905-1982]**CLC 11; DAM POP**

See also Queen, Ellery
See also CA 1-4R; 107; CANR 1, 39; DLB 137; MTCW
**D'Annunzio, Gabriele** [1863-1938] **TCLC 6, 40**
See also CA 104; 155
**Danois, N. le**
See Gourmont, Remy (-Marie-Charles) de
**Dante** [1265-1321] .. **CMLC 3, 18; DA; DAB; DAC; DAM MST, POET; PC 21; WLCS**
**d'Antibes, Germain**
See Simenon, Georges (Jacques Christian)
**Danticat, Edwidge** [1969-] ................. **CLC 94**
See also CA 152
**Danvers, Dennis** [1947-] .................... **CLC 70**
**Danziger, Paula** [1944-] ..................... **CLC 21**
See also AAYA 4; CA 112; 115; CANR 37; CLR 20; JRDA; MAICYA; SATA 36, 63; SATA-Brief 30
**Dario, Ruben** [1867-1916] .... **TCLC 4; DAM MULT; HLC; PC 15**
See also CA 131; HW; MTCW
**Darley, George** [1795-1846] ............. **NCLC 2**
See also DLB 96
**Darrow, Clarence (Seward)** [1857-1938] **TCLC 81**
See also CA 164
**Darwin, Charles** [1809-1882] ......... **NCLC 57**
See also DLB 57, 166
**Daryush, Elizabeth** [1887-1977] ...**CLC 6, 19**
See also CA 49-52; CANR 3; DLB 20
**Dasgupta, Surendranath** [1887-1952] **T C L C 81**
See also CA 157
**Dashwood, Edmee Elizabeth Monica de la Pasture** [1890-1943]
See Delafield, E. M.
See also CA 119; 154
**Daudet, (Louis Marie) Alphonse** [1840-1897] **NCLC 1**
See also DLB 123
**Daumal, Rene** [1908-1944] ............. **TCLC 14**
See also CA 114
**Davenport, Guy (Mattison, Jr.)** [1927-] **C L C 6, 14, 38; SSC 16**
See also CA 33-36R; CANR 23; DLB 130
**Davidson, Avram** [1923-]
See Queen, Ellery
See also CA 101; CANR 26; DLB 8
**Davidson, Donald (Grady)** [1893-1968] **C L C 2, 13, 19**
See also CA 5-8R; 25-28R; CANR 4; DLB 45
**Davidson, Hugh**
See Hamilton, Edmond
**Davidson, John** [1857-1909] ........... **TCLC 24**
See also CA 118; DLB 19
**Davidson, Sara** [1943-] ....................... **CLC 9**
See also CA 81-84; CANR 44, 68; DLB 185
**Davie, Donald (Alfred)** [1922-1995]**CLC 5, 8, 10, 31**
See also CA 1-4R; 149; CAAS 3; CANR 1, 44; DLB 27; MTCW
**Davies, Ray(mond Douglas)** [1944-]. **CLC 21**
See also CA 116; 146
**Davies, Rhys** [1901-1978] ................. **CLC 23**
See also CA 9-12R; 81-84; CANR 4; DLB 139, 191
**Davies, (William) Robertson** [1913-1995]**CLC 2, 7, 13, 25, 42, 75, 91; DA; DAB; DAC; DAM MST, NOV, POP; WLC**
See also BEST 89:2; CA 33-36R; 150; CANR 17, 42; DLB 68; INT CANR-17; MTCW
**Davies, W(illiam) H(enry)** [1871-1940]**T C L C 5**
See also CA 104; DLB 19, 174
**Davies, Walter C.**

See Bradley, Marion Zimmer
**Dexter, Martin**
　See Faust, Frederick (Schiller)
**Dexter, Pete** [1943-] **CLC 34, 55; DAM POP**
　See also BEST 89:2; CA 127; 131; INT 131;
　MTCW
**Diamano, Silmang**
　See Senghor, Leopold Sedar
**Diamond, Neil** [1941-] ...................... **CLC 30**
　See also CA 108
**Diaz del Castillo, Bernal** [1496-1584] . **LC 31**
**di Bassetto, Corno**
　See Shaw, George Bernard
**Dick, Philip K(indred)** [1928-1982] . **CLC 10, 30, 72; DAM NOV, POP**
　See also AAYA 24; CA 49-52; 106; CANR 2,
　16; DLB 8; MTCW
**Dickens, Charles (John Huffam)** [1812-1870]
　**NCLC 3, 8, 18, 26, 37, 50; DA; DAB; DAC; DAM MST, NOV; SSC 17; WLC**
　See also AAYA 23; CDBLB 1832-1890; DLB
　21, 55, 70, 159, 166; JRDA; MAICYA; SATA
　15
**Dickey, James (Lafayette)** [1923-1997] **CLC 1, 2, 4, 7, 10, 15, 47, 109; DAM NOV, POET, POP**
　See also AITN 1, 2; CA 9-12R; 156; CABS 2;
　CANR 10, 48, 61; CDALB 1968-1988; DLB
　5, 193; DLBD 7; DLBY 82, 93, 96, 97; INT
　CANR-10; MTCW
**Dickey, William** [1928-1994] ......... **CLC 3, 28**
　See also CA 9-12R; 145; CANR 24; DLB 5
**Dickinson, Charles** [1951-] ................ **CLC 49**
　See also CA 128
**Dickinson, Emily (Elizabeth)** [1830-1886]
　**NCLC 21; DA; DAB; DAC; DAM MST, POET; PC 1; WLC**
　See also AAYA 22; CDALB 1865-1917; DLB
　1; SATA 29
**Dickinson, Peter (Malcolm)** [1927-] **CLC 12, 35**
　See also AAYA 9; CA 41-44R; CANR 31, 58;
　CLR 29; DLB 87, 161; JRDA; MAICYA;
　SATA 5, 62, 95
**Dickson, Carr**
　See Carr, John Dickson
**Dickson, Carter**
　See Carr, John Dickson
**Diderot, Denis** [1713-1784] .................. **LC 26**
**Didion, Joan** [1934-] **CLC 1, 3, 8, 14, 32; DAM NOV**
　See also AITN 1; CA 5-8R; CANR 14, 52;
　CDALB 1968-1988; DLB 2, 173, 185;
　DLBY 81, 86; MTCW
**Dietrich, Robert**
　See Hunt, E(verette) Howard, (Jr.)
**Dillard, Annie** [1945-] **CLC 9, 60; DAM NOV**
　See also AAYA 6; CA 49-52; CANR 3, 43, 62;
　DLBY 80; MTCW; SATA 10
**Dillard, R(ichard) H(enry) W(ilde)** [1937-]
　**CLC 5**
　See also CA 21-24R; CAAS 7; CANR 10; DLB
　5
**Dillon, Eilis** [1920-1994] .................... **CLC 17**
　See also CA 9-12R; 147; CAAS 3; CANR 4,
　38; CLR 26; MAICYA; SATA 2, 74; SATA-
　Obit 83
**Dimont, Penelope**
　See Mortimer, Penelope (Ruth)
**Dinesen, Isak** .............. **CLC 10, 29, 95; SSC 7**
　See also Blixen, Karen (Christentze Dinesen)
**Ding Ling** ......................................... **CLC 68**
　See also Chiang, Pin-chin
**Disch, Thomas M(ichael)** [1940-] . **CLC 7, 36**
　See also AAYA 17; CA 21-24R; CAAS 4;
　CANR 17, 36, 54; CLR 18; DLB 8;
　MAICYA; MTCW; SAAS 15; SATA 92

**Disch, Tom**
　See Disch, Thomas M(ichael)
**d'Isly, Georges**
　See Simenon, Georges (Jacques Christian)
**Disraeli, Benjamin** [1804-1881] . **NCLC 2, 39**
　See also DLB 21, 55
**Ditcum, Steve**
　See Crumb, R(obert)
**Dixon, Paige**
　See Corcoran, Barbara
**Dixon, Stephen** [1936-] ....... **CLC 52; SSC 16**
　See also CA 89-92; CANR 17, 40, 54; DLB 130
**Doak, Annie**
　See Dillard, Annie
**Dobell, Sydney Thompson** [1824-1874] **NCLC 43**
　See also DLB 32
**Doblin, Alfred** ................................... **TCLC 13**
　See also Doeblin, Alfred
**Dobrolyubov, Nikolai Alexandrovich** [1836-1861] .......................................... **NCLC 5**
**Dobson, Austin** [1840-1921] .......... **TCLC 79**
　See also DLB 35; 144
**Dobyns, Stephen** [1941-] .................... **CLC 37**
　See also CA 45-48; CANR 2, 18
**Doctorow, E(dgar) L(aurence)** [1931-] **CLC 6, 11, 15, 18, 37, 44, 65, 113; DAM NOV, POP**
　See also AAYA 22; AITN 2; BEST 89:3; CA
　45-48; CANR 2, 33, 51; CDALB 1968-1988;
　DLB 2, 28, 173; DLBY 80; MTCW
**Dodgson, Charles Lutwidge** [1832-1898]
　See Carroll, Lewis
　See also CLR 2; DA; DAB; DAC; DAM MST,
　NOV, POET; MAICYA; YABC 2
**Dodson, Owen (Vincent)** [1914-1983] **CLC 79; BLC 1; DAM MULT**
　See also BW 1; CA 65-68; 110; CANR 24; DLB
　76
**Doeblin, Alfred** [1878-1957] .......... **TCLC 13**
　See also Doblin, Alfred
　See also CA 110; 141; DLB 66
**Doerr, Harriet** [1910-] ........................ **CLC 34**
　See also CA 117; 122; CANR 47; INT 122
**Domecq, H(onorio) Bustos**
　See Bioy Casares, Adolfo; Borges, Jorge Luis
**Domini, Rey**
　See Lorde, Audre (Geraldine)
**Dominique**
　See Proust, (Valentin-Louis-George-Eugene-)
　Marcel
**Don, A**
　See Stephen, SirLeslie
**Donaldson, Stephen R.** [1947-] **CLC 46; DAM POP**
　See also CA 89-92; CANR 13, 55; INT CANR-
　13
**Donleavy, J(ames) P(atrick)** [1926-] **CLC 1, 4, 6, 10, 45**
　See also AITN 2; CA 9-12R; CANR 24, 49, 62;
　DLB 6, 173; INT CANR-24; MTCW
**Donne, John** [1572-1631] **LC 10, 24; DA; DAB; DAC; DAM MST, POET; PC 1**
　See also CDBLB Before 1660; DLB 121, 151
**Donnell, David** [1939(?)-] .................. **CLC 34**
**Donoghue, P. S.**
　See Hunt, E(verette) Howard, (Jr.)
**Donoso (Yanez), Jose** [1924-1996] . **CLC 4, 8, 11, 32, 99; DAM MULT; HLC**
　See also CA 81-84; 155; CANR 32; DLB 113;
　HW; MTCW
**Donovan, John** [1928-1992] ............. **CLC 35**
　See also AAYA 20; CA 97-100; 137; CLR 3;
　MAICYA; SATA 72; SATA-Brief 29
**Don Roberto**
　See Cunninghame Graham, R(obert) B(ontine)
**Doolittle, Hilda** [1886-1961] **CLC 3, 8, 14, 31, 34, 73; DA; DAC; DAM MST, POET; PC**

**5; WLC**
　See also H. D.
　See also CA 97-100; CANR 35; DLB 4, 45;
　MTCW
**Dorfman, Ariel** [1942-] ... **CLC 48, 77; DAM MULT; HLC**
　See also CA 124; 130; CANR 67; HW; INT 130
**Dorn, Edward (Merton)** [1929-] **CLC 10, 18**
　See also CA 93-96; CANR 42; DLB 5; INT 93-
　96
**Dorris, Michael (Anthony)** [1945-1997] **C L C 109; DAM MULT, NOV**
　See also AAYA 20; BEST 90:1; CA 102; 157;
　CANR 19, 46; DLB 175; NNAL; SATA 75;
　SATA-Obit 94
**Dorris, Michael A.**
　See Dorris, Michael (Anthony)
**Dorsan, Luc**
　See Simenon, Georges (Jacques Christian)
**Dorsange, Jean**
　See Simenon, Georges (Jacques Christian)
**Dos Passos, John (Roderigo)** [1896-1970]
　**CLC 1, 4, 8, 11, 15, 25, 34, 82; DA; DAB; DAC; DAM MST, NOV; WLC**
　See also CA 1-4R; 29-32R; CANR 3; CDALB
　1929-1941; DLB 4, 9; DLBD 1, 15; DLBY
　96; MTCW
**Dossage, Jean**
　See Simenon, Georges (Jacques Christian)
**Dostoevsky, Fedor Mikhailovich** [1821-1881]
　**NCLC 2, 7, 21, 33, 43; DA; DAB; DAC; DAM MST, NOV; SSC 2; WLC**
**Doughty, Charles M(ontagu)** [1843-1926]
　**TCLC 27**
　See also CA 115; DLB 19, 57, 174
**Douglas, Ellen** ..................................... **CLC 73**
　See also Haxton, Josephine Ayres; Williamson,
　Ellen Douglas
**Douglas, Gavin** [1475(?)-1522] ........... **LC 20**
　See also DLB 132
**Douglas, George**
　See Brown, George Douglas
**Douglas, Keith (Castellain)** [1920-1944]
　**TCLC 40**
　See also CA 160; DLB 27
**Douglas, Leonard**
　See Bradbury, Ray (Douglas)
**Douglas, Michael**
　See Crichton, (John) Michael
**Douglas, (George) Norman** [1868-1952]
　**TCLC 68**
　See also CA 119; 157; DLB 34, 195
**Douglas, William**
　See Brown, George Douglas
**Douglass, Frederick** [1817(?)-1895] **NCLC 7, 55; BLC 1; DA; DAC; DAM MST, MULT; WLC**
　See also CDALB 1640-1865; DLB 1, 43, 50,
　79; SATA 29
**Dourado, (Waldomiro Freitas) Autran** [1926-]
　**CLC 23, 60**
　See also CA 25-28R; CANR 34
**Dourado, Waldomiro Autran**
　See Dourado, (Waldomiro Freitas) Autran
**Dove, Rita (Frances)** [1952-] ..... **CLC 50, 81; BLCS; DAM MULT, POET; PC 6**
　See also BW 2; CA 109; CAAS 19; CANR 27,
　42, 68; DLB 120
**Doveglion**
　See Villa, Jose Garcia
**Dowell, Coleman** [1925-1985] ........... **CLC 60**
　See also CA 25-28R; 117; CANR 10; DLB 130
**Dowson, Ernest (Christopher)** [1867-1900]
　**TCLC 4**
　See also CA 105; 150; DLB 19, 135
**Doyle, A. Conan**
　See Doyle, Arthur Conan

**Doyle, Arthur Conan** [1859-1930] .. **TCLC 7; DA; DAB; DAC; DAM MST, NOV; SSC 12; WLC**
See also AAYA 14; CA 104; 122; CDBLB 1890-1914; DLB 18, 70, 156, 178; MTCW; SATA 24

**Doyle, Conan**
See Doyle, Arthur Conan

**Doyle, John**
See Graves, Robert (von Ranke)

**Doyle, Roddy** [1958(?)-] .................... **CLC 81**
See also AAYA 14; CA 143; DLB 194

**Doyle, Sir A. Conan**
See Doyle, Arthur Conan

**Doyle, Sir Arthur Conan**
See Doyle, Arthur Conan

**Dr. A**
See Asimov, Isaac; Silverstein, Alvin

**Drabble, Margaret** [1939-]CLC 2, 3, 5, 8, 10, 22, 53; **DAB; DAC; DAM MST, NOV, POP**
See also CA 13-16R; CANR 18, 35, 63; CDBLB 1960 to Present; DLB 14, 155; MTCW; SATA 48

**Drapier, M. B.**
See Swift, Jonathan

**Drayham, James**
See Mencken, H(enry) L(ouis)

**Drayton, Michael** [1563-1631] ... **LC 8; DAM POET**
See also DLB 121

**Dreadstone, Carl**
See Campbell, (John) Ramsey

**Dreiser, Theodore (Herman Albert)** [1871-1945] .. **TCLC 10, 18, 35, 83; DA; DAC; DAM MST, NOV; SSC 30; WLC**
See also CA 106; 132; CDALB 1865-1917; DLB 9, 12, 102, 137; DLBD 1; MTCW

**Drexler, Rosalyn** [1926-] ................. **CLC 2, 6**
See also CA 81-84; CANR 68

**Dreyer, Carl Theodor** [1889-1968] ... **CLC 16**
See also CA 116

**Drieu la Rochelle, Pierre(-Eugene)** [1893-1945] **TCLC 21**
See also CA 117; DLB 72

**Drinkwater, John** [1882-1937] ....... **TCLC 57**
See also CA 109; 149; DLB 10, 19, 149

**Drop Shot**
See Cable, George Washington

**Droste-Hulshoff, Annette Freiin von** [1797-1848] ....................................... **NCLC 3**
See also DLB 133

**Drummond, Walter**
See Silverberg, Robert

**Drummond, William Henry** [1854-1907] **TCLC 25**
See also CA 160; DLB 92

**Drummond de Andrade, Carlos** [1902-1987] **CLC 18**
See also Andrade, Carlos Drummond de
See also CA 132; 123

**Drury, Allen (Stuart)** [1918-] ............ **CLC 37**
See also CA 57-60; CANR 18, 52; INT CANR-18

**Dryden, John** [1631-1700]LC 3, 21; **DA; DAB; DAC; DAM DRAM, MST, POET; DC 3; WLC**
See also CDBLB 1660-1789; DLB 80, 101, 131

**Duberman, Martin (Bauml)** [1930-] ... **CLC 8**
See also CA 1-4R; CANR 2, 63

**Dubie, Norman (Evans)** [1945-] ........ **CLC 36**
See also CA 69-72; CANR 12; DLB 120

**Du Bois, W(illiam) E(dward) B(urghardt)** [1868-1963] ............................................ **CLC 1, 2, 13, 64, 96; BLC 1; DA; DAC; DAM MST, MULT, NOV; WLC**
See also BW 1; CA 85-88; CANR 34; CDALB

1865-1917; DLB 47, 50, 91; MTCW; SATA 42

**Dubus, Andre** [1936-]CLC 13, 36, 97; **SSC 15**
See also CA 21-24R; CANR 17; DLB 130; INT CANR-17

**Duca Minimo**
See D'Annunzio, Gabriele

**Ducharme, Rejean** [1941-] ................. **CLC 74**
See also CA 165; DLB 60

**Duclos, Charles Pinot** [1704-1772] ........ **LC 1**

**Dudek, Louis** [1918-] .................... **CLC 11, 19**
See also CA 45-48; CAAS 14; CANR 1; DLB 88

**Duerrenmatt, Friedrich** [1921-1990]CLC 1, 4, 8, 11, 15, 43, 102; **DAM DRAM**
See also CA 17-20R; CANR 33; DLB 69, 124; MTCW

**Duffy, Bruce** [(?)-] .............................. **CLC 50**

**Duffy, Maureen** [1933-] .................... **CLC 37**
See also CA 25-28R; CANR 33, 68; DLB 14; MTCW

**Dugan, Alan** [1923-] ........................ **CLC 2, 6**
See also CA 81-84; DLB 5

**du Gard, Roger Martin**
See Martin du Gard, Roger

**Duhamel, Georges** [1884-1966] ........... **CLC 8**
See also CA 81-84; 25-28R; CANR 35; DLB 65; MTCW

**Dujardin, Edouard (Emile Louis)** [1861-1949] **TCLC 13**
See also CA 109; DLB 123

**Dulles, John Foster** [1888-1959] .... **TCLC 72**
See also CA 115; 149

**Dumas, Alexandre (Davy de la Pailleterie)** [1802-1870] **NCLC 11; DA; DAB; DAC; DAM MST, NOV; WLC**
See also DLB 119, 192; SATA 18

**Dumas (fils), Alexandre** [1824-1895] . **N C L C 71; DC 1**
See also AAYA 22; DLB 192

**Dumas, Claudine**
See Malzberg, Barry N(athaniel)

**Dumas, Henry L.** [1934-1968] ....... **CLC 6, 62**
See also BW 1; CA 85-88; DLB 41

**du Maurier, Daphne** [1907-1989] **CLC 6, 11, 59; DAB; DAC; DAM MST, POP; SSC 18**
See also CA 5-8R; 128; CANR 6, 55; DLB 191; MTCW; SATA 27; SATA-Obit 60

**Dunbar, Paul Laurence** [1872-1906]TCLC 2, 12; **BLC 1; DA; DAC; DAM MST, MULT, POET; PC 5; SSC 8; WLC**
See also BW 1; CA 104; 124; CDALB 1865-1917; DLB 50, 54, 78; SATA 34

**Dunbar, William** [1460(?)-1530(?)] ...... **LC 20**
See also DLB 132, 146

**Duncan, Dora Angela**
See Duncan, Isadora

**Duncan, Isadora** [1877(?)-1927] .... **TCLC 68**
See also CA 118; 149

**Duncan, Lois** [1934-] ........................ **CLC 26**
See also AAYA 4; CA 1-4R; CANR 2, 23, 36; CLR 29; JRDA; MAICYA; SAAS 2; SATA 1, 36, 75

**Duncan, Robert (Edward)** [1919-1988]CLC 1, 2, 4, 7, 15, 41, 55; **DAM POET; PC 2**
See also CA 9-12R; 124; CANR 28, 62; DLB 5, 16, 193; MTCW

**Duncan, Sara Jeannette** [1861-1922]TCLC 60
See also CA 157; DLB 92

**Dunlap, William** [1766-1839] ........... **NCLC 2**
See also DLB 30, 37, 59

**Dunn, Douglas (Eaglesham)** [1942-]CLC 6, 40
See also CA 45-48; CANR 2, 33; DLB 40; MTCW

**Dunn, Katherine (Karen)** [1945-] ..... **CLC 71**
See also CA 33-36R

**Dunn, Stephen** [1939-] ...................... **CLC 36**

See also CA 33-36R; CANR 12, 48, 53; DLB 105

**Dunne, Finley Peter** [1867-1936] ... **TCLC 28**
See also CA 108; DLB 11, 23

**Dunne, John Gregory** [1932-] .......... **CLC 28**
See also CA 25-28R; CANR 14, 50; DLBY 80

**Dunsany, Edward John Moreton Drax Plunkett** [1878-1957]
See Dunsany, Lord
See also CA 104; 148; DLB 10

**Dunsany, Lord** ...................... **TCLC 2, 59**
See also Dunsany, Edward John Moreton Drax Plunkett
See also DLB 77, 153, 156

**du Perry, Jean**
See Simenon, Georges (Jacques Christian)

**Durang, Christopher (Ferdinand)** [1949-] **CLC 27, 38**
See also CA 105; CANR 50

**Duras, Marguerite** [1914-1996]CLC 3, 6, 11, 20, 34, 40, 68, 100
See also CA 25-28R; 151; CANR 50; DLB 83; MTCW

**Durban, (Rosa) Pam** [1947-] ............. **CLC 39**
See also CA 123

**Durcan, Paul** [1944-]CLC 43, 70; **DAM POET**
See also CA 134

**Durkheim, Emile** [1858-1917] ........ **TCLC 55**

**Durrell, Lawrence (George)** [1912-1990]CLC 1, 4, 6, 8, 13, 27, 41; **DAM NOV**
See also CA 9-12R; CANR 40; CDBLB 1945-1960; DLB 15, 27; DLBY 90; MTCW

**Durrenmatt, Friedrich**
See Duerrenmatt, Friedrich

**Dutt, Toru** [1856-1877] ................... **NCLC 29**

**Dwight, Timothy** [1752-1817] ........ **NCLC 13**
See also DLB 37

**Dworkin, Andrea** [1946-] .................. **CLC 43**
See also CA 77-80; CAAS 21; CANR 16, 39; INT CANR-16; MTCW

**Dwyer, Deanna**
See Koontz, Dean R(ay)

**Dwyer, K. R.**
See Koontz, Dean R(ay)

**Dye, Richard**
See De Voto, Bernard (Augustine)

**Dylan, Bob** [1941-] ........... **CLC 3, 4, 6, 12, 77**
See also CA 41-44R; DLB 16

**Eagleton, Terence (Francis)** [1943-]
See Eagleton, Terry
See also CA 57-60; CANR 7, 23, 68; MTCW

**Eagleton, Terry** .................................... **CLC 63**
See also Eagleton, Terence (Francis)

**Early, Jack**
See Scoppettone, Sandra

**East, Michael**
See West, Morris L(anglo)

**Eastaway, Edward**
See Thomas, (Philip) Edward

**Eastlake, William (Derry)** [1917-1997]CLC 8
See also CA 5-8R; 158; CAAS 1; CANR 5, 63; DLB 6; INT CANR-5

**Eastman, Charles A(lexander)** [1858-1939] **TCLC 55; DAM MULT**
See also DLB 175; NNAL; YABC 1

**Eberhart, Richard (Ghormley)** [1904-]CLC 3, 11, 19, 56; **DAM POET**
See also CA 1-4R; CANR 2; CDALB 1941-1968; DLB 48; MTCW

**Eberstadt, Fernanda** [1960-] ............. **CLC 39**
See also CA 136; CANR 69

**Echegaray (y Eizaguirre), Jose (Maria Waldo)** [1832-1916] ................................ **TCLC 4**
See also CA 104; CANR 32; HW; MTCW

**Echeverria, (Jose) Esteban (Antonino)** [1805-1851] .......................................................
**NCLC 18**

Ferguson, Samuel [1810-1886] ...... **NCLC 33**
See also DLB 32
Fergusson, Robert [1750-1774] ........... **LC 29**
See also DLB 109
Ferling, Lawrence
See Ferlinghetti, Lawrence (Monsanto)
Ferlinghetti, Lawrence (Monsanto) [1919(?)-]
**CLC 2, 6, 10, 27, 111; DAM POET; PC 1**
See also CA 5-8R; CANR 3, 41; CDALB 1941-
1968; DLB 5, 16; MTCW
Fernandez, Vicente Garcia Huidobro
See Huidobro Fernandez, Vicente Garcia
Ferrer, Gabriel (Francisco Victor) Miro
See Miro (Ferrer), Gabriel (Francisco Victor)
Ferrier, Susan (Edmonstone) [1782-1854]
**NCLC 8**
See also DLB 116
Ferrigno, Robert [1948(?)-] .............. **CLC 65**
See also CA 140
Ferron, Jacques [1921-1985] .. **CLC 94; DAC**
See also CA 117; 129; DLB 60
Feuchtwanger, Lion [1884-1958] ..... **TCLC 3**
See also CA 104; DLB 66
Feuillet, Octave [1821-1890] .......... **NCLC 45**
See also DLB 192
Feydeau, Georges (Leon Jules Marie) [1862-
1921] .......................................................
**TCLC 22; DAM DRAM**
See also CA 113; 152; DLB 192
Fichte, Johann Gottlieb [1762-1814]**NCLC 62**
See also DLB 90
Ficino, Marsilio [1433-1499] ............... **LC 12**
Fiedeler, Hans
See Doeblin, Alfred
Fiedler, Leslie A(aron) [1917-] **CLC 4, 13, 24**
See also CA 9-12R; CANR 7, 63; DLB 28, 67;
MTCW
Field, Andrew [1938-] ........................ **CLC 44**
See also CA 97-100; CANR 25
Field, Eugene [1850-1895] ................ **NCLC 3**
See also DLB 23, 42, 140; DLBD 13; MAICYA;
SATA 16
Field, Gans T.
See Wellman, Manly Wade
Field, Michael [1915-1971] ............. **TCLC 43**
See also CA 29-32R
Field, Peter
See Hobson, Laura Z(ametkin)
Fielding, Henry [1707-1754]**LC 1; DA; DAB;
DAC; DAM DRAM, MST, NOV; WLC**
See also CDBLB 1660-1789; DLB 39, 84, 101
Fielding, Sarah [1710-1768] ........... **LC 1, 44**
See also DLB 39
Fields, W. C. [1880-1946] ................ **TCLC 80**
See also DLB 44
Fierstein, Harvey (Forbes) [1954-] . **CLC 33;
DAM DRAM, POP**
See also CA 123; 129
Figes, Eva [1932-] ............................. **CLC 31**
See also CA 53-56; CANR 4, 44; DLB 14
Finch, Anne [1661-1720] ........... **LC 3; PC 21**
See also DLB 95
Finch, Robert (Duer Claydon) [1900-]**CLC 18**
See also CA 57-60; CANR 9, 24, 49; DLB 88
Findley, Timothy [1930-]**CLC 27, 102; DAC;
DAM MST**
See also CA 25-28R; CANR 12, 42, 69; DLB
53
Fink, William
See Mencken, H(enry) L(ouis)
Firbank, Louis [1942-]
See Reed, Lou
See also CA 117
Firbank, (Arthur Annesley) Ronald [1886-
1926] ......................................... **TCLC 1**
See also CA 104; DLB 36
Fisher, M(ary) F(rances) K(ennedy) [1908-

1992] ..................................... **CLC 76, 87**
See also CA 77-80; 138; CANR 44
Fisher, Roy [1930-] ........................... **CLC 25**
See also CA 81-84; CAAS 10; CANR 16; DLB
40
Fisher, Rudolph [1897-1934]**TCLC 11; BLC 2;
DAM MULT; SSC 25**
See also BW 1; CA 107; 124; DLB 51, 102
Fisher, Vardis (Alvero) [1895-1968] ... **CLC 7**
See also CA 5-8R; 25-28R; CANR 68; DLB 9
Fiske, Tarleton
See Bloch, Robert (Albert)
Fitch, Clarke
See Sinclair, Upton (Beall)
Fitch, John IV
See Cormier, Robert (Edmund)
Fitzgerald, Captain Hugh
See Baum, L(yman) Frank
FitzGerald, Edward [1809-1883] .... **NCLC 9**
See also DLB 32
Fitzgerald, F(rancis) Scott (Key) [1896-1940]
**TCLC 1, 6, 14, 28, 55; DA; DAB; DAC;
DAM MST, NOV; SSC 6, 31; WLC**
See also AAYA 24; AITN 1; CA 110; 123;
CDALB 1917-1929; DLB 4, 9, 86; DLBD 1,
15, 16; DLBY 81, 96; MTCW
Fitzgerald, Penelope [1916-] **CLC 19, 51, 61**
See also CA 85-88; CAAS 10; CANR 56; DLB
14, 194
Fitzgerald, Robert (Stuart) [1910-1985]**C L C
39**
See also CA 1-4R; 114; CANR 1; DLBY 80
FitzGerald, Robert D(avid) [1902-1987]**C L C
19**
See also CA 17-20R
Fitzgerald, Zelda (Sayre) [1900-1948] **T C L C
52**
See also CA 117; 126; DLBY 84
Flanagan, Thomas (James Bonner) [1923-]
**CLC 25, 52**
See also CA 108; CANR 55; DLBY 80; INT
108; MTCW
Flaubert, Gustave [1821-1880] .**NCLC 2, 10,
19, 62, 66; DA; DAB; DAC; DAM MST,
NOV; SSC 11; WLC**
See also DLB 119
Flecker, Herman Elroy
See Flecker, (Herman) James Elroy
Flecker, (Herman) James Elroy [1884-1915]
**TCLC 43**
See also CA 109; 150; DLB 10, 19
Fleming, Ian (Lancaster) [1908-1964]**CLC 3,
30; DAM POP**
See also CA 5-8R; CANR 59; CDBLB 1945-
1960; DLB 87; MTCW; SATA 9
Fleming, Thomas (James) [1927-] .... **CLC 37**
See also CA 5-8R; CANR 10; INT CANR-10;
SATA 8
Fletcher, John [1579-1625] ....... **LC 33; DC 6**
See also CDBLB Before 1660; DLB 58
Fletcher, John Gould [1886-1950] . **TCLC 35**
See also CA 107; DLB 4, 45
Fleur, Paul
See Pohl, Frederik
Flooglebuckle, Al
See Spiegelman, Art
Flying Officer X
See Bates, H(erbert) E(rnest)
Fo, Dario [1926-]**CLC 32, 109; DAM DRAM**
See also CA 116; 128; CANR 68; DLBY 97;
MTCW
Fogarty, Jonathan Titulescu Esq.
See Farrell, James T(homas)
Folke, Will
See Bloch, Robert (Albert)
Follett, Ken(neth Martin) [1949-] .. **CLC 18;
DAM NOV, POP**

See also AAYA 6; BEST 89:4; CA 81-84; CANR
13, 33, 54; DLB 87; DLBY 81; INT CANR-
33; MTCW
Fontane, Theodor [1819-1898] ...... **NCLC 26**
See also DLB 129
Foote, Horton [1916-] ...... **CLC 51, 91; DAM
DRAM**
See also CA 73-76; CANR 34, 51; DLB 26; INT
CANR-34
Foote, Shelby [1916-] .. **CLC 75; DAM NOV,
POP**
See also CA 5-8R; CANR 3, 45; DLB 2, 17
Forbes, Esther [1891-1967] ............... **CLC 12**
See also AAYA 17; CA 13-14; 25-28R; CAP 1;
CLR 27; DLB 22; JRDA; MAICYA; SATA 2
Forche, Carolyn (Louise) [1950-]**CLC 25, 83,
86; DAM POET; PC 10**
See also CA 109; 117; CANR 50; DLB 5, 193;
INT 117
Ford, Elbur
See Hibbert, Eleanor Alice Burford
Ford, Ford Madox [1873-1939] **TCLC 1, 15,
39, 57; DAM NOV**
See also CA 104; 132; CDBLB 1914-1945;
DLB 162; MTCW
Ford, Henry [1863-1947] ................ **TCLC 73**
See also CA 115; 148
Ford, John [1586-(?)] ............................ **DC 8**
See also CDBLB Before 1660; DAM DRAM;
DLB 58
Ford, John [1895-1973] .................... **CLC 16**
See also CA 45-48
Ford, Richard [1944-] ................. **CLC 46, 99**
See also CA 69-72; CANR 11, 47
Ford, Webster
See Masters, Edgar Lee
Foreman, Richard [1937-] ................. **CLC 50**
See also CA 65-68; CANR 32, 63
Forester, C(ecil) S(cott) [1899-1966] **CLC 35**
See also CA 73-76; 25-28R; DLB 191; SATA
13
Forez
See Mauriac, Francois (Charles)
Forman, James Douglas [1932-] ....... **CLC 21**
See also AAYA 17; CA 9-12R; CANR 4, 19,
42; JRDA; MAICYA; SATA 8, 70
Fornes, Maria Irene [1930-] ....... **CLC 39, 61**
See also CA 25-28R; CANR 28; DLB 7; HW;
INT CANR-28; MTCW
Forrest, Leon (Richard) [1937-1997] **CLC 4;
BLCS**
See also BW 2; CA 89-92; 162; CAAS 7; CANR
25, 52; DLB 33
Forster, E(dward) M(organ) [1879-1970]**CLC
1, 2, 3, 4, 9, 10, 13, 15, 22, 45, 77; DA; DAB;
DAC; DAM MST, NOV; SSC 27; WLC**
See also AAYA 2; CA 13-14; 25-28R; CANR
45; CAP 1; CDBLB 1914-1945; DLB 34, 98,
162, 178, 195; DLBD 10; MTCW; SATA 57
Forster, John [1812-1876] .............. **NCLC 11**
See also DLB 144, 184
Forsyth, Frederick [1938-]**CLC 2, 5, 36; DAM
NOV, POP**
See also BEST 89:4; CA 85-88; CANR 38, 62;
DLB 87; MTCW
Forten, Charlotte L. .......... **TCLC 16; BLC 2**
See also Grimke, Charlotte L(ottie) Forten
See also DLB 50
Foscolo, Ugo [1778-1827] ................ **NCLC 8**
Fosse, Bob .............................................. **CLC 20**
See also Fosse, Robert Louis
Fosse, Robert Louis [1927-1987]
See Fosse, Bob
See also CA 110; 123
Foster, Stephen Collins [1826-1864]**NCLC 26**
Foucault, Michel [1926-1984]**CLC 31, 34, 69**
See also CA 105; 113; CANR 34; MTCW

**Fouque, Friedrich (Heinrich Karl) de la Motte** [1777-1843] .................. **NCLC 2**
See also DLB 90

**Fourier, Charles** [1772-1837] ......... **NCLC 51**

**Fournier, Henri Alban** [1886-1914]
See Alain-Fournier
See also CA 104

**Fournier, Pierre** [1916-] .................... **CLC 11**
See also Gascar, Pierre
See also CA 89-92; CANR 16, 40

**Fowles, John** [1926-] **CLC 1, 2, 3, 4, 6, 9, 10, 15, 33, 87; DAB; DAC; DAM MST**
See also CA 5-8R; CANR 25; CDBLB 1960 to Present; DLB 14, 139; MTCW; SATA 22

**Fox, Paula** [1923-] ............................ **CLC 2, 8**
See also AAYA 3; CA 73-76; CANR 20, 36, 62; CLR 1, 44; DLB 52; JRDA; MAICYA; MTCW; SATA 17, 60

**Fox, William Price (Jr.)** [1926-] ........ **CLC 22**
See also CA 17-20R; CAAS 19; CANR 11; DLB 2; DLBY 81

**Foxe, John** [1516(?)-1587] ................... **LC 14**
See also DLB 132

**Frame, Janet** [1924-] **CLC 2, 3, 6, 22, 66, 96; SSC 29**
See also Clutha, Janet Paterson Frame

**France, Anatole** .................................. **TCLC 9**
See also Thibault, Jacques Anatole Francois
See also DLB 123

**Francis, Claude** [19(?)-] ...................... **CLC 50**

**Francis, Dick** [1920-] **CLC 2, 22, 42, 102; DAM POP**
See also AAYA 5, 21; BEST 89:3; CA 5-8R; CANR 9, 42, 68; CDBLB 1960 to Present; DLB 87; INT CANR-9; MTCW

**Francis, Robert (Churchill)** [1901-1987] **CLC 15**
See also CA 1-4R; 123; CANR 1

**Frank, Anne(lies Marie)** [1929-1945] **TCLC 17; DA; DAB; DAC; DAM MST; WLC**
See also AAYA 12; CA 113; 133; CANR 68; MTCW; SATA 87; SATA-Brief 42

**Frank, Bruno** [1887-1945] .............. **TCLC 81**
See also DLB 118

**Frank, Elizabeth** [1945-] .................... **CLC 39**
See also CA 121; 126; INT 126

**Frankl, Viktor E(mil)** [1905-1997] ... **CLC 93**
See also CA 65-68; 161

**Franklin, Benjamin**
See Hasek, Jaroslav (Matej Frantisek)

**Franklin, Benjamin** [1706-1790] **LC 25; DA; DAB; DAC; DAM MST; WLCS**
See also CDALB 1640-1865; DLB 24, 43, 73

**Franklin, (Stella Maria Sarah) Miles (Lampe)** [1879-1954] .......................... **TCLC 7**
See also CA 104; 164

**Fraser, (Lady) Antonia (Pakenham)** [1932-] **CLC 32, 107**
See also CA 85-88; CANR 44, 65; MTCW; SATA-Brief 32

**Fraser, George MacDonald** [1925-] ... **CLC 7**
See also CA 45-48; CANR 2, 48

**Fraser, Sylvia** [1935-] ........................ **CLC 64**
See also CA 45-48; CANR 1, 16, 60

**Frayn, Michael** [1933-] **CLC 3, 7, 31, 47; DAM DRAM, NOV**
See also CA 5-8R; CANR 30, 69; DLB 13, 14, 194; MTCW

**Fraze, Candida (Merrill)** [1945-] ..... **CLC 50**
See also CA 126

**Frazer, J(ames) G(eorge)** [1854-1941] **TCLC 32**
See also CA 118

**Frazer, Robert Caine**
See Creasey, John

**Frazer, Sir James George**
See Frazer, J(ames) G(eorge)

**Frazier, Charles** [1950-] .................. **CLC 109**
See also CA 161

**Frazier, Ian** [1951-] ............................ **CLC 46**
See also CA 130; CANR 54

**Frederic, Harold** [1856-1898] ........ **NCLC 10**
See also DLB 12, 23; DLBD 13

**Frederick, John**
See Faust, Frederick (Schiller)

**Frederick the Great** [1712-1786] ......... **LC 14**

**Fredro, Aleksander** [1793-1876] ...... **NCLC 8**

**Freeling, Nicolas** [1927-] .................. **CLC 38**
See also CA 49-52; CAAS 12; CANR 1, 17, 50; DLB 87

**Freeman, Douglas Southall** [1886-1953] **TCLC 11**
See also CA 109; DLB 17

**Freeman, Judith** [1946-] .................... **CLC 55**
See also CA 148

**Freeman, Mary Eleanor Wilkins** [1852-1930] **TCLC 9; SSC 1**
See also CA 106; DLB 12, 78

**Freeman, R(ichard) Austin** [1862-1943] **TCLC 21**
See also CA 113; DLB 70

**French, Albert** [1943-] ...................... **CLC 86**

**French, Marilyn** [1929-] **CLC 10, 18, 60; DAM DRAM, NOV, POP**
See also CA 69-72; CANR 3, 31; INT CANR-31; MTCW

**French, Paul**
See Asimov, Isaac

**Freneau, Philip Morin** [1752-1832] **NCLC 1**
See also DLB 37, 43

**Freud, Sigmund** [1856-1939] .......... **TCLC 52**
See also CA 115; 133; CANR 69; MTCW

**Friedan, Betty (Naomi)** [1921-] ........ **CLC 74**
See also CA 65-68; CANR 18, 45; MTCW

**Friedlander, Saul** [1932-] .................. **CLC 90**
See also CA 117; 130

**Friedman, B(ernard) H(arper)** [1926-] **CLC 7**
See also CA 1-4R; CANR 3, 48

**Friedman, Bruce Jay** [1930-] ... **CLC 3, 5, 56**
See also CA 9-12R; CANR 25, 52; DLB 2, 28; INT CANR-25

**Friel, Brian** [1929-] ....... **CLC 5, 42, 59; DC 8**
See also CA 21-24R; CANR 33, 69; DLB 13; MTCW

**Friis-Baastad, Babbis Ellinor** [1921-1970] **CLC 12**
See also CA 17-20R; 134; SATA 7

**Frisch, Max (Rudolf)** [1911-1991] **CLC 3, 9, 14, 18, 32, 44; DAM DRAM, NOV**
See also CA 85-88; 134; CANR 32; DLB 69, 124; MTCW

**Fromentin, Eugene (Samuel Auguste)** [1820-1876] ........................................ **NCLC 10**
See also DLB 123

**Frost, Frederick**
See Faust, Frederick (Schiller)

**Frost, Robert (Lee)** [1874-1963] **CLC 1, 3, 4, 9, 10, 13, 15, 26, 34, 44; DA; DAB; DAC; DAM MST, POET; PC 1; WLC**
See also AAYA 21; CA 89-92; CANR 33; CDALB 1917-1929; DLB 54; DLBD 7; MTCW; SATA 14

**Froude, James Anthony** [1818-1894] **NCLC 43**
See also DLB 18, 57, 144

**Froy, Herald**
See Waterhouse, Keith (Spencer)

**Fry, Christopher** [1907-] **CLC 2, 10, 14; DAM DRAM**
See also CA 17-20R; CAAS 23; CANR 9, 30; DLB 13; MTCW; SATA 66

**Frye, (Herman) Northrop** [1912-1991] **CLC 24, 70**
See also CA 5-8R; 133; CANR 8, 37; DLB 67, 68; MTCW

**Fuchs, Daniel** [1909-1993] ............ **CLC 8, 22**
See also CA 81-84; 142; CAAS 5; CANR 40; DLB 9, 26, 28; DLBY 93

**Fuchs, Daniel** [1934-] ........................ **CLC 34**
See also CA 37-40R; CANR 14, 48

**Fuentes, Carlos** [1928-] **CLC 3, 8, 10, 13, 22, 41, 60, 113; DA; DAB; DAC; DAM MST, MULT, NOV; HLC; SSC 24; WLC**
See also AAYA 4; AITN 2; CA 69-72; CANR 10, 32, 68; DLB 113; HW; MTCW

**Fuentes, Gregorio Lopez y**
See Lopez y Fuentes, Gregorio

**Fugard, (Harold) Athol** [1932-] **CLC 5, 9, 14, 25, 40, 80; DAM DRAM; DC 3**
See also AAYA 17; CA 85-88; CANR 32, 54; MTCW

**Fugard, Sheila** [1932-] ...................... **CLC 48**
See also CA 125

**Fuller, Charles (H., Jr.)** [1939-] **CLC 25; BLC 2; DAM DRAM, MULT; DC 1**
See also BW 2; CA 108; 112; DLB 38; INT 112; MTCW

**Fuller, John (Leopold)** [1937-] .......... **CLC 62**
See also CA 21-24R; CANR 9, 44; DLB 40

**Fuller, Margaret** ............................ **NCLC 5, 50**
See also Ossoli, Sarah Margaret (Fuller marchesa d')

**Fuller, Roy (Broadbent)** [1912-1991] **CLC 4, 28**
See also CA 5-8R; 135; CAAS 10; CANR 53; DLB 15, 20; SATA 87

**Fulton, Alice** [1952-] .......................... **CLC 52**
See also CA 116; CANR 57; DLB 193

**Furphy, Joseph** [1843-1912] .......... **TCLC 25**
See also CA 163

**Fussell, Paul** [1924-] .......................... **CLC 74**
See also BEST 90:1; CA 17-20R; CANR 8, 21, 35, 69; INT CANR-21; MTCW

**Futabatei, Shimei** [1864-1909] ....... **TCLC 44**
See also CA 162; DLB 180

**Futrelle, Jacques** [1875-1912] ........ **TCLC 19**
See also CA 113; 155

**Gaboriau, Emile** [1835-1873] ......... **NCLC 14**

**Gadda, Carlo Emilio** [1893-1973] .... **CLC 11**
See also CA 89-92; DLB 177

**Gaddis, William** [1922-] **CLC 1, 3, 6, 8, 10, 19, 43, 86**
See also CA 17-20R; CANR 21, 48; DLB 2; MTCW

**Gage, Walter**
See Inge, William (Motter)

**Gaines, Ernest J(ames)** [1933-] **CLC 3, 11, 18, 86; BLC 2; DAM MULT**
See also AAYA 18; AITN 1; BW 2; CA 9-12R; CANR 6, 24, 42; CDALB 1968-1988; DLB 2, 33, 152; DLBY 80; MTCW; SATA 86

**Gaitskill, Mary** [1954-] ...................... **CLC 69**
See also CA 128; CANR 61

**Galdos, Benito Perez**
See Perez Galdos, Benito

**Gale, Zona** [1874-1938] **TCLC 7; DAM DRAM**
See also CA 105; 153; DLB 9, 78

**Galeano, Eduardo (Hughes)** [1940-] **CLC 72**
See also CA 29-32R; CANR 13, 32; HW

**Galiano, Juan Valera y Alcala**
See Valera y Alcala-Galiano, Juan

**Galilei, Galileo** [1546-1642] ................. **LC 45**

**Gallagher, Tess** [1943-] ... **CLC 18, 63; DAM POET; PC 9**
See also CA 106; DLB 120

**Gallant, Mavis** [1922-] **CLC 7, 18, 38; DAC; DAM MST; SSC 5**
See also CA 69-72; CANR 29, 69; DLB 53; MTCW

**Gallant, Roy A(rthur)** [1924-] .......... **CLC 17**
See also CA 5-8R; CANR 4, 29, 54; CLR 30; MAICYA; SATA 4, 68

**Gallico, Paul (William)** [1897-1976] .. **CLC 2**
　See also AITN 1; CA 5-8R; 69-72; CANR 23;
　DLB 9, 171; MAICYA; SATA 13

**Gallo, Max Louis** [1932-] ................... **CLC 95**
　See also CA 85-88

**Gallois, Lucien**
　See Desnos, Robert

**Gallup, Ralph**
　See Whitemore, Hugh (John)

**Galsworthy, John** [1867-1933] . **TCLC 1, 45;**
　**DA; DAB; DAC; DAM DRAM, MST,**
　**NOV; SSC 22; WLC 2**
　See also CA 104; 141; CDBLB 1890-1914;
　DLB 10, 34, 98, 162; DLBD 16

**Galt, John** [1779-1839] ...................... **NCLC 1**
　See also DLB 99, 116, 159

**Galvin, James** [1951-] ........................ **CLC 38**
　See also CA 108; CANR 26

**Gamboa, Federico** [1864-1939] ..... **TCLC 36**

**Gandhi, M. K.**
　See Gandhi, Mohandas Karamchand

**Gandhi, Mahatma**
　See Gandhi, Mohandas Karamchand

**Gandhi, Mohandas Karamchand** [1869-1948]
　**TCLC 59; DAM MULT**
　See also CA 121; 132; MTCW

**Gann, Ernest Kellogg** [1910-1991] ... **CLC 23**
　See also AITN 1; CA 1-4R; 136; CANR 1

**Garcia, Cristina** [1958-] .................... **CLC 76**
　See also CA 141

**Garcia Lorca, Federico** [1898-1936]**TCLC 1,**
　**7, 49; DA; DAB; DAC; DAM DRAM,**
　**MST, MULT, POET; DC 2; HLC; PC 3;**
　**WLC**
　See also CA 104; 131; DLB 108; HW; MTCW

**Garcia Marquez, Gabriel (Jose)** [1928-]**C L C**
　**2, 3, 8, 10, 15, 27, 47, 55, 68; DA; DAB;**
　**DAC; DAM MST, MULT, NOV, POP;**
　**HLC; SSC 8; WLC**
　See also AAYA 3; BEST 89:1, 90:4; CA 33-
　36R; CANR 10, 28, 50; DLB 113; HW;
　MTCW

**Gard, Janice**
　See Latham, Jean Lee

**Gard, Roger Martin du**
　See Martin du Gard, Roger

**Gardam, Jane** [1928-] ........................ **CLC 43**
　See also CA 49-52; CANR 2, 18, 33, 54; CLR
　12; DLB 14, 161; MAICYA; MTCW; SAAS
　9; SATA 39, 76; SATA-Brief 28

**Gardner, Herb(ert)** [1934-] .............. **CLC 44**
　See also CA 149

**Gardner, John (Champlin), Jr.** [1933-1982]
　**CLC 2, 3, 5, 7, 8, 10, 18, 28, 34; DAM NOV,**
　**POP; SSC 7**
　See also AITN 1; CA 65-68; 107; CANR 33;
　DLB 2; DLBY 82; MTCW; SATA 40; SATA-
　Obit 31

**Gardner, John (Edmund)** [1926-] ... **CLC 30;**
　**DAM POP**
　See also CA 103; CANR 15, 69; MTCW

**Gardner, Miriam**
　See Bradley, Marion Zimmer

**Gardner, Noel**
　See Kuttner, Henry

**Gardons, S. S.**
　See Snodgrass, W(illiam) D(e Witt)

**Garfield, Leon** [1921-1996] .............. **CLC 12**
　See also AAYA 8; CA 17-20R; 152; CANR 38,
　41; CLR 21; DLB 161; JRDA; MAICYA;
　SATA 1, 32, 76; SATA-Obit 90

**Garland, (Hannibal) Hamlin** [1860-1940]
　**TCLC 3; SSC 18**
　See also CA 104; DLB 12, 71, 78, 186

**Garneau, (Hector de) Saint-Denys** [1912-1943]
　**TCLC 13**
　See also CA 111; DLB 88

**Garner, Alan** [1934-] ... **CLC 17; DAB; DAM**
　**POP**
　See also AAYA 18; CA 73-76; CANR 15, 64;
　CLR 20; DLB 161; MAICYA; MTCW; SATA
　18, 69

**Garner, Hugh** [1913-1979] ................ **CLC 13**
　See also CA 69-72; CANR 31; DLB 68

**Garnett, David** [1892-1981] ................ **CLC 3**
　See also CA 5-8R; 103; CANR 17; DLB 34

**Garos, Stephanie**
　See Katz, Steve

**Garrett, George (Palmer)** [1929-] **CLC 3, 11,**
　**51; SSC 30**
　See also CA 1-4R; CAAS 5; CANR 1, 42, 67;
　DLB 2, 5, 130, 152; DLBY 83

**Garrick, David** [1717-1779] ..... **LC 15; DAM**
　**DRAM**
　See also DLB 84

**Garrigue, Jean** [1914-1972] ........... **CLC 2, 8**
　See also CA 5-8R; 37-40R; CANR 20

**Garrison, Frederick**
　See Sinclair, Upton (Beall)

**Garth, Will**
　See Hamilton, Edmond; Kuttner, Henry

**Garvey, Marcus (Moziah, Jr.)** [1887-1940]
　**TCLC 41; BLC 2; DAM MULT**
　See also BW 1; CA 120; 124

**Gary, Romain** ...................................... **CLC 25**
　See Kacew, Romain
　See also DLB 83

**Gascar, Pierre** ...................................... **CLC 11**
　See also Fournier, Pierre

**Gascoyne, David (Emery)** [1916-] .... **CLC 45**
　See also CA 65-68; CANR 10, 28, 54; DLB 20;
　MTCW

**Gaskell, Elizabeth Cleghorn** [1810-1865]
　**NCLC 70; DAB; DAM MST; SSC 25**
　See also CDBLB 1832-1890; DLB 21, 144, 159

**Gass, William H(oward)** [1924-] **CLC 1, 2, 8,**
　**11, 15, 39; SSC 12**
　See also CA 17-20R; CANR 30; DLB 2; MTCW

**Gasset, Jose Ortega y**
　See Ortega y Gasset, Jose

**Gates, Henry Louis, Jr.** [1950-] ...... **CLC 65;**
　**BLCS; DAM MULT**
　See also BW 2; CA 109; CANR 25, 53; DLB
　67

**Gautier, Theophile** [1811-1872] **NCLC 1, 59;**
　**DAM POET; PC 18; SSC 20**
　See also DLB 119

**Gawsworth, John**
　See Bates, H(erbert) E(rnest)

**Gay, Oliver**
　See Gogarty, Oliver St. John

**Gaye, Marvin (Penze)** [1939-1984] .. **CLC 26**
　See also CA 112

**Gebler, Carlo (Ernest)** [1954-] ......... **CLC 39**
　See also CA 119; 133

**Gee, Maggie (Mary)** [1948-] .............. **CLC 57**
　See also CA 130

**Gee, Maurice (Gough)** [1931-] .......... **CLC 29**
　See also CA 97-100; CANR 67; SATA 46

**Gelbart, Larry (Simon)** [1923-] . **CLC 21, 61**
　See also CA 73-76; CANR 45

**Gelber, Jack** [1932-] ........... **CLC 1, 6, 14, 79**
　See also CA 1-4R; CANR 2; DLB 7

**Gellhorn, Martha (Ellis)** [1908-1998]**CLC 14,**
　**60**
　See also CA 77-80; 164; CANR 44; DLBY 82

**Genet, Jean** [1910-1986]**CLC 1, 2, 5, 10, 14, 44,**
　**46; DAM DRAM**
　See also CA 13-16R; CANR 18; DLB 72;
　DLBY 86; MTCW

**Gent, Peter** [1942-] ............................ **CLC 29**
　See also AITN 1; CA 89-92; DLBY 82

**Gentlewoman in New England, A**
　See Bradstreet, Anne

**Gentlewoman in Those Parts, A**
　See Bradstreet, Anne

**George, Jean Craighead** [1919-] ...... **CLC 35**
　See also AAYA 8; CA 5-8R; CANR 25; CLR 1;
　DLB 52; JRDA; MAICYA; SATA 2, 68

**George, Stefan (Anton)** [1868-1933]**TCLC 2,**
　**14**
　See also CA 104

**Georges, Georges Martin**
　See Simenon, Georges (Jacques Christian)

**Gerhardi, William Alexander**
　See Gerhardie, William Alexander

**Gerhardie, William Alexander** [1895-1977]
　**CLC 5**
　See also CA 25-28R; 73-76; CANR 18; DLB
　36

**Gerstler, Amy** [1956-] ........................ **CLC 70**
　See also CA 146

**Gertler, T.** ........................................... **CLC 34**
　See also CA 116; 121; INT 121

**Ghalib** ................................................ **NCLC 39**
　See also Ghalib, Hsadullah Khan

**Ghalib, Hsadullah Khan** [1797-1869]
　See Ghalib
　See also DAM POET

**Ghelderode, Michel de** [1898-1962]**CLC 6, 11;**
　**DAM DRAM**
　See also CA 85-88; CANR 40

**Ghiselin, Brewster** [1903-] ................ **CLC 23**
　See also CA 13-16R; CAAS 10; CANR 13

**Ghose, Aurabinda** [1872-1950] ...... **TCLC 63**
　See also CA 163

**Ghose, Zulfikar** [1935-] .................... **CLC 42**
　See also CA 65-68; CANR 67

**Ghosh, Amitav** [1956-] ...................... **CLC 44**
　See also CA 147

**Giacosa, Giuseppe** [1847-1906] ....... **TCLC 7**
　See also CA 104

**Gibb, Lee**
　See Waterhouse, Keith (Spencer)

**Gibbon, Lewis Grassic** ...................... **TCLC 4**
　See also Mitchell, James Leslie

**Gibbons, Kaye** [1960-]**CLC 50, 88; DAM POP**
　See also CA 151

**Gibran, Kahlil** [1883-1931]**TCLC 1, 9; DAM**
　**POET, POP; PC 9**
　See also CA 104; 150

**Gibran, Khalil**
　See Gibran, Kahlil

**Gibson, William** [1914-] **CLC 23; DA; DAB;**
　**DAC; DAM DRAM, MST**
　See also CA 9-12R; CANR 9, 42; DLB 7; SATA
　66

**Gibson, William (Ford)** [1948-] **CLC 39, 63;**
　**DAM POP**
　See also AAYA 12; CA 126; 133; CANR 52

**Gide, Andre (Paul Guillaume)** [1869-1951]
　**TCLC 5, 12, 36; DA; DAB; DAC; DAM**
　**MST, NOV; SSC 13; WLC**
　See also CA 104; 124; DLB 65; MTCW

**Gifford, Barry (Colby)** [1946-] ......... **CLC 34**
　See also CA 65-68; CANR 9, 30, 40

**Gilbert, Frank**
　See De Voto, Bernard (Augustine)

**Gilbert, W(illiam) S(chwenck)** [1836-1911]
　**TCLC 3; DAM DRAM, POET**
　See also CA 104; SATA 36

**Gilbreth, Frank B., Jr.** [1911-] ......... **CLC 17**
　See also CA 9-12R; SATA 2

**Gilchrist, Ellen** [1935-] ... **CLC 34, 48; DAM**
　**POP; SSC 14**
　See also CA 113; 116; CANR 41, 61; DLB 130;
　MTCW

**Giles, Molly** [1942-] ........................... **CLC 39**
　See also CA 126

**Gill, Patrick**
　See Creasey, John

Gilliam, Terry (Vance) [1940-] ......... **CLC 21**
  See also Monty Python
  See also AAYA 19; CA 108; 113; CANR 35;
  INT 113
Gillian, Jerry
  See Gilliam, Terry (Vance)
Gilliatt, Penelope (Ann Douglass) [1932-1993]
  **CLC 2, 10, 13, 53**
  See also AITN 2; CA 13-16R; 141; CANR 49;
  DLB 14
Gilman, Charlotte (Anna) Perkins (Stetson)
  [1860-1935] ........... **TCLC 9, 37; SSC 13**
  See also CA 106; 150
Gilmour, David [1949-] .................... **CLC 35**
  See also CA 138, 147
Gilpin, William [1724-1804] .......... **NCLC 30**
Gilray, J. D.
  See Mencken, H(enry) L(ouis)
Gilroy, Frank D(aniel) [1925-] ............ **CLC 2**
  See also CA 81-84; CANR 32, 64; DLB 7
Gilstrap, John [1957(?)-] ................. **CLC 99**
  See also CA 160
Ginsberg, Allen [1926-1997]**CLC 1, 2, 3, 4, 6,
  13, 36, 69, 109; DA; DAB; DAC; DAM
  MST, POET; PC 4; WLC 3**
  See also AITN 1; CA 1-4R; 157; CANR 2, 41,
  63; CDALB 1941-1968; DLB 5, 16, 169;
  MTCW
Ginzburg, Natalia [1916-1991]**CLC 5, 11, 54,
  70**
  See also CA 85-88; 135; CANR 33; DLB 177;
  MTCW
Giono, Jean [1895-1970] ................ **CLC 4, 11**
  See also CA 45-48; 29-32R; CANR 2, 35; DLB
  72; MTCW
Giovanni, Nikki [1943-]**CLC 2, 4, 19, 64; BLC
  2; DA; DAB; DAC; DAM MST, MULT,
  POET; PC 19; WLCS**
  See also AAYA 22; AITN 1; BW 2; CA 29-32R;
  CAAS 6; CANR 18, 41, 60; CLR 6; DLB 5,
  41; INT CANR-18; MAICYA; MTCW; SATA
  24
Giovene, Andrea [1904-] ..................... **CLC 7**
  See also CA 85-88
Gippius, Zinaida (Nikolayevna) [1869-1945]
  See Hippius, Zinaida
  See also CA 106
Giraudoux, (Hippolyte) Jean [1882-1944]
  **TCLC 2, 7; DAM DRAM**
  See also CA 104; DLB 65
Gironella, Jose Maria [1917-] .......... **CLC 11**
  See also CA 101
Gissing, George (Robert) [1857-1903] **T C L C
  3, 24, 47**
  See also CA 105; DLB 18, 135, 184
Giurlani, Aldo
  See Palazzeschi, Aldo
Gladkov, Fyodor (Vasilyevich) [1883-1958]
  **TCLC 27**
Glanville, Brian (Lester) [1931-] ........ **CLC 6**
  See also CA 5-8R; CAAS 9; CANR 3; DLB 15,
  139; SATA 42
Glasgow, Ellen (Anderson Gholson) [1873-
  1945] ......................... **TCLC 2, 7**
  See also CA 104; 164; DLB 9, 12
Glaspell, Susan [1882(?)-1948] ...... **TCLC 55**
  See also CA 110; 154; DLB 7, 9, 78; YABC 2
Glassco, John [1909-1981] ................... **CLC 9**
  See also CA 13-16R; 102; CANR 15; DLB 68
Glasscock, Amnesia
  See Steinbeck, John (Ernst)
Glasser, Ronald J. [1940(?)-] ............ **CLC 37**
Glassman, Joyce
  See Johnson, Joyce
Glendinning, Victoria [1937-] .......... **CLC 50**
  See also CA 120; 127; CANR 59; DLB 155
Glissant, Edouard [1928-]**CLC 10, 68; DAM
  MULT**
  See also CA 153
Gloag, Julian [1930-] ...................... **CLC 40**
  See also AITN 1; CA 65-68; CANR 10
Glowacki, Aleksander
  See Prus, Boleslaw
Gluck, Louise (Elisabeth) [1943-] **CLC 7, 22,
  44, 81; DAM POET; PC 16**
  See also CA 33-36R; CANR 40, 69; DLB 5
Glyn, Elinor [1864-1943] ................ **TCLC 72**
  See also DLB 153
Gobineau, Joseph Arthur (Comte) de [1816-
  1882] .......................... **NCLC 17**
  See also DLB 123
Godard, Jean-Luc [1930-] ................ **CLC 20**
  See also CA 93-96
Godden, (Margaret) Rumer [1907-]. **CLC 53**
  See also AAYA 6; CA 5-8R; CANR 4, 27, 36,
  55; CLR 20; DLB 161; MAICYA; SAAS 12;
  SATA 3, 36
Godoy Alcayaga, Lucila [1889-1957]
  See Mistral, Gabriela
  See also BW 2; CA 104; 131; DAM MULT;
  HW; MTCW
Godwin, Gail (Kathleen) [1937-]**CLC 5, 8, 22,
  31, 69; DAM POP**
  See also CA 29-32R; CANR 15, 43, 69; DLB
  6; INT CANR-15; MTCW
Godwin, William [1756-1836] ........ **NCLC 14**
  See also CDBLB 1789-1832; DLB 39, 104, 142,
  158, 163
Goebbels, Josef
  See Goebbels, (Paul) Joseph
Goebbels, (Paul) Joseph [1897-1945]**TCLC 68**
  See also CA 115; 148
Goebbels, Joseph Paul
  See Goebbels, (Paul) Joseph
Goethe, Johann Wolfgang von [1749-1832]
  **NCLC 4, 22, 34; DA; DAB; DAC; DAM
  DRAM, MST, POET; PC 5; WLC 3**
  See also DLB 94
Gogarty, Oliver St. John [1878-1957] **T C L C
  15**
  See also CA 109; 150; DLB 15, 19
Gogol, Nikolai (Vasilyevich) [1809-1852]
  **NCLC 5, 15, 31; DA; DAB; DAC; DAM
  DRAM, MST; DC 1; SSC 4, 29; WLC**
  See also DLB 198
Goines, Donald [1937(?)-1974]**CLC 80; BLC
  2; DAM MULT, POP**
  See also AITN 1; BW 1; CA 124; 114; DLB 33
Gold, Herbert [1924-] ......... **CLC 4, 7, 14, 42**
  See also CA 9-12R; CANR 17, 45; DLB 2;
  DLBY 81
Goldbarth, Albert [1948-] ............. **CLC 5, 38**
  See also CA 53-56; CANR 6, 40; DLB 120
Goldberg, Anatol [1910-1982] .......... **CLC 34**
  See also CA 131; 117
Goldemberg, Isaac [1945-] ................ **CLC 52**
  See also CA 69-72; CAAS 12; CANR 11, 32;
  HW
Golding, William (Gerald) [1911-1993] **C L C
  1, 2, 3, 8, 10, 17, 27, 58, 81; DA; DAB;
  DAC; DAM MST, NOV; WLC**
  See also AAYA 5; CA 5-8R; 141; CANR 13,
  33, 54; CDBLB 1945-1960; DLB 15, 100;
  MTCW
Goldman, Emma [1869-1940] ........ **TCLC 13**
  See also CA 110; 150
Goldman, Francisco [1954-] ............. **CLC 76**
  See also CA 162
Goldman, William (W.) [1931-] ....**CLC 1, 48**
  See also CA 9-12R; CANR 29, 69; DLB 44
Goldmann, Lucien [1913-1970] ........ **CLC 24**
  See also CA 25-28; CAP 2
Goldoni, Carlo [1707-1793] ........**LC 4; DAM
  DRAM**

Goldsberry, Steven [1949-] ............... **CLC 34**
  See also CA 131
Goldsmith, Oliver [1728-1774] .... **LC 2; DA;
  DAB; DAC; DAM DRAM, MST, NOV,
  POET; DC 8; WLC**
  See also CDBLB 1660-1789; DLB 39, 89, 104,
  109, 142; SATA 26
Goldsmith, Peter
  See Priestley, J(ohn) B(oynton)
Gombrowicz, Witold [1904-1969]**CLC 4, 7, 11,
  49; DAM DRAM**
  See also CA 19-20; 25-28R; CAP 2
Gomez de la Serna, Ramon [1888-1963]**C L C
  9**
  See also CA 153; 116; HW
Goncharov, Ivan Alexandrovich [1812-1891]
  **NCLC 1, 63**
Goncourt, Edmond (Louis Antoine Huot) de
  [1822-1896] ................ **NCLC 7**
  See also DLB 123
Goncourt, Jules (Alfred Huot) de [1830-1870]
  **NCLC 7**
  See also DLB 123
Gontier, Fernande [19(?)-] ................ **CLC 50**
Gonzalez Martinez, Enrique [1871-1952]
  **TCLC 72**
  See also CA 166; HW
Goodman, Paul [1911-1972] ... **CLC 1, 2, 4, 7**
  See also CA 19-20; 37-40R; CANR 34; CAP 2;
  DLB 130; MTCW
Gordimer, Nadine [1923-]**CLC 3, 5, 7, 10, 18,
  33, 51, 70; DA; DAB; DAC; DAM MST,
  NOV; SSC 17; WLCS**
  See also CA 5-8R; CANR 3, 28, 56; INT CANR-
  28; MTCW
Gordon, Adam Lindsay [1833-1870]**NCLC 21**
Gordon, Caroline [1895-1981]**CLC 6, 13, 29,
  83; SSC 15**
  See also CA 11-12; 103; CANR 36; CAP 1;
  DLB 4, 9, 102; DLBY 81; MTCW
Gordon, Charles William [1860-1937]
  See Connor, Ralph
  See also CA 109
Gordon, Mary (Catherine) [1949-]**CLC 13, 22**
  See also CA 102; CANR 44; DLB 6; DLBY
  81; INT 102; MTCW
Gordon, N. J.
  See Bosman, Herman Charles
Gordon, Sol [1923-] ......................... **CLC 26**
  See also CA 53-56; CANR 4; SATA 11
Gordone, Charles [1925-1995]**CLC 1, 4; DAM
  DRAM; DC 8**
  See also BW 1; CA 93-96; 150; CANR 55; DLB
  7; INT 93-96; MTCW
Gore, Catherine [1800-1861] ......... **NCLC 65**
  See also DLB 116
Gorenko, Anna Andreevna
  See Akhmatova, Anna
Gorky, Maxim [1868-1936] ..**TCLC 8; DAB;
  SSC 28; WLC**
  See also Peshkov, Alexei Maximovich
Goryan, Sirak
  See Saroyan, William
Gosse, Edmund (William) [1849-1928]**T C L C
  28**
  See also CA 117; DLB 57, 144, 184
Gotlieb, Phyllis Fay (Bloom) [1926-] **CLC 18**
  See also CA 13-16R; CANR 7; DLB 88
Gottesman, S. D.
  See Kornbluth, C(yril) M.; Pohl, Frederik
Gottfried von Strassburg [fl. c. 1210-]**C M L C
  10**
  See also DLB 138
Gould, Lois ......................................**CLC 4, 10**
  See also CA 77-80; CANR 29; MTCW
Gourmont, Remy (-Marie-Charles) de [1858-
  1915] ......................... **TCLC 17**

See also Greve, Felix Paul (Berthold Friedrich)
See also DLB 92
**Grubb**
See Crumb, R(obert)
**Grumbach, Doris (Isaac)** [1918-]**CLC 13, 22, 64**
See also CA 5-8R; CAAS 2; CANR 9, 42; INT CANR-9
**Grundtvig, Nicolai Frederik Severin** [1783-1872] ............................................
**NCLC 1**
**Grunge**
See Crumb, R(obert)
**Grunwald, Lisa** [1959-] ..................... **CLC 44**
See also CA 120
**Guare, John** [1938-]**CLC 8, 14, 29, 67; DAM DRAM**
See also CA 73-76; CANR 21, 69; DLB 7; MTCW
**Gudjonsson, Halldor Kiljan** [1902-1998]
See Laxness, Halldor
See also CA 103; 164
**Guenter, Erich**
See Eich, Guenter
**Guest, Barbara** [1920-] ..................... **CLC 34**
See also CA 25-28R; CANR 11, 44; DLB 5, 193
**Guest, Judith (Ann)** [1936-]**CLC 8, 30; DAM NOV, POP**
See also AAYA 7; CA 77-80; CANR 15; INT CANR-15; MTCW
**Guevara, Che** ........................... **CLC 87; HLC**
See also Guevara (Serna), Ernesto
**Guevara (Serna), Ernesto** [1928-1967]
See Guevara, Che
See also CA 127; 111; CANR 56; DAM MULT; HW
**Guild, Nicholas M.** [1944-] ............... **CLC 33**
See also CA 93-96
**Guillemin, Jacques**
See Sartre, Jean-Paul
**Guillen, Jorge** [1893-1984] .... **CLC 11; DAM MULT, POET**
See also CA 89-92; 112; DLB 108; HW
**Guillen, Nicolas (Cristobal)** [1902-1989]**C L C 48, 79; BLC 2; DAM MST, MULT, POET; HLC; PC 23**
See also BW 2; CA 116; 125; 129; HW
**Guillevic, (Eugene)** [1907-] ................ **CLC 33**
See also CA 93-96
**Guillois**
See Desnos, Robert
**Guillois, Valentin**
See Desnos, Robert
**Guiney, Louise Imogen** [1861-1920]**TCLC 41**
See also CA 160; DLB 54
**Guiraldes, Ricardo (Guillermo)** [1886-1927]
**TCLC 39**
See also CA 131; HW; MTCW
**Gumilev, Nikolai (Stepanovich)** [1886-1921]
**TCLC 60**
See also CA 165
**Gunesekera, Romesh** [1954-] ............ **CLC 91**
See also CA 159
**Gunn, Bill** ....................................... **CLC 5**
See also Gunn, William Harrison
See also DLB 38
**Gunn, Thom(son William)** [1929-] **CLC 3, 6, 18, 32, 81; DAM POET**
See also CA 17-20R; CANR 9, 33; CDBLB 1960 to Present; DLB 27; INT CANR-33; MTCW
**Gunn, William Harrison** [1934(?)-1989]
See Gunn, Bill
See also AITN 1; BW 1; CA 13-16R; 128; CANR 12, 25
**Gunnars, Kristjana** [1948-] .............. **CLC 69**

See also CA 113; DLB 60
**Gurdjieff, G(eorgei) I(vanovich)** [1877(?)-1949]
**TCLC 71**
See also CA 157
**Gurganus, Allan** [1947-]**CLC 70; DAM POP**
See also BEST 90:1; CA 135
**Gurney, A(lbert) R(amsdell), Jr.** [1930-]**C L C 32, 50, 54; DAM DRAM**
See also CA 77-80; CANR 32, 64
**Gurney, Ivor (Bertie)** [1890-1937] **TCLC 33**
**Gurney, Peter**
See Gurney, A(lbert) R(amsdell), Jr.
**Guro, Elena** [1877-1913] ................ **TCLC 56**
**Gustafson, James M(oody)** [1925-] **CLC 100**
See also CA 25-28R; CANR 37
**Gustafson, Ralph (Barker)** [1909-] .. **CLC 36**
See also CA 21-24R; CANR 8, 45; DLB 88
**Gut, Gom**
See Simenon, Georges (Jacques Christian)
**Guterson, David** [1956-] ................... **CLC 91**
See also CA 132
**Guthrie, A(lfred) B(ertram), Jr.** [1901-1991]
**CLC 23**
See also CA 57-60; 134; CANR 24; DLB 6; SATA 62; SATA-Obit 67
**Guthrie, Isobel**
See Grieve, C(hristopher) M(urray)
**Guthrie, Woodrow Wilson** [1912-1967]
See Guthrie, Woody
See also CA 113; 93-96
**Guthrie, Woody** .................................. **CLC 35**
See also Guthrie, Woodrow Wilson
**Guy, Rosa (Cuthbert)** [1928-] ........... **CLC 26**
See also AAYA 4; BW 2; CA 17-20R; CANR 14, 34; CLR 13; DLB 33; JRDA; MAICYA; SATA 14, 62
**Gwendolyn**
See Bennett, (Enoch) Arnold
**H. D.** ................ **CLC 3, 8, 14, 31, 34, 73; PC 5**
See also Doolittle, Hilda
**H. de V.**
See Buchan, John
**Haavikko, Paavo Juhani** [1931-] **CLC 18, 34**
See also CA 106
**Habbema, Koos**
See Heijermans, Herman
**Habermas, Juergen** [1929-] ............. **CLC 104**
See also CA 109
**Habermas, Jurgen**
See Habermas, Juergen
**Hacker, Marilyn** [1942-]**CLC 5, 9, 23, 72, 91; DAM POET**
See also CA 77-80; CANR 68; DLB 120
**Haeckel, Ernst Heinrich (Philipp August)** [1834-1919] ................................ **TCLC 83**
See also CA 157
**Haggard, H(enry) Rider** [1856-1925] **T C L C 11**
See also CA 108; 148; DLB 70, 156, 174, 178; SATA 16
**Hagiosy, L.**
See Larbaud, Valery (Nicolas)
**Hagiwara Sakutaro** [1886-1942]**TCLC 60; PC 18**
**Haig, Fenil**
See Ford, Ford Madox
**Haig-Brown, Roderick (Langmere)** [1908-1976]
**CLC 21**
See also CA 5-8R; 69-72; CANR 4, 38; CLR 31; DLB 88; MAICYA; SATA 12
**Hailey, Arthur** [1920-] .. **CLC 5; DAM NOV, POP**
See also AITN 2; BEST 90:3; CA 1-4R; CANR 2, 36; DLB 88; DLBY 82; MTCW
**Hailey, Elizabeth Forsythe** [1938-] .. **CLC 40**
See also CA 93-96; CAAS 1; CANR 15, 48;

INT CANR-15
**Haines, John (Meade)** [1924-] .......... **CLC 58**
See also CA 17-20R; CANR 13, 34; DLB 5
**Hakluyt, Richard** [1552-1616] ............. **LC 31**
**Haldeman, Joe (William)** [1943-] ..... **CLC 61**
See also CA 53-56; CAAS 25; CANR 6; DLB 8; INT CANR-6
**Haley, Alex(ander Murray Palmer)** [1921-1992] **CLC 8, 12, 76; BLC 2; DA; DAB; DAC; DAM MST, MULT, POP**
See also BW 2; CA 77-80; 136; CANR 61; DLB 38; MTCW
**Haliburton, Thomas Chandler** [1796-1865]
**NCLC 15**
See also DLB 11, 99
**Hall, Donald (Andrew, Jr.)** [1928-]**CLC 1, 13, 37, 59; DAM POET**
See also CA 5-8R; CAAS 7; CANR 2, 44, 64; DLB 5; SATA 23, 97
**Hall, Frederic Sauser**
See Sauser-Hall, Frederic
**Hall, James**
See Kuttner, Henry
**Hall, James Norman** [1887-1951] .. **TCLC 23**
See also CA 123; SATA 21
**Hall, (Marguerite) Radclyffe** [1886-1943]
**TCLC 12**
See also CA 110; 150
**Hall, Rodney** [1935-] .......................... **CLC 51**
See also CA 109; CANR 69
**Halleck, Fitz-Greene** [1790-1867] . **NCLC 47**
See also DLB 3
**Halliday, Michael**
See Creasey, John
**Halpern, Daniel** [1945-] ..................... **CLC 14**
See also CA 33-36R
**Hamburger, Michael (Peter Leopold)** [1924-]
**CLC 5, 14**
See also CA 5-8R; CAAS 4; CANR 2, 47; DLB 27
**Hamill, Pete** [1935-] ........................... **CLC 10**
See also CA 25-28R; CANR 18
**Hamilton, Alexander** [1755(?)-1804]**NCLC 49**
See also DLB 37
**Hamilton, Clive**
See Lewis, C(live) S(taples)
**Hamilton, Edmond** [1904-1977] ......... **CLC 1**
See also CA 1-4R; CANR 3; DLB 8
**Hamilton, Eugene (Jacob) Lee**
See Lee-Hamilton, Eugene (Jacob)
**Hamilton, Franklin**
See Silverberg, Robert
**Hamilton, Gail**
See Corcoran, Barbara
**Hamilton, Mollie**
See Kaye, M(ary) M(argaret)
**Hamilton, (Anthony Walter) Patrick** [1904-1962] ........................................... **CLC 51**
See also CA 113; DLB 10
**Hamilton, Virginia** [1936-] .... **CLC 26; DAM MULT**
See also AAYA 2, 21; BW 2; CA 25-28R; CANR 20, 37; CLR 1, 11, 40; DLB 33, 52; INT CANR-20; JRDA; MAICYA; MTCW; SATA 4, 56, 79
**Hammett, (Samuel) Dashiell** [1894-1961]**CLC 3, 5, 10, 19, 47; SSC 17**
See also AITN 1; CA 81-84; CANR 42; CDALB 1929-1941; DLBD 6; DLBY 96; MTCW
**Hammon, Jupiter** [1711(?)-1800(?)]**NCLC 5; BLC 2; DAM MULT, POET; PC 16**
See also DLB 31, 50
**Hammond, Keith**
See Kuttner, Henry
**Hamner, Earl (Henry), Jr.** [1923-].... **CLC 12**
See also AITN 2; CA 73-76; DLB 6
**Hampton, Christopher (James)** [1946-]**CLC 4**

**Hearne, Vicki** [1946-] .......................... **CLC 56**
See also CA 139
**Hearon, Shelby** [1931-] ...................... **CLC 63**
See also AITN 2; CA 25-28R; CANR 18, 48
**Heat-Moon, William Least** ................ **CLC 29**
See also Trogdon, William (Lewis)
See also AAYA 9
**Hebbel, Friedrich** [1813-1863] ..... **NCLC 43;**
**DAM DRAM**
See also DLB 129
**Hebert, Anne** [1916-] ... **CLC 4, 13, 29; DAC;**
**DAM MST, POET**
See also CA 85-88; CANR 69; DLB 68; MTCW
**Hecht, Anthony (Evan)** [1923-]**CLC 8, 13, 19;**
**DAM POET**
See also CA 9-12R; CANR 6; DLB 5, 169
**Hecht, Ben** [1894-1964] ........................ **CLC 8**
See also CA 85-88; DLB 7, 9, 25, 26, 28, 86
**Hedayat, Sadeq** [1903-1951] .......... **TCLC 21**
See also CA 120
**Hegel, Georg Wilhelm Friedrich** [1770-1831]
**NCLC 46**
See also DLB 90
**Heidegger, Martin** [1889-1976] ......... **CLC 24**
See also CA 81-84; 65-68; CANR 34; MTCW
**Heidenstam, (Carl Gustaf) Verner von** [1859-
1940] .................................................................
**TCLC 5**
See also CA 104
**Heifner, Jack** [1946-] .......................... **CLC 11**
See also CA 105; CANR 47
**Heijermans, Herman** [1864-1924] . **TCLC 24**
See also CA 123
**Heilbrun, Carolyn G(old)** [1926-] .... **CLC 25**
See also CA 45-48; CANR 1, 28, 58
**Heine, Heinrich** [1797-1856] ...... **NCLC 4, 54**
See also DLB 90
**Heinemann, Larry (Curtiss)** [1944-] **CLC 50**
See also CA 110; CAAS 21; CANR 31; DLBD
9; INT CANR-31
**Heiney, Donald (William)** [1921-1993]
See Harris, MacDonald
See also CA 1-4R; 142; CANR 3, 58
**Heinlein, Robert A(nson)** [1907-1988]**CLC 1,**
**3, 8, 14, 26, 55; DAM POP**
See also AAYA 17; CA 1-4R; 125; CANR 1,
20, 53; DLB 8; JRDA; MAICYA; MTCW;
SATA 9, 69; SATA-Obit 56
**Helforth, John**
See Doolittle, Hilda
**Hellenhofferu, Vojtech Kapristian z**
See Hasek, Jaroslav (Matej Frantisek)
**Heller, Joseph** [1923-]**CLC 1, 3, 5, 8, 11, 36, 63;**
**DA; DAB; DAC; DAM MST, NOV, POP;**
**WLC**
See also AAYA 24; AITN 1; CA 5-8R; CABS
1; CANR 8, 42, 66; DLB 2, 28; DLBY 80;
INT CANR-8; MTCW
**Hellman, Lillian (Florence)** [1906-1984]**C L C**
**2, 4, 8, 14, 18, 34, 44, 52; DAM DRAM;**
**DC 1**
See also AITN 1, 2; CA 13-16R; 112; CANR
33; DLB 7; DLBY 84; MTCW
**Helprin, Mark** [1947-]**CLC 7, 10, 22, 32; DAM**
**NOV, POP**
See also CA 81-84; CANR 47, 64; DLBY 85;
MTCW
**Helvetius, Claude-Adrien** [1715-1771] **LC 26**
**Helyar, Jane Penelope Josephine** [1933-]
See Poole, Josephine
See also CA 21-24R; CANR 10, 26; SATA 82
**Hemans, Felicia** [1793-1835] .......... **NCLC 71**
See also DLB 96
**Hemingway, Ernest (Miller)** [1899-1961]**CLC**
**1, 3, 6, 8, 10, 13, 19, 30, 34, 39, 41, 44, 50,**
**61, 80; DA; DAB; DAC; DAM MST, NOV;**
**SSC 25; WLC**

See also AAYA 19; CA 77-80; CANR 34;
CDALB 1917-1929; DLB 4, 9, 102; DLBD
1, 15, 16; DLBY 81, 87, 96; MTCW
**Hempel, Amy** [1951-] ........................ **CLC 39**
See also CA 118; 137
**Henderson, F. C.**
See Mencken, H(enry) L(ouis)
**Henderson, Sylvia**
See Ashton-Warner, Sylvia (Constance)
**Henderson, Zenna (Chlarson)** [1917-1983]
**SSC 29**
See also CA 1-4R; 133; CANR 1; DLB 8; SATA
5
**Henley, Beth** .............................. **CLC 23; DC 6**
See also Henley, Elizabeth Becker
See also CABS 3; DLBY 86
**Henley, Elizabeth Becker** [1952-]
See Henley, Beth
See also CA 107; CANR 32; DAM DRAM,
MST; MTCW
**Henley, William Ernest** [1849-1903] **TCLC 8**
See also CA 105; DLB 19
**Hennissart, Martha**
See Lathen, Emma
See also CA 85-88; CANR 64
**Henry, O.** .............. **TCLC 1, 19; SSC 5; WLC**
See also Porter, William Sydney
**Henry, Patrick** [1736-1799] ................... **LC 25**
**Henryson, Robert** [1430(?)-1506(?)] ... **LC 20**
See also DLB 146
**Henry VIII** [1491-1547] ........................ **LC 10**
**Henschke, Alfred**
See Klabund
**Hentoff, Nat(han Irving)** [1925-] ...... **CLC 26**
See also AAYA 4; CA 1-4R; CAAS 6; CANR
5, 25; CLR 1, 52; INT CANR-25; JRDA;
MAICYA; SATA 42, 69; SATA-Brief 27
**Heppenstall, (John) Rayner** [1911-1981]**C L C**
**10**
See also CA 1-4R; 103; CANR 29
**Heraclitus** [c. 540B.C.-c. 450B.C.] **CMLC 22**
See also DLB 176
**Herbert, Frank (Patrick)** [1920-1986]**CLC 12,**
**23, 35, 44, 85; DAM POP**
See also CA 53-56; 118; CANR 5,
43; DLB 8; INT CANR-5; MTCW; SATA 9,
37; SATA-Obit 47
**Herbert, George** [1593-1633] .. **LC 24; DAB;**
**DAM POET; PC 4**
See also CDBLB Before 1660; DLB 126
**Herbert, Zbigniew** [1924-] **CLC 9, 43; DAM**
**POET**
See also CA 89-92; CANR 36; MTCW
**Herbst, Josephine (Frey)** [1897-1969]**CLC 34**
See also CA 5-8R; 25-28R; DLB 9
**Hergesheimer, Joseph** [1880-1954] **TCLC 11**
See also CA 109; DLB 102, 9
**Herlihy, James Leo** [1927-1993] ........ **CLC 6**
See also CA 1-4R; 143; CANR 2
**Hermogenes** [fl. c. 175-] ................... **CMLC 6**
**Hernandez, Jose** [1834-1886] .......... **NCLC 17**
**Herodotus** [c. 484B.C.-429B.C.] .... **CMLC 17**
See also DLB 176
**Herrick, Robert** [1591-1674]**LC 13; DA; DAB;**
**DAC; DAM MST, POP; PC 9**
See also DLB 126
**Herring, Guilles**
See Somerville, Edith
**Herriot, James** [1916-1995] ... **CLC 12; DAM**
**POP**
See also Wight, James Alfred
See also AAYA 1; CA 148; CANR 40; SATA
86
**Herrmann, Dorothy** [1941-] .............. **CLC 44**
See also CA 107
**Herrmann, Taffy**
See Herrmann, Dorothy

**Hersey, John (Richard)** [1914-1993]**CLC 1, 2,**
**7, 9, 40, 81, 97; DAM POP**
See also CA 17-20R; 140; CANR 33; DLB 6,
185; MTCW; SATA 25; SATA-Obit 76
**Herzen, Aleksandr Ivanovich** [1812-1870]
**NCLC 10, 61**
**Herzl, Theodor** [1860-1904] .......... **TCLC 36**
**Herzog, Werner** [1942-] .................... **CLC 16**
See also CA 89-92
**Hesiod** [c. 8th cent. B.C.-] ................. **CMLC 5**
See also DLB 176
**Hesse, Hermann** [1877-1962]**CLC 1, 2, 3, 6, 11,**
**17, 25, 69; DA; DAB; DAC; DAM MST,**
**NOV; SSC 9; WLC**
See also CA 17-18; CAP 2; DLB 66; MTCW;
SATA 50
**Hewes, Cady**
See De Voto, Bernard (Augustine)
**Heyen, William** [1940-] ............... **CLC 13, 18**
See also CA 33-36R; CAAS 9; DLB 5
**Heyerdahl, Thor** [1914-] .................... **CLC 26**
See also CA 5-8R; CANR 5, 22, 66; MTCW;
SATA 2, 52
**Heym, Georg (Theodor Franz Arthur)** [1887-
1912] ........................................... **TCLC 9**
See also CA 106
**Heym, Stefan** [1913-] .......................... **CLC 41**
See also CA 9-12R; CANR 4; DLB 69
**Heyse, Paul (Johann Ludwig von)** [1830-1914]
**TCLC 8**
See also CA 104; DLB 129
**Heyward, (Edwin) DuBose** [1885-1940]**TCLC
59**
See also CA 108; 157; DLB 7, 9, 45; SATA 21
**Hibbert, Eleanor Alice Burford** [1906-1993]
**CLC 7; DAM POP**
See also BEST 90:4; CA 17-20R; 140; CANR
9, 28, 59; SATA 2; SATA-Obit 74
**Hichens, Robert (Smythe)** [1864-1950]**T C L C
64**
See also CA 162; DLB 153
**Higgins, George V(incent)** [1939-] **CLC 4, 7,**
**10, 18**
See also CA 77-80; CAAS 5; CANR 17, 51;
DLB 2; DLBY 81; INT CANR-17; MTCW
**Higginson, Thomas Wentworth** [1823-1911]
**TCLC 36**
See also CA 162; DLB 1, 64
**Highet, Helen**
See MacInnes, Helen (Clark)
**Highsmith, (Mary) Patricia** [1921-1995]**C L C
2, 4, 14, 42, 102; DAM NOV, POP**
See also CA 1-4R; 147; CANR 1, 20, 48, 62;
MTCW
**Highwater, Jamake (Mamake)** [1942(?)-]**CLC
12**
See also AAYA 7; CA 65-68; CAAS 7; CANR
10, 34; CLR 17; DLB 52; DLBY 85; JRDA;
MAICYA; SATA 32, 69; SATA-Brief 30
**Highway, Tomson** [1951-] ..... **CLC 92; DAC;**
**DAM MULT**
See also CA 151; NNAL
**Higuchi, Ichiyo** [1872-1896] .......... **NCLC 49**
**Hijuelos, Oscar** [1951-]**CLC 65; DAM MULT,**
**POP; HLC**
See also AAYA 25; BEST 90:1; CA 123; CANR
50; DLB 145; HW
**Hikmet, Nazim** [1902(?)-1963] .......... **CLC 40**
See also CA 141; 93-96
**Hildegard von Bingen** [1098-1179]**CMLC 20**
See also DLB 148
**Hildesheimer, Wolfgang** [1916-1991]**CLC 49**
See also CA 101; 135; DLB 69, 124
**Hill, Geoffrey (William)** [1932-]**CLC 5, 8, 18,**
**45; DAM POET**
See also CA 81-84; CANR 21; CDBLB 1960
to Present; DLB 40; MTCW

See also DLB 133

**Inchbald, Elizabeth** [1753-1821] ... **NCLC 62**
See also DLB 39, 89

**Inclan, Ramon (Maria) del Valle**
See Valle-Inclan, Ramon (Maria) del

**Infante, G(uillermo) Cabrera**
See Cabrera Infante, G(uillermo)

**Ingalls, Rachel (Holmes)** [1940-] ...... **CLC 42**
See also CA 123; 127

**Ingamells, Rex** [1913-1955] ........... **TCLC 35**

**Inge, William (Motter)** [1913-1973]**CLC 1, 8, 19; DAM DRAM**
See also CA 9-12R; CDALB 1941-1968; DLB 7; MTCW

**Ingelow, Jean** [1820-1897] ............. **NCLC 39**
See also DLB 35, 163; SATA 33

**Ingram, Willis J.**
See Harris, Mark

**Innaurato, Albert (F.)** [1948(?)-] **CLC 21, 60**
See also CA 115; 122; INT 122

**Innes, Michael**
See Stewart, J(ohn) I(nnes) M(ackintosh)

**Innis, Harold Adams** [1894-1952] . **TCLC 77**
See also DLB 88

**Ionesco, Eugene** [1909-1994]**CLC 1, 4, 6, 9, 11, 15, 41, 86; DA; DAB; DAC; DAM DRAM, MST; WLC**
See also CA 9-12R; 144; CANR 55; MTCW; SATA 7; SATA-Obit 79

**Iqbal, Muhammad** [1873-1938] ..... **TCLC 28**

**Ireland, Patrick**
See O'Doherty, Brian

**Iron, Ralph**
See Schreiner, Olive (Emilie Albertina)

**Irving, John (Winslow)** [1942-]**CLC 13, 23, 38, 112; DAM NOV, POP**
See also AAYA 8; BEST 89:3; CA 25-28R; CANR 28; DLB 6; DLBY 82; MTCW

**Irving, Washington** [1783-1859]**NCLC 2, 19; DA; DAB; DAM MST; SSC 2; WLC**
See also CDALB 1640-1865; DLB 3, 11, 30, 59, 73, 74, 186; YABC 2

**Irwin, P. K.**
See Page, P(atricia) K(athleen)

**Isaacs, Jorge Ricardo** [1837-1895] **NCLC 70**

**Isaacs, Susan** [1943-] .... **CLC 32; DAM POP**
See also BEST 89:1; CA 89-92; CANR 20, 41, 65; INT CANR-20; MTCW

**Isherwood, Christopher (William Bradshaw)** [1904-1986] . **CLC 1, 9, 11, 14, 44; DAM DRAM, NOV**
See also CA 13-16R; 117; CANR 35; DLB 15, 195; DLBY 86; MTCW

**Ishiguro, Kazuo** [1954-]**CLC 27, 56, 59, 110; DAM NOV**
See also BEST 90:2; CA 120; CANR 49; DLB 194; MTCW

**Ishikawa, Hakuhin**
See Ishikawa, Takuboku

**Ishikawa, Takuboku** [1886(?)-1912]**TCLC 15; DAM POET; PC 10**
See also CA 113; 153

**Iskander, Fazil** [1929-] ...................... **CLC 47**
See also CA 102

**Isler, Alan (David)** [1934-] ................ **CLC 91**
See also CA 156

**Ivan IV** [1530-1584] ........................... **LC 17**

**Ivanov, Vyacheslav Ivanovich** [1866-1949] **TCLC 33**
See also CA 122

**Ivask, Ivar Vidrik** [1927-1992] ......... **CLC 14**
See also CA 37-40R; 139; CANR 24

**Ives, Morgan**
See Bradley, Marion Zimmer

**J. R. S.**
See Gogarty, Oliver St. John

**Jabran, Kahlil**

See Gibran, Kahlil

**Jabran, Khalil**
See Gibran, Kahlil

**Jackson, Daniel**
See Wingrove, David (John)

**Jackson, Jesse** [1908-1983] ................ **CLC 12**
See also BW 1; CA 25-28R; 109; CANR 27; CLR 28; MAICYA; SATA 2, 29; SATA-Obit 48

**Jackson, Laura (Riding)** [1901-1991]
See Riding, Laura
See also CA 65-68; 135; CANR 28; DLB 48

**Jackson, Sam**
See Trumbo, Dalton

**Jackson, Sara**
See Wingrove, David (John)

**Jackson, Shirley** [1919-1965]**CLC 11, 60, 87; DA; DAC; DAM MST; SSC 9; WLC**
See also AAYA 9; CA 1-4R; 25-28R; CANR 4, 52; CDALB 1941-1968; DLB 6; SATA 2

**Jacob, (Cyprien-)Max** [1876-1944] . **TCLC 6**
See also CA 104

**Jacobs, Harriet A(nn)** [1813(?)-1897] **NCLC 67**

**Jacobs, Jim** [1942-] ........................... **CLC 12**
See also CA 97-100; INT 97-100

**Jacobs, W(illiam) W(ymark)** [1863-1943] **TCLC 22**
See also CA 121; DLB 135

**Jacobsen, Jens Peter** [1847-1885] .. **NCLC 34**

**Jacobsen, Josephine** [1908-] ..... **CLC 48, 102**
See also CA 33-36R; CAAS 18; CANR 23, 48

**Jacobson, Dan** [1929-] .................... **CLC 4, 14**
See also CA 1-4R; CANR 2, 25, 66; DLB 14; MTCW

**Jacqueline**
See Carpentier (y Valmont), Alejo

**Jagger, Mick** [1944-] ......................... **CLC 17**

**Jahiz, Al-** [c. 776-869] .................... **CMLC 25**

**Jahiz, al-** [c. 780-c. 869] ................. **CMLC 25**

**Jakes, John (William)** [1932-]**CLC 29; DAM NOV, POP**
See also BEST 89:4; CA 57-60; CANR 10, 43, 66; DLBY 83; INT CANR-10; MTCW; SATA 62

**James, Andrew**
See Kirkup, James

**James, C(yril) L(ionel) R(obert)** [1901-1989] **CLC 33; BLCS**
See also BW 2; CA 117; 125; 128; CANR 62; DLB 125; MTCW

**James, Daniel (Lewis)** [1911-1988]
See Santiago, Danny
See also CA 125

**James, Dynely**
See Mayne, William (James Carter)

**James, Henry Sr.** [1811-1882] ........ **NCLC 53**

**James, Henry** [1843-1916]**TCLC 2, 11, 24, 40, 47, 64; DA; DAB; DAC; DAM MST, NOV; SSC 8; WLC**
See also CA 104; 132; CDALB 1865-1917; DLB 12, 71, 74, 189; DLBD 13; MTCW

**James, M. R.**
See James, Montague (Rhodes)
See also DLB 156

**James, Montague (Rhodes)** [1862-1936] **TCLC 6; SSC 16**
See also CA 104

**James, P. D.** .............................. **CLC 18, 46**
See also White, Phyllis Dorothy James
See also BEST 90:2; CDBLB 1960 to Present; DLB 87

**James, Philip**
See Moorcock, Michael (John)

**James, William** [1842-1910] ..... **TCLC 15, 32**
See also CA 109

**James I** [1394-1437] ........................... **LC 20**

**Jameson, Anna** [1794-1860] .......... **NCLC 43**
See also DLB 99, 166

**Jami, Nur al-Din 'Abd al-Rahman** [1414-1492] **LC 9**

**Jammes, Francis** [1868-1938] ........ **TCLC 75**

**Jandl, Ernst** [1925-] ........................... **CLC 34**

**Janowitz, Tama** [1957-] **CLC 43; DAM POP**
See also CA 106; CANR 52

**Japrisot, Sebastien** [1931-] ................ **CLC 90**

**Jarrell, Randall** [1914-1965]**CLC 1, 2, 6, 9, 13, 49; DAM POET**
See also CA 5-8R; 25-28R; CABS 2; CANR 6, 34; CDALB 1941-1968; CLR 6; DLB 48, 52; MAICYA; MTCW; SATA 7

**Jarry, Alfred** [1873-1907]**TCLC 2, 14; DAM DRAM; SSC 20**
See also CA 104; 153; DLB 192

**Jarvis, E. K.**
See Bloch, Robert (Albert); Ellison, Harlan (Jay); Silverberg, Robert

**Jeake, Samuel, Jr.**
See Aiken, Conrad (Potter)

**Jean Paul** [1763-1825] ...................... **NCLC 7**

**Jefferies, (John) Richard** [1848-1887] **NCLC 47**
See also DLB 98, 141; SATA 16

**Jeffers, (John) Robinson** [1887-1962]**CLC 2, 3, 11, 15, 54; DA; DAC; DAM MST, POET; PC 17; WLC**
See also CA 85-88; CANR 35; CDALB 1917-1929; DLB 45; MTCW

**Jefferson, Janet**
See Mencken, H(enry) L(ouis)

**Jefferson, Thomas** [1743-1826] ..... **NCLC 11**
See also CDALB 1640-1865; DLB 31

**Jeffrey, Francis** [1773-1850] .......... **NCLC 33**
See also DLB 107

**Jelakowitch, Ivan**
See Heijermans, Herman

**Jellicoe, (Patricia) Ann** [1927-] ........ **CLC 27**
See also CA 85-88; DLB 13

**Jen, Gish** .............................................. **CLC 70**
See also Jen, Lillian

**Jen, Lillian** [1956(?)-]
See Jen, Gish
See also CA 135

**Jenkins, (John) Robin** [1912-] .......... **CLC 52**
See also CA 1-4R; CANR 1; DLB 14

**Jennings, Elizabeth (Joan)** [1926-]**CLC 5, 14**
See also CA 61-64; CAAS 5; CANR 8, 39, 66; DLB 27; MTCW; SATA 66

**Jennings, Waylon** [1937-] ................. **CLC 21**

**Jensen, Johannes V.** [1873-1950] ... **TCLC 41**

**Jensen, Laura (Linnea)** [1948-] ........ **CLC 37**
See also CA 103

**Jerome, Jerome K(lapka)** [1859-1927]**TCLC 23**
See also CA 119; DLB 10, 34, 135

**Jerrold, Douglas William** [1803-1857]**NCLC 2**
See also DLB 158, 159

**Jewett, (Theodora) Sarah Orne** [1849-1909] **TCLC 1, 22; SSC 6**
See also CA 108; 127; DLB 12, 74; SATA 15

**Jewsbury, Geraldine (Endsor)** [1812-1880] **NCLC 22**
See also DLB 21

**Jhabvala, Ruth Prawer** [1927-]**CLC 4, 8, 29, 94; DAB; DAM NOV**
See also CA 1-4R; CANR 2, 29, 51; DLB 139, 194; INT CANR-29; MTCW

**Jibran, Kahlil**
See Gibran, Kahlil

**Jibran, Khalil**
See Gibran, Kahlil

**Jiles, Paulette** [1943-] ................. **CLC 13, 58**
See also CA 101

NCLC 3
See also DLB 150

**Karapanou, Margarita** [1946-] ......... **CLC 13**
See also CA 101

**Karinthy, Frigyes** [1887-1938] ....... **TCLC 47**

**Karl, Frederick R(obert)** [1927-] ...... **CLC 34**
See also CA 5-8R; CANR 3, 44

**Kastel, Warren**
See Silverberg, Robert

**Kataev, Evgeny Petrovich** [1903-1942]
See Petrov, Evgeny
See also CA 120

**Kataphusin**
See Ruskin, John

**Katz, Steve** [1935-] ........................... **CLC 47**
See also CA 25-28R; CAAS 14, 64; CANR 12;
DLBY 83

**Kauffman, Janet** [1945-] ................... **CLC 42**
See also CA 117; CANR 43; DLBY 86

**Kaufman, Bob (Garnell)** [1925-1986]**CLC 49**
See also BW 1; CA 41-44R; 118; CANR 22;
DLB 16, 41

**Kaufman, George S.** [1889-1961] ... **CLC 38;**
**DAM DRAM**
See also CA 108; 93-96; DLB 7; INT 108

**Kaufman, Sue** ...................................... **CLC 3, 8**
See also Barondess, Sue K(aufman)

**Kavafis, Konstantinos Petrou** [1863-1933]
See Cavafy, C(onstantine) P(eter)
See also CA 104

**Kavan, Anna** [1901-1968] ....... **CLC 5, 13, 82**
See also CA 5-8R; CANR 6, 57; MTCW

**Kavanagh, Dan**
See Barnes, Julian (Patrick)

**Kavanagh, Patrick (Joseph)** [1904-1967]**CLC**
**22**
See also CA 123; 25-28R; DLB 15, 20; MTCW

**Kawabata, Yasunari** [1899-1972]**CLC 2, 5, 9,**
**18, 107; DAM MULT; SSC 17**
See also CA 93-96; 33-36R; DLB 180

**Kaye, M(ary) M(argaret)** [1909-] ..... **CLC 28**
See also CA 89-92; CANR 24, 60; MTCW;
SATA 62

**Kaye, Mollie**
See Kaye, M(ary) M(argaret)

**Kaye-Smith, Sheila** [1887-1956] .... **TCLC 20**
See also CA 118; DLB 36

**Kaymor, Patrice Maguilene**
See Senghor, Leopold Sedar

**Kazan, Elia** [1909-] .................. **CLC 6, 16, 63**
See also CA 21-24R; CANR 32

**Kazantzakis, Nikos** [1883(?)-1957]**TCLC 2, 5,**
**33**
See also CA 105; 132; MTCW

**Kazin, Alfred** [1915-] .................. **CLC 34, 38**
See also CA 1-4R; CAAS 7; CANR 1, 45; DLB
67

**Keane, Mary Nesta (Skrine)** [1904-1996]
See Keane, Molly
See also CA 108; 114; 151

**Keane, Molly** ....................................... **CLC 31**
See also Keane, Mary Nesta (Skrine)
See also INT 114

**Keates, Jonathan** [1946(?)-] .............. **CLC 34**
See also CA 163

**Keaton, Buster** [1895-1966] .............. **CLC 20**

**Keats, John** [1795-1821]**NCLC 8; DA; DAB;**
**DAC; DAM MST, POET; PC 1; WLC**
See also CDBLB 1789-1832; DLB 96, 110

**Keene, Donald** [1922-] ....................... **CLC 34**
See also CA 1-4R; CANR 5

**Keillor, Garrison** ............................... **CLC 40**
See also Keillor, Gary (Edward)
See also AAYA 2; BEST 89:3; DLBY 87; SATA
58

**Keillor, Gary (Edward)** [1942-]
See Keillor, Garrison

See also CA 111; 117; CANR 36, 59; DAM
POP; MTCW

**Keith, Michael**
See Hubbard, L(afayette) Ron(ald)

**Keller, Gottfried** [1819-1890]**NCLC 2; SSC 26**
See also DLB 129

**Keller, Nora Okja** ............................. **CLC 109**

**Kellerman, Jonathan** [1949-] **CLC 44; DAM**
**POP**
See also BEST 90:1; CA 106; CANR 29, 51;
INT CANR-29

**Kelley, William Melvin** [1937-] ......... **CLC 22**
See also BW 1; CA 77-80; CANR 27; DLB 33

**Kellogg, Marjorie** [1922-] ................... **CLC 2**
See also CA 81-84

**Kellow, Kathleen**
See Hibbert, Eleanor Alice Burford

**Kelly, M(ilton) T(erry)** [1947-] ......... **CLC 55**
See also CA 97-100; CAAS 22; CANR 19, 43

**Kelman, James** [1946-] ................ **CLC 58, 86**
See also CA 148; DLB 194

**Kemal, Yashar** [1923-] ................ **CLC 14, 29**
See also CA 89-92; CANR 44

**Kemble, Fanny** [1809-1893] ........... **NCLC 18**
See also DLB 32

**Kemelman, Harry** [1908-1996] .......... **CLC 2**
See also AITN 1; CA 9-12R; 155; CANR 6;
DLB 28

**Kempe, Margery** [1373(?)-1440(?)] ....... **LC 6**
See also DLB 146

**Kempis, Thomas a** [1380-1471] .......... **LC 11**

**Kendall, Henry** [1839-1882] ........... **NCLC 12**

**Keneally, Thomas (Michael)** [1935-]**CLC 5, 8,**
**10, 14, 19, 27, 43; DAM NOV**
See also CA 85-88; CANR 10, 50; MTCW

**Kennedy, Adrienne (Lita)** [1931-] .. **CLC 66;**
**BLC 2; DAM MULT; DC 5**
See also BW 2; CA 103; CAAS 20; CABS 3;
CANR 26, 53; DLB 38

**Kennedy, John Pendleton** [1795-1870]**NCLC**
**2**
See also DLB 3

**Kennedy, Joseph Charles** [1929-]
See Kennedy, X. J.
See also CA 1-4R; CANR 4, 30, 40; SATA 14,
86

**Kennedy, William** [1928-] **CLC 6, 28, 34, 53;**
**DAM NOV**
See also AAYA 1; CA 85-88; CANR 14, 31;
DLB 143; DLBY 85; INT CANR-31;
MTCW; SATA 57

**Kennedy, X. J.** ................................... **CLC 8, 42**
See also Kennedy, Joseph Charles
See also CAAS 9; CLR 27; DLB 5; SAAS 22

**Kenny, Maurice (Francis)** [1929-] .. **CLC 87;**
**DAM MULT**
See also CA 144; CAAS 22; DLB 175; NNAL

**Kent, Kelvin**
See Kuttner, Henry

**Kenton, Maxwell**
See Southern, Terry

**Kenyon, Robert O.**
See Kuttner, Henry

**Kepler, Johannes** [1571-1630] ............. **LC 45**

**Kerouac, Jack** ...... **CLC 1, 2, 3, 5, 14, 29, 61**
See also Kerouac, Jean-Louis Lebris de
See also AAYA 25; CDALB 1941-1968; DLB
2, 16; DLBD 3; DLBY 95

**Kerouac, Jean-Louis Lebris de** [1922-1969]
See Kerouac, Jack
See also AITN 1; CA 5-8R; 25-28R; CANR 26,
54; DA; DAB; DAC; DAM MST, NOV,
POET, POP; MTCW; WLC

**Kerr, Jean** [1923-] ............................. **CLC 22**
See also CA 5-8R; CANR 7; INT CANR-7

**Kerr, M. E.** ..................................... **CLC 12, 35**
See also Meaker, Marijane (Agnes)

See also AAYA 2, 23; CLR 29; SAAS 1

**Kerr, Robert** ...................................... **CLC 55**

**Kerrigan, (Thomas) Anthony** [1918-]**CLC 4, 6**
See also CA 49-52; CAAS 11; CANR 4

**Kerry, Lois**
See Duncan, Lois

**Kesey, Ken (Elton)** [1935-]**CLC 1, 3, 6, 11, 46,**
**64; DA; DAB; DAC; DAM MST, NOV,**
**POP; WLC**
See also AAYA 25; CA 1-4R; CANR 22, 38,
66; CDALB 1968-1988; DLB 2, 16; MTCW;
SATA 66

**Kesselring, Joseph (Otto)** [1902-1967] . **C L C**
**45; DAM DRAM, MST**
See also CA 150

**Kessler, Jascha (Frederick)** [1929-] .... **CLC 4**
See also CA 17-20R; CANR 8, 48

**Kettelkamp, Larry (Dale)** [1933-] .... **CLC 12**
See also CA 29-32R; CANR 16; SAAS 3; SATA
2

**Key, Ellen** [1849-1926] ................... **TCLC 65**

**Keyber, Conny**
See Fielding, Henry

**Keyes, Daniel** [1927-] .... **CLC 80; DA; DAC;**
**DAM MST, NOV**
See also AAYA 23; CA 17-20R; CANR 10, 26,
54; SATA 37

**Keynes, John Maynard** [1883-1946]**TCLC 64**
See also CA 114; 162, 163; DLBD 10

**Khanshendel, Chiron**
See Rose, Wendy

**Khayyam, Omar** [1048-1131]**CMLC 11; DAM**
**POET; PC 8**

**Kherdian, David** [1931-] .................. **CLC 6, 9**
See also CA 21-24R; CAAS 2; CANR 39; CLR
24; JRDA; MAICYA; SATA 16, 74

**Khlebnikov, Velimir** ......................... **TCLC 20**
See also Khlebnikov, Viktor Vladimirovich

**Khlebnikov, Viktor Vladimirovich** [1885-1922]
See Khlebnikov, Velimir
See also CA 117

**Khodasevich, Vladislav (Felitsianovich)** [1886-
1939] ...............................................
**TCLC 15**
See also CA 115

**Kielland, Alexander Lange** [1849-1906]
**TCLC 5**
See also CA 104

**Kiely, Benedict** [1919-] ................ **CLC 23, 43**
See also CA 1-4R; CANR 2; DLB 15

**Kienzle, William X(avier)** [1928-] .. **CLC 25;**
**DAM POP**
See also CA 93-96; CAAS 1; CANR 9, 31, 59;
INT CANR-31; MTCW

**Kierkegaard, Soren** [1813-1855] ... **NCLC 34**

**Killens, John Oliver** [1916-1987] ..... **CLC 10**
See also BW 2; CA 77-80; 123; CAAS 2; CANR
26; DLB 33

**Killigrew, Anne** [1660-1685] ................. **LC 4**
See also DLB 131

**Kim**
See Simenon, Georges (Jacques Christian)

**Kincaid, Jamaica** [1949-]**CLC 43, 68; BLC 2;**
**DAM MULT, NOV**
See also AAYA 13; BW 2; CA 125; CANR 47,
59; DLB 157

**King, Francis (Henry)** [1923-] .... **CLC 8, 53;**
**DAM NOV**
See also CA 1-4R; CANR 1, 33; DLB 15, 139;
MTCW

**King, Kennedy**
See Brown, George Douglas

**King, Martin Luther, Jr.** [1929-1968]**CLC 83;**
**BLC 2; DA; DAB; DAC; DAM MST,**
**MULT; WLCS**
See also BW 2; CA 25-28; CANR 27, 44; CAP
2; MTCW; SATA 14

**King, Stephen (Edwin)** [1947-]CLC 12, 26, 37, 61, 113; DAM NOV, POP; SSC 17
See also AAYA 1, 17; BEST 90:1; CA 61-64; CANR 1, 30, 52; DLB 143; DLBY 80; JRDA; MTCW; SATA 9, 55

**King, Steve**
See King, Stephen (Edwin)

**King, Thomas** [1943-] CLC 89; DAC; DAM MULT
See also CA 144; DLB 175; NNAL; SATA 96

**Kingman, Lee** ............................. CLC 17
See also Natti, (Mary) Lee
See also SAAS 3; SATA 1, 67

**Kingsley, Charles** [1819-1875] ....... NCLC 35
See also DLB 21, 32, 163, 190; YABC 2

**Kingsley, Sidney** [1906-1995] ........... CLC 44
See also CA 85-88; 147; DLB 7

**Kingsolver, Barbara** [1955-]CLC 55, 81; DAM POP
See also AAYA 15; CA 129; 134; CANR 60; INT 134

**Kingston, Maxine (Ting Ting) Hong** [1940-] CLC 12, 19, 58; DAM MULT, NOV; WLCS
See also AAYA 8; CA 69-72; CANR 13, 38; DLB 173; DLBY 80; INT CANR-13; MTCW; SATA 53

**Kinnell, Galway** [1927-]CLC 1, 2, 3, 5, 13, 29
See also CA 9-12R; CANR 10, 34, 66; DLB 5; DLBY 87; INT CANR-34; MTCW

**Kinsella, Thomas** [1928-] .............. CLC 4, 19
See also CA 17-20R; CANR 15; DLB 27; MTCW

**Kinsella, W(illiam) P(atrick)** [1935-]CLC 27, 43; DAC; DAM NOV, POP
See also AAYA 7; CA 97-100; CAAS 7; CANR 21, 35, 66; INT CANR-21; MTCW

**Kipling, (Joseph) Rudyard** [1865-1936]TCLC 8, 17; DA; DAB; DAC; DAM MST, POET; PC 3; SSC 5; WLC
See also CA 105; 120; CANR 33; CDBLB 1890-1914; CLR 39; DLB 19, 34, 141, 156; MAICYA; MTCW; YABC 2

**Kirkup, James** [1918-] ........................ CLC 1
See also CA 1-4R; CAAS 4; CANR 2; DLB 27; SATA 12

**Kirkwood, James** [1930(?)-1989] ........ CLC 9
See also AITN 2; CA 1-4R; 128; CANR 6, 40

**Kirshner, Sidney**
See Kingsley, Sidney

**Kis, Danilo** [1935-1989] ..................... CLC 57
See also CA 109; 118; 129; CANR 61; DLB 181; MTCW

**Kivi, Aleksis** [1834-1872] ................. NCLC 30

**Kizer, Carolyn (Ashley)** [1925-] CLC 15, 39, 80; DAM POET
See also CA 65-68; CAAS 5; CANR 24; DLB 5, 169

**Klabund** [1890-1928] ...................... TCLC 44
See also CA 162; DLB 66

**Klappert, Peter** [1942-] ...................... CLC 57
See also CA 33-36R; DLB 5

**Klein, A(braham) M(oses)** [1909-1972] CLC 19; DAB; DAC; DAM MST
See also CA 101; 37-40R; DLB 68

**Klein, Norma** [1938-1989] ................ CLC 30
See also AAYA 2; CA 41-44R; 128; CANR 15, 37; CLR 2, 19; INT CANR-15; JRDA; MAICYA; SAAS 1; SATA 7, 57

**Klein, T(heodore) E(ibon) D(onald)** [1947-] CLC 34
See also CA 119; CANR 44

**Kleist, Heinrich von** [1777-1811]NCLC 2, 37; DAM DRAM; SSC 22
See also DLB 90

**Klima, Ivan** [1931-] ...... CLC 56; DAM NOV
See also CA 25-28R; CANR 17, 50

**Klimentov, Andrei Platonovich** [1899-1951]
See Platonov, Andrei
See also CA 108

**Klinger, Friedrich Maximilian von** [1752-1831] NCLC 1
See also DLB 94

**Klingsor the Magician**
See Hartmann, Sadakichi

**Klopstock, Friedrich Gottlieb** [1724-1803] NCLC 11
See also DLB 97

**Knapp, Caroline** [1959-] ................... CLC 99
See also CA 154

**Knebel, Fletcher** [1911-1993] ............ CLC 14
See also AITN 1; CA 1-4R; 140; CAAS 3; CANR 1, 36; SATA 36; SATA-Obit 75

**Knickerbocker, Diedrich**
See Irving, Washington

**Knight, Etheridge** [1931-1991]CLC 40; BLC 2; DAM POET; PC 14
See also BW 1; CA 21-24R; 133; CANR 23; DLB 41

**Knight, Sarah Kemble** [1666-1727] ...... LC 7
See also DLB 24, 200

**Knister, Raymond** [1899-1932] ...... TCLC 56
See also DLB 68

**Knowles, John** [1926-]CLC 1, 4, 10, 26; DA; DAC; DAM MST, NOV
See also AAYA 10; CA 17-20R; CANR 40; CDALB 1968-1988; DLB 6; MTCW; SATA 8, 89

**Knox, Calvin M.**
See Silverberg, Robert

**Knox, John** [c. 1505-1572] .................. LC 37
See also DLB 132

**Knye, Cassandra**
See Disch, Thomas M(ichael)

**Koch, C(hristopher) J(ohn)** [1932-] . CLC 42
See also CA 127

**Koch, Christopher**
See Koch, C(hristopher) J(ohn)

**Koch, Kenneth** [1925-] .. CLC 5, 8, 44; DAM POET
See also CA 1-4R; CANR 6, 36, 57; DLB 5; INT CANR-36; SATA 65

**Kochanowski, Jan** [1530-1584] ........... LC 10

**Kock, Charles Paul de** [1794-1871]NCLC 16

**Koda Shigeyuki** [1867-1947]
See Rohan, Koda
See also CA 121

**Koestler, Arthur** [1905-1983] CLC 1, 3, 6, 8, 15, 33
See also CA 1-4R; 109; CANR 1, 33; CDBLB 1945-1960; DLBY 83; MTCW

**Kogawa, Joy Nozomi** [1935-] CLC 78; DAC; DAM MST, MULT
See also CA 101; CANR 19, 62

**Kohout, Pavel** [1928-] ...................... CLC 13
See also CA 45-48; CANR 3

**Koizumi, Yakumo**
See Hearn, (Patricio) Lafcadio (Tessima Carlos)

**Kolmar, Gertrud** [1894-1943] ........ TCLC 40

**Komunyakaa, Yusef** [1947-] ...... CLC 86, 94; BLCS
See also CA 147; DLB 120

**Konrad, George**
See Konrad, Gyoergy

**Konrad, Gyoergy** [1933-] ....... CLC 4, 10, 73
See also CA 85-88

**Konwicki, Tadeusz** [1926-] ..... CLC 8, 28, 54
See also CA 101; CAAS 9; CANR 39, 59; MTCW

**Koontz, Dean R(ay)** [1945-] .. CLC 78; DAM NOV, POP
See also AAYA 9; BEST 89:3, 90:2; CA 108; CANR 19, 36, 52; MTCW; SATA 92

**Kopernik, Mikolaj**
See Copernicus, Nicolaus

**Kopit, Arthur (Lee)** [1937-] .. CLC 1, 18, 33; DAM DRAM
See also AITN 1; CA 81-84; CABS 3; DLB 7; MTCW

**Kops, Bernard** [1926-] ........................ CLC 4
See also CA 5-8R; DLB 13

**Kornbluth, C(yril) M.** [1923-1958] . TCLC 8
See also CA 105; 160; DLB 8

**Korolenko, V. G.**
See Korolenko, Vladimir Galaktionovich

**Korolenko, Vladimir**
See Korolenko, Vladimir Galaktionovich

**Korolenko, Vladimir G.**
See Korolenko, Vladimir Galaktionovich

**Korolenko, Vladimir Galaktionovich** [1853-1921] ...................... TCLC 22
See also CA 121

**Korzybski, Alfred (Habdank Skarbek)** [1879-1950] ......................
TCLC 61
See also CA 123; 160

**Kosinski, Jerzy (Nikodem)** [1933-1991] C L C 1, 2, 3, 6, 10, 15, 53, 70; DAM NOV
See also CA 17-20R; 134; CANR 9, 46; DLB 2; DLBY 82; MTCW

**Kostelanetz, Richard (Cory)** [1940-] CLC 28
See also CA 13-16R; CAAS 8; CANR 38

**Kostrowitzki, Wilhelm Apollinaris de** [1880-1918]
See Apollinaire, Guillaume
See also CA 104

**Kotlowitz, Robert** [1924-] ................... CLC 4
See also CA 33-36R; CANR 36

**Kotzebue, August (Friedrich Ferdinand) von** [1761-1819] .............................. NCLC 25
See also DLB 94

**Kotzwinkle, William** [1938-] .. CLC 5, 14, 35
See also CA 45-48; CANR 3, 44; CLR 6; DLB 173; MAICYA; SATA 24, 70

**Kowna, Stancy**
See Szymborska, Wislawa

**Kozol, Jonathan** [1936-] .................... CLC 17
See also CA 61-64; CANR 16, 45

**Kozoll, Michael** [1940(?)-] ................. CLC 35

**Kramer, Kathryn** [19(?)-] ................. CLC 34

**Kramer, Larry** [1935-] CLC 42; DAM POP; DC 8
See also CA 124; 126; CANR 60

**Krasicki, Ignacy** [1735-1801] ........... NCLC 8

**Krasinski, Zygmunt** [1812-1859] ..... NCLC 4

**Kraus, Karl** [1874-1936] .................. TCLC 5
See also CA 104; DLB 118

**Kreve (Mickevicius), Vincas** [1882-1954]
TCLC 27

**Kristeva, Julia** [1941-] ...................... CLC 77
See also CA 154

**Kristofferson, Kris** [1936-] ............... CLC 26
See also CA 104

**Krizanc, John** [1956-] ....................... CLC 57

**Krleza, Miroslav** [1893-1981] ............ CLC 8
See also CA 97-100; 105; CANR 50; DLB 147

**Kroetsch, Robert** [1927-]CLC 5, 23, 57; DAC; DAM POET
See also CA 17-20R; CANR 8, 38; DLB 53; MTCW

**Kroetz, Franz**
See Kroetz, Franz Xaver

**Kroetz, Franz Xaver** [1946-] ............. CLC 41
See also CA 130

**Kroker, Arthur (W.)** [1945-] .............. CLC 77
See also CA 161

**Kropotkin, Peter (Alekseievich)** [1842-1921]
TCLC 36
See also CA 119

**Krotkov, Yuri** [1917-] ........................ CLC 19
See also CA 102

**Krumb**
See Crumb, R(obert)
**Krumgold, Joseph (Quincy)** [1908-1980]**CLC 12**
See also CA 9-12R; 101; CANR 7; MAICYA; SATA 1, 48; SATA-Obit 23
**Krumwitz**
See Crumb, R(obert)
**Krutch, Joseph Wood** [1893-1970] ... **CLC 24**
See also CA 1-4R; 25-28R; CANR 4; DLB 63
**Krutzch, Gus**
See Eliot, T(homas) S(tearns)
**Krylov, Ivan Andreevich** [1768(?)-1844] **NCLC 1**
See also DLB 150
**Kubin, Alfred (Leopold Isidor)** [1877-1959] **TCLC 23**
See also CA 112; 149; DLB 81
**Kubrick, Stanley** [1928-] ................. **CLC 16**
See also CA 81-84; CANR 33; DLB 26
**Kumin, Maxine (Winokur)** [1925-]**CLC 5, 13, 28; DAM POET; PC 15**
See also AITN 2; CA 1-4R; CAAS 8; CANR 1, 21, 69; DLB 5; MTCW; SATA 12
**Kundera, Milan** [1929-]**CLC 4, 9, 19, 32, 68; DAM NOV; SSC 24**
See also AAYA 2; CA 85-88; CANR 19, 52; MTCW
**Kunene, Mazisi (Raymond)** [1930-] . **CLC 85**
See also BW 1; CA 125; DLB 117
**Kunitz, Stanley (Jasspon)** [1905-] **CLC 6, 11, 14; PC 19**
See also CA 41-44R; CANR 26, 57; DLB 48; INT CANR-26; MTCW
**Kunze, Reiner** [1933-] ....................... **CLC 10**
See also CA 93-96; DLB 75
**Kuprin, Aleksandr Ivanovich** [1870-1938] **TCLC 5**
See also CA 104
**Kureishi, Hanif** [1954(?)-] ................. **CLC 64**
See also CA 139; DLB 194
**Kurosawa, Akira** [1910-] ....... **CLC 16; DAM MULT**
See also AAYA 11; CA 101; CANR 46
**Kushner, Tony** [1957(?)-] ....... **CLC 81; DAM DRAM**
See also CA 144
**Kuttner, Henry** [1915-1958] ........... **TCLC 10**
See also Vance, Jack
See also CA 107; 157; DLB 8
**Kuzma, Greg** [1944-] .......................... **CLC 7**
See also CA 33-36R
**Kuzmin, Mikhail** [1872(?)-1936] ... **TCLC 40**
**Kyd, Thomas** [1558-1594] ........ **LC 22; DAM DRAM; DC 3**
See also DLB 62
**Kyprianos, Iossif**
See Samarakis, Antonis
**La Bruyere, Jean de** [1645-1696] ........ **LC 17**
**Lacan, Jacques (Marie Emile)** [1901-1981] **CLC 75**
See also CA 121; 104
**Laclos, Pierre Ambroise Francois Choderlos de** [1741-1803] ................................ **NCLC 4**
**La Colere, Francois**
See Aragon, Louis
**Lacolere, Francois**
See Aragon, Louis
**La Deshabilleuse**
See Simenon, Georges (Jacques Christian)
**Lady Gregory**
See Gregory, Isabella Augusta (Persse)
**Lady of Quality, A**
See Bagnold, Enid
**La Fayette, Marie (Madelaine Pioche de la Vergne Comtes** [1634-1693] ......... **LC 2**
**Lafayette, Rene**

See Hubbard, L(afayette) Ron(ald)
**Laforgue, Jules** [1860-1887]**NCLC 5, 53; PC 14; SSC 20**
**Lagerkvist, Paer (Fabian)** [1891-1974]**CLC 7, 10, 13, 54; DAM DRAM, NOV**
See also Lagerkvist, Par
See also CA 85-88; 49-52; MTCW
**Lagerkvist, Par** ........................ **SSC 12**
See also Lagerkvist, Paer (Fabian)
**Lagerloef, Selma (Ottiliana Lovisa)** [1858-1940] ......................................
**TCLC 4, 36**
See also Lagerlof, Selma (Ottiliana Lovisa)
See also CA 108; SATA 15
**Lagerlof, Selma (Ottiliana Lovisa)**
See Lagerloef, Selma (Ottiliana Lovisa)
See also CLR 7; SATA 15
**La Guma, (Justin) Alex(ander)** [1925-1985] **CLC 19; BLCS; DAM NOV**
See also BW 1; CA 49-52; 118; CANR 25; DLB 117; MTCW
**Laidlaw, A. K.**
See Grieve, C(hristopher) M(urray)
**Lainez, Manuel Mujica**
See Mujica Lainez, Manuel
See also HW
**Laing, R(onald) D(avid)** [1927-1989]**CLC 95**
See also CA 107; 129; CANR 34; MTCW
**Lamartine, Alphonse (Marie Louis Prat) de** [1790-1869]**NCLC 11; DAM POET; PC 16**
**Lamb, Charles** [1775-1834] .. **NCLC 10; DA; DAB; DAC; DAM MST; WLC**
See also CDBLB 1789-1832; DLB 93, 107, 163; SATA 17
**Lamb, Lady Caroline** [1785-1828] **NCLC 38**
See also DLB 116
**Lamming, George (William)** [1927-]**CLC 2, 4, 66; BLC 2; DAM MULT**
See also BW 2; CA 85-88; CANR 26; DLB 125; MTCW
**L'Amour, Louis (Dearborn)** [1908-1988]**CLC 25, 55; DAM NOV, POP**
See also AAYA 16; AITN 2; BEST 89:2; CA 1-4R; 125; CANR 3, 25, 40; DLBY 80; MTCW
**Lampedusa, Giuseppe (Tomasi) di** [1896-1957] **TCLC 13**
See also Tomasi di Lampedusa, Giuseppe
See also CA 164; DLB 177
**Lampman, Archibald** [1861-1899] **NCLC 25**
See also DLB 92
**Lancaster, Bruce** [1896-1963] ........... **CLC 36**
See also CA 9-10; CAP 1; SATA 9
**Lanchester, John** .................................. **CLC 99**
**Landau, Mark Alexandrovich**
See Aldanov, Mark (Alexandrovich)
**Landau-Aldanov, Mark Alexandrovich**
See Aldanov, Mark (Alexandrovich)
**Landis, Jerry**
See Simon, Paul (Frederick)
**Landis, John** [1950-] ........................ **CLC 26**
See also CA 112; 122
**Landolfi, Tommaso** [1908-1979] . **CLC 11, 49**
See also CA 127; 117; DLB 177
**Landon, Letitia Elizabeth** [1802-1838]**NCLC 15**
See also DLB 96
**Landor, Walter Savage** [1775-1864]**NCLC 14**
See also DLB 93, 107
**Landwirth, Heinz** [1927-]
See Lind, Jakov
See also CA 9-12R; CANR 7
**Lane, Patrick** [1939-] **CLC 25; DAM POET**
See also CA 97-100; CANR 54; DLB 53; INT 97-100
**Lang, Andrew** [1844-1912] ............. **TCLC 16**
See also CA 114; 137; DLB 98, 141, 184; MAICYA; SATA 16

**Lang, Fritz** [1890-1976] ........... **CLC 20, 103**
See also CA 77-80; 69-72; CANR 30
**Lange, John**
See Crichton, (John) Michael
**Langer, Elinor** [1939-] ...................... **CLC 34**
See also CA 121
**Langland, William** [1330(?)-1400(?)] **LC 19; DA; DAB; DAC; DAM MST, POET**
See also DLB 146
**Langstaff, Launcelot**
See Irving, Washington
**Lanier, Sidney** [1842-1881] .. **NCLC 6; DAM POET**
See also DLB 64; DLBD 13; MAICYA; SATA 18
**Lanyer, Aemilia** [1569-1645] ......... **LC 10, 30**
See also DLB 121
**Lao Tzu** ............................................. **CMLC 7**
**Lapine, James (Elliot)** [1949-] .......... **CLC 39**
See also CA 123; 130; CANR 54; INT 130
**Larbaud, Valery (Nicolas)** [1881-1957]**TCLC 9**
See also CA 106; 152
**Lardner, Ring**
See Lardner, Ring(gold) W(ilmer)
**Lardner, Ring W., Jr.**
See Lardner, Ring(gold) W(ilmer)
**Lardner, Ring(gold) W(ilmer)** [1885-1933] **TCLC 2, 14**
See also CA 104; 131; CDALB 1917-1929; DLB 11, 25, 86; DLBD 16; MTCW
**Laredo, Betty**
See Codrescu, Andrei
**Larkin, Maia**
See Wojciechowska, Maia (Teresa)
**Larkin, Philip (Arthur)** [1922-1985]**CLC 3, 5, 8, 9, 13, 18, 33, 39, 64; DAB; DAM MST, POET; PC 21**
See also CA 5-8R; 117; CANR 24, 62; CDBLB 1960 to Present; DLB 27; MTCW
**Larra (y Sanchez de Castro), Mariano Jose de** [1809-1837] ............................. **NCLC 17**
**Larsen, Eric** [1941-] .......................... **CLC 55**
See also CA 132
**Larsen, Nella** [1891-1964] . **CLC 37; BLC 2; DAM MULT**
See also BW 1; CA 125; DLB 51
**Larson, Charles R(aymond)** [1938-] **CLC 31**
See also CA 53-56; CANR 4
**Larson, Jonathan** [1961-1996] .......... **CLC 99**
See also CA 156
**Las Casas, Bartolome de** [1474-1566] **LC 31**
**Lasch, Christopher** [1932-1994] ..... **CLC 102**
See also CA 73-76; 144; CANR 25; MTCW
**Lasker-Schueler, Else** [1869-1945] **TCLC 57**
See also DLB 66, 124
**Laski, Harold** [1893-1950] ............. **TCLC 79**
**Latham, Jean Lee** [1902-1995] ......... **CLC 12**
See also AITN 1; CA 5-8R; CANR 7; CLR 50; MAICYA; SATA 2, 68
**Latham, Mavis**
See Clark, Mavis Thorpe
**Lathen, Emma** ...................................... **CLC 2**
See also Hennissart, Martha; Latsis, Mary J(ane)
**Lathrop, Francis**
See Leiber, Fritz (Reuter, Jr.)
**Latsis, Mary J(ane)** [1927(?)-1997]
See Lathen, Emma
See also CA 85-88; 162
**Lattimore, Richmond (Alexander)** [1906-1984] **CLC 3**
See also CA 1-4R; 112; CANR 1
**Laughlin, James** [1914-1997] ........... **CLC 49**
See also CA 21-24R; 162; CAAS 22; CANR 9, 47; DLB 48; DLBY 96, 97
**Laurence, (Jean) Margaret (Wemyss)** [1926-1987] **CLC 3, 6, 13, 50, 62; DAC; DAM**

MST; SSC 7
  See also CA 5-8R; 121; CANR 33; DLB 53;
  MTCW; SATA-Obit 50
**Laurent, Antoine** [1952-] .................. **CLC 50**
**Lauscher, Hermann**
  See Hesse, Hermann
**Lautreamont, Comte de** [1846-1870] . **N C L C**
  **12; SSC 14**
**Laverty, Donald**
  See Blish, James (Benjamin)
**Lavin, Mary** [1912-1996]**CLC 4, 18, 99; SSC 4**
  See also CA 9-12R; 151; CANR 33; DLB 15;
  MTCW
**Lavond, Paul Dennis**
  See Kornbluth, C(yril) M.; Pohl, Frederik
**Lawler, Raymond Evenor** [1922-] .... **CLC 58**
  See also CA 103
**Lawrence, D(avid) H(erbert Richards)** [1885-
  1930] ......................................................
  **TCLC 2, 9, 16, 33, 48, 61; DA; DAB; DAC;**
  **DAM MST, NOV, POET; SSC 4, 19; WLC**
    See also CA 104; 121; CDBLB 1914-1945;
    DLB 10, 19, 36, 98, 162, 195; MTCW
**Lawrence, T(homas) E(dward)** [1888-1935]
  **TCLC 18**
    See also Dale, Colin
    See also CA 115; DLB 195
**Lawrence of Arabia**
  See Lawrence, T(homas) E(dward)
**Lawson, Henry (Archibald Hertzberg)** [1867-
  1922] ......................................................
  **TCLC 27; SSC 18**
    See also CA 120
**Lawton, Dennis**
  See Faust, Frederick (Schiller)
**Laxness, Halldor** .................................. **CLC 25**
  See also Gudjonsson, Halldor Kiljan
**Layamon** [fl. c. 1200-] ................... **CMLC 10**
  See also DLB 146
**Laye, Camara** [1928-1980]**CLC 4, 38; BLC 2;**
  **DAM MULT**
    See also BW 1; CA 85-88; 97-100; CANR 25;
    MTCW
**Layton, Irving (Peter)** [1912-] .... **CLC 2, 15;**
  **DAC; DAM MST, POET**
    See also CA 1-4R; CANR 2, 33, 43, 66; DLB
    88; MTCW
**Lazarus, Emma** [1849-1887] ........... **NCLC 8**
**Lazarus, Felix**
  See Cable, George Washington
**Lazarus, Henry**
  See Slavitt, David R(ytman)
**Lea, Joan**
  See Neufeld, John (Arthur)
**Leacock, Stephen (Butler)** [1869-1944]**T C L C**
  **2; DAC; DAM MST**
    See also CA 104; 141; DLB 92
**Lear, Edward** [1812-1888]................ **NCLC 3**
    See also CLR 1; DLB 32, 163, 166; MAICYA;
    SATA 18
**Lear, Norman (Milton)** [1922-] ........ **CLC 12**
    See also CA 73-76
**Leautaud, Paul** [1872-1956] ........... **TCLC 83**
    See also DLB 65
**Leavis, F(rank) R(aymond)** [1895-1978]**C L C**
  **24**
    See also CA 21-24R; 77-80; CANR 44; MTCW
**Leavitt, David** [1961-] .. **CLC 34; DAM POP**
    See also CA 116; 122; CANR 50, 62; DLB 130;
    INT 122
**Leblanc, Maurice (Marie Emile)** [1864-1941]
  **TCLC 49**
    See also CA 110
**Lebowitz, Fran(ces Ann)** [1951(?)-] **CLC 11,**
  **36**
    See also CA 81-84; CANR 14, 60; INT CANR-
    14; MTCW

**Lebrecht, Peter**
  See Tieck, (Johann) Ludwig
**le Carre, John** .................... **CLC 3, 5, 9, 15, 28**
    See also Cornwell, David (John Moore)
    See also BEST 89:4; CDBLB 1960 to Present;
    DLB 87
**Le Clezio, J(ean) M(arie) G(ustave)** [1940-]
  **CLC 31**
    See also CA 116; 128; DLB 83
**Leconte de Lisle, Charles-Marie-Rene** [1818-
  1894] ......................................................
  **NCLC 29**
**Le Coq, Monsieur**
  See Simenon, Georges (Jacques Christian)
**Leduc, Violette** [1907-1972] .............. **CLC 22**
    See also CA 13-14; 33-36R; CANR 69; CAP 1
**Ledwidge, Francis** [1887(?)-1917] . **TCLC 23**
    See also CA 123; DLB 20
**Lee, Andrea** [1953-]..**CLC 36; BLC 2; DAM**
  **MULT**
    See also BW 1; CA 125
**Lee, Andrew**
  See Auchincloss, Louis (Stanton)
**Lee, Chang-rae** [1965-] ...................... **CLC 91**
    See also CA 148
**Lee, Don L.** .............................................. **CLC 2**
    See also Madhubuti, Haki R.
**Lee, George W(ashington)** [1894-1976] **C L C**
  **52; BLC 2; DAM MULT**
    See also BW 1; CA 125; DLB 51
**Lee, (Nelle) Harper** [1926-]**CLC 12, 60; DA;**
  **DAB; DAC; DAM MST, NOV; WLC**
    See also AAYA 13; CA 13-16R; CANR 51;
    CDALB 1941-1968; DLB 6; MTCW; SATA
    11
**Lee, Helen Elaine** [1959(?)-] .............. **CLC 86**
    See also CA 148
**Lee, Julian**
  See Latham, Jean Lee
**Lee, Larry**
  See Lee, Lawrence
**Lee, Laurie** [1914-1997]**CLC 90; DAB; DAM**
  **POP**
    See also CA 77-80; 158; CANR 33; DLB 27;
    MTCW
**Lee, Lawrence** [1941-1990] .............. **CLC 34**
    See also CA 131; CANR 43
**Lee, Manfred B(ennington)** [1905-1971]**C L C**
  **11**
    See also Queen, Ellery
    See also CA 1-4R; 29-32R; CANR 2; DLB 137
**Lee, Shelton Jackson** [1957(?)-] .... **CLC 105;**
  **BLCS; DAM MULT**
    See also Lee, Spike
    See also BW 2; CA 125; CANR 42
**Lee, Spike**
  See Lee, Shelton Jackson
    See also AAYA 4
**Lee, Stan** [1922-] ................................ **CLC 17**
    See also AAYA 5; CA 108; 111; INT 111
**Lee, Tanith** [1947-] ............................ **CLC 46**
    See also AAYA 15; CA 37-40R; CANR 53;
    SATA 8, 88
**Lee, Vernon** .......................................... **TCLC 5**
    See also Paget, Violet
    See also DLB 57, 153, 156, 174, 178
**Lee, William**
  See Burroughs, William S(eward)
**Lee, Willy**
  See Burroughs, William S(eward)
**Lee-Hamilton, Eugene (Jacob)** [1845-1907]
  **TCLC 22**
    See also CA 117
**Leet, Judith** [1935-] .......................... **CLC 11**
**Le Fanu, Joseph Sheridan** [1814-1873]**NCLC**
  **9, 58; DAM POP; SSC 14**
    See also DLB 21, 70, 159, 178

**Leffland, Ella** [1931-] ........................ **CLC 19**
    See also CA 29-32R; CANR 35; DLBY 84; INT
    CANR-35; SATA 65
**Leger, Alexis**
  See Leger, (Marie-Rene Auguste) Alexis Saint-
  Leger
**Leger, (Marie-Rene Auguste) Alexis Saint-
  Leger** [1887-1975] **CLC 4, 11, 46; DAM**
  **POET; PC 23**
    See also CA 13-16R; 61-64; CANR 43; MTCW
**Leger, Saintleger**
  See Leger, (Marie-Rene Auguste) Alexis Saint-
  Leger
**Le Guin, Ursula K(roeber)** [1929-]**CLC 8, 13,**
  **22, 45, 71; DAB; DAC; DAM MST, POP;**
  **SSC 12**
    See also AAYA 9; AITN 1; CA 21-24R; CANR
    9, 32, 52; CDALB 1968-1988; CLR 3, 28;
    DLB 8, 52; INT CANR-32; JRDA; MAICYA;
    MTCW; SATA 4, 52
**Lehmann, Rosamond (Nina)** [1901-1990]**CLC
  5**
    See also CA 77-80; 131; CANR 8; DLB 15
**Leiber, Fritz (Reuter, Jr.)** [1910-1992]**CLC 25**
    See also CA 45-48; 139; CANR 2, 40; DLB 8;
    MTCW; SATA 45; SATA-Obit 73
**Leibniz, Gottfried Wilhelm von** [1646-1716]
  **LC 35**
    See also DLB 168
**Leimbach, Martha** [1963-]
  See Leimbach, Marti
    See also CA 130
**Leimbach, Marti** ................................. **CLC 65**
    See also Leimbach, Martha
**Leino, Eino** .......................................... **TCLC 24**
    See also Loennbohm, Armas Eino Leopold
**Leiris, Michel (Julien)** [1901-1990] .. **CLC 61**
    See also CA 119; 128; 132
**Leithauser, Brad** [1953-] .................... **CLC 27**
    See also CA 107; CANR 27; DLB 120
**Lelchuk, Alan** [1938-] ......................... **CLC 5**
    See also CA 45-48; CAAS 20; CANR 1
**Lem, Stanislaw** [1921-] .......... **CLC 8, 15, 40**
    See also CA 105; CAAS 1; CANR 32; MTCW
**Lemann, Nancy** [1956-]....................... **CLC 39**
    See also CA 118; 136
**Lemonnier, (Antoine Louis) Camille** [1844-
  1913] ...................................... **TCLC 22**
    See also CA 121
**Lenau, Nikolaus** [1802-1850] ......... **NCLC 16**
**L'Engle, Madeleine (Camp Franklin)** [1918-]
  **CLC 12; DAM POP**
    See also AAYA 1; AITN 2; CA 1-4R; CANR 3,
    21, 39, 66; CLR 1, 14; DLB 52; JRDA;
    MAICYA; MTCW; SAAS 15; SATA 1, 27,
    75
**Lengyel, Jozsef** [1896-1975] ................ **CLC 7**
    See also CA 85-88; 57-60
**Lenin** [1870-1924]
  See Lenin, V. I.
    See also CA 121
**Lenin, V. I.** ......................................... **TCLC 67**
    See also Lenin
**Lennon, John (Ono)** [1940-1980] **CLC 12, 35**
    See also CA 102
**Lennox, Charlotte Ramsay** [1729(?)-1804]
  **NCLC 23**
    See also DLB 39
**Lentricchia, Frank (Jr.)** [1940-] ........ **CLC 34**
    See also CA 25-28R; CANR 19
**Lenz, Siegfried** [1926-] ...................... **CLC 27**
    See also CA 89-92; DLB 75
**Leonard, Elmore (John, Jr.)** [1925-]**CLC 28,**
  **34, 71; DAM POP**
    See also AAYA 22; AITN 1; BEST 89:1, 90:4;
    CA 81-84; CANR 12, 28, 53; DLB 173; INT
    CANR-28; MTCW

Leonard, Hugh ...................... CLC 19
See also Byrne, John Keyes
See also DLB 13
Leonov, Leonid (Maximovich) [1899-1994]
CLC 92; DAM NOV
See also CA 129; MTCW
Leopardi, (Conte) Giacomo [1798-1837]
NCLC 22
Le Reveler
See Artaud, Antonin (Marie Joseph)
Lerman, Eleanor [1952-] ................... CLC 9
See also CA 85-88; CANR 69
Lerman, Rhoda [1936-] ..................... CLC 56
See also CA 49-52
Lermontov, Mikhail Yuryevich [1814-1841]
NCLC 47; PC 18
Leroux, Gaston [1868-1927] ........... TCLC 25
See also CA 108; 136; CANR 69; SATA 65
Lesage, Alain-Rene [1668-1747] .......... LC 28
Leskov, Nikolai (Semyonovich) [1831-1895]
NCLC 25
Lessing, Doris (May) [1919-]CLC 1, 2, 3, 6, 10,
15, 22, 40, 94; DA; DAB; DAC; DAM MST,
NOV; SSC 6; WLCS
See also CA 9-12R; CAAS 14; CANR 33, 54;
CDBLB 1960 to Present; DLB 15, 139;
DLBY 85; MTCW
Lessing, Gotthold Ephraim [1729-1781]LC 8
See also DLB 97
Lester, Richard [1932-] ...................... CLC 20
Lever, Charles (James) [1806-1872]NCLC 23
See also DLB 21
Leverson, Ada [1865(?)-1936(?)] ... TCLC 18
See also Elaine
See also CA 117; DLB 153
Levertov, Denise [1923-1997]CLC 1, 2, 3, 5, 8,
15, 28, 66; DAM POET; PC 11
See also CA 1-4R; 163; CAAS 19; CANR 3,
29, 50; DLB 5, 165; INT CANR-29; MTCW
Levi, Jonathan ..................................... CLC 76
Levi, Peter (Chad Tigar) [1931-] ...... CLC 41
See also CA 5-8R; CANR 34; DLB 40
Levi, Primo [1919-1987]CLC 37, 50; SSC 12
See also CA 13-16R; 122; CANR 12, 33, 61;
DLB 177; MTCW
Levin, Ira [1929-] ........ CLC 3, 6; DAM POP
See also CA 21-24R; CANR 17, 44; MTCW;
SATA 66
Levin, Meyer [1905-1981]CLC 7; DAM POP
See also AITN 1; CA 9-12R; 104; CANR 15;
DLB 9, 28; DLBY 81; SATA 21; SATA-Obit
27
Levine, Norman [1924-] .................... CLC 54
See also CA 73-76; CAAS 23; CANR 14; DLB
88
Levine, Philip [1928-] CLC 2, 4, 5, 9, 14, 33;
DAM POET; PC 22
See also CA 9-12R; CANR 9, 37, 52; DLB 5
Levinson, Deirdre [1931-] ................. CLC 49
See also CA 73-76
Levi-Strauss, Claude [1908-] ............ CLC 38
See also CA 1-4R; CANR 6, 32, 57; MTCW
Levitin, Sonia (Wolff) [1934-] ......... CLC 17
See also AAYA 13; CA 29-32R; CANR 14, 32;
JRDA; MAICYA; SAAS 2; SATA 4, 68
Levon, O. U.
See Kesey, Ken (Elton)
Levy, Amy [1861-1889] ................... NCLC 59
See also DLB 156
Lewes, George Henry [1817-1878] NCLC 25
See also DLB 55, 144
Lewis, Alun [1915-1944] ................... TCLC 3
See also CA 104; DLB 20, 162
Lewis, C. Day
See Day Lewis, C(ecil)
Lewis, C(live) S(taples) [1898-1963]CLC 1, 3,
6, 14, 27; DA; DAB; DAC; DAM MST,

NOV, POP; WLC
See also AAYA 3; CA 81-84; CANR 33;
CDBLB 1945-1960; CLR 3, 27; DLB 15,
100, 160; JRDA; MAICYA; MTCW; SATA
13
Lewis, Janet [1899-] ......................... CLC 41
See also Winters, Janet Lewis
See also CA 9-12R; CANR 29, 63; CAP 1;
DLBY 87
Lewis, Matthew Gregory [1775-1818] N C L C
11, 62
See also DLB 39, 158, 178
Lewis, (Harry) Sinclair [1885-1951]TCLC 4,
13, 23, 39; DA; DAB; DAC; DAM MST,
NOV; WLC
See also CA 104; 133; CDALB 1917-1929;
DLB 9, 102; DLBD 1; MTCW
Lewis, (Percy) Wyndham [1882(?)-1957]
TCLC 2, 9
See also CA 104; 157; DLB 15
Lewisohn, Ludwig [1883-1955] ..... TCLC 19
See also CA 107; DLB 4, 9, 28, 102
Lewton, Val [1904-1951] ................ TCLC 76
Leyner, Mark [1956-] ....................... CLC 92
See also CA 110; CANR 28, 53
Lezama Lima, Jose [1910-1976] . CLC 4, 10,
101; DAM MULT
See also CA 77-80; DLB 113; HW
L'Heureux, John (Clarke) [1934-] .... CLC 52
See also CA 13-16R; CANR 23, 45
Liddell, C. H.
See Kuttner, Henry
Lie, Jonas (Lauritz Idemil) [1833-1908(?)]
TCLC 5
See also CA 115
Lieber, Joel [1937-1971] ...................... CLC 6
See also CA 73-76; 29-32R
Lieber, Stanley Martin
See Lee, Stan
Lieberman, Laurence (James) [1935-]CLC 4,
36
See also CA 17-20R; CANR 8, 36
Lieh Tzu [fl. 7th cent. B.C.-5th cent. B.C.]
CMLC 27
Lieksman, Anders
See Haavikko, Paavo Juhani
Li Fei-kan [1904-]
See Pa Chin
See also CA 105
Lifton, Robert Jay [1926-] ................. CLC 67
See also CA 17-20R; CANR 27; INT CANR-
27; SATA 66
Lightfoot, Gordon [1938-] ................. CLC 26
See also CA 109
Lightman, Alan P(aige) [1948-] ........ CLC 81
See also CA 141; CANR 63
Ligotti, Thomas (Robert) [1953-] ... CLC 44;
SSC 16
See also CA 123; CANR 49
Li Ho [791-817] .................................... PC 13
Liliencron, (Friedrich Adolf Axel) Detlev von
[1844-1909] ............................... TCLC 18
See also CA 117
Lilly, William [1602-1681] ................... LC 27
Lima, Jose Lezama
See Lezama Lima, Jose
Lima Barreto, Afonso Henrique de [1881-1922]
TCLC 23
See also CA 117
Limonov, Edward [1944-] .................. CLC 67
See also CA 137
Lin, Frank
See Atherton, Gertrude (Franklin Horn)
Lincoln, Abraham [1809-1865] ...... NCLC 18
Lind, Jakov ...................... CLC 1, 2, 4, 27, 82
See also Landwirth, Heinz
See also CAAS 4

Lindbergh, Anne (Spencer) Morrow [1906-]
CLC 82; DAM NOV
See also CA 17-20R; CANR 16; MTCW; SATA
33
Lindsay, David [1878-1945] .......... TCLC 15
See also CA 113
Lindsay, (Nicholas) Vachel [1879-1931]TCLC
17; DA; DAC; DAM MST, POET; PC 23;
WLC
See also CA 114; 135; CDALB 1865-1917;
DLB 54; SATA 40
Linke-Poot
See Doeblin, Alfred
Linney, Romulus [1930-] ................... CLC 51
See also CA 1-4R; CANR 40, 44
Linton, Eliza Lynn [1822-1898] ..... NCLC 41
See also DLB 18
Li Po [701-763] .................................. CMLC 2
Lipsius, Justus [1547-1606] ............... LC 16
Lipsyte, Robert (Michael) [1938-] .. CLC 21;
DA; DAC; DAM MST, NOV
See also AAYA 7; CA 17-20R; CANR 8, 57;
CLR 23; JRDA; MAICYA; SATA 5, 68
Lish, Gordon (Jay) [1934-] . CLC 45; SSC 18
See also CA 113; 117; DLB 130; INT 117
Lispector, Clarice [1925-1977] ......... CLC 43
See also CA 139; 116; DLB 113
Littell, Robert [1935(?)-] .................... CLC 42
See also CA 109; 112; CANR 64
Little, Malcolm [1925-1965]
See Malcolm X
See also BW 1; CA 125; 111; DA; DAB; DAC;
DAM MST, MULT; MTCW
Littlewit, Humphrey Gent.
See Lovecraft, H(oward) P(hillips)
Litwos
See Sienkiewicz, Henryk (Adam Alexander
Pius)
Liu, E [1857-1909] ........................... TCLC 15
See also CA 115
Lively, Penelope (Margaret) [1933-]CLC 32,
50; DAM NOV
See also CA 41-44R; CANR 29, 67; CLR 7;
DLB 14, 161; JRDA; MAICYA; MTCW;
SATA 7, 60
Livesay, Dorothy (Kathleen) [1909-] . CLC 4,
15, 79; DAC; DAM MST, POET
See also AITN 2; CA 25-28R; CAAS 8; CANR
36, 67; DLB 68; MTCW
Livy [c. 59B.C.-c. 17] ...................... CMLC 11
Lizardi, Jose Joaquin Fernandez de [1776-
1827] ...................................... NCLC 30
Llewellyn, Richard
See Llewellyn Lloyd, Richard Dafydd Vivian
See also DLB 15
Llewellyn Lloyd, Richard Dafydd Vivian [1906-
1983] .........................................................
CLC 7, 80
See also Llewellyn, Richard
See also CA 53-56; 111; CANR 7; SATA 11;
SATA-Obit 37
Llosa, (Jorge) Mario (Pedro) Vargas
See Vargas Llosa, (Jorge) Mario (Pedro)
Lloyd, Manda
See Mander, (Mary) Jane
Lloyd Webber, Andrew [1948-]
See Webber, Andrew Lloyd
See also AAYA 1; CA 116; 149; DAM DRAM;
SATA 56
Llull, Ramon [c. 1235-c. 1316] ....... CMLC 12
Locke, Alain (Le Roy) [1886-1954]TCLC 43;
BLCS
See also BW 1; CA 106; 124; DLB 51
Locke, John [1632-1704] ................. LC 7, 35
See also DLB 101
Locke-Elliott, Sumner
See Elliott, Sumner Locke

Macdonald, Ross ........ **CLC 1, 2, 3, 14, 34, 41**
See also Millar, Kenneth
See also DLBD 6
**MacDougal, John**
See Blish, James (Benjamin)
**MacEwen, Gwendolyn (Margaret)** [1941-1987]
**CLC 13, 55**
See also CA 9-12R; 124; CANR 7, 22; DLB
53; SATA 50; SATA-Obit 55
**Macha, Karel Hynek** [1810-1846] . **NCLC 46**
**Machado (y Ruiz), Antonio** [1875-1939]
**TCLC 3**
See also CA 104; DLB 108
**Machado de Assis, Joaquim Maria** [1839-1908]
**TCLC 10; BLC 2; SSC 24**
See also CA 107; 153
**Machen, Arthur** .................. **TCLC 4; SSC 20**
See also Jones, Arthur Llewellyn
See also DLB 36, 156, 178
**Machiavelli, Niccolo** [1469-1527] .. **LC 8, 36;**
**DA; DAB; DAC; DAM MST; WLCS**
**MacInnes, Colin** [1914-1976] ........ **CLC 4, 23**
See also CA 69-72; 65-68; CANR 21; DLB 14;
MTCW
**MacInnes, Helen (Clark)** [1907-1985]**CLC 27,**
**39; DAM POP**
See also CA 1-4R; 117; CANR 1, 28, 58; DLB
87; MTCW; SATA 22; SATA-Obit 44
**Mackay, Mary** [1855-1924]
See Corelli, Marie
See also CA 118
**Mackenzie, Compton (Edward Montague)**
[1883-1972] ................................................
**CLC 18**
See also CA 21-22; 37-40R; CAP 2; DLB 34,
100
**Mackenzie, Henry** [1745-1831] ...... **NCLC 41**
See also DLB 39
**Mackintosh, Elizabeth** [1896(?)-1952]
See Tey, Josephine
See also CA 110
**MacLaren, James**
See Grieve, C(hristopher) M(urray)
**Mac Laverty, Bernard** [1942-] ......... **CLC 31**
See also CA 116; 118; CANR 43; INT 118
**MacLean, Alistair (Stuart)** [1922(?)-1987]
**CLC 3, 13, 50, 63; DAM POP**
See also CA 57-60; 121; CANR 28, 61; MTCW;
SATA 23; SATA-Obit 50
**Maclean, Norman (Fitzroy)** [1902-1990]**C L C**
**78; DAM POP; SSC 13**
See also CA 102; 132; CANR 49
**MacLeish, Archibald** [1892-1982] . **CLC 3, 8,**
**14, 68; DAM POET**
See also CA 9-12R; 106; CANR 33, 63; DLB
4, 7, 45; DLBY 82; MTCW
**MacLennan, (John) Hugh** [1907-1990]**CLC 2,**
**14, 92; DAC; DAM MST**
See also CA 5-8R; 142; CANR 33; DLB 68;
MTCW
**MacLeod, Alistair** [1936-] .... **CLC 56; DAC;**
**DAM MST**
See also CA 123; DLB 60
**Macleod, Fiona**
See Sharp, William
**MacNeice, (Frederick) Louis** [1907-1963]
**CLC 1, 4, 10, 53; DAB; DAM POET**
See also CA 85-88; CANR 61; DLB 10, 20;
MTCW
**MacNeill, Dand**
See Fraser, George MacDonald
**Macpherson, James** [1736-1796] ......... **LC 29**
See also Ossian
See also DLB 109
**Macpherson, (Jean) Jay** [1931-] ....... **CLC 14**
See also CA 5-8R; DLB 53
**MacShane, Frank** [1927-] ................. **CLC 39**

See also CA 9-12R; CANR 3, 33; DLB 111
**Macumber, Mari**
See Sandoz, Mari(e Susette)
**Madach, Imre** [1823-1864] ............. **NCLC 19**
**Madden, (Jerry) David** [1933-] ..... **CLC 5, 15**
See also CA 1-4R; CAAS 3; CANR 4, 45; DLB
6; MTCW
**Maddern, Al(an)**
See Ellison, Harlan (Jay)
**Madhubuti, Haki R.** [1942-]**CLC 6, 73; BLC**
**2; DAM MULT, POET; PC 5**
See also Lee, Don L.
See also BW 2; CA 73-76; CANR 24, 51; DLB
5, 41; DLBD 8
**Maepenn, Hugh**
See Kuttner, Henry
**Maepenn, K. H.**
See Kuttner, Henry
· **Maeterlinck, Maurice** [1862-1949] . **TCLC 3;**
**DAM DRAM**
See also CA 104; 136; DLB 192; SATA 66
**Maginn, William** [1794-1842] .......... **NCLC 8**
See also DLB 110, 159
**Mahapatra, Jayanta** [1928-] . **CLC 33; DAM**
**MULT**
See also CA 73-76; CAAS 9; CANR 15, 33, 66
**Mahfouz, Naguib (Abdel Aziz Al-Sabilgi)**
[1911(?)-]
See Mahfuz, Najib
See also BEST 89:2; CA 128; CANR 55; DAM
NOV; MTCW
**Mahfuz, Najib** ............................. **CLC 52, 55**
See also Mahfouz, Naguib (Abdel Aziz Al-
Sabilgi)
See also DLBY 88
**Mahon, Derek** [1941-] ........................ **CLC 27**
See also CA 113; 128; DLB 40
**Mailer, Norman** [1923-]**CLC 1, 2, 3, 4, 5, 8, 11,**
**14, 28, 39, 74, 111; DA; DAB; DAC; DAM**
**MST, NOV, POP**
See also AITN 2; CA 9-12R; CABS 1; CANR
28; CDALB 1968-1988; DLB 2, 16, 28, 185;
DLBD 3; DLBY 80, 83; MTCW
**Maillet, Antonine** [1929-] ....... **CLC 54; DAC**
See also CA 115; 120; CANR 46; DLB 60; INT
120
**Mais, Roger** [1905-1955] ................... **TCLC 8**
See also BW 1; CA 105; 124; DLB 125; MTCW
**Maistre, Joseph de** [1753-1821] ..... **NCLC 37**
**Maitland, Frederic** [1850-1906] ..... **TCLC 65**
**Maitland, Sara (Louise)** [1950-] ....... **CLC 49**
See also CA 69-72; CANR 13, 59
**Major, Clarence** [1936-]**CLC 3, 19, 48; BLC 2;**
**DAM MULT**
See also BW 2; CA 21-24R; CAAS 6; CANR
13, 25, 53; DLB 33
**Major, Kevin (Gerald)** [1949-]**CLC 26; DAC**
See also AAYA 16; CA 97-100; CANR 21, 38;
CLR 11; DLB 60; INT CANR-21; JRDA;
MAICYA; SATA 32, 82
**Maki, James**
See Ozu, Yasujiro
**Malabaila, Damiano**
See Levi, Primo
**Malamud, Bernard** [1914-1986]**CLC 1, 2, 3, 5,**
**8, 9, 11, 18, 27, 44, 78, 85; DA; DAB; DAC;**
**DAM MST, NOV, POP; SSC 15; WLC**
See also AAYA 16; CA 5-8R; 118; CABS 1;
CANR 28, 62; CDALB 1941-1968; DLB 2,
28, 152; DLBY 80, 86; MTCW
**Malan, Herman**
See Bosman, Herman Charles; Bosman, Herman
Charles
**Malaparte, Curzio** [1898-1957] ..... **TCLC 52**
**Malcolm, Dan**
See Silverberg, Robert
**Malcolm X** ............... **CLC 82; BLC 2; WLCS**

See also Little, Malcolm
**Malherbe, Francois de** [1555-1628] ...... **LC 5**
**Mallarme, Stephane** [1842-1898]**NCLC 4, 41;**
**DAM POET; PC 4**
**Mallet-Joris, Francoise** [1930-] ........ **CLC 11**
See also CA 65-68; CANR 17; DLB 83
**Malley, Ern**
See McAuley, James Phillip
**Mallowan, Agatha Christie**
See Christie, Agatha (Mary Clarissa)
**Maloff, Saul** [1922-] ........................... **CLC 5**
See also CA 33-36R
**Malone, Louis**
See MacNeice, (Frederick) Louis
**Malone, Michael (Christopher)** [1942-] **C L C**
**43**
See also CA 77-80; CANR 14, 32, 57
**Malory, (Sir) Thomas** [1410(?)-1471(?)] .. **L C**
**11; DA; DAB; DAC; DAM MST; WLCS**
See also CDBLB Before 1660; DLB 146; SATA
59; SATA-Brief 33
**Malouf, (George Joseph) David** [1934-] **C L C**
**28, 86**
See also CA 124; CANR 50
**Malraux, (Georges-)Andre** [1901-1976] **C L C**
**1, 4, 9, 13, 15, 57; DAM NOV**
See also CA 21-22; 69-72; CANR 34, 58; CAP
2; DLB 72; MTCW
**Malzberg, Barry N(athaniel)** [1939-] . **CLC 7**
See also CA 61-64; CAAS 4; CANR 16; DLB
8
**Mamet, David (Alan)** [1947-] **CLC 9, 15, 34,**
**46, 91; DAM DRAM; DC 4**
See also AAYA 3; CA 81-84; CABS 3; CANR
15, 41, 67; DLB 7; MTCW
**Mamoulian, Rouben (Zachary)** [1897-1987]
**CLC 16**
See also CA 25-28R; 124
**Mandelstam, Osip (Emilievich)** [1891(?)-
1938(?)] ................................................
**TCLC 2, 6; PC 14**
See also CA 104; 150
**Mander, (Mary) Jane** [1877-1949] **TCLC 31**
See also CA 162
**Mandeville, John** [fl. 1350-] .......... **CMLC 19**
See also DLB 146
**Mandiargues, Andre Pieyre de** .......... **CLC 41**
See also Pieyre de Mandiargues, Andre
See also DLB 83
**Mandrake, Ethel Belle**
See Thurman, Wallace (Henry)
**Mangan, James Clarence** [1803-1849]**N C L C**
**27**
**Maniere, J.-E.**
See Giraudoux, (Hippolyte) Jean
**Manley, (Mary) Delariviere** [1672(?)-1724]
**LC 1**
See also DLB 39, 80
**Mann, Abel**
See Creasey, John
**Mann, Emily** [1952-] ..............................**DC 7**
See also CA 130; CANR 55
**Mann, (Luiz) Heinrich** [1871-1950] **TCLC 9**
See also CA 106; 164; DLB 66
**Mann, (Paul) Thomas** [1875-1955]**TCLC 2, 8,**
**14, 21, 35, 44, 60; DA; DAB; DAC; DAM**
**MST, NOV; SSC 5; WLC**
See also CA 104; 128; DLB 66; MTCW
**Mannheim, Karl** [1893-1947] ......... **TCLC 65**
**Manning, David**
See Faust, Frederick (Schiller)
**Manning, Frederic** [1887(?)-1935] **TCLC 25**
See also CA 124
**Manning, Olivia** [1915-1980] ........ **CLC 5, 19**
See also CA 5-8R; 101; CANR 29; MTCW
**Mano, D. Keith** [1942-] .................. **CLC 2, 10**
See also CA 25-28R; CAAS 6; CANR 26, 57;

DLB 6

**Mansfield, Katherine** TCLC 2, 8, 39; DAB; SSC 9, 23; WLC
See also Beauchamp, Kathleen Mansfield
See also DLB 162

**Manso, Peter** [1940-] ......................... CLC 39
See also CA 29-32R; CANR 44

**Mantecon, Juan Jimenez**
See Jimenez (Mantecon), Juan Ramon

**Manton, Peter**
See Creasey, John

**Man Without a Spleen, A**
See Chekhov, Anton (Pavlovich)

**Manzoni, Alessandro** [1785-1873] . NCLC 29

**Mapu, Abraham (ben Jekutiel)** [1808-1867]
NCLC 18

**Mara, Sally**
See Queneau, Raymond

**Marat, Jean Paul** [1743-1793] ............. LC 10

**Marcel, Gabriel Honore** [1889-1973] CLC 15
See also CA 102; 45-48; MTCW

**Marchbanks, Samuel**
See Davies, (William) Robertson

**Marchi, Giacomo**
See Bassani, Giorgio

**Margulies, Donald** ............................... CLC 76

**Marie de France** [c. 12th cent. -] CMLC 8; PC 22

**Marie de l'Incarnation** [1599-1672] .... LC 10

**Marier, Captain Victor**
See Griffith, D(avid Lewelyn) W(ark)

**Mariner, Scott**
See Pohl, Frederik

**Marinetti, Filippo Tommaso** [1876-1944]
TCLC 10
See also CA 107; DLB 114

**Marivaux, Pierre Carlet de Chamblain de**
[1688-1763] ......................... LC 4; DC 7

**Markandaya, Kamala** ..................... CLC 8, 38
See also Taylor, Kamala (Purnaiya)

**Markfield, Wallace** [1926-] ................. CLC 8
See also CA 69-72; CAAS 3; DLB 2, 28

**Markham, Edwin** [1852-1940] ....... TCLC 47
See also CA 160; DLB 54, 186

**Markham, Robert**
See Amis, Kingsley (William)

**Marks, J**
See Highwater, Jamake (Mamake)

**Marks-Highwater, J**
See Highwater, Jamake (Mamake)

**Markson, David M(errill)** [1927-] .... CLC 67
See also CA 49-52; CANR 1

**Marley, Bob** ......................................... CLC 17
See also Marley, Robert Nesta

**Marley, Robert Nesta** [1945-1981]
See Marley, Bob
See also CA 107; 103

**Marlowe, Christopher** [1564-1593] ... LC 22;
DA; DAB; DAC; DAM DRAM, MST; DC 1; WLC
See also CDBLB Before 1660; DLB 62

**Marlowe, Stephen** [1928-]
See Queen, Ellery
See also CA 13-16R; CANR 6, 55

**Marmontel, Jean-Francois** [1723-1799] LC 2

**Marquand, John P(hillips)** [1893-1960] C L C 2, 10
See also CA 85-88; DLB 9, 102

**Marques, Rene** [1919-1979] .. CLC 96; DAM MULT; HLC
See also CA 97-100; 85-88; DLB 113; HW

**Marquez, Gabriel (Jose) Garcia**
See Garcia Marquez, Gabriel (Jose)

**Marquis, Don(ald Robert Perry)** [1878-1937]
TCLC 7
See also CA 104; 166; DLB 11, 25

**Marric, J. J.**

See Creasey, John

**Marryat, Frederick** [1792-1848] ...... NCLC 3
See also DLB 21, 163

**Marsden, James**
See Creasey, John

**Marsh, (Edith) Ngaio** [1899-1982] CLC 7, 53; DAM POP
See also CA 9-12R; CANR 6, 58; DLB 77; MTCW

**Marshall, Garry** [1934-] ..................... CLC 17
See also AAYA 3; CA 111; SATA 60

**Marshall, Paule** [1929-] CLC 27, 72; BLC 3; DAM MULT; SSC 3
See also BW 2; CA 77-80; CANR 25; DLB 157; MTCW

**Marsten, Richard**
See Hunter, Evan

**Marston, John** [1576-1634] ...... LC 33; DAM DRAM
See also DLB 58, 172

**Martha, Henry**
See Harris, Mark

**Marti, Jose** [1853-1895] ...... NCLC 63; DAM MULT; HLC
See also DLB 118; DLB 65

**Martial** [c. 40-c. 104] ........................... PC 10

**Martin, Ken**
See Hubbard, L(afayette) Ron(ald)

**Martin, Richard**
See Creasey, John

**Martin, Steve** [1945-] ......................... CLC 30
See also CA 97-100; CANR 30; MTCW

**Martin, Valerie** [1948-] ..................... CLC 89
See also BEST 90:2; CA 85-88; CANR 49

**Martin, Violet Florence** [1862-1915] TCLC 51

**Martin, Webber**
See Silverberg, Robert

**Martindale, Patrick Victor**
See White, Patrick (Victor Martindale)

**Martin du Gard, Roger** [1881-1958] TCLC 24
See also CA 118; DLB 65

**Martineau, Harriet** [1802-1876] .... NCLC 26
See also DLB 21, 55, 159, 163, 166, 190; YABC 2

**Martines, Julia**
See O'Faolain, Julia

**Martinez, Enrique Gonzalez**
See Gonzalez Martinez, Enrique

**Martinez, Jacinto Benavente y**
See Benavente (y Martinez), Jacinto

**Martinez Ruiz, Jose** [1873-1967]
See Azorin; Ruiz, Jose Martinez
See also CA 93-96; HW

**Martinez Sierra, Gregorio** [1881-1947] TCLC 6
See also CA 115

**Martinez Sierra, Maria (de la O'LeJarraga)**
[1874-1974] ............................... TCLC 6
See also CA 115

**Martinsen, Martin**
See Follett, Ken(neth Martin)

**Martinson, Harry (Edmund)** [1904-1978]
CLC 14
See also CA 77-80; CANR 34

**Marut, Ret**
See Traven, B.

**Marut, Robert**
See Traven, B.

**Marvell, Andrew** [1621-1678] LC 4, 43; DA; DAB; DAC; DAM MST, POET; PC 10; WLC
See also CDBLB 1660-1789; DLB 131

**Marx, Karl (Heinrich)** [1818-1883] NCLC 17
See also DLB 129

**Masaoka Shiki** ................................... TCLC 18
See also Masaoka Tsunenori

**Masaoka Tsunenori** [1867-1902]
See Masaoka Shiki

See also CA 117

**Masefield, John (Edward)** [1878-1967] C L C 11, 47; DAM POET
See also CA 19-20; 25-28R; CANR 33; CAP 2; CDBLB 1890-1914; DLB 10, 19, 153, 160; MTCW; SATA 19

**Maso, Carole** [19(?)-] ......................... CLC 44

**Mason, Bobbie Ann** [1940-] CLC 28, 43, 82; SSC 4
See also AAYA 5; CA 53-56; CANR 11, 31, 58; DLB 173; DLBY 87; INT CANR-31; MTCW

**Mason, Ernst**
See Pohl, Frederik

**Mason, Lee W.**
See Malzberg, Barry N(athaniel)

**Mason, Nick** [1945-] ........................... CLC 35

**Mason, Tally**
See Derleth, August (William)

**Mass, William**
See Gibson, William

**Masters, Edgar Lee** [1868-1950] TCLC 2, 25; DA; DAC; DAM MST, POET; PC 1; WLCS
See also CA 104; 133; CDALB 1865-1917; DLB 54; MTCW

**Masters, Hilary** [1928-] ..................... CLC 48
See also CA 25-28R; CANR 13, 47

**Mastrosimone, William** [19(?)-] ........ CLC 36

**Mathe, Albert**
See Camus, Albert

**Mather, Cotton** [1663-1728] ................. LC 38
See also CDALB 1640-1865; DLB 24, 30, 140

**Mather, Increase** [1639-1723] ............. LC 38
See also DLB 24

**Matheson, Richard Burton** [1926-] .. CLC 37
See also CA 97-100; DLB 8, 44; INT 97-100

**Mathews, Harry** [1930-] ............... CLC 6, 52
See also CA 21-24R; CAAS 6; CANR 18, 40

**Mathews, John Joseph** [1894-1979] CLC 84; DAM MULT
See also CA 19-20; 142; CANR 45; CAP 2; DLB 175; NNAL

**Mathias, Roland (Glyn)** [1915-] ........ CLC 45
See also CA 97-100; CANR 19, 41; DLB 27

**Matsuo Basho** [1644-1694] ..................... PC 3
See also DAM POET

**Mattheson, Rodney**
See Creasey, John

**Matthews, Greg** [1949-] ..................... CLC 45
See also CA 135

**Matthews, William (Procter, III)** [1942-1997]
CLC 40
See also CA 29-32R; 162; CAAS 18; CANR 12, 57; DLB 5

**Matthias, John (Edward)** [1941-] ....... CLC 9
See also CA 33-36R; CANR 56

**Matthiessen, Peter** [1927-] CLC 5, 7, 11, 32, 64; DAM NOV
See also AAYA 6; BEST 90:4; CA 9-12R; CANR 21, 50; DLB 6, 173; MTCW; SATA 27

**Maturin, Charles Robert** [1780(?)-1824]
NCLC 6
See also DLB 178

**Matute (Ausejo), Ana Maria** [1925-] CLC 11
See also CA 89-92; MTCW

**Maugham, W. S.**
See Maugham, W(illiam) Somerset

**Maugham, W(illiam) Somerset** [1874-1965]
CLC 1, 11, 15, 67, 93; DA; DAB; DAC; DAM DRAM, MST, NOV; SSC 8; WLC
See also CA 5-8R; 25-28R; CANR 40; CDBLB 1914-1945; DLB 10, 36, 77, 100, 162, 195; MTCW; SATA 54

**Maugham, William Somerset**
See Maugham, W(illiam) Somerset

See Wilde, Oscar (Fingal O'Flahertie Wills)
**Meltzer, Milton** [1915-] ...................... **CLC 26**
See also AAYA 8; CA 13-16R; CANR 38; CLR 13; DLB 61; JRDA; MAICYA; SAAS 1; SATA 1, 50, 80
**Melville, Herman** [1819-1891]**NCLC 3, 12, 29, 45, 49; DA; DAB; DAC; DAM MST, NOV; SSC 1, 17; WLC**
See also AAYA 25; CDALB 1640-1865; DLB 3, 74; SATA 59
**Menander** [c. 342B.C.-c. 292B.C.] . **CMLC 9; DAM DRAM; DC 3**
See also DLB 176
**Mencken, H(enry) L(ouis)** [1880-1956]**TCLC 13**
See also CA 105; 125; CDALB 1917-1929; DLB 11, 29, 63, 137; MTCW
**Mendelsohn, Jane** [1965(?)-] ............. **CLC 99**
See also CA 154
**Mercer, David** [1928-1980] ...... **CLC 5; DAM DRAM**
See also CA 9-12R; 102; CANR 23; DLB 13; MTCW
**Merchant, Paul**
See Ellison, Harlan (Jay)
**Meredith, George** [1828-1909] **TCLC 17, 43; DAM POET**
See also CA 117; 153; CDBLB 1832-1890; DLB 18, 35, 57, 159
**Meredith, William (Morris)** [1919-]**CLC 4, 13, 22, 55; DAM POET**
See also CA 9-12R; CAAS 14; CANR 6, 40; DLB 5
**Merezhkovsky, Dmitry Sergeyevich** [1865-1941] ......................................... **TCLC 29**
**Merimee, Prosper** [1803-1870] **NCLC 6, 65; SSC 7**
See also DLB 119, 192
**Merkin, Daphne** [1954-] ..................... **CLC 44**
See also CA 123
**Merlin, Arthur**
See Blish, James (Benjamin)
**Merrill, James (Ingram)** [1926-1995] **CLC 2, 3, 6, 8, 13, 18, 34, 91; DAM POET**
See also CA 13-16R; 147; CANR 10, 49, 63; DLB 5, 165; DLBY 85; INT CANR-10; MTCW
**Merriman, Alex**
See Silverberg, Robert
**Merriman, Brian** [1747-1805] ........ **NCLC 70**
**Merritt, E. B.**
See Waddington, Miriam
**Merton, Thomas** [1915-1968]**CLC 1, 3, 11, 34, 83; PC 10**
See also CA 5-8R; 25-28R; CANR 22, 53; DLB 48; DLBY 81; MTCW
**Merwin, W(illiam) S(tanley)** [1927-]**CLC 1, 2, 3, 5, 8, 13, 18, 45, 88; DAM POET**
See also CA 13-16R; CANR 15, 51; DLB 5, 169; INT CANR-15; MTCW
**Metcalf, John** [1938-] ....................... **CLC 37**
See also CA 113; DLB 60
**Metcalf, Suzanne**
See Baum, L(yman) Frank
**Mew, Charlotte (Mary)** [1870-1928] **TCLC 8**
See also CA 105; DLB 19, 135
**Mewshaw, Michael** [1943-] ................. **CLC 9**
See also CA 53-56; CANR 7, 47; DLBY 80
**Meyer, June**
See Jordan, June
**Meyer, Lynn**
See Slavitt, David R(ytman)
**Meyer-Meyrink, Gustav** [1868-1932]
See Meyrink, Gustav
See also CA 117
**Meyers, Jeffrey** [1939-] ...................... **CLC 39**
See also CA 73-76; CANR 54; DLB 111

**Meynell, Alice (Christina Gertrude Thompson)** [1847-1922] ................................. **TCLC 6**
See also CA 104; DLB 19, 98
**Meyrink, Gustav** ............................... **TCLC 21**
See also Meyer-Meyrink, Gustav
See also DLB 81
**Michaels, Leonard** [1933-]**CLC 6, 25; SSC 16**
See also CA 61-64; CANR 21, 62; DLB 130; MTCW
**Michaux, Henri** [1899-1984] ......... **CLC 8, 19**
See also CA 85-88; 114
**Micheaux, Oscar** [1884-1951] ........ **TCLC 76**
See also DLB 50
**Michelangelo** [1475-1564] ................ **LC 12**
**Michelet, Jules** [1798-1874] ............ **NCLC 31**
**Michener, James A(lbert)** [1907(?)-1997]**CLC 1, 5, 11, 29, 60, 109; DAM NOV, POP**
See also AITN 1; BEST 90:1; CA 5-8R; 161; CANR 21, 45, 68; DLB 6; MTCW
**Mickiewicz, Adam** [1798-1855] ....... **NCLC 3**
**Middleton, Christopher** [1926-] ....... **CLC 13**
See also CA 13-16R; CANR 29, 54; DLB 40
**Middleton, Richard (Barham)** [1882-1911] **TCLC 56**
See also DLB 156
**Middleton, Stanley** [1919-] ............ **CLC 7, 38**
See also CA 25-28R; CAAS 23; CANR 21, 46; DLB 14
**Middleton, Thomas** [1580-1627]**LC 33; DAM DRAM, MST; DC 5**
See also DLB 58
**Migueis, Jose Rodrigues** [1901-] ...... **CLC 10**
**Mikszath, Kalman** [1847-1910] ..... **TCLC 31**
**Miles, Jack** ..................................... **CLC 100**
**Miles, Josephine (Louise)** [1911-1985]**CLC 1, 2, 14, 34, 39; DAM POET**
See also CA 1-4R; 116; CANR 2, 55; DLB 48
**Militant**
See Sandburg, Carl (August)
**Mill, John Stuart** [1806-1873] .. **NCLC 11, 58**
See also CDBLB 1832-1890; DLB 55, 190
**Millar, Kenneth** [1915-1983] . **CLC 14; DAM POP**
See also Macdonald, Ross
See also CA 9-12R; 110; CANR 16, 63; DLB 2; DLBD 6; DLBY 83; MTCW
**Millay, E. Vincent**
See Millay, Edna St. Vincent
**Millay, Edna St. Vincent** [1892-1950]**TCLC 4, 49; DA; DAB; DAC; DAM MST, POET; PC 6; WLCS**
See also CA 104; 130; CDALB 1917-1929; DLB 45; MTCW
**Miller, Arthur** [1915-]**CLC 1, 2, 6, 10, 15, 26, 47, 78; DA; DAB; DAC; DAM DRAM, MST; DC 1; WLC**
See also AAYA 15; AITN 1; CA 1-4R; CABS 3; CANR 2, 30, 54; CDALB 1941-1968; DLB 7; MTCW
**Miller, Henry (Valentine)** [1891-1980]**CLC 1, 2, 4, 9, 14, 43, 84; DA; DAB; DAC; DAM MST, NOV; WLC**
See also CA 9-12R; 97-100; CANR 33, 64; CDALB 1929-1941; DLB 4, 9; DLBY 80; MTCW
**Miller, Jason** [1939(?)-] ....................... **CLC 2**
See also AITN 1; CA 73-76; DLB 7
**Miller, Sue** [1943-] ........ **CLC 44; DAM POP**
See also BEST 90:3; CA 139; CANR 59; DLB 143
**Miller, Walter M(ichael, Jr.)** [1923-]**CLC 4, 30**
See also CA 85-88; DLB 8
**Millett, Kate** [1934-] .......................... **CLC 67**
See also AITN 1; CA 73-76; CANR 32, 53; MTCW
**Millhauser, Steven (Lewis)** [1943-].. **CLC 21, 54, 109**

See also CA 110; 111; CANR 63; DLB 2; INT 111
**Millin, Sarah Gertrude** [1889-1968] **CLC 49**
See also CA 102; 93-96
**Milne, A(lan) A(lexander)** [1882-1956]**TCLC 6; DAB; DAC; DAM MST**
See also CA 104; 133; CLR 1, 26; DLB 10, 77, 100, 160; MAICYA; MTCW; YABC 1
**Milner, Ron(ald)** [1938-] .... **CLC 56; BLC 3; DAM MULT**
See also AITN 1; BW 1; CA 73-76; CANR 24; DLB 38; MTCW
**Milnes, Richard Monckton** [1809-1885] **NCLC 61**
See also DLB 32, 184
**Milosz, Czeslaw** [1911-]**CLC 5, 11, 22, 31, 56, 82; DAM MST, POET; PC 8; WLCS**
See also CA 81-84; CANR 23, 51; MTCW
**Milton, John** [1608-1674]**LC 9, 43; DA; DAB; DAC; DAM MST, POET; PC 19; WLC**
See also CDBLB 1660-1789; DLB 131, 151
**Min, Anchee** [1957-] ......................... **CLC 86**
See also CA 146
**Minehaha, Cornelius**
See Wedekind, (Benjamin) Frank(lin)
**Miner, Valerie** [1947-] ....................... **CLC 40**
See also CA 97-100; CANR 59
**Minimo, Duca**
See D'Annunzio, Gabriele
**Minot, Susan** [1956-] ......................... **CLC 44**
See also CA 134
**Minus, Ed** [1938-] ............................. **CLC 39**
**Miranda, Javier**
See Bioy Casares, Adolfo
**Mirbeau, Octave** [1848-1917] ........ **TCLC 55**
See also DLB 123, 192
**Miro (Ferrer), Gabriel (Francisco Victor)** [1879-1930] ................................. **TCLC 5**
See also CA 104
**Mishima, Yukio** [1925-1970]**CLC 2, 4, 6, 9, 27; DC 1; SSC 4**
See also Hiraoka, Kimitake
See also DLB 182
**Mistral, Frederic** [1830-1914] ........ **TCLC 51**
See also CA 122
**Mistral, Gabriela** .................... **TCLC 2; HLC**
See also Godoy Alcayaga, Lucila
**Mistry, Rohinton** [1952-] ........ **CLC 71; DAC**
See also CA 141
**Mitchell, Clyde**
See Ellison, Harlan (Jay); Silverberg, Robert
**Mitchell, James Leslie** [1901-1935]
See Gibbon, Lewis Grassic
See also CA 104; DLB 15
**Mitchell, Joni** [1943-] ......................... **CLC 12**
See also CA 112
**Mitchell, Joseph (Quincy)** [1908-1996] **CLC 98**
See also CA 77-80; 152; CANR 69; DLB 185; DLBY 96
**Mitchell, Margaret (Munnerlyn)** [1900-1949] **TCLC 11; DAM NOV, POP**
See also AAYA 23; CA 109; 125; CANR 55; DLB 9; MTCW
**Mitchell, Peggy**
See Mitchell, Margaret (Munnerlyn)
**Mitchell, S(ilas) Weir** [1829-1914] **TCLC 36**
See also CA 165
**Mitchell, W(illiam) O(rmond)** [1914-1998] **CLC 25; DAC; DAM MST**
See also CA 77-80; 165; CANR 15, 43; DLB 88
**Mitchell, William** [1879-1936] ....... **TCLC 81**
**Mitford, Mary Russell** [1787-1855] **NCLC 4**
See also DLB 110, 116
**Mitford, Nancy** [1904-1973] .............. **CLC 44**
See also CA 9-12R; DLB 191

See also CA 41-44R; CANR 14; JRDA; SATA 5, 77

Nexo, Martin Andersen [1869-1954]TCLC 43

Nezval, Vitezslav [1900-1958] ........ TCLC 44
See also CA 123

Ng, Fae Myenne [1957(?)-] ................ CLC 81
See also CA 146

Ngema, Mbongeni [1955-] ................ CLC 57
See also BW 2; CA 143

Ngugi, James T(hiong'o) ........... CLC 3, 7, 13
See also Ngugi wa Thiong'o

Ngugi wa Thiong'o [1938-] CLC 36; BLC 3;
DAM MULT, NOV
See also Ngugi, James T(hiong'o)
See also BW 2; CA 81-84; CANR 27, 58; DLB 125; MTCW

Nichol, B(arrie) P(hillip) [1944-1988]CLC 18
See also CA 53-56; DLB 53; SATA 66

Nichols, John (Treadwell) [1940-] .... CLC 38
See also CA 9-12R; CAAS 2; CANR 6; DLBY 82

Nichols, Leigh
See Koontz, Dean R(ay)

Nichols, Peter (Richard) [1927-]CLC 5, 36, 65
See also CA 104; CANR 33; DLB 13; MTCW

Nicolas, F. R. E.
See Freeling, Nicolas

Niedecker, Lorine [1903-1970] .. CLC 10, 42;
DAM POET
See also CA 25-28; CAP 2; DLB 48

Nietzsche, Friedrich (Wilhelm) [1844-1900]
TCLC 10, 18, 55
See also CA 107; 121; DLB 129

Nievo, Ippolito [1831-1861] ........... NCLC 22

Nightingale, Anne Redmon [1943-]
See Redmon, Anne
See also CA 103

Nik. T. O.
See Annensky, Innokenty (Fyodorovich)

Nin, Anais [1903-1977]CLC 1, 4, 8, 11, 14, 60;
DAM NOV, POP; SSC 10
See also AITN 2; CA 13-16R; 69-72; CANR 22, 53; DLB 2, 4, 152; MTCW

Nishida, Kitaro [1870-1945] .......... TCLC 83

Nishiwaki, Junzaburo [1894-1982] ..... PC 15
See also CA 107

Nissenson, Hugh [1933-] ................ CLC 4, 9
See also CA 17-20R; CANR 27; DLB 28

Niven, Larry .......................... CLC 8
See also Niven, Laurence Van Cott
See also DLB 8

Niven, Laurence Van Cott [1938-]
See Niven, Larry
See also CA 21-24R; CAAS 12; CANR 14, 44, 66; DAM POP; MTCW; SATA 95

Nixon, Agnes Eckhardt [1927-] ........ CLC 21
See also CA 110

Nizan, Paul [1905-1940] ................. TCLC 40
See also CA 161; DLB 72

Nkosi, Lewis [1936-] . CLC 45; BLC 3; DAM MULT
See also BW 1; CA 65-68; CANR 27; DLB 157

Nodier, (Jean) Charles (Emmanuel) [1780-1844] ......................... NCLC 19
See also DLB 119

Noguchi, Yone [1875-1947] ........... TCLC 80

Nolan, Christopher [1965-] .............. CLC 58
See also CA 111

Noon, Jeff [1957-] ........................ CLC 91
See also CA 148

Norden, Charles
See Durrell, Lawrence (George)

Nordhoff, Charles (Bernard) [1887-1947]
TCLC 23
See also CA 108; DLB 9; SATA 23

Norfolk, Lawrence [1963-] ............... CLC 76
See also CA 144

Norman, Marsha [1947-] ....... CLC 28; DAM DRAM; DC 8
See also CA 105; CABS 3; CANR 41; DLBY 84

Normyx
See Douglas, (George) Norman

Norris, Frank [1870-1902] .............. SSC 28
See also Norris, (Benjamin) Frank(lin, Jr.)
See also CDALB 1865-1917; DLB 12, 71, 186

Norris, (Benjamin) Frank(lin, Jr.) [1870-1902]
TCLC 24
See also Norris, Frank
See also CA 110; 160

Norris, Leslie [1921-] ...................... CLC 14
See also CA 11-12; CANR 14; CAP 1; DLB 27

North, Andrew
See Norton, Andre

North, Anthony
See Koontz, Dean R(ay)

North, Captain George
See Stevenson, Robert Louis (Balfour)

North, Milou
See Erdrich, Louise

Northrup, B. A.
See Hubbard, L(afayette) Ron(ald)

North Staffs
See Hulme, T(homas) E(rnest)

Norton, Alice Mary
See Norton, Andre
See also MAICYA; SATA 1, 43

Norton, Andre [1912-] ..................... CLC 12
See also Norton, Alice Mary
See also AAYA 14; CA 1-4R; CANR 68; CLR 50; DLB 8, 52; JRDA; MTCW; SATA 91

Norton, Caroline [1808-1877] ........ NCLC 47
See also DLB 21, 159, 199

Norway, Nevil Shute [1899-1960]
See Shute, Nevil
See also CA 102; 93-96

Norwid, Cyprian Kamil [1821-1883]NCLC 17

Nosille, Nabrah
See Ellison, Harlan (Jay)

Nossack, Hans Erich [1901-1978] ....... CLC 6
See also CA 93-96; 85-88; DLB 69

Nostradamus [1503-1566] ..................... LC 27

Nosu, Chuji
See Ozu, Yasujiro

Notenburg, Eleanora (Genrikhovna) von
See Guro, Elena

Nova, Craig [1945-] ...................... CLC 7, 31
See also CA 45-48; CANR 2, 53

Novak, Joseph
See Kosinski, Jerzy (Nikodem)

Novalis [1772-1801] ........................ NCLC 13
See also DLB 90

Novis, Emile
See Weil, Simone (Adolphine)

Nowlan, Alden (Albert) [1933-1983]CLC 15;
DAC; DAM MST
See also CA 9-12R; CANR 5; DLB 53

Noyes, Alfred [1880-1958] ................ TCLC 7
See also CA 104; DLB 20

Nunn, Kem .............................. CLC 34
See also CA 159

Nye, Robert [1939-] CLC 13, 42; DAM NOV
See also CA 33-36R; CANR 29, 67; DLB 14; MTCW; SATA 6

Nyro, Laura [1947-] ....................... CLC 17

Oates, Joyce Carol [1938-]CLC 1, 2, 3, 6, 9, 11, 15, 19, 33, 52, 108; DA; DAB; DAC; DAM MST, NOV, POP; SSC 6; WLC
See also AAYA 15; AITN 1; BEST 89:2; CA 5-8R; CANR 25, 45; CDALB 1968-1988; DLB 2, 5, 130; DLBY 81; INT CANR-25; MTCW

O'Brien, Darcy [1939-] ................... CLC 11
See also CA 21-24R; CANR 8, 59

O'Brien, E. G.

See Clarke, Arthur C(harles)

O'Brien, Edna [1936-]CLC 3, 5, 8, 13, 36, 65;
DAM NOV; SSC 10
See also CA 1-4R; CANR 6, 41, 65; CDBLB 1960 to Present; DLB 14; MTCW

O'Brien, Fitz-James [1828-1862] .. NCLC 21
See also DLB 74

O'Brien, Flann ............. CLC 1, 4, 5, 7, 10, 47
See also O Nuallain, Brian

O'Brien, Richard [1942-] ................. CLC 17
See also CA 124

O'Brien, (William) Tim(othy) [1946-]CLC 7, 19, 40, 103; DAM POP
See also AAYA 16; CA 85-88; CANR 40, 58; DLB 152; DLBD 9; DLBY 80

Obstfelder, Sigbjoern [1866-1900] .. TCLC 23
See also CA 123

O'Casey, Sean [1880-1964]CLC 1, 5, 9, 11, 15, 88; DAB; DAC; DAM DRAM, MST; WLCS
See also CA 89-92; CANR 62; CDBLB 1914-1945; DLB 10; MTCW

O'Cathasaigh, Sean
See O'Casey, Sean

Ochs, Phil [1940-1976] ..................... CLC 17
See also CA 65-68

O'Connor, Edwin (Greene) [1918-1968]C L C 14
See also CA 93-96; 25-28R

O'Connor, (Mary) Flannery [1925-1964]CLC 1, 2, 3, 6, 10, 13, 15, 21, 66, 104; DA; DAB; DAC; DAM MST, NOV; SSC 1, 23; WLC
See also AAYA 7; CA 1-4R; CANR 3, 41; CDALB 1941-1968; DLB 2, 152; DLBD 12; DLBY 80; MTCW

O'Connor, Frank .................... CLC 23; SSC 5
See also O'Donovan, Michael John
See also DLB 162

O'Dell, Scott [1898-1989] ................. CLC 30
See also AAYA 3; CA 61-64; 129; CANR 12, 30; CLR 1, 16; DLB 52; JRDA; MAICYA; SATA 12, 60

Odets, Clifford [1906-1963] .. CLC 2, 28, 98;
DAM DRAM; DC 6
See also CA 85-88; CANR 62; DLB 7, 26; MTCW

O'Doherty, Brian [1934-] ................. CLC 76
See also CA 105

O'Donnell, K. M.
See Malzberg, Barry N(athaniel)

O'Donnell, Lawrence
See Kuttner, Henry

O'Donovan, Michael John [1903-1966] C L C 14
See also O'Connor, Frank
See also CA 93-96

Oe, Kenzaburo [1935-]CLC 10, 36, 86; DAM NOV; SSC 20
See also CA 97-100; CANR 36, 50; DLB 182; DLBY 94; MTCW

O'Faolain, Julia [1932-] . CLC 6, 19, 47, 108
See also CA 81-84; CAAS 2; CANR 12, 61; DLB 14; MTCW

O'Faolain, Sean [1900-1991]CLC 1, 7, 14, 32, 70; SSC 13
See also CA 61-64; 134; CANR 12, 66; DLB 15, 162; MTCW

O'Flaherty, Liam [1896-1984]CLC 5, 34; SSC 6
See also CA 101; 113; CANR 35; DLB 36, 162; DLBY 84; MTCW

Ogilvy, Gavin
See Barrie, J(ames) M(atthew)

O'Grady, Standish (James) [1846-1928]
TCLC 5
See also CA 104; 157

O'Grady, Timothy [1951-]................ CLC 59

See Codrescu, Andrei

**Parini, Jay (Lee)** [1948-] ................... **CLC 54**
See also CA 97-100; CAAS 16; CANR 32

**Park, Jordan**
See Kornbluth, C(yril) M.; Pohl, Frederik

**Park, Robert E(zra)** [1864-1944] ... **TCLC 73**
See also CA 122; 165

**Parker, Bert**
See Ellison, Harlan (Jay)

**Parker, Dorothy (Rothschild)** [1893-1967]
**CLC 15, 68; DAM POET; SSC 2**
See also CA 19-20; 25-28R; CAP 2; DLB 11, 45, 86; MTCW

**Parker, Robert B(rown)** [1932-]**CLC 27; DAM NOV, POP**
See also BEST 89:4; CA 49-52; CANR 1, 26, 52; INT CANR-26; MTCW

**Parkin, Frank** [1940-] ..................... **CLC 43**
See also CA 147

**Parkman, Francis, Jr.** [1823-1893] **NCLC 12**
See also DLB 1, 30, 186

**Parks, Gordon (Alexander Buchanan)** [1912-]
**CLC 1, 16; BLC 3; DAM MULT**
See also AITN 2; BW 2; CA 41-44R; CANR 26, 66; DLB 33; SATA 8

**Parmenides** [c. 515B.C.-c. 450B.C.]**CMLC 22**
See also DLB 176

**Parnell, Thomas** [1679-1718] ................ **LC 3**
See also DLB 94

**Parra, Nicanor** [1914-] .... **CLC 2, 102; DAM MULT; HLC**
See also CA 85-88; CANR 32; HW; MTCW

**Parrish, Mary Frances**
See Fisher, M(ary) F(rances) K(ennedy)

**Parson**
See Coleridge, Samuel Taylor

**Parson Lot**
See Kingsley, Charles

**Partridge, Anthony**
See Oppenheim, E(dward) Phillips

**Pascal, Blaise** [1623-1662] ................... **LC 35**

**Pascoli, Giovanni** [1855-1912] ....... **TCLC 45**

**Pasolini, Pier Paolo** [1922-1975]**CLC 20, 37, 106; PC 17**
See also CA 93-96; 61-64; CANR 63; DLB 128, 177; MTCW

**Pasquini**
See Silone, Ignazio

**Pastan, Linda (Olenik)** [1932-]**CLC 27; DAM POET**
See also CA 61-64; CANR 18, 40, 61; DLB 5

**Pasternak, Boris (Leonidovich)** [1890-1960]
**CLC 7, 10, 18, 63; DA; DAB; DAC; DAM MST, NOV, POET; PC 6; SSC 31; WLC**
See also CA 127; 116; MTCW

**Patchen, Kenneth** [1911-1972] **CLC 1, 2, 18; DAM POET**
See also CA 1-4R; 33-36R; CANR 3, 35; DLB 16, 48; MTCW

**Pater, Walter (Horatio)** [1839-1894]**NCLC 7**
See also CDBLB 1832-1890; DLB 57, 156

**Paterson, A(ndrew) B(arton)** [1864-1941]
**TCLC 32**
See also CA 155; SATA 97

**Paterson, Katherine (Womeldorf)** [1932-]
**CLC 12, 30**
See also AAYA 1; CA 21-24R; CANR 28, 59; CLR 7, 50; DLB 52; JRDA; MAICYA; MTCW; SATA 13, 53, 92

**Patmore, Coventry Kersey Dighton** [1823-1896] ........................................... **NCLC 9**
See also DLB 35, 98

**Paton, Alan (Stewart)** [1903-1988]**CLC 4, 10, 25, 55, 106; DA; DAB; DAC; DAM MST, NOV; WLC**
See also CA 13-16; 125; CANR 22; CAP 1; MTCW; SATA 11; SATA-Obit 56

**Paton Walsh, Gillian** [1937-]
See Walsh, Jill Paton
See also CANR 38; JRDA; MAICYA; SAAS 3; SATA 4, 72

**Patton, George S.** [1885-1945] ....... **TCLC 79**

**Paulding, James Kirke** [1778-1860] **NCLC 2**
See also DLB 3, 59, 74

**Paulin, Thomas Neilson** [1949-]
See Paulin, Tom
See also CA 123; 128

**Paulin, Tom** ......................................... **CLC 37**
See also Paulin, Thomas Neilson
See also DLB 40

**Paustovsky, Konstantin (Georgievich)** [1892-1968] ............................................
**CLC 40**
See also CA 93-96; 25-28R

**Pavese, Cesare** [1908-1950] **TCLC 3; PC 13; SSC 19**
See also CA 104; DLB 128, 177

**Pavic, Milorad** [1929-] ...................... **CLC 60**
See also CA 136; DLB 181

**Payne, Alan**
See Jakes, John (William)

**Paz, Gil**
See Lugones, Leopoldo

**Paz, Octavio** [1914-1998]**CLC 3, 4, 6, 10, 19, 51, 65; DA; DAB; DAC; DAM MST, MULT, POET; HLC; PC 1; WLC**
See also CA 73-76; 165; CANR 32, 65; DLBY 90; HW; MTCW

**p'Bitek, Okot** [1931-1982] . **CLC 96; BLC 3; DAM MULT**
See also BW 2; CA 124; 107; DLB 125; MTCW

**Peacock, Molly** [1947-] ...................... **CLC 60**
See also CA 103; CAAS 21; CANR 52; DLB 120

**Peacock, Thomas Love** [1785-1866]**NCLC 22**
See also DLB 96, 116

**Peake, Mervyn** [1911-1968] .......... **CLC 7, 54**
See also CA 5-8R; 25-28R; CANR 3; DLB 15, 160; MTCW; SATA 23

**Pearce, Philippa** .................................. **CLC 21**
See also Christie, (Ann) Philippa
See also CLR 9; DLB 161; MAICYA; SATA 1, 67

**Pearl, Eric**
See Elman, Richard (Martin)

**Pearson, T(homas) R(eid)** [1956-] .... **CLC 39**
See also CA 120; 130; INT 130

**Peck, Dale** [1967-] ............................. **CLC 81**
See also CA 146

**Peck, John** [1941-] ............................. **CLC 3**
See also CA 49-52; CANR 3

**Peck, Richard (Wayne)** [1934-] ......... **CLC 21**
See also AAYA 1, 24; CA 85-88; CANR 19, 38; CLR 15; INT CANR-19; JRDA; MAICYA; SAAS 2; SATA 18, 55, 97

**Peck, Robert Newton** [1928-] .. **CLC 17; DA; DAC; DAM MST**
See also AAYA 3; CA 81-84; CANR 31, 63; CLR 45; JRDA; MAICYA; SAAS 1; SATA 21, 62

**Peckinpah, (David) Sam(uel)** [1925-1984]
**CLC 20**
See also CA 109; 114

**Pedersen, Knut** [1859-1952]
See Hamsun, Knut
See also CA 104; 119; CANR 63; MTCW

**Peeslake, Gaffer**
See Durrell, Lawrence (George)

**Peguy, Charles Pierre** [1873-1914] **TCLC 10**
See also CA 107

**Peirce, Charles Sanders** [1839-1914]**TCLC 81**

**Pena, Ramon del Valle y**
See Valle-Inclan, Ramon (Maria) del

**Pendennis, Arthur Esquir**

See Thackeray, William Makepeace

**Penn, William** [1644-1718] ................... **LC 25**
See also DLB 24

**PEPECE**
See Prado (Calvo), Pedro

**Pepys, Samuel** [1633-1703]**LC 11; DA; DAB; DAC; DAM MST; WLC**
See also CDBLB 1660-1789; DLB 101

**Percy, Walker** [1916-1990]**CLC 2, 3, 6, 8, 14, 18, 47, 65; DAM NOV, POP**
See also CA 1-4R; 131; CANR 1, 23, 64; DLB 2; DLBY 80, 90; MTCW

**Perec, Georges** [1936-1982] .............. **CLC 56**
See also CA 141; DLB 83

**Pereda (y Sanchez de Porrua), Jose Maria de** [1833-1906] ............................. **TCLC 16**
See also CA 117

**Pereda y Porrua, Jose Maria de**
See Pereda (y Sanchez de Porrua), Jose Maria de

**Peregoy, George Weems**
See Mencken, H(enry) L(ouis)

**Perelman, S(idney) J(oseph)** [1904-1979]**CLC 3, 5, 9, 15, 23, 44, 49; DAM DRAM**
See also AITN 1, 2; CA 73-76; 89-92; CANR 18; DLB 11, 44; MTCW

**Peret, Benjamin** [1899-1959] .......... **TCLC 20**
See also CA 117

**Peretz, Isaac Loeb** [1851(?)-1915] **TCLC 16; SSC 26**
See also CA 109

**Peretz, Yitzhok Leibush**
See Peretz, Isaac Loeb

**Perez Galdos, Benito** [1843-1920] . **TCLC 27**
See also CA 125; 153; HW

**Perrault, Charles** [1628-1703] .............. **LC 2**
See also MAICYA; SATA 25

**Perry, Brighton**
See Sherwood, Robert E(mmet)

**Perse, St.-John**
See Leger, (Marie-Rene Auguste) Alexis Saint-Leger

**Perutz, Leo** [1882-1957] ................. **TCLC 60**
See also DLB 81

**Peseenz, Tulio F.**
See Lopez y Fuentes, Gregorio

**Pesetsky, Bette** [1932-] ...................... **CLC 28**
See also CA 133; DLB 130

**Peshkov, Alexei Maximovich** [1868-1936]
See Gorky, Maxim
See also CA 105; 141; DA; DAC; DAM DRAM, MST, NOV

**Pessoa, Fernando (Antonio Nogueira)** [1898-1935] ............................................
**TCLC 27; HLC; PC 20**
See also CA 125

**Peterkin, Julia Mood** [1880-1961] .... **CLC 31**
See also CA 102; DLB 9

**Peters, Joan K(aren)** [1945-] ............. **CLC 39**
See also CA 158

**Peters, Robert L(ouis)** [1924-] ........... **CLC 7**
See also CA 13-16R; CAAS 8; DLB 105

**Petofi, Sandor** [1823-1849] ............. **NCLC 21**

**Petrakis, Harry Mark** [1923-] ............ **CLC 3**
See also CA 9-12R; CANR 4, 30

**Petrarch** [1304-1374]**CMLC 20; DAM POET; PC 8**

**Petrov, Evgeny** ................................... **TCLC 21**
See also Kataev, Evgeny Petrovich

**Petry, Ann (Lane)** [1908-1997] **CLC 1, 7, 18**
See also BW 1; CA 5-8R; 157; CAAS 6; CANR 4, 46; CLR 12; DLB 76; JRDA; MAICYA; MTCW; SATA 5; SATA-Obit 94

**Petursson, Halligrimur** [1614-1674] ..... **LC 8**

**Phaedrus** [18(?)B.C.-55(?)] ............ **CMLC 25**

**Philips, Katherine** [1632-1664] ............ **LC 30**
See also DLB 131

See also CA 107; 145; CANR 33, 61; MTCW

**Pound, Ezra (Weston Loomis)** [1885-1972]
**CLC 1, 2, 3, 4, 5, 7, 10, 13, 18, 34, 48, 50, 112; DA; DAB; DAC; DAM MST, POET; PC 4; WLC**
See also CA 5-8R; 37-40R; CANR 40; CDALB 1917-1929; DLB 4, 45, 63; DLBD 15; MTCW

**Povod, Reinaldo** [1959-1994] ........... **CLC 44**
See also CA 136; 146

**Powell, Adam Clayton, Jr.** [1908-1972] **C L C 89; BLC 3; DAM MULT**
See also BW 1; CA 102; 33-36R

**Powell, Anthony (Dymoke)** [1905-]**CLC 1, 3, 7, 9, 10, 31**
See also CA 1-4R; CANR 1, 32, 62; CDBLB 1945-1960; DLB 15; MTCW

**Powell, Dawn** [1897-1965] ................. **CLC 66**
See also CA 5-8R; DLBY 97

**Powell, Padgett** [1952-] ................ **CLC 34**
See also CA 126; CANR 63

**Power, Susan** [1961-] ......................... **CLC 91**

**Powers, J(ames) F(arl)** [1917-]**CLC 1, 4, 8, 57; SSC 4**
See also CA 1-4R; CANR 2, 61; DLB 130; MTCW

**Powers, John J(ames)** [1945-]
See Powers, John R.
See also CA 69-72

**Powers, John R.** ............................... **CLC 66**
See also Powers, John J(ames)

**Powers, Richard (S.)** [1957-] ............ **CLC 93**
See also CA 148

**Pownall, David** [1938-] ...................... **CLC 10**
See also CA 89-92; CAAS 18; CANR 49; DLB 14

**Powys, John Cowper** [1872-1963] . **CLC 7, 9, 15, 46**
See also CA 85-88; DLB 15; MTCW

**Powys, T(heodore) F(rancis)** [1875-1953]
**TCLC 9**
See also CA 106; DLB 36, 162

**Prado (Calvo), Pedro** [1886-1952] . **TCLC 75**
See also CA 131; HW

**Prager, Emily** [1952-] ......................... **CLC 56**

**Pratt, E(dwin) J(ohn)** [1883(?)-1964]**CLC 19; DAC; DAM POET**
See also CA 141; 93-96; DLB 92

**Premchand** ........................................ **TCLC 21**
See also Srivastava, Dhanpat Rai

**Preussler, Otfried** [1923-] ................. **CLC 17**
See also CA 77-80; SATA 24

**Prevert, Jacques (Henri Marie)** [1900-1977]
**CLC 15**
See also CA 77-80; 69-72; CANR 29, 61; MTCW; SATA-Obit 30

**Prevost, Abbe (Antoine Francois)** [1697-1763]
**LC 1**

**Price, (Edward) Reynolds** [1933-] . **CLC 3, 6, 13, 43, 50, 63; DAM NOV; SSC 22**
See also CA 1-4R; CANR 1, 37, 57; DLB 2; INT CANR-37

**Price, Richard** [1949-] .................... **CLC 6, 12**
See also CA 49-52; CANR 3; DLBY 81

**Prichard, Katharine Susannah** [1883-1969]
**CLC 46**
See also CA 11-12; CANR 33; CAP 1; MTCW; SATA 66

**Priestley, J(ohn) B(oynton)** [1894-1984]**C L C 2, 5, 9, 34; DAM DRAM, NOV**
See also CA 9-12R; 113; CANR 33; CDBLB 1914-1945; DLB 10, 34, 77, 100, 139; DLBY 84; MTCW

**Prince** [1958(?)-] ................................. **CLC 35**

**Prince, F(rank) T(empleton)** [1912-] **CLC 22**
See also CA 101; CANR 43; DLB 20

**Prince Kropotkin**

See Kropotkin, Peter (Aleksieevich)

**Prior, Matthew** [1664-1721] ................... **LC 4**
See also DLB 95

**Prishvin, Mikhail** [1873-1954] ....... **TCLC 75**

**Pritchard, William H(arrison)** [1932-]**CLC 34**
See also CA 65-68; CANR 23; DLB 111

**Pritchett, V(ictor) S(awdon)** [1900-1997]**CLC 5, 13, 15, 41; DAM NOV; SSC 14**
See also CA 61-64; 157; CANR 31, 63; DLB 15, 139; MTCW

**Private 19022**
See Manning, Frederic

**Probst, Mark** [1925-] ......................... **CLC 59**
See also CA 130

**Prokosch, Frederic** [1908-1989]....**CLC 4, 48**
See also CA 73-76; 128; DLB 48

**Prophet, The**
See Dreiser, Theodore (Herman Albert)

**Prose, Francine** [1947-] ...................... **CLC 45**
See also CA 109; 112; CANR 46

**Proudhon**
See Cunha, Euclides (Rodrigues Pimenta) da

**Proulx, Annie**
See Proulx, E(dna) Annie

**Proulx, E(dna) Annie** [1935-] **CLC 81; DAM POP**
See also CA 145; CANR 65

**Proust, (Valentin-Louis-George-Eugene-) Marcel** [1871-1922]**TCLC 7, 13, 33; DA; DAB; DAC; DAM MST, NOV; WLC**
See also CA 104; 120; DLB 65; MTCW

**Prowler, Harley**
See Masters, Edgar Lee

**Prus, Boleslaw** [1845-1912] ........... **TCLC 48**

**Pryor, Richard (Franklin Lenox Thomas)** [1940-] ...................................... **CLC 26**
See also CA 122

**Przybyszewski, Stanislaw** [1868-1927]**T C L C 36**
See also CA 160; DLB 66

**Pteleon**
See Grieve, C(hristopher) M(urray)
See also DAM POET

**Puckett, Lute**
See Masters, Edgar Lee

**Puig, Manuel** [1932-1990]**CLC 3, 5, 10, 28, 65; DAM MULT; HLC**
See also CA 45-48; CANR 2, 32, 63; DLB 113; HW; MTCW

**Pulitzer, Joseph** [1847-1911] ......... **TCLC 76**
See also CA 114; DLB 23

**Purdy, A(lfred) W(ellington)** [1918-]**CLC 3, 6, 14, 50; DAC; DAM MST, POET**
See also CA 81-84; CAAS 17; CANR 42, 66; DLB 88

**Purdy, James (Amos)** [1923-]**CLC 2, 4, 10, 28, 52**
See also CA 33-36R; CAAS 1; CANR 19, 51; DLB 2; INT CANR-19; MTCW

**Pure, Simon**
See Swinnerton, Frank Arthur

**Pushkin, Alexander (Sergeyevich)** [1799-1837]
**NCLC 3, 27; DA; DAB; DAC; DAM DRAM, MST, POET; PC 10; SSC 27; WLC**
See also SATA 61

**P'u Sung-ling** [1640-1715] ....... **LC 3; SSC 31**

**Putnam, Arthur Lee**
See Alger, Horatio, Jr.

**Puzo, Mario** [1920-]**CLC 1, 2, 6, 36, 107; DAM NOV, POP**
See also CA 65-68; CANR 4, 42, 65; DLB 6; MTCW

**Pygge, Edward**
See Barnes, Julian (Patrick)

**Pyle, Ernest Taylor** [1900-1945]
See Pyle, Ernie

See also CA 115; 160

**Pyle, Ernie** [1900-1945] ................. **TCLC 75**
See also Pyle, Ernest Taylor
See also DLB 29

**Pyle, Howard** [1853-1911] ............. **TCLC 81**
See also CA 109; 137; CLR 22; DLB 42, 188; DLBD 13; MAICYA; SATA 16

**Pym, Barbara (Mary Crampton)** [1913-1980]
**CLC 13, 19, 37, 111**
See also CA 13-14; 97-100; CANR 13, 34; CAP 1; DLB 14; DLBY 87; MTCW

**Pynchon, Thomas (Ruggles, Jr.)** [1937-]**C L C 2, 3, 6, 9, 11, 18, 33, 62, 72; DA; DAB; DAC; DAM MST, NOV, POP; SSC 14; WLC**
See also BEST 90:2; CA 17-20R; CANR 22, 46; DLB 2, 173; MTCW

**Pythagoras** [c. 570B.C.-c. 500B.C.]**CMLC 22**
See also DLB 176

**Q**
See Quiller-Couch, SirArthur (Thomas)

**Qian Zhongshu**
See Ch'ien Chung-shu

**Qroll**
See Dagerman, Stig (Halvard)

**Quarrington, Paul (Lewis)** [1953-]... **CLC 65**
See also CA 129; CANR 62

**Quasimodo, Salvatore** [1901-1968] ..**CLC 10**
See also CA 13-16; 25-28R; CAP 1; DLB 114; MTCW

**Quay, Stephen** [1947-] ........................**CLC 95**

**Quay, Timothy** [1947-] ......................**CLC 95**

**Queen, Ellery** .................................... **CLC 3, 11**
See also Dannay, Frederic; Davidson, Avram; Lee, Manfred B(ennington); Marlowe, Stephen; Sturgeon, Theodore (Hamilton); Vance, John Holbrook

**Queen, Ellery, Jr.**
See Dannay, Frederic; Lee, Manfred B(ennington)

**Queneau, Raymond** [1903-1976]**CLC 2, 5, 10, 42**
See also CA 77-80; 69-72; CANR 32; DLB 72; MTCW

**Quevedo, Francisco de** [1580-1645] ....**LC 23**

**Quiller-Couch, SirArthur (Thomas)** [1863-1944] ...................................... **TCLC 53**
See also CA 118; 166; DLB 135, 153, 190

**Quin, Ann (Marie)** [1936-1973] .......... **CLC 6**
See also CA 9-12R; 45-48; DLB 14

**Quinn, Martin**
See Smith, Martin Cruz

**Quinn, Peter** [1947-] .........................**CLC 91**

**Quinn, Simon**
See Smith, Martin Cruz

**Quiroga, Horacio (Sylvestre)** [1878-1937]
**TCLC 20; DAM MULT; HLC**
See also CA 117; 131; HW; MTCW

**Quoirez, Francoise** [1935-] .................**CLC 9**
See also Sagan, Francoise
See also CA 49-52; CANR 6, 39; MTCW

**Raabe, Wilhelm** [1831-1910] .......... **TCLC 45**
See also DLB 129

**Rabe, David (William)** [1940-] **CLC 4, 8, 33; DAM DRAM**
See also CA 85-88; CABS 3; CANR 59; DLB 7

**Rabelais, Francois** [1483-1553] ... **LC 5; DA; DAB; DAC; DAM MST; WLC**

**Rabinovitch, Sholem** [1859-1916]
See Aleichem, Sholom
See also CA 104

**Rachilde** [1860-1953] ..................... **TCLC 67**
See also DLB 123, 192

**Racine, Jean** [1639-1699]**LC 28; DAB; DAM MST**

**Radcliffe, Ann (Ward)** [1764-1823] **NCLC 6, 55**

See also DLB 39, 178

**Radiguet, Raymond** [1903-1923] ... **TCLC 29**
See also CA 162; DLB 65

**Radnoti, Miklos** [1909-1944] ......... **TCLC 16**
See also CA 118

**Rado, James** [1939-] ......................... **CLC 17**
See also CA 105

**Radvanyi, Netty** [1900-1983]
See Seghers, Anna
See also CA 85-88; 110

**Rae, Ben**
See Griffiths, Trevor

**Raeburn, John (Hay)** [1941-] .......... **CLC 34**
See also CA 57-60

**Ragni, Gerome** [1942-1991] ............. **CLC 17**
See also CA 105; 134

**Rahv, Philip** [1908-1973] .................. **CLC 24**
See also Greenberg, Ivan
See also DLB 137

**Raimund, Ferdinand Jakob** [1790-1836]
**NCLC 69**
See also DLB 90

**Raine, Craig** [1944-] .................. **CLC 32, 103**
See also CA 108; CANR 29, 51; DLB 40

**Raine, Kathleen (Jessie)** [1908-] ... **CLC 7, 45**
See also CA 85-88; CANR 46; DLB 20; MTCW

**Rainis, Janis** [1865-1929] .............. **TCLC 29**

**Rakosi, Carl** [1903-] .......................... **CLC 47**
See also Rawley, Callman
See also CAAS 5; DLB 193

**Raleigh, Richard**
See Lovecraft, H(oward) P(hillips)

**Raleigh, Sir Walter** [1554(?)-1618] **LC 31, 39**
See also CDBLB Before 1660; DLB 172

**Rallentando, H. P.**
See Sayers, Dorothy L(eigh)

**Ramal, Walter**
See de la Mare, Walter (John)

**Ramon, Juan**
See Jimenez (Mantecon), Juan Ramon

**Ramos, Graciliano** [1892-1953] ..... **TCLC 32**

**Rampersad, Arnold** [1941-] ............. **CLC 44**
See also BW 2; CA 127; 133; DLB 111; INT
133

**Rampling, Anne**
See Rice, Anne

**Ramsay, Allan** [1684(?)-1758] .............. **LC 29**
See also DLB 95

**Ramuz, Charles-Ferdinand** [1878-1947]
**TCLC 33**
See also CA 165

**Rand, Ayn** [1905-1982]**CLC 3, 30, 44, 79; DA;**
**DAC; DAM MST, NOV, POP; WLC**
See also AAYA 10; CA 13-16R; 105; CANR
27; MTCW

**Randall, Dudley (Felker)** [1914-]**CLC 1; BLC**
**3; DAM MULT**
See also BW 1; CA 25-28R; CANR 23; DLB
41

**Randall, Robert**
See Silverberg, Robert

**Ranger, Ken**
See Creasey, John

**Ransom, John Crowe** [1888-1974]**CLC 2, 4, 5,**
**11, 24; DAM POET**
See also CA 5-8R; 49-52; CANR 6, 34; DLB
45, 63; MTCW

**Rao, Raja** [1909-] ... **CLC 25, 56; DAM NOV**
See also CA 73-76; CANR 51; MTCW

**Raphael, Frederic (Michael)** [1931-] **CLC 2,**
**14**
See also CA 1-4R; CANR 1; DLB 14

**Ratcliffe, James P.**
See Mencken, H(enry) L(ouis)

**Rathbone, Julian** [1935-] .................. **CLC 41**
See also CA 101; CANR 34

**Rattigan, Terence (Mervyn)** [1911-1977]**C L C**

**7; DAM DRAM**
See also CA 85-88; 73-76; CDBLB 1945-1960;
DLB 13; MTCW

**Ratushinskaya, Irina** [1954-] ............ **CLC 54**
See also CA 129; CANR 68

**Raven, Simon (Arthur Noel)** [1927-] **CLC 14**
See also CA 81-84

**Ravenna, Michael**
See Welty, Eudora

**Rawley, Callman** [1903-]
See Rakosi, Carl
See also CA 21-24R; CANR 12, 32

**Rawlings, Marjorie Kinnan** [1896-1953]
**TCLC 4**
See also AAYA 20; CA 104; 137; DLB 9, 22,
102; JRDA; MAICYA; YABC 1

**Ray, Satyajit** [1921-1992] **CLC 16, 76; DAM**
**MULT**
See also CA 114; 137

**Read, Herbert Edward** [1893-1968] .. **CLC 4**
See also CA 85-88; 25-28R; DLB 20, 149

**Read, Piers Paul** [1941-] ........ **CLC 4, 10, 25**
See also CA 21-24R; CANR 38; DLB 14; SATA
21

**Reade, Charles** [1814-1884] ............. **NCLC 2**
See also DLB 21

**Reade, Hamish**
See Gray, Simon (James Holliday)

**Reading, Peter** [1946-] ...................... **CLC 47**
See also CA 103; CANR 46; DLB 40

**Reaney, James** [1926-] **CLC 13; DAC; DAM**
**MST**
See also CA 41-44R; CAAS 15; CANR 42; DLB
68; SATA 43

**Rebreanu, Liviu** [1885-1944] ......... **TCLC 28**
See also CA 165

**Rechy, John (Francisco)** [1934-]**CLC 1, 7, 14,**
**18, 107; DAM MULT; HLC**
See also CA 5-8R; CAAS 4; CANR 6, 32, 64;
DLB 122; DLBY 82; HW; INT CANR-6

**Redcam, Tom** [1870-1933] .............. **TCLC 25**

**Reddin, Keith** .................................... **CLC 67**

**Redgrove, Peter (William)** [1932-]**CLC 6, 41**
See also CA 1-4R; CANR 3, 39; DLB 40

**Redmon, Anne** ................................... **CLC 22**
See also Nightingale, Anne Redmon
See also DLBY 86

**Reed, Eliot**
See Ambler, Eric

**Reed, Ishmael** [1938-]**CLC 2, 3, 5, 6, 13, 32, 60;**
**BLC 3; DAM MULT**
See also BW 2; CA 21-24R; CANR 25, 48; DLB
2, 5, 33, 169; DLBD 8; MTCW

**Reed, John (Silas)** [1887-1920] ........ **TCLC 9**
See also CA 106

**Reed, Lou** ......................................... **CLC 21**
See also Firbank, Louis

**Reeve, Clara** [1729-1807] ............... **NCLC 19**
See also DLB 39

**Reich, Wilhelm** [1897-1957] .......... **TCLC 57**

**Reid, Christopher (John)** [1949-] ..... **CLC 33**
See also CA 140; DLB 40

**Reid, Desmond**
See Moorcock, Michael (John)

**Reid Banks, Lynne** [1929-]
See Banks, Lynne Reid
See also CA 1-4R; CANR 6, 22, 38; CLR 24;
JRDA; MAICYA; SATA 22, 75

**Reilly, William K.**
See Creasey, John

**Reiner, Max**
See Caldwell, (Janet Miriam) Taylor (Holland)

**Reis, Ricardo**
See Pessoa, Fernando (Antonio Nogueira)

**Remarque, Erich Maria** [1898-1970]**CLC 21;**
**DA; DAB; DAC; DAM MST, NOV**
See also CA 77-80; 29-32R; DLB 56; MTCW

**Remizov, A.**
See Remizov, Aleksei (Mikhailovich)

**Remizov, A. M.**
See Remizov, Aleksei (Mikhailovich)

**Remizov, Aleksei (Mikhailovich)** [1877-1957]
**TCLC 27**
See also CA 125; 133

**Renan, Joseph Ernest** [1823-1892] **NCLC 26**

**Renard, Jules** [1864-1910] ............. **TCLC 17**
See also CA 117

**Renault, Mary** .......................... **CLC 3, 11, 17**
See also Challans, Mary
See also DLBY 83

**Rendell, Ruth (Barbara)** [1930-]**CLC 28, 48;**
**DAM POP**
See also Vine, Barbara
See also CA 109; CANR 32, 52; DLB 87; INT
CANR-32; MTCW

**Renoir, Jean** [1894-1979] .................. **CLC 20**
See also CA 129; 85-88

**Resnais, Alain** [1922-] ...................... **CLC 16**

**Reverdy, Pierre** [1889-1960] ............. **CLC 53**
See also CA 97-100; 89-92

**Rexroth, Kenneth** [1905-1982]**CLC 1, 2, 6, 11,**
**22, 49, 112; DAM POET; PC 20**
See also CA 5-8R; 107; CANR 14, 34, 63;
CDALB 1941-1968; DLB 16, 48, 165;
DLBY 82; INT CANR-14; MTCW

**Reyes, Alfonso** [1889-1959] ............. **TCLC 33**
See also CA 131; HW

**Reyes y Basoalto, Ricardo Eliecer Neftali**
See Neruda, Pablo

**Reymont, Wladyslaw (Stanislaw)** [1868(?)-
1925] ......................................... **TCLC 5**
See also CA 104

**Reynolds, Jonathan** [1942-] .......... **CLC 6, 38**
See also CA 65-68; CANR 28

**Reynolds, Joshua** [1723-1792] ............ **LC 15**
See also DLB 104

**Reynolds, Michael Shane** [1937-] ..... **CLC 44**
See also CA 65-68; CANR 9

**Reznikoff, Charles** [1894-1976] ......... **CLC 9**
See also CA 33-36; 61-64; CAP 2; DLB 28, 45

**Rezzori (d'Arezzo), Gregor von** [1914-]**C L C**
**25**
See also CA 122; 136

**Rhine, Richard**
See Silverstein, Alvin

**Rhodes, Eugene Manlove** [1869-1934]**T C L C**
**53**

**Rhodius, Apollonius** [c. 3rd cent. B.C.-]
**CMLC 28**
See also DLB 176

**R'hoone**
See Balzac, Honore de

**Rhys, Jean** [1890(?)-1979]**CLC 2, 4, 6, 14, 19,**
**51; DAM NOV; SSC 21**
See also CA 25-28R; 85-88; CANR 35, 62;
CDBLB 1945-1960; DLB 36, 117, 162;
MTCW

**Ribeiro, Darcy** [1922-1997] ............... **CLC 34**
See also CA 33-36R; 156

**Ribeiro, Joao Ubaldo (Osorio Pimentel)** [1941-
] ............................................. **CLC 10, 67**
See also CA 81-84

**Ribman, Ronald (Burt)** [1932-] .......... **CLC 7**
See also CA 21-24R; CANR 46

**Ricci, Nino** [1959-] ............................ **CLC 70**
See also CA 137

**Rice, Anne** [1941-] ........ **CLC 41; DAM POP**
See also AAYA 9; BEST 89:2; CA 65-68; CANR
12, 36, 53

**Rice, Elmer (Leopold)** [1892-1967]**CLC 7, 49;**
**DAM DRAM**
See also CA 21-22; 25-28R; CAP 2; DLB 4, 7;
MTCW

**Rice, Tim(othy Miles Bindon)** [1944-]**CLC 21**

              

DLB 48; MTCW
**Sharp, William** [1855-1905] .......... **TCLC 39**
See also CA 160; DLB 156
**Sharpe, Thomas Ridley** [1928-]
See Sharpe, Tom
See also CA 114; 122; INT 122
**Sharpe, Tom** ........................................ **CLC 36**
See also Sharpe, Thomas Ridley
See also DLB 14
**Shaw, Bernard** .................................. **TCLC 45**
See also Shaw, George Bernard
See also BW 1
**Shaw, G. Bernard**
See Shaw, George Bernard
**Shaw, George Bernard** [1856-1950] **TCLC 3,
9, 21; DA; DAB; DAC; DAM DRAM,
MST; WLC**
See also Shaw, Bernard
See also CA 104; 128; CDBLB 1914-1945;
DLB 10, 57, 190; MTCW
**Shaw, Henry Wheeler** [1818-1885] **NCLC 15**
See also DLB 11
**Shaw, Irwin** [1913-1984] **CLC 7, 23, 34; DAM
DRAM, POP**
See also AITN 1; CA 13-16R; 112; CANR 21;
CDALB 1941-1968; DLB 6, 102; DLBY 84;
MTCW
**Shaw, Robert** [1927-1978] .................... **CLC 5**
See also AITN 1; CA 1-4R; 81-84; CANR 4;
DLB 13, 14
**Shaw, T. E.**
See Lawrence, T(homas) E(dward)
**Shawn, Wallace** [1943-] .................... **CLC 41**
See also CA 112
**Shea, Lisa** [1953-] .............................. **CLC 86**
See also CA 147
**Sheed, Wilfrid (John Joseph)** [1930-] **CLC 2,
4, 10, 53**
See also CA 65-68; CANR 30, 66; DLB 6;
MTCW
**Sheldon, Alice Hastings Bradley** [1915(?)-1987]
See Tiptree, James, Jr.
See also CA 108; 122; CANR 34; INT 108;
MTCW
**Sheldon, John**
See Bloch, Robert (Albert)
**Shelley, Mary Wollstonecraft (Godwin)** [1797-
1851] ..............................................................
**NCLC 14, 59; DA; DAB; DAC; DAM MST,
NOV; WLC**
See also AAYA 20; CDBLB 1789-1832; DLB
110, 116, 159, 178; SATA 29
**Shelley, Percy Bysshe** [1792-1822] **NCLC 18;
DA; DAB; DAC; DAM MST, POET; PC
14; WLC**
See also CDBLB 1789-1832; DLB 96, 110, 158
**Shepard, Jim** [1956-] ........................ **CLC 36**
See also CA 137; CANR 59; SATA 90
**Shepard, Lucius** [1947-] .................... **CLC 34**
See also CA 128; 141
**Shepard, Sam** [1943-] **CLC 4, 6, 17, 34, 41, 44;
DAM DRAM; DC 5**
See also AAYA 1; CA 69-72; CABS 3; CANR
22; DLB 7; MTCW
**Shepherd, Michael**
See Ludlum, Robert
**Sherburne, Zoa (Morin)** [1912-] ....... **CLC 30**
See also AAYA 13; CA 1-4R; CANR 3, 37;
MAICYA; SAAS 18; SATA 3
**Sheridan, Frances** [1724-1766] .............. **LC 7**
See also DLB 39, 84
**Sheridan, Richard Brinsley** [1751-1816]
**NCLC 5; DA; DAB; DAC; DAM DRAM,
MST; DC 1; WLC**
See also CDBLB 1660-1789; DLB 89
**Sherman, Jonathan Marc** .................. **CLC 55**
**Sherman, Martin** [1941(?)-] .............. **CLC 19**

See also CA 116; 123
**Sherwin, Judith Johnson** [1936-] . **CLC 7, 15**
See also CA 25-28R; CANR 34
**Sherwood, Frances** [1940-] ................ **CLC 81**
See also CA 146
**Sherwood, Robert E(mmet)** [1896-1955]
**TCLC 3; DAM DRAM**
See also CA 104; 153; DLB 7, 26
**Shestov, Lev** [1866-1938] ................ **TCLC 56**
**Shevchenko, Taras** [1814-1861] ..... **NCLC 54**
**Shiel, M(atthew) P(hipps)** [1865-1947] **T C L C
8**
See also Holmes, Gordon
See also CA 106; 160; DLB 153
**Shields, Carol** [1935-] ..... **CLC 91, 113; DAC**
See also CA 81-84; CANR 51
**Shields, David** [1956-] ........................ **CLC 97**
See also CA 124; CANR 48
**Shiga, Naoya** [1883-1971] ... **CLC 33; SSC 23**
See also CA 101; 33-36R; DLB 180
**Shilts, Randy** [1951-1994] ................ **CLC 85**
See also AAYA 19; CA 115; 127; 144; CANR
45; INT 127
**Shimazaki, Haruki** [1872-1943]
See Shimazaki Toson
See also CA 105; 134
**Shimazaki Toson** [1872-1943] ......... **TCLC 5**
See also Shimazaki, Haruki
See also DLB 180
**Sholokhov, Mikhail (Aleksandrovich)** [1905-
1984] ..............................................................
**CLC 7, 15**
See also CA 101; 112; MTCW; SATA-Obit 36
**Shone, Patric**
See Hanley, James
**Shreve, Susan Richards** [1939-] ........ **CLC 23**
See also CA 49-52; CAAS 5; CANR 5, 38, 69;
MAICYA; SATA 46, 95; SATA-Brief 41
**Shue, Larry** [1946-1985] ........ **CLC 52; DAM
DRAM**
See also CA 145; 117
**Shu-Jen, Chou** [1881-1936]
See Lu Hsun
See also CA 104
**Shulman, Alix Kates** [1932-] ......... **CLC 2, 10**
See also CA 29-32R; CANR 43; SATA 7
**Shuster, Joe** [1914-] ............................ **CLC 21**
**Shute, Nevil** ........................................ **CLC 30**
See also Norway, Nevil Shute
**Shuttle, Penelope (Diane)** [1947-] ....... **CLC 7**
See also CA 93-96; CANR 39; DLB 14, 40
**Sidney, Mary** [1561-1621] ............. **LC 19, 39**
**Sidney, Sir Philip** [1554-1586] **LC 19, 39; DA;
DAB; DAC; DAM MST, POET**
See also CDBLB Before 1660; DLB 167
**Siegel, Jerome** [1914-1996] ................ **CLC 21**
See also CA 116; 151
**Siegel, Jerry**
See Siegel, Jerome
**Sienkiewicz, Henryk (Adam Alexander Pius)**
[1846-1916] ................................ **TCLC 3**
See also CA 104; 134
**Sierra, Gregorio Martinez**
See Martinez Sierra, Gregorio
**Sierra, Maria (de la O'LeJarraga) Martinez**
See Martinez Sierra, Maria (de la O'LeJarraga)
**Sigal, Clancy** [1926-] .......................... **CLC 7**
See also CA 1-4R
**Sigourney, Lydia Howard (Huntley)** [1791-
1865] ................................ **NCLC 21**
See also DLB 1, 42, 73
**Siguenza y Gongora, Carlos de** [1645-1700]
**LC 8**
**Sigurjonsson, Johann** [1880-1919] **TCLC 27**
**Sikelianos, Angelos** [1884-1951] .... **TCLC 39**
**Silkin, Jon** [1930-] .................... **CLC 2, 6, 43**
See also CA 5-8R; CAAS 5; DLB 27

**Silko, Leslie (Marmon)** [1948-] . **CLC 23, 74;
DA; DAC; DAM MST, MULT, POP;
WLCS**
See also AAYA 14; CA 115; 122; CANR 45;
65; DLB 143, 175; NNAL
**Sillanpaa, Frans Eemil** [1888-1964] . **CLC 19**
See also CA 129; 93-96; MTCW
**Sillitoe, Alan** [1928-] **CLC 1, 3, 6, 10, 19, 57**
See also AITN 1; CA 9-12R; CAAS 2; CANR
8, 26, 55; CDBLB 1960 to Present; DLB 14,
139; MTCW; SATA 61
**Silone, Ignazio** [1900-1978] ................ **CLC 4**
See also CA 25-28; 81-84; CANR 34; CAP 2;
MTCW
**Silver, Joan Micklin** [1935-] .............. **CLC 20**
See also CA 114; 121; INT 121
**Silver, Nicholas**
See Faust, Frederick (Schiller)
**Silverberg, Robert** [1935-] **CLC 7; DAM POP**
See also AAYA 24; CA 1-4R; CAAS 3; CANR
1, 20, 36; DLB 8; INT CANR-20; MAICYA;
MTCW; SATA 13, 91
**Silverstein, Alvin** [1933-] .................... **CLC 17**
See also CA 49-52; CANR 2; CLR 25; JRDA;
MAICYA; SATA 8, 69
**Silverstein, Virginia B(arbara Opshelor)** [1937-
] ..............................................................
**CLC 17**
See also CA 49-52; CANR 2; CLR 25; JRDA;
MAICYA; SATA 8, 69
**Sim, Georges**
See Simenon, Georges (Jacques Christian)
**Simak, Clifford D(onald)** [1904-1988] **CLC 1,
55**
See also CA 1-4R; 125; CANR 1, 35; DLB 8;
MTCW; SATA-Obit 56
**Simenon, Georges (Jacques Christian)** [1903-
1989] ..............................................................
**CLC 1, 2, 3, 8, 18, 47; DAM POP**
See also CA 85-88; 129; CANR 35; DLB 72;
DLBY 89; MTCW
**Simic, Charles** [1938-]. **CLC 6, 9, 22, 49, 68;
DAM POET**
See also CA 29-32R; CAAS 4; CANR 12, 33,
52, 61; DLB 105
**Simmel, Georg** [1858-1918] ........... **TCLC 64**
See also CA 157
**Simmons, Charles (Paul)** [1924-] ...... **CLC 57**
See also CA 89-92; INT 89-92
**Simmons, Dan** [1948-] .. **CLC 44; DAM POP**
See also AAYA 16; CA 138; CANR 53
**Simmons, James (Stewart Alexander)** [1933-]
**CLC 43**
See also CA 105; CAAS 21; DLB 40
**Simms, William Gilmore** [1806-1870] **NCLC 3**
See also DLB 3, 30, 59, 73
**Simon, Carly** [1945-] ........................ **CLC 26**
See also CA 105
**Simon, Claude** [1913-1984] **CLC 4, 9, 15, 39;
DAM NOV**
See also CA 89-92; CANR 33; DLB 83; MTCW
**Simon, (Marvin) Neil** [1927-] **CLC 6, 11, 31,
39, 70; DAM DRAM**
See also AITN 1; CA 21-24R; CANR 26, 54;
DLB 7; MTCW
**Simon, Paul (Frederick)** [1941(?)-] ... **CLC 17**
See also CA 116; 153
**Simonon, Paul** [1956(?)-] .................. **CLC 30**
**Simpson, Harriette**
See Arnow, Harriette (Louisa) Simpson
**Simpson, Louis (Aston Marantz)** [1923-] **CLC
4, 7, 9, 32; DAM POET**
See also CA 1-4R; CAAS 4; CANR 1, 61; DLB
5; MTCW
**Simpson, Mona (Elizabeth)** [1957-] . **CLC 44**
See also CA 122; 135; CANR 68
**Simpson, N(orman) F(rederick)** [1919-] **C L C**

**29**
See also CA 13-16R; DLB 13
**Sinclair, Andrew (Annandale)** [1935-]**CLC 2, 14**
See also CA 9-12R; CAAS 5; CANR 14, 38; DLB 14; MTCW
**Sinclair, Emil**
See Hesse, Hermann
**Sinclair, Iain** [1943-] .......................... **CLC 76**
See also CA 132
**Sinclair, Iain MacGregor**
See Sinclair, Iain
**Sinclair, Irene**
See Griffith, D(avid Lewelyn) W(ark)
**Sinclair, Mary Amelia St. Clair** [1865(?)-1946]
See Sinclair, May
See also CA 104
**Sinclair, May** [1863-1946] .......... **TCLC 3, 11**
See also Sinclair, Mary Amelia St. Clair
See also CA 166; DLB 36, 135
**Sinclair, Roy**
See Griffith, D(avid Lewelyn) W(ark)
**Sinclair, Upton (Beall)** [1878-1968]**CLC 1, 11, 15, 63; DA; DAB; DAC; DAM MST, NOV; WLC**
See also CA 5-8R; 25-28R; CANR 7; CDALB 1929-1941; DLB 9; INT CANR-7; MTCW; SATA 9
**Singer, Isaac**
See Singer, Isaac Bashevis
**Singer, Isaac Bashevis** [1904-1991]**CLC 1, 3, 6, 9, 11, 15, 23, 38, 69, 111; DA; DAB; DAC; DAM MST, NOV; SSC 3; WLC**
See also AITN 1, 2; CA 1-4R; 134; CANR 1, 39; CDALB 1941-1968; CLR 1; DLB 6, 28, 52; DLBY 91; JRDA; MAICYA; MTCW; SATA 3, 27; SATA-Obit 68
**Singer, Israel Joshua** [1893-1944] . **TCLC 33**
**Singh, Khushwant** [1915-] ................. **CLC 11**
See also CA 9-12R; CAAS 9; CANR 6
**Singleton, Ann**
See Benedict, Ruth (Fulton)
**Sinjohn, John**
See Galsworthy, John
**Sinyavsky, Andrei (Donatevich)** [1925-1997] **CLC 8**
See also CA 85-88; 159
**Sirin, V.**
See Nabokov, Vladimir (Vladimirovich)
**Sissman, L(ouis) E(dward)** [1928-1976] **C L C 9, 18**
See also CA 21-24R; 65-68; CANR 13; DLB 5
**Sisson, C(harles) H(ubert)** [1914-] ..... **CLC 8**
See also CA 1-4R; CAAS 3; CANR 3, 48; DLB 27
**Sitwell, Dame Edith** [1887-1964]**CLC 2, 9, 67; DAM POET; PC 3**
See also CA 9-12R; CANR 35; CDBLB 1945-1960; DLB 20; MTCW
**Siwaarmill, H. P.**
See Sharp, William
**Sjoewall, Maj** [1935-] .......................... **CLC 7**
See also CA 65-68
**Sjowall, Maj**
See Sjoewall, Maj
**Skelton, Robin** [1925-1997] .............. **CLC 13**
See also AITN 2; CA 5-8R; 160; CAAS 5; CANR 28; DLB 27, 53
**Skolimowski, Jerzy** [1938-] .............. **CLC 20**
See also CA 128
**Skram, Amalie (Bertha)** [1847-1905]**TCLC 25**
See also CA 165
**Skvorecky, Josef (Vaclav)** [1924-]**CLC 15, 39, 69; DAC; DAM NOV**
See also CA 61-64; CAAS 1; CANR 10, 34, 63; MTCW
**Slade, Bernard** ......................... **CLC 11, 46**

See also Newbound, Bernard Slade
See also CAAS 9; DLB 53
**Slaughter, Carolyn** [1946-] ................. **CLC 56**
See also CA 85-88
**Slaughter, Frank G(ill)** [1908-] ......... **CLC 29**
See also AITN 2; CA 5-8R; CANR 5; INT CANR-5
**Slavitt, David R(ytman)** [1935-] ...**CLC 5, 14**
See also CA 21-24R; CAAS 3; CANR 41; DLB 5, 6
**Slesinger, Tess** [1905-1945] ............. **TCLC 10**
See also CA 107; DLB 102
**Slessor, Kenneth** [1901-1971] ........... **CLC 14**
See also CA 102; 89-92
**Slowacki, Juliusz** [1809-1849] ........ **NCLC 15**
**Smart, Christopher** [1722-1771] **LC 3; DAM POET; PC 13**
See also DLB 109
**Smart, Elizabeth** [1913-1986] ........... **CLC 54**
See also CA 81-84; 118; DLB 88
**Smiley, Jane (Graves)** [1949-] ... **CLC 53, 76; DAM POP**
See also CA 104; CANR 30, 50; INT CANR-30
**Smith, A(rthur) J(ames) M(arshall)** [1902-1980] ........................ **CLC 15; DAC**
See also CA 1-4R; 102; CANR 4; DLB 88
**Smith, Adam** [1723-1790] ..................... **LC 36**
See also DLB 104
**Smith, Alexander** [1829-1867] ....... **NCLC 59**
See also DLB 32, 55
**Smith, Anna Deavere** [1950-] ............ **CLC 86**
See also CA 133
**Smith, Betty (Wehner)** [1896-1972] . **CLC 19**
See also CA 5-8R; 33-36R; DLBY 82; SATA 6
**Smith, Charlotte (Turner)** [1749-1806]**NCLC 23**
See also DLB 39, 109
**Smith, Clark Ashton** [1893-1961] ..... **CLC 43**
See also CA 143
**Smith, Dave** .................................. **CLC 22, 42**
See also Smith, David (Jeddie)
See also CAAS 7; DLB 5
**Smith, David (Jeddie)** [1942-]
See Smith, Dave
See also CA 49-52; CANR 1, 59; DAM POET
**Smith, Florence Margaret** [1902-1971]
See Smith, Stevie
See also CA 17-18; 29-32R; CANR 35; CAP 2; DAM POET; MTCW
**Smith, Iain Crichton** [1928-] ............. **CLC 64**
See also CA 21-24R; DLB 40, 139
**Smith, John** [1580(?)-1631] ................... **LC 9**
See also DLB 24, 30
**Smith, Johnston**
See Crane, Stephen (Townley)
**Smith, Joseph, Jr.** [1805-1844] ....... **NCLC 53**
**Smith, Lee** [1944-] ...................... **CLC 25, 73**
See also CA 114; 119; CANR 46; DLB 143; DLBY 83; INT 119
**Smith, Martin**
See Smith, Martin Cruz
**Smith, Martin Cruz** [1942-] .. **CLC 25; DAM MULT, POP**
See also BEST 89:4; CA 85-88; CANR 6, 23, 43, 65; INT CANR-23; NNAL
**Smith, Mary-Ann Tirone** [1944-] ..... **CLC 39**
See also CA 118; 136
**Smith, Patti** [1946-] ........................... **CLC 12**
See also CA 93-96; CANR 63
**Smith, Pauline (Urmson)** [1882-1959] **T C L C 25**
**Smith, Rosamond**
See Oates, Joyce Carol
**Smith, Sheila Kaye**
See Kaye-Smith, Sheila
**Smith, Stevie** ............ **CLC 3, 8, 25, 44; PC 12**

See also Smith, Florence Margaret
See also DLB 20
**Smith, Wilbur (Addison)** [1933-] ...... **CLC 33**
See also CA 13-16R; CANR 7, 46, 66; MTCW
**Smith, William Jay** [1918-] ................. **CLC 6**
See also CA 5-8R; CANR 44; DLB 5; MAICYA; SAAS 22; SATA 2, 68
**Smith, Woodrow Wilson**
See Kuttner, Henry
**Smolenskin, Peretz** [1842-1885] ..... **NCLC 30**
**Smollett, Tobias (George)** [1721-1771] . **LC 2**
See also CDBLB 1660-1789; DLB 39, 104
**Snodgrass, W(illiam) D(e Witt)** [1926-]**CLC 2, 6, 10, 18, 68; DAM POET**
See also CA 1-4R; CANR 6, 36, 65; DLB 5; MTCW
**Snow, C(harles) P(ercy)** [1905-1980]**CLC 1, 4, 6, 9, 13, 19; DAM NOV**
See also CA 5-8R; 101; CANR 28; CDBLB 1945-1960; DLB 15, 77; MTCW
**Snow, Frances Compton**
See Adams, Henry (Brooks)
**Snyder, Gary (Sherman)** [1930-]**CLC 1, 2, 5, 9, 32; DAM POET; PC 21**
See also CA 17-20R; CANR 30, 60; DLB 5, 16, 165
**Snyder, Zilpha Keatley** [1927-] ......... **CLC 17**
See also AAYA 15; CA 9-12R; CANR 38; CLR 31; JRDA; MAICYA; SAAS 2; SATA 1, 28, 75
**Soares, Bernardo**
See Pessoa, Fernando (Antonio Nogueira)
**Sobh, A.**
See Shamlu, Ahmad
**Sobol, Joshua** ......................................... **CLC 60**
**Socrates** [469B.C.-399B.C.] .......... **CMLC 27**
**Soderberg, Hjalmar** [1869-1941] ... **TCLC 39**
**Sodergran, Edith (Irene)**
See Soedergran, Edith (Irene)
**Soedergran, Edith (Irene)** [1892-1923]**T C L C 31**
**Softly, Edgar**
See Lovecraft, H(oward) P(hillips)
**Softly, Edward**
See Lovecraft, H(oward) P(hillips)
**Sokolov, Raymond** [1941-] .................. **CLC 7**
See also CA 85-88
**Solo, Jay**
See Ellison, Harlan (Jay)
**Sologub, Fyodor** ................................. **TCLC 9**
See also Teternikov, Fyodor Kuzmich
**Solomons, Ikey Esquir**
See Thackeray, William Makepeace
**Solomos, Dionysios** [1798-1857] .... **NCLC 15**
**Solwoska, Mara**
See French, Marilyn
**Solzhenitsyn, Aleksandr I(sayevich)** [1918-]**CLC 1, 2, 4, 7, 9, 10, 18, 26, 34, 78; DA; DAB; DAC; DAM MST, NOV; WLC**
See also AITN 1; CA 69-72; CANR 40, 65; MTCW
**Somers, Jane**
See Lessing, Doris (May)
**Somerville, Edith** [1858-1949] ....... **TCLC 51**
See also DLB 135
**Somerville & Ross**
See Martin, Violet Florence; Somerville, Edith
**Sommer, Scott** [1951-] ........................ **CLC 25**
See also CA 106
**Sondheim, Stephen (Joshua)** [1930-]**CLC 30, 39; DAM DRAM**
See also AAYA 11; CA 103; CANR 47, 68
**Song, Cathy** [1955-] ............................. **PC 21**
See also CA 154; DLB 169
**Sontag, Susan** [1933-]**CLC 1, 2, 10, 13, 31, 105; DAM POP**
See also CA 17-20R; CANR 25, 51; DLB 2,

67; MTCW
**Sophocles** [496(?)B.C.-406(?)B.C.] . **CMLC 2;
DA; DAB; DAC; DAM DRAM, MST; DC
1; WLCS**
See also DLB 176
**Sordello** [1189-1269] ...................... **CMLC 15**
**Sorel, Julia**
See Drexler, Rosalyn
**Sorrentino, Gilbert** [1929-]**CLC 3, 7, 14, 22, 40**
See also CA 77-80; CANR 14, 33; DLB 5, 173;
DLBY 80; INT CANR-14
**Soto, Gary** [1952-]**CLC 32, 80; DAM MULT;
HLC**
See also AAYA 10; CA 119; 125; CANR 50;
CLR 38; DLB 82; HW; INT 125; JRDA;
SATA 80
**Soupault, Philippe** [1897-1990] ........ **CLC 68**
See also CA 116; 147; 131
**Souster, (Holmes) Raymond** [1921-] . **CLC 5,
14; DAC; DAM POET**
See also CA 13-16R; CAAS 14; CANR 13, 29,
53; DLB 88; SATA 63
**Southern, Terry** [1924(?)-1995] .......... **CLC 7**
See also CA 1-4R; 150; CANR 1, 55; DLB 2
**Southey, Robert** [1774-1843] ........... **NCLC 8**
See also DLB 93, 107, 142; SATA 54
**Southworth, Emma Dorothy Eliza Nevitte**
[1819-1899] ...............................................
**NCLC 26**
**Souza, Ernest**
See Scott, Evelyn
**Soyinka, Wole** [1934-] . **CLC 3, 5, 14, 36, 44;
BLC 3; DA; DAB; DAC; DAM DRAM,
MST, MULT; DC 2; WLC**
See also BW 2; CA 13-16R; CANR 27, 39; DLB
125; MTCW
**Spackman, W(illiam) M(ode)** [1905-1990]
**CLC 46**
See also CA 81-84; 132
**Spacks, Barry (Bernard)** [1931-] ...... **CLC 14**
See also CA 154; CANR 33; DLB 105
**Spanidou, Irini** [1946-] ..................... **CLC 44**
**Spark, Muriel (Sarah)** [1918-]**CLC 2, 3, 5, 8,
13, 18, 40, 94; DAB; DAC; DAM MST,
NOV; SSC 10**
See also CA 5-8R; CANR 12, 36; CDBLB 1945-
1960; DLB 15, 139; INT CANR-12; MTCW
**Spaulding, Douglas**
See Bradbury, Ray (Douglas)
**Spaulding, Leonard**
See Bradbury, Ray (Douglas)
**Spence, J. A. D.**
See Eliot, T(homas) S(tearns)
**Spencer, Elizabeth** [1921-] ................ **CLC 22**
See also CA 13-16R; CANR 32, 65; DLB 6;
MTCW; SATA 14
**Spencer, Leonard G.**
See Silverberg, Robert
**Spencer, Scott** [1945-] ...................... **CLC 30**
See also CA 113; CANR 51; DLBY 86
**Spender, Stephen (Harold)** [1909-1995] **C L C
1, 2, 5, 10, 41, 91; DAM POET**
See also CA 9-12R; 149; CANR 31, 54; CDBLB
1945-1960; DLB 20; MTCW
**Spengler, Oswald (Arnold Gottfried)** [1880-
1936] ........................................................
**TCLC 25**
See also CA 118
**Spenser, Edmund** [1552(?)-1599] ... **LC 5, 39;
DA; DAB; DAC; DAM MST, POET; PC
8; WLC**
See also CDBLB Before 1660; DLB 167
**Spicer, Jack** [1925-1965]**CLC 8, 18, 72; DAM
POET**
See also CA 85-88; DLB 5, 16, 193
**Spiegelman, Art** [1948-] ..................... **CLC 76**
See also AAYA 10; CA 125; CANR 41, 55

**Spielberg, Peter** [1929-] ...................... **CLC 6**
See also CA 5-8R; CANR 4, 48; DLBY 81
**Spielberg, Steven** [1947-] ................... **CLC 20**
See also AAYA 8, 24; CA 77-80; CANR 32;
SATA 32
**Spillane, Frank Morrison** [1918-]
See Spillane, Mickey
See also CA 25-28R; CANR 28, 63; MTCW;
SATA 66
**Spillane, Mickey** .............................. **CLC 3, 13**
See also Spillane, Frank Morrison
**Spinoza, Benedictus de** [1632-1677] ...... **LC 9**
**Spinrad, Norman (Richard)** [1940-] **CLC 46**
See also CA 37-40R; CAAS 19; CANR 20; DLB
8; INT CANR-20
**Spitteler, Carl (Friedrich Georg)** [1845-1924]
**TCLC 12**
See also CA 109; DLB 129
**Spivack, Kathleen (Romola Drucker)** [1938-]
**CLC 6**
See also CA 49-52
**Spoto, Donald** [1941-] ........................ **CLC 39**
See also CA 65-68; CANR 11, 57
**Springsteen, Bruce (F.)** [1949-] ......... **CLC 17**
See also CA 111
**Spurling, Hilary** [1940-] .................... **CLC 34**
See also CA 104; CANR 25, 52
**Spyker, John Howland**
See Elman, Richard (Martin)
**Squires, (James) Radcliffe** [1917-1993] **C L C
51**
See also CA 1-4R; 140; CANR 6, 21
**Srivastava, Dhanpat Rai** [1880(?)-1936]
See Premchand
See also CA 118
**Stacy, Donald**
See Pohl, Frederik
**Stael, Germaine de** [1766-1817]
See Stael-Holstein, Anne Louise Germaine
Necker Baronn
See also DLB 119
**Stael-Holstein, Anne Louise Germaine Necker
Baronn** [1766-1817] ................... **NCLC 3**
See also Stael, Germaine de
See also DLB 192
**Stafford, Jean** [1915-1979] **CLC 4, 7, 19, 68;
SSC 26**
See also CA 1-4R; 85-88; CANR 3, 65; DLB 2,
173; MTCW; SATA-Obit 22
**Stafford, William (Edgar)** [1914-1993]**CLC 4,
7, 29; DAM POET**
See also CA 5-8R; 142; CAAS 3; CANR 5, 22;
DLB 5; INT CANR-22
**Stagnelius, Eric Johan** [1793-1823]**NCLC 61**
**Staines, Trevor**
See Brunner, John (Kilian Houston)
**Stairs, Gordon**
See Austin, Mary (Hunter)
**Stannard, Martin** [1947-] ................... **CLC 44**
See also CA 142; DLB 155
**Stanton, Elizabeth Cady** [1815-1902] **T C L C
73**
See also DLB 79
**Stanton, Maura** [1946-] ....................... **CLC 9**
See also CA 89-92; CANR 15; DLB 120
**Stanton, Schuyler**
See Baum, L(yman) Frank
**Stapledon, (William) Olaf** [1886-1950]**T C L C
22**
See also CA 111; 162; DLB 15
**Starbuck, George (Edwin)** [1931-1996] **C L C
53; DAM POET**
See also CA 21-24R; 153; CANR 23
**Stark, Richard**
See Westlake, Donald E(dwin)
**Staunton, Schuyler**
See Baum, L(yman) Frank

**Stead, Christina (Ellen)** [1902-1983]**CLC 2, 5,
8, 32, 80**
See also CA 13-16R; 109; CANR 33, 40;
MTCW
**Stead, William Thomas** [1849-1912]**TCLC 48**
**Steele, Richard** [1672-1729] ................. **LC 18**
See also CDBLB 1660-1789; DLB 84, 101
**Steele, Timothy (Reid)** [1948-] .......... **CLC 45**
See also CA 93-96; CANR 16, 50; DLB 120
**Steffens, (Joseph) Lincoln** [1866-1936]**T C L C
20**
See also CA 117
**Stegner, Wallace (Earle)** [1909-1993] **CLC 9,
49, 81; DAM NOV; SSC 27**
See also AITN 1; BEST 90:3; CA 1-4R; 141;
CAAS 9; CANR 1, 21, 46; DLB 9; DLBY
93; MTCW
**Stein, Gertrude** [1874-1946]**TCLC 1, 6, 28, 48;
DA; DAB; DAC; DAM MST, NOV, POET;
PC 18; WLC**
See also CA 104; 132; CDALB 1917-1929;
DLB 4, 54, 86; DLBD 15; MTCW
**Steinbeck, John (Ernst)** [1902-1968]**CLC 1, 5,
9, 13, 21, 34, 45, 75; DA; DAB; DAC; DAM
DRAM, MST, NOV; SSC 11; WLC**
See also AAYA 12; CA 1-4R; 25-28R; CANR
1, 35; CDALB 1929-1941; DLB 7, 9; DLBD
2; MTCW; SATA 9
**Steinem, Gloria** [1934-] ...................... **CLC 63**
See also CA 53-56; CANR 28, 51; MTCW
**Steiner, George** [1929-] **CLC 24; DAM NOV**
See also CA 73-76; CANR 31, 67; DLB 67;
MTCW; SATA 62
**Steiner, K. Leslie**
See Delany, Samuel R(ay, Jr.)
**Steiner, Rudolf** [1861-1925] ........... **TCLC 13**
See also CA 107
**Stendhal** [1783-1842]**NCLC 23, 46; DA; DAB;
DAC; DAM MST, NOV; SSC 27; WLC**
See also DLB 119
**Stephen, Adeline Virginia**
See Woolf, (Adeline) Virginia
**Stephen, SirLeslie** [1832-1904] ...... **TCLC 23**
See also CA 123; DLB 57, 144, 190
**Stephen, Sir Leslie**
See Stephen, SirLeslie
**Stephen, Virginia**
See Woolf, (Adeline) Virginia
**Stephens, James** [1882(?)-1950] ....... **TCLC 4**
See also CA 104; DLB 19, 153, 162
**Stephens, Reed**
See Donaldson, Stephen R.
**Steptoe, Lydia**
See Barnes, Djuna
**Sterchi, Beat** [1949-] ......................... **CLC 65**
**Sterling, Brett**
See Bradbury, Ray (Douglas); Hamilton,
Edmond
**Sterling, Bruce** [1954-] ...................... **CLC 72**
See also CA 119; CANR 44
**Sterling, George** [1869-1926] ......... **TCLC 20**
See also CA 117; 165; DLB 54
**Stern, Gerald** [1925-] ................ **CLC 40, 100**
See also CA 81-84; CANR 28; DLB 105
**Stern, Richard (Gustave)** [1928-] . **CLC 4, 39**
See also CA 1-4R; CANR 1, 25, 52; DLBY 87;
INT CANR-25
**Sternberg, Josef von** [1894-1969] ..... **CLC 20**
See also CA 81-84
**Sterne, Laurence** [1713-1768]**LC 2; DA; DAB;
DAC; DAM MST, NOV; WLC**
See also CDBLB 1660-1789; DLB 39
**Sternheim, (William Adolf) Carl** [1878-1942]
**TCLC 8**
See also CA 105; DLB 56, 118
**Stevens, Mark** [1951-] ....................... **CLC 34**
See also CA 122

Swift, Jonathan [1667-1745]LC 1; DA; DAB; DAC; DAM MST, NOV, POET; PC 9; WLC
See also CDBLB 1660-1789; DLB 39, 95, 101; SATA 19

Swinburne, Algernon Charles [1837-1909] TCLC 8, 36; DA; DAB; DAC; DAM MST, POET; WLC
See also CA 105; 140; CDBLB 1832-1890; DLB 35, 57

Swinfen, Ann ........................................ CLC 34

Swinnerton, Frank Arthur [1884-1982] C L C 31
See also CA 108; DLB 34

Swithen, John
See King, Stephen (Edwin)

Sylvia
See Ashton-Warner, Sylvia (Constance)

Symmes, Robert Edward
See Duncan, Robert (Edward)

Symonds, John Addington [1840-1893]NCLC 34
See also DLB 57, 144

Symons, Arthur [1865-1945] .......... TCLC 11
See also CA 107; DLB 19, 57, 149

Symons, Julian (Gustave) [1912-1994]CLC 2, 14, 32
See also CA 49-52; 147; CAAS 3; CANR 3, 33, 59; DLB 87, 155; DLBY 92; MTCW

Synge, (Edmund) J(ohn) M(illington) [1871-1909] ......................
TCLC 6, 37; DAM DRAM; DC 2
See also CA 104; 141; CDBLB 1890-1914; DLB 10, 19

Syruc, J.
See Milosz, Czeslaw

Szirtes, George [1948-] ...................... CLC 46
See also CA 109; CANR 27, 61

Szymborska, Wislawa [1923-] .......... CLC 99
See also CA 154; DLBY 96

T. O., Nik
See Annensky, Innokenty (Fyodorovich)

Tabori, George [1914-] ...................... CLC 19
See also CA 49-52; CANR 4, 69

Tagore, Rabindranath [1861-1941] TCLC 3, 53; DAM DRAM, POET; PC 8
See also CA 104; 120; MTCW

Taine, Hippolyte Adolphe [1828-1893]N C L C 15

Talese, Gay [1932-] ............................ CLC 37
See also AITN 1; CA 1-4R; CANR 9, 58; DLB 185; INT CANR-9; MTCW

Tallent, Elizabeth (Ann) [1954-] ....... CLC 45
See also CA 117; DLB 130

Tally, Ted [1952-] ............................... CLC 42
See also CA 120; 124; INT 124

Tamayo y Baus, Manuel [1829-1898]NCLC 1

Tammsaare, A(nton) H(ansen) [1878-1940] TCLC 27
See also CA 164

Tam'si, Tchicaya U
See Tchicaya, Gerald Felix

Tan, Amy (Ruth) [1952-] ........ CLC 59; DAM MULT, NOV, POP
See also AAYA 9; BEST 89:3; CA 136; CANR 54; DLB 173; SATA 75

Tandem, Felix
See Spitteler, Carl (Friedrich Georg)

Tanizaki, Jun'ichiro [1886-1965] CLC 8, 14, 28; SSC 21
See also CA 93-96; 25-28R; DLB 180

Tanner, William
See Amis, Kingsley (William)

Tao Lao
See Storni, Alfonsina

Tarassoff, Lev
See Troyat, Henri

Tarbell, Ida M(inerva) [1857-1944]TCLC 40
See also CA 122; DLB 47

Tarkington, (Newton) Booth [1869-1946] TCLC 9
See also CA 110; 143; DLB 9, 102; SATA 17

Tarkovsky, Andrei (Arsenyevich) [1932-1986] CLC 75
See also CA 127

Tartt, Donna [1964(?)-] ...................... CLC 76
See also CA 142

Tasso, Torquato [1544-1595] .................. LC 5

Tate, (John Orley) Allen [1899-1979]CLC 2, 4, 6, 9, 11, 14, 24
See also CA 5-8R; 85-88; CANR 32; DLB 4, 45, 63; MTCW

Tate, Ellalice
See Hibbert, Eleanor Alice Burford

Tate, James (Vincent) [1943-] .. CLC 2, 6, 25
See also CA 21-24R; CANR 29, 57; DLB 5, 169

Tavel, Ronald [1940-] ........................... CLC 6
See also CA 21-24R; CANR 33

Taylor, C(ecil) P(hilip) [1929-1981].. CLC 27
See also CA 25-28R; 105; CANR 47

Taylor, Edward [1642(?)-1729] .. LC 11; DA; DAB; DAC; DAM MST, POET
See also DLB 24

Taylor, Eleanor Ross [1920-] .............. CLC 5
See also CA 81-84

Taylor, Elizabeth [1912-1975] .. CLC 2, 4, 29
See also CA 13-16R; CANR 9; DLB 139; MTCW; SATA 13

Taylor, Frederick Winslow [1856-1915]TCLC 76

Taylor, Henry (Splawn) [1942-] ........ CLC 44
See also CA 33-36R; CAAS 7; CANR 31; DLB 5

Taylor, Kamala (Purnaiya) [1924-]
See Markandaya, Kamala
See also CA 77-80

Taylor, Mildred D. ............................. CLC 21
See also AAYA 10; BW 1; CA 85-88; CANR 25; CLR 9; DLB 52; JRDA; MAICYA; SAAS 5; SATA 15, 70

Taylor, Peter (Hillsman) [1917-1994] CLC 1, 4, 18, 37, 44, 50, 71; SSC 10
See also CA 13-16R; 147; CANR 9, 50; DLBY 81, 94; INT CANR-9; MTCW

Taylor, Robert Lewis [1912-] ............. CLC 14
See also CA 1-4R; CANR 3, 64; SATA 10

Tchekhov, Anton
See Chekhov, Anton (Pavlovich)

Tchicaya, Gerald Felix [1931-1988]CLC 101
See also CA 129; 125

Tchicaya U Tam'si
See Tchicaya, Gerald Felix

Teasdale, Sara [1884-1933] .............. TCLC 4
See also CA 104; 163; DLB 45; SATA 32

Tegner, Esaias [1782-1846] ............... NCLC 2

Teilhard de Chardin, (Marie Joseph) Pierre [1881-1955] ............................... TCLC 9
See also CA 105

Temple, Ann
See Mortimer, Penelope (Ruth)

Tennant, Emma (Christina) [1937-] CLC 13, 52
See also CA 65-68; CAAS 9; CANR 10, 38, 59; DLB 14.

Tenneshaw, S. M.
See Silverberg, Robert

Tennyson, Alfred [1809-1892] NCLC 30, 65; DA; DAB; DAC; DAM MST, POET; PC 6; WLC
See also CDBLB 1832-1890; DLB 32

Teran, Lisa St. Aubin de ..................... CLC 36
See also St. Aubin de Teran, Lisa

Terence [195(?)B.C.-159B.C.]CMLC 14; DC 7

Teresa de Jesus, St. [1515-1582] ......... LC 18

Terkel, Louis [1912-]
See Terkel, Studs
See also CA 57-60; CANR 18, 45, 67; MTCW

Terkel, Studs ...................................... CLC 38
See also Terkel, Louis
See also AITN 1

Terry, C. V.
See Slaughter, Frank G(ill)

Terry, Megan [1932-] ......................... CLC 19
See also CA 77-80; CABS 3; CANR 43; DLB 7

Tertullian [c. 155-c. 245] ............... CMLC 29

Tertz, Abram
See Sinyavsky, Andrei (Donatevich)

Tesich, Steve [1943(?)-1996] ....... CLC 40, 69
See also CA 105; 152; DLBY 83

Teternikov, Fyodor Kuzmich [1863-1927]
See Sologub, Fyodor
See also CA 104

Tevis, Walter [1928-1984] .................. CLC 42
See also CA 113

Tey, Josephine ................................... TCLC 14
See also Mackintosh, Elizabeth
See also DLB 77

Thackeray, William Makepeace [1811-1863] NCLC 5, 14, 22, 43; DA; DAB; DAC; DAM MST, NOV; WLC
See also CDBLB 1832-1890; DLB 21, 55, 159, 163; SATA 23

Thakura, Ravindranatha
See Tagore, Rabindranath

Tharoor, Shashi [1956-] .................... CLC 70
See also CA 141

Thelwell, Michael Miles [1939-] ....... CLC 22
See also BW 2; CA 101

Theobald, Lewis, Jr.
See Lovecraft, H(oward) P(hillips)

Theodorescu, Ion N. [1880-1967]
See Arghezi, Tudor
See also CA 116

Theriault, Yves [1915-1983] . CLC 79; DAC; DAM MST
See also CA 102; DLB 88

Theroux, Alexander (Louis) [1939-]CLC 2, 25
See also CA 85-88; CANR 20, 63

Theroux, Paul (Edward) [1941-]CLC 5, 8, 11, 15, 28, 46; DAM POP
See also BEST 89:4; CA 33-36R; CANR 20, 45; DLB 2; MTCW; SATA 44

Thesen, Sharon [1946-] ...................... CLC 56
See also CA 163

Thevenin, Denis
See Duhamel, Georges

Thibault, Jacques Anatole Francois [1844-1924]
See France, Anatole
See also CA 106; 127; DAM NOV; MTCW

Thiele, Colin (Milton) [1920-] ........... CLC 17
See also CA 29-32R; CANR 12, 28, 53; CLR 27; MAICYA; SAAS 2; SATA 14, 72

Thomas, Audrey (Callahan) [1935-] . CLC 7, 13, 37, 107; SSC 20
See also AITN 2; CA 21-24R; CAAS 19; CANR 36, 58; DLB 60; MTCW

Thomas, D(onald) M(ichael) [1935-]CLC 13, 22, 31
See also CA 61-64; CAAS 11; CANR 17, 45; CDBLB 1960 to Present; DLB 40; INT CANR-17; MTCW

Thomas, Dylan (Marlais) [1914-1953] T C L C 1, 8, 45; DA; DAB; DAC; DAM DRAM, MST, POET; PC 2; SSC 3; WLC
See also CA 104; 120; CANR 65; CDBLB 1945-1960; DLB 13, 20, 139; MTCW; SATA 60

Thomas, (Philip) Edward [1878-1917]T C L C 10; DAM POET

**Truffaut, Francois** [1932-1984] **CLC 20, 101**
See also CA 81-84; 113; CANR 34

**Trumbo, Dalton** [1905-1976] ............. **CLC 19**
See also CA 21-24R; 69-72; CANR 10; DLB 26

**Trumbull, John** [1750-1831] ......... **NCLC 30**
See also DLB 31

**Trundlett, Helen B.**
See Eliot, T(homas) S(tearns)

**Tryon, Thomas** [1926-1991]**CLC 3, 11; DAM POP**
See also AITN 1; CA 29-32R; 135; CANR 32; MTCW

**Tryon, Tom**
See Tryon, Thomas

**Ts'ao Hsueh-ch'in** [1715(?)-1763] ......... **LC 1**

**Tsushima, Shuji** [1909-1948]
See Dazai Osamu
See also CA 107

**Tsvetaeva (Efron), Marina (Ivanovna)** [1892-1941] ......................................................

**TCLC 7, 35; PC 14**
See also CA 104; 128; MTCW

**Tuck, Lily** [1938-] ............................ **CLC 70**
See also CA 139

**Tu Fu** [712-770] ....................................... **PC 9**
See also DAM MULT

**Tunis, John R(oberts)** [1889-1975] ... **CLC 12**
See also CA 61-64; CANR 62; DLB 22, 171; JRDA; MAICYA; SATA 37; SATA-Brief 30

**Tuohy, Frank** ..................................... **CLC 37**
See also Tuohy, John Francis
See also DLB 14, 139

**Tuohy, John Francis** [1925-]
See Tuohy, Frank
See also CA 5-8R; CANR 3, 47

**Turco, Lewis (Putnam)** [1934-] ... **CLC 11, 63**
See also CA 13-16R; CAAS 22; CANR 24, 51; DLBY 84

**Turgenev, Ivan** [1818-1883] .. **NCLC 21; DA; DAB; DAC; DAM MST, NOV; DC 7; SSC 7; WLC**

**Turgot, Anne-Robert-Jacques** [1727-1781]**LC 26**

**Turner, Frederick** [1943-] ................. **CLC 48**
See also CA 73-76; CAAS 10; CANR 12, 30, 56; DLB 40

**Tutu, Desmond M(pilo)** [1931-]**CLC 80; BLC 3; DAM MULT**
See also BW 1; CA 125; CANR 67

**Tutuola, Amos** [1920-1997] ... **CLC 5, 14, 29; BLC 3; DAM MULT**
See also BW 2; CA 9-12R; 159; CANR 27, 66; DLB 125; MTCW

**Twain, Mark**TCLC **6, 12, 19, 36, 48, 59; SSC 6, 26; WLC**
See also Clemens, Samuel Langhorne
See also AAYA 20; DLB 11, 12, 23, 64, 74

**Tyler, Anne** [1941-]CLC **7, 11, 18, 28, 44, 59, 103; DAM NOV, POP**
See also AAYA 18; BEST 89:1; CA 9-12R; CANR 11, 33, 53; DLB 6, 143; DLBY 82; MTCW; SATA 7, 90

**Tyler, Royall** [1757-1826] ................. **NCLC 3**
See also DLB 37

**Tynan, Katharine** [1861-1931] ......... **TCLC 3**
See also CA 104; DLB 153

**Tyutchev, Fyodor** [1803-1873] ....... **NCLC 34**

**Tzara, Tristan** [1896-1963]....**CLC 47; DAM POET**
See also CA 153; 89-92

**Uhry, Alfred** [1936-] **CLC 55; DAM DRAM, POP**
See also CA 127; 133; INT 133

**Ulf, Haerved**
See Strindberg, (Johan) August

**Ulf, Harved**

See Strindberg, (Johan) August

**Ulibarri, Sabine R(eyes)** [1919-] ..... **CLC 83; DAM MULT**
See also CA 131; DLB 82; HW

**Unamuno (y Jugo), Miguel de** [1864-1936] **TCLC 2, 9; DAM MULT, NOV; HLC; SSC 11**
See also CA 104; 131; DLB 108; HW; MTCW

**Undercliffe, Errol**
See Campbell, (John) Ramsey

**Underwood, Miles**
See Glassco, John

**Undset, Sigrid** [1882-1949] ..... **TCLC 3; DA; DAB; DAC; DAM MST, NOV; WLC**
See also CA 104; 129; MTCW

**Ungaretti, Giuseppe** [1888-1970]**CLC 7, 11, 15**
See also CA 19-20; 25-28R; CAP 2; DLB 114

**Unger, Douglas** [1952-] .................... **CLC 34**
See also CA 130

**Unsworth, Barry (Forster)** [1930-] .. **CLC 76**
See also CA 25-28R; CANR 30, 54; DLB 194

**Updike, John (Hoyer)** [1932-]CLC **1, 2, 3, 5, 7, 9, 13, 15, 23, 34, 43, 70; DA; DAB; DAC; DAM MST, NOV, POET, POP; SSC 13, 27; WLC**
See also CA 1-4R; CABS 1; CANR 4, 33, 51; CDALB 1968-1988; DLB 2, 5, 143; DLBD 3; DLBY 80, 82, 97; MTCW

**Upshaw, Margaret Mitchell**
See Mitchell, Margaret (Munnerlyn)

**Upton, Mark**
See Sanders, Lawrence

**Urdang, Constance (Henriette)** [1922-] **C L C 47**
See also CA 21-24R; CANR 9, 24

**Uriel, Henry**
See Faust, Frederick (Schiller)

**Uris, Leon (Marcus)** [1924-]CLC **7, 32; DAM NOV, POP**
See also AITN 1, 2; BEST 89:2; CA 1-4R; CANR 1, 40, 65; MTCW; SATA 49

**Urmuz**
See Codrescu, Andrei

**Urquhart, Jane** [1949-] ........... **CLC 90; DAC**
See also CA 113; CANR 32, 68

**Ustinov, Peter (Alexander)** [1921-] ..... **CLC 1**
See also AITN 1; CA 13-16R; CANR 25, 51; DLB 13

**U Tam'si, Gerald Felix Tchicaya**
See Tchicaya, Gerald Felix

**U Tam'si, Tchicaya**
See Tchicaya, Gerald Felix

**Vachss, Andrew (Henry)** [1942-] .... **CLC 106**
See also CA 118; CANR 44

**Vachss, Andrew H.**
See Vachss, Andrew (Henry)

**Vaculik, Ludvik** [1926-] ...................... **CLC 7**
See also CA 53-56

**Vaihinger, Hans** [1852-1933] ......... **TCLC 71**
See also CA 116; 166

**Valdez, Luis (Miguel)** [1940-] **CLC 84; DAM MULT; HLC**
See also CA 101; CANR 32; DLB 122; HW

**Valenzuela, Luisa** [1938-]CLC **31, 104; DAM MULT; SSC 14**
See also CA 101; CANR 32, 65; DLB 113; HW

**Valera y Alcala-Galiano, Juan** [1824-1905] **TCLC 10**
See also CA 106

**Valery, (Ambroise) Paul (Toussaint Jules)** [1871-1945]TCLC **4, 15; DAM POET; PC 9**
See also CA 104; 122; MTCW

**Valle-Inclan, Ramon (Maria) del** [1866-1936] **TCLC 5; DAM MULT; HLC**
See also CA 106; 153; DLB 134

**Vallejo, Antonio Buero**

See Buero Vallejo, Antonio

**Vallejo, Cesar (Abraham)** [1892-1938]T C L C **3, 56; DAM MULT; HLC**
See also CA 105; 153; HW

**Vallette, Marguerite Eymery**
See Rachilde

**Valle Y Pena, Ramon del**
See Valle-Inclan, Ramon (Maria) del

**Van Ash, Cay** [1918-] ........................ **CLC 34**

**Vanbrugh, Sir John** [1664-1726]LC **21; DAM DRAM**
See also DLB 80

**Van Campen, Karl**
See Campbell, John W(ood, Jr.)

**Vance, Gerald**
See Silverberg, Robert

**Vance, Jack** ......................................... **CLC 35**
See also Kuttner, Henry; Vance, John Holbrook
See also DLB 8

**Vance, John Holbrook** [1916-]
See Queen, Ellery; Vance, Jack
See also CA 29-32R; CANR 17, 65; MTCW

**Van Den Bogarde, Derek Jules Gaspard Ulric Niven** [1921-]
See Bogarde, Dirk
See also CA 77-80

**Vandenburgh, Jane** ............................ **CLC 59**

**Vanderhaeghe, Guy** [1951-] .............. **CLC 41**
See also CA 113

**van der Post, Laurens (Jan)** [1906-1996]CLC **5**
See also CA 5-8R; 155; CANR 35

**van de Wetering, Janwillem** [1931-] **CLC 47**
See also CA 49-52; CANR 4, 62

**Van Dine, S. S.** ................................... **TCLC 23**
See also Wright, Willard Huntington

**Van Doren, Carl (Clinton)** [1885-1950]T C L C **18**
See also CA 111

**Van Doren, Mark** [1894-1972] ...... **CLC 6, 10**
See also CA 1-4R; 37-40R; CANR 3; DLB 45; MTCW

**Van Druten, John (William)** [1901-1957] **TCLC 2**
See also CA 104; 161; DLB 10

**Van Duyn, Mona (Jane)** [1921-]CLC **3, 7, 63; DAM POET**
See also CA 9-12R; CANR 7, 38, 60; DLB 5

**Van Dyne, Edith**
See Baum, L(yman) Frank

**van Itallie, Jean-Claude** [1936-] ......... **CLC 3**
See also CA 45-48; CAAS 2; CANR 1, 48; DLB 7

**van Ostaijen, Paul** [1896-1928] ...... **TCLC 33**
See also CA 163

**Van Peebles, Melvin** [1932-]CLC **2, 20; DAM MULT**
See also BW 2; CA 85-88; CANR 27, 67

**Vansittart, Peter** [1920-] .................... **CLC 42**
See also CA 1-4R; CANR 3, 49

**Van Vechten, Carl** [1880-1964] ........ **CLC 33**
See also CA 89-92; DLB 4, 9, 51

**Van Vogt, A(lfred) E(lton)** [1912-] ...... **CLC 1**
See also CA 21-24R; CANR 28; DLB 8; SATA 14

**Varda, Agnes** [1928-] ......................... **CLC 16**
See also CA 116; 122

**Vargas Llosa, (Jorge) Mario (Pedro)** [1936-] **CLC 3, 6, 9, 10, 15, 31, 42, 85; DA; DAB; DAC; DAM MST, MULT, NOV; HLC**
See also CA 73-76; CANR 18, 32, 42, 67; DLB 145; HW; MTCW

**Vasiliu, Gheorghe** [1881-1957]
See Bacovia, George
See also CA 123

**Vassa, Gustavus**
See Equiano, Olaudah

**NOV, POP**
See also AITN 1; CA 1-4R; 132; CAAS 1; CANR 1, 27; INT CANR-27; MTCW

**Wallant, Edward Lewis** [1926-1962] **CLC 5, 10**
See also CA 1-4R; CANR 22; DLB 2, 28, 143; MTCW

**Walley, Byron**
See Card, Orson Scott

**Walpole, Horace** [1717-1797] ................ **LC 2**
See also DLB 39, 104

**Walpole, Hugh (Seymour)** [1884-1941]**T C L C 5**
See also CA 104; 165; DLB 34

**Walser, Martin** [1927-] ...................... **CLC 27**
See also CA 57-60; CANR 8, 46; DLB 75, 124

**Walser, Robert** [1878-1956]**TCLC 18; SSC 20**
See also CA 118; 165; DLB 66

**Walsh, Jill Paton** .............................. **CLC 35**
See also Paton Walsh, Gillian
See also AAYA 11; CLR 2; DLB 161; SAAS 3

**Walter, Villiam Christian**
See Andersen, Hans Christian

**Wambaugh, Joseph (Aloysius, Jr.)** [1937-]
**CLC 3, 18; DAM NOV, POP**
See also AITN 1; BEST 89:3; CA 33-36R; CANR 42, 65; DLB 6; DLBY 83; MTCW

**Wang Wei** [699(?)-761(?)] ..................... **PC 18**

**Ward, Arthur Henry Sarsfield** [1883-1959]
See Rohmer, Sax
See also CA 108

**Ward, Douglas Turner** [1930-] .......... **CLC 19**
See also BW 1; CA 81-84; CANR 27; DLB 7, 38

**Ward, Mary Augusta**
See Ward, Mrs. Humphry

**Ward, Mrs. Humphry** [1851-1920] **TCLC 55**
See also DLB 18

**Ward, Peter**
See Faust, Frederick (Schiller)

**Warhol, Andy** [1928(?)-1987] ............ **CLC 20**
See also AAYA 12; BEST 89:4; CA 89-92; 121; CANR 34

**Warner, Francis (Robert le Plastrier)** [1937-]
**CLC 14**
See also CA 53-56; CANR 11

**Warner, Marina** [1946-] .................... **CLC 59**
See also CA 65-68; CANR 21, 55; DLB 194

**Warner, Rex (Ernest)** [1905-1986] ... **CLC 45**
See also CA 89-92; 119; DLB 15

**Warner, Susan (Bogert)** [1819-1885]**NCLC 31**
See also DLB 3, 42

**Warner, Sylvia (Constance) Ashton**
See Ashton-Warner, Sylvia (Constance)

**Warner, Sylvia Townsend** [1893-1978]**CLC 7, 19; SSC 23**
See also CA 61-64; 77-80; CANR 16, 60; DLB 34, 139; MTCW

**Warren, Mercy Otis** [1728-1814] ... **NCLC 13**
See also DLB 31, 200

**Warren, Robert Penn** [1905-1989]**CLC 1, 4, 6, 8, 10, 13, 18, 39, 53, 59; DA; DAB; DAC; DAM MST, NOV, POET; SSC 4; WLC**
See also AITN 1; CA 13-16R; 129; CANR 10, 47; CDALB 1968-1988; DLB 2, 48, 152; DLBY 80, 89; INT CANR-10; MTCW; SATA 46; SATA-Obit 63

**Warshofsky, Isaac**
See Singer, Isaac Bashevis

**Warton, Thomas** [1728-1790] .. **LC 15; DAM POET**
See also DLB 104, 109

**Waruk, Kona**
See Harris, (Theodore) Wilson

**Warung, Price** [1855-1911] ............. **TCLC 45**

**Warwick, Jarvis**
See Garner, Hugh

**Washington, Alex**
See Harris, Mark

**Washington, Booker T(aliaferro)** [1856-1915]
**TCLC 10; BLC 3; DAM MULT**
See also BW 1; CA 114; 125; SATA 28

**Washington, George** [1732-1799] ........ **LC 25**
See also DLB 31

**Wassermann, (Karl) Jakob** [1873-1934]
**TCLC 6**
See also CA 104; DLB 66

**Wasserstein, Wendy** [1950-] **CLC 32, 59, 90; DAM DRAM; DC 4**
See also CA 121; 129; CABS 3; CANR 53; INT 129; SATA 94

**Waterhouse, Keith (Spencer)** [1929-]**CLC 47**
See also CA 5-8R; CANR 38, 67; DLB 13, 15; MTCW

**Waters, Frank (Joseph)** [1902-1995] **CLC 88**
See also CA 5-8R; 149; CAAS 13; CANR 3, 18, 63; DLBY 86

**Waters, Roger** [1944-] ...................... **CLC 35**

**Watkins, Frances Ellen**
See Harper, Frances Ellen Watkins

**Watkins, Gerrold**
See Malzberg, Barry N(athaniel)

**Watkins, Gloria** [1955(?)-]
See hooks, bell
See also BW 2; CA 143

**Watkins, Paul** [1964-] .................... **CLC 55**
See also CA 132; CANR 62

**Watkins, Vernon Phillips** [1906-1967]**CLC 43**
See also CA 9-10; 25-28R; CAP 1; DLB 20

**Watson, Irving S.**
See Mencken, H(enry) L(ouis)

**Watson, John H.**
See Farmer, Philip Jose

**Watson, Richard F.**
See Silverberg, Robert

**Waugh, Auberon (Alexander)** [1939-] **CLC 7**
See also CA 45-48; CANR 6, 22; DLB 14, 194

**Waugh, Evelyn (Arthur St. John)** [1903-1966]
**CLC 1, 3, 8, 13, 19, 27, 44, 107; DA; DAB; DAC; DAM MST, NOV, POP; WLC**
See also CA 85-88; 25-28R; CANR 22; CDBLB 1914-1945; DLB 15, 162, 195; MTCW

**Waugh, Harriet** [1944-] ...................... **CLC 6**
See also CA 85-88; CANR 22

**Ways, C. R.**
See Blount, Roy (Alton), Jr.

**Waystaff, Simon**
See Swift, Jonathan

**Webb, (Martha) Beatrice (Potter)** [1858-1943]
**TCLC 22**
See also Potter, (Helen) Beatrix
See also CA 117

**Webb, Charles (Richard)** [1939-] ....... **CLC 7**
See also CA 25-28R

**Webb, James H(enry), Jr.** [1946-] .... **CLC 22**
See also CA 81-84

**Webb, Mary (Gladys Meredith)** [1881-1927]
**TCLC 24**
See also CA 123; DLB 34

**Webb, Mrs. Sidney**
See Webb, (Martha) Beatrice (Potter)

**Webb, Phyllis** [1927-] ........................ **CLC 18**
See also CA 104; CANR 23; DLB 53

**Webb, Sidney (James)** [1859-1947] **TCLC 22**
See also CA 117; 163; DLB 190

**Webber, Andrew Lloyd** ...................... **CLC 21**
See also Lloyd Webber, Andrew

**Weber, Lenora Mattingly** [1895-1971]**CLC 12**
See also CA 19-20; 29-32R; CAP 1; SATA 2; SATA-Obit 26

**Weber, Max** [1864-1920] ................. **TCLC 69**
See also CA 109

**Webster, John** [1579(?)-1634(?)] **LC 33; DA; DAB; DAC; DAM DRAM, MST; DC 2; WLC**
See also CDBLB Before 1660; DLB 58

**Webster, Noah** [1758-1843] ............ **NCLC 30**

**Wedekind, (Benjamin) Frank(lin)** [1864-1918]
**TCLC 7; DAM DRAM**
See also CA 104; 153; DLB 118

**Weidman, Jerome** [1913-] .................... **CLC 7**
See also AITN 2; CA 1-4R; CANR 1; DLB 28

**Weil, Simone (Adolphine)** [1909-1943]**T C L C 23**
See also CA 117; 159

**Weinstein, Nathan**
See West, Nathanael

**Weinstein, Nathan von Wallenstein**
See West, Nathanael

**Weir, Peter (Lindsay)** [1944-] ........... **CLC 20**
See also CA 113; 123

**Weiss, Peter (Ulrich)** [1916-1982] **CLC 3, 15, 51; DAM DRAM**
See also CA 45-48; 106; CANR 3; DLB 69, 124

**Weiss, Theodore (Russell)** [1916-]**CLC 3, 8, 14**
See also CA 9-12R; CAAS 2; CANR 46; DLB 5

**Welch, (Maurice) Denton** [1915-1948] **T C L C 22**
See also CA 121; 148

**Welch, James** [1940-] .. **CLC 6, 14, 52; DAM MULT, POP**
See also CA 85-88; CANR 42, 66; DLB 175; NNAL

**Weldon, Fay** [1931-]**CLC 6, 9, 11, 19, 36, 59; DAM POP**
See also CA 21-24R; CANR 16, 46, 63; CDBLB 1960 to Present; DLB 14, 194; INT CANR-16; MTCW

**Wellek, Rene** [1903-1995] .................. **CLC 28**
See also CA 5-8R; 150; CAAS 7; CANR 8; DLB 63; INT CANR-8

**Weller, Michael** [1942-] .............. **CLC 10, 53**
See also CA 85-88

**Weller, Paul** [1958-] ........................ **CLC 26**

**Wellershoff, Dieter** [1925-] ............... **CLC 46**
See also CA 89-92; CANR 16, 37

**Welles, (George) Orson** [1915-1985]**CLC 20, 80**
See also CA 93-96; 117

**Wellman, John McDowell** [1945-]
See Wellman, Mac
See also CA 166

**Wellman, Mac** [1945-] ...................... **CLC 65**
See also Wellman, John McDowell; Wellman, John McDowell

**Wellman, Manly Wade** [1903-1986] . **CLC 49**
See also CA 1-4R; 118; CANR 6, 16, 44; SATA 6; SATA-Obit 47

**Wells, Carolyn** [1869(?)-1942] ....... **TCLC 35**
See also CA 113; DLB 11

**Wells, H(erbert) G(eorge)** [1866-1946]**T C L C 6, 12, 19; DA; DAB; DAC; DAM MST, NOV; SSC 6; WLC**
See also AAYA 18; CA 110; 121; CDBLB 1914-1945; DLB 34, 70, 156, 178; MTCW; SATA 20

**Wells, Rosemary** [1943-] .................... **CLC 12**
See also AAYA 13; CA 85-88; CANR 48; CLR 16; MAICYA; SAAS 1; SATA 18, 69

**Welty, Eudora** [1909-]**CLC 1, 2, 5, 14, 22, 33, 105; DA; DAB; DAC; DAM MST, NOV; SSC 1, 27; WLC**
See also CA 9-12R; CABS 1; CANR 32, 65; CDALB 1941-1968; DLB 2, 102, 143; DLBD 12; DLBY 87; MTCW

**Wen I-to** [1899-1946] ...................... **TCLC 28**

**Wentworth, Robert**
See Hamilton, Edmond

**Werfel, Franz (Viktor)** [1890-1945] **TCLC 8**
See also CA 104; 161; DLB 81, 124

Williams, Norman [1952-] ................ **CLC 39**
See also CA 118
Williams, Sherley Anne [1944-]**CLC 89; BLC 3; DAM MULT, POET**
See also BW 2; CA 73-76; CANR 25; DLB 41; INT CANR-25; SATA 78
Williams, Shirley
See Williams, Sherley Anne
Williams, Tennessee [1911-1983]**CLC 1, 2, 5, 7, 8, 11, 15, 19, 30, 39, 45, 71, 111; DA; DAB; DAC; DAM DRAM, MST; DC 4; WLC**
See also AITN 1, 2; CA 5-8R; 108; CABS 3; CANR 31; CDALB 1941-1968; DLB 7; DLBD 4; DLBY 83; MTCW
Williams, Thomas (Alonzo) [1926-1990]**C L C 14**
See also CA 1-4R; 132; CANR 2
Williams, William C.
See Williams, William Carlos
Williams, William Carlos [1883-1963]**CLC 1, 2, 5, 9, 13, 22, 42, 67; DA; DAB; DAC; DAM MST, POET; PC 7; SSC 31**
See also CA 89-92; CANR 34; CDALB 1917-1929; DLB 4, 16, 54, 86; MTCW
Williamson, David (Keith) [1942-] ... **CLC 56**
See also CA 103; CANR 41
Williamson, Ellen Douglas [1905-1984]
See Douglas, Ellen
See also CA 17-20R; 114; CANR 39
Williamson, Jack .................................. **CLC 29**
See also Williamson, John Stewart
See also CAAS 8; DLB 8
Williamson, John Stewart [1908-]
See Williamson, Jack
See also CA 17-20R; CANR 23
Willie, Frederick
See Lovecraft, H(oward) P(hillips)
Willingham, Calder (Baynard, Jr.) [1922-1995]
**CLC 5, 51**
See also CA 5-8R; 147; CANR 3; DLB 2, 44; MTCW
Willis, Charles
See Clarke, Arthur C(harles)
Willy
See Colette, (Sidonie-Gabrielle)
Willy, Colette
See Colette, (Sidonie-Gabrielle)
Wilson, A(ndrew) N(orman) [1950-] **CLC 33**
See also CA 112; 122; DLB 14, 155, 194
Wilson, Angus (Frank Johnstone) [1913-1991]
**CLC 2, 3, 5, 25, 34; SSC 21**
See also CA 5-8R; 134; CANR 21; DLB 15, 139, 155; MTCW
Wilson, August [1945-]**CLC 39, 50, 63; BLC 3; DA; DAB; DAC; DAM DRAM, MST, MULT; DC 2; WLCS**
See also AAYA 16; BW 2; CA 115; 122; CANR 42, 54; MTCW
Wilson, Brian [1942-] ........................ **CLC 12**
Wilson, Colin [1931-] ..................... **CLC 3, 14**
See also CA 1-4R; CAAS 5; CANR 1, 22, 33; DLB 14, 194; MTCW
Wilson, Dirk
See Pohl, Frederik
Wilson, Edmund [1895-1972]**CLC 1, 2, 3, 8, 24**
See also CA 1-4R; 37-40R; CANR 1, 46; DLB 63; MTCW
Wilson, Ethel Davis (Bryant) [1888(?)-1980]
**CLC 13; DAC; DAM POET**
See also CA 102; DLB 68; MTCW
Wilson, John [1785-1854] ................. **NCLC 5**
Wilson, John (Anthony) Burgess [1917-1993]
See Burgess, Anthony
See also CA 1-4R; 143; CANR 2, 46; DAC; DAM NOV; MTCW
Wilson, Lanford [1937-]**CLC 7, 14, 36; DAM DRAM**
See also CA 17-20R; CABS 3; CANR 45; DLB 7
Wilson, Robert M. [1944-] ............... **CLC 7, 9**
See also CA 49-52; CANR 2, 41; MTCW
Wilson, Robert McLiam [1964-] ....... **CLC 59**
See also CA 132
Wilson, Sloan [1920-] ........................ **CLC 32**
See also CA 1-4R; CANR 1, 44
Wilson, Snoo [1948-] ......................... **CLC 33**
See also CA 69-72
Wilson, William S(mith) [1932-] ....... **CLC 49**
See also CA 81-84
Wilson, (Thomas) Woodrow [1856-1924]
**TCLC 79**
See also CA 166; DLB 47
Winchilsea, Anne (Kingsmill) Finch Counte [1661-1720]
See Finch, Anne
Windham, Basil
See Wodehouse, P(elham) G(renville)
Wingrove, David (John) [1954-] ....... **CLC 68**
See also CA 133
Wintergreen, Jane
See Duncan, Sara Jeannette
Winters, Janet Lewis .......................... **CLC 41**
See also Lewis, Janet
See also DLBY 87
Winters, (Arthur) Yvor [1900-1968]**CLC 4, 8, 32**
See also CA 11-12; 25-28R; CAP 1; DLB 48; MTCW
Winterson, Jeanette [1959-] .. **CLC 64; DAM POP**
See also CA 136; CANR 58
Winthrop, John [1588-1649] ................ **LC 31**
See also DLB 24, 30
Wiseman, Frederick [1930-] ............. **CLC 20**
See also CA 159
Wister, Owen [1860-1938] ............. **TCLC 21**
See also CA 108; 162; DLB 9, 78, 186; SATA 62
Witkacy
See Witkiewicz, Stanislaw Ignacy
Witkiewicz, Stanislaw Ignacy [1885-1939]
**TCLC 8**
See also CA 105; 162
Wittgenstein, Ludwig (Josef Johann) [1889-1951] .................
**TCLC 59**
See also CA 113; 164
Wittig, Monique [1935(?)-] ................ **CLC 22**
See also CA 116; 135; DLB 83
Wittlin, Jozef [1896-1976] ................. **CLC 25**
See also CA 49-52; 65-68; CANR 3
Wodehouse, P(elham) G(renville) [1881-1975]
**CLC 1, 2, 5, 10, 22; DAB; DAC; DAM NOV; SSC 2**
See also AITN 2; CA 45-48; 57-60; CANR 3, 33; CDBLB 1914-1945; DLB 34, 162; MTCW; SATA 22
Woiwode, L.
See Woiwode, Larry (Alfred)
Woiwode, Larry (Alfred) [1941-] . **CLC 6, 10**
See also CA 73-76; CANR 16; DLB 6; INT CANR-16
Wojciechowska, Maia (Teresa) [1927-] . **C L C 26**
See also AAYA 8; CA 9-12R; CANR 4, 41; CLR 1; JRDA; MAICYA; SAAS 1; SATA 1, 28, 83
Wolf, Christa [1929-] ............. **CLC 14, 29, 58**
See also CA 85-88; CANR 45; DLB 75; MTCW
Wolfe, Gene (Rodman) [1931-]**CLC 25; DAM POP**
See also CA 57-60; CAAS 9; CANR 6, 32, 60; DLB 8

Wolfe, George C. [1954-] ...... **CLC 49; BLCS**
See also CA 149
Wolfe, Thomas (Clayton) [1900-1938] **T C L C 4, 13, 29, 61; DA; DAB; DAC; DAM MST, NOV; WLC**
See also CA 104; 132; CDALB 1929-1941; DLB 9, 102; DLBD 2, 16; DLBY 85, 97; MTCW
Wolfe, Thomas Kennerly, Jr. [1931-]
See Wolfe, Tom
See also CA 13-16R; CANR 9, 33; DAM POP; DLB 185; INT CANR-9; MTCW
Wolfe, Tom .................. **CLC 1, 2, 9, 15, 35, 51**
See also Wolfe, Thomas Kennerly, Jr.
See also AAYA 8; AITN 2; BEST 89:1; DLB 152
Wolff, Geoffrey (Ansell) [1937-] ....... **CLC 41**
See also CA 29-32R; CANR 29, 43
Wolff, Sonia
See Levitin, Sonia (Wolff)
Wolff, Tobias (Jonathan Ansell) [1945-]**C L C 39, 64**
See also AAYA 16; BEST 90:2; CA 114; 117; CAAS 22; CANR 54; DLB 130; INT 117
Wolfram von Eschenbach [c. 1170-c. 1220]
**CMLC 5**
See also DLB 138
Wolitzer, Hilma [1930-] ...................... **CLC 17**
See also CA 65-68; CANR 18, 40; INT CANR-18; SATA 31
Wollstonecraft, Mary [1759-1797] ........ **LC 5**
See also CDBLB 1789-1832; DLB 39, 104, 158
Wonder, Stevie ................................... **CLC 12**
See also Morris, Steveland Judkins
Wong, Jade Snow [1922-] .................. **CLC 17**
See also CA 109
Woodberry, George Edward [1855-1930]
**TCLC 73**
See also CA 165; DLB 71, 103
Woodcott, Keith
See Brunner, John (Kilian Houston)
Woodruff, Robert W.
See Mencken, H(enry) L(ouis)
Woolf, (Adeline) Virginia [1882-1941]**T C L C 1, 5, 20, 43, 56; DA; DAB; DAC; DAM MST, NOV; SSC 7; WLC**
See also CA 104; 130; CANR 64; CDBLB 1914-1945; DLB 36, 100, 162; DLBD 10; MTCW
Woolf, Virginia Adeline
See Woolf, (Adeline) Virginia
Woollcott, Alexander (Humphreys) [1887-1943]
**TCLC 5**
See also CA 105; 161; DLB 29
Woolrich, Cornell [1903-1968] ......... **CLC 77**
See also Hopley-Woolrich, Cornell George
Wordsworth, Dorothy [1771-1855] **NCLC 25**
See also DLB 107
Wordsworth, William [1770-1850]**NCLC 12, 38; DA; DAB; DAC; DAM MST, POET; PC 4; WLC**
See also CDBLB 1789-1832; DLB 93, 107
Wouk, Herman [1915-] . **CLC 1, 9, 38; DAM NOV, POP**
See also CA 5-8R; CANR 6, 33, 67; DLBY 82; INT CANR-6; MTCW
Wright, Charles (Penzel, Jr.) [1935-] **CLC 6, 13, 28**
See also CA 29-32R; CAAS 7; CANR 23, 36, 62; DLB 165; DLBY 82; MTCW
Wright, Charles Stevenson [1932-] **CLC 49; BLC 3; DAM MULT, POET**
See also BW 1; CA 9-12R; CANR 26; DLB 33
Wright, Jack R.
See Harris, Mark
Wright, James (Arlington) [1927-1980] **C L C 3, 5, 10, 28; DAM POET**

# Literary Criticism Series
# Cumulative Topic Index

This index lists all topic entries in Gale's *Classical and Medieval Literature Criticism, Contemporary Literary Criticism, Literature Criticism from 1400 to 1800, Nineteenth-Century Literature Criticism,* and *Twentieth-Century Literary Criticism.*

Topic Index

Topic Index

Topic Index

# Twentieth-Century Literary Criticism
## Cumulative Nationality Index

Nationality Index

# *TCLC-80* Title Index